Industrial Organization

Contemporary Theory
and Empirical Applications

Fifth Edition

Lynne Pepall

Dan Richards

George Norman

WILEY

VICE PRESIDENT & EXECUTIVE PUBLISHER	George Hoffman
EXECUTIVE EDITOR	Joel Hollenbeck
CONTENT EDITOR	Jennifer Manias
ASSISTANT EDITOR	Courtney Luzzi
SENIOR EDITORIAL ASSISTANT	Erica Horowitz
DIRECTOR OF MARKETING	Amy Scholz
ASSISTANT MARKETING MANAGER	Puja Katariwala
MARKETING ASSISTANT	Mia Brady
SENIOR PRODUCT DESIGNER	Allison Morris
SENIOR PRODUCTION MANAGER	Janis Soo
ASSOCIATE PRODUCTION MANAGER	Joel Balbin
PRODUCTION EDITOR	Eugenia Lee
COVER PHOTO CREDIT	Jerry Horbert/iStockphoto

This book was set in 10/12pt TimesLTStd by Laserwords Private Limited, Chennai, India.

Founded in 1807, John Wiley & Sons, Inc. has been a valued source of knowledge and understanding for more than 200 years, helping people around the world meet their needs and fulfill their aspirations. Our company is built on a foundation of principles that include responsibility to the communities we serve and where we live and work. In 2008, we launched a Corporate Citizenship Initiative, a global effort to address the environmental, social, economic, and ethical challenges we face in our business. Among the issues we are addressing are carbon impact, paper specifications and procurement, ethical conduct within our business and among our vendors, and community and charitable support. For more information, please visit our website: www.wiley.com/go/citizenship.

Evaluation copies are provided to qualified academics and professionals for review purposes only, for use in their courses during the next academic year. These copies are licensed and may not be sold or transferred to a third party. Upon completion of the review period, please return the evaluation copy to Wiley. Return instructions and a free of charge return mailing label are available at www.wiley.com/go/returnlabel. If you have chosen to adopt this textbook for use in your course, please accept this book as your complimentary desk copy. Outside of the United States, please contact your local sales representative.

To order books or for customer service please, call 1-800-CALL WILEY (225-5945).

Library of Congress Cataloging-in-Publication Data

Pepall, Lynne, 1952-
   Industrial organization : contemporary theory and empirical applications / Lynne Pepall, Dan Richards, George Norman.–Fifth edition.
      pages cm
   Includes bibliographical references and index.
   ISBN 978-1-118-25030-3 (pbk. : alk. paper) 1. Industrial organization. I. Richards, Daniel Jay.
II. Norman, George, 1946- III. Title.
   HD31.P377 2014
   658.1–dc23

                                                                    2013032338

Printed in the United States of America
10 9 8 7 6 5 4

Contents

About The Authors

Lynne Pepall is Professor of Economics and Dean of the Graduate School of Arts and Sciences at Tufts University. Professor Pepall received her undergraduate degree in mathematics and economics from Trinity College, University of Toronto, and her Ph.D. in economics from the University of Cambridge in England. She has written numerous papers in industrial organization, appearing in *The Journal of Industrial Economics*, *International Journal of Industrial Organization*, *Journal of Economics and Management Strategy*, *Economic Journal*, *Journal of Finance*, *Canadian Journal of Economics*, *Economica*, and the *American Journal of Agricultural Economics*. She has taught industrial organization and microeconomics at both the graduate and undergraduate levels at Concordia University, Queens University, and Tufts. Professor Pepall lives in Newton, Massachusetts, with her husband, a co-author of this book, and their dog, Churchill.

Dan Richards is Professor and current Chair of Economics at Tufts University. Professor Richards received his A.B. in economics and history from Oberlin College and his Ph.D. in economics at Yale University. Professor Richards has written numerous articles in both macroeconomics and industrial organization, appearing in the *American Economic Review*, *Quarterly Journal of Economics*, *Journal of Industrial Economics*, *Economica*, the *B. E. Journals in Economic Analysis and Policy*, *Canadian Journal of Economics*, the *Journal of Money, Credit, and Banking*, and the *American Journal of Agricultural Economics*. He served as Director of the Graduate Program in Economics from 1989 through 1998, and has also served as a consultant to the Federal Trade Commission. From 1996 to 2005 he taught Applied Economics in the Sloan Fellows Program at MIT's Sloan School of Management. Professor Richards lives in Newton, Massachusetts, with his wife, a co-author of this book, and their dog, Churchill.

George Norman holds the Cummings Family Chair of Entrepreneurship and Business Economics at Tufts University. He came to Tufts in 1995 from Edinburgh University, where he had served as head of the department of economics. Prior to that, Professor Norman was the Tyler Professor of Economics at the University of Leicester (England). Professor Norman attended the University of Dundee (Scotland) where he was awarded the MA in Economics with first class honors. He received his Ph.D. in economics from the University of Cambridge, England. His more than 70 published articles have appeared in such professional journals as the *American Economic Review*, *Review of Economic Studies*, *Quarterly Journal of Economics*, *Journal of Industrial Economics*, and *International Journal of Industrial Organization*. He is currently an Associate Editor for two journals, the *Bulletin of Economic Research* and *Regional Science and Urban Economics*. He is also on the editorial board of the *BE Journals in Economic Analysis and Policy*. In addition to this book, Professor Norman has written and edited, either alone or in collaboration with others, 17 other books. Professor Norman has taught courses in industrial organization and microeconomic theory at both the graduate and undergraduate levels. He has also taught introductory economics, corporate strategy, international economics, and entrepreneurship. Professor Norman lives in Newbury, Massachusetts, with his wife Margaret who, while *not* a co-author, has provided invaluable support and assistance in his work on this book.

Preface to the Fifth Edition

We are greatly pleased by the publication of the fifth edition of *Industrial Organization: Contemporary Theory and Practice*. It is gratifying to have such continued market confirmation of our conceptualization of the field and its major contributions—in particular, that the application of rigorous thinking about strategic interaction yields important and testable insights into real world events. We believe that this edition of our textbook renews this message.

Overall, the organization of the book is roughly the same as the previous edition but there are important changes. The two chapters on price-fixing and anti-trust policy vis-à-vis collusion (Chapters 14 and 15 in the fourth edition) have been streamlined and combined into one chapter. The same is true for the formerly two separate chapters on advertising (Chapters 20 and 21 in the fourth edition). More importantly, we have added a new chapter on strategic interaction as it applies to international competition and the scope this introduces for strategic trade policies. The net change is one less chapter and a more concise text.

The two most substantive changes, however, are: 1) the inclusion of a somewhat extended discussion of a single empirical study in each chapter; and 2) the shift of all calculus derivations to chapter appendices. The first of these builds on the innovation in the fourth edition in which we included an empirical study in roughly every other chapter. Finding studies that are both appropriate for each chapter's subject matter and also well suited to the statistical training of the variety of students using the text is not an easy task. However, we believe that we have done a good job in this respect. This includes the inclusion of a straightforward empirical comparison of antitrust enforcement across countries in the introductory first chapter.

Shifting the calculus sections to the appendix will, we hope, make the book more usable for those teaching classes without a strong mathematics prerequisite while still making that material available for those who want a more formal approach. This is not to say that there is no math in the current text. We still include a lot of algebra and derive a lot of results from the first order condition of marginal revenue equal to marginal cost. Algebraic analysis is also prevalent in the empirical applications of each chapter. However, those seeking a formal calculus presentation fully integrated into the primary text may be better served by the quantitative alternative version, *Contemporary Industrial Organization: A Quantitative Approach*.

ACKNOWLEDGMENTS

Our students at Tufts and elsewhere have been extremely helpful and we owe each of them a great deal of thanks. Special recognition in this regard is due to Sonia Jaffe and Kevin Proulx, who provided incredible assistance with the chapter problems, power point slides, and much more. In addition, the comments of formal reviewers, instructors, and simply those who wished to be helpful have been very insightful. Among this group, we wish to give particular thanks to:

Sheri Aggarwal, University of Virginia
Simon Anderson, University of Virginia
David Audretsch, Indiana University
Vassilios Bardis, York University
Emek Basker, University of Missouri
Gary Biglaiser, University of North Carolina
Giacomo Bonanno, University of California/Davis
Stacey Brook, University of Iowa
Erik Brynjolfsson, MIT
Sam Bucovetsky, York University
Giacomo Calzolari, University of Bologna
Marcelo Celani, Torcuato di Tello University
Darlene Chisholm, Suffolk University
Henry W. Chappell, Jr., University of South Carolina
Yongmin Chen, University of Colorado
Carlos Cinquetti, São Paolo University
John R. Conlon, University of Mississippi
James Dana, Northeastern University
Richard Dagen, Federal Trade Commission
Larry DeBrock, University of Illinois
George Deltas, University of Illinois
Greg Ellis, University of Washington
Glenn Ellison, MIT
Sara Fisher Ellison, MIT
Stephen Erfle, Dickinson College
Gianni De Fraja, University of Leicester
Robert M. Feinberg, American University
Ann Harper Fender, Gettysburg College
Mark R. Frascatore, Clarkson University
Luke Froeb, Vanderbilt University
Shailendra Gajanan, University of Pittsburgh
Ian Gale, Georgetown University
Paolo Garella, University of Milan

Christos Genakos, Selwyn College, Cambridge
Gerald Granderson, Miami University of Ohio
Arne Hallam, Iowa State University
Justine Hastings, Brown University
Mehdi Haririan, Bloomsburg University
Oliver Hart, Harvard University
Barry Haworth, University of Louisville
Hugo A. Hopenhayn, UCLA
Peter Huang, University of Colorado
Hugo A. Hopenhayn, UCLA
Peter Huang, University of Colorado
Stanley Kardasz, University of Waterloo
Phillip King, San Francisco State University
John Kwoka, Northeastern University
Nicola Lacetera, University of Toronto
Robert Lawrence, Harvard University
John Logan, ANU
Nancy Lutz, National Science Foundation
Howard Marvel, Ohio State University
Catherine Matraves, FCC
Jaime Maya, University of San Francisco de Quito
Jill McCluskey, Washington State University
Deborah Menegotto, Tufts University
Eugenio J. Miravete, University of Texas
Erich Muehlegger, Kennedy School
Wallace Mullin, George Washington University
Jon Nelson, Pennsylvania State University
Craig Newmark, North Carolina State University
David Ong, Peking University
Debashis Pal, University of Cincinnati
Nicola Persico, University of Pennsylvania
Russell Pittman, Department of Justice

Raymond Raab, University of Minnesota
James Reitzes, The Brattle Group
Vasco Rodrigues, Catholic University, Portugal
Steve Rubb, Bentley College
Michael Salinger, Boston University
Tim Sass, Georiga State University
Nicholas Schmitt, Simon Fraser University
John Sessions, University of Bath
Danny Shapiro, Simon Fraser University
Jay Shimshack, Tulane University

Chris Snyder, Dartmouth College
Dan Spulber, Northwestern University
Sarah Stafford, William and Mary
Chad Syverson, University of Chicago
David Weiskopf, CompassLexecon
Greg Werden, Department of Justice
William C. Wood, James Madison University
James Zinser, Oberlin College
Zenon Zyginont, Western Oregon University

Here at Tufts, Debra Knox, Caroline Kalogeropoulos, and Linda Casey have given us outstanding secretarial assistance and support. The editorial staff at Wiley-Blackwell, especially George Lobell and Courtney Luzzi, have provided excellent and much-needed editorial guidance. Eugenia Lee's production editing has been outstanding.

Of course, we owe the greatest debts to our family members. Lynne and Dan are thankful for the help, support, and inspiration from their increasingly independent sons, Ben and William. They also wish to thank Dan's brother, David Richards, whose professional integrity, clear judgment, and openness to new ideas continue to guide their writing. George would like to thank his wife Margaret for her patience, help, and humor, which are indispensable to his work. For these and countless other reasons, we affectionately dedicate this book to our loved ones.

Part One
Foundations

We begin our study of industrial organization by reviewing the basic building blocks of market analysis. The first chapter provides a road map for the entire enterprise. Here, we describe the central aim of industrial organization, namely, the investigation of firm behavior and market outcomes in settings of less than perfect competition. We emphasize that an understanding of strategic interaction is a critical component of this analysis. We end the chapter with a study by Nicholson (2008) relating the strength of active antitrust policy to exposure to trade and measures of economic development.

In Chapter 2, we review the basic microeconomics of the two polar textbook cases of perfect competition and pure monopoly. This permits the introduction of basic supply and demand analysis, as well as the notions of consumer surplus, producer surplus, and total surplus necessary for welfare evaluation of market outcomes. In addition, we introduce intertemporal considerations, discounting, and the Coase durable goods conjecture. We conclude with a review of the Chevalier and Goolsbee (2009) paper testing the rational forward-looking behavior reflected in student textbook purchasing decisions.

Chapter 3 focuses on how we might identify those markets where market power is likely to be a problem. This is an obvious place to introduce such measures as the n-firm concentration ratio and the Herfindahl-Hirschman Index. However, we also take the additional step of introducing the most explicit measure of monopoly price distortions, namely, the Lerner Index. This includes an extended empirical application explaining the many attempts at measuring the economy-wide welfare loss from such distortions beginning with Harberger (1954).

Finally, in Chapter 4, we turn to a discussion of some of the reasons that markets may exhibit the structural conditions that make perfect competition unlikely. Chief among these are cost considerations, and it is in this chapter that we explore cost concepts most formally. We review the notion of marginal cost that has already been introduced and then turn our attention to those remaining cost concepts that most directly relate to market structure such as sunk costs, average cost, and both scale and scope economies. We also explore the implications of endogenous sunk cost as emphasized by Sutton (1991). Chapter 4 also includes an empirical application based on the early work of Pulley and Braunstein (1992), investigating scale and scope economies in the banking sector.

1

Industrial Organization: What, How, and Why

A sample of business press from just the last few years includes the following items: the emergence of a price war in the e-reader market involving Amazon's *Kindle* and Barnes & Noble's *Nook* and even Apple's *iPad*; guilty pleas from ten (so far) real estate investors admitting that they colluded to rig bids at public foreclosure auctions in California; widespread evidence that hospitals charge different prices for the same procedure depending on who the patient is (including evidence that the uninsured are often charged *higher* prices); and the filing of a suit by the US Department of Justice to block a proposed merger between two large mobile phone companies, AT&T and T-Mobile.

Students often feel that there is a considerable gap between stories like those just described and the economics they study in the classroom. This is so despite the fact that most modern texts include real world applications. Indeed, it is difficult to think of a contemporary economics textbook that does not include examples drawn from the practical business experience. Nevertheless, it is still far from unusual to hear remarks such as "economics is too abstract" or "this wasn't covered in the microeconomics that I studied."

This book is very much in keeping with the modern practice of illustrating the applications of economic theory. Our aim is, however, more ambitious than just showing that economics can illuminate the everyday events of the business world. Our goal is to develop a way of thinking about such experiences—a mental framework that permits students to form hypotheses about the mechanisms underlying such events and to consider how to test those hypotheses against empirical evidence. Of course, we cannot offer a single framework for analyzing all economic phenomena, but we can develop one that applies to a large class of events including the ones described above. That framework lies at the heart of the field that economists call industrial organization.

1.1 WHAT IS INDUSTRIAL ORGANIZATION?

What is industrial organization? Certainly for those outside the economics profession, the answer to that question is far from clear. In fact, probably no subfield of economics has a less informative name. Unlike those working in international trade, environmental economics, and most other economics fields with highly self-explanatory titles, those of us working in industrial organization can rarely expect non-economists to understand what we do from the name of the field alone. One possible answer to the question is that industrial organization has to do with how market production is arranged. Another is that it is really applied business economics. Yet while each of these responses has a grain of truth, each is also wide of the mark. In our view, the simplest and most direct answer is that the field of industrial organization is that branch of economics that is concerned with the study of imperfect competition with the further qualification that this is done almost exclusively in a partial equilibrium framework.

Given that you are reading this book, the chances are very good that you have had some economics classes, especially microeconomics classes, already. As a result, you have probably been exposed to the concept of perfect competition—that somewhat utopian vision of markets populated by numerous small firms and characterized by economic efficiency. You are also likely to have read about the most obvious counter example, pure monopoly. The case of a market dominated by one firm alone offers a clear contrast to the ideal of perfect competition. But what happens when the truth lies, as it almost always does, between these two polar extremes? What happens when there are two, or three, or several firms? How do competitive forces play out when each firm faces only a limited number of rivals? Will prices be driven to (marginal) costs, or will advertising and other promotional tactics avert this outcome? Will research and development of new products be the major source of competitive pressure? If so, how do monopolies come about? If firms can obtain monopoly power, can they also devise strategies to maintain such power? Is it possible to keep new competitors from coming into the market?

Industrial organization forms the analytical core that economists use to answer these and many other related questions. Economists long ago worked out the analytics of perfect competition. What happens under the more common setting of imperfect competition—how close to or how far from working like the perfectly competitive market—is much less settled. This less settled domain is the field of industrial organization.

There is a good reason that industrial organization does not yield clear and simple answers regarding what happens in imperfectly competitive markets. When we describe a market as less than perfectly competitive, that still leaves open a wide range of possibilities. It could be a duopoly market with only two firms, or perhaps a market dominated by one large firm competing with many very small ones. The products of the different firms may be identical, as in the case of cement manufacturers, or perhaps highly differentiated, as in the case of cosmetics. Entry by new firms may be easy, as in the restaurant business, or difficult, as in the automobile industry. This variety of possible market characterizations makes it very difficult to make broad, unambiguous statements about imperfectly competitive markets.

Matters become even more complicated when we consider the decisions that the management of an imperfectly competitive firm must make. Start with perhaps a simple case such as a florist setting the price for a dozen roses. Should the price rise on Valentine's Day? Should the price for a dozen be exactly twelve times the price of a single rose? Or should the prospective buyer of flowers get a break if he or she buys in quantity?

Consider Jody Adams, the chef at one of the Boston area's top restaurants, *Rialto*. Jody must choose the complete menu of entrees and appetizers that the restaurant will serve at the start of each season as well as set the price of each menu entry. In making this choice, she must evaluate the cost and availability of different ingredients. For example, what seafood and vegetables are in season and can be served fresh? What price should she set for a la carte items and for the fixed price meal? Should she make available special dishes for those patrons with food allergies? How extensive a wine list should she maintain? These decisions make clear that product design decisions are just as important as pricing decisions. A critical design choice by Microsoft to package its Web browser, *Internet Explorer* with its *Windows* operating system and to sell the two as one product was perhaps the primary reason for *Internet Explorer's* success against *Netscape*. It also played a major role in the government's later decision to pursue antitrust charges against Microsoft.

Price and product design choices are not the only decisions that firms make, however. Another choice concerns promotional effort. For example, in September 2011, the soft-drink giant Pepsi announced that it had completed a new deal as an official sponsor of the National Football League extending from 2012 through the 2022 season. Under this deal, *Pepsi Max* will continue as the official soft drink of the NFL and *Gatorade* will continue its ubiquitous presence along the field sidelines of both teams. Pepsi also keeps the right to use the logos of the Super Bowl and other league properties in ads, signs, and banners. However, the deal is estimated to have cost Pepsi more than $2.3 billion over its ten-year life or a little over $200 million per year. What economic rationale can justify this expenditure?

Somewhat similarly, September 2011 also witnessed the introduction of Amazon's *Kindle Fire* as a direct competitor to Apple's *iPad*. What made this the right time for Amazon's entry into this market? What tactics might Amazon use to insure the success of this venture?

Firms make tough decision like the ones just discussed on a daily basis. Industrial organization economists analyze those decisions and try to derive some predictions from that analysis to help us understand market outcomes. We also try to test those predictions using modern statistical analysis. This is the heart of what industrial organization is.

1.2   HOW WE STUDY INDUSTRIAL ORGANIZATION

One reason that analyzing imperfect competition is difficult is because of the interdependence that characterizes the firms' decisions in their markets. When Amazon introduces the *Kindle Fire*, it has to recognize that this will have a non-trivial effect on the other makers of smart tablets. They may react by cutting prices, or by changing their installed applications, or perhaps by cutting back on production so as to avoid a glut on the market. Similarly, when Pepsi thinks about putting in a high bid to become the National Football League's official soft drink, it has to wonder how Coke will respond. Will it bid even higher or pursue a similar contract with an alternative sports league? Will it instead "punish" Pepsi by launching a price war in the soft drink market?

As these examples indicate, imperfect competition is played out against a background of interdependence or, what economists call, a setting of strategic interaction. This means that determining a firm's optimal behavior can also be difficult. Because the firms are likely to be aware of the interdependency of their actions, each firm will wish to take into account its rivals' response to its action. Yet that response will also depend on how the rivals think the first firm will react to their reaction and so on. A firm in this situation needs to put itself in its rival's shoes to see how the rival will respond to different actions that the firm could take. The firm must do this to figure out what its best course of action is. To understand the logic of strategic interaction, we use game theory. Game theory provides us with the necessary framework for an analysis of settings in which the participants or players recognize that what they do affects other players and, in turn, what other players do affects them. It is for this reason that much of the recent work in industrial organization uses game theory to understand market outcomes under imperfect competition. While not all of the analysis in this book relies on game theory, a good bit of our discussion is aimed at developing and applying the logic of game theory to market settings.

The ability of game theory to permit a clear and logically consistent analysis of strategic interaction makes it an indispensable tool in industrial organization. It is equally important, however, to recognize that game theory and, more generally, the understanding of strategic interaction serves a broader goal of understanding how industrial organization analysis is conducted. This perhaps is best expressed by reference to a quote from John Maynard Keynes who wrote insightfully, "the theory of economics does not furnish a body of settled conclusions immediately applicable to policy. It is a method rather than a doctrine, an

Reality Checkpoint
Show Time!

Perhaps no example of strategic interaction is more common than the annual or even seasonal game television networks play in scheduling their programming. The objective is to get the highest "average audience" rating as calculated by the A. C. Nielsen Company and defined as the percentage of homes with a television that are tuned to a program during an average minute of prime time viewing. This value determines the advertising fees that a network can charge and, hence, is crucial to the network's profit. Indeed, scheduling strategy is understood throughout the broadcast industry as a crucial element in network success and a variety of well-known tactics have emerged over the years. These include: 1) *quick openers*—starting the evening with one's strongest shows to set up the rest of the viewing night; 2) *infant protection*—the avoidance of scheduling promising new shows to compete with strong rival programming and/or using an existing strong network show to serve as a lead-in for the new one; 3) *counterprogramming*—scheduling say a police show in a slot where the major competition is a comedy; and 4) *bridging*—scheduling shows an hour long or longer so that competing shows of an hour's length begin in the middle of the scheduled program.

For a long time, the undisputed ratings champ on network television was Fox's *American Idol*. Recently though, *Idol* has been overtaken by NBC's *The Voice*, a similar musical competition show. Given the popularity of *The Voice* NBC decided to premier its new 2012 series, *Smash*, right after it on Monday nights. In contrast, CBS first moved its popular sitcom, *The Big Bang Theory*, to Thursday nights and then followed that by subsequently moving a second sitcom, *Two-and-a-Half Men*, to Thursday right afterwards. The idea appears to be the creation of a super comedy hour that attracts lots of viewers to CBS's Thursday programming because advertisers highly value that night as the one in which consumers make weekend travel and spending plans.

All of these scheduling tactics though have been thrown into uncertainty with the rise of non-network show producers, such as Netflix and Amazon. In 2013, for example, Netflix offered a new mini-series, *House of Cards*, starring Kevin Spacey. Because this series could be downloaded and "streamed," viewers could watch it on their own schedule—not that set by the networks.

Sources: B. Carter, "For Fox Rivals, 'American Idol' Remains a Schoolyard Bully." *New York Times*, 20 February, 2007, p. C1.
B. Carter, "'The Voice' Keeps Up Super Bowl Momentum; 'Smash' Results Are Mixed," *New York Times*, 7 February, 2012, p. B7.
B. Stelter, B. Carter, and B. Elliott, "'Two and a Half Men' Aims to Lift Thursday," *New York Times*, 17 May, 2012, p. B9.

apparatus of the mind, a technique of thinking which helps its possessor to draw correct conclusions."[1] The same can be said for modern industrial organization. Investigating imperfect competition requires a technique of thinking. To be precise, it requires a way of thinking strategically and applying the insights to market behavior and outcomes.

Of course, no model is a complete description of reality. A complete detailing of each aspect of the actual marketplace would be far too lengthy and unwieldy to be of much use. Instead, any market model is like a road map. It is a deliberate simplification of a very complicated terrain, omitting some features and thereby emphasizing others. The aim of the model is to capture and make transparent the essential features of the interaction among firms. In this light, to say that the real world is more complicated than the model is no criticism. Indeed, if the modeling achieves its aim of making clear the underlying structure and the principles governing the market outcome, then its abbreviated portrait of the real world is its strength.

Whether or not a particular theoretical model is a good proxy for real world outcomes can be determined by testing the predictions of the model against actual data and observational evidence. Armed with ever-increasingly sophisticated statistical techniques, such testing has also become an essential part of the field of modern industrial organization. Throughout this book, you will find numerous Reality Checkpoints designed to illustrate the applicability of the concepts in question. In addition, you will find a number of recent empirical studies offering evidence on the validity of the various models. This combination of theory and evidence provide a useful guide to the likely outcome of strategic interaction in a variety of settings. In each such case studied, the basic interpretation of the model and associated data is that "this is how to think about what happens in an imperfectly competitive market when . . ." This is how we do industrial organization.

1.3   WHY: ANTITRUST AND INDUSTRIAL ORGANIZATION THEORY

The text of the principal US antitrust statutes is given in the Appendix to this chapter. Suffice it to say at this point that such legislation came early to the United States with the passage of the first major antitrust law—the Sherman Act—in 1890. This predates much of the formal modeling of imperfect competition and certainly its dissemination. However, economists had had an intuitive grasp of the potential problems of monopoly power as far back as Adam Smith. In his classic *The Wealth of Nations* (1776), Smith had written on both collusion among ostensibly rival firms and on the raw exercise of monopoly power:

> People of the same trade seldom meet together, even for merriment or diversion, but the conversation ends in a conspiracy against the public, or in some contrivance to raise prices . . .
>   The monopolists, by keeping the market constantly understocked, by never fully supplying the effectual demand, sell their commodities much above the natural price . . . .

Within the United States, a sizable popular sentiment against monopoly became clear in the Jacksonian era. By the second half of the 19th century, this sentiment had grown large enough that political parties officially calling themselves the Anti-Monopoly Party emerged

---

[1]   Keynes (1935).

in many states and even formed a national party in 1884.[2] By this time, many Americans had become convinced that a few large firms and trusts, such as Standard Oil and American Tobacco, had exploited their market power in just the ways Smith had forecast. A consensus emerged—one that has endured throughout the history of antitrust legislation—that some form of legal framework was needed to maintain competition in the market place.

Thus, it was popular sentiment reinforced by shrewd Smithian insight that led to the enactment of the first US antitrust law, the 1890 Sherman Act. Indeed, it is somewhat remarkable just how directly the concerns of Adam Smith are reflected in the two primary sections of the Sherman Act. Section 1 prohibits contracts, combinations, and conspiracies "in restraint of trade." Section 2 makes illegal any attempt to monopolize a market. The view that government institutions were necessary to achieve these aims was also later reflected in the Clayton and Federal Trade Commission Acts.

Antitrust policy, in the beginning, focused primarily on prosecuting and preventing collusive agreements to raise prices under the authority of Section 1. Early cases such as the *Trans-Missouri Freight Association* and the *Addyston Pipe* case of 1897 and 1898, respectively, established this tradition. It remains a centerpiece of antitrust policy to this day,[3] as evidenced by the successful prosecution in the past fifteen years of agricultural products giant Archer Daniels Midland; the world's two largest auction houses, Sotheby's and Christie's, the international pharmaceutical giant Hoffman-LaRoche; the LCD manufacturers AU Optronics, LG Display, and Samsung; and the largest publishing houses with respect to their pricing of e-books.

However, unlike the Section 1 statute, the enforcement of Section 2 on monopolization has been more limited. Despite wide public perception that many of the giant firms emerging from the Industrial Revolution had abused and exploited their monopoly power, it was twelve years before one of these, the Standard Oil Company of New Jersey, was prosecuted under Section 2.[4] That case eventually led to the famous Supreme Court ruling in 1911 that Standard Oil had illegally monopolized the petroleum refining industry. Similar findings against other trusts, including most notably the Tobacco Trust,[5] followed quickly. Yet unlike the price-fixing cases, these monopolization decisions were less clear about what actions were illegal. In particular, the court established a "rule of reason" framework for monopolization cases that permitted the courts to examine not only whether monopolization of an industry had occurred but, if so, what the market context was surrounding the formation of that monopoly and the business practices used to achieve it. Only if this additional inquiry found an explicit intent to monopolize or an obvious exploitation of monopoly power was there a true violation.

Practically speaking, the rule of reason approach meant that there was a lot of ambiguity in exactly what actions were illegal. This had two important results. First, those who feared that such a legal framework might weaken antitrust enforcement were motivated to pursue additional reforms so that Section 2 of the Sherman Act would not become a "paper-toothed tiger."[6] This led in 1914 to the passage of the Clayton Act meant to stop monopolization

---

[2]   See Ritter's (1997) excellent book for a history of the anti-monopoly sentiment in 19th century America.

[3]   *United States v. Trans-Missouri Freight Association* 166 U.S. 290 (1897) and *United States v. Addyston Pipe & Steel Co.*, 85 F. 271 (6 Cir. 1898).

[4]   *Standard Oil Co. of New Jersey v. United States*, 221 U.S. 1 (1911). See also, Posner (1970).

[5]   *United States v. American Tobacco Co.*, U.S. 221 U.S. 106 (1911).

[6]   Berki, Sylvester (1966), ix.

in its incipiency by limiting the use of a number of business practices such as rebates, tying, and exclusive contracts that were used by Standard Oil in establishing its dominance. Section 7, which was later amended in the 1950s, was passed to prevent anticompetitive mergers.

The same fear also led to the passage of the Federal Trade Commission Act in 1914 that established an administrative agency, the Federal Trade Commission (FTC), endowed with powers of investigation and adjudication to handle Clayton Act violations. As later amended, this act also outlawed "unfair methods of competition" and "unfair and deceptive acts or practices." Creation of the FTC gave antitrust policy a second arm of law enforcement in addition to that provided by the Justice Department (DOJ).

The second major result stemming from adoption of a rule of reason approach emerged later with the *U.S. Steel* case of 1920. In that case, the Court made clear that in its view "the law does not make mere size an offense or the existence of unexerted power an offense—it does not compel competition nor require all that is possible."[7] As a result, the Court found U.S. Steel—a firm that through a series of mergers had grown to control over 70 percent of US steel-making capacity—innocent of any antitrust violations.

The U.S. Steel decision had a major impact on both the steel industry and the US legal framework. For our purposes, however, the reason that this case was so important is that it served as a major intellectual stimulus to the field of industrial organization. For the conclusion to which many analysts were led by the 1920 decision was that without a good economic road map by which to understand imperfect competition, the making of antitrust policy was a difficult proposition at best. It was the subsequent effort to provide the road map that initiated the field that we now call industrial organization.

Economists such as Edward Chamberlin (1933) and Edward Mason (1939), both at Harvard, led the way. In their view, the microeconomics of the time offered little guidance either to policy makers or the legal system as to what evidence might be useful in determining the likely outcome that a market would produce. The Supreme Court's dismissal of the government charges of monopolization in the U.S. Steel case was based on an argument that no exploitation of monopoly power or intent to monopolize had been shown. Only U.S. Steel's large market share had been documented and, *"the law does not make mere size an offense"* [emphasis added]. Unless there was good reason to believe that a large market share offered strong evidence of monopolization, or until there was a coherent argument that identified other observable characteristics that in turn implied illegal behavior, the court's decision had a fair bit of justification.

More generally, economists at that time realized that any informed legal judgment would require some practical way to determine from observable evidence whether the industry in question was closer to perfect competition or closer to monopoly. Accordingly, they viewed the highest priority of industrial economics to be the determination of whether and how one could infer illegal behavior from either firm size or other structural features. It was to provide this policy guide that the field of industrial organization began to emerge. The very name of the field—industrial organization—dates from this time.

Early work therefore focused on a set of key questions: how is the production of the industry organized? How is the market structured? How many firms are there and how large are they relative to each other? Are there clear barriers to entry? It was recognized from

---

[7]   *United States v. United States Steel Corporation*, 251 U.S. 417 (1920).

the outset, however, that answering these questions would not be enough to provide the legal framework needed by legislators and courts to determine whether or not the antitrust laws had been violated. Achieving this goal required not only that an industry's structural features be revealed but that clear links between structure and market outcomes also be identified. That is, industrial economists needed to obtain data on prices, profits, and market structure, and then use these data to identify statistical relationships between various market structures, on the one hand, and industrial performance, on the other.

This was the agenda explicitly announced by Edward Mason who in 1939 wrote, "The problem, as I see it, is to reduce the voluminous data concerning industrial organization to some sort of order through a classification of market structures. Differences in market structure are ultimately explicable in terms of technological factors. The economic problem, however, is to explain, through an examination of the structure of markets and the organization of firms, differences in competitive practices including price, production and investment policies."[8] In sum, the early industrial organization economists viewed their goal as one of establishing links between both market structure and the conduct of firms in the market. In turn, that conduct would determine the likely outcome or performance of the market in terms of economic efficiency or general social welfare. For this reason, this early approach is typically referred to as the Structure-Conduct-Performance (or SCP) approach. Presumably, if the outcome for a particular industry given its structure was sufficiently bad, legal action was justified either to alter the conduct that structure would otherwise generate or, if necessary, to change the structure itself.

The basic principle behind the SCP paradigm was that perfect competition and monopoly are usefully viewed as opposite ends of a spectrum of market structures along which all markets lie. One natural measure of market structure is the degree of concentration, or the percentage of market output produced by the largest firms in that industry. Accordingly, the practice of industrial economics at that time became one of, first, accurately describing the structure of different markets and, second, deriving empirical relations between structures and outcomes in terms of price–cost margins, innovative efforts, and other performance measures. Research focused on examining statistically the broad hypotheses on market structure and performance implied by the SCP paradigm. Here, structure was often identified with the degree of concentration or the percentage of total market output accounted for by the few largest firms. Finding a road map for policy was interpreted to mean providing numerical answers to questions such as how much would a bit more concentration or a bit higher entry barriers raise price above cost.

In pursuit of the SCP quest, the 1930s and 1940s witnessed numerous studies attempting to document and to measure the link between industrial performance, say profitability, and an industry's structural features, such as concentration. In some respects, this goal was met. For example, the research appeared to establish a positive link between a measure of industrial concentration and industry profit and a similarly positive link between advertising and profitability. The first finding gave support to the view that an industry in which there was more than one but still just a few large firms was indeed somewhat close to the monopoly pole. The second finding was interpreted as evidence that firms used advertising to build customer loyalty and, thus, to deter other firms from entering the market. In turn, this permitted the incumbent firms to enjoy monopoly power and profit.

---

[8]   Mason (1939), 61–74.

1.3.1   The "New" Sherman Act and the Dominance of Structure-Based Analysis

The early findings of SCP scholars increasingly seemed to suggest that perhaps a firm's "mere size" *could* imply a legal offense if it is sufficiently large. The practical question then became whether or not these developments would influence antitrust law. This question was answered in the affirmative with the 1945 Supreme Court case against Alcoa.

Alcoa was by far the largest aluminum manufacturer in North America. It had been prosecuted for antitrust violations a number of times prior to the 1945 case. In fact, so large a number of Supreme Court justices in 1945 had had previous litigation experience with Alcoa that they could not participate in this proceeding, with the result that the Supreme Court lacked a quorum to hear the case. For this reason, the 1945 decision was issued by a special panel of three circuit court judges. In a key decision, this panel overturned the finding of innocence by the lower district court and found Alcoa guilty of monopolization under Section 2 of the Sherman Act. An explicit consideration for the Court was the issue of size.[9] Alcoa's market share depended critically on how one measured the market, and much attention was given to this issue. Ultimately, the Court defined Alcoa's relevant market to be primary aluminum ingot production. Using this definition, the Court found that Alcoa supplied 90 percent of the market. In effect, this decision was a major policy validation of the SCP approach.

Other cases also reflecting a newly found concern over market domination by large firms soon followed. In 1946, the Supreme Court found the big three tobacco companies—American Tobacco, Ligget & Myers, and R. J. Reynolds, which controlled 75 percent of domestic cigarette production—guilty of monopolization.[10] A number of similar cases continued over the next twenty years, culminating with such well-known ones as the 1962 *Brown Shoe* case and the 1964 case against the Grinnell Corporation. All of these cases gave increasing weight to market structure as an indictment of proposed or past actions.[11] The (in)famous price discrimination case of *Utah Pie* (1967) may also be read as an indictment of any outcome in which a few large firms come to dominate the market.[12] In that case, the Court viewed the pricing strategies of the bigger nationwide companies to be evidence of predatory intent against a smaller firm primarily because the shares of the larger firms grew over a four-year period. In short, the period from 1945 into the late 1960s reflects the growing dominance of the SCP framework as the major intellectual influence on antitrust policy.[13]

1.3.2   The Tide Changes—The Chicago School and Beyond

Matters began to change in the 1970s. In part, this reflected a growing awareness among academic scholars that the SCP paradigm had important failings. One of these was that the vast array of empirical findings that the SCP researchers had amassed was actually subject

---

[9]   *United States v. Aluminum Co. of America (ALCOA)*, 148 F.2d 416 (2 Cir. 1945).
[10]   *American Tobacco Company v. United States*, 328 U.S. 781 (1946).
[11]   *Brown Shoe Co. v. United States*, 370 U.S. 294 (1962) and *United States v. Grinnell Corp.*, 236 F.Supp. 244 (D.R.I. 1964).
[12]   *Utah Pie Co. v. Continental Baking Co., et al.*, 386 U.S. 685 (1967).
[13]   For an excellent survey of antitrust history see Mueller (1996).

to different interpretations. For example, consider the frequent finding that firms with large market shares tend to earn greater profit. This could be taken as a verification of the basic SCP view that the larger a firm's market share, the greater the monopoly power and the higher its profit. However, a more benign interpretation of this evidence is also possible. It could be that the most efficient, or the lowest cost, firm gains the largest share of the market, so that both large size and healthy profit are simply reflections of a firm's superior technology or talent.[14]

What was really unsatisfactory about the SCP approach, however, was that in considering its middle link—firm conduct—little or no attention was paid to strategic interaction. A consideration of strategic interaction forces one to face a critical failure in the SCP paradigm. That failure is that it treats structure as exogenous—a factor that determines firm behavior but is not determined by it. Yet it is clear that firm conduct has important effects on market structure. For example, intense price competition among incumbent firms may make entry unattractive with the result that we may find industries with relatively high concentration to be precisely the industries with competitive pricing—a result not easily squared with the basic SCP approach.

To be sure, some of those working in the SCP tradition—notably Joe Bain (1956)—understood this limitation. Bain, in particular, was among the first who understood that entry considerations had to become a part of industrial economics. This important insight played a central role in the "contestability" theory developed much later by Baumol, Panzar, and Willig (1982). It is however a two-edged sword. The ease with which new firms can enter is at least partially the result of actions taken by the firms already in the market. That is, incumbent firms can pursue strategic actions meant to influence the entry decisions of other, potential rivals. Within the SCP paradigm, one could not easily address this issue.

The weaknesses in the SCP paradigm were accompanied by a discomfort that many felt concerning the more aggressive antitrust enforcements mentioned above. In the *Brown Shoe* case, for example, the Court disallowed the merger of two firms (Brown and Kinney) even though they only controlled about five percent of the national market (though a greater percentage of individual local markets). Similarly, the *Utah Pie* case seemed to be a decision that did more to protect a specific competitor (Utah Pie) than to protect competitive forces.

The rising concern over flaws in both the SCP approach and the public policy it had fostered made possible a counter movement led by lawyers and economists from the Chicago School such as Richard Posner, Robert Bork, and Sam Peltzman. These and other scholars began to point out that many of the practices that the courts had been viewing as harmful to competition and economic welfare could, when viewed through the lens of corporate strategy and tactics, be seen as actually improving economic efficiency and benefitting consumers. This work initially focused on the vertical relationships either between a firm and its suppliers or between a firm and its distributors. Many such vertical contracts include restrictions such as those that grant franchisees exclusive territories,

---

[14]   As shown later, this is a standard result in a Cournot model in which costs differ across firms. Specifically, if P is market price, η is the market demand elasticity at that price, and c_i and s_i are the ith firm's unit cost and market share, respectively, then it must be the case that: $\dfrac{P - c_i}{P} = \dfrac{s_i}{\eta}$. Lower cost firms will have larger market shares, larger profit margins, and larger total profit.

or that require distributors to sell at some minimum price. Chicago School economists argued that there were good economic reasons for these practices and that these restrictions actually brought benefits to consumers. Over time, these arguments were successful and many practices that had been previously found to be *per se* or outright illegal the court now began to review for their "reasonability" on a case-by-case method.[15]

The Chicago School influence on vertical relationships soon spread to more of antitrust policy. In 1974, the US Supreme Court rejected the government's efforts to block a large merger in a case involving the General Dynamics Corporation.[16] Many mergers that would previously have been prevented soon followed, justified on both grounds of cost savings and the potential for new entrants to constrain any attempt by the newly merged firm to exercise monopoly power. The government also lost several key cases accusing large firms such as Kodak and IBM of monopolization in violation of the Sherman Act. In addition, the precedent of the *Utah Pie* case was firmly rejected during these subsequent years. It became increasingly clear—most notably in the case involving a complaint by Zenith Corporation charging that seven Japanese television manufacturers had attempted to drive out competitors—that in the courts' view, efforts to eliminate rivals by pricing below cost rarely made sense.[17]

The Chicago School's contributions are difficult to underestimate and its legal influence is felt to this day. These scholars were right to point out the need to examine the logic and reasonability of a firm's conduct. However, they were hampered by the fact that, as of that time, no language or framework in which to view such strategic behavior on a consistent basis had yet been developed. Yet such a framework was emerging. Building on the work of Von Neumann and Morgenstern (1944) and Nash (1951), Nobel Prize laureates Reinhard Selten, John Harsanyi, Michael Spence, and Thomas Schelling all made a number of crucial contributions that permitted game theory to become the language for modeling strategic interaction. As we noted earlier, the past two decades have witnessed the rapid spread of game theory to analyze virtually every aspect of imperfect competition. As a result, the field of industrial organization has again been transformed and now reflects, at least in part, what some call a post-Chicago view and what others simply refer to as the "new IO."[18]

We have already noted that there is much to be said for pursuing a game-theoretic understanding of the strategic interaction of firms. What is important to note at this point is that it was game theory that allowed us a way to model and analyze firm behavior in imperfectly competitive markets. Moreover, as game theoretic analysis spread through modern industrial organization its insights have, to some extent, led to a diminishment of the Chicago School's impact. However, it would be wrong to identify the advent of game theory models and the new post-Chicago approach as a total rejection of the Chicago School's work. For example, the Merger Guidelines adopted jointly by the Federal Trade Commission and the Justice Department have deep roots in the Cournot-Nash game theoretic model that we describe more fully in Chapter 15. While these guidelines are far

---

[15]   See *Continental T.V. Inc. v. GTE Sylvania, Inc.*, 433 U.S. 36 (1977) and, more recently, *State Oil v.Khan, et al*, 522 U.S. 3 (1997) and *Leegin Creative Leather Products, Inc. v. PSKS, Inc.*, 551 U. S. 877 (2007).

[16]   *United States v. General Dynamics Corp.* 415 U.S. (1974).

[17]   *Matsuhita Electric Industrial Co. v. Zenith Radio Corp.*, 475 U.S. 574 (1986).

[18]   Schmalensee (1988) provides a survey of the then "new IO" that is still relevant. Kovacic and Shapiro (2000) survey the influence of game theory on modern antitrust policy. Kwoka and White (2004) offer a discussion of recent antitrust cases.

from permissive, they still allow for many more mergers than would ever have legally occurred in the "New Sherman Act" years of the 1950s and 1960s.

The major point of this brief review is that since its inception, industrial organization has been associated with antitrust policy. More than that, however, industrial organization has emerged as the locus of work on strategic interaction among firms. In this regard, its goal is to understand business tactics and the market implications of corporate strategies. It therefore provides considerable insight into business life, and to some extent this understanding has become a goal in itself. We want to know how firms compete when they have market power, what implication that competition has, what the role of public policy might be in helping imperfectly competitive markets achieve outcomes closer to the competitive ideal, and what counter-tactics firms may employ. Finding the answers to these questions is why we study industrial organization.

1.4   EMPIRICAL APPLICATION: ANTITRUST AROUND THE GLOBE

As noted, a major motivation for the study of industrial organization on imperfect competition is the insights that it provides for antitrust policy. Industrial organization tools will be useful wherever antitrust is an active concern of government. To what nations does this apply? How extensively and to what depth are antitrust laws applied around the world?

Economist Michael Nicholson (2008) has provided some recent answers to the above questions by creating an Antitrust Law Index measuring the extent of anti-monopoly laws in fifty-two different countries as of 2005. For each of these countries, Nicholson (2008) examines three broad areas of antitrust concern: 1) collusive behavior to raise prices or otherwise restrain trade; 2) abuse of monopoly power such as below-cost pricing to drive out competitors; and 3) mergers. To this he adds a consideration of what remedies the laws specify and whether private parties can initiate antitrust actions. Within each of these areas, Nicholson looks for the presence of explicit laws; the country in question receives a score of 1 if it has such a law and 0 otherwise. For example, if a country has a law requiring (large) firms to pre-notify the authorities that they intend to merge, one point is added to its overall antitrust score while it gets 0 if it does not. Similarly, the presence of an explicit law against price-fixing also results in the award of 1 point. Over all such categories, the highest possible score is 31.

As mentioned, Nicholson (2008) constructs his Antitrust Law Index for fifty-two separate countries. Across these countries the Index ranges in value from 4 in Malta and Chile to 21 in the United States. The median value across all countries is about 14. The full set of index values by country is shown in Table 1.1.

Nicholson (2008) also briefly explores the source of these differences in each country. One point that seems clear is that emerging economies often adopt extensive antitrust laws, especially when they hope to eventually join an international trade group such as the European Union that already has strong antitrust laws. More explicitly, Nicholson presents evidence that the Antitrust Law Index initially falls with GNP, but ultimately rises with it. As a result, small economies and large economies will have a higher Antitrust Law Index than will medium-sized ones.

Table 1.1 Index of antitrust laws around the world; maximum score possible is 32

United States	21	Italy	15	Denmark	12
Ukraine	20	Czech Republic	14	Brazil	11
Turkey	19	Israel	14	Costa Rica	11
Belgium	18	Korea	14	Finland	11
Latvia	18	Slovenia	14	Norway	11
Poland	18	Taiwan	14	Germany	10
Romania	18	Venezuela	14	Jamaica	10
Argentina	17	Zambia	14	New Zealand	10
Lithuania	17	Australia	13	Panama	10
South Africa	17	Canada	13	Sri Lanka	10
Uzbekistan	17	Indonesia	13	Tunisia	10
France	16	Macedonia	13	Japan	9
Ireland	16	Mexico	13	United Kingdom	9
Kenya	16	Peru	13	Yugoslavia	8
Slovakia	16	Spain	13	Netherlands	7
Sweden	16	Thailand	13	Chile	4
Croatia	15	Armenia	12	Malta	4
Estonia	15				

Summary

Industrial organization is the study of imperfect competition. Industrial economists are interested in markets that we actually encounter in the real world. However, these real world markets come in many shapes and flavors. For example, some are comprised of a few large firms; some have one large firm and many smaller ones. In some, the products are greatly differentiated while in others they are nearly identical. Some firms compete largely by trying to keep prices as low as possible. In other markets, advertising and other forms of non-price competition are the dominant tactics. This range of possibilities has meant that over time, industrial organization has become a field rich with practical insights regarding real business behavior and public policy. This book is all about these developments.

Firms in imperfectly competitive industries need to make strategic decisions—that is, decisions that will have an identifiable impact on other participants in the market, be they rival firms, suppliers, or distributors. As a result, making any such choice must inevitably involve some consideration of how these other players in the game will react. Examples of such strategic choice variables include price, product design, decisions to expand capacity, and whether or not to invest heavily in research and development of a new product. This book presents the modern analysis of market situations involving such strategic interaction—an analysis that is rooted in non-cooperative game theory. We use this analysis to examine such issues as why there are so many varieties of cereals, or how firms maintain a price-fixing agreement, or how advertising and product innovation affect the nature of competition. We also describe how the predictions of these models have been tested.

Our interest is more than just determining the profit-maximizing strategies that firms in a particular market context should adopt. As economists we are interested in the market outcomes that result when firms adopt such strategies, and whether those outcomes are close to those of the competitive ideal. If not, we then need to ask whether and how public policy can improve market allocations. Our hope is to convey the value of economic research and the gains from learning "to think like an economist." More generally, we hope to demonstrate the vitality and relevance of industrial organization, both in theory and in practice.

Problems

1. List three markets that you think are imperfectly competitive. Explain your reasoning.

2. Explain why a perfectly competitive market does not reflect a setting of strategic interaction.

3. The Appendix to this chapter lists the current, major antitrust laws of the US. Review Sections 2 and 7 of the Clayton Act. What potential threats to competition do these sections address?

4. Suppose that sophisticated statistical research provides clear evidence that, all else equal, worker productivity increases as industrial concentration increases. How would you interpret this finding?

5. Why do you think that the US courts have consistently disallowed any form of price-fixing agreements among different firms but have been more tolerant of market dominance by one firm?

References

Bain, Joseph. 1956. *Barriers to New Competition*. Cambridge: Harvard University Press.

Baumol, W. J., J. C. Panzar, and R. D. Willig. 1982. *Contestable Markets and the Theory of Market Structure*. New York: Harcourt, Brace, Jovanovich.

Berki, Sylvester, ed. 1996. *Antitrust Policy: Economics and Law*. Boston: D.C. Heath and Company.

Chamberlin, E. H. 1933. *The Theory of Monopolistic Competition*. Cambridge: Harvard University Press.

Keynes, J. M. 1935. *The General Theory of Employment, Interest and Money*. New York: Harcourt Brace and Company.

Kovacic, W. E., and C. Shapiro. 2000. "Antitrust Policy: A Century of Legal and Economic Thinking." *Journal of Economic Perspectives*, 14:43–60.

Kwoka, J. E., and L. J. White. 2004. *The Antitrust Revolution: Economics, Competition, and Policy*. 4th Edition. Oxford: Oxford University Press.

Mason, E. S. 1939. "Price and Production Policies of Large Scale Enterprise." *American Economic Review*, 29:61–74.

Mueller, Dennis C. 1996. "Lessons from the United State's Antitrust History." *International Journal of Industrial Organization*, 14:415–45.

Nash, J. 1951. "Noncooperative Games." *Annals of Mathematics*, 54:286–95.

Nicholson, M. W. 2008. "An Antitrust Law Index for Empirical Analysis of International Competition Policy." *Journal of Competition Law and Economics*, 4 (December): 1009–1029.

Posner, Richard. 1970. "A Statistical Study of Antitrust Enforcement." *Journal of Law and Economics*, 13 (October): 365–419.

Ritter, G. 1997. *Goldbugs and Greenbacks: The AntiMonopoly Tradition and the Politics of Finance in America, 1865–1896*. Cambridge: Cambridge University Press.

Schelling, T. 1959. *The Strategy of Conflict*. New York: Oxford University Press.

Schmalensee, R. 1988. "Industrial Economics: An Overview." *Economic Journal*, 98:643–81.

Smith, A. 1776. *An Inquiry into the Nature and Causes of the Wealth of Nations*. (Reprint). Oxford: Oxford University Press, 1993.

Von Neumann, J., and O. Morgenstern. 1944. *Theory of Games and Economic Behavior*. Princeton: Princeton University Press.

Appendix

Excerpts from Key Antitrust Statutes

THE SHERMAN ACT

Sec. 1. Every contract, combination in the form of trust or otherwise, or conspiracy, in restraint of trade or commerce among the several States, or with foreign nations, is declared to be illegal. Every person who shall make any contract or engage in any combination or conspiracy hereby declared to be illegal shall be deemed guilty of a felony, and, on conviction thereof, shall be punished by fine not exceeding $100,000,000 if a corporation, or, if any other person, $350,000, or by imprisonment not exceeding three years, or by both said punishments, in the discretion of the court.

   Sec. 2. Every person who shall monopolize, or attempt to monopolize, or combine or conspire with any other person or persons, to monopolize any part of the trade or commerce among the several States, or with foreign nations, shall be deemed guilty of a felony, and, on conviction thereof, shall be punished by fine not exceeding $100,000,000 if a corporation, or, if any other person, $350,000, or by imprisonment not exceeding three years, or by both said punishments, in the discretion of the court.

THE CLAYTON ACT, INCLUDING KEY AMENDMENTS OF THE ROBINSON-PATMAN ACT AND CELLER-KEFAUVER ACT

Sec. 2.

(a) Price; selection of customers

It shall be unlawful for any person engaged in commerce, in the course of such commerce, either directly or indirectly, to discriminate in price between different purchasers of commodities of like grade and quality, where either or any of the purchases involved in such discrimination are in commerce, where such commodities are sold for use, consumption, or resale within the United States or any Territory thereof or the District of Columbia or any insular possession or other place under the jurisdiction of the United States, and where the effect of such discrimination may be substantially to lessen competition or tend to create a monopoly in any line of commerce, or to injure, destroy, or prevent competition with any person who either grants or knowingly receives the benefit of such discrimination, or with customers of either of them: Provided, That nothing herein contained shall prevent differentials which make only due allowance for differences in the cost of manufacture, sale, or delivery resulting from the differing methods or quantities in which such commodities are to such purchasers sold or delivered: Provided, however, That the Federal Trade Commission may, after due investigation and hearing to all interested parties, fix and establish quantity limits, and revise the same as it finds necessary, as to particular commodities or classes of commodities, where it finds that available purchasers in greater quantities are so few as to render differentials on account thereof unjustly discriminatory or promotive of monopoly in any line of commerce; and the foregoing shall then not be construed to permit differentials based on differences in quantities greater than those so fixed and established: And provided further, That nothing herein contained shall prevent persons engaged in selling goods, wares, or merchandise in commerce from selecting their own customers in bona fide transactions and not in restraint of trade: And provided further, That nothing herein contained shall prevent price changes from time to time where in response to changing conditions affecting the market for or the marketability of the goods concerned, such as but not limited to actual or imminent deterioration of perishable goods, obsolescence of seasonal goods, distress sales under court process, or sales in good faith in discontinuance of business in the goods concerned.

(b) Burden of rebutting prima-facie case of discrimination

Upon proof being made, at any hearing on a complaint under this section, that there has been discrimination in price or services or facilities furnished, the burden of rebutting the prima-facie case thus made by showing justification shall be upon the person charged with a violation of this section, and unless justification shall be affirmatively shown, the Commission is authorized to issue an order terminating the discrimination: Provided, however, That nothing herein contained shall prevent a seller rebutting the prima-facie case thus made by showing that his lower price or the furnishing of services or facilities to any purchaser or purchasers was made in good faith to meet an equally low price of a competitor, or the services or facilities furnished by a competitor.

(c) Payment or acceptance of commission, brokerage, or other compensation

It shall be unlawful for any person engaged in commerce, in the course of such commerce, to pay or grant, or to receive or accept, anything of value as a commission, brokerage, or other compensation, or any allowance or discount in lieu thereof, except for services rendered in connection with the sale or purchase of goods, wares, or merchandise, either to the other party to such transaction or to an agent, representative, or other intermediary therein where such intermediary is acting in fact for or in behalf, or is subject to the direct or indirect control, of any party to such transaction other than the person by whom such compensation is so granted or paid.

(d) Payment for services or facilities for processing or sale

It shall be unlawful for any person engaged in commerce to pay or contract for the payment of anything of value to or for the benefit of a customer of such person in the course of such commerce as compensation or in consideration for any services or facilities furnished by or through such customer in connection with the processing, handling, sale, or offering for sale of any products or commodities manufactured, sold, or offered for sale by such person, unless such payment or consideration is available on proportionally equal terms to all other customers competing in the distribution of such products or commodities.

(e) Furnishing services or facilities for processing, handling, etc.

It shall be unlawful for any person to discriminate in favor of one purchaser against another purchaser or purchasers of a commodity bought for resale, with or without processing, by contracting to furnish or furnishing, or by contributing to the furnishing of, any services or facilities connected with the processing, handling, sale, or offering for sale of such commodity so purchased upon terms not accorded to all purchasers on proportionally equal terms.

(f) Knowingly inducing or receiving discriminatory price

It shall be unlawful for any person engaged in commerce, in the course of such commerce, to be a party to, or assist in, any transaction of sale, or contract to sell, which discriminates to his knowledge against competitors of the purchaser, in that, any discount, rebate, allowance, or advertising service charge is granted to the purchaser over and above any discount, rebate, allowance, or advertising service charge available at the time of such transaction to said competitors in respect of a sale of goods of like grade, quality, and quantity; to sell, or contract to sell, goods in any part of the United States at prices lower than those exacted by said person elsewhere in the United States for the purpose of destroying competition, or eliminating a competitor in such part of the United States; or, to sell, or contract to sell, goods at unreasonably low prices for the purpose of destroying competition or eliminating a competitor.

Sec. 3.

Sale, etc., on agreement not to use goods of competitor

It shall be unlawful for any person engaged in commerce, in the course of such commerce, to lease or make a sale or contract for sale of goods, wares, merchandise, machinery, supplies, or other commodities, whether patented or unpatented, for use, consumption, or resale within the United States or any Territory thereof or the District of Columbia or any insular possession or other place under the jurisdiction of the United States, or fix a price charged therefore, or discount from, or rebate upon, such price, on the condition, agreement, or understanding that the lessee or purchaser thereof shall not use or deal in the goods, wares, merchandise, machinery, supplies, or other commodity of a competitor or competitors of the lessor seller, where the effect of such lease, sale, or contract for sale or such condition, agreement, or understanding may be to substantially lessen competition or tend to create a monopoly in any line of commerce.

Sec. 7.

No person engaged in commerce or in any activity affecting commerce shall acquire, directly or indirectly, the whole or any part of the stock or other share capital and no person subject to the jurisdiction of the Federal Trade Commission shall acquire the whole or any part of the assets of another person engaged also in commerce or in any activity affecting commerce, where in any line of commerce or in any activity affecting commerce in any section of the country, the effect of such acquisition may be substantially to lessen competition, or to tend to create a monopoly.

2

Basic Microeconomics

Considerable time passed before Adam Smith's original and intuitive insights regarding the nature of market behavior and market outcomes were translated into formal models. It then took even more time for that formal understanding to make its way into a standard professional literature. Yet by the late nineteenth century, a rigorous understanding of the benefits of competition versus monopoly had been established as evidenced in particular by the publication of Alfred Marshall's **Principles of Economics, Vol. 1** (1890). While we are ultimately interested in modeling the gray area that lies between competition and monopoly, a sound understanding of the perfectly competitive and pure monopolized markets is nevertheless quite insightful. Indeed, these models continue to provide useful starting points for interpreting much of what one reads about in the daily business press. They also reveal the primary intellectual force behind public policies designed to limit monopoly power. For all these reasons, we undertake in this chapter a brief review of the basic models of perfect competition and monopoly.

2.1   COMPETITION VERSUS MONOPOLY: THE POLES OF MARKET PERFORMANCE

We focus on firm profit-maximizing behavior and the resultant market outcome that such behavior implies. We take as given the derivation of an aggregate consumer demand for the product that defines the market of interest. This market demand curve describes the relationship between how much money consumers are willing to pay per unit of the good and the aggregate quantity of the good consumed. Figure 2.1 shows an example of a market demand curve—more specifically, a linear market demand curve that can be described by the equation $P = A - BQ$. When we write the demand curve in this fashion with price on the left-hand side, it is often called an inverse demand curve.[1] The vertical intercept A is

---

[1]   The reason for this terminology is that traditionally in microeconomics, we think of quantity demanded as being the dependent variable, (left-hand side of the equation) and price, the independent variable, (right-hand side of the equation). However, when firms choose quantities and price adjusts to clear the market, it is preferable to put market price on the left-hand side, hence, the inverse demand function. Our discussion should make clear that the market demand curve can be thought of as the horizontal summation of the individual demand curve of each consumer. It is not, however, the horizontal summation of the demand curve facing each firm.

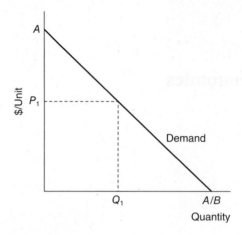

Figure 2.1 Market demand curve

The price P_1 is the marginal consumer valuation of an additional unit of output when current output is Q_1.

the maximum willingness to pay, or maximum reservation demand price that any consumer is willing to pay to have this good. At a market price greater than A, no one in this market wants to buy any of the product. As the market price falls below A, demand for the product increases. For example, if the market price of the good is P_1, then consumers will desire to purchase a quantity Q_1 of the good. Alternatively, we may view P_1 as consumer willingness to pay at the margin. That is, P_1 is the most any consumer would pay for the last or the Q_1th unit of the good.

When we draw a demand curve, we are implicitly thinking of some period of time over which the good is consumed. For example, we may want to look at consumer demand for the product per week, per quarter, or per year. Similarly, when we talk about firms producing the good, we want to consider their corresponding weekly, quarterly, or annual production of the good. The temporal period over which we define consumer demand and firm production typically affects what production technologies are available to the firm for producing the good. The shorter the time period, the fewer options any firm has for altering its production. Following the tradition in microeconomics, we distinguish between two general time periods: the short run and the long run. The short run is a sufficiently short time period for the industry so that no new production facilities—no new plant and equipment—can be brought on line. In the short run, neither the number of firms nor the fixed capital at each firm can be changed. By contrast, the long run is a production period sufficiently long so that firms can build new production facilities to meet market demand.

For either the short-run or the long-run scenario, we are interested in determining when a market is in equilibrium. By this we mean finding an outcome at which the market is "at rest." A useful interpretation of a market equilibrium is a situation in which no consumer and no firm in the market has an incentive to change its decision on how much to buy or how much to sell. To be sure, the precise meaning of this definition may vary depending on whether we consider the short run or the long run. Yet in either case, the essential feature is the same. Equilibrium requires that no one has an incentive to change his or her trading decision.

2.1.1   Perfect Competition

A perfectly competitive firm is a "price taker." The price of its product is not something that the perfectly competitive firm chooses. Instead, that price is determined by the interaction of all the firms and consumers in the market for this good, and it is beyond the influence of any one of the perfectly competitive firms. This characterization only makes sense if each firm's potential supply of the product is "small" relative to market demand for the product. If a firm's supply of a good were large relative to the market, we would expect that that firm could influence the price at which the good was sold. An example of a "small" firm would be a wheat farmer in Kansas or, alternatively, a broker on the New York Stock Exchange trading IBM stock. Each is so small that any feasible change in their behavior leaves the prices of wheat and IBM stock, respectively, unchanged.

Because a perfectly competitive firm cannot influence the market price at which the good trades, the firm perceives that it can sell as much, or as little, as it wants to at that price. If the firm cannot sell as much as it wants to at the market price, then the implication is that selling more would require a fall in the price. Because this would imply that the firm has some power over the market price, such a firm would not be a perfect competitor. The fact that the firm cannot affect the market price also means that its actions do not affect other producers. In turn, this means that perfectly competitive firms do not strategically interact with any of their numerous rivals.

Because the output decision of a perfectly competitive firm does not affect the going price, a graph of the inverse demand curve facing such a firm appears as a horizontal line at the current market price. No matter how much or how little the firm produces, that price remains unchanged. Note that this is the case even though the market demand curve describing the demand faced by the entire industry is downward-sloping.[2] That market demand curve indicates that if the aggregate output of all firms increases in any material way, the market price will fall. Again, though, the distinguishing feature of a perfectly competitive firm is that it is so small that its output choice has no such material impact on total industry output—or where the industry is on the market demand curve.

Like all firms, the perfectly competitive ones will each choose that output level which maximizes their individual profit. Profit is defined as the difference between the firm's revenue and its total costs. Revenue is just market price, P, times the firm's output, q. The firm's total cost is assumed to rise with the level of the firm's production according to some function, $C(q)$. It is important to understand that the firm's costs include the amount necessary to pay the owners of the firm's capital (that is, its stockholders) a normal or competitive return. This is a way of saying that input costs are properly measured as opportunity costs. That is, each input must be paid at least what that input could earn in its next best alternative employment. This is true for the capital employed by the firm as much as it is true for the labor and raw materials that the firm also uses. Generally speaking, the opportunity cost for the firm's capital is measured as the rate of return that the capital could earn if invested in other industries. This cost is then included in our measure of total cost, $C(q)$. In other words, the concept of profit we are using is that of economic profit. It reflects net revenue above what is necessary to pay all of the firm's inputs at least what they could

---

[2] This follows from the definition of a perfect competitor. One may wonder how each firm can face a horizontal demand curve while industry demand is downward sloped. The answer is that the demand curve facing the industry reflects the summation of the individual demand presented by each consumer—not the individual demand facing each firm.

earn in alternative employment. This point is important because it makes clear that when a firm earns no economic profit it does not mean that its stockholders go away empty-handed. It simply means that those stockholders do not earn more than a normal return on their investment.

A necessary first order condition for profit maximization is that the firm chooses an output level such that the revenue received for the last unit produced, or the marginal revenue, just equals the cost incurred to produce that last unit, or the marginal cost. This condition for profit maximization holds for the output choice of any firm, be it a perfectly competitive one, or a monopoly. Since total revenue depends on the amount produced, marginal revenue is also dependent on q as described by the marginal revenue function, $MR(q)$. Because the perfectly competitive firm can sell as much as it likes at the going market price, each additional unit of output produced and sold generates additional revenue exactly equal to the current market price. That is, the marginal revenue function for a competitive firm is just $MR(q) = P$. Similarly, because total cost is a function of total output, q, the marginal cost function also depends on q, according to the function $MC(q)$. This function describes the additional cost incurred by the firm for each successive unit of output produced.

Diagrams like those shown in Figures 2.2(a) and 2.2(b), respectively, are often used to illustrate the standard textbook model of the perfectly competitive firm and the perfectly competitive market in which the firm sells. For any market to be in equilibrium, the necessary condition mentioned earlier must hold for each firm. For a competitive market, this means that for each firm the price received for a unit of output exactly equals the cost of producing that output at the margin. This condition is illustrated in Figures 2.2(a) and 2.2(b). The initial industry demand curve is D_1 and the market price is P_C. A firm producing output q_C incurs a marginal cost of production $MC(q_C)$ just equal to that price. Producing one more unit would incur an extra cost, as indicated by the marginal cost curve MC that exceeds the price at which that unit would sell. Conversely, producing less than q_C would save less in cost than it would sacrifice in revenue. When the firm produces q_C and sells it at market price, P_C, it is maximizing profit. It therefore has no incentive to change its choice of output. Hence, in a competitive equilibrium each firm must produce at a point where its marginal cost is just equal to the price.

Total market supply, Q_C, is the sum of each firm's output, q_C. Because each firm is maximizing profit, the condition $P = MC(q_C)$, will hold for each firm. If demand for the product increases and the market price rises to say P_1, each firm will revise its production decision and increase output to q_1, where $P_1 = MC(q_1)$. This will increase total production to Q_1. Indeed, because the firms' production decisions are governed by costs at the margin, the marginal cost curve of each firm provides the basis for determining the total industry supply at any given market price. As the price rises, we work out how each firm adjusts its profit-maximizing output by moving up its marginal cost function to a point where $P = MC(q)$ at this new price. Then we add up all the firms' revised decisions and compute the total output now supplied. Repeating this exercise for various prices reveals the industry supply function indicating the total output supplied at any given market price. It is illustrated by the curve S_1 in Figure 2.2(b). Because for each firm price is equal to its marginal cost, it must be the case that at each point on the supply function for every firm the incremental cost of the last unit produced is just equal to that price.

Consider a simple linear example where each firm's marginal cost curve is linear instead of curved, as shown in Figure 2.2(a). Specifically, let the marginal cost of each firm be: $MC(q) = 4q + 8$. Given a market price P, the optimal output for any one competitive firm

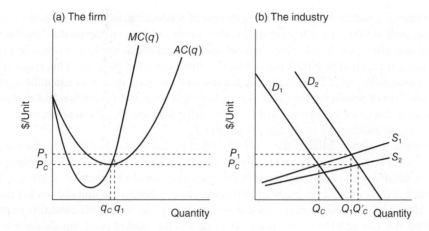

Figure 2.2   The long-run competitive equilibrium

Price P_1 is consistent with a short-run equilibrium in which each firm produces at a point where its marginal cost is equal to P_1. However, at P_1 price exceeds average cost and each firm earns a positive economic profit. This will encourage entry by new firms, shifting out the supply curve as shown in (b). The long-run competitive equilibrium occurs at price P_C, in which each firm produces output level q_C and price equals both average and marginal cost.

is then q such that $4q + 8 = P$, implying that the optimal output for each such firm satisfies $q = \dfrac{P}{4} - 2$.

If there are 80 such firms, total industry production Q at price P is 80 times q or $Q^S = 20P - 160$. Solving for P writes the resultant supply curve in the form implied by Figures 2.2(a) and 2.2(b) in which price appears on the vertical axis. This yields $P = 0.05Q^S + 8$. At a price of 8 or less, each firm will produce zero output. Industry output will also be zero. A rise in P to 12 will induce each firm to raise its output to 1 unit, increasing industry output to 80. A further rise to $P = 16$ will lead every firm to raise its output to 2 units, implying a total supply of 160. We could repeat this exercise many times over, each time choosing a different price. Plotting the industry output against each such price yields the industry supply curve. The important point to understand is that the derivation of that supply curve reflects the underlying first order condition for profit maximization—that is, each competitive firm choose a profit-maximizing level of output such that $P = MC(q)$.

In the example shown in Figures 2.2(a) and 2.2(b), the market initially clears at the price, P_C. Given the demand curve D_1, this equilibrium is consistent with the first order condition that each firm produce an output such that $P = MC(q)$. The requirement that each firm produces where marginal cost equals the market price is almost all that is required for a competitive equilibrium in the short run.[3] However, there is an additional condition that must be met in order for this to be a long-run competitive equilibrium. The condition is that in a long-run equilibrium, each firm earns zero economic profit. This condition is also met in the initial equilibrium illustrated in Figure 2.2(a).

---

[3]   We say almost because there may be a distinction between average variable cost and marginal cost. No production will occur at all in the short run if the firm cannot produce at a level that will cover its average variable cost.

At output q_C, each firm is just covering its cost of production, including the cost of hiring capital as well as labor and other inputs. In other words, a long-run competitive equilibrium requires that firms just "break even" and not earn any economic profit—revenue in excess of the amount required to attract the productive inputs into the industry. This requirement can be stated differently. In the long run, the price of the good must just equal the average or per unit cost of producing the good. Again, both this zero-profit condition and the further requirement that price equal marginal cost are satisfied in the initial equilibrium in which the industry demand curve is D_1 and the price is P_C.

If demand suddenly shifts to the level described by the demand curve, D_2, the existing industry firms will respond by increasing output. In so doing, these firms maximize profit by again satisfying the basic requirement that they each produce where $P = MC(q)$. This leads each firm to expand its production from q_C to q_1, thereby raising the market output to Q_1. However, this short-run response does not satisfy the zero profit condition required for a long-run competitive equilibrium. At price P_1, the market price equals each firm's marginal cost but exceeds each firm's average cost. Hence, each firm earns a positive economic profit of $P_1 - AC(q_1)$ on each of the q_1 units it sells.

Such profit either induces new firms to enter the industry or existing firms to expand production. This expansion shifts the industry supply curve outward until the equilibrium price again just covers average cost. Figure 2.2(b) illustrates this by the shift in the industry supply curve to S_2. As drawn, this shift reestablishes the initial price, P_C. Each firm again produces output q_C at which the industry price equals both the firm's marginal cost and its average cost. Of course, total industry output is now higher at Q'_C. While each firm is producing the output q_C, there are now more firms. These examples illustrate a central element in our definition of an equilibrium—namely, that no firm has the incentive to change its production plan. In the long run, this includes the idea that no firm wishes either to leave or to enter the market.

2.1

Practice Problem

Assume that the manufacturing of cellular phones is a perfectly competitive industry. The market demand for cellular phones is described by a linear demand function: $Q^D = \dfrac{6000 - 50P}{9}$. There are fifty manufacturers of cellular phones. Each manufacturer has the same production costs. These are described by long-run total and marginal cost functions of $TC(q) = 100 + q^2 + 10q$, and $MC(q) = 2q + 10$.

a. Show that a firm in this industry maximizes profit by producing $q = \dfrac{P - 10}{2}$.
b. Derive the industry supply curve and show that it is $Q^S = 25P - 250$.
c. Find the market price and aggregate quantity traded in equilibrium.
d. How much output does each firm produce? Show that each firm earns zero profit in equilibrium.

2.1.2   Monopoly

In a perfectly competitive market, each firm's production of the good is tiny relative to the market total. What would happen, though, if all of these tiny sellers become consolidated into one firm, i.e., what would happen if the market were monopolized? Because this

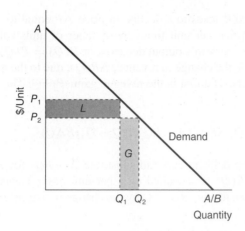

Figure 2.3   The marginal revenue from increased production for a monopolist

An increase in production from Q_1 to Q_2 causes a gain in revenues approximated by area G, and a loss in revenues approximated by area L. The net change or marginal revenue is therefore $G - L$. Note, because the firm is a monopolist, this is also the net revenue gain generated by cutting the price from P_1 to P_2.

single firm would be the only supplier of the good, its demand curve is identical with the market demand curve. In complete contrast to the competitive firm, this monopoly firm can decisively influence the price in this market because its choices decisively alter the total supply. Recognizing this effect, the monopolist's profit-maximizing behavior will differ from that of a competitive firm and so will change the market equilibrium.

Because the monopolist's demand curve slopes downward, any increased production by the monopolist will lead to a price reduction. Consider, for instance, Figure 2.3. Here, a monopolist who is considering selling either Q_1 or Q_2 units faces the following dilemma. If production is restricted to Q_1 units, the market price will be P_1. If instead production is set at Q_2 however, the market price will fall to P_2. Accordingly, the monopolist is very different from the competitive firm that reckons that every additional unit sold will bring in revenue equal to the current market price. Instead, the monopolist knows that every unit sold will bring in marginal revenue less than the existing price. Because the additional output can be sold only if the price declines, the marginal revenue from an additional unit sold is not market price but something less.

In Figure 2.3, the components of marginal revenue for a monopolist are illustrated by the shaded areas G and L. These areas reflect the two forces affecting the monopolist's revenue when the monopolist increases output from Q_1 to Q_2, and thereby causes the price to fall from P_1 to P_2. Area G is equal to the new price P_2 times the rise in output, $Q_2 - Q_1$. It is the revenue gain that comes from selling more units. Area L equals the amount by which the price falls, $P_1 - P_2$, times the original output level, Q_1. This reflects the revenue lost on the initial Q_1 units as a result of cutting the price to P_2. The net change in the monopolist's revenue is the difference between the gain and the loss, or $G - L$.

We can be more precise about this. Let $\Delta Q = Q_2 - Q_1$, and $\Delta P = P_1 - P_2$. The slope of the monopolist's (inverse) demand curve may then be expressed as $\dfrac{\Delta P}{\Delta Q}$. If we describe this demand curve (which of course is also the market demand curve) as a linear relation, $P = A - BQ$, that slope is also equal to the term, $-B$, i.e., $\dfrac{\Delta P}{\Delta Q} = -B$. In other words, an increase in output ΔQ^4 leads to a decline in price ΔP equal to $-B\Delta Q$. Because total revenue is defined as price per unit times the number of units sold, we can write total revenue as a function of the firm's output decision, or $R(Q) = P(Q)Q = (A - BQ)Q$. As just shown in Figure 2.3, the change in revenue, $\Delta R(Q)$, due to the increase in output, ΔQ, is the sum of two effects. The first is the revenue gain, $P_2\Delta Q$. The second is the revenue loss, $Q_1\Delta P$. Hence,

$$\Delta R(Q) = P_2\Delta Q - Q_1\Delta P = (A - BQ_2)\Delta Q - Q_1(B\Delta Q) \tag{2.1}$$

where we have used the demand curve to substitute $A - BQ_2$ for P_2 in the first term on the right-hand side. $MR(Q)$ is measured on a per-unit basis. Hence, we must divide the change in revenue shown in equation (2.1) by the change in output, ΔQ, to obtain marginal revenue. This yields

$$MR(Q) = \frac{\Delta R(Q)}{\Delta Q} = A - BQ_2 - BQ_1 \approx A - 2BQ \tag{2.2}$$

Here we have used the approximation, $B(Q_1 + Q_2) \approx 2BQ$. This will be legitimate so long as we are talking about small changes in output, i.e., so long as Q_2 is fairly close to Q_1.

Equation (2.2)—sometimes referred to as the "twice as steep rule"—is very important, and we will make frequent reference to it throughout the text. It not only illustrates that the monopolist's marginal revenue is less than the current price but, for the case of linear demand, also demonstrates the precise relationship between price and marginal revenue. The equation for the monopolist's marginal revenue function, $MR(Q) = A - 2BQ$, has the same price intercept A as the monopolist's demand curve but twice the slope, $-2B$ versus just $-B$. In other words, when the market demand curve is linear, the monopolist's marginal revenue curve starts from the same vertical intercept as that demand curve, but is everywhere twice as steeply sloped. It follows that the monopolist's marginal revenue curve must then lie everywhere below the inverse demand curve.

In Figure 2.4, we show both the market demand curve and the corresponding marginal revenue curve facing the monopolist. Again, profit maximization requires that a firm produce up to the point where the marginal revenue associated with the last unit of output just covers the marginal cost of producing that unit. This is true for the monopoly firm as well as for the perfectly competitive firm. The key difference here is that for the monopoly firm, marginal revenue is less than price. For the monopoly firm, the profit-maximizing rule of marginal revenue equal to marginal cost, or $MR(Q) = MC(Q)$, holds at the output Q_M. The monopolist therefore produces at this level and sells each unit at the price P_M. Observe that, at this output level, the revenue received from selling the last unit of output MR is less than the price at which that output is sold, $MR(Q_M) < P_M$. It is this fact that leads the monopolist to produce an output below the (short-run) equilibrium output of a competitive industry, Q_C.

We have also drawn the average cost function for the monopoly firm in Figure 2.4. The per-unit cost of producing output Q_M, described on the average cost curve by $AC(Q_M)$, is less than the price P_M at which the monopolist sells the good. This means, of course, that

---

4   Under perfect competition, firm output is different from industry output. So we use a lower case q to refer to firm output and an upper case Q for industry output. Under monopoly, firm output is the market output and so we use Q to describe both.

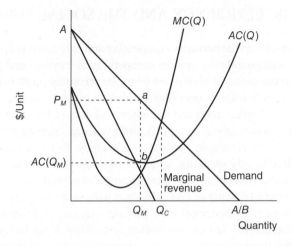

Figure 2.4   The textbook monopoly case

The monopolist maximizes profit by choosing the output, Q_M, at which marginal revenue equals marginal cost. The price at which this output can be sold is identified by the demand curve as P_M, which exceeds marginal cost. Profit is $P_M abAC(Q_M)$. The competitive industry would have instead produced Q_C, at which point price equals marginal cost.

total revenue exceeds total cost, and the monopolist earns a positive economic profit. This profit is shown as the rectangle $P_M abAC(Q_M)$. Furthermore, because the monopolist is the only firm in this market, and because we assume that no other firm can enter and supply this good, this market outcome is a long-run equilibrium. Each consumer buys as much as he wants to at price P_M and, given these cost demand conditions, the monopolist has no incentive to sell more or to sell less.

2.2

Suppose that the cellular phone market described in Practice Problem 2.1, is monopolized. The monopolist has 50 identical plants to run, each with the same cost function as described in that problem. Hence, the marginal cost function for the multiplant monopolist[5] is described by $MC(Q) = 10 + Q/25$. The market demand is also assumed to be the same as in Practice Problem 2.1. Recall $Q^D = \dfrac{6000 - 50P}{9}$

a.   Show that the monopolist's marginal revenue function is $MR(Q) = 120 - 18Q/50$.
b.   Show that the monopolist's profit-maximizing output level is $Q_M = 275$. What price does the monopolist set to sell this level of output?
c.   What is the profit earned at each one of the monopolist's plants?

Practice Problem

---

[5]   Cost minimization for any multiplant firm requires that the marginal unit be produced at the plant with the lowest marginal cost. With divisible output, this implies that the profit-maximizing monopolist will want to allocate total production across the fifty plants in such a way that the marginal cost of producing the last unit of output is the same in each plant. Therefore, the monopolist derives the overall marginal cost function in a manner similar to how we constructed the supply function for the competitive industry. See Chapter 4, footnote 3 and the Appendix.

2.2   ECONOMIC EFFICIENCY AND THE SOCIAL SURPLUS

Now that we have described the perfectly competitive and pure monopoly market outcomes, it is time to try to understand why perfect competition is extolled and pure monopoly is judged harshly by economists. In both cases firms are driven by profit maximization. Also, in both cases the firms sell to consumers who decide how much they want to buy at any given price. What makes one market good and the other market not? The answer to this question does not reflect any concern about too much profit or firms "ripping off" consumers. The answer instead lies in the economic concept of efficiency. In economics, efficiency has a very precise meaning. Briefly speaking, a market outcome is said to be efficient when it is impossible to find some small change in the allocation of capital, labor, goods, or services that would improve the well being of one individual without hurting any others.[6] If the only way we can make somebody better off is by making someone else worse off, then there is really no slack or inefficiency in how the market is working. If, on the other hand, we can imagine changes that would somehow allow one person to have more goods and services while nobody else has less, then the current market outcome is not efficient. As it turns out, that is precisely the case for a monopolized market. One can think of changes to the monopoly outcome that would yield more for at least one individual and no less for any other.

It is readily apparent that to implement our efficiency criterion we need some measure of how well off consumers and firms are in any market outcome. For this purpose, we use the notions of consumer surplus and producer surplus. The consumer surplus obtained from consuming one unit of the good is defined as the difference between the maximum amount a consumer is willing to pay for that unit and the amount the consumer actually does pay. Total consumer surplus in a market is then measured by summing this difference over each unit of the good bought in the market. Analogously, the producer surplus obtained from producing a single unit of the good is the difference between the amount the seller receives for that unit of the good and the cost of producing it. Total producer surplus in a market is then measured by summing up this difference over each unit of the good sold.

2.2.1   Economic Efficiency and Surplus in a Competitive Market

We illustrate these concepts in Figure 2.5. In the competitive outcome, Q_C units of the good are bought and sold. The maximum amount a consumer is willing to pay for the last unit, the Q_Cth unit, is just the equilibrium price P_C. However, the maximum amount a consumer is willing to pay for the first, the second, the third, and so on, up to the Q_Cth unit is greater than P_C. We know this because, at a given sales volume, the demand curve is a precise measure of the maximum amount any consumer is willing to pay for one more unit. Hence, the area under the demand curve but above the market equilibrium price P_C is surplus to consumers. It is a measure of how much they were willing to pay less what they actually did pay in the competitive outcome. This is shown in Figure 2.5 as area *abc*.

---

[6]   This notion of efficiency is often referred to as Pareto Optimality after the great Italian social thinker of the late nineteenth and early twentieth centuries, Vilfredo Pareto.

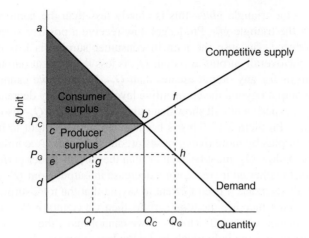

Figure 2.5   Competition maximizes the total surplus

At the competitive price P_C and output Q_C, consumers enjoy a surplus equal to triangle *abc*. Producers enjoy a surplus equal to triangle *cbd*. This is the maximum. Producing less would lose some of the total surplus given by triangle *abd*. Subsidizing production to output Q_G reduces the price to P_G. The required subsidy is *gfh*. Consumers gain additional surplus *cbge*. However, this amount represents a transfer of surplus from producers to consumers and thus, no net gain in total surplus. Consumers also gain the triangle *gbh*, but this is more than offset by the funds required for the needed subsidy. The remaining part of the subsidy equal to triangle *bfh* is a deadweight loss as resources valued more highly in alternative uses are transferred to the industry in question where the marginal value of output is only P_G.

For competitive producers, the supply curve tells us the marginal cost of producing each unit.[7] Similar to consumer surplus, we can construct a measure of producer surplus. For each unit of the good sold, producer surplus is measured by the difference between market price P_C and the corresponding reservation supply price on the supply curve. By adding up this difference for each value of output up to the competitive output, we obtain total producer surplus. This is illustrated by the area *cbd* in Figure 2.5.

Note that when the equilibrium quantity, Q_C, of the good is produced and sold at price P_C, the total surplus or welfare to consumers and producers is given by the area *abd*.[8]

Suppose that an output greater than Q_C, say Q_G, was produced in this market. For consumers to buy this quantity of the good, the price must fall to P_G. This rise in production and sales results in an increase in consumer surplus. Specifically, consumer surplus increases to *aeh*. Producer surplus, however, falls. Moreover, it falls by more than the increase in consumer surplus. Much of the rise in consumer surplus that results from moving to output Q_G—in particular, the shaded area *cbge*—is not an increase in total surplus. It simply reflects a transfer of surplus from producers to consumers. As for the additional increase in

---

7   Again, remember that the market supply curve is the horizontal summation of each competitive firm's marginal cost curve, and so the supply curve tells us exactly what is the opportunity cost to the firm of producing and selling each unit of the good.

8   Observe that the unit of measurement of the areas of consumer and producer surplus is the dollar. To work out the areas you must take $/unit, as measured on the vertical axis, times units on the horizontal axis. This gives you a measure in dollars, which is a money measure of the welfare created by having this good produced at output level Q_C and sold at price P_C.

consumer surplus—the triangle *gbh*—this is clearly less than the additional decrease in producer surplus—the triangle *gfh*. Producers now receive a positive surplus only on the first Q' units produced. Because the gain in consumer surplus is less than the loss in producer surplus, the overall surplus at output Q_G is less than that at output Q_C. It is easy to repeat this analysis for any output greater than Q_C. In short, we cannot increase total surplus by raising output beyond the competitive level; we can only decrease it.

A similar thought experiment will show that output levels below Q_C also reduce the total surplus (see Practice Problem 2.3). This is because restricting output to be less than Q_C reduces consumer surplus by more than it raises producer surplus. Accordingly, the overall surplus at an output below Q_C must be smaller than the surplus under perfect competition. Note that saying that neither an increase nor a decrease in output from Q_C can increase the total surplus but only decrease it is equivalent to saying that the total surplus is maximized at Q_C. Yet if we cannot increase the total surplus then we cannot make anyone better off without making someone worse off. That is, if we cannot make the size of the pie bigger, we can only give more to some individuals by giving less to others. Because this is the case under perfect competition, the perfectly competitive output is efficient.[9]

2.3

Practice Problem

Return to the cellular phone industry when it was organized as a perfectly competitive industry. Use the information in Practice Problem 2.1 to work out consumer surplus and producer surplus in a competitive equilibrium.

a. Show that when $Q^C = 500$ units and $P^C = \$30$ per unit then consumer surplus is equal to \$22,500 and producer surplus is equal to \$5,000. This results in a total surplus equal to \$27,500.
b. Show that when an output of 275 units is produced in this industry, the sum of consumer and producer surplus falls to \$21,931.25.

2.2.2   The Monopolist and the Social Surplus

Now consider the monopoly outcome. If this is inefficient, it must be possible to show that by producing an output level different from the monopoly output Q_M, the total surplus rises. The way to show this is similar to the solution to Practice Problem 2.3 and is shown in Figure 2.6. This figure shows the competitive output and price, Q_C and P_C respectively, much as in Figure 2.5. However, in Figure 2.6 we also show what happens when the industry is monopolized. The monopolist produces output Q_M and sets price P_M. Consumer surplus is then the triangle *jax*. The monopolist's profit at Q_M is measured by area *jxzk*. The sum of these two surpluses is *axzk*. This is clearly smaller than the area *ayk*, which measures the total surplus obtained in the perfectly competitive outcome.

It is worth noting that while the total surplus is greater under perfect competition than it is under monopoly, the opposite holds true for producer surplus. True, a move from monopoly to competition gains the producer surplus *wyz*. But to achieve this gain requires

---

[9] We focus here on the concept of allocational or static efficiency, in which we examine the best way to allocate resources for the production of a given set of goods and services with a given technology. Dynamic efficiency, which considers the allocation of resources so as to promote the development of new goods and new production techniques, is addressed explicitly in Chapter 20.

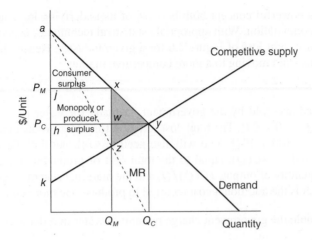

Figure 2.6   The deadweight loss of monopoly

The monopolist produces Q_M units and sells each at price P_M. A competitive industry produces Q_C units and each sells at a price of P_C. The deadweight loss caused by a move from competition to monopoly is triangle *xyz*.

setting the competitive price P_C and the consequent loss of the firm's surplus, *hjxw*. The loss is greater than the gain.

Note that the reduction in consumer surplus that monopoly causes is not purely the result of an increase in the monopolist's surplus. Quite the contrary, the decline in total surplus alerts us to the fact that the monopolist's gain is less than the consumer's loss. In other words, as a result of moving from a competitive industry to one of monopoly, consumers lose more than the profit that the monopolist earns. They also lose an additional amount—the area *xwy* in Figure 2.6—beyond that part of their surplus that is transferred to the monopolist.

The area of the shaded triangle *xyz* is an exact measure of inefficiency under monopoly. The upper boundary of this triangle comprises points that lie on the consumers' demand curve. Every point on this boundary indicates the marginal value that consumers place on successive increases in output beyond Q_M. The lower boundary of this triangle traces out the marginal cost of producing this additional output. The triangle *xyz* thus reflects all the trades that generate a surplus but that do not take place under monopoly. Within this triangle, the price that consumers would willingly pay exceeds the cost of producing extra units, and this difference is the surplus lost—that is, earned by no one—due to monopolization of the industry. If this additional output were produced, there would be a way to distribute it and make one person better off without lowering the profit of the monopolist or the welfare of any other individual. The triangle *xyz* is often referred to as the deadweight loss of monopoly. It is also a good approximation of the gains to be had by restructuring the industry to make it a competitive one.

Again, it is worth repeating that the deadweight loss in Figure 2.6 is not due to the excess profit of the monopolist. From the viewpoint of economic efficiency, we do not care whether the surplus generated in a market goes to consumers—as it does under perfect competition—or to producers. The welfare triangle in Figure 2.6 is a loss because it reflects the potential surplus that would have gone to someone—consumers or producers—had the efficient output been produced. It is not the division of the surplus but its total amount that is addressed by economic efficiency.

Efficiency is a powerful concept both because of its underlying logic and because it is open to explicit computation. With appropriate statistical techniques, economists can try to calculate the deadweight loss of Figure 2.6 for a given industry. Hence, they can estimate the potential gains from moving to a more competitive market.

2.4

Practice Problem

Water is produced and sold by the government. Demand for water is represented by the linear function $Q = 50 - 2P$. The total cost function for water production is also a linear function: $TC(Q) = 100 + 10Q$. You will also need to work out both the average cost of production, denoted by $AC(Q)$, equal to the total cost of producing a quantity of output divided by that quantity of output, $TC(Q)/Q$, and the marginal cost of production, denoted by $MC(Q)$, which is the additional cost incurred to produce one more unit.

a. What fee should the government charge per unit of water in order to reach the efficient allocation?

b. How much should it charge if it wishes to maximize profit from the sale of water?

c. What is the value of the efficiency loss that results from charging the price in part b rather than the price determined in part a?

2.3   INTERTEMPORAL CONSIDERATIONS AND CONSTRAINTS ON MONOPOLY POWER

Both the competition and the monopoly models described in the previous section are somewhat vague with respect to time. While some distinction is made between the short run and the long run, neither concept explicitly confronts the notion of a unit of time such as a day, a week, a month, or a year, or of how many such units constitute say, the long run. To maximize profit in the long run requires, for example, only that the firm make all necessary adjustments to its inputs in order to produce at the optimum level, and then repeatedly choose this input–output combination in every individual period. From the standpoint of decision making then, the long run is envisioned as a single market period and the assumption that the firm will seek to maximize profit is unambiguous in its meaning.

However, the recognition that the long run is a series of individual, finite time periods extending far into the future also raises the possibility that each such period will not be the same. The choice may well be between taking an action that yields profit immediately versus taking an action that yields perhaps greater profit but not until many periods later. In such a setting, the meaning of maximizing profit is less clear. Is it better or worse to have more profit later and less profit now? How does one compare profit in one period with profit in another? Such questions must be answered if we are to provide a useful analysis of the strategic interaction among firms over time.

Sacrificing profit today means incurring a cost. Hence, the problem just described arises anytime that a cost is incurred in the present in return for benefits to be realized much later. Firms often face such a trade-off. A classic example is the decision to build a new manufacturing plant. If the plant is constructed now, the firm will immediately incur the expense of hiring architects and construction workers and the buying of building materials, machinery, and equipment. It will only be sometime later—after the plant is built and running smoothly—that the firm will actually begin to earn some profit or return on this investment.

2.3.1   Discounting, Present Value, and Intertemporal Trades

In order to understand how firms make decisions in which the costs and benefits are experienced not just in one period but instead over time, we borrow some insights from financial markets. After all, the comparison of income received (or foregone) at different points in time is really what financial markets are all about. Think for a moment. If one buys some stock in, say, Microsoft, one has to give up some funds today—namely, the price of a share in Microsoft times the number of shares bought. Of course, investors do this every day. Thousands of Microsoft shares are bought every day of the week. These investors are thus sacrificing some of their current wealth—which could alternatively be used to purchase a Caribbean vacation, wardrobe, or other consumer goods—to buy these shares. Why do investors do this? The answer is that they do so in the expectation that those shares will pay dividends and will also appreciate in value over time. That is, stockholders buy shares of stock and incur the associated investment expense now, in the hope that the ownership of those shares will generate income later in the form of dividends and capital gains.

In short, the financial markets are explicitly involved in trading current for future income. Accordingly, we can use the techniques of those markets to evaluate similar trades of current versus future profit that a firm might make. The key insight that we borrow from financial markets is the notion of present value or discounting. To understand the concept of discounting, imagine that a friend has asked to borrow $1,000 for twelve months. Suppose further that for you to lend her money requires that you withdraw $1,000 from your checking account, an account that pays 3 percent interest per year. In other words, you will have to lose about $30 of interest income by making this withdrawal. Although you like your friend very much, you may not see precisely why you should make her a gift of $30. Therefore, you agree to lend her the $1,000 today if, a year from now, she pays you not only the $1,000 of principal but also an additional $30 in interest. Your friend will likely agree. After all, if she borrowed from the bank directly she would have to pay at least as much. The bank cannot afford to pay you 3 percent per year if it does not charge an interest rate at least as high when it loans those funds out. In fact, the bank will probably charge an interest rate a bit higher to cover its expenses. Therefore, it makes sense for your friend to agree that you give her $1,000 today and that she give you $1,030 in twelve months.

Quite explicitly, you and your friend have just negotiated a trade of present funds for future funds. In fact, you have established the exact terms at which such a trade can take place. One thousand dollars today may be exchanged for $1,030 one year from now. Of course, matters would have been a bit different if the interest rate that your bank paid on deposits had been 5 percent. In that case, you would have asked your friend for $50 (5 percent of $1,000) in repayment beyond the $1,000 originally borrowed. That would have been the only repayment that would truly compensate you for your loss of the interest on your bank deposit. In general, if we denote the interest rate as r, then we have that $1,000 today exchanges for $(1 + r)$ times $1,000 in one year. If we now become even more general and consider an initial loan amount different from $1,000, say of Y, we will quickly see that the same logic implies that Y today trades for $(1 + r)Y$ paid in twelve months.

There is, however, an alternative way to view the transactions just described. Instead of asking how much money one will receive in a year for giving up $1,000 (or Y) now, we can reverse the question. That is, we can ask instead how much we have to pay today in order to get a particular payment one year from the present. For example, we could ask how much it would cost right now to buy a contract requiring that the other party to the deal pay us $1,030 in a year. If the interest rate is 3 percent, the answer is easy. It is simply $1,000.

In fact, this is the contract with your friend that we just considered. You essentially paid $1,000 to purchase a promise from your friend to pay you $1,030 in one year. The intuition is that at an interest rate of 3 percent, the banks and the financial markets are saying that in return for a deposit of $1,000 they promise to pay $1,030 in one year. In other words, we can buy the contract we are thinking about for exactly $1,000 from the banks. There's no sense in paying more for it from anyone else, and no one else is going to accept less. Therefore, when the interest rate is 3 percent, the market is saying that the current price of a contract promising to pay $1,030 in one year is exactly $1,030/(1.03) or $1,000. Because price is just the economist's term for value, we call this the present value or, more completely, the present discounted value of $1,030 due in twelve months.

More generally, the present value of a piece of paper (e.g., a loan contract or share of stock) promising its owner a payment of Z in one period is just $Z/(1 + r)$. The term $1/(1 + r)$ is typically referred to as the discount factor and is often presented just as R. In other words, $R = 1/(1 + r)$. Hence, the present value of Z dollars one year from now is often written as RZ. The source of the adjective discount should be clear. Income that does not arrive until a year from now is not as valuable as income received today. Instead, the value of such future income is discounted. This has nothing to do with inflation and any possible cheapening of the currency over time. It simply reflects the fact that individuals prefer to have their consumption now and have to be paid a premium—an interest rate return—in order to be persuaded to wait.

What if the term of the loan had been for two years? Let us return again to our original example of a $1,000 loan at 3 percent interest. If your friend had initially asked to borrow the funds for two years, your reasoning might have gone as follows. Making a two-year loan to my friend requires that I take $1,000 out of my checking account today. Not making the loan means that the $1,000 stays in the bank. In this case, I will earn 3 percent over the next twelve months and, accordingly, start the next year with $1,030 in the bank. I will then earn 3 percent on this amount over the next or second year. Accordingly, by refusing my friend and keeping the funds in the bank, I will have on deposit $1,030(1.03) = $1,060.90 in two years. Therefore, I will only lend my friend the funds for two years if she in turn promises to pay me $1,060.90—the same as I could have earned at the bank—when the loan expires twenty-four months from now. Note that the amount $1,060.90 can be alternatively expressed as $1,000(1.03)(1.03) = $1,000(1.03)^2$. In general, a loan today of amount Y will yield $Y(1 + r)^2$ or YR^{-2} in two years. By extension, a loan of Y dollars for t years will yield an amount of $Y(1 + r)^t$ or YR^{-t} when it matures t years from now.

As before, we can turn the question around and ask how much we need to pay currently in order to receive an amount of Z dollars at some date t periods into the future. The answer follows immediately from our work above. It is $R^t Z$. How do we know this? If we put the amount $R^t Z$ dollars in an interest-bearing account today, then the amount that can be withdrawn in t periods is, by our previous logic, $(R^t Z)R^{-t} = Z$. So, clearly, the present discounted value of an amount Z to be received t periods in the future is just $R^t Z$.

The only remaining question is how to value a claim that provides different amounts at different dates in the future. For example, consider the construction of a plant that will, after completion in one year, generate Z_1 in net revenue; a net revenue of Z_2 two years from now; Z_3 three years from now; and so on. What is the present value of this stream of future net revenues?

The present value of Z_1 in one period is, as we know, RZ_1. Similarly, the present value of the Z_2 to be received in two periods is $R^2 Z_2$. If we continue in this manner, we will work out the present value of the income received at each particular date. The present value of this entire stream will then simply be the sum of all these individual present values. In general, the present value PV of a stream of income receipts to be received at different dates extending T periods into the future is:

$$PV = RZ_1 + R^2 Z_2 + R^3 Z_3 + \ldots + R^T Z^T = \sum_{t=1}^{T} R^t Z_t \qquad (2.3)$$

A special case of equation (2.3) occurs when the income received in each period Z_t is the same, that is, when $Z_1 = Z_2 = \ldots = Z_T = \overline{Z}$. In that case, the present value of the total stream is:

$$PV = \frac{\overline{Z}}{(1 - R)}(R - R^{T+1}) \qquad (2.4)$$

An even more special case occurs when not only is the income receipt constant at $Z = \overline{Z}$, but also the stream persists into the indefinite future so that the terminal period T approaches infinity. In that case, because the discount factor R is less than one, the term R^{T+1} in equation (2.4) goes to zero. Hence, when the stream is both constant and perpetual, the present value formula becomes:

$$PV = \overline{Z}\left(\frac{R}{1 - R}\right) = \frac{\overline{Z}}{r} \qquad (2.5)$$

Thus, if the interest rate r were 3 percent, a promise to pay a constant \$30 forever would have a present value of $PV = \$30/0.03 = \$1,000$. Note that for all our present value formulas, an increase in the real interest rate r implies a decrease in the discount factor R. In turn, this means that a rise in the interest rate implies a decrease in the present value of any given future income stream.

Again, it is important to remember the context in which these equations have been developed. Often firm decision-making has a temporal dimension. Indeed, our focus on long-run equilibria implies that we are considering just such decisions. Hence, we need to consider trade-offs that are made over time. An expense may need to be incurred now in order to reap additional profit at some future date or dates. The simple dictum maximize profit does not have a clear meaning in such cases. The only way of evaluating the desirability of such a trade-off over time is to discount, that is, translate the future dollar inflows into a current or present value that may then be compared with the current expense necessary to secure those future receipts. If the present value of the future income is not at least as great as the value of the necessary expense, then the trade-off is not favorable. If, for instance, a plant costs \$3 million to build, and will generate future profit with a discounted present value of only \$2 million, it is not a desirable investment, and we would not expect a rational firm to undertake it.[10] In short, our assumption that firms maximize profit must now be qualified to mean that firms maximize the present value of all current and future profit. Of course, for one-period problems, this is identical with the assumption that firms simply maximize profit. However, we will need to be familiar with the idea of discounting and the present value of future profits in the second half of the book when we take up such issues as collusion, research, and development, which often have a multiperiod dimension.

[10] We have treated the problem as one of current expenses versus future receipts. Of course, future costs should be discounted as well.

Reality Checkpoint
Ticket Discounts

A recent study by the National Highway Traffic Safety Administration reveals that nearly 80 percent of drivers admit to speeding within the last month and 25 percent admit to speeding that day. Given attitudes regarding what truly constitutes speeding and willingness to admit to illegal behavior, a prudent guess is that something like 50 percent of the drivers are driving above the posted speed limits on multi-lane interstate highways at any time.

Of course, the prospect of being pulled over and ticketed by the police is a deterrent to overly fast driving. Fines vary by state but a fine of $200 for those going 15 miles over the posted limit is common, and that fine is just part of the cost. Another major part is the impact of a speeding conviction on one's auto insurance. In Massachusetts, for example, one speeding ticket adds 30 percent to the cost of insurance in four areas: 1) bodily injury, 2) property damage, 3) personal injury, and 4) collision for a total of $300 extra in annual insurance cost for at least three years. Assuming a discount factor of $R = 0.97$ (an interest rate of about 3 percent), the cost of a speeding ticket is: $200 + $300 + R$300 + $R^2$300 = 1073.

Not all speeders are caught. Rough evidence from Massachusetts and Virginia suggests that a typical driver averaging 10–15 miles over the speed limit has about a 15 percent chance of being ticketed every year. Hence, over a three-year period, the average driver, for whom the probability of a second speeding ticket is basically zero, has an expected speeding cost of: $0.15*$1073 + 0.15R$1073 + 0.15R^2$1073 = 469. This cost can be avoided though by purchasing a high quality radar (and lidar) detector such as Escort's Passport 9500i, Cobra's XR5-R9G, or the Beltronics Bel STi Driver. These retail for $450 to $500 and last about three years before they either become overly sensitive and give so many false warnings that drivers turn them off or police update their technologies to make that generation of detectors obsolete.

So, the net benefit of buying a detector for a typical driver is small. For the true super-speeders, though, who regularly push the pedal to the metal and who therefore face substantially higher probabilities of getting a ticket, purchasing a detector may well seem a good investment . . . but slowing down may be cheaper.

Source: J. Welsh "No Radar Detectors Give Speed Freaks a Rush," *Wall Street Journal*, January 10, 2008, p. D1. National Highway Traffic Safety Administration, *National Survey of Speeding and Unsafe Driving Attitudes & Behaviors*, (2003).

Practice Problem

2.5

Suite Enterprises is a large restaurant supply firm that dominates the local market. It does, however, have one rival: Loew Supplies. Because of this competition, Suite earns a profit of $100,000 per year. It could, however, cut its prices to cost and drive out Loew. To do this, Suite would have to forego all profit for one year and earn zero. After that year, Loew would be gone forever and Suite could earn $110,000 per year. The interest rate Suite confronts is 12 percent per annum, and thus the discount factor $R = 0.8929$.

a. Is driving Loew out of the market a good "investment" for Suite?
b. Consider the alternative strategy in which Suite buys Loew for $80,000 today and then operates the newly combined firm, Suite & Loew, as a monopoly earning $110,000 in all subsequent periods. Is this a good investment?

2.3.2 Time and the Evolution of Industry Structure

Considerations of time also introduce some potential constraints on the exercise of monopoly power and, consequently, on the amount of welfare loss that accompanies such power. One such mechanism reflects the dynamics of industrial structure. In our textbook analysis above, we simply assumed that the market had either a competitive or monopoly structure. We did not ask how that structure was achieved or whether it is stable. In this sense, the analysis is short run in character. This is not to say that it is inaccurate. The welfare loss associated with monopoly pricing is real. There may be some question, though, as to whether it will be long lasting. Whether or not this is the case depends in part on whether the economic profit or surplus that the monopoly firm earns will attract entry and competition over time.

As noted earlier, a sensible requirement for a long-run equilibrium is that there is no incentive for the industry structure to change. In other words, there should be no incentive for any firm to exit or enter the industry. There are many ways to impose this condition. The most common one however is to assume that it requires that each firm in the industry earn zero economic profit.[11] In other words, for each firm, total revenue Pq_i equals total cost $C(q_i)$. Dividing each side by the firm's output, q_i, reveals that this is equivalent to imposing the constraint that firms exit or enter until the market price equals average cost, where average cost is defined as the ratio of total cost to total production or cost per unit.

We will return to a more complete discussion of average (and marginal) cost again in Chapter 4 when we discuss the production technology and its implications for the firm's costs in some detail. For now, we simply note that imposing the long-run equilibrium condition that price equals average cost provides a way to determine the equilibrium structure of the industry. To the extent that that structure has more than one firm in it, that is, to the extent that the market permits entry by rivals over time, the monopolist's ability to sustain a price far above marginal cost will be lessened. Indeed, even if the market only has one firm, the ability of that firm to price above marginal cost may be sharply curtailed by the threat of potential entrants who would come into the market readily and undercut such pricing. This in fact is the fundamental idea behind the idea of contestable markets.[12]

At the same time, it is important to recognize that a firm with monopoly power may be able to take actions that protect that power against rival entrants over time, and that push the evolution of market structure toward the monopoly pole. In short, market structure at any point in time may not be an accurate gauge of the intensity of competition in an industry. Even a monopolist can be constrained by the prospect of actual or potential entry. It is equally important to recognize that because both entry and entry deterrence typically require that a cost be incurred today in return for higher profits in the future, analysis of these issues inevitably involves comparison of profits at different points of time and the use of the discounting techniques just discussed.

2.3.3 Durable Goods and the Coase Conjecture

A second way in which attention to time considerations may reveal a constraint on monopoly power arises in connection with durable goods. Unlike, say, food, many goods such as household appliances and automobiles last a number of years. In turn, this means that a

---

[11] An alternative approach would be to require that each firm within the industry earns nonnegative profits (and so have no incentive to leave) while any firm not in the industry would earn nonpositive profit if it entered (and so have no incentive to do so).

[12] See, for example, Baumol, Panzar, and Willig (1982).

monopolist has to think carefully about the price initially set and the volume sold today. That supply will still be around to influence market outcomes one or two periods later. Nobel laureate Ronald Coase argued nearly 40 years ago (Coase 1972) that this durability might greatly reduce if not eliminate the ability of the monopolist to set prices above the efficient level even in the current period.

Consider the following example. The time frame has two discrete periods. A monopolist has two units of a durable good that will provide services to an owner in each of the two periods with no loss due to depreciation. There are two such potential consumers. One values the services of the good at $50 per period. The other values these services at $30 per period. Thus, for the high-value consumer the present value of services from the good is $50 + R\$50 = (1 + R)\$50$, while for the low-value consumer it is $(1 + R)\$30$. Because the monopolist has the two units already, marginal production cost is zero. In turn, this implies that the maximum total surplus available in this market is $(1 + R)\$80$. Any outcome that yields this surplus is efficient, but any outcome that yields a total surplus less than $(1 + R)\$80$ is inefficient.

Of course, the monopolist seeks to maximize his own surplus, not the total surplus. In doing so, he will recognize the following constraints. First, any first period price below $(1 + R)\$30$ will result in both consumers purchasing the good in the first period and the market process will effectively end, i.e., there will be no more sales in period 2. The monopolist has nothing left to sell in the second period and both consumers continue to enjoy the services of the good then because it is durable. Second, any price above $(1 + R)\$30$ will result in the sale of either one unit in the first period, if the price is less than $(1 + R)\$50$, or no units if it is higher. In the first case, the monopolist will enter the second period with one unit left, which can then be sold to the low-value consumer for $30. In the second case, the monopolist will face the choice between selling either both units at a price of $30 or one unit at a price of $50. Clearly, the best option in this case is to sell both at $30 for a total second-period profit of $60.

An important implication of the foregoing analysis is that any and all second period sales must take place at a price of $30. There is simply no way that the monopolist can make a credible first-period commitment to any second-period price above this amount. Given this, we can now consider the strategy of making one first-period sale to the high-value consumer at a price of $(1 + R)\$50$ from the viewpoint of that consumer. The difficulty with this strategy is then immediately apparent. Confronted with a first-period price of $(1 + R)\$50$, the high-value consumer can either buy in the first period—and earn zero surplus—or defer the purchase to the second-period knowing that the price will then be $30, and that there will therefore be a surplus of $R\$20$ in present value terms. The high-value consumer will obviously choose the latter. It follows that the monopolist cannot hope to make a first-period sale at $(1 + R)\$50$. The fact that the second-period price must be $30 makes this impossible.

What about a price below $(1 + R)\$50$ but above $(1 + R)\$30$? Consider the first-period price, $(1 + R)\$(30 + \varepsilon)$, where ε is a small positive constant. Such a price gives the high-value consumer a surplus of $(1 + R)\$(20 - \varepsilon)$. If the consumer instead waits and purchases the good next period at $30, there will be a surplus with present value $R\$20$. Thus, in order for the monopolist to sell to this consumer in the first period, it must be the case that the monopolist offers a price such that

$$(1 + R)\$(20 - \varepsilon) > R\$20 \rightarrow \varepsilon \leq \frac{\$20}{1 + R} \tag{2.6}$$

In other words, the maximum price that the monopolist can set in the first period in order to sell just one unit is $(1 + R)\left(\$30 + \dfrac{\$20}{1 + R}\right) = (1 + R)\$30 + \$20$.

In light of the above, we can now greatly simplify the monopolist's problem. Either sell two units in the first period each at a price of $(1 + R)\$30$; or one unit in the first period at a price of $(1 + R)\$30 + \$20$ and a second unit in the following period at a price of $\$30$; or no units in the first period but both units in the second period at a price of $\$30$. The corresponding profits are shown in Table 2.1.

A little algebra will confirm that the first row option in Table 2.1 gives the greatest profit in present value terms. That is, the monopolist will maximize profit by setting a first-period price of $(1 + R)\$30$ and selling both units immediately, one to each consumer. The monopolist will then earn a surplus of $2(1 + R)\$30$. The high-value consumer will earn a surplus of $(1 + R)\$20$, while the low-value consumer will earn zero surplus. The total surplus will thus be $2(1 + R)\$30 + (1 + R)\$20 = (1 + R)\$80$, the maximum amount possible. In other words, the durable feature of the good has constrained the monopolist to set efficient prices—ones that maximize the surplus. This is Coase's conjecture. It is the supposition that durability constrains monopoly pricing so as to eliminate any deadweight loss.

However, just as the efficacy of entry as a discipline on monopoly behavior can be weakened, so too can the impact of durability. Consider how the above example would have been altered had the low-value consumer only valued the services of the durable good at $\$20$ per period or $(1 + R)\$20$ in total. In this case, it is now no longer the case that any and all second-period sales must take place at the maximum price of the low-value consumer, which is now $\$20$. If the monopolist sells no units in the first-period and enters the second-period with two units to sell, it will be preferable to sell just one unit to the high-value consumer at $\$50$ rather than both units at $\$20$ a piece. It follows that the high-value consumer can no longer bargain so aggressively in the first period. This consumer will now prefer any price of $(1 + R)\$(50 - \varepsilon)$ in the first period that provides a surplus of $(1 + R)\$\varepsilon$ to a price of $\$50$ in the second-period that provides a surplus of zero. Thus, by making ε arbitrarily small, the monopolist can induce the high-value consumer to buy in the first period, and then sell at a price of $\$20$ to the low-value consumer in the second period. Neither consumer will enjoy any surplus, while the monopolist will earn a profit of $(1 + R)\$50 + R\$20$. As can be easily verified, the maximum surplus available in this case is $(1 + R)\$70$, which is $\$20$ greater than the surplus actually realized. Here, durability has not eliminated the deadweight loss of monopoly.

The difference in the two cases reflects the distribution of consumer valuations. In both cases, this distribution is discrete. However, the jump from one valuation to the next is more substantial in the second case. Heuristically, valuations are less continuous in that setting. This points to a generalization regarding the Coase conjecture. The more that

Table 2.1   Price options and corresponding profit for the durable goods monopolist

First-Period Price	Second-Period Price	Present Value of Profits
$(1 + R)\$30$	NA	$2(1 + R)\$30$
$(1 + R)\$30 + \$20$	$\$30$	$(1 + R)\$30 + \$20 + R\$30$
$> (1 + R)\$50$	$\$30$	$2R\$30$

consumer valuations are continuous, the more that durability constrains monopoly pricing of durable goods to be efficient. Indeed, as the distribution becomes perfectly continuous, the monopolist may be forced to set competitive prices. In general, durability will, like potential entry, impose some limits on the exploitation of monopoly power and the extent of the associated welfare loss.[13]

2.3.4   The Nonsurplus Approach to Economic Efficiency[14]

Let us return to the second example in the discussion of the Coase conjecture above in which the Coase conjecture fails. Recall that the efficient first-period price is $(1 + R)\$20$ resulting in a total surplus of $(1 + R)\$70$, but that the monopolist instead sets an initial price of $(1 + R)\$50$ and a subsequent second-period price of $\$20$, resulting in a deadweight loss of $\$20$. We may ask now how matters might be different had there been fifty high-value consumers and fifty low-value ones again assuming that the monopolist has just two units.

The first thing to note is that the total surplus now available on the market is $2(1 + R)\$50$. At a first-period price of $(1 + R)\$50$, two units will be sold to two of the 50 high-value consumers and all of this surplus will go to the monopolist. In fact, no other price is possible. None would buy at a higher price. Moreover, at any lower price, the high-value consumers would actively compete with higher bids until again the price rose to $(1 + R)\$50$. Here is another case in which profit maximization by the monopolist is consistent with efficient resource allocation.

Why does this happen here? Why is it that now, despite the sizeable differences in consumer valuations between the two groups, monopoly pricing involves no deadweight loss? The answer lies in considering more deeply just what that deadweight loss of monopoly signifies. The deadweight loss of monopoly is really just the additional surplus that the monopolist could generate if output were increased to the efficient level. The problem for the monopolist in the conventional setting, e.g., Figure 2.2(b), is that the monopolist cannot appropriate the full value of this marginal surplus. As the additional output is sold and price moves down the demand curve, units are sold at a lower price. Even if the monopolist captures all the surplus on the marginal units, the net gain is less than this because less is now earned on infra-marginal units.

It is the inability of the monopolist to appropriate all the surplus that production generates that lies at the heart of the welfare loss of monopoly. When there are fifty high-value consumers, however, and the monopolist only has two units to sell, this problem no longer exists. The monopolist can sell the efficient amount without lowering the price to any infra-marginal consumer. Within the feasible range of sales, the monopolist generates $(1 + R)\$50$ of surplus for each unit sold and acquires and keeps all this surplus.

When there are fifty high-value consumers, the monopolist's output potential is small relative to the total market. At the margin, the decision to increase or decrease sales by one unit and sell it at $(1 + R)\$50$, leaves the surplus of all other market participants unaffected. The marginal consumer earns a surplus of zero in either case. Note that this is similar to the perfectly competitive case. There, too, each firm is sufficiently small relative to the market that it has no effect on the surplus earned by all other participants. The profit of a

---

[13]   Stokey (1981) offers a formal derivation of the Coase Conjecture. See also Thepot (1998).

[14]   This section and the previous one make extensive use of the nonsurplus approach developed in Makowski and Ostroy (1995). It has had an important influence on our understanding of market participation. It also plays a central role in the business strategies advocated by Brandenburger and Nalebuff (1996).

single competitive firm at the margin is zero and this is precisely the same as that firm's contribution to the surplus or welfare created by market trading. The same can be true for a monopolist if it is small relative to the overall market.

The understanding that the crucial factor giving rise to inefficient outcomes is that there are market participants able, at the margin, to alter the surplus of other participants is known as the non-surplus approach to economic analysis. For our purposes, it makes the important point that it is not the number of sellers but their size relative to the market that gives rise to a welfare loss. In other words, it is not the fact that the monopolist is the only seller but the fact that the monopolist is large relative to the market that leads to inefficient outcomes.[15]

2.4   EMPIRICAL APPLICATION: TESTING THE COASE DURABLE GOODS MODEL

Coase's argument that monopolists selling durable goods may still face market pressure to price competitively rests on a very rational model of consumer behavior in which consumers are assumed to be forward-looking when making today's buying decisions. Whether buyers are really that rational, though, is open to question. Judith Chevalier and Austan Goolsbee (2009) examine this issue by analyzing the college textbook market. Their intuition is straightforward: If the standard model accurately describes consumer behavior, then students buying a textbook should consider the likelihood that a new edition will come out after the student is done with it and wants to sell it back on the used book market. In particular, the prospect that a new edition will come out soon should depress the student demand for the book, as this will make it harder to sell a used version.

To investigate this issue, Chevalier and Goolsbee collected data for textbooks in biology, economics, and psychology for the years 1997 through 2001 by semester and by class. For each class, they know the assigned textbook and how many people were in the class. They also know the aggregate new book sales of each text and also the total sales of used versions of the assigned text through college bookstores. For any textbook i in year t, let N_{it} be the number of students who bought the text new and A_{it} be the total number of students in classes in which the book was assigned. Then $S1_{it} = N_{it}/A_{it}$ is the share of the potential academic class market that bought the book new. Similarly, let $S2_{it}$ be the share of students who bought a used version at the college bookstore. Finally, let $S3_{it}$ be the share of students who did not buy the assigned text at all. The variable $S1_{it}/S3_{it}$ is then a measure of the demand for a new, unused book relative to not buying the book in any form. It is tempting to relate this linearly to the price p_{it} of a new book and some other independent variables X_{it}, to give the simple linear:

$$S1_{it}/S3_{it} = \beta X_{it} - \alpha_1 p_{it} + u_{it} \tag{2.7}$$

Here, β is a vector of coefficients on the X_{it} variables, which include such things as whether the book is an introductory or advanced text, whether it comes shrink-wrapped with a study guide and other ancillaries, and the book's level of difficulty, while α_1 measures the effect of the book price on student purchases of new, unused texts. However, Chevalier

---

[15]   The nonsurplus approach is developed in Makowski and Ostroy (1995). It has had an important influence on our understanding of market participation. It also plays a central role in the business strategies advocated by Brandenburger and Nalebuff (1996).

and Goolsbee recognize that because both $S1_{it}$ and $S3_{it}$ are positive fractions, their ratio must also always be positive. Yet it is possible that the data may give rise to estimates of β and α_1 that predict values below zero. Further, the simple relationship expressed in equation (2.7) allows no direct test of whether students are forward-looking in their textbook purchases.

Chevalier and Goolsbee (2009) therefore make two alterations to the simple model above. First, they make what is known as a logit transformation by using the natural log of the dependent variable, i.e., by using $\ln(S1_{it}/S3_{it}) = \ln(S1_{it}) - \ln(S3_{it})$. Because logarithms can be negative, this allows the data to "speak freely." Second, they include a second price variable $= .5(1 - D_{it})p_{it}$, where D_{it} is a 1, 0 dummy variable that takes the value 1 in any semester in which a new edition of the book is coming out one semester later, and zero otherwise. The idea behind this second modification is simple. The true price of buying a new textbook is the price paid for it initially, p_{it}, less the discounted price for which students can sell the book back at the end of the term. Chevalier and Goolsbee find that this resale price is typically on the order of 50 to 75 percent of the initial price, or $0.5p_{it}$, reflecting a rule of thumb for buybacks that almost all bookstores follow. However, if a new version of the text is about to come out ($D_{it} = 1$), then the resale price falls to zero. Thus, the true price of purchasing a new book is given by: $p_{it} - R0.5(1 - D_{it})p_{it}$. Here, R reflects the discount factor that students apply to the money they will receive in the future when they sell the book—a variable that is not directly observed.

With these modifications, equation (2.7) becomes:

$$\ln(S1_{it}) - \ln(S3_{it}) = \beta X_{it} - \alpha_1[p_{it} - R0.5(1 - D_{it})p_{it}] + u_{it} \tag{2.8}$$

or, more generally,

$$\ln(S1_{it}) - \ln(S3_{it}) = \beta X_{it} - \alpha_1 p_{it} + \alpha_2(1 - D_{it})p_{it} + u_{it} \tag{2.9}$$

Note that the value of $\alpha_2 = \alpha_1 0.5R$ and that it indicates whether or not students are forward-looking. If $\alpha_2 = 0$, then students are myopic and consider only the initial price. However, if α_2 is not zero, then students do consider a text's future resale value in their original purchase decision, except in years when $D_{it} = 1$ so that future resale value is zero. Note as well that we can define the ratio $\lambda = \alpha_2/\alpha_1 = 0.5R$. Hence, if we have estimates of α_1 and α_2, we can infer the typical student's discount factor R.

Chevalier and Goolsbee (2009) estimate equation (2.9) with alternative regression techniques (OLS and GMM) including in each case several additional independent variables (X_{it}). These are time dummies to capture general shifts in textbook demand from one year to the next, for the particular field that the text is in, whether it is bundled with additional software; the fraction of the time that the book was required for the class and not just assigned (which is greater than 0.90 for all of the books considered); the average SAT score of students assigned the book; the age of the edition; and whether it is a paperback.[16] For the purposes of testing the Coase view and, specifically, the underlying assumption that

[16]   Students with a knowledge of econometrics may recognize that the price variable is endogenous and that therefore an instrumental variables (IV) approach is warranted. Chevalier and Goolsbee do indeed adopt an IV approach, including a dummy variable indicating if a book is published by a non-profit publisher, the share of non-profit publishers among textbooks designed for the same course, and the Herfindahl index for publishers for the course in the year in which the textbook was published.

Table 2.2 Estimated effects of current price and future resale price on textbook demand (standard errors in parentheses)

Coefficient	OLS Estimation	GMM Estimation
α_1	−0.060 (0.008)	−0.061 (0.012)
α_2	0.033 (0.003)	0.037 (0.003)
λ	0.55 (0.092)	0.61 (0.15)

students are forward-looking, we present only their basic results for the price variables. These are shown in Table 2.2.

These results confirm both the model and the hypothesis that students are definitely forward-looking. The current price has a highly significant and negative effect on new textbook demand, while the resale price has a significantly positive effect just as it should for forward-looking consumers. Indeed, the estimates of λ imply estimated student discount factors that exceed 1. If this were literally true, it would mean that far from being myopic, students care more about the future resale value than the initial purchase price in buying a text. However, the estimate of λ is not so precise that one can rule out more normal, one-semester discount factors of say $R = 0.98$.

In short, the Chevalier and Goolsbee (2009) estimates imply that consumers, or at least college students taking biology, economics, and psychology classes, are forward-looking. Indeed, the difference in price sensitivity of these students differs dramatically in years in which a new version of the text is not anticipated ($D_{it} = 0$) and years in which one is ($D_{it} = 1$). In the former case, the estimates in Table 2.2 imply that a 10 percent rise in the initial purchase price will decrease initial sales by only 16.3 percent because they plan on getting half of that price increase back at the end of the term. In contrast, for students expecting no resale because of an anticipated new edition, a 10 percent price rise on the initial purchase leads to a nearly 40 percent decline in sales. Perhaps somewhat paradoxically, then, the presence of a resale market leads to higher initial prices as students are more willing to pay those prices if they believe that can resell the book later.

As authors of a textbook ourselves, we know that it is widely believed among students that new editions are introduced to raise profits by eliminating competition from used books. Yet Chevalier and Goolsbee (2009) show that their estimates imply that there is no such incentive for economics textbooks because given how forward-looking students are and how sensitive they are to a book's expected resale value, the expected sales revenue for economics texts varies little with the frequency of revision. Faster revisions means lower initial sales in a manner that basically cancels out any gain from eliminating used book competition. This evidence thus lends fairly strong support to Coase's argument regarding the pricing constraints facing a durable goods monopolist.

Summary

We have formally presented the basic microeconomic analysis of markets characterized by either perfect competition or perfect monopoly. In both cases, the goal of any firm is assumed to be to maximize profit. The necessary condition for profit maximization is that the firm produce at a level at which marginal revenue equals marginal cost. Because firms in competitive markets take market price as a given, price equals marginal revenue for the competitive firm. As a result, the competitive market equilibrium is one in which price is set equal to marginal cost. In turn, this implies that the competitive market equilibrium is efficient in that it maximizes the sum of producer and consumer surplus.

The pure monopoly case does not yield an efficient outcome. The monopoly firm understands that it can affect the market price and this implies that marginal revenue will be less than the price for a monopoly firm. If the market demand curve is linear, this difference is reflected in the fact that the monopolist's marginal revenue curve has the same price intercept but is twice as steeply sloped as its demand curve. A monopoly firm equating marginal revenue with marginal cost, as required for profit maximization, yields an output inefficiently below that of the competitive equilibrium. Resources are misallocated because too few resources are employed in the production of the monopolized commodity. The inefficiency that results is often called the deadweight or welfare loss of monopoly.

There are, however, some natural limits to monopoly power. To begin with, monopoly profits will attract entry so that firms with substantial market shares may be forced to price relatively close to competitive levels by potential entrants who will swoop in and steal customers away

(perhaps permanently) should the incumbent firm materially abuse its market power. In addition, monopolists of durable goods face competition from still-surviving units of their own earlier production. This creates a difficult pricing tension that can again discipline the firm's pricing and, depending on the distribution of consumer reservation prices, even force it to charge perfectly competitive prices. To be sure, this discipline requires that consumers are forward-looking and that they consider future used good prices when they make their initial purchase. Evidence from the market for student textbooks tends to confirm that this is the case.

Perfect competition and monopoly form the two polar cases of market structure. The behavior of firms and the nature of market outcomes in these two cases are fairly well understood. The remaining question is what happens in the far more common cases of something between these two extremes. Before we directly address that issue, however, we need to have a more rigorous way of characterizing the market setting and a deeper understanding of the technological and cost features that give rise to particular market structures. These are the topics to be addressed in the next two chapters.

Problems

1. Suppose that the annual demand for prescription antidepressants such as Prozac, Paxil, and Zoloft is, in inverse form, given by: $P = 1000 - 0.025Q$. Suppose that the competitive supply curve is given by: $P = 150 + 0.033Q$.
    a. Calculate the equilibrium price and annual quantity of antidepressants.
    b. Calculate i) producer surplus; and ii) consumer surplus in this competitive equilibrium.

2. Assume that the dairy industry is initially in a perfectly competitive equilibrium. Assume that, in the long run, the technology is such that average cost is constant at all levels of output. Suppose that producers agree to form an association and behave as a

profit-maximizing monopolist. Explain clearly in a diagram the effects on (a) market price, (b) equilibrium output, (c) economic profit, (d) consumer surplus, and (e) efficiency.

3. Suppose that the total cost of producing pizzas for the typical firm in a local town is given by: $C(q) = 2q + 2q^2$. In turn, marginal cost is given by: $MC = 2 + 4q$. (If you know calculus, you should be able to derive this expression for marginal cost.)
    a. Show that the competitive supply behavior of the typical pizza firm is described by: $q = \dfrac{P}{4} - \dfrac{1}{2}$.
    b. If there are 100 firms in the industry, each acting as a perfect competitor,

show that the market supply curve is, in inverse form, given by: $P = 2 + Q/25$.

4. Let the market demand for widgets be described by $Q = 1000 - 50P$. Suppose further that widgets can be produced at a constant average and marginal cost of \$10 per unit.
   a. Calculate the market output and price under perfect competition and under monopoly.
   b. Define the point elasticity of demand ε_D at a particular price and quantity combination as the ratio of price to quantity times the slope of the demand curve, $\Delta Q/\Delta P$, all multiplied by -1. That is, $\eta_D = -\dfrac{P}{Q}\dfrac{\Delta Q}{\Delta P}$. What is the elasticity of demand in the competitive equilibrium? What is the elasticity of demand in the monopoly equilibrium?
   c. Denote marginal cost as MC. Show that in the monopoly equilibrium, the following condition is satisfied:
   $$\frac{P - MC}{P} = -\frac{1}{\eta_D}.$$

5. Suppose that the inverse demand for clothes hangers is given by: $P = 3 - Q/16{,}000$. Suppose further that the marginal cost of producing hangers is constant at \$1.
   a. What is the equilibrium price and quantity of hangers if the market is competitive?

   b. What is the equilibrium price and quantity of hangers if the market is monopolized?
   c. What is the deadweight or welfare loss of monopoly in this market?

6. A single firm monopolizes the entire market for single-lever, ball-type faucets which it can produce at a constant average and marginal cost of $AC = MC = 10$. Originally, the firm faces a market demand curve given by $Q = 60 - P$.
   a. Calculate the profit-maximizing price and quantity for the firm. What is the firm's profit?
   b. Suppose that the market demand curve shifts outward and becomes steeper. Market demand is now described as $Q = 45 - 0.5P$. What is the firm's profit-maximizing price and quantity combination now? What is the firm's profit?
   c. Instead of the demand function assumed in part b, assume that market demand shifts outward and becomes flatter. It is described by $Q = 100 - 2P$. Now what is the firm's profit-maximizing price and quantity combination? What is the firm's profit?
   d. Graph the three different situations in parts a, b, and c. Based on what you observe, explain why there is no supply curve for a firm with monopoly power.

References

Baumol, W. J., J. C. Panzar, and R. D. Willig. 1982. *Contestable Markets and the Theory of Market Structure*. New York: Harcourt, Brace, Jovanovich.

Brandenburger, A., and B. Nalebuff. 1996. *Co-opetition*. Cambridge: Harvard University Press.

Chevalier, J., and A. Goolsbee. 2009. "Are Durable Goods Consumers Forward-Looking? Evidence from College Textbooks," *Quarterly Journal of Economics* 124 (November): 1853–84.

Coase, R. L. 1972. "Durability and Monopoly," *Journal of Law & Economics* 15 (April): 143–50.

Makowski, L., and J. Ostroy. 1995. "Appropriation and Efficiency: A Revision of the First Theorem of Welfare Economics," *American Economic Review* 85: 808–27.

Marshall, Alfred. 1890. *Principals of Economics*, London: Macmillan Publishers.

Stokey, Nancy L. 1981. "Rational Expectations and Durable Goods Pricing," *Bell Journal of Economics* 12 (Spring): 112–28.

Thepot, Jacques. 1998. "A Direct Proof of the Coase Conjecture," *Journal of Mathematical Economics* 29 (January): 57–66.

Appendix

The Calculus of Competition

The competitive firm's problem may be solved by first writing the firm's profit π as a function of its output, $\pi(q)$ in turn defined as revenue $R(q)$ less cost $C(q)$. Price-taking behavior implies $R(q) = Pq$. Hence:

$$\pi(q) = R(q) - C(q) = Pq - C(q) \tag{2.A1}$$

Standard maximization then yields:

$$\frac{d\pi}{dq} = P - C'(q) = 0 \tag{2.A2}$$

P = marginal cost $C'(q)$ under perfect competition.

For the monopoly firm, its output is the same as industry output Q, that gives $P(Q)$, via the inverse demand curve. Hence, the monopolist's profit maximization problem is to choose output Q so as to maximize:

$$\pi(Q) = R(Q) - C(Q) = P(Q)Q - C(Q) \tag{2.A3}$$

Again, standard maximization techniques yield:

$$\frac{d\pi}{dQ} = P(Q) + QP'(Q) - C'(Q) = 0 \tag{2.A4}$$

$P(Q) + QP'(Q)$, is the firm's marginal revenue. The monopolist will maximize profit by producing where marginal cost equals marginal revenue. For a linear demand curve of the form of $P(Q) = A - BQ$ we have $P'(Q) = -B$. In this case, the firm's marginal revenue is $A - BQ - BQ$, or $A - 2BQ$. The monopolist's marginal revenue curve has the same intercept as its demand curve twice the slope.

Note that the profit-maximizing condition above can also be written as

$$P(Q) - C'(Q) = -QP'(Q) \tag{2.A5}$$

Dividing both sides by $P(Q)$, we then have

$$\frac{P(Q) - C'(Q)}{P(Q)} = -\frac{QP'(Q)}{P(Q)} = \frac{1}{\eta} \tag{2.A6}$$

where η is what economists call the elasticity of demand—a measure of how responsive the quantity demanded is to price movements. It is formally defined as:

$$-\eta = \frac{P(Q)}{Q} \frac{1}{P'(Q)} \tag{2.A7}$$

3

Market Structure and Market Power

Early industrial economics, working in the Structure-Conduct-Performance framework, examined firms' decisions given the industrial structure. More modern analysis, however, recognizes that firms' strategic behavior will in fact be a major determinant of market structure. Yet despite this change in perspective, it is clear that contemporary industrial economics must still address the issue of market structure, or the way the industry's producers are organized. In turn, this requires that market structure—and its close cousin market power—be well understood in a way that allows distinction between different structures or different degrees of market power.

We know, for example, that markets work well when the market consists of numerous firms, each with a minimal market share. Yet such markets are relatively rare in the real world. Some markets have just two or three firms. Some have ten or twelve of unequal size. In what ways is this difference important? If there are twenty firms, does it matter if one firm has 60 percent of the market and the other nineteen have just a bit more than 2 percent each? Alternatively, can we measure market structure in such a way that enables us to make some inference of market power? Can we create an index that allows us to say how close or how far a market structure is from the competitive ideal? Because such a roadmap could be of great use to policy makers, it is worthwhile to explore the question at some length.

3.1 DESCRIBING MARKET STRUCTURE

One way to think about an industry's structure is to undertake the following simple procedure. First, take all the firms in the industry and rank them by some measure of size from largest to smallest—one, denoting largest; two, the next largest; etc. Suppose for example that we use production as a measure of size. We could then calculate the fraction of the industry's total output that is accounted for by the largest firm, then the two largest firms combined, then the three largest firms combined, and so on. This gives us the cumulative fraction of the industry's total output as we include progressively smaller firms. Plotting this relationship yields what we call a concentration curve. It is called a concentration curve because it describes the extent to which output is concentrated in the hands of just a few firms.

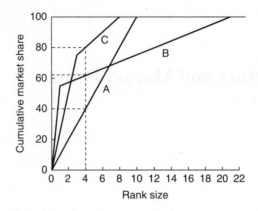

Figure 3.1 Some possible concentration curves

Figure 3.1 displays concentration curves for each of three representative industries: A, B, and C. The firms' ranked sizes are measured along the horizontal axis, again with the first firm being the largest. The cumulative market share is measured on the vertical axis. For example, Industry A has ten firms, each with a 10 percent market share. Industry B has twenty-one firms, the largest of which has a 55 percent market share. The remaining twenty firms each have a 2.25 percent share. Finally, in Industry C, there are three firms each with a market share of 25 percent and five firms each with a market share of 5 percent. For Industry B, the vertical coordinates corresponding to the horizontal values 1 and 2 on the concentration curve are 55 and 57.25, respectively. This reflects the fact that the largest firm has 55 percent of the market and the largest two firms have 57.25 percent between them.

Concentration curves are a useful illustrative device.[1] They permit one to get a quick sense of how industry production is allocated across firms from a swift visual inspection. However, often we need to summarize industrial structure with just a single parameter or index. One such measure that is frequently used is the four-firm concentration ratio, CR_4, or the percent of industry sales accounted for by the top four firms. For the three hypothetical industries described above, we can identify the CR_4 concentration very easily. All we need to do is draw a vertical line from the value 4 on the horizontal axis to the relevant concentration curve, and from that point read horizontally to the vertical axis coordinate. As can be seen, CR_4 is 40, 61.75, and 80, for A, B, and C, respectively. A similar exercise yields the eight-firm ratio CR_8 that also is often reported. Its value for markets A, B, and C is 80, 70.75, and 100, respectively.

Thus, for any n, we can define CR_n as the n-firm concentration ratio. A little thought will then quickly reveal that CR_n corresponds to a particular point on the industry's concentration curve. It follows that the principal drawback to such a measure is that it omits the other information in the curve. Compare for example the four-firm and eight-firm concentration

[1]   Those familiar with the GINI Coefficient typically used to measure income inequality will recognize the concentration curve as the industrial structure analog of the Lorenz Curve from which the GINI Coefficient is derived. For further details, see Damgaard (2007).

ratios just given for the A, B, and C industries. Industry A appears more concentrated than does industry B using the CR_8 measure, but less concentrated when evaluated with the CR_4 index.

An alternative to CR_n that attempts to reflect more fully the information in the concentration curve is the Herfindahl-Hirschman Index or, more simply, the HI. For an industry with N firms, this is defined as follows:

$$HI = \sum_{i=1}^{N} s_i^2 \qquad\qquad (3.1)$$

where s_i is the market share of the ith firm. In other words, the HI is the sum of the squares of the market shares of all of the firms in the industry. Table 3.1 illustrates the calculation of the HI for industry C in our example. If we measure market share in decimal terms so that a firm with 25 percent of the market has a share $s_i = 0.25$, the HI for industry C is 0.20. Compare this to a maximum value of HI = 1.0, which would be the HI if the industry were a pure monopoly with one firm accounting for all the output. However, the practice is often to measure the shares in percentage terms in which case the HI for industry C is 2000, which compares with a maximum, pure monopoly value of HI = 10,000 when shares are measured in this way. For industries A and B, similar calculations yield HI = 1,000 and HI = 3,126.25, respectively.

Like a concentration ratio, the HI measure has its drawbacks. However, it does have one very strong advantage over a measure such as CR_4 or CR_8. This is that the HI reflects the combined influence of both unequal firm sizes and the concentration of activity in a few large firms. That is, rather than just reflect a single point on the concentration curve, the HI provides, in a single number, a more complete sense of the shape of that curve. It is this ability to reflect both average firm size and inequality of size between firms that leads economists to prefer the HI to simple concentration ratios such as CR_4. In our example, Industry B gets the highest HI value because it is the one with the greatest disparity in firm sizes.

Table 3.1   Calculation of the HI for industry C

Firm Rank	Market Share (%) s_i	Squared Market Share s_i^2
1	25	625
2	25	625
3	25	625
4	5	25
5	5	25
6	5	25
7	5	25
8	5	25
Sum:	100	2000 (HI)

3.1

Consider two industries, each comprising ten firms. In industry A, the largest firm has a market share of 49 percent. The next three firms have market shares of 7 percent each, and the remaining six firms have equal shares of 5 percent each. In industry B, the top four firms share the bulk of the market with 19 percent apiece. The next largest firm accounts for 14 percent, and the smallest five firms equally split the remaining 10 percent of the industry.

a. Compute the four-firm concentration ratio and HI for each industry. Compare these measures across the two industries. Which industry do you think truly exhibits a more competitive structure? Which measure do you think gives a better indication of this? Explain.

b. Now let the three second largest firms in industry A merge their operations while holding onto their combined 21 percent market share. Recalculate the HI for industry A.

3.1.1   Measurement Matters: What Is a Market?

Whether one uses CR_4 or HI as an overall measure of a market's structure, it should be clear that the ability to make such measurements at all is predicated upon our ability to identify a well-defined market in the first place. In truth, this is not often easy to do. Consider, for example, the soft drink Pepsi. Does Pepsi compete only against other carbonated beverages, or should we also include such products as fruit juices, iced teas, and flavored milk in thinking about this market? Alternatively, think about multi-use products such as the *Xbox* that, among other capabilities, can function as a DVR and a platform for streaming services such as Netflix and HBO GO. Is the relevant market for *Xbox* simply that of video games, or does it also include products such as TiVo? Unless we have a clear procedure for answering such questions, any summary measure of market structure such as HI will become an arbitrary statistic capable of being manipulated either upward or downward at the whim of the researcher. An analyst can then make CR_4 or HI arbitrarily small or large by defining the market either broadly or narrowly.

One commonly used set of market definitions is the set maintained by the US Census Bureau (in collaboration with other agencies) known as the North American Industry Classification System (NAICS). The Bureau begins by first categorizing the output of business units in the United States into broad sectors of the economy, such as manufacturing, primary metals, agriculture, and forestry products, each of which receives a numeric code. These sectors are then subdivided further, and each is given a two-digit code. The manufacturing sector, for example, is covered by codes 31–33, while retail is covered by codes 44–45, and finance by 52. In each case, the two-digit codes are further disaggregated into the three-digit, four-digit, five-digit, and six-digit levels. Each additional digit represents a further subdivision of the initial classification. The Bureau surveys companies and assigns each plant to a specific six-digit industry, defined primarily on the basis of similarity of production processes. For plants that produce more than one product, the Bureau makes an assignment based on the plant's primary product, as measured by sales. Once all the establishments are so assigned at the most disaggregated level, it is easy to add up to the higher levels. It is also straightforward to work out the market shares and concentration indices according to who owns which plants for any industry at any level of aggregation.

Table 3.2   Concentration measures for selected industries

Industry	CR_4	HI
Breakfast Cereals	80.4	2425.5
Footwear Manufacturing	40.9	602.8
Automobiles	67.6	1448.8
Textile Mills	19.6	160.2
Paper Manufacturing	24.0	227.8
Petroleum Refineries	47.5	806.5
Pesticides	58.2	1109.1
Pharmaceuticals	29.5	359.1
Soap & Detergent Manufacturing	67.1	2025.3
Aluminum Sheet/Plate/Foil	70.5	1995.3
Computers & Peripherals	63.4	2030.7
Electric Light Bulbs & Parts	75.4	2258.3
Dolls, Toys, & Games	33.6	388.8
Aircraft	81.3	2652.2
Battery Manufacturing	58.1	1079.1
Telephone Apparatus	60.5	2078.5
Farm Machinery	59.0	1828.5
Tire Manufacturing	72.8	1539.6
Soft Drink Manufacturing	58.1	1094.5
Medical Equipment & Supplies	19.2	167.6

Source: "Concentration Ratios in Manufacturing," Bureau of the Census, 2007 Census of Manufacturing, January 2011.

These data are published regularly by the Census Bureau. Table 3.2 shows both CR_4 and HI for a sample of well-known NAICS industries.[2]

The two measures of industrial concentration, CR_4 and HI, are highly correlated, implying that each gives roughly the same description of an industry's structure. Yet while the CR_4 and HI measures often tell the same story, the crucial question is whether or not it is the right story.[3] As a little consideration quickly confirms, there is in fact reason to doubt that this is the case.

The source of the potential dissatisfaction with NAICS-based measures of industry structure is that these measures are based more on commonality of production technologies and less on whether the output of the different establishments considered really do compete with each other. Generally speaking, we would like to include production establishments in the same market if the goods that they produce are close substitutes in consumption. Yet as noted, the NAICS procedure is based more on a similarity of production techniques. For example, while wood flooring, resilient floor covering (e.g., linoleum tile), and ceramic tile are all flooring products, the NAICS categorization places them in different industries at the three-digit and all higher levels (321 for wood flooring, 326 for resilient flooring, and 327 for ceramic tile). In addition, the industries identified by the NAICS data calculate market shares on the basis of the national market when in fact practical considerations for a number

[2] Further details are available online at http://www.census.gov/epcd/www/naics.html.
[3] A quite readable discussion of the advantages and disadvantages of each ratio is available in Sleuwaegen and Dehandschutter (1986) and Sleuwaegen, Dehandschutter, and DeBondt (1989).

Reality Checkpoint
Concentrating on Concentration

Just as we can measure the fraction of an industry's output accounted for by its largest firms, so we can measure the fraction of the economy's entire output, GDP, accounted for by its largest corporations. However, while it may make some sense to speak of a concentration index based on just the top four to eight firms when speaking of a single industry, such a small number of firms would account for much too little of GDP to seriously consider. So, in the case of aggregate economic activity, we consider concentration ratios such as CR_{50} or CR_{200}. Such measures can be constructed using data from the Census Bureau's Census of Manufactures. Economist Lawrence White (2002) made such calculations for the US for various years up to the end of the 20th century. Some of his results are shown below.

Aggregate Concentration for Manufacturing (Value Added Basis); Selected Years, 1947–97

Year	CR_{50}	CR_{100}	CR_{200}
1947	17%	23%	30%
1958	23	30	38
1967	25	33	42
1977	24	33	44
1987	25	33	43
1992	24	32	42
1997	24	32	40

These data suggest that, at least since the 1950s, aggregate concentration in manufacturing has shown no increasing or decreasing trend. It was approximately the same in 1997 as it was in 1958 whether one looks at the top 50, 100, or 200 largest firms. White shows that somewhat similar results can be obtained if one looks at all nonfinancial corporations or focuses on shares of employment or profit.

This of course does not mean that firms are not getting bigger. If each firm grows at the same rate as the economy, each of us will find ourselves employed in larger and larger organizations over time even though concentration is stable. White shows that this too has been happening and that the size of the average firm has, correspondingly, grown.

More recently, Elaine Tan (2008) has estimated both trends in concentration and trends in firm size inequality over a slightly longer time period than White (2002), namely, from 1931 to 2000, using total assets to measure firm size and assuming that the distribution of firm sizes is generated by a Champernowne distribution. Like its close cousin, the logistic distribution, the Champernowne distribution is like the normal distribution except that it has "fatter tails." Rather than look at the four-firm concentration ratio, Tan (2008) looks at the asset share of the largest 500 US firms both for all corporations and limited to non-financial corporations. In both cases, Tan finds that the share of total assets owned by the top 500 firms increased from 1931 to the middle of the second world war but then fluctuated with the end result that the share was about the same in 2000 (55 percent) as it was in 1942, although that share rose steadily during the 1990s. She also finds that the inequality among firm sizes has grown. Both of these results are consistent with White's earlier findings.

Sources: L. White. 2002. "Trends in Aggregate Concentration in the United States," *Journal of Economic Perspectives* (Fall): 137–60; and E. S. Tan. 2008. "Champernowne Model Estimates of Aggregate Concentration in the US, 1931–2000," *Working Paper*, University of London, Royal Halloway.

of goods, such as newspapers and ready-mix concrete, imply that inter-firm competition is only local or regional while for others such as passenger aircraft or automobile manufacture competition in international.

If true product markets are defined by the substitutability between the various goods sold, then one would ideally like to define such substitutes on the basis of a direct measure of such substitutability. A formal measure that captures this relationship is what economists call the cross-price elasticity of demand η_{ij}. This is defined as the percentage change in demand for good i that occurs when there is a 1 percent change in the price of another good j. The mathematical definition of this elasticity is

$$\eta_{ij} = \frac{\Delta q_i}{\Delta p_j} \frac{p_j}{q_i} \tag{3.2}$$

In brief, if η_{ij} is large and positive then goods i and j would be considered to be reasonably close substitutes.[4] Precisely what values of η_{ij} ought to be considered large and positive, though, is not immediately clear.

A practical approach to market definition that implicitly embodies the cross-elasticity measure is that employed by the Department of Justice and the Federal Trade Commission in evaluating mergers.[5] This is typically referred to as the SSNIP standard. This is an acronym for a "small but significant and non-transitory increase in price." Essentially, the authorities start with the narrowest possible definition of the market. For example, they might consider grocery stores selling natural, organic products such as Whole Foods. In that case, the SSNIP test would be whether, if all such natural foods grocery stores were monopolized, the monopolist could profitably raise the price of any of the goods by some small amount—usually 5 percent. If the answer is yes, then these grocery stores by themselves constitute a relevant product market. The intuition is that the hypothetical monopolist could only profitably raise prices if other stores left out of this market did not offer close substitutes and therefore the market analyzed is well-defined. If the answer to the SSNIP test is no, however, then the potential market is widened perhaps to all grocery stores natural or not, and the test of a profitable price increase by a hypothetical monopolist is repeated. If the answer is still no, then this process continues through ever wider definitions of the retail food market until the "yes" moment is realized.

While the SSNIP standard is clear however, its implementation is not. For example, in the early 2000s, Oracle, People-Soft, and SAP were the three leading firms engaged in developing, manufacturing, marketing, and servicing the complicated software used by businesses to manage their large organizations. This software is often further subdivided into separate modules for a corporation's many parts. Thus, there is a software module for human resources management (HRM), for financial management (FM), for supply chain management (SCM), and customer relations management (CRM). Besides the three firms already mentioned, there were also many smaller firms specializing in just one of these modules. The DOJ filed suit to block the proposed merger of Oracle and People-Soft. In its suit, the Justice Department argued that the relevant market based on an SSNIP test was the

---

[4] However, a high monopoly price may inflate the cross-elasticity measure, a point originally emphasized by Stocking and Mueller (1955). Because the marginal consumer may look for substitutes when faced with a high monopoly price that would not be sought if the good were priced competitively, the cross price elasticity measured at the current industry price may be unduly large.

[5] Since 1997, the European Commission has also explicitly recognized this standard as a tool for market definition.

market for high-end business software of the type sold to large and complex firms including major universities such as Stanford and Princeton, major banks such as Bank of America, and large government agencies such as the Department of Defense. The DOJ argued that competition to provide such complex firms with business software took place in auction markets in which only the three largest vendors could participate because each firm required a very detailed and uniquely configured software plan. The many smaller firms did not, and could not compete for these contracts because they focused on selling and servicing simple, standardized products that, while appropriate for much smaller firms, could never serve the needs of the large complex enterprises. The DOJ argued that an SSNIP test confirmed this market definition. However, Oracle disagreed and argued that a proper application of the SSNIP standard would indicate that a much broader market definition including all those firms preparing business software was appropriate.[6] Thus, while the standard may be clear, the proper way to impose it is more ambiguous.

3.1.2   More Measurement Matters: Geography and Vertical Relations

The application of the SSNIP standard above depended on what products define the market. Which products are included in the market and which are not? Clearly however, there is an equal need to define the market's geographic space. Consider for example the newspapers that serve the same city. Assuming that printed news media is determined to be a relevant product market, we still need to determine which printed media constitute the citywide newspaper market. Is it just newspapers printed and sold within the city? Or do national newspapers that are printed far beyond the city such as the *New York Times* and *USA Today* also constitute some of the market?

Alternatively, consider a region with a number of software producers who sell to a global market. If most of these firms' customers live outside the region then the geographic boundaries must be expanded. Similarly, it could be the case that local producers sell to a broad regional or even global market. As a result, although most local consumers buy from local producers, the presence of many consumers outside the local area means that the relevant geographic market extends beyond the local region.

In principle, an SSNIP test could be used to define the locations that constitute a geographic market just as it is used to define the goods that determine a specific product market. That is, once we have defined the relevant product market, we can define a region such as the local city and ask whether a firm that monopolized production within this area—say of newspapers or software—could impose small but significant and non-transitory increases in price. If the answer is yes, then the city does define a relevant geographic market. If the answer is no, then a wider geographic region needs to be considered.

In fact, the merger guidelines put out by the DOJ and the FTC point to exactly that kind of test. In practice however, alternative approaches are often used to define the relevant geographic market. A common test in this regard is the Elzinga-Hogarty (1978) test. This test considers two features of a geographic region to determine whether it represents a legitimate regional market. The first is LIFO (Little in from Outside) defined as 1 minus the fraction of all the products consumed within a region that are produced outside the region. Returning to our newspaper example, if 20 percent of all newspaper subscriptions within a local area are national newspapers, then LIFO would be 80 percent. The other measure of the Elzinga-Hogarty (1978) test is LOFI (Little out from Inside). This is calculated as

---

[6]   31 F. Supp. 2d 1098; 2004–2 Trade Cas. (CCH) ¶4,542. In the main, the court accepted Oracle's view and the merger was allowed to proceed.

1 minus the fraction of production within the region that is shipped to consumers outside the region. In other words, LIFO is a rough measure of 1 minus the fraction imported while LOFI is roughly 1 minus the fraction exported. Based on a review of historical evidence, Elzinga and Hogarty (1978) suggest that for regions in which either the LIFO and LOFI measures both exceed 75 percent, or where their average exceeds 90 percent, the presumption that the region is a well-defined geographic market is strong.

Yet while the Elzinga and Hogarty (1978) standard is easy to understand and measure, the threshold value needed to establish a definite market is not. As noted, Elzinga and Hogarty (1978) suggest a 75/90 threshold as a practical rule of thumb. Yet this critical value is based on economic intuition and a rough sense of what is workable—not on any probability distribution that would allow us to construct confidence intervals or test for statistical significance. It is not entirely clear, for example, why thresholds of 65 and 80 would not be better at capturing actual market boundaries. Note too that the definition of the product market has implications for the definition of the geographic market and vice versa. In the Oracle case, for example, the LIFO and LOFI measures vary depending on whether the product market consists of just the individualized business software sold by the big three firms or all business software sold by any firm.

A further issue with both product and market definitions relates to the relationships between firms operating at different stages of the production process. The delivery of a final good or service to the customer often represents the last of many steps. These include the acquisition of the raw materials, their transformation into a semi-finished good, the refinement of the semi-finished good into a final consumer product, and thereafter, the retailing. In economics jargon, the initial raw materials phase is typically described as the upstream phase after which the product flows "downstream" through the various stages toward its final sale to the consumer. The relationship between upstream and downstream phases is therefore a vertical one, and there are several forms that this relationship can take. An upstream producer may own all the subsequent phases in which case we say the firm is vertically integrated. Alternatively, an upstream producer may offer franchising agreements or long-term contracts to downstream sellers. The existence and variability of such relationships can cause difficulty in measuring the structure of the market at any one stage of production. For instance, there are many bottling companies so that conventional measures of market concentration in the bottled can and soft drink industry are rather low. In turn, this suggests a fairly competitive market. However, the reality is that most bottling companies do not compete with each other but, instead, are tied through strict contractual agreements to use one of the national upstream suppliers, such as Coca-Cola or Pepsi.[7] As a result, there may be much less competition among bottlers than the concentration measure would suggest.

In sum, the interpretation of structural market measures such as CR_4 and HI is greatly complicated by a variety of factors beginning with the fact that any such structure is endogenous. Much of our data collection organizes markets on the basis of similar production techniques rather than on a measure of substitution. Implementing more appropriate market measures such as SSNIP requires careful application and interpretation of the evidence, and this can be problematical. Geographic definitions such as the Elzinga and Hogarty (1978) standard are easy to understand, but it is not obvious which values of that standard should serve as a threshold of market determination. The point is that while much of the theoretical work covered in this text will take the market at hand to be well understood, the real world measurement of actual markets is fraught with difficulties.

---

[7] Some authors, for example, Gort (1962) and, more recently, Davies and Morris (1995), have tried to obtain a precise, quantitative measure of the extent of vertical integration.

At the same time, one should not overstate the case. For example, categorizing industries on the basis of closeness of shared production techniques does not necessarily indicate the substitutability necessary for competition. However, it has the advantage that it likely does group firms with similar production costs. This is important because any analysis that links an industry's configuration to the underlying structure of its technology and costs only makes sense if the production technologies are sufficiently similar that we can make general, industry-wide statements about a typical firm's cost structure.

3.2   MEASURING MARKET POWER

Throughout this chapter, we have been thinking about market structure in the quite literal sense of how the industry's production of output is allocated across different firms. We have seen how summary statistics such as the CR_4 or HI attempt to describe this configuration of firms in an industry much as a census taker might use similar statistics to describe the number and size of families in a geographic region. A large part of the motivation for these measures is the desire to summarize succinctly just where an industry might lie relative to the ideal of perfect competition. There is nothing wrong with this structural approach so long as one clear caveat is kept in mind: that a particular structure does not necessarily imply a particular outcome.

When we say that an industry is highly concentrated we are saying that the industry output is dominated by a few firms, in contrast to the configuration that we associate with the competitive model. Does that necessarily mean then that prices charged in this industry are above what would prevail in a perfectly competitive market? The answer is not so straightforward. As we shall see in subsequent chapters, markets with even just two or three firms may sometimes come quite close to duplicating the competitive or efficient outcome.

The Lerner Index is one way to measure how well a market performs from an efficiency point of view. The Lerner Index, LI, measures how far the outcome is from the competitive ideal in the following way:

$$LI = \frac{P - MC}{P} \tag{3.3}$$

Because the Lerner Index directly reflects the discrepancy between price and marginal cost it captures much of what we are interested when it comes to the *exercise* of market power. For a competitive firm, the Lerner Index is zero because such a firm prices at marginal cost. For a pure monopolist, on the other hand, the Lerner Index can be shown to be the inverse of the elasticity of demand—the less elastic the demand the greater the price-marginal cost distortion. (See the Appendix of Chapter 2 for a formal derivation.) To see this, recall that for a monopolist the marginal revenue of selling an additional unit of output can be written as $MR = P + \frac{\Delta P}{\Delta Q} Q$. For profit maximization we set marginal revenue equal to marginal cost, or $P + \frac{\Delta P}{\Delta Q} Q = MC$. Rearranging and dividing by price P we obtain

$$\frac{P - MC}{P} = -\frac{\Delta P}{\Delta Q} \frac{Q}{P} = \frac{1}{\eta} \tag{3.4}$$

where $1/\eta$ is the inverse of the elasticity of demand. The less elastic is demand, or the smaller is η, the greater is the difference between market price and marginal cost of production in the monopoly outcome. To drive the point home, recall that the perfectly competitive firm faces an infinitely elastic or horizontal demand curve. When such a large value is substituted for the elasticity term, equation (3.4) implies a Lerner Index of 0. Again, the perfectly competitive firm sells at a price equal to marginal cost. Note too that the Lerner Index can never exceed 1 and that it can only hit this maximum value if marginal cost is 0.

For an industry of more than one but not a large number of firms, measuring the Lerner Index is more complicated and requires obtaining some average index of marginal cost. A particularly straightforward case in this regard is that in which the commodity in question is homogenous so that all firms must sell at exactly the same price. If this is so, then we can measure a market-wide Lerner Index as:

$$LI = \frac{P - \sum_{i=1}^{N} s_i MC_i}{P} \tag{3.5}$$

Here, as before, s_i is the market share of the ith firm and N is the total number of firms.

The Lerner Index is a very useful conceptual tool and we will make reference to it throughout the remainder of this book. Like the CR_4 or the HI, the Lerner Index is a summary measure. The difference is that the Lerner Index is not so much a measure of how an industry's production is structured as it is a measure of the market outcome. The greater the Lerner Index, the farther the market outcome lies from the competitive case—and the more market power is being exploited. In this sense, the Lerner Index is a direct and useful gauge of the extent of market competition.

For example, Ellison (1994) tries to get evidence on game-theoretic models of cartel behavior. For this purpose, he studies railroad prices over time in the late nineteenth century. He estimates that, apart from price war periods, the Lerner Index was about 85 percent of what it would be under pure monopoly pricing. In other words, the collusive behavior of railroads at this time was capable of coming within 15 percent of the pure monopoly price distortion.

However, much like the structural indices, the Lerner Index also has its problems. To begin with, calculating the Lerner Index for an industry runs into the problem of market definition. Further, even when the market definition is reasonably clear, the Lerner Index is still difficult to measure. It is one thing to count the number and estimate the sizes of the various firms in an industry. Measuring the elasticity of demand is trickier. Measuring marginal cost is even more difficult. Unfortunately, even small changes in the assumptions one makes about the data can lead to sizable differences in estimated price–cost margins. For example, Ellison's (1994) study relied on data studied earlier by Porter (1983). Yet Porter's (1983) estimate of the price distortion during collusive periods is only half as large as Ellison's (1994) estimate.

Moreover, even when the Lerner Index is accurately measured its interpretation can remain ambiguous. Suppose for example that each firm in an industry has to incur a one-time sunk cost F associated with setting up its establishment. Assume further that each firm's marginal cost is constant. Because each firm needs to earn enough operating profit to cover its sunk cost, the equilibrium price level will need to rise above marginal cost. That is, the Lerner Index will need to be positive. However, the more positive that difference is—the greater is the price–cost margin—the greater the number of firms that can cover the one time sunk cost. As a result, we might observe a high Lerner Index in a setting in which there are numerous firms, none of which is very large. In such a case, the high Lerner

Index might erroneously indicate little competition even though no firm has any significant market power.[8]

Conversely, the Lerner Index might underestimate market power in settings in which cost-reducing innovations are important. Suppose for example that an industry has an old and not very efficient incumbent firm with high marginal cost. As long as demand is somewhat elastic, such a firm may have no choice but to price relatively close to marginal cost. At the same time, the incumbent has a great incentive to take whatever actions it can that will keep a low-cost rival from entering the market. In this case, the Lerner Index deceptively indicates a fair bit of competition because price is low relative to the incumbent's marginal cost when the relevant but unavailable comparison is the price with the potential rival's lower marginal cost.[9]

3.3   EMPIRICAL APPLICATION: MONOPOLY POWER—HOW BAD IS IT?

A recurrent question in antitrust policy is just how costly imperfect competition is for the economy overall. If the losses from monopoly power are not large, then devoting any significant resources to antitrust enforcement to prevent such losses is probably not worthwhile. Such scarce resources would be better used in, say, increasing homeland security or providing relief to hurricane victims. If the economic costs of market power are large, however, then allocating resources to combat the abuse of that power is likely to be warranted. Hence, it would be useful if economists had some sense of just how serious the losses from monopoly power actually are.

In principle, economists have a clear measure of the economic loss caused by monopoly power. It is the deadweight loss or triangle that results from prices above marginal cost. In practice, however, measuring this loss is not so easy. This is because it requires getting estimates of cost and/or demand but, as with any estimate, these values are subject to some error. Unfortunately, rather small changes in the estimates can lead to rather large changes in the estimated welfare cost.

To understand the issues involved, let us start with the basic measurement of the welfare or deadweight loss that results from pricing above marginal cost. As shown in Chapter 2, this is the area whose height is given by the difference between price P and marginal cost MC, and whose base is given by the difference between the competitive output Q^C that would sell if $P = MC$ and the actual market output Q that sells at the actual price P. Hence, the welfare loss WL is:

$$WL = \frac{1}{2}(P - MC)(Q^C - Q) \tag{3.6}$$

It is convenient to express this welfare loss as a proportion of total sales revenue PQ to yield

$$WL' = \frac{WL}{PQ} = \frac{1}{2}\frac{(P - MC)}{P}\frac{(Q^C - Q)}{Q} \tag{3.7}$$

---

[8]   See, for example, Elzinga (1989).
[9]   Hovenkamp (1994), among others, has made this argument.

Remember that the elasticity of demand η is the proportionate increase in output in response to a given proportionate decrease in price. If the price were to fall from its current P level to the competitive level of $P = MC$, then output would rise to the competitive level of Q^C. That is:

$$\eta = \frac{(Q^C - Q)/Q}{(P - MC)/P} \quad \Rightarrow \quad \frac{(Q^C - Q)}{Q} = \eta \frac{(P - MC)}{P} \tag{3.8}$$

Because we also know that the industry Lerner Index is $(P - MC)/P$, we can rewrite equation (3.7) as:

$$WL' = \frac{WL}{PQ} = \frac{1}{2}\eta(LI)^2 \tag{3.9}$$

Now recall from equation (3.4) earlier in the chapter that, for a pure monopolist, the Lerner Index is given by: $LI = (P - MC)/P = 1/\eta$. Then, in this case, the deadweight loss relative to industry sales will be:

$$WL' = \frac{WL}{PQ} = \frac{1}{2}\frac{1}{\eta} \tag{3.10}$$

That is, for the perfect monopoly case, the deadweight loss as a fraction of current industry sales is simply one-half the Lerner Index or one over twice the elasticity of demand. The intuition is that as the demand elasticity increases, the welfare loss shrinks because other goods are increasingly viewed as substitutes to the monopolized commodity. Note further the sensitivity of the welfare loss to the elasticity estimate. An estimate that $\eta = 1.5$ produces a welfare loss equal to 33 percent of revenue. An estimate of $\eta = 2$ reduces this amount to 25 percent of revenue. That is, a 0.5 change in the elasticity estimate yields an eight percent change in the welfare loss.

The first person to make calculations along the foregoing lines on a large scale was Arnold Harberger (1954). Using a sample of 73 manufacturing industries, Harberger (1954) took the difference in the five-year average industry rate of return and the five-year average for manufacturing overall as an approximation of LI. Because he worked with industry data, and because none of the industries was a pure monopoly, Harberger (1954) could not assume that his LI estimate is the inverse of elasticity of demand, as we did in equation (3.10). Instead, he combined his LI estimates with an assumed demand elasticity of $\eta = 1$ in equation (3.9). The dollar value of these estimated distortions is then given by multiplying WL' by industry sales PQ. When Harberger (1954) added these dollar values up and extrapolated the results across the entire economy he found a surprisingly small welfare cost of monopoly—on the order of one-tenth of one percent of Gross Domestic Product. The low value of Harberger's (1954) estimate thus raised a serious question about the cost-effectiveness of antitrust policy and litigation.

Harberger's (1954) approach, however, did not go uncriticized. Bergson (1973) noted that Harberger's (1954) procedure essentially used a partial equilibrium framework to obtain a general equilibrium measure. He demonstrated that, in principle, this could mean that Harberger's (1954) estimate considerably understated the actual loss. Cowling and Mueller (1978) used firm-level data for 734 companies in the United States and 103 companies in the United Kingdom. The use of firm-level data means that Cowling and Mueller (1978) could apply equation (3.10) directly. Their estimated monopoly welfare costs range from 4 to 13 percent of GDP in the United States and from 4 to 7 percent in the United Kingdom—far larger than Harberger's (1954) estimates.

Table 3.3 Hall's (1988) estimated Lerner Index for selected industries

Industry	Lerner Index
Food & Kindred Products	0.811
Tobacco	0.638
Textile Mill Products	−0.214
Apparel	0.444
Lumber and Wood	0.494
Furniture and Fixtures	0.731
Paper and Allied Products	0.930
Printing	0.950
Rubber & Plastic	0.337
Leather Products	0.524
Stone, Clay, and Glass	0.606
Primary Metals	0.540
Fabricated Metals	0.394
Machinery	0.300
Electric Equipment	0.676
Instruments	0.284
Miscellaneous Mfg	0.777
Communication	0.972
Electric, Gas & Sanitary Services	0.921
Motor Vehicles	0.433
Average	0.57

Robert Hall (1988) used a production theory approach to derive estimates of the Lerner Index for twenty broad manufacturing sectors in the United States. These are shown in Table 3.3. Domowitz, Hubbard, and Petersen (1988) obtained similar but generally lower estimates of the Index using Hall's (1988) approach corrected for changes in raw material usage. Whereas Hall (1988) found an average price–cost margin of 0.577, Domowitz, Hubbard, and Petersen (1988) estimate the average to be only 0.37. Even this lower value, however, indicates a substantial degree of welfare loss in the manufacturing sector due to non-competitive pricing.

An important source of variation in Cowling and Mueller's (1978) analysis is how advertising costs are treated in measuring *LI*. This calls attention to the critical importance of the marginal cost measure in determining welfare losses. This issue has been addressed more recently by Aiginger and Pfaffermayr (1997). They start by recognizing that without the pressure of perfect competition, firms can operate in an industry with different cost efficiencies. Thus, the average industry marginal cost $\overline{MC}$ is very likely not the minimum average cost that would be enforced if perfect competition were the rule. Aiginger and Pfaffermayr (1997) then make use of a result (one that we shall derive in Chapter 9) from a standard oligopoly model. The result is that the industry price-cost margin measure using $\overline{MC}$ is equal to the industry Herfindahl Index *HI* (scaled from 0 to 1), divided by the elasticity of industry demand. That is:

$$\frac{P - \overline{MC}}{P} = \frac{HI}{\eta} \quad \Rightarrow \quad \eta = HI\left(\frac{P}{P - \overline{MC}}\right) \tag{3.11}$$

Substituting this result into equation (3.9), we obtain:

$$WL' = \frac{WL}{PQ} = \frac{1}{2} \left(\frac{P - MC}{P} \right) \left(\frac{P - MC}{P - \overline{MC}} \right) HI \qquad (3.12)$$

Note that the term $\left(\dfrac{P - MC}{P - \overline{MC}} \right)$ is greater than one because MC is the marginal cost that would prevail under competition. Aiginger and Pfaffermayr (1997) measure this competitive MC as the marginal cost of the most efficient firm in the industry under the assumption that this is the cost efficiency that would be required for competitive firms to survive. Effectively, their approach permits them to decompose the welfare cost of market power into two parts. One is the traditional welfare loss measure due to prices not equal to *industry* average marginal cost, $P - \overline{MC}$. The other is due to the fact that market power allows the survival of firms with higher than minimum costs, $\overline{MC} - MC$. Using data from 10,000 cement and paper firms in the European Union, Aiginger and Pfaffermayr (1997) find that the total welfare loss of market power in these industries is on the order of 9 to 11 percent of industry sales. Perhaps not surprisingly, they find that these welfare losses are largely due to the cost inefficiencies that imperfect competition permits. Thus, their estimate of the traditional welfare loss measure is on the order of 2 to 3 percent, while the cost inefficiency loss is on the order of 7 to 7.5 percent. Extrapolating these estimates to the entire economy would yield results that are considerably closer to the Cowling and Mueller estimates (1978) than those obtained by Harberger (1954).

In evaluating all of these estimates, it is useful to bear in mind at least two caveats. First, an implicit assumption in all these calculations is that it is feasible to have perfect competition in all industries. As we shall see in the next chapter, however, costs and technology make this an unlikely outcome. In this sense, the estimates of welfare losses due to monopoly price distortions are too high as there is no way in which all industries could be freed of such market power. Second, the measures are taken from data in which active antitrust enforcement has been the norm. In this sense, the measures are an understatement of the potential for monopoly-induced welfare losses. Had there been no antitrust enforcement, there would have presumably been more market power abuses and the associated welfare losses would have been greater.

Summary

This chapter has focused on the measurement of market structure and market power. We are very often interested in summarizing the extent to which an industry departs from the competitive ideal in a single number or index. The issue then becomes whether and how we can construct such a summary measure.

Concentration indices, such as the CR_4 or HI, are explicit measures of a market's structure. Both look at firm shares as a fraction of the industry's total output. Both encounter important problems, such as the difficulty of accurately defining the relevant market. The HI, however, is generally preferred by economists since it not only reflects the top firm shares but also the differences in relative firm sizes.

An explicit measure of market power is the Lerner Index. Because it is based on a comparison of price and marginal cost, this index directly addresses the extent to which the market outcome deviates from the competitive ideal. However, the need to measure marginal cost accurately, along with other measurement issues, makes the Lerner Index as difficult to employ as the structural indices. Estimates of the Lerner Index also serve as a useful starting point to estimate the actual efficiency costs of monopoly power. Many efforts have been made to do this for the entire economy in an attempt to get a general view as to how serious the problem of market power really is. These empirical studies have yielded a wide range of estimates of the aggregate deadweight loss as a percentage of GDP. The lower bound estimate is that monopoly power imposes only a small inefficiency cost of a few tenths of one percent of GDP. However, upper bound estimates range as high as 14 percent. A crucial parameter in such studies is the elasticity of demand assumed to be typical.

As long as the foregoing problems are recognized, the CR_4, HI, and Lerner Index measures are useful starting points to characterize an industry's competitive position. However, an industry's degree of concentration and price–cost margin do not materialize out of thin air. Instead, these indices all derive from the interaction of a number of factors. One of those factors is the nature of production costs. The role that technology and cost play in shaping the industrial outcome is examined in the next chapter.

Problems

1. The following table gives US market share data in percentages for three paper product markets in 1994.

Facial Tissue		Toilet Paper		Paper Towels	
Company	% Share	Company	% Share	Company	% Share
Kimberly-Clark	48	Proctor & Gamble	30	Proctor & Gamble	37
Proctor & Gamble	30	Scott	20	Scott	18
Scott	7	James River	16	James River	12
Georgia Pacific	6	Georgia Pacific	12	Georgia Pacific	11
Other	9	Kimberly-Clark	5	Scott	4
		Other	16	Other	18

   a. Calculate the four-firm concentration ratio for each industry.
   b. Calculate each industry's HI Index.
   c. Which industry do you think exhibits the most concentration?

2. Consider a market comprised of three firms. Firm 1 produces and sells 23 units per period. Firm produces and sells 19 units per period, while firm 3's periodic production and sales are 15 units. The (inverse) market demand is estimated to be: $P = 100 - Q$, where $Q =$ total output $= q_1 + q_2 + q_3$. Determine the market price and the elasticity of market demand as well as the market share of each firm. Now use equation (3.5) to determine each firm's marginal cost. What relation do you find between marginal cost and market share?

3. Monopoly Air is on record with the local transportation authority arguing that there is no market need and no market room for an additional air service because even now, Monopoly Air planes are flying with only 60 percent of the seats typically booked. Hence, it argues that the market is not large enough to sustain two efficient-sized air carriers.

   Evaluate this argument. Why might Monopoly Air flights be so under-booked? Does this prove that there is no "market room" for a new competitor?

4. We defined the Lerner Index as $LI = 1/\mu$ where μ is the absolute value of the elasticity of demand. We also showed that LI can be alternatively expressed as $(P - MC)/P$. Use these relationships to show that LI can never exceed 1. What does this imply is the minimum demand elasticity we should ever observe for a monopolist?

References

Aiginger and Pfaffermayr. 1997. "Looking at the Cost Side of Monopoly," *Journal of Industrial Economics* 44 (September): 245–67.

Bergson, A. 1973. "On Monopoly Welfare Losses," *American Economic Review* 63 (December): 853–70.

Cowling, K., and D. C. Mueller. 1978. "The Social Cost of Monopoly Power," *Economic Journal* 88 (December): 727–48.

Damgaard, C. 2007. "Lorenz Curve." From *MathWorld*–A Wolfram Web Resource, created by Eric W. Weisstein. http://mathworld .wolfram.com/LorenzCurve.html

Davies, S. W., and C. Morris. 1995. "A New Index of Vertical Integration: Some Estimates for UK Manufacturing," *International Journal of Industrial Organization* 13:151–78.

Domowitz, I., R. G. Hubbard, and B. Petersen. 1988. "Market Structure and Cyclical Fluctuations in Manufacturing," *Review of Economics and Statistics* 70 (February): 55–66.

Ellison, G. 1994. "Theories of Cartel Stability and the Joint Executive Committee," *Rand Journal of Economics* 25 (Spring): 37–57.

Elzinga, K. 1989. "Unmasking Monopoly Power: Four Types of Economic Evidence," in R. Larner and J. Meehan, Jr., eds., *Economics and Antitrust Policy*. Westport, CT: Greenwood Press.

Elzinga, K., and Hogarty. 1978. "The Problem of Geographic Market Delineation Revisited: The Case of Coal," *Antitrust Bulletin* 23 (Spring): 1–18.

Gort, M. 1962. *Diversification and Integration in American Industry*. Princeton: Princeton University Press.

Hall, R. 1988. "The Relation Between Price and Marginal Cost in U. S. Industry," *Journal of Political Economy* 96 (October): 921–47.

Harberger, A. 1954. "Monopoly and Resource Allocation," *American Economic Review* 45 (May): 77–87.

Hovenkamp, H. J. 1994. *Federal Antirust Law Policy: The Law of Competition and Its Practice*. St. Paul: West Publishing.

Porter, R. 1983. "A Study of Cartel Stability: The Joint Executive Committee, 1880–1886," *Bell Journal of Economics* 14 (Autumn): 301–14.

Sleuwaegen, L., and W. V. Dehandschutter. 1986. "The Critical Choice between the Concentration Ratio and the H-Index in Assessing Industry Performance," *Journal of Industrial Economics* 35 (December):193–208.

Sleuwaegen, L., W. V. Dehandschutter, and R. DeBondt. 1989. "The Herfindahl Index and Concentration Ratios Revisited," *Antitrust Bulletin* 34 (Fall): 625–40.

Stocking, G., and W. Mueller. 1955. "The Cellophane Case and the New Competition," *American Economic Review* 45 (March): 29–63.

4

Technology and Cost

In late 2001, Microsoft introduced its first *Xbox* video game console. The relatively simple model for which only a few games were available sold at a retail price of $300. By 2004, the price had fallen to $150 despite technical improvements, as Microsoft prepared to launch the new *Xbox 360* series. The base or *Core* model 360 emerged in 2005 at a price of $300—a price that fell to $200 in 2008 as the *Core* model was replaced by the *Arcade* series with initially a 60GB hard drive. That price fell further over the next two years, even as the hard drive capacity grew to 250GB and more features and games were added. As this text is going to press, an *Xbox 360S* series along with a *Kinect* scanner that allows full-body gaming is selling as a bundle for $250. In sum, the price of an *Xbox* game console has declined over the last decade—especially if the vastly improved technical features are considered—despite the fact that the prices of other consumer goods have risen over 25 percent (about 2.6 percent per year) in that same time period.

Clearly, Microsoft's pricing strategy reflects in part its rivalry with other video game platform producers such as Sony and Nintendo. Yet the above prices must also reflect *Xbox* production costs because the profitability of any price choice will depend critically on the cost of producing each unit of the total sold at that price. More generally, production costs affect both firm behavior and industrial structure. The four firms—General Mills, Kellogg, General Foods (Post), and Quaker Oats currently account for about 80 percent of sales in the US ready-to-eat breakfast cereal industry. By contrast, the largest four manufacturers of games and toys account for 35 to 45 percent of these products—less if video games are included. In this chapter, we introduce key cost concepts that are relevant to understanding such dramatic differences in industry structure.[1]

4.1 PRODUCTION TECHNOLOGY AND COST FUNCTIONS FOR SINGLE PRODUCT FIRMS

What is a firm's technology? For our purposes, the firm's technology is a production relationship that describes how a given quantity of inputs is transformed into the firm's output. In this sense, we adopt the traditional neoclassical approach in which a firm is solely

---

[1] Panzar (1989) presents a more extended review of this topic.

envisioned as a production unit. The goal of this production unit is profit maximization, which, in turn, implies minimizing the cost of making any given level of output.

The neoclassical approach is not without its weaknesses. While it does indicate how the firm's production plans change in response to changes in input and output prices, it says little about how that plan is actually implemented or managed. In other words, it says little about what happens inside the firm, and more specifically, about how the various competing interests of management, workers, and shareholders are reconciled in the design and implementation of a production plan.[2]

Moreover, whatever happens within a firm, it is clear that these internal relationships are different from the external ones that exist between the firm and those outside the firm such as customers and suppliers. A market typically mediates these external relationships. Customers and suppliers buy from and sell to the firm at market prices. Inside the firm, however, relationships are organized by non-market methods, such as hierarchical control. Thus, as eloquently argued by Nobel laureate Ronald Coase (1937), the boundary of the firm is really the boundary between the use of non-market business transactions and market ones. The question Coase then raised is what determines this boundary. Why is it that production of a good is distributed across many different firms instead of a few large ones? Indeed, what limits are there to having all production organized by one or a few giant, multidivisional, and multiplant firms?

The questions raised by Coase (1973) cannot be answered within the simple neoclassical view of the firm. This is not to say though that economics cannot address these issues at all. Over the years, a large number of scholars have developed theories of the firm typically rooted in the recognition of two facts. First, it is typically not possible to write contracts that cover all possible contingencies. Contracts must therefore be incomplete. Second, information is often asymmetric. Managers have information that is not accessible to shareholders. Employees know things that managers do not.

The fact that contracts cannot be complete may require an authority relationship, typically within a firm as a means of dealing with all the contingencies not covered by the contract (Williamson 1975). This is particularly true when specialized investments are required that will only be profitable if the two contracting parties, say a firm and its supplier, continue working together. Otherwise, once such an investment is made, the party that paid for it may find itself at a disadvantage in setting contract terms, e.g., the supply price because it has little alternative use for these assets (Williamson 1975, Grossman and Hart 1986, Hart and Moore 1990, and Hart 1995). Likewise, the fact of asymmetric information can give rise to free-riding and moral hazard problems that can only be resolved by an organizational structure that includes someone who monitors the work efforts of others and, in return, receives a residual payment to insure that there is an incentive to do this job efficiently (Alchian and Demsetz 1972, Holmstrom 1982, and Holmstrom and Milgrom 1994). These and related issues concerning the nature of the firm continue to be important topics of economic research, as evidenced by Daniel Spulber's recent book (2009).

Yet while the neoclassical approach to firm size and market structure is not without its limitations, the approach does remain insightful. For our purposes, it is useful to be aware of the issues raised by the agency and transactions cost literature, but to explore those concerns at all satisfactorily would take us beyond the boundary of this book. As long as its limitations are recognized, the neoclassical view of the firm will permit us to accomplish many of our objectives. Therefore keep in mind throughout the following discussion that

---

[2]   See Milgrom and Roberts (1992) for a classic discussion of these issues.

a firm is interpreted as simply a profit-maximizing production unit and not a complex organization.

4.1.1   Key Cost Concepts

Standard microeconomic theory describes a firm in terms of its production technology. A firm producing the quantity q of a single product is characterized by its production function $q = f(x_1, x_2, \ldots, x_k)$. This function specifies the quantity q that the firm produces from using k different inputs at levels x_1 for the first input, x_2 for the second input, and so on through the kth input of which x_k is used. The technology is reflected in the precise form of the function, $f(\ )$. In turn, the nature of this technology will be a central determinant of the firm's costs.

The firm is treated as a single decision-making unit that chooses output q and the associated inputs $x_1, x_2, \ldots, x_k$ to maximize profits. It is convenient to approach this choice by first identifying the relationship between a firm's output and its resulting production costs—which is simply the firm's cost function. That is, for any specific output $\overline{q}$ and given the prices $w_1, w_2, \ldots, w_k$ of the k inputs, there is a unique way to choose the level of each input $x_1, x_2, \ldots, x_k$ so as to minimize the total cost of producing $\overline{q}$. The firm obtains this solution by choosing the input combination that solves the problem:

$$\underset{x_i}{Minimize} \sum_{i=1}^{k} w_i x_i \tag{4.1}$$

subject to the constraint $f(x_1, x_2, \ldots, x_k) = \overline{q}$.

If we solve this problem for different levels of output $\overline{q}$, we will obtain the minimum cost of each possible production level per unit of time. This relationship between costs and output is what is described by the cost function for the firm. We typically denote the firm's cost function by the expression $C(q) + F$, from which we can then derive three key cost concepts: fixed cost, average or unit cost, and marginal cost.

1. *Fixed cost*: The fixed cost concept is reflected in the term F. This term represents a given amount of expenditure that the firm must incur each period and that is unrelated to how much output the firm produces. That is, the firm must incur F whether it produces zero or a thousand units, hence the term, fixed. This is distinct from the variable cost portion described by $C(q)$ that does vary as output changes. Costs that may be fixed include interest costs associated with financing a particular size of plant and advertising costs. Note, however, that often these costs may be fixed only in the short run. Over a longer period of time, the firm can adjust what plant size it wants to operate and its promotional efforts. If this is true, then these costs are not fixed over a longer period of time.

2. *Average cost*: The firm's average cost is simply a measure of the expenditure per unit of production and is given by total cost divided by total output. This cost measure does depend on output, hence its algebraic representation is $AC(q)$. Formally, $AC(q) = [C(q) + F]/q$. We may also decompose average cost into its fixed and variable components. Average fixed cost is simply total fixed cost per unit of output, or F/q. Average variable cost $AVC(q)$ is similarly just the total variable cost per unit of output, $C(q)/q$. Alternatively, average variable cost is just average cost less average fixed cost, $AVC(q) = AC(q) - F/q$.

3. *Marginal cost*: The firm's marginal cost $MC(q)$ is calculated as the addition to total cost that is incurred in increasing output by one unit. Alternatively, marginal cost can be defined as the savings in total cost that is realized as the firm decreases output by one unit.[3]

We now add a fourth key cost concept—*sunk cost*. Like fixed cost, sunk cost is a cost that is unrelated to output. However, unlike fixed costs, which are incurred every period, sunk cost is a cost that is only incurred prior to a specific date—often prior to the entry date. For example, a doctor will need to acquire a license to operate. Similarly, a firm may need to do market and product research or install highly specialized equipment before it enters a market. The cost of the license, the research expenditures, and the expenditures on specialized assets are likely to be unrelated to subsequent output, so in this sense they are fixed. More importantly, should the doctor or firm subsequently decide to close down, only part of these specialized expenditures will be recoverable. It will be difficult to sell the license to another doctor and certainly not at the price that the first doctor paid. Similarly, the research expenditures are unrecoverable on exit and it will not be possible to sell the specialized assets for anything close to their initial acquisition costs. For example, the kilns that are needed to manufacture cement have almost no alternative use other than as scrap metal. Much of the capital cost that Toyota incurred in building its US car manufacturing plants—production lines, robots, and other highly specialized machinery—likewise have no other uses. By contrast, the airplanes used by JetBlue to open up a new route, say between Boston and Miami, can be redeployed if passenger traffic on that route turns out to be insufficient to continue its operation. Sunk costs, in other words, are initial entry costs that are unrecoverable if the firm chooses later to exit the market.

4.1.2   Cost Variables and Output Decisions

Figure 4.1 depicts a standard textbook average cost function, $AC(q)$, and its corresponding marginal cost function, $MC(q)$. As discussed in Chapter 2, profit maximization over any period of time requires that the firm produce where marginal revenue is equal to marginal

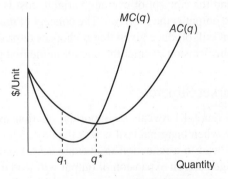

Figure 4.1   Typical average and marginal cost curves

---

[3]   Formally, marginal cost is the slope of the total cost function and so is defined by the derivative term, $MC(q) = dC(q)/dq$. (See Appendix.) Note that in the case of a multiplant firm, shifting one unit of production to plant i from plant j while leaving total output unchanged, would change total cost by an amount: $MC_i - MC_j$. It follows that if $C(q)$ is a minimized, marginal cost is equalized across all plants.

cost. Thus, with one important caveat, marginal cost is the relevant cost concept to determine how much the firm should produce. That caveat is that marginal cost is important for determining how much to produce *given* that the firm is going to produce any output at all.

Suppose, for example, that demand is very weak. In such a case, equating marginal cost to marginal revenue may result in the price falling below average cost. If price is below average cost, the firm loses money on every unit that it sells. It cannot continue to do this in the long run. Hence, the firm will eventually shut down if price stays below average cost. Whether this shutdown happens sooner or later will depend on the relation between price and average variable cost, $AVC(q)$. If price exceeds average variable cost, the firm will continue to operate in the short run. If price is above average variable cost, the firm can make some operating profit on each unit that it sells and this provides funds to cover at least some of its fixed cost. However, if price is below average variable cost, then the firm will simply shut down immediately.

Consideration of price and average cost also allows us to identify the role played by sunk cost in the firm's decision-making. Again, profit per unit in any period is simply price less average cost, $P - AC(q)$. Total profit in any period is just the profit per unit times the number of units, $[P - AC(q)]q$. Before entering an industry, a firm must expect at least to break even. If entry incurs a sunk cost, such as a licensing fee or research expense, then the firm will have to believe that it will earn enough profit in subsequent periods to cover that initial sunk cost. Otherwise, it will not enter the market. Formally, the discounted present value of the expected future profits must be at least as great as the sunk cost of entry. Note though, that once it has entered, the sunk cost is no longer relevant. Once the entry decision has been made and the sunk cost incurred, the best that the firm can do is to follow the prescription above: produce where marginal revenue equals marginal cost so long as in the short run price is greater than average variable cost, otherwise shut down. In the long run, produce where marginal revenue equals marginal cost so long as price is greater than average cost, otherwise exit. Sunk cost affects the entry decision—not the decision on how much to produce after entry has occurred nor the decision to exit.

In sum, the concept of average cost is relevant to whether the firm will produce positive output in the long run, and the concept of average variable cost is relevant to whether the firm will produce positive output in the short run. The concept of marginal cost is relevant to how much output the firm will produce given that it chooses to produce a positive amount. Sunk cost is relevant to the decision to enter the market in the first place.

4.1.3   Costs and Market Structure

Closer consideration of Figure 4.1 reveals an important relationship between average and marginal costs. Note that when marginal cost is less than average cost, as at output q_1, an expansion of output will lead to a reduction in average cost. Conversely, when marginal cost is greater than average cost, an expansion of output will lead to an increase in average cost. In the figure, marginal cost is less than average cost for all outputs less than q^*, the range through which average cost constantly falls. Conversely, marginal cost is greater than average cost for outputs greater than q^*, the range through which average cost constantly rises. This feature is true for all cost functions. Average cost falls whenever marginal cost is less than average cost, and rises whenever marginal cost exceeds average cost. It follows immediately that marginal cost and average cost are equal when average cost is minimized.

Table 4.1 Average and marginal cost

Output	Total Cost ($)	Average Cost ($/Output)	Marginal Cost (Δ$/Δ Output)	Scale Economy Index (S)
5	725	145	–	–
6	816	136	96	1.42
7	917	131	104	1.26
8	1024	128	113	1.13
9	1143	127	123	1.03
10	1270	127	132	0.96
11	1408	128	151	0.85
12	1572	131	–	–

The basic cost relationships are illustrated with a hypothetical example in Table 4.1 (the parameter S in this table is explained below). This table provides measures of total, average, and marginal cost data for an imaginary firm.[4] The table documents the point made above that average cost falls when it lies above marginal cost, rises when it is below marginal cost, and (because the numbers are a discrete approximation) is essentially equal to marginal cost at the minimum average cost value. The Appendix to this chapter presents a formal derivation of cost measures and cost functions.

As noted above, firms have to expect to break even in order for production to be profitable. This means that both average cost and sunk cost play a role in determining market structure. We consider average cost first.

When average cost falls as output increases, it means that the cost per unit of output declines as the scale of operations rises. It is natural to describe this state of affairs as one in which there are economies of scale. If, however, unit costs rise as production increases, we say that there are diseconomies of scale. Fundamentally, the presence of scale economies or scale diseconomies reflects the underlying technology. Some factors of production simply cannot be scaled down to small levels of production. For example, provision of passenger rail service between Omaha and Lincoln, Nebraska, will require approximately sixty miles of track whether the number of trains per day is one or twenty. As a result, a passenger train firm renting the track from the freight company that currently owns it will have to pay the same rent whether it has many passengers or just a few.

Yet it is not just the presence of large fixed costs that gives rise to scale economies. For many productive processes, there are efficiencies that come about just as a result of being larger. To begin with, size permits a greater division of labor, as Adam Smith noted over 200 years ago.[5] This in turn permits specialization and more efficient production. Sometimes, the simple mathematics of the activity give rise to important scale effects. It is well known, for example, that the cost of a container will rise roughly in proportion to its surface area (essentially, the radius squared), whereas its capacity rises roughly in proportion to its volume (essentially, the radius cubed). Thus, while a 10x10x10 cube will hold 1,000 cubic feet, a 20x20x20 cube holds 8,000 cubic feet. Because the cost in terms of materials and labor depends on surface area but output depends on volume, it follows

---

[4] In Table 4.1, marginal cost is calculated as the average of the increase in cost associated with producing one unit more and the decrease in cost associated with producing one unit less.

[5] Smith's classic, *The Wealth of Nations*, includes a famous chapter on the division of labor and the productivity enhancement that this yielded at a pin factory.

that as container size increases there is a less-than-proportional rise in the cost. In turn, this implies that unit cost declines as output increases. Specifically, unit cost will fall by about 3 percent for every 10 percent increase in output.[6] For a variety of processes, such as distributing natural gas via a pipeline or manufacturing glass products in which molten glass is kept in large ovens, this relationship suggests that it will be less expensive per unit to operate at a large volume.[7]

Whatever the source of the scale economies, the fact that scale economies are indicated by a falling average cost gives us a precise way to measure their presence. For we know that a declining average cost can only be observed if marginal cost is below average cost. Likewise, the presence of scale diseconomies or rising average cost requires that marginal cost be above average cost. Hence, we can construct a precise index of the extent of scale economies by defining the measure S to be the ratio of average to marginal cost. That is:

$$S = \frac{AC(q)}{MC(q)} = \frac{[C(q) + F]/q}{MC(q)} = \frac{C(q) + F}{qMC(q)} \tag{4.2}$$

The more that S exceeds 1, the greater is the extent of scale economies. In such a setting, a 1 percent increase in output is associated with a less than 1 percent increase in costs. Conversely, when $S < 1$, diseconomies of scale are present. Increasing output by 1 percent now leads to more than a 1 percent increase in costs. Finally, when $S = 1$, neither economies nor diseconomies of scale are present. In this case, we say that the production technology exhibits constant returns to scale.

We define *minimum efficient scale* as the lowest level of output at which economies of scale are exhausted or, in other words, at which $S = 1$. In Figure 4.1 the minimum efficient scale is q^*.

In Table 4.1, we can approximate the value of S at $q = 6$ as follows. The addition to total cost of increasing output from 6 to 7 is \$101. The reduction in total cost of decreasing q by one unit is \$91. So, an approximate measure of marginal cost at exactly $q = 6$ is the mean of these two numbers, or \$96. Average cost at $q = 6$ is \$136. Accordingly, $S = 136/96 = 1.42$. S can also be estimated by dividing the percentage increase in total output by the percentage increase in total cost. For example, when output is increased from 6 to 7, the percentage increase is given by:

$$\frac{1}{6} \times 100\% = 16.67\%$$

Meanwhile, this output rise induces a percentage increase in total cost of:

$$\frac{917 - 816}{816} \times 100\% = 12.37\%$$

The ratio of these two percentages is then $16.67\%/12.37\% = 1.35\%$. This is not far from the measure of S ($= 1.42$) that we obtained using the ratio of average to marginal

---

[6] The classic study by Chenery (1949) on natural gas pipelines is an example of this technical relationship.

[7] The technical explanations given here reflect the shortcomings of the neoclassical approach in that they do not make clear why the scale economies associated with a specific production technology must be exploited within a single firm. For example, two or more firms can own pipelines jointly. Indeed, there is growing support for the use of co-ownership, or cotenancy, as an alternative to direct regulation in the case of natural monopoly. See Gale (1994).

cost. Indeed, if we could vary production more continuously and so consider the cost of producing 6.5 units, or 6.25 units, and so on, the two measures would be equal.

The ratio of the percentage change in total cost with respect to the percentage change in output is called the elasticity of cost with respect to output. What we have just shown is that the inverse of this ratio—the percentage change in output divided by the percentage change in cost—is a good indicator of scale economies. In other words, S measures the proportionate increase in output one obtains for a given proportionate increase in costs.

4.1

Confirm that at an output of $q = 11$, the scale economy index in Table 4.1 is indeed 0.85.

Practice Problem

How is the behavior of average cost or the extent of scale economies related to industry structure? Going back to Figure 4.1, we see that $S > 1$ for any level of output less than q^*. Scale economies are present at every output level in this range. By contrast, $S < 1$ for all outputs greater than q^*. Now suppose that we have other information indicating that demand conditions are such that the maximum extent of the market is less than q^* even if price falls to zero. We can then state that scale economies are present throughout the relevant range of production. Put another way, economies of scale are global in such a market.

If scale economies are global then the market is a natural monopoly. The term "natural" is meant to reflect the implication that monopoly is an (almost) inevitable outcome for this market because it is cheaper in such cases for a single firm to supply the entire market than for two or more firms to do so. For example, the least expensive way to produce the quantity q^* in Figure 4.1 is to have one firm produce the entire amount. If instead, two firms divided this production equally so that each produces an output $q_1 = q^*/2$, each of these two firms would have higher average costs than would the single firm producing q^*.

The role of scale economies in determining market structure should now be clear. If scale economies are global, there will be no more than one firm in an efficient market. Even if they are not global but simply quite large, efficiency may still require that all the production be done in one firm. More generally, the greater the extent of scale economies—the larger the output at which average cost is minimized—the fewer are the firms that can operate efficiently in the market. Thus, large scale economies will tend to result in concentrated markets.

4.2

Consider the following cost relationship: $C = 50 + 2q + 0.5q^2$.

a. Derive an expression for average cost. Plot the value of average cost for $q = 4$, $q = 8$, $q = 10$, $q = 12$, and $q = 15$.
b. Marginal cost can be approximated by the rise in cost, ΔC, that occurs when output increases by one unit, $\Delta q = 1$. However, it can also be approximated by the fall in cost that occurs when output is decreased by one unit, $\Delta q = -1$. Because these two measures will not be quite the same, we often use their average. Show that for the above cost relation, this procedure produces an estimate of marginal cost equal to $MC = 2 + q$.
c. Compute the index of scale economies, S. For what values of q is it the case that $S > 1$, $S = 1$, and $S < 1$?

Practice Problem

Reality Checkpoint
Hotel Phone Costs May Be Fixed

Business travelers stopping at the Hampton Inn in Salt Lake City often find themselves powering down their cell phones and just relying on their room phone even though this is far more expensive. At some hotels, the cost of using the in-room phone can run as high as $2 per minute or even more for domestic calls and ten or more times that amount for international calls. This compares with a near zero charge for cell phone calls. So, why does anyone use a hotel room phone?

The main answer is that cell phones do not always work. Reception can be poor and getting cell phone service simply may not be possible. For many travelers, the need to be in phone contact with others is such that they are willing to pay the high prices of hotel room phones. In turn, those high prices are necessary in part because of the fixed costs the hotels incur whether the phone is used a lot, a little, or not at all. These costs include a fixed rental fee for each line, the expense of employing operators, and the cost of maintaining equipment, all of which is incurred regardless of the intensity with which room phones are used. The hotels charge a hefty fee, well above marginal cost, to earn those fixed costs back.

Unfortunately for the hotels, the advent of cell phones has sharply cut into their room phone revenue. In fact, operating profits per room phone per year in the United States fell from $644 in 2000 to $152 in 2004. This loss in revenue and profit may have led some hotels to go to rather unusual lengths to beat the cell phone competition. In 2003, the Scottish newspaper the *Daily Record* reported evidence that a local firm, Electron Electrical Engineering Services, was selling cell phone jamming devices to hotels and bed-and-breakfast establishments for between $135 and $200 a piece. These devices have the ability to block cell phone reception without the cell phone customer realizing it. All the customer will see is a message that "service is unavailable" in the location from which they are calling. Loreen Haim-Cayzer, the director of marketing and sales for Netline Communications Technologies in Tel Aviv, also acknowledged that her company had sold hundreds of cell phone jammers to hotels around the world, though none in the United States as far as she knew.

Of course, savvy phone users have another option. They can carry a phone card for use whenever their cell phone cannot get a signal. Those who do not, however, will have to rely on the in-room phone . . . and pay the associated fees. These customers may perhaps be forgiven then if they suspect that it is more than just the cost of such phones that's fixed.

Source: C. Elliot, "Mystery of the Cell Phone that Doesn't Work at the Hotel," *New York Times*, 7 September, 2004, p. C8, and C. Page "Mobile Phones Jam Scam," *The Daily Record*, 26 August, 2003, p1.

4.2   SUNK COST AND MARKET STRUCTURE

Sunk costs also play a role in influencing market structure in a way that is conceptually similar to the role of scale economies. Again, firms only enter a market if they believe that they can at least break even. This means that if there are positive sunk costs associated with entry, then firms must earn positive profits in each subsequent period of actual operation to cover those entry costs. If this is the case, entry will occur. This view leads naturally to a definition of long-run equilibrium. Firms will stop entering the industry—and therefore the number of firms will be at its equilibrium level—when the profit from operating each period just covers the initial sunk cost that entry requires.

The foregoing logic permits us to see clearly the role of sunk cost in determining market structure. Imagine for example a market in which each firm produces an identical good and in which the elasticity of demand is exactly one, or $\eta = 1$, throughout the demand curve. This means that the total consumer expenditure for the product is constant because a 1 percent decrease in price is balanced by a 1 percent increase in quantity sold. Denote then this constant total expenditure as E. If P is the market price and Q is total market output, we then have: $E = PQ$. However, total output Q is also equal to the output of each firm q_i times the number of firms, N, that is, $Q = Nq_i$. Putting these two relationships together we then obtain:

$$q_i = E/NP \tag{4.3}$$

Now recall the Lerner Index that was discussed in Chapter 3. If we assume that all firms are identical and that each has a constant marginal (and average) production cost c, then this index LI is given by: $(P - c)/P$. Because this index is a measure of the extent of monopoly power in the industry, it is natural to assume that it declines as the number of firms, N, gets larger. We formalize this idea by assuming that the industry Lerner Index is negatively related to the number of firms N as follows:

$$(P - c)/P = A/N^\alpha \tag{4.4}$$

where A and α are both arbitrary positive constants. Finally, let's assume that firms only operate one period so that to break even requires that: $(P - c)q_i = F$, where F is the sunk entry cost.[8] Substituting this break-even requirement into equation (4.3) and combining that equation with equation (4.4) then yields that the equilibrium number of firms N^e at which each entrant just covers its sunk entry cost F, is given by:

$$N^e = \left[\frac{AE}{F}\right]^{\frac{1}{1+\alpha}} \tag{4.5}$$

Clearly, N^e declines as F rises. While the precise results of equation (4.5) reflect the particular assumptions made for our example, the intuition underlying those results is fairly general. Industry structure is likely to be more concentrated in markets where sunk entry costs are a high proportion of consumer expenditures.

4.3   COSTS AND MULTIPRODUCT FIRMS

Because scale economies are a description of the behavior of costs as output increases, investigating their existence in any industry requires that we measure the output of the firms in that industry. This is not always so easy. Consider, for instance, the case of a railroad. One possible measure of output is the rail ton-mile, defined as the number of tons transported times the average number of miles each ton travels. However, not all railroads carry the same type of freight. Some carry mainly mining and forestry products, some carry manufactured goods, and some carry agricultural products. In addition, through the first half of this century, many private US railroads carried passengers as well as freight.

---

[8]   Alternatively, we could assume that F is the annualized value of the sunk entry costs.

Elsewhere in the world, this is still the case. Because all of these different kinds of services have different carrying costs, aggregating each railroad's output into a simple measure such as total ton-miles will confuse any cost analysis. Such aggregation does not allow us to identify whether cost differences between railroads are due to differences in scale or to differences in the kinds of transport being provided.

The railroad example points to a gap in our analysis of the firm. In particular, it implies the need to extend the analysis to cover firms producing more than one type of good, that is, to investigate costs for multiproduct firms. This need is perhaps more important today than ever before. Bernard, Redding, and Schott (2009), for example, find that 39 percent of US manufacturing firms produce more than one major product and that these firms account for 87 percent of total US production. Thus, the major automobile firms also produce trucks and buses. Microsoft produces both the *Windows* operating systems and several applications written for that system. Consumer electronics firms produce TVs, stereos, game consoles, and so on. Measuring the total output of these firms in a single index is clearly less than straightforward. If we are to use the technological approach to the firm to gain some understanding of industry structure, we clearly need to extend that approach to handle multiproduct companies. In other words, we need to develop an analysis of costs for the multiproduct firm. The question then becomes whether we can derive average cost and scale economy measures for multiproduct firms that are as precise and clear as the analogous concepts developed for the single product case.

4.3.1   Multiproduct Scale and Scope Economies

The answer to the foregoing question is that, subject to some restrictions, yes we can. This is one of the major contributions of Baumol, Panzar, and Willig (1982). These authors show that the restriction is simply that we measure average cost for a given mix of products, say two units of freight service for every one unit of passenger service in the railroad case. We can then measure average cost at any production level so long as we keep these proportions constant. This is what Baumol, Panzar, and Willig (1982) call Ray Average Cost (RAC). They further show that we can derive a measure of scale economies based on the RAC measure that is conceptually quite similar to the scale economies measure for the single-product case.

To understand the basic idea of Ray Average Cost, consider a firm with two products, q_1 and q_2. Let us imagine that these two products may be combined to create a composite good called $q = q_1 + q_2$. However, this composite good will be different depending on how much of each good we have. A composite good made up of one unit of product 1 and five units of product 2 is very different from one comprised of three units of product 1 and one unit of product 2. Because we want to consider costs for a specific product, we choose a production ray along which the two goods are always produced in the same proportion. A possible production ray, for example, is one in which the production of good 1 is always twice that of good 2, that is, $q_1 = 2q_2$. Now we can consider the behavior of costs for all output levels in which this proportion is maintained—for $q_1 = 2$ and $q_2 = 1$; $q_1 = 20$ and $q_2 = 10$; and so on. By focusing on a specific production ray, we isolate the change in cost that is due only to changing the level of output and not that due to changes in the product mix.

Continuing with our example, suppose that $q_1 = 60$ so that $q_2 = 30$. Then it follows that $q = q_1 + q_2 = 90$. Note that we could write this alternatively as $q_1 = (60/90)q$ and $q_2 = (30/90)q$. More generally, for a given product mix or production ray, we can write $q_1 = \lambda q$ and $q_2 = (1 - \lambda)q$, where $\lambda/(1 - \lambda)$ is the fixed proportions of the product mix along the production ray being considered. In our example, $\lambda = 2/3$ and $1 - \lambda = 1/3$, so that $\lambda/(1 - \lambda) = 2$.

We denote the total cost of producing both products at any level as $C(q_1, q_2) + F = C[\lambda q, (1 - \lambda)q] + F = C(q) + F$. We denote the marginal cost of goods 1 and 2, respectively, as MC_1 and MC_2. Recall that for the single product case, our scale economy measure was the ratio of average cost to marginal cost [equation (4.2)]. Analogously, we define a measure of multi-product (in our case, two-product) scale economies as:

$$S^M = \frac{C(q_1, q_2) + F}{q_1 MC_1 + q_2 MC_2} \tag{4.6}$$

Having an explicit definition for scale economies in the multiproduct case is, as we shall see, very helpful. Perhaps a more important insight of Baumol, Panzar, and Willig (1982), however, is their introduction of an equally critical measure called economies of *scope*. Economies of scope are said to be present whenever it is less costly to produce a set of goods in one firm than it is to produce that set in two or more firms. Let the total cost of producing two goods, q_1 and q_2, be given by $C(q_1, q_2) + F$. For the two-product case, scope economies exist if $C(q_1, \ 0) + F_1 + C(0, \ q_2) + F_2 - [C(q_1, \ q_2) + F] > 0$. The first two terms in this equation are the total costs of producing product 1—the variable costs associated with just this one good plus the fixed cost if only this good is produced. The next two terms are the analogous cost measures when only good 2 is produced. The last terms are of course the total cost of having these products produced by the same firm. If the difference is positive, then scope economies exist. If it is negative, there are diseconomies of scope. If it is 0, then there are neither economies nor diseconomies of scope. The degree of such economies S^C is defined by the ratio:

$$S^C = \frac{C(q_1, \ 0) + F_1 + C(0, \ q_2) + F_2 - [C(q_1, \ q_2) + F]}{C(q_1, \ q_2) + F} \tag{4.7}$$

The concept of scope economies is a crucial one that provides the central technological reason for the existence of multiproduct firms. Such economies can arise for two main reasons. The first of these is that particular outputs share common inputs. This is the source of economies of scope in the railroad example where the common input is the track. Another example would include a firm's advertising expenditures that benefit all of the products carrying that same brand name.

An alternative source of scope economies is the presence of cost complementarities. Cost complementarities occur when producing more of one good lowers the cost of producing a second good. There are numerous ways in which such interactions can take place. For example, the exploration and drilling of an oil well often yields not just oil but also natural gas. Hence, engaging in crude oil production will likely lower the cost of gas exploration. Similarly, a firm that manufactures computer software may also find it easy to provide computer-consulting services.

Scope economies have likely become stronger in recent decades following the introduction of new manufacturing techniques, referred to as flexible manufacturing systems. They can be defined as "production unit(s) capable of producing a range of discrete products with a minimum of manual intervention" (U.S. Office of Technology Assessment, 1984, p. 60). The idea here is that production processes should be capable of switching easily from one variant of a product to another without a significant cost penalty.

Reality Checkpoint

An Arm and a Leg . . . Scope Economies and Hospital Consolidation

The health care industry has been in transformation since at least the 1990s. As health care expenditures have risen steadily—from 6 or 7 percent of GDP thirty years ago to nearly 18 percent today—patients, insurance companies, and the doctors and hospital service providers themselves have all been forced to adjust to new market pressures. One manifestation of this transformation has been a continuing wave of hospital mergers and consolidation. Since 1997, the average Herfindahl Index for hospital services in metropolitan areas has increased from 4200 to nearly 4800 today. Because the DOJ/FTC Merger Guidelines define any market with an index over 2500 to be highly concentrated and any increase over 100 points in such markets to be significant, these data show that the typical urban hospital market is one in which hospitals may have considerable and growing market power.

Cost efficiency has been a major motivation behind the hospital merger wave and scope economies are likely an important source for any such cost savings. There may, for example, be important scope economies between serving patients needing surgery and follow-up in-hospital care such as amputees and those receiving hip or knee replacements, with serving patients needing continuing disease control and/or rehabilitation because many of the nursing and monitoring services required are the same. Similar scope economies may exist between inpatient and outpatient care. In addition, scope economies may be realized by combining in one hospital both those who specialize in various functional areas with generalists who treat diseases that affect those areas and others. For example, because prostate and colorectal are two of the most common kinds of cancers, it may be less costly to house proctology and urology specialists in the same hospital as oncologists.

Of course, acquiring market power may be another motivation behind the hospital merger wave. These issues came to a head recently when the Federal Trade Commission blocked a merger between Pro Medica Health System and St. Luke's Hospital in Toledo, Ohio. The merging hospitals argued that their joining was necessary to coordinate care and controlling costs especially in light of the changes instituted by the Affordable Care Act. The FTC provided data showing that this consolidation would substantially increase concentration in the Toledo area hospital market. It also gave evidence implying that Pro Medica's hospitalization fees were among the highest. FTC officials saw the merger as a classic case of an attempt to eliminate (buy out) a low-cost rival. In the FTC's view, even if the scope economies were realized there was no guarantee that these savings would be passed on to the public given the market power the newly merged firm would have. The FTC was not against saving lives and limbs more efficiently. It just wanted to make sure that it did not end up costing patients an arm and a leg.

Source: R. Pear, "Regulator Orders Hospitals to Undo a Merger in Ohio," *New York Times*, April 3, 2012, p. A11.

Consider, for example, the popular clothing manufacturer, Benetton. This Italian family firm has over 2,500 retail outlets around the globe. Each is equipped with special cash registers that collect and transmit information regarding which items are selling, and in what colors, sizes, and styles. This information is sent to the central manufacturing facilities. These, together with numerous small sub-contracting firms, then respond quickly to these market signals. Benetton's famous coloring is the final step of the process, as the dyeing of the goods is done at the last moment just before shipment to the stores. All of this is made possible via Benetton's extensive use of computer-assisted-design/computer-assisted-manufacturing (CAD/CAM) technology, which allows it to produce a wide array of differentiated (by color) products.

4.3.2   Different Products versus Different Versions

So far, our discussion of multiproduct firms has not distinguished between situations in which the two outputs are somewhat related, as is the case with passenger and freight rail service, and those in which the two goods are substantially different products, say cologne and shirts. In the latter case, the two products use quite different production processes and the presence of scope economies seems less compelling. It seems more likely that scope economies will be found when the goods being produced use similar production techniques because then we are more likely to find shared inputs and cost complementarities.

An issue that arises in this regard is the distinction between different goods and different versions of the same good. Campbell's produces both canned soup and canned beverages, principally, *V8*. While this may reflect some scope effects, the real source of scope economies at Campbell's is undoubtedly the fact that it is cheaper to manufacture of Campbell's thirty-plus types of canned soup at one firm rather than having over thirty separate firms each producing one of those varieties. Likewise, there are almost certainly some strong scope economies at work that lead L'Oreal to offer over more than fifty shades of its *Riche Lipstick*, as well as offering other cosmetics, including lipsticks, through its subsidiaries, Maybelline and Lancôme.

Because firms so often market multiple varieties within a product category as well as possibly marketing more than one distinct good, it is useful to have a way of modeling markets in which the basic good is sold in many differentiated versions. One way to do this is to imagine that some particular characteristic is the critical distinguishing feature between different versions of the good. In the case of cars, this characteristic could be speed or acceleration. In the case of soft drinks, it could be sugar content. We can then construct an index to measure this feature. Each point on the index, ranging from low to high acceleration capacity, low to high sugar content, and so on, represents a different product variety. Some consumers will prefer a car that accelerates rapidly or a very sweet beverage, while others will favor cars that are easier to drive because they are capable of less acceleration or beverages with very low sugar content.

As an example, imagine a soft-drink company considering the marketing of three versions of its basic cola: (1) Diet or sugar free; (2) Super, with full sugar content; and (3) LX, an intermediate cola with just half the sugar content of Super. In this case, the distinctive feature separating each product type is sugar content, and thus we want to construct an index of such content. It is customary to normalize such an index so that it ranges from 0 to 1. The spectrum of products for our imaginary company, therefore, ranges from Diet, located at point 0 on our index, to Super, located at point 1, with LX positioned, let's say, squarely in the middle at point 0.5. This is illustrated in Figure 4.2.

The spectrum shown in Figure 4.2 may be alternatively interpreted as a street. In turn, we may regard consumers as being located at different "addresses" on this street. Consumers who really like sugar will have addresses close to the Super product line. In contrast, consumers who really need to watch their calorie intake will have addresses near the Diet product line. Similarly, consumers who favor more than a medium amount of sugar but

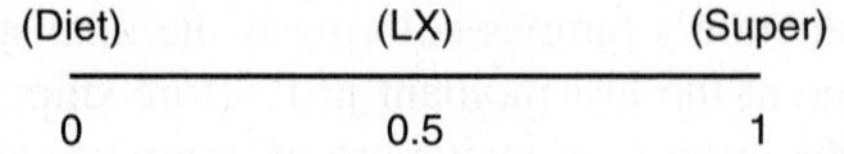

(Diet)	(LX)	(Super)
0	0.5	1

Figure 4.2   Location of cola products along the sugar content line

not quite so much as that contained in the Super variety will have addresses somewhere between the LX and Super points.

If scope economies exist, firms have a strong incentive to exploit them. If we extend this logic to the case of multiple varieties within a product category, then the implication is that firms in such markets ought to produce a wide range of product types. This logic has been formalized by Eaton and Schmitt (1994). These authors present a formal model of flexible manufacturing in which there are k possible versions of the good. They show that when scope economies are very strong, it will be natural for each firm in the industry to produce the entire range of k products.

The same incentive applies of course to scope economies across truly different product categories. Indeed, a critical insight of the analysis of multiproduct production is that it is the presence of *scope* economies as identified by equation (4.7) that makes it possible to exploit the multiproduct *scale* economies identified by equation (4.6). The airline industry offers another good example. For many years, major air carriers have organized their services around the hub-and-spoke system. Under this system, central large airports, designated as hubs, act as collector stations. Hub-to-hub flights are typically served by large aircraft for which the cost per passenger mile is low when they are filled to near capacity. Spoke airports, in contrast, serve as "feeders" that use relatively small aircraft to fly passengers from many different locations to a hub where they can all be collected and put on hub-to-hub flights to generate the passenger volume necessary to exploit the efficiencies of the larger aircraft. The multi-product scale economies can thus only be realized by operating in both the spoke and the hub markets.

Overall then, significant scope economies lead to more concentrated market structures in two ways. First, the scope effects by definition create incentives to consolidate the production of different products and different product versions within one firm rather than many separate firms. Second, strong scope economies also give rise to important multiproduct scale economies, leading firms to be large relative to market size.[9]

4.4   LEARNING-BY-DOING AND EXPERIENCE CURVES

Scale economies reflect the lower unit cost that comes from operating on a larger scale as defined by the volume of production per unit of time. If there are significant scale economies in automobile production, then General Motors will have a lower unit cost in 2013 if it produces say 3.8 million cars that year instead of 3.4 million. There is, however, another size factor that may influence a firm's cost. This is its total, cumulative output over its entire

---

[9]   See Panzar (1989) for a good discussion of cost issues in general. See Evans and Heckman (1986) and Roller (1990) for evidence of scope economies in the telephone industry; Cohn, Rhine, and Santos (1989) and DeGroot, McMahon, and Volkwein (1991) for evidence of scope economies in higher education; and Gilligan, Smirlock, and Marshall (1984) and Pulley and Braunstein (1992) for evidence of scope economies in finance.

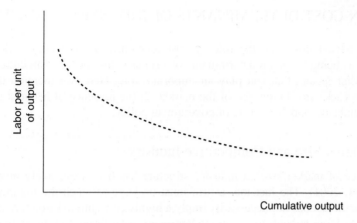

Figure 4.3   Hypothetical experience or learning curve

history. If this factor is important, then a firm that produces only 3.4 million cars might still have relatively low unit cost if it has produced a lot of cars in previous years.

Like any organization, firms and their employees can learn with experience. There are typically many ways of organizing design, production, and sales, and the best ways can only be learned by trial-and-error. As the cumulative experience of the firm grows, more such trials can be made and the insights from that experience can be used to raise productivity in the future. Based on a survey of the then-existing literature, Argote and Epple (1990) find that for the typical US manufacturing firm, labor costs fall by 20 percent as its cumulative output doubles. Ramanarayanan (2006) finds that for cardiac surgeons, each additional coronary artery bypass performed lowers the probability of death for subsequent patients by 0.14 percent. These results imply that cost reductions due to organizational learning are important, as illustrated by Figure 4.3.

Yet if organizations can learn, they can also forget. As older workers retire or quit and institutional memories are lost, firms may move backwards and unit costs may rise. Benkard (2000, 2004) finds evidence of both learning and forgetting in aircraft production. As firms learn and forget, the dynamics of industry structure become complicated.

However, the basic intuition regarding how important learning effects may affect market structure is relatively straightforward. Essentially, learning-by-doing leads to more concentrated market structures because it provides further advantage to first movers or early entrant firms, as these firms will typically have had the longest time to learn. Strategic considerations are likely to reinforce this result. Faced with possible new rivals, an incumbent firm will often find it optimal to price artificially low so as to sell more units. This not only helps the incumbent move down the learning curve itself but also makes it harder for rivals to do the same. Further, the prospect that whatever it learns may be forgotten gives a further incentive for the incumbent to price low and thereby acquire more experiences so that even if it loses some of its knowledge, it still has an advantage. Thus, both in and of itself and because of the strategic responses it induces, learning-by-doing will likely lead to more concentrated markets in which early incumbents maintain and even extend their dominance.[10]

---

[10]   See Besanko, et al, (2010) for an extended examination of these issues.

4.5   NON-COST DETERMINANTS OF INDUSTRY STRUCTURE

So far, we have focused on the role of cost relationships, especially scale and scope economies, as being the main determinants of firm size and industry structure. There are, however, other factors that can play an important role. Here, we mention three factors specifically. These are: 1) the size of the market, 2) the presence of network externalities on the demand side, and 3) the role of government policy.

4.5.1   Market Size and Competitive Industry

The influence of market size on industry structure has been extensively investigated by Sutton (1991, 2001). The fact that a firm must be large to reach the minimum efficient scale of operations does not necessarily imply a highly concentrated structure if the market in question is large enough to accommodate many such firms. Similarly, the fact that it is cheaper to produce many different products (or many versions of the same product) in one firm rather than in several firms does not necessarily imply a market dominated by a few firms. Most farms produce more than one crop. Yet farming is a very competitively structured industry in part because the market for agricultural products is so extensive.

Just how big does a market have to be in order to avoid domination by a few firms? The answer is: it depends. When scale economies are extensive, for example when sunk or fixed costs associated with indivisible inputs are relatively large, the market will need to be greater to accommodate more firms. Thus, the relationship between market structure and market size will vary according to the specific market being examined.

If scale economies are exhausted at some point and if sunk entry costs do not rise with the size of the market, then we ought to see that concentration declines as market size grows sufficiently large. Some direct evidence of this effect is provided by Bresnahan and Reiss (1991). They gathered data on a number of professions and services from over 200 towns scattered across the western United States. They find that a town of about 800 or 900 will support just one doctor. As the town grows to a population of roughly 3,500, a second doctor will typically enter. It takes a town of over 9,000 people to generate an industry of five doctors. The same positive relationship between market size and the number of firms is also found in other professions. For tire dealers, for example, Bresnahan and Reiss find that a town of only 500 people is needed to support one tire dealer and that five tire dealers will emerge when the town reaches a population of 6,000. The smaller market requirements needed to support a given number of tire dealers instead of doctors probably reflects, among other things, the fact that doctors have higher fixed/sunk costs than do the tire dealers.

Sutton (1991, 2001) however, provides an important qualification to the idea that concentration will decline with the size of the market. He notes that such a relationship does not appear to hold in a number of industries, particularly in industries that compete heavily using either advertising, such as processed foods, or R&D, such as pharmaceuticals. Sutton argues that these expenditures are not only sunk but also endogenous. They are sunk in that once the expenditures for a promotional campaign or product design have been incurred, they cannot be recovered. They are endogenous in that in these kinds of industries, sunk cost F is not fixed but in fact increases as the market size grows.

The logic of the Sutton argument can be seen by focusing on the sunk entry cost term F in equation (4.5). Assume that this term reflects advertising and/or R&D expenditures. However, rather than simply assuming that such expenditures are equal to some exogenous level F, assume instead that they are related to market size. For example, we may assume a linear relationship of the form:

$$F = K + \beta(AE) \tag{4.8}$$

where recall that A is a constant (K is also a constant) and E is aggregate consumer expenditure in the industry.

Using (4.8), equation (4.5) now may be written as:

$$N^e = \left[\frac{1}{\left(\frac{K}{AE}\right) + \beta} \right]^{\frac{1}{1+\alpha}} \tag{4.9}$$

Equation (4.9) says that the equilibrium number of firms in the industry will grow as market size AE grows but that this process has an asymptotic limit. Specifically, the number of firms will never exceed $(1/\beta)^{1/(1+\alpha)}$ no matter how large the market gets. For example, suppose that $\alpha = 1$ and $\beta = 0.0625$. If this is the case, then the equilibrium number of firms in the industry will never exceed four, regardless of market size.[11]

Somewhat similarly, our initial derivation of equation (4.5) assumed that price cost margins declined as a result of an increase in the number of firms as described by: $(P - c)/P = A/N^a$. However, there may be systematic differences between industries in the relationship between the price cost margin and the population of firms. In particular, markets in which firms sell a homogenous product and in which they can quickly alter production to meet demand may have very small price cost margins. This is because in such homogenous good markets, the firm with the lowest price gets all the customers, especially if it can readily adjust output to meet that demand. Algebraically, this means that the parameter α above will differ across markets. It will be larger in those markets in which competition is naturally more intense. In such markets, the equilibrium number of firms will be correspondingly smaller.

4.5.2   Network Externalities and Market Structure

It is not news to anyone reading this book that Microsoft's *Windows* has an approximate 85 percent of the operating systems market for desktop and laptop computers with virtually all of the remaining 15 percent going to Apple's *Mac* products.[12] *Microsoft Word* and *Microsoft Excel* have similarly large, dominant market shares of the word-processing and spreadsheet markets, respectively. Scale and scope economies are undoubtedly part of the explanation for the highly concentrated nature of these markets. Once the costs have been sunk to design the basic program for the operating systems or application software, the cost of reproducing the product many times over is quite trivial. It is also highly likely that there will be a large common component to these design costs. However, as many witnesses testified at the Microsoft antitrust case of 1999–2000, an additional critical factor behind Microsoft's dominance is the presence of *network externalities*. Such network effects reflect the fact that for some products, a consumer's willingness to pay for a good or service increases as the number of other consumers buying the product rises.

---

[11]   See Baldwin (1995) for some evidence on this point.
[12]   www.statowl.com/operating_system_market_share.php.

Network effects can be *direct* or *indirect*. Telephone service exhibits direct network externalities. The usefulness or value of a single consumer connecting to a telephone system is essentially nil. Yet, as more people sign on to the system, the number of potential calls and hence the utility of owning a phone increases as well. Operating systems, platforms such as Amazon's *Kindle*, and credit card services each exhibit more indirect network effects due to complementarities with other products. In the case of operating systems, for example, the significant scale economies that characterize the design and production of applications means that firms marketing computer apps want to make them compatible with as large a network as possible. Likewise, consumers want to use an operating system for which the number of available applications is largest. This establishes a positive feedback loop. As *Windows'* market share grows, more applications firms will want to design their applications to run on the *Windows* operating system. As more applications are written for *Windows*, demand for the *Windows* system rises and with it, *Windows'* market share. Likewise as more books are offered on *Kindle* and as more retailers accept *American Express* cards, the more consumers want to use *Kindle* readers and *Amex* credit cards, which in turn, increases the market shares of these firms.

We address the topic of network externalities more extensively in Chapter 22. However, from the brief discussion above, it should be relatively easy to see that markets with important network externalities are likely to be ones populated by a few very large firms. In other words, they are likely to have a highly concentrated structure—even if scale economies are not present on the cost side. Indeed, many analysts view network externalities as a case of scale economies that exist on the demand side of the market.

4.5.3   The Role of Government Policy

From 1934 to the mid 1990s, the number of medallions authorizing legal ownership of a taxicab in Boston was fixed at 1,525. Not a single additional medallion was issued in all that time despite the fact that the regional population increased by over 50 percent and the level of income and economic activity doubled several times over. Costs and technology were not the source of this fixed industrial structure. The primary reason for the limited entry into the Boston taxi industry was government policy. City and state officials deliberately limited the number of taxi medallions, largely to the benefit of those lucky taxi owners who obtained the first batch of medallions. A court order in the mid-1990s led to an increase of nearly 300 medallions over the subsequent five years. Yet this was not enough to keep the price of medallion from rising dramatically.[13]

A similar phenomenon prevailed from the 1930s through the 1970s when the number of so-called trunk airlines flying interstate routes never exceeded sixteen and fell to ten by the end of the 70s. Not only was the total number of airlines small on a national scale, it was even smaller for individual city-pair markets. Many of these were often served by only one or two carriers. Here again, the primary cause was government policy. In this case, that policy was implemented by the Civil Aeronautics Board (CAB), the federal agency established in 1938 as the economic regulator of the airline industry. Throughout its existence, the CAB deliberately limited entry and sustained a high concentration level in the US domestic airline industry. Indeed, this forty-year period witnessed numerous applications by freight and charter airlines to be granted the right to offer scheduled passenger services, as well as frequent applications of existing airlinesto enter new city-pair markets. Virtually all

---

[13]   C. Berdik, "Boston's Fare Game," *Boston Magazine*, September 2004: 19.

of these requests were turned down. The CAB argued that this policy was necessary to promote the stability and healthy development of the airline industry. Whether it achieved its perceived goals, and whether such goals were appropriate, are questions to be answered elsewhere. The central point illustrated by both the taxicab and airline examples is that explicit government policies often play an important role in determining market structure.

More often than not, the role of government policy has been to increase market concentration as both of the examples above illustrate. However, some government policies do work to increase the number of firms in an industry. The Robinson-Patman Act that prohibits price discounts to large firms if such discounts are deemed anticompetitive reflects a conscious effort to keep independent retailers in business. These are typically small firms that otherwise would have been driven out of the market by the large retail chains. Similarly, the decision of the US government after World War II to force the Alcoa Company to sell some of its wartime aluminum plants to the Kaiser and Reynolds corporations was clearly an effort to promote a more competitive structure. Perhaps most obviously, antitrust policies that lead either the Federal Trade Commission or the Justice Department to block mergers also increase the equilibrium number of firms in an industry.

4.6 EMPIRICAL APPLICATION: SCALE AND SCOPE ECONOMIES IN BANKING

Because the underlying technology and associated cost implications are central determinants of industrial structure, economists have been interested in getting evidence on cost relationships for a long time. Unfortunately, we rarely have direct evidence on the production technology. Thus estimating firm cost functions can be a tricky business. However, application of basic microeconomic theory can greatly facilitate the process.

The basic idea is clear enough. A profit-maximizing firm will choose inputs to produce a given output level at the lowest cost given the set of input prices. For single product firms, this will imply that cost is simply a function of its total output and the prices of its inputs (See the Appendix for a formal derivation of this relationship). With a data set in which these variables vary either across firms at a point in time or for the same firm at different times (or both), we can estimate this relationship to measure how total costs vary with output and, hence, to estimate the extent of any scale economies. For instance, with one output Q, and two inputs, capital and labor, whose input prices are r and w, respectively, we might estimate the simple logarithmic relationship below:

$$\ln C = \text{Constant} + \delta_1 \ln r + \delta_2 \ln w + \delta_3 \ln Q \tag{4.10}$$

In this case, the coefficient δ_3 is a direct measure of the elasticity of total cost with respect to output. Therefore, $1/\delta_3$ is a measure of single-product scale economies.

A very simple extension of equation (4.10) to handle a firm with two outputs, q_1 and q_2, we might instead assume a cost function of the form:

$$\ln C = \text{Constant} + \delta_1 \ln\ r + \delta_2 \ln\ w + \delta_3 \ln q_1 + \delta_4 \ln q_2 + \delta_5 (\ln q_1)(\ln q_2) \tag{4.11}$$

Here, the final term allows for interaction between the two outputs and thus allows for possible scope economies. A more complicated extension of equation (4.10) that is potentially consistent with a very large range of underlying production functions is the translog cost function, which in this case is written as:

$$\ln C = \text{Constant} + \delta_1 \ln r + \delta_2 \ln w + \delta_3 \ln q_1 + \delta_4 \ln q_2 + \delta_5 (\ln q_1)(\ln q_2)$$
$$+ \delta_6 (\ln r)(\ln w) + \delta_7 (\ln r)^2 + \delta_8 (\ln w)^2 + \delta_9 (\ln q_1)^2 + \delta_{10} (\ln q_2)^2$$
$$+ \delta_{11} (\ln r)(\ln q_1) + \delta_{12} (\ln w)(\ln q_1) + \delta_{13} (\ln r)(\ln q_2) + \delta_{14} (\ln w)(\ln q_2) \quad (4.12)$$

Note that equation (4.12) includes equations (4.11) and (4.10) as special cases.

Once the cost function parameters (the δs) have been estimated, it is straightforward, in principle, to derive the scale economy and scope economy measures described in the text. Christensen and Green (1976) use this approach to find important scale economies in electricity generation, while also finding that most power-generating firms are sufficiently large that these scale economies have been fully exploited. DeGroot, McMahon, and Volkwein (1991) use this translog approach to model the cost structure of American research universities, assuming three university outputs: 1) undergraduate education, 2) graduate education, and 3) research. They find that for the product mix of the typical university there were significant unexploited scale economies (declining Ray Average Cost). However, this was not true for the less student-intensive product mix of the top private schools for which they found little if any scale economies. They also found significant scope economies between graduate and undergraduate education but, somewhat surprisingly, no scope economies between graduate education and research.

Pulley and Braunstein (1992) apply this same approach to commercial banking firms with one important modification. Consider again the two-output case. Remember that the measure of scope economies in this case is $\{[C(q_1, 0) + F_1 + C(0, q_2) + F_2] - [C(q_1, q_2) + F]\}/[C(q_1, q_2) + F]$. It may turn out, however, that there are no firms in the sample that produce only one output. Thus, any estimates of scope economies will have to be based on hypothetical cases for which there are no actual counterparts. For this reason, Pulley and Braunstein (1992) introduce a measure of *quasi*-scope economies. To understand this concept, consider the two-variable case. While no firms may actually specialize completely in one product, some may come relatively close by devoting 90 percent of their effort to a single output and 10 percent to the remaining output. We might therefore consider the cost disadvantage that these firms face as: $\{[C(0.9q_1, 0.1q_2) + F_1 + C(0.1q_1, 0.9q_2) + F_2] - [C(q_1, q_2) + F]\}/[C(q_1, q_2) + F]$. More generally, if ε is the fraction devoted to the minor activity, then Pulley and Braunstein (1992) define *quasi*-scope economies in the two-output case as:

$$\text{quasi-}S^C = \{[C((1 - \varepsilon)q_1, \ \varepsilon q_2) + F_1 + C(\varepsilon q_1, (1 - \varepsilon)q_2) + F_2]$$
$$- [C(q_1, q_2) + F]\}/[C(q_1, q_2) + F] \quad (4.13)$$

By using different values of ε, Pulley and Braunstein (1992) can infer a robust estimate of the importance of scope effects in banking.

For this purpose, Pulley and Braunstein (1992) define four banking outputs. These are: 1) demand deposits plus savings and small time deposits, 2) real estate loans, 3) commercial and industrial loans, and 4) installment and credit card loans. Table 4.2 below shows some of the (quasi) scope and scale estimates they obtain for different variations of the underlying cost equation and different values of ε.

Table 4.2   Estimates of (Quasi) scope and scale economies in US commercial banking (standard errors in parentheses)

	Composite Cost Function Quasi-Scope Economies	Translog Cost Function Quasi-Scope Economies
$\varepsilon = 0.10$	0.23 (0.06)	0.18 (0.28)
$\varepsilon = 0.15$	0.19 (0.05)	0.15 (0.13)
$\varepsilon = 0.20$	0.16 (0.05)	0.15 (0.05)
Scale Economy Estimate	0.04 (0.01)	0.06 (0.02)

The Pulley and Braunstein (1992) estimates indicate that there are sizable and statistically significant advantages of scope in US commercial banking. Combining all four activities in one firm reduces costs by 15 to 23 percent relative to the costs of producing these outputs at four separate and much more specialized banks. Statistically significant but relatively small scale effects are also found. Very large banks save only about 5 percent in costs relative to small ones—not trivial, but perhaps not enough to offset the bad effects of having large banks with a lot of market power—and that may need to be bailed out by the government if they are "too large to fail."

Summary

This chapter has focused on technology, key cost concepts, and the implications they have for industrial structure. Scale economies tend to increase market concentration. Economies of scope have a similar effect of concentrating the production of different products within a single firm. Scope economies also typically give rise to important multiproduct scale economies. This is particularly the case when the various products are not truly different goods but, instead, different versions of the same goods. In such product-differentiated markets, the presence of scope and scale economies will again imply a more concentrated structure. A further cost-related factor is captured by the experience or learning curve that characterizes some industries, such as aircraft manufacturing. In such markets, firms learn valuable, cost-saving techniques as their total production over time rises. This too will tend to result in somewhat concentrated markets as early entrants have a cost advantage over later rivals because these incumbents will be farther down the learning curve.

Other factors influence market structure as well. One of these is market size. Because a large market has room for a number of firms, larger markets tend to be less concentrated than smaller ones. However, increasing market size does not lead to less concentration in markets in which sunk costs also increase with size. These are typically markets in which advertising or research and development costs play a major role.

Another important determinant of market structure comes from the demand side of the market in the form of network externalities. Network externalities imply that the value of a product to any one consumer increases as other consumers use it. Such externalities act much like scale economies on the demand side and they foster increased market concentration.

Government policy is also a very important determinant of market structure. Regulations such as those long applied to local taxi markets and the airline industry typically reduce the ability of new firms to enter the market. Antitrust policy can raise the number of firms in a market by blocking a proposed merger.

Careful application of economic theory can generate clear implications for the statistical measurement of cost relationships. Such work has been extremely useful in identifying scale and scope economies. For example, regression analysis based on the theory of production costs has found significant scope economies between different banking activities but little evidence of

significant scale economies. Other studies have found important scale effects in electric power generation and important economies of scope between graduate and undergraduate education.

Problems

1. Let the cost function be $C = 100 + 4q + 4q^2$. Derive an expression for average cost. Derive an expression for marginal cost. Is there any range of production characterized by scale economies? At what production level are scale economies exhausted?

2. An urban rapid-transit line runs crowded trains (200 passengers per car) at rush hours, but nearly empty trains (10 passengers per car) at off-peak hours. A management consultant argues that the cost of running a car for one trip on this line is about $50 regardless of the number of passengers. Hence, the consultant concludes that the per passenger cost is about 25 cents at rush hour but rises to $5 in off-peak hours. Consequently, the consultant advises that it would be better to discourage the off-peak business. Is the consultant a good economist? Why or why not?

3. Consider the following cost relationships for a single-product firm:

   $C(q) = 50 + 0.5q$ for $q \leq 7$

   $C(q) = 7q$ for $q > 7$

   a. Derive average and marginal cost for all integer outputs less than or equal to 7.
   b. What are the average and marginal cost for all outputs above 7?

4. In the problem above, is there a minimum efficient scale of plant implied by these cost relationships? If so, what is it?

5. Let P be industry price and Q be total industry output. If the industry demand curve is $P = 84 - 0.5Q$, use the data in question 3 to determine what is the maximum number of efficient-sized firms that the industry can sustain.

6. How would your answer to question 5 be changed if industry demand were instead $P = 14 - 0.5Q$? Explain.

7. Some estimates for the cement industry suggest the following relationship between capacity and average cost:

Capacity (Thousands of Tons)	Average Cost
250	28.78
500	25.73
750	23.63
1,000	21.63
1,250	21.00
1,500	20.75
1,750	20.95
2,000	21.50

   a. At what production level are scale economies exhausted?
   b. Calculate the scale economy index for the production levels 500, 750, 1,000, 1,500, and 1,750.

8. A recent article (J. Peder Zane, "It Ain't for the Meat; It's for Lotion," *New York Times*, Sunday May 5, 1996: E5) presented the following data for a cow brought to market:

Part	Use	Price/lb ($)
Horns	Gelatin Collagen	0.42
Cheek	Sausage Baloney	0.55
Adrenal Gland	Steroids	2.85
Meat	Beef	1.05
Lips	Taco Filling	0.19
Hide	Footwear Clothing	0.75

   Comment on the scope economies illustrated by this example. What is the source of such economies? What does the existence of such economies imply about the supply of such products as leather skins, beef, and gelatin powder?

References

Alchian, A. A., and Demsetz, H. 1972. "Production, Information Costs, and Economic Organization," *American Economic Review* 62(December): 772–95.

Argote, L., and D. Epple. 1990. "Learning Curves in Manufacturing," *Science* 247 (February 23, 1990): 920–24.

Baldwin, John R. 1995. *The Dynamics of Industrial Competition: A North American Perspective*. Cambridge: Cambridge University Press.

Baumol, W. J., J. C. Panzar, and R. D. Willig. 1982. Contestable Markets and the Theory of Industry Structure. New York: Harcourt, Brace, Jovanovich.

Benkard, L. 2000. "Learning and Forgetting: The Dynamics of Aircraft Production," *American Economic Review* 90 (December): 1034–54.

———. 2004. "A Dynamic Analysis of the Market for Wide-bodied Commercial Aircraft," *Review of Economic Studies* 71: 581–611.

Bernard, A., S. J. Redding, and P. K. Schott. 2009. "Products and Productivity," *Scandinavian Journal of Economics* 111 (December): 681–709.

Besanko, D., U. Doraszelski, Y. Kryukov, and M. Satterwaite. 2010. "Learning-By-Doing, Organizational Forgetting, and Industry Dynamics," (with Ulrich Doraszelski, Yaroslav Kryukov, and Mark Satterthwaite); *Econometrica*, 78 (March): 453–508.

Bresnahan, T., and P. Reiss. 1991. "Entry and Competition in Concentrated Markets," *Journal of Political Economy* 99 (October): 977–1009.

Caves, D., L. Christensen, and M. W. Tretheway. 1980. "Flexible Cost Functions for Multiproduct Firms," *Review of Economics and Statistics* 62 (August):477–81.

Chenery, H. 1949. "The Engineering Production Function," *Quarterly Journal of Economics* 63 (May):507–31.

Christensen, L., and W. Greene. 1976. "Economies of Scale in U.S. Electric Power Generation," *Journal of Political Economy* 84 (August): 655–76.

Coase, R. H. 1937. "The Nature of the Firm," *Economica* 4 (March):386–405.

Cohn, E., S. L. Rhine, and M. C. Santos. 1989. "Institutions of Higher Education as Multi-Product Firms: Economies of Scale and

Scope," *Review of Economics and Statistics* 71 (May):284–90.

De Groot, H., W. McMahon, and J. F. Volkwein. 1991. "The Cost Structure of American Research Universities," *Review of Economics and Statistics* 73 (August):424–31.

Eaton, B. C., and N. Schmitt. 1994. "Flexible Manufacturing and Market Structure," *American Economic Review* 84 (September):875–88.

Evans, D., and J. Heckman. 1986. "A Test for Subadditivity of the Cost Function with Application to the Bell System," *American Economic Review* 74 (September):615–623.

Gale, I. 1994. "Price Competition in Noncooperative Joint Ventures," *International Journal of Industrial Organization* 12:53–69.

Gilligan, T., M. Smirlock, and W. Marshall. 1984. "Scale and Scope Economies in the Multi-Product Banking Firm," *Journal of Monetary Economics* 13 (May):393–405.

Grossman, S. J., and , O. D. Hart. (1986), 'The Costs and Benefits of Ownership: A Theory of Vertical and Lateral Integration," *Journal of Political Economy* 94: 691–719.

Hart, O. 1995. *Firms, Contracts, and Financial Structure*. New York: Oxford University Press.

Hart, O., and J. Moore. 1990. "Property Rights and the Nature of the Firm," *Journal of Political Economy* 98 (December):1119–58.

Holmström, B. 1982. "Moral Hazard in Teams," *Bell Journal of Economics* 13 (Autumn): 324–40.

Holmström, B., and P. Milgrom, 1994. "The Firm as an Incentive System," *American Economic Review* 84 (September): 972–91.

Milgrom, P., and J. Roberts. 1992. *Economics, Organization, and Management*. Upper Saddle River, NJ: Prentice Hall.

Panzar, J. C. 1989. "Technological Determinants of Firm and Industry Structure." In R. Schmalensee and R. Willig, eds., *Handbook of Industrial Organization. Vol. 1*. Amsterdam: North-Holland, 3–60.

Pulley, L. B., and Y. M. Braunstein. 1992. "A Composite Cost Function for Multiproduct Firms with an Application to Economies of Scope in Banking," *Review of Economics and Statistics* 74 (May):221–30.

Ramanarayanan S. 2006. "Does Practice Make Perfect?: An Empirical Analysis of Learning-By-Doing in Cardiac Surgery." Working Paper, UCLA Anderson School of Management.

Roller, L. 1990. "Proper Quadratic Cost Functions with Application to the Bell System," *Review of Economics and Statistics* 72 (May):202–10.

Smith, Adam. 1776. *The Wealth of Nations.*

Spulber, Daniel. 2009. *The Theory of the Firm: Microeconomics with Endogenous Entrepreneurs, Firms, Markets, and Organizations.* Cambridge: Cambridge University Press.

Sutton, John. 1991. *Sunk Costs and Market Structure.* Cambridge, MA: The MIT Press.

_____, 2001. *Technology and Market Structure.* Cambridge, MA: The MIT Press.

Williamson, O. E. 1975. *Markets and Hierarchies: Analysis and Antitrust Implications.* New York: Free Press.

Appendix

AVERAGE COST, MARGINAL COST, AND COST MINIMIZATION

Average cost is defined to be $AC(q) = [C(q) + F]/q$. Differentiate this with respect to output to yield:

$$\frac{dAC(q)}{dq} = \frac{q\frac{dC(q)}{dq} - [C(q) + F]}{q^2} = \frac{q\left(MC(q) - \frac{[C(q)+F]}{q}\right)}{q^2} = \frac{[MC(q) - AC(q)]}{q} \quad (4.A1)$$

The denominator is positive. So, if marginal cost exceeds average cost, the slope is positive. Raising output raises average cost. If average cost exceeds marginal cost, the slope is negative. Raising output lowers average cost. Minimizing average cost curve requires that the AC slope be zero, or that average cost and marginal cost are equal.

Derivation of total and average cost functions assumes that firms produce each output level at minimum cost. A necessary condition for such minimization is that the following equation be satisfied for any pair of inputs i and j:

$$\frac{MP_i}{MP_j} = \frac{w_i}{w_j}; \text{ which is equivalent to } \frac{MP_i}{w_i} = \frac{MP_j}{w_j} \quad (4.A2)$$

In other words, inputs should be used up to the point where the marginal product of the last dollar spent on input i equals the marginal product of the last dollar spent on input j.

THE SCALE ECONOMY INDEX AND THE ELASTICITY OF TOTAL COST

The standard definition of the elasticity η_C of costs with respect to output is the proportionate increase in total cost that results from a given proportionate increase in output. This can be written as:

$$\eta_C = \frac{d(C(q) + F)}{C(q) + F} \Big/ \frac{dq}{q} = \left(\frac{dC(q) + F}{dq}\right)\left(\frac{q}{C(q) + F}\right) = \frac{MC(q)}{AC(q)} \quad (4.A3)$$

As the scale economy index S is defined as the ratio of average cost to marginal cost, it follows that: $S = 1/\eta_C$.

RAY AVERAGE COST AND MULTIPRODUCT SCALE ECONOMIES

Scale economies are indicated by declining average cost, or declining Ray Average Cost (RAC) for a multiproduct firm. If a firm has 2 products so that its cost function is $C(q_1, q_2) + F$ we may implicitly define total output q by the equations $q_1 = \lambda_1 q$, and $q_2 = \lambda_2 q$, where λ_1 and λ_2 sum to unity. Then ray average cost is:

$$RAC(q) = \frac{C(\lambda_1 q, \lambda_2 q) + F}{q} \tag{4.A4}$$

Multiproduct scale economies imply that RAC declines as output expands or that

$$\frac{dRAC(q)}{dq} = \frac{q(\lambda_1 MC_1 + \lambda_2 MC_2) - C(\lambda_1 q, \lambda_2 q) - F}{q^2} < 0 \tag{4.A5}$$

where MC_i is the marginal cost of producing good i. It follows immediately that the sign of $dRAC(q)/dq$ is determined by the sign of the numerator of this expression. In other words, if $q_1 MC_1 + q_2 MC_2 > C(q_1, q_2) + F$ then $dRAC(q)/dq > 0$, while if $q_1 MC_1 + q_2 MC_2 < C(q_1, q_2) + F$ then $dRAC(q)/dq < 0$. Now define the ratio

$$S^M = \frac{C(q_1, q_2) + F}{q_1 MC_1 + q_2 MC_2} \tag{4.A6}$$

If $S^M > 1$ ray average cost decreases with output and so exhibits multiproduct increasing returns to scale. If $S < 1$, ray average cost is increasing, and so exhibits multiproduct decreasing returns to scale. If $S = 1$, neither scale economies nor diseconomies exist for the multiproduct firm.

FORMAL COST FUNCTION ANALYSIS AND EMPIRICAL ESTIMATION: THE COBB-DOUGLAS CASE

Assume that production is generated from capital K and labor L inputs via a Cobb-Douglas production function:

$$Q = K^\alpha L^\beta \tag{4.A7}$$

If r is the rental price of capital and w is the wage rate of labor, then total cost $C = rK + wL$. Cost minimization requires choosing the capital and labor inputs that minimize cost for achieving a given level of output. If we denote the target output level as $\overline{Q}$, the firm's problem then becomes:

Minimize $C = rK + wL$ subject to $\overline{Q} = K^\alpha L^\beta$

Since the production relation implies: $L = \overline{Q}^{\frac{1}{\beta}} K^{-\frac{\alpha}{\beta}}$, the cost function becomes $C = rK + w\overline{Q}^{\frac{1}{\beta}} K^{-\frac{\alpha}{\beta}}$. Minimizing this with respect to capital and solving for K yields:

$$K = \left(\frac{\alpha}{\beta}\frac{w}{r}\right)^{\frac{\beta}{\alpha+\beta}} \overline{Q}^{\frac{1}{\alpha+\beta}} \tag{4.A8}$$

Substituting this value into the labor input implied by the production constraint, the cost-minimizing labor input is:

$$L = \left(\frac{\beta}{\alpha}\frac{r}{w}\right)^{\frac{\beta}{\alpha+\beta}} \overline{Q}^{\frac{1}{\alpha+\beta}} \tag{4.A9}$$

Together, the optimal K and L equations imply that the minimal cost for producing any given level of output $\overline{Q}$ is:

$$C = w\left(\frac{\beta}{\alpha}\frac{r}{w}\right)^{\frac{\beta}{\alpha+\beta}} \overline{Q}^{\frac{1}{\alpha+\beta}} + r\left(\frac{\alpha}{\beta}\frac{w}{r}\right)^{\frac{\beta}{\alpha+\beta}} \overline{Q}^{\frac{1}{\alpha+\beta}} = \left[\left(\frac{\alpha}{\beta}\right)^{\frac{\beta}{\alpha+\beta}} + \left(\frac{\beta}{\alpha}\right)^{\frac{\alpha}{\alpha+\beta}}\right] r^{\frac{\alpha}{\alpha+\beta}} w^{\frac{\beta}{\alpha+\beta}} \overline{Q}^{\frac{1}{\alpha+\beta}} \tag{4.A10}$$

The exponents for each factor price, r and w, sum to unity so that the cost function is homogeneous of degree one in factor prices. Since the exponent on the output level is $1/(\alpha + \beta)$ there will be constant returns to scale if $\alpha + \beta = 1$; scale economies if $\alpha + \beta > 1$; and scale diseconomies if $\alpha + \beta < 1$.

$$\ln C = \ln\left[\left(\frac{\alpha}{\beta}\right)^{\frac{\beta}{\alpha+\beta}} + \left(\frac{\beta}{\alpha}\right)^{\frac{\alpha}{\alpha+\beta}}\right] + \left(\frac{\alpha}{\alpha+\beta}\right)\ln r + \left(\frac{\beta}{\alpha+\beta}\right)\ln w + \left(\frac{1}{\alpha+\beta}\right)\ln \overline{Q} \tag{4.A11}$$

For estimation purposes, this can easily be translated into: $\ln C = \text{Constant} + \delta_1 \ln r + \delta_2 \ln w + \delta_3 \ln Q$. With observations on input prices and output levels, estimation of the coefficients δ_i allow us to recover the underlying production parameters, α and β.

If the assumption of Cobb-Douglas technology is incorrect, the estimated coefficients will not satisfy theoretical restrictions. Hence, empirical analysis often employs a more flexible specification that includes Cobb-Douglas as a special case. One such specification is the translog cost function. For the two-input case above, this function is:

$$\ln C = \text{Constant} + \delta_1 \ln r + \delta_2 \ln w + 0.5[\delta_{11}(\ln r)^2 + \delta_{12}(\ln w)(\ln r)$$

$$+ \delta_{21}(\ln w)(\ln r) + \delta_{22}(\ln w)^2] + \delta_3 \ln Q$$

$$+ \delta_{31}(\ln Q)(\ln r) + \delta_{32}(\ln Q)(\ln w) + 0.5\delta_{33}(\ln Q)^2 \tag{4.A12}$$

As before, we expect δ_1 and δ_2 to be positive fractions that sum to unity. However, the measure of scale economies $S = 1/\frac{\partial \ln C}{\partial \ln Q}$ now depends on the level of output. That is we now have: $S = 1/\frac{\partial \ln C}{\partial \ln Q} = 1/(\delta_3 + \delta_{33}\ln Q + \delta_{31}\ln r + \delta_{32}\ln w)$. Only if $\delta_{31} = \delta_{32} = \delta_{33} = 0$, will the index of scale economies be independent of the level of Q.

Part Two
Monopoly Power in Theory and Practice

In Part Two, we consider the pure monopoly case in much more detail than the simple, textbook case presented in Chapter 2. In particular, we consider a single firm facing a downward-sloping demand curve and the price and non-price tactics that it may use. While focusing on a single firm omits much strategic interaction, there are some cases in which this is realistic. In many regions, for example, there is just one ski lift operator within a radius of fifty miles and only one amusement park serving an even greater area. Second, and more importantly, the tactics discussed such as quantity discounts and bundling are also available in a setting of multiple rivals. However, it is much easier to understand the role of such measures in this more competitive environment *after* seeing them used by a single firm with no strategically-linked rival.

Chapter 5 begins with an examination of linear price discrimination tactics, such as market segmentation. It also includes an analysis of the 2003 study of price discrimination in new car sales by Scott-Morton, Zettelmeyer, and Silva-Risso. This is followed by a discussion of nonlinear price discrimination techniques, e.g., two-part tariffs, in Chapter 6. That chapter also includes a discussion of the evidence on airline price discrimination presented by Stavins (2001).

In Chapter 7, we explore the choice of product quality. This allows us to introduce the two concepts of horizontal differentiation, in which consumers disagree about what makes a high-quality product (but may agree on the value of higher quality), and vertical differentiation, in which consumers agree about the quality ranking of different goods (but typically disagree about quality's marginal value). Both of these concepts, but especially that of horizontal differentiation, will be used extensively in subsequent chapters. We also present the empirical analysis of Berry and Waldfogel (2010) linking newspaper quality to market size.

Chapter 8 reviews the classic techniques of bundling and tie-in sales. Here we consider not only the surplus-extracting aspects of such tactics, but also their potential for leveraging market power from one market to another. This permits a discussion of the related (and extensive) developments in antitrust policy. The chapter concludes with an illustration of the basic, profit-enhancing effects that bundling can have based on the empirical study by Crawford (2008) of bundling in cable TV.

5

Price Discrimination and Monopoly:
Linear Pricing

The standard definition of price discrimination is that a seller sells the same product to different buyers at different prices. Examples of price discrimination abound. Consider, for example, the market for prescription and generic drugs. Both casual and formal empirical evidence finds that brand name prescription drug prices are on average lower in Canada than in the United States. Table 5.1 demonstrates this with evidence from two recent studies, one by Skinner and Rovere (2008) and the other by Quon, Firszt, and Eisenberg (2005). While the precise drugs covered by each study differ somewhat, the basic conclusion in each is the same. US consumers pay between 24 percent and 57 percent more for prescription drugs on average than do their Canadian neighbors.

The case of prescription drugs is far from an isolated example. Passenger airline companies and hotel chains are past masters at what they euphemistically call "yield management," as any frequent traveler can readily attest. In the great majority of business-to-business transactions, prices are arrived at through prolonged negotiation. Sophisticated travelers who visit the Grand Bazaar in Istanbul know that all prices are negotiable—and are typically lower if the traveler happens to be accompanied by a native of Istanbul who does the negotiating! Nearer to home, purchasing a pre-owned automobile usually involves equally intensive negotiation. In each of these cases of negotiated prices, there is no reason to believe that the price offered to one buyer will be the same as the price offered to another.

The extensive use of price discrimination by sellers raises two sets of questions. First, what market conditions make price discrimination feasible? Second, what makes price discrimination profitable? It is, after all, difficult to believe that discriminatory pricing is extensively employed but unprofitable! Essentially, our task in this and upcoming chapters is to analyze the methods firms can use to implement price discrimination in a way that increases profits relative to charging the same price to everyone.

This raises another important issue. Any increased profit that price discrimination generates must come either from a reduction in consumer surplus, improved market efficiency, or some combination of the two. From a policy perspective, it matters a great deal which of these is the case. As a result, we also want to explore the welfare implications of price discrimination. Finally, it is worthwhile noting that discriminatory prices can also affect market competition. This occurs when the buyers are not final consumers but instead, retailers such as drug stores. If large drug store chains are charged different wholesale prices than are small, independent pharmacies, then retail competition between these two

Table 5.1   Comparison of US and Canadian prescription prices, selected drugs

Brand Name	Percent Canadian Reduction from US Price [Skinner & Rove (2008)]	Percent Canadian Reduction from US Price [Quon, Firszt, and Eisenberg (2005)]
Accupril	43%	17%
Altace	54%	40%
Arthrotec	67%	——
Ativan	88%	——
Avandia	——	27%
Celebrex	62%	53%
Coversyl	57%	——
Crestor	57%	21%
Diovan HCT	54%	27%
Flomax	——	40%
Fosomax	——	30%
Lipitor	40%	34%
Lopressor	96%	——
Neurontin	——	14%
Prozac	——	50%
Vasotec	21%	——
Viagra	——	−37%
Zestril	46%	——
Average	**57.08%**	**26.33%**

groups will not be conducted on a level playing field. We address these issues in the next group of chapters.

5.1   FEASIBILITY OF PRICE DISCRIMINATION

A firm with market power faces a downward sloping demand curve. So if the firm charges the same price to each consumer—the standard case of non-discriminatory pricing—the marginal revenue it gets from selling an additional unit of output is less than the price charged. In order to sell the additional unit, the firm must lower its price not only to the consumer who buys the additional unit, but to all its other consumers as well. Having to lower the price for all its customers in order to gain an additional consumers weakens the monopolist's incentive to serve more consumers. As a result, the textbook monopoly undersupplies its product relative to the efficient outcome.

Non-discriminatory pricing by a monopolist is not just a source of potential inefficiency. It is also a constraint on the firm's ability to convert consumer surplus into profit, particularly from those consumers willing to pay a lot for its product. Price discrimination is a powerful technique that can greatly increase firm profits. In some cases, moreover, price discrimination may induce the monopolist to sell more output thereby coming closer to the competitive outcome and enhancing market efficiency.

While a monopolist can increase profit through price discrimination, it is important to realize that price discrimination is not always easily accomplished. There is a reason that the standard textbook case assumes that each customer pays the same price. To discriminate successfully, the monopolist must overcome two main obstacles. The first of these is the *identification problem*: the firm needs to be able to identify who is who on its market demand curve. The second is the problem of *arbitrage*: being able to prevent those who are offered a low price from reselling to those charged a high price.

In considering the identification problem, it is useful to recall a common assumption in the textbook monopoly model: that the firm knows the quantity demanded at each price. Without this knowledge the firm would not know its marginal revenue curve and, hence, would not be able to determine the profit-maximizing output. Let's examine more carefully what this assumption means in practice.

For some products such as bicycles, TVs, DVD players, or haircuts, each consumer purchases at most one unit of the good over a given period of time. The firm's market demand curve is then an explicit ordering of consumers by their reservation prices—the top price each is willing to pay. For these goods, knowledge of the demand curve means that the monopolist knows that the top part of the demand curve is made up of those consumers willing to pay a relatively large amount for the one unit they will purchase, whereas the bottom part of the demand curve is made up of those willing to pay only a little.

For other products, such as movies, CDs, refreshments, and tennis lessons, the construction of the market demand curve is slightly more complex. This is because each individual consumer can be expected to purchase an increasing (decreasing) quantity of the good as the price is reduced (increased). As a result, for these goods the market demand curve reflects not only differences in the willingness to pay across consumers, but also differences in the willingness to pay as any one consumer buys more of the product.

When the monopolist practices uniform pricing, these distinctions are not relevant. In that case, the assumption that the firm knows its demand curve means only that it knows how willingness to pay for the good *in the overall market* varies with the quantity of the good sold. To be able to practice price discrimination, the monopolist must be able to acquire and exploit more information about consumers than is assumed in the standard model. The monopolist must know how the market demand curve has been constructed from the individual consumer demand curves. In other words, the monopolist must know how different kinds of consumers differ in their demands for its good.

This is easier for some sellers than for others. For example, tax accountants effectively sell one unit of their services to each client in any given year. Further, they know exactly how much their clients earn and, more importantly, how much they save their clients by way of reduced tax liabilities. They can certainly use this information to identify their clients' willingness-to-pay. Similarly, a car dealer typically sells one car to a customer. The dealer may be able to identify those buyers with the greatest or least willingness to pay by asking potential buyers where they live, work, or shop and more generally through the process of negotiation. The same is often true for realtors, dentists, and lawyers.

Sellers of retail merchandise, however, face a more anonymous market. Various schemes such as varying the price depending on time of purchase—"early-bird" specials or Saturday morning sales—or offering coupons that take time to collect, can help retailers identify "who's who" on their demand curve. Nevertheless, the identification problem is still difficult to overcome. Moreover, even if weekend sales or coupon schemes do successfully identify the firm's different consumers, such schemes may be too costly to implement.

Even when a monopolist can solve the identification problem, there is still the second obstacle to price discrimination: arbitrage. As was noted previously, to discriminate successfully the monopolist must be able to prevent those consumers who are offered a low price from reselling their purchases to other consumers to whom the monopolist wants to charge a high price. Again, this is more easily accomplished for some goods and services than for others. Medical, legal, and educational services are not easily resold. One consumer can't sell her appendectomy to another! Similarly, a senior citizen cannot easily resell a discounted movie theater ticket to a teenager. For other markets, particularly consumer durables such as bicycles and automobiles, resale—or sale across different markets—is difficult to prevent. This is an important part of the drug pricing story noted at the start of this chapter. Pharmaceutical companies can only price discriminate successfully if they can keep the American and Canadian markets separate, in other words, only if they can prevent arbitrage.

To sum up, we expect firms with monopoly power to try to price discriminate. In turn, this implies that we should expect these firms to develop techniques by which they can identify the different types of consumers who buy their goods and prevent resale or consumer arbitrage among them. The ability to do this and the best strategy for achieving price discrimination will vary from firm to firm and from market to market.

We now turn to the practice of price discrimination and investigate some of the more popularly practiced techniques. The tradition in economics has been to classify these techniques into three broad classes: first degree, second degree, and third degree price discrimination.[1] More recently, these types of pricing schemes have been referred to respectively as personalized pricing, menu pricing, and group pricing.[2] In this chapter, we focus on third-degree price discrimination, or group pricing.

5.2   THIRD-DEGREE PRICE DISCRIMINATION OR GROUP PRICING

Third-degree price discrimination, or group pricing, is defined by three key features. First, there is some easily observable characteristic such as age, income, geographic location, or education status by which the monopolist can group consumers in terms of their willingness to pay for its product. Second, the monopolist can prevent arbitrage across the different groups. In the prescription drug case with which we started this chapter, this implies that it is possible to prevent the re-importation to the United States of prescription drugs initially exported from the United States to Canada. Finally, a central feature of third-degree price discrimination is that, while the monopolist quotes different unit prices to different groups, all consumers *within* a particular group are quoted the same unit price. Consumers in each group then decide how much to purchase at their quoted price.

Group pricing is an example of price discrimination precisely because the price quoted to one group of consumers is not the same as the price quoted to another group *for the same good*. This type of pricing policy is the one most commonly found in economics textbooks and is referred to in the industrial organization literature as *linear pricing*—hence the title of this chapter. Consumers within a group are free to buy as much as they like at the quoted price, so that the average price per unit paid by each consumer is the same as the marginal price for the last unit bought.

---

[1]   Price discrimination is a fascinating topic and its interest to economists goes well beyond the field of industrial organization. The distinction between first, second, and third degree discrimination follows the work of Pigou (1920). A more modern treatment appears in Phlips (1983).

[2]   These terms were first coined by Shapiro and Varian (1999).

Table 5.2   Annual membership dues for the
American Economic Association

Annual Income	Subscription Price
Less than $70,000	$20
$70,000 to $105,000	$30
Above $105,000	$40

The world is full of examples of third-degree price discrimination. Senior discounts and "kids are free" programs are both examples. An interesting case that is familiar to economists is the fee schedule for membership in the *American Economic Association*, the major professional organization for economists in the United States. Payment of the fee entitles a member to receive professional announcements, newsletters, and three very important professional journals, *The American Economic Review, The Journal of Economic Perspectives*, and *The Journal of Economic Literature*, each of which is published quarterly.

The 2012 fee schedule is shown in Table 5.2. As can be seen, the aim is to price discriminate on the basis of income. A particularly interesting feature of this scheme is that the Association makes no attempt to check the veracity of the income declared by a prospective member. What they appear to rely upon is that economists will be either honest or even boastful in reporting their income. In addition, the Association must also hope to avoid the arbitrage problem whereby junior faculty members who pay a low subscription fee resell to senior faculty members who pay a high one. Casual observation suggests such reselling is rare.

The practice of the American Economic Association is not unique. Many academic journals charge a different price to institutions such as university libraries than to individuals. The print and online 2012 subscription rate to the *Journal of Economics and Management Strategy*, for example, is $59 for an individual but $446 for an institution.

Airlines are particularly adept at applying third-degree price discrimination. It has sometimes been suggested that the number of different fares charged to Economy class passengers on a particular flight is approximately equal to the number of passengers! A common feature of this type of price discrimination is that it is implemented by restrictions on the characteristics of the ticket. These include constraints upon the time in advance by which the flight must be booked, whether flights can be changed, the number of days between departure and return, whether the trip involves staying over a Saturday night, and so on. We return to the airline case later in this chapter.

Other examples of third-degree price discrimination are restaurant "early bird specials" and supermarket discounts to shoppers who clip coupons. Similarly, department stores that lower their apparel prices at the end of the season are attempting to charge a different price based on the observable characteristic of the time of purchase.[3] Segmenting consumers by time of purchase is also evident in other markets. Consumers typically pay more to see a film at a first-run theater when the film is newly released than to see it at a later date at a second-run cinema or, still later, as a downloaded film at home.

---

[3]   Discounting over time in a systematic fashion runs the risk that if consumers know prices will fall in the future, they will delay their purchases. If the number of customers that postpone is "too" large, seasonal discounts will not be a very good strategy.

An essential feature of all third-degree price discrimination schemes is that the monopolist has some easily observed characteristic that serves as a good proxy for differences in consumer willingness to pay. This characteristic can be used effectively to divide the market into two or more groups, each of which will be charged a different price. The monopolist must next be able to ensure that resale of the product by those who are offered a low price to those who are offered a high one is not feasible. Consider the airline example again. The requirement to stay over a Saturday night is designed to discriminate between those consumers who are traveling on business and those who are not. Senior discounts typically require proof of age but this in itself is not necessarily sufficient to prevent arbitrage. Suppose, for example, that a local supermarket were to offer a senior discount. Forty- and fifty-somethings who have a senior parent living nearby would then have an incentive to have their parent purchase the groceries. This is why most senior discounts require both proof of age *and* proof of consumption (e.g., theater or movie tickets).

Once the different consumer groups have been identified and separated, the general rule that characterizes third-degree price discrimination is easily stated. *Consumers for whom the elasticity of demand is low should be charged a higher price than consumers for whom the elasticity of demand is relatively high.*

5.3 IMPLEMENTING THIRD-DEGREE PRICE DISCRIMINATION OR GROUP PRICING

The logic underlying the pricing rule is fairly straightforward. Here, we illustrate it with a simple example and defer formal presentation to the Appendix at the end of this chapter.

Suppose that the publishers of J.K Rowling's final volume in the Harry Potter series, *Harry Potter and the Deathly Hallows*, estimate that inverse demand for this book in the United States is $P_U = 36 - 4Q_U$ and in Europe is $P_E = 24 - 4Q_E$. In each case, prices are measured in dollars and quantities in millions of books sold at publication of the first edition of the book. Marginal cost is assumed to be the same in each market and equal to $4 per book. The publisher also incurs other costs such as cover design and promotion, but we treat these as fixed and independent of sales volume and so ignore them in our analysis.

As a benchmark, suppose that the publisher treats the two markets as a single, integrated market and so quotes the same, nondiscriminatory price to consumers in the United States and Europe. To work out the profit maximizing price, the publisher first needs to calculate aggregate market demand at any price P. This means that they need to add the two market demand curves *horizontally*. In the United States, we have $P = 36 - 4Q_U$, which can be inverted to give $Q_U = 9 - P/4$ provided, of course, that $P \leq \$36$. In Europe we have $P = 24 - 4Q_E$ so that $Q_E = 6 - P/4$ provided $P \leq \$24$. This gives us the aggregate demand equation:

$$Q = Q_U + Q_E = 9 - P/4 \qquad \text{for } \$36 \geq P \geq \$24$$
$$Q = Q_U + Q_E = 15 - P/2 \qquad \text{for } P < \$24 \tag{5.1}$$

We can write this in the more normal inverse form as:

$$P = 36 - 4Q \qquad \text{for } \$36 \geq P \geq \$24$$
$$P = 30 - 2Q \qquad \text{for } P < \$24 \tag{5.2}$$

This demand relationship is illustrated in Figure 5.1. The kink in the aggregate demand function at a price of $24 and a quantity of 3 million occurs because at any price above $24 books will be sold only in the United States whereas once the price drops below $24 both markets are active. The marginal revenue function associated with this demand function satisfies the usual "twice as steep" rule:

$$MR = 36 - 8Q \qquad \text{for } Q < 3$$
$$MR = 30 - 4Q \qquad \text{for } Q > 3 \tag{5.3}$$

This is also illustrated in Figure 5.1. The jump in the marginal revenue function at a quantity of 3 million arises because when price falls from just above $24 to just below $24, the inactive European market becomes active. That is, when the price falls to just below $24, it brings in a new set of consumers.

We can use equations (5.1)–(5.3) to calculate the profit maximizing price, aggregate quantity, and quantity in each market. Equating marginal revenue with marginal cost, assuming that both markets are active, we have $30 - 4Q = 4$ so that $Q^* = 6.5$ million. From the aggregate demand curve (5.2) this gives a price of $P^* = \$17$. It follows from the individual market demands (5.1) that 4.75 million books will be sold in the United States and 1.75 million books in Europe. Aggregate profit (ignoring all the fixed and other set-up costs) is $(17 - 4)*6.5 = \$84.5$ million.

That this pricing strategy is not the best that the monopolist can adopt is actually clear from Figure 5.1. At the equilibrium we have just calculated, the marginal revenue on the last book sold in Europe is greater than marginal cost whereas marginal revenue on the last book sold in the United States is less than marginal cost (it is actually negative in this example!). Transferring some of the books sold in the United States to the European market will, therefore, lead to an increase in profit.

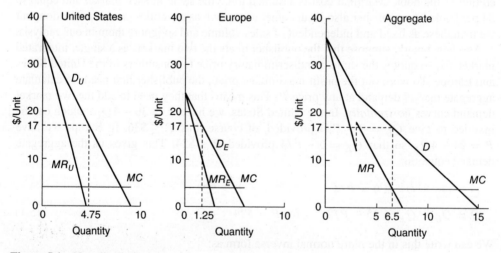

Figure 5.1   Non-discriminatory pricing—constant marginal cost
The firm identifies aggregate demand and the associated marginal revenue. It chooses total output where marginal revenue equals marginal cost and the non-discriminatory price from the aggregate demand function. Output in each market is the market clearing output.

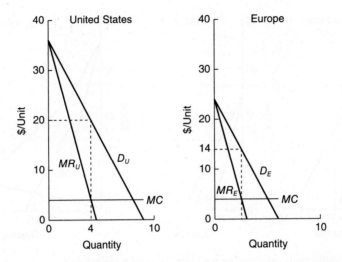

Figure 5.2 Third-degree price discrimination or group pricing—constant marginal cost
The firm sets output where marginal revenue equals marginal cost in each market and sets the market clearing price in each market.

We can make this more explicit. A necessary condition for profit maximization under third-degree price discrimination is that marginal revenue must equal marginal cost in *each* market that the monopolist serves. If this were not the case in a particular market, then the last unit sold in that market would be generating either more or less in cost than it is earning in revenue. Cutting back or increasing total production in that market would therefore raise profits. If marginal cost in serving each market is identical, as in our case, then this condition implies that marginal revenue be the same on the last unit sold in each market. If this condition does not hold, the monopolist can raise revenue and profit with no increase in production (and hence, no increase in costs), simply by shifting sales from the low marginal revenue market to the high one.

The application of these principles to our example is illustrated in Figure 5.2. Recall that demand in the United States market is $P_U = 36 - 4Q_U$, and in Europe it is $P_E = 24 - 4Q_E$. This means that marginal revenue in the United States is $MR_U = 36 - 8Q_U$ and in Europe is $MR_E = 24 - 8Q_E$. Now apply the rule that marginal revenue equals marginal cost in each market. This gives a profit-maximizing output in the United States of $Q_U^* = 4$ million books at a price of $P_U^* = \$20$, and in Europe a profit-maximizing output of $Q_E^* = 2.5$ million books at a price of $P_E^* = \$14$. Profit from sales in the Unites States is \$64 million and in Europe is \$25 million, giving aggregate profit (again ignoring all the fixed and other set-up costs) of \$89 million, an increase of \$4.5 million over the nondiscriminatory profit.

How does this outcome relate to the elasticity rule that we presented above? An important property of linear demand curves is that the elasticity of demand falls smoothly from infinity to zero as we move down the demand curve. This means that, for any price less than \$24 (and greater than zero) the elasticity of demand in the United States market is lower than in the European market. (You can check this by evaluating the demand elasticity in the two markets at any price for which both markets are active.) Our rule then states that we should find a higher price in the United States than in Europe, precisely as in our example.

How is our analysis affected if marginal cost is not constant? The same basic principles apply with one important change. If marginal production costs are not constant, we cannot

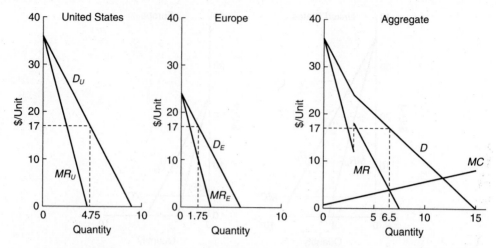

Figure 5.3   Non-discriminatory pricing with non-constant marginal cost

The firm identifies aggregate demand and the associated marginal revenue. It chooses total output where marginal revenue equals marginal cost and the non-discriminatory price from the aggregate demand function. Output in each market is the market clearing output

treat the two markets independently. Whatever output the monopolist chooses to supply to the United States, for example, affects the marginal cost of supplying Europe. As a result we need to look at the different markets together. Nevertheless, we still have simple rules that guide the monopolist's pricing decisions in these markets.

To illustrate this point, suppose that the publisher of *Harry Potter and the Deathly Hallows* has a single printing facility that produces books for both the United States and European markets and that marginal cost is given by $MC = 0.75 + Q/2$, where Q is the total number of books printed.

Figure 5.3 illustrates the profit-maximizing behavior if the monopolist chooses not to price discriminate. The basic analytical steps in this process are as follows:

1. Calculate aggregate market demand as above.
2. Identify the marginal revenue function for this aggregate demand function. From our example, if $Q > 3$ so that both markets are active, this is $MR = 30 - 4Q$.
3. Equate marginal revenue with marginal cost to determine aggregate output. Thus we have $0.75 + Q/2 = 30 - 4Q$ giving $Q^* = 6.5$ million books.
4. Identify the equilibrium price from the aggregate demand function. Because both markets are active, the relevant part of the aggregate demand function is $P = 30 - 2Q$, giving an equilibrium price of $P^* = \$17$.
5. Calculate demand in each market at this price: 4.75 million books in the United States and 1.75 million books in Europe.

Now suppose that the monopolist chooses to price discriminate. This outcome is illustrated in Figure 5.4. The underlying process is clearly different, and the steps in implementing profit maximizing price discrimination are as follows:

1. Derive marginal revenue in each market and add these *horizontally* to give aggregate marginal revenue. Marginal revenue in the United States is $MR = 36 - 8Q_U$ for any

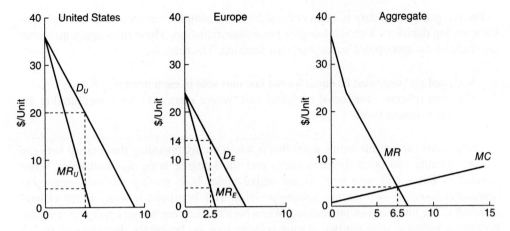

Figure 5.4   Third-degree price discrimination or group pricing with non-constant marginal cost
The firm calculates aggregate marginal revenue and equates this with marginal cost. Output in each market
equates marginal revenue with aggregate marginal cost. Price in each market is the market-clearing price.

marginal revenue under $36. In Europe, $MR = 24 - 8Q_E$ for marginal revenue below
$24. Inverting these gives $Q_U = 4.5 - MR/8$ and $Q_E = 3 - MR/8$. Summing these
gives an aggregate marginal revenue:

$$Q = Q_U + Q_E = 4.5 - MR/8 \quad \text{for } Q \le 1.5$$
$$Q = Q_U + Q_E = 7.5 - MR/4 \quad \text{for } Q > 1.5 \tag{5.4}$$

This can be inverted to give aggregate marginal revenue its more usual form

$$MR = 36 - 8Q \qquad \text{for } Q \le 1.5$$
$$MR = 30 - 4Q \qquad \text{for } Q > 1.5 \tag{5.5}$$

Note how this step differs from the non-discriminatory case. In the latter both markets
are treated as one, so we start with aggregate demand and derive its associated marginal
revenue. In the discriminatory pricing case, by contrast, the markets are supplied
separately, with the profit maximizing condition that $MC = MR$ in both markets so we
need aggregate marginal revenue, not aggregate demand.

2. Equate aggregate marginal revenue with marginal cost to identify the equilibrium
    aggregate quantity *and* marginal revenue. So we have $30 - 4Q = 0.75 + 2Q$ giving
    $Q^* = 6.5$. As a result, the equilibrium marginal revenue is $4, which is equal to the
    marginal cost of the last unit produced.
3. Identify the equilibrium quantities in each market by equating individual market
    marginal revenue with the equilibrium marginal revenue and marginal cost. In the
    United States this gives $36 - 8Q_U = 4$ or $Q_U^* = 4$ million books and in Europe
    $24 - 8Q_U = 4$ or $Q_E^* = 2.5$ million books.
4. Identify the equilibrium price in each market from the individual market demand
    functions, giving a price of $20 in the United States and $14 in Europe.

The foregoing procedure is again derived from two simple rules that guide the monopolist's pricing decisions with third-degree price discrimination. These rules apply no matter the shape of the monopolist's marginal cost function. The rules are:

1. Marginal revenue must be equal for the last unit sold in each market.
2. Marginal revenue must equal marginal cost, where marginal cost is measured at the *aggregate* output level.

There is one further interesting point that is worth noting regarding the contrast between uniform pricing (no price discrimination) and third-degree price discrimination. When demand is linear and both markets are active under both pricing schemes, *aggregate demand is identical with the two pricing policies*. This is proved formally in the chapter Appendix. The intuition is simple to see. When both markets are active, aggregate marginal revenue is identical with the two pricing policies (we are below the discontinuity in *MR* in Figure 5.3). So equating aggregate marginal revenue with aggregate marginal cost must give the same aggregate output. The reason that third-degree price discrimination is more profitable in this case is that the aggregate output is allocated more profitably across the two markets—to ensure that marginal revenue on the last unit sold in each market is equal.

We complete our discussion of third-degree price discrimination in this section by making explicit the relationship between the price set and the elasticity of demand in any specific market segment. Our review of monopoly and market power in Chapters 2 and 3 explained how we could express the firm's marginal revenue in any market in terms of price and the point elasticity of demand at that price. Specifically, marginal revenue in market i is given by $MR_i = P_i \left(1 - \dfrac{1}{\eta_i} \right)$ where η_i is (the absolute value of) the elasticity of demand. The larger is η_i the more elastic is demand in this market. Now recall that third-degree price discrimination requires that the profit-maximizing aggregate output must be allocated such that marginal revenue is equalized across each market (and, of course, equal to marginal cost). For example, if there are two markets this says that $MR_1 = MR_2$. Substituting from the equations above, we then know that $MR_1 = P_1 \left(1 - \dfrac{1}{\eta_1} \right) = MR_2 = P_2 \left(1 - \dfrac{1}{\eta_2} \right)$. We can solve this for the ratio of the two prices to give:

$$\frac{P_1}{P_2} = \frac{(1 - 1/\eta_2)}{(1 - 1/\eta_1)} = \frac{\eta_1 \eta_2 - \eta_1}{\eta_1 \eta_2 - \eta_2}. \tag{5.6}$$

From this, it is clear that price will indeed be lower in the market with the higher elasticity of demand. The intuition is that prices must be lower in those markets in which consumers are sensitive to price. Such price sensitivity means that raising the price will lose too many customers, and this loss more than offsets any gain in surplus per customer. To put it differently, when consumers are price sensitive, the strategy of lowering price can actually raise the monopolist's total surplus because it brings in many additional purchases. We encourage you to reinterpret the various examples with which we motivated our analysis in terms of demand elasticities. For example, is it reasonable to think that business travelers will have a lower elasticity of demand for air travel at a particular time than vacation travelers?

The manager of a local movie theater believes that demand for a film depends on when the movie is shown. Early moviegoers who go to films before 5 pm are more sensitive to price than are evening moviegoers. With some market research, the manager discovers that the demand curves for daytime (D) and evening (E) moviegoers are $Q_D = 100 - 10P_D$ and $Q_E = 140 - 10P_E$, respectively. The marginal cost of showing a movie is constant and equal to $3 per customer no matter when the movie is shown. This includes the costs of ticketing and cleaning.

a. What is the profit maximizing pricing policy if the manager charges the same price for daytime and evening attendance? What is attendance in each showing and what is aggregate profit per day?
b. Now suppose that the manager adopts a third-degree price discrimination scheme, setting a different day and evening price. What are the profit maximizing prices? What is attendance at each session? Confirm that aggregate attendance is as in (a). What is aggregate profit per day?

5.4   PRODUCT VARIETY AND THIRD-DEGREE PRICE DISCRIMINATION OR GROUP PRICING

We have thus far defined price discrimination as occurring whenever a firm sells an identical product to two or more buyers at different prices. But what if the products are not identical? Ford, for example, offers several hundred (perhaps even several thousand) varieties of the Ford *Taurus* with slightly different features. Procter and Gamble offers a wide range of toothpastes in different tastes, colors, and claimed medicinal qualities. Kellogg's offers dozens of breakfast cereals that vary in terms of grain, taste, consistency, and color.

Many examples of what looks like third-degree price discrimination or group pricing arise when the seller offers such *differentiated* products. For example, books are first released as expensive hardcover editions and only later as cheap paperbacks. Hotels in a ski area are more expensive in winter than in summer. First class air travel costs more than coach. The common theme of these examples is that they all involve variations of a basic product. This is a phenomenon that we meet every day in buying restaurant meals, refrigerators, electronic goods, and many other goods and services. In each of these situations, what we observe is a firm selling different varieties of the same good—distinguished by color, material, or design. As a brief reflection on the typical restaurant menu will reveal, what we also usually observe is that the different varieties are aimed at different groups and sold at different prices.

In considering these as applications of price discrimination we have to be careful. After all, the cost incurred in producing goods of different types, such as hardback and paperback books, or first class versus coach flights, is different. Philips (1983) provides perhaps the best definition of third-degree price discrimination or group pricing once we allow for product differentiation: "Price discrimination should be defined as implying that two varieties of a commodity are sold (by the same seller) to two buyers at different *net* prices, the net price being the price (paid by the buyer) corrected for the cost associated with the product differentiation."

Using this definition, it would not be discriminatory to charge $750 extra for a car with antilock brakes if it costs $750 extra to assemble a car with such brakes. By contrast, the difference in price between a coach class fare of $450 and a first class fare of $8,000 for service between Boston and London must be seen as almost entirely reflecting price discrimination because the additional cost of providing first class service per passenger is well below the $7,550 difference in price. In other words, price discrimination among different versions of the same good exists only if the difference in prices is not justified by differences in underlying costs: this is what Philips means by the *net price*.

Consideration of product variety leads to a very important question. Does offering different varieties of a product enhance the monopolist's ability to charge different net prices? That is, does a firm with market power increase its ability to price discriminate by offering different versions of its product? As we shall see, the general answer is yes.

We can obtain at least some insight into this issue by recalling the two problems that successful discrimination must overcome, namely, identification and arbitrage. In order to price discriminate, the firm must determine who is who on its demand curve and then be able to prevent resale between separate consumers. By offering different versions or models of its product, the monopolist may be able to solve these two problems. Different consumers may buy different versions of a good and therefore reveal who they are through their purchase decisions. Moreover, because different customers are purchasing different varieties, the problem of resale is considerably reduced.

As an example of the potential for product differentiation to enhance profit, consider an airline that we will call Delta Airlines (DA), operating direct passenger flights between Boston and Amsterdam. DA knows that there are three types of customers for these flights: those who prefer to travel first class, those who wish to travel business class, and those who are reconciled to having to travel coach. One part of the arbitrage problem is, of course, easily solved: in order to sit in a first class seat you need a first class ticket. However, there is another aspect to this problem. If the difference in price is great enough relative to the value a consumer places on a higher class of travel, a business class traveler, for example, might choose to fly coach. For simplicity, we assume that this arbitrage, or self-selection problem does not arise. That is, we assume that first class passengers prefer not to travel rather than sit in business or coach, and business class passengers similarly will not consider coach travel—they place sufficiently high values on the differences in quality between the types of seat that they will not trade down. (See end-of-chapter problem 5 for an example of this case).[4]

DA's market research indicates that daily demand for first class travel on this route is $P_F = 18,500 - 1,000Q_F$, for business class travel is $P_B = 9,200 - 250Q_B$, and for Coach travel is $P_C = 1500 - 5Q_C$. The marginal cost is estimated to be $100 for a coach passenger, $200 for a business class passenger, and $500 for a first class passenger.

The profit maximizing third-degree price discrimination scheme for differentiated products of this type satisfies essentially the same rules as for homogeneous products. Simply put, DA should identify the quantity that equates marginal revenue with marginal cost for each class of seat and then identify the equilibrium price from the relevant demand function. For first class passengers this requires $MR_F = 18,500 - 2,000Q_F = 500$, or $Q_F^* = 9$. The resulting first class fare is $P_F^* = \$9,500$. In business class, we have

---

[4]   There is also the possibility that coach or business travelers would want to trade up. The equilibrium prices that we derive in the example preclude such a possibility.

Reality Checkpoint

Variations on a Theme—Broadway Ticket Prices

In New York, over 20,000 people attend Broadway shows each night. As avid theatergoers know, prices for these tickets have been rising inexorably. The top price for Broadway shows has risen 31 percent between 1998 and 2004 and has more than doubled since then. However, discounts offered through coupons, two-for-one deals, special student prices, and then TKTS booth in Times Square, significantly reduce this price impact.

Why so much discounting? The value of a seat in a theater, like a seat on an airplane, is highly perishable. Once the show starts or the plane takes off, a seat is worth next to nothing. So, it's better to fill the seat at a low price than not fill it at all.

Stanford economist Phillip Leslie investigated Broadway ticket price discrimination using detailed data for a 1996 Broadway play, *Seven Guitars*. Over 140,000 people saw this play, and they bought tickets in seventeen price categories. While some of the difference was due to seat quality—opera versus mezzanine versus balcony, a large amount of price differentials remained even after quality adjustments. The average difference of two tickets chosen at random on a given night was about 40 percent of the average price. This is comparable to the price variation in airline tickets.

Leslie used advanced econometric techniques to estimate the values that different income groups put on the various categories of tickets. He found that Broadway producers do a pretty good job, in general, at maximizing revenue. He found the average price set for *Seven Guitars* was about $55 while, according to Mr. Leslie's estimates, the value that would maximize profit was a very close $60. His data also indicated that the optimal uniform price would be a little over $50. Again, price discrimination is less about the average price charged and more about varying the price in line with the consumer's willingness to pay. In this connection, Leslie found that optimal price discrimination drew in over 6 percent more patrons than would optimal uniform pricing.

Source: P. Leslie. "Price Discrimination in Broadway Theatre," *Rand Journal of Economics* 35 (Autumn, 2004): 520–41.

$MR_B = 9,200 - 500Q_B = 200$, or $Q_B^* = 18$ and $P_B^* = \$4,700$. Finally, in coach we have $1500 - 10Q_C = 100$, giving $Q_C^* = 140$ and $P_C^* = \$800$.

The example we have just presented resolved the arbitrage problem by assuming that different types of travelers are committed to particular classes of travel. Of course, this may not always be the case. For example, the downturn in economic activity through 2011 has encouraged many businesses to seek ways to cut costs. In particular, business travelers increasingly are required by their companies to fly coach. It remains the case that these types of travelers are willing to pay more (though not as much more as before) for air travel than casual or vacation travelers. Now, however, the airline's ability to exploit the difference in willingness to pay faces a potentially severe arbitrage problem.

To see this more clearly, let's simplify the problem and suppose that the airline has just two types of customers, business people and vacationers. Business people are known to have a high reservation price, or willingness to pay, for a return ticket, which we will denote as V^B. Vacationers, by contrast, have a low reservation price, denoted as V^V. By assumption, $V^B > V^V$, and the airline would obviously like to exploit this difference by charging business customers a high price and vacationers a low one. However, the airline cannot simply impose this distinction. A policy of explicitly charging business customers more than vacationers would quickly lead to every customer claiming to be on holiday and not on business. To be sure, the airline could try to identify which passengers really are on holiday, but this would be costly and likely to alienate customers.

If this were the end of our story, it would appear that the airline has no choice but to sell its tickets at a single, uniform price. It would then face the usual textbook monopoly dilemma. A high price will earn a large surplus from every customer that buys a ticket but clearly leads to a smaller, mostly business set of passengers. By contrast, a low price will encourage many more people to fly but, unfortunately, leave the company with little surplus from any one consumer.

Suppose, however, that business and holiday travelers differ in another respect as well as in their motives for flying. To be specific, suppose that business travelers want to complete their trip and return home within three days, whereas vacationers want to be away for at least one week. Suppose also that the airline learns (through surveys and other market research) that business travelers are willing to pay a premium beyond a normal ticket price if they can be guaranteed a return flight within their preferred three-day span. In this case, product differentiation by means of offering two differentiated tickets—one with a minimum time away of a week and another with no minimum stay—will enable the airline to extract considerable surplus from each type of consumer.

The complete strategy would be as follows: First, set a low price of V^V for tickets requiring a minimum of one week before returning. Because holiday travelers do not mind staying away seven days, and because the ticket price does not exceed their reservation price, they will willingly purchase this ticket. Because such travelers are paying their reservation price, the airline has extracted their entire consumer surplus and converted it into profit for itself.[5]

Second, the airline should set a price as close to V^B as possible for flights with no minimum stay. The limit on its ability to do this will be such factors as the cost of paying for a hotel for extra nights, the price of alternative transportation capable of returning individuals in three days, and related considerations. Denote the dollar value of these other factors as M. Business people wanting to return quickly will gladly pay a premium over the one week price V^V up to the value of M, so long as their total fare is less than V^B. (The precise condition is $V^V + M < V^B$.) Using such a scheme enables the airline to extract considerable surplus from business customers, while simultaneously extracting the entire surplus from vacationers.

In short, even if the airline cannot squeeze out the entire consumer surplus from the market, it can nevertheless improve its profits greatly by offering two kinds of tickets. This is undoubtedly the reason that the practice just described is so common among airlines and other transportation companies. (See Reality Checkpoint.) Such companies offer different varieties of their product as a means of having their customers self-select into different groups. Automobile and appliance manufacturers us a similar strategy—offering different product lines meant to appeal to consumers of different incomes or otherwise different willingness to pay. Stiglitz (1977) labels such mechanisms as *screening devices* because

---

[5]   An alternative and frequently used distinction is to require that the traveler stay over a Saturday night in order to qualify for a cheap fare. Presumably a corporation will not want to finance the lodgings of its employees when they are not on company business. Further, business travelers will typically want to spend weekends with family and loved ones. On both counts, the Saturday night requirement works as a self-separating device.

Reality Checkpoint
You Can't Go Before You Come Back

It is not uncommon to find that a coach fare to fly out on Tuesday and return quickly on Thursday costs well over twice the coach fare to fly out on Tuesday and return a week later. So, for travelers wanting to return in two days, an obvious strategy is to buy two round trip tickets—one, say, that departs on Thursday the 10th and returns on Thursday the 17th, and another that departs on Tuesday the 15th and returns on Tuesday the 22nd. The passenger can use the outgoing half of the second ticket on Tuesday the 15th and then fly back on the return flight of the first ticket that flies on the 17th. Unfortunately for such savvy travelers—and for the students and other needy consumers who could use the unused portions of each flight—airlines are alert to such practices. In particular, when a passenger checks in for a flight, the airline checks to see if the passenger has an unused portion of a return flight. If so, the fee is automatically adjusted to the higher fare. The airlines have a great incentive to make sure that those who are willing to pay a substantial premium to return in two days really do pay it.

Los Angeles resident Peter Szabo found this out the hard way. He had planned a trip that would take him first to Boston, then to New York, and then to Philadelphia. He paid $435 dollars for a US Airways flight to Boston with a return flight from Philadelphia, with an intermediate bus trip from Boston to Philadelphia that stopped in Manhattan. A week or so before his departure, however, a business firm in New York that was interested in making a deal with Szabo asked to meet with him and offered to fly him to New York for free. So, Szabo amended his itinerary to go to New York first, then Boston, and then return from Philadelphia using the second half of the original ticket. He soon discovered that this was not possible. Because he had not used the first half, he could not use the second half. If he wanted to fly from Philadelphia now, he would have to purchase a new, one-way ticket *plus* a $150 ticket-change fee.

Sources: "Why It Doesn't Pay to Change Planes or Plans," *London Daily Telegraph* 11 March, 2000, p. 27; D. Lazarus. "Using Just Half of a Round Trip Ticket Can Be Costly," *Los Angeles Times* 11 January, p. B3.

they screen or separate customers precisely along the relevant dimension of willingness to pay.

A rather curious kind of screening is illustrated by Wolfram Research, manufacturers of the *Mathematica®* software package. In making its student version of the software, Wolfram disables a number of functions that are available in the full academic or commercial versions. In 2011, Wolfram offered the full version of *Mathematica®* at around $2,495, the academic version at around $1,095, and the student version at around $140. There is little doubt that this is a case involving substantial differences in net prices.

The motivation behind this screening by means of product differentiation seems equally clear. Wolfram realizes that some customers do not need—or at least do not want to pay very much for—the full version of their software. Wolfram markets the low-priced version of *Mathematica®* for these consumers, and then sells the extended version to customers with a high willingness to pay for the improved product. Note that the two products must really differ in some important respect (to consumers at least). If Wolfram did not reduce the capabilities of the student version, it would have to worry about arbitrage between the two customer groups, with students buying for their professors!

The Wolfram example just described is a type of screening referred to by marketing experts as "crimping the product." Deneckere and McAffee (1996) argue that crimping, or deliberately damaging a product to enhance the ability to price discriminate, has been a frequent practice of manufacturers throughout history. Among the examples that they cite are (1) IBM's *Laser Printer E*, an intentionally slower version of the company's higher-priced top-of-the-line laser printer and (2) simple cooking wine, which is ordinary table wine with so much salt added that it is undrinkable. Some people have even argued that the US Post Office deliberately reduces the quality of its standard, first class service so as to raise demand for its two-day priority and overnight mail services.

Each of these examples is a clear case of a difference in net prices. The lower-quality product sells for a lower price, yet—because it starts as a high-quality product and then requires the further cost of crimping—the lower-quality product is actually more expensive to make. Why do firms crimp a high-quality product to produce a low-quality one instead of simply producing a low-quality one in the first place? The most obvious answer relates to costs of production. Given that a firm with monopoly power such as Wolfram knows that there are consumers of different types willing to buy different varieties of its product, the firm must decide how these consumer types can be supplied with products "close" to those that they most want at least cost. It may well be cheaper to produce the student version of *Mathematica*® by crimping the full version rather than to set up a separate production line dedicated to manufacturing different versions of the software package.

The final type of product differentiation that we consider in this chapter is differentiation by *location of sale*.[6] In many cases, a product for sale in one location is not the same as the otherwise identical product for sale in another location. A prescription drug such as *Lipitor*® for sale in Wisconsin is not identical to the same prescription drug for sale in New York state. Even with the advent of sophisticated Internet search engines, a new automobile for sale in one state is not identical to the same new automobile for sale in another state.

To illustrate why this type of product differentiation can lead to price discrimination, suppose that there is a company, Boston Sea Foods (BSF), which sells a proprietary brand of clam chowder. BSF knows that demand for its chowder in Boston is $P_B = A - BQ_B$ and in Manhattan is $P_M = A - BQ_M$, where quantities are measured in thousands of pints. In other words, the firm believes that these two markets have identical demands. BSF has constant marginal costs of c per thousand pints of chowder. Transport costs to reach the Boston market are negligible but it costs BSF an amount t to transport a thousand pints of chowder to Manhattan.

How does BSF maximize its profits from these two markets, given that BSF employs linear pricing? BSF should apply the rules that we have already developed. It should equate marginal revenue with marginal cost in each market. In the Boston market this requires that $A - 2BQ_B = c$, so that $Q_B^* = (A - c)/2B$ and the Boston price is $P_B^* = (A + c)/2$. In the Manhattan market we have, by contrast, $A - 2BQ_M = c + t$, so that $Q_M^* = (A - c - t)/2B$ and the Manhattan price is $P_M^* = (A + c + t)/2$.

Why is this outcome an example of third-degree price discrimination? Recall our definition of price discrimination with differentiated products. For there to be *no* such discrimination, any difference in price should be equal to the difference in the costs of

---

[6]   We return to spatial differentiation in more detail in Chapter 7.

product differentiation. In our BSF example, it costs BSF t per thousand pints to send chowder from Boston to Manhattan but the difference in price in the two markets is only $t/2$. In other words, BSF is price discriminating by absorbing 50 percent of the transport costs of sending its chowder to Manhattan.

What about the arbitrage problem in the BSF example? Manhattanites might want to buy their chowder directly in the Boston market, but it is economic for them to do so only if they have access to a transport technology that is at least 50 percent cheaper than that employed by BSF, a very tall order other than for those who choose to vacation in Boston.

Returning to our prescription drug example in Table 5.1, one possible explanation for the difference in prices in the three United States regions might be differences in costs of supplying these three regions. Another, of course, would be differences in demands in the three regions arising from differences in these regions' demographics or incomes.

5.2

Practice Problem

NonLegal Seafoods (NS) sells its excellent clam chowder in Boston, New York, and Washington. NS has estimated that the demands in these three markets are respectively $Q_B = 10,000 - 1,000P_B$, $Q_{NY} = 20,000 - 2,000P_{NY}$ and $Q_W = 15,000 - 1,500P_W$, where quantities are pints of clam chowder per day. The marginal cost of making a pint of clam chowder in their Boston facility is \$1. In addition, it costs \$1 per pint to ship the chowder to New York and \$2 per pint to ship to Washington.

a.   What are the profit maximizing prices that NS should set in these three markets? How much chowder is sold per day in each market?
b.   What profit does NS make in each market?

5.5   THIRD-DEGREE PRICE DISCRIMINATION OR GROUP PRICING AND SOCIAL WELFARE

The term "price discrimination" suggests inequity and, from a social perspective, sounds like a "bad thing." Is it? To answer this question, we must recall the economist's approach to social welfare and the problem raised by the standard monopoly model. Economists view arrangements as less than socially optimal whenever there are potential trades that could make both parties better off. This is the reason that a standard monopoly is sub-optimal. The textbook monopolist practicing uniform pricing restricts output. At the margin, consumers value the product *more* than it costs the monopolist to produce it. A potentially mutually beneficial trade exists but under uniform pricing such a trade will not occur.

The question that we consider in this section is whether third-degree price discrimination worsens or reduces this monopoly distortion. The intuitive reason that third-degree discrimination may reduce efficiency relative to the uniform pricing case is essentially that such a policy amounts to uniform pricing within two or more separate markets. It thus runs the risks of compounding the output-reducing effects of monopoly power.

We can be more specific regarding the welfare effects of third-degree price discrimination by drawing on the work of Schmalensee (1981). This is illustrated for the case of two

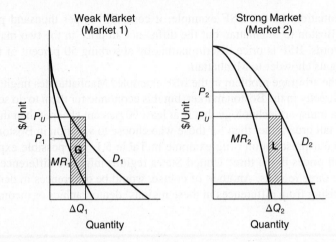

Figure 5.5   Welfare effects of third-degree price discrimination or group pricing
The upper limit on the welfare gain is area G and the lower limit on welfare loss is area L. The upper limit of the net welfare impact is G—L and is positive only if aggregate output is greater with discriminatory pricing than with nondiscriminatory pricing.

markets in Figure 5.5. In this figure, P_1 and P_2 are the profit maximizing discriminatory prices—obtained by equating marginal revenue with marginal cost in each market—while P_U is the optimal nondiscriminatory price. Market 2 is referred to as the strong market because the discriminatory price is higher than the uniform price while market 1 is the weak market. ΔQ_1 and ΔQ_2 are respectively the difference between the discriminatory output and the nondiscriminatory output in the weak and the strong market. It follows, of course, that $\Delta Q_1 > 0$ and $\Delta Q_2 < 0$.

Our normal definition of welfare is the sum of consumer plus producer surplus. Using this definition, an upper limit on the increase in surplus that follows from third-degree price discrimination in Figure 5.5 is the area G minus the area L. This gives us the following equation. (In writing equation (5.7) we have used the property that $\Delta Q_2 < 0$.)

$$\Delta W \leq G - L = (P_U - MC)\Delta Q_1 + (P_U - MC)\Delta Q_2 = (P_U - MC)(\Delta Q_1 + \Delta Q_2) \quad (5.7)$$

Extending this analysis to n markets, we have

$$\Delta W \leq (P_U - MC)\sum_{i=1}^{n} \Delta Q_i \quad (5.8)$$

It follows from equation (5.8) that for $\Delta W \geq 0$ it is necessary that $\sum_{i=1}^{n} \Delta Q_i \geq 0$. In other words, a necessary condition for third-degree price discrimination to increase welfare is that it increases total output.

We know from the Harry Potter example (and from the more general presentation in the Appendix) that when demands in the various markets are linear, total output is identical with discriminatory and non-discriminatory pricing. It follows that with linear demands third-degree price discrimination must reduce total welfare. The increase in profit is more than offset by the reduction in consumer surplus. Schmalensee states:

> "If one thinks that demand curves are about as likely to be concave as convex ... (this) ... might lead one to the conclusion that monopolistic third-degree price discrimination should be outlawed." (Schmalensee 1981, 246) See also Shih, Mai and Lui (1988).

However, before jumping to the suggested conclusion, we need to note an important caveat. Our analysis implicitly assumes that the same markets are served with and without price discrimination. This may very well not be the case. In particular, one property of price discrimination that we have not yet considered is that it can make it profitable to serve markets that will not be served with non-discriminatory prices. If this is the case, then the additional welfare from the new markets that third-degree price discrimination introduces more than offsets any loss of welfare in the markets that were previously being served.

A simple example serves to make this point. Suppose that monthly demand for a patented AIDS drug treatment in North America is $P_N = 100 - Q_N$ and in Sub-Saharan Africa is $P_S = \alpha 100 - Q_S$ with $\alpha < 1$ reflecting the assumption that African consumers have a lower demand because their income is so much smaller. Further assume that the marginal cost of producing each month's treatment is constant at $c = 20$ per unit and that transport costs to the African market are negligible.

Now assume that the patent holder is constrained from price discriminating across the two markets. As before, we start by inverting the demand functions to give $Q_N = 100 - P$ and $Q_S = \alpha 100 - P$. If the price is low enough to attract buyers in both markets then aggregate demand is: $Q = (1 + \alpha)100 - 2P$ or $P = (1 + \alpha)50 - Q/2$, and marginal revenue is $MR = (1 + \alpha)50 - Q$. Equating marginal revenue with marginal cost $c = 20$, gives the equilibrium output, $Q = (1 + \alpha)50 - 20 = 30 + \alpha 50$, and price $P = 35 + 25\alpha$.

Now recall our assumption that both markets are active without price discrimination. For this assumption to hold it must be that the equilibrium price when there is no discrimination is less than the maximum price—$\alpha 100$—that Sub-Saharan African consumers are willing and able to pay. That is, for our assumption to hold it must be the case that $35 + 25\alpha < \alpha 100$. In turn, this implies that for both markets to be active with no price discrimination it is necessary that $\alpha > 35/75$ or $\alpha > 0.466$. In other words, for the Sub-Saharan African market to be served it is necessary that the maximum willingness to pay for AIDS drugs in that market be at least 47 percent of the maximum willingness to pay in North America.

Moreover, even if $\alpha > 0.466$, the Sub-Saharan African market may not be served. From the patent-holding firm's perspective, it is not quite enough that the maximum willingness to pay exceeds the price charged if it serves both markets. This is because the monopolist always has the option of choosing a higher price and serving only the North American market. In the end-of-chapter problem 6, you are asked to show that $\alpha > 0.531$ for it to be profitable for the firm to serve both markets when price discrimination is for some reason prohibited.

Why might allowing the firm to price discriminate in this example lead to an increase in total welfare? Whether or not the monopolist is allowed to price discriminate, the firm will set the monopoly price in the United States so there is no change on total surplus in the United States. What about the Sub-Saharan market? For the monopolist to be willing to supply this market all that is needed now is that the reservation price 100α be greater than marginal cost of $20, or $\alpha > 0.2$. If this condition is satisfied, total surplus is increased by third-degree price discrimination because a market is opened up that would otherwise not be served.

5.3

Return to practice problem 5.1 and confirm that total welfare is greater with nondiscriminatory pricing than with third-degree price discrimination.

Practice Problem

5.6 EMPIRICAL APPLICATION: PRICE DISCRIMINATION IN THE NEW CAR MARKET

As we have seen, a firm with market power has a very strong interest in discriminating in the price it charges to different consumers—getting the most from those with the greatest willingness to pay and concluding a sale to those with lower valuations of the good at a lower price. As we have seen, an explicit pricing rule such as time-of-day pricing can sometimes be used to this effect. However, in a number of cases, the actual price paid is not the result of an explicit pricing schedule but, instead, reflects the outcome of a bargaining process between seller and buyer. New car purchases are a good example.

Automobiles come with a Manufacturer's Suggested Retail Price (MSRP) but the actual price paid by any consumer is typically the outcome of a bargaining process between the buyer and the car dealer. As a result, different consumers will end up paying different prices. In part, this will depend on factors that affect the dealer's willingness to reduce price, such as an end-of-the-month sales bonus or the number of rival dealerships nearby. Controlling for these factors, however, variations in the price paid should reflect variations in consumer demand elasticity. Consumers with incomes well above the average are likely to pay more while consumers who are well-informed about car prices at other dealers, i.e., those with low search costs, will be more price sensitive and negotiate a lower price. There may also be overt discrimination based on other factors such as gender and race.

Scott Morton, Zettelmeyer, and Silva-Risso (2003) (hereafter SZS) examine actual new car prices for over 671,000 transactions at over 3,500 dealers during a 14 month period beginning on January 1, 1999 and ending on February 28, 2000. Working with a market research firm, the authors were able to collect data for each of these transactions regarding the price paid, the make, model, and trim level of the car, the financing and any trade-in values that accompanied the deal, the dealership that made the sale, the name, address, and age of the buyer and, very importantly, whether the buyer used the online car-referral service, Autobytel.

SZS can match the name and address of each buyer to a specific census block group, which is a precise neighborhood of 1,100 people that comprises about one-fourth of the geographic tracts compiled by the US Census Bureau. For each such census block, the authors have data on the percentage of the population that is black, Hispanic, and Asian (and hence, the percentage that is in none of these racial groups). They also have data on other socioeconomic variables for the block such as median household income, the percentage that own their homes, the percentage that completed college, and the occupational breakdown between professionals, business executives, blue collar workers, and technicians.

SZS then identify 834 specific "cars" depending on the make, model, and trim involved. For each such car, they measure the net price paid by the buyer as the transaction price less any manufacturer's rebate and also less any excess value given for a trade-in as measured by the difference between the value assigned the trade-in vehicle and that car's book value. Because they cannot control for all option features, they include a variable that should indicate additional special features called DVehCost. This is measured as the difference between the vehicle's recorded invoice (dealer cost) and the average cost for that type of car. As noted, SZS also control for the number of nearby rival dealers, the "hotness" of the car (how long since it was first introduced), end-of-month sales, and various other dealer characteristics. The first of the main results of the SZS research for our purposes are shown in Table 5.3. For ease of interpretation, all coefficient estimates have been multiplied by 100.

Because the dependent variable is the natural log of the net purchase price, the coefficients are naturally interpreted as percentage price effects. In this light, first note that the dealer control variables generally have the right sign and are statistically significant. For example, the inclusion of unobserved features that raise the vehicle cost above the dealer's average also raise the final price, as does the presence of a trade-in as dealers try to recover some of the trade-in value paid. Competition as measured by the number of rival dealers nearby significantly lowers the price.

Table 5.3 Determinants of new car prices actually paid

Variable	Estimated Coefficient	Standard Error
%Black	0.015	(0.00054)*
%Hispanic	0.011	(0.001)*
%Asian	−0.004	(0.00096)*
Female	0.210	(0.01)*
Age	0.005	(0.00063)*
Age > 64	−0.170	(0.03)*
Median Income	−0.00002	(1.39e-06)*
(Median Income)^2	1.3e-10	(7.58e-12)*
%College Grad	−0.0031	(0.00095)*
%<High School	0.0039	(0.0013)*
%HomeOwner	−0.0027	(0.00045)*
%Professional	0.0046	(0.0014)*
%Executives	−0.00013	(0.0015)
%Blue Collar	0.00018	(0.001)
%Technicians	0.0046	(0.0035)
Median Home Value	2.7e-06	(1.28e-07)*
End of Month	−0.3500	(0.015)*
Weekend	0.1100	(0.016)*
DVehCost	88	(0.13)*
Competition	−0.02	(0.0035)*
Any Trade	0.31	(0.01)*
Constant	1,001	(0.13)*
R^2	0.97	

*Significant at 1% level.

For our immediate concern with price discrimination, the first thing to note is that those buyers with the most elastic demands and therefore those who pay the lowest prices tend to be those from census blocks with typically low incomes or high education levels. Thus, the coefficients on the two income variables imply that the price rises sharply as the median household income of the buyer's census block increases above $80,000. The price is also notably higher for someone likely to have less than a high school education and falls significantly for those with a college degree. The interpretation of these factors is straightforward. Those with relatively high incomes have high search costs because the value of their time is high. Hence, they are willing to pay a high price for a car rather than spend more time seeking a better deal. Similarly, those with little education are willing to pay a higher price, all else equal, because they find searching difficult.

SZS pay particular attention to the race and gender effects. Because the race variable is the percentage of the census block of a specific race, one may take this as an estimate of the probability that the buyer from that block is also of that race. Thus, if we set either %Black or %Hispanic to 100, the coefficient will indicate the price differential paid by a black or Hispanic buyer relative to a white person. The data therefore indicate that Hispanic and black car buyers pay 1.1% and 1.5% more, respectively, than do white buyers.

Turning to the gender variable (which is assigned primarily on a name basis), the initial estimate suggests that women pay 0.2% more for a new car than do men. SZS feel that this may underestimate the gender effect because often a brother, father, boyfriend, or husband is present in those cases in which the buyer is recorded officially as a woman. They therefore look separately at the purchase of minivans for which 98 percent of the buyers are married couples relative to the purchase of compact and sporty cars for which only 48 percent of the buyers are married couples. The female price premium essentially disappears for the case of minivans but rises to over four-tenths of a percent for compact car purchases.

Given an average car price of $23,000, the price premia that SZS estimate for minorities ($253–$345) and women ($98) translate into nontrivial dollar amounts. It is natural to ascribe these extra charges to racial and gender bias. SZS however suggest that it is not so much bias on the part of dealers as it is the case that the race and gender variables capture the further measure of search cost difficulty. Recall that the authors also have data indicating whether or not the buyer used the Internet service, Autobytel, to submit their purchase request. For this group of buyers—just under 3 percent of all buyers—search costs should be decidedly smaller. Thus, this group of buyers should pay a lower price, all else equal. More importantly, if the premium paid by women and minorities is due mainly to search costs, then use of Autobytel should be particularly helpful to these buyers.

Table 5.4 below shows the effects that SZS estimate for the impact of Autobytel use both by itself and when it is interacted with each of the important buyer groups. Here, SZS also include the market research firm's race assignment (Hispanic or Asian) to supplement the census block data so as to get as complete an estimate of the internet effect as possible.

Clearly, the use of Autobytel's Internet service helps reduce prices. Most notably though, these effects are particularly important for women and minorities. The coefficients above suggest that for those black and Hispanic buyers who used Autobytel, the earlier premiums they paid of 1.1 to 1.5 percent are virtually eliminated. For women who use this service, the effect is smaller but still very significant.

In short, the SZS results confirm our analysis that consumers with high search costs have less elastic demands and therefore end up paying higher prices. In the case of car buyers, this includes in particular those with higher incomes and less education. It also includes minority and female buyers. As a result, it is particularly these buyers who benefit from use of an Internet-based car-buying service.

Table 5.4 Impact of internet use (Autobytel) on actual car prices paid

Variable	Estimated Coefficient	Standard Error
Autobytel	−0.88	0.045[†]
Autobytel Franchise	−0.46	0.015[†]
Autobytel * %Black	−0.12	0.0028[†]
— * %Hispanic	−0.02	0.0038[†]
— * %Asian	−0.007	0.0033[†]
— * Hispanic	−0.57	0.15[†]
— * Asian	0.14	0.16
— * Female	−0.12	0.058

[*]Significant at 5% level.
[†]Significant at 1% level.

Summary

We started this chapter with a discussion of prescription drug price differentials that seem not to be related to costs. In a well-functioning market, such differentials can only occur if there is something that allows a firm with market power to set different prices to different groups of consumers. We showed that a firm with monopoly power can increase its profits if the firm can figure out a way to separate its consumers by type and charge different prices to the different types. Our analysis has concentrated on third-degree price discrimination or group pricing, in which the firm offers different prices to different consumer groups, but leaves it up to consumers to determine how much they will purchase at the quoted prices. This is often referred to as linear pricing.

In order to implement third-degree price, discrimination the firm has to solve two problems. First, it needs some observable characteristic by which it can identify the different groups of consumers: the identification problem. Second, the firm must be able to prevent consumers who pay a low price from selling to consumers offered a high price: the arbitrage problem. Provided that both problems can be overcome, there is then a simple principle that guides the monopolist in setting prices. Set a high price in markets in which elasticity of demand is low and a low price in markets in which elasticity of demand is high. When the firm makes a single homogeneous product, this implies that different groups of consumers will be paying different prices for

the same good. If the firm sells differentiated products, it implies that the prices of different varieties will vary by something other than the difference in their marginal production costs.

Recent empirical evidence on new car purchases provides support for the hypothesis that the negotiated auto price will vary inversely with the buyer's elasticity which, in turn, varies inversely with the buyer's search costs. Buyers whose search costs are low either because they are well educated, have a low opportunity cost of time or, in particular, use Internet buying programs tend to pay significantly lower net prices for new cars. This last mechanism is particularly important for minorities and women who otherwise tend to pay 0.2 to 1.5 percent more for a new care relative to other groups.

While third-degree price discrimination or group pricing is undoubtedly profitable, it is less clear that it is socially desirable. Again there is a simple principle that can guide us. For third-degree price discrimination to increase social welfare it is necessary, but not sufficient, that it lead to an increase in output. This makes intuitive sense. After all, we know that under uniform pricing or nondiscrimination a monopolist makes profit by restricting output. If price discrimination leads to increased output it might reduce the monopoly distortion. This is, however, a tall order, usually requiring some very restrictive conditions regarding the shapes of the demand functions in the different markets. For example, it is a condition that is *never* satisfied when demands are linear and the same markets are served with and without price discrimination.

The qualification regarding the same markets being served is, however, important. There may be cases in which group price discrimination has the beneficial effect of encouraging the monopolist to serve markets that would otherwise have been left unserved. For example, markets populated by very low income groups might not be supplied if the monopolist were not able to set discriminatory prices. When price discrimination leads the monopolist to serve additional markets, the likelihood that it increases social welfare is greatly increased.

We conclude by noting one limitation of focusing on third-degree price discrimination. Restricting the monopolist to simple, linear forms of price discrimination is qualitatively the same as allowing it to charge a monopoly price in each of its separate markets. Yet we know that in any given market, charging a monopoly price reduces the surplus. The monopolist knows this too and, therefore, cannot help but wonder if a more complicated—that is, a nonlinear pricing strategy—might permit the monopolist to capture more of the potential surplus as profit. It is to this question that we turn in the next chapter.

Problems

1. TRUE or FALSE: Price discrimination always increases economic efficiency relative to what would be achieved by a single, uniform monopoly price.

2. A nearby pizza parlor offers pizzas in three sizes: small, medium, and large. Its corresponding price schedule is: $6, $8, and $10. Do these data indicate that the firm is price discriminating? Why or why not?

3. A monopolist has two sets of customers. The inverse demand for Group 1 is described by $P = 200 - X$. For Group 2, the inverse demand is $P = 200 - 2X$. The monopolist faces constant marginal cost of 40.
   a. Show that the monopolist's total demand, if the two markets are treated as one is:

   $X = 0$; $\qquad\qquad$ $P \geq 200$
   $X = 200 - P$; $\qquad\quad$ $100 < P \leq 200$
   $X = 300 - (3/2)P$; $\quad 0 < P \leq 100$

   b. Show that the monopolist's profit maximizing price is $P = 120$ if both groups are to be charged the same price. At this price, how much is sold to members of Group 1 and how much to members of Group 2? What is the consumer surplus of each group? What are total profits?

4. Now suppose that the monopolist in #3 can separate the two groups and charge separate, profit-maximizing prices to each group
   a. What will these prices be? What is consumer surplus? What are total profits?

   b. If total surplus is consumer surplus plus profit, how has price discrimination affected total surplus?

5. Suppose that Coca-Cola uses a new type of vending machine that charges a price according to the outside temperature. On "hot" days—defined as days in which the outside temperature is 25 degrees Celsius or higher—demand for vending machine soft drinks is: $Q = 300 - 2P$. On "cool" days—when the outside temperature is below 25 degrees Celsius—demand is: $Q = 200 - 2P$. The marginal cost of a canned soft drink is 20 cents.
   a. What price should the machine charge for a soft drink on "hot" days? What price should it charge on "cool" days?
   b. Suppose that half of the days are "hot" and the other half are "cool." If Coca-Cola uses a traditional machine that is programmed to charge the same price regardless of the weather, what price should it set?
   c. Compare Coca-Cola's profit from a weather-sensitive machine to the traditional, uniform pricing machine.

6. Return to the final example of section 5.5, in which the demand for AIDS drugs was $Q_N = 100 - P$ in North America and $Q_S = \alpha 100 - P$ in Sub-Saharan Africa. Show that with marginal $cost = 20$ for such drugs, it must be the case that $\alpha > 0.531$ if the drug manufacturer is to serve both markets while

charging the same price in each market. (HINT: Calculate the total profit if it serves only North America and then calculate the total profit if it serves both markets. Then determine the value of α for which the profit from serving both markets is at least as large.)

7. Frank Buckley sells his famous bad tasting but very effective cough medicine in Toronto and Montreal. The demand functions in these two urban areas, respectively, are: $P_T = 18 - Q_T$ and $P_M = 14 - Q_M$. Buckley's plant is located in Kingston, Ontario, which is roughly midway between the two cities. As a result, the cost of producing and delivering cough syrup to each town is: $2 + 3Q_i$ where $i = T, M$.

   a. Compute the optimal price of Buckley's cough medicine in Toronto and Montreal if the two markets are separate.

   b. Compute the optimal price of Buckley's medicine if Toronto and Montreal are treated as a common market.

8. The Mount Sunburn Athletic Club has two kinds of tennis players, Acers and Netters, in its membership. A typical Ace has a weekly demand for hours of $Q_A = 6 - P$. A typical Netter has a weekly demand of $Q_N = 3 - P/2$. The marginal cost of a court is zero and there are one thousand players of each type. If the MSAB charges the same price per hour regardless of who plays, what price should it charge if it wishes to maximize club revenue?

References

Deneckere, R., and R. P. McAffee. 1996. "Damaged Goods," *Journal of Economics and Management Strategy* 5 (Summer): 149–74.

Leslie, P. 2004. "Price Discrimination in Broadway Theatre," *Rand Journal of Economics* 35 (Autumn): 520–41.

Quon, B., R. Firszt, and M. Eisenberg. 2005. "A Comparison of Brand Name Drug Prices between Canadian-Based Internet Pharmacies and Major U.S. Drug Chain Pharmacies," *Annals of Internal Medicine*, 143: 397–403.

Philips, L. 1983. *The Economics of Price Discrimination*. Cambridge: Cambridge University Press.

Pigou, A. C. 1920. *The Economics of Welfare*. London: MacMillan.

Schmalensee, R. 1981. "Output and Welfare Implications of Monopolistic Third-Degree Price Discrimination," *American Economic Review* 71 (March): 242–47.

Scott Morton, F., F. Zettelmeyer, and J. Silva-Risso. 2003. "Consumer Information and Discrimination: Does the Internet Affect the Pricing of New Cars to Women and Minorities?" *Quantitative Marketing and Economics* 1 (March): 65–92.

Skinner, B., and M. Rovere. (2008). *Seniors and Drug Prices in Canada and the United States*. Fraser Alert, Fraser Institute, Canada.

Stiglitz, J. 1977. "Monopoly, Nonlinear Pricing, and Imperfect Information: The Insurance Market," *Review of Economic Studies* 44 (October): 407–30.

Shapiro, C. and H. R. Varian. 1999. *Information Rules*. Boston: Harvard Business School Press.

Shih, J., and C. Mai, and J. Liu. 1988. "A General Analysis of the Output Effect under Third-Degree Price Discrimination," *Economic Journal* (March): 149–58.

Appendix

DISCRIMINATORY AND NONDISCRIMINATORY PRICING

Let a monopolist supply two groups of consumers with inverse demand given by:

$$P_1 = A_1 - B_1 Q_1$$
$$P_2 = A_2 - B_2 Q_2 \hspace{3cm} (5.A1)$$

We assume that $A_1 > A_2$ so that group 1 is the "high demand" group whose demand is the less elastic at any given price. Inverting the inverse demands gives the direct demands at some price P:

$$Q_1 = (A_1 - P)/B_1; \quad Q_2 = (A_2 - P)/B_2 \tag{5.A2}$$

Aggregate demand is:

$$Q = Q_1 + Q_2 = \frac{A_1 B_2 + A_2 B_1}{B_1 B_2} - \frac{B_1 + B_2}{B_1 B_2} P \tag{5.A3}$$

Of course, this holds only for any price less that A_2. Aggregate inverse demand for the two groups, again for any price less than A_2 is:

$$P = \frac{A_1 B_2 + A_2 B_1}{B_1 + B_2} - \frac{B_1 B_2}{B_1 + B_2} Q \tag{5.A3}$$

The marginal revenue associated with this aggregate demand is:

$$MR = \frac{A_1 B_2 + A_2 B_1}{B_1 + B_2} - 2 \frac{B_1 B_2}{B_1 + B_2} Q \tag{5.A4}$$

Without loss of generality, assume that marginal cost is zero. Equilibrium aggregate output Q^U and price P^U with uniform pricing is then:

$$Q^U = \frac{A_1 B_2 + A_2 B_1}{2 B_1 B_2}; \quad P^U = \frac{A_1 B_2 + A_2 B_1}{2(B_1 + B_2)} \tag{5.A5}$$

Substituting this price into the individual demands then gives equilibrium output in each market

$$Q_1^U = \frac{(2A_1 - A_2)B_1 + A_1 B_2}{2B_1(B_1 + B_2)}; \quad Q_2^U = \frac{(2A_2 - A_1)B_2 + A_2 B_1}{2B_2(B_1 + B_2)} \tag{5.A6}$$

With third-degree price discrimination, marginal revenue equals marginal cost for each group. Hence:

$$Q_1^D = \frac{A_1}{2B_1}; \quad Q_2^D = \frac{A_2}{2B_2}. \tag{5.A7}$$

Comparison of (5.A6) and (5.A7) confirms that 1) $Q_1^D < Q_1^U$; and 2) $Q_2^D > Q_2^U$.

6

Price Discrimination and Monopoly: Nonlinear Pricing

If you buy the *New Yorker* magazine at the newsstand, you will pay $4.99 per issue, or $234.53 if you buy all forty-seven issues. If instead you purchase an annual subscription you will pay $69.99 for forty-seven issues—a savings of approximately 70 percent over the newsstand price. Similarly, if you are a baseball fan you know that the price per ticket on a season pass is much less than the price per ticket on a game-by-game basis. When you go grocery shopping you find that a 24-pack of Coca-Cola costs less on a price-per-can basis than a six-pack or than a single can. These are all examples of price discrimination that reflect quantity discounts—the more you buy the cheaper it is on a per-unit basis.

Quantity discounting is just a way of saying that firms are employing *nonlinear* prices. The price per unit is not constant but rather varies with some feature of the buying arrangement depending, perhaps, on the consumer's income, value of time, the quantity bought or other characteristics. Such a pricing strategy differs from the linear price discrimination methods discussed in Chapter 5. The goal of nonlinear pricing is to allow the seller to convert as much of the individual consumer's willingness to pay into revenues and profits as possible. We shall see that such techniques are generally more profitable than third-degree price discrimination or linear pricing, precisely because they permit the seller to set a price closer to willingness to pay *of each consumer*. As a result, nonlinear pricing helps the monopolist to earn more profit.

The design and implementation of nonlinear pricing strategies are this chapter's focus. We explore how and under what circumstances a firm with market power can implement such pricing schemes and examine their welfare properties. Traditionally, nonlinear pricing is divided into two general categories: first-degree price discrimination and second-degree price discrimination or, as Shapiro and Varian (1999) categorize them, personalized pricing and menu pricing. See both Pigou (1920) and Philips (1983) for an elaboration of price discrimination categories.

6.1 FIRST-DEGREE PRICE DISCRIMINATION OR PERSONALIZED PRICING

First-degree, or perfect price discrimination is practiced when the monopolist is able to charge the maximum price each consumer is willing to pay for *each* unit of the product sold. Suppose that you have inherited five antique cars, each a classic Ford *Model T*, and that you want to sell them to finance your college education. They are of no other value to you. Your market research tells you that there are several collectors interested in buying a *Model T*. When you rank these collectors in terms of their willingness to pay for a car, you estimate that the keenest collector is willing to pay up to $10,000, the second up to $8,000, the third up to $6,000, the fourth $4,000, and the fifth $2,000. First-degree price discrimination means that you are able sell the first car for $10,000, the second for $8,000, the third for $6,000, the fourth for $4,000, and the fifth car for $2,000. The revenue from such a discriminatory pricing policy is $30,000. Not surprisingly, this strategy is also called personalized pricing.

What if, on the other hand, you chose to sell your antiques at the same, uniform price? It is easy to calculate that the best you can do is to set a price of $6,000 at which you sell three cars for a total revenue (and profit) of $18,000. Any higher or lower price generates lower revenues. In short, under uniform pricing your highest possible revenue is $18,000 while successful first-degree price discrimination yields a much higher revenue of $30,000. Why? Very simply because first-degree price discrimination enables you to extract the entire surplus that selling your car generates. No consumer surplus remains if you can successfully discriminate to this extent whereas with a uniform price the keenest buyer has consumer surplus of $4,000 and the second keenest buyer has consumer surplus of $2,000.

Because first-degree price discrimination, or personalized pricing, redirects surplus from consumers to the firm, it should be expected to increase the monopolist's profit-maximizing output. In fact, as we shall see, with first-degree price discrimination the monopolist chooses the socially efficient output: the output that would be achieved under perfect competition. In our *Model T* example, no mutually beneficial trades are left unmade: all five cars are sold. By contrast, with uniform pricing only three cars are sold leaving two of the cars in the "wrong" hands: there are two potential buyers who value the cars much more highly than you do.

The same is true in more general cases. For a monopolist able to practice first-degree price discrimination, selling an additional unit never requires lowering the price on other units. Each additional unit sold generates additional revenue exactly equal to the price at which it is sold. Hence, with first-degree price discrimination marginal revenue is equal to price. Accordingly, for such a monopolist, the profit maximizing rule that marginal revenue equals marginal cost yields an output level at which price equals marginal cost as well. As we know, this is the output level that would be generated by a competitive industry.

Suppose that a monopoly seller knows that his or her demand curve is linear, and knows that at a price of $40, five units can be sold, while at a price of $25, 10 units are sold.

a. If each potential consumer buys only one unit, what is the reservation price of the consumer with the greatest willingness to pay?

b. Suppose that the monopolist discovers that the demand curve worked out in (a) applies only to the first unit a consumer buys and that, in fact, each consumer will buy a second unit at a price $8 below the price at which they purchase just one. How many units will be sold at a price of $34? (Use whole dollar amounts.)

At first glance it might seem that first-degree discrimination is little more than a theoretical curiosity. How could a monopolist ever have sufficient information about potential buyers and the ability to prevent arbitrage so as to effectively implement a pricing scheme in which a different, personalized price is charged to each buyer and for each unit bought? The problems of identification and arbitrage prevention seem insurmountable. However, in some cases the monopolist seller may indeed have the ability to achieve the personalized pricing outcome. A tax accountant knows the financial situation of his or her clients. Management consultants typically negotiate their fees with individual clients. Another example, rather closer to home, is the fees paid by students who apply to any of the (expensive) private universities in the United States. When they apply for financial aid, they are required to complete a detailed statement of financial means. The universities of course can use this information, as well SAT scores and other data, to determine the aid to be granted and so the net tuition that each prospective student is required to pay. Look around you. If you break down the total tuition on a per class basis, chances are that many of your classmates are paying a different fee for this class than you are!

Of course, the accountant, consultant, and university examples are somewhat special because often the fee is set *after* the customer has contracted to purchase the service. What we now consider is whether there are pricing strategies that permit the seller to achieve the same effect even when fees must be announced in advance. The answer is yes, in some circumstances. One such strategy is a *two-part* pricing scheme. Another is *block pricing*. We discuss each in turn.

Reality Checkpoint

The More *You* Shop the More *They* Know

Before Facebook, could sell shares in the company on the public stock markets, it had to reveal its business model showing its assets and sources of income. Advertising revenue of course tops the bill, but it is really access that Facebook sells. Facebook makes money by selling ad space to companies that want to reach a targeted audience. Advertisers choose key words or characteristics for focus such as relationship status, location, activities, favorite books, and employment. Then, Facebook runs the ads for the targeted groups within its millions of users. If you reveal a taste for wine, live in certain neighborhoods, and host parties, then the local liquor store can place an ad on your page.

Of course, Facebook is not alone. Other e-commerce retailers such as Amazon.com and Wine.com constantly track your purchases. This allows them to tailor both ads and special promotional offers to their individual consumers. Third-party trackers are also important. NebuAd, for example, contracts with Internet service providers to monitor user activities in e-mail, web searches, and

Internet purchases. All this information is collected and sold to advertisers with a view to creating more effective advertising. Health product promotions can be more appropriately aimed at those of the right age, gender, and with a specific history of web searches. Different vacation package offerings can be shown to different consumers again depending on age, location, and Internet history. Spokeo gathers data both for advertising and for reselling to others such as potential employers. Indeed, one of its services invites women, for a fee, to submit their boyfriends' e-mail address and offers in return to provide the information necessary for a woman to find out if "He's Cheating on You." Whatever one's relationships status on Facebook, however, there is no doubt that each of our cyber selves is intimately known.

Source: Shapiro and Varian. 1999. *Information Rules: A Strategic Guide to the Internet Economy*, Harvard Business School Press: Boston.
L. Andrews, "Facebook is Using You," *New York Times* February 5, 2012, p SR7.

6.1.1   Two-Part Pricing

A two-part pricing scheme is a pricing strategy that consists of: 1) a fixed fee, such as a membership fee, that entitles the consumer to buy the good or service but which is independent of the quantity that the buyer actually purchases; and 2) a price or usage fee charged for each unit the consumer actually buys. Many clubs use such two-part pricing. They charge a flat annual fee for membership in the club (which is sometimes differentiated by age or some other member characteristic), and additional per-unit fees to use particular facilities or buy particular goods or services. Country clubs, athletic clubs, and discount shopping clubs are all good examples of organizations that use this kind of pricing. A related example of two-part pricing is that used by theme parks under which a flat fee is charged to enter the park and additional fees (sometimes set to zero) are charged on a per ride or per amusement basis.[1]

To see how two-part pricing can work to achieve first-degree price discrimination, let us consider a ski resort in Colorado owned and operated by a local monopolist. Assume that the resort's clients are of two types, old and young. A typical old client's inverse demand curve to use the resort's ski lifts is:

$$P = V_O - Q_O \tag{6.1}$$

while from each young client has the inverse demand curve:

$$P = V_Y - Q_Y \tag{6.2}$$

Reality Checkpoint

Call Options

Nonlinear pricing is an increasingly common feature of everyday life. Consider the packages available for cell phone service offered by the four major providers in the US, AT&T/Cingular, Verizon, Sprint/Nexus, and T-Mobile. Virtually all of these involve some variant of two-part pricing and quantity discounts. Family plans, for example, offer two lines for a fixed monthly fee. After that, each minute of calling is free up to a specified maximum. Low level plans offer something like 700 minutes for free at a monthly fee of, say, $70 while higher use plans offer roughly twice as many free monthly minutes for a fee of about $90. There is also a 3,000 minute

plan that usually sells for about $150. Additional phones can be added to a family plan at a fee of $10 per month. There are also single line plans and even pay-as-you-go plans. The latter are essentially calling card plans that sell say, 30 minutes or 90 minutes of phone time for $15 or $25, respectively. They are clearly for those who cannot be induced to make more than a few calls even with a hefty discount.

Sources: L. Magid, "BASICS: Plain Cellphones Can Overachieve, with a Little Help," *New York Times*, January 25, 2007, p. c14; and "The Bottom Line on Calling Plans," *Consumer Reports*, February, 2004, pp. 11–18.

---

[1]   Versions of such a scheme are used, for example, at parks such as Disney World. See Oi (1971) for the seminal discussion. As Ekelund (1970) notes, much modern analysis was anticipated by the work of 19th century French economist and engineer, Jules Dupuit. Varian (1989) provides an extensive survey of the price discrimination strategies discussed in this chapter.

where Q_i is the number of ski lift rides bought by a client of type i (O or Y), P is the price per lift ride and V_i is the maximum amount a client of type Q_i will pay for just one lift ride. We assume that young clients are willing to pay more for a given number of lift rides than are old clients, i.e., $V_O < V_Y$. After all, they are younger and probably fitter. We further assume that the ski resort owner incurs a marginal cost of c dollars per lift ride taken plus a fixed cost F of operating the resort each day. That is, the daily total cost function for the resort is:

$$C(Q) = F + cQ \qquad (6.3)$$

where Q is the number of lift rides sold and taken.

This example is illustrated in Figure 6.1. The demand curve for a typical skier starts at V_i and declines with slope -1 until it hits the quantity axis. The constant marginal cost curve is a horizontal line through the value c.

We assume that the ski resort owner can identify the true type of each skier, perhaps by checking their IDs, and can prevent arbitrage, perhaps by selling the different types of skier ski lift rides of different colors. Suppose first that the owner employs third-degree price discrimination. Entry to the resort is free, the resort owner sets a price per ski lift ride to each type of skier, and the skiers decide how many lift rides to buy at that price.

We simply apply the principles that we developed in Chapter 5. The resort owner maximizes profit using the usual two-stage process. First equate marginal revenue with marginal cost for each type of skier to identify the quantity of lift rides that the owner wants to sell to each type of skier. Second, identify the prices that can be charged for these quantities from the demand functions in equation (6.1) and equation (6.2).

Using the standard "twice as steep" rule, we know from equations (6.1) and (6.2) that the relevant marginal revenues are:

$$\text{Young}: MR_Y = V_Y - 2Q_Y$$

$$\text{Old}: MR_O = V_O - 2Q_O \qquad (6.4)$$

Setting marginal revenue equal to marginal cost c the profit-maximizing output—number of lift rides—to be sold to each type of skier is:

$$\text{Young}: MR_Y = V_Y - 2Q_Y = c \Rightarrow Q_Y = \frac{V_Y - c}{2}$$

$$\text{Old}: MR_O = V_O - 2Q_O = c \Rightarrow Q_O = \frac{V_O - c}{2} \qquad (6.5)$$

Substituting these quantities into the demand functions gives the profit-maximizing price per lift ride for each type of skier:

$$\text{Young}: P_Y = V_Y - \frac{V_Y - c}{2} = \frac{V_Y + c}{2}$$

$$\text{Old}: P_O = V_O - \frac{V_O - c}{2} = \frac{V_O + c}{2} \qquad (6.6)$$

Because by assumption $V_O < V_Y$ we have the result, as we found in Chapter 5, that the high-demand group—in this case the young skiers—pay more per unit than the low-demand group—the older skiers. Profit from each type of skier with this pricing policy is:

$$\text{Young} : \pi_Y = (P_Y - c)Q_Y = \frac{(V_Y - c)^2}{4}$$

$$\text{Old} : \pi_O = (P_O - c)Q_O = \frac{(V_O - c)^2}{4} \tag{6.7}$$

These are the areas *bdhi* and *fgjk*, respectively, in Figure 6.1.

For example, if V_o is \$12, V_Y is \$16, and c is \$4, then the optimal prices per ski lift ride are \$10 to each young skier and \$8 to each old skier. Young skiers each buy six lift rides and old skiers each buy four lift rides. Under this strategy, the resort owner earns a profit of (\$10 − \$4)*6 = \$36 from each young skier and (\$8 − \$4)*4 = \$16 from each old skier. If there were 100 old and 100 young skiers per day, the ski resort owner would earn a profit of \$5,200 each day less any fixed costs F that are incurred.

To see that the ski resort owner can improve on this outcome, first note that at the prices given by equation (6.6) every client of the ski resort enjoys some consumer surplus. Each young skier has consumer surplus given by the triangle *abd* in Figure 6.1(a) and each old skier has consumer surplus given by area *efg* in Figure 6.1(b). These areas are, by standard geometric techniques:

$$\text{Young} : CS_Y = (V_Y - P_Y)Q_Y = \frac{1}{2}(Q_Y)^2 = \frac{(V_Y - c)^2}{8}$$

$$\text{Old} : CS_O = (V_O - P_O)Q_O = \frac{1}{2}(Q_O)^2 = \frac{(V_O - c)^2}{8} \tag{6.8}$$

In our numerical example, each young client has consumer surplus of \$18 and each old client has consumer surplus of \$8. This is a measure of the surplus that the resort owner has failed to extract. The owner will clearly prefer any pricing scheme that appropriates at least some, or even better, all of this surplus.

One possibility is for the resort owner to switch to a nonlinear pricing scheme that has two parts—a cover charge that allows skiers to enter the resort and an additional charge for every lift ride bought. This pricing design is often referred to as a two-part tariff. Each

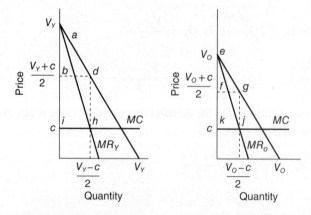

Figure 6.1   No price discrimination
Not price discriminating leaves both types of consumers with consumer surplus that the monopolist would like to convert to profit.

old skier is charged an entry fee $E_O = \dfrac{(V_O - c)^2}{8}$, whereas each young skier is charged an entry fee of $E_Y = \dfrac{(V_Y - c)^2}{8}$. The entry fee is the first, fixed part of the two-part tariff. The second part is the price per lift ride to each type of skier, which is either P_O or P_Y. In our numerical example, each old skier is charged an entry fee of $8 and each young skier is charged an entry fee of $18. Lift rides are sold at $8 each to the old skiers and $10 each to the young skiers. Checking IDs on entry to the resort and when using the ski lifts solves both arbitrage and identification problems.[2] Moreover, the skiers will still be willing to patronize the resort. Paying the entry fee reduces their surplus to zero but does not make it negative. The surplus is a measure of their willingness to pay. Finally, because the entry fee is independent of the number of lift rides each skier actually buys, each customer will also continue to buy the same number of lift rides as before. Because the entry fee is equal to the consumer surplus each skier previously enjoyed under the discriminatory but linear pricing policy, the immediate effect of this two-part tariff is to extract the entire consumer surplus and to convert it into profit for the resort owner. This implies a profit increase of E_O per old skier and E_Y per young skier. Again, in our example, this represents a profit increase of $8 per old skier and $18 per young one.

While the entry fees and unit prices we have calculated certainly increase the resort owner's profit, they are far from the best that the resort owner can do. By *reducing* the price of a lift ride the resort owner increases the potential consumer surplus each skier has. This permits the resort owner to increase the entry fees to extract this additional surplus, further increasing profit. The profit-maximizing two-part pricing scheme is illustrated in Figure 6.2. It has the following properties[3]:

1. Set the price per unit (per lift ride) equal to marginal cost c.
2. Set the entry fee for each type of client equal to that client's consumer surplus at the price given by 1.

In our ski resort example, the price per lift ride is set at c no matter the type of skier. The areas of the triangles *abd* and *efg* describe the consumer surplus at this price for young skiers and for old skiers, respectively. These areas are $CS_O = \dfrac{1}{2}(V_O - c)^2$ and $CS_Y = \dfrac{1}{2}(V_Y - c)^2$. As a result, the ski resort owner can now increase the entry fee to CS_O for old skiers and CS_Y for young skiers.

Under this optimal pricing scheme, the profit per lift ride from each skier is zero, because lift rides are sold at cost. This pricing strategy has the advantage of encouraging the skiers to purchase many lift rides, thereby yielding more consumer surplus. In turn, the resort owner can appropriate that surplus by imposing the optimal entry fee. The funds generated by the entry fees *are* profit, indeed, they are the resort owner's only source of profit in our

---

[2]   We assume that the cost of falsifying IDs and make-up to age a skier is more than the surplus young skiers lose by paying the higher price.

[3]   To see why these properties hold, denote the fixed portion of the two-part tariff for a particular type of consumer as T and the user charge as p. Express the demand curve for this type of consumer in inverse form, $p = D(q)$ and assume that the firm's total cost function is $C(q)$. The monopolist's problem is to choose the production level for this type of consumer, q^*, implying a price $p^* = D(q^*)$, that maximizes profits, $\Pi(q)$, where $\Pi(q)$ is given by: $\Pi(q) = \int_0^q D(x)dx - C(q)$. Standard calculus then reveals that maximizing this profit always requires setting a price or user charge equal to marginal cost, and a fixed charge T equal to the consumer surplus generated at that price.

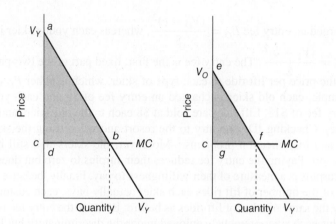

Figure 6.2   First-degree price discrimination with a two-part tariff
The monopolist sets a unit price to each type of consumer equal to marginal cost. The monopolist then charges each consumer an entry or membership fee equal to the resulting consumer surplus.

example. Total profit has, therefore, been increased to:

$$\Pi_f = n_O \frac{(V_O - c)^2}{2} + n_Y \frac{(V_Y - c)^2}{2} - F \tag{6.9}$$

where n_O is the number of old skiers and n_Y is the number of young skiers per day.

In our example, the price per lift ride is set at \$4. Old skiers purchase eight rides and young skiers twelve rides. The entry fee, and profit per old skier, is now \$32 while the entry fee and profit per young skier is \$72. This is a considerable increase over the \$36 and \$16 profit earned without any fixed fee or even the \$54 and \$24 earned with the "wrong" two-part tariff. This is a hefty profit increase.[4]

While the increase in profit is sizable and important, the two-part tariff has had another result that is equally significant. Note that each client is now buying the quantity of lift rides, $V_O - c$ for the typical old client and $V_Y - c$ for the typical young one, that each would have bought if the lift rides had been priced competitively at marginal cost. The ability to practice first-degree price discrimination leads the monopolist to expand output to the competitive level. That is, the market outcome is now efficient. The total surplus is maximized—and that total surplus is claimed entirely by the monopolist.

Practice Problem

Consider an amusement park operating as a monopoly. Figure 6.3 shows the demand curve of a typical consumer at the park. There are no fixed costs. The marginal cost associated with each ride is constant. It is comprised of two parts, each also a constant. There is the cost per ride of labor and equipment, k, and there is the cost per ride of printing and collecting tickets, c. A management consultant has suggested two alternative pricing policies for the park. Policy A: Charge a fixed admission fee, T, and a fee per ride of r. Policy B: Simply charge a fixed admission fee, say T', and a zero fee per ride.

---

[4]   It is also easy to show that the ski resort owner's profit would be smaller than that achieved by the two-part tariff if a uniform, linear pricing policy were adopted. We leave you to show this for yourselves.

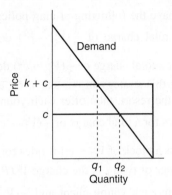

Figure 6.3   Diagram for the amusement park problem

a.   For Pricing Policy A, show on the graph the admission fee, T, and the per ride price, p, that will maximize profits.

b.   For Pricing Policy B, show on the graph the single admission fee, T', that will maximize profits.

c.   Compare the two policies. What are the relative advantages of each policy? What determines which policy leads to higher profits?

6.1.2   Block Pricing

There is a second nonlinear pricing strategy by which the ski resort owner can achieve the same level of profit. This scheme is block pricing. Using this type of pricing a seller *bundles* the quantity that he or she is willing to sell with the total charge wished to be set for that quantity. In our ski resort example, the owner sets a pricing policy of the form "Entry plus X ski lift rides for Y dollars." In order to earn maximum profit and appropriate all potential consumer surplus, two simple rules determine the optimal block-pricing strategy:

1.   Set the number of ski lift rides offered to each consumer type equal to the amount that type of consumer would buy at competitive pricing, that is, the quantity bought at a price equal to marginal cost;

2.   Set a fixed charge for each consumer type at the total willingness to pay for the quantity identified in (1).

Let's examine how this would work in our ski resort example. Applying rule 1, we know that each young client would buy $V_Y - c$ lift rides and each old client would buy $V_O - c$ lift rides if the lift rides were priced at marginal cost. The total willingness to pay for these quantities by young and old clients respectively is the area under the relevant demand curve at these quantities. These are:

$$\text{Young}: WTP_Y = \frac{1}{2}(V_Y - c)^2 + (V_Y - c)c = \frac{1}{2}(V_Y^2 - c^2)$$

$$\text{Old}: WTP_O = \frac{1}{2}(V_O - c)^2 + (V_O - c)c = \frac{1}{2}(V_O^2 - c^2) \qquad (6.10)$$

Applying rule 2, we then have the following pricing policy. Offer each old client entry plus $V_O - c$ lift rides for a total charge of $\frac{1}{2}(V_O^2 - c^2)$ dollars and each young client entry plus $V_Y - c$ lift rides for a total charge of $\frac{1}{2}(V_Y^2 - c^2)$ dollars.

How would we implement this strategy in our ski resort example? One way would be to ID each client at entry to the resort, then offer each young client a package of "Entry plus a block of $V_Y - c$ lift rides for a total charge of $\frac{1}{2}(V_Y^2 - c^2)$ dollars" and offer each old client a package of "Entry plus a block of $V_O - c$ lift rides for a total charge of $\frac{1}{2}(V_O^2 - c^2)$ dollars." Profit from a customer of type i is the charge WTP_i minus the cost of the rides, $c(V_i - c)$, or $\frac{1}{2}(V_Y - c)^2$ from each young client and $\frac{1}{2}(V_O - c)^2$ from each old client, exactly as in the two-part pricing system.

In our example, this amounts to offering each young skier a package of "Entry plus twelve ski lift rides for $120" and each old skier a package of "Entry plus eight ski lift rides for $64." Profit from each young skier package is $120 - 48 = $72 and from each old skier package is $64 - 32 = $32 as in the two-part pricing strategy.

Before leaving this section, we can point out a further interesting feature of the two types of first-degree price discrimination that we have discussed. Both the two-part tariff and the block pricing schemes result in the ski resort owner selling each old client entry plus $V_O - c$ lift rides for a total charge of $\frac{1}{2}(V_O^2 - c^2)$ and each young client entry plus $V_Y - c$ lift rides for a total charge of $\frac{1}{2}(V_Y^2 - c^2)$. Therefore, in each case, the average price paid per lift ride by an old client is $\frac{1}{2}(V_O^2 - c^2)/(V_O - c) = \frac{1}{2}(V_O + c)$. Similarly, each young client pays an average price per lift ride of $\frac{1}{2}(V_Y + c)$. You can easily check from equation (6.6) that these are exactly the same prices per lift ride that would be levied if the ski resort owner were to apply third-degree price discrimination. Yet the profit outcome is different.

The reason that first-degree and third-degree price discrimination lead to very different profits, despite the fact that the average price is the same in each case, lies in the very different nature of the two pricing schemes.[5] Recall that each point on a demand function measures the marginal benefit that a consumer obtains from consuming that unit. The quantity demanded equates marginal benefit with the marginal cost to the consumer of buying the last unit where, of course, marginal cost to the consumer is just the price for that last unit. With third-degree price discrimination, or linear pricing, the price paid for the last unit (indeed, every unit) is greater than marginal cost, which is how the resort owner makes profit with this pricing scheme. More importantly, while the price charged for the last lift ride sold under third degree price discrimination is equal to its marginal benefit, the price charged for every other lift ride sold is less than its marginal benefit: there is money (willingness to pay) "left on the table." By contrast, with the nonlinear two-part pricing scheme the ski resort owner sets the unit price of a lift ride to marginal cost, greatly increasing the owner's sales of ski rides. This creates consumer surplus, but the fixed charge

---

[5]   That average prices are the exactly same under the two pricing schemes is, of course, a result of our assumption that demand functions are linear. But this does not alter the fact that first-degree price discrimination is much more profitable than third-degree price discrimination or no price discrimination.

converts this consumer surplus into profit: there is no money "left on the table." With block pricing a buyer is not offered a price per unit. Rather, quantity and total charge are bundled in a package of "X units for a total charge of Y dollars," with the package being designed to extract the total willingness to pay for the X units. Again, there is no money "left on the table."

6.2   SECOND-DEGREE PRICE DISCRIMINATION OR MENU PRICING

First-degree price discrimination, or personalized pricing, is possible for the ski resort owner for two reasons. First, the resort's different types of customers are distinguishable by means of a simple, observable characteristic. Secondly, the resort owner has the ability to deny access to those not paying the entry charge designed for them. Not all services can be marketed in this way. For example, if instead of a ski resort the monopoly seller is a refreshment stand located in a campus center then limiting access by means of a cover charge is not feasible.

Even in the ski resort case, first-degree discrimination by means of a two-part tariff is not possible if the difference in consumer willingness to pay is attributable to some characteristic that the resort owner cannot observe. For example, suppose that what differentiates high-demand and low-demand clients is not age but income. In our numerical example, the ski resort will now find that any attempt to implement the first-degree price discrimination scheme of charging high-income patrons an entry fee of \$72 and low-income patrons an entry fee of \$32 is not likely to succeed. Every client would claim to have low income in order to pay the lower entry charge and there is no obvious (or legal) method by which the resort owner can enforce the higher fee.

What about the block pricing strategy of offering entry plus twelve ski lift rides for \$120 and entry plus eight ski lift rides for \$64? Will that work? Again, the answer is no. It is easy to show that high income clients are willing to pay up to \$96 for entry plus eight ski lift rides. Thus they derive \$32 of consumer surplus from the (eight rides, \$64) package but no consumer surplus from the (twelve rides, \$120) package. They will prefer to pretend to be low income in order to pay the lower charge and enjoy some surplus rather than confess to being high income, even though this means that they get fewer lift rides.

The monopolist could, of course, decide to limit entry only to high-income clients by setting the entry charge at \$72 or offering only the (twelve rides, \$120) package but this loses business (and profit) from low-income clients. Suppose, for instance, that there are N_O low-income clients and N_Y high-income clients. The profit from selling to only the high-income clients is $\$72N_Y$. Setting the lower entry fee or offering only the (eight rides, \$64) package in order to attract both types of client gives profit of $\$32(N_Y + N_O)$. Clearly, the latter strategy is more profitable if $32N_O > 40N_Y$. In other words, if the ratio of low-income to high-income clients (N_O/N_Y) is more than 1.25:1 (the per skier profit difference divided by profit per young skier) the policy of setting the higher entry fee or offering only the (twelve rides, \$120) package generates less profit than offering just the lower entry fee or the (eight rides, \$64) package to all customers.

The point is that once we reduce either the seller's ability to identify different types of buyers or to prevent arbitrage among them (or both), complete surplus extraction by means of perfect price discrimination is no longer possible. Both the two-part and block pricing mechanisms can still be used to raise profit above that earned by linear pricing but they cannot earn as much as they did previously. Solving the identification and arbitrage problem has now become costly. It is still possible that the monopolist can design a pricing scheme that will induce customers to reveal who they are and keep them separated by their purchases, but the only way to do this incurs some cost—a cost reflected in less surplus extraction. Such a pricing scheme is called second-degree price discrimination, or menu pricing.

Second-degree price discrimination is most usually implemented by offering quantity discounts targeted to different consumer types. To see how it works, let's continue with our ski resort example illustrated in Figure 6.4 for the numerical example. Again, the high-demand customers have (inverse) demand $P_h = 16 - Q_h$ and the low-demand customers have (inverse) demand $P_l = 12 - Q_l$. Now, however, the ski resort owner has no means of distinguishing who is who because the source of the difference between consumers is inherently unobservable. All the owner knows is that two such different types of consumer exist and they both wish to frequent the ski resort.

Any attempt to implement a differentiated two-part tariff will not work in this case. Both types of customer will claim to be low-demand types when entering the resort in order to pay the lower entry fee of $32. Only *after* they are in the resort will the different consumers reveal who they are. Because the price per ski lift ride is set at marginal cost of $4, the high-demand customers will buy twelve rides and reveal themselves to be high demanders whereas the low-demand customers will buy eight rides and reveal themselves as such.

You might be tempted to think that the resort owner could implement first-degree price discrimination using the following strategy. When entering the resort, skiers are allowed to purchase some defined maximum number of ski lift rides. If they pay an entry charge of $32 they will be allowed to purchase up to eight ski lift rides, while if they pay $72 they will be allowed to purchase up to twelve rides. Yet this approach will not work either, and for the same reason that the block pricing strategy of offering (twelve rides, $120) and (eight rides, $64) packages failed. High-demand customers again have every reason to pretend to be low-demand customers and pay an entry charge of only $32, thereby buying eight ski lift rides at $4 each for a total expenditure of $64. Because, as can be seen from Figure 6.4(a), their total willingness to pay for the eight ski lift rides is $96, high-demand consumers will enjoy a surplus of $32 from this deception. By contrast, they will enjoy no surplus if they pay the entry charge of $72 and buy twelve rides because their total expenditure will be then $120, which exactly equals their willingness to pay for twelve ski lift rides. As a result, it remains the case that the high-demand customers are better off by pretending to be low-demand even though this constrains the number of ski lift rides that they can buy.

While unsuccessful, the idea of offering different entry and lift ride combinations as different packages does contain the hint of a strategy that the ski resort owner can use to increase profit. The point is to employ a variant on the *block pricing* strategy described earlier. The difference is that, because there is no easy way to identify and separate the different types of customers, the block pricing strategy itself must be designed to achieve this purpose. This imposes a new constraint or cost on the resort owner and so will not yield as much profit as first-degree price discrimination. However, it will substantially improve on simply offering all customers a ($64, eight lift rides) package that yields a profit of $32 from each.

To see how one might use block pricing to achieve the identification and separation necessary for price discrimination let us start with the low-demand customers. The ski resort owner knows that these customers are willing to pay a total of $64 for eight lift rides. In other words, the resort owner can offer a package of entry plus eight lift rides at

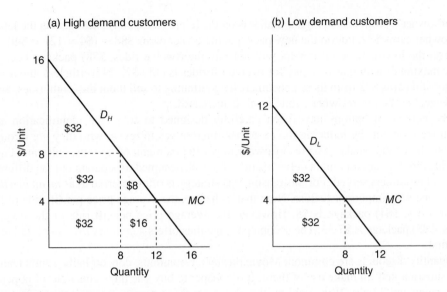

Figure 6.4   Second-degree price discrimination

Low demand customers are willing to pay $64 for entry plus 8 drinks. High demand customers are willing to pay up to $96 for entry plus 8 drinks, and so get $32 surplus from the 8-drinks, $64-package. They will therefore be willing to buy a 12-drinks, $88-package, which also gives them a $32 surplus.

a price of $64 for the package. This package will be attractive to low-demand customers, effectively extracting the $32 surplus from each of them. The problem is that high-demand customers will also be willing to buy this package because their willingness to pay for entry and eight lift rides is $96. While the resort owner also gets $32 in profit from the high-demand customers buying this package, those customers themselves still enjoy a surplus of $96 − $64 = $32.

The resort owner's optimal strategy at this point is to offer a second package targeted to high-demand consumers. The owner knows that the high-demand customers are willing to pay a total of $120 for entry plus twelve lift rides. Yet the owner also knows that he cannot charge $120 for twelve lift rides because the high-demand customers will not be willing to pay this much, given that they can buy the (eight rides, $64) package and enjoy a consumer surplus of $32. For an alternative package to be attractive to high-demand consumers it has to be what economists call *incentive compatible* with the (eight rides, $64) package. This means that any alternative package must also allow the high-demand customers to enjoy a surplus of at least $32.

A package that meets this requirement but that also generates some additional profit for the club owner is a package of entry plus twelve lift rides for a total charge of $88. We know that the high-demand customers value entry plus twelve lift rides at $120. By offering this deal at a price of $88, the resort owner permits these customers to get $32 of surplus when they buy this package, just enough to get them to switch from the (eight rides, $64) package.[6] And while the high-demand consumers get a $32 surplus on this package, the

---

[6]   We are working in round numbers to keep things neat. What the ski resort owner might actually do is price the package of entry plus twelve lift rides at $87.99 to ensure that the high-demand customers will strictly prefer this to the (eight rides, $64) package.

resort owner's profit is also higher than it is on the (eight rides, $64) package. On the latter, the owner earns $32, but on the new package, the owner earns $88 − ($4 × 12) = $40. Of course, the low-demand customers will not buy the (twelve rides, $88) package because their maximum willingness to pay for twelve lift rides is only $72. Nevertheless, the resort owner still earns $32 from these consumers by continuing to sell them the (eight rides, $64) package. So, the resort owner's total profit is increased.

The two menu options have been carefully designed to solve the identification and arbitrage problems by inducing the customers themselves to reveal who they are through the purchases they make. The resort owner now offers a menu of options, entry and eight lift rides for $64 or entry and twelve lift rides for $88, designed to separate out the different types of customers served. For this reason, this strategy is often referred to as *menu pricing*. It has one very important feature. Note that as before, the average price per lift ride of the (eight rides, $64) package is $8. However, the average price per lift ride of the (twelve rides, $88) package is $7.33. The second package thus offers a *quantity discount* relative to the first.

Quantity discounts are common. Movie theaters, restaurants, concert halls, sports teams, and supermarkets all make use of them. It is cheaper to buy one huge container of popcorn than many small ones. Wine sold by the glass is more expensive per unit than wine sold by the bottle. A 24-pack of Coca-Cola is cheaper than twenty-four individual bottles. It is cheaper per game to buy a season's subscription to your favorite football team's home games than to buy passes to each individual game. As we have just seen, a full-day pass at a ski resort will reflect a lower price per run than will a half-day lift ride. In these and many other cases, the sellers are using a quantity discount to woo the high-demand consumers.

There is another twist to consider. What if the ski resort owner now decides to offer a lower number of lift rides, say seven, in the package designed for the low-demand customers? The maximum willingness to pay for entry plus seven lift rides by a low-demand customer is $59.50, so this new package will be (seven rides, $59.50). The profit it generates from each customer is $31.50, which is 50 cents less than the (eight rides, $64) package. But now consider the high-demand customers. Their maximum willingness to pay for seven rides is $87.50, so buying this new package gives them consumer surplus of $28. As a result, the ski resort owner can increase the price of the twelve lift-ride package. Rather than pricing it so that it gives the high-demand customers $32 of consumer surplus, the owner can now price it so that it gives them only $28 of surplus. In other words, the price of the second package (entry plus 12 lift rides) can now be raised to $120 − 28 = $92, increasing the owner's profit from each such package to $44.

The example illustrates the importance of the incentive compatibility constraint. Any package designed to attract low-demand customers constrains the ability of the monopolist to extract surplus from high-demand customers. Again, this is because the high-demand customers cannot be prevented from buying the package designed for low-demand customers, and thus will always enjoy some consumer surplus from doing so. As a result, the monopolist will find it more profitable to reduce the number of units offered to low-demand customers because this will allow the price charges for the package targeted to the high-demand customers to be increased. There may even be circumstances in which the monopolist would prefer to push this logic to the extreme and not serve low-demand customers at all because of the constraint serving them imposes on the prices that can be charged to other customers.

Whether or not the monopolist has an incentive to serve the low-demand consumers will depend on the number of low-demand consumers relative to high-demand ones. The fewer low-demand consumers there are relative to high-demand ones, the less desirable it is to serve low-demand consumers because any effort to do so imposes an incentive compatibility constraint on the extraction of surplus from high-demand ones.

When we extend our analysis to a more general case with more than two types of consumers the profit-maximizing second-degree price discrimination, or menu pricing, scheme will exhibit some key features. In particular, if consumer willingness to pay can be unambiguously ranked by type then any optimal second-degree price discrimination scheme will:

1. Extract the entire consumer surplus of the lowest demand type served but leave some consumer surplus for all other types;
2. Contain a quantity that is less than the socially optimal quantity for all consumer types other than the highest-demand type;
3. Exhibit quantity discounting.

Second-degree discrimination enhances the ability of the monopolist to convert consumer surplus into profit, but does so less effectively than first-degree discrimination. With no costless way to distinguish the different types of consumers, the monopolist must rely on some sort of block pricing scheme to solve the identification and arbitrage problems. However, the incentive compatibility constraints that such a scheme must satisfy restrict the firm's ability to extract all of the consumer surplus. Instead, the firm is forced to make a compromise between setting a high charge that loses sales to low-demand buyers, and a low charge that foregoes the significant surplus that can be earned from the high-demand buyers. And contrary to what many consumers may think, the lower price charged for a larger quantity is entirely unrelated to scale economies. If in our example the ski resort owner has no fixed costs there are no economies of scale. Nevertheless, the owner finds it profitable to offer a quantity discount to high-demand customers.

6.3

Assume that the customers a monopolist serves are of two types, low-demand customers whose inverse demand is $P_l = 12 - Q_l$ and high-demand customers whose demand is $P_h = 16 - Q_h$. However, the monopolist does not know which type of customer is which. The production costs are \$4 per unit.

a. Complete the Table below for this example.
b. Assume that there are the same numbers of high-demand and low-demand customers. What is the profit-maximizing number of units that should be offered in the package aimed at the low-demand customers?
c. Now assume that there are twice as many low-demand customers as high-demand customers. What is the profit-maximizing pair of packages for the monopolist?
d. The monopolist is considering offering two packages, one containing six units and the other twelve units. What are the charges at which these packages will be offered? What is the ratio of high-demand to low-demand customers above which it will be better for the monopolist to supply only the high-demand customers?

Practice Problem

Low-Demand Customers			High-Demand Customers			
Number of Units in the Package	Charge for the Package*	Profit per Package	Consumer Surplus from Low-Demand Package	Maximum Willingness to Pay for 12 units	Charge for Package of 12 Units	Profit from each Package of 12 Units
0	0	0	0	$120.00		$72.00
1	$11.50		$4.00	$120.00	$116.00	
2		$14.00	$8.00	$120.00		$64.00
3						
4	$40.00	$24.00		$120.00		
5	$47.50	$27.50	$20.00	$120.00	$100.00	$52.00
6	$54.00			$120.00		$48.00
7	$59.50	$31.50	$28.00	$120.00	$92.00	$44.00
8	$64.00	$32.00	$32.00	$120.00	$88.00	$40.00
9						
10	$70.00	$30.00	$40.00	$120.00		
11						
12	$72.00		$48.00	$120.00	$72.00	

*This is the low-demand customer's maximum willingness to pay for the number of units in the package.

6.3   SOCIAL WELFARE WITH FIRST- AND SECOND-DEGREE PRICE DISCRIMINATION

One way to understand the welfare effects of price discrimination is to consider a particular consumer group i. Suppose each consumer in this group has inverse demand:

$$P = P_i(Q) \tag{6.11}$$

Assume also that the monopolist has constant marginal costs of c per unit. Now let the quantity that each consumer in group i is offered with a particular pricing policy be Q_i. Then the total surplus—consumer surplus plus profit—generated for each consumer under this pricing policy is just the area between the inverse demand function and the marginal cost function up to the quantity Q_i, as illustrated in Figure 6.5.

The pricing policy chosen by the firm affects the quantity offered to each type of consumer, and it alters the distribution of total surplus between profit and consumer surplus. The first effect has an impact on welfare, whereas the second effect does not imply a change in total welfare, but rather a transfer of surplus between consumers and producers. As a result, *price discrimination increases (decreases) the social welfare of consumer group* i *if it increases (decreases) the quantity offered to that group.*

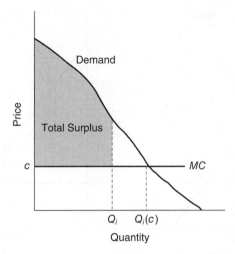

Figure 6.5   Total surplus
When the total quantity consumed is Q_i total surplus is given by the shaded area. Total surplus is maximized at quantity $Q_i(c)$.

It follows immediately that first-degree price discrimination always increases social welfare even though it extracts all consumer surplus. With this pricing policy we have seen that the monopoly seller supplies each consumer group with the socially efficient quantity (the quantity that would be chosen if price were set to marginal cost). Hence first-degree discrimination always increases the total quantity to a level [$Q_i(c)$ in Figure 6.5] that exceeds that which would have been sold under uniform pricing.

With second-degree price discrimination matters are not so straightforward. As we have seen, this type of price discrimination leads to high-demand groups being supplied with quantities "near to" the socially efficient level. However, we have also seen that the seller will want to restrict the quantity supplied to lower-demand groups and, in some cases, not supply these groups at all. The net effect on output is therefore not clear a priori.

The impact on social welfare of second-degree price discrimination can nevertheless be derived using much the same techniques that we used in Chapter 5. By way of illustration, suppose that there are two consumer groups with demands illustrated in Figure 6.6 (i.e., Group 2 is the high-demand group). In this figure, P^U is the nondiscriminatory uniform price, and Q_1^U and Q_2^U are the quantities sold to each consumer in the relevant group at this price. By contrast, Q_1^s and Q_2^s are the quantities supplied to the two groups with second-degree price discrimination.[7] We define the terms:

$$\Delta Q_1 = Q_1^s - Q_1^U; \quad \Delta Q_2 = Q_2^s - Q_1^U \tag{6.12}$$

In the case illustrated we have $\Delta Q_1 < 0$ and $\Delta Q_2 > 0$. This tells us that an upper limit on the increase in total surplus that follows from second-degree price discrimination is the area G minus the area L. This gives us the equation:

$$\Delta W \leq G - L = (P_U - MC)\Delta Q_1 + (P_U - MC)\Delta Q_2 = (P_U - MC)(\Delta Q_1 + \Delta Q_2) \tag{6.13}$$

---

[7]   Because Group 2 is the high-demand group, we know that $Q_2^s = Q_2(c)$.

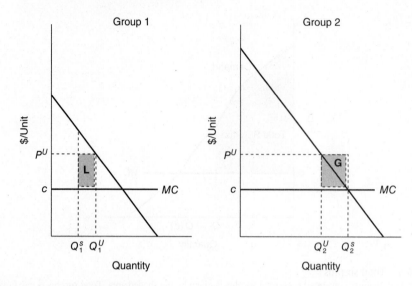

Figure 6.6   Impact of second-degree price discrimination on welfare

An upper limit on the change in total surplus that arises from second-degree price discrimination is the upper limit on the gain, G, minus the lower limit on the loss, L.

Extending the analysis to n markets, we then have:

$$\Delta W \leq (P_U - MC) \sum_{i=1}^{n} \Delta Q_i \tag{6.14}$$

It follows that for $\Delta W \geq 0$ it is necessary that $\sum_{i=1}^{n} \Delta Q_i \geq 0$. In other words, a necessary condition for second-degree price discrimination to increase welfare is that it increases total output when compared to uniform pricing.

We know from the previous chapter that this requirement is generally not met in the case of third-degree price discrimination and linear demands because then the monopolist supplies the same total quantity as with uniform pricing, so third-degree price discrimination does not increase welfare. By contrast, it could be the case that second-degree price discrimination leads to an increase in the quantity supplied to both markets and this would increase social welfare. In the ski resort owner's case, for example, this will be the case if there are equal number of high-demand and low-demand customers. (You are asked to show this in the end-of-chapter problem 7.)

6.4   EMPIRICAL APPLICATION: PRICE DISCRIMINATION AND MONOPOLY VERSUS IMPERFECT COMPETITION

We have set our discussion of price discrimination in both the current and previous chapter in the framework of a monopolized market. Yet as students frequently point out, many of the discriminatory practices we describe are observed in markets that are far from monopolies such as airlines, restaurants, hotels, and even theme parks. Of course, in each of these cases, the firms employing price discrimination tactics have to have some degree of market power even though they do confront rival sellers. Perfectly competitive firms by definition must take the market price as given and therefore cannot manipulate that price in any way or extract any additional surplus. Imperfectly competitive firms, though, do have discriminatory power. Moreover, it turns out that it is precisely in a setting of imperfect competition that there is additional pressure for firms to price discriminate beyond the surplus extraction consideration that motivates a pure monopolist.

When firms are imperfect rivals, the nature of that competition will often result in discriminatory prices as part of their competitive strategy. This point, first emphasized by Borenstein (1985), can be illustrated with a simple example. Consider a monopolist who owns the only two surfboard shops in Minnesota—one in Minneapolis and the other in St. Paul. The proximity of the two towns is such that transport costs are not a factor for any consumer in choosing which store to patronize. The $2N$ potential customers are evenly distributed between the two towns and each is willing to pay as much as V for a surfboard. However, while consumers are alike in their willingness to pay, they are different in one other respect. Half of the consumers are inexplicably loyal to their town's shop. That is, one-fourth of the consumers will always buy from the Minneapolis store and one-fourth will always buy from the St. Paul store so long as the price is less than V, and without regard to the price at the other shop. The remaining N consumers are just the opposite. While willing to pay as much as V, these consumers always shop wherever the price is lowest.

A little economic reasoning should convince you that our hypothetical monopolist will set a price of V at both shops and serve all the $2N$ customers. Clearly the price cannot be higher than this or no customer will buy the product. However, there is no need to reduce the price. The first set of consumers will not consider the price at any location other than their local store. The second group will look for a lower price but, because the price is V at each shop, this group also splits evenly between the two stores. The monopolist would then make a total profit of $2(V - c)N$ divided evenly between the two stores. No amount of price discrimination can increase this value.

Now consider what would happen if the two stores are instead owned by two different firms, firm 1 and firm 2. Each store has $N/2$ customers who are totally locked-in to that shop and who the store would like to charge V. There may, however, be competition for the second group of consumers who care about price. If firm 1 in Minneapolis charges V to this group, firm 2 in St. Paul can attract all their patronage by charging a price $1 lower, i.e., by charging $V - 1$. In response, the Minneapolis store might lower its price to $V - 2$, which would induce further cuts in St. Paul and so on. Ultimately, then, competition for the N price-conscious consumers pushes prices closer to marginal cost at both stores. The question is whether each store can somehow prevent this competition from spilling over to its locked-in consumers. The answer of course is that, yes, firm 1 and firm 2 can each continue to charge their intensely loyal customers a high price provided two familiar conditions are met. These are the identification and no-arbitrage conditions we derived in Chapter 5. If the non—price-sensitive consumers can be identified and separated in a meaningful way from the price-conscious ones, then each store can continue to charge these consumers V for a surfboard while selling at price c to everyone else.

It is important to emphasize that it is competition—imperfect as it is—that leads to the differential pricing strategy. Again, had the market been monopolized, no price discrimination would have emerged. The price would have been V to all consumers. This is what we mean when we say that imperfectly competitive markets create an additional force evoking discriminatory prices. Price discrimination permits competing actively for those consumers who perceive alternatives to the firm's product while still charging a high price to those that do not. In our example, there is only one other store, so the pricing is bifurcated. Some customers pay V while others pay c. We might expect that if there had instead been three or four stores, there might be fewer locked-in consumers as some might regard another Minneapolis or another St. Paul store an acceptable substitute. In this case, we might see more and more complicated price breaks.

The foregoing intuition lies at the heart of the paper by Stavins (2001), which examines the influence of competition on the use of discriminatory pricing in the airline industry. For this purpose, she looked at price and other information for 5,804 rides over twelve different routes on a specific Thursday in September, 1995. Selecting a single day is useful because it eliminates any price differentials due to flying on other days of the week, especially weekend days. A September choice also avoids both peak summer and winter demand periods. The key characteristics that Stavins (2001) looks at are: 1) whether a Saturday night stay-over was required and 2) whether a 14-day advance purchase was required.

As discussed in Chapter 5, each of these restrictions serves as a means for airlines to identify and separate customers based on how they value their time and their need for flexibility. Prices for rides requiring a Saturday night stay-over or that had to be purchased 14 days prior to departure should sell for less than other rides. The hypothesis to be tested is that the price discount on these restricted rides gets bigger the more competition there is on the route. Stavins (2001) constructs a Herfindahl-Hirschman Index HI for each route to serve as a rough measure of that market's competitive pressure.

To test this hypothesis, Stavins (2001) runs two sets of regressions. The first of these serves to confirm that ride restrictions do indeed translate into discriminatory price differentials. It takes the basic form:

$$p_{ijk} = \beta_0 + \beta_1 R_{ijk} + \beta_2 HI_i + \beta_3 S_{ij} + \beta_4 First_{ijk} + \beta_5 Days_{ijk} + \beta_6 Z_i + \varepsilon_{ijk} \tag{6.15}$$

Here, p_{ijk} is the (log of the) price of the kth ride sold by airline j in city-pair market i. R_{ijk} is a dummy variable equal to 1 if there was a restriction on the flight (Saturday night stay-over or pre-purchase requirement) and 0 otherwise. HI_i is the Herfindahl-Hirschman Index for the ith market. S_{ij} is the market share of airline i in market j. $First_{ijk}$ is a dummy variable equal to 1 if the ride was for first-class fare and 0 otherwise. $Days_{ijk}$ is the number of days prior to departure that the fare for that ride was last offered. Z_i is a vector of other market i characteristics such as average income and population. The error term ε_{ijk} is assumed to be normally distributed with a mean of 0.

If ride restrictions serve as a means of implementing price discrimination then the coefficient β_1 on R_{ijk} should be negative. This would imply that passengers flying the same flight on the same airline paid lower prices if they accepted a requirement that they stay over Saturday night or that they purchase the ride in advance.

However, simply finding that β_1 is negative only shows that price discrimination occurs. It does not tell us if there is any connection between the extent of such discrimination and the degree of competition in the market. To test this hypothesis, Stavins (2001) runs regressions of the basic form:

$$p_{ijk} = \beta_0 + \beta_1 R_{ijk} + \beta_2 HI_i + \beta_3 (HI_i x R_{ijk}) + \beta_4 S_{ij}$$
$$+ \beta_5 First_{ijk} + \beta_6 Days_{ijk} + \beta_7 z_i + \varepsilon_{ijk} \tag{6.16}$$

This is exactly the same as the previous regression except that it now includes the interactive term $(HI_i x R_{ijk})$, the product of the concentration index and the restricted travel variables.

Table 6.1 Ride restrictions and air fares

Variable	Coefficient	t-statistic	Coefficient	t-Statistic	Coefficient	t-Statistic	Coefficient	t-statistic
Saturday-Night Stay-Over Required	−0.249	−2.50	—	—	−0.408	−4.05	—	—
Saturday-Night Stay- Over x HI	—	—	—	—	0.792	3.39	—	—
Advance Purchase Requirement	—	—	−0.007	−2.16	—	—	−0.023	−5.53
Advance Purchase Requirement x HI	—	—	—	—	—	—	0.098	8.38

If the coefficient on this term is positive, it says that the discount associated with, say, a Saturday night stay-over requirement declines as the level of concentration rises. Stavins' (2001) results are shown in Table 6.1.

The first four columns indicate that passengers do indeed pay different prices depending on the restrictions applied to their rides. These effects are both statistically significant and economically substantial. For example, passengers who accepted the requirement that they not return until after Saturday night paid 25 percent less on average than those who did not accept this restriction even though they were otherwise getting the same flight service.

However, the real issue is how these discounts vary as the extent of competition in the market as measured by *HI* varies. This is where the next four columns become relevant as they show what happens when the term interacting competition or concentration and ride restrictions is included. In both cases, the estimated coefficient on the interaction term is positive. This indicates that while ride restrictions still lead to price reductions, this effect diminishes as the airline route becomes less competitive or has high concentration.

Given the range of *HI* values observed over the twelve routes Stavins (2001) studies, she estimates that in the most competitive markets, a Saturday night stay-over requirement led to a price reduction of about $253, whereas in the least competitive ones the same restriction led to a price reduction of only $165. Likewise, an advance purchase requirement was associated with a price reduction of $111 in the most competitive markets but a cut of only $41 in the least competitive markets.

Summary

In this chapter, we have extended our analysis of price discrimination to cases in which firms employ more sophisticated, nonlinear pricing schemes. Our focus has been on commonly observed examples of such nonlinear pricing schemes. These are: 1) two-part pricing in which the firm charges a fixed fee plus a price per unit and 2) block pricing in which the firm bundles the quantity being offered with the total charge for that quantity. Both schemes have the same objective, to increase the monopolist's profit either by increasing the surplus on existing sales or by extending sales to new markets, or both.

The most perfect form of price discrimination, first-degree price discrimination or personalized pricing, can only be practiced when the firm can costlessly solve the identification and arbitrage problems. The firm needs to be able to identify the different types of consumers and must also be able to keep them apart. If this is possible, then two-part tariffs and block pricing can, in principle, convert *all* consumer surplus into revenues for the firm. The positive side to this is that the firm supplies the socially efficient level of output to each consumer type. The negative side is that there are potentially severe distributional inequities in that all social surplus takes the form of profit.

If the requirements necessary to practice perfect price discrimination are not met, then the monopoly seller cannot achieve such a large profit. However, the monopolist can employ second-degree price discrimination or menu pricing, another form of nonlinear pricing. Second-degree price discrimination differs from both first- and third-degree in that it relies on the pricing mechanism itself—usually block pricing that exhibits quantity discounts—to induce consumers to *self-select* into groups that reveal their identity or who they are on the demand curve.

The use of a quantity discount to sort or screen consumers must always satisfy an *incentive compatibility* constraint across the different consumer types. This constraint weakens the monopolist's ability to extract consumer surplus. Because the incentive compatibility constraint adversely affects profits, the monopolist may choose to avoid it by refusing to serve low-demand markets, with the result that the low-demand type

consumers are clearly worse off. As a consequence, the welfare effects of second-degree price discrimination are not clear. Yet unlike the case of third-degree discrimination (with linear demand curves at least), second-degree pricing strategies do have some positive probability of making things better.

Market power is a necessary requirement for price discrimination. Perfectly competitive firms take the market price as a given and must charge that price to all customers. It is for this reason that we have set our discussion of price discrimination in a monopoly context. Yet while a monopoly framework is convenient, all that is strictly required is a setting of imperfect competition. In this regard, it is noteworthy that the use of price discrimination by firms may also be a means of implementing competition when firms are imperfectly competitive rivals. Price discrimination permits firms with market power to offer price cuts to customers of a rival brand without offering such price cuts to those among its current customers who are not price sensitive. Supporting evidence for this view may be found in many studies, including that by Stavins (2001) on airline competition. Together, this theory and evidence suggest that price discrimination as a tool for inter-firm rivalry can push imperfect competition closer to the competitive ideal.

Problems

1. Many universities allocate financial aid to undergraduate students on the basis of some measure of need. Does this practice reflect charity or price discrimination? If it reflects price discrimination, do you think it lies closer to first-degree discrimination or third-degree discrimination?

2. A food co-op sells a homogenous good called groceries, denoted g. The co-op's cost function is described by: $C(g) = F + cg$; where F denotes fixed cost and c is the constant per unit variable cost. At a meeting of the co-op board, a young economist proposes the following marketing strategy: Set a fixed membership fee M and a price per unit of groceries p_M that members pay. In addition, set a price per unit of groceries p_N higher than p_M at which the co-op will sell groceries to non-members.

a. What must be true about the demand of different customers for this strategy to work?
b. What kinds of price discrimination does this strategy employ?

3. At Starbuck's coffee shops, coffee drinkers have the option of sipping their lattes and cappuccinos while surfing the Internet on their laptops. These connections are made via a connection typically provided by a wireless firm such as T-Mobile. Using a credit card, customers can buy Internet time in various packages. A one-hour package currently goes for an average price of $6. A day pass that is good for any time in the next 24 hours sells for $10. A seven-day pass sells for about $40. Briefly describe the pricing tactics reflected in these options.

4. A night-club owner has both student and adult customers. The demand for drinks by a typical student is $Q^S = 18 - 3P$. The demand for drinks by a typical adult is $Q^A = 10 - 2P$. There are equal numbers of students and adults. The marginal cost of each drink is $2.

   a. What price will the club owner set if it is not possible to discriminate between the two groups? What will the total profit be at this price?

   b. If the club owner could separate the groups and practice third-degree price discrimination, what price per drink would be charged to members of each group? What would be the club owner's profit in this case?

5. If the club owner in problem 4 can "card" patrons and determine who among them is a student and who is not and, in turn, can serve each group by offering a cover charge and a number of drink tokens to each group, what will the cover charge and number of tokens be for students? What will be the cover charge and number of tokens given to adults? What is the club owner's profit under this regime?

6. A local phone company has three family plans for its wireless service. Under each of these plans, the family gets two lines (phones) and can make local and long distance (within the United States and Canada) calls for free so long as the total number of minutes used per month does not exceed the plan maximum. The price and maximum minutes per month for each plan are: Plan 1: 500 minutes for $50; Plan 2: 750 minutes for $62.50; and Plan 3: 1000 minutes for $75.00. Assuming that there are equal numbers of consumers in each group and that the value of a marginal minute for each group declines at the rate of $0.0004 per minute used, work out the demand curves consistent with this pricing. What surplus will each consumer group enjoy?

7. Now return to our ski resort owner in the text in which low-demand consumers have an inverse demand of: $P = 12 - Q$, while high-demand consumers have an inverse demand of: $P = 16 - Q$. Marginal cost per lift ride is again $4. Assume that there are N_h high-demand customers and N_l low-demand customers but that the ski resort owner does not know the type of each skier. Show that under these circumstances the firm will only serve low-demand customers, i.e., will only offer both packages if there are at least as many low-demand consumers as high-demand ones. In other words, $\frac{N_h}{N_l} \leq 1$ in order for low-demand consumers to be served.

References

Borenstein, S. 1985. "Price Discrimination in Free-Entry Markets," *Rand Journal Economics* 16 (Autumn): 380–97.

Ekelund, R. 1970. "Price Discrimination and Product Differentiation in Economic Theory: An Early Analysis," *Quarterly Journal of Economics* 84 (February): 268–78.

Oi, W. 1971. "A Disneyland Dilemma: Two-part Tariffs for a Mickey Mouse Monopoly," *Quarterly Journal of Economics* 85 (February): 77–96.

Philips, L. 1983. *The Economics of Price Discrimination*, Cambridge: Cambridge University Press.

Pigou, A. C. 1920. *The Economics of Welfare*, London: Macmillan Publishing.

Shapiro, C., and H. Varian. 1999. *Information Rules: A Strategic Guide to the Internet Economy*, Boston: Harvard Business School Press.

Schmalensee, R. 1981. "Output and Welfare Implications of Monopolistic Third-Degree Price Discrimination," *American Economic Review* 71 (March): 242–47.

Stavins, J. 2001. "Price Discrimination in the Airline Market: The Effect of Market Concentration," *Review of Economics and Statistics* 83 (February): 200–02.

Varian, H. "Price Discrimination." in *The Handbook of Industrial Organization, Vol. 1*, R. Schmalensee and R. Willig, eds., Amsterdam: North-Holland (1989), 597–654.

7

Product Variety and Quality Under Monopoly

Most firms sell more than one product. Microsoft offers not only an operating system and an Internet browser but also a number of other products, most notably, the word-processing package *Word*, the spreadsheet software *Excel*, and the presentation package *PowerPoint*. High-tech firms such as Apple sell a wide range of computers including a tablet computer, a music player, and a mobile telephone. Major automobile manufacturers such as Toyota offer a bewildering array of mid-range automobiles and a range of higher-end autos under other brand names, such as *Lexus*. Companies such as Comcast offer telephone, television, and Internet services. Fashion designers such as Ralph Lauren offer a broad range of apparel from sportswear to haute couture, for both women and men.

Indeed, even the most cursory examination of consumer markets suggests that the multi-product firm is likely to be the norm rather than the exception. Take a company such as Kellogg's. Is there any flavor, color, or texture of breakfast cereal that they do not market? Or consider Procter & Gamble, a large consumer product company that offers more than a dozen varieties of their *Head and Shoulders* shampoo and even more varieties of their *Crest* toothpaste.

This leads us to the question of exactly how much variety a firm should aim to offer. Indeed Procter & Gamble asked itself the same question when it reexamined its product strategy in the early 1990s. By 1996, the company had reduced its list of products by one-third as compared with 1991. All the evidence suggests, however, that the past decade has seen the company once more expand its product range.

A firm's incentive to offer many varieties of what is essentially the same product—breakfast foods, hair or tooth care—is simple enough to understand. It is a way for the firm to appeal and sell to consumers with very different tastes. Because we as consumers differ in our most preferred color, flavor, or texture, selling successfully to many consumers requires offering something a little different to each of them. Specifically, to induce a consumer to make a purchase the firm must market a product that is reasonably close to the version that the consumer most prefers. When a firm offers a variety of products in response to different consumer tastes, it is adopting a strategy that we refer to as *horizontal product differentiation*.

There are other cases in which consumers agree on the product features that make for a "good" product. For example, all consumers likely agree that a car with antilock brakes is better than one without such a stopping mechanism. Similarly, all probably agree that while a *3 Series* BMW is an attractive car, it pales in comparison to the *7 Series*. Everyone is likely to agree that flying from Boston to San Francisco first class is a better than flying coach. Where consumers differ in these cases is not in what features they consider to be desirable but, instead, in how much a desired feature is worth to them. In other words, consumers differ not in their rankings of product quality but rather in how much they are willing to pay for antilock brakes, a better BMW, or first class airfare. When a firm responds to differences in consumer willingness to pay for quality of a product by offering different qualities of the same product, it is called *vertical product differentiation*.

In this chapter, we analyze the horizontal and vertical product differentiation strategies of a monopoly firm, focusing in particular on how product differentiation may be used by the firm to increase profitability. We also consider the welfare properties of these strategies.

7.1   A SPATIAL APPROACH TO HORIZONTAL PRODUCT DIFFERENTIATION

We begin by considering a market in which consumers agree both on the quality of the product being considered, whether this be breakfast cereal, hair treatment, or an automobile, and on their willingness to pay for this product. However, consumers differ with respect to the specific features of the product that make the product attractive to them: they may differ, for example, in their most preferred taste, color, or location of the product. In other words, all consumers may agree on the quality of and their willingness to pay for a product, perhaps a margherita pizza, if it is sold at a shop close to their home. However, not all consumers are equidistant from the shop. Some are close and some are far away. Given the time and effort required to travel, the willingness to pay of those who live far from the shop will be lower. By contrast, those who live close—and who therefore do not have to incur travel expenses—will be willing to pay a higher price. The fact that a product sold close to home is different from one that is sold far away is a good example of horizontal product differentiation. Such differentiation is characterized by the property that each consumer has his or her own preferred location of the shop or product, namely, one close to the consumer's own address.

When the consumer market is differentiated by geographic location, a firm can vary its product strategy through its choice of where the product is sold. The firm may choose to sell its product only in one central location to which all shoppers must come: high-end designers such as Giorgio Armani or Burberry for example, do this. Alternatively, it may decide to offer the product at many locations spaced throughout the city: McDonald's, Dunkin' Donuts, and Subway are obvious examples. Customers are not indifferent between these alternative strategies. If the firm sells only at one central location, those who do not live in the middle of town have to incur travel costs to come to the store. These costs are greatest for those living farthest from the center. The alternative strategy of selling at many different locations allows more consumers to purchase the good without going too far out of their way.

When geography is taken into account and traveling is costly, consumers are willing to pay more for a product marketed close to their own geographic location. In this case, products are differentiated by the locations at which they are sold. This setting is known as the *spatial model of product differentiation*, pioneered by Hotelling (1929).[1]

---

[1]   Hotelling (1929) was concerned with analyzing competition between two stores whereas we consider here the case in which the stores are owned by the same firm and so act cooperatively.

Before presenting the model formally, there is a very important feature of the model that must be emphasized. It proves convenient to develop the model using a geographic representation that can easily be interpreted. With just a little imagination, however, geographic space can be transformed into a "product" or, more properly "characteristics space." In such a space, each consumer's "location" reflects that consumer's most preferred set of product characteristics such as color, style, or other features. Recall our earlier discussion in Chapter 4 of a soft-drink firm offering a product line differing in terms of sugar content. That example made use of precisely this type of horizontal or spatial differentiation.

Extending the analogy, the travel cost of the geographic model can be interpreted as a psychic or utility cost that the consumer incurs if she must purchase a good whose characteristics are "distant" from her most preferred type. Just as consumers prefer to go to video stores close to their home, so they prefer to buy clothes that are "close" to their individual preferred style, or soft drinks close to their preferred amount of sugar content. In fact, Hotelling suggested just this interpretation in his seminal article:

> Distance, as we have used it for illustration, is only a figurative term for a great congeries of qualities. Instead of sellers of an identical commodity separated geographically we might have considered two ... cider merchants ... one selling a sweeter liquid than the other. If consumers of cider are thought of as varying by infinitesimal degrees in the sourness they desire, we have much the same situation as before. The measure of sourness now represents distance, while instead of transportation costs there are degrees of disutility resulting from the consumer getting cider more or less different from what he wants. (Hotelling, 1929, 54)

7.2   MONOPOLY AND HORIZONTAL DIFFERENTIATION

Assume that there is a town spread out along a single road, call it Main Street, that is one mile in length. There are N consumers who live spaced evenly along this road from one end of town to the other. A firm that has a monopoly in, for example, fast food must decide how to serve these consumers at the greatest profit. What this means is that the monopolist must choose the number of retail outlets or shops that it will operate, where these should be located on Main Street, and what prices should be charged. In the product differentiation analogy to drinks of different sweetness, the monopolist has to decide how many different drinks it should offer, what their precise degrees of sweetness should be, and what their prices should be. More generally, what range of products should the monopolist bring to the market and how should they be priced? In what follows we use the geographic interpretation of the model for clarity, but we again emphasize that you should always bear in mind its much wider interpretation.

In this section, we consider cases in which the monopolist does not price discriminate among the consumers that are served.[2] When a consumer travels to a retail outlet in order to buy a product the consumer incurs transport costs. We assume that the transportation cost is t per unit of distance (there-and-back) traveled. Except for their addresses or their locations, consumers are identical to each other. We further assume that in each period each consumer is willing to buy exactly one unit of the product sold by the monopolist provided that the price paid, including transport costs, which we call the *full price*, is less than the reservation price, which we denote by V.

---

[2]   The case in which the monopolist price discriminates is developed in section 7.4.

Suppose that the monopolist decides to operate only a single retail outlet. Then it makes sense to locate this outlet at the center of Main Street. Now consider the monopolist's pricing decision. The essentials of the analysis are illustrated in Figure 7.1. The westernmost resident (residing at the left end of the diagram) has an address of $z = 0$, the easternmost resident has an address of $z = 1$, and the shop is located at $z = 1/2$.

The vertical axis in Figure 7.1 measures the price. A price of V in this diagram is the reservation price for each consumer. The full price that each consumer pays is comprised of two parts. First, there is the price p_1 actually set by the monopolist. Secondly, there is the additional cost consumers incur in getting to the shop (and back home). Measured per unit of distance there and back, the *full price* actually paid by a consumer who lives a distance x from the center of town is the monopolist's price plus the transport cost, or $p_1 + tx$. This full price is indicated by the Y-shaped set of lines in Figure 7.1. It indicates that the full price paid by a consumer at the center of town—one who incurs no transport cost—is just p_1. However, as the branches of the Y indicate, the full price rises steadily above p_1 for consumers both east and west of the town center. So long as distance from the shop is less than x_1, the consumer's reservation price V exceeds the full price $p_1 + tx$ and such a consumer buys the monopolist's product. However, for distances beyond x_1 the full price exceeds V and these consumers do not buy the product. In other words, the monopolist serves all those who live within a distance of x_1 units of the town center.

How is the distance x_1 determined? Consumers who reside distance x_1 from the shop are just indifferent between buying the product and not buying it at all. For them, the full price $p_1 + tx_1$ is equal to V so we have:

$$p_1 + tx_1 = V \text{ which implies that } x_1 = \frac{V - p_1}{t} \tag{7.1}$$

It is important to note that x_1 is just a fraction. Because the town is one mile long, x_1 is a fraction of a mile and the retail outlet sells to a fraction $2x_1$ of the whole town—because it sells to consumers that fall to the left and to the right of the market center so long as they live no further than x_1 from the shop. Recall that we assume that there are N consumers evenly distributed over Main Street. Accordingly, there are $2x_1 N$ consumers who each are willing to buy one unit of the product if it is priced at p_1. By substituting the expression for x_1 from

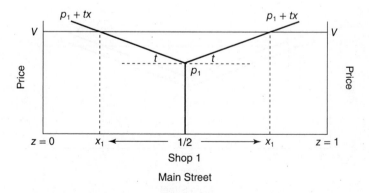

Figure 7.1   The full price of the shop on Main Street
The full price, including transport cost, rises as consumers live farther from the shop.

equation (7.1) into the number of customers served by the monopolist, $2x_1 N$ at price p_1, we find that the total demand for the monopolist's product given that it operates just one shop is:

$$Q(p_1, 1) = 2x_1 N = \frac{2N}{t}(V - p_1) \tag{7.2}$$

Equation (7.2) tells us something interesting. Even though we have assumed that each consumer buys exactly one unit or none of the monopolist's product, the demand function of equation (7.2) shows that aggregate demand smoothly increases as the monopolist lowers its price. The reason is illustrated in Figure 7.2. When the shop price is reduced from p_1 to p_2 demand increases because *more consumers are willing to buy the product at the lower price*. Now all consumers within distance x_2 of the shop buy the product.

This raises an important question. Suppose that the monopolist wants to sell to every customer in town. What is the *highest* price that the monopolist can set and still be able to sell to all N consumers? The answer must be the price at which the consumers who live furthest from the shop, i.e., those who are half a mile away, are just willing to buy. At any shop price p these consumers pay a full price of $p + t/2$ and so will buy only if $p + t/2 \leq V$. What this tells us is that with a single retail outlet located at the market center, the maximum price that the monopolist can charge and still supply the entire market of N consumers with its one store is $p(N, 1)$ given by:

$$p(N, 1) = V - \frac{t}{2} \tag{7.3}$$

Suppose that the monopolist's marginal production costs are c per unit sold. Suppose also that there are set-up costs of F for each retail outlet. These set-up costs could be associated with the cost of buying a site, commissioning the building, and so on. In the product differentiation analogy, the setup costs might be the costs of designing and marketing the new product. Whatever the framework, the monopolist's profit with a single retail outlet that supplies the entire market is:

$$\pi(N, 1) = N[p(N, 1) - c] - F = N\left(V - \frac{t}{2} - c\right) - F \tag{7.4}$$

We can now confirm that this single shop should indeed be located in the center of town. Very simply, this is the location that makes it possible for the single outlet to supply the

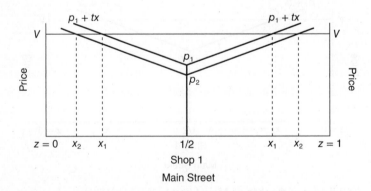

Figure 7.2 Lowering the price at the shop on Main Street
A fall in the shop price brings additional customers from both east and west.

entire market at the highest possible price. To see why, note that at the price $p = V - \dfrac{t}{2}$, a move a little to the east will not gain any new customers on the east end of town (there are no more to gain) but will lose some of those at the extreme west end of town. In other words, if the firm moves from the center, the only way it can continue to serve the entire town is by cutting its price below $V - \dfrac{t}{2}$. Only by locating its single outlet at the center can it reach all customers with a price as high as $V - \dfrac{t}{2}$.

Of course, there is no reason to believe that the monopolist will actually want to operate a single outlet. What happens when there are two, or three, or n outlets along Main Street? As before, we continue to assume that unit cost at each shop is c per unit sold and that the set-up cost for each outlet is F. In other words there are no scope economies from operating multiple outlets. We start by asking what happens if the number of retail outlets is increased to two. Because each segment of the market along Main Street is the same and each shop has the same costs, the monopolist will choose to set the same price at each shop. Moreover the monopolist will want to coordinate the location of these two shops so as to maximize the price charged at a shop while still reaching the entire market. In other words, the same intuition that justifies a central location with one outlet can be used to show that the optimal location strategy with two outlets is to locate one of the two $1/4$ mile from the left-hand end and the other $1/4$ mile from the right-hand end of Main Street, as in Figure 7.3.[3]

With two retail outlets located as we have just discussed, the maximum distance that any consumer has to travel to a shop is $1/4$ mile—much less than the $1/2$ mile when there is only one retail outlet. As a result, the highest price that the monopolist can charge and supply the entire market is:

$$p(N, 2) = V - \frac{t}{4} \tag{7.5}$$

which is higher than the price with a single retail outlet. The monopolist's profit is now:

$$\pi(N, 2) = N\left(V - \frac{t}{4} - c\right) - 2F \tag{7.6}$$

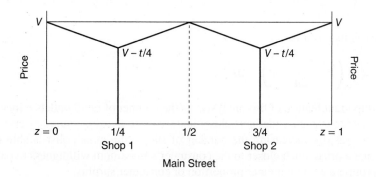

Figure 7.3   Opening two shops on Main Street
The maximum price is higher with two shops than it is with one.

---

[3]   For the interested reader, a formal proof of this result is given in Mathematical Appendix 1 to this chapter.

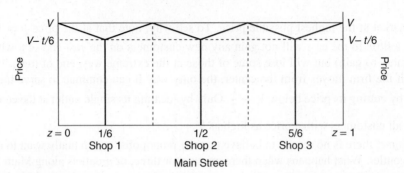

Figure 7.4   Opening three shops on Main Street

Now suppose that the monopolist decides to operate three shops. By exactly the same argument as above, these shops should be located symmetrically at 1/6, 1/2, and 5/6 miles from the left-hand end of the market so that each supplies 1/3 of the market, as illustrated in Figure 7.4. The maximum distance that any consumer has to travel now is 1/6 mile, so the price at each shop (again assuming, of course, that all consumers are to be served) is:

$$p(N, 3) = V - \frac{t}{6} \tag{7.7}$$

While profit is now

$$\pi(N, 3) = N\left(V - \frac{t}{6} - c\right) - 3F \tag{7.8}$$

There is, in fact, a general rule emerging. If the monopolist has n retail outlets to serve the entire market, they will be located symmetrically at distances $1/2n, 3/2n, 5/2n, \ldots, (2i - 1)/2n, \ldots, (2n - 1)/2n$ from the left-hand end of the market. The maximum distance that any consumer has to travel to a shop is $1/2n$ miles, so the price that the monopolist can charge at each shop while supplying the entire market is

$$p(N, n) = V - \frac{t}{2n} \tag{7.9}$$

At this price, its profit is

$$\pi(N, n) = N\left(V - \frac{t}{2n} - c\right) - nF \tag{7.10}$$

Note an important feature of this analysis. As the number of retail outlets n increases, the monopolist's price at each outlet gets closer and closer to the consumer's reservation price V. In other words, by increasing the number of shops, the monopolist is able to charge each consumer a price much closer to the consumer's maximum willingness to pay, V, and thereby appropriate a much greater proportion of consumer surplus.

The moral of the foregoing analysis is clear—especially when we remember to interpret the geographic space of Main Street as a more general product space. Even if no scope economies are present, a monopolist has an incentive to offer many varieties of a good. Doing so allows the monopolist to exploit the wide variety of consumer tastes, charging each consumer a high price because each is being offered a variety that is very close to the consumer's specific most preferred type. It is not surprising, therefore, that we see such extensive product proliferation in real-world markets such as those for cars, soft drinks, toothpastes, hair shampoos, cameras, and so on.[4]

However, there must be some factor limiting this proliferation of varieties or outlets. We do not observe a McDonald's on every street corner, or a personally customized Ford *Focus*, or each person's custom-designed breakfast cereals or soft drinks! We therefore need to think about what constrains the monopolist from adding more and more retail outlets or product variants. Equation (7.10) gives the clue. Admittedly, adding additional retail outlets allows the monopolist to increase its prices. However, the establishment of each additional new shop or new product variant also incurs an additional set-up cost. If, for example, the monopolist decides to operate $n + 1$ retail outlets its profit is

$$\pi(N, n + 1) = N \left(V - \frac{1}{2(n + 1)} - c \right) - (n + 1)F \tag{7.11}$$

This additional shop, or variety of drink, or new product variant increases profit if and only if $\pi(N, n + 1) > \pi(N, n)$, which requires that:

$$\frac{t}{2n}N - \frac{t}{2(n + 1)}N - F > 0$$

This simplifies to:

$$n(n + 1) < \frac{tN}{2F} \tag{7.12}$$

Suppose, for example, that there are 5 million consumers in the market so that $N = 5{,}000{,}000$ and that there is a fixed cost $F = \$50{,}000$ associated with each shop. Suppose further that the transport cost $t = \$1$. Hence, $tN/2F = 50$. Then if n is less than or equal to 6, equation (7.12) is satisfied, indicating that it is profitable to add a further shop. However, once the monopolist sets up $n = 7$ shops, equation (7.12) is no longer satisfied, indicating that it is not profitable to add any more shops. (You can easily check that the monopolist should operate exactly 7 shops for any value of $tN/2F$ greater than 42 but less than 56.)

If we ignore the fact that the number of retail outlets n has to be an integer, we can be even more precise about the profit maximizing number of retail outlets (or number of product variants). We show in the Appendix to this chapter that the monopolist maximizes profit as given by equation (7.10) with respect to the number of retail outlets n by setting

$$n^* = \sqrt{\frac{tN}{2F}} \tag{7.13}$$

Equations (7.12) and (7.13) actually have a simple and appealing intuition. The monopolist has to balance the increase in price and revenues that results from increased product variety against the additional setup costs that offering increased variety entails. What this tells us is that we would expect to find greater product variety in markets where there are many consumers (N is large), or where the set-up costs of increasing product variety are low

---

[4] See Shapiro and Varian (1999) for a similar argument regarding product variety in e-commerce markets.

(F is small), or where consumers have strong and distinct preferences regarding product characteristics (t is large).

The first two conditions should be obvious. It tells us why there are many more retail outlets in Chicago than in Peoria; why we see many franchise outlets of the same fast-food chain but not of a gourmet restaurant; and why we see many more Subway outlets in a city than Marriott hotels. What does the third condition mean? For a given number of shops, n, equation (7.12) tells us that an additional ($n + 1$) shop will be increasingly desirable the greater that transportation cost t is. Thus, as t increases, so will the monopolist's optimal number of outlets or degree of product variety.

The intuition is that when t is high consumers incur very large costs if they are not offered their most preferred brand. That is, a large value of t implies that consumers are very strongly attached to their preferred product type or location and are unwilling to purchase products that deviate significantly from this type—or travel very far to buy the product—unless they are offered a significant price discount. If the monopolist is to continue to attract consumers while maintaining high prices it must tailor its products more closely to each consumer's unique demand, which requires that it offer a wider range of product variants—or operate more retail outlets.

To summarize, in this kind of market, adding a new shop or a new product variant does not necessarily mean increasing the total supply of the good. Instead, it means replacing some of an existing variety with an alternative variety that more closely matches the specific tastes of some customers. As we have seen, this also allows the firm to charge a higher price. Yet this advantage does not come free. The firm must incur the set-up cost F for each new outlet or product variant.

This raises another important question. Is it actually profitable for the monopolist to serve the entire market? To answer this question we need to identify the condition that determines whether the monopolist will prefer to supply only part of the market rather than the whole market.

If only part of the market is served then each retail outlet is effectively a "stand alone" shop whose market area does not touch that of the remaining outlets, as in Figure 7.5. Again, we use the mathematical appendix to show that the profit-maximizing price when only part of the market is served is $p^* = (V + c)/2$, which does not depend on the number of outlets or product variants the monopolist has. This leads to a simple rule that determines whether or not the entire market is to be served. Suppose that there are n retail outlets. Then we know from equation (7.9) that the price at which the entire market can be served is $p(N, n) = V - t/2n$. Serving the entire market is therefore better than supplying only part of the market provided $p(N, n) > p^*$. In turn, this requires:

$$V - \frac{t}{2n} > \frac{V + c}{2} \Rightarrow V > c + \frac{t}{n} \tag{7.14}$$

We can put this rule another way. What equation (7.14) tells us is that the monopolist's optimal pricing policy can be described as follows:

1. If marginal production cost plus per unit transport cost divided by the number of retail outlets, $c + t/n$, is greater than the consumers' reservation price V, the monopolist should set a price at each shop of $p* = (V + c)/2$ and supply only part of the market.
2. If marginal production plus per unit transport cost divided by the number of retail outlets, $c + t/n$, is less than the consumers' reservation price V, the monopolist should set a price at each shop of $p(N, n) = V - t/2n$ and supply the entire market.

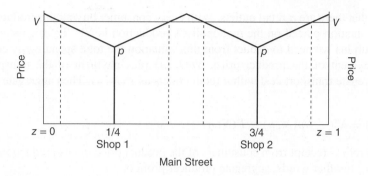

Figure 7.5   Non-competing retail shops on main street

The intuition behind this rule is relatively straightforward. When the consumer reservation price is low relative to production and transportation costs and when there are few outlets, trying to supply the entire market gives the monopolist a very low margin over operating costs and could even lead to selling at a loss. By contrast, when the consumer reservation price is high relative to the cost of production and transportation and there are many outlets, a price that allows the monopolist to supply the entire market offers a reasonable margin over costs. In these latter circumstances, the monopolist will not wish to set a high price that sacrifices any sales. Because the marginal revenue of every unit sold significantly exceeds the production cost, the monopolist will wish to sell all the units it can.

7.3   IS THERE TOO MUCH PRODUCT VARIETY?

Our analysis in the previous section implies that a profit-maximizing firm with market power may have an incentive to create a large number of outlets or product varieties so as to provide each consumer with something close to the consumer's most preferred product and thereby extract a high price. It is easy to think of real-world firms that, while not pure monopolists, have substantial market power and employ this strategy. For instance, automobile manufacturers market many varieties of compact, midsize, and large luxury-class cars. Franchise operations such as McDonald's or Subway grant exclusive geographic rights so as to space their outlets evenly over an area and avoid competition between neighboring franchises. Digital cameras come in a bewildering variety of styles and colors. Soft drink, cereal, and ice cream companies offer a wide array of minimally differentiated goods.

The sometimes overwhelming degree of product variety that we frequently observe raises the question whether the incentive to offer a wide variety of product types is too strong. Does the monopolist provide the degree of product variety that is consistent with maximizing social welfare? Or are the incentives so strong that the monopolist provides too much product variety? To answer this question, we first need to describe the socially optimal degree of product variety. Although the argument can be made in general terms, it is easiest to see the answer for the case in which the entire market is served.

We use the efficiency criterion to determine the optimality of the variety of products offered. This requires that we choose the degree of product variety that maximizes total surplus, which is defined, as usual, as aggregate consumer surplus plus producer profit.

Suppose that there are n retail outlets. With every consumer buying the product, the total consumer valuation placed on the monopolist's production is NV. To calculate aggregate consumer surplus we need to deduct from this valuation the total spending by consumers, which is payment of the product price, $Np(N, n)$ plus payment of the transport costs. Denote aggregate transport cost with n retail outlets as $T(N, n)$. Then aggregate consumer surplus is

$$CS(N, n) = NV - Np(N, n) - T(N, n) \tag{7.15}$$

Aggregate profit is receipt from consumers of the product price minus production costs and set-up costs.[5] In other words, aggregate producer profit is

$$\Pi(N, n) = Np(N, n) - Nc - nF \tag{7.16}$$

Summing these gives total surplus:

$$TS(N, n) = NV - Nc - T(N, n) - nF \tag{7.17}$$

Note that the first two terms of $TS(N, n)$ are independent of the number of retail outlets the firm establishes. In fact, once all N consumers are served, only two factors change as more stores or product varieties are added. One of these is the transport cost incurred by a typical or average consumer. Clearly, as more shops are added, more consumers find themselves closer to a store and this cost falls. That's the good news. The bad news is that adding more shops also incurs the additional setup cost of F per shop. Our question about whether the monopolist provides too many (or too few) shops thus comes down to determining whether it is the good news or the bad news that dominates.

More formally, when all consumers are served, the total surplus is the total value NV, minus the total production cost Nc, minus the total transportation and setup costs. Because the first two terms are fixed independent of the number of shops, maximizing the total surplus is equivalent to minimizing the sum of transportation and setup costs. Does the monopolist's strategy achieve this result?

One feature of the monopoly outcome makes answering this question a little easier. The monopolist always spaces its shops evenly along Main Street no matter how many it operates. That is, a single shop is located at the center, two shops are located at 1/4 and 3/4, and so on. This greatly simplifies the calculation of total transportation cost that consumers incur for any number of shops n.

Consider Figure 7.6, which shows both the full price and the transportation cost paid by those consumers buying from a particular outlet, shop i. As before, the top Y-shaped figure shows that a consumer located right next to the store has no transport cost and pays a price of $p = V - \dfrac{t}{2n}$. As we consider consumers farther from the shop, the branches of the Y show that the full price rises because these consumers incur greater and greater transportation costs. The lower branches in the figure provide a direct measurement of this transportation cost for each such consumer. Again, the transportation cost for a consumer located right next to the store is zero. It rises gradually to $t/2n$—the transportation cost paid by a consumer who lives the maximum distance from the shop. Total transportation cost for the consumers of shop i is the sum of the individual transportation cost of each consumer.

---

[5]   Transportation costs are paid by consumers and so do not figure into the profit calculation.

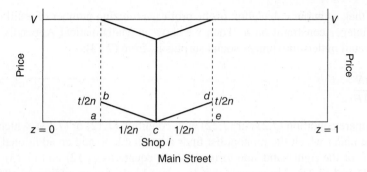

Figure 7.6   Costs of serving customers when there are n shops

This is indicated by the areas of the symmetric triangles abc and cde in Figure 7.6. Each of these triangles has a height of $t/2n$. Each also has a base $1/2n$. Hence, the area of each is $t/8n^2$. Remember though that the base reflects the fraction of the total N consumers that shop i serves in either direction. This means that to translate this area into actual dollars of transportation costs that the consumers of shop i pay, we have to multiply through by N. The result is that the customers who patronize shop i from the east pay a total transportation cost of $tN/8n^2$ as do those who patronize it from the west. The total transportation costs incurred by all consumers of shop i is therefore the sum of these two amounts, or $tN/4n^2$. If we now multiply this by the number of shops n, we find that the total transportation costs associated with all n shops is simply $T(N, n) = tN/4n$. The same exercise tells us that the total setup costs for all n shops is nF. Accordingly, the aggregate transportation plus setup costs associated with serving all N customers and operating n shops are:

$$C(N, n) = \frac{tN}{4n} + nF \tag{7.18}$$

By the same argument, aggregate transportation plus setup costs with $(n + 1)$ shops are

$$C(N, n + 1) = \frac{tN}{4(n + 1)} + (n + 1)F \tag{7.19}$$

Recall that our goal is to minimize this total cost. Therefore, we want to add an additional shop so long as doing so results in a reduction in total costs. Comparison of equations (7.19) and (7.18) indicates that this will be the case, that is, $C(n + 1) < C(n)$, if:

$$\frac{tN}{4n} - \frac{tN}{4(n + 1)} > F \tag{7.20}$$

Simplification of this inequality tells us that it will be socially beneficial to add one more shop or one more product variant beyond the n existing ones so long as:

$$n(n + 1) < \frac{tN}{4F} \tag{7.21}$$

Suppose that, as in our calculation of the profit-maximizing number of retail outlets, we ignore the integer constraint on n. Then we show in Mathematical Appendix 4 that the number of retail outlets maximizes social surplus is, from (7.14):

$$n^o = \sqrt{\frac{tN}{4F}} \qquad\qquad (7.22)$$

Now compare condition (7.21) or (7.22) with condition (7.12) or (7.13), which describes the situation under which the monopolist finds it profitable to add an additional shop. The denominator of the right-hand-side term is $2F$ in equations (7.12) and (7.13) while it is $4F$ in (7.21) and (7.22). This means that it is less likely for an additional shop to meet the requirement of equation (7.21) and be socially desirable than it is for it to meet the requirement of equation (7.12) and enhance the monopolist's profit. In other words, the monopolist has an incentive to expand product variety even when the social gains from doing so have been exhausted. The monopolist chooses too great a degree of product variety. [See Spence (1976).]

Taking the same example that we had earlier in which $t = \$1$, $N = 5,000,000$, and $F = \$50,000$. We then have that $tN/4F = 25$. In this case, equation (7.21) implies that the socially optimal number of shops is five. However, we have already shown that the monopolist would like to operate seven shops or offer seven product varieties in this market.

Casual evidence supports the "too much variety" hypothesis. Look at the myriad of ready-to-eat breakfast cereals offered by the major cereal firms, the multitude of options available on automobiles, and the vast array of finely distinguished perfumes and lipsticks available at department stores around the country. Admittedly, the producers of these goods are not pure monopolists, but they do exercise considerable market power and so they are likely subject to many of the same influences that we have just been considering.

The basic reason why a monopolist offers too much variety is that the firm maximizes profit, not total surplus. When deciding to add another shop, the monopolist balances the additional setup cost against the additional revenues that it can earn from being able to increase prices. However, from the viewpoint of efficiency this additional revenue is not a net gain. It is just a transfer of surplus from consumers to the monopolist. The true social optimum balances the setup cost of an extra shop against the reduction in transportation costs that results. Clearly, this criterion will lead to the establishment of fewer shops than will the criterion used by the monopolist.

Operating additional shops is attractive to a monopolist because this is the easiest way to reach what would otherwise be distant consumers. The monopolist operating just one shop at the center of Main Street can only sell to customers at the eastern and western ends of town by greatly reducing the price *to all customers*. The incentive to operate additional shops is that it permits reaching consumers without so significant a price reduction.

This raises another issue that takes us back to the discussion in Chapters 5 and 6. If somehow the firm could charge a price to distant consumers that they are willing to pay *without* lowering the price to nearby ones, then reaching these distant consumers from just a few shops or with just a few varieties might be more attractive. That is, if the monopolist could price discriminate, the tendency to oversupply variety might be much less strong. We now examine this possibility.

7.4 MONOPOLY AND HORIZONTAL DIFFERENTIATION WITH PRICE DISCRIMINATION

In our discussion thus far, we have been assuming that the monopolist does not price discriminate between its customers. This makes sense when customers travel to the shop to purchase the good and so do not reveal their addresses, or who they are to the monopolist. Suppose instead that the monopolist controls delivery of the product, and so knows who is who by their address in the market. What pricing policy might we expect the monopoly firm to adopt?

It should be clear that when the monopolist controls delivery it will charge every consumer the consumer's reservation price V. This is a pricing policy known as *uniform delivered pricing*. A firm adopting such a pricing policy charges all consumers the same prices and absorbs the transportation costs in delivering the product to them. This is discriminatory pricing because even though consumers pay the same price, this price does not reflect the true costs of supplying consumers in different locations. By way of analogy, charging a consumer in San Francisco the same price as a consumer in New York for a product manufactured in New York is just as much discriminatory pricing as charging a different price for this product to two different New York residents.

As in the no-price-discrimination case, we should check whether the monopoly firm actually wants to supply every consumer. Suppose that, as before, the firm operates n retail outlets evenly spaced along Main Street. Then the transportation and production costs that the firm incurs in supplying the consumers located furthest away from a retail outlet are $c + t/2n$. There is profit to be made from such sales provided that:

$$V > c + t/2n \tag{7.23}$$

Notice that this is a weaker condition than equation (7.14) without price discrimination. This is another example of a typical property of price discrimination. It allows the monopolist to serve consumers who might otherwise be left unserved.

Now consider how many shops (or product varieties) the price-discriminating monopolist will choose to operate. Given that the firm is supplying the entire market and is charging every consumer the consumer's reservation price of V, the firm's total revenue is fixed at NV. Total costs are variable production costs, which are fixed at Nc, plus the transport costs that the firm absorbs $T(N, n)$ and the set-up costs nF. These two latter costs are just the total costs $C(N, n)$ from equation (7.18). Thus the profit of the price-discriminating monopolist is:

$$\pi(N, n) = NV - Nc - \left(\frac{tN}{4n} + nF \right) \tag{7.24}$$

How does the monopolist maximize profit in this case? Because the first two terms in (7.24) are fixed, independent of n, profit maximization is achieved by minimizing the costs $C(N, n)$. But this means that *the discriminating monopolist chooses to offer the socially efficient degree of product variety.*

If you recall our discussion of price discrimination in Chapter 5, you should not find this too surprising. We saw in that chapter that a monopolist who engages in first-degree price discrimination extracts all consumer surplus and therefore wants to produce the efficient amount of output. The result just obtained extends that finding to the case of a product differentiated market. In such a market, a firm that can achieve first-degree price discrimination not only produces the socially efficient output but also the socially efficient amount of product variety. With perfect price discrimination the firm expropriates all consumer surplus. As a result, the degree of product variety that maximizes total profit is just the degree of product variety that maximizes total surplus. The incentive to go beyond the socially optimal degree of product variety does not exist.

Price discrimination in a geographic spatial model has a clear interpretation—the monopoly firm incurs the delivery cost and in doing so charges different net prices for the same good. How do we interpret price discrimination in a product characteristics space rather than a geographic one? Alternatively, how can a monopolist control "delivery" of products that are differentiated by characteristics rather than by location? MacLeod, Norman, and Thisse (1988) [See also Borenstein (1985).] provide the analogy:

> In the context of product differentiation, price discrimination arises when the producer begins with a "base product" and then redesigns this product to the customers' specifications. This means that the firm now produces a *band* of horizontally differentiated products ... instead of a single product ... Transport cost is no longer interpreted as a utility loss, but as an additional cost incurred by the firm in adapting its product to the customers' requirements ... (So) long as product design is under the control of the producer— equivalent to the producer controlling transportation—he need not charge the full cost of design change. (1988, pp. 442–3)

Consider, for example, buying a Ford *Taurus*. On the one hand you might choose one of the standard variants. Alternatively, the salesperson might persuade you into taking a different sound system, different wheels, an attractive stripe along the side that makes the car sportier, and so on. Effectively, what the salesperson is doing is making you reveal your actual "address" through the options you choose, with perhaps the intention of also separating you from more of your money.

But how easy is it for firms to offer this type of product customization? After all, customization would seem to imply the sacrifice of economies of scale and so increase costs. You might be surprised to learn that it is becoming easier and less costly by the day. The ability to offer this type of product range is what distinguishes *flexible manufacturing systems*, defined as "production units capable of producing a range of discrete products with a minimum of manual intervention" (US Office of Technology Assessment, 1984, p. 60). We discussed the properties of these types of manufacturing processes in Chapter 4, and they are becoming increasingly common. Companies such as Levi Strauss, Custom Shoe, Italian ceramic tile manufacturers, Ford, Mitsubishi, and Hitachi all operate flexible manufacturing systems. Any of you who regularly use web retailers such as Amazon.com will have noticed that the initial page you see upon entering the site changes over time to reflect your buying habits. You eventually have your very own, customized entry page resulting in your very own, customized prices.[6]

---

[6] A clear, if brief, expression of the view that e-commerce firms greatly facilitate price discrimination may be found in P. Krugman, "Reckonings: What Price Fairness," *New York Times*, October 4, 2000, p. A16.

Practice Problem

7.1

Henry Shortchap is the only blacksmith in the small village of Chestnut Tree. The village is composed of twenty-one households evenly distributed one-tenth of a mile apart along the main street of the town. Each such household uses at most one unit of smithing services per month. In addition, each household incurs a there-and-back-again transport cost of $0.50 for every tenth of a mile it lives from Shortchap's smithery. The reservation price of each household for such services is $10. Henry's cost of providing smithing services is $2 per unit. However, he can operate only one shop at most. Where should Henry locate his shop and what price should he charge? Suppose instead that Henry could operate a mobile smithy that allowed him to offer his services at his customers' homes. However, it would cost him $0.75 there-and-back-again transport costs for every tenth of a mile he has to move his smithy. Should he switch to this mobile service?

7.5   VERTICAL PRODUCT DIFFERENTIATION

The distinguishing feature of horizontal product differentiation is that consumers do not agree on what is the preferred variety of product. So, if two different varieties are offered at the same price, some consumers are likely to buy one variety and other consumers will buy the other. *Vertical differentiation* is different. In this case, all consumers agree on what is the preferred or best product, the next to best product, and so on. If a high- and a low-quality good are offered at the same price, all consumers will buy the high-quality good. Lower quality goods will find a market only if they are offered at sufficiently lower prices. A Chevrolet costs much less than a Cadillac. No-frills airlines such as JetBlue and Southwest attract customers because their flights are offered at large discounts relative to the larger carriers such as United and American. The Empire Hotel in New York charges much less than the Waldorf Astoria. However, while all consumers agree in their ranking of products from highest to lowest quality, they differ in their willingness to pay for quality. This may occur because consumers have very different incomes or simply because they have different attitudes regarding what quality is worth.

We would like to understand the incentives a monopoly firm has to offer different qualities of a product and the prices that it will charge for them. The analysis we use for this purpose is a simplified one. Nevertheless, it captures much of the flavor of more general treatments.[7]

7.5.1   Price and Quality Choice with Just One Product

We first consider how changes in quality affect consumer demand when the firm offers just one product and each consumer buys at most one unit of the good. This will give us some idea of how quality or product design can be used to enhance a firm's profit. We next examine how the firm might increase its profit by offering more than one quality of a product. The firm knows that there is some feature, or set of features, that can be used to measure the product quality valued by consumers. The firm's ability to choose these features means that it can choose the quality of product as well as its price.

---

[7]   The first and classic treatment of this problem is Mussa and Rosen (1978). Unfortunately, this is also a rather complex analysis.

Suppose, then, that the firm knows that each consumer is willing to pay something extra to get a higher quality product, but the precise amount extra varies across consumers. Some consumers place a high value on quality and will gladly pay a considerable premium for a quality improvement. Others are less concerned with quality and, unless the accompanying price increase is minimal, such consumers do not buy a better quality but higher priced good. In other words, each consumer examines the price and quality of the product and the utility obtained from consuming it. If the consumer places a value on the quality of product offered that is greater than the price being charged, the consumer purchases the good—say a CD player. If not, the consumer simply refrains from buying altogether.

The demand curve facing the monopolist depends on the precise quality of the product marketed. This is reflected in the inverse demand function, denoted by $P = P(Q, z)$, where the market clearing price P depends not only on how much the firm produces Q but also on the quality z of these units. To put it somewhat differently, an increase in quality z raises the market-clearing price for any given quantity, Q. The demand curve shifts out (or up) as product quality z increases.

It is useful to distinguish between two different ways that an increase in quality can shift the inverse demand curve $P(Q, z)$. Each is illustrated in Figure 7.7. To better understand this diagram, note that because consumers vary in terms of their willingness to pay for a good of given quality z, and because each consumer buys at most one unit of the good, the demand curve really reflects a ranking of consumers in terms of their reservation prices for a good of a specific quality z. The reservation price of the consumer most willing to pay for the good is the intercept term. The reservation price of the consumer next most willing to pay is the next point on the demand curve as we move to the right, and so on. In both Figures 7.7(a) and 7.7(b), the initial quantity produced is Q_1 and the initial quality is z_1. The market-clearing price for this quantity–quality combination is P_1. From what we have just said, this price must be the willingness to pay or the reservation price of the Q_1th consumer. At price P_1, this consumer is just indifferent between buying the good and not buying it at all given that it is of quality z_1. This consumer is called the marginal consumer. Consumers to the left—those consumers who also buy the product—are called *infra*marginal consumers.

Figure 7.7(a) shows how the inverse demand curve shifts when there is an increase in quality that raises the willingness to pay of the inframarginal consumers by more than it

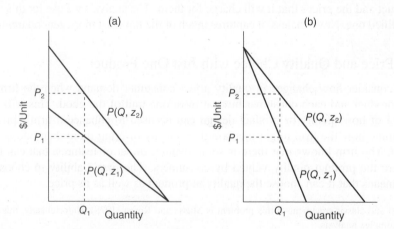

Figure 7.7   Impact of quality on demand

raises the willingness to pay of the marginal consumer. An increase in quality from z_1 to z_2 raises the price at which the quantity Q_1 sells from P_1 to P_2. However, the increase in the reservation price is greatest for consumers who were already purchasing the product so that the demand curve shifts by "sliding along" the price axis. Figure 7.7(b) illustrates the alternative case. Here, the increase in quality from z_1 to z_2 increases the willingness to pay of the Q_1th or marginal consumer by proportionately more than it raises the reservation price of the inframarginal consumers. Once again, this quality increase raises the market price of quantity Q_1 from P_1 to P_2. However, the demand curve now shifts by "sliding along" the quantity axis.[8]

Whether demand is described by Figure 7.7(a) or 7.7(b), we can see that for the monopolist the choice of quality really amounts to a decision as to which demand curve it faces. Increases in quality are attractive because they rotate the demand curve and so increase the firm's revenue at any given price. However, it is normally costly to increase product quality. Therefore what the monopolist has to do is balance the benefits in increased revenue that improved quality generates against the increased costs that increased quality incurs. More precisely, the monopolist choosing quality should think through the profit-maximizing calculus in a way similar to that used when choosing output or price. For any given choice of output, the monopolist should choose the level of quality at which the marginal revenue from increasing quality equals the marginal cost of increasing quality. In other words, the monopolist that controls both quality and quantity of its product has *two* profit maximizing conditions to satisfy. These are:

1. For a given choice of quality, the marginal revenue from the last unit sold should equal the marginal cost of making that unit at that quality;
2. For a given choice of quantity, the marginal revenue from increasing quality of each unit of output should equal the additional (marginal) cost of increasing the quality of that quantity of output.

We illustrate the quality or product design choice by assuming demand is of the type shown in Figure 7.7(a). More specifically, assume that the demand function is given by the equation:

$$P = z(50 - Q) = 50z - zQ \tag{7.25}$$

Equation (7.25) says that regardless of the quality of the product, at a price of zero a total of 50 units will be sold but increased quality causes the demand function to rotate clockwise about the point $Q = 50$.

Let us also keep the example simple by assuming that the cost of improving quality is a sunk design cost so that marginal *production* cost is independent of the quality of the product. A better film or software package may require say, more expensive script or programming, respectively, but the actual costs of showing the film or printing the CD are independent of how good it is. To make matters even simpler, let us further assume that production costs are not only constant but also zero. Design costs, however, rise with the quality level chosen. Specifically, we shall assume that design costs are:

$$F(z) = 5z^2 \tag{7.26}$$

---

[8] For models based on the case illustrated in Figure 7.7(b), some care must be taken to limit the ultimate size of the market. That is, quality increases cannot indefinitely expand the quantity demanded at a given price.

which implies that the marginal cost of increasing product quality is $10z$ (see Appendix 5).[9] We can now write the firm's profit to be:

$$\pi(Q, z) = P(Q, z)Q - F(z) = z(50 - Q)Q - 5z^2 \tag{7.27}$$

Consider first the profit-maximizing choice of output. This turns out to be very simple in this case. As usual, marginal revenue has the same intercept as the demand function but twice the slope. So with the demand function $P = 50z - zQ$ we know that marginal revenue is $MR = 50z - 2zQ = z(50 - 2Q)$. Equating this with marginal cost gives the profit-maximizing output condition: $z(50 - 2Q) = 0$. Hence, the profit-maximizing output is: $Q^* = 50/2 = 25$.

In this simple example, the monopolist's quantity choice is independent of the quality choice. The profit-maximizing output remains constant at $Q^* = 25$ no matter the choice of quality. Going back to the demand function, the profit-maximizing price is given by $P^* = z(50 - Q^*)$ so that the optimal price is: $P^* = 25z$. Unlike output, the profit-maximizing price *is* affected by the choice of quality. Moreover, the quality choice also affects the firm's design costs. A higher quality design z permits the monopolist to raise price and earn more revenue but it also raises the firm's costs. This is the tradeoff that the monopolist must evaluate.

To choose the profit-maximizing quality the monopolist must compare the additional revenue resulting from an increase in z with the increase in design cost that the higher quality requires. Because the quantity sold is constant at $Q^* = 25$, the additional revenue of an increase in quality is just this output level times the difference in price that can be charged following the rise in quality. In our example, we can see from equation (7.20) that the firm's revenue PQ at product quality z when it charges the profit-maximizing price $P^* = 25z$, is:

$$P^* Q^* = 25z25 = 625z \tag{7.28}$$

So, increasing product quality by one "unit" increases revenue by \$625, which is therefore the marginal revenue from increased quality. We know also from equation (7.25) that the marginal cost of increased quality is $10z$. Equating marginal revenue with marginal cost then gives the profit-maximizing quality choice:

$$z^* = 625/10 = 62.5 \tag{7.29}$$

An interesting question that arises in connection with the monopolist's choice of quality is how that choice compares with the socially optimal one. Does the monopolist produce too

---

[9] For an intuitive understanding, recall that marginal cost is measured at a precise value of z, e.g., we can think of the marginal cost of quality at $z = 2$, or at $z = 8$. Wherever marginal cost is measured however, it is meant to capture *both* the cost increment of increasing quality by a small amount and the cost savings from decreasing quality by a small amount. In principle, the answer to either of these questions should be the same. However, if we consider a one-unit increase in quality, the change in cost is: $5(z + 1)^2 - 5z^2 = 5(2z + 1)$, whereas if we consider a one-unit decrease in quality, the cost savings is: $5z^2 - 5(z - 1)^2 = 5(2z - 1)$. Because we get a slightly different answer depending on whether we measure marginal cost as an increase from raising quality or a decrease from reducing it, and because we want to have just one answer, we simply take the average of the two to get a marginal cost of higher quality $= 5 \times 2z = 10z$.

high or too low a quality of good? Looking at Figure 7.7(a) you might be able to work out that in this case the monopolist's quality choice is too low. The reason is straightforward. An increase in z rotates the demand curve upward and increases the total surplus earned from the 25 units that are always sold. The social optimum requires that quality be increased so long as this gain in total surplus exceeds the extra design cost. However, the monopolist only gets to keep the increase in producer surplus that a quality increase generates. As a result, profit maximization leads the monopoly firm to increase quality only so long as the extra producer surplus covers the additional design cost. Because the producer surplus is less than the total surplus, the monopolist will stop short of producing the socially optimal quality. Of course, the monopolist holds quantity below the optimal amount, too.

Our primary objective however is not to determine whether firms with monopoly power choose to market products of either too low or too much quality. The main point is to show that for such firms the quality choice matters. By carefully choosing product quality jointly with product price, the monopolist can again extract further surplus from the market.

7.2

Will Barret is the only lawyer in the small country town of Percyville. The weekly demand for his legal services depends on the quality of service he provides as reflected by his inverse demand curve: $P = 4 - Q/z$. Here, P is the price per case; Q is the number of cases or clients; and z is the quality of service Will provides. Will's costs are independent of how many cases he actually takes, but they do rise with quality. More specifically, Will's costs are given by: $C = z^2$.

a. Draw Will's demand curve for a given quality, z. How do increases in z affect the demand curve?

b. Consider the three options: $z = 1, z = 2$, and $z = 3$. Derive the profit maximizing output for each of these choices.

c. Compute the market price and profit—net of quality costs—for each of the three choices above. Which quality choice leads to the highest profits?

Practice Problem

7.5.2   Offering More than One Product in a Vertically Differentiated Market

Now that we have worked through the basics of how product quality can affect market demand, let's consider a multi-product strategy. To make it simple, suppose that the monopolist knows there are only two different types of consumer, distinguished by their willingness to pay for quality. Each consumer type buys at most one unit of the firm's product per period. In deciding which quality of product to buy, a consumer buys the quality of product yielding the greatest consumer surplus. For consumer type i the consumer surplus obtained from consuming a product of quality z at price p is:

$$V_i = \theta_i(z - \underline{z}_i) - p \quad (i = 1,2) \tag{7.30}$$

In this equation, θ_i is a measure of the value that consumers of type i places on quality and $\underline{z}_i$ is the lower bound on quality below which a consumer of type i chooses not to

---

Reality Checkpoint

Room Service? We'd like a baby and a bottle of your best champagne!

Although hospitals are always under pressure to rein in costs, they are also always on the lookout for ways to raise quality—at least for those who are willing to pay for it. Offering high-end rooms and service to those who have a taste for such amenities and a willingness to pay for it is a way to attract more revenue from the wealthiest of patients. As a result, the last decade has seen a very healthy splurge in spending on deluxe units. For example, in a growing number of maternity wards, moms-to-be who are willing to pay a little more can get private suites, whirlpool baths, Internet access, and top culinary food. For an extra fee, St. Vincent's Hospital in Indianapolis throws in a massage and the services of a professional photographer. Robert Wood Johnson Hospital in New Jersey allows patients to order from a restaurant-style menu and serves a "high tea" daily at 3:00 p.m. Offering such services reflects a trend that began some years ago as a means to attract customers, especially wealthy ones. Matilda Hospital in Hong Kong is one of a number of hospitals that particularly courts those interested in a luxury hospital stay. Their three-day maternity package includes four-star cuisine meal service with champagne while staying in a beautiful private room with molding-trimmed high ceilings, cherry-finished wood floors, and a balcony overlooking the sea for only $1,800 per night. Likewise, for a mere $2,400 per night, Greenberg 14 South, the elite, penthouse wing of New York Presbyterian/Weill Cornell hospital also offers marble bathrooms, luxuriant beds, and full room service complete with a butler as patients look out through magnificent floor-length windows to a beautiful view of the city and the East River 200 feet below. Talk about vertical differentiation!

Source: See J. Barshay, "Luxury Rooms Are Latest Fads for Private Hospitals in Asia," *Wall Street Journal*, January 26, 2001, p. A1 and P. Davies, "Hospitals Build Deluxe Wings for New Moms," *Wall Street Journal*, February 8, 2005; and N. Bernstein, "Chefs, Butlers, Marble Baths: Chefs Vie for the Affluent," *New York Times*, January 22, 2012, p. A1.

---

buy the product. We assume that $\theta_1 > \theta_2$. That is, type 1 consumers place a higher value on quality than type 2 consumers, perhaps because type 1 consumers have higher incomes than type 2 consumers or more generally because they have more intense preferences for quality. We also assume that $\underline{z}_1 > \underline{z}_2 = 0$. In other words, type 1 consumers will not buy the monopolist's product unless it is at least of quality $\underline{z}_1$. These are consumers who "wouldn't be seen dead" flying in coach, eating in fast-food joints, or shopping in discount stores. By contrast, type 2 consumers are willing to buy the monopolist's product of any quality provided, of course, that consumer surplus is non-negative. Unfortunately for the firm, while it knows that these different consumer types exist, it has no objective measure by which it can distinguish the different types.

Similar to second-degree price discrimination, the monopolist would like to choose a product line that identifies and separates customers of different types. The monopolist would like to induce type 1 consumers to buy a product of high quality z_1 at a high price while simultaneously inducing type 2 consumers to purchase a product of low quality z_2 at a lower price, which is equal to their willingness to pay. Suppose that the firm is able to produce any quality in the quality range $[\underline{z}, \overline{z}]$. To keep the analysis (reasonably) simple, further assume that the marginal costs of production are constant and identical across all qualities of product, and are set equal to zero.[10] Finally, we make the following important assumption (explained below):

Assumption 1 : $\bar{z} > \dfrac{\theta_1 \underline{z}_1}{(\theta_1 - \theta_2)}$

Note that Assumption 1 is most easily satisfied when the difference between θ_1 and θ_2 is relatively large.

Let's look first at a consumer of type 2, a consumer with a low willingness to pay for quality. What the firm will do is charge this consumer a price that is just low enough for the consumer to be willing to purchase the low-quality product. From equation (7.30), and given that $z_2 = 0$, consumer type 2 will buy z_2 if $p_2 \leq \theta_2 z_2$, implying a good 2 price of

$$p_2 = \theta_2 z_2 \tag{7.31}$$

Now consider a consumer of type 1 with a stronger preference for quality. This consumer can, of course, buy the low-quality product. So in pricing the high-quality product, the firm faces the same type of *incentive compatibility constraint* that we met when discussing second-degree price discrimination. (There is also the constraint that type 2 consumers buy the low-quality rather than the high-quality product. See below.) For a type 1 consumer to buy the high-quality product, it is necessary that:

$$\theta_1(z_1 - \underline{z}_1) - p_1 \geq \theta_1(z_2 - \underline{z}_1) - p_2$$
$$\theta_1(z_1 - \underline{z}_1) - p_1 \geq 0 \tag{7.32}$$

The first expression in (7.32) says that the consumer surplus that a type 1 consumer obtains from buying the high-quality product must be greater than or equal to the consumer surplus that could be obtained if the type 1 consumer bought the low-quality good. The second expression states that the consumer surplus that a type 1 consumer obtains from purchasing the high-quality good must be non-negative.

Substituting $p_2 = \theta_2 z_2$ from (7.31) into the first expression in (7.32) we find that:

$$p_1 \leq \theta_1 z_1 - (\theta_1 - \theta_2)z_2 \tag{7.33}$$

Equation (7.33) says that the maximum price p_1 that can be charged for the high-quality product is $p_1 \leq \theta_1 z_1 - (\theta_1 - \theta_2)z_2$. This price is greater the higher are the values θ_1 and θ_2 that the two types of consumers place on quality, and the higher is the quality differential between z_1 and z_2. That is, quality can be priced more highly when it is valued more highly by all consumers. Further, because the monopolist is effectively competing with itself by offering two products of different qualities, the monopolist has an incentive to increase the quality differential between the products, i.e., to make two goods more differentiated. Doing so weakens the competition between products and allows the firm to increase the price of its high-quality product. Note that when $p_1 \leq \theta_1 z_1 - (\theta_1 - \theta_2)z_2$ the condition that consumers of type 1 receive non-negative surplus when they buy the high-quality good can now be written as $\theta_1(z_1 - \underline{z}_1) - p_1 \geq 0 \Rightarrow (\theta_1 - \theta_2)z_2 - \theta_1 \underline{z}_1 \geq 0$. Given our Assumption

---

[10]   It might be, for example, that the majority of the firm's costs are set-up costs and that crimping higher quality products makes lower quality products. Relaxing this assumption doesn't change much, and having it makes the analysis a bit easier.

1 that $\bar{z} > \dfrac{\theta_1 \underline{z}_1}{(\theta_1 - \theta_2)}$ it follows that the condition of non-negative consumer surplus can be satisfied by some $z_2 \leq \bar{z}$.

It is easy to check that the incentive compatibility constraint is always satisfied for type 2 consumers. For this type of consumer *not* to want to buy the high-quality product it must be the case that $\theta_2 z_1 - p_1 < 0$. Given that $p_1 \leq \theta_1 z_1 - (\theta_1 - \theta_2)z_2$ this implies $-(\theta_1 - \theta_2)z_1 + (\theta_1 - \theta_2)z_2 < 0$. Because $z_1 > z_2$ and $\theta_1 > \theta_2$ this must be true. In other words, the prices given by (7.30) and (7.32) guarantee that type 1 consumers buy the high-quality product and type 2 consumers buy the low-quality product.

Now assume that there are N_i consumers of each type. Furthermore, suppose that variable costs of production do not depend on quality and so for simplicity we set the unit production costs of each good $c_1 = c_2 = 0$. Again for simplicity assume that there are no fixed costs as well. Given that $p_1 = \theta_1 z_1 - (\theta_1 - \theta_2)z_2$ and $p_2 = \theta_2 z_2$ the firm's total profit is:

$$\Pi = N_1 p_1 + N_2 p_2 = N_1 \theta_1 z_1 - N_1(\theta_1 - \theta_2)z_2 + N_2 \theta_2 z_2$$
$$= N_1 \theta_1 z_1 - (N_1 \theta_1 - (N_1 + N_2)\theta_2)z_2 \tag{7.34}$$

The issue that we want to address now is what quality of goods, z_1 and z_2, will maximize the firm's profit. It is clear from equation (7.34) that the coefficient on z_1 is positive, given by $N_1 \theta_1$. That is, profit rises as z_1 rises, so the firm should set z_1 as high as possible; that is:

$$z_1^* = \bar{z} \tag{7.35}$$

The firm should set the quality of its highest quality product at the maximum quality level possible.

For z_2 matters are not quite as straightforward. The impact of z_2 upon the monopolist's profit depends upon the sign of the coefficient, $N_1 \theta_1 - (N_1 + N_2)\theta_2$. When this term is positive, the monopolist's profit decreases as z_2 increases. When it is negative, profit increases as z_2 increases. We need to examine these two cases separately.

Case 1: $N_1 \theta_1 < (N_1 + N_2)\theta_2$

If $N_1 \theta_1 < (N_1 + N_2)\theta_2$ then it follows from (7.34) that profit is increasing in z_2. In this case the firm should set $z_2 = z_1 = \bar{z}$. In other words, the firm should offer only one product and that product should be of the highest possible quality. The question now becomes whether the firm in this case should price the high-quality product to sell to both types of consumer or price it to sell only to type 1 consumers.

Selling to both types of consumer requires that the product be priced at $p^* = \theta_2 \bar{z}$. Type 2 consumers have all their consumer surplus extracted but, given Assumption 1, type 1 consumers enjoy some consumer surplus. The firm earns a total profit of $(N_1 + N_2)\theta_2 \bar{z}$. If, instead, the monopolist chooses to sell only to type 1 consumers, the product can be priced at $p = \theta_1(\bar{z} - \underline{z}_1)$, extracting all consumer surplus from each type 1 consumer by not supplying type 2 consumers. This strategy gives the firm a total profit of $N_1 \theta_1(\bar{z} - \underline{z}_1)$. Comparing these two strategies tells us that that selling to both types of consumers is more profitable if:

$$N_1 \theta_1(\bar{z} - \underline{z}_1) < (N_1 + N_2)\theta_2 \bar{z} \Rightarrow N_1 \theta_1 < (N_1 + N_2)\theta_2 \frac{\bar{z}}{(\bar{z} - \underline{z}_1)} \tag{7.36}$$

Note that this case is defined by the condition that $N_1\theta_1 < (N_1 + N_2)\theta_2$. Further note that $\dfrac{\overline{z}}{\overline{z} - \underline{z}_1} > 1$. In other words, equation (7.35) holds. We can conclude that in Case 1, for which $N_1\theta_1 < (N_1 + N_2)\theta_2$, the monopolist offers a single product of quality $\overline{z}$ and prices it at $p^* = \theta_2\overline{z}$ in order to sell to both types of consumer.

Case 2: $N_1\theta_1 > (N_1 + N_2)\theta_2$

From (7.34) it is clear that in this case profit is decreasing in z_2 and so the firm has an incentive to offer two qualities that are as differentiated as possible. The firm will choose $z_1^* = \overline{z}$ and set z_2 as low as is feasible. This does not mean, however, that z_2 can be reduced to its minimum of $\underline{z}_2$. Remember that we must also satisfy the constraint that type 1 consumers receive non-negative consumer surplus from buying the high-quality good. That is, $\theta_1(z_1^* - \underline{z}_1) - p_1 \geq 0$. But we know that $z_1^* = \overline{z}$ and, from (7.33), $p_1 = \theta_1 z_1^* - (\theta_1 - \theta_2)z_2$. Substituting these into the non-negativity constraint gives $(\theta_1 - \theta_2)z_2 - \theta_1\underline{z}_1 \geq 0$. In other words the monopolist chooses:

$$z_2^* = \frac{\theta_1\underline{z}_1}{\theta_1 - \theta_2} \tag{7.37}$$

It is here that we see the impact of the assumption that the monopolist cannot distinguish the two consumer types. The monopolist would like to set z_2 even lower than is implied by equation (7.37) but cannot do so if the monopolist is to offer products that make the consumers self-select into their true types.

We can now work out the profit-maximizing prices for the two goods. Substituting (7.37) in (7.31) we find $p_2^* = \dfrac{\theta_2\theta_1\underline{z}_1}{\theta_1 - \theta_2}$. Similarly substituting (7.37) and $z_1^* = \overline{z}$ into $p_1 = \theta_1 z_1^* - (\theta_1 - \theta_2)z_2$, we find that $p_1^* = \theta_1(\overline{z} - \underline{z}_1)$. In other words, type 1 consumers are charged their maximum willingness to pay for the highest quality possible, $\overline{z}$, and type 2 consumers are charged their maximum willingness to pay for the lower quality $z_2^* = \dfrac{\theta_1\underline{z}_1}{\theta_1 - \theta_2}$. In offering both goods, the monopolist extracts all the consumer surplus but has to compromise on the qualities that are offered. Aggregate profit is:

$$\Pi = N_1\theta_1(\overline{z} - \underline{z}_1) + N_2\frac{\theta_2\theta_1\underline{z}_1}{\theta_1 - \theta_2} \tag{7.38}$$

In comparing the prices that the monopolist sets in the two cases, we can identify the intuition behind the result that in one case the monopolist wants to offer only one (high-) quality good while in the other the firms wants to offer both a high-quality and a low-quality good.

We saw that when only one, high-quality good is offered it is priced at $p^* = \theta_2\overline{z}$ in order to have it sell to both types of consumer. When a high-quality and low-quality good are offered, the high-quality good is priced at $p_1^* = \theta_1(\overline{z} - \underline{z}_1)$ while the low-quality good is priced at $p_2^* = \dfrac{\theta_2\theta_1\underline{z}_1}{\theta_1 - \theta_2}$. It follows immediately from Assumption 1 that $p_1^* > p^*$ and $p_2^* < p^*$. Offering two quality-differentiated goods allows the monopolist to charge a higher price to type 1 consumers but forces the monopolist to lower the price it charges to type 2 consumers. For this strategy to be profitable, there needs to be "sufficiently many" type 1 consumers as compared to type 2. This is exactly the property captured by the condition that the two-product strategy should be adopted only if $N_1\theta_1 > (N_1 + N_2)\theta_2$.

General Foods is a monopolist and knows that its market for Bran Flakes contains two types of consumers. Type A consumers have indirect utility functions $V_a = 20(z - z_1)$ while type B consumers have indirect utility functions $V_b = 10z$. In each case z is a measure of product quality, which can be chosen from the interval [0,2]. There are N consumers in the market, of which General Foods knows that a fraction η is of type A and the remainder is of type B.

a. Suppose that General Foods can tell the different consumer types apart and so can charge them different prices for the same quality of breakfast cereal. What is the profit maximizing strategy for General Foods?

Now suppose that General Foods does not know which type of consumer is which.

b. Show how its profit maximizing strategy is determined by η.
c. What is the profit maximizing strategy when $z_1 = 0$?

7.6 EMPIRICAL APPLICATION: PRODUCT QUALITY AND MARKET SIZE

One important insight that comes from formal consideration of vertically differentiated markets is that quality tends to increase as the market size grows. The intuition behind this insight is most easily seen in our initial discussion of a vertical quality market in which the inverse demand curve is of the general form:

$$P = z(K - Q) \tag{7.39}$$

The advantage of this specification is that the market size is totally captured by the parameter K. Thus, if $K = 50$, as in our earlier example, the maximum market demand at $P = \$0$ is $Q = 50$. However, if $K = 100$, the maximum demand at $P = \$0$ is $Q = 100$. We can repeat this comparison at all other prices and the same relative result will emerge. Holding quality z constant, total demand in the market at any price P is greater the larger is K.

Consider now our earlier example in which the marginal production cost was independent of quality z and for convenience set to zero, while the overhead design cost was quadratic, that is, $F(z) = 5z^2$. As before, we can solve for the optimal quantity by recognizing that marginal revenue is given by: $MR = zK - 2zQ$. Equating this to the assumed marginal cost value of zero, yields:

$$Q = \frac{K}{2} \Rightarrow P = z\frac{K}{2} \tag{7.40}$$

In turn, this means that the firm's profit is given by:

$$\pi(z) = \frac{K^2}{4}z - 5z^2 \tag{7.41}$$

Thus, every increment in quality z raises revenue by $K^2/4$, and we know from before, that every such increase in quality has a marginal cost of $10z$. Equating this marginal revenue and marginal cost then yields

$$z = \frac{K^2}{40} \tag{7.42}$$

Again, it is easy to check that when $K = 50$, this yields $z = 62.5$ as we found in our initial example. More generally though, note that the profit-maximizing choice of z increases with our measure of market size, K.

The foregoing intuition is quite general. It also applies when the marginal production cost rises with quality. In fact, it holds when there is competition so that different firms offer different quality products though here it typically means that it is the quality of the best product that will rise with market size.

In short, there is a general prediction that larger markets ought to offer better quality products. It is this prediction that Berry and Waldfogel (2010) test in a recent paper. For this purpose they look at two sets of local markets—those for newspapers and those for restaurants—where each local market corresponds to one of 283 metropolitan statistical areas defined by the US Census Bureau. We focus on their newspaper results here because this market is closest in spirit to the intuitive argument above.

Berry and Waldfogel (2010) define newspaper quality in a number of ways. Because more content should mean better quality, one measure is simply the number of pages the newspaper has. For a collection of different newspapers, we might instead take the average number of pages (AVEPAGE) or, in line with our analysis above, the number of pages in the largest newspaper (MAXPAGE). An alternative, input-based measure of quality is the number of reporters on staff, again averaged across all papers (AVESTAFF) or taken at its largest value for a given community (MAXSTAFF). The number of staff reporters may be particularly important at the local level, as it is likely to reflect the extent to which the paper covers local news as opposed to printing syndicated, national reports.[11]

The various measures of newspaper quality are then regressed on a measure of the metropolitan area population, as a measure of market size, along with other variables meant to control for various factors that may influence the quality choice—the metropolitan median income; the percent of the population with some college education; the percent that are young (under age thirty-five); and the percent that are old (over age sixty-five). The Berry and Waldfogel (2010) results are shown in Table 7.1 below for regressions that use the natural logarithm of the quality and market size variables so that the estimated coefficients are naturally treated as elasticities, i.e., as a ratio of percentage changes.

The estimates across the first row strongly confirm the hypothesis that product quality rises with market size. Thus, as the population grows by 10 percent, the number of pages in the average and largest metropolitan area grows by 2 and 3 percent, respectively, and each result is statistically significant at the 1 percent level. Similarly, as the metropolitan population grows by 10 percent, the number of staff reporters on the average and largest newspaper grows by 48 and 56 percent, respectively. Again, these results are very statistically significant.

Moreover, the highest quality paper is also the one with the largest market share. For example, New York's paper with the most pages is the *New York Times* and its metropolitan market share is essentially the same as the shares of the next two largest papers—the *Daily*

---

[11]   Averages were circulation-weighed averages.

Table 7.1   Newspaper quality and market size*

	Dependent Variable			
	ln(AVEPAGE)	*ln(AVESTAFF)*	*ln(MAXPAGE)*	*ln(MAXSTAFF)*
ln(POP)	0.208	0.475	0.287	0.560
	(0.021)	(0.025)	(0.015)	(0.025)
Median Income	−0.001	0.009	0.005	0.025
	(0.005)	(0.006)	(0.004)	(0.006)
% College	1.106	0.900	1.025	0.961
	(0.388)	(0.479)	(0.275)	(0.477)
% Young (< 35)	2.387	1.73	1.119	0.428
	(1.115)	(1.380)	(0.790)	(1.375)
% Old (> 65)	2.480	0.183	1.982	0.006
	(1.113)	(1.377)	(0.789)	(1.371)
Constant	2.59	2.611	3.165	3.010
	(0.549)	(0.680)	(0.389)	(0.677

*Standard errors in parentheses.

News and the *Post*—combined. Thus, the highest quality choice is invariably the decision of the firm with the most market share, which is a bit more in the spirit of the analysis in this chapter.[12] Overall then, the newspaper quality and market size seem to be very positively correlated.

Summary

This chapter has investigated product-differentiated strategies that a monopolist may employ when it sells to consumers with diverse tastes. By offering a line of products, the firm can better expropriate consumer surplus and increase profit. First we considered horizontal product differentiation. In this scenario, consumers differ in their preferences for specific product characteristics. Some prefer yellow, some black, some soft, some hard, some sweet, and some sour. By selling different varieties of the product, the monopolist expands its market and simultaneously enhances its ability to charge customers higher prices in return for selling a variety of product that is close to their most preferred flavor, color, or design.

A feature of this kind of market is that the monopolist tends to offer too much variety—a prediction for which there is a good bit of supportive casual evidence. However, the monopolist's incentive to over-supply variety is mitigated if the firm is able to price discriminate. Indeed, perfect or first-degree price discrimination encourages the firm to offer consumers the same amount of variety as the socially optimal case.

We also investigated the monopolist's strategy when products are vertically differentiated. In this case, all consumers agree that higher quality is better, where quality is measured by some observable feature, or set of features of the product. Consumers, however, differ in their willingness to pay for quality. In the case in which the monopolist offers only one type of product and quality is costly, we found that the monopolist may choose too low a quality. The monopolist may also have in the vertically differentiated case an incentive to offer a range of different qualities in order to exploit the differences in consumers' preferences. In doing so, however, the firm faces an incentive compatibility constraint and must choose quality and price such that the different types of consumer will purchase the quality targeted to their type. These constraints encountered in

[12]   However, recall our warning from Chapter 1 that structure (and market shares) are endogenous. The high quality of a paper is as much responsible for that paper's market share as the firm's market power is responsible for the paper's high quality.

second-degree price discrimination in Chapter 6. One empirical prediction that emerges from this analysis is that in vertically differentiated products, the quality of the best product will tend to rise as the market size increases to allow a fuller exploitation of any scale economies in making a better product. Evidence from urban newspaper markets where quality is measured in terms of variables such as average staff size or average number of pages confirms this hypothesis.

We have cast our theoretical discussion mainly in the context of monopoly. Yet the practices we have described are often employed by companies that are far from perfect monopolists

without significant rivals. This reflects the fact that imperfectly competitive firms often have a very powerful incentive to offer a range of differentiated products, whether they are horizontally or vertically differentiated. Indeed, imperfectly competitive firms often have a very strong incentive to pursue such differentiation as an important tactic to deal with rivals. We will discuss this point in subsequent chapters. Here we simply note that the empirical study of urban newspaper markets reported in this chapter also tends to confirm this view. Two papers in the same city rarely offer readers the same quality of news coverage.

Problems

1. A monopolist faces the following inverse demand curve: $P = (36 - 2Q)z$; where P is price; Q is her total output; and z is the quality of product sold. z can take on only one of two values. The monopolist can choose to market a low-quality product for which $z = 1$. Alternatively, the monopolist can choose to market a high-quality product for which $z = 2$. Marginal cost is independent of quality and is constant at zero. Fixed cost, however, depends on the product design and increases with the quality chosen. Specifically, fixed cost is equal to $65z^2$.

    a. Find the monopolist's profits if profits are maximized *and* a low-quality design is chosen.

    b. Find the monopolist's profits if profits are maximized *and* a high-quality design is chosen

    c. Comparing your answers to 1(a) and 1(b), what quality choice should the monopolist make?

2. In the early 1970s, the six largest manufacturers of ready-to-eat breakfast cereals shared 95 percent of the market. Over the preceding twenty years, these same manufacturers introduced over eighty new varieties of cereals. How would you evaluate this strategy from the viewpoint of the Hotelling spatial model described earlier in the chapter?

3. Crepe Creations is considering franchising its unique brand of crepes to stall-holders on Hermoza Beach, which is five miles long.

CC estimates that on an average day there are 1,000 sunbathers evenly spread along the beach and that each sunbather will buy one crepe per day provided that the price plus any disutility cost does not exceed $5. Each sunbather incurs a disutility cost of getting up from resting to get a crepe and returning to their beach spot of 25 cents for every $1/4$ mile the sunbather has to walk to get to the CC stall. Each crepe costs $0.50 to make and CC incurs a $40 overhead cost per day to operate a stall. How many franchises should CC award given that it determines the prices the stall holders can charge and that it will have a profit-sharing royalty scheme with the stall holders? What will be the price of a crepe at each stall?

4. Return to Problem 3 above. Suppose now that CC requires that each stall holder deliver the crepes in its own designated territory. How many franchises should now be awarded if we make the standard assumption that the effort costs of the stall holders are the same as those of the sun bathers? How would your answer change if the stall holders instead incurred effort costs half as much as those of the sun bathers, that is, if their costs were 12.5 cents for every quarter mile of distance?

5. Imagine that Dell is considering two versions of a new laptop. One version will meet high performance standards. The other will only meet medium performance standards. To make the second, Dell uses cheaper

materials and then crimps the keyboard of the high-performance machine with the result that the marginal cost of the each product is an identical $500. There are two types of consumers for the new laptop. "Techies" have the (indirect) utility function $V_t = 2000(z - 1)$. "Norms" have the (indirect) utility function $V_n = 1000z$, where z is a measure of product quality. Dell can choose the quality level z for each machine from the interval (1,3), subject only to the restriction that the medium-performance machine have a lower z quality than the high-performance machine. If Dell knows that there are N_t Techies and N_n Norms, and if Dell also can identify which type any consumer is, what is its optimum price and product quality strategy?

6. Return to Problem 5, above. Suppose Dell cannot identify each customer but only knows the numbers of each type. Show that Dell's profit-maximizing strategy is determined by the relative numbers of each type.

7. A monopolist faces an inverse demand curve given by: $P = 22 - Q/100z$, where z is an index of quality. The monopolist incurs a cost per unit of: $c = 2 + z^2$.

    a. How do increases in product quality z affect demand?

    b. Imagine that the firm must choose one of three quality levels: $z = 1$, $z = 2$, and $z = 3$. Which quality choice will maximize the firm's profit? What profit-maximizing output and price are associated with this profit-maximizing quality level?

8. Return to Problem 7, above. What is the quality choice that will maximize the social welfare? If the monopolist were constrained to produce this socially optimal quality, what price would the monopolist charge?

References

Berry, S., and J. Waldfogel. 2010. "Product Quality and Market Size," *Journal of Industrial Economics* 58 (March): 1–31.

Hotelling, H. 1929. "Stability in Competition," *Economic Journal* 39 (January): 41–57.

Macleod, W. B., G. Norman, and J. F. Thisse. 1988. "Price Discrimination and Equilibrium in Monopolistic Competition," *International Journal of Industrial Organization* 6 (December), 429–46.

Mussa, M., and S. Rosen. 1978. "Monopoly and Product Quality," *Journal of Economic Theory* 18: 301–17.

Appendix

LOCATION CHOICE WITH TWO SHOPS

Shops have identical costs. Symmetry implies each is located a distance d from each market endpoint.

1. $d \leq 1/4$: If d is less than $1/4$, then the maximum full price that can be charged if all consumers are to be served is determined by the consumers at the market center ($x = 1/2$) and is equal to a price p such that when transport costs are included, they pay a full price equal to V. Hence, the maximum price is:

$$p(d) + t\left(\frac{1}{2} - d\right) = V \Rightarrow p(d) = V - t\left(\frac{1}{2} - d\right) \tag{7.A1}$$

Aggregate profit at this price is also a function of d and is given by:

$$\pi(d) = [p(d) - c]N = \left(V + td - \frac{t}{2} - c\right)N \tag{7.A2}$$

This profit increases as d gets larger. It follows therefore that d should never be less than $1/4$.

2. $d > 1/4$. If d is greater than $1/4$, the maximum price if all consumers are to be served is determined by consumers at the market endpoints $(x = 0,1)$. The maximum price now satisfies:

$$p(d) + td = V \Rightarrow p(d) = V - td \tag{7.A3}$$

Aggregate profit is now

$$\pi(d) = [p(d) - c]N - (V - td - c)N \tag{7.A4}$$

This is decreasing in d. Hence, d should never exceed $1/4$. Given that d should also never be less than $1/4$, that profit maximization implies that $d = 1/4$ exactly.

THE PROFIT MAXIMIZING NUMBER OF RETAIL OUTLETS

Recall that the profit to the firm if it has n outlets (or product variants) is:

$$\pi(N, n) = N\left(V - \frac{t}{2n} - c\right) - nF \tag{7.A5}$$

If we ignore the integer constraint on n we can find the profit-maximizing number of retail outlets by differentiating (7.A5) with respect to the number of retail outlets n to give the first-order condition:

$$\frac{\partial \pi(N, n)}{\partial n} = \frac{Nt}{2n^2} - F = 0 \tag{7.A6}$$

Solving for n gives the profit-maximizing number of retails outlets

$$n^* = \sqrt{\frac{Nt}{2F}} \tag{7.A7}$$

OPTIMAL PARTIAL MARKET PRICE

Assume that the left-hand shop is located $1/4$ mile from the left-hand end of the market. At a price p this shop sells to consumers located within distance r on each side such that $p + tr = V$, or $r = (V - p)/t$. Total demand to this shop is, as before, $2rN$. Profit to this shop is, therefore:

$$\pi = 2N(p - c)(V - p)/t \tag{7.A8}$$

Differentiating with respect to p gives the first order condition:

$$\frac{\partial \pi}{\partial p} = \frac{2N}{t}(V - 2p + c) = 0 \tag{7.A9}$$

Solving for the optimal price p^* then gives:

$$p^* = (V + c)/2 \tag{7.A10}$$

At this price, profit to each retail outlet is:

$$\pi = \frac{N}{2t}(V - c)^2 \tag{7.A11}$$

THE SOCIALLY OPTIMAL NUMBER OF RETAIL OUTLETS

The optimal number of retail outlets (product variants) minimizes total transportation and set-up costs:

$$C(N, n) = \frac{tN}{4n} + nF \tag{7.A12}$$

Minimizing (7.A12) with respect to the number of retail outlets n yields:

$$n^o = \sqrt{\frac{Nt}{4F}} \tag{7.A14}$$

OPTIMAL CHOICE OF OUTPUT AND QUALITY

Let demand be given by:

$$P = z(\theta - Q) \tag{7.A15}$$

Let marginal production costs be zero but the design cost be quadratic in quality z so that:

$$C(Q, z) = \alpha z^2 \tag{7.A16}$$

It follows that the firm's profit function is:

$$\pi(Q, z) = PQ - C(Q, z) = z(\theta - Q)Q - \alpha z^2 \tag{7.A17}$$

Solving for the optimal output Q^* then gives:

$$Q^* = \theta/2 \tag{7.A19}$$

Now differentiate the profit function with respect to quality choice z to give the first-order condition:

$$\frac{\partial \pi(Q, z)}{\partial z} = (\theta - Q)Q - 2\alpha z = 0 \tag{7.A20}$$

Substituting the optimal quantity Q^* from (7.A19) in (7.A20) gives:

$$z^* = \theta^2/8\alpha \tag{7.A21}$$

8

Commodity Bundling and Tie-In Sales

On November 5, 1999, Judge Thomas Penfield Jackson issued his "Findings of Fact" in the Microsoft antitrust trial that served subsequently as the basis for Judge Jackson's guilty verdict in the trial five months later on April 3, 2000. Among other things, Judge Jackson concluded that Microsoft's *Windows* operating system and its *Internet Explorer* web browser constituted separate products that could, in principle, stand alone but that Microsoft had bundled together as one package. Judge Jackson's focus was on the use of such bundling as an illegal tying of the two products aimed at extending Microsoft's operating systems monopoly to the browser market. Any defense against this charge must offer an explanation for such bundling that is not related to extending monopoly power.

The remedy that Judge Jackson ordered was that Microsoft be broken into two separate companies, one that would produce the operating system and the other that would produce software components such as Microsoft *Office* and *Internet Explorer*. Judge Jackson's judgment was reversed on appeal, with the proposed settlement being that Microsoft share its application programming interfaces, making it easier for competitors seeking to offer *Windows*-based applications to ensure that their software would operate seamlessly on the *Windows* platform.

A subsequent complaint was brought by the European Commission, accusing Microsoft of abusing its dominant position by bundling *Windows Media Player* (*WMP*) with the *Windows* operating system. A preliminary judgment in 2003 required Microsoft to offer a version of *Windows* without *WMP* and to provide the information necessary for a competitor to offer a media player that would operate effectively on the *Windows* platform. Microsoft was also fined €497 million, a fine that was increased to a further €860 million in 2012 based on the finding that Microsoft had delayed implementing the 2004 judgment.

Is Microsoft's behavior unique to that technology company? Far from it. The truth is that most firms—both those with market power and those without it—sell more than one good, and bundling or tying between a firm's different products is frequently observed. What are the possible gains to the firm from tying together the sale of its products? Are they solely the anti-competitive, entry-deterring motives that worried Judge Jackson and the European Commission? Does bundling raise both profit and efficiency, or does it earn profit at the expense of efficiency? Do consumers win or lose from these bundling and tying tactics? These are the questions we investigate in this chapter.

That consumers might actually gain from bundling seems possible when we examine the prices that Microsoft charges, not for its *Windows* operating system but for its software applications. The Microsoft *Office* suite is one of the most popular applications packages. *Office Professional* 2010 contains the *Word, Excel, Outlook, PowerPoint, Access*, and *OneNote* programs, priced in September 2012 at $400. You can buy the individual components separately, *Word, Excel, Outlook*, and *Access* selling for $140 each and *OneNote* for $80, a total of $780. In other words, there is a bundle discount of $380. The question then becomes: what incentive does Microsoft have to engage in such bundling? How does offering the *Office* bundle help raise Microsoft's profit?

Before proceeding we should make our analysis a bit more precise. In some cases, firms like Microsoft market two or more products as an explicit bundle comprised of fixed amounts of the individual components. Thus, the *Office* suite contains exactly one copy of each of the constituent programs; a fixed price menu at a restaurant contains one of each of the included courses; and a holiday travel package might specify *one* return flight to London, *five* nights' accommodation, and *three* West End plays.

There is an alternative to bundling, commonly referred to as tying. Under this strategy a firm *ties* the sale of one product to the purchase of another but does not control the proportions in which the two products are consumed. Under a tying strategy the purchase of some amount of one good (the tying good) requires that the buyer purchase a second product (the tied good). For example, in the early days of business machines and computers IBM sold its machines under the requirement that the buyer also use IBM-produced tabulating cards. In other words, the purchase of the machine was tied to the additional purchase of IBM cards.[1] We differentiate this from commodity bundling because IBM did not specify the number of cards that the consumer had to purchase.

More recent examples of tied sales are not difficult to find. If you buy a computer printer you also commit yourself to buying the unique ink cartridges that fit into that printer. Hewlett-Packard cartridges do not fit Canon printers nor vice versa. Similarly, Sony's *Play Station* game cartridges do not work on either a Nintendo *Wii* or a Microsoft *Xbox* system. What is tied in all these cases is the brand (and seller) of the associated product, not its quantity. You can always reduce your demand for Hewlett-Packard ink cartridges by being very strict with yourself on how many drafts of a term paper you actually print out! These modern examples of tie-in sales are *technology* based rather than *contractual* as in the IBM case. Yet, whether contractual or technical, the issues we wish to address are the motivations for and the implications of both tying and bundling practices. It is to a more formal analysis of these questions that we now turn.

8.1   COMMODITY BUNDLING AND CONSUMER VALUATION

We begin with a story told almost thirty years ago by Nobel laureate, George Stigler, who was one of the first to understand bundling as a means of exploiting differences in consumer valuations of the goods on offer.[2] At the time that he published his brief analysis he was responding to a recent Supreme Court case involving the movie industry. Throughout the 1950s and 1960s, airing older Hollywood films was a substantial part of television fare. Film distributors who owned the rights to the films sold presentation rights for a fee to local

---

[1]   This tying policy was challenged as a violation of the Clayton Act in *International Business Machines* v. *U.S.*, 298 U.S. 131 (1936). Similar charges arose repeatedly in the many private antitrust suits against IBM in the following decades.

[2]   Stigler (1968).

television stations. However, they rarely sold films individually. Instead, they sold them in packages typically combining screen gems such as *Casablanca* and *Treasure of the Sierra Madre* with such "grade B" losers as *Gorilla Man* and *Tear Gas Squad*.[3] Stigler's insight was to recognize that while every television station valued the first two films (or others of similar quality) more than the last two films, the relative valuations of the two types of movies might well vary from station to station. Such differences provide a motive for the observed bundling.

A modified version of Stigler's example goes as follows. Suppose that there are two films, X and Y, and two stations (located in different cities), A and B. Each station's reservation prices for the two films are as follows:

	Maximum Willingness to Pay for Film X	Maximum Willingness to Pay for Film Y
Station A	$8,000	$2,500
Station B	$7,000	$4,000

As you may recall from earlier chapters, the film distributor can exploit these different valuations by applying discriminatory prices. However, as you may also recall, price discrimination must surmount the twin problems of identifying which station is which and then avoiding arbitrage between stations. Suppose that this is not possible. Then the distributor must charge a uniform price for each film, in which case its best bet is to charge $7,000 for film X and $2,500 for film Y. At these prices, both stations buy both films, and the distributor's total revenue is $19,000.

Bundling, however, permits further revenues to be earned. Instead of selling the two films separately, suppose that the distributor offers the films in a bundle to the two stations for a combined price of $10,500. Because both stations value the bundle at least this highly, the distributor sells both films to both stations. Its revenue now rises to $21,000.

The reason that bundling raises revenue is straightforward. It reduces the variation in consumers' willingness to pay. In turn, this reduction in variance effectively makes the demand curve more elastic with the result that a relatively small price reduction will generate a substantial demand increase. In the film example above, selling a second unit of film X requires a price drop of $1,000 while selling a second unit of film Y requires a price drop of $1,500 when each is sold separately. When offered as a bundle however, selling a second packaged unit requires a price drop of only $500. Bundling works because the variation in the willingness to pay for individual products is likely to be reduced when those products are packaged together.

Stigler's insight into bundling is surely valid. However, his analysis is incomplete on a number of fronts. First, his model implies that for bundling to be profitable consumer valuations must be distributed in a particular way. Suppose, for example that Station B also has a value for film Y of $2,500. Then the bundle price is $9,500, implying a total revenue of $19,000 with bundling which does no better than offering the films separately. In this case, there is no variation in the willingness to pay for film Y and bundling is not a profit-enhancing strategy. Second, Stigler's analysis does not address the central concern of the US Department of Justice and the European Commission: bundling as an entry deterring

---

[3]   See *United States v. Loew's Inc.*, 371 U.S. 38 (1962).

strategy. Third, Stigler's model fails to consider the strategy of *mixed bundling*—that is, selling both products individually as well as in a bundle. It is to these issues that we now turn.

To do so we begin with a variant of a (relatively) simple model developed by Nalebuff (2007). Assume that there are two goods, labeled 1 and 2. Each of these goods is produced with constant marginal (and average) cost that for the moment we assume to be zero. In other words, we assume that there are no cost advantages of multiproduct production. In particular, there are no scope economies of the type discussed in Chapter 4. Accordingly, the marginal cost of producing a bundle or a package consisting of one unit of each good is also zero.

We assume that each consumer buys exactly one unit of each good per unit of time provided that the price charged is less than the reservation price for that good. The consumer's reservation price, or maximum willingness to pay, for good 1 is R_1 and for good 2 is R_2. We further assume that the consumer's reservation price for a commodity bundle consisting of one unit of each good is $R_B = R_1 + R_2$. This assumption, that the reservation price for the bundle is the sum of the reservation prices for the individual goods, is a common one (and one made by Stigler as well). Yet the assumption is, at least in some circumstances, restrictive. If the two goods are complementary goods, such as nuts and bolts, the assumption is almost certainly false. We expect that the willingness to pay for bolts is quite low in the absence of any nuts and vice versa. In other words, for complementary goods the reservation price for the bundle is likely to be higher than the sum of the separate reservation prices for each good consumed separately. Yet while the assumption that $R_B = R_1 + R_2$ is restrictive, it is also useful. It permits us to focus explicitly on the profit and other motives for bundling. We return to the case of complementary goods in section 8.3.

Suppose that consumers differ in their separate valuations of the two goods—that is, the values of R_1 and R_2 (and so R_B) vary across consumers. Some consumers have a high R_1 and a low R_2; for others just the reverse is true. Some place a high value on both goods. For others, R_1 and R_2 are both quite low. If we draw a quadrant with R_1 on the horizontal axis and R_2 on the vertical axis as in Figure 8.1, then our assumptions allow us to define each

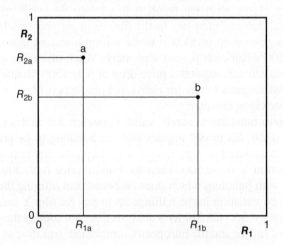

Figure 8.1   Consumer reservation prices

consumer's type by a point in the (R_1, R_2) quadrant. For example, consumers of type a in Figure 8.1 have reservations prices R_{1a} for good 1 and R_{2a} for good 2 while consumers of type b have reservations prices R_{1b} for good 1 and R_{2b} for good 2.

We make two further assumptions. First, we assume that that consumer valuations R_1 and R_2 are distributed on the range $[0, 1]$ so that the "market" can be described by the unit square as in Figure 8.1. Secondly, we assume that consumers are uniformly distributed at density D over this market. In other words, there are as many consumers of type a as there are of type b or of any other type in the market. These might on first sight appear to be limiting assumptions, but Nalebuff (2007) shows that if anything they understate the power of bundling to increase profit and deter entry.

8.1.1   Bundling and Profitability

Suppose first that the firm prices its two products separately, setting a price p_1 for good 1 and p_2 for good 2 as in Figure 8.2. It follows that all consumers with reservation prices $R_1 \geq p_1$ buy good 1 and all consumers with reservation prices $R_2 \geq p_2$ buy good 2. In Figure 8.2, all consumers in region A buy only good 1, those in region B buy only good 2, those in region C buy both goods 1 and 2, while those in region D buy neither good. This non-italicized D implies a portion of the market space while the italicized D implies market density. Aggregate demand for good 1 is the number of consumers in the rectangle A + C and for good 2 is the number of consumers in the rectangle B + C. In other words, $q_1 = D(1 - p_1)$ and $q_2 = D(1 - p_2)$.

Writing these demand functions in our familiar inverse form we have:

$$p_1 = 1 - q_1/D; \ p_2 = 1 - q_2/D \tag{8.1}$$

from which we derive the marginal revenues:

$$MR_1 = 1 - 2q_1/D; \ MR_2 = 1 - 2q_2/D \tag{8.2}$$

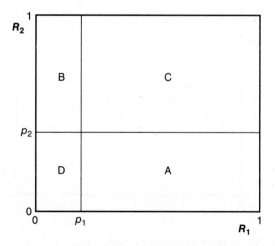

Figure 8.2 Consumers' reservation prices and simple monopoly pricing

At monopoly prices p_1 and p_2 Group A buys only product 1, Group B buys only product 2, Group C buys both goods, and Group D buys neither.

Equating marginal revenue with marginal cost (assumed equal to zero) gives

$$q_1 = q_2 = D/2$$

and from (8.1)

$$p_1 = p_2 = 1/2.$$

These are just the monopoly prices for the two products when they are sold separately. Profit from this non-bundling strategy is:

$$\pi_{nb} = 0.5D$$

Assume instead that the firm decides to offer the two products only as a bundle, with the bundle priced at $p_B < 1$. [4] This is illustrated in Figure 8.3.

Now consumers are partitioned into two groups. Each consumer in region E has reservation prices for the two goods the sum of which is greater than p_B and so buys the bundle. By contrast, each consumer in region F has reservation prices for the two goods the sum of which is less than p_B and so does not buy the bundle. Aggregate demand for the bundle is the number of consumers in region E, which is the total numer of potential consumers D minus the number of consumers in the triangle F. In other words, aggregate demand for the bundle at price p_B is

$$q_B(p_B) = D - Dp_B^2/2 = D(1 - p_B^2/2) \qquad (8.3)$$

Profit from this bundling strategy is (recall that marginal costs are assumed to be zero):

$$\pi_B(p_B) = p_B D(1 - p_B^2/2) \qquad (8.4)$$

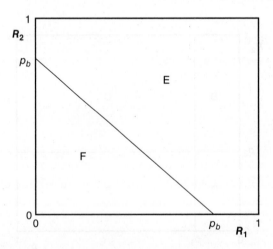

Figure 8.3   Monopoly pricing of a pure bundle of goods 1 and 2

At the bundle price p_B consumers in Group E buy the bundle and consumers in Group F do not.

---

[4]   As shown below, the optimal bundle price is always less than sum of the non-bundled monopoly prices.

Table 8.1   Profit from bundling

Bundle Price p_B	Profit
1	$0.5D$
0.9	$0.536D$
0.8	$0.544D$
0.7	$0.529D$
0.6	$0.492D$
0.5	$0.438D$

Table 8.1 evaluates this profit function for a range of bundle prices, from which we can conclude that the optimal bundle price is approximately $p_B = 0.8$. (We show in the Appendix to this chapter that the profit maximizing bundle price is actually $p_B = 0.816$ and that the resulting profit from the bundling strategy is $0.5443D$.)

As you can see, bundling increases profit by approximately 8.8 percent, not bad but perhaps not a lot to write home about or cause concern to the anti-trust authorities. Which brings us to the other possibility: that bundling is an entry-deterring device.

8.1.2   Bundling and Entry Deterrence

We continue with our simple model but now assume that the incumbent firm faces the threat of entry by a potential challenger that, by incurring fixed entry costs of F, can offer a perfect substitute for the incumbent's product 2. The incumbent remains the sole producer of product 1 whether or not entry takes place.[5]

Suppose first that the incumbent does not adopt a bundling strategy. Because it faces no challenge in its market for product 1, its price for that product is unaffected at $p_1 = 1/2$ and its profit from selling product 1 remains $D/4$. By contrast, in its product 2 market the incumbent has to identify a price that will deter entry. Suppose that the incumbent sets a price of $p_2 < 1/2$. The best strategy for the potential entrant is to just undercut that price, thereby stealing all of the incumbent's product 2 consumers. In Figure 8.4, consumers in regions A and C buy product 1 from the incumbent, while those in regions B and C switch to purchase product 2 from the entrant provided only that the entrant sets a price $p_2 - \varepsilon$ "just less" than p_2.

Profit to the entrant is

$$\pi_E = Dp_2(1 - p_2) - F \tag{8.5}$$

In order to deter entry, the incumbent has to set p_2 to ensure that $\pi_E < 0$. Define $f = F/D$, so that f is entry cost per consumer. We show in the Appendix that the entry-deterring price for the incumbent is

$$p_2^{nd} = \frac{1}{2}(1 - \sqrt{1 - 4f}) \tag{8.6}$$

---

[5]   Assuming that the entrant can offer only one product replicates our Microsoft example. Nalebuff (2007) assumes that the entrant can randomly produce either good 1 or good 2, which introduces complications that we would rather avoid. We address the credibility of entry deterrence in a two-product case in subsequent chapters.

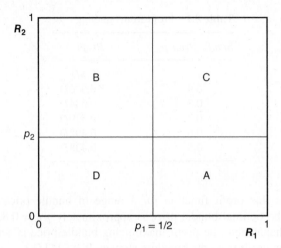

Figure 8.4   An incumbent threatened by entry—no bundling
The entrant sells product 2 to consumers is Groups B and C; the incumbent sells product 1 to consumers in Groups A and C.

Rather than use calculus, however, we adopt a simpler approach. Equation (8.5) can be used to identify, for a range of product 2 prices, the entry cost per consumer above which entry is unprofitable and so is deterred. Suppose, for example, that the incumbent sets price $p_2 = 0.4$. Then, from equation (8.5), the entrant, by just undercutting this price, earns profit $0.4D(1 - 0.4) - F = 0.24D - F$. This is negative, and entry is deterred, for $f = F/D \geq 0.24$. The results for this analysis are presented in Table 8.2.

Now think of this another way. Suppose that entry cost per consumer is $f = 0.24$. Then from Table 8.2 we can see that the incumbent can deter entry by setting its product 2 price at "just less" than 0.4: a price that completely limits entry. By applying such a *limit price* the incumbent earns aggregate profit $D(0.25 + 0.24) = 0.49D$. The first term in brackets is the monopoly profit from product 1 and the second is profit from product 2 given that price is set to deter entry. More generally, we can see from Table 8.2 that if the entrant's entry cost per consumer is f, entry deterrence gives the incumbent aggregate profit $D(0.25 + f)$.

This kind of entry deterrence is always profitable for the incumbent provided only that $f > 0$. Note also that entry is actually blockaded—not possible even if the incumbent adopts the simple monopoly price for product 2 —provided that $f > 0.25$.

Table 8.2   Entry deterrence—no product bundling

Incumbent Price for Product 2	Entry Deterring Cost per Consumer f	Aggregate Incumbent Profit
0.5	0.25	0.5D
0.4	0.24	0.49D
0.3	0.21	0.46D
0.2	0.16	0.41D
0.1	0.09	0.34D

Now suppose that the incumbent adopts a product bundling strategy, setting the bundle price at $p_B \leq 1$ and assume that the potential entrant sets its product 2 price at p_2. Consumers face three choices: continue to buy the bundle; switch to buying product 2 from the entrant, as a result of which the consumer cannot buy product 1; buy nothing. The consumer, as usual, picks the option that maximizes consumer surplus.

Consider a consumer with reservation prices (R_1, R_2). If this consumer buys the bundle from the incumbent the consumer surplus is $CS_B = R_1 + R_2 - p_B$ while if the consumer switches to buying only product 2 (from the entrant) the consumer surplus is $CS_2 = R_2 - p_2$. The consumers that switch to the entrant have reservation prices that satisfy two constraints:

$$CS_2 > CS_B \Rightarrow R_2 - p_2 > R_1 + R_2 - p_B \Rightarrow R_1 < p_B - p_2 \qquad (8.7)$$

$$CS_2 > 0 \Rightarrow R_2 > p_2 \qquad (8.8)$$

Constraint (8.7) ensures that the consumer prefers to purchase product 2 from the entrant rather than the bundle of product 1 and product 2 from the incumbent, while constraint (8.8) ensures that the consumer prefers to purchase product 2 from the entrant than to purchase nothing.

These constraints tell us that the consumers that switch from buying the bundle to buying product 2 from the entrant are consumers (i) with relatively low reservation prices for product 1—the product that they give up—and (ii) relatively high reservation prices for product 2—the product that they continue to purchase. Intuitively, the entrant in competing with the incumbent's bundled product is most likely to capture those consumers who really like product 2 but place a low valuation on product 1.

These constraints are illustrated in Figure 8.5. Constraint (8.8) is simply illustrated. Now consider constraint (8.7). Because the line $p_B p_B$ has slope -1, the distance ab equals the distance bc and both ab and $bc = p_B - p_2$. Thus all consumers with reservation prices to the left of the vertical line dce satisfy constraint (8.7) and all consumers in the region A + B satisfy *both* constraints (8.7) and (8.8).

In the absence of entry, consumers in regions B, C, and D purchase the bundle while consumers in regions A, E, and F do not. Post-entry, consumers in regions A and B purchase product 2 from the entrant, consumers in regions C and D continue to buy the bundle from the incumbent, while consumers in regions E and F buy neither the bundle nor the entrant's product 2.

It is here that we see the beginning of an explanation for why bundling might be an entry-deterring strategy. Suppose that the incumbent, instead of bundling, had priced the two products separately, with product 2 priced at p_2 and product 1 priced at $p_1 = p_B - p_2$ in Figure 8.5. If the entrant had priced product 2 at "Just less" than p_2 as in our analysis above, the entrant would have gained all consumers in regions A, B, and C, many more consumers than are gained when the incumbent bundles.

We can make this more precise. As we have seen in Figure 8.5, given that the incumbent sets the bundle price at p_B the entrant, setting its product 2 price at p_2, gains consumers in region A + B, whose area is $(1 - p_2)(p_B - p_2)$. Profit to the entrant is then:

$$\pi_E = Dp_2(1 - p_2)(p_B - p_2) - F \qquad (8.9)$$

A comparison with equation (8.5) indicates that, as we just suggested, the bundling strategy by the incumbent makes entry much less profitable, in other words, easier to deter.

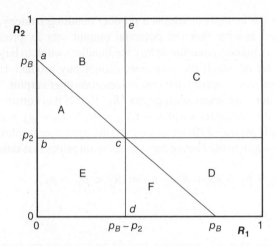

Figure 8.5   An incumbent threatened by entry—pure bundling
Post-entry consumers in Groups A and B buy product 2 from the entrant, consumers in Groups C and D buy the bundle from the incumbent, consumers in Groups E and F do not buy from either the incumbent or the entrant.

   With bundling, the incumbent actually has to go through a two-stage thought process in formulating its entry-deterring strategy. First, for any bundle price, the incumbent should expect the entrant to choose its entry price to maximize its profit as given by equation (8.9). We derive the optimal price for the entrant in the Appendix. Second, given this price for the entrant, the incumbent has to identify the bundle price that just deters entry.

   Rather than take this analytical approach, however, we mirror the non-bundling case by presenting a simplified numerical analysis. Table 8.3 gives the potential entrant's profit, *ignoring its entry costs*, for a range of combinations of the bundle price p_B and the entrant's price p_2. Given our analysis in the previous section, we can confine our attention to bundle prices less than 0.8.

   Suppose first that the incumbent acts as a monopolist facing no entry threat and sets a bundle price of 0.8. Then Table 8.3 tells us that the best the entrant can do is set a price for product 2 of approximately 0.3, giving the entrant profit of $0.105D - F$. This tells us that entry is blockaded with the bundling strategy for any entry cost per consumer $f > 0.105$. Contrast this with the non-bundling strategy. We saw there that for entry to be blockaded requires that $f > 0.25$. In other words, bundling significantly increases the range of entry

Table 8.3   Entrant's gross profit—product bundling

	Bundle Price p_B			
p_2	0.8	0.7	0.6	0.5
0.35	0.102	0.080	0.057	0.034
0.3	0.105	0.084	0.063	0.042
0.25	0.103	0.0844	0.066	0.047
0.2	0.096	0.08	0.064	0.048
0.15	0.083	0.07	0.057	0.045
Incumbent Profit	0.544D	0.529D	0.492D	0.438D

costs for which the incumbent is free of the threat of entry without the need to adopt a specific entry-deterring price.

We can repeat this analysis for different incumbent prices for the bundle. Suppose, for example, that the bundle is priced at 0.7. Then the entrant will set its product price p_2 to approximately 0.25, earning profit $0.0844D - F$. We can put this another way. Suppose that entry cost per consumer is $f = 0.0844$. Then the incumbent can deter entry by setting a bundle price "just less" than 0.7, earning profit $0.529D$. Similarly, if entry cost per consumer is $f = 0.066$, the incumbent can deter entry by setting the bundle price "just less" than 0.6, earning profit $0.492D$, and if entry cost per consumer is $f = 0.048$ entry is deterred by a bundle price of 0.5, giving the incumbent profit of $0.438D$.

We summarize these results in Table 8.4 from which we can see the real strategic power of bundling as an entry deterring device. If $f > 0.25$, entry is blockaded whether or not the incumbent bundles and bundling increases profit, but only by 8.8 percent. If $0.25 > f > 0.105$, entry is feasible without bundling but blockaded by bundling. Product bundling increases profit by up to 53 percent. At lower entry costs per consumer, bundling is less profitable, but even with f as low as 0.048 bundling increases profit by 47 percent.

The conclusion to be drawn from this analysis is straightforward. Product bundling is indeed a potent entry-deterring strategy, justifying the concerns that the anti-trust authorities have with this strategy.

8.1.3   Mixed Bundling

While Microsoft attempted to apply a pure bundling strategy with respect to the sale of its *Windows* operating system (bundling *Windows* with *Explorer* and *Windows Media Player*), it applies a rather different strategy with respect to its *Office* suite of programs. As we noted above, consumers can purchase the full suite of *Office* programs *or* they can purchase some but not necessarily all of the individual programs. This is an example of *mixed bundling*.

A possible explanation for the difference in strategy can be suggested. Microsoft had an effective monopoly on operating systems with its *Windows* program and so had the potential to leverage that monopoly into browsers and media player software. By contrast, Microsoft faces competition from established companies offering word processing, spreadsheet, and presentation programs. The best that it can do is to adopt some kind of profit maximizing strategy, mixed bundling being one such strategy.

Table 8.4   Bundling and entry-deterrence

Entry Cost per Consumer F	Incumbent Entry-Deterring Profit		Profit Increase from Bundling
	Non-Bundling	Bundling	
0.25	$0.5D$	$0.544D$	8.8%
0.20	$0.45D$	$0.544D$	20.9%
0.15	$0.40D$	$0.544D$	36%
0.105	$0.355D$	$0.544D$	53.2%
0.0844	$0.3344D$	$0.529D$	58.2%
0.066	$0.316D$	$0.492D$	55.7%
0.048	$0.298D$	$0.438D$	47%

Returning to our simple model of the last two sections, the monopolist applying a mixed bundling strategy offers to sell the two goods separately at specified prices, respectively, of p_1 and p_2 (which are not necessarily the monopoly prices) and also sells them as a bundle at price p_B (again not necessarily the monopoly pure bundle price). Of course, for this to make sense, it must again be the case that $p_B < p_1 + p_2$. Otherwise, no consumer would ever purchase the bundle. Figure 8.6 illustrates such a strategy. The monopolist offers consumers the possibility of buying either product 1 or product 2 individually at the stated prices or buying them as a bundle at price p_B.

We now show that consumers are partitioned by this strategy into four groups. To do so, we need to determine the conditions under which a consumer will prefer to buy only one of the two goods or the bundle or nothing.

Clearly, anyone who values good 1 at more than p_1 and good 2 at more than p_2, that is, anyone who is willing to buy both goods at the individual prices, will buy the bundle because its price is less than the sum of the individual prices. Consider now a consumer whose reservation price for good 1 is less than p_1. If this consumer buys anything, the consumer will buy either the bundle or only good 2. Of course, the consumer will make the choice that gives the greater consumer surplus. Suppose then that the corresponding reservation prices are R_1 for good 1 and R_2 for good 2. If the bundle is purchased, the consumer pays p_B and gets a consumer surplus of $CS_B = R_1 + R_2 - p_B$. If only good 2 is bought, the consumer gets a consumer surplus of $CS_2 = R_2 - p_2$.

This type of consumer will buy only good 2 if two conditions are satisfied. First, $CS_2 > CS_B$, which requires that $R_1 < p_B - p_2$. Second, $CS_2 > 0$, which requires that $R_2 > p_2$. We have already seen these conditions in our discussion of entry deterrence: see Figure 8.5. It follows that all consumers in the region *hef* in Figure 8.6, such as consumer y, buy only good 2.

By exactly the same argument, a consumer will buy only good 1 if two conditions are satisfied: first $R_2 < p_B - p_1$ and second $R_1 > p_1$. The difference $p_B - p_1$ is illustrated in Figure 8.6 by the line *jad* and all points to the right of *ab* represent consumers for whom $R_1 > p_1$. Therefore, all consumers with reservation prices in the region *dab*, such as consumer x, will buy only good 1.

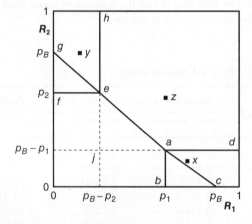

Figure 8.6 Monopoly pricing with mixed bundling

The firm sets prices p_1 for product 1, p_2 for product 2, and p_B for the bundle. Consumers in *dab* buy only product 1, consumers in *hef* buy only product 2, consumers in *daeh* buy the bundle, and consumers in *feab* buy nothing.

Now consider a consumer for whom $R_2 > p_B - p_1$ and $R_1 > p_B - p_2$. This is a consumer whose reservation price for good 1 is to the right of *jeh* and for good 2 is above *jad*. If such a consumer buys anything at all it will be the bundle, as this gives more consumer surplus than either only good 1 or only good 2. For this consumer to buy the bundle it is then necessary that $R_1 + R_2 > p_B$, which means that the reservation prices must put the consumer above the line *caeg* in Figure 8.6. In other words, all consumers in the region *daeh*, such as consumer *z*, will buy the bundle.

This leaves only the region *feab*. What will be the choice of these types of consumers? Their reservation prices are less than the individual prices of the two goods, so they will not buy either good individually. In addition, the sum of their reservation prices is less than the bundle price, so they will not buy the bundle. Consumers in *feab* do not buy anything.

Derivation of the optimal individual and bundle prices for our "simple" model is actually very complex. For the interested reader the derivation is provided in this chapter's Appendix. It turns out that for this model these prices are $p_1 = p_2 = 2/3$ and $p_B = 0.862$, giving the monopolist aggregate profit $0.549D$, greater than either simple monopoly pricing or pure bundling.

8.1.4 A Worked Example

When we compare either pure or mixed bundling with simple monopoly pricing, it is clear that mixed bundling always increases the monopolist's *sales*. What is less clear is whether bundling will increase the monopolist's *profits*. What we should expect is that the profit impact of commodity bundling will depend upon the distribution of consumer preferences for the goods being offered and the costs of making those goods, issues that our formal model has not really considered. An example will serves to illustrate this and some of the other ideas introduced so far.

Assume that the monopolist knows that it has four consumers, A, B, C, and D, each interested in buying the two goods, 1 and 2. The marginal cost of good 1 is $c_1 = \$100$ and of good 2 is $c_2 = \$150$. Each consumer has reservation prices for these two goods, as given in Table 8.5, and buys exactly one unit of either good in any period so long as its price is less than the reservation price for that good. Each consumer will consider buying the goods as a bundle provided that the bundle price is less than the sum of the reservation prices.

Suppose that the monopolist decides to sell the goods unbundled and adopts simple monopoly pricing. Table 8.6 allows us to identify the profit-maximizing monopoly prices for the two goods. Profit from good 1 is maximized at $450 by setting a price of $250 and selling to consumers B, C, and D. Profit from good 2 is maximized at $300 by setting a price of $450 and selling only to consumer A. Total profit from simple monopoly pricing is, therefore, $750.

Table 8.5 Consumer reservation prices

Consumer	Reservation Price for Good 1	Reservation Price for Good 2	Sum of Reservation Prices
A	50	450	500
B	250	275	525
C	300	220	520
D	450	50	500

Table 8.6 Determination of simple monopoly prices

Price	Quantity Demanded	Total Revenue ($)	Profit ($)	Price	Quantity Demanded	Total Revenue ($)	Profit ($)
450	1	450	350	450	1	450	300
300	2	600	400	275	2	550	250
250	3	750	450	220	3	660	210
50	4	200	−200	50	4	200	−400

Now consider the pure bundling strategy. The firm can: 1) choose a bundle price of $525, which will attract only consumer B; 2) choose a bundle price of $520, which will attract consumers B and C; or 3) choose a bundle price of $500, which will attract all four consumers. The third strategy is preferable because it yields a total profit of 4($500 − $100 − $150), or $1,000. Pure bundling is, in this case, preferable to simple monopoly pricing. However, under bundling, consumer A is able to consume good 1 and consumer D is able to consume good 2 even though they each value the relevant good at less than its marginal production costs. (This is also a feature of pure bundling in the previous model if we introduce non-zero marginal costs to that model.)

Can a mixed bundling strategy do better? Suppose first that the monopolist merely combines the simple monopoly and pure bundling strategies. That is, the firm sets a price of $250 for good 1, $450 for good 2, and $500 for the bundle. How will consumers respond to this pricing and product offering? Consumer A will not buy just good 1, and is indifferent between buying the bundle or only good 2 because in either case, the consumer earns zero surplus. However, the firm is definitely not indifferent. The firm makes a profit of $300 if consumer A buys just good 2 but only $250 if consumer A buys the bundle. Hence, the firm would like to find a way to encourage consumer A to opt only for good 2.

Now consider Consumer D. This consumer earns the greatest surplus if only good 1 is purchased, in which case consumer surplus is $200. Therefore, Consumer D will buy only good 1 and the profit to the monopolist from that sale will be $150. In this consumer's case, the monopolist would actually prefer that Consumer D buy the bundle at $500 from which the monopolist earns a profit of $250. Finally, consider consumers B and C. They are each unwilling to buy either good separately at the stated prices. However, each will buy the bundle giving a combined profit to the monopolist from both sales of $500.

Adding up the sales and related profits, we find that the proposed mixed bundling strategy gives the monopolist a total profit of $900 or $950, depending upon whether consumer A buys the bundle or only good 2. This is certainly better than simple monopoly pricing profit derived earlier of $750. But it is not as good as the profit of $1,000 earned in the pure bundling case of selling only the bundle at a price of $500.

However, with a little thought, it is easy to see how the monopolist can alter the current mixed bundling strategy to raise profits further. The insight is to change the prices to sort customers into different purchase choices. We have already noted that Consumer A is indifferent to buying just good 2 or the bundle at the current prices. A slight rise in the bundle price say, to $520, will definitely tilt this consumer to purchasing just good 2. Suppose that in addition the firm also raises the price of good 1 to $450, so that the new price configuration is: $p_B = \$520$, $p_1 = \$450$, and $p_2 = \$450$. Consumer A will now buy good 2. Consumer D will continue to buy good 1 and Consumers B and C will continue to buy the bundle. However, the price increases for good 1 and the bundle, respectively, let the monopolist earn an additional profit of $200 on its sale of good 1 to Consumer D, and $40 on its two bundle sales to Consumers B and C, while guaranteeing profit of $300 from Consumer A. Total profit is $300 + $270 + $270 + $350 = $1,190, which *does* exceed our pure bundling maximum.

This is actually the best that the monopolist can do in this example. The monopolist has extracted the entire consumer surplus of consumers A, C, and D and all but $5 of the consumer surplus of consumer B. In other words, the monopolist has done nearly as well as it would have done if it had been able to adopt first-degree price discrimination.

Mixed bundling (in which the bundle price is less than the price of buying each component separately) is always at least as profitable as pure bundling. The reason is simple enough to see. The worst that a mixed bundling strategy can do is to replicate the pure bundling strategy by setting arbitrarily high individual prices and a bundle price equal to the pure bundle price. However, it will usually be possible to improve on this by setting individual component prices that are sufficiently low to attract those who really just want the one item but high enough to earn more profit than can be earned from the bundle.

We should note, though, that while mixed bundling must always improve profits relative to pure bundling, it is not always the case that some sort of bundling is more profitable than no bundling at all. A drawback to bundling—one illustrated in the previous example—is that it can lead to an outcome in which some of the consumers who buy the bundle actually have a reservation price for one of the goods that is less than marginal production cost. This is inefficient and so the firm too would prefer a different pricing scheme. Our example also demonstrates that bundling, whether pure or mixed, is likely to be profitable only when the variation in consumer valuations of the goods is significant. In our example, consumers A and D—who buy a single good—have very different valuations of the individual goods. In contrast, consumers B and C—who buy the bundled good—have very similar valuations. Adams and Yellen (1976) made clear that the gains from bundling arise from the differences in consumer valuations.

> Some people may value an appetizer relatively highly (soup on a cold day), others may value dessert relatively higher (Baked Alaska, unavailable at home), but all may wish to pay roughly the same amount for a complete dinner. The à la carte menu is designed to capture consumer surplus from those gastronomes with extremely high valuations of particular dishes, while the complete dinner is designed to retain those with lower variance. (Adams and Yellen 1976, 488)

We can see the same basic point in the context of the Stigler example with which we started. If station A valued both movies at $8,000 and station B valued both at $3,500, the differences in the relative valuation of the products would vanish. In that case, bundling would no longer be a profitable strategy.

Note also that because the bundle price p_B is less than the sum of the individual prices $p_1 + p_2$ commodity bundling can be viewed as discriminatory pricing. The lower bundle price serves to attract consumers who place a relatively low value on one or other of the two goods but are willing to pay a reasonable sum for the bundle. The two separate prices serve to extract surplus from those customers who have a great willingness to pay for only one of the products. We would therefore expect most multiproduct firms with monopoly power to engage in some sort of mixed bundling.

Mixed bundling is in fact a common practice. Restaurants serve combination platters and also offer items individually. Resorts often offer food and lodging both separately and as a package. Software companies sell individual products but also offer packages consisting of several applications, such as Microsoft's *Office* package. Some of this surely reflects price discrimination efforts.

8.1

A cable company has two services. One service is the Basic Service channel. The other is the Walt Disney Movie channel. The potential subscribers for the services—students, families, hotels, schools, young adults, and retirees—regard the two services as separate alternatives, that is, not as complementary products. So, the demands for the two services are completely unrelated for each and every consumer. Each buyer is characterized by a pair of reservation prices as shown in the table below. The marginal cost of each service is $3. Assume there are equal numbers of consumers in each category.

a. If the services are sold separately and not offered as a bundle, what price should the cable operator set for each service? What profits will be earned? Which consumers will subscribe to which service?
b. Suppose that the operator decides to pursue a mixed bundling strategy. What price should be set for the bundled service? What price should be set for each service if purchased individually? Which consumers buy which options, and what are the cable operator's profits?
c. How would your answers to the first two questions be changed if the marginal cost of producing each service had been $10 instead of $3?

Reservation Prices for Each Cable Service by Type of Subscriber

	Basic Service ($)	Disney Channel ($)
Students	5	15
Families	11	9
Hotels	14	6
Schools	4	16
Young Adults	0	17
Retirees	17	0

8.2   REQUIRED TIE-IN SALES

Tie-in sale arrangements differ from bundling in that they tie together the purchase of two or more products without prescribing the amount that must be bought of at least one of these products. A further difference commonly but not always observed is that the tied goods typically exhibit a complementary relationship with each other whereas bundled goods need not. We now turn to a somewhat magical example to illustrate why tying is often an effective marketing strategy.

Consider an imaginary product called a *Magicam* that is produced by only one firm, Rowling Corp. A *Magicam* is much like an ordinary camera with one exception—the figures in a *Magicam* photograph can actually move and even wave back at the picture viewer because of Rowling's patented, magical method of placing the images on film. In all other respects, however, the *Magicam* is essentially identical to a typical real-world camera. In particular, both a *Magicam* and a regular camera can be used to make anywhere from one to a very large number of pictures per day or per month. It is up to the owner to decide how many pictures to take per period of time.

This fact does not mean that every consumer who has a *Magicam* will take a huge number of snapshots. After all, they have to pay for the film cartridge and spend time taking pictures rather than doing other things. Presumably, consumers differ in this regard. Suppose that there are one thousand low-demand consumers each with a monthly demand for pictures described by $Q = 12 - P$, and one thousand high-demand consumers each with a monthly demand for pictures given by $Q = 16 - P$. In other words, if cartridges of film were free, the first group of consumers would each take twelve pictures per month and the second group sixteen pictures. Unfortunately, Rowling Corp. has no way, magical or otherwise, of identifying these different types.

Because of the sensitive nature of the technology incorporated in *Magicams* we assume that Rowling Corp. does not sell the cameras but rather uses its monopoly power to offer them on monthly lease agreements that include servicing the camera to maintain its magical properties.[6] Given that the lease fee is set such that each of the two thousand consumers will lease a *Magicam* the manufacturing costs of the cameras become effectively fixed costs for Rowling Corp. The same is not true for the camera film. Suppose that film production takes place under competitive conditions and that the marginal cost of producing film is $2 per photograph that the film can take. This means, of course, that film will be priced at the competitive price of $2 per picture. Now consider Rowling Corp.'s potential strategies for leasing its cameras.

If a *Magicam* and camera film are all that is needed for producing the wonderful pictures, Rowling Corp. might find the situation somewhat frustrating. Because the firm cannot tell one type of consumer from another, the firm cannot easily lease its *Magicams* at different prices to each type. About the best that Rowling Corp. can do is to charge a monthly lease rate of $50. Why? Because this is the consumer surplus earned by a low-demand consumer faced with a film price of $2 per picture and Rowling Corp. cannot price discriminate across the two consumer types. (You should check that this is indeed the consumer surplus for a low-demand consumer when film is priced at $2 per picture.)

Both types of consumer will lease the camera. High-demand consumers will use it to take fourteen pictures per month while low-demand consumers will take ten pictures per month. Rowling earns a monthly profit of $50 on each of the 2,000 cameras leased—1,000 to the low-demand and 1,000 to the high-demand types—or $100,000 per month.

The situation is not desperate, but like any good profit-maximizer, Rowling wonders if somehow the firm can do better. After thinking a bit, Rowling management realizes that with some redesigning of the camera and a bit of clever marketing it can tie the lease of a *Magicam* to the use of its own *Magifilm*. This gives Rowling an idea. Why not implement a tying strategy and sell *Magifilm* cartridges at $4 per exposure?

Both low- and high-demand consumers now pay $4 at the margin for a picture. The low-demand consumers will therefore reduce their monthly demand for *Magicam* photos to just eight. And if low-demand consumers pay the $4 per picture price of *Magifilm*, they will enjoy a surplus of $32. Thus this surplus is the rental rate at which Rowling can lease the *Magicam*. (Notice the connection between this and our discussion of two-part pricing in

---

[6]   This is actually the strategy that IBM, Kodak. and Xerox used initially with their machines.

Chapter 6.) As a result, Rowling earns $32 from each of the 1,000 low-demand consumers in camera rentals and $16 from each in cartridge sales, giving a total profit of $48,000 from the low-demand customers.

High-demand consumers will also lease the *Magicam* at $32. However, at $4 per picture in film costs, these consumers will shoot twelve photos per month. Hence, Rowling earns a profit of $32 on cameras and $24 on film cartridges from each of the 1,000 high-demand customers, giving a total profit from this group of $56,000. In total, Rowling now earns a combined profit of $104,000 —greater than the $100,000 it earned without the tie-in. It has achieved this profit increase by exploiting its ability to *tie* the use of its camera to the use of its film.

To understand the way that tying helps Rowling, first note that high demand consumers receive a quantity discount under either of the two regimes. When the *Magicam* is leased for $50 and the film is purchased competitively at $2 per photo, high-demand consumers take fourteen photos and pay only $5.57 per shot, while low-demand consumers take ten pictures and pay $7 for each. Under the tied film arrangement, high-demand consumers pay a total charge of $80 for twelve pictures, or $6.67 per photo. By contrast, low-demand consumers pay a total of $64 and take only eight pictures per month, or $8 per photo. Thus, the tied sale is not attractive solely because it permits a quantity discount.

What tying does accomplish is to permit Rowling to solve the identification and arbitrage problems by exploiting its post-lease position as the monopoly seller of *Magifilm*. Now, the high-demand consumers are revealed by their film purchases to Rowling and the quantity discount is put to work in a profit-increasing way. Nor is arbitrage capable of undoing the discrimination. After all, both the camera and the film are readily available to all consumers at the same prices. Given that a single *Magicam* can serve either a low-demand consumer or a high-demand consumer equally well, solving the identification and arbitrage problems can only be achieved by tying its use to another product whose volume does change depending on the consumer's type. No consumer will ever lease more than one *Magicam*, but they will differ in terms of how much *Magifilm* they purchase.

Now let's take Rowling's case one step further. The low- and high-demand functions we have used may look familiar to you. They are the same ones we used in Chapter 6 in our discussion of quantity discounts with second-degree price discrimination. If you look back at that earlier example, you may get an idea of how Rowling can redesign and package the camera to do even better. For example, suppose that Rowling redesigns the *Magicam* so that the cartridge of *Magifilm* becomes an integral part of the camera that only Rowling's film developers can take out without destroying the camera.

Rowling can then design two varieties of its new, integrated *Magicam*, one of which has a ten-shot capacity and the other a fourteen-shot capacity.[7] The firm can offer to lease the ten-shot *Magicam* for $70 per month and the fourteen-shot *Magicam* for $88 per month. In both cases, the lease agreement also offers free developing as well as the free replacement of the cartridge. From our analysis in Chapter 6, we know what will happen in this case. Low-demand consumers will lease the ten-shot *Magicam* while high-demand consumers will lease the fourteen-shot *Magicam*. Rowling will then earn an even greater profit of $50,000 + $58,000 = $108,000. This technological integration plus the monthly leasing agreement has enabled Rowling to identify and separate the different customers even more profitably.

---

[7]   With marginal film costs of $2, these are the socially efficient quantities to offer.

Consider the *Magicam* story in the text. Again, let there be 1,000 high-demand and 1,000 low-demand consumers and let them have inverse demand functions of $P = 16 - Q$ and $P = 12 - Q$, respectively. Show that the price of \$4 per photo is, indeed, the profit-maximizing price for *Magifilm* when the film is sold separately from the camera. Now suppose that Rowling Corp. produces the integrated camera plus film cartridge in eight-shot and fourteen-shot varieties. What rental rates will be charged for the two varieties? What are Rowling Corp.'s profits? Finally, suppose that there are 1,000 low-demand consumers and N_h high-demand consumers. How many high-demand consumers would there have to be for Rowling to wish to manufacture only the fourteen-shot variety of integrated *Magicam* given that the other variety is

a.   ten-shot;
b.   eight-shot.

We have seen that, like bundling, tie-ins can be used to implement price discrimination schemes. This is no doubt one reason that tie-ins are frequently used, especially in situations where one of the components, like our fictitious *Magicam*, is capable of different intensities of use covering a very large range. Some tying is contractual, as in the case of IBM requiring the use of its punch cards for users of its punch card machines in the early days of computing. Some tying is technologically forced as in the *Magicam* and *Magifilm* example, or in the real-world case where Polaroid instant picture cameras used only Polaroid film. *Nintendo 64* players and *Game Boys* use only Nintendo or Nintendo-licensed games. Every manufacturer of computer printers designs their printers so that they use only their own ink cartridges. Again, these can be very useful product design strategies for extracting surplus from the market.

Price discrimination is not the only reason, however, that we may observe bundling and tying practices. As Judge Stevens made clear, an additional reason is that such practices may enhance monopoly power. At the same time, we also need to recognize that bundling and tying based on actual cost considerations will be observed in relatively competitive markets where they have little to do with discriminatory practices. We turn to these issues shortly, after first considering some aspects of complementary goods pricing.

8.3   COMPLEMENTARY GOODS, NETWORK EXTERNALITIES, AND MONOPOLY PRICING

The *Magicam* and *Magifilm* are complementary goods. In the days before the advent of digital cameras, there was no point in buying a camera—magical or otherwise—unless one also bought some film. Today, there is little point in owning a CD player without also purchasing CDs, an e-book reader without buying e-books, a PC without buying some software applications, or in buying bolts without buying nuts. In passenger airline manufacturing, it is necessary to have both engines and avionics equipment.

Sometimes the market for at least one of the complementary goods is reasonably competitive. Other times, the same firm may control both goods. However, there is a third possibility. This is that each of the complementary goods is produced by a different monopolist. There might be just one camera corporation and one separate film company.

Reality Checkpoint
The Bundled Skies

If you have purchased an airline ticket in the past year or two, you will have noticed that it is no longer a simple choice of aisle, center, or window, even if you restrict yourself to coach travel. These days air passengers can also select from options such as "Choice Plus," "Cabin Express," "Ascend," or "Lift." Airlines are rapidly becoming highly skilled at bundling choices in packages just as the cable companies, carmakers, and others have before them.

For example, American Airlines now offers both a *Choice Essential* and a *Choice Plus* travel option. For an extra $68, the first option permits one free checked bag and assigns the passenger to the first group to board. The second includes the privileges of *Choice Essential* but adds in an alcoholic beverage plus 50 percent extra frequent flyer miles, now for an additional $88. Delta's *Ascend* package costs $42 extra but gives the passenger priority boarding and free wi-fi. For just $120, JetBlue offers an *Even More Space* bundle of coach ticket, extra legroom, priority boarding, and express security clearance.

Originally, these options were offered as "extras" on airline websites. A passenger trying to obtain a ticket would first see the regular coach price and then each additional perk and the extra fee it required. Increasingly, however, the airlines are simply offering the bundles right up front. Thus, a visit to the American website in search of a Boston-to-LA flight may not find the generic coach ticket at all. Instead, the customer will see the various options—*Choice Essential, Choice Plus*, and so on—and have to pick one. Delta in fact is taking this bundling practice to the next level by tracking a customer's choice and designing a consumer-specific bundle for that person the next time he or she travels. Thus, having flown on Delta once already, a returning business customer may be targeted with an option that includes free wi-fi and a rental car on return.

As one might expect, these bundling efforts appear to have paid off. A number of estimates suggest that they have raised airline revenues by 10 percent. Those extra profits may be the biggest bundle of them all.

Source: S. McCartney, "Bundles of Travel Deals for Fliers," *Wall Street Journal*, January 31, 2013, p. D1.

As the French mathematical economist, Augustin Cournot, recognized over 150 years ago, this last situation may have particularly bad implications for both profit and efficiency.

Cournot's (1838) basic insight can be shown fairly simply. Suppose that the two complementary goods in question are nuts and bolts. A separate monopoly firm produces each and, to keep things simple, marginal production cost for each firm is zero. (We provide in the Appendix an alternative solution in which we allow the two firms to have different marginal costs.) The two goods are perfect complements. A consumer who wants to purchase 100 bolts also wants to purchase 100 nuts. In other words, the two goods are always consumed in the fixed proportion of one-to-one. For this reason, consumers care only about the combined price, $P_B + P_N$, in determining their demand. As you can see, the demands for the two products are clearly interrelated. The price of bolts will affect the demand for nuts and vice versa.

Suppose that the demand for nut and bolt pairs is given by the demand function

$$Q = 12 - (P_B + P_N) \tag{8.10}$$

Because consumers always buy the two goods together—one nut for every bolt—equation (8.10) also describes the separate demand facing each monopolist. That is, the bolt producer and the nut producer each face demand curves

$$Q_B = 12 - (P_B + P_N) \quad \text{Bolt Demand Curve}$$

$$Q_N = 12 - (P_B + P_N) \quad \text{Nut Demand Curve} \tag{8.11}$$

The problem with separate production is easy to see. The nut producer's pricing decision affects the bolt producer's demand curve, and vice versa. A change in the price of nuts not only changes the quantity demanded in the nut market but also in the bolt market. This implies that each firm's pricing decision has profit implications not just for itself but for the other firm as well. In other words, the pricing policy of either of the two firms imposes an externality on the other firm. In this situation, we might reasonably expect that a merger or creation of a business network to coordinate the pricing decisions of the two firms will offer significant advantages for them by at least partially correcting the market failure associated with the externality. Less obviously, but as we shall see nonetheless true, it is also possible that consumers will gain from such coordination.

Let's calculate the profit-maximizing decisions of the two firms, first without and then with coordination between them. We can rewrite the demand curves of equation (8.11) in inverse form.

$$P_B = (12 - P_N) - Q_B \quad \text{Inverse Demand Curve for Bolts}$$

$$P_N = (12 - P_B) - Q_N \quad \text{Inverse Demand Curve for Nuts} \tag{8.12}$$

From this we know that the marginal revenue curve facing each firm is

$$MR_B = (12 - P_N) - 2Q_B \quad \text{Bolt Marginal Revenue}$$

$$MR_N = (12 - P_B) - 2Q_N \quad \text{Nut Marginal Revenue} \tag{8.13}$$

Not surprisingly, just as each firm's demand curve depends on the other firm's price, so each firm's marginal revenue is affected by the other firm's price. When each firm independently maximizes its profit then each firm will choose an output where marginal revenue equals marginal cost, here assumed to be zero. So, setting each of the equations in (8.13) to zero and solving for Q_B and Q_N gives

$$Q_B = (12 - P_N)/2 \quad \text{Bolt Production}$$

$$Q_N = (12 - P_B)/2 \quad \text{Nut Production} \tag{8.14}$$

If we now substitute these outputs into the individual demand curves, we obtain each firm's optimal price as a function of the other firm's price, as follows:

$$P_B = (12 - P_N)/2 \quad \text{Bolt Price Rule}$$

$$P_N = (12 - P_B)/2 \quad \text{Nut Price Rule} \tag{8.15}$$

These equations show that each producer's corresponding profit-maximizing price depends on the price set by the other firm. Alternatively, the equations identify each firm's profit-maximizing choice of price given the price of the other firm's good. Whatever price is being charged by the nut firm is communicated to the bolt firm through the effect on the demand curve facing the bolt producer. If nut prices are high, the demand curve will be low. Alternatively, if nut prices are low, bolt demand will be strong. Taking the demand curve as given, the bolt producer simply picks the price–quantity combination that maximizes profits using the familiar profit-maximizing $MR = MC$ rule.

We can identify what the price equilibrium in the two markets will be by graphing equations (8.15) in a diagram with the two prices P_B and P_N on the axes. This is done in Figure 8.7. The more gently sloped line gives the bolt company's best choice of P_B for every nut price, P_N. For example, if the nuts were priced at zero, the profit-maximizing bolt price would be $6. If the nut price rises to somewhere near $12, the profit-maximizing bolt price falls to near zero. Higher nut prices reduce bolt demand and lower the bolt firm's profit-maximizing price. The more steeply sloped line describes the same strategic choices from the perspective of the nut company. This line describes the profit-maximizing choice of P_N for every choice of P_B.

Equilibrium occurs at the intersection. At this point, each firm has selected a price that is best given the price choice of the other firm. Accordingly, neither has an incentive to change. In order to identify this equilibrium, we substitute the equation for the nut price, for example, into the equation for the bolt price. This gives

$$P_B = \frac{1}{2}(12 - P_N) = \frac{1}{2}\left(12 - \frac{1}{2}(12 - P_B)\right) = \frac{12}{4} + \frac{P_B}{4} \text{ so that } \frac{3P_B}{4} = 3 \text{ or } P_B = 4$$

(8.16)

This tells us that the profit-maximizing bolt price is $P_B = \$4$. Substituting into equation (8.15) gives the profit-maximizing nut price as $P_N = \$4$. As a result, the combined nut/bolt price is $P_B + P_N = \$8$, and from the demand equation (8.10), the number of bolt and nut pairs sold is four. The bolt firm makes profits of $P_B Q_B = \$16$, as does the nut producer.

Now consider what happens if the two firms merge and the newly combined firm markets a single, "bundled nut-and-bolt" product. Such a firm faces the joint demand curve of equation (8.10) and so recognizes that the relevant price to customers is the sum of individual bolt and nut prices, or the total price paid for the bundled nut-and-bolt product. The marginal

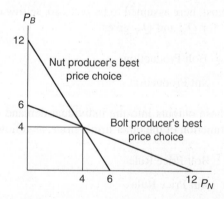

Figure 8.7   Pricing of complementary goods: the nuts and bolts case

revenue curve associated with the demand curve of equation (8.10) is $MR = 12 - 2Q$, where Q is the number of nut-and-bolt pairs sold. Equating marginal revenue with marginal cost identifies the optimal quantity of nut-and-bolt pairs to sell. Because we have assumed that marginal cost is zero, it is easy to see that the optimal quantity of nut-and-bolt pairs that the merged monopolist should offer for sale is $Q^* = 6$. The demand function then tells us that each pair can be sold at a combined price of $P^* = \$6$ (or separate prices of \$3 each). The merged firm's total profit is $P^*Q^* = \$36$.

Comparing these values with those obtained earlier, when the firms set their prices independently of each other, shows that a merger of the two firms leads to lower prices and more output than when the two firms act separately. This is because the merged firm understands the interaction of demands between the two products. As a result of coordinating nut and bolt production and pricing, consumers are made better off by this merger. Moreover, the profit of the combined firm exceeds the sum of profits earned by the two separate firms. This was Cournot's basic point.[8] By internalizing the interdependence of the two firms, both consumers and producers gain.

Merger is not the only way to achieve this outcome. Alternative means of coordinating the separate decisions of the two firms exist. For example, they could decide to form a product network. Examples include Automatic Teller Machine (ATM) networks, airline computerized reservation systems (CRS), real estate multiple-listing services (MLS), markets for interactive components such as computer CPUs and peripherals, and long-distance and local telephone services. Where they exist, such networks have been created by the joint action of many firms with the aim of taking better account of the interactions between the demands for the firms' complementary products.

Alternatively, we might hope for one or both markets to become competitive. If this happened in only one of the two markets, say bolts, then the bolt price would fall to marginal cost, which in this case was assumed equal to zero. Each firm in the bolt market would be so small that it could not possibly impose any external effects on the nut-producing monopoly. Given a zero price for bolts, equations (8.15) imply that the profit maximizing price for nuts—and therefore of a nut-and-bolt combination—would be \$6. Accordingly, this outcome would duplicate that which occurs under merger. If both markets were to become competitive, then bolt price and the nut price would each fall to marginal cost. This, of course, would yield the maximum total surplus and all of that surplus would accrue to consumers.

There is a factor that can work against the emergence of competition in markets for complementary goods. That factor is the presence of network externalities. For some goods and services, there is a scale economy effect that operates on the demand side of the market. For example, the more consumers that are connected to a phone system, the more valuable the phone system is to existing and new consumers. Each consumer who connects to the phone system generates an external benefit to all those already connected and makes the system more attractive to potential consumers. Sometimes this feature is described as a positive feedback.

Product complementarities of the sort we have been discussing here can also give rise to a positive feedback. Consider the Microsoft case. Microsoft's operating system *Windows* serves as the platform from which software applications such as word processing packages,

---

[8]   Allen (1938) made the same point with regard to the price-reducing effects of merging two complementary-goods monopolies. A calculus-based presentation of a more general form of our analysis is provided in the Appendix.

computer games, and graphic arts programs can be launched. A technical aspect of this relationship is that the code for a particular application must include an applications program interface (API) in order to work with the operating system. Typically, the API that works with one operating system will not work with another. In other words, applications such as *Stata* or *Mathematica* must be written to work on a specific operating system such as *Windows*, *Mac OS*, or *Linux*. The two products, the applications and the operating system, are therefore complements.

Two additional features of the design and production of applications programs are also important. First, their production exhibits substantial scale economies. The cost is almost entirely in the design phase. Once the underlying source code is written, the program can be put on CD-ROMs (or websites) and sold (or downloaded) to millions of consumers almost costlessly. Second, there is a network externality in that the more people use the application, the more consumers will want to use it. It is convenient to know that I can put my presentation graphics on a memory stick or in an e-mail attachment and have it read by a colleague miles away because we both use the same graphics software. For both of these reasons, firms that make these software applications have an incentive to design them to work with the most widely used operating systems because this permits the firms to exploit these supply-side and demand-side scale economies more effectively.

By exactly the same reasoning, the operating system that consumers will want the most is the one for which there are the most applications. The complementary relationship between applications and operating system has resulted in a very favorable positive feedback for Microsoft's *Windows*. As *Windows* became the dominant operating system, applications were increasingly written to run on it. In turn, this ever-expanding menu of applications greatly fortified the position of *Windows* as the dominant system. This interaction is sometimes called the *applications barrier to entry*. The idea is that any would-be rival operating system will have a great deal of difficulty entering the market. Applications producers will not have an incentive to design their products to run on the alternative system until it has a significant market share. Yet the system will never get any sizable market share unless applications are written for it.

What this analysis suggests is that there is a countervailing force to the benefits from closer coordination in the production and marketing of complementary products. Although it is generally true that coordination is profitable and, as our nut and bolt example indicates, is beneficial for consumers, when there is monopoly power in the production of the complementary goods the network effects, and the positive feedback that they generate means that monopoly power can be enhanced. This is one way in which monopoly power in one product line could be extended or leveraged to others.

8.4   ANTITRUST, BUNDLING, AND TIE-IN SALES

We are now in a better position to consider the antitrust issues raised by bundling and tie-ins. The main question is whether such practices may be used by firms with significant market power either to sustain or to extend that power against competitors or potential competitors. We illustrate these issues first with a review of the Microsoft case with which we opened this chapter. We then briefly discuss other cases and legal developments in this area. (See Economides and Salop (1992) for a more complete discussion.)

8.4.1   Bundling and the Microsoft Case

A central issue in the government's case against Microsoft was the claim that Microsoft had integrated or bundled its browser, *Internet Explorer*, directly into its operating system *Windows* as a means to eliminate the rival browser, Netscape's *Navigator*, from the market. The argument was that because Microsoft had monopoly power in the operating systems market, every consumer of *Windows* would now find *Internet Explorer* as the default browser thereby eliminating or greatly reducing Netscape's market share. To prove its claim and demonstrate a violation of the antitrust laws, the government would have to show 1) that Microsoft did possess monopoly power, 2) that an operating system and a browser were two related but distinct products that did not need to be tightly bundled, and 3) that Microsoft's practices constituted an abuse of its power motivated by the firm's desire to maintain or extend its dominant position.

In light of the foregoing, it is worthwhile recalling Judge Jackson's three key findings of fact. First, the judge found that Microsoft is indeed a monopoly in the sense of the Sherman Act. The evidence for this finding appears reasonably strong. At the time of the trial, *Windows* had over 90 percent of the operating systems market and had maintained that share of the market for well over a decade. Additionally, Microsoft's use of mixed bundling and other price discriminatory practices provided further evidence of something less than a competitive market. Both the structural and behavioral evidence provided some support to Judge Jackson's finding that Microsoft possessed monopoly power.

The judge's second finding was that an operating system and an Internet browser are two separate albeit complementary products. Microsoft had argued that a browser was really just an integrated part of a modern operating system. Just as flash bulbs that used to be sold separately had become technologically embedded in cameras themselves, Microsoft claimed that similar technological developments had led it to make its browser, *Internet Explorer*, an integral part of its *Windows* operating system. Microsoft further alleged that separation of the two could not be achieved without damaging at least one of them. However, the fact remained that Netscape still marketed its *Navigator* browser independently, suggesting that consumers did not demand an integrated operating system and browsing experience. In addition, evidence was presented at the trial showing that it was relatively easy to separate *Internet Explorer* from the operating system with which Microsoft had bundled it, without harming either product. Therefore, Judge Jackson's finding that *Windows* and *Internet Explorer* are separate products could also be justified.

In light of these first two findings, Microsoft's only remaining defense is that even though it possesses monopoly power, its practice of bundling its distinct operating system and browser products did not amount to "acting badly." In other words, arguing that its integration of *Windows* and *Internet Explorer* was not done with a view to hurt competition but instead to help consumers in order to avoid a finding that it had violated the antitrust laws. One way to make such a defense would be to pursue the coordination argument that we discussed above. That is, Microsoft might argue that the complementarity between an operating system and a browser requires coordination of the marketing of the two products in order to ensure that consumers receive both goods at low prices. Microsoft could then make a case that its behavior was in fact pro consumer.

As we saw in the previous section, the existence of a complementary relationship between two products can lead to serious inefficiencies if each product is produced by a separate monopoly. This was arguably the case in the software industry. Microsoft's *Windows* controlled the lion's share of the operating systems market and Netscape's *Navigator* dominated the complementary browser market. There was a good case to be made that some mechanism for coordinating the marketing of these two products was desirable. One way to achieve this coordination is by means of a merger of the two firms.[9] What happens, however, if one of the firms does not want to merge?

For example, suppose that Netscape feels that, as a much smaller company, any merger would amount to its being swallowed up by Microsoft and losing all its managerial independence. Its management might then decide to reject a merger proposal and to continue the separate marketing of its browser. In these circumstances, we can imagine that Microsoft might decide to create its own browser and bundle it with its operating system.

We can illustrate how the market outcome might evolve, again using our simple nut/bolt example. Suppose that the demand by consumers who want both an operating system and a web browser is given by

$$Q = 12 - (P_O + P_B). \tag{8.17}$$

where the subscripts "O" and "B" now indicate operating system and browser, respectively. Again, let us also simplify by assuming that marginal costs for both products are zero. (We noted earlier that for software, this assumption is actually quite realistic.)

Our nut/bolt example above tells us that, when operating independently, Microsoft will sell its operating systems at $P_O = \$4$ and Netscape will sell its browser at $P_B = \$4$, so that the price of a combined operating system and browser service is $8. We also know that this is an inefficient outcome. If the two firms coordinate or become one firm, the price of a combined system falls to $6. Total profit of the two firms would simultaneously rise.

If a merger with Netscape is rejected, Microsoft might then develop its own browser, which we also assume can be produced at a marginal cost of zero. It would then appear that Microsoft could offer the operating system at $3 and the browser at $3, or a package price of $6. However, this ignores the competition from Netscape. If Microsoft proceeds with this plan, Netscape can no longer offer its browser at a price of $4. It could, however, offer to sell its browser at a price of $2. After all, this is still well above marginal cost. Moreover, this price is sufficiently low that consumers would then be attracted to the Netscape browser while still buying Microsoft's operating system at the price of $3. Of course, Microsoft would then want to reduce the price of its browser, perhaps to $1.95. Netscape would then respond by selling its browser at perhaps $1.80, and so on.

What we have just described is an outbreak of price competition in the browser market. The ultimate effect of this price competition will be to drive the browser price to marginal cost—in this case to zero. This is certainly bad news for Netscape. What about Microsoft? A review of its optimal pricing strategy as given by equations (8.17) implies that when the browser price falls to zero, Microsoft's optimal price for operating systems rises to $6. Further, a browser price of 0 implies that $6 is also the best price for a combined operating system and browser package—exactly as would occur if the two firms merged. Moreover, the profit increase that a merger would bring is also realized, although it now goes entirely to Microsoft. In other words, a merger is not the only way to solve the coordination problem. Competition in one of the markets will remove the inefficiency that would otherwise result when each market is monopolized and the monopolists fail to coordinate their pricing. Prices are lower and both consumer and producer surplus have increased.

---

[9]   In June of 1995, Microsoft did in fact offer to work cooperatively with Netscape in the browser market and, allegedly, even suggested a merger—a proposal that was rejected by Netscape.

It is insightful to note that the outcome of the "browser war" just described involves a final browser price of zero. That is, in equilibrium Microsoft sells its operating system for $6 and then throws in its browser for free. This looks very much like bundling, the only complicating factor being that Netscape is also offering a free browser and so can be expected to retain a share of the browser market.

Review of the foregoing scenario should make clear that the accusation that Microsoft bundled its browser with its operating system to exploit its monopoly power and harm competitors can be challenged. Microsoft could legitimately argue that it has simply acted in a way that promotes price competition and that the lower browser prices are just a reflection of this fact. In this view, Microsoft's actions have been pro-competitive, not anti-competitive.

There is, however, an additional aspect to the case that we must consider. This involves the interaction between complementary products and network externalities. The complementarity between operating systems and the applications written for them has created a substantial positive feedback loop for Microsoft. Because *Windows* had a monopoly in operating systems, the majority of applications were written to run on *Windows*. In turn, because most applications were written for *Windows*, no other operating system could challenge the *Windows* dominance. Internet browsers, however, offered a potential way around this problem. The advent of the JAVA programming language developed by Sun Microsystems and other technical advances make it possible to run applications on an Internet browser. The browser itself therefore can serve as a platform from which to launch applications.

If *Navigator* can serve as an applications platform, then even after the development of *Internet Explorer*, *Navigator* would be expected to retain a reasonable share of the browser market. In turn, the existence of this alternative platform with a substantial market share means that design firms could begin to write their applications to run on an alternative to *Windows*. As this happened, *Navigator* would benefit from the same positive feedback that *Windows* enjoyed. As more applications could be run from the browser, the browser would become more popular and still more applications would be written for it. Clearly, such a development would strike at the core of Microsoft's success by leading to fierce competition in the platform market. Testimony at the trial revealed that Microsoft management was both aware and fearful of this development.

In light of the foregoing, Microsoft's explicit bundling of *Internet Explorer* with its *Windows* operating system takes on a different light. Instead of a competitive act that reduces a coordination inefficiency between complementary products, Microsoft's bundling can also be viewed as a deliberate effort to reduce Netscape's share of the browser market so that the Netscape browser becomes an unattractive alternative to applications designers. In turn, this would eliminate Netscape as a threat to Microsoft's operating system monopoly. Indeed, Microsoft initially required that PC manufacturers such as Compaq and Dell, who installed *Windows* as their operating system also install *Internet Explorer* as the default browser appearing on the *Windows* desktop. They did this presumably on the supposition that most consumers want only one browser even if a second can be obtained for free. The subsequent integration of *Internet Explorer* into the *Windows* software could be viewed as an attempt to replace contractual bundling with technological bundling.

Whatever the type of bundling, however, the foregoing analysis sees the motive as the same—namely the prevention of Netscape developing a viable competitor to Microsoft. This alternative interpretation of Microsoft's behavior does imply a violation of the antitrust laws because it alleges that Microsoft abused its power primarily to sustain its monopoly, that is, to hurt competition. In support of this argument, the Justice Department offered much suggestive evidence only a portion of which we can summarize here.

First, there were internal Microsoft documents revealing management's concern over the potential threat that Netscape might pose to the dominance of *Windows* as the applications platform. Second, some additional evidence of malicious intent was that in addition to its bundling strategy that effectively required *Windows* users to acquire *Internet Explorer* as their default browser, Microsoft also pressured Macintosh to support *Internet Explorer* as its default browser. It did so by refusing to develop applications, such as its *Office* products, for the Macintosh computers unless Macintosh complied. Because Macintosh computers do not use the *Windows* operating system, this action was hard to justify as reflecting a technical improvement to *Windows* in the way that an internal flash device was an improvement to cameras. Finally, and perhaps even more damaging, was the fact that Microsoft actually paid Internet service providers such as America-On-Line (AOL) to adopt its browser and even gave AOL a space on the *Windows* desktop. Because AOL competed directly with Microsoft's own Internet service, this action is again hard to understand except as a way to foreclose the AOL market to Netscape. [See also Rubinfeld (2003)]

Ultimately, Judge Jackson found the evidence compelling that Microsoft abused its market power and used bundling to extend its dominance to the browser market. To some extent, this is what the appellate court later found as well. However, that court differed strongly with Judge Jackson regarding his opinion that the appropriate remedy for violation was to break up Microsoft into separate companies much as John D. Rockefeller's Standard Oil was broken up ninety years earlier. Instead, the court remanded the case to Judge Colleen Kollar-Kotelly who worked out a less drastic remedy based on restrictions on Microsoft's actions along with monitoring to ensure that those restrictions were enforced.[10] While this settlement went forward and the case is now over, the issues it raised remain to this day. As we noted in the introduction to this chapter, Microsoft continued to be the object of European antitrust lawsuits most notably in connection with its audio-visual software, *Media Player*. Likewise, both Google and its Android operating systems have been the focus of antitrust investigations rooted in bundling/tying and complementarities, e.g., the Android operating system and its several mobile applications.

8.4.2   Antitrust Policy, Bundling, and Tying: Additional Developments

The issues raised in the Microsoft case are not new. The fear that large, established firms could abuse their market power and prevent or eliminate competition is what lies at the heart of antitrust policy. As noted in Chapter 1, Section 1 of the Sherman Act explicitly proscribes monopoly power whenever its exercise weakens competition. Moreover, the subsequent Clayton Act speaks rather directly to the issue of bundling or tying: "It shall be unlawful . . . to lease (or sell) goods . . . on the condition, agreement, or understanding that the lessee or purchaser thereof shall not use or deal in the goods . . . of a competitor or competitors of the lessor or seller, where the effect . . . may be *to substantially lessen competition or tend to create a monopoly in any line of commerce*" [emphasis added]. While we postpone a formal analysis of anti-competitive tactics until Chapters 12 and 13, now is a good time to consider antitrust policy responses to the anticompetitive potential of bundling and tying.

Two key cases established a clear legal presumption against tie-in requirements. The first was the United Shoe case of 1922. As a result of over fifty mergers, the United Shoe company had emerged as the dominant maker of shoe-manufacturing machinery in the early twentieth century with a market share on the order of 80 to 90 percent. Shoe-making uses a number of machines, however, and United Shoe faced competition in at least some of these lines. In leasing its machines to shoe manufacturers, it stipulated that the manufacturers could not use any United Shoe machines in combination with those of other rival manufacturers and also that the shoe manufacturers had to buy certain supplies exclusively from United Shoe. Twenty-five years later, the court confronted a similar case with the International Salt Company. That company refused to lease its salt processing machines unless the lessee also agreed to purchase all of its salt from International Salt. In this case, the court inferred International Salt's monopoly power largely from the fact that the company had a patent on its machines. The court found that both the United Shoe and International Salt tying requirements violated the antitrust statutes.[10] In these cases and others (including one involving IBM), the court emphasized the defendant firm's monopoly power in the tying good. As a result, the conventional legal wisdom was that tying requirements imposed by large, dominant firms would almost constitute a *per se* violation of the antitrust laws.

Over the years, the court's views on tying mellowed. In part, this was the result of an important insight of the Chicago School. This insight was that tying contracts as a means of leveraging a firm's power in one market to power in another would make little sense in a wide class of cases. Recall our nut and bolt example. Assume that bolts are monopolized but nuts are competitive. As we showed earlier, the bolt monopolist would then set a price of $6 and earn a profit of $36. Suppose now that this monopoly bolt firm uses a tying clause to require the use of its own nuts and thereby extends its monopoly power to this second market, as well. We know that this would allow the firm to raise the price of nuts to say, $2. However, if it does this, the firm will need to lower the bolt price to $4 because what consumers really want is the nut-and-bolt combination and the profit-maximizing price for that combination is still $6, and the maximum profit earned is still $36. The point of this Chicago School argument is that there is a potential maximum monopoly profit in these two markets and the monopolist can get all of the profit in the bolt market if the nut market is competitive, thereby removing any incentive to extend its monopoly to nuts via a tying requirement.

As both the Nalebuff (2007) theoretical model and the historical practice revealed by the Microsoftcase shows, however, there is a qualification to this argument. When the market for the tied good involves substantial scale or scope economies, an incumbent can use tying (and bundling) and so leverage power from one market into another and can do so profitably. Strategic use of these practices by an incumbent can serve to deny these economies to rivals and potential entrants and thereby weaken or eliminate their ability to compete in either of the tied good markets. As a result, the incumbent can preserve and increase its profits by reaping those economies for itself.

Recognition that the leverage of market power may sometimes be anticompetitive has led the court to move cautiously in relaxing its earlier strict rules against tying and bundling. In 1960, the Supreme Court accepted the use of a tied-sales clause in a case involving Jerrold Electronics Corporation, a pioneer in cable television systems and the community antenna television (CATV) industry, because it felt that this was a legitimate way of guaranteeing quality performance of a service in the early, developmental stage of an

---

[10] *United Shoe Machinery Corp.* v. *United States*, 258 U.S. 451 *International Salt Co.* v. *United States*, 332 U.S. 392 (1947). Peterman (1979) argues that the fact that firms were allowed to use salt from producers other than International Salt if it was cheaper suggests that the real purpose of the tying was to reveal to International Salt the pricing practices of its rivals.

industry.[11] Subsequently, in the 1984 *Jefferson Parish* case, the Supreme Court attempted to articulate a clear set of guidelines under which any such arrangement would be *per se* illegal. The case involved a requirement by the Jefferson Parish Hospital that to use its surgical services it was necessary to use the group of anesthesiologists with whom the hospital had an exclusive contract. In its decision, which found for the hospital, the Court stated three conditions, all of which would have to be met for the tie-in to violate antitrust laws.[12] These are

1. the existence of two distinct products, the tying product and the tied one;
2. the firm tying the products must have sufficient monopoly power in the tying market to force the purchase of the tied good; and
3. the tying arrangement must foreclose, or have the potential to foreclose, a substantial volume of trade.

The logic behind these conditions is clear enough. It would be wrong, for example, to consider a computer and its power cord as two separate products and then claim illegal tying. Likewise, the anticompetitive abuse of market power is only plausible if a firm has such power in the first place. Yet the result of these efforts in practice has been a curious mixture of *per se* and rule of reason standards. On the one hand, the *Jefferson Parish* standards are meant to establish conditions under which bundling and tying are *per se* illegal. On the other hand, the interpretation of those standards is open to enough variation that a sort of rule of reason has emerged about whether they apply. Despite this ambiguity, it remains the case that tying arrangements tend to be viewed more harshly than bundling arrnagements by the anti-trust authorities. One result has been that plaintiffs may attempt to argue that a bundling pratice is actually a tying arrangement.

One troubling feature of the foregoing judicial history is that so little attention has been paid to cost-based reasons for bundling and tying. Yet there can be little doubt that such cost-efficiencies are present. This is because we see bundling and tying requirements in many competitive situations where neither price discrimination nor the extension of monopoly power can be the motive. This point has been particularly emphasized in a series of papers by Evans and Salinger (2005) and Evans (2006).

To understand the intuition of the Evans and Salinger (2005) argument, consider the case of head cold remedies. Some cold sufferers primarily endure headaches and sore throats. For these consumers, the main treatment they want is pain relief. Others, however, find sinus congestion and irritation to be the main aggravating symptoms. These consumers want a decongestant in their cold remedy. Of course, there is also a third group that wants both a pain reliever and a decongestant.

As a specific example, let us assume that there are 50 people in each of the first two groups and 100 in the third. Members of each group have a sufficiently high reservation price that they will always buy the product. Let us also assume that to produce, package, and market each cold remedy drug for this market incurs a fixed cost of $300. Further, assume that the marginal cost of producing and packaging either a bottle of pain relief medicine or a package of decongestants is $4, but that there are some marginal cost savings in putting the two in one pill so that the marginal cost of a combined, pain reliever and

[11] *United States v. Jerrold Corporation*, 187 F. Supp. 545 (1960), affirmed *per curiam* at 363 U.S. 567 (1961).
[12] *Hyde v. Jefferson Parish Hospital District No. 2, et al.*, 466 U.S. 2, 15–18 (1984).

decongestant product is just $7. Finally, rather than assume a perfectly competitive market, we will assume that there is just one firm. However, we will also assume that entry is easy and costless so that that firm is constrained to offer products at prices that just permit it to break even. Table 8.7, below shows the possible product offerings and the associated zero-profit prices.

Let's first think about our firm just offering the pain reliever and the decongestant separately. The first group of consumers will buy the pain reliever, the second will buy the decongestant, and the third group will want to buy both products. So, demand for each product is 150 implying an average fixed cost for each drug of $300/150 = $2. When added to the marginal cost of $4, the break-even price is $6. However, this outcome is not an equilibrium. Any firm could enter the market and sell just the bundle for $10.00. This would attract all of the 100 consumers who want a combined medication, because they currently pay $6 + $6 = $12 to get both types of relief. In turn, the loss of these customers would make the continued offering of the two separate products at a price of $6 impossible as the average cost of each of these would now rise to $10. Indeed, because this price is the same as the bundle price, we might imagine that some of these consumers will actually buy the bundle as it gives them the relief they want plus a little something extra. As this happens, however, the bundle price falls further due to additional fixed cost savings while the individual prices must rise further. This will push all 200 customers to buy the bundle at which point the break-even price for the bundle drops to $8.50. This is, in fact, the only sustainable price and product combination. It is therefore the equilibrium in this imperfectly competitive but contestable market.[13]

The scenario just described is worth some reflection. Competitive pressures police the market and force prices to equal costs. Even so, the firm in the market offers only the two goods, pain reliever and decongestant, together in one package. No consumer can buy this firm's pain relief medicine without also buying its decongestant. This is definitely a case of tying. Yet the tying is not done either to price discriminate or to extend monopoly power. It is simply another result of the competitive pressure to offer low-cost medication.

The idea that competition underlies much of the tying and bundling we observe is precisely the point that Evans and Salinger (2005) and Evans (2006) make. In their view,

Table 8.7 Pure bundling as the sustainable equilibrium

Demand Volume	Product		
	Pain Relief 50	Decongestant 50	Bundle 100
Costs			
Fixed Cost	$300	$300	$300
Marginal Cost	$4	$4	$7
Possible Prices Under:			
Separate Goods	$6	$6	—
Pure Bundling	—	—	$8.5
Mixed Bundling	$10	$10	$10
Bundle and Good 1	$10	—	$9
Bundle and Good 2	—	$10	$9

[13] A review of Table 8.7 will make it clear why either mixed bundling or offering a bundle and one good separately also cannot be an equilibrium.

these practices are far too common to be explained either by price discrimination or monopolization motives. They note as well that even when price discrimination is the cause, the market outcome does not merit policy intervention. Hence, the only time that tying or bundling is definitely harmful is when it is used for leveraging market power. Given that some large scale and possibly scope economies are required to make the leveraging argument powerful, these authors and others have argued that all attempts at a *per se* illegal rule is misguided. Instead, they call for an explicit use of a rule of reason with a general presumption that the tying is legal unless the intent and ability to extend market power is explicitly shown.

8.5   EMPIRICAL APPLICATION: BUNDLING IN CABLE TV

As we have seen, the enhanced profitability that a firm with market power can gain from bundling stems from reducing the variation in consumers' willingness to pay. As a result, selling the bundle to a large range of consumers requires a much smaller price reduction than selling each product individually to an equally large group. In other words, bundling makes demand more sensitive to prices—more price elastic.

The prediction that bundling makes demand more elastic and that, as a result, it can be used to enhance a firm's profit is examined in recent work by economist Gregory Crawford (2008) in the specific case of cable television. The intuition is straightforward. Any one cable channel is likely to have some viewers who like it a lot and are willing to pay a great deal for it and others who do not value it very much and are not willing to pay much at all for its inclusion as part of a cable service. Hence, by combining more stations in its Basic Service offering, the cable service provider eliminates the extreme values and shrinks the dispersion of the customer population's willingness to pay for the overall bundle.

For example, a useful measure of dispersion of a variable is the coefficient of variation defined as the ratio of a variable's standard deviation to its mean. Let consumer i have a willingness to pay for network j be of α_{ij} and let this be distributed normally across the population of consumers with a mean $\overline{\alpha}$ and variance σ^2, common to all networks. For a cable service that includes n networks, consumer i's willingness to pay for the entire cable service V_i is therefore:

$$V_i = \sum_{j=1}^{n} \alpha_{ij} \tag{8.18}$$

Of course, the average willingness to pay for the cable network will just be: $\overline{V} = n\overline{\alpha}$.

If we assume that each α_{ij} is distributed independently, then the standard deviation of the total willingness to pay V_i will be given by $\sigma \sqrt{n}$. Hence, the coefficient of variation for the V_i will be:

$$\text{Coefficient of Variation} = \frac{\sigma \sqrt{n}}{n\overline{\alpha}} = \frac{\sigma}{\overline{\alpha}\sqrt{n}} \tag{8.19}$$

This clearly shrinks as the number n of cable stations bundled together in the package increases. Moreover, this shrinkage will be even greater if, instead of independent station valuations, the valuations for at least some of the stations are negatively correlated. That is, if those customers who tend to have either very high or very low valuations for say, station 1, have inversely, very low or very high valuations for station 2, then putting these two stations together in one cable package will shrink the variation of the bundle even more.

Crawford (2008) investigates these effects using data from 1,159 cable systems offered across the United States in 1996. Cable service operators typically offer different types of bundled packages. One of these is a Basic Service package that usually includes the major broadcast networks such as ABC, CBS, FOX, and NBC as well as cable networks such as ESPN, CNN, and MTV. In more recent years, the Basic Services package has been further differentiated into one limited bundle that hast just a subset of broadcast and cable networks, and an Expanded Basic Services that includes a larger collection of such networks. In addition, cable operators also typically offer unbundled premium channels such as HBO to which customers may subscribe in addition to either a Basic or Expanded Basic Service. However, it is the fixed bundle of which the component stations are only accessible as part of that complete package that is the focus of Crawford's (2008) investigation.

Specifically, Crawford (2008) estimates a demand for cable services equation with a view to testing two hypotheses. First, does demand grow more elastic as additional networks are added to the bundle? Second, is the increase in elasticity particularly large when a network whose valuations are likely to be negatively correlated with those of other networks are added to the bundle?

The essential details of Crawford's (2008) approach are as follows. For the period covered by his data, the fifteen most important cable networks are: WTBS, the Discovery Channel, ESPN, USA, CSPAN, TNT, the Family Channel, the Nashville Channel, Lifetime, CNN, A&E, the Weather Channel, QVC, the Learning Channel, and MTV. Most Basic Service (or Expanded Basic Service) packages offer some of these in addition to broadcast networks. Some offer all of them. Note that some of these cable networks are not general interest stations but instead appeal to a narrow consumer interest. Thus, MTV caters to young adults while Lifetime focuses primarily on the concerns of adult women. It is these special interest channels for which consumer values are most likely to be negatively related to the consumer valuations of the general interest stations. Thus, it is especially as these stations are included that the elasticity of demand ought to increase.

Crawford (2008) therefore specifies a cable service demand equation as follows:

$$w^*_{sn} = X'_{sn}\beta + D'_n\theta_s + (\alpha_s + X'_{sn}\gamma + D'_n\theta^p)p_{sn} + u_{sn} \tag{8.20}$$

Here, w^*_{sn} is a measure of the share of consumers in market n who subscribe to cable system s; X'_{sn} is a vector indicating which of the fifteen important cable networks system s carries; D'_n measures demographic characteristics of the population in market n, such as age, education, etc.; p_{sn} is the price of service s in market n; and u_{sn} is a random error term reflecting unobserved factors that affect demand for cable services. Note that the individual stations—the X'_{sn}—have two effects on demand. They shift the *level* of demand, as indicated by the coefficients in the vector β, as well as materially alter the effect that impact that the system price p_{sn} has on cable demand via the coefficient vector γ. If the addition of a cable station makes demand more elastic—more sensitive to price—then the γ estimates should be negative. Crawford's (2008) basic estimates and their implications for demand elasticity are shown in Table 8.8 below. The values in bold indicate the statistically significant estimates.

Of course, changes in the level of demand and changes in the slope will each affect the estimated price elasticity. For our purposes then, the third column of Table 8.7 is the critical one. It shows the ultimate impact on the demand elasticity when both the level and slope

Table 8.8   Impact of cable stations on elasticity of demand for bundled cable services (basic or expanded basic services (standard errors in parentheses)*

Variable	Level Effect	Slope Effect	Elasticity Effect
WTBS	**1.14**	**−0.06**	**−0.53**
	(0.19)	(0.01)	(0.11)
Discovery	0.07	−0.01	−0.04
	(0.12)	(0.01)	(0.07)
ESPN	**0.58**	**−0.06**	**−0.40**
	(0.23)	(0.02)	(0.05)
USA	−0.19	0.01	0.10
	(0.14)	(0.01)	(0.09)
CSPAN	**0.47**	**−0.03**	**−0.22**
	(0.23)	(0.01)	(0.10)
TNT	**0.28**	**−0.02**	**−0.14**
	(0.13)	(0.01)	(0.06)
Family	0.02	−0.01	−0.02
	(0.15)	(0.01)	(0.08)
Nashville	0.10	−0.01	**−0.12**
	(0.13)	(0.01)	(0.07)
Lifetime	**0.28**	**−0.02**	**−0.25**
	(0.17)	(0.01)	(0.07)
CNN	**0.32**	**−0.03**	**−0.23**
	(0.14)	(0.01)	(0.08)
A&E	−0.33	0.01	0.07
	(0.23)	(0.01)	(0.09)
Weather	−0.10	0.00	0.01
	(0.14)	(0.01)	(0.04)
QVC	0.09	−0.01	**−0.18**
	(0.20)	(0.01)	(0.09)
Learning	**0.71**	**−0.05**	**−0.47**
	(0.33)	(0.02)	(0.15)
MTV	−0.23	0.01	0.00
	(0.25)	(0.01)	(0.13)
Other Networks	−0.14	—	—
	(0.03)		
Bundle Size	—	0.72	—
		(0.18)	
Average Top 15 Effect	**0.21**	**−0.02**	**−0.16**
	(0.03)	(0.00)	(0.04)

*Instrumental variables used for the potentially endogenous price term.

effects are taken into account. Here, the price elasticity of demand is taken as a negative number. So, anything that makes that elasticity significantly more negative makes demand more sensitive to price—precisely the hypothesized effect for bundling.

It is easy to see that eleven of the fifteen major cable offerings increase the price elasticity of cable service demand and that for nine of these this effect is statistically significant.

This is of course precisely what is predicted by the bundling literature. Overall, the average effect across all of the top fifteen stations is to raise the absolute value of elasticity by 0.16.

It is also noteworthy that the strongest elasticity-raising effects come from those cable stations catering to specialized tastes. Crawford (2008) identifies TBS, USA, TNT, Family Channel, A&E, and the Nashville Network as largely general interest channels, while Discovery, ESPN, Lifetime, the Weather Channel, QVC, MTV, and the Learning Channel all serve consumers with more specialized interests. Indeed, Crawford's (2008) estimates imply that the average elasticity effect of adding one of the specialized networks to the basic cable service is to increase (in absolute terms) the elasticity by a very significant 0.197. In contrast, adding one of the general interest stations has a much more modest and insignificant effect of increasing that elasticity by 0.1. Again, this is precisely what the theory predicts.

In short, Crawford's (2008) analysis suggests that cable service companies know what they are doing when they bundle channels together and offer them as either a Basic Services or Expanded Basic Services package. Moreover, this bundling pays off. Recall our simple model of consumer preferences and willingness to pay for each of the separate stations.

Crawford's next step is to take the elasticity effects shown in Table 8.7 above and to work out the ultimate profit and consumer surplus that are consistent with each of those effects. Given his estimates, he focuses this exercise on the effects of adding one of the top, special interest cable interest networks to the cable operator's bundle. He finds that this typically raises the firm's profit by 4.7 percent while reducing consumer surplus by 5 percent. Thus, as with most price discrimination schemes, producers gain and consumers lose. In Crawford's model, producer surplus is a bit larger to begin with so the overall surplus increases slightly. Bundling hurts those consumers who really only care about access to a few stations but who end up buying the entire bundle to get them. Again, this is what economic theory predicts.

Summary

In this chapter, we have shown that a firm with monopoly power in more than one product line may have additional opportunities to price discriminate. By bundling its two goods together as a package or, more generally, by tying the sale of one good to the purchase of the other, the firm can induce customers to sort themselves out by their purchase and *ex post* identify who is who. This permits charging a higher net price to those consumers with a greater willingness to pay.

In the case of two complementary products for which a fall in the price of one good raises the quantity demanded of both, sales coordination may occur for reasons other than price discrimination. In the absence of such coordination through a merger or a business network, for example, the separate production and marketing of two complementary products will typically raise prices, reduce output, and reduce profits. By taking account of the interrelationship between the demand for each product, coordination potentially offers benefits to both consumers and firms alike.

There can, however, be a downside to both bundling and tie-in sales. In cases in which large scale economies are present, these strategies may enable a firm to extend its market power in one product to another product line. Indeed, our analysis shows that bundling can be a powerful and credible entry-deterring practice. This was the charge against Microsoft, and it is the central issue in antitrust cases involving tie-in requirements.

However, it is worthwhile recognizing that some fairly strong market conditions have to be met for this outcome to prevail. It is equally worthwhile to remember that much of the tying and bundling occurs in fairly competitive markets. In such cases, there is some presumption that the practices are cost efficient. It follows that when we observe firms with market power using the same tactics, the goal of cost minimization may again be the reason.

So far, our analysis has focused on the strategic choices of a monopoly firm either acting alone or interacting in a second market that is also monopolized. The next step is to consider firms' strategies in the context of imperfect competition where there are just a few firms interacting as opposed to one or many. In such a setting, a firm can no longer simply address the issue of how to extract greater surplus from consumers. Each firm must now also consider how its production and pricing strategies affect not just consumers but the other rival firms. This is the stuff of game theory and it is to this topic that we turn next.

Problems

1. A university has determined that its students fall into two categories when it comes to room and board demand. University planners call these two types Sleepers and Eaters. The reservation prices for a dormitory room and the basic meal plan of the two types are as follows:

	Sleepers	Eaters
Dorm Room	$5,500	$3,000
Meal Plan	$2,500	$6,000

   Currently, the university offers students the option of selecting just the dorm room at $3,000, just the meal plan at $2,500, or both for a total price of $5,500. An economic consultant advises the university to stop offering the two goods separately and, instead, to sell them only as a single, combined room and board package. Explain the consultant's strategy and determine what price the university should set for the combined product.

2. Bundling is not always superior to non-bundling. To see this, consider a telecommunications firm that offers both phone service and a high-speed modem service. It has two types of consumers who differ in their willingness to pay a monthly rental fee for either service.

	Talkers	Hackers
Phone Service	$30	$a
High-Speed Connection	$16	$24

   Determine for what values of a bundling would be more profitable than not bundling.

3. Many years ago, the major alternative to xerography in copying was the Electrofax copying process. Electrofax machines used a special paper coated with a heavy wax film. Like Xerox, the Electrofax companies charged a low price for the use of the machine but set a paper price per page of 4 cents. The actual and marginal cost of manufacturing the paper was, in fact, only 1 cent per page.

   a. Explain the pricing policy of the Electrofax producers.

   b. The high markup on Electrofax paper soon attracted new firms offering to supply the paper at a much lower price than the Electrofax producers. How do you think Electrofax would respond to this competition?

4. Computer software, S, and hardware, H, are complementary products used to produce computer services. Customers make a one-time purchase of hardware, but buy various amounts of software. That is, once the hardware is purchased, the price of additional computer services is P_S, the price of a unit of software. The software market is competitive. However, the hardware market is monopolized by the firm, HAL, Inc. The cost of producing software and hardware is c_S and c_H, respectively:

   a. Assume that all users of computer services are alike, that is, have the same demand curve for computer services. Use a graph to describe the profit-maximizing price HAL can charge.

   b. Would HAL gain anything by buying software at the competitive price, branding it as its own, and then selling its hardware only to customers who use the HAL-brand software?

5. LRW runs a railroad line from New York to Philadelphia, the LRW line. At present, fixed costs are reasonably large, making it difficult for others to enter the market. Later, Nat Skape discovers that there is a market for travel from Philadelphia to Washington that is sufficiently large to permit offering passenger service between these two cities. His service is called the NSRR. Over time, both the LRW Line and the NSRR learn that many, though not all, of the customers riding from Philadelphia to Washington are actually passengers who originated in New York.

    a. What pricing issues arise between the LRW Line and the NSRR?

    b. Imagine that once it has incurred the sunk costs of setting up the Philadelphia to Washington line, it is possible that with a little experience, NSRR may be able to enter successfully the New York to Philadelphia market. Imagine further that before such entry occurs, the LRW Line builds an extension to Washington and offers riders from New York the advantage of service to Washington without the need to change trains. How should antitrust policy makers respond to this development?

6. Return to Table 8.6. What would be the equilibrium product offering and associate prices if:

    a. All values were unchanged except that there are now 100 consumers in each of the first two groups and only 50 in the group that wants both a pain reliever and a decongestant?

    b. All values were unchanged except that there are now 100 consumers who want pain relief, 100 who want both pain relief and a decongestant, but just 50 who want only a decongestant?

7. Return to the Nalebuff model. Assume that marginal cost of producing products 1 and 2 are both c per unit and of producing the bundle is $2c$ per unit.

    a. Derive the monopoly prices with no bundling and with pure bundling.

    b. Identify a constraint on c such that $p_B < 1$.

    c. Compare profits with and without pure bundling.

References

Adams, W. J., and J. Yellen. 1976. "Commodity Bundling and the Burden of Monopoly," *Quarterly Journal of Economics* 90 (May): 475–98.

Allen, R. G. D. 1938. *Mathematical Analysis for Economists*. New York: St. Martin's Press.

Cournot, A. 1838. Researches into the Mathematical Principles of the Theory of Wealth, Paris: Hachette, (English Translation by N.T. Bacon, New York: Macmillan,1897).

Crawford, Gregory. 2008. "The Discriminatory Incentives to Bundle in the Cable Television Industry," *Quantitative Marketing and Economics* 6 (March): 41–78.

Economides, N., and S. Salop. 1992. "Competition and Integration among Complements, and Network Market Structure," *Journal of Industrial Economics* 40 (March): 105–23.

Evans, D. 2006."Tying: The Poster Child for Antitrust Modernization," in R. Hahn, ed., *Antitrust Policy and Vertical Restraints*. Washington, D.C.: Brookings Institution Press, 65–88.

_____, and M. Salinger. 2005. "Why Do Firms Bundle and Tie? Evidence from Competitive Markets and Implications For Tying Law," *Yale Journal on Regulation* 22 (Winter).

Nalebuff, Barry. 2007. "Bundling as an Entry Barrier," *Quarterly Journal of Economics* 119 (February): 159–87.

Peterman, J. 1979. "The International Salt Case," *Journal of Law and Economics* 22:351–64.

Rubinfeld, Daniel. 2003. "Maintenance of Monopoly: *U.S. v. Microsoft* (2001)" in J. E. Kwoka, Jr., and L. J. White, *The Antitrust Revolution: Economics, Competition, and Policy*, 4th ed. Oxford, Oxford University Press.

Stigler, G. 1968. "Note on Block Booking," in *The Organization of Industry*. Homewood, IL: Irwin.

Appendix

Bundling, Entry Deterrence, and Optimal Pricing

OPTIMAL PURE BUNDLE PRICE

From equation (8.3)

$$q_B(p_B) = D - Dp_B^2/2 = (1 - p_B^2/2) \tag{8A.1}$$

and profit from the pure bundling strategy from equation (8.4)

$$\pi_B(p_B) = Dp_B(1 - p_B^2/2) \tag{8A.2}$$

Maximization of π_B with respect to p_B yields: $p_B = \sqrt{2/3} = 0.816$.

ENTRY-DETERRING LIMIT PRICE

From equation (8.5) the profit of the entrant is:

$$\pi_E = Dp_2(1 - p_2) - F \tag{8A.3}$$

Equating this to zero using the substitution $f = F/D$ gives:

$$p_2^2 - p_2 + f = 0$$

The solution to this consistent with the constraint $p_2 < 1$:

$$p_2^{nd} = \frac{1 - \sqrt{1 - 4f}}{2} = \frac{1}{2}(1 - \sqrt{1 - 4f}) \tag{8A.4}$$

OPTIMAL ENTRY PRICE WITH PURE BUNDLING

If the incumbent adopts pure bundling with bundle price p_B, the entrant's profit equation (8.9) is:

$$\pi_E = Dp_2(1 - p_2)(p_B - p_2) - F. \tag{8.A5}$$

Maximizing this with respect to p_2 again yields a quadratic equation with relevant solution:

$$p_2^b = \frac{1}{3}(1 + p_b - \sqrt{1 - p_b + p_b^2}) \tag{8A.6}$$

OPTIMAL MIXED BUNDLING PRICES

From Figure 8.6, mixed bundling splits consumers into four groups: those who purchase only product 1, those who purchase only product 2, those who purchase the bundle and those who purchase nothing.

Consumers who purchase only product 1 are those in the rectangle *dab* whose area is $(1 - p_1)(p_b - p_1)$. Consumers who purchase only product 2 are those in the rectangle *hef* whose area is $(1 - p_2)(p_b - p_2)$. Consumers who purchase the bundle lie in the market area *deah*, which is defined by the rectangle of area $(1 - (p_b - p_1))(1 - (p_b - p_2))$ minus the triangle of area $(p_1 - (p_b - p_2))(p_2 - (p_b - p_1))/2$. It follows that the profit from mixed bundling is given by:

$$\pi_{mb} = D \left[\begin{array}{l} p_1 \left(1 - p_1\right) \left(p_b - p_1\right) + \\ p_2(1 - p_2)(p_b - p_2) + \\ p_b((1 - (p_b - p_1))(1 - (p_b - p_2)) - (p_1 - (p_b - p_2))(p_2 - (p_b - p_1))/2) \end{array} \right]$$

(8A.7)

Differentiating with respect to p_1, p_2, and p_b gives the three first-order conditions

$$\frac{\partial \pi_{mb}}{\partial p_1} = (p_b - p_1)(2 - 3p_1) = 0$$

$$\frac{\partial \pi_{mb}}{\partial p_2} = (p_b - p_2)(2 - 3p_2) = 0$$

$$\frac{\partial \pi_{mb}}{\partial p_b} = \frac{1}{2}(2 + 4p_1 - 3p_1^2 + 4p_2 - 3p_2^2 - 8p_b + 3p_b^2) = 0$$

(8A.8)

The first two equations imply $p_1 = p_2 = 2/3$. Substitution into the third equation then implies:

$$\frac{3p_b^2}{2} - 4p_b + \frac{7}{3} = 0$$

(8A.9)

which gives the bundle price $p_b = (4 - \sqrt{2})/3 = 0.862$ implying that profit $= 0.549D$.

FIRMS WITH COMPLEMENTARY GOODS AND NONZERO MARGINAL COSTS

Let demand for nuts and bolts be: $Q_N = Q_B = A - P_N - P_B$. Let marginal cost of the nut and bolt production be c_N and c_B respectively. With separate production, profit of the nut producer is: $\pi_N = (P_N - c_N)Q_N = (P_N - c_N)(A - P_N - P_B)$. Maximization with respect P_N yields:

$$P_N = (A + c_N - P_B)/2$$

(8A.10)

By symmetry it follows immediately that the profit-maximizing bolt-pricing rule is:

$$P_B = (A + c_B - P_N)/2 \tag{8A.11}$$

Jointly solving (8A.10) and (8A.11) yields:

$$P_N = \frac{A + 2c_N - c_B}{3}; \quad \text{and} \quad P_B = \frac{A + 2c_B - c_N}{3} \tag{8A.12}$$

If the two firms merge, their joint profit is:

$$\pi_M = (P - c_N - c_B)(A - P) \tag{8A.13}$$

Maximization with respect to P yields:

$$P = \frac{A + c_n + c_B}{2} \tag{8A.14}$$

Comparison of this price P with the sum of P_N and P_B in (8A.12) reveals that P is lower by $\dfrac{A - c_n - c_B}{6}$, while profits are higher. Both consumers and producers gain from coordinating the prices of these two complementary goods.

Part Three
Strategic Interaction and Basic Oligopoly Models

In the next three chapters, we present our analysis of markets populated by just a few firms, that is, oligopolies. In such a setting, the actions of any one firm can change the market environment, for example the market price, not just for itself but for all firms. Thus, such actions will induce reactions that will in turn prompt further actions, and so on. This interaction is of course recognized by each firm and plays a crucial role in determining each firm's strategic choices. Because game theory is the formal framework for analysis of strategic interaction, the next three chapters present the basic game theoretic models of oligopoly behavior.

In Chapter 9, we present the Nash equilibrium concept. We then develop the Cournot model of quantity competition and show that it is consistent with the Nash equilibrium concept, even as the number of firms expands beyond two and differences in costs emerge between them. We conclude with an empirical application based on the Brander and Zhang (1990) paper that supports the modeling of airline competition as consistent with the Cournot predictions.

An important insight of game theory is that the outcome of any game is heavily dependent on the rules of the game. In the Cournot model, firms compete in quantities or production levels. Chapter 10 therefore presents the major rival to the Cournot model, namely, the Bertrand model, which assumes firms compete in prices. Because price competition can be particularly fierce when firms sell homogenous goods, the Bertrand assumption also gives firms an important motivation for differentiating their products. Hence, we also use this chapter to introduce price competition in the spatial setting first considered by Hotelling (1929). We explore price competition in a setting of differentiated consumer tastes by reviewing Hasting's (2004) empirical study of gasoline prices in southern California in the 1990s.

Finally, in Chapter 11, we consider a different alteration of the Cournot analysis, namely, the order of play. The Stackelberg model of Chapter 11 retains the Cournot assumption of quantity competition but now assumes that one firm plays first, i.e., chooses its production level before its rivals. This permits consideration of the benefits of incumbency and first mover advantages, more generally. We then discuss the experimental work of Huck Müller, and Normann (2001), providing experimental evidence on the Stackelberg versus the Cournot model.

9

Static Games and Cournot Competition

One of the most successful companies in the history of business is Coca-Cola. Indeed, "Coca-Cola" is said to be the second most well-known phrase in the world, the first being "okay."[1] Yet despite its iconic status in American popular culture, Coca-Cola is not a monopoly. Coca-Cola shares the carbonated soft drink market share with its archrival PepsiCo. An ongoing battle for market share has engaged these two companies for almost 100 years. The cola wars have been fought with a number of strategies, one of which is the frequent introduction of new soft drink products. Pepsi launched *Pepsi Vanilla* in the summer of 2003 in response to the year-earlier introduction of *Vanilla Coke*. In 2006, Coke initiated its biggest new brand campaign in twenty-two years for its new diet drink, *Coke Zero*. This followed Pepsi's revitalization of its *Pepsi One* brand made with Splenda sweetener instead of Aspartame.

In fighting these cola wars, each company must identify and implement the strategy that it believes is best suited to gaining a competitive advantage in the soft drink industry. If Coca-Cola were a monopoly, it would not have to worry about any rivals. Nebbither does a perfectly competitive firm. The pure monopolist has no rivals and the company in a perfectly competitive market has no effect on its rivals. Each such firm is so small that its decisions have no effect at all on the industry.

However, Coke, Pepsi, and many if not the majority of other real world firms live in the middle ground of *oligopoly*, in which firms have visible rivals with whom strategic interaction is a fact of life. Each firm is aware that its actions affect others, and therefore, prompt *re*actions. Each firm must, therefore, take these interactions into account when making a decision about prices, output, or other business actions. *Game theory* is the analytic framework used to formally analyze strategic interaction. As a result, game theory and the study of oligopoly are closely intertwined. In this chapter we introduce some basic game theoretic analysis to show how it may be used to understand oligopoly markets.

Game theory itself is divided into two branches: *noncooperative* and *cooperative* game theory.[2] The essential difference between these two branches is that in noncooperative

---

[1] "Coca-Cola is okay" has been claimed to be understood in more places by more people than any other sentence (Tedlow 1996).
[2] A good textbook that offers a more formal treatment of game theory and its applications to economics is Rasmusen (2007).

games, the unit of analysis is the individual decision-maker or player, for example, the firm. By contrast, cooperative game theory takes the unit of analysis to be a group or a coalition of players, for example, a group of firms. We will focus almost exclusively on noncooperative game theory. The individual player will be the firm. The *rules of the game* will define how competition between the different players or firms takes place. The noncooperative setting means that each player is concerned only with doing as well as possible for himself or herself, and not in advancing a more general group interest. As we shall see though, such noncooperative behavior can sometimes look very much like cooperative behavior because cooperation sometimes turns out to maximize the well-being of each individual player, as well.

Two basic assumptions underlie the application of noncooperative game theory to oligopoly. The first is that *firms are rational*. They pursue well-defined goals, principally profit maximization. The second basic assumption is that firms apply their rationality to the process of *reasoning strategically*. That is, in making its decisions, each firm uses all the knowledge it has to form expectations regarding how other firms will behave. The motivation behind these assumptions is that our ultimate goal is to understand and predict how real firms will act. We assume that firms are rational and reason strategically because we suspect that real firms do precisely this or will be forced to do so by market pressures. Hence, understanding what rational and strategic behavior implies ought to be useful for understanding and predicting real world outcomes.

There is one caution that any introduction to the study of oligopoly must include. It is that, unlike the textbook competition and monopoly cases, there is no single, standard oligopoly model. Differences in the rules of the game such as the number of players, the information available to the various players, and the timing of each player's actions all conspire to yield a number of possible scenarios. Yet while there is not a single theory or model of oligopoly, common themes and insights from the various models of oligopoly do emerge. Understanding these broad concepts is our goal for the next three chapters. Moreover, we should add that the lack of one single oligopoly model is not entirely a disadvantage. Rather, it means that one has a rich assortment of models from which to choose for any particular investigation. One model will be appropriate for some settings, a different model for other settings. Because the real business world environment is quite diverse, it is useful to have a variety of analyses from which to draw. We will present three different oligopoly models. In this chapter we introduce the Cournot (1836) model of oligopoly, in the next chapter the Bertrand model, and then in Chapter 11 the Stackelberg model.

9.1   STRATEGIC INTERACTION: INTRODUCTION TO GAME THEORY

In game theory, each player's decision or plan of action is called a *strategy*. A list of strategies showing one particular strategy choice for each player is called a *strategy combination*. Any given strategy combination determines the *outcome* of the game, which describes the payoffs or final net gains earned by each player. In the context of oligopoly theory, these payoffs are naturally interpreted as each firm's profit.

For a game to be interesting, at least one player must be able to choose from more than one strategy so that there will be more than one possible *strategy combination*, and thus more than one possible outcome to the game. Yet while there may be many possible outcomes, not all of these will be *equilibrium* outcomes. By equilibrium we mean a *strategy combination* such that no firm has an incentive to *change* the strategy it is currently using given that no other firm changes its current strategy. If this is the case, then the combination of strategies across firms will remain unaltered because no one is changing his or her behavior. The market or game will come to rest. Nobel Laureate John Nash developed this notion of an equilibrium strategy combination for a noncooperative game. In his honor, it is commonly referred to as the Nash equilibrium concept.[3]

In the oligopoly models studied in the next three chapters, a firm's strategy focuses on either its price choice or its output choice. Each firm chooses either the price it will set for its product or how much of that product to produce. A corresponding Nash equilibrium will, therefore, be either a set of prices, one for each firm, or a set of production levels, again one for each firm, for which no firm wishes to change its price (quantity) decision given those of all the other firms.

We note parenthetically here that, unlike the monopoly case, the price strategy outcome differs from the quantity strategy outcome in oligopoly models. For a monopolist, the choice of price implies—via the market demand curve—a unique output. In other words, the monopolist will achieve the same market outcome whether the profit-maximizing price or the profit-maximizing output is chosen.[4] Matters are different in an oligopoly setting. When firms interact strategically, the market outcome obtained when each firm chooses the price will usually differ from the outcome obtained when each firm chooses its output level. The fact that the outcome depends on whether the rules of the game specify a price strategy or a quantity strategy is just one of the reasons that the study of oligopoly does not yield a unique set of theoretical predictions.

Because interaction is the central fact of life for an oligopolist, rational strategic action requires that such interaction be recognized. For example, when one firm in an oligopoly market lowers its price, its rivals will notice the effect as they lose customers to the price-cutter. If these firms then lower their price too, they may win back their original customers. Because prices have fallen throughout the industry, the quantity demanded at each firm will increase. However, each firm will now be meeting that demand at a lower price that earns a lower mark-up. Our assumption that the oligopoly firm is a rational strategic actor means that the firm will understand and anticipate this chain of events *and* that the firm will include this information in making the decision of whether or not to lower prices in the first place.

Our opening story about carbonated beverages is an example of such an interaction, except that instead of a price decision, Coca-Cola and Pepsi were making product design choices. In doing so, each forms some idea as to how its rival will react. It would be *irrational* for Coke to anticipate no reaction from Pepsi, when, in fact, Coke understands that not reacting is not in Pepsi's interest. Similarly, if Coke lowers the price of its soft drinks, it doesn't make sense for Coke to hope that Pepsi will continue to charge a high price if Coke knows that Pepsi would do better to match its price reduction.

How can an oligopolist anticipate what the response of its rivals will be to any specific action? The best way to make such a prediction is to have information regarding the structure of the market and the strategy choices available to other firms. In a symmetric

[3]   Nash shared the 1994 prize with two other game theorists, R. Selten and J. Harsanyi. The award to the three game theorists served as widely publicized recognition of the importance game theory has achieved as a way of thinking in economic analysis. See Schelling's (1960) seminal work for much of the intuitive foundation of strategic analysis.

[4]   Competitive firms have no option as to which choice variable—price or quantity—to select. Competitive firms by definition cannot make a price choice. They are price-takers and can only choose the quantity of output they sell.

situation in which all firms are identical, such information is readily available. Any one firm can proceed by asking itself, "What would I do if I were the other player?" Sometimes, even when firms are not symmetric, they will still have enough experience, business "savvy," or other information to be fairly confident regarding their rivals' behavior. As we shall see later, precisely what information firms have about each other is a crucial element determining the final outcome of the game.

Another crucial element in determining the outcome of the game is the time-dimension of the strategic interaction. In a two-firm oligopoly or *duopoly*, such as Coca-Cola and Pepsi, we can imagine that one firm, say Coca-Cola, makes its choice to introduce *Vanilla Coke* first. Then in the next period, the other firm, Pepsi, follows with its choice. In that case, the strategic interaction is *sequential*. Each firm moves in order and each, when its turn comes, must think strategically about how the course of action it is about to choose will affect the future action of the other firm and how those *re*actions will then feed back on its own future choices. Chess and Checkers are each a classic example of a two-person, sequential game. Sequential games are often called dynamic games.

Alternatively, both players might make their choices *simultaneously*, thereby acting without knowledge as to what the other player has actually done.[5] Yet even though the other player's choice is unknown, knowledge of the strategy choices available to the other player permits a player to think rationally and strategically about what other players will choose. The childhood game, "Rock-Paper-Scissors" is an example of a simultaneous two-person game. Such simultaneous games are often called static games.

Whether the game is sequential or simultaneous, the requirement that the strategic firm rationally predicts the choices of its rivals is the same. Once it has done this, the firm may then choose what action is in its own best interest. In other words, being rational means that the firm's choice of strategy is the optimal (profit-maximizing) choice against the anticipated optimal actions of its rivals. When each firm does this, and when each has, as a result of rational strategizing, correctly predicted the choice of the others, we will obtain a Nash equilibrium. In this chapter we will focus on solving for Nash equilibria in simultaneous or static games.

9.2 DOMINANT AND DOMINATED STRATEGIES

Sometimes Nash equilibria are rather easy to determine. This is because some of a firm's possible strategies may be *dominated*. For example, suppose that we have two firms in a market, A and B, and that one of A's strategies is such that it is *never* a profit-maximizing strategy regardless of the choice made by B. That is, there is always an alternative strategy for firm A that yields higher profits than does the strategy in question. Then we say that the strategy in question is dominated. It will never rationally be chosen. Player A would never choose a dominated strategy because to do so would be to guarantee that A's profit was not maximized. No matter what B does, the dominated strategy does worse for A than one of A's other strategies. In turn, this means that in determining the game's equilibrium, we do not have to worry about any strategy combinations that include the dominated strategy. Because these will never occur, they cannot possibly be part of the equilibrium outcome.

---

[5]   The important aspect of simultaneous games is not that the firms involved actually make their decisions at the same time. Rather, it is that no firm can *observe* any other firm's choice before making its own. This lack of information makes the actions of each firm effectively simultaneous.

Dominated strategies can be eliminated one by one. Once the dominated strategies for one firm have been eliminated, we can turn to the other firms to see if any of their strategies are dominated given the strategies still remaining for the first firm that we examined. We can proceed firm-by-firm, eliminating all dominated strategies until only non-dominated ones remain available to each player. Often but not always, this iterative procedure of eliminating dominated strategies leaves one or more players with only one strategy choice remaining.[6] It is then a simple matter to determine the game's outcome because, for such firms, their course of action is clear.

As an example, consider the case of two airlines, Delta and American, each offering a daily flight from Boston to Budapest. We assume that each firm has already set a price for the flight but that the departure time is still undecided. Departure time is the strategy choice in this game. We also assume that the two firms choose departure times simultaneously. Neither can observe the departure time selected by the other before it makes its own departure time selection. Managers for each airline do realize, however, that at the very time American's managers are meeting to make their choice, Delta's managers are as well. The two firms are engaged in a strategic game of simultaneous moves.

In part, the choice of departure time will depend upon consumer preferences. Suppose that market research has shown that 70 percent of the potential clientele for the flight would prefer to leave Boston in the evening and arrive in Budapest the next morning. The remaining 30 percent prefer a morning Boston departure and arrival in Budapest late in the evening of the same day. Both firms know this distribution of consumer preferences. Both also know that, if the two airlines choose the same flight time, they split the market. Profits at each carrier are directly proportional to the number of passengers carried so that each wishes to maximize its share of the market.

If they are rational and strategic, Delta's managers will reason as follows: If American flies in the morning, then we at Delta can either fly at night and serve 70 percent of the market or, like American, depart in the morning in which case we (Delta) will serve 15 percent of the market (half of the 30 percent served by the two carriers in total). On the other hand, if American chooses an evening flight time, then we at Delta may choose either a night departure as well, and serve 35 percent (half of 70 percent) of the market or, instead, offer a morning flight and fly 30 percent of the market.

A little reflection will make clear that Delta does better by scheduling an evening flight *no matter which departure time American chooses*. In other words, choosing a *morning* departure time is a dominated strategy. If Delta is interested in maximizing profits, it will never select the morning flight option. But of course, American's managers will reason similarly. They will recognize that flying at night is their best choice regardless of Delta's selection. The only equilibrium outcome for this game is to have both airlines choose an evening departure time.

Table 9.1 illustrates the logic just described. The table shows four entries, each consisting of a pair of values. These entries describe the payoffs, or market shares, associated with the four feasible strategy combinations of the game. American's strategy choices are shown as the columns, while Delta's choices are shown as the rows. The pair of values at each row-column intersection gives the payoffs to each carrier if that particular strategy combination occurs. The first (left-hand) value of each pair is the payoff—the percent of

---

[6]   If the process continues until only one strategy remains for each player, then we have found an iterated dominance equilibrium.

Table 9.1 Strategy combinations and firm payoffs in the flight departure game

		American	
		Morning	Evening
Delta	Morning	(15, 15)	(30, 70)
	Evening	(70, 30)	(35, 35)

the total potential passenger market—that goes to Delta. The second (right-hand) value is the payoff to American.

Now we put ourselves in the shoes of Delta's managers and ask first what Delta should do if American chooses a morning flight. The answer is obvious. If Delta also chooses a morning flight then Delta's market share will be 15 percent, whereas if Delta chooses an evening flight its market share will be 70 percent. The evening flight is clearly the better choice. Now consider Delta's response should American choose an evening flight. If Delta opts for a morning departure, its market share is 30 percent, whereas if it goes for an evening departure its market share is 35 percent. Once again, the evening departure is the better choice. In other words, no matter what American does, Delta will never choose to depart in the morning. Whatever the equilibrium outcome is, it must involve Delta choosing an evening flight.

If we now place ourselves in American's shoes, we get the same result. A morning flight is never American's rational choice. Just as it was for Delta, flying in the morning is a dominated strategy for American. Hence, just like Delta, American will always choose the evening departure time.

The outcome of the game is now fully determined. Both carriers will choose an evening departure and share equally the 70 percent of the potential Boston-to-Budapest flyers who prefer that time. That this is a Nash equilibrium is easy to see by virtue of the dominated strategy argument. Clearly, neither carrier has an incentive to change its choice from evening to morning because neither carrier would ever choose a morning flight time in any case.

Solving the flight departure game was easy because each carrier had only two strategies and for each player one of the strategies—the morning flight—was dominated. To put it another way, we might refer to the evening departure strategy as *dominant*. A dominant strategy is one that outperforms all of a firm's other strategies *no matter what its rivals do*. That is, it leads to higher profits (or sales, or growth, or whatever the objective is) than any other strategy the firm might pursue regardless of the strategies selected by the firm's rivals. This does not imply that a dominant strategy will lead a firm to earn higher profits than its competitors. It only means that the firm will do the best it possibly can if it chooses such a strategy. Whether its payoff is as good as, or better than the payoffs obtained by its rivals depends on the structure of the game.

Except when the number of strategy choices is two, a firm may have some *dominated* strategies—choices that are never good ones because better ones are available—but not have any *dominant* strategies, or a choice that always yields better results than all others. Sometimes, a firm will have neither a dominant nor a dominated strategy. But for a firm that has a dominant strategy, the choice is clear. Use it! Such a firm really does not have to think very much about what other firms do.

Table 9.2   Strategy combinations and firm payoffs in the modified flight departure game

		American	
		Morning	Evening
Delta	Morning	(18, 12)	(30, 70)
	Evening	(70, 30)	(42, 28)

Let's rework the departure time game so that at least one firm has no dominated or dominant strategy. To do this, we will now suppose that because of a frequent flyer program, some of the potential Boston-to-Budapest flyers prefer Delta even if the two carriers fly at the same time. Specifically, assume now that departing at the same time does not yield an even split of customers between the two carriers. Instead, whenever the two carriers schedule identical departure times, Delta gets 60 percent of the passengers and American gets only 40 percent. Table 9.2 depicts the new payoffs for each strategy combination.

As can be seen from the table, an evening flight is still the dominant strategy for Delta. It always carries more passengers by choosing an evening flight than it would by choosing a morning flight, regardless of what American does. However, American's strategy choices are no longer so clear. If Delta chooses a morning flight, American should fly at night. But if Delta chooses an evening departure time, American does better by flying in the morning.

Assuming that each carrier knows the payoffs described by Table 9.2, however, the game's outcome remains clear. Looking at the table, American can readily determine that Delta will always select an evening flight. Knowing that Delta will choose an evening departure, it is then an easy matter for American to select a morning departure as its best response. The equilibrium outcome for this modified departure time game is therefore just as transparent as that for the earlier version. In this case, the equilibrium involves Delta choosing an evening flight and American opting to fly in the morning. Again, it is easily verified that this equilibrium satisfies the Nash criteria.

In solving both the previous games, we made extensive use of the ability to rule out dominated strategies and, when possible, to focus on dominant ones.[7] We showed that the outcomes obtained by this process were Nash equilibrium outcomes. However in many games no dominated or dominant strategies can be found. In such cases, the Nash equilibrium concept becomes more than just a criterion to check our analysis. It becomes part of the solution procedure itself. This is because rational, strategic firms will use the Nash concept to determine the reactions of their rivals to their own strategic choice. In the modified departure time game just described, for instance, Delta can work out that if it selects an evening departure, then its rival American will choose a morning flight. Delta can therefore deduce that the strategy combination of both carriers flying at night can never be an equilibrium—in the Nash sense—because if that outcome occurred, American would have a clear incentive to change its choice.

---

[7]   Some care needs to be taken in ruling out dominated strategies. While one can eliminate *strictly* dominated strategies as a rational choice, *weakly* dominated strategies cannot be so ruled out. A strategy is *weakly* dominated if there exists some other strategy, which is possibly better but never worse, yielding a higher payoff in some strategy combinations and never yielding a lower payoff. The Nash equilibrium may be affected by the order of exclusion of *weakly* dominated strategies. See Mas-Colell, et al. (1995), 238–41.

9.3   NASH EQUILIBRIUM AS A SOLUTION CONCEPT

In order to understand more deeply how to use the Nash equilibrium concept to solve a game, let's change the Boston-to-Budapest game to a game in prices.

Although many price strategies are available to each firm in reality, let's limit ourselves here to just three—a low, medium, and high price. This yields nine possible strategy combinations. We will assume that the payoffs (in this case profits) for each such combination are described by the new airfare game matrix shown in Table 9.3. As is now our convention, the payoff entries in each row-column intersection show the profit of the row player (Delta) as the first entry in each case.

We could in principle check each cell of the matrix in Table 9.3 to determine if it satisfies the Nash equilibrium requirement that neither airline wants to change its strategy. For example, examination of the upper left-hand corner cell quickly reveals that the strategy combination $P_D = P_A = Low$ is not a Nash equilibrium, because each airline in that case would want to switch to a medium price. Similarly, the middle cell of the left-hand column with $P_D = Medium$ and $P_A = Low$ is not a Nash equilibrium. While Delta cannot improve its profit given that American is charging a low fare, American would do better by raising its own fare to the medium level given that Delta is already doing just that. If American followed this inclination, however, it would move the game into the $P_A = P_D = Medium$ cell in the middle of the matrix, and it is easy to see that that strategy combination *is* a Nash equilibrium. Indeed, following this same procedure for all other cells would reveal that $P_A = P_D = Medium$ is the unique Nash equilibrium for this game.

A more appealing approach is to start by identifying that the strategy of setting a high price is never the best strategy for either firm. That is, $P_D = High$ and $P_A = High$ are each dominated strategies for Delta and American, respectively. We can therefore eliminate the third column and third row cells from consideration. Having done that, we are left with the simple 2×2 game in which each firm sets either a low or medium price. Within those choices however, we now find that $P_D = Low$ and $P_A = Low$ are each dominated by, respectively, $P_D = Medium$ and $P_A = Medium$. Thus, peeling off the dominated strategies as suggested earlier allows us to reach the result that $P_D = P_A = Medium$ is the unique Nash equilibrium for this game.

The fact that there are a number of ways of identifying the Nash equilibrium for any game suggests that behind each is a common but deeper meaning of the Nash concept. This more fundamental insight may be made clear by noting that if players are rational, we would not expect the game above to evolve along the path suggested by our first solution technique in which both firms start by setting $P_D = P_A = Low$, followed by Delta choosing $P_D = Medium$ and then American doing the same thing. Instead, given the fact that both players know the above payoff matrix and the rules of the game, each should choose a medium price right from the start. Why? Consider again Delta's management. Looking at

Table 9.3   Payoff matrix for the airfare game

		American		
		$P_A = Low$	$P_A = Medium$	$P_A = High$
	$P_D = Low$	$15,000 $15,000	$25,000 $22,000	$40,000 $20,000
Delta	$P_D = Medium$	$22,000 $25,000	$35,000 $35,000	$38,000 $33,000
	$P_D = High$	$20,000 $40,000	$33,000 $38,000	$30,000 $30,000

the game, they can see that American will never set $P_A = High$. Thus, recognizing that $P_A = High$ is a dominated strategy allows Delta to restrict American's possible choices to either $P_A = Low$ or $P_A = Medium$. However, further consideration reveals that American would only ever choose $P_A = Low$ if it thought that Delta was going to set $P_D = High$, for if Delta chooses a low or medium price, American does better by choosing a medium price as well. Yet it is not rational for American ever to think that Delta would choose $P_D = High$ because looking at the same table, American can see that whether it sets a low or medium price, Delta always does best by choosing $P_D = Medium$. Therefore, it would be foolish for American ever to set $P_A = Low$. Thus, Delta can set $P_D = Medium$ with a complete confidence that American will do the same thing and, more importantly, that when Delta's choice of a medium price is revealed, the predicted American strategy of $P_A = Medium$ is in fact precisely the choice American would want to make given Delta's choice of $P_D = Medium$. Of course, American can follow the exact same reasoning. As a result, each firm will select a medium pricing strategy from the start. There will be no action and reaction that eventually converge to the $P_D = P_A = Medium$ combination. It is this deeper logical consistency—the fact that each firm's strategy choice reflects its best response to the choice predicted for its rival which, in turn, is the rival's best response to the firm's own selected strategy—that gives the Nash equilibrium concept its true power.

Firm 1 and Firm 2 are movie producers. Each has the option of producing a blockbuster romance or a blockbuster suspense film. The payoff matrix displaying the payoffs for each of the four possible strategy combinations (in thousands) is shown below, with Firm 1's payoff listed first. The game is played simultaneously. Determine the Nash equilibrium outcome.

		Firm 2	
		Romance	Suspense
Firm 1	Romance	($900, $900)	($400, $1,000)
	Suspense	($1,000 $400)	($750, $750)

9.4   STATIC MODELS OF OLIGOPOLY: THE COURNOT MODEL

All the games of the previous section are single period or static. Delta and American, for example, are assumed to choose either their departure times or their airfares simultaneously and without regard to the possibility that, at some later date, they might play the game again. This is a feature of earlier work on modeling oligopoly markets. Firms in these models "meet only once" and the market clears once-and-for-all. There is no sequential movement over time and no repetition of the interaction. These may be limitations. Yet the analysis is still capable of generating important insights. Moreover, studying such static models is a good preparation for later examining dynamic models.

The most well known static oligopoly models are the Cournot and Bertrand models, each named after its respective author. Both works were completed in the 19th century, hence these models were not expressed in the formal language of modern game theory. Nevertheless, the equilibrium proposed by the author of each model fully anticipates the

Nash concept. Indeed, for this reason one often sees that outcome referred to as the Cournot-Nash or the Bertrand-Nash equilibrium in tribute to these two early scholars and their anticipation of Nash's result. Presenting both models also helps us to underscore a critical point that should be recognized by game theory students everywhere, namely, that the rules of the game matter . . . a lot. The rules for the Cournot and Nash game are identical in all respects except for the variable of strategic choice. In the Cournot model, that variable is the firm's output level, whereas in the Bertrand model it is price. Yet this seemingly small change has enormous implications for the outcome of the game.

Augustin Cournot, a French mathematician, published his model in 1836. Although its insights remained largely unrecognized for the next 100 years, it is now at the foundation of models of oligopolistic markets. The story that Cournot told to motivate his analysis went as follows. Assume a single firm wishes to enter a market currently supplied by a monopoly. The entrant is able to offer a product that is identical in all respects to that of the incumbent monopolist and to produce it at the same unit cost. Entry is attractive because under the assumption of constant and identical costs, we know that the monopolist is producing where price is greater than marginal cost, which means that the price also exceeds the marginal cost of the would-be entrant. Hence, the entrant firm will see that it can profitably sell some amount in this market. However the new entrant will, Cournot reasoned, choose an output level that maximizes its profit, *after taking account of the output being sold by the monopolist.*

Of course, if entry occurred and the new firm produced its chosen output, the monopolist would react. Before entry, the monopolist chose a profit-maximizing output assuming no other rivals. Now, the former monopolist will have to re-optimize and choose a new level. In so doing, the monopolist will (as did the new entrant previously) choose an output level that maximizes profits *given the output sold by the new rival firm.*

This process of each firm choosing an output conditional on the other's output choice is to be repeated—at least as a mental exercise. For every output choice by the incumbent, firm 1, the entrant, firm 2, is shown to have a unique, profit-maximizing response and vise-versa. Cournot called the graph representations of these responses Reaction Curves. Each firm has its own Reaction Curve that can be graphed in the q_1q_2 quadrant. That Cournot anticipated Nash is evidenced by the fact that he described the equilibrium outcome of this process as that pair of output levels at which each firm's output choice is the profit-maximizing response to the other's quantity. Otherwise, Cournot reasoned, at least one firm would wish to change its production level. A further appealing aspect of Cournot's duopoly model is that the equilibrium price resulting from the output choices of the two firms is below that of the pure monopoly outcome. Yet it is also greater than that which would occur if there were not two firms but many firms and pure competition prevailed. In other words, the Cournot model carries the intuitive implication that more competition is better than less.

To present Cournot's analysis more formally we assume that the industry *inverse* demand curve[8] is linear, and can be described by:

$$P = A - BQ = A - B(q_1 + q_2) \tag{9.1}$$

where Q is the sum of each firm's production, i.e., the total amount sold on the market; q_1 is the amount of output chosen by firm 1, the incumbent firm; and q_2 is the amount of

---

[8]   See Green and Newberry (1992) for a model in which firms compete in supply schedules relating the volume of output offered to a specific price. See also Wolfram (1999).

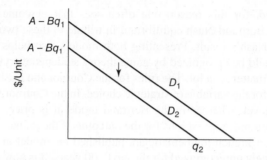

Figure 9.1   Firm 2's demand curve in the Cournot duopoly game depends on firm 1's output
An increase in q_1 to q_1' shifts D_2, the demand curve facing Firm 2, downwards.

output chosen by firm 2, the new competitor. As noted earlier, we shall also assume that each firm faces the same, constant marginal cost of production, c.

If we now consider firm 2 alone, and take firm 1's output, q_1, as given, the inverse demand curve, facing firm 2 is:

$$P = A - Bq_1 - Bq_2 \tag{9.2}$$

which is formally identical to (9.1). However, from firm 2's perspective, the first two terms on the right-hand side are not part of its decision-making, and can be taken as given. In other words, those two terms together form the intercept of firm 2's perceived demand curve so that firm 2 understands that the only impact *its* output choice has on price is given by the last term of the equation, namely, $-Bq_2$. Note, however, that any change in the anticipated output choice of the firm would be communicated to firm 2 by means of a shift in firm 2's perceived demand curve. Figure 9.1 illustrates this point.

As we can see from Figure 9.1, a different choice of output by firm 1 will imply a different demand curve for firm 2 and, correspondingly, a different profit-maximizing output for firm 2. Thus, for each choice of q_1 there will be a different optimal level of q_2. We can solve for this relationship algebraically, as follows. Associated with each demand curve illustrated in Figure 9.1 there is a marginal revenue curve that is twice as steeply sloped as discussed in Chapter 2. That is, firm 2's marginal revenue curve is also a function of q_1 given by:

$$MR_2 = (A - Bq_1) - 2Bq_2 \tag{9.3}$$

Marginal cost for each firm is constant at c. Setting marginal revenue MR_2 equal to marginal cost c, as required for profit-maximization, and solving for q_2^* yields firm 2's Reaction Curve. Thus we have $MR_2 = c$, which implies that $A - Bq_1 - 2Bq_2^* = c$ or $2Bq_2^* = A - c - Bq_1$. Further simplification then gives the Reaction Curve for firm 2:

$$q_2^* = \frac{(A - c)}{2B} - \frac{q_1}{2} \tag{9.4}$$

Equation (9.4) describes firm 2's best output choice, q_2^*, for every choice of q_1. Note that the relationship is a negative one. Every increase in firm 1's output lowers firm 2's demand and marginal revenue curves and, with a constant marginal cost, also lowers firm 2's profit-maximizing output.

Of course, matters work both ways. We may symmetrically re-work the industry demand curve to show that firm 1's individual demand depends similarly on firm 2's choice of output, so that as q_2 changes, so does the profit-maximizing choice of q_1. Then, we may analogously derive firm 1's Reaction Curve giving its best choice of q_1 for each alternative possible value of q_2. By symmetry with firm 2, this is given by:

$$q_1^* = \frac{(A-c)}{2B} - \frac{q_2}{2} \tag{9.5}$$

As was the case for firm 2, firm 1's profit maximizing output level q_1^* falls as q_2 increases.[9] The Reaction Curve for each firm is shown in Figure 9.2 in which the strategic variables for each firm and firm outputs are on the axes.

Consider first, the Reaction Curve of firm 1, the initial monopolist. This curve says that if firm 2 produces nothing, then firm 1 should optimally produce quantity $\dfrac{(A-c)}{2B}$, which is, in fact, the pure monopoly level, at which we assumed firm 1 to be producing in the first place. Now consider the Reaction Curve for firm 2. That curve shows that if firm 1 were producing at the assumed level of $\dfrac{(A-c)}{2B}$, then firm 2's best bet is to produce at level $\dfrac{(A-c)}{4B}$, that is, firm 2 should enter the market. However, if firm 2 does choose that level, then firm 1 will no longer do best by producing the monopoly level. Instead, firm 1 will maximize profits by selecting quantity $q_1 = \dfrac{3(A-c)}{8B}$.

As Cournot understood, none of the output or strategy combinations just described corresponds to an equilibrium outcome. In each case, the reaction of one firm is based upon a choice of output for the other firm that is not, itself, that other firm's best reaction to the initial chooser's selection. For the outcome to be an equilibrium, it must be the case that each firm is responding optimally to the (optimal) choice of its rival. For that to be the case

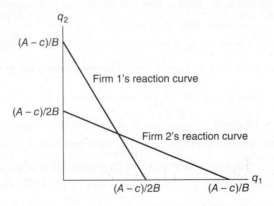

Figure 9.2   Best response (Reaction) curves for the Cournot duopoly model

---

[9]   We could alternatively solve for q_2^* by writing firm 2's profit function, Π^2, as revenue less cost, or: $\Pi_2(q_1, q_2) = (A - Bq_1 - Bq_2)q_2 - cq_2 = (A - Bq_1 - c)q_2 - Bq_2^2$. When we differentiate this expression with respect to q_2 and set the result equal to 0, (first order condition for maximization), and then solve for q_2^*, we get the same result as equation (9.4). A similar procedure may be used to obtain q_1^*.

though, requires that *both* firms be on their respective Reaction Curves. This happens at only one point in Figure 9.2, namely, the intersection of the two Reaction Curves.

To see how this works, recall the Reaction Function for firm 2: $q_2^* = \dfrac{(A-c)}{2B} - \dfrac{q_1}{2}$. We know and firm 2 knows that in an equilibrium, firm 1 must also be on its Reaction Curve, or that $q_1^* = \dfrac{(A-c)}{2B} - \dfrac{q_2}{2}$. Substituting this into firm 2's Reaction Curve allows firm 2 (and also us) to solve for:

$$q_2^* = \frac{A-c}{2B} - \frac{1}{2}\left(\frac{A-c}{2B} - \frac{q_2^*}{2}\right) = \frac{A-c}{4B} + \frac{q_2^*}{4} \tag{9.6}$$

so that $\dfrac{3q_2^*}{4} = \dfrac{A-c}{4B}$. In turn, this implies: $q_2^* = \dfrac{(A-c)}{3B}$. Because the two firms are formally identical, it follows that $q_1^* = \dfrac{(A-c)}{3B}$ as well. Total output for this market is $Q^* = \dfrac{2(A-c)}{3B}$. Substituting this into the demand function gives the equilibrium price: $P = A - BQ = \dfrac{A+2c}{3}$. Profit for each firm is total revenue less total cost, which can be solved as $\pi_i = \dfrac{(A-c)^2}{9B}$.

As Figure 9.2 makes clear, the Cournot duopoly model just presented has a unique Nash equilibrium. Unfortunately, Cournot's original discussion somewhat obscures the underlying Nash insight that we emphasized earlier. In particular, Cournot's story suggests a kind of trial-by-error learning process by which the two firms act and react and thereby move along their Reaction Curves until the equilibrium is achieved. But the power of the Nash equilibrium is that it makes it unnecessary to play out such an iterative procedure in real time. If the entrant, firm 2, is rational and strategic then in choosing its own production level, it *must anticipate* that the incumbent, firm 1, will do whatever maximizes its profits. An expectation, for instance, by firm 2 that the incumbent will continue to produce the monopoly output $\dfrac{(A-c)}{2B}$ after firm 2 enters and produces $\dfrac{(A-c)}{4B}$ is not a rational expectation as that is not firm 1's best response to the production choice by firm 2. That is, firm 2 ought never to predict $q_1 = \dfrac{(A-c)}{2B}$. The only rationally prediction that firm 2 can possibly make is in fact that $q_1 = \dfrac{(A-c)}{3B}$ the value of q_1 in the Nash equilibrium. For if firm 2 predicts q_1 to be equal to $\dfrac{(A-c)}{3B}$, then firm 2 will *optimally* choose that output level, too. In turn, this output choice by firm 2 is such that firm 1 should indeed produce at the level of $\dfrac{(A-c)}{3B}$ if it wishes to maximize its profits. Of course, the same holds true for firm 1's expectations of firm 2's output. In other words, for each firm the only logically consistent expectation is that its rival will produce $\dfrac{(A-c)}{3B}$ in which case each firm will also choose to produce exactly that amount and thereby fulfill the expectation. Rationally strategic firms can work through the Cournot model as a pure thought experiment, and select the unique Nash equilibrium output $q_i^* = \dfrac{(A-c)}{3B}$ without any time-consuming real world trials and errors. For this reason, many economists, including the authors of this book, prefer to use the term "*best response function*" instead of "Reaction Curve." The point is to emphasize that the correct Nash interpretation of the Cournot model is not one of action and reaction but one in which equilibrium is achieved directly by each seller's recognition that its choices be logically consistent.[10]

As a numeric example, consider two firms, Untel and Cyrox, who supply the market for computer chips for toaster ovens. Untel's chips are perfect substitutes for Cyrox's chips and vice versa. Market demand for chips is estimated to be $P = 120 - 20Q$, where Q is the total quantity (in millions) of chips bought. Both firms have a constant marginal cost equal to 20 per unit of output. Untel and Cyrox independently choose what quantity of output to produce. The price then adjusts to clear the market of the total quantity of chips produced. What quantity of output will Untel produce? What quantity of output will Cyrox produce? What will be the price of computer chips and how much profit will each firm make?

Let's put ourselves on the management team at Untel to see the problem from its perspective. The demand curve that Untel faces can be written as $P = 120 - 20q_c - 20q_u$, where q_c is the output of Cyrox and q_u is the output of Untel. Untel's marginal revenue curve is $MRu = 120 - 20q_c - 40q_u$. To maximize profit, Untel chooses a quantity of output q_u^* such that its marginal revenue is equal to marginal cost. That is, $120 - 20q_c - 40q_u^* = 20$. This condition for profit maximization implies that:

$$q_u^* = \frac{120 - 20}{40} - \frac{20}{40}q_c \ \ or \ \ q_u^* = \frac{5}{2} - \frac{1}{2}q_c \tag{9.7}$$

This is Untel's best response function describing its optimal choice for any given level of output by Cyrox. In addition however, Untel knows that Cyrox is also a profit maximizer, and so Untel anticipates that Cyrox will want to produce q_c^* to satisfy the same best response condition for its profit maximization. That is, by precisely the same argument that we have just gone through, Untel knows that Cyrox's best response function is similarly: $q_c^* = \frac{120 - 20}{40} - \frac{20}{40}q_u \ \ or \ \ q_c^* = \frac{5}{2} - \frac{1}{2}q_u$. Untel can recognize that Cyrox's choice of output depends on Untel's. Untel also knows that Cyrox knows that Untel is a profit-maximizer, and that Cyrox will anticipate that Untel will choose a profit-maximizing level of output q_u^*. Therefore, Untel predicts that Cyrox will choose $q_c^* = \frac{5}{2} - \frac{1}{2}q_u^*$. Substituting this prediction into Untel's best response function, equation (9.6), leads Untel to produce

$$q_u^* = \frac{5}{2} - \frac{1}{2}q_c^* = \frac{5}{2} - \frac{1}{2}\left(\frac{5}{2} - \frac{1}{2}q_u^*\right) \Rightarrow q_u^* = \frac{5}{3}$$

Now let's put ourselves on the management team at Cyrox and repeat the exercise. Because the two firms are *identical* there is no reason why Cyrox would do anything different from Untel, and so we can quickly jump to the conclusion that Cyrox will also produce $q_c^* = \frac{5}{3}$. Note that when Untel produces $\frac{5}{3}$, Cyrox's best response is to produce $q_c^* = \frac{5}{3}$, and similarly when Cyrox produces $\frac{5}{3}$, Untel's best response is to produce $q_u^* = \frac{5}{3}$. Aggregate market output therefore is $Q^* = \frac{10}{3}$, and so the price that clears the market

---

[10] Friedman (1977) includes a brief discussion of these issues, particularly valuable to those interested in the history of economic thought. He notes that Cournot's fate was not quite one of total obscurity owing to his friendship with the father of the French economist Walras. The English economist Marshall apparently was also well aware of and influenced by Cournot's work.

is $P^* = 120 - 20\left(\dfrac{10}{3}\right) = \$53.33$. For each firm the margin of price over unit cost is $33.33 so that each firm makes a profit of $55.55.

9.2

Assume that there are two identical firms serving a market in which the inverse demand function is given by $P = 100 - 2Q$. The marginal costs of each firm are $10 per unit. Calculate the Cournot equilibrium outputs for each firm, the product price, and the profits of each firm.

Practice Problem

9.5   VARIATIONS ON THE COURNOT THEME: MANY FIRMS AND DIFFERENT COSTS

Cournot's model is insightful in its treatment of the interaction among firms and remarkably modern in its approach. Yet these are not its only strengths. Cournot's analysis has the further advantage that, as noted earlier, the results also blend well with economic intuition. In the simple Cournot duopoly model described above, each firm produces its Nash equilibrium output of $\dfrac{(A - c)}{3B}$, implying that total industry output is $\dfrac{2(A - c)}{3B}$. This is clearly greater than the monopoly output for the industry, which would be $Q^M = \dfrac{(A - c)}{2B}$. Yet it is also less than the perfectly competitive output, $Q^C = \dfrac{(A - c)}{B}$, where price equals marginal cost. Accordingly, the market-clearing price in Cournot's model $P = \dfrac{(A + 2c)}{3}$ is less than the monopoly price $P^M = \dfrac{(A + c)}{2}$ but it is higher than the competitive price, c, which is equal to marginal cost. That is, Cournot's duopoly model has the intuitively plausible result that the interaction of two firms yields more industry output at a lower price than would occur under a monopoly, but less output at a higher price than results under perfect competition.

It is natural to ask if the foregoing result generalizes to the Cournot model when the number of firms grows to three, four, or N. That is, would introducing a third firm bring the industry still closer to the competitive ideal and, if so, would a fourth bring us closer still? Is the Cournot model consistent with the notion that when there are many firms the price converges to marginal cost?

The answer to this question is straightforward in the linear demand framework we have been using. To see this, assume that instead of two there are N identical firms, each producing the same homogenous good and each with the same, constant marginal cost c. Industry demand is again given by $P = A - BQ$ where Q is aggregate output. However, now we have that $Q = q_1 + q_2 + \dots + q_N = \sum_{i=1}^{N} q_i$ so that $P = A - B\sum_{i=1}^{N} q_i$, where q_i is the output of the ith firm. In turn, this means that we can write the demand curve facing just a single firm, say firm 1, as: $P = (A - Bq_2 - Bq_3 - \dots - Bq_N) - Bq_1$. The parenthetical expression reflects the fact that for firm 1, this sum is beyond its control and merely appears as the intercept in firm 1's demand curve. It is convenient to use the notation Q_{-1} as a shorthand method of denoting the sum of all industry output *except* that of firm 1's. Using this notation, we can write firm 1's demand curve even more simply as: $P = A - BQ_{-1} - Bq_1$. Clearly, firm 1's profits depend on both Q_{-1}, over which it has no control, and its own production level, q_1, which it is free to choose. Given its constant unit cost of c, firm 1's profits Π^1 can be written as: $\Pi^1(Q_{-1}, q_1) = (A - BQ_{-1} - Bq_1)q_1 - cq_1$. In turn, the twice-as-steep rule implies that firm 1's marginal revenue is given by $A - BQ_{-1} - 2Bq_1$. Hence, the condition $MR = MC$ necessary for profit maximization implies:

$$(A - BQ_{-1}) - 2Bq_1^* = c \tag{9.8}$$

Solving this equation for q_1^* gives us the *best response* function for firm 1:

$$q_1^* = \frac{(A - c)}{2B} - \frac{Q_{-1}}{2} \tag{9.9}$$

Because all firms are identical, we can extend this same logic to develop the best response function for any firm. Using the same shorthand notation, we can use Q_{-i} to mean the total industry production excluding that of firm i. The best response function for any firm i is:

$$q_i^* = \frac{(A - c)}{2B} - \frac{Q_{-i}}{2} \tag{9.10}$$

In a Nash equilibrium, each firm i chooses a best response, q_i^*, that reflects a correct prediction of the outputs that the other $N - 1$ firms will choose. Denote by Q_{-i}^* the sum of all the outputs excluding q_i^* when each element in that sum is *each firm's best output response decision*. Then an algebraic representation of the Nash equilibrium is:

$$q_i^* = \frac{(A - c)}{2B} - \frac{Q_{-i}^*}{2}; \quad \text{for } i = 1, 2, \ldots N \tag{9.11}$$

However, since the N firms are identical, each will produce in equilibrium the *same* output, that is, $q_1^* = q_2^* = \ldots = q_N^*$, or just $q*$ for short. Hence, for any firm i, we must have $Q_{-i}^* = (N - 1)q^*$. Therefore, we can write equation (9.11) as:

$$q^* = \frac{(A - c)}{2B} - \frac{(N - 1)q^*}{2} \tag{9.12}$$

from which it follows that the equilibrium output for each firm in the Cournot-Nash equilibrium is:

$$q^* = \frac{(A - c)}{(N + 1)B} \tag{9.13}$$

If each of the N firms produces q^* as given by equation (9.13), then we may easily derive the Cournot-Nash equilibrium industry output, $Q^* = Nq^*$, and the Cournot-Nash equilibrium industry price, $P^* = A - BQ^*$, as:

$$Q^* = \frac{N(A - c)}{(N + 1)B}; \quad P^* = \frac{A}{(N + 1)} + \frac{N}{(N + 1)}c \tag{9.14}$$

Examine the two equations in (9.14) carefully. Recall that $\dfrac{(A-c)}{B}$ is the competitive industry output. Thus, for the linear demand and constant cost case, the N-firm Cournot model industry output is $\left(\dfrac{N}{N+1}\right)$ times the competitive output. This rule, sometimes called the $\left(\dfrac{N}{N+1}\right)$ rule predicts (correctly) that the monopoly output is $1/2$ of the competitive output. As we move to a duopoly, the rule says that industry output rises to 2/3 of the competitive output. At three firms, the proportion rises to 3/4 and so on. In other words, our earlier result does generalize. The Cournot market output rises progressively closer to the competitive output as the number of firms N rises. Likewise close inspection of the price equation (9.14) reveals that the equilibrium Cournot price correspondingly moves progressively closer to the competitive equilibrium price $P = c$ as N rises.

In short, the Cournot model implies that as the number of identical firms in the market grows, the industry equilibrium gets closer and closer to that prevailing under perfect competition. That is, for this symmetric case, the Cournot model has the appealing feature that it predicts market outcomes will improve as market concentration falls.

What if the firms competing in the market are not identical? Specifically, what if each firm has a different marginal cost? We first handle this question for the case of two firms. Assume that the marginal costs of firm 1 are c_1 and of firm 2 are c_2. We use the same approach as before with the duopoly model, starting with the demand function for firm 1, which we can write as:

$$P = (A - Bq_2) - Bq_1$$

The associated marginal revenue function is $MR_1 = (A - Bq_2) - 2Bq_1$.

As before, firm 1 maximizes profit by equating marginal revenue with marginal cost. Thus setting $MR_1 = c_1$ and solving for q_1 gives the best response function for firm 1 as:

$$q_1^* = \frac{(A - c_1)}{2B} - \frac{q_2}{2} \qquad (9.15a)$$

By an exactly symmetric argument, the best response function for firm 2 is:

$$q_2^* = \frac{(A - c_2)}{2B} - \frac{q_1}{2} \qquad (9.15b)$$

Notice that the only difference from our initial analysis of the Cournot model is that now each firm's best response function reflects its own specific marginal cost.

An important feature of these best response functions that is obscured when the firms are identical is that the *position* of each firm's best response function is affected by its marginal cost. For example, if the marginal cost of firm 2 increases from say, c_2 to c_2', its best response curve will shift inwards.

Figure 9.3 illustrates this point. It shows the best response function for each firm assuming initially that each firm has identical costs as in Figure 9.2. It then shows what happens when firm 2's unit cost rises. As equation (9.15b) makes clear, this cost increase *lowers* firm 2's best output response for any given level of q_1. That is, it shifts firm 2's best response curve inward. This change in firm 2's best response function affects the equilibrium outputs that the two firms will choose. As you can see from the diagram, an increase in firm 2's

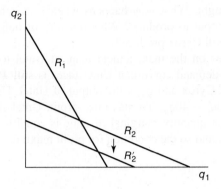

Figure 9.3 The Cournot duopoly model with different costs across firms
A rise in Firm 2's unit cost shifts the Firm 2 Best Response Function downward from R_2 to R_2'. In the new equilibrium, Firm 1 produces more and Firm 2 produces less than previously.

marginal cost leads to a new equilibrium in which firm 1 produces more than it did in the initial equilibrium and firm 2 produces less. This makes intuitive sense. We should expect that low-cost firms will generally produce more than high-cost firms. The changes are not offsetting, however. Firm 2's output falls by more than firm 1's production rises so that the new equilibrium is characterized by less output in total than was the original equilibrium. (Can you say why?)

The Cournot-Nash equilibrium can be obtained as before by substituting the expression for q_2^* into firm 1's best response to solve for q_1^*. Then we may use this value to solve for q_2^*. In other words, we have:

$$q_1^* = \frac{(A - c_1)}{2B} - \frac{1}{2}\left(\frac{(A - c_2)}{2B} - \frac{q_1^*}{2}\right)$$

which can be solved for q_1 to give the equilibrium:

$$q_1^* = \frac{(A + c_2 - 2c_1)}{3B} \tag{9.16a}$$

By an exactly symmetric argument, the equilibrium output for firm 2 is:

$$q_2^* = \frac{(A + c_1 - 2c_2)}{3B} \tag{9.16b}$$

It is easy to check that the relative outputs of these two firms are determined by the relative magnitudes of their marginal costs. The firm with the lower marginal costs will have the higher output.

Let's return to our Untel and Cyrox example of the two firms who produce computer chips for toaster ovens but now change this story a bit. While we still assume that Untel's chips are perfect substitutes for Cyrox's chips and vice versa, we no longer assume that they have identical costs. Instead, we now assume that Untel is the low-cost firm with a constant unit cost of 20, and Cyrox is the high-cost producer with a constant unit cost of 40. Market demand for chips is still estimated to be $P = 120 - 20Q$, where Q is the total quantity (in millions) of chips bought. What now happens when Untel and Cyrox independently choose the quantity of output to produce? What quantity of output will Untel produce? What quantity of output will Cyrox produce?

Again we put ourselves on the management team at Untel to see the problem from Untel's perspective. The demand curve that Untel faces is still $P = 120 - 20q_c - 20q_u$, where q_c is the output of Cyrox and q_u is the output of Untel. Untel's marginal revenue is again $MR_u = 120 - 20q_c - 40q_u$. To maximize profit, Untel should sell a quantity of output q_u^* such that at that quantity marginal revenue is equal to marginal cost. That is, $120 - 20q_c - 40q_u^* = 20$, and so the condition for profit maximization implies that:

$$q_u^* = \frac{5}{2} - \frac{1}{2}q_c \qquad (9.17)$$

Untel's profit-maximizing choice of output still depends on the output that the higher cost rival, Cyrox, chooses to produce. Equally importantly, a comparison of equation (9.16) with (9.6) indicates that Untel's best response function is unaffected by the assumed increase in Cryox's marginal cost. What about Cryox? By the same argument, the demand curve that Cryox faces is $P = 120 - 20q_u - 20q_c$ and its marginal revenue curve is $MR_c = 120 - 20q_u - 40q_c$. Equating this with marginal cost of 40 and solving for q_c gives the best response function for Cryox of $q_c^* = \frac{120 - 40}{40} - \frac{20}{40}q_u$ or $q_c^* = 2 - \frac{1}{2}q_u$. As we expected, the best response function for Cryox is shifted downward by the assumed increase in its marginal cost.

Untel knows that higher cost Cyrox is also a profit maximizer and therefore anticipates that Cyrox will want to produce q_c^* that maximizes its profit. It is also the case, as it was before, that Untel knows that Cyrox knows that Untel is a profit-maximizer, and so knows that Cyrox will anticipate that Untel will choose a profit-maximizing level of output q_u^*. All of this implies that Untel predicts that Cyrox will choose $q_c^* = 2 - \frac{1}{2}q_u^*$. Substituting this new prediction into Untel's best response function leads Untel to produce $q_u^* = \frac{5}{2} - \frac{1}{2}q_c^* = \frac{5}{2} - \frac{1}{2}\left(2 - \frac{1}{2}q_u^*\right) \Rightarrow q_u^* = 2$.

Now we put ourselves on the management team at Cyrox and repeat the exercise. To cut to the chase, we know that Cyrox's best response is $q_c^* = 2 - \frac{1}{2}q_u$. Moreover we know that Cyrox will predict that Untel will produce a best response that is based on a prediction that Cyrox will also produce a best response. That is, Cryox predicts that Untel will produce $q_u^* = \frac{5}{2} - \frac{1}{2}q_c^*$. Substituting this prediction into Cyrox's best response function leads to: $q_c^* = 2 - \frac{1}{2}q_u^* = 2 - \frac{1}{2}\left(\frac{5}{2} - \frac{1}{2}q_c^*\right) \Rightarrow q_c^* = 1$. Again note that when Untel produces 2, Cyrox's best response is to produce $q_c^* = 1$, and similarly when Cyrox produces 1, Untel's best response is to produce $q_u^* = 2$.

Although the foregoing analysis is limited to just two firms, it still yields important insights. First, there is a disadvantage to being a high-cost firm. It means a smaller market share and less profit. Second, while the disadvantage is real it is not fatal. A high-cost firm is not driven out of business, It is simply less successful than its ost rival. Finally, when costs vary across firms, the equilibrium Cournot output Q^* is not only too low (i.e., less than the competitive level), it is also produced inefficiently. As we know from

Chapter 4, efficient production among two or more firms would allocate output such that, in the final configuration, each firm's marginal cost is the same. This would be the outcome, for example, if the industry were comprised of a single, profit maximizing multiplant monopolist. It will also obtain under perfect competition. However, the non-cooperative feature of the Cournot-Nash equilibrium means that firms' marginal costs are not equalized.[11] Hence, the output allocation at equilibrium when costs are different is not an efficient one.

What is aggregate output, market price, Untel's profit, and Cyrox's profit for the above case in which Untel is the low-cost producer and Cyrox the high-cost one? Compare your answers to the ones you work out when the two firms are identical and have a constant unit cost of 20.

9.6   CONCENTRATION AND PROFITABILITY IN THE COURNOT MODEL

Let's now try to combine the case of many firms together with the assumption of *non-identical* costs. That is, let's analyze the Cournot model with N firms, each with its own (constant) marginal cost such that the marginal cost of firm i is c_i. We can use the first order condition for profit-maximization for each firm i, equation (9.8), and substitute c_i for c in this equation. This gives us the following:

$$A - BQ_{-i} - 2Bq_i^* - c_i = 0 \qquad (9.18)$$

where Q_{-i} again is shorthand for the industry production accounted for by all firms other than the ith one.

In a Nash equilibrium, the equilibrium output q_i^* *for each firm i* must satisfy the first-order profit-maximizing condition. Hence, in the Nash equilibrium, the term Q_{-i} must be the sum of the *optimal* outputs q_j^* for each of the "not i" firms. Denote this equilibrium sum as Q_{-i}^*. Then we can rewrite (9.18) as:

$$A - BQ_{-i}^* - 2Bq_i^* - c_i = 0 \qquad (9.19)$$

By definition, the total equilibrium output, Q^*, equals the sum of Q_{-i}^* and q_i^*. Hence, (9.19) implies that

$$A - B(Q^* - q_i^*) - 2Bq_i^* - c_i = 0$$

which can be reorganized to give:

$$A - BQ^* - c_i = Bq_i^* \qquad (9.20)$$

---

[11]   Our example assumed constant but different marginal costs across firms. The same insight could be easily obtained for the more general presentation in which the marginal cost of firm i, c_i, is a general function of its output, q_i, as in $c_i = c_i(q_i)$.

We also know that the Nash equilibrium price, P^*, is obtained by substituting the Nash equilibrium output into the industry demand curve yielding, $P^* = A - BQ^*$. Substitution into equation (9.20) then yields:

$$P^* - c_i = Bq_i^*$$ (9.21)

Dividing both sides of equation (9.21) by P^* and multiplying the right-hand side by $\dfrac{Q^*}{Q^*}$, we obtain:

$$\frac{P^* - c_i}{P^*} = \frac{BQ^*}{P^*} s_i^*$$ (9.22)

where $s_i^* = \dfrac{q_i^*}{Q^*}$ is the ith firm's market share in equilibrium.

Let's consider equation (9.22) step-by-step. The left-hand-side term is the difference between the price and firm i's marginal cost as a proportion of market price. This is just the *Lerner Index of Monopoly Power* that we met in Chapter 3. The notion is that the greater firm i's market power, the greater its ability to keep price above marginal cost.

The right-hand-side of (9.22) has two terms. The first is the slope of industry demand curve times the ratio of industry output to price. But the slope is just $B = -\Delta P / \Delta Q$ so that we have $\dfrac{BQ^*}{P^*} = -\dfrac{\Delta P}{\Delta Q} \cdot \dfrac{Q^*}{P^*}$. Recall the definition of the price elasticity of demand: $\eta = -\dfrac{\Delta Q}{\Delta P} \cdot \dfrac{P}{Q}$. So the first term on the right-hand side of equation (9.22) is just the inverse of the price elasticity of demand. The second term is just the market share of the ith firm, that is, its output relative to total industry output. Hence, equation (9.22) may be rewritten as:

$$\frac{P^* - c_i}{P^*} = \frac{s_i^*}{\eta}$$ (9.23)

where η is the price elasticity of industry demand.

Equation (9.23) is a further implication of the Cournot model, now extended to allow for many firms with differing costs. What it says is this: A firm that produces in an industry where demand is relatively inelastic and where it has a relatively large market share will also be a firm with a substantial degree of market power as measured by the Lerner Index or the firm's price-marginal cost distortion.

The relationship described in equation (9.23) tells us about market power at the level of the firm. In Chapter 3, we discussed the structure-conduct-performance (SCP) paradigm in industrial organization that linked market power, as measured by the Lerner Index, to the structure of the *industry*. The question that remains is whether we can extend the relationship in equation (9.23) at the firm level to the level of the entire industry.

To see how, let's first multiply each side of equation (9.23) by the firm's market share, s_i^*. Then add together the modified equation for firm 1 with that for firm 2 and that for firm 3 and so on until we add together all N modified (9.23) equations. The left-hand side of this sum of N equations is:

$$\sum_{i=1}^{N} s_i^* \left(\frac{P^* - c_i}{P^*} \right) = \frac{\left(\sum_{i=1}^{N} s_i^* P^* - \sum_{i=1}^{N} s_i^* c_i \right)}{P^*} = \frac{P^* - \bar{c}}{P^*}$$

Reality Checkpoint

Cournot Theory and Public Policy: The 1982 Merger Guidelines

In our review of antitrust policy in Chapter 1, we noted the dramatic change in policy regarding the treatment of mergers that occurred in 1982. In that year, the Department of Justice issued a new version of its *Horizontal Merger Guidelines*. This version replaced the original guidelines issued in 1968. Like that first set of guidelines, the 1982 document specified the conditions under which the government would challenge horizontal mergers. Unlike their predecessor, however, the new guidelines were based explicitly on the Herfindahl Index. Specifically, they stated that a merger would not be challenged if the industry Herfindahl Index was less than 1,000. A merger would also not be challenged if the index was over 1,000 but less than 1,800

and if the merger did not raise the Herfindahl Index by over 100 points. If the Herfindahl Index exceeded 1,800 points, then any merger that raised the index by over 50 points would cause concern and likely be challenged.

We will discuss these guidelines and their more recent modifications again in Chapter 15. For now, the point to note is that the explicit use of the Herfindahl Index may be viewed as a bow to the Cournot model which, as shown in the text, directly connects that index to the price-cost margin measure of monopoly power.

Source: Department of Justice, *Horizontal Merger Guidelines* (1982, 1984).

where $\bar{c}$ is the weighted average unit cost of production, the weights being the market shares of the firms in the industry. The right-hand side of the summed N equations is:

$$\frac{\sum_{i=1}^{N} (s_i^*)^2}{\eta} = \frac{HI}{\eta}$$

where HI is the Herfindahl Index that we defined as a measure of concentration in Chapter 4 (here expressed using fractional shares, e.g., a 10 percent share is recorded as $s_i = 0.10$). Therefore equation (9.23) aggregated at the level of the industry implies that:

$$\frac{(P^* - \bar{c})}{P^*} = \frac{HI}{\eta} \tag{9.24}$$

Our generalized Cournot model thus gives theoretical support for the view that as concentration (here measured by the industry's Herfindahl Index) increases, prices also rise further and further above marginal cost.

A variant of the relationship in equation (9.24) was tested in Marion et al. (1979) for food products. They collected price data for a basket of ninety-four grocery products, and market share data for thirty-six firms operating in thirty-two US Standard Metropolitan Statistical Areas, and found that price is significantly higher in markets with a higher Herfindahl Index. Likewise, Marvel (1989) found that for twenty-two US cities, concentration in the retail market for gasoline, as measured by the Herfindahl Index, had a significant impact on the average price of gasoline.

9.7   EMPIRICAL APPLICATION: COURNOT COMPETITION IN AN AIRLINE DUOPOLY

The examples above suggest that at least some of the implications of the Cournot model are consistent with real world data. However, such results might also be compatible with other models as well that differ in an important respect from the precise assumptions of the Cournot model presented in this chapter. One such difference concerns the Cournot firm's understanding of how rivals will react to its output choice.

Consider again the basic duopoly model with a linear demand curve: $P = A - BQ$. As before, assume as well that each firm has a constant marginal cost c_i. As we described above, the industry demand perceived by each firm is described by $P = A - Bq_1 - Bq_2$. Consider firm 1. The Cournot model hypothesis is that in calculating the impact of changes in its output, i.e., in calculating its marginal revenue, firm 1 assumes that firm 2's output is unchanged. Hence, as in equation (9.3), the profit-maximizing output for firm 1 satisfies $MR_1 = A - Bq_2 - 2Bq_1 = c$. However, we want to write this equation slightly differently to make a key point of the Cournot model. Recognizing that $A - Bq_1 - Bq_2 = P$, we can rewrite firm 1's profit-maximizing condition as follows:

$$P - q_1 B = c \qquad (9.25)$$

The term $B = -\left(\dfrac{\Delta P}{\Delta Q}\right)$ is of course the slope term that simply characterizes the (negative) effect on the industry price of changes in industry output. Its presence reflects the fact that when firm 1 makes a small marginal increase in its own output, Δq_1, the Cournot assumption that q_2 does not change implies that $\Delta Q = \Delta q_1$ so that the resultant fall in price is B. Multiplying this over firm 1's current output then captures the downside of further increases in q_1. Similarly, the Cournot model assumes firm 2 also expects no reaction to a small change in its output q_2 so that it perceives $\Delta Q = \Delta q_2$.

It is possible, however, that instead of no response each firm anticipates that its rival will adjust its output as the initial firm changes its own production. That is, firm 1 may believe that $\Delta q_2 = v\Delta q_1$ so that when firm 1 changes its output, the total change in industry output is now $\Delta Q = (1 + v)\,\Delta q_1$. Likewise, firm 2 may believe that $\Delta Q = (1 + v)\,\Delta q_2$. As a result, the movement in price from a small increase at the margin in firm 1's output will be $B(1 + v)$. Hence, the profit-maximizing first-order condition in equation (9.25) now becomes:

$$P - q_1 B(1 + v) = c \qquad (9.26a)$$

Symmetrically, firm 2's profit maximizing condition is now:

$$P - q_2 B(1 + v) = c \qquad (9.26b)$$

Because the parameter v reflects the firm's conjecture regarding the output response their own choices will induce, it is often referred to as the conjectural variations parameter. With a little intuition, we can use equations (9.26a) and (9.26b) to put some bounds on the values that v can take. In this regard, observe that if $v = -1$, the two equations imply $P = c$. That is, $v = -1$ corresponds to perfect competitive behavior in which price is driven to marginal cost. To see the implication if $v = 1$, recall from Chapter 2 that the monopoly output is $Q^M = \dfrac{A-c}{2B}$, so that the monopoly price is $P^M = \dfrac{A+c}{2}$. Assume that each firm produces half the monopoly output as would be the case if the firms acted like a cartel. Hence, $q_1 = q_2 = \dfrac{A-c}{4B}$. Then our adjusted equations each yield $P = \dfrac{A+c}{2}$, i.e., the monopoly price. Thus, our conjectural variations parameter must lie between a lower bound of $v = -1$ reflecting perfectly competitive behavior and an upper bound of $v = +1$ reflecting cartel or monopoly behavior. The intermediate value of $v = 0$ reflects Cournot behavior.

Table 9.4 Estimated conjectural variation parameter v for American airlines and United airlines in 33 city markets paired with Chicago

Pair City	American v Estimate	United v Estimate
Grand Rapids	0.82	1.02
Indianapolis	−0.11	1.95
Columbus	1.46	0.41
Des Moines	1.50	0.34
Omaha	1.74	0.02
Buffalo	0.39	0.35
Rochester	0.39	0.81
Tulsa	0.00	1.08
Wichita	0.25	0.90
Syracuse	0.19	0.59
Baltimore	0.62	0.16
Oklahoma	0.17	0.82
Albany	−0.10	0.82
New York	0.20	0.48
Charleston	−0.50	−0.62
Hartford	0.79	0.01
Dallas	−0.39	1.33
Providence	−0.14	0.28
Austin	−0.72	−1.43
San Antonio	−0.13	−0.20
Albuquerque	−0.78	−0.31
Phoenix	−0.08	−0.70
Tucson	−0.79	−0.17
Las Vegas	−0.75	−1.15
Reno	−0.80	−0.77
Ontario, CA	−0.28	−0.49
San Diego	−0.28	−0.58
Seattle	−0.11	−0.32
Los Angeles	−0.16	0.02
Portland	−0.84	−0.35
Sacramento	−0.08	−0.31
San Jose	0.33	0.04
San Francisco	0.26	−0.20
Mean	**0.06**	**0.23**
Overall Mean	**0.09**	

Let us now allow for the two firms to have different marginal costs c_i and therefore different market shares s_i. Then recognizing that firm i's output $q_i = s_i Q$ we may generalize equations (9.25a) and (9.25b) as follows:

$$P - s_i QB(1 + v_i) = c_i; \ i = 1,2 \tag{9.27}$$

Solving for v_i and recognizing that $B = -\left(\dfrac{\Delta P}{\Delta Q}\right)$ so that $\dfrac{1}{BQ} = \dfrac{\eta}{P}$, where η is the elasticity of demand (expressed as a positive number), equation (9.27) may be rewritten as:

$$v_i = \left(\frac{P - c_i}{P}\right)\frac{\eta}{s_i} - 1 \tag{9.28}$$

Brander and Zhang (1990) use data from thirty-three airline routes emanating from Chicago in the 1980s that were served by just the two carriers, American Airlines and United Airlines. Their baseline case uses an assumed elasticity of $\eta = 1.6$ (based on other research) and marginal cost estimates derived from the operating expenses for each firm (including an allowance for marginal cost to vary with the length of the flight with an elasticity of 0.5). Their calculated v_i values for each firm in each market are shown in Table 9.4 above.

The rough calculation behind these measures implies that they will include a fair bit of noise. Even so, the overwhelming majority or 57 of the 66 estimated v_i parameters lie within the theoretical upper and lower bounds of 1 and -1. More importantly, the estimated mean is very close to 0 for both firms and across the entire sample. Classical statistical tests would reject the null hypothesis that v equals either 1 or -1 They would not reject the Cournot hypothesis that $v = 0$. Thus, this rough exercise gives fairly strong support to the Cournot model as a useful description of real world behavior.

Summary

For industries populated by a relatively small number of firms, strategic interaction is a fact of life. Each firm is aware of the fact that its decisions have a significant impact on its rivals. Each firm will want to take account of the anticipated response of its rivals when determining its course of action. It is reasonable to believe that firms' anticipations or expectations are rational.

Game theory is the modern formal technique for studying rational strategic interaction. Each player in a game has a set of strategies to choose from. A strategy combination is a set of strategies—one for each player. Each such strategy combination implies a particular payoff or final outcome for each player. A Nash equilibrium is a strategy combination such that each player is maximizing his or her own payoff *given* the strategies chosen by all other players. In a

Nash equilibrium, no player has an incentive to change behaviors unilaterally.

In this chapter, we presented the well-known Cournot model of competition. It is a static or single market period model of oligopoly. Although this model was developed prior to the development of formal game theory, the outcome proposed by Cournot captures basic game theoretic principles, specifically the Nash equilibrium solution.

The Cournot model makes clear the importance of firms recognizing and understanding their interdependence. The model also has the nice intuitive implication that the degree of departure from competitive pricing may be directly linked to the structure of the industry as measured by the Herfindahl Index. While the Cournot model is not the only game-theoretic model of imperfect competition, a number of its predictions are borne out by empirical evidence.

It is important to remember though that, as pointed out in Chapter 4, market structure is endogenous. Strategies that generate above normal profits for existing firms will induce new firms to enter. At the same time, incumbent firms may be able to take actions that deter such entry. We need to extend our analysis in ways that allow us to examine these issues.

Further, the Cournot model studied in this chapter has firms interacting only once. The reality, of course, is that firms are involved in strategic interactions repeatedly. In such a setting, issues such as learning, establishing a reputation, and credibility can become quite important. We turn to a consideration of how the nature of strategic interaction over time affects market structure in Chapters 11–13.

Problems

1. Harrison and Tyler are two students who met by chance the last day of exams before the end of the spring semester and the beginning of summer. Fortunately, they liked each other very much. Unfortunately, they forgot to exchange addresses. Fortunately, each remembers that they spoke of attending a campus party that night. Unfortunately, there are two such parties. One party is small. If each attends this party, they will certainly meet. The other party is huge. If each attends this one, there is a chance they will not meet because of the crowd. Of course, they will certainly not meet if they attend separate parties. Payoffs to each depending on the combined choice of parties are shown below, with Tyler's payoffs listed first.

		Harrison	
		Go to Small Party	Go to Large Party
Tyler	Go to Small Party	(1,000, 1,000)	(0, 0)
	Go to Large Party	(0, 0)	(500, 500)

   a. Identify the Nash equilibria for this problem.
   b. Identify the Pareto optimal outcome for this "two party" system.

2. Suppose that the small party of Problem 1 is hosted by the "Outcasts," twenty men and women students trying to organize alternatives to the existing campus party establishment. All twenty Outcasts will attend the party. But many other students—not unlike Harrison and Tyler—only go to a party to

which others (no one in particular, just people in general) are expected to come. As a result, total attendance A at the small party depends on just how many people X everyone *expects* to show up. Let the relationship between A and X be given by: $A = 20 + 0.6X$
   a. Explain this equation. Why is the intercept 20? Why is the relation between A and X positive?
   b. If the equilibrium requires that partygoers' expectations be correct, what is the equilibrium attendance at the Outcasts' party?

3. A game known well to both academics and teenage boys is "Chicken." Two players each drive their car down the center of a road in opposite directions. Each chooses either STAY or SWERVE. Staying wins adolescent admiration and a big payoff *if* the other player chooses SWERVE. Swerving loses face and has a low payoff when the other player stays. Bad as that is, it is still better than the payoff when both players choose STAY in which case they each are badly hurt. These outcomes are described below with Player A's payoffs listed first.

		Player B	
		Stay	Swerve
Player A	Stay	(−6, −6)	(2, −2)
	Swerve	(−2, 2)	(1, 1)

   a. Find the Nash equilibria in this game.
   b. This is a good game to introduce mixed strategies. If Player A adopts the strategy STAY one-fifth of the time, and SWERVE four-fifths of the time, show

that Player B will then be indifferent between either strategy, STAY or SWERVE.

c.   If *both* players use this probability mix, what is the chance that they will both be badly hurt?

4.   You are a manager of a small "widget"-producing firm. There are only two firms, including yours, that produce "widgets." Moreover your company and your competitor's are identical. You produce the same good and face the same costs of production described by the following total cost function: Total Cost $= 1500 + 8q$ where q is the output of an individual firm. The market-clearing price, at which you can sell your widgets to the public, depends on how many widgets both you and your rival choose to produce. A market research company has found that market demand for widgets can be described as: $P = 200 - 2Q$ where $Q = q_1 + q_2$, where q_1 is your output and q_2 is your rivals. The Board of Directors has directed you to choose an output level that will *maximize* the firm's profit. How many widgets should your firm produce in order to achieve the profit-maximizing goal? Moreover you must present your strategy to the Board of Directors and explain to them why producing this amount of widgets is the profit-maximizing strategy.

5.   You are still a manager of a small widget-producing firm. Now however there are fourteen such firms (including yours) in the industry. Each firm is identical; each one produces the same product and has the same costs of production. Your firm, as well as each one of the other firms, has the same total cost function, namely: Total Cost $= 200 + 50q$ where q is the output of an individual firm. The price at which you can sell your widgets is determined by market demand, which has been estimated as: $P = 290 - \frac{1}{3}Q$ where Q is the sum of all the individual firms producing in this industry. So, for example, if 120 widgets are produced in the industry then the market-clearing price will be 250, whereas if 300 widgets are produced then the market-clearing price will be 190. The Board of Directors has directed you to choose an output level that maximizes the

firm's profit. You have an incentive to maximize profits because your job and salary depend upon the profit performance of this company. Moreover you should also be able to present your profit-maximizing strategy to the Board of Directors and explain to them why producing this amount maximizes the firm's profit.

6.   The inverse market demand for fax paper is given by $P = 400 - 2Q$. There are two firms who produce fax paper. Each firm has a unit cost of production equal to 40, and they compete in the market in quantities. That is, they can choose any quantity to produce, and they make their quantity choices simultaneously.

a.   Show how to derive the Cournot-Nash equilibrium to this game. What are firms' profits in equilibrium?

b.   What is the monopoly output, i.e., the one that maximizes total industry profit? Why isn't producing one-half the monopoly output a Nash equilibrium outcome?

7.   Return to Problem 6, but suppose now that firm 1 has a cost advantage. Its unit cost is constant and equal to 25 whereas firm 2 still has a unit cost of 40. What is the Cournot outcome now? What are the profits for each firm?

8.   We can use the Cournot model to derive an equilibrium industry structure. For this purpose, we will define an equilibrium as that structure in which no firm has an incentive to leave or enter the industry. If a firm leaves the industry, it enters an alternative competitive market in which case it earns zero (economic) profit. If an additional firm enters the industry when there are already n firms in it, the new firm's profit is determined by the Cournot equilibrium with $n + 1$ firms. For this problem, assume that each firm has the cost function: $C(q) = 256 + 20q$. Assume further that market demand is described by: $P = 100 - Q$.

a.   Find the long-run equilibrium number of firms in this industry.

b.   What industry output, price, and firm profit levels will characterize the long-run equilibrium?

References

Abraham, C. 1999. "Measuring Duopoly Power in the British Electricity Spot Market," *American Economic Review* 89 (September), 804–26.

Brander, J., and A. Zhang. 1990. "Market Conduct in the Airline Industry: An Empirical Investigation," *Rand Journal of Economics* 4 (Winter): 567–83.

Cournot, A. 1836. *Researches into the Mathematical Principles of the Theory of Wealth*, Paris: Hachette. (English Translation by N.T. Bacon, 1897, New York: Macmillan.)

Friedman, J. 1977. *Oligopoly Theory*, Amsterdam: North Holland Press.

Green, R. J., and D. Newberry. 1992. "Competition in the British Electricity Spot Market," *Journal of Political Economy* 100 (October): 929–53.

Marion, B.W., W.F Mueller, R.W. Cotterill, F.E. Geithman, and J.R. Schmelzer. 1979. *The Food Retailing Industry Market Structure, Profits and Prices*, New York: Praeger.

Marvel, H. 1989. "Concentration and Price in Gasoline Retailing," in Leonard Weiss (ed.), *Concentration and Price*, Cambridge, MA: MIT Press.

Mas-Colell, A., M.D. Whinston, and J. Green, 1995. *Microeconomic Theory*, New York: Oxford University Press.

Rasmusen, E., 2007. *Games and Information, An Introduction to Game Theory*, 4th ed. Cambridge: Basil Blackwell.

Schelling, T. 1960. *The Strategy of Conflict*, Cambridge Mass.: Harvard University Press.

Tedlow, R. 1996. *New and Improved: The Story of Mass Marketing in America*. Boston: Harvard Business School Press, 2nd ed.

Wolfram, C. 1999. *Measuring Duopoly Power in the British Electricity Spot Market: American Economic Review*, 89 (September), 805–26.

10

Oligopolistic Price Competition

In 2007, Amazon introduced its first *Kindle* e-reader at a price of $399. The product was a quick success. However, in the face of an announcement by Barnes & Noble that it would soon launch its own *Nook* e-reader, the price was reduced in 2008 to $259. In 2009, when the *Nook* was launched, the competition intensified and Amazon dropped the price to $199. In March of 2010, Apple began taking orders for its new *iPad* product, which also included e-reading capabilities. As this text is being written, both the *Kindle Touch* and the *Nook Simple Touch* are selling for $99, while the latest top-of-the-line *Kindle Fire* that also serves as a viewer and game platform is being offered at a sale price of $139. This rapid fall of e-reader prices has been all the more remarkable in that it has been accompanied by an almost equally rapid rise in their quality. Relative to the initial products, the current *Kindle* and *Nook* are more than 50 percent lighter, have a battery life more than twice as long, and a storage capacity as much as 100 times greater.

The digital and mobile technology markets are similar to many markets, including restaurants, electricians, moving companies, consulting firms, and financial services, in which consumers favor those products that best match their preferences at the lowest price. In these markets, it is in fact the firm's price choice that largely determines its demand and its profit, and each firm may set a different price. While this may seem eminently plausible, it is quite different from the way competition works in the Cournot model. There each firm independently chooses a level of production. It is only afterwards that the market price adjusts so that consumers will buy the combined output of all the firms at a price that is the same for each company.

In a monopolized market, it would of course make no difference whether the firm initially set a price and then produced whatever amount consumers demanded at that price or, instead, first chose its production and let the price settle at whatever level was necessary to sell that output. When a profit-maximizing monopolist optimally sets price, that choice will imply, via the demand curve, a specific output level. That same optimal price is precisely the price that would have emerged if instead the monopolist had initially chosen its profit-maximizing production.

Once we leave the world of monopoly, however, the equivalence of price and output strategies vanishes. In oligopolistic markets, it matters very much whether firms compete in terms of quantities, as in Cournot, or in prices like the e-reader firms above. To understand these differences, we begin as we did with the Cournot model by examining the simple duopoly case in which the two firms sell an identical good but now compete by first setting prices instead of production levels. This is known as the Bertrand model. Later in the chapter we allow the products to be less than perfect substitutes, or to be differentiated. As in Chapter 9, we also focus on static or simultaneous models of price competition limited to a single market period.

10.1   THE BERTRAND DUOPOLY MODEL

The standard duopoly model, recast in terms of price strategies rather than quantity strategies, is typically referred to as the Bertrand model. Joseph Bertrand was a French mathematician who in 1883 reviewed and critiqued Cournot's work nearly fifty years after its publication in the *Journal des Savants*. Bertrand was critical of mathematical modeling in economics, and to prove his point he analyzed the Cournot model in terms of prices rather than quantities. The legacy of Bertrand is not, however, his criticism of what he termed "pseudo-mathematics" in economics. Instead, Bertrand's contribution was the recognition that outcome of the strategic interaction depends critically on the nature of the strategic variable—in this case, quantity versus price. This is just a way of expressing the point made at the start of the previous chapter. The rules of the game matter . . . a lot.

Therefore, consider the simple duopoly model of Chapter 9, but now let each firm choose the price it will charge rather than the quantity it will produce. All other assumptions, however, remain unchanged. Each firm produces the same good at the same constant marginal cost c, and the firms choose their strategies simultaneously. Each firm knows the structure of market demand and its rival's cost, as well as the fact that total demand is: $P = A - BQ$. In this case, it is more convenient to write the demand function with output as the dependent variable.[1] Hence:

$$Q = a - bP; \quad \text{where} \quad a = \frac{A}{B} \quad \text{and} \quad b = \frac{1}{B} \tag{10.1}$$

Consider the pricing problem first from firm 2's perspective. In order to determine its best price response to its rival, firm 2 must first work out the demand for its product *conditional* on both its own price, denoted by p_2, and firm 1's price, denoted by p_1. Rationally speaking, firm 2's reasoning would go as follows. If $p_2 > p_1$, firm 2 will sell no output. The product is homogenous so that consumers always buy from the cheapest source. Setting a price above that of firm 1 therefore means that firm 2 will serve no customers. The opposite is true if $p_2 < p_1$. When firm 2 sets the lower price, it will supply the entire market, and firm 1 will sell nothing. Finally, if $p_2 = p_1$, the two firms will split the market evenly. When both firms charge identical prices, we will assume that each firm's demand is one half the total market demand at that price.

The foregoing reasoning tells us that demand for firm 2's output, q_2, may be described as follows:

$$q_2 = 0 \qquad \text{if } p_2 > p_1$$

$$q_2 = \frac{a - bp_2}{2} \qquad \text{if } p_2 = p_1 \tag{10.2}$$

$$q_2 = a - bp_2 \qquad \text{if } p_2 < p_1$$

---

[1]   When firms choose quantities (as in Cournot's model) it is often easier to work with the inverse demand curve and treat price as the dependent variable. When firms select prices, as in Bertrand's analysis, it is often best to let quantity be the dependent variable.

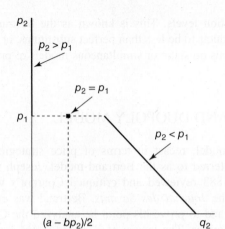

Figure 10.1   Firm 2's demand curve in the Bertrand model
Industry demand equal to $a - bp_2$ is the same as firm 2's demand for all p_2 less than p_1. If $p_2 = p_1$, then the two firms share equally the total demand. For $p_2 > p_1$, firm 2's demand falls to zero.

As Figure 10.1 shows, this demand function is *not* continuous. For any p_2 greater than p_1, demand for q_2 is zero. But when p_2 falls and becomes exactly equal to p_1, demand jumps from zero to $\dfrac{a - bp_2}{2}$. When p_2 then falls still further so that it is below p_1, demand then jumps again to $a - bp_2$.

This discontinuity in firm 2's demand curve was not present in the Cournot model of quantity competition, and it turns out to make a crucial difference in terms of firms' strategies. The discontinuity in demand carries over into a discontinuity in profits. Firm 2's profit, Π_2, as a function of p_1 and p_2 is:

$$\Pi_2(p_1, p_2) = 0 \qquad\qquad \text{if } p_2 > p_1$$

$$\Pi_2(p_1, p_2) = (p_2 - c)\frac{a - bp_2}{2} \qquad \text{if } p_2 = p_1 \qquad\qquad (10.3)$$

$$\Pi_2(p_1, p_2) = (p_2 - c)(a - bp_2) \qquad \text{if } p_2 < p_1$$

To find firm 2's *best response* function, we need to find the price p_2 that maximizes firm 2's profits $\Pi_2(p_1, p_2)$ for any given choice of p_1. For example, suppose firm 1 chooses a very high price—higher even than the pure monopoly price, which in this case is $p^M = \dfrac{a + bc}{2b}$.[2] Because firm 2 could capture the entire market by selecting any price lower than p_1, its best response would be to choose the pure monopoly price p^M, and thereby earn the pure monopoly profits.

Conversely, what if firm 1 set a very low price, say one below its unit cost c? This would be an unusual choice, but if we wish to construct a complete *best response* function for firm 2, we must determine its value for *all* the possible values p_1 can take. If $p_1 < c$, then firm 2 is best setting its price a level above p_1. This will mean that firm 2 will sell nothing

---

[2]   This is, of course, the same monopoly price as we showed in Chapter 8 for the quantity version of the model with the notational change that $a = A/B$, and $b = 1/B$.

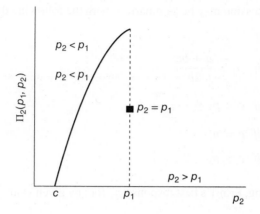

Figure 10.2   Firm 2's profits as a function of p_2 when firm 1 prices above cost but below the pure monopoly price
Firm 2's profits rise continuously as its price rises from the level of marginal cost, c, to just below firm 1's price. When p_2 equals p_1, firm 2's profits fall relative to those earned when p_2 is just below p_1. For p_2 greater than p_1, firm 2 earns zero profits.

and earn zero profits. The alternative of setting $p_2 \leq p_1 < c$ will lead to *negative* profits: firm 2 sells a positive amount of output, but at a price below unit cost so that it loses money on each unit sold.

What about the more likely case in which firm 1 sets its price above marginal cost c but either equal to or below the pure monopoly price p^M? How should firm 2 optimally respond in these circumstances? The simple answer is that it should set a price *just a bit less than p_1*. The intuition behind this strategy is illustrated in Figure 10.2, which shows firm 2's profit given a price p_1, satisfying the relationship $\dfrac{a + bc}{2b} \geq p_1 > c$.

Note that firm 2's profits rise continuously as p_2 rises from c to just below p_1. Whenever p_2 is less than p_1, firm 2 is the only company that sells anything. However, when p_1 is less than or equal to p^M, the monopoly power that firm 2 obtains from undercutting p_1 is constrained. In particular, the firm cannot sell at the pure monopoly price, p^M, and earn the associated profit because at that price, firm 2 would lose all its customers. Still, the firm will wish to get as close to that result as possible. It could, of course, just match firm 1's price exactly. But whenever it does so, it shares the market equally with its rival. If, instead, firm 2 just *slightly* reduces its price below p_1 level, it will double its sales while incurring only an infinitesimal decline in its profit margin per unit sold. This is a trade well worth the making, as Figure 10.2 makes clear. In turn, the implication is that for any p_1 such that $p^M \geq p_1 > c$, firm 2's best response is to set $p_2^* = p_1 - \varepsilon$, where ε is an arbitrarily small amount.

The last case to consider is the case in which firm 1 prices at cost so that $p_1 = c$. Clearly, firm 2 has no incentive to undercut this value of p_1. To do so would only lead to losses for firm 2. Instead, firm 2 will do best to set p_2 either equal to or above p_1. If it prices above p_1, firm 2 will sell nothing and earn zero profits. If it matches p_1, it will enjoy positive sales but break even on every unit sold. Accordingly, firm 2 will earn zero profits in this latter case, too. Thus, when $p_1 = c$, firm 2's *best response* is to set p_2 either greater than or equal to p_1.

Our preceding discussion may be summarized with the following description of firm 2's best price response:

$$p_2^* = \frac{a + bc}{2b} \qquad if \ \ p_1 > \frac{a + bc}{2b}$$

$$p_2^* = p_1 - \varepsilon \qquad if \ \ c < p_1 \leq \frac{a + bc}{2b} \tag{10.4}$$

$$p_2^* \geq p_1 \qquad if \ \ c = p_1$$

$$p_2^* > p_1 \qquad if \ \ c > p_1 \geq 0$$

By similar reasoning, firm 1's best response p_1^* for any given value of p_2 would be given by:

$$p_1^* = \frac{a + bc}{2b} \qquad if \ \ p_2 > \frac{a + bc}{2b}$$

$$p_1^* = p_2 - \varepsilon \qquad if \ \ c < p_1 \leq \frac{a + bc}{2b} \tag{10.5}$$

$$p_1^* \geq p_2 \qquad if \ \ c = p_2$$

$$p_1^* > p_2 \qquad if \ \ c > p_2 \geq 0$$

We may now determine the Nash equilibrium for the duopoly game when played in prices. We know that a Nash equilibrium is one in which neither firm has an incentive to change its strategy. For example, the strategy combination $\left[p_1 = \dfrac{a + bc}{2b}, p_2 = \dfrac{a + bc}{2b} - \varepsilon \right]$ *cannot* be an equilibrium. This is because in that combination, firm 2 undercuts firm 1's price and sells at a price just below the monopoly level. However, in such a case, firm 1 would have no customers and earn zero profit. Because firm 1 could earn a substantial profit by lowering its price to just below that set by firm 2, it would wish to do so. Accordingly, this strategy cannot be a Nash equilibrium. To put it another way, firm 2 could never expect firm 1 to set the monopoly price of $p_1 = (a + c)/2b$ precisely because firm 1 would know that so doing would lead to zero profit as firm 2 would undercut that price by a small amount ε and steal all of firm 1's customers.

As it turns out, there is one and only one Nash equilibrium for the Bertrand duopoly game described above. It is the price pair, $(p_1^* = c, p_2^* = c)$.[3] If firm 1 sets this price in the expectation that firm 2 will do so, and if firm 2 acts in precisely the same manner, neither will have an incentive to change. Hence, the outcome of the Bertrand duopoly game is that the market price equals marginal cost. This is, of course, exactly what occurs under perfect competition. The only difference is that here, instead of many small firms, we have just two firms, each of which is large relative to the market.

It is no wonder that Bertrand made note of the different outcome obtained when price replaces quantity as the strategic variable. Far from being a cosmetic or minor change, this alternative specification has a dramatic impact. It is useful, therefore, to explore the nature and the source of this powerful effect more closely.

---

[3]   This outcome assumes that prices can be varied continuously.

Practice Problem

10.1

Let the market demand for carbonated water be given by $Q^D = 100 - 5P$. Let there be two firms producing carbonated water, each with a constant marginal cost of 2.

a. What is the market equilibrium price and quantity when each firm behaves as a Cournot duopolist choosing quantities? What profit does each firm earn?

b. What is the market equilibrium price and quantity when each firm behaves as a Bertrand duopolist choosing price? What firm profit does each firm earn now?

10.2   BERTRAND RECONSIDERED

Like its Cournot cousin, the Bertrand analysis of a duopoly market is not without its critics. One chief source of criticism with the Bertrand model is its assumption that *any* price deviation between the two firms leads to an immediate and complete loss of demand for the firm charging the higher price. It is, of course, this assumption that gives rise to the discontinuity in both firms' demand and profit functions. It is also this assumption that underlies our derivation of each firm's best response function and their intersection at $P = MC$.

There are two very sound reasons that a firm's decision to charge a price higher than its rival may not result in the complete loss of all its customers. One reason is that typically the rival firm does not have the capacity to serve all of the customers who demand the product or service at its low price.[4] The second is that consumers may not view the two products as perfect substitutes.

To see the importance of capacity constraints, consider the fictional case of a small New England area with two ski resorts, Pepall Ridge and Snow Richards, each located on different sides of Mount Norman. Skiers regard the services at these resorts to be the same and will choose when possible to ski at the resort that quotes the lowest lift ticket price. Pepall Ridge and Snow Richards are roughly the same size and each can handle 1,800 skiers a day. We will further assume that the overall demand for skiing at Mount Norman is: $Q = 6000 - 60P$, where P is the price of a daily lift ticket and Q is number of skiers per day.

The two resorts compete in price. Suppose that the marginal cost of providing lift services is the same at each resort and is equal to $10 per skier. However, the outcome in which each resort sets a price equal to marginal cost *cannot* be a Nash equilibrium. Demand when the price of a lift ticket is equal to $10 would be equal to 5,400 skiers, far exceeding the total capacity of the two resorts. To be sure, if each resort had understood the extent of demand, each might have built additional lifts, ski runs, and parking facilities in order to increase capacity. Nevertheless, it is still not likely that the Nash equilibrium will end up with each resort charging a lift ticket price equal to the marginal cost of $10 per skier. Why? Think of it this way. If Pepall Ridge sets a price of $11, Snow Richards will only find it profitable to undercut this price—say, charge $10.90 for a lift ticket—if it can serve all the skiers who would come at this lower price. Yet because total demand at $P = \$10.90$ is $Q = 5346$ it clearly cannot do so with its current capacity of 1,800.

---

[4]   Edgeworth (1925) was one of the first economists to investigate the impact of capacity constraints on Bertrand analysis.

We might then ask how each resort ended up with a capacity of just 1,800. Wouldn't it have been profitable for each to expand their capacity precisely because this would then enable either to undercut the other's price and gain more profit? The answer to this question, however, is no. Consider an initial capacity choice by each firm of 5,400. Clearly, such a choice is required for each firm to make a credible threat of cutting its price to $10. Yet if each firm did cut its price to this marginal cost, each would only serve half the market, i.e., 2,700 skiers per day. Given that building capacity is expensive, neither firm will choose an initial capacity of 5,400 because this would imply an equilibrium in which each firm sets a price equal to marginal cost = $10 and in which each would serve only 2,700 skiers and have an equal amount of costly but unused capacity.

We can see then that when capacity constraints are binding, a firm charging a higher price than its rival only loses all its customers if its rival has the capacity to serve them. We can also see that such a capacity choice for both firms is not likely in the range of P = marginal cost = $10. Hence, once capacity constraints are considered, Bertrand's proposed solution that $p_1 = p_2$ = marginal cost is no longer a Nash equilibrium. This leaves open, though, the question of precisely what capacity choice for each firm does make sense, i.e., what is the Nash equilibrium capacity choice?

When capacity constraints come into play, the game between the two firms really becomes a two-stage one. In the first stage, the two firms choose capacity levels. In the second, they compete in price. Viewed in this light, it is straightforward to show that the outcome is likely to be close to the Cournot solution despite the fact that competition is in prices as Bertrand proposed.[5] To see this point more clearly, let's return to the ski resort competition between Pepall Ridge and Snow Richards. We assume that at any price at which a resort has demand beyond its maximum capacity, the skiers that the resort serves are those skiers who are the most eager and who have the highest willingness to pay.[6] Suppose, for instance, that each resort sets a lift price of $30. Then total market demand is 4,200, well beyond the total capacity of 3,600 across both firms. Therefore, each resort will need somehow to ration or choose which skiers will actually ski. Our assumption, sometimes called the efficient rationing assumption, is that the resorts will do this by serving customers in order of their willingness to pay. Pepall Ridge, for example, will serve the 1,800 potential skiers with the 1,800 highest willingesses to pay. In turn, the assumption of efficient rationing allows us to derive the residual demand curve facing Snow Richards at any price.

A price of particular interest is $40. Suppose then that both resorts have set $p_1 = p_2 =$ $40. At these prices, total demand is equal to 3,600, which is just equal to the total capacity of the two resorts. Is this a Nash equilibrium? We can answer this question by using the logic above to determine the demand function facing Snow Richards when Pepall Ridge sets a price equal to $40. Under our assumption of efficient rationing, this is shown in Figure 10.3. It is the original demand curve shifted to the left by 1,800 units, i.e. it is $Q = 4200 - 60P$ (or, in inverse form, $P = 70 - Q/60$). The associated marginal revenue curve— $MR = 70 - Q/30$—is also shown.

Note though that while changes in its price also change its quantity demanded, Snow Richards is always constrained to serve no more than its capacity of 1,800. This is why Figure 10.3 shows the residual demand and marginal revenue curves truncated at that output level. More importantly, note that when Pepall Ridge sets a price of $40, Snow Richards

---

[5] This result is formally modeled in a two-stage game in Kreps and Scheinkman (1983).

[6] We also implicitly assume that in the first stage, installing capacity of any amount is costless but that, once installed, that capacity cannot be expanded in the second stage.

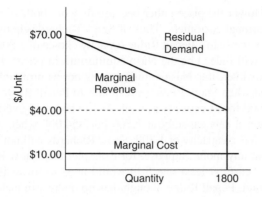

Figure 10.3   Snow Richards residual demand curve

finds that $MR = MC$ at an output exactly equal to its capacity of 1,800, implying that this is indeed the best response for Snow Richards. It also implies a price of $40 for this resort as well. In turn, both firms charging a price of $40 also leads to the full utilization of the 1,800 skiers per day capacity at Pepall Ridge. There can be no doubt then that price = $40 for both firms is a Nash equilibrium if both choose capacity of 1,800. But is this the right capacity level? Given Pepall Ridge's choice, would Snow Richards have preferred to have a greater or lesser capacity?

Suppose for instance that Snow Richards initially chose a capacity of 1,700 while, as noted, Pepall Ridge had chosen 1,800. In this case, $40 could no longer be the price at both firms because then the total demand (3,600) would exceed the total capacity (3,500). What would the new price equilibrium be? Start by noting what happens if the price set by both firms is $41.67, i.e., the price point at which total demand would equal the capacity of 3,500. If each firm charges $41.67 per lift ticket, Pepall Ridge will serve 1,800 skiers per day, Snow Richards will serve 1,700, and the market will clear. If just one firm raises its price, it loses no customers to its rival (which is working at capacity) but it does lose marginal consumers who are not willing to pay any more for a lift ticket. That is, for each firm, we can again work out the residual demand curve and associated marginal revenue curve given the price and capacity choice of its rival. These are:

Snow Richards   —Residual Demand : $P = 70 - Q/60$

—Residual Marginal Revenue : $MR = 70 - Q/30$

Pepall Ridge   —Residual Demand : $P = 71.67 - Q/60$

—Residual Marginal Revenue : $MR = 71.67 - Q/30$

Profit maximization implies that each firm will want to expand its output and lower its price so long as marginal revenue exceeds marginal cost and so long as there is spare capacity. It is straightforward to show, though, that at the capacity limit of each firm (1,700 and 1,800, respectively), the marginal revenue for each firm exceeds or equals its marginal cost so that each will want to produce at least to capacity. To put it another way, with each firm setting a price of $41.67 and each working to capacity, neither will want to raise its price because to do so would lose more in revenue than it would save in costs. Of course, neither firm wants to lower the price either because they are both working at capacity and cannot serve any additional customers. Thus, if Snow Richards chooses instead the lower capacity of 1,700 in response to a Pepall Ridge capacity choice of 1,800, each firm charging $41.67 per lift ticket will indeed be the Nash equilibrium in prices. From the perspective of Snow Richards, however, this Nash equilibrium is not as profitable as the equilibrium that we earlier derived when Snow Richards responds to Pepall Ridge's capacity choice of 1,800 by selecting 1,800 for its capacity as well. As can be readily verified, Snow Richards earns $53,833.33 when it sets capacity at 1,700 but $54,000 when it sets it at 1,800. In short, if Pepall Ridge has a capacity of 1,800, Snow Richards will not want any less.

It will also not want any more. Suppose, for example, that Snow Richards had a 1,900 skier capacity. In this case, at least one firm would need to lower its price to $38.33 in order to clear the market. Pepall Ridge, though, has no interest in making such a price cut. If it keeps its price at $40, it will serve its capacity of 1,800 skiers regardless of the Snow Richards price because that firm can only serve 1,900 skiers. Thus, there is no reason for Pepall Ridge to cut its price if Snow Richards expands its capacity by 100 units. This means that Snow Richards faces exactly the same situation as in the original Nash equilibrium, except that now its residual marginal revenue curve, $MR = 70 - Q/30$, extends to an output of 1,900 before it is truncated. Yet that marginal revenue falls below the marginal cost of $10 as soon as the firm's output exceeds 1,800 units. If Snow Richards had the additional capacity, it would not want to use it. Hence, there is no point in installing the extra 100 units of capacity in the first place.

Obviously, the foregoing argument is symmetric so that just as Snow Richards wants neither to expand nor contract its capacity from 1,800, neither does Pepall Ridge. It follows that each firm choosing a capacity of 1,800 and setting a price of $40 is the Nash equilibrium for this price competition game. More importantly, this outcome is exactly the same as the Cournot outcome in a market without capacity constraints but in which each firm has a constant marginal cost of 10 and market demand is described by $Q = 6000 - 60P$. That is, once capacity constraints are considered and assuming efficient rationing, Bertrand price competition yields Cournot quantity competition outcomes. This is in fact a fairly general result, again, conditional on the key assumptions. Of course, in reality, capacity may be more expandable than assumed here and rationing may not be efficient. Nevertheless, the analysis provides a strong counter argument to the dramatic marginal-cost pricing implication of the simple Bertrand model.

10.2

Practice Problem

Suppose now that market demand for skiing increases to $Q^D = 9000 - 60P$. However, because of environmental regulations neither Pepall Ridge nor Snow Richards can increase their capacities and serve more skiers beyond their current level of 1,800. What is the Nash equilibrium price outcome for this case?

10.3   BERTRAND IN A SPATIAL SETTING

There is a second reason that the simple Bertrand efficient outcome of price equal to marginal cost may not occur. This is that the two firms often do not, as Bertrand assumed, produce identical products. Think of hair salons, for example. No two hair stylists cut and style hair in exactly the same way. Nor will the salons have exactly the same sort of equipment or furnishings. Also, as long as the two firms are not side by side, they will differ in their locations. This is often sufficient by itself to generate a preference by some consumers for one salon or the other even when different prices are charged. In short, differences in locations, furnishings, or cutting styles can each be sufficient to permit one salon to price somewhat higher than its rival without immediately losing all of its customers.

We presented a spatial model of product differentiation in Chapter 7. There our aim was to understand the use of such differentiation by a monopoly firm to extract additional surplus from its customers. The same model, however, may also be used to understand the nature of price competition when competing firms market differentiated products. Let's review the basic setup presented earlier. There is a line of unit length (say one mile) along which consumers are uniformly distributed. This market is supplied by two stores. This time though, the same company does not operate the two stores. Rival firms operate them. One firm—located at the west end of town—has the address $x = 0$. The other—located at the east end of town—has the location, $x = 1$. Each of the firms has the same constant unit cost of production c.

We define a consumer's "location" in this market to be that consumer's most preferred product, or style. Thus "consumer x" is located distance x from the left-hand end of the market, where distance may be geographic in a spatial model or measured in terms of characteristics in a more general product differentiation sense. While consumers differ regarding which variant or location of the good they consider to be the best, they are identical in their reservation price V for their most preferred product. We further assume that the reservation price V is substantially greater than the unit cost of production c. Each consumer buys at most one unit of the product. If consumer x purchases a good that is not an ideal product, the consumer incurs a utility loss. Specifically, consumer x incurs the cost tx if good 1 (located at $x = 0$) is consumed, and the cost $t(1 - x)$ if good 2 (located at $x = 1$) is consumed. If the consumer buys good 1 at price p_1, the consumer enjoys consumer surplus $V - p_1 - tx$; if good 2 at price p_2 is purchased, there will be a consumer surplus of $V - p_2 - t(1 - x_2)$. Of course, the consumer will purchase the good that offers the greater consumer surplus provided that this is greater than zero. Figure 10.4 describes this market setting.

It bears reemphasizing that the concept of location that we have introduced here serves as a metaphor for all manner of qualitative differences between products. Instead of having two stores geographically separated, we can think of two products marketed by two different firms that are differentiated by some characteristic, such as sugar content in the case of soft drinks, fat content in the case of fast food, or fuel efficiency in the case of automobiles. Our unit line in each case represents the spectrum of products differentiated by this characteristic and each consumer has a most preferred product specification on this line. For the case of soft drinks our two firms could be Pepsi and Coca-Cola. In the case of fast food, our two firms could be McDonald's and Burger King, whereas for automobiles, our two firms could be Ford and GM.

As in the simple Bertrand model, the two firms compete for customers by setting prices p_1 and p_2, respectively. These are chosen simultaneously, and we want to solve for a Nash

Firm 1   x   Firm 2

Figure 10.4   The "main street" spatial model once again

equilibrium solution to the game. If $V > c$ then in equilibrium it must be the case that both firms have a positive market share. Because any equilibrium will require that firms charge at least c per unit and because customers always prefer the closer shop at any common price, there is no way that either firm can steal all the customers from its rival. Here, we assume not only that $V > c$, but also that V is sufficiently large that the entire market is served. That is, the market outcome is such that every consumer buys one unit of the product from either firm 1 or firm 2.[7] When V is large, each customer can be charged a price sufficiently high to make each such sale profitable.

When the entire market is served, then it must be the case that there is some consumer, called the marginal consumer x^m, who is indifferent between buying from either firm 1 or firm 2. That is, this consumer enjoys the same consumer surplus either way. Algebraically, this means that for consumer x^m:

$$V - p_1 - tx^m = V - p_2 - t(1 - x^m) \tag{10.6}$$

Equation 10.6 may be solved to find the address or the location of the marginal consumer, x^m. This is:

$$x^m(p_1, p_2) = \frac{(p_2 - p_1 + t)}{2t} \tag{10.7}$$

At any set of prices p_1 and p_2, all consumers to the left of x^m buy from firm 1. All those to the right of x^m buy from firm 2. In other words, x^m is the fraction of the market that buys from firm 1 and $(1 - x^m)$ is the fraction that buys from firm 2. If the total number of consumers is N and they are uniformly distributed over the market space, the demand function facing firm 1 at any price combination (p_1, p_2) in which the entire market is served is:[8]

$$D^1(p_1, p_2) = x^m(p_1, p_2) = \frac{(p_2 - p_1 + t)}{2t}N \tag{10.8}$$

Similarly, firm 2's demand function is:

$$D^2(p_1, p_2) = (1 - x^m(p_1, p_2)) = \frac{(p_1 - p_2 + t)}{2t}N \tag{10.9}$$

These demand functions make sense in that each firm's demand is decreasing in its own price but increasing in its competitor's price. Notice also that, unlike the simple Bertrand duopoly model in Section 10.1, the demand function facing either firm here is continuous in both p_1 and p_2. This is because when goods are differentiated, a decision by say firm 1 to set p_1 a little higher than its rival's price p_2 does not cause firm 1 to lose all of its customers. Some of its customers still prefer to buy good 1 even at the higher price simply because they prefer that version of the good to the style (or location) marketed by firm 2.[9]

---

[7]   Refer to Figure 7.3 in Chapter 7 for a discussion of this point.

[8]   We are using N here to refer to the *number of consumers* in the market.

[9]   Our assumption that the equilibrium is one in which the entire market is served is critical to the continuity result.

The continuity in demand functions carries over into the profit functions. Firm 1's profit function is:

$$\Pi^1(p_1, p_2) = (p_1 - c)\frac{(p_2 - p_1 + t)}{2t}N \tag{10.10}$$

Similarly, firm 2's profits are given by:

$$\Pi^2(p_1, p_2) = (p_2 - c)\frac{(p_1 - p_2 + t)}{2t}N \tag{10.11}$$

In order to work out firm 1's best response pricing strategy we need to work out how firm 1's profit changes as the firm varies price p_1 in response to a given price p_2 set by firm 2. The most straightforward way to do this is to take the derivative of the profit function (10.10) with respect to p_1. When we set the derivative equal to zero we can then solve for the firm's best response price p_1^* to a given price p_2 set by firm 2.[10]

However, careful application of the alternative solution method of converting firm 1's demand curve into its inverse form and solving for the point at which marginal revenue equals marginal cost will also work. From (10.7), we can write firm 1's inverse demand curve for a given value of firm 2's price p_2 as $p_1 = p_2 + t - \frac{2t}{N}q_1$. Hence firm 1's marginal revenue curve is $MR_1 = p_2 + t - \frac{4t}{N}q_1$. Equating firm 1's marginal revenue with its marginal cost gives the first-order condition for profit maximization, $p_2 + t - \frac{4t}{N}q_1 = c$. Solving for the optimal value of firm 1's output, again given the price chosen by firm 2, we then obtain:

$$q_1^* = \frac{N}{4t}(p_2 + t - c) \tag{10.12}$$

When we substitute the value of q_1^* from equation (10.12) into firm 1's inverse demand curve, we find the optimal price for firm 1 to set given the value of the price set by firm 2. This is by definition firm 1's best response function:

$$p_1^* = \frac{p_2 + c + t}{2} \tag{10.13}$$

where t is the per unit distance transportation or utility cost incurred by a consumer. Of course, we can replicate this procedure for firm 2. Because the firms are symmetric, the best response function of each firm is the mirror image of that of its rival. Hence, firm 2's best price response function is:

$$p_2^* = \frac{p_1 + c + t}{2} \tag{10.14}$$

The best response functions described in (10.13) and (10.14) for the two firms are illustrated in Figure 10.5. They are upward sloping. The Nash equilibrium set of prices is, of course, where these best response functions intersect. In other words, the Nash equilibrium

[10]   Setting $\partial\Pi^1(p_1, p_2)/\partial p_1 = 0$ in equation (10.10) yields immediately: $p_1^* = (p_2 + c + t)/2$.

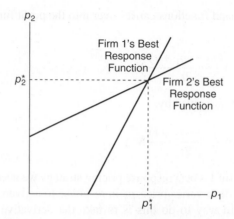

Figure 10.5   Best response functions for price competition with imperfect substitutes

is a pair of prices (p_1^*, p_2^*) such that p_1^* is firm 1's best response to p_2^* and p_2^* is firm 2's best response to p_1^*. Thus, we may replace p_1 and p_2 on the right-hand-side of the equations in (10.13) and (10.14) with p_1^* and p_2^*, respectively. Solving jointly for the Nash equilibrium pair (p_1^*, p_2^*) yields:

$$p_1^* = p_2^* = c + t \tag{10.15}$$

In equilibrium, each firm charges a price that is equal to the unit production cost *plus* an amount t, the utility cost per unit of distance a consumer incurs in buying a good that is at some distance from the preferred good. At these prices, the firms split the market. The marginal consumer is located at the address $x = 1/2$. The profit earned by each firm is the same, and equal to $(p_i^* - c)N/2 = tN/2$.

By way of example, consider the two hair salons located one mile apart on Main Street. All the potential customers live along this stretch of Main Street and are uniformly spread out. Each consumer is willing to pay at most $50 for a haircut done at the consumer's home. However, if a consumer has to travel to get a haircut a round-trip travel cost of $5 per mile will be incurred. Each of the hair salons can cut hair at a constant unit cost of $10 per cut, and each wants to set a price per haircut that maximizes the salon's profit. Our model predicts that the equilibrium price of a haircut in this town will be $15, a price that is greater than the marginal cost of a haircut.

Two points are worth making in connection with these results. First, note the role that the parameter t plays. It is a measure of the value each consumer places on obtaining the most preferred version of the product. The greater t is, the less willing the consumer is to buy a product "far away" from the favorite location, product, or style. That is, a high t value indicates consumers have strong preferences for their most desired product and incur a high utility loss from having to consume a product that is less than ideal. The result is that neither firm has much to worry about when charging a high price because consumers prefer to pay that price rather than buy a low-price alternative that is "far away" from their preferred style. When t is large, the price competition between the two firms is softened. In other words, a large value of t means that product differentiation makes price competition much less intense.

Reality Checkpoint

Unfriendly Skies: Price Wars in Airline Markets

Following the euphoria that accompanied deregulation in 1977, the major airlines have been in for a bumpy ride with generally lower and more volatile profits. One source of this downward trend has been the persistent recurrence of price wars. Morrison and Winston (1996) define such conflicts as any city-pair route market in which the average airfare declines by 20 percent or more within a single quarter. Based on this definition, they estimate that over 81 percent of airline city-pair routes experienced such wars in the 1979–95 time period. In the wars so identified, the average fare in fact typically falls by over 37 percent and sometimes falls by as much as 79 percent. While these conflicts abated in the last part of the 1990s, new wars had emerged by the early 2000s and continued through the decade leading to more than six bankruptcies and a number of mergers. The continued price pressure largely stemmed from two forces. First, the growth of low-cost airlines such as

Southwest and JetBlue placed continued pressure on fares. Berry and Jia (2010) document that this pressure was increasingly strong as consumers grew to view the low-cost carriers as close substitutes for the more established ones. Second, in the wake of the recessions associated with the dot-com bubble and, later, the sub-prime mortgage collapses, business demand became substantially more price sensitive. These factors push prices closer to marginal cost and raise consumer surplus, but this is not much comfort to airline executives.

Source: S. Morrison and C. Winston, 1996. "Causes and Consequences of Airline Fare Wars," *Brookings Papers on Economic Activity*, Microeconomics: 85–124.; M. Maynard, "Yes, It Was a Dismal Year for Airlines; Now for the Bad News," *New York Times*, December 16, 2002, p. C2.; S. Berry and P. Jia, 2010. "Tracing the Woes: An Empirical Analysis of the Airline Industry," *American Economic Journal* 2 (August): 1–43.

However, as t falls consumers place less value on obtaining their most preferred styles, and become more sensitive to lower prices. This intensifies price competition. In the limit, when $t = 0$, product differentiation is of no value to consumers. They treat all goods as essentially identical. Price competition becomes fierce and, in the limit, drives prices to marginal cost just as in the original Bertrand model.

The second point concerns the location of the firms. We simply assumed that the two firms were located at either end of town. However, the location or product design of the firm is also part of a firm's strategy. Allowing the two firms to choose simultaneously *both* their price and their location strategies makes the model too complicated to solve here. Still, the intuition behind location choice is instructive. There are two opposing forces affecting the choice of price and location. On the one hand, the two firms will wish to avoid locating at the same point because to do so eliminates all differences between the two products. Price competition in this case will be fierce, as in the original Bertrand model. On the other hand, each firm also has some incentive to be located near the center of town. This enables a firm to reach as large a market as possible. Evaluating the balance of these two forces is what makes the solution of the equilibrium outcome so difficult.[11]

---

[11]   There is a wealth of literature on this topic with the outcome often depending on the precise functional forms assumed. See, for example, Eaton (1976); D'Aspremont, Gabszewicz, and Thisse (1979); Novshek (1980); and Economides (1989).

Imagine that the two hair salons located on Main Street no longer have the same unit cost. In particular, one salon has a constant unit cost of $10 whereas the other salon has a constant unit cost of $20. The low-cost salon, we'll call it Cheap-Cuts, is located at the west end of town, $x = 0$. The high-cost salon, The Ritz, is located at the east end, $x = 1$. There are 100 potential customers who live along the mile stretch, and they are uniformly spread out along the mile. Consumers are willing to pay $50 for a haircut done at their home. If a consumer has to travel to get a haircut, then a travel cost of $5 per mile is incurred. Each salon wants to set a price for a haircut that maximizes the salon's profit.

a. The demand functions facing the two salons are not affected by the fact that now one salon is high cost and the other is low cost. However the salons' best response functions are affected. Compute the best response function for each salon. How does an increase the unit cost of one salon affect the other salon's best response?

b. Work out the Nash equilibrium in prices for this model. Compare these prices to the ones derived in the text for the case when the two salons had the same unit cost equal to $10. Explain why prices changed in the way they did. It may be helpful in your explanation to draw the best response functions when the salons are identical and compare them to those when the salons have different costs.

10.4   STRATEGIC COMPLEMENTS AND SUBSTITUTES

Best response functions in simultaneous-move games are extremely useful tools for understanding what we mean by a Nash equilibrium outcome. But an analysis of such functions also serves other useful purposes. In particular, examining the properties of best response functions can aid our understanding of how strategic interaction works and how that interaction can be made "more" or "less" competitive.

Figure 10.6 shows both the best response functions for the standard Cournot duopoly model and the best response functions for the Bertrand duopoly model with differentiated

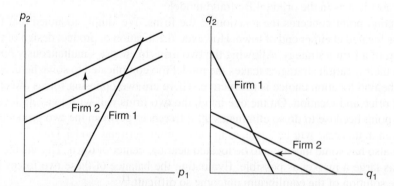

Figure 10.6   Best response functions for the Cournot (quantity) case and the Bertrand (price) case
A rise in firm 2's cost shifts its response function inwards in the Cournot model but outwards in the Bertrand model. Firm 1 reacts aggressively to increase its market share in the Cournot case. It reacts mildly in the Bertrand price by *raising* its price.

products. One feature in the diagram is immediately apparent. The best response functions for the Cournot quantity model are *negatively* sloped—firm 1's best response to an increase in q_2 is to *decrease* q_1. But the best response functions in the Bertrand price model are *positively* sloped. Firm 1's best response to an increase in p_2 is to increase p_1, as well.

Whether the best response functions are negatively or positively sloped is quite important. The slope reveals much about the nature of competition in the product market. To see this, consider the impact of an increase in firm 2's unit cost c_2. Our analysis of the Cournot model indicated that the effect of a rise in c_2 would be to shift *inward* firm 2's best response curve. As Figure 10.6 indicates, this leads to a new Nash equilibrium in which firm 2 produces less and firm 1 produces more than each did before c_2 rose. That is, in the Cournot quantity model, firm 1's response to firm 2's bad luck is a rather aggressive one in which it seizes the opportunity to expand its market share at the expense of firm 2.

Consider now the impact of a rise in c_2 in the context of the differentiated goods Bertrand model. The rise in this case shifts firm 2's best response function *upwards*. Given the rise in its cost, firm 2 will choose to set a higher p_2 than it did previously in response to any given value of p_1. How does firm 1 respond? Unlike the Cournot case, firm 1's reaction is less aggressive. Firm 1—seeing that firm 2 is now less able to set a low price—realizes that the price competition from firm 2 is now less intense. Hence, firm 1 now reacts by raising p_1.

When the best response functions are upward sloping, we say that the strategies (prices in the Bertrand case) are *strategic complements*. When we have the alternative case of downward sloping best response functions, we say that the strategies (quantities in the Cournot case) are *strategic substitutes*.[12] What should be clear at this point is that the choice of modeling firm competition in terms of variables that are strategic substitutes or complements is a crucial one. If we are interested in understanding the competitive dynamics of a particular industry, we need to know the underlying features of that industry that will determine that strategic variable choice. For example, in those industries in which firms set their production schedules far in advance of putting the goods on the market for sale, there is a good case to assume that firms compete in quantities. Examples include aircraft producers, coffee-growers, and automobile manufacturers. In many service industries—such as banking, insurance, and air travel—in which production levels can be quickly adjusted, it is much more natural to think in terms of price competition.

10.5   EMPIRICAL APPLICATION: BRAND COMPETITION AND CONSUMER PREFERENCES—EVIDENCE FROM THE CALIFORNIA RETAIL GASOLINE MARKET

Gasoline is typically produced by refiners and then shipped to a central distribution point. The gasoline is then bought either by an unbranded independent retailer such as RaceTrac, or by service stations selling a branded product such as an Exxon or a Chevron station. In the latter case, a special additive unique to the brand has to be added. That is, to sell "Chevron" gasoline, a station has to have added *Techronas*[TM] to the fuel. Thus, each specific brand is differentiated by the use of its own additive. Independent stations, however, simply sell the basic gasoline without any additive. Here, we briefly describe a paper by Justine

---

[12]   This terminology comes from Bulow, Geanakopolos, and Klemperer (1985) and reflects similar terminology in consumer demand theory.

Hastings (2004) that examines the nature of price competition in the retail gasoline market in Southern California.

The background to the study is as follows. In June of 1997, the Atlantic Richfield Company (ARCO), a well-known refiner and retail brand, acquired control of about 260 gasoline stations that formerly had been operated by the independent retailer, Thrifty, in and around Los Angeles and San Diego. ARCO then converted these to ARCO stations—a process that was essentially completed by September of that same year. Thus, the ARCO-Thrifty acquisition resulted in the exit of a large number of independent service stations in Southern California, as these were replaced in part by ARCO sellers.

Hastings (2004) asks what effect the ARCO-Thrifty deal had on retail gasoline prices. In principle, the effect could be either positive or negative, depending on consumer preferences. If consumers identify brands with higher quality and independents with lower quality, then conversion of the unbranded (low-quality) stations to the ARCO brand would mean that these stations now sell a closer substitute to the other branded products. This would intensify price competition and *lower* branded gasoline prices. However, if a large pool of consumers is unresponsive to brand labels because their willingness to pay for higher quality is limited and they only want to buy gasoline as cheaply as possible, then the loss of the Thrifty stations removes this low-cost alternative and *raises* gasoline prices.

To isolate the effect of the ARCO-Thrifty merger, Hastings (2004) looked at how prices charged by gasoline stations in the Los Angeles and San Diego areas differed depending on whether they competed with a Thrifty or not. Her data cover the prices charged by 699 stations measured at four different times: February 1997, June 1997, October 1997, and December 1997. Notice that the first two dates are for prices before the conversion while the last two dates are for prices after the conversion. She then defines submarkets in which each station's competitors are all the other stations within one mile's driving distance. A simple regression that might capture the effect of the merger would be:

$$p_{it} = Constant + \alpha_i + \beta_1 X_{it} + \beta_2 Z_{it} + e_{it} \tag{10.16}$$

where p_{it} is the price charged by station i at time t; α_i is a firm-specific dummy that lets the intercept be different for each service station; X_{it} is a dummy variable that has the value 1 if station i competes with an independent (Thrifty) at time t and 0 otherwise; likewise Z_{it} is 1 if a competitor of station i has become a station that is owned by a major brand as opposed to a station that operates as a franchisee or lessee of a major brand, and 0 otherwise. This last variable, Z_{it} is meant to capture the impact of any differential effects depending on the contractual relationship between a major brand and the station that sells that brand. The key variable of interest however is X_{it}. We want to know whether the estimated coefficient β_1 is negative, which would indicate that having independent rivals generally leads to lower prices—or is positive, which would indicate that the presence of independents softens competition and raises prices.

However, there is a potentially serious problem with estimating equation (10.16). The problem is that over the course of 1997, gasoline prices were rising generally throughout Southern California. Equation (10.16) does not allow for this general rising trend. Consider our key variable X_{it}. In the data, this will be 1 for a lot more stations before the merger in February and June than it will be in October and December. As a result, the coefficient β_1 will likely be negative because prices were lower in February and June (when there were a lot more independents) than in September and December (after the merger removed the Thrifty stations). That is, β_1 will be biased because it will pick up time effects as well as the effects of independents. The solution to this problem is to include variables that explicitly isolate this time effect so that what is left after this effect is removed is a pure measure of the impact of having an independent gasoline retailers on market prices. Accordingly, Hastings (2004) puts in location specific time dummies for February, June, and September. (The effect of December is of course captured in the regression constant.) That is, she estimates an equation something like:

$$p_{it} = Constant + \alpha_i + \beta_1 X_{it} + \beta_2 Z_{it} + \beta_3 T_i + e_{it} \qquad (10.17)$$

where T_i or time is captured not as a continuous variable but, again, by dummy variables capturing the sequence of specific times in each location. Her results, both with and without the time dummies (but suppressing the firm specific intercepts) are shown in Table 10.1, below.

Consider first the column of results for the equation that includes the location time dummies. Here, the estimate of β_1, the coefficient on having a Thrifty or independent rival in a station's local market, implies that this led the station to lower its price by about five cents per gallon. The standard error on this estimate is very small, so we can be very confident of this measure. Note too how this contrasts with the effect measured in the regression results shown in the first column that leaves out the time effects. That estimate suggests a much larger effect a ten cents per gallon decline when a station has independent rivals. Again, this is because in leaving out the time effects, the regression erroneously attributes the general rise in gasoline prices throughout the region to the merger, when in fact prices were clearly rising for other reasons as well. We should also note that the coefficient estimate for β_2 is not significant in either equation. So, the type of ownership by a major brand does not seem to be important for retail gasoline prices.

One picture is often worth a large number of words. The graph below in Figure 10.7 illustrates the behavior of Southern California gasoline prices over the period covered by Hastings's data for each of two groups: 1) the treatment group that competed with a Thrifty station; and 2) the control group of stations that did not.

Notice the general rise in prices in both groups through October. Clearly, this is a phenomenon common to the gasoline market in general and not the result of the merger per

Table 10.1 Brand competition and gasoline prices

Variable	Without location-time dummies Coefficient (Standard Error)	With location-time dummies Coefficient (Standard Error)
Constant	1.3465 (0.0415)	1.3617 (0.0287)
X_{it}	−0.1013 (0.0178)	−0.0500 (0.0122)
Z_{it}	−0.0033 (0.0143)	−0.0033 (0.0101)
LA*February		0.0180 (0.0065)
LA*June		0.0243 (0.0065)
LA*December		0.1390 (0.0064)
SD*February		−0.0851 (0.0036)
SD*June		−0.0304 (0.0036)
SD*December		0.0545 (0.0545)
R^2	0.3953	0.7181

Dependent Variable = price per gallon of regular unleaded

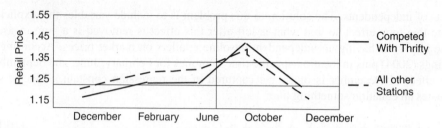

Figure 10.7 "Thrifty" competition and gasoline prices in Southern California

se. However, a close look at the data does reveal that the merger did have some impact. In the months before the merger, stations that competed with a Thrifty had prices that were two to three cents *lower* than those in the control group. Starting about the time of the merger in June, however, and continuing afterwards, these same stations had prices two to three cents *higher* than those in the control group. It is this roughly five-cent effect that is being picked up in the final column of the preceding table.[13] For both groups, those that initially competed with a Thrifty prior to the merger and those that did not, prices differ between the beginning of 1997 and the end. To isolate the effects of the merger, we need to look at how these differences over time were different between the two groups. If we recall that for the treatment group stations $X_{it} = 1$ at first but 0 after the merger, while it is always zero for firms in the control group, the price behavior for the two groups is:

	Before Merger	After Merger	Difference
Treatment group:	$\alpha_i + \beta_1$	$\alpha_i + time\ effects$	$-\beta_1 + time\ effects$
Control Group:	α_j	$\alpha_j + time\ effects$	$time\ effects$

Thus, β_1 in our regression reflects the difference between the difference over time in the treatment group and that in the control group. For this reason, β_1 is often referred to as a *difference-in-differences* estimator.

Summary

In the Bertrand model, firms compete in prices. In the simple model of Bertrand competition, prices are pushed to marginal cost even if there are just two firms. This result stands in sharp contrast with the outcome under quantity or Cournot competition in which prices remain substantially above marginal cost so long as the number of firms is not large. In addition, high-cost firms can survive in Cournot competition whereas they will be forced out of business in the simple Bertrand

model. In short, Bertrand's initial analysis predicts competitive and efficient market outcomes even when the number of firms is quite small.

However, the efficient outcomes predicted by the simple Bertrand model depend upon two key assumptions. The first is that firms have extensive capacity so that it is possible to serve all of a rival's customers after undercutting the rival's price. The second key assumption is that the firms produce identical products so that relative price

---

[13]   More recently, C. Taylor, N. Kreisle, and P. Zimmerman, (2010) use an alternative data set that suggests the impact of the merger was to raise prices by much less than the effect found by Hastings (2004).

is all that matters to consumers when choosing between brands. If either of these assumptions is relaxed, the efficiency outcomes of the simple Bertrand model can no longer be obtained. If firms must choose production capacities in advance, the outcome with Bertrand price competition becomes closer to what occurs in the Cournot model. If products are differentiated, prices are again likely to remain above marginal cost. Indeed, given the fierceness of price competition, firms have a real incentive to differentiate their products.

A useful model of product differentiation is the Hotelling (1929) spatial model, which we first introduced in Chapter 4. This model uses geographic location as a metaphor for more general distinctions between different versions of the same product. It thereby makes it possible to consider price competition between firms selling differentiated products. The model makes it clear that Bertrand competition with differentiated products does not result in efficient marginal cost pricing. It also makes clear that the deviation from such pricing depends on how much consumers value variety. The greater value that the typical consumer places on getting his or her most preferred brand or version of the product, the higher prices will rise above marginal cost.

Ultimately, the differences between Cournot and Bertrand competition reflect underlying differences between quantities and prices as strategic variables. The quantities chosen by Cournot firms are strategic substitutes—increases in one firm's production lead to decreases in the rival's output. In contrast, the prices chosen by Bertrand competitors are strategic complements. A rise in one firm's price permits its rival to raise price, too. To be accurate, analysis of any industry requires familiarity with those industry features that determine whether the competitive rivalry is played out in a setting of strategic substitutes or strategic complements.

Models of price competition based on consumer preferences and perceived quality have provided an extremely useful framework for academicians and policy makers alike. It is important in this regard to identify the precise mechanism in which consumers' preferences for specific brands and designs are modeled. For instance, depending on the nature of consumer preferences, a merger between a high-quality and a low-quality firm that results in the transformation of the low-quality firm outlets to high-quality ones could either weaken competition because it removes a low-quality competitor or intensify competition because it adds to the high-quality supply. In the case of retail gasoline markets in Southern California, work by Hastings (2004) finds that a merger leading to removal of a low-quality firm raised prices, although subsequent work by Taylor, Kreisle, and Zimmerman (2010) offers some contrasting evidence.

Problems

1. Suppose firm 1 and firm 2 each produce the same product and face a market demand curve described by $Q = 5000 - 200P$. Firm 1 has a unit cost of production c_1 equal to 6 whereas firm 2 has a higher unit cost of production c_2 equal to 10.

   a. What is the Bertrand-Nash equilibrium outcome?

   b. What are the profits of each firm?

   c. Is this outcome efficient?

2. Suppose that market demand for golf balls is described by $Q = 90 - 3P$, where Q is measured in kilos of balls. There are two firms that supply the market. Firm 1 can produce a kilo of balls at a constant unit cost of $15 whereas firm 2 has a constant unit cost equal to $10.

   a. Suppose the firms compete in quantities. How much does each firm sell in a Cournot equilibrium? What is the market price and what are the firms' profits?

   b. Suppose the firms compete in price. How much does each firm sell in a Bertrand equilibrium? What is market price and what are the firms' profits?

3. Refer again to the golf ball market described in problem 2.

   a. Would your answer in 2b change if there were three firms, one with unit cost = $20 and two with unit cost = $10? Explain why or why not.

b. Would your answer in 2b change if firm 1's golf balls were green and endorsed by Tiger Woods, whereas firm 2's were plain and white? Explain why or why not.

4. In Tuftsville, everyone lives along Main Street, which is 10 miles long. There are 1,000 people uniformly spread up and down Main Street, and every day they each buy a fruit smoothie from one of the two stores located at either end of Main Street. Customers ride their motor scooters to and from the store using $0.50 worth of gas per mile. Customers buy their smoothies from the store offering the lowest price, which is the store's price plus the customer's travel expenses getting to and from the store. Ben owns the store at the west end of Main Street and Will owns the store at the east end of Main Street.

a. If both Ben and Will charge $1 per smoothie, how many will each of them sell in a day? If Ben charges $1 per smoothie and Will charges $1.40, how many smoothies will each sell in a day?

b. If Ben charges $3 per smoothie, what price would enable Will to sell 250 smoothies per day? 500 smoothies per day? 750 smoothies per day? 1,000 smoothies per day?

c. If Ben charges p_1 and Will charges p_2, what is the location of the customer who is indifferent between going to Ben's or Will's shop? How many customers go to Will's store and how many go to Ben's store? What are the demand functions that Ben and Will face?

d. Rewrite Ben's demand function with p_1 on the left-hand side. What is Ben's marginal revenue function?

e. Assume that the marginal cost of a smoothie is constant and equal to $1 for both Ben and Will. In addition, each of them pays Tuftsville $250 per day for the right to sell smoothies. Find the equilibrium prices, quantities sold, and profits net of the $250 license fee.

5. Return to Main Street in Tuftsville. Now suppose that George would like to open another store at the midpoint of Main Street. He must pay Tuftsville an addional $250 per day to operate this new store.

a. If Ben and Will do not change their prices, what is the best price for George to charge? How much profit would he earn?

b. What do you think would happen if George did open another store in the middle of Main Street? Would Ben and Will have an incentive to change their prices? Their locations? Would one or both leave the market?

6. Suppose that there are two firms, firm B and firm N, that produce complementary goods, say bolts and nuts. The demand curve for each firm is described as follows:

$$Q_B = Z - P_B - P_N \text{ and } Q_N = Z - P_N - P_B$$

For simplicity, assume further that each firm faces a constant unit cost of production, $c = 0$.

a. Show that the profits of each firm may be expressed as $\Pi^B = P_B = (P_B)(Z - P_B - P_N)$ and $\Pi^N = P_N(Z - P_B - P_N)$.

b. Show that each firm's optimal price depends on the price chosen by the other as given by the optimal response functions: $P_B^* = (Z - P_N)/2$ and $P_N^* = (Z - P_B)/2$.

c. Graph these functions. Show that the Nash equilibrium prices are: $P_B = P_N = Z/3$.

d. Are the prices set by each of the two firms either strategic complements or strategic substitutes?

7. Assume that two firms sell differentiated products and face the following demand curves:

$$q_1 = 15 - p_1 + 0.5p_2 \text{ and } q_2 = 15 - p_2 + 0.5p_1;$$

a. Derive the best response function for each firm. Do these indicate that prices are strategic substitutes or strategic complements?

b. What is the equilibrium set of prices in this market? What profits are earned at those prices?

References

Berry, S., and P. Jia, 2010. "Tracing the Woes: An Empirical Analysis of the Airline Industry," *American Economic Journal* 2 (August): 1–43.

Bertrand, J. 1883. "Review," *Journal des Savants* 68: 499–508, reprinted in English translation by James Friedman in A.F. Daughety (ed.) 1988. *Cournot Oligopoly*, Cambridge: Cambridge University Press.

Bulow, J., J. Geanakopolos, and P. Klemperer, 1985. "Multimarket Oligopoly: Strategic Substitutes and Complements." *Journal of Political Economy* 93 (June): 488–511.

D'Aspremont, C., J. Gabszewicz, and J. Thisse, 1979. "On Hotelling's Stability in Competition," *Econometrica* 47 (September): 1145–50.

Eaton, B. C. 1976. "Free Entry in One-Dimensional Models: Pure Profits and Multiple Equilibrium," *Journal of Regional Science* 16 (January): 21–33.

Economides, N. 1989. "Symmetric Equilibrium Existence and Optimality in Differentiated Products Markets," *Journal of Economic Theory* 27 (February): 178–94.

Edgeworth, F.Y. 1925. *"The Pure Theory of Monopoly"*, in Papers Relating to Political Economy Volume I, London: McMillan, 111–142.

Hastings, J. 2004. "Vertical Relationships and Competition in Retail Gasoline Markets: Empirical Evidence from Contract Changes in Southern California," *American Economic Review* 94 (March): 317–28.

Hotelling, H. 1929. "Stability in Competition," *Economic Journal* 39 (January): 41–57.

Kreps, D., and J. Scheinkman. 1983. "Quantity Precommitment and Bertrand Competition Yield Cournot Outcomes," *Bell Journal of Economics* 14 (Autumn): 326–37.

Morrison, S., and Winston, C. 1996. "Causes and Consequences of Airline Fare Wars," *Brookings Papers on Economic Activity: Microeconomics*: 85–124.

Novshek, W. 1980. "Equilibrium in Simple Spatial (or Differentiated Products) Models," *Journal of Economic Theory* 22 (June): 313–26.

Taylor, C., N. Kreisle, and P. Zimmerman. 2010. "Vertical Relationships and Competition in Retail Gasoline Markets: Empirical Evidence from Contract Changes in Southern California: Comment," *American Economic Review* 100 (June): 1269–76.

11

Dynamic Games and First and Second Movers

In 2007, Apple introduced its first *iPhone*. While other advanced, wireless phones already existed (principally, RIM's *Blackberry*), the *iPhone* was the first to allow input through a multi-touch screen rather than with a stylus or keypad, and the first to be compatible with downloadable applications. Its music playing and web browsing capacities were also far superior to anything that then existed. In short, this was the first of the modern "smart" phones.

Competition was not long in coming. In 2008, Google released the operating system *Android* as an open-source platform available to other hardware and software producers. T-Mobile was first with its *HTC Dream* phone but Motorola and Samsung soon began marketing their own *Android*-based phones. As this text is being written, Apple still retains its dominant position (within the United States, at least) as the leading smartphone manufacturer. However, the *Android* operating system now powers more smartphones across all manufacturers combined.[1]

An essential feature of the above strategic interaction between Apple and its rivals is its sequential nature. That is, unlike the simultaneous games discussed in the previous two chapters, this rivalry evolved dynamically over time. First, Apple took an action, and then—after that action was taken and observed—its rivals, principally Google, responded with their own action. Such dynamic games are the focus of this chapter. In principal, these games can have many rounds of play, sometimes called stages. Here, we concentrate mostly on games with just two stages and, for convenience, just two firms. Typically, one firm will play in the first round, the first mover, and the other will play in the second round, the second mover.

Popular business literature is replete with stories about first movers.[2] Many of these focus on specific cases in which, like the Apple smartphone example, the first mover is an early entrant who gains a dominant position and subsequently faces competition from later entrants. In the late nineteenth century, for example, Campbell's emerged as the dominant maker of canned soup in North America. Similarly, Heinz was the first entrant in the UK canned-soup market. Later, Campbell's entered the UK market after Heinz, and similarly Heinz entered the US market after Campbell's. Yet the first mover in each market continues

[1] Nielsen Media Research, "Mobile Media Report: Q3 2011."
[2] Lieberman and Montgomery (1988).

to dominate. Campbell's has roughly 63 percent of the US market, but only 9 percent of the UK market, whereas Heinz has a 41 percent market share in the United Kingdom and a relatively minor market share in the United States.[3]

Sequential entry and dynamic games merit explicit economic analysis, partly because they are so common but also because, as the Campbell's and Heinz cases illustrate, they suggest important advantages for the first entrant into a market in facing competition from later entrants. Remember, entry is a key part of the competitive market's success story as an allocative mechanism. It is entry—or the threat of entry—that erodes the market power of an established firm and that transforms otherwise monopolized markets into competitive ones. This enforcement mechanism will, however, be weakened if there is any asymmetry between established firms and later rivals. Understanding such asymmetry is therefore an important issue in industrial economics.

In the next two chapters, we explore the entry process in detail when the firms—the entrants and the incumbents—are strategic players in the market place. At this juncture, the point to realize is that entry is a sequential process—some firms enter early and some enter late. Thus developing an understanding of dynamic games is good groundwork for our later investigation of entry and entry deterrence in oligopoly markets.

We first examine quantity and price competition when firms move sequentially rather than simultaneously. We will discover again that price and quantity competition are different, and depending on the kind of competition, there can be first-mover or second-mover advantages. This raises the interesting question of whether and how a firm can become either a first- or second-mover. Often the key to achieving the desired position and the associated higher profits is the ability of the firm to make a credible commitment to its strategy when the market opens for trade. We examine what credibility means in game theory and how it affects our equilibrium solution concept for dynamic models.

Simultaneous games, such as the traditional Cournot or Bertrand model, describe a once-and-for-all market interaction between the rival firms. In some sequential games as well there is only one market period where trade takes place, although this might occur in several stages. However, the more likely scenario is that rival firms interact and trade today in the market and then interact again in the future. Moreover, the competing firms understand the likelihood of future interactions today. Repeating the market interaction over and over again gives rise to a somewhat different type of dynamic game, usually called a repeated game. We defer our discussion of repeated games until Chapter 14.

11.1   THE STACKELBERG MODEL OF QUANTITY COMPETITION

The duopoly model of Stackelberg (1934) is similar to the Cournot model except for one critically important difference. The two firms now choose quantities *sequentially* rather than *simultaneously*. The firm that moves first and chooses its output level first is the leader firm. The firm that moves second is the follower firm. The sequential choice of output is what makes the game dynamic. However, the firms trade their goods on the market only once and their interaction yields a "once-and-for-all" market-clearing outcome.

Let market demand again be represented by a linear inverse demand function $P = A - BQ$. Firm 1 is the leader who moves first and firm 2 is the follower who chooses its output *after* the choice of the leader is made. Each firm has the same constant unit

---

[3]   See, for example, Sutton (1991).

cost of production c. Total industry output Q equals the sum of the outputs of each firm, $Q = q_1 + q_2$.

Firm 1 acts first and chooses q_1. How should it make this choice? Both firms are rational and strategic and both firms know this, and know that each other knows this. As a result, firm 1 will make its choice taking into account its best guess as to firm 2's rational response to its choice of q_1. In other words, firm 1 will work out firm 2's best response to each value of q_1, incorporate that best response into its own decision-making, and then choose the q_1 which, given firm 2's best response, maximizes firm 1's profit.

We can solve for firm 2's best response function q_2^* exactly as we did in the Cournot model in Chapter 9. For any choice of output q_1, firm 2 faces the inverse demand and marginal revenue curves:

$$P = (A - Bq_1) - Bq_2$$
$$MR_2 = (A - Bq_1) - 2Bq_2 \tag{11.1}$$

Setting marginal revenue equal to marginal cost yields firm 2's best response q_2^* as the solution to the first-order condition:

$$A - Bq_1 - 2Bq_2^* = c \tag{11.2}$$

from which we obtain:

$$q_2^* = \frac{(A - c)}{2B} - \frac{q_1}{2} \tag{11.3}$$

If firm 1 is rational, firm 1 will understand that equation (11.3) describes what firm 2 will do in response to each possible choice of q_1. We can summarize equation (11.3) by $q_2^*(q_1)$. Anticipating this behavior by firm 2, firm 1 can substitute $q_2^*(q_1)$ for q_2 in its demand function so that its inverse demand function may be written as:

$$P = A - Bq_2^*(q_1) - Bq_1 = \frac{A + c}{2} - \frac{B}{2}q_1, \tag{11.4}$$

In turn, this implies that its profit function is:

$$\Pi_1(q_1, q_2^*(q_1)) = \left(\frac{A + c}{2} - \frac{B}{2}q_1 - c \right) q_1 = \left(\frac{A - c}{2} - \frac{B}{2}q_1 \right) q_1 \tag{11.5}$$

Note that this substitution results in firm 1's demand and profits being dependent only on its own output choice, q_1. This is because firm 1 effectively sets q_2 as well, by virtue of the fact that q_2 is chosen by firm 2 in response to q_1 according to firm 2's best response function, *and firm 1 anticipates this*. In other words, the first-mover correctly predicts the second-mover's best response and incorporates this prediction into its decision-making calculus.

To solve for firm 1's profit-maximizing output q_1^* we find the marginal revenue curve associated with firm 1's demand curve in (11.4), that is, $MR_1 = \dfrac{A + c}{2} - Bq_1$, and find the output q_1^* at which marginal revenue is equal to marginal cost. Alternatively, we could maximize the profit function of equation (11.5) with respect to q_1^*. Either way we find that:

$$q_1^* = \frac{(A - c)}{2B} \qquad (11.6)$$

Given this output choice by firm 1, firm 2 selects its best response as given by equation (11.3), which yields:

$$q_2^* = \frac{(A - c)}{4B} \qquad (11.7)$$

Together, equations (11.6) and (11.7) describe the Stackelberg-Nash equilibrium production levels of each firm. Note that the leader's output is exactly equal to the level of output chosen by a simple uniform-pricing monopolist. This is a well-known feature of the Stackelberg model when demand is linear and costs are constant.

The total industry production is of course the sum of the two outputs shown in equations (11.6) and (11.7). This sum is: $Q^S = \dfrac{3(A - c)}{4B}$. Compare this market output with the earlier Cournot-Nash equilibrium industry output $Q^C = \dfrac{2(A - c)}{3B}$. Clearly, the Stackelberg model yields a greater industry output. Accordingly, the equilibrium price is lower in the Stackelberg model than it is in the Cournot model. The price and output results are illustrated in Figure 11.1.

A central feature of the Stackelberg model is the difference in the relative outcome of the two firms. Recall that from the standpoint of both consumer preferences and production techniques, the firms are identical. They produce identical goods and do so at the same constant unit cost. Yet, because one firm moves first, the outcome for the two firms is different. Comparing q_1^* and q_2^* reveals that the leader gets a far larger market share and earns a much larger profit than does the follower. Moving first clearly has advantages. Alternatively, entering the market late has its disadvantages.

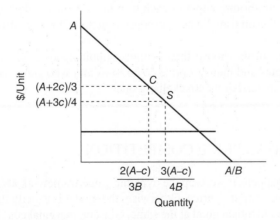

Figure 11.1   The Cournot and Stackelberg outcomes compared
C = Cournot Equilibrium; S = Stackelberg Equilibrium

An interesting additional aspect of the disadvantaged outcome for firm 2 in the Stackelberg model is that this outcome occurs even though firm 2 has full information regarding the output choice of q_1. Indeed, firm 2 actually observes that choice before selecting q_2. In the Cournot duopoly model, firm 2 did not have such concrete information. Because the Cournot model is based upon simultaneous moves, each firm could only make a (rational) guess as to its rival's output choice. Paradoxically, firm 2 does worse when it has complete information about firm 1's choice (the Stackelberg case) than it does when its information is less than perfect (the Cournot case). This is because saying the information is concrete amounts to saying that firm 1's choice—at the time that firm 2 observes it—is irreversible. In the Stackelberg model, by the time firm 2 moves, firm 1 is already fully committed to $q_1 = \dfrac{(A-c)}{2B}$. In the Cournot context, $q_1 = \dfrac{(A-c)}{2B}$ is *not* a best response to the choice $q_2 = \dfrac{(A-c)}{4B}$ and so firm 2 would not anticipate that firm 1 would produce that quantity. In contrast, in the Stackelberg model we do not derive firm 1's choice as a best response to $q_2 = \dfrac{(A-c)}{4B}$. Instead, we derived firm 1's output choice as the profit-maximizing output when firm 1 correctly anticipates that firm 2's decision is to choose its best value of q_2 *conditional upon* the output choice already made by firm 1. It is this fact that reflects the underlying assumption of sequential moves that distinguishes the Stackelberg model.

Stackelberg's modification to the basic Cournot model is important. It is a useful way to capture the observed phenomenon that one firm often has a dominant or leadership position in a market. The Stackelberg model reveals that moving first can have its advantage and therefore can be an important aspect of strategic interaction.

11.1

Practice Problem

Consider the following game. Firm 1, the leader, selects an output q_1, after which firm 2, the follower, observes the choice of q_1 and then selects its own output q_2. The resulting price is one satisfying the industry demand curve $P = 200 - q_1 - q_2$. Both firms have zero fixed costs and a constant marginal cost of 60.

a. Derive the equation for the follower firm's best response function. Draw this equation on a graph with q_2 on the vertical axis and q_1 on the horizontal axis. Indicate the vertical intercept, horizontal intercept, and slope of the best response function.

b. Determine the equilibrium output of each firm in the leader-follower game. Show that this equilibrium lies on firm 2's best response function. What are firm 1's profits in the equilibrium?

c. Now let the two firms choose their outputs simultaneously. Compute the Cournot equilibrium outputs and industry price. Who loses and who gains when the firms play a Cournot game instead of the Stackelberg one?

11.2 SEQUENTIAL PRICE COMPETITION

Now consider what happens if we keep the dynamic game framework above but change the strategic variable from output to price. Otherwise, the model is exactly the same as before. Each firm produces an identical good at the same, constant marginal cost, c, and consumers will purchase the good from the lowest-priced firm. If they set the same prices, then each firm will serve half the market.

In setting its price, firm 1 must of course anticipate firm 2's best response. Clearly firm 2 will have an incentive to price slightly below firm 1's price whenever firm 1 sets a price greater than unit cost c and less than or equal to the monopoly price. In that case, by undercutting, firm 2 will serve the entire market and earn all the potential profits. On the other hand, if firm 1 sets a price less than unit cost c, then firm 2 will not match or undercut firm 1's price because firm 2 has no interest in making any sales when each unit sold loses money. Finally, if firm 1 sets a price equal to unit cost c, firm 2's best response is to match it. The anticipated behavior of firm 2 in stage 2 puts firm 1 in a tight bind. Any price greater than unit cost c results in zero sales and there is no sense in setting a price less than c. The best firm 1 can do then is set a price equal to unit cost c. Firm 2's best response in the next stage is to match firm 1's price.

As we saw in Chapter 10, however, matters are very different if the two firms are not selling identical products. In this case, not all consumers buy from the lower-priced firm. Product differentiation changes the outcome of price competition. To illustrate the nature of price competition with differentiated products, recall the spatial model of product differentiation that we developed previously. There is a product spectrum of unit length along which consumers are uniformly distributed. Two firms supply this market. One firm has the address or product design $x = 0$ on the line whereas the other has location $x = 1$. Each of the firms has the same constant unit cost of production c.

A consumer's location in this market refers to the consumer's most preferred product or style. "Consumer x" is located distance x from the left-hand end of the market. Consumers differ regarding which variant or location of the good they consider to be the best, or their ideal product, but are identical in their reservation price V for their most preferred product. We assume that the reservation price V is substantially greater than the unit cost of production c. Each consumer buys at most one unit of the product. If consumer x purchases a good that is not the ideal product, a utility loss of tx is incurred if good 1 (located at $x = 0$) is consumed; a utility loss of $t(1 - x)$ is incurred if good 2 (located at $x = 1$) is incurred.

The two firms compete for customers by setting prices, p_1 and p_2, respectively. However, unlike the simple Bertrand model, firm 1 sets its price p_1 first, and then firm 2 follows by setting p_2. In order to find the demand facing the firms at prices p_1 and p_2 we proceed as in the previous chapter by identifying the marginal consumer x^m, who is indifferent between buying from either firm 1 or firm 2. Indifference means that consumer x^m gets the same consumer surplus from either product and so satisfies the condition:

$$V - p_1 - tx^m = V - p_2 - t(1 - x^m) \qquad (11.8)$$

From equation (11.8) we find that the address of the marginal consumer x^m is:

$$x^m (p_1, p_2) = \frac{(p_2 - p_1 + t)}{2t} \qquad (11.9)$$

At any set of prices, p_1 and p_2, all consumers to the left of x^m buy from firm 1, and all those to the right of x^m buy from firm 2. In other words, x^m is the fraction of the market buying from firm 1 and $(1 - x^m)$ is the fraction buying from firm 2. If the total number of consumers is denoted by N and they are uniformly distributed over the product spectrum, the demand function facing firm 1 at any price combination (p_1, p_2) is:

$$D^1(p_1, p_2) = x^m(p_1, p_2) = \frac{(p_2 - p_1 + t)}{2t} N \qquad (11.10)$$

Similarly, firm 2's demand function is:

$$D^2 = (p_1, p_2) = (1 - x^m(p_1, p_2)) = \frac{(p_1 - p_2 + t)}{2t} N \tag{11.11}$$

Firm 1 acts first and sets its price p_1. In doing so, firm 1 anticipates firm 2's best response to the price p_1 that firm 1 sets. In other words, firm 1 works out firm 2's best response to each possible price p_1, and then chooses its profit-maximizing price p_1 given firm 2's best response to that price. We can solve for firm 2's best response function p_2^* exactly as we did in Section 3 of Chapter 10 [equation (10.14)]. It is

$$p_2^* = \frac{p_1 + c + t}{2} \tag{11.12}$$

Firm 1 knows that equation (11.12) describes what firm 2 will do in response to each price p_1 that firm 1 could set. We can summarize equation (11.12) by $p_2^*(p_1)$. Firm 1 knows that if it sets first a price p_1, then firm 2 will set a price $p_2^*(p_1)$. As a result, firm 1's demand (11.10) becomes:

$$D^1(p_1, p_2^*(p_1)) = q_1 = \frac{(p_2^*(p_1) - p_1 + t)}{2t} N = \frac{N}{4t}(c + 3t - p_1) \tag{11.13}$$

Firm 1's inverse demand curve is therefore:

$$p_1 = c + 3t - \frac{4t}{N} q_1 \tag{11.14}$$

By the twice-as-steep rule, firm 1's marginal revenue is given by: $MR = c + 3t - \frac{8t}{N} q_1$.

Equating this with marginal cost c then yields firm 1's optimal output as $q_1^* = \frac{3N}{8}$. In turn, this implies that firm 1's profit-maximizing price is:

$$p_1^* = c + \frac{3t}{2} \tag{11.15}$$

Given this choice of price by firm 1, firm 2 uses equation (11.12) to choose its best price:

$$p_2^* = c + \frac{5t}{4} \tag{11.16}$$

Recall that in Section 10.3, when we analyzed this market with simultaneous price competition the result was the symmetric outcome in which each firm set the same prices $p_1^* = p_2^* = c + t$, and each served half the market. Things change, however, in the sequential game. Both firms now charge higher prices but the prices are no longer equal. The price leader, firm 1, now sets a higher price than the follower, firm 2. As a result, firm 2 now serves the larger market share—5/8 relative to the 3/8 served by firm 1.

Note that firm 1's price leadership has helped both firms. In the simultaneous game, each earned a profit of $Nt/2$. Now, firm 1 earns a profit equal to $9Nt/16$, while firm 2 earns an even greater profit equal to $25Nt/32$. That is, while both firms are better off under the price leadership game (and consumers are worse off), it is the second or follower firm that gains the most. There is then an important first-mover *dis*advantage in this price game. Once firm 1 commits to a price, it becomes a fixed target for firm 2 to undercut. Yet because goods are differentiated it is difficult for firm 2 to steal all of firm 1's customers unless it prices really low. Knowing that this is not profitable and that firm 2 will therefore not undercut its price too much is what leads firm 1 to set a fairly high—and more profitable—price to begin with. If consumers regarded the goods as perfect substitutes so that the parameter $t = 0$, prices would again fall to marginal cost as in the original Bertrand model, and there would be no first- or second-mover advantage.

11.2

Practice Problem

Let there be two hair salons located on Main Street, which is one mile long. One is located at the east end of town, $x = 0$, and the other is located at the east end, $x = 1$. There are 100 potential customers who live along the mile stretch, and they are uniformly spread out along the mile. Consumers are willing to pay $50 for a haircut done at their home. If a consumer has to travel there and back to get a haircut then a travel cost of $5 per mile is incurred. Each salon has the same unit cost equal to $10 per haircut.

a. Suppose the East End Salon posts its price for a haircut first and then the West End Salon posts its price for a haircut. What prices will the two salons set? How many customers does each salon serve? What are the profits?
b. Compare the prices to the ones we found when the two salons set their prices simultaneously [Chapter 10, equation (10.15)]. Explain why prices changed in the way they did.

Firms generally seem to do better when they compete sequentially in prices than when they compete sequentially in output. The average price is higher and both firms earn higher profits when price competition is sequential rather than simultaneous. In contrast, the industry price falls and only one firm earns higher profit when quantity competition becomes sequential rather than simultaneous. This difference is related to another distinction: whereas it is the first mover who has the clear advantage in the quantity game, in the price game, it is the firm who moves last that does best.[4]

It is important to understand the central reason that the dynamic games above yield such different outcomes from their simultaneous counterparts. Again, the reason is that sequential play means that when the follower moves, firm 1's move is taken as irreversible or given. To put it differently, the game only becomes truly sequential if firm 1 can make a *credible commitment* not to alter its choice after firm 2 has played. If for example, firm 1 could alter its output or price after firm 2 moves, the Nash equilibrium in either the output or price games discussed above would be the same as in the simultaneous games of Chapters 9 and 10. Because credibility is so important, we should expect that the firms playing dynamic games will also distinguish between credible strategies and non-credible ones. So, we need to understand what makes strategies credible in dynamic games.

We explore dynamic credibility in the next section. We do so in the context of a market entry game. This is a game that has been of great interest to industrial organization economists. In this game, the incumbent firm announces a strategy promising its reaction to actual entry. The entrant then moves by deciding whether or not to enter, taking account the incumbent's threatened reaction. The question is what threats are credible.

---

[4]   This would not be the case if the market were instead vertically differentiated and the first mover was also the firm with the highest quality good.

Reality Checkpoint

First-Mover Advantage in the TV Market: More Dishes and Higher Prices

When a firm markets a new good or service, consumers understand that it may take time to learn how to use it in such a way that one gets full use of all the product's features. For example, it takes experience to learn the full use of an Apple *iPhone* or how to trade on e-Bay. Gabszewicz, Pepall, and Thisse (GPT) (1992) develop a two-stage model to show how consumer learning may confer a first-mover advantage to the first firm to market a new product. Firm 1 leads with its version of a new good. Firm 2 enters in stage two with its own variant of the same good. GPT argue that those consumers who bought firm 1's product in stage 1 will know now how to use it effectively but they will not know that for firm 2's product. As a result, they will tend to prefer firm 1's good even if firm 2 sells at a lower price.

GPT show that the pricing implications can be quite novel. Foreseeing the advantage that learning confers against a later entrant, firm 1 has an incentive to price very low in the first stage so as to induce a lot of consumers to try and to become experienced with its product before firm 2 enters. This creates a large group of captive consumers willing to pay a higher price for firm 1's product in stage 2 now that they know how the product works. Thus when firm 2 enters, firm 1 actually raises its price and still retains a large number of consumers who cannot be bothered to learn how to use the entrant's different version of the good. Not only is there a first-mover advantage but prices rise at the very time that new competition emerges—the opposite of what simple textbook analysis often implies.

The rivalry between cable and dish TV may illustrate this point. Cable was generally first in this market and spread fast with over 70 percent of American homes now receiving cable service. Direct broadcast satellite (DBS) TV that consumers receive through a satellite dish followed. Textbook analysis would suggest that DBS competition would lead to lower cable prices. However, Goolsbee and Petrin (2004) found that, to the contrary, the spread of dish TV led to an increase in the annual cable fee of about $34.68, precisely the first-mover advantage noted by Gabszewicz, Pepall, and Thisse.

Source: Gabszewicz, J., Pepall, L. and J-F. Thisse, 1992. "Sequential Entry with Brand Loyalty Caused by Consumer Learning-By-Doing," *Journal of Industrial Economics* 60 (December): 397–416; and Goolsbee, A., and A. Petrin, 2004. "The Consumer Gains from Direct Broadcast Satellite and Competition with Cable TV," *Econometrica* 72 (March): 351–81.

11.3   CREDIBILITY OF THREATS AND NASH EQUILIBRIA FOR DYNAMIC GAMES

We begin by introducing a concept that is critical to all dynamic games, namely, that of a subgame. A subgame is a part of an entire game that can stand alone as a game in itself. A proper subgame is a game within a game. Simultaneous games cannot have subgames, but dynamic games can. An example of a subgame in a two period model is the competition in the second period, which is a one-shot game within the larger two-period game.

Closely related to the notion of subgame is the concept of subgame perfection, first introduced by Nobel Prize winner Reinhard Selten (1978). It is the concept of subgame perfection that permits us to understand whether a firm's strategy is credible in a dynamic game. The term sounds very technical but it is actually quite simple. Basically, subgame perfection means that if a strategy chosen at the start of a game is optimal, it must be optimal to stick with that strategy at every later juncture in the game as play progresses.

It is easier to understand the concept of subgame perfection by seeing its application in practice. Imagine then a dynamic game between two software firms, one a giant called Microhard who is the incumbent firm in the market and the other an upstart firm, Newvel, who wishes to enter the market. In this game the potential entrant, Newvel, chooses either to enter Microhard's market or to stay out. If Newvel stays out it earns a normal profit from being somewhere else in the economy, say $\Pi = 1$, and Microhard continues to earn a monopoly profit in the software market, say $\Pi = 5$. If Newvel enters the market then Microhard can choose either to accommodate the new entrant and share the market or to fight the new entrant by slashing prices. If Microhard accommodates Newvel's entry, then each firm earns a profit $\Pi = 2$. If, on the other hand, Microhard fights, then neither firm makes any profit so each firm earns $\Pi = 0$.

Dynamic games with moves in sequence require more care in presentation than single-period, simultaneous games. In a simultaneous game, a firm moves once and simultaneously and so its *action* is the same as its *strategy*. For a dynamic game, a firm's strategy is a complete set of instructions that tell the firm what *actions* to pick at every conceivable situation in the game. However, we can begin the analysis of this entry game between Microhard and Newvel using a payoff matrix of the type introduced in Chapter 9. For the game at hand, this matrix is shown in Table 11.1.

Start with the combination (Enter, Fight). This *cannot* correspond to an equilibrium. Enter will lead Newvel to come into the market. If Microhard has adopted the Fight strategy, it must respond to such an entry very aggressively. Yet, as the payoff matrix makes clear, such an aggressive action is not Microhard's best response to entry by Newvel. Now try (Enter, Accommodate). This *is* a Nash equilibrium in strategies. If Newvel chooses to Enter and if Microhard has adopted the strategy, Accommodate, the associated outcome is a best response for both Newvel and Microhard. That is, if Microhard has adopted a strategy to Accommodate, then Enter is the best response for Newvel and if Newvel enters accommodating is a best response for Microhard. Therefore the combination (Enter, Accommodate) is a Nash equilibrium.

What about the combination (Stay Out, Fight)? It also satisfies the Nash definition. If Newvel chooses Stay Out, then the Fight strategy is a best response for Microhard, while if Microhard has chosen its Fight strategy, then Stay Out is a best response for Newvel. Therefore, (Stay Out, Fight) is also a Nash equilibrium in strategies. We leave it for the reader to show that the strategy combination (Stay Out, Accommodate) is not a Nash equilibrium.

Again, it is important to understand that a Nash equilibrium is defined in terms of strategies that are best responses to each other. In the second Nash equilibrium (Stay Out, Fight), Microhard never actually takes or implements a fighting action. Instead, it relies

Table 11.1 Payoff matrix for the Newvel-Microhard entry game

		Microhard	
		Fight	Accommodate
Newvel	Enter	(0, 0)	(2, 2)
	Stay Out	(1, 5)	(1, 5)

fully on the *threat* to do so as a device to deter Newvel from entering. The Nash equilibrium concept is not based on what actions are actually observed in the market place, but rather upon what thinking or strategizing underlies what we observe. This is what is meant when we say we need to define a Nash equilibrium in terms of firms' strategies.

It appears then that there are two Nash equilibria to this game. There is, however, something troubling about one of these, namely, the Nash equilibrium (Stay Out, Fight). It is true that if Microhard has fully committed itself to the strategy, "Fight," then Newvel's best strategy is "Stay Out." But Newvel might question whether such a commitment is really possible. By adopting the Fight strategy, Microhard essentially says to Newvel, "I am going to price high as long as you stay out, but, if you enter my market, I will cut my price and smash you." The problem is that this threat suffers a serious *credibility* problem. We already know that once Newvel has entered the market, taking action to fight back is not in Microhard's best interest. It does much better by accommodating such an entry. Consequently, Microhard does not have an incentive to carry out its threat. So, why should Newvel believe that threat in the first place?

What we have really just discovered is that any Nash equilibrium strategy combination based on non-credible threats is not very satisfactory. This means that we need to strengthen our definition of Nash equilibrium to rule out such strategy combinations. This is where the notion of subgame perfection, or a subgame perfect Nash equilibrium, becomes important. A Nash equilibrium is considered to be subgame perfect only if at that point in the game when a player is called upon to make good on a promise or a threat, doing exactly that and fulfilling the promise or threat is what would be the player's best response. In other words, if any promises or threats are made in one period, carrying them out is still part of a Nash equilibrium in a later period should the occasion arise to do so. If Microhard adopts a strategy that includes the threat of a fight if entry occurs, then if the strategy is subgame perfect it must be optimal for Microhard to fight in the event that Newvel enters, i.e., in the subgame set in period 2 after Newvel has made its entry decision. Because it is not, any outcome that includes Fight cannot be part of a subgame perfect Nash equilibrium.

Generally speaking, it is more difficult to test for subgame perfection using the matrix representation of the game. This is the reason we originally found two Nash equilibria in the game above. For dynamic games, we prefer instead to use an extensive or tree representation of the game.

The extensive form of a game is comprised of branches, nodes, and vectors of payoffs. The nodes are the decision points of the game. The extensive form of the entry game between Newvel and Microhard is shown in Figure 11.2. Here, the nodes are labeled N (Newvel) or M (Microhard), depending on which firm makes the move at that position. The

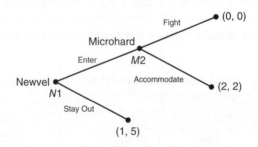

Figure 11.2   The extensive form of the Microhard-Newvel game

branches that are drawn from a node represent the choice of actions available to the player at that node. Each branch points either to another node, where further action takes place, or to a vector of payoffs (Newvel's payoff shown first), which means that this particular action has ended the game. Finally, at any node players know about the course of play that has led to that node.

When we represent a sequential game in extensive form it is easy to identify a subgame. A subgame is defined as a single node and all the actions that flow from that node. In the extensive game illustrated in Figure 11.2, there are two subgames. There is the full game starting from node $N1$ (the full game is always a subgame). Then there is the subgame starting at node $M2$, and including all subsequent actions that flow from this node. A strategy combination is subgame perfect if the strategy for each player is a best response against the strategies of the other players for every subgame of the entire game. In the case at hand, it is readily apparent that for the subgame beginning at node $M2$, the best response strategy for Microhard is Accommodate and *not* Fight. Hence, the strategy combination (Stay Out, Fight) cannot correspond to a subgame perfect equilibrium. The only such equilibrium in this case is that of (Enter, Accommodate).

There is an important technique for solving games with a finite number of nodes. In such games, the simplest way to identify the subgame perfect equilibria is to work backwards, eliminating branches that will not be taken until we have reduced the game tree to having a single branch from each node. This takes advantage of the property that a subgame perfect equilibrium strategy combination must be a Nash equilibrium in each subgame. In our example, we start at node $M2$. We have already seen that we can eliminate the "Fight" branch, leaving only the single "Accommodate" branch from node $M2$. Now pass down the tree to node $N1$. Newvel now knows that Stay Out leads to a payoff of 1, while Enter leads to $M2$ and to Accommodate by Microhard, giving Newvel a payoff of 2. So the Stay Out branch can be eliminated. The game tree now has a single branch from $N1$ and a single branch from $M2$, so we have solved the game. Newvel chooses to Enter and Microhard chooses to Accommodate. In other words, this procedure has eliminated the combination (Stay Out, Fight) as a perfect Nash equilibrium.

11.3

Practice Problem

Centipede is a well-known variant of games involving a chance to "grab a dollar." The game is played as between two players, as follows. A neutral third party, call it Nature, puts $1 on the table. Player 1 can either "grab" this dollar or "wait." If player 1 takes the dollar, the game is over and player 1 gets $1 and player 2 obviously gets nothing. However, it is completely understood that, if player 1 waits, Nature will *triple* the amount on the table to $3. At that point, it becomes player 2's turn to move. Player 2's options are as follows: either take the entire $3 or share the money equally with player 1.

a. Construct the 2×2 payoff matrix for this game taking player 1's actions to be either Grab or Wait, and player 2's actions to be either Grab (the whole $3) or Share. Assume the payoffs are equal to the amount of money the player receives.

b. Draw the game in its extensive form.

c. Suppose that player 2 promises player 1 to choose Share if player 1 chooses Wait. Is this promise credible? Why or why not?

11.4   THE CHAIN STORE PARADOX

In the Microhard and Newvel game, there is just one market and one potential entrant, and fighting the entrant was not an optimal response to entry. However, what if Microhard faced more than one entrant? Perhaps fighting one entrant builds a reputation for aggressive behavior that will scare off later entrants. The consideration of the reputational effects of fighting may change Microhard's optimal strategy. Taking predatory action against a rival—costly though it is—could be useful *if* it serves to make the threat credible against *other* rivals, either those in other markets or those who may appear later in time. If we introduce this possibility into our example, could Microhard's threat to fight become credible because the subsequent gains in other markets from establishing a reputation as a fighter are sufficiently large? In other words, could reputation effects make Fight credible and the strategy combination (Stay Out, Fight) subgame perfect?

The fact that extension of the above game to many markets (distributed over time or space) and to other rivals may *not* lead to a different outcome is a famous result dubbed by Selten as "The Chain-Store Paradox."[5] To see the logic of this puzzling result, consider a situation in which Microhard has established operating units in each of twenty markets, perhaps twenty different cities. In each city, Microhard faces potential entry by a single, small competitor. At the moment, none of these potential competitors has the capital to start operations. However, as time goes on, one after another will raise the necessary funds. To make matters simple, assume that the pay-offs in each of the twenty markets are just as in the pay-off matrix of the previous section. The question facing Microhard is how to react to this sequence of potential entrants. In particular, should Microhard adopt an aggressive response to the first entrant and drive it out of business? Will this tactic earn Microhard a reputation for ruthlessness such that subsequent entrants in its other markets will get the message and choose not to enter?

Again, working backwards can help us identify a subgame perfect strategy. So, let's start with one possible scenario in which Microhard is facing the last potential entrant in the final, twentieth market. It is possible that Microhard has followed through on its threat to cut price and drive out any entrant not just in the first market, but also in all previous nineteen markets. This is a possible path in the game and we are interested if such an aggressive response to entry can convince the last potential entrant to stay out, so that Microhard would be spared a fight in this final case.

However, consider the viewpoint of the entrant to the twentieth market. This firm will realize that because there are no subsequent entrants, it is playing a game that is exactly the one-period game we discussed above. Hence, this last entrant will understand that Microhard has no incentive to Fight in this last market. Microhard's profit is greater if it follows a "live and let live" strategy in this last case[6] because it cannot gain from any further demonstration of its ruthlessness. There are no other entrants left to impress! In other words, (Enter, Accommodate) must be the Nash equilibrium for this final subgame.

One might think that just because Microhard cannot credibly deter entry in the twentieth market, it is still possible to deter the entry of earlier rivals by means of the threat to Fight. To see why this is not possible, however, consider the potential entrant in the nineteenth

---

[5]   Selten (1978). We have obviously limited ourselves here to consideration of finitely repeated games only. Infinitely repeated games are considered in the next chapter.

[6]   Implicit here is the presumption that accommodating an entrant is in the short run more profitable than engaging in a price war.

rather than the twentieth market. Once again, let's take the extreme case in which Microhard has taken predatory or fighting action in the prior eighteen markets. Now the potential entrant in the nineteenth market can reason as well as we can. As a result, this firm will work out the logic of the preceding case and rightfully conclude that Microhard will not fight in the twentieth market. The entrant in the nineteenth or next-to-last market will then reason as follows: "Microhard will let the last rival firm survive because it is more profitable to do so. Yet this implies that both Microhard and I know that the entry of the last rival will not be challenged no matter what happens in this, the nineteenth market. It follows then that there is no reason for Microhard to act tough here. Its only reason to do so would be to convince the entrant in the next market. Because this is not possible, the only justification for fighting in market nineteen has been removed." Once again, Microhard's promise to fight is not credible. It gains Microhard nothing by way of a demonstration to the next rival. Absent such a reputation effect, Microhard's best response to entry in the nineteenth market is again to accommodate. Knowing this, the potential entrant in market nineteen will enter.

We can continue in this fashion repeatedly, bringing us back all the way to the initial market. At every stage, we will find that a strategy to fight after entry occurs is not in Microhard's interest. Accordingly, any strategy that includes the threat to Fight if entry occurs is not credible and therefore not subgame perfect. This is true at each node, from that at the twentieth market to that at the nineteenth market, and so on all the way back to the complete game starting with the very first market. Within this simple model, there is no way for the incumbent to credibly threaten an aggressive low-price response to entry.

If this were the end of the story, our interest in the predatory conduct would certainly be very low. Why should we worry about an event that presumably never occurs? The answer is that there may be ways to make the threat to fight credible other than actual fighting, itself.[7] In the next two chapters we will examine tactics by which firms may make their predatory threats credible and deter entry significantly.

11.5   EMPIRICAL APPLICATION: STACKELBERG BEATS COURNOT

The oligopoly models studied in this and the previous chapters—Cournot, Bertrand, and Stackelberg—are just that: They are models and therefore simplified abstractions of a very complicated reality. Often students learning these models ask whether anyone really thinks this way, i.e., whether anyone really works through the models to derive their optimal choices in the way game theory implies.

It is difficult of course to understand or to prove exactly what happens inside someone's mind. However, we can make intelligent inferences about their thought process by observing their behavior in different settings. A relatively recent method for doing this is to conduct experiments with real people in a controlled setting. An example of such work is the paper "Stackelberg Beats Cournot: On Collusion and Efficiency in Experimental Markets" by Huck, Müller, and Normann (2001).

In brief, Huck, Müller, and Normann (2001) divide 134 students into pairs to play simulated Cournot and Stackelberg two-person games. In each case, each of the two student players is told that they are one of two firms, each of which must choose how much to

---

[7]   Schelling (1960) contains early and lasting contributions to developing equilibrium notions for dynamic games. See also Tirole (1988) and Rasmusen (2007).

produce of an identical product at a constant marginal cost of $c = 6$, and facing the inverse market demand curve:

$$P(Q) = P(q_1 + q_2) = 30 - Q; \text{ for } Q \le 30; \text{ otherwise } 0 \tag{11.17}$$

In the Stackelberg games, one student is assigned the role of follower and plays only after observing the student assigned the leader role. In the Cournot games, each student chooses without knowing the choice of the other so that play is effectively simultaneous. Before the start of any game, players were also given a payoff table showing for each and every possible strategy combination the profit to each firm as measured in a fictitious currency called a "Taler." A single game between two players actually consisted of ten rounds in which the players would make the output choices ten successive times to allow for learning. Player motivation to maximize profit was provided by the fact that players knew that two of the ten rounds would be chosen at random and that they would then receive real money (Euros) at the rate of one unit for every ten Talers of profit. In the results below, we focus on the outcomes for games in which the rival players were assigned randomly before the start of each complete game.

Given the demand and cost structure, you should recognize that the standard Stackelberg outcome is for the leader to produce twelve units while the follower produces six, and that the standard Cournot outcome is for each firm to produce eight units. In turn, these outcomes also carry the implication that total output in the Stackelberg market will exceed that in the Cournot market. What happened in the laboratory experiments?

Table 11.2 shows the average outcomes across the sample of games along with the theoretical predictions for each scenario. A few findings are readily observable. First, the outcomes in the Cournot experiments are very close to those predicted by economic theory, with each Cournot student-firm typically choosing an output very close to eight units. Second, the Stackelberg experiments yield results that, while still preserving the greater output and first-mover advantage for the leader firm, depart somewhat from the Stackelberg theoretical model in that the leader's output is smaller than predicted while the follower's output is larger than predicted. Third, despite this latter finding, the typical Stackelberg game nevertheless still results in more total output than the typical Cournot game, again as theory predicts.

Huck Müller, and Normann (2001) explore the difference between the actual and theoretical Stackelberg predictions somewhat further by first comparing the best-response function implied by the actual players' behavior with that predicted by theory. The latter

Table 11.2 Actual and predicted outcomes for Stackelberg and Cournot experiments

	Stackelberg		Cournot	
	Actual *Leader/Follower*	*Predicted* *Leader/Follower*	*Actual* *Each Duopolist*	*Predicted* *Each Duopolist*
Individual Firm Output	10.19/8.32	12/6	8.07	8
Total Market Output	18.51	18	16.14	16
Total Combined Profit	93.48	108	116.60	128
Total Consumer Surplus	175.37	162	135.38	108
Total Welfare	268.85	270	251.98	236

is of course: $q_F = 12 - 0.5q_L$. Using linear regression, the authors find that the followers in their random pair experiments instead are best described as having a response function given by:

$$q_F = 10.275 - 0.178q_L \tag{11.18}$$

The slope of this estimated behavior is much flatter than predicted, implying that follower firms do not reduce their output as much as predicted in response to an output choice by the leader. For example, at the predicted leader output of 12, the response function in (11.18) implies a follower output of 8.35—well above the 6 units predicted by the theoretical best response function.

In short, Huck, Müller, and Normann (2001) find that followers are more aggressive than theory predicts. They hypothesize then that this is because followers have an *inequality aversion* in that they care not just about their own profit but also about the inequality between the profits of the leader and the follower. In particular, the authors suggest that instead of maximizing profit, follower players may instead be maximizing the following utility function:

$$U(\pi_F, \pi_L) = \pi_F - \alpha \ \max(\pi_L - \pi_F, 0) - \beta \ \max(\pi_F - \pi_L, 0) \tag{11.19}$$

Here α and β are typically taken to be positive fractions. Thus, equation (11.19) implies that if the leader and the follower have the same profit, $\pi_F = \pi_L$, the follower player cares only about maximizing his or her own profit as in the conventional model. However, if either $\pi_L > \pi_F$ or $\pi_F > \pi_L$ the follower loses some utility. Hence, the follower will be willing to sacrifice some profit depending on how large α and β are. Usually, it is assumed that $\alpha > \beta$, implying that the follower cares more about the leader being the one to earn the greater profit.

Consider for example, the typical leader output of 10.19 found in the experiments. If this output is taken as given, then the follower firm faces an inverse demand curve of: $P = 19.81 - q_a$ and therefore a marginal revenue curve of MR $= 19.81 - 2q_F$. Equating this with its marginal cost of 6, the follower would maximize its profit at $q_F = 6.9$, implying that 12.91 is the price. However, this would mean that $\pi_L - \pi_F = 70.41 - 47.68 = 22.73$, and this inequality in profits would reduce the followers utility if $\alpha > 0$. Note though that the follower is in a position of doing something about this. If the follower increases output a bit, this will lower the price and reduce the leader's profit. It will also lower the follower's profit but not as much as the leader's precisely because the follower's output is increasing while the leader's output is, by assumption, given. Therefore, increasing its output will reduce the profit difference between the two firms.

Because β is not relevant when $\pi_L > \pi_F$, we can now write the follower's utility function as:

$$U(\pi_F, \pi_L) = (1 + \alpha)\pi_F - \alpha\pi_L \tag{11.20}$$

It follows that the change in utility ΔU satisfies:

$$\Delta U = (1 + \alpha)\Delta\pi_F - \alpha\Delta\pi_L \tag{11.21}$$

At the optimal point, the follower is just balancing the greater profit equality its output increase is bringing against the actual profit loss that increase causes. Hence, $\Delta U = 0$ at the optimum implying that α satisfies:

$$\frac{\alpha}{1+\alpha} = \frac{\Delta \pi_F}{\Delta \pi_L} \qquad (11.22)$$

It is straightforward to show that at the observed experimental average outputs in the Stackelberg experiments, $\Delta \pi_F / \Delta \pi_L = 0.277$, i.e., an increase in the follower's output would lower its profit by about 28 percent as much as it would lower the leader's output. From this, we can infer that for this "representative" case, $\alpha = 0.3845$. In other words, the follower players felt that having each firm have the same profit was about 40 percent as important as having its own individual profit maximized. It is this rather sizable preference for equal profit outcomes that Huck, Müller, and Normann (2001) deem responsible for the more aggressive follower behavior they observe. Whether that preference also characterizes real-world business people as opposed to experimental student players is an open question. Even with that possible qualification, however, it is still notable how closely the experimental outcomes follow the theoretical predictions for the relative Stackelberg and Cournot outcomes.

Summary

Sequential market games are different from simultaneous ones. Moreover, the effect of changing from simultaneous to sequential play differs depending on whether the strategic variable of choice is quantity or price. The basic sequential quantity game, typically referred to as the Stackelberg model, confers a large advantage to the firm that chooses production first. In the linear demand and cost case, the first mover in a Stackelberg game produces the monopoly output. The follower produces only half this much. Prices are lower than in the basic Cournot model, but the large market share of the first mover gives that firm an increase in profit over what it would earn in the simultaneous production game.

In contrast, a sequential price game with differentiated products yields higher profits for both firms than either would earn if prices were set simultaneously. Moreover, in this case, it is the firm that sets price last that does best if products are horizontally differentiated. Sequential price games are thus an example of games that have a second-mover as opposed to a first-mover advantage.

How close theoretical models correspond to economic reality is always a question. However, experimental evidence relying on classroom "laboratory" test runs with students playing Cournot and Stackelberg duopoly games suggests that these players do respond largely in the manner predicted by these models. This is true even though the actual monetary reward earned by these students averaged only about $9. If such small motivations are enough to get student players to largely duplicate the theoretical predictions, one might argue that actual business leaders for whom the stakes of "getting it right" are much higher might come that much closer to the hypothesized ideal behavior.

Crucial to any sequential game is the issue of commitment. How do firms establish themselves as leaders or followers? How can a firm commit to its output or price strategy in a way that a rival finds credible? This issue is best explored by considering the game in its extended form and identifying strategy combinations that are subgame perfect, i.e., strategies that call for actions at later points in the game in which those actions continue to be optimal when the time comes to take them, given the history of play up to that date.

Threats and promises of later punishments and rewards are particularly important in games in which one firm is trying to prevent another from entering its market (or perhaps trying to induce it to leave). The question again is whether such threats and promises can be made credible. If they can, then incumbent firms may be able to maintain their dominant position in an industry and not fear competitive entry. This is the subject of our next chapter.

Problems

1. Consider a Stackelberg game of quantity competition between two firms. Firm 1 is the leader and firm 2 is the follower. Market demand is described by the inverse demand function $P = 1000 - 4Q$. Each firm has a constant unit cost of production equal to 20.
   a. Solve for Nash equilibrium outcome.
   b. Suppose firm 2's unit cost of production is $c < 20$. What value would c have so that in the Nash equilibrium the two firms, leader and follower, had the same market share?

2. Let's return to Tuftsville (Chapter 10) where everyone lives along Main Street, which is 10 miles long. There are 1,000 people uniformly spread up and down Main Street, and every day they each buy fruit smoothie from one of the two stores located at either end of the street. Customers ride their motor scooters to and from the store, using $0.50 worth of gas per mile. Customers buy their smoothies from the store offering the lowest price, which is the store's price plus the customer's travel expenses getting to and from the store. Ben owns the store at the west end of Main Street and Will owns the store at the east end of Main Street. The marginal cost of a smoothie is constant and equal to $1 for both Ben and Will. In addition, each of them pays Tuftsville $250 per day for the right to sell smoothies.
   a. Ben sets his price p_1 first and then Will sets his price p_2. After the prices are posted consumers get on their scooters and buy from the store with the lowest price including travel expenses. What prices will Ben and Will set?
   b. How many customers does each store serve and what are their profits?

3. In Centipede[8] there are two players: player 1 moves first, player 2 moves second. After at most two moves, the game ends. The game begins with $1 sitting on a table. Player 1 can either take the $1 or wait. If player 1 takes the $1 the game is over, and player 1 gets to keep the $1. If player 1 waits, the $1 quadruples to $4. Now it is player 2's turn.

Player 2 can either take the entire $4 or split the $4 evenly with player 1.
   a. Draw the extensive form for the game of Centipede.
   b. What is the equilibrium to this game? Can player 2's strategy of splitting the money ever be a part of an equilibrium outcome to the game?
   c. Now suppose that Centipede has three moves. Player 2 can now either wait, split the money, or take the $4. If player 2 waits then the money on the table quadruples again and player 1 can either take it all or split it. Draw the extensive form for the new game and solve for the equilibrium outcome.

4. Dry Gulch has two water suppliers. One is Northern Springs, whose water is crystal clear but not carbonated. The other is Southern Pelligrino, whose water is naturally carbonated but also somewhat "hard." The marketing department of each firm has worked out the following profit matrix depending on the price per 2-gallon container charged by each firm. Southern Pelligrino's profits are shown as the first entry in each pair.

Northern Springs Price:

Southern Pelligrino's Price:		3	4	5	6
	3	24,24	30,25	36,20	42,12
	4	25,30	32,32	41,30	48,24
	5	20,36	30,41	40,40	50,36
	6	12,42	24,48	36,50	48,48

   a. What is the Nash equilibrium if the two firms set prices simultaneously?
   b. What is the Nash equilibrium if Northern Springs must set its price first and stick with it, and Southern Pelligrino is free to respond as best it can to Northern Springs's price?
   c. Show that choosing *price* first is a disadvantage for Northern Springs. Why is this the case?

---

[8] This game was first introduced by Rosenthal (1981).

5. Suppose that firm 1 can choose to produce good A, good B, both goods, or nothing. Firm 2, on the other hand, can produce only good C or nothing. Firms' profits corresponding to each possible scenario of goods for sale are described in the following table:

Product Selection	Firm 1's Profit	Firm 2's Profit
A	20	0
A,B	18	0
A,B,C	2	−2
B,C	−3	−3
C	0	10
A,C	8	8
B	11	0

a. Set up the normal form game for when the two firms simultaneously choose their product sets. What is the Nash equilibrium (or equilibria)?

b. Now suppose that firm 1 can commit to its product choice before firm 2. Draw the extensive form of this game and identify its subgame perfect Nash equilibrium. Compare your answer to (a) and explain.

c. The game is like the one in (b), only now suppose that firm 1 can reverse its decision after observing firm 2's choice and this possibility is common knowledge. Does this affect the game? If so, explain the new outcome. If not, explain why not.

6. Find three examples of different ways individual firms or industries can make the strategy "This offer is good for a limited time only" a credible strategy.

7. The Gizmo Company has a monopoly on the production of gizmos. Market demand is described as follows: at a price of $1,000 per gizmo, 25,000 units will be sold whereas at a price of $600, 30,000 will be sold. The only costs of production are the initial sunk costs of building a plant. Gizmo Co. has already invested in capacity to produce up to 25,000 units.

a. Suppose an entrant to this industry could capture 50 percent of the market if it invested in $10 million to construct a plant. Would the firm enter? Why or why not?

b. Suppose Gizmo could invest $5 million to expand its capacity to produce 40,000 gizmos. Would this strategy be a profitable way to deter entry?

References

Gabszewicz, J., Pepall, L., and J.F. Thisse. 1992. "Sequential Entry with Brand Loyalty Caused by Consumer Learning-By-Doing," *Journal of Industrial Economics* 60 (December): 397–416.

Goolsbee, A., and A. Petrin. 2004. "The Consumer Gains from Direct Broadcast Satellite and Competition with Cable TV," *Econometrica* 72 (March): 351–81.

Huck, S., W. Müller, and H. T. Normann 2001. "Stackelberg Beats Cournot: On Collusion and Efficiency in Experimental Markets," *The Economic Journal* 111 (October): 749–65.

Lieberman, Marvin. B., and David. B. Montgomery, 1988. "First Mover Advantages," *Strategic Management Journal* 9 (Summer): 41–49.

Rasmusen, E. 2007. *Games and Information*, 4th ed. Cambridge, MA: Basil Blackwell, Inc.

Rosenthal, R. W. 1981. "Games of Perfect Information, Predatory Pricing, and the Chain Store Paradox," *Journal of Economic Theory* 25 (August): 92–100.

Schelling, T. 1960. *The Strategy of Conflict*, Cambridge Mass.: Harvard University Press.

Selten, R. 1978. "The Chain Store Paradox," *Theory and Decision* 9 (April): 127–59.

Stackelberg, H. von, 1934. *Marktform und Gleichgewicht*, Berlin and Vienna. English translation by A.T. Peacock, (1952) London: William Hodge.

Sutton, J. 1991. *Sunk Cost and Market Structure*, Cambridge, MA: The MIT Press.

Tirole, J. 1988. *The Theory of Industrial Organization*, Cambridge: MIT Press.

Part Four
Anticompetitive Behavior and Antitrust Policy

The chapters in this section build on the game theoretic analysis of the previous three chapters to explore the tactics that firms can employ to blunt competitive pressures and thereby earn supracompetitive profits. In Chapter 12, we consider various tactics that exploit the first-mover advantage of the incumbent relative to a new entrant, such as the excess capacity investment stressed by Dixit (1980) and the bundling techniques discussed earlier in Chapter 8. We also present some empirical evidence regarding the use of excess capacity based on the Conlin and Kadiyali (2006) study of the Texas hotel industry.

In Chapter 13, we extend the analysis of so-called predatory behavior to include tactics that exploit either the information advantage that the incumbent has, as in the classic Milgrom and Roberts (1982) limit pricing paper, or the disadvantage that a small entrant might have vis-à-vis its creditors, as in the paper by Bolton and Scharfstein (1990). We then examine the use of long-term contracts to "tie up" consumers and deny a new entrant the customer base necessary to exploit scale economies. The empirical application for this chapter is based on the Ellison and Ellison (2011) study of the advertising decisions of pharmaceutical firms faced with potential new generic competitors as their key patents expire.

Finally, in Chapter 14, we consider the ability of firms to collude and suppress competitive pressures. Such price-fixing is a major concern of the antitrust laws. Indeed, the last fifteen years have witnessed the successful prosecution of a record number of price-fixing cartels. We begin with an analysis of the difficulties that must be overcome by cartel members if collusion is to succeed. We then show how collusion can become an equilibrium outcome in games of indefinite duration. This gives rise to the well-known Folk Theorem describing the conditions under which those obstacles can be overcome. This permits a discussion of antitrust policy including the recent practice of granting leniency to the first cartel members who cooperate with the authorities, and how important this has been in breaking international cartels. The chapter concludes with a discussion of Kwoka's (1997) empirical analysis of the impact of a real estate cartel that rigged auctions in the Washington, D.C., area.

12

Entry Deterrence and Predation

Elementary textbook presentations of microeconomics, such as our presentation in Chapter 2, often represent monopoly power as a transient phenomenon. The argument is that whenever a firm acquires market power and earns super-normal profit, entry will occur and the new entrants will reestablish a competitive market. Those who follow actual markets, however, know that this scenario may be more the exception than the rule. Campbell's, for example, has held a dominant position with 60 percent or more of the US canned canned soup sales for over a hundred years. For twenty years, Microsoft's *Windows* has maintained a share of over 90 percent in the market for personal computer operating systems, although this share drops to closer to 80 percent if tablet computers are included.[1] Despite recent expansion by Chinese and other emerging economy firms, Sotheby's and Christie's have together controlled roughly 55 percent of the world's fine art auction market for two decades, and as much as 70 percent of that market during many of those years.[2] Such instances of sustained dominance are common. Moreover, such anecdotal evidence is buttressed by formal analysis such as that by Baldwin (1995) and Geroski and Toker (1996). These authors find that, on average, the number one firm in an industry retains that rank for somewhere between seventeen and twenty-eight years. In short, there is abundant evidence that, in contrast to the textbook analysis, market power is lasting. This raises the question then as to how such firms can sustain their profit-winning position. Why don't new rivals emerge to compete away that market share and profit? Are there strategies that the dominant firms can adopt to prevent this from happening? If so, what are these strategies and what are their implications for market outcomes?

The questions just raised are the focus of this chapter. They are of much more than mere academic interest. The potential for large incumbent firms to eliminate or prevent the entry of rivals was a major motivation behind the enactment of antitrust laws in the first place. That concern has persisted through many antitrust cases ever since, including the dramatic Microsoft antitrust case in 2000.[3] Section 2 of the Sherman Act deems it illegal to "monopolize or attempt to monopolize ... any part of the trade or commerce." It follows

[1] Gartner Press Release, "Windows 7 Will Become Leading Operating System in 2011," http://www.gartner.com/it/page.jsp? id=17626149 (August, 2011).

[2] Art Market Monitor, "Art World Expansion Erodes Sotheby's/Christie's Market Share," http://artmarketmonitor.com (June 23, 2011).

[3] *United States v. Microsoft Corp.*, 87 F. Supp. 2d 30 (D.D.C. 2000).

that enforcement of this provision requires an understanding of what a firm can do in order to "monopolize" the market.

Employing tactics that are only profitable if they deter rival firms from competing in a market is what economists call *predatory* conduct.[4] A firm engaging in predatory conduct wants to influence the behavior of its rivals—either those currently in the market or those thinking of entering it. Predatory conduct often involves the making of threats and, if necessary, actually implementing the threats in a way that ensures such threats are *credible*. Credibility is absolutely essential for predatory conduct to be successful. After all, as we learned from the Chain Store Paradox in the last chapter, "talk is cheap." A threat aimed at dissuading a rival from entering one's market will only have the desired effect if it is credible. Such threats work when the rival or prey believes that the predator really "means business" and will pursue the predatory conduct *if the rival chooses to ignore the threat*.

In this chapter, we examine conduct designed either to deter rivals from entering an incumbent's market or to induce existing rivals to exit. Fear over such conduct was a fundamental motivation behind the initial antitrust provisions, which focused on efforts "to monopolize ... any part of the trade or commerce" and to "materially reduce competition."[5] The basis for this legislative concern is, of course, the fear that with existing rivals and the threat of entry removed, a dominant firm will pursue monopoly practices that reduce efficiency. In this chapter, we limit ourselves to cases of complete information. We defer the examination of predatory conduct under incomplete information or uncertainty until the next chapter.

12.1   MARKET STRUCTURE OVER TIME: RANDOM PROCESSES & STYLIZED FACTS

Before we begin to model incumbent firm strategies to deter rivals' entry and encourage rivals' exit, we need to consider more fully what theory and evidence can tell us about how an industry's structure might evolve over time. As a simple example, consider an industry comprised of 256 firms, each with sales of $10 million. Suppose that in any period, sales at each firm will decline by 30 percent with probability 0.25, stay the same with probability 0.5, or return to their prior level with probability 0.25 for any firm of any size. (If these rates of growth or decline seem large, think of a period as say three or four years long.) Table 12.1 shows the evolution of firm size over just four periods. We can see that even over this short amount of time, the distribution of firm sizes is becoming very unequal. The largest firm is now nine times as large as the smallest and the top nine firms account for roughly the same amount of output as the bottom forty. This inequality will grow even larger as we let the process run over more periods of time.

The trend toward increasing inequality is a common feature of any process in which growth in any period is a random variable independent of firm size and previous growth rates. It is broadly referred to as Gibrat's Law after Robert Gibrat (1931) who made the following formal argument. Let X_t be a firm's size at time t. Let this be related to its size at $t - 1$ by the following stochastic process:

$$X_t = (1 + v_t)X_{t-1} \tag{12.1}$$

---

[4]   See, for example, Fisher (1991).
[5]   Our definition is also similar to that of Ordover and Willig (1981).

Table 12.1   Size distribution of firms after four years starting with 256 equal-sized firms

	Sales (Millions)								
	$2.40	$3.43	$4.90	$7.00	$10.00	$13.00	$16.90	$21.97	$28.56
Period 0	0	0	0	0	256	0	0	0	0
Period 1	0	0	0	64	128	64	0	0	0
Period 2	0	0	16	64	96	64	16	0	0
Period 3	0	4	24	60	80	60	24	4	0
Period 4	1	8	28	56	70	56	28	8	1

Here v_t is a random disturbance term that we assume is normally distributed and has mean μ and variance σ^2. Next, take the natural log of both sides. If the time interval between t and $t-1$ is short, we may use the approximation that $\ln(1 + v_t) \approx v_t$, where we uses lower case letters to denote logs. Hence, we may now write:

$$x_t = x_{t-1} + v_t \tag{12.2}$$

Denoting x at time $t = 0$ as x_0, repeated substitution yields:

$$x_t = v_t + v_{t-1} + v_{t-2} + v_{t-3} + \ldots + x_0 \tag{12.3}$$

This last equation says that the logarithm of the firm's size at time t will just be a random variable reflecting the accumulation of all the random growth shocks it has experienced up to that time. Each shock is itself a random variable drawn from the normal distribution. Thus over k time periods, as the importance of x_0 approaches zero, x_t will converge to a random variable with mean $k\mu$ and variance $k\sigma^2$. In turn, this implies that the variance of firm size itself will be $e^{k(2\mu+\sigma^2)}(e^{k\sigma^2} - 1)$, which of course is far larger than $k\sigma^2$. Indeed, over a long time period the sum of all those accumulated shocks is also a normal random variable. Recall however that logarithms reflect exponential power. As the log of a firm's assets doubles, the actual volume of those assets is squared. So, although the log of firm size may be normally distributed, the distribution of actual firm sizes will be skewed. Those firms with above average values for the log of firm size will have many times above average values when size is measured without logs.

As mentioned previously, the outcome described above in which a market concentration increases endogenously over time is usually referred to as Gibrat's Law after its originator Robert Gibrat (1931). It has generated enormous interest in part because it suggests that oligopoly or even monopoly are natural market outcomes. In a rough way, it is consistent with the evidence cited earlier that dominant firms retain their market power for a considerable length of time. In fact, in an early study motivated by Gibrat's work, Kalecki (1945) produced some evidence that was very supportive of this natural concentrating tendency.

To a large extent, however, the subsequent research on Gibrat's Law focuses primarily on what that analysis leaves out rather than what it keeps in. This is because the Gibrat process is very mechanistic. There is no talk of research and cost-saving innovations that enhance a firm's growth. There is no consideration of mergers and firm combinations over time. Perhaps most relevant for our present purpose, there is no discussion of new firms entering an industry or older firms leaving, or what strategic interaction may lie behind such entry and exit. Subsequent research has tried to remedy these omissions and to develop theoretical models of industry evolution that build in these features [See, for example, Jovanovic (1982), Nelson and Winter (1982), Sutton (1997), and Klepper (2002).]

Of course, any theoretical model must ultimately confront the real world facts. Over the last twenty-five years, economists have worked hard to review the data and to document any empirical regularities or stylized facts that appear. A survey of these studies suggests that there are four stylized facts that any theory of industrial evolution must explain.

The first is that *entry is common*. Dunne et al. (1988, 1989), using US census data between 1963 and 1982, computed rates of entry in a wide cross section of two-digit SIC manufacturing industries. Their estimate of the average entry rate in manufacturing—defined as the number of *new* firms over a five-year period relative to the number of incumbent firms at the start of that period—ranged between 41.4 percent and 51.8 percent (about 8 to 10 percent on an annual basis). For the United Kingdom, Geroski (1995) estimated somewhat smaller but still significant annual rates of entry for a sample of 87 three-digit manufacturing industries. These ranged between 2.5 percent and 14.5 percent over the period 1974 to 1979. Cable and Schwalbach (1991) show that similar rates of entry exist across a wide range of developed countries. More recently, Jarmin et al. (2004) showed that rates of entry are even higher in the retail sector and may reach well over 60 percent, especially during periods of economic prosperity.[6]

The second stylized fact is that when entry occurs it is, by and large, *small-scale entry*. The studies by Dunne et al. (1988, 1989) showed that the collective market share of entrants in an industry ranged between 13.9 and 18.8 percent, again over a five-year interval.[7] Similarly, in Geroski's (1995) UK study, the market share of a new entrant was found to be quite modest, ranging from 1.45 to 6.35 percent. In the United States, Cable and Schwalbach (1991) find that while new entrants typically constitute 7.7 percent of an industry's firms in any year, they account for only 3.2 percent of its output. The typical share of entrants in retailing is noticeably larger, say closer to 25 percent, according to Jarmin et al. (2004), but they also find that this value has been declining over recent years.

The third stylized fact is that the *new entrant survival rate is relatively low*. Dunne et al. (1988, 1989) find that roughly 61.5 percent of all entrant firms exited within five years of entry and 79.6 percent exited within ten years. The corresponding exit rates found in retailing by Jarmin et al. (2004) are a very similar, between 59 percent and 82 percent. Birch (1987) used Dun and Bradstreet data for all sectors in the United States including, but not limited to, manufacturing and found that about 50 percent of all new entrant firms fail within the first five years.

Our final stylized fact that appears to hold in every study is that while rates of entry and exit vary across industries, *industries with high entry rates also have high exit rates*. In other words, entry and exit rates are strongly correlated. To take just one clear example, Cable and Schwalbach (1991) found that corresponding to an entry rate of 7.7 percent accounting for 3.2 percent of industry output, the exit rate is 7.0 percent and similarly it accounts for 3.3 percent of industry output. This finding is a little surprising because it does not appear consistent with the hypothesis that entry occurs in response to above-normal profit or that

---

[6] The Dunne et al. (1988, 1989) entry (and exit) estimates are generally higher than those obtained by other researchers owing to the fact that they explicitly recognize the multiproduct and multiplant nature of firms.

[7] Dunne et al. (1988) did find that existing firms who enter a new market through diversification typically enter at a larger scale than new, or *de novo*, entrants do.

exit reflects a below-normal profit. If profit is high, and therefore entry attractive, there is no reason for firms to leave. Similarly, if profit is so low that firms are induced to leave the industry, there ought to be little incentive for new entrants to emerge.

Taken together, the stylized facts reported above can be read as suggesting a sort of revolving-door setting in which mostly small firms enter, eventually fail, and exit, only to be replaced by a new cohort of small-scale entrants. In this view, the major difference across industries would be the pace at which this entry-fail-exit cycle proceeds. One interpretation of this evidence is that it reflects repeated attempts and, just as often, repeated failures of small firms to penetrate the markets dominated by large incumbents. This may help explain the correlation between entry and exit rates. Incumbents in markets that seem the most tempting targets may be those firms that fight the hardest against new entrants.

More formal support for this revolving door interpretation is offered by Urban et al. (1984) on the benefits of incumbency. They studied 129 frequently purchased brands of consumer products in twelve US markets and found that market shares were a decreasing function of the order of entry of the brand. Earlier entrants enjoyed larger market shares, all else equal. Similar results have been found by Lambkin (1988), Mitchell (1991), and Brown and Lattin (1994).[8]

A more recent analysis that combines an underlying theoretical random process with actual market data is Sutton's (2007) examination of forty-five Japanese industries over a twenty-three year period. Given the initial distribution of market shares and the variance of shocks to those shares, Sutton (2007) can calculate the expected number of initial industry leaders that will have lost their position due to random shocks after say fifteen or twenty years. In both cases, he finds that the actual number of such leadership losses is significantly less than what one would expect, i.e., market leaders retain their position significantly more than one would anticipate given the normal randomness those shares exhibit. Thus, this finding also suggests that leading firms retain their dominance longer than one would normally expect.

To be sure, the persistence of market dominance may well reflect the superior cost efficiency or higher product quality of those firms that emerge as market leaders early on. However, it is frequently alleged (especially by failed rival entrants) that the ability of early entrants to sustain a dominant industry position also reflects deliberate behavior aimed either at driving new entrants out or preventing their entry in the first place. This is the primary issue addressed in this and the subsequent chapter.

12.2   PREDATORY CONDUCT AND LIMIT PRICING

As noted above, there is a difference between a rational competitive response to rival entry and truly predatory behavior. We know, for example, that both the static Cournot and Bertrand models predict that when a second firm enters a previously monopolized market, the initial incumbent's response will lead to a (possibly dramatic) fall in price. While this may make the entry less profitable, it does not reflect anything other than a normal competitive response to competitive pressure. For true predation to occur, economists

---

[8]   As Caves (1998) notes, though, there is regression toward the mean in firm growth rates. That is, really large firms tend to grow more slowly than do small ones. This feature blunts the ever-increasing concentration tendency implied by Gibrat's Law.

require that the actions taken by a firm are profitable *only if* they drive existing rivals out of the market or deter potential rivals from coming in to the market.

To put it somewhat loosely, predatory conduct must appear on the surface to reduce the predator firm's profit and seem to be "irrational." The rationality for such conduct would be the additional profit the predator earns *if and only if* the conduct is successful at limiting the competition.

When the "irrational" or predatory action in question is the firm's setting an ultra-low price that drives rival firms out of business it is called *predatory pricing*. Historically, accusations of such predatory pricing are among the most common cases of alleged predation. However, setting a low price that instead deters potential rivals from entering the market in the first place can also be predatory. The entry-limiting price is typically referred to as the *limit price*. If output is the strategic variable, we will refer to the analogous entry-deterring output as the *limit output*. We start the important work of this chapter by reviewing two approaches to limit pricing. The first one is an earlier approach predating the advent of a game theoretic treatment of the subject. The second approach takes the insight of the first but derives a more fundamental explanation of such entry deterrence rooted in a dynamic game between the incumbent and the entrant.

12.2.1   An Informal Model of Entry Deterrence

The traditional limit-pricing story of entry deterrence is told in the work of Bain (1956) and later modeled in Sylos-Labini (1962). These earlier industrial organization economists were shrewd observers of everyday business practices and had reasons to believe that predatory pricing and entry-deterring behavior occurred. We can illustrate the essence of the limit pricing strategy using a simple variant of the Stackelberg model. Recall from the previous chapter that the strategic variable in the Stackelberg model is quantity. So, the analysis we present might more properly be labeled a limit output model, rather than a limit price one. Yet the basic idea of setting the strategic variable so as to deter entry is the same in either case—especially because the dominant firm's output choice will greatly influence the industry price. That is, we might regard the resulting price in our model as the limit price.

Figure 12.1 illustrates the essential features of the model. The incumbent firm is the Stackelberg leader and is allowed to choose its output first. We begin by making a simple and yet strong assumption that whatever this choice is, the entrant believes that its own entry into the market will not alter the leader's choice of output. That is, the entrant regards the incumbent as irrevocably committed to its output choice. A further crucial assumption is that the entrant's average cost declines over at least the initial range of low levels of production. When both of these assumptions hold, then by the correct choice of its pre-entry output level, the incumbent can manipulate the entrant's profit calculation and discourage entry.

In Figure 12.1, the appropriate production level to which the incumbent must commit to deter entry is $\overline{Q}$. If the entrant stays out, this implies a market price $\overline{P}$. What would happen to market price if the entrant now produced any positive output? The answer is also shown in Figure 12.1. Because the entrant believes that the incumbent will maintain $\overline{Q}$, the demand the new entrant faces at any price P is the total quantity that is demanded at that price, $D(P)$, less $\overline{Q}$. That is, the entrant faces a *residual demand curve* R^e that, in this case, is simply the market demand curve $D(P)$ shifted inward along the horizontal axis by the amount $\overline{Q}$. Corresponding to this residual demand curve is the entrant's marginal revenue curve MR^e. The entrant maximizes its profit by selecting output q^e at which its marginal revenue just

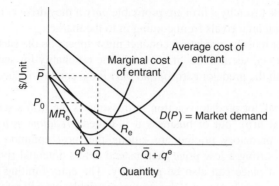

Figure 12.1   The limit output model

By producing at $\overline{Q}$, the incumbent can preclude profitable entry.

equals its marginal cost. As shown in Figure 12.1, this output is such that when it is added to the output $\overline{Q}$ of the incumbent firm market price becomes P_0 and this price barely covers the entrant's average cost. In other words, by committing to the output $\overline{Q}$, the incumbent firm removes any profit incentive for the entrant to actually participate in the market.

12.1

Practice Problem

Suppose that market demand is described by $P = 100 - (Q + q)$, where P is the market price, Q is the output of the incumbent firm, and q is the output of a potential entrant to the market. The incumbent firm's total cost function is $TC(Q) = 40Q$, whereas the cost function of the entrant is $C(q) = 100 + 40q$, where 100 is a sunk cost incurred to enter the market.

a.   If the entrant observes the incumbent producing Q_0 units of output and expects this output level to be maintained, write down the equation for the residual demand curve that the entrant firm faces.

b.   If the entrant firm maximizes profit given the residual demand curve in (a) what output q^e will the entrant produce? (Your answer should be a function of Q_0.)

c.   How much output would the incumbent firm have to produce to just keep the entrant out of the market? That is, solve for the limit output $\overline{Q}$. At what price will the incumbent sell the limit output?

It should be clear that successful predation of the type just described depends crucially on the entrant's belief that the incumbent is truly committed to its action. In the language of the last chapter, the strategy must be subgame perfect. The issue then becomes whether this is possible. Can the incumbent truly commit to produce output $\overline{Q}$ even if the entrant enters the market?

Earlier scholars such as Bain (1956) and Sylos-Labini (1962) did not formally address the credibility issue. Nevertheless, they do appear to have understood that in order deter entry the incumbent firm had to commit or "lock in" to the predatory behavior. They assumed that such commitment was achieved by further supposing that the incumbent's output $\overline{Q}$ was "very" costly to adjust. Hence, the potential entrant was correct to assume that the incumbent's output would remain at $\overline{Q}$ because it was too costly to change. In other words, the presence of adjustment costs once the incumbent is already producing at a particular level acted as a mechanism to commit the incumbent to the output $\overline{Q}$ even in the face of entry.

The idea sounds plausible and may well be true. Unfortunately, as stated, it is a little *ad hoc*. Without a full specification of how such costs are generated and how they fit into a complete analysis of strategic interaction between the two firms, the adjustment cost story amounts to little more than a statement that the incumbent's output is given because it is given. Producing $\overline{Q}$ is truly credible only if $\overline{Q}$ is the incumbent's best response to the entrant coming into the market and choosing an output level to produce. Limit pricing can only work if the incumbent firm can commit to producing the limit output even if entry occurs.

12.2.2 Capacity Expansion as a Credible Entry-Deterring Commitment

In a key article, Spence (1977) recognized that what may make limit pricing a credible deterrent strategy is the incumbent firm's ability to make a prior and irrevocable investment in production capacity, and specifically an investment in the *capacity* to produce the limit output $\overline{Q}$. Spence's work was followed by Dixit (1980) who worked out a precise mechanism by which the incumbent could guarantee that in the post-entry market, it would produce an output equal to its pre-entry capacity [See also Gilbert and Harris (1984) and Gilbert (1989)]. As a result, the potential entrant's belief that this will occur is reasonable, i.e., the strategy is subgame perfect. We present the essentials of Dixit's model below. We warn the reader in advance that this model is hard work. While no one piece of the analysis is difficult, considerable care is required in putting all the pieces together.

The game Dixit posits between the two firms is a dynamic, two-stage one in the spirit of those covered in the previous chapter. In the first stage, the incumbent firm is alone and chooses a capacity level that we will denote as $\overline{K_1}$. This commits the firm to a fixed cost of $r\overline{K_1}$ where r is the cost per unit of capacity. One unit of capacity provides one unit of the input K needed to produce one unit of output. Hence, by investing in capacity $\overline{K_1}$ in the first stage of the game, the incumbent firm has the capability of producing any output less than or equal to $\overline{K_1}$ when the second stage of the game begins. However, the incumbent's capacity can be further increased in stage two of the game. Again, this will cost r per unit. The difference is that this is a marginal decision at that time. One can add just one unit of the input K or many at a cost of r apiece. In contrast, the initial $\overline{K_1}$ units of capacity cannot be reduced. They represent a fixed cost in stage two, for which the firm will pay $r\overline{K_1}$ regardless of what its production level is.

The potential entrant observes the incumbent's capacity choice in stage one. It is only after that observation that the potential entrant makes its entry decision in stage two. If entry does occur then, in the second stage of the game, the two firms play a Cournot game in output. Market demand for the product in stage two is described by $P = A - B(q_1 + q_2)$. It is very important to note that the two firms simultaneously choose both their outputs (q_1, q_2) and their levels of input $K(K_1, K_2)$ in stage two. For the incumbent, this input choice is constrained because its capacity in the second stage cannot be less than the capacity chosen in the first stage, i.e., $K_1 \geq \overline{K_1}$. The incumbent firm can increase its capacity in stage two but not decrease it below the precommitted level.

We will denote any sunk costs incurred by the incumbent other than those associated with its capacity choice $\overline{K_1}$ as F_1. For simplicity, we will further assume that every unit produced requires the input of one unit of labor as well as a unit of input K. If labor can be hired at the wage w, then the incumbent's marginal cost of production in stage two for output if $K_1 \leq \overline{K}_1$ is just w. However, if the incumbent wishes to produce an output greater than q_1 then it must expand capacity by hiring additional units of K, again at the price of r per unit, as well as hire more labor at a cost of w per unit. That is, every unit of output above $\overline{K}_1$ has marginal cost $w + r$. These relationships are reflected in the following description of the incumbent's cost function in stage two of the game:

$$C_1(q_1, \overline{K}_1, w, r) = F_1 + r\overline{K}_1 + wq_1; \quad \text{for } q_1 \leq \overline{K}_1 \text{ Marginal Cost} = w$$

$$C_1(q_1, \overline{K}_1, w, r) = F_1 + r\overline{K}_1 + r(q_1 - \overline{K}_1) + wq_1, \text{ for } q_1 > \overline{K}_1 \text{ Marginal Cost} = w + r$$

(12.4)

The incumbent's marginal cost is w for output up to $\overline{K}_1$ but $w + r$ for higher levels. Now denote any sunk cost the entrant incurs as result of participating in the market as F_2. The entrant's cost function implies that its marginal cost is always $w + r$ no matter what output it chooses, as shown below:

$$C_2(q_2, w, r) = F_2 + (r + w)q_2 \text{ Marginal Cost} = w + r \tag{12.5}$$

Note that for any output q that fully utilizes its capacity equal to $\overline{K}_1$, the incumbent's total cost will be the same as cost incurred by the entrant to produce that same output, namely, $(w + r)q$. That is, the incumbent's initial capacity investment does not give it an advantage in terms of total cost. Instead, what that investment does achieve is a change in the composition of the incumbent's cost. Up to production level $\overline{K}_1$, that cost now reflects an additional fixed cost of $r\overline{K}_1$, and variable cost of just wq_1. In particular, firm 1's advantage is that up to any output less than or equal to $\overline{K}_1$, its *marginal* cost is just w in stage two whereas the entrant faces a marginal cost of $w + r$ for all output levels. This difference is reflected in Figure 12.2, where we draw the marginal cost curve for both firms. The diagram suggests why investment in capacity can have a commitment value. The incumbent's commitment to produce at least as much as $\overline{K}_1$ is made more believable by the fact that up to that production level, its marginal cost is *relatively* low.

In a sequential game, we begin by working out what happens in the last stage in order to work out the incumbent firm's optimal move in the first stage. To solve for a subgame perfect equilibrium strategy for the incumbent firm, we need to determine how the incumbent's choice of capacity in stage one affects the market outcome when the two firms compete in stage two. So, we start by working out what happens in stage two for any particular level

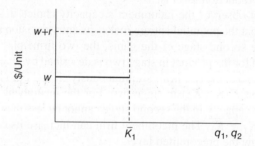

Figure 12.2   The effect of previously acquired capacity on current marginal cost

The incumbent has previously acquired capacity $\overline{K}_1$ and therefore incurs a marginal cost of only w up to this level of production. For greater levels, its marginal cost is $w + r$. The entrant has no previously acquired capacity. Its marginal cost is $w + r$ for all production levels.

of capacity chosen in stage one. We then determine what happens in stage one by choosing the capacity that maximizes the incumbent's profits in stage two.

In stage two, the firms are playing a Cournot game in quantities. From our analysis in Chapter 9, we know that the marginal revenue for each firm is given by:

Incumbent Marginal Revenue : $MR_1 = A - 2Bq_1 - Bq_2$

Entrant Marginal Revenue : $MR_2 = A - Bq_1 - 2Bq_2$ (12.6)

As always, the profit-maximizing output choice for each firm is to produce where marginal revenue equals marginal cost. For the entrant, the implication of this rule is clear. Because the entrant's marginal cost is always $w + r$, its optimal output choice will always be given by the best response function:

$$q_2^* = \frac{(A - w - r)}{2B} - \frac{q_1}{2}$$ (12.7)

Recall, however, that the incumbent's marginal cost depends on whether or not the firm is producing beyond its initial capacity investment $\overline{K}_1$. Hence, the incumbent's best response function will also depend on where its production lies relative to $\overline{K}_1$. In particular, we have:

$$q_1^* = \frac{(A - w)}{2B} - \frac{q_2}{2} \quad \text{when } q_1^* \leq \overline{K}_1; \text{ and}$$

$$q_1^* = \frac{(A - w - r)}{2B} - \frac{q_2}{2} \quad \text{when } q_1^* > \overline{K}_1$$ (12.8)

This means that the incumbent firm's best response function jumps at the output level $q_1^* = \overline{K}_1$. We can see the jump more clearly when we draw the incumbent's best response function in the second stage of the game. We do this in Figure 12.3, where the best response function when marginal cost is just w is shown as $L'L$, while the best response curve when marginal cost is $w + r$ is shown as $N'N$. Again, the incumbent's actual best response curve is a composite of these two line segments that switches from the low-cost curve $L'L$ to the high-cost curve $N'N$ at $\overline{K}_1$, the incumbent's capacity that is given in stage two but chosen in stage one of the game.

One point worth stressing before going further is that the entrant's best response function (12.7) applies on the condition that the entrant chooses to produce any output at all, i.e., so long as $q_2 > 0$. The best response function is derived using the marginal conditions and therefore does *not* take account of the sunk cost F_2 that the potential entrant incurs should it actually decide to enter. The intercept of equation (12.7) with the q_2 axis, namely, $(A - w - r)/2B$ is the entrant's optimal output if the incumbent somehow decided to produce nothing. That would correspond to the entrant being a monopoly and would almost certainly imply positive profits (otherwise we could rule out entry from the start). However, as one moves from left to right along the entrant's best response function, the entrant's output becomes successively smaller as it adjusts to larger and larger output choices by the incumbent. This decline limits the volume over which the entrant's fixed cost F_2 may be spread. As a result, firm 2's average total cost rises as its output falls. It is quite possible that, at some point where the incumbent's output q_1 is sufficiently large, the market price implied by the combined output of both firms will not cover the entrant's average cost *even when it produces the profit-maximizing output implied by its best response curve*. If those

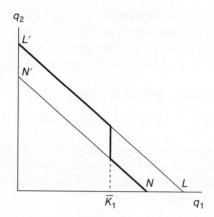

Figure 12.3 The best response function of the incumbent firm depends on its first-stage choice of capacity

For output less than $\overline{K}_1$, the incumbent will have a low marginal cost and operate on the higher response function $L'L$. For output greater than $\overline{K}_1$, the incumbent will have a high marginal cost and operate on the lower best response function $N'N$.

fixed costs had already been incurred they would be sunk and the entrant would continue to produce. Yet because the cost F_2 is only incurred if entry occurs, firm 2 can avoid this expense by choosing not to enter. Obviously, it will do this if it foresees that the Nash equilibrium if it does enter will not generate an operating profit sufficient to cover that cost F_2. We will return to this point below.

Now consider the incumbent's initial capacity choice $\overline{K}_1$. It is clear that this choice will critically affect the Nash equilibrium in stage two. The larger is $\overline{K}_1$, the more likely it is that the state 2 equilibrium will occur along the best response function of the incumbent that is further to the right, i.e., at a point at which the incumbent has a marginal cost of w instead of $w + r$. How should the incumbent make this choice in stage 1?

A little reflection on our analysis in Chapter 11 should convince you that the incumbent's choice for $\overline{K}_1$ will never be less than the Stackelberg leader's choice for output when it has a marginal cost of $w + r$. From that chapter we know that output level is $q_1 = \dfrac{(A - w - r)}{2B}$ and we will now denote this output level as M_1. We also know that if firm 1 does produce this level, firm 2's best response is to set $q_2 = \dfrac{(A - w - r)}{4B}$, an output level we will now denote as M_2. It is actually rather straightforward to understand why the incumbent will never choose an initial capacity less than M_1.

Consider the following. If the incumbent produces at the Stackelberg leader level, the entrant will either stay out of the market entirely or, enter and produce its best response to the Stackelberg output, namely, M_2. The decision to stay out will reflect the fact that if it does enter, the entrant's fixed cost is sufficiently high that it will still lose money even if it produces its best response to the incumbent's Stackelberg output, i.e., when it produces M_2. In other words, if the incumbent's production of M_1 creates enough downward pressure on price that the entrant cannot enter profitably at any output of M_2 or less, then the incumbent will be alone in the market as a monopolist. However, this means that the incumbent will be producing exactly the right amount because we know that the Stackelberg leader output M_1 *is* precisely the output level chosen by a monopolist. Indeed, that is why we designated this output level as M_1. Note that there is no real predation in this case. The incumbent is

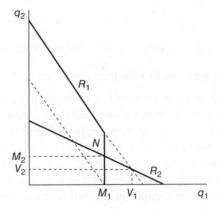

Figure 12.4   Possible incumbent capacity choices and entrant responses
The incumbent will make an initial capacity investment somewhere between points M and V, i.e., in the interval M_1 to V_1. The incumbent will choose the Stackelberg/monopoly capacity of M_1 if: 1) the entrant cannot break even at an output less than M_2; or 2) the entrant can break even at output levels lower than V_2. In the first case, the incumbent is acting as a non-predatory profit-maximizing monopoly. In the second, entry can only be limited—not prevented—by choosing the Stackelberg output. Predatory entry deterrence can occur when the entrant can break even at output levels less than M_2 but greater than V_2 while on its best response curve R_2. Here, the incumbent's investment in initial capacity in excess of M_1 may prevent entry.

simply acting as the monopolist it is by producing the monopoly output and that in itself is enough to block entry and confirm the incumbent's monopoly status.

In the event that entry does occur, the incumbent will face an actual rival in stage 2. Yet if entry cannot be prevented altogether it can still be limited. Moreover, the Stackelberg leader output $M_1 = \dfrac{(A - w - r)}{2B}$ is by definition the best output choice for this purpose. It limits the entrant to $M_2 = \dfrac{(A - w - r)}{4B}$.

Note that for either of the two events above to be subgame perfect outcomes, the incumbent's commitment to producing the Stackelberg output M_1 must be credible. In particular, that output must be a best response to the entrant's choice. Because M_1 is the monopoly output, this is clearly the case if the entrant does not enter. Yet unlike the conventional Cournot model in which the incumbent faces a constant marginal cost of $w + r$ and therefore wishes to reduce its output below M_1 when the rival produces M_2, the *ex ante* investment in capacity also makes M_1 a best response to the entrant's choice of M_2 here. This is shown in Figure 12.4. In this diagram, the sloping dashed lines reflect the incumbent's best response curve under different marginal costs. The inner dashed curve reflects a high marginal cost of $w + r$. The outer dashed line reflects the lower part of the incumbent's best response curve when it has a low marginal cost w. The rest of that best response is reflected in the solid line extension of the outer dashed line. That solid line together with the vertical solid line through output $q_1 = M_1$ together describe the incumbent's best response function, R_1. The entrant's best response function R_2 is less complicated as it reflects the high marginal cost $w + r$ for all output choices.

Note that by investing in capacity $\overline{K}_1 = M_1$ *ex ante*, the incumbent guarantees itself an *ex post* marginal cost of just w up to the output level M_1. This is why we say that R_1 includes the vertical portion through the output level $M_1 = \dfrac{(A - w - r)}{2B}$ implying that this is a best response to a variety of entrant production levels, including the entrant's best response of $M_2 = \dfrac{(A - w - r)}{4B}$ to the incumbent's choice of M_1. As a result, the incumbent's commitment to M_1 is credible and the output combination $q_1 = \dfrac{(A - w - r)}{2B}$, $q_2 = \dfrac{(A - w - r)}{4B}$ is a subgame perfect Nash equilibrium.

We have just shown that the incumbent will never invest in initial capacity $\overline{K}_1 < M_1$. In addition to this lower bound on its initial investment there is also an upper bound. This is the output level shown in Figure 12.4 as V_1, corresponding to the Nash equilibrium when the incumbent has the low marginal cost w throughout its production. The reason should be clear. While it is feasible for the incumbent to set $\overline{K}_1 > V_1$, such higher outputs cannot be part of a Nash equilibrium in a post-entry game. There is no point to the right of V at which the best response function of the incumbent R_1 will intersect the best response function of the entrant R_2. Because the incumbent will never wish to produce more than V_1 it will never wish to invest in $\overline{K}_1 > V_1$ initial capacity.

So far, we have shown that the incumbent will never make a stage one investment in capacity either less than M_1 or greater than V_1, i.e., we must have $M_1 \leq \overline{K}_1 \leq V_1$. The remaining question is whether the incumbent will ever choose an initial capacity $\overline{K}_1$ somewhere in between this upper and lower bound. That is, is it possible to have a subgame perfect equilibrium in which $\overline{K}_1$ exceeds M_1 but is less than V_1? To see why this is possible, consider Figure 12.4 again in which we have assumed an initial capacity choice of exactly $\overline{K}_1 = M_1 = \dfrac{(A - w - r)}{2B}$. This choice in turn implies that the stage two equilibrium will be at point M (the Stackelberg point) with firm 1 producing at capacity M_1 and firm 2 producing at $M_2 = 0.5M_1$. Suppose though that in this equilibrium the entrant's output M_2 generates just enough operating profit to cover its fixed cost F_2. Hence, in this equilibrium the entrant breaks even, i.e., the market price just covers the entrant's average total cost.

Starting from this point, it is clear from equation (12.7) that if the incumbent increased its output by one unit to $M_1 + 1$, the entrant's output would fall by $1/2$ unit. So, total output would rise by a $1/2$ unit implying that the market price would fall. Yet because it would now be spreading its fixed overhead cost F_2 over a smaller volume, the entrant's average cost will have risen. It follows that if it had just been breaking even in the previous market outcome, the entrant will now be losing money because the price per unit has fallen and the cost per unit has risen. Foreseeing this, however, the entrant would not enter in the first place. It is better not to enter and earn zero rather than to enter and actually lose money. In other words, this is a situation in which, by committing to an output of $M_1 + 1$, the incumbent can deter the entrant from entering the market at all. To be sure, the output $M_1 + 1$ is a little higher than the profit-maximizing monopoly output of $M_1 = \dfrac{(A - w - r)}{2B}$. However, as we have seen, the commitment to a higher output level is what makes monopoly possible in the first place. The lower output choice of M_1 allows the entrant in to compete as a Stackelberg follower. In the case at hand, that rivalry will reduce the incumbent's profit more than the cost of choosing slightly more capacity than it would have had it been a monopoly not facing entry. In other words, the incumbent's choice comes down to this: commit to producing $M_1 = \dfrac{(A - w - r)}{2B}$ units which will permit the entrant to enter and produce $M_2 = \dfrac{(A - w - r)}{4B}$ units so that the incumbent earns the profit of a Stackelberg leader, or commit to $M_1 + 1$ units which will prevent the entrant from coming into the market at all and leave the incumbent with the monopoly profit from producing $M_1 + 1$ units, which is a little less than a pure monopolist facing no entry. It should be clear that the latter choice will often be preferable. Indeed, even if it has to increase its initial capacity investment to $M_1 + 2$, or $M_1 + n$ in order to deter entry, the incumbent may find it profitable to do so, so long as n is not so large that the incumbent commits to a level of output greater than V_1.

In sum, there are three possibilities in the Dixit (1980) model. One is that the entrant's fixed cost F_2 is sufficiently high that it cannot operate profitably at any point along its best response curve that has an output less than or equal to that of a Stackelberg follower ($\leq M_2$ in Figure 12.4). A second possible outcome is that the entrant's fixed cost F_2 is sufficiently low that it can profitably enter even in a Nash equilibrium (point V in Figure 12.4), in which the incumbent's marginal cost is just w reflecting only its labor input, so that the entrant's output is very low (V_2 or lower in Figure 12.4). In either of these cases, the incumbent will find it optimal to commit to a capacity level of $\overline{K}_1 = M_1 = \dfrac{(A - w - r)}{2B}$. If the entrant cannot enter, this is the right value because it is the output that a monopolist would choose. If the entrant cannot be blocked, this is the output level that best limits the extent of entry. However, there is a range of entrant fixed cost F_2 not so large that the incumbent's commitment to a capacity level $\overline{K}_1 > M_1 = \dfrac{(A - w - r)}{2B}$ will deter entry but large enough such that commitment to capacity $\overline{K}_1$ satisfying $V_1 \geq \overline{K}_1 > M_1$ will imply losses for the entrant even if it makes its best response to the incumbent's choice because it will not achieve sufficient scale economies. In this case, predatory entry deterrence *is* possible. We say predatory because the incumbent would not normally choose an initial capacity of $\overline{K}_1 > M_1$ except for the fact that this deters all entry, i.e., the action is profitable only because of its entry deterring effect. This is the common definition of market predatory behavior. Practice Problem 12.2 provides a numerical example of this analysis. Formal analysis of the Dixit (1980) model may be found in the Appendix to this chapter.

12.2

Suppose that the inverse demand function is described by $P = 120 - (q_1 + q_2)$, where q_1 is the output of the incumbent firm and q_2 is the output of the entrant. Let both the labor cost and capital cost per unit be 30, i.e., $w = r = 30$. In addition, let each firm have a fixed cost of $F_1 = F_2 = 200$. (See Figure 12.5 for illustration.)

a. Suppose that in stage one the incumbent invests in capacity $\overline{K}_1$. Show that in stage two the incumbent's best response function is $q_1 = 45 - \dfrac{1}{2}q_2$ when $q_1 \leq \overline{K}_1$, and $q_1 = 30 - \dfrac{1}{2}q_2$ when $q_1 > \overline{K}_1$.

b. Show that the entrant's best response function in stage two is $q_2 = 30 - \dfrac{1}{2}q_1$.

c. Show that the monopoly or Stackelberg leader's output is equal to 30. If the incumbent commits to a production capacity of $\overline{K}_1 = 30$ show that in stage two the entrant will come in and produce an output equal to 15. Show that in this case firm 2, the entrant, earns a profit equal to $25, whereas the incumbent earns a profit of $250.

Practice Problem

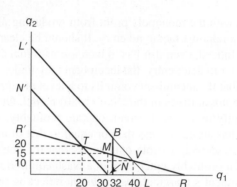

Figure 12.5 An example of entry deterrence

By initially investing in capacity of 32 in stage one, the incumbent firm insures that it will operate on the response function $L'L$ up to this output level in stage two. It also signals the potential entrant that the incumbent will produce an output of $q_1 \geq 32$ in this later stage. The entrant's best response to this production level is to set $q_2 = 14$. However, the entrant will not cover its cost even with this best response. Therefore, by committing to an output of $q_1 = 32$, the incumbent deters any actual entry.

    d.   Now show that if the incumbent chooses a $\overline{K}_1 = 32$ in stage one then the entrant in stage two can not earn a positive profit if it enters the market. In this case, the incumbent produces slightly more output than the monopolist and earns a profit equal to \$632, which is far greater than the profit earned in part (c).

The Dixit (1980) model makes clear that the incumbent firm has an advantage. More importantly, the model reveals precisely the source of that advantage. It is the incumbent's ability to commit credibly to a particular output level in stage two by means of its choice of capacity in stage one. Effectively, the incumbent commits to producing at least as much as the initial capacity it installs because to produce any less amounts to throwing away some of that investment, which is costly. In this respect, two further aspects of the model are worth noting. First, when the incumbent deters entry it does so by deliberately *over*-investing in initial capacity. That is, installing an initial capacity greater than M_1 would not be profitable were it not for the fact that doing so eliminates the competition. Therefore, such capacity expansion is predatory in the usual sense of the word.

Second, note that capacity expansion is credible as a deterrent strategy only to the extent that capacity, once in place, is a sunk cost. If unused plant capacity can be sold off for a fee r, then capacity is truly flexible and acquiring it does not reflect any real commitment on the part of the firm. When such flexibility is not possible, which is often the case, then capacity investment is a much more effective way to deter strategy than simply a promise to set a low price. A price commitment is much less credible precisely because it may easily be changed. Making a real commitment is typically costly. In the Dixit model, this cost reflects the fact that the incumbent operates at a level of output above the profit-maximizing choice of a pure monopoly. Yet it is precisely the act of making that commitment and incurring that cost that makes monopoly possible. Practice Problem 12.3 offers another model of predation by way of commitment.

Now think back to the empirical evidence on entry that we reviewed at the beginning of the chapter. Two of the stylized facts are: (1) entry is commonly observed in a wide

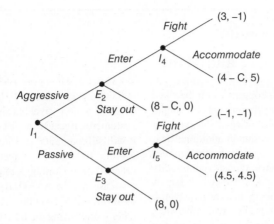

Figure 12.6 Extensive form for practice problem 12.3

At nodes labeled I it is the incumbent's turn to move. At nodes labeled E it is the entrant's turn.

cross-section of industries, and (2) market penetration as measured by market share is relatively low for the entrants. These stylized facts are consistent with this model. The incumbent has a strategic advantage in being the first to invest in capacity, and can use this advantage strategically to limit the impact of entry into its market—perhaps eliminating it altogether.

12.3

The extensive form for a dynamic game between an incumbent and an entrant firm is described in Figure 12.6. The incumbent firm moves first and chooses whether or not to spend C as a means of enhancing its ability to be aggressive. The entrant moves next and decides whether or not to enter the market. If the entrant enters then the incumbent decides whether to accommodate its new rival or to fight. If the entrant does not enter, the incumbent earns 8 minus C if it has made that expenditure, and 8 if it has not. If the entrant does enter, the incumbent's payoffs depend on whether it fights or accommodates. Fighting when the expenditure C has been sunk yields a payoff of 3. Fighting is bloodier when the incumbent has not spent C. Accommodation when C has been spent wastes that investment. The final payoffs are described in parentheses, the first being the incumbent's payoff and the second the entrant's.

a. Show that for C greater than or equal to 1, the incumbent will always fight *if* it has invested in the capacity to do so—that is, if it has initially made the expenditure C.
b. Show that for C greater than or equal to 3.5, the incumbent will not make the initial investment C.

Practice Problem

12.3   PREEMPTION AND BUNDLING

A central force that drives the Dixit (1980) model is the presence of scale economies. The fixed cost F_2 of the entrant must be spread over a sufficiently large volume of output in order for its average cost to be sufficiently low. This is often the case because the scale of a

Reality Checkpoint
Take-or-Pay ... and Win!

Firms typically have contracts with their key suppliers that stipulate the amount of the input to be bought and the price to be paid for the coming year. A common additional feature of such contracts, especially for supplies of natural gas, electricity, and commodity raw materials, is a "take-or-pay" clause. A contract that includes a take-or-pay clause requires that the purchasing firm either uses all the amount of the input initially contracted or, that if it orders less than that amount, it still pays some amount, usually less than the full contract price, for the additional amount remaining.

Take-or-pay contracts stabilize both the production schedule and the revenues of supplier firms. However, as you should recognize, they also serve another purpose. They are a straightforward way to implement the Dixit entry deterrence strategy.

For example, Corning is one of the leading manufacturers of fiber optic cables. One of its key suppliers is Praxair, a major producer of specialty gases. Suppose that Corning signs a contract with Praxair that calls for Corning to purchase 1,000,000 cubic feet of helium (which is used as a coolant in the production of fiber optic cable) at $400 per 1,000 cubic feet. The contract also includes a take-or-pay contract where Corning has to pay $300 per cubic feet for any amount of the 1,000,000 that it does not use. What this does is effectively transform the structure of Corning's costs. If Corning orders all of the 1,000,000 cubic feet, its helium bill will be: ($400/1000) × 1,000,000 = $400,000. Suppose though that Corning only uses 900,000 cubic feet of helium (perhaps because a new rival steals some Corning customers). Because of the take or pay clause, it will still pay $300 per thousand cubic feet for the 100,000 cubic feet that it did not order. Hence, Corning's total helium cost in this case will be: ($400/1000) × 900,000 + ($300/1000) × 100,000 = $390,000.   In other words, using the last 100,000 cubic feet of helium only raises Corning's total helium bill by $10,000. Effectively, the contract has changed the marginal cost of helium for Corning from $400 to $100 per thousand cubic feet. Note that it has not changed the total cost of using one million cubic feet of helium. The contract has simply transformed some of those costs into fixed costs so that up to the one million volume, Corning has a very low marginal cost.

There is of course a downside to the take-or-pay contract. This is that if another large rival, e.g., the British fiber optic producer Marconi, already exists and both firms sign take-or-pay contracts with their helium suppliers, the industry could find itself in a nasty price war in which prices fall to the low levels of marginal cost via Bertrand competition. Some believe that this is part of what happened in the fiber optic market following the burst of the telecommunications bubble.

Sources: A. M. Brandenburger and B. J. Nalebuff, 1996. *Co-opetition*. New York: Doubleday; and F. Norris, "Disaster at Corning: At Least the Balance Sheet is Strong," *New York Times*, July 13 2001, p. C2.

plant or plant capacity is frequently not a continuous but a discrete variable—available only in specific, fixed amounts. This same scale economy feature also plays a role in other entry deterring strategies but ones that while similar, are logically distinct from the mechanism of the Dixit (1980) model. Two of these strategies include an investment timing tactic generally referred to as preemption and the strategic use of bundling. We discuss each in turn.

12.3.1 Preemption

While the intuition underlying the preemption analysis has long been understood, the first formal analysis is due to Eaton and Lipsey (1979), and is set in a spatial market framework of the type introduced in Chapters 4, 7, and 10. We illustrate the basic idea here using a simple numerical Cournot example.

Consider a monopolist facing current demand given by: $Q = 30 - P$, so that inverse demand is $P = 30 - Q$. Operating in this market requires a plant, and these come only in one size. Specifically, each plant can product any output up to a capacity of 15 units. Such a plant can be built and utilized instantaneously and it will last forever, but acquiring a plant of this capacity requires a one-time cost of $150. For simplicity, we assume all other costs are zero. Hence, once the plant is built, the firm has a marginal cost of zero. By either the twice-as-steep rule (Chapter 2) or the Cournot $N/(N + 1)$ rule (Chapter 9) with $N = 1$, it should be easy to see that the monopolist's profit maximizing output is $Q^M = 15$, implying a monopoly price of $P^M = \$15$ and an operating profit of $225, or a net monopoly profit of $\pi_1^M = \$75$, after the cost of building the necessary plant is included.

We now complicate this setting with two additional features. The first of these is that there is a potential entrant against whom the monopolist will compete as a Cournot duopolist should entry actually occur. The second is that there is a subsequent market period in which demand will grow to: $Q = 42 - P$, i.e., it is known that the market will increase by 40 percent over time. If this seems like very rapid growth, think of a period as say ten years so that it reflects an annual growth rate of 3.4 percent. Of course, this time element implies that discounting is relevant. We will assume a periodic interest rate of 50 percent (4.1 percent a year if a period is ten years). This implies that the discount factor $R = 0.67$.

In the absence of the entry threat the incumbent would reason as follows. If it does not add capacity by building another plant, it will sell 15 units in period two. Given the increased demand, these units will sell at a price of $27 each and the firm will earn a profit of $405. Given the discount factor, the present value of this profit is $R\$405 = \$270$. Alternatively, the firm can acquire a second plant for $150 either now or in the second period. From a present value perspective, the latter option is clearly better as the present value of the cost is then just $R\$150 = \$100$. If it has a capacity of 30 units, then again, use of the $\left(\dfrac{N}{N + 1}\right)$ rule (Section 9.5) implies that with $N = 1$, the monopoly output in period two is 21 units implying a price of $21, and a revenue of $441. In present value terms, this has value of $R\$441 = \$294$. Thus, the present value of adding a second plant to expand capacity is $294 - $100 = 194. Because this is less than the present value ($405) of simply producing at the current capacity of 15, the incumbent would not add any capacity in the absence of any entry threat.

We now turn to the potential entrant. This firm observes the incumbent in period one and decides then whether or not to enter in period two. To do so obviously requires that this firm make the $150 investment in a plant. However, it has a choice about when it should do this. It can invest in the plant now and pay a present value of $150 or wait one period and pay a present value of $R\$150 = \$100$. As a Cournot duopolist in the second period, the $N/(N + 1)$ rule implies that both the entrant and the incumbent will produce 14 units in period two. This will lead to a second period price of $14. Therefore, the present value of the operating profit each firm will make is $R\$196 = \$130.67$. Clearly, this is not enough to cover the cost of investing in a plant today but is enough to cover the cost if investment is delayed one period. Accordingly, the entrant will wait until the second period to acquire the necessary plant to enter the market.

We now return to the incumbent. It understands the logic of the above analysis and can see that the entrant will enter invest and enter in period two, which will end its monopoly position. Is there a strategy that the incumbent can use to prevent this?

Here we make one further assumption. This is that while the two firms compete as symmetric Cournot duopolists if they invest at the same time, each with a marginal cost of zero, this is not the case if one firm builds capacity before the other. More specifically, if one firm adds capacity before the other, it gains all the consumers it can serve up to its new capacity. Only if demand is more than that expanded maximum will its rival gain any customers. This may be because by being first, the firm can sign up consumers to a contract before its rival, or for other reasons. In a spatial model setting, it reflects the fact that once a firm has staked out a market position it cannot move. Whatever the reason, however, it now gives the incumbent an incentive to invest in period one—to preempt the entrant's later expansion—and so to keep its monopoly position.

The logic of the incumbent's new strategy is straightforward. There is clearly no point in investing in new capacity in period two because the entrant will still find it profitable to enter at that time. Thus, the incumbent's choice comes down to either not investing at all as per its original strategy or expanding capacity in period one. In the former case, the entrant will enter and the incumbent will earn a second period duopoly operating profit of $196. The present value of its profit over time will then be: $-\$150 + \$225 + R\$196 = \$205.66$. Alternatively, the incumbent can expand capacity now by initially building two plants giving it a capacity of 30—more than enough to serve all the output demanded at the duopoly price of $14. As a result, the entrant will see that entry is not profitable and the incumbent will keep its monopoly position. Now, with a capacity of 30 in period two, the incumbent will produce the profit-maximizing output of 21 units, implying a price of $21 and an operating profit of $441. The present value of its cash flow in this case is: $-\$300 + \$225 + R\$441 = \$219$. It is evident then that investing in additional capacity today is the more profitable strategy. Therefore, the incumbent will add an additional plant in period one as a means to preempt the entrant and maintain its monopoly power.

The reason that the incumbent can afford to expand capacity in period one while the entrant cannot is straightforward. The incumbent is fighting to protect monopoly profit while the best that the entrant can hope for is a duopoly profit. Thus, the payoff to early capacity expansion is greater for the incumbent than it is for the entrant.

Note two further features of the preemptive capacity expansion just described. First, the strategy implies that in period one the incumbent will operate with a lot of excess capacity. Specifically, it will have a capacity of 30 units and yet produce only half that amount. Second, and even more important, note that the incumbent's first-period capacity expansion would not be profitable—and the incumbent would not do it—except for the fact that the investment works to prevent entry. Viewed in this light, this preemptive strategy is truly predatory.

12.3.2   Bundling to Deter Entry

In Chapter 8, we presented the use of bundling as both a price discrimination technique and as a predatory tactic with particular reference to the Microsoft case. The underlying analysis of this second role, due to Nalebuff (2004) among others, is worth reviewing briefly here with a simple numerical example. To this end, consider the following valuation of two different goods, A and B, by each of ten potential buyers.

Consumer	Value of Product A	Value of Product B	Value of Both Products
1	0.5	5.0	5.5
2	1.0	8.0	9.0
3	1.5	6.0	7.5
4	2.0	3.0	5.0
5	2.5	3.9	6.4
6	3.0	4.0	7.0
7	3.4	3.9	7.3
8	4.0	6.0	10.0
9	4.5	8.0	12.5
10	5.0	10.0	15.0

The current incumbent has a marginal cost of $1 per unit of each good. Each consumer will buy at most one unit of either commodity, depending on whether the price exceeds or is less than the consumer's valuation. As a little experimentation will quickly reveal, the profit-maximizing values for the two prices P_A and P_B if they are sold separately are $P_A = \$3$ and $P_B = \$3.9$. At these prices, five consumers will buy product A and nine will buy product B. As a result, the incumbent will earn an operating profit of $10 in market A and $26.1 in market B for a total profit of $36.1. If instead the firm bundles the two products as one packaged combination, the profit-maximizing bundle price is $6.4 at which price eight consumers will buy the package. Because the production cost of the bundle is $2, this strategy will lead to an operating profit of $8 \times (\$6.4 - \$2) = \$35.2$. Because this is less than $36.1, this is a case in which the incumbent would not engage in pure bundling.

However, the potential entry of a rival might change matters. Suppose that a more efficient rival for the A market emerges. This rival offers a perfect substitute for the incumbent's product A and does so at a lower cost. Specifically, the rival has the same fixed cost of $5 but a marginal cost of zero. Clearly, if this firm enters, it can set a price P_A of (just under) $1, and steal all of the incumbent's market A customers. The incumbent will still earn an operating profit of $26.1 from its B product line but nothing from its A product line. Meanwhile, by selling nine units of A at a price of $1, the entrant would earn $9 in revenue, which is more than enough to cover its variable cost ($0) and its fixed cost ($5).

Bundling may offer a means of preventing this entry. As noted in Chapter 8, bundling allows the firm to attract those potential A consumers who also place a large value on product B. If it can attract enough of these, it can make it impossible for the entrant to cover its fixed overhead cost. For example, suppose that the incumbent offers goods A and B together as a bundle for a bundle price of $6, while the entrant continues to offer good A at price $P_A = \$1$. Each consumer now has the choice of buying either just product A from the entrant at a price of $1 or products A and B together in a bundle offered by the incumbent at a price of $6. Because consumers maximize the surplus they get from any purchase, consumer 1 will buy neither alternative, while consumers 4 through 7 buy product A alone. The resultant revenue of $4, however, is not enough to cover the entrant's fixed cost and so entry would not occur (if it did it would soon be followed by exit). This leaves the incumbent selling the bundle for $6 which, in the absence of any rival goods, will now sell to eight consumers implying a net profit of $8(\$6 - \$2) = \$32$. Because this profit is more than the incumbent earns if it accepts the rival's entry and simply sets the profit-maximizing price of $3.9 in the B market, the incumbent will now find it profitable to bundle.

It is important to remember that the incumbent's decision to bundle in the foregoing example is only profitable because it keeps out new entrants. In the initial market setup with no threat of entry the incumbent did not find bundling profitable. It is the ability of bundling to prevent entry (or drive out existing rivals) that makes it a profitable strategy. Again, this is what economists mean when they talk about predatory behavior.

12.4   PREDATORY ENTRY DETERRENCE: HISTORICAL CASES

Both the Dixit-Spence and the preemption models discussed in the preceding sections suggest that dominant firms may expand capacity rapidly as a means to deter entry. In one case, this reflects a change in the cost structure that allows the firm to commit to aggressive pricing if entry does occur. In the other case, it serves as a preemptive claim on future customers. Is there any evidence that such capacity expansion motivated by rival entry actually occurs?

The answer to this question is, "It depends." It would be inaccurate to say that the available evidence supports the view that incumbents generally engage in such behavior. For example, Lieberman (1987) examines the capital investment behavior of incumbent and entrant firms in thirty-eight chemical industries in the face of excess capacity and market growth. He finds no difference in the behavior of the two types of firms. This suggests that the incumbents are not engaging in any capital investment for the purpose of discouraging entry. Moreover, because investment commitment strategies are more likely to occur in more capital-intensive industries, one might expect profitability to be higher in such industries, all else equal, if preemptive expansion is the norm. However, an early study by Caves and Ghemawat (1986) does not find support for this result.

Yet there is a difference between finding no evidence that capacity expansion motivated by entry deterrence is an empirical regularity and finding no evidence that such behavior ever occurs at all. To begin with, different conditions across markets have different implications for what entry deterring behavior is to be expected. For example, while the models described above have been set in a duopoly context, the reality is that there is often more than one such potential rival. One possibility in this case is a free rider problem in which successful entry by one firm will lead to many more entrants that erode that first entrant's profitability. In such a setting, it may take very little capacity expansion on the part of the incumbent to deter any entry. So, the fact that we do not see such much excess capital investment in such markets does not necessarily mean that entry deterrence is not taking place if there are many potential entrants. A second free rider problem arises if there is more than one incumbent. If one firm's capacity expansion is enough to deter entry, each incumbent may decide to let its current rivals take on that cost with the result that the observed excess investment in entry-deterring capacity is again small.[9]

The difficulties in formally testing a generalized model of entry deterrence via capacity expansion suggest that we must instead rely on the alternative approach of looking for such behavior in specific, well-defined markets. This is the approach we take here. In the following section, we present formal analysis based on evidence from hotel chains operating in Texas.

---

[9]   See Gilbert and Vives (1986) for a contrary view in which capacity expansion grows as concentration falls in a Cournot setting.

Perhaps the clearest case of capacity expansion to deter entry is provided by the Alcoa case of 1945 [*U.S. v. Aluminum Co. of America*, 148 F. 2d 416 (1945)]. As the court noted in finding Alcoa guilty of illegal monopolization, the dominant aluminum refiner expanded capacity eight-fold between 1912 and 1934. The court felt that this prevented all but two attempts to enter the industry both of which failed for lack of sufficient market share.

Weiman and Levin (1994) find that preemptive investment was an explicit tactic of Southern Bell Telephone (SBT) in its effort to monopolize the local phone service market in the central southern and eastern southern regions of the United States. Those markets had become intensely competitive after the expiration of the Bell patents so that by 1902, independent firms accounted for 60 percent of the local phone service in the region from Virginia to Alabama and Florida. Weiman and Levin (1994) provide a detailed review of company archival records showing that SBT's leader, Edward J. Hall, launched an aggressive capital expansion program to build a regional toll network in anticipation of market development and with the explicit goal of preempting rivals. Within four years, SBT had increased the geographic reach of its system from 2,000 to 8,600 pole miles. Even more impressively, its calling capacity as measured by toll wire coverage grew from 5,000 to over 55,000 miles. All this was accompanied by an aggressive price-cutting campaign both in markets where it faced competition and those where it expected it. Among other features, this had the effect of restricting the investment funds available to competitors for their own expansion whereas SBT was able to rely on heavy financing from its parent firm, AT&T. The plan worked. By 1912, SBT had virtually complete control of the southern local telephone market.

A third example is set in the town of Edmonton, Alberta, during the 1960s and early 1970s. The major retail grocer in Edmonton at that time was Safeway. However, in the early 1960s other grocery chains began to enter the Edmonton market. These included two Ontario firms, Loblaws and Dominion, and one Western Canada firm, Tom Boy. Between 1960 and 1963, these three firms opened twelve new stores in the Edmonton area. By 1964, they were operating a total of twenty-one stores—not far behind Safeway's then total of twenty-five. Safeway could clearly see that continued entry by these and other firms was a real possibility and it rapidly responded. It opened four new stores in 1963–64, another four new stores in 1965–66, and then added five new stores in 1968. Moreover, Safeway chose the locations of these new stores quite carefully. It located them in areas where due to increasing population and the fact that no other store was currently close by, it looked like a site of potential entry. In addition, just to drive home the seriousness of its intentions, Safeway also located some of its new stores almost right next to locations where its rivals also had a store. The strategy worked. By 1973, Safeway was operating thirty-five stores in the Edmonton area whereas, due to closings, its three major rivals were operating just ten.[10]

Our final case comes from the market for titanium dioxide. This is a chemical additive used as a whitener in such products as paint, paper, and plastics. At the time of our story, it could be produced by any of three processes. One of these is a sulfate procedure that uses ilmenite ore. One is a chloride process that uses rutile ore. Both of these processes were known and available to all producers. The third process, however, is a special chloride process that because of legal restrictions was known and available for use only by DuPont. Like the sulfate process, DuPont's procedure uses ilmenite ore. Yet like the generic chloride

---

[10]   Safeway was charged with monopolizing the Edmonton market in 1972 and, in late 1973, signed a consent decree that, among other things, prohibited it from expanding its total square footage in Edmonton for three-and-a-half-years. See von Hohenbalken and West (1986).

process, DuPont's method emits little pollution. This is not the case with the sulfate procedure, which has bad pollution affects.

Seven domestic firms were active in the titanium dioxide market during the 1970s. DuPont was the largest of these with about 34 percent of the market, but NL industries—which used the sulfate procedure—was a close second. Then, two events happened in the early 1970s that gave DuPont a decided advantage. First, rutile ore became more expensive, implying that other producers using the generic chloride technique might have to cut back. Second, strict pollution controls were imposed that made the sulfate process very expensive. Suddenly, DuPont's proprietary chloride technique based on ilmenite ore gave the company an edge with respect to costs. A strategic firm would lose no time in exploiting that edge. It would know that those producers using sulfate were not likely to expand. It might also recognize that rutile could someday become cheap again (it did). If in addition the firm expected, as did all participants in the titanium oxide market, that demand would grow, a firm in DuPont's position might wish to expand capacity immediately. This would preclude those rivals using the rutile-based technique from expanding production when and if rutile prices dropped and thus, permit the firm to capture the gap caused by market growth and the declining sulfate-based production entirely for itself.

In fact, DuPont increased its capacity by over 60 percent in the next five years while the industry in general stagnated. By 1977, DuPont's market share had risen to 46 percent. Moreover, when rival Kerr-McGee began to construct a new plant in 1974, just before DuPont got its planned expansion going, DuPont began trumpeting its plans to the whole industry. This seemed deliberately aimed at curtailing any expansion rival beyond that of Kerr-McGee's.[11]

In short, there appear to be a number of individual cases that support the use of capacity expansion to deter entry. Recall moreover that the role of capacity expansion in the Dixit model is to change the structure of a firm's costs as opposed to its total costs. There may be contractual and other ways to achieve this same result (see Reality Checkpoint, "Take or Pay"). Thus, one cannot easily rule out the possibility that firms engage in some such efforts.

We will turn to an explicit econometric analysis of capacity expansion in the next section. Before doing so, however, we ask whether there is also evidence on the use of bundling as an entry deterrent. Here again, the answer is again individualized to specific cases. Clearly, the issue of a large firm using bundling to damage a rival was at the heart of the Microsoft case of 2000.[12] The critical argument there was that by bundling its own web browser, *Internet Explorer*, into its general *Windows* operating system at essentially a zero price, Microsoft made it nearly impossible for the *Netscape Navigator* browser to survive. The issue also arose in connection with Microsoft's *Media Player*, which the European Commission also found harmful to competition.[13]

It is useful in this regard to note that bundling (and tying) can work in rather sophisticated ways. For example, Goolsbee and Syverson (2008) document that airlines flying routes on which the probability that discount airline Southwest has a high probability of entering cut

---

[11]   See Ghemawat (1984). See also Hall (1990) for evidence that DuPont's action was consistent with the Dixit model.

[12]   The judge's decision in *United States v. Microsoft Corp.* 97 F. Supp. 2d 59 (D.D.C. 2000) was explicit in its findings of an illegal tying violation of the Sherman Act.

[13]   In its ruling in 2004, the European Commission found Microsoft guilty of illegal tying and fined the company €497 million ($613 million). It also ordered Microsoft to share technical documents with rivals and market a version of Windows without *Media Player*. See *Microsoft Corp. v. Commission of the European Communities, T-201/04*, March 24, 2004.

prices dramatically in advance of any actual entry. Given airline frequent flyer programs this not only expands the incumbents' market demand immediately but also in the future. In effect, frequent flyer programs may be thought of as the bundling of two goods differentiated by time, namely, air travel today and air travel in the future. By locking in future air passengers, this tactic may again make Southwest's actual entry more difficult.

12.5   EMPIRICAL APPLICATION: EXCESS CAPACITY EXPANSION IN TEXAS HOTELS

Because the use of entry-deterring tactics reflects strategic consideration, we will not observe its use by perfectly competitive firms. Moreover, entry deterrence efforts may be limited even in less than perfectly competitive markets, given that each incumbent is tempted to free ride on the entry deterring actions of others. Only when an incumbent has a large market share will it find it worthwhile to engage in entry-deterring behavior. The overall intuition then is that entry-deterring tactics ought to be more commonly employed in more concentrated markets[14] and by larger firms.

Conlin and Kadiyali (2006) apply the foregoing insight to hotel markets across 254 counties in Texas over the years 1991 through 1997. Following the intuition of the Dixit (1980) and Eaton and Lipsey (1979) models above, they identify entry deterrence with excess capacity.[15] Their basic hypothesis is therefore that there will be more excess capacity—a higher percentage of unoccupied rooms—in more concentrated markets and for firms with larger market shares.

Conlin and Kadiyali (2006) apply four different definitions of the local hotel market. One is simply the county: all hotels in Anderson county form one hotel market. A second is the more local city market: all hotels in Houston form one market. Variations on each of these two basic definitions come from considering which of three specific hotel segments—Full Service, Limited Service, or Extended Stay—forms the core of the hotel's business. Again, examples would include the Anderson County Full Service hotel market and the Houston Limited Service hotel market. With these data, Conlin and Kadiyali (2006) create a Herfindahl Index for each such market. They also measure the percentage excess capacity in each market in each year, defined as $100\% \times (1 - the\ average\ occupancy\ rate)$. They then estimate the following regression for each market group across all the sample years:

$$\text{Percentage Excess Capacity}_{m,t} = \alpha_t + \beta(\text{Herfindahl Index})_{m,t} + \varphi X_{m,t} + \varepsilon_{m,t} \quad (12.9)$$

The dependent variable is the percentage excess capacity in market m and year t. The intercept varies over time to allow for the general economic conditions of each year. The expectation is that the Herfindahl Index for market m in year t will have a positive effect on market excess capacity, i.e., β will be positive reflecting the hypothesis that more concentrated markets will exhibit more entry-deterring behavior. However, the authors control for a variety of other influences on excess capacity such as unemployment, per capita income, population, taxes, etc., by including the vector of variables $X_{m,t}$. Of course, there is also a random error term $\varepsilon_{m,t}$ associated with each regression observation. The

[14]   See Gilbert and Vives (1986) for an alternative view in which entry-deterring capacity expansion falls with concentration.

[15]   Bulow et al. (1985) show that the incumbent in the Dixit model will have excess capacity when demand is nonlinear.

Table 12.2   Effect of market concentration on excess capacity in local texas hotel markets

Market Definition	Herfindahl Index Estimated Coefficient	Standard Error
County	0.478*	(0.167)
County-Sector	0.159	(0.154)
City	0.345*	(0.129)
City-Sector	0.240**	(0.129)

*Significant at 1% level;
**Significant at 10% level

estimates of the key parameter β for each of the four different market definition regressions are shown above in Table 12.2.

The results tend to confirm the hypothesis that increased concentration is associated with increased excess capacity in Texas hotel markets. All four of the estimated concentration coefficients are positive and three are statistically significant. Thus, these results offer support for the view that firms with market power pursue capacity expansion as an entry deterrent.

Yet while supportive of the basic hypothesis, Conlin and Kadiyali (2006) recognize that these findings are far from conclusive. The reason is that while, as noted, they have controlled for many other observable differences between markets, such as unemployment, population, and so on, there may be other, unobservable differences that are driving these results. For example, the presence of excess capacity may cause hotels to exit a local market. Moreover, it may be the smallest hotels that leave first. As these small hotels exit, market concentration increases giving rise to a positive correlation between excess capacity and concentration that does not at all reflect an entry-deterring strategy. Similarly, it may be that highly concentrated markets permit tacit collusion among firms to a greater extent than anticipated when their capacity was first installed with the result that suppressing output now yields excess capacity. Once again the data would then show a positive correlation between concentration and excess capacity that should not be attributed to entry deterrence.

One way to deal with the unobservable differences across markets is to put in a "fixed effects" term, which amounts to letting the regression intercept be different for each market. These fixed effects terms will pick up all the differences between markets—observed or unobserved, unrelated to time. The bad news, though, is that this means that the identification of a concentration effect comes from the variation over time within a market and not from the differences in concentration across market. This variation is not sufficiently large to yield useful estimates if these "fixed effects" are included in the regression model of equation (12.9). Therefore, Conlin and Kadiyali (2006) turn to an alternative specification that looks at the relation between an individual firm's excess capacity and that firm's market share.

Specifically, using i to index firms; m to index market; and t to index time, Conlin and Kadiyali (2006) estimate the following regression:

$$\text{Excess Capacity} y_{i,m,t} = \text{Constant}_{m,t} + \gamma \text{Market Share}_{i,m,t}$$

$$+ \rho(\text{Share in Total Capacity of Related Hotels})_{i,m,t}$$

$$+ \eta(\text{Incumbent Expansion})_{i,m,t} + \theta(\text{Entrant Expansion})_{i,m,t} + u_{i,m,t}$$

$$(12.10)$$

Table 12.3   Effect of market share on excess capacity in local texas hotels

Market Definition	Market Share Estimated Coefficient	Standard Error
County	0.4115*	(0.027)
County-Sector	0.177*	(0.035)
City	0.106*	(0.022)
City-Sector	0.157*	(0.300)

*Significant at 1% level.

The first term in equation (12.10) directly addresses the hypothesized effect. If large firms keep excess capacity as part of an entry deterring strategy, the estimate of γ will be positive. The other variables pick up: 1) whether or not the firm is affiliated with other firms in the market, e.g., Holiday Inn is affiliated with Holiday Express; 2) whether the firm is an incumbent that has recently expanded; or 3) whether the firm is an entrant that has recently expanded. Because the estimation is conducted at the firm level and there is a lot of variation in a firm's share of a specific market over time, this equation *can* be estimated using the fixed effects estimator. The results are shown in Table 12.3 below.

Here again, the effects are supportive of the use of excess capacity as an entry-deterring device. Excess capacity rises significantly with an increase in a firm's market share. Overall, the marginal effect of an increase of 10 percentage points in the firm's market share is an increase of 1.2 percentage points in a firm's excess capacity. While again, there may be other explanations behind these findings other than entry deterrence, the results in Table 12.3 when added to those in Table 12.2 offer fairly compelling evidence that entry deterrence is at least part of the explanation.

Summary

This chapter has investigated the ability of firms to maintain a dominant market position in their industry for a prolonged period of time. Both anecdotal and formal evidence indicate that such sustained market power is a widespread feature. In turn, this implies that the entry of new rivals who can compete away an incumbent firm's profits is not as powerful in the real world as it is suggested to be in basic microeconomic texts. Something permits an incumbent to preserve its market position and successfully defend itself against rival entry.

By itself, a finding that market structures have evolved in a manner that maintains or even strengthens the dominance of initial firms over time is not evidence of entry deterrence. Random processes such as Gibrat's Law suggest that asymmetrically dominated markets are the norm. Richer theoretical models such as Klepper's (2002), in which innovation becomes easier as firms get larger and more experienced, also yield oligopoly as their equilibrium outcome. Yet the additional evidence that when entry does occur it is on a small scale and often doomed to failure, along with the experiences that motivated the antitrust laws initially and the numerous court cases and anecdotal observations that have followed, all coalesce into a clear enough pattern that one cannot help but be suspicious that entry is being deterred. That suspicion can only be confirmed or denied, however, if one has a logically consistent model in which such predation is rational and formal evidence that supports that analysis.

Spence (1977), Eaton and Lipsey (1979), Dixit (1980), and Nalebuff (2004) are all examples of modern efforts to develop formal models of entry deterrence. These models hinge on the ability of incumbent firms to commit to a large output in the face of entry, typically by making a substantial capital investment. Numerous case studies suggest that firms such as Alcoa and DuPont have used such entry-deterring tactics. Statistical documentation of this behavior as an empirical regularity is more difficult, but work such as Conlin and Kadiyali (2006) does suggest a clear linkage between market power and excess capital capacity, consistent with models of entry deterring behavior. Thus, there is reason to believe that such tactics are common among real-world firms. Still it must be recognized that it is often difficult to distinguish predation from normal competitive behavior.

In both theory and practice, there is a distinction between preventing the entry of new firms and driving existing ones out of business. In this chapter we have focused on the issue of entry deterrence, or predatory conduct, and done so in a setting of complete information. While some of these tactics will apply equally well to driving rivals out rather than just not letting them in, we will address explicit efforts to force rivals to exit in the next chapter. We will also extend our analysis of incumbent response to entry in the context of incomplete information.

Problems

1. Let the domestic market for small, specialized calculators and similar office equipment be currently served by one firm, called firm I. The firm has the following cost schedules: $TC(q_I) = 0.025q_I^2$ and $MC(q_I) = .05q_I$. Market demand is $P = 50 - 0.1Q$, and right now q is equal to q_I because the only firm in the market is the incumbent firm I.

    a. If the incumbent acts as a simple monopolist, what price will it charge and what level of output will it produce?

    b. Suppose now that a foreign producer of calculators is considering exporting to the US market. Because of transportation costs and tariffs this foreign firm faces some cost disadvantage vis-à-vis the domestic incumbent. Specifically the foreign firm's cost schedules are: $TC(q_E) = 10q_E + 0.025$ and $MC(q_E) = 10 + .05q_E$. Suppose that the incumbent firm is committed to the monopoly level of output. What is the demand curve faced by the potential entrant? Write it down. Facing this demand, what level of output will the foreign firm actually export to the domestic market? What will be the new industry price?

    c. To what level of output would the incumbent firm have to commit in order to deter the foreign firm from entering the market? (Hint: You must solve for output level $q*$ with the property that if the entrant believes that the incumbent will produce $q*$, then the

    entrant's profit-maximizing response will be to produce such that $= 0$.) What is the incumbent firm's profit?

2. Return to Problem 1. Suppose that the incumbent and the entrant instead will play a Cournot game if and when the entrant enters. What are firms' profits in this case? Is it reasonable to believe that the incumbent will try and commit to $q*$ in order to deter entry? Why?

3. Suppose that the inverse demand function is described by: $P = 100 - 2(q_1 + q_2)$, where q_1 is the output of the incumbent firm and q_2 is the output of the entrant. Let the labor cost per unit $w = 20$ and capital cost per unit be $r = 20$. In addition, let each firm have a fixed cost of $F_1 = F_2 = \$100$.

    a. Suppose that in stage one the incumbent invests in capacity $\overline{K}_1$. Show that in stage two the incumbent's best response function is $q_1 = 20 - q_2/2$ when $q_1 \le \overline{K}_1$; and $q_1 = 15 - q_2/2$ when $q_1 > \overline{K}_1$.

    b. Show that the entrant's best response function in stage two is $q_2 = 15 - q_1/2$.

4. Return to Problem 3. Now show that if the incumbent commits to a production capacity of $=15$, the entrant will do best by producing 7.5 and earn a profit of \$12.5, while the incumbent earns a profit of \$125.

    a. Show that if the incumbent instead commits in stage one to a production capacity $= 16$ then the entrant's best stage two response is to produce

$q_2 = 7$, at which output the entrant does not earn a positive profit.

b. In light of your answer to 2(d), show that committing to a production capacity of 16, gives the incumbent a profit of $348.

5. Two firms, firm 1 and 2, must decide whether to enter a new industry. Industry demand is described by $P = 900 - Q$, where $Q = q_1 + q_2, q_j \geq 0$. To enter the industry a firm must build a production facility of one of two types: small or large. A small facility requires an investment of $50,000 and allows the firm to produce as many as 100 units of the good at a unit production cost of zero. Alternatively, the firm can pay $175,000 to construct a large facility that will allow the firm to produce any number of units of output at zero unit cost. A firm with a small production facility is capacity constrained whereas a firm with a large facility is not. Firm 1 makes the entry decision first. It must choose whether to enter and, if it enters, what kind of production facility to build. After observing firm 1's action, firm 2 chooses from the same set of alternatives. If only one firm enters the industry then it selects a quantity of output and sells it at the corresponding price. If both firms are in the industry they compete as Cournot firms. All output decisions in the market stage are subject to the capacity constraints of the production facilities. The market lasts for only one period.

a. Draw the extensive tree that represents the entry game being played between 1 and 2.

b. What is the outcome? Does firm 1 enter and at what size? Does firm 2 enter and at what size?

6. Let the demand for hand-blown glass vases be given by $q = 70000 - 2000P$, where q is the quantity of glass vases consumed per year and P is the dollar price of a vase. Suppose that there are 1000 identical small sellers of these glass vases. The marginal cost function of such a seller is $MC(q) = q + 5$, where q is the firm's output.

a. Assuming that each small seller acts as a price taker in this market derive the market supply curve, and the equilibrium price and quantity traded.

b. Suppose that a new mechanized technique of producing vases is discovered and monopolized by some firm, call it firm B for "BIG." Using this technique, vases can be produced at a constant average and marginal cost of $15 per vase. Consumers cannot tell the difference between vases produced by the old and the new technique. Given the existence of the fringe of small sellers what is the demand curve facing firm B?

c. Facing this demand curve, what is the profit-maximizing quantity produced by firm B? What is the price that it sets and the overall amount of vases traded in the market?

7. There are ten consumers in the markets for widgets and gadgets. Consumer valuations for each good are positively correlated, as shown in the tables below, and consumers will buy at most one unit of either good. The incumbent has a monopoly in each product. Producing each incurs a marginal cost of $40. There is also a fixed cost of $20 associated with the production of each good.

Consumer	Willingness to Pay For a Widget	Willingness to Pay For a Gadget
1	$10	$10
2	$20	$20
3	$30	$30
4	$40	$40
5	$50	$50
6	$60	$60
7	$70	$70
8	$80	$80
9	$90	$90
10	$100	$100

a. Show that the prices $P_{Widget} = P_{Gadget} = \$70$ will maximize the firm's profit if the goods are sold separately.

b. Show that there is no incentive for the incumbent to bundle the goods and sell them as a package of one widget and one gadget.

c. Imagine that there is a potential entrant in the gadget market selling an identical product to the incumbent's and competing in price. If the entrant has a marginal cost of $30 per unit and a fixed cost of $20, can the entrant enter and compete successfully against the incumbent in the gadget market if the incumbent sells gadgets separately from widgets?

d. Show that if the incumbent sells widgets and gadgets only as a bundle of one unit of each good at a price of $100 it will successfully keep the entrant out. Is this strategy profitable for the incumbent?

8. [Calculus] Suppose that two firms are in a race to enter a new market. For each firm, there is an advantage to taking time and perfecting its product because then consumers will pay more for it and it will be more profitable. However, there is also a disadvantage in waiting, in that this has an interest opportunity cost of r. Let the time to enter t vary from 0 to 1 (year), and denote the choice of firm 1's entry and firm 2's entry as t_1 and t_2, respectively. The (symmetric) profit functions are:

$$\pi^1(t_1, t_2) = \begin{cases} e^{(1-r)t_1}; & \text{if } t_1 < t_2 \\ e^{\left(\frac{1}{2}rt_1\right)}; & \text{if } t_1 = t_2 \\ e^{(1-t_2)-rt_1}; & \text{if } t_1 > t_2 \end{cases}$$

$$\pi^2(t_1, t_2) = \begin{cases} e^{(1-r)t_2}; & \text{if } t_2 < t_1 \\ e^{\left(\frac{1}{2}rt_2\right)}; & \text{if } t_2 = t_1 \\ e^{(1-t_1)-rt_2}; & \text{if } t_2 > t_1 \end{cases}$$

Show that the Nash equilibrium entry times are $t_1 = t_2 = 1/2$.

References

Bain, J., 1956. *Barriers to New Competition: Their Character and Consequences in Manufacturing Industries*, Cambridge, MA: Harvard University Press.

Baldwin, J. 1995. *The Dynamics of Industrial Competition*, Cambridge: Cambridge University Press.

Birch, D. 1987. *Job Creation in America: How Our Smallest Companies Put the Most People to Work*, New York: MacMillan, Free Press.

Brandenburger, A. B., and B. J. Nalebuff. 1996. *Co-opetition*, New York: Doubleday.

Brown, C., and J. Lattin. 1994. "Investigating the Relationship between Time in Market and Pioneering Advantage," *Management Science* 40 (October): 1361–69.

Bulow, J. J. Geanakoplos, and P. Klemperer. 1985. "Holding Idle Capacity to Deter Entry." *The Economic Journal*, 95 (March), 178–82.

Cable, J., and J. Schwalbach, 1991. "International Comparisons of Entry and Exit," in P. Geroski and J. Schwalbach, eds., *Entry and Market Contestability*, Oxford: Blackwell Publishers.

Caves, R. E. 1998. "Industrial Organization and New Findings on the Turnover and Mobility of Firms," *Journal of Economic Literature* 36 (December): 1947–82.

Caves, R. E., and P. Ghemawat. 1986. "Capital Commitment and Profitability: An Empirical Investigation," *Oxford Economic Papers* 38 (July): 94–110.

Conlin, M., and V. Kadiyali. 2006. "Entry Deterring Capacity in the Texas Lodging Industry," *Journal of Economics and Management Strategy* 15 (Spring): 167–85.

Dixit, A. 1980. "The Role of Investment in Entry Deterrence," *The Economic Journal* 90 (January): 95–106.

Dunne, T., M. J. Roberts, and L. Samuelson. 1988. "Patterns of firm entry and exit in U.S. Manufacturing Industries," *RAND Journal of Economics* 19 (Winter): 495–515.

———,1989. "The Growth and Failure of U.S. Manufacturing Plants," *Quarterly Journal of Economics* 104 (November): 671–98.

Eaton, B. C., and R. Lipsey. 1979. "The Theory of Market Preemption: The Persistence of Excess Capacity and Monopoly in Growing Spatial Market,." *Economica* 46 (February): 149–58.

Fisher, F. 1991. *Industrial Organization, Economics and the Law*, Cambridge MA: MIT Press.

Kalecki, M. 1945. "On the Gibrat Distribution," *Econometrica* 13 (April): 161–70.

Geroski, P.A. 1995. "What do we know about entry?", *International Journal of Industrial Organization* 13 (December): 421–440.

Geroski, P.A., and S. Toker. 1996. "The Turnover of Market Leaders in UK Manufacturing Industries, 1979–86," *International Journal of Industrial Organization* 14 (June): 141–58.

Ghemawat, P. 1984. "Capacity Expansion in the Titanium Dioxide Industry," *Journal of Industrial Economics* 33 (December): 145–63.

Gibrat, P. 1931. *Les inegalities economiques; applications: aux inegalities des richesses, a la concentration des enterprises, aux populations des villes, aux statistiques des familles, etc., d'une loi nouvelle, la loi de l'effet proportionnel*, Paris: Librairie du Recueill Sirey.

Gilbert, R. 1989. "Mobility Barriers and the Value of Incumbency," *Handbook of Industrial Organization, Vol. 1*, R. Schmalensee and R. Willig, eds. Amsterdam: North-Holland, 575–435.

Gilbert and R. Harris. 1984. "Competition with Lumpy Investment," *Rand Journal of Economics*, 15 (Summer): 197–212.

Gilbert, R., and X. Vives. 1986. "Entry Deterrence and the Free Rider Problem," *Review of Economic Studies* 53 (January): 71–83.

Goolsbee, A., and C. Syverson. 2008. "How Do Incumbents Respond to the Threat of Entry? Evidence from the Major Airlines," *Quarterly Journal of Economics* 123 (November): 1611–33.

Hall, E. A. 1990. "An Analysis of Preemptive Behavior in the Titanium Dioxide Industry," *International Journal of Industrial Organization* 8 (September): 469–84.

Hohenbalken von, B., and D. West. 1986. "Empirical Tests for Predatory Reputation," *Canadian Journal of Economics* 19 (February): 160–78.

Jarmin, R. S., S. D. Klimek, and J. Miranda. 2004. "Firm Entry and Exit in the U. S. Retail Sector: 1977–1997," Working Paper 04–17, Center for Economic Studies, Bureau of the Census.

Jovanovic, B. 1982. "Selection and the Evolution of Industry," *Econometrica* 50 (May): 649–70.

Klepper, S. 2002. "Firms Survival and the Evolution of Oligopoly," *Rand Journal of Economics* 33 (Summer): 37–61.

Lambkin, M. 1988. "Order of Entry and Performance in New Markets," *Management Science* 9 (Summer): 127–40.

Lieberman, M. 1987. "Excess Capacity as a Barrier to Entry: An Empirical Appraisal." *Journal of Industrial Economics*, 35 (December), 607–27.

Mitchell, W. 1991. "Dual Clocks: Entry Order Influences on Incumbent and Newcomer Market Share and Survival When Specialized Assets Retain Their Value," *Strategic Management Journal*, 12 (February): 85–100.

Nalebuff, B. 2004. "Bundling as an Entry Barrier," *Quarterly Journal of Economics* 119 (February): 159–88.

Nelson, R., and S. G. Winter. 1982. *An Evolutionary Theory of Economic Change*, Cambridge, MA, Harvard University Press.

Ordover, J., and R. Willig. 1981. "An Economic Definition of Predation: Pricing and Product Innovation," *Yale Law Journal* 91: 8–53.

Spence, A. M. 1977. "Entry, Investment, and Oligopolistic Pricing," *Bell Journal of Economics*, 8 (Fall): 534–44.

Sylos-Labini, P. 1962. *Oligopoly and Technical Progress*, Cambridge, MA: Harvard University Press.

Sutton, J. 1997. "Gibrat's Legacy," *Journal of Economic Literature* 35 (March): 40–59.

Sutton, J. 2007. "Market Share Dynamics and the "Persistence of Leadership" Debate." *American Economic Review* 97(March): 222–41.

Urban, G., T. Carter, S. Gaskin, and Z. Mucha, 1984. "Market Share Rewards to Pioneering Brands," *Management Science* 32 (June): 645–59.

Weiman, D., and R. C. Levin. 1994. "Preying for Monopoly? The Case of Southern Bell Telephone Company, 1894–1912," *Journal of Political Economy* 102 (February): 103–26.

Appendix

Wee present the formal analysis behind the Dixit (1980) model of entry prevention assuming the linear demand and cost relations given in the text.

Market inverse demand is given by $P = A - Q = A - (q_1 + q_2)$ where q_1 is the output of the incumbent and q_2 is the output of the entrant. Production of one unit of output by firm i requires one unit of capacity input K and one unit of a variable input L. These are available at the cost of r and w per unit, respectively.

The game has two stages. In the first stage, the incumbent makes an initial capacity choice $\overline{K}_1$. The incumbent's capacity can be further increased in stage two of the game but cannot be reduced.

The potential entrant observes the incumbent's stage one capacity choice and makes its entry decision in stage two. It is only after that observation that the potential entrant makes its entry decision in stage two. If entry occurs then stage two is characterized by simultaneous quantity competition. Market demand in stage two is described by $P = A - (q_1 + q_2)$. Both firms simultaneously choose both outputs (q_1, q_2) and their *final* capacity levels (K_1, K_2) in stage two. For the incumbent, however, $K_1 \geq \overline{K}_1$. Hence, the incumbent's cost function in stage two of the game:

$$C_1(q_1, q_2; \overline{K}_1) = F_1 + wq_1 + r\overline{K}_1 \quad \text{for } q_1 \leq \overline{K}_1;$$
$$= F_1 + (w + r)q_1, \quad \text{for } q_1 > \overline{K}_1; \tag{12.A1}$$

The entrant makes no initial capacity investment in stage one. Hence, its cost function in stage two is:

$$C_2(q_2) = F_2 + (w + r)q_2; \tag{12.A2}$$

implying a constant marginal cost of $w + r$ at all levels of production.

The incumbent firm's operating profit (revenue less variable cost) in stage 2 is:

$$\pi_1(q_1, q_2, \overline{K}_1) = [A - (q_1 + q_2)]q_1 - wq_1 \quad \text{for } q_1 \leq \overline{K}_1 \tag{12.A3a}$$

$$\pi_1(q_1, q_2, \overline{K}_1) = [A - (q_1 + q_2)]q_1 - wq_1 - r(q_1 - \overline{K}_1) \quad \text{for } q_1 > \overline{K}_1 \tag{12.A3b}$$

Maximizing either (12.A13a) or (12.A3b) with respect to q_1 yields the incumbent's best response function:

$$q_1^* = \frac{(A - w)}{2} - \frac{q_2}{2} \quad \text{when } q_1^* \leq \overline{K}_1, \text{ and} \tag{12.A4a}$$

$$q_1^* = \frac{(A - w - r)}{2} - \frac{q_2}{2} \quad \text{when } q_1^* > \overline{K}_1 \tag{12.A4b}$$

The incumbent's best response function makes a discrete shift at $q_1 = \overline{K}_1$ due to a change in marginal cost. Total cost remains: $wq_1 + r\overline{K}_1 + F_1$ regardless of the value of $\overline{K}_1$.

If it enters, the entrant's total profit in stage two is:

$$\pi_2(q_1, q_2, \overline{K}_1) = [A - (q_1 + q_2)]q_2 - [(w + r)q_2 + F_2] \tag{12.A5}$$

Maximization with respect to q_2 yields entrant's best response function is:

$$q_2^* = \frac{(A - w - r)}{2} - \frac{q_1}{2} \tag{12.A6}$$

Equation (12.A6) applies only so long as $\pi_2(q_1^*, q_2^*, \overline{K_1}) = [A - (q_1^* + q_2^*)]q_2 - [(w + r)q_2^* - F_2] \geq 0$. If instead $\pi_2(q_1^*, q_2^*, \overline{K_1}) \leq 0$, the entrant will not enter and firm 1 will be a monopoly.

For any choice of $\overline{K}_1$ satisfying $\dfrac{A - w - r}{3} \leq \overline{K}_1 \leq \dfrac{A - w - r}{2}$ the incumbent can commit to a second-period output of $q_1 = \overline{K}_1$. The best choice within this range is for the incumbent to commit to the Stackelberg leader output of $q_1 = \overline{K}_1 = \dfrac{A - w - r}{2}$. Hence, the entrant (if it enters) will produce $q_2 \leq \dfrac{A - w - r}{4}$. This gives rise to thee cases.

Case 1: F_2 is sufficiently large that the entrant earns a negative profit at $q_2^* \leq \dfrac{(A - w - r)}{4}$. Entry is not possible. The incumbent will choose the monopoly output $q^M = \dfrac{A - w - r}{2}$.

Case 2: F_2 is sufficiently small that the entrant earns a nonnegative profit at an output of $q_2^* \leq \dfrac{A - w - 2r}{3}$. No credible choice of initial capacity can prevent entry. However, the entry can be limited by the profit-maximizing choice of $\overline{K}_1$ equal to the monopoly output $\overline{K}_1 = q^M = \dfrac{A - w - r}{2}$.

Case 3: F_2 is sufficiently small that the entrant can earn positive profit at $q_2 = \dfrac{A - w - 2r}{3}$ but not at $q_2 = \dfrac{A - w - r}{4}$. There is an initial capacity choice $\overline{K}_1^{**}$ satisfying $\dfrac{A - w - r}{2} \leq \overline{K}_1^{**} \leq \dfrac{A - w + r}{3}$, such that the entrant's best response to $q_1 = \overline{K}_1^{**}$, i.e., $q_2 = \dfrac{A - w - r}{2} - \dfrac{\overline{K}_1^{**}}{2}$ yields non-positive profit. Hence, the incumbent can prevent entry by choosing initial capacity $\overline{K}_1^{**}$. It will do so if operating at $q_1 = \overline{K}_1^{**}$ as a monopoly yields more profit than operating as a Stackelberg leader at $q_1 = \dfrac{A - w - r}{2}$.

13

Predatory Conduct: More Recent Developments

At one level, predatory actions can be conceptually divided into two classifications: those aimed at preventing potential rivals from entering a market, and those aimed at driving existing rivals out of a market. Our discussion in Chapter 12 was largely framed in terms of the first of these categories, i.e., deterrence of potential rivals from entering. Yet it should be clear that while these two categories are conceptually distinct, in actual practice it is very difficult to distinguish them. Tactics used to prevent entry will often be identical to tactics that drive existing rivals to exit. Bundling may be a useful entry-deterring tactic. Yet it was the devastating effect on its actual rival Netscape that raised concern over Microsoft's bundling *Internet Explorer* with its *Windows* operating system. Indeed, from the 1911 *Standard Oil* case on, the vast bulk of antitrust litigation over predatory behavior has centered on cases alleging that a dominant firm abused its power to drive out competitors.

There are at least two reasons that the legal history surrounding charges of predatory behavior is so heavily dominated by cases alleging efforts of one firm to drive its rivals out of business rather than to prevent them from entering in the first place. One is that to be effective, entry deterrence requires credibility. When a firm operates in many markets or faces a number of potential entrants over time in a single market, it may be necessary (and worthwhile) to take on the expense of driving an existing rival from the market in order to establish its commitment to defend its market and thereby discourage any further entry.

A second and perhaps even more important reason, is that to accuse a firm of predatory behavior is to charge it with a criminal offense. Such a charge is a lot easier to prosecute when there is an actual victim whose losses are demonstrable rather than a potential victim whose losses may appear to be merely hypothetical. Yet this motivation also serves to point out a risk in using legal action to address claims of predatory tactics. As the data reviewed in Chapter 12 demonstrate, the truth is that life on the corporate battlefield is tough, and many firms will fail not because of predation but because they are inefficient, and/or produce low quality products. In considering claims of predation therefore, we must recognize the motivation that any unsuccessful firm has to claim that its failure is due to "bad" behavior on the part of a rival rather than its own incompetence. Accordingly, we must pay some attention to the conditions under which predatory actions to drive existing rivals out of business are truly rational if we want to separate instances of true predation from cases in which an inefficient firm is simply blaming someone else for its failure.

The most commonly alleged predation aimed at eliminating existing rivals is pricing below cost with a view to raising prices later when the competition has left. Supreme Court

Justice Louis Brandeis, a member of the *Standard Oil* court, was a particularly eloquent exponent of this theory of "predatory pricing." Brandeis warned in 1913 that:

> "Americans should be under no illusion as to the value of price-cutting. It is the most potent weapon of monopoly—a means of killing the small rival to which the great trusts have resorted most frequently. Far-seeing organized capital secures by this means the cooperation of the shortsighted consumer to his own undoing. Thoughtless or weak, he yields to the temptation of trifling immediate gain; and selling his birthright for a mess of pottage, becomes himself an instrument of monopoly."[1]

That the predatory pricing scenario Brandeis feared sometimes happens is largely beyond doubt. In the late 19th and early 20th century, the Mogul Steamship Company appears to have maintained its market power in trade with China by quoting shipping rates so low that rivals were forced from the business.[2] Likewise, the American Sugar Refining Company, also known as the Sugar Trust, responded to any significant entry attempt with a price war that drove the sugar price below cost. At the same time, it must be recognized that the logic of dynamic games emphasized earlier—and particularly the requirement for subgame perfection—casts some doubt on the rationality of the predatory pricing strategy. The predator's rival must somehow be convinced of the predator's commitment to pursue the tactic in order to induce the rival to exit. Even if the rival does leave, then what? Any attempt by the predator to raise prices may well attract new rivals, negating the whole purpose of the predation. For this reason, more recent charges of predatory pricing against modern firms such as Wal-Mart,[3] AT&T,[4] Toyota and Mazda,[5] and American Airlines have provoked skeptical responses.

This chapter follows the work of Chapter 12 by further investigating strategies aimed at limiting the number of rivals. Because of its prominence, we start with the debate over predatory pricing. Thereafter, we investigate the logic of predation more deeply and, in particular, focus on the credible commitment that predation requires. As it turns out, information, specifically "who knows what," plays a key role in predatory behavior. To understand predatory strategies, it is important to examine very carefully the information that each player has about the other players and about the market. We therefore start with a careful analysis of the predatory pricing argument. We examine both its basic intuition and whether that intuition meets the formal rationality requirements and, in particular, the requirement of subgame perfection. We then consider variations of this theme and the ideas developed in Chapter 12 on entry deterrence and inducing the exit of rivals. One key difference between the strategies considered here and those analyzed in Chapter 12 is that virtually all of the models analyzed in this chapter are set in an environment of imperfect information so that the results of specific actions are uncertain *ex ante*.

---

[1] Brandeis, L., 1913. "Cutthroat prices-the competition that kills," *Harper's Weekly* 15 (November): 10–12, cited in Holmes, (1996). See Ordover and Saloner (1989) for a discussion of a broad range of entry deterrence strategies, including predatory pricing.

[2] This case is discussed in Yamey (1972) and more recently in Scott-Morton (1997).

[3] "Slinging Pebbles at Wal-Mart," *The Economist*, 10-23-93.

[4] *Wall Street Journal*, "AT&T Discounts Signal a National Price War," *Wall Street Journal*, 5-80-96, B1.

[5] Note though that the International Trade Commission subsequently ruled that US auto makers were not in fact harmed by the pricing policies of Toyota and Mazda.

13.1   PREDATORY PRICING: MYTH OR REALITY?

For many economists, the term predatory pricing conjures up the image of John Rockefeller and Standard Oil. The famed antitrust case against Standard Oil occurred at the turn of the century. Between the years 1870 and 1899, Standard Oil built a dominant 90 percent market share in the US petroleum refining industry. It did this by acquiring more than 120 rival companies. The conventional story is that Rockefeller would first make an offer to acquire a rival refiner and, when rebuffed, would cut prices until the rival exited the market.[6] After achieving its market dominance in oil refining capacity and distribution, Standard raised prices to oil producers. This eventually led to its federal prosecution and dissolution in 1911 under the Sherman Antitrust Act of 1890.

On the face of it there seems little doubt that Standard Oil did engage in fierce price competition with its rivals, and that rival firms in the refining business did leave the market. There is some doubt, however, whether this is in fact evidence of *predatory* pricing. Such doubt has foundations in both theory and evidence. There are two arguments that imply predatory pricing is not an optimal strategy, and therefore we should not expect a firm to practice it. The first argument is basically that predatory pricing, as in the Chain Store Paradox, is not subgame perfect.

To understand the power of this argument we will review the Microhard Newvel game that we introduced in Chapter 11. However, we will add some new twists that make the game more like the real world setting, facing a dominant incumbent firm such as Standard Oil and a smaller rival. The game is again a two period one. Rather than a potential entrant however, we will assume that the upstart Newvel has already entered the market in period 1, but that Microhard—perhaps based on its long-established record in other markets—nevertheless retains a first mover advantage in terms of deciding whether or not to engage in predatory practices in this first period. One important new twist is that now we assume that each firm incurs a fixed cost of $115 million in each market period. This amount must be paid up front at the start of each period. Unlike Microhard, which has internal retained earnings from its long experience in other markets, Newvel has no internal funds. Therefore, Newvel must borrow such funds from a competitive banking sector.

Next we introduce some uncertainty into the market. Independent of Microhard's actions, there is a 50 percent chance in any period that Newvel will be successful and enjoy a high operating profit of $200 million. There is also a 50 percent chance that it will not be successful and earn a lower operating profit of $100 million. In the former case, Newvel's net profit for the period is $200 million less what it must pay to the bank for its loan. In the second case, Newvel does not earn enough to repay even the loan's principal of $115 million. As a result, Newvel will simply default and turn over the $100 million it earned to the bank.

Because the banking sector is competitive, any bank should expect to earn roughly zero profit on the loan it makes to Newvel. We assume that the discount factor R between periods is equal to one (the interest rate $r = 0$). To earn zero profit, the bank, or more generally the investor, must ask for a repayment of $130 million when Newvel's operating profit is high and $100 million when its profit is low. With such a contract, the bank will be paid $130

---

[6]   There is an extensive literature on the varied business practices used by Standard Oil during this period. Other practices include securing discriminatory rail freight rates and rebates, foreclosing crude oil supplies to competitors by buying up local pipelines, and allegedly blowing up competing pipelines. See Yergin (1991).

million half of the time and $100 million the other half of the time when Newvel defaults. On average, such a contract would result in the bank earning $115 million and hence just covering its loan. To give the bank some incentive to take on the risk however, it may need to do a bit better than this. So, we assume that it can demand a repayment of $132.5 million in the event that Newvel's operating profit is high. This gives the bank an expected net return of $0.5[\$132.5 + \$100] - \$115 = \$1.25$ million each period. In contrast, Newvel will either net $(\$200 - \$132.5) = \$67.5$ million with probability 0.5, or nothing, also with probability 0.5. Hence, Newvel's expected net income in any period is $33.75 million.

Now consider the incumbent Microhard. Suppose that in any period that Newvel is in the market Microhard earns an operating profit of $150 million, but that it would earn a monopoly profit of $325 million if Newvel exits. Suppose further that by cutting prices and sacrificing $30 million of profit in any period, Microhard could raise the probability to 70 percent that Newvel is not successful and hence would earn only $100 million in that same period. Will Microhard have an incentive to cut prices and worsen Newvel's chances?

Let's begin by analyzing the second period of the game. First, Microhard will not engage in predation and cut prices in period two. As there is no "next period," this would only sacrifice profit with no prospect of recovering the loss at a later date. Hence, if Newvel stays after the first round, the outcome in the last period has to be a duopoly in which each earns an expected $150 million in operating or gross profit. Thus, regardless of what happened in the first period Newvel will be able to get a loan for its fixed cost at the start of the second period. Even if Newvel defaulted in the first period and the bank lost $15 million, Newvel and the bank would still have an incentive to renegotiate another loan for the second period. Because Microhard will not engage in predation, the bank has an expectation of earning $1.25 million, which will at least help a little in covering its first period loss rather than not making the loan and earning nothing. Similarly, Newvel can expect to earn $33.75 million.

Will Microhard engage in predation and try to drive Newvel out of the market in the first period? Again the answer is no. No matter what happens in the first period, we know that Newvel will want to stay for the second period. Hence, no amount of predation by Microhard in the first period can prevent Newvel from operating in the second. Microhard will recognize that Newvel intends to stay, in which case there is no reason to pursue predatory pricing and lose revenue in the first period. Predation will not occur.

13.1

Suppose that Newvel's chance of success worsens and the probability that it will earn a high operating profit of $200 million falls to 40 percent. For a loan of $115 million, what would be the contingent contract demanded by a bank in a competitive banking sector? In other words, how much repayment would the bank demand when operating profits were high and when they were low? Does the worsening of Newvel's prospects affect Microhard's incentive to price low in the first period? Explain why or why not.

Practice Problem

If the foregoing scenario is close to capturing the reality of the corporate battlefield, then predatory tactics such as selling below cost don't seem to make sense, and so should not be observed in practice. The argument is even stronger than that just presented because we simply assumed that if Microhard were somehow successful in driving out Newvel then it would enjoy full monopoly power. Yet there is no reason to believe that a new rival would not emerge at that time. If such later entry is a possibility, then there is even less for Microhard to gain from predation.

Beyond the reasoning that predation is not a subgame perfect strategy, there is a second argument implying that predatory strategies should not be used. This argument is credited to the economist John McGee (1958, 1980) who reviewed the *Standard Oil* case extensively and argued that the firm was *not* engaged in predation. In his classic 1958 article, "Predatory Price Cutting: The Standard Oil Case," McGee argued that predatory pricing only makes sense if two conditions are met. The first is that the increase in post-predatory profit (in present value terms) is sufficient to compensate the predator for the loss incurred during the predatory price war. This amounts, of course, to a requirement that the predation be subgame perfect. However, if this requirement were met, McGee also noted that there was a second requirement that a predation strategy would have to meet. This is that there is *no more profitable strategy* to achieve the same outcome. It was this second point that drew McGee's attention. He argued that a merger is always more profitable than predatory pricing. Hence, predatory pricing should not occur.

McGee's reasoning is straightforward and can also be understood in a game theoretic framework. Basically the point is that predatory pricing is a dominated strategy and hence, one that will never be used. We can illustrate this point using the Stackelberg model. The Stackleberg leader is the potential predator, and the follower is the intended prey. Suppose that each firm has a constant average and marginal cost c. The inverse market demand curve is: $P = A - BQ = A - B(q_L + q_F)$. Here, q_L is the output of the Stackelberg leader and q_F is the output of the follower. In Chapter 12 we found that the Nash equilibrium outcome is $q_L = (A - c)/2B$, and $q_F = (A - c)/4B$, which leads to an industry price $p = (A + 3c)/4$. At this price, each firm earns a positive profit. The leader earns the profit $(A - c)^2/8B$, while the follower earns half this amount. Large as it may be however, the leader's profit is still less than that earned by a pure monopolist, namely, $(A - c)^2/4B$.

The leader would obviously prefer to be alone in the market. Let's now allow for two market periods, thus giving scope to the leader to engage in predatory behavior. All we need to do is imagine that for the first market period the leader is fully committed to producing an output so large that all of it can only be sold at a price just equal to its average cost of c. Because the follower can only sell additional units by driving the market price below c, and therefore losing money, the follower will exit or not enter. If we suppose that this experience is enough to keep the follower out forever, it will mean that in the second market period, the leader is now a monopolist and can set the monopoly price and earn the monopoly profit, $(A - c)^2/4B$.

Apart from the issue of subgame perfection, the trouble with this strategy, as McGee pointed out, is that a better one is available. Under the predatory strategy just described, the leader or predator earns a stream of profit of 0 in the first market period and then $(A - c)^2/4B$ in the second. The follower or victim can look forward to a stream of 0 profit in both periods. McGee's point is that it would be more profitable for the leader to buy out or merge with the follower at the start of the first period. The merged firms can then act as a monopoly and earn the monopoly profit $(A - c)^2/4B$ in both market periods. Even if the leader has to share its first period profit with the follower, say on a fifty-fifty basis, *both* firms still do better than they would under predation when both the predator and prey earned a zero profit in period one. Because the second period profit is unchanged by the merger, it seems clear that the merger strategy dominates the predatory one.

McGee's (1958) argument that predation is a dominated strategy is straightforward and compelling. Coupled with the possibility that predation may not be subgame perfect, McGee's analysis would seem to cast serious doubt on any allegation of predatory pricing.

However, there are some weaknesses in the McGee (1958) argument. To begin with, any merger between rival firms is a public event. In particular, the antitrust authorities will know about the merger and may easily file suit to prevent it. Indeed, the authorities may well be more concerned about a merger than they would be about predatory pricing because the merger would eliminate even the short, predatory period in which consumer prices are low. A second, and perhaps more important, weakness in the logic of McGee's merging strategy arises when we extend the analysis to include additional potential entrants. Once a dominant firm such as Standard Oil is seen as willing to buy out any rival, it will likely face a stream of entrants who enter just for the profitability of being purchased.[7] That is, the merger tactic may actually encourage entry—the last thing the dominant firm wishes to do. In this light, predatory pricing may be more attractive because it not only encourages existing rivals to exit but can deter subsequent entrants as well.[8]

13.2

Practice Problem

Suppose that there are two firms in a market. One firm is a dominant firm and behaves like a Stackelberg leader. The other rival firm is the follower. The firms compete in quantities and face market demand described by $P = 100 - Q$. Assume that marginal production cost is constant and equal to 10.

a. Solve for the single market period equilibrium outcome, that is, the quantity produced by each firm and the firms' respective profits.

b. Now consider a two market period game. One possibility is that the two firms play the Stackelberg game twice, once in each market period. The other possibility is that the dominant firm chooses an output level so great in the first market period that the rival firm exits the market or sells zero output. In the second market period the dominant firm is alone in the market and acts like a monopoly. Solve for the dominant firm's first and second market period output choices under this scenario, and the firm's overall profit.

c. Suppose that we allow the dominant firm the option of making an offer to the rival firm to buy it out at the beginning of the first market period. What is the maximum amount the dominant firm will have to pay the rival firm to buy it out? Show that the dominant firm is better off buying out its rival in the first period and monopolizing the market through merging than through predation.

Although there are some qualifications to McGee's reasoning, the existence of a less costly alternative means of eliminating rivals and doubt about the credibility of predatory pricing are two good reasons to be suspicious of rivals alleging predatory pricing by a

---

[7] Rasmusen (2007) explores this possibility.

[8] This point was made by Yamey (1972): "the aggressor will, moreover, be looking beyond the immediate problem of dealing with its current rival. Alternative strategies for dealing with that rival may have different effects on the flow of future rivals."

Reality Checkpoint
Pay for Delay—McGee on Drugs

In the 1990's two major drugs emerged to treat the millions of Americans who suffer from high blood pressure. *Cardizem CD*, produced by Sanofi (formerly Aventis), and *Hytrin*, produced by Abbott Laboratories, were both initially protected by patents. However, the 1984 Hatch-Waxman Act permits a generic producer to market its own drug by filing an Abbreviated New Drug Application (ANDA) in which the generic firm only has to show that its drug is the bioequivalent of the patented brand without replicating all the safety and efficacy tests of the original drug. The only requirement is that the generic applicant must show either that the original patent was not valid or that the new drug does not truly infringe the patent rights of the name brand product. Generic drug makers regularly do this and, of course, the patent holders reject such claims and file a countersuit claiming patent infringement. In that case, the Food and Drug Administration (FDA) cannot approve the new generic for at least thirty months or until the claim is resolved, whichever comes first.

Despite this legal hurdle, generic drugmakers still frequently challenge patents and enter the market mainly because there is the further incentive that the *first* generic to obtain approval is granted a 180-day exclusivity period vis-à-vis all other generics. Once one firm begins to sell a generic substitute, no other generic firm is allowed to do so for at least 180 days. This is exactly what happened when Andrx applied for permission to market a generic substitute for *Cardizem CD* and Geneva Pharmaceuticals requested authorization to market a generic substitute for *Hytrin*. Both Aventis and Abbott sued, and the automatic thirty month delay began. Yet as that period drew to a close and with no resolution in sight, each incumbent was faced with the imminent entry of a rival. Presumably, each firm could have pursued predatory pricing to deter entry. Instead each went the route proposed by McGee. They bought out the potential competitor.

Aventis agreed to pay Andrx $10 million per quarter in return for *not* selling the *Cardizem* substitute as well as an additional $60 million per year from 1998 until the end of the ongoing patent trial. A similar agreement was reached between Abbott and Geneva. Under the law, signing such an agreement means that the generic firm loses its 180-day exclusivity. However, that exclusivity does not then pass to the next generic entrant. So, any later generic entrant must worry about competition from still more entrants.

The *Cardizem* and *Hytrin* agreements were both ultimately held to be illegal [*In re Cardizem CD Antitrust Litig., 332 F.3d 896, 908 6th Cir. 2003*]. However, court opinion soon turned. In several cases of generic entry, including those involving the major breast cancer drug *Tamoxifen* and the super antibiotic *Cipro*, the courts approved such "pay for delay" agreements arguing that such payments might actually encourage more generic entry. However, the Federal Trade Commission (FTC) has consistently opposed these deals from the start. Its internal 2010 study estimated that the net effect of such agreements is to suppress competition with an estimated annual cost to consumers of $3.5 billion. A new change came in July of 2012, when the Third Circuit Court of Appeals sided with the FTC and overturned a lower court ruling that had approved an agreement between Merck's Schering-Plough division and the generic firm Upsher-Smith paying to delay entry of Upsher's generic treatment for hypokalemia. The case is now headed to the Supreme Court. If it upholds the appellate decision, the large pharmaceutical companies may need some painkillers.

Source: J. Guidera and R. T. King, Jr., "Abbott Labs, Novartis Unit near Pact with FTC over Agreement on Hytrin," *Wall Street Journal* 14 March 2000, p. B6; "Pay-for-Delay: How Drug Company Payoffs Cost Consumers Billions," www.ftc.gov; and E. Wyatt, "For Big Drug Companies, a Headache Looms," *New York Times*, July 27 2012, p. B1.

dominant firm. There is also a third reason. As noted above, unsuccessful rivals always have an incentive to claim that they are victims of predation rather than victims of their own inefficiencies. Hence, claims of predation that come from failed rivals must be taken with a grain of salt.

For example, consider the famous *Utah Pie*[9] case decided by the US Supreme Court in 1967. Utah Pie was a producer of frozen dessert pies operating out of Salt Lake City and selling to supermarkets in Utah and surrounding states. In 1957, it had over two-thirds of the Salt Lake City market. However, three national firms—Continental Bakeries, Pet, and Carnation—all began to compete vigorously in the Salt Lake City area. Over the next three years, this resulted in prices falling by over a third and Utah Pie's market share declining to as low as 33 percent, though it later climbed to nearly 45 percent. Utah Pie filed suit arguing that the three national firms were selling at prices in the Salt Lake City market below those that they charged in other cities and that the three firms were therefore engaged in illegal price discrimination with a predatory objective.

However, Utah Pie's sales grew steadily throughout the period of alleged predation, as did its net worth. Moreover, except for the first year of the intensified competition, Utah Pie also continued to earn a positive net income. To many economists, it appeared that Utah Pie's real complaint was more about preserving its initial near monopoly position and the high prices that monopoly power permitted, than it was about predatory tactics. In the end, however, the Supreme Court found in favor of Utah Pie in a decision that was widely decried and since then, largely repudiated. Yet the point remains. Company officials will inevitably wish to claim that the cause of their profit and market share decline is illegal activity by rivals who are "not playing fairly" rather than confess their own inefficiencies. For that reason, charges of predatory pricing must be taken with at least a few grains of salt.

The deep skepticism that predation, especially predatory pricing, ever occurs is a view closely associated with the Chicago School. This view has had a profound effect on both public policy and court judgments regarding predatory pricing cases. However, over the last twenty-five years or so, a new view—sometimes called the post-Chicago School—has emerged. In this alternative view, while predation claims are rightly treated with caution, there is no *a priori* dismissal of such charges because it is recognized that predatory tactics are not a theoretical impossibility and real world predation should not be viewed as an idle threat.

13.2   PREDATION AND IMPERFECT INFORMATION

Much of the post-Chicago literature on the topic of predation is based on two period games in which one firm knows something and the other firm does not, and both firms understand that there is asymmetry in information.[10] In this section, we present two important models that build on this feature of asymmetric information. The first is due to Bolton and Scharfstein (1990) and focuses on the informational asymmetry between the new rival, such as Newvel, and the bank from which it borrows. The second is due to Milgrom and Roberts (1982) and focuses on the information asymmetry between the new rival, in our case Newvel, and the dominant incumbent rival Microhard.

---

[9]   *Utah Pie Co. v. Continental Baking Co. et al.* 386 U.S. 685 (1967).
[10] Early important papers in this vein included Milgrom and Roberts (1982), Benoit (1984), and Fudenberg and Tirole (1986).

13.2.1   Predatory Pricing and Financial Constraints

Recall the two-period model above in which Microhard is the incumbent and Newvel is the new firm that must borrow $115 million at the start of each period in order to operate. Following Bolton and Schaferstein (1990) we make one important fundamental change. We now assume that at the end of any period *only* Newvel, and *not* its bank or lender, knows whether Newvel's operating profit is $100 million or $200 million. To make clear how this informational asymmetry affects both Newvel's incentives in its dealing with the bank and the bank's incentive to lend to Newvel, we introduce the bank as an explicit player in the game. Figure 13.1 illustrates the interaction between the Bank and Newvel for just a single market period. The Bank first makes a loan. Then Nature chooses whether Newvel's profit is high or low. Subsequently, Newvel chooses whether to report high or low operating profit. For each outcome, the net profit both to the Bank and to Newvel are shown. Because the Bank moved first, its payoff is shown first.

Focusing on the game for just one period is insightful because, as Figure 13.1 makes clear, the Bank would never lend Newvel the required $115 million if the game were only one period long. The reason is straightforward. At the end of the period, only Newvel knows what its profit is. Accordingly, it has every incentive to say that it was only $100 million, pay that amount to the bank and default on any remaining amount. Obviously, if operating profit really was $100 million, this is all Newvel can do. However, if actual profit were $200 million, lying and reporting that profit was only $100 million allows Newvel to walk away with $100 million for itself. In other words, because only Newvel knows the truth, it has an incentive to exploit this informational asymmetry to its own advantage. Anticipating this, however, the Bank would realize that in a one-period setting it would never get more than $100 million in return for the $115 million that it lent. Therefore, it would never agree to the loan.

The one-period analysis carries two immediate insights for a two-period model. The first is that whatever repayment R the Bank gets at the end of the first period, it can never get more than $100 million at the end of the second period. When the second period comes about, it will simply be a replay of the one-period game just described. The other and related insight is that if the Bank is actually to make a loan, it will have to write a contract that extends over both periods. Two one-period contracts will just run into the same problem

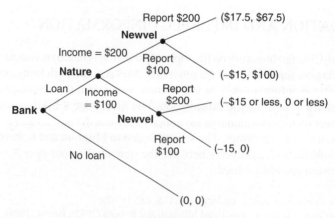

Figure 13.1   The bank and Newvel for just one period

twice. Somehow, the Bank and Newvel will have to agree on a contract that links the repayment over both market periods.

Bolton and Scharfstein (1990) show that the optimal contract has the following terms. First, recognizing that it will never get paid more than $100 million at the end of period two, the Bank will contract for a high repayment at the end of period one. Second, to give Newvel an incentive to report a high income at the end of the first period, the Bank will cut funding, i.e., refuse to make a loan for the second period if Newvel reports low first-period income. Because Newvel will only ever pay $100 million to the Bank at the end of the second period, it can therefore expect to earn $150 − $100 = $50 million at that time, and this contractual feature gives Newvel a real interest in making sure that the second period happens.

In our example the lending contract might look as follows. The Bank loans the required $115 million at the start of the first period. At the end of that period, if Newvel reports the higher profit of $200 million, then it is required to repay $150 million—its average profit. When it does so, the Bank will lend the $115 million necessary to operate in the second period. At the end of that second period, the Bank is paid $100 million despite what happens by virtue of the earlier argument about a one-period loan. Alternatively, if at the end of the first period Newvel reports only the lower profit of $100 million, the Bank is paid that amount but *no* further loans are made. Newvel in this case does not survive into the second period.

Figure 13.2 describes the nature of the loan contract. After the Bank makes an initial loan, Nature's choice of profit outcome occurs. This is not shown in the diagram because at the end of the first period Newvel's incentive is to report Nature's draw accurately, and the Bank understands this. If it is low, the loan is terminated and Newvel exits. If it is high, the loan is extended for a second period, after which Nature again draws a profit outcome. As we know, at the end of the second period Newvel has an incentive always to report a low profit. The payoff pair shows the total payoff for the Bank and Newvel over the two periods, with the Bank's shown first.

Note that both parties do well with this contract. Consider the Bank. If first period profits are low, Newvel is liquidated, and the Bank walks away with only $100 million for a loss of $15 million. If, on the other hand, first period profits are high, the Bank is paid $150 million, thereby netting $35 million. However, it is then obligated to lend out $115 million for a second time. At the end of the second period the Bank receives only $100 million because at that point Newvel never reports a high income. Because good luck and bad luck happen with equal probability, the Bank's expected net profit from the two-period

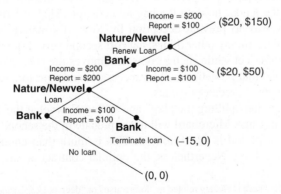

Figure 13.2   The decision tree in the two-period loan contract

contract is: $0.5[\$100 - \$115] + 0.5[(\$150 - \$115) + (\$100 - \$115)] = \$2.5$ million. Note that this is exactly the profit the Bank earned with two, one-period contracts when it was fully informed of Newvel's income.

Newvel also earns a positive expected profit. At the end of the first period, it either receives a net payment of [$200 − $150] or nothing, each with probability 0.5 so that the expected payment at the end of the first period is $25 million. Similarly, at the end of the second period, Newvel receives a net payment of either [$200 − $100] million or again zero, each with probability 0.5, for an expected second-period income of $50 million. Because the *ex ante* probability of reaching the second period is just 0.5, the firm's *ex ante* expected profit for the second period is another $25 million so that the overall expected profit over both periods is $50 million.

Yet while both players earn profit under the contract, there is a flaw. Half the time, Newvel fails after the first period and no second period loan is made. This is inefficient because that investment does have an expected profit of $35 million. Again, such inefficiency is the result of the asymmetric information that characterizes the relationship between the Bank and Newvel. The only way to prevent Newvel from exploiting its informational advantage is to include a promise to stop funding Newvel should it perform badly in the first period.

Now let's think about adding Microhard to the game. Suppose again that Microhard's duopoly profit is $150 million, its monopoly profit is $325 million, and by preying and cutting prices below cost, its profit is reduced by $30 million. By cutting prices low Microhard can raise the probability that Newvel will fail from 50 to 70 percent. Because now Newvel exits whenever it fails to earn a first period profit of $200 million, predation results in raising Microhard's chance of being a monopolist in the second period by 20 percent. Its expected profit then rises from $0.5 \times \$150$ million $+ 0.5 \times \$325$ million $= \$237.5$ to $0.3 \times \$150 + 0.7 \times \$325 = \$272.5$, a gain of $35 million—more than enough to cover the $30 million cost of predation. Unlike our earlier case, predation is now rational and therefore should be expected to occur.[11]

The intuition as to why the outcome is different with asymmetric information from what it was in our earlier analysis is straightforward. Newvel can report low first period profits for one of two reasons. Either profits really are low because it has had bad luck including being a possible victim of predation, or profits are really high but Newvel's management has hidden them by spending them on lavish offices, expensive business trips, and excessive compensation. In the absence of a contract like the one described, the lender cannot easily know the truth. If it simply believes whatever Newvel says, the lender will quickly find that Newvel constantly reports low profits in every period and blames this on bad luck and predation—leaving the lender holding the bag at a cost of ($115 − $100) or $15 million each time. The only way to prevent deception by Newvel's management is to write a two-period contract that, among other things, cuts off second period funding in the wake of a poor first period profit. Yet while such a contract removes the potential for dishonesty, it increases the likelihood that predation will be successful and therefore raises the incentive for Microhard to engage in predatory tactics.

It is worth repeating that "pulling the plug" and killing Newvel at the start of the second period is inefficient. Because Microhard will never predate in the second period, Newvel's expected profit in that period is $150 million. This is more than enough to pay off the needed loan of $115 million. Nevertheless, the optimal contract is a two-period one that

---

[11]   The predation story told here is closely related to "long purse" or "deep pockets" models. See, e.g., Philips (1995).

cannot look at the second period alone. As a result, this contract must call for Newvel's premature death if it does not report a good outcome in period one in order to keep Newvel honest.[12]

13.3

Practice Problem

In the above example, it is worthwhile for Microhard to engage in predatory behavior because such behavior increases the odds of Newvel failing in the market from 50 percent to 70 percent, an increase of 20 percent. What is the lowest increase in unfavorable odds that will induce Microhard to engage in predatory behavior?

13.2.2   Asymmetric Information and Limit Pricing

In the Bolton and Scharfstein (1990) model, the upstart rival firm Newvel knows a lot about the market. Newvel knows not only its own profitability, but it understands the profits and incentives facing Microhard as well. In reality, this is often unlikely to be the case. A new firm can typically only guess at the profits and costs of the rival incumbent. In their classic paper, Milgrom and Roberts (1982) present a model in which the assumption that the rival entrant firm is perfectly informed is relaxed. Specifically, they assume that the rival entrant firm does not know the incumbent firm's cost of production. In this context charging a low price to keep the entrant out may no longer be an empty bluff. We now turn to the classic Milgrom and Roberts (1982) limit pricing model, noting that in this model we return to strategies aimed at preventing the entry of a rival and not ones aimed at eliminating an existing rival.

The setting is again a two period game in which there is a long-standing incumbent and a *potential* entrant. At the risk of repetition, let's again call the incumbent Microhard and the potential entrant Newvel. There is no lender or other player. Microhard is alone in the market in the first period. During that time, Newvel observes Microhard's behavior, specifically the price that Microhard chooses to set for that period, and then Newvel decides whether or not to enter the market in the second period. As before, we assume the interest rate is zero so that we do not have to worry about discounting future profits.

Newvel knows its own unit cost and the market demand in each period, but Newvel does not know Microhard's unit cost. Microhard, on the other hand, knows its unit cost, Newvel's unit cost, as well as market demand in each period. Each firm also knows that the other also understands all of this. From Newvel's perspective, Microhard's unit cost could be either high or low, depending on factors such as the expertise of management, the quality of equipment, or the input prices that Microhard has negotiated with its suppliers. These are all features of production costs that are in fact not easily ascertained by outsiders. And while Newvel does not know Microhard's unit cost, it does know something about how likely it is that Microhard is a high-cost or low-cost type. Specifically, Newvel knows that there is a probability ρ that Microhard has a low cost and a probability $(1 - \rho)$ that it has a high cost.

In the interest of making the model easier to understand, we will again work through a specific numeric example. Let's assume that when Microhard has low costs and acts like a profit-maximizing monopoly in the first period, it sets a relatively low price but, because

---

[12]   Strictly speaking, the contract described is only optimal if it is unobserved by Microhard. If Microhard can observe the details of the loan, the contract may be written in a way that deters predation.

of its low costs, earns a profit equal to $100 million. In contrast, if it were a less efficient high-cost monopoly, Microhard's profit-maximizing price would be higher, but again due to its cost inefficiency, it would earn less profit at that price, namely, $60 million. Finally, we assume that if Microhard were a high-cost firm but, nevertheless, chose the price that is optimal for a low-cost incumbent, its profit would fall still further to $40 million.

Microhard's second period profits depend both on its unit cost and on whether or not Newvel comes into the market. We will assume that if Microhard is alone in the second period, it simply sets the monopoly price appropriate for its cost structure because entry is no longer a worry. It then earns either $100 million (low-cost monopoly profit) or $60 million (high-cost monopoly profit) in the second period when no entry occurs. We also assume that the potential entrant Newvel earns a profit of 0 whenever it stays out of the market.

If entry occurs in the second period, Microhard's profit suffers. If it is a low-cost firm, it earns only $50 million in the second period when Newvel is present. If Microhard is a high-cost firm, it is able to compete less and earns only $20 million. If Newvel enters and competes against an inefficient, high-cost incumbent, it earns a positive profit of $20 million. But if the incumbent turns out to be a low-cost type, then entry results in a *loss* of $20 million for Newvel.

The extensive form for this example of the entry game is shown in Figure 13.3. Newvel's uncertainty about Microhard's cost is modeled by introducing the player Nature who moves first and chooses the cost of the incumbent firm. With probability ρ Nature chooses a low-cost incumbent and with probability $(1 - \rho)$ Nature chooses a high-cost incumbent. Microhard moves next and sets either a high or low price when it sells output in the first period. Then Newvel decides whether to enter and to compete in period two or to stay out. At the end of each path, we show the total payoffs for each firm over the two periods depending on the choices about prices and entering. Microhard's total profit is the sum of its profit in each period. Newvel's profit is just that which it earns in the market for the final period.

Figure 13.3 shows three possibilities for Microhard. The first is that it is a high-cost firm and sets a first-period monopoly price that corresponds to being high cost. The second possibility is that it is again a high-cost firm but now chooses to set the lower price

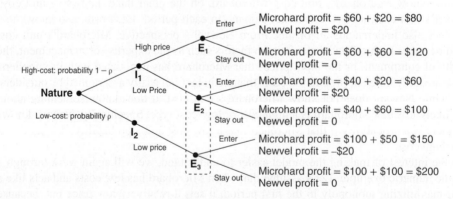

Figure 13.3 Extensive form of the sequential entry game with asymmetric information on cost

appropriate for a more cost-efficient firm. Finally, the third possibility is that Microhard is truly a low-cost firm and sets the lower monopoly price corresponding to being low cost. Note that we have ruled out the possibility of a low-cost Microhard charging the high-cost monopoly price. We will see in a moment that a low-cost Microhard has no incentive to do so. One important point to understand is that we have captured the asymmetry of information, or who knows what, by circling together the nodes E_2 and E_3. This is meant to indicate that when the entrant Newvel observes a low price in the first period, it does not know whether that corresponds to node E_2 or E_3, and Microhard, the incumbent, knows that the entrant firm does not know at which node it is.

You may ask at this point why a high-cost incumbent firm would ever set a sub-optimally low price that would lead to a lower level of profit. The answer is that this may influence the entrant's decision to enter in the second period. Newvel might, for instance, reason as follows: "If Microhard charges a high price during the first period, it must be an inefficient, high-cost firm and I will enter. However, if Microhard charges a low price, it must be a cost-efficient firm, and I best stay out of the market." In this setting, there is a considerable incentive for a high-cost incumbent initially to play against type and set the low monopoly price in the first period. True, this will mean that it earns only a profit of $40 million instead of the $60 million during the first period. Yet given the entrant firm's reasoning, this sacrifice pays off in the second period because it deters entry and thereby permits Microhard then to earn a profit of $60 million rather than the $20 million it would have earned had it initially set a high price that would have encouraged entry.

This same reasoning helps explain our assertion above that a low-cost incumbent firm will never initially set the high-cost monopoly price. Such a choice is not profit-maximizing in the short run and, in addition, serves to attract entry.

Our analysis so far makes clear that what happens in this game is sensitive to the nature of the beliefs that Newvel holds based on the behavior of Microhard observed in the first period. What we have just said above is that if Newvel believes "low price means low-cost, high price means high-cost," its entry decision will be easily manipulated by Microhard. Accordingly, this may not be a very reasonable sort of belief for Newvel to hold. We should therefore expect that Newvel will also realize this and will adopt an alternative way to interpret the evidence observed in the first period.

The important question here is what beliefs are reasonable. Suppose that Newvel—recognizing the foregoing argument—thinks in a different way. Because Newvel understands that it is possible for both a high-cost and a low-cost type firm to play a low-price strategy, it reasons that observing a low first period price really gives no useful information as to the type of incumbent it is facing. Instead, when Newvel observes a low initial price it simply uses what it knows about the probabilities associated with different cost types. Specifically, when Newvel observes a low price, it simply concludes that Microhard is a low-cost firm with probability ρ and a high-cost one with probability $(1 - \rho)$. However, because a low-cost firm never has an incentive to charge a high price, Newvel does continue to believe that a high price in the first period means that Microhard has high costs. In other words, Newvel's conditional inferences are as follows:

If Microhard sets a low price in period 1, it has a low unit cost with probability ρ and a high unit cost with probability $(1 - \rho)$. Accordingly, second period entry will yield an expected profit of $[(1 - \rho)\$20 - \rho\$20]$ million.

If Microhard sets a high price in period 1, it has a high unit cost. Second-period entry will yield a certain profit of $20 million.

The foregoing beliefs are rational. Note, however, that they imply that if Newvel observes a low first-period price and then enters, its *expected profit* when it enters is: $-\$20\rho + \$20(1 - \rho) = 20 - 40\rho$ (in millions). If Nature's draw or the probability that Microhard is a low-cost firm is high enough, in our example, if $\rho > 1/2$, then Newvel's *expected profit* from entering is negative. Consequently, it will not enter if it observes a low price. Microhard can work this out, too. It will therefore recognize that if the probability of being a low-cost firm $\rho > 1/2$, it will do better by pretending to be a low-cost firm and setting a low price in the first period even if, in reality, it is a high-cost firm. Once again, this will lead to a profit of \$40 million initially and then, in the second period when the firm is a secure monopoly, a profit of \$60 million, for a total profit of \$100 million. This is better than the alternative strategy of initially charging a high price that would reveal its type to the potential entrant, invite entry, and lead to the lower total profit of \$80 million. That is, when $\rho > 1/2$, a high-cost Microhard will set a limit price—one lower than its true profit-maximizing price—in order to deter an imperfectly informed entrant from entering the market. This again is what we mean by predatory conduct.[13]

In sum, both the Bolton and Scharfstein (1990) and the Milgrom and Roberts (1982) models show how pricing below cost or predatory pricing can be rational or, more formally, part of a subgame perfect strategy in a dynamic game. When the players, either investors or rivals, have incomplete information, the incumbents may find that they can manipulate or exploit that information asymmetry in a way that eliminates rival firms.

Now recall McGee's (1958) claim that predatory pricing is dominated by the alternative strategy of eliminating rivals by buying them out. As we noted earlier, there are weaknesses in this argument, perhaps most notably the fact that buying out any rival is likely to encourage more and more rivals to enter just for the privilege of being bought out. Yet ignoring those issues for the moment, it does seem reasonable to ask if the profitability of predatory tactics in the informationally asymmetric settings just described is indeed less than the profitability of merging in these environments.

The simple answer is that it is difficult to say without more information. There are numerous private lawsuits filed by alleged victims of predatory tactics and few of these plaintiffs appear to have had the option of merging. This suggests that the issues raised earlier about the feasibility of McGee's "buy out your rival" strategy are real. Yet there is also a more complex answer, which is that the two tactics are not mutually exclusive. Indeed, predatory pricing and corporate acquisition may both be part of the same overall

---

[13]   We can complicate the story by introducing uncertainty on both sides of the game. Suppose, for instance, that Newvel does not know what Microhard's payoff is from fighting an entrant, and Microhard does not know a potential entrant's pay-off from entering. Specifically, from an entrant's point of view, Microhard can be one of two types: with probability p^0 Microhard is believed to be "tough" (i.e., low-cost), which means that its pay-offs are such that it will always fight in every market; and with probability $1 - p^0$ Microhard is believed to be "weak" (i.e., high-cost) and more accommodating of entry. Similarly, each potential entrant is believed by Microhard to be "tough" with probability q^0, in which case the entrant will always enter no matter what Microhard does; and to be "weak" with probability $1 - q^0$, in which case the entrant's pay-offs are as in the current example. The "tough" version of Microhard always fights and so is of no interest to us. What *is* of interest is that a Microhard that knows itself to be "weak", will, as before, still have an incentive to fight entry in order to develop a reputation in the minds of potential entrants that it might, in fact, be "tough." The willingness of a "weak" incumbent to fight is an increasing function of p^0 and a decreasing function of q^0. More generally, the greater the number of markets there are the lower is the probability p^0 necessary for entry to be deterred. Simply put, a "weak" incumbent is more likely to fight entry if there are "many" of its markets remaining in which entry has not taken place than if there are "fewer."

strategy. This is the idea in the take-over game analyzed by Saloner (1987) that is somewhat similar to the Bolton and Scharfstein (1990) model. In that game, the incumbent may cut prices low to reduce the profitability of the entrant precisely because by making the entrant less profitable, the incumbent can buy this rival at a lower cost.

Burns (1986) offers evidence that American Tobacco used the predatory pricing tactic exactly in this manner to acquire many of the forty-three rival firms that it ultimately bought. Specifically, Burns (1986) finds that after identifying the target rival it wished to eliminate, American Tobacco would then introduce a competing brand at a low price in the target's market. The resultant drop in the target firm's profit would induce it to settle for a lower acquisition price—25 percent lower by Burns' (1986) estimates.[14] Brevoort and Marvel (2004) report similar tactics by the National Cash Register (NCR) company, except that in this case, price reductions on specialized product lines were accompanied by harassing lawsuits charging the rival with violating NCR's patent rights. Brevoort and Marvel (2004) find one case that particularly stands out, namely, NCR's purchase of a rival named The Ideal Register Co. After repeated price cuts and legal challenges, Ideal eventually consented to being acquired by NCR for about $12,000 despite the fact that internal company documents suggested that NCR was willing to pay as much as $125,000 for Ideal.

13.3 CONTRACTS AS A BARRIER TO ENTRY

Our discussion of preemption in the previous chapter suggested that early building of plant capacity might be useful in persuading buyers to contract for purchases later. This suggests that part of the preemption story is related to the nature of contracts. Experience confirms this intuition. For example, while much of the Microsoft antitrust trial has focused on Microsoft's practice of bundling its *Internet Explorer* web browser in with its *Windows* operating system, that was not the only issue of concern. Another crucial question in the case was whether or not Microsoft was able, through its contracts with PC makers, to foreclose other rivals from entering the operating systems market in which Microsoft had a virtual monopoly.

Indeed, concerns that contractual requirements may be used to exclude rivals have been an important issue in antitrust litigation for well over 100 years. The troubling contract provisions and the attendant antitrust concerns over this time span are perhaps best illustrated by the cases involving the United Shoe Machinery (USM) company. The first of these was decided in 1918, the next in 1922, and the most well known in 1953.

USM was created in 1899 as a result of the merger of seven separate shoe machine firms. In general, these firms produced machines related either to different types of shoes or to different parts of the shoe-making business, i.e., they were mostly complementary machines. Nevertheless, the new USM started with control of 60 to 70 percent of all North American shoe machine manufacturing. From the very beginning, USM followed a policy of not selling but only leasing its machines to shoe-making companies. It was the terms of these lease contracts that repeatedly landed the company in the courts.

---

[14] In 1911, immediately following the Standard Oil decision, the Supreme Court found American Tobacco guilty of monopolizing the cigarette and tobacco product market, and cited predation to induce rivals to sell out as evidence of illegal monopolistic intent. A district court ordered that American Tobacco be dissolved and reconstituted as separate firms, the big three being American Tobacco, Ligget and Myers, and Lorillard.

To begin with, USM leases were long, lasing seventeen years. If the shoe company using the machine needed to add capacity, it had to lease another USM machine. Typically the shoe-maker needed different types of machines, and the contracts required that if the firm leased one type of USM machine, it had to use other USM machines for other kinds of work. Conversely, if a shoe manufacturer violated the terms of its contract for one type of machine, USM had the right to terminate the firm's leases for all of its USM machines. It may seem clear that some or all of these provisions were aimed at foreclosing the market to rival shoe-machine makers. Nevertheless, the Supreme Court initially sided with USM and permitted the lease only policy and the terms of the leases to remain. In reaching this judgment, the Court relied largely on a simple point. If these restrictions were harmful to shoemakers, why did they sign the contracts? This is an important question. If a shoe manufacturer understands that there is an alternative machine producer that will come on line soon, why should it sign a contract with USM that will prevent it from later contracting with this alternative supplier?

Prominent Chicago School scholars such as Bork (1978) and Posner (1976) have used the voluntary nature of restrictive contracts as a major reason to be skeptical that such contracts are a predatory device. In their view, any contract signed must give not just the supplier but also the buyer some benefit—say by way of increased service or repair. In turn, this implies that the deal ratified by the contract must be a step toward greater efficiency. These proponents of the Chicago School emphasize the efficiency grounds for observed contracts rather than the predatory motive. As we shall see, however, more recent theory has provided consistent arguments supporting the view that predation can occur in this rational world. We present two basic analyses showing that buyers may voluntarily sign contracts with suppliers that, in fact, are predatory and inefficient. The first is due to Aghion and Bolton (1987). The second is due to Rasmussen, Rasmeyer, and Wiley (1991). We briefly present a numerical example illustrating each model in turn.

13.3.1   Long-Term Exclusive Contracts as Predatory Instruments

Aghion and Bolton (1987) consider a market for some essential intermediate good that extends over two periods. In the first period, there is an incumbent monopoly seller of the good whose unit cost we will assume is $50. Each buyer of this good uses exactly one unit of the input per period and is willing to pay up to $100 for the product. In the second period there is the possible arrival of a new entrant. This is recognized by all parties at the start of the first period. However, neither a buyer in the second period nor the monopoly seller initially in the market knows the unit cost c of this second period potential entrant. All that these initial participants know is that c is distributed randomly but uniformly on the interval between $0 and $100.

We begin by considering matters from the viewpoint of a buyer looking forward to the second period. We assume that if the entrant actually enters the market at that time, Bertrand or price competition will emerge between the initial monopoly supplier and the new rival. If the entrant's unit cost c exceeds $50, however, it will lose this competition. With $c > $50, the incumbent can always underbid the entrant. The entrant obviously knows this. Hence, if the entrant finds that its cost $c > $50, no entry will occur. In this case, which by our assumption happens with probability 1/2, the incumbent remains a monopolist and can charge a buyer its full reservation price of $100 for the good.

However, if $c \leq $50, then entry will occur. In this case, the competition between the entrant and the incumbent will bid the price down to $50, at which point the incumbent will drop out. Once this happens, however, the entrant is under no additional pressure to lower its price so a buyer will end up paying $50 for the good for any case in which $c \leq \$50$. This too happens with probability 1/2. Notice that once again there is an element of uncertainty as well as some asymmetry. For $0 \leq c \leq 50$, only the entrant will know its true cost as the buyer will be charged $50 no matter the cost.

One of the two scenarios just outlined must happen. Therefore, in the absence of any contract obligating a buyer to purchase from the initial incumbent, the buyer's expected price for the intermediate good in the second period is:

$$1/2 \times \$50 + 1/2 \times \$100 = \$75 \tag{13.1}$$

Note that equation (13.1) also implies that because a buyer values the product at $100, the buyer should expect a surplus of $25 in the absence of any contract with the initial monopolist supplier. To put it another way, any contract that the incumbent offers the buyer must promise the buyer an expected surplus of at least $25 in the second period, or the buyer will not sign it. The question then is whether the monopolist can and will offer such a contract. If it will, we would also like to know the efficiency aspects of such an arrangement.

One long-term contract that a buyer might find attractive is the following. In the first period, the buyer agrees to make its second-period purchase of the good from the incumbent at a price of $75 with only one possible exception. The exception is that the buyer can instead make its second-period purchase from the new entrant so long as it pays the initial incumbent a $50 breach-of-contract fee.

There are several features of this proposed contract that deserve emphasis. First, observe that the entrant will now only enter the market if its cost $c \leq \$25$. The reason is that in the second period, a buyer can either buy from the incumbent for $75 or from the entrant at some price p plus the breach-of-contract fee of $50. Hence, a buyer will prefer to fulfill the contract rather than switch to the alternative supplier unless that supplier charges a price of $25 or less. However, the only way that the entrant can do this is when cost $c \leq \$25$. Accordingly, the entrant will only enter the market when $c \leq \$25$. Notice that this also implies that the contract restricts entry. Without the contract, entry occurred with probability 1/2. With the contract, entry will only occur when $c \leq \$25$, which happens only with probability 1/4.

Will the buyer actually sign the proposed contract? This is where the second noteworthy feature of the agreement becomes relevant. The contract is such that no matter what happens, the buyer will pay $75 for the good. Three-fourths of the time, the potential rival will not enter and the buyer will pay the stipulated $75 to the initial incumbent. One-fourth of the time, the rival will have a cost $c \leq \$25$. In this case, it will enter and charge the buyer the highest price it can while still making a sale, namely, $25 (or just a penny less). A buyer will then switch and purchase the good from the new entrant at $25 but, in addition, pay a $50 breach-of-contract fee to the initial incumbent. Again, the buyer's total payment is $75, leaving it a surplus of $25. Thus, a buyer's expected (in fact guaranteed) surplus with this contract is $25. Because this is also its expected profit or surplus without the contract, a buyer will be willing to sign the agreement.

The next question is whether or not the incumbent monopoly seller will actually find it worthwhile to offer the agreement. Here again the answer is yes. To see this, we now need to consider the monopoly seller's expected profit both without and with the contract.

Reality Checkpoint
Coke Takes Out a Contract on Texas Rivals

Dangerfield, Texas, gets awfully hot. The summertime temperature can regularly top 100 degrees Fahrenheit and shade is hard to find. That's probably one reason that Dangerfield residents and their neighbors drink a lot of soft drinks every year. Indeed, for convenience stores in the area, it is estimated that as much as half of their sales are from beverages. In the years just before 1992, the stores received their soft-drink supplies from a number of small, soft-drink firms and bottlers, as well as from Coca-Cola and Pepsi. However, that all began to change after 1992.

Bruce Hackett, a former Coke employee and owner of Hackett Beverages, supplied ice-filled barrels to a number of stores that were also stoked with his soft-drink bottles. The barrels were usually displayed just outside the cash register line so that customers could easily grab a cold beverage and pay for it on the way out. However, starting in 1992, Hackett found more and more of his barrels turned upside down and left at the side of the road. In four years, he went from having barrels in fifty-two stores to barrels in just two. Other independent bottlers and small beverage firms had similar experiences. They found stores abandoning the refrigerator units they gave them to display their products, dumping their fresh soda dispensing and vending machines, and even refusing them any shelf space.

The reason for these changes was easy to find. Coca-Cola had started an aggressive marketing campaign in which it paid store owners to display its products *exclusively* and refused to give them access even to non-Coke drinks handled by Coca-Cola bottlers if they did not. Thus, one contract offered a bonus of $2 million to a regional supermarket chain Brookshire's in return for just selling Coke products alone. Another contract required that "Coca-Cola products will occupy a minimum of 100 percent of total soft-drink space" in the store.

The case went to trial before a Texas court in 2000. Coke's defense was that the stores wanted the contract deals it was offering. They argued that the stores felt they had little to offer in the soft-drink category unless they offered the national Coke brand at the best terms possible. Coke argued that the contracts it offered allowed the stores to do just that. However, it was indisputable that as the smaller firms were driven from the market, Coke prices went up. At Nu-Way, a popular Dangerfield convenience store that still offers Royal Crown Cola, a 20-ounce container of the Royal Crown product sells for 69 cents while the same size container of Coke sells for 92 cents. However, at another convenience store E Z Mart a short distance away, there is no Royal Crown alternative and Coke sells for $1.09. Whether this was a case of predation or not is a question of judgment. However, a comment by Coca-Cola spokesperson Polly Howes probably did not help Coke's cause. In a widely distributed statement, Ms. Howes said that far from "a lack of competition. There was too much competition." The Texas jury found Coca-Cola guilty of violating the antitrust laws.

Source: C. Hays, "How Coke Pushed Rivals Off the Shelf," *New York Times*, August 6, 2003, Section 3, p. 1.

In the absence of any agreement, the incumbent monopolist will sell to a buyer at a price of $100 half the time. The other half of the time it will be underbid by the new entrant. When it does sell at $100, the incumbent makes a profit of $50. Because this happens with probability 1/2, the monopoly seller's expected profit in the second period without the contract is $1/2 \times \$50 = \$25$ per customer.

With the contract, the calculation of the incumbent's profit is slightly more complicated. With probability 3/4, the monopolist will still sell to the buyer at the pre-specified price of $75. Because the monopolist has a unit cost of $50, such a sale generates a profit of $25. With probability 1/4, however, the monopolist makes no sale because the buyer breaks the contract and switches to the new entrant. This is not bad news, however. The switch means that the monopolist no longer has to incur the $25 unit production cost. Moreover, the buyer's breach of contract entitles the seller to a $50 fee in the one-fourth of the time that the contract is broken. In short, the contract offers the initial incumbent seller an expected surplus in period two of:

$$3/4 \times (\$75 - \$50) + 1/4 \times \$50 = \$31.25 > \$25 \qquad (13.2)$$

As equation (13.2) makes clear, the monopoly seller's expected profit with the contract is $31.25, an amount that definitely exceeds its expected profit of $25 without the contract. Moreover, we have already shown that a typical buyer's expected surplus is the same whether the agreement is in force or not. In other words, the incumbent monopolist is made better off and the buyer is made no worse off by the contract. Accordingly, with one party desiring the contract and the other indifferent, we expect that the contract will be offered and signed.

From a social viewpoint, however, the contract is inefficient. To be sure, it does increase the expected surplus of the buyer and seller together from $50 (= $25 + $25) to $56.25 (= $25 + $31.25) for a net gain of $6.25. However, it reduces the entrant's expected surplus by more than this amount. Why?

Without the contract, the entrant will stay out of the market half the time and enter the other half. When it does enter, the entrant will sell at a price of $50 per unit. In such cases, the entrant's unit cost c will range from 0 to $50 or $25, on average. This implies that the entrant has an expected profit of $1/2 \times (\$50 - \$25) = \$12.50$ when there is no contract. When the incumbent binds a second period buyer with a contract, the potential rival only enters the market with probability 1/4 and sells at a price of only $25. Its unit cost in such cases will range from 0 to $25, or $12.50 on average. So, once the contract is signed, the potential rival's expected profit is only $1/4 \times (\$25 - \$12.50) = \$3.13$. From this, we can see that the issuance of a contract reduces the potential entrant's expected surplus from $12.50 to $3.13, or by $9.37. As noted, this reduction exceeds the joint gains to the buyer and seller ($6.25), so the total social surplus is less with the contract than without it.

The intuition behind the foregoing result, however, is subtle. From the buyer's perspective, the problem is that without the contract, the new entrant will never sell at a price less than $50—even if it has a cost of $0. Ideally, the buyer would like to benefit more in such cases where the entrant has such a particularly low cost. Yet, in the absence of the contract, nothing compels the new entrant to engage in such sharing. Once the price falls to $50, the initial incumbent drops out of the market, and the entrant faces no further pressure to reduce its price. By offering the contract, the incumbent monopolist effectively enables the buyer to force the seller never to charge a price above $25. The buyer is, as just noted, willing to pay for this service.

The point is that even though a contract may bring benefits to a monopoly supplier and its buyers, the contract is still inefficient if it achieves these gains only by reducing the surplus of the new entrant by an even greater amount. The inefficiency reflects the fact that under the contract regime, some desirable entry is prevented. Specifically, entry does not occur when the new rival has a cost c satisfying $\$25 < c \leq \$50$ despite the fact that within this range, the entrant is more efficient than the initial monopoly seller. Because of the breach-of-contract clause in the long-term contract, the entrant cannot break into the market.

13.3.2   Naked Exclusion

The Rasmusen, Ramseyer, and Wiley (1991) model differs from the above in so far as it focuses on an externality in the contract rather than on an uncertainty. Suppose again that there is one supplier with a unit cost of $50, and, say, three buyers. As before, each buyer will pay up to $100 for one unit of the input. There is also an entrant with a unit cost of $40 waiting to enter the market next period. However, the entrant also has a sunk cost—say due to market research or promotional activities—of $60. Hence, to underbid the incumbent and cover its sunk cost, the entrant has to serve at least two customers. If the new entrant serves three customers, it can charge each a price as low as $60. The $20 total that it earns in operating profit from each customer will, in total, cover the firm's overhead. If it serves two customers, the entrant can still underbid the incumbent, but it must now charge a price no lower than $70. If it serves only one customer, the entrant must charge a price of $100 to acquire the $60 needed to cover its sunk cost. In this case, the entrant will not find entry attractive.

The incumbent can of course match any of the entrant's price offers in the second period. Still, the incumbent has to recognize that if the entrant comes in at a price of $70 and the incumbent has to match that price, the incumbent's profit will fall to $60 even if it keeps all three customers. The incumbent, therefore, has some incentive to stop the entrant from acquiring two or more clients with a long-term contract. To sell this contract, the incumbent engages in the following tactic. It tells two customers that each of them will be able to buy the input at $70 if, and only if, each signs an exclusive contract promising not to buy from any other supplier. Why might this work?

Each buyer offered an exclusive contract with a purchase price of $70 now has to worry. Once two sign the contract, no offer needs to be made to the third because once two buyers are bound to the incumbent, the entrant cannot profitably underbid the incumbent's price. Therefore, the third buyer may well face a price of $100 once the other two have signed. In an effort to avoid such an outcome, each buyer will rush to sign the contract. In fact, by playing buyers against each other in this way, the incumbent may be able to sign exclusive deals even if it offers a small price reduction to only $90.

Here again the contract inefficiently blocks entry. The potential entrant is a more efficient producer. The problem is that each buyer looks only to the effect that the contract has on that buyer's profit. Each ignores the impact that signing the contract has on overall competition and the profitability of other buyers (perhaps some of whom are rivals to the buyer in the downstream market).

13.3.3   Tying Contracts

We discussed bundling as an entry-deterring strategy in both Chapters 4 and 12. As tying is more or less a generalization of bundling, it should not be surprising that similar arguments apply to tying contracts as well. Of course, the Chicago School's "only one profit" approach eloquently presented by Posner (1976) and Bork (1978) among others, rejects the use of bundling or tying as part of a predatory strategy. In that view, centered on complementary products such as cameras and film, or food and lodging, what consumers really value is the combined good—e.g., a room and a meal. In that case, any rise in the price of, say, a meal will only lower the price that can be charged for a room. In this view, a monopoly hotel owner on a small resort island, for example, has little incentive to try to monopolize the local restaurant market.[15]

There are, however, at least three responses to the Chicago School analysis. First, while visiting tourists may be interested in both food and lodging, there are likely local residents who are interested only in restaurant meals. If this segment of the meals market is large, then we really have two independent goods and correspondingly, two independent markets. In this case, there is not "one monopoly profit" but effectively two—one for each market. As a result, tying can be profitable if it helps the hotel owner establish a monopoly in this second, largely unrelated market—say by denying an upstart restaurant enough consumers from those who value both goods such that the entrant cannot cover its average cost.

A second reason that the hotel owner (or the camera maker, etc.) may want to use tying or bundling to exclude rivals in a second market is that failure to do so may eventually lead to the loss of monopoly in the basic commodity. Thus, if the hotel owner does not eliminate rival restaurants on the island, one of these may eventually build a motel.

Finally, as we saw in Chapter 8, both tying and bundling are also techniques of price discrimination. While such price discrimination may eliminate a competitive film market (recall Microsoft and Netscape), it must nevertheless be acknowledged that if the price discrimination motivation is paramount, the incumbent firm will pursue it independent of the presence of any rival. Hence, this is not predation. Moreover, to the extent that this price discrimination expands the market, it tends to raise welfare.

In short, there are good practical and theoretical reasons to believe that bundling/tying are often part of an entry-deterring or exit-encouraging strategy. Yet there are equally good reasons to see these tactics as part of sophisticated price discrimination techniques. While the early Chicago "only one profit" analysis likely fails to hold, the welfare implications of bundling and tying remain complicated. They can be resolved only on a case-by-case basis built on careful analysis of each market setting.

13.4   PREDATION AND REPUTATION

There is one other point that we wish to make about the profitability of predation. This is that firms rarely operate in just one market or for just one period. Whatever competition it faces in one market today, a firm can usually count on potential rivals emerging in its other markets or even the same market in the future. In such cases, the gains from predatory activity may include the establishment of a reputation that also deters these potential rivals in other markets and times.

For example, consider again our limit pricing game between Microhard and Newvel but with one change. This is that when Microhard is a high-cost firm and sets the low-cost optimal price as a monopolist, its profits really suffer. In particular, its profits fall from $60 million to just $19 million, i.e., the cost of misrepresentation is now $41 million.

If this were the only change, the incumbent would no longer find it worthwhile to try to fool the entrant that it is a low-cost firm. The cost now is too high. As a high-cost firm with a second period monopoly, it earns $60 million, while as a high cost duopolist it earns $20 million. Thus, by persuading the entrant to stay out, the firm preserves $40 million of profit. Yet, as just noted, our new assumption implies that to deter entry by initially pricing as a low-cost firm even though it is a high-cost one, the incumbent now incurs a cost of $41 million. So, the gain would not appear worth the cost.

However, the foregoing analysis neglects the fact that later rival entrants or entrants in other markets in which the incumbent operates are also watching. They too will use the incumbent's behavior at this time in this market to infer its type and therefore its behavior in later periods and/or other markets. Thus, by acting as a low-cost firm the incumbent gains a reputation for aggressive pricing that may be enough to deter these other rivals. If this is the case, the gains from "acting tough" in the current market and period in question include the profit increases the incumbent enjoys from keeping its position in these other periods and markets.

Needless to say, the advantage gained by establishing a reputation as a tough competitor is independent of whether that reputation is earned as a result of low pricing, insisting on long-term contracts, tying purchases, or other means. All of the predatory tactics we have discussed have enhanced value to the extent that they deter rivals in markets beyond the ones in which they are applied.

The favorable effect of a reputation for toughness are clearly evident in the history of the National Cash Register (NCR) company in the late 19th and early 20th centuries, documented by Brevoort and Marvel (2004). The cash register was a major advance at this time. Not only was it able to store money like the common till, but it was also able both to display the precise charge to customers in large visible digits and, most importantly, keep a running record of all the day's transactions—keeping clerks honest and providing valuable information to managers.

John Henry Patterson quickly saw the cash register's value. He bought the patent rights from the machine's creator, James Ritty, and established NCR in 1884, complete with an expanded sales force to promote the product. Sales and profits grew rapidly and, of course, soon attracted rival cash register firms. Patterson's response was to create a special division called the Competition Department. The purpose of this division was simple: use promotions and other tactics—including threats of patent infringement lawsuits and sabotage of rival machines—to suppress these rivals. A particularly widely used strategy was to have an NCR agent visit a customer using a rival machine and surreptitiously insert a piece of metal or other object to make the machine malfunction. As the owner examined and attempted to repair the machine, the NCR representative would appear and offer to replace the machine with an NCR model typically referred to as a "knocker." NCR knockers were typically low-end NCR models often modified to look like those of other firms to match customers' specific tastes. NCR sold the knockers at well below cost, especially when considering the salary and expenses of paying the NCR representatives selling them. In this way, NCR was able to cut prices selectively against rivals in any region that they appeared, rather than cut prices across the board.[15]

The results of NCR's aggressive campaigns against rivals were clear. By 1900, the company had 90 percent or more of the cash register market. Newsletters at the time suggested that over 95 percent of the cash register companies formed in the prior decade had gone out of business. Equally important for our purposes is the fact that there were virtually no new entrants into the business for the next twenty years, and the entry that began to occur after 1920 was due to NCR's signing a consent decree in court to limit its aggressive behavior. In short, NCR appears to have consciously engaged in predatory tactics and established a reputation for doing so with the goal of suppressing competition.

---

[15] See Whinston (1990) for a complete and illuminating discussion for these issues.

13.5 PREDATION AND ANTITRUST POLICY

In the wake of the Great Depression—a period of falling prices and many small firm bankruptcies—and with the history of the aggressive tactics of firms such as Standard Oil and NCR still fresh, it was perhaps natural that a wide consensus formed that predatory pricing was widespread and harmful. The most visible manifestation of that view was the passage of the Robinson-Patman Act of 1936 which, among other things, prevented selective price discounts by large firms that would disadvantage smaller firms. Over time however, this legislation was seen as less protective of competitive markets and more protective of specific competitors against more efficient rivals. Subsequently, against a history of cases such as *Utah Pie*, the work of McGee (1958, 1980), Koller (1971), Posner (1976), Bork (1978), Easterbrook (1984), and others of the Chicago School reflected a necessary corrective. Many firms achieve dominance not because of predation but because of their superior competitive skill. Hence, policies that constrain "bigness" would have adverse incentive effects on competitive behavior. A corollary to this view is that market dominance will not persist if it is due to any factor not related to superior skill or efficiency. Indeed, these very arguments were later made by Microsoft during its 1998–2001 trial and appeal. As a result of the force of these arguments, the Chicago School perspective on predatory behavior became increasingly influential. It received an official blessing in the 1986 *Matsuhita* case when the Supreme Court wrote, "For this reason, there is a consensus among commentators that predatory pricing schemes are rarely tried, and even more rarely successful."[16] A few years later in the *Brooke* case of 1993, the Court went even further and outlined stringent evidentiary standards that had to be met before a predation claim would be supported.[17]

The Brooke Group (also known as Ligget) was a small cigarette manufacturer that began selling a generic brand in 1980, at prices well below those of the major brands. When consumers responded favorably to the introduction of these cheap cigarettes, Brown & Williamson and other large tobacco companies responded with vigorous price cuts. In its effort to undersell Brooke, it seems clear that Brown cut prices so low that it sustained millions of dollars of losses over a period as long as a year or more. Ultimately, however, Brooke could not keep pace. It raised the price on its cigarettes. Almost immediately thereafter, Brown & Williamson and other cigarette manufacturers did the same.

The Supreme Court did not find the foregoing evidence conclusive. In the wake of the Chicago School revival, the Court had moved to a view that there was an economics consensus that predatory pricing was irrational. The Court did, however, take the opportunity to establish two broad requirements for the successful prosecution of a predatory pricing case. The first was evidence of selling below some measure of cost. The second and really new element introduced by the court was evidence that the predator had a reasonable expectation of recouping the losses endured during the predatory period. Just how strong the new requirements were can be seen in the fact that there was not one successful prosecution of predatory action in the first forty cases that followed the Brooke decision. It was not until the important case of Microsoft that there was a finding of criminal guilt.

In our view, the consensus to which the Supreme Court referred in *Matsuhita* no longer exists—if it ever did. Commitment via capacity expansion, asymmetric information, and

---

[16] *Brooke Group v. Brown & Williamson Tobacco* 509 U.S. 209 (1993). Interestingly enough, Brooke actually won the initial jury trial but lost in subsequent appeals to the federal courts.

[17] See Scherer's (1976) exchange with Areeda and Turner (1976) on this and other points.

contractual exclusions are all features that can be combined to make a coherent argument for the rationality of predatory actions. Here, the reputation effects of successful predation in one market are particularly important. In measuring the ability of a firm to recover its losses, one has to include in the calculations all the profits secured by the deterrent effect that the firm's reputation has on other would-be entrants in other markets and time periods.

However, the Court's statement of necessary evidence does speak to an important issue. The recognition that predation can be rational and can happen does not carry any clear policy implications unless we have a clear standard by which predatory actions can be identified and distinguished from conduct that is truly procompetitive. Any entry will generally evoke some reaction from the incumbent firms. Typically, this may come in the form of lower prices or other expanded consumer benefits. Most such responses are not predatory in nature. To the contrary, they are exactly the conduct that we expect and hope that markets will promote. Similarly, when any firm, large or small, first comes into a market as a new entrant, it may want to set a low initial price, lower than the short-term, profit-maximizing one, as a way to induce consumers to forego their usual brand and try the entrant's relatively unknown product. Once established, the firm may then raise price. Clearly, the intent of this kind of promotional pricing is not to drive a rival from the market. Yet it may be difficult empirically to distinguish this pricing strategy from predatory pricing.

In other words, to the extent that antitrust enforcement seeks to prevent predatory practices, policy makers need to create workable legal standards that are able to distinguish procompetitive from anticompetitive conduct. Ideally, we would like such policy to be governed by a simple rule that could be used to detect the presence of predation. This would permit all parties to understand just what is and what is not legal. Yet in the area of predation simple rules rarely work.

Of the various rules that have been proposed, the most famous is that of Areeda and Turner (1975), which essentially finds any price to be predatory if it is below the firm's short-run average variable cost standing in as a proxy for marginal cost. Unfortunately, it is not a very good proxy. In actual practice, average variable cost can be significantly less than short-run marginal cost so that a firm could set a price below its current marginal cost yet still above its average cost. In so doing, the firm would be acting within the legal range permitted by the Areeda and Turner rule even though a price below short-run marginal cost would likely be judged as predatory by many economists. Hence, as Scherer (1976) was quick to point out, the use of the average cost standard could still permit serious predation.[18] Moreover, if there are important learning curve effects so that average cost falls with a firm's cumulative production over time (as opposed to scale economies in which average cost falls with the volume of production per unit of time), predation can occur by means of a vigorous output expansion without prices ever falling below cost.[19]

Another problem is that the rule ignores the strategic aspect of predatory pricing. To take a simple example, consider a market in which there is one firm operating as a monopoly. Suppose that if a new firm enters it will produce an identical good to that of the monopolist and that the game is one of Bertrand or price competition. As we saw in Chapter 10, the equilibrium of this game is that prices fall immediately to their marginal cost. By Areeda and Turner's rule, this would not be predatory. Yet if the entrant foresees this outcome, the existence of any sunk entry cost will be enough to induce it to stay out. Here again,

[18] See Cabral and Riordan (1997) for an elaboration of this point.
[19] See, for example, his decision in *Barry Wright Corporation v. ITT Grinnell Corporation, et al.*, 724F. 2d 227 (1st Cir. 1983).

the Areeda and Turner rule might permit entry-deterring behavior. Whenever the threat of "cutthroat pricing" is sufficiently credible that it never is actually used, the evidence Areeda and Turner look for will not be found.

Despite its shortcomings, the Areeda and Turner rule has been applied in many US antitrust cases. It has been frequently relied upon by Supreme Court Justice, Stephen Breyer. It was also used to exonerate IBM against predatory price-cutting charges in *California Computer Products, Inc., et al. v. International Business Machines* [613 F. 2d 727 (9th Cir. 1979)]. Perhaps the clearest statement is that of Judge Kaufman who, in *Northeastern Telephone Company v. American Telephone and Telegraph Company et al.*, [651 F. 2d 76 (2nd Cir. 1981)], wrote: "We agree with Areeda and Turner that in the general case, at least, the relationship between a firm's prices and its marginal costs provides the best single determinant of predatory pricing."

Nevertheless, the weaknesses in the Areeda and Turner rule have led many economists to propose modified alternatives. Some of these are like the Areeda and Turner approach in that they focus essentially on the behavior of a single variable. Baumol (1979), for example, focuses primarily on the behavior of the incumbent's price before entry and after exit of a rival. Essentially, this rule requires that any price reduction by a dominant firm in the face of entry be required to be "quasi-permanent," say for a period of five years. If the price reduction that entry induced is quickly reversed following the entrant's exit, Baumol's (1979) rule would find the pricing behavior predatory.

In a later updating of this work, Baumol (1996) also suggests comparing the predator's price with a measure of Average Avoidable Cost (AAC). AAC is a measure of the cost that the alleged predator could have avoided had it not engaged in the predatory increase in output. Thus, if the predatory action lasted for a year, AAC would be the total amount of extra costs incurred in that year divided by the extra quantity produced. In a similar vein, Williamson (1977) suggests looking at the incumbent's *output* before and after entry. The idea is that a rapid expansion of output after entry would be a sign of possible predation. This rule has two advantages. First, because of the suspicion raised by expansion after entry, the incumbent might well expand output earlier. In turn, this eliminates some of the monopoly distortion that would otherwise occur when the incumbent is alone in the market. Second, Williamson's rule may also prevent capacity expansion as an entry-deterring strategy by making the threat to expand once entry is no longer credible.

While both the Baumol (1979) and Williamson (1977) rules are insightful, both are also limited by focusing on a single variable to indicate predation. As we have emphasized, predatory conduct is part of an often complicated corporate strategy. As a result, it is unlikely to be reflected accurately in the behavior of a single variable. The Dixit (1980) model of capacity deterrence does not involve pricing at all and so would go undetected by both the Areeda-Turner and the Baumol tests. Similarly, Williamson's test would not prevent deterrence by preemption. None of these tests involve any consideration as to whether the strategic environment actually permits predation.

Joskow and Klevorick (1979) were among the first to suggest a more complete assessment of alleged predation within a strategic framework. Their rule combines the separate criteria mentioned above—below-cost pricing, output expansion, and price reversal—but requires as well that there be evidence that such actions were or at least could have been conceived as part of an overall strategy. In particular, Joskow and Klevorick (1979) propose to examine company documents to determine whether or not a firm was intentionally pursuing the aggressive policies. These authors would also examine the industry's structural features to see whether the conditions for predatory pricing exist.

Ordover and Willig (1981) and Bolton, Brodley, and Riordan (2001) also try to present a comprehensive framework for evaluating predatory accusations. The Ordover and Willig (1981) paper is important for its clear and modern definition of predatory conduct as any action for which the profitability is dependent on driving the rival out or preventing it from entering in the first place. In this view, predatory pricing is but one of a number of predation tactics. Both papers argue that an important first step is to check the market structure for the preconditions necessary to make predation worthwhile. The structural conditions so identified are that the accused predator really has significant market power and that entry be difficult so that if a rival is forced to exit, it is not subsequently replaced. Brodley, Bolton, and Riordan (2001) also argue that recoupment can be demonstrated by relating the predator's actions to a clear and evidence-supported strategy of predation. In the case of predatory pricing, these authors would rely on an Average Avoidable Cost measure as a benchmark.

None of the proposed predatory standards is simple or easily translated into a courtroom proceeding. The difficulty of distinguishing between good, fierce competition, on the one hand, and predatory efforts, on the other, is substantial. Moreover, as tough as this distinction is to make in the case of pricing, it may be even more difficult to achieve in considering other actions.

For example, consider the alleged predatory product innovations key to two well-known cases, *Telex v. IBM*, and *Berkey v. Kodak*. In the former, the issue at hand was the claim by Telex (and others) that IBM, which at the time admittedly controlled the market for mainframe computers but faced serious competition in markets for peripheral equipment, began to develop new equipment designs so that only new IBM peripherals were compatible with IBM mainframes (a tying arrangement). In the *Berkey* case, Berkey was a photo-finisher and camera manufacturer that claimed that Kodak should have given it advance notice of Kodak's introduction of a new 110 camera film so as to permit Berkey to redesign its cameras and remain viable in the market. In both cases, the courts eventually ruled against the plaintiffs and in favor of IBM and Kodak, respectively. There is perhaps good reason to believe that the technological alterations reflected in these two cases truly were motivated by predatory considerations. However, there is also a legitimate fear that punishing such actions could have a chilling effect on all innovation.

13.6   EMPIRICAL APPLICATION: ENTRY DETERRENCE IN THE PHARMACEUTICAL INDUSTRY

We noted that legal cases concerning predatory and entry deterring behavior often founder for lack of a clear standard defining predation. It is equally difficult to find clear evidence of such efforts in formal econometric studies. To be sure, the case histories such as Weiman and Levin (1994) concerning AT&T and the Brevoort and Marvel (2004) paper studying NCR offer clear specific examples. In a widely-cited paper on shipping cartels, Scott-Morton (1997) does find some formal evidence that established cartels in the late 19th and early 20th century engaged in predatory pricing to deter new shipping entrants, especially when the entrants were small and/or had poor financial resources. However, in another paper, Scott-Morton (2000) Morton finds very little statistical evidence that pharmaceutical firms successfully use advertising to deter generic entry as the end of the incumbent's patent nears.

The unfortunate truth is that the formal econometric requirements necessary to identify consistently any systematic predatory behavior across a set of market data points are fairly

Reality Checkpoint
Cut-rate or Cutthroat Fares?

In 1994, Sun Jet Airlines began offering service between Dallas-Fort Worth airport and a select few other cities including Tampa, Florida, and Long Beach, California. Its entry was subsequently followed by that of Vanguard Airlines flying between Dallas and Kansas City, and Western Pacific offering flights between Dallas and Colorado Springs. All three airlines are small startup carriers whose operating costs are widely recognized to be well below those of the major, established airlines. Indeed, it was this cost advantage that gave these small startups their only hope of surviving in the Dallas-Fort Worth market. This is because the Dallas-Fort Worth airport is a central hub for American Airlines. American carries 70 percent of all the passengers who travel from any city nonstop to Dallas and 77 percent of all those nonstop passengers originating in Dallas. It has concessions from local businesses and has already sunk the costs necessary to operate its gates, ticketing desks, and so on. Internal documents obtained from American by the Justice Department reveal that these and other advantages made the firm confident that its dominance would not be challenged by another major airline. However, those same documents suggest that American was concerned

about the entry of low-cost startups, especially after observing how much market share such firms had taken from other major carriers at their hub airports.

American responded aggressively to the three startups. It greatly expanded its flight offerings in the challenged markets and lowered its fares. In each of the three markets shown, this strategy ultimately led the startup to exit the market. Immediately thereafter, American cut its flights and raised fares back to or above earlier levels. This is shown for the case of three markets in the table below.

Was this a case of predatory pricing? The Justice Department thought so. It claimed that during the battle with the startups, American lost money on each flight. The actual losses are claimed to be even greater because to offer the additional flights, aircraft were diverted from profitable routes to these unprofitable ones. American won an initial decision in district court. In July 2003, a three-judge Appeals Court upheld the lower court's decision.

Source: D. Carney and W. Zellner, "Caveat Predator: The Justice Department is Cracking Down on Predatory Pricing," *Business Week*, May 22, 2000, p. 116.

	Before Entry		During Conflict		After Exit	
	# Daily Flights	Price	# Daily Flights	Price	# Daily Flights	Price
Kansas City	8	$108	14	$80	11	$147
Long Beach	0	—	3	$86	0	—
Colorado Springs	5	$150	7	$81	6	$137

demanding. One reason for this is that such work must somehow identify cases where an incumbent both regarded entry as a real threat *and* felt that there was a way to prevent it. Suppose, for instance, that the data set includes two kinds of markets. One type is characterized by a high likelihood of entry by several new firms and that by taking a costly action X the incumbent can reduce the number of entrants. The other market type is characterized by a very low probability of entry and by one new rival at most. Finally, suppose that post-entry competition is Cournot so that the fewer new entrants the better from the viewpoint of the incumbent.

In such a setting, we may find that incumbents only take action X in the first type of market because entry is so unlikely in the second kind of market that incurring the cost of action X is not worthwhile. If this is so, the data will be divided into two groups. In one set of cases, the incumbent takes action X and there is some entry (though less than otherwise would have been the case). In the other set of cases, the incumbent does not take action X, yet there is no entry. Thus, on balance, the data will show that there is *more* entry when the predatory tactic X is used than when it is not. Unless care is taken to identify such markets *a priori*, it will be hard to conclude from such data that predation is a serious threat.

Another difficulty that the researcher must overcome is identifying the entry-deterring strategy. This too is trickier than it may at first appear. Consider the first-mover, consumer learning-by-doing model of Gabszewicz, Pepall, and Thisse (1992) discussed in Chapter 11. Recall that in the first period of that model when the incumbent is alone, the incumbent prices low to "buy up" a cohort of customers who will be loyal to its product after the second-period entry of a rival because these customers have learned how to work with the incumbent's brand. On the one hand, then, such aggressive pricing may seem as if it deters entry because it limits the number of customers for whom the later entrant can compete. On the other hand, however, the fact that it has such a loyal and price-insensitive cohort encourages the incumbent to charge a high price when entry occurs, and this allows the entrant to gain more consumers at a high price as well. Of course, this latter effect makes entry more likely.

A recent paper that nicely illustrates these issues is Ellison and Ellison (2011). They look at the advertising and pricing behavior of pharmaceutical companies in the case of sixty-four drugs about to lose their patents over the years 1986–92. They first do a simple regression to determine which markets are most vulnerable to entry. For this purpose, they code each market as to whether or not there was any generic entry within three years after the expiration of the incumbent's patent. This procedure creates a 1, 0 variable for each market called Entry, where the variable is 1 if there was entry and 0 if there was not. Ellison and Ellison (2011) then try to explain this entry variable with an equation that includes three right-hand-side variables that should be related to entry. These are: Rev_i, the average annual revenue earned by the incumbent over the three years prior to patent expiration; $Hosp_i$, the fraction of revenues from the drug due to hospital sales in the year prior to patent expiration; and Chronic/$Acute_i$, which takes on the value 0 if the drug treats an acute condition but 1 if it treats a chronic condition. Their estimated equation then is:

$$Entry_i = constant + \beta_1 Rev_i + \beta_2 Hosp_i + \beta_3 Chronic/Acute_i + \varepsilon_i \tag{13.3}$$

where ε_i represents random factors that may affect entry in the ith market.

Because the dependent variable is not continuous but instead either 1 or 0, equation (13.3) cannot be efficiently estimated by ordinary least squares (OLS) regression. The linear feature of OLS means that it is quite likely that for plausible values of the independent variables the OLS estimates of the β_k coefficients will predict a value for entry outside the [0,1] interval.

Instead, Ellison and Ellison (2011) use an alternative regression procedure called Probit. This procedure effectively transforms the data so that for any value of the right-hand-side variables, the coefficient estimates give rise to a value for $Entry_i$ that lies between 0 and 1. This predicted value is then a measure of the probability of entry given the market features.

In turn, this allows them to classify each of their sixty-four markets as one of three types: 1) low probability of entry; 2) intermediate probability of entry; and 3) high probability of entry.

Ellison and Ellison (2011) next consider the strategic use of advertising to deter entry in these markets. They start by noting that in these cases advertising by one firm has considerable spillover to the products of another. In particular, advertising by an incumbent calls attention to the specific functions of the drug, its potential benefits, its proper use, and so on, in a way that is likely to inform consumers of the benefit of later generic rivals. This is particularly the case with drugs because doctors are smart enough to realize that the active ingredients in branded medications and generics are chemically identical. It is even more the case in those states in which pharmacies are required by law to fill a prescription with a cheaper generic medication if one is available and the doctor has not explicitly forbidden it. In other words, Ellison and Ellison (2011) assume that advertising by an incumbent today will *help* tomorrow's generic entrant. Hence, if incumbents wish to deter entry, they should *reduce* advertising in the period prior to the expected emergence of a rival. Note how this implies a further complication in evaluating the evidence on entry deterrence. The other strategies we considered, e.g., capacity expansion and price-cutting, are actions that are expensive for the firm. By reducing advertising, however, the firm also lowers its expense.

Of course, whether or not incumbents will wish to deter entry will depend in part on how likely entry is. A key insight of the Ellison and Ellison (2011) paper is that the relationship between the probability of entry and strategic deterrence efforts is likely to be nonmonotonic. This is because entry deterrence is probably not worth the cost either in markets where entry is highly probable or in ones where it is very unlikely. In the first case, no amount of deterrence is likely to prevent entry. In the second case, no deterrence is really necessary. Thus, Ellison and Ellison (2011) predict that deterrence efforts will first rise (relative to what they would otherwise be) as the probability of entry rises from a low value to an intermediate one, and then fall, as the probability of entry rises still further to a high value. In terms of advertising, this means that incumbents will *lower* their advertising in those markets that their Probit regression results characterize as having an intermediate probability of entry but exhibit no advertising response to the threat of entry in either low or high probability of entry markets. Again, this is because Ellison and Ellison (2011) assume that advertising by the incumbent also has strong benefits for the generic entrant. Reducing advertising prior to the period of potential entry can then make that entry less likely. To some extent, this is precisely what they find.

Consider so-called detail advertising. By this we mean the promotional efforts of pharmaceuticals to influence physicians' prescribing practices by visiting doctors and health care providers and making direct presentations in their offices. Ellison and Ellison (2011) look at the time trend in the value of detail advertising relative to its average in the three years prior to patent expiration for each month starting 36 months before that expiration and continuing for 12 months after by estimating the regression equation:

$$\frac{Advertising_{it}}{Average\ Advertising_i} - 1 = (\beta_1 LowEntry_i + \beta_2 IntermedEntry_i + \beta_3 HighEntry_i)Time + \varepsilon_{it}$$

$$(13.4)$$

Table 13.1   Detail advertising trend by category of entry probability, 64 pharmaceutical markets

Coefficient	Estimated Value	Standard Error
β_1	−0.007	0.013
β_2	−0.032	0.009
β_3	0.009	0.007

The *Time* variable is just a trend term that increases by one as one moves a month closer to expiration date. The dependent variable is the ratio of advertising in the ith market in month t relative to average monthly detail advertising in that market. LowEntry, IntermedEntry, and HighEntry are each a 1,0 dummy variable indicating what entry category market i is in. The hypothesis is that β_2 will be significantly less than either β_1 or β_2, reflecting the efforts of incumbents in these markets to reduce advertising as a means of deterring entry. The estimated results are shown in Table 13.1 above.

As you can see, the estimate of β_2 is noticeably smaller (algebraically) than either of the other two coefficients. That is, the results imply that while the incumbent's detail advertising declines by less than 1 percent per month relative to the norm in high entry markets (β_1) and actually rises a bit in low entry markets (β_3), it falls by over 3 percent per month in markets with an intermediate chance of entry. Thus, Ellison and Ellison (2011) provide some interesting evidence of strategic deterrence efforts in US pharmaceutical markets in the late 1980s.

Summary

Allegations of pricing below cost to drive out a competitor and other comparable predatory strategies have been met in the last part of the twentieth century with increasing skepticism by the courts. This reflects the Chicago School view that predation is irrational. In the language of game theory, the Chicago view is that predation is not a subgame perfect strategy and it is typically dominated by other choices. Accordingly, few charges of predatory activity have been successfully prosecuted in the last twenty years or so.

At the same time, there appear to be clear historical cases of actual predatory conduct. As a result, an important question in contemporary industrial organization theory has been whether we can construct plausible models in which predatory actions are rational. The answer turns out to be yes and numerous game theoretic models have now been developed that overturn the logic of the Chain Store Paradox.

An important common feature in many of these models is asymmetric information. Asymmetries between a lender and a firm regarding the firm's true profitability, or between an established firm and an upstart regarding the incumbent's cost can make predation a feasible and attractive strategy. Even without such uncertainty, long-term and/or tying contracts can also be used to deny rivals a market. Yet while the viability of predation in both theory and practice seems clear, the proper role of public policy remains clouded.

The principal problem is one of distinguishing aggressive pricing and other competitive strategies from ones that are truly predatory—profitable only if they succeed in driving a rival out of business. Some antitrust enforcement—especially those cases prosecuted under the Robinson-Patman Act in the first thirty-five years after it was passed—appear to have been misguided efforts to protect competitors and not competition. Both economists and the courts continue to struggle with the implementation of a workable definition of predation. Empirical work testing systematic entry deterrence has been challenged by the data requirements necessary to identify predatory behavior across a set of market data points. Nevertheless this is an active research area in empirical industrial organization, holding promise for policy makers seeking to implement and enforce antitrust laws on predatory behavior.

Problems

1. Return to the Microhard Newvel game as discussed in section 13.1. Suppose now that Newvel's fixed costs are only $80 million per period. What would be the loan contract that a bank in a competitive banking industry would accept to loan Newvel $80 million in each period? Now suppose that the worst case scenario facing Newvel worsens. Specifically there is a 50 percent chance of earning $200 million and a 50 percent chance of earning only $40 million. Fixed costs are $80 million per period. Now what would be the loan contract that a bank in a competitive banking industry would accept to loan Newvel $80 million in each period?

2. Two firms are contending for a local market. The incumbent has a cost function of: $C(q_I) = 800 + 40q_I$. The upstart entrant has a cost function given by: $C(q_E) = 1300 + 36q_E$. The industry inverse demand function is given by: $P = 100 - Q$, where Q is total industry output. Prior to the upstart's entry, the incumbent acted like a profit-maximizing, uniform pricing monopolist. What price was it setting? What profit net of fixed cost did it earn? Upon the entry of the upstart rival, the incumbent quickly dropped its price to $63. How do you think the entrant will respond to this price? Does the incumbent's price-cutting constitute predation? Why or why not?

3. Suppose a buyer is willing to pay up to $200 for one unit of some good. There is currently only one supplier of the good and its cost of supplying one unit of the good is $100. Next period, a rival supplier may appear in the market. The rival's cost of supplying the good is not known. It is assumed to be uniformly distributed on the interval [50,150]. Describe a long-term contract that the current supplier can offer the buyer that will be attractive to the buyer and that at the same time will strengthen the monopoly power of the current supplier.

4. An incumbent firm has a cost function given by: $C_I = 100 + 1.5q_I^2$. Hence, its marginal cost is given by: $MC_I = 3q_I$. A recently entered rival has the cost function: $C_E = 100 + 75q_E$. Suppose the incumbent sets a price of 74 and meets demand at that price, where market (inverse) demand is given by: $P = 100 - Q$.
   a. Does the incumbent's behavior violate the Areeda-Turner rule of selling below marginal cost?
   b. Does the incumbent's behavior violate the Areeda-Turner rule when average variable cost is used as a proxy for marginal cost? Why or why not?

References

Aghion, P., and P. Bolton. 1987. "Contracts as a Barrier to Entry," *American Economic Review* 77 (June): 388–401.

Areeda, P. E., and D. F. Turner. 1975. "Predatory pricing and related practices under section 2 of the Sherman Act," *Harvard Law Review* 88 (February): 697–733.

Areeda, P. E., and D. F. Turner. 1976. "Scherer on Predatory Pricing: A Reply," *Harvard Law Review* 89 (March): 891–900.

Baumol, W. J. 1979. "Quasi-Permanence of Price Reductions: A Policy for Prevention of Predatory Pricing," *Yale Law Journal* 89: 1–26.

Baumol, W. J. 1996. "Predation and the Logic of the Average Variable Cost Test," *Journal of Law & Economics* 39 (April): 49–72.

Benoit, J. P. 1984. "Financially Constrained Entry in a Game with Incomplete Information," *Rand Journal of Economics* 15 (Winter): 490–9.

Bolton, P., and D. Scharfstein. 1990. "A Theory of Predation Based on Agency Problems in Financial Contracting," *American Economic Review*, 80 (March): 93–106.

Bork, R. 1978. *The Antitrust Paradox*, New York: Basic Books.

Brandeis, L. 1913. "Cutthroat prices-the competition that kills," *Harper's Weekly* 15 (November): 10–12.

Brevoort, K., and H. Marvel. (2004). "Successful Monopolization through Predation: The National Cash Register Company," *Research in Law and Economics* 21 (January): 85–125.

Brodley, J., P. Bolton, and M. Riordan. 2001. "Predatory Pricing: Strategic Theory and Legal Policy," *Georgetown Law Review* 88 (August): 2239–330

Burns, M. R. 1986. "Predatory pricing and the acquisition cost of competitors," *Journal of Political Economy* 94 (April): 266–96.

Cabral, L. M. B., and M. J. Riordan. 1997. "The Learning Curve, Predation, Antitrust, and Welfare," *Journal of Industrial Economics* 45 (June):155–69.

Easterbrook, F. H. 1984. "The Limits of Antitrust," *The Texas Law Review* 63 (January): 1–40.

Ellison, G., and S. Ellison. 2011. "Strategic Entry Deterrence and the Behavior of Pharmaceutical Incumbents Prior to Patent Expiration," *American Economic Journal* 3 (January): 1–36.

Dixit (1980)

Fudenberg, D., and J. Tirole. 1986. "A Signal-Jamming Theory of Predation," *Rand Journal of Economics* 17 (Autumn): 366–76.

Gabszewicz, Pepall, and Thisse (1992)

Genesove, D., and W. Mullin. 1998. "Testing Static Oligopoly Models: Conduct and Cost in the Sugar Industry, 1890–1914," *Rand Journal of Economics* 14 (Summer): 355–77.

Holmes (1996)

Joskow, P. L., and A. K. Klevorick. 1979. "A Framework for Analyzing Predatory Pricing Policy," *Yale Law Journal* 89 (December): 213–70.

Koller, R. H. II. 1971. "The Myth of Predatory Pricing: An Empirical Study," *Antitrust Law & Economics Review* 4 (Summer): 105–43.

Koller (1969)

McGee, J. S. 1958. "Predatory Price Cutting: the Standard Oil (N.J.) case," *Journal of Law and Economics* 1 (April):137 –169.

McGee, J. S. 1980. "Predatory pricing revisited," *Journal of Law and Economics* 23 (October): 289–330.

Milgrom, P., and J. Roberts. 1982. "Limit Pricing and Entry under Incomplete Information: An Equilibrium Analysis," *Econometrica* 50 (March): 443–60.

Ordover, J. A., and G. Saloner. 1989. "Predation, Monopolization and Antitrust," in *Handbook of Industrial Organization, Vol. 1*, R. Schmalensee and R. Willig, eds. Amsterdam: North-Holland, 537–95.

Ordover, J. A., and R. Willig, 1981. "An Economic Definition of Predation: Pricing and Product Innovation," *Yale Law Journal* 91 (1981): 8–53.

Posner, R. 1976. *Antitrust Law: An Economic Perspective*, University of Chicago Press.

Philips, L. 1995. *Competition Policy: A Game Theoretic Analysis*. Cambridge: Cambridge University Press.

Rasmusen, E. 2007. *Games and Information*, 4th ed. Cambridge, MA: Basil Blackwell, Inc.

Rasmusen, E., J. M. Ramseyer, and J. Wiley. 1991. "Naked Exclusion," *American Economic Review* 81 (December): 113745.

Saloner, G. 1987. "Predation, Mergers and Incomplete Information," *Rand Journal of Economics* 18 (Summer): 165–186.

Scherer, F. M. 1976. "Predatory Pricing and the Sherman Act: A Comment," *Harvard Law Review* 89 (March): 869–90.

Scott-Morton, F. 1997. "Entry and Predation: British Shipping Cartels, 1879–1929," *Journal of Economics and Management Strategy* 6 (Winter): 679–724.

Scott-Morton, F. 2000. "Barriers to Entry, Brand Advertising, and Generic Entry in the U.S. Pharmaceutical Industry," *International Journal of Industrial Organization* 18 (October): 1085–124.

Weiman and Levin (1994)

Whinston, M. 1990. "Tying, Foreclosure, and Exclusion," *American Economic Review* 80 (September): 837–59.

Williamson, O. E. 1977. "Predatory Pricing: A Strategic and Welfare Analysis," *Yale Law Journal* 87 (December): 284–340.

Yamey, B., S. 1972. "Predatory price cutting: notes and comments," *Journal of Law and Economics* 15 (April): 129–42.

Yergin, D., 1991. *The Prize*, New York: Simon and Schuster.

14

Price Fixing, Repeated Games, and Antitrust Policy

On December 5, 2012, the European Commission announced the fines totalling €1.5 billion ($1.92 billion) on seven firms that had participated in two related, but distinct illegal cartels. This is the largest single price-fixing fine ever imposed by the Commission and the firms involved include some of world's largest electronics firms such as LG Electronics, Philips, Samsung, Panasonic, and Toshiba.[1] Notably, in this last case, the fine imposed on Asahi/AGC was reduced by 50 percent to €113.5 million in return for that firm's cooperation with the cartel investigation and its providing information that helped expose the cartel.

The European case was related to an earlier case in the United States involving the liquid crystal displays used in flat panel TVs and computer screens. That case also involved several major electronics firms including Hitachi, Sharp, Samsung, and Toshiba. Settlements with these firms in late 2011 and early 2012 resulted in fines totaling $1.1 billion. That was before the final fine levied on Au Optronics of $500 million in September of 2012. That fine matched the largest single fine the US authorities had ever levied on any price-fixing firm.

The good news is that the above conspiracies were caught and prosecuted. The bad news is that such collusive agreements are not uncommon. Early in 2012, the United States levied fines and prison sentences on three Japanese firms operating in the US that conspired to fix the prices of key auto parts such as heater control panels. In November 2009, the European Union Competition Directorate jointly fined Akzo, Ciba, Elf Aquitaine, and seven others €173 million ($260 million at the time) for fixing the price of plastic additives. In 2007, European regulators fined five elevator manufacturers a total of €992 million (approximately $1.4 billion) for operating a cartel that controlled prices in Germany, Belgium, Luxembourg, and the Netherlands. The elevator case came just one month after another case involving gas-insulated switch-gear products in which the Commission imposed fines totaling €750 million on eleven companies for their parts in a price-fixing cartel. A few years earlier, the US Department of Justice imposed a total of more than $732 million on companies operating a cartel to control the pricing of dynamic random access memory (DRAM).

Tables 14.1 and 14.2 show that these conspiracies are not isolated events. Since 1995, the US Department of Justice has detected and successfully prosecuted thirty-eight cartels in which the final fine was $50 million or more. If we extend the list to include fines

---

[1] Details of the European Union cases can be obtained at http://ec.europa.eu/comm/competition/antitrust/cases/index.html.

Table 14.1 US price-fixing violations yielding a corporate fine of $50 million or more since 1995

Defendant(s) & Year	Product(s)	Fine ($Million)
Au Optronics Corporation (2012)	Liquid Crystal Display Panels	$500
F. Hoffmann-La Roche, Ltd. (1999)	Vitamins	$500
Yazaki Corporation (2012)	Automobile Parts	$470
LG Display (2009)	Liquid Crystal Display Panels	$400
Air France / KLM (2008)	Air Transportation (Cargo)	$350
Korean Air Lines Co., Ltd. (2007)	Air Transportation (Cargo/Passenger)	$300
British Airways (2007)	Air Transportation (Cargo/Passenger)	$300
Samsung Electronics & Semiconductor (2006)	Dram	$300
BASF AG (1999)	Vitamins	$225
Chi Mei Optoelectronics Corporation (2010)	Liquid Crystal Display Panels	$220
Furukawa Electric Co. Ltd. (2012)	Automotive Wire Harnesses & Like Goods	$200
Hynix Semiconductor Inc. (2005)	Dram	$185
Infineon Technologies Ag (2004)	Dram	$160
SGL Carbon Ag (1999)	Graphite Electrodes	$135
Mitsubishi Corp. (2001)	Graphite Electrodes	$134
Sharp Corporation (2009)	Liquid Crystal Display Panels	$120
Cargolux Airlines S.A. (2009)	Air Transportation (Cargo)	$119
Japan Airlines Co. Ltd (2008)	Air Transportation (Cargo)	$110
UCAR, Inc. (1998)	Graphite Electrodes	$110
Lan Cargo S.A./Aerolinhas Brasileiras S.A. (2009)	Air Transportation (Cargo)	$109
Archer Daniels Midland Co. (1996)	Lysine & Citric Acid	$100
Embraco North America (2011)	Compressors	$ 92
Elpida Memory, Inc. (2006)	Dram	$ 84
Dupont Dow Elastomers L.L.C. (2005)	Chloroprene Rubber	$ 84
Denso Corporation (2012)	Automobile Parts	$ 78
All Nippon Airways Co., Ltd. (2011)	Air Transportation (Cargo & Passenger)	$ 73
Takeda Chemical Industries, Ltd. (1999)	Vitamins	$ 72
Bayer Ag (2004)	Rubber Chemicals	$ 66
Chunghwa Picture Tubes, Ltd. (2009)	Liquid Crystal Display Panels	$ 65
Qantas Airways Limited (2008)	Air Transportation (Cargo)	$ 61
Cathay Pacific Airways Limited (2008)	Air Transportation (Cargo)	$ 60
Bilhar Establishment (2002)	Construction	$ 54
Daicel Chemical Industries, Ltd. (2000)	Sorbates	$ 53
Abb Middle East & Africa Participations Ag (2001)	Construction	$ 53
SAS Cargo Group, A/S (2008)	Air Transportation (Cargo)	$ 52
Crompton (2004)	Rubber Chemicals	$ 50
Haarmann & Reimer Corp. (1997)	Citric Acid	$ 50
Asiana Airlines Inc. (2009)	Air Transportation (Cargo & Passenger)	$ 50

Source: US Department of Justice, Antitrust Division, www.usdoj.gov/atr.

Table 14.2   Cartel cases decided by the European
Commission since 1990 and associated fines in €millions

Period	Cases	Total Fines
1990—94	10	€ 344
1995—99	10	€ 271
2000—04	30	€ 3,157
2005—09	33	€ 8,430
2010—12	16	€ 5,358

of $10 million or more, the number grows to nearly 100. Table 14.2 shows that the European case is similar. Since 1990 the European Commission has imposed fines in nearly 100 cases running the total fines levied to close to €18 billion.

In short, cartels happen. There appears to be no shortage of firms that enter into collusive agreements to fix prices and avoid competition. However, forming and maintaining a cartel is not easy for two, closely related reasons. The first is that such agreements are *per se* illegal.[2] That is, there is no justification that the courts will find acceptable. Both the antitrust laws of the United States and the legal framework established in Europe's Treaty of Rome, as well as the laws of most other nations, are explicit in making any and all collusion illegal and punishable by fines and (in the United States) possible imprisonment of corporate officers.[3]

The second obstacle is that the automatic illegality of collusive agreements means that the implicit contracts among the conspiring firms cannot be legally enforced. If one of the cartel members decides to price below the cartel-agreed level or to produce more than its cartel-authorized output quota, the other members cannot sue or take other legal action to curtail the renegade firm. Hence, a cartel's success requires that it find some extra-legal means of enforcing its agreement.

In this chapter, we explore the formation of cartels. This includes determining the techniques cartels may use to maintain their agreement and the conditions under which such techniques are most likely to be successful. In addition, we also address how antitrust authorities may best detect and prevent cartels.

14.1   THE PRISONER'S DILEMMA, REPEATED GAMES, AND THE FOLK THEOREM

The central issue that a potential cartel must face is clear. There are extra profits to be earned if each firm cooperates and holds production off the market to approximate more closely the monopoly outcome. Unfortunately, the price/output choices necessary for this are not typically part of a Nash equilibrium.[4]

---

[2]   Some regulatory agencies have power to grant antitrust immunity from *per se* illegality.

[3]   If anything, the language of European Union law is even stronger in that it also treats "concerted practices" based upon a "concordance of wills" as *per se* illegal. In practice, however, the US and European policy is nearly identical.

[4]   A terrific guide to the intuition underlying the cartel problem and, indeed, all of game theory is Schelling (1960).

Consider, for example the simple Bertrand model of price competition with identical products. As we know, the Nash equilibrium for that case is for both firms to set price equal to marginal cost. Obviously, they could both set the monopoly price and this would greatly enhance the profit of each. The problem though is that with, say, firm 1 setting the monopoly price, firm 2's best response in *not* to set that price but to undercut it. Alternatively, consider the Cournot model. We know from Chapter 9 that if demand is given by $P = A - BQ = A - B(q_1 + q_2)$ and each firm has a constant marginal cost of c, the monopoly output is $Q^M = (A - c)/2B$. Hence, to achieve the monopoly outcome each duopolist would need to produce $q_1 = q_2 = (A - c)/4B$. Unfortunately for these firms, we also know that the best response function for each is: $q_i = (A - c)/2B\text{-}q_j/2$ ($i, j = 1,2;\ i \neq j$). Hence, if one firm cooperates and produces one half of the total monopoly output, the best response of the rival is not to do the same but instead to produce three-fourths of the monopoly output, thereby driving the price below the monopoly level.[5]

We illustrate the foregoing Bertrand and Cournot cases for the specific case of a market in which demand is described by $P = 150 - Q = 150 - (q_1 + q_2)$ and in which each firm has a constant marginal cost of $c = \$30$. In each case, if the firms enter into a price-fixing agreement, they will earn maximum industry profit by agreeing to cooperate to achieve the monopoly price of $90. At that price, market demand is 60 units which we assume is shared equally between the two firms so that each earns a profit of $\pi_i{}^M = \$1,800$. In the Bertrand case, cheating on the agreement by either firm is very attractive as the assumption of identical products means that only a trivial price cut is necessary for either firm to steal the entire monopoly market from its rival and so double its profits to $3,600.

The temptation to defect from the agreement is weaker in the Cournot case but, nevertheless, very real. Here, if, say, firm 1 produces its share of the monopoly output or 30 units, firm 2's best response is to produce 45 units. With a total output of 75 units, the price falls to $75. Hence, each firm now makes $75 - \$30 = \$45$ on each unit with the result that by cheating, firm 2 now earns $2,025, a 12.5 percent increase over its profits in the joint monopoly outcome. Of course, defection by both firms is tantamount to the noncooperative

Table 14.3(a)   Payoffs ($ thousands) to cooperation (M) and defection (D) in the Bertrand duopoly game

		Strategy for Firm 2	
		Cooperate (M)	Defect (D)
Strategy for Firm 1	Cooperate (M)	($1.8, $1.8)	($0, $3.6)
	Defect (D)	($3.6, $0)	(ε, ε)

Table 14.3(b)   Payoffs ($ thousands) to cooperation (M) and defection (D) in the Cournot duopoly game

		Strategy for Firm 2	
		Cooperate (M)	Defect (D)
Strategy for Firm 1	Cooperate (M)	($1.8, $1.8)	($1.35, $2.025)
	Defect (D)	($2.025, $1.35)	($1.6, $1.6)

[5] Throughout this and succeeding chapters, we restrict our analysis to pure strategies. The reader should be aware, however, that the analysis can be extended, with some qualifications, to include mixed strategies: see, for example, Harsanyi (1973).

Reality Checkpoint

Milking the Consumer—British Retail Dairy Prices

On September 20, 2007, Britain's Office of Fair Trading (OFT) announced that it was actively pursuing charges of price fixing for milk and cheese products at Britain's four largest supermarkets—Asda, Tesco, Morrison's (Safeway) and Sainsbury's—and four of its largest dairy firms—McLelland, Dairy Crest, The Cheese Company, and Wiseman. The charge was based on coordinated price setting during the years 2002 and 2003. Ultimately, all of the firms except Tesco agreed to pay a fine of £50 ($82 million) in August of 2011. The case is interesting for at least three reasons. First, while the collusion involved the milk retailers and their dairy suppliers of cheese and fresh liquid milk, the initial push came from the dairy farmers. Because UK dairy price supports are a European Union policy, they are expressed in Euros. As the pound strengthened against the Euro in the late 1990s and early 2000s, UK farmers found the real value of raw milk prices declining and by protests and letter campaigns, pushed for payments from the dairies. Of course, the dairies could only pay the farmers a higher price if they could charge a higher price to grocery chains which, in turn, required higher retail prices.

The second point of interest is the means by which the coordination took place. The retail supermarkets were clearly aware that they could not meet directly with each other. However, each retailer did hold regular and perfectly legal meetings with their suppliers—the dairies. Soon these meetings became the locus of indirect coordination. At a meeting of its suppliers, a retailer such as Safeway would reveal that it was willing to increase its price by a certain amount provided the other retailers did the same. The date of the increase would also be discussed. Subsequently, this information was passed on to the other grocery chains when they met with those same suppliers. The result was a set of coordinated retail price increases for milk and cheese products on the order of 10 to 20 percent. About one-third of these increases were passed on to the dairy firms. Perhaps not surprisingly though, it does not appear that any of retail and wholesale price increases ever translated into higher raw milk prices for farmers.

The third interesting feature of the case is that Arla, a large dairy firm with a six percent market share, escaped any paying any fines because it was the cartel member that disclosed the price-fixing operation to OFT. This is part of the United Kingdom's leniency program designed to induce members of a cartel to come forward before they are caught. The bulk of the fines were imposed on the retailers, roughly £10 million on Sainsbury's, Tesco, and Asda, and £6 million on Morrison's. Among the dairies, Dairy Crest was fined over £7 million, Wiseman over £3 million, and The Cheese Company and McLelland a little over £1 million each.

Source: C. Binham, "Supermarkets Fined £50 Million for Price Fixing," *Financial Times* August 11, 2011; and Office of Fair Trading, "Investigation into Certain Large Supermarkets and Dairy Processors Regarding Retail Pricing Practices for Certain Dairy Products," http://www.oft.gov.uk/shared_oft/ca-and-cartels/dairy-decision.pdf.

Nash equilibrium in both the Bertrand and the Cournot cases. Tables 14.3(a) and 14.3(b) show the payoff matrices for these two games.

In short, cartel cooperation is not "natural" despite the large potential profit that it can bring because cooperation is not a Nash equilibrium for either firm. Instead, each firm's best response is always to defect from the agreement even if the rival continues to keep to it.

These situations are in fact examples of many games in which players share possibilities for mutual gain that cannot be realized because of a conflict of interest. Such games are often referred to as "prisoners' dilemma" games because one of the earliest illustrations of this case involved dealings between a prosecutor and two suspects. (See Practice Problem 14.1.)

The prisoners' dilemma is clearly a real problem for any potential cartel. Unless there is some way to overcome this conflict, it would appear that antitrust policy need not be terribly worried about cartels because logically they should not happen. Yet as we have seen cartels do happen. The evidence is compelling that collusive agreements are not uncommon and firms do pursue cooperative strategies. The prisoners' dilemma argument cannot be the full story. There must be some way that firms can create incentives that will sustain cartel agreements among them.

14.1

Practice Problem

Jacoby and Myers are two attorneys suspected of mail fraud in the small principality of Zenda. In an effort to obtain a confession, Sergeant First Brigadier Morse has had the two suspects brought in and subjected to separate questioning. Each is given the following options: (1) Confess (and implicate the other), or (2) Do Not Confess. Morse indicates to each suspect that if only one suspect confesses, she will be released in return for providing evidence against the other and spend no time in jail. The one not confessing in this case will "have the book thrown at her" and do ten years. If both confess, Morse indicates that he will be a bit more lenient and each will spend six years behind bars. When asked what will happen if neither confesses, Morse responds that he will find some small charge that he knows will stick, so that, in this case, each will do at least one year.

Using Confess and Do Not Confess as the possible actions of either Jacoby or Myers, derive the payoff matrix and Nash equilibrium for the game between these prisoners of Zenda.

In the last thirty years, economists have come to understand that there is a clear way around the logic of the prisoners' dilemma. The trick is for firms to look at their strategic interaction from a more dynamic perspective than that of the static Cournot and Bertrand models. Specifically, the firms need to recognize that their interaction is likely to be repeated over time. This allows firms to base their choice in any one period on how it will affect outcomes not only in the present but in future periods as well. With this modification it becomes possible for the firms that are party to a collusive agreement to reward "good" behavior by sticking with the agreement and to punish "bad" behavior by guaranteeing a breakdown in the cartel. However, in order to understand such a strategy we need to analyze what is called a repeated game—games in which a simultaneous market interaction is repeated, perhaps for many times. By moving from one period to many, we are changing the rules of the game.

14.2   REPEATED GAMES

Refer to the game of Table 14.3(a). Collusion between the two firms to produces the monopoly output is unsustainable in that it is not a Nash equilibrium to the single period game. Now suppose that firm 2 thinks forward a bit, knowing that its interactions with firm 1 are going to occur several, perhaps many, times. Suppose further that firm 1 has indicated that it will play cooperatively so long as firm 2 does, but that once firm 2 defects, firm 1 will never cooperate again. In that case, firm 2 might calculate as follows: "If I cheat on the cartel my profits go up to $2,025 and I gain a one-off increase in profits of $225. But then the cartel falls apart, and we revert to the noncooperative, Cournot equilibrium with profits to me of $1,600 per period, so that I earn $200 less per period than if I had not cheated in the first place. Is it worth my while to cheat?"

Quite possibly, the answer is no. Depending on how firm 2 discounts future profits and how credible firm 1's punishment actually is, the short, one-period gain of $225 from defecting may be offset by the loss of $200 every period thereafter. Whether or not this is in fact the case—whether or not firm 2's cooperation is fully reasonable—remains to be seen. Nevertheless, one can see that moving from a static one-period game to a repeated game may alter a firm's thinking in a manner that dramatically raises the profitability of cooperative, cartel behavior. When the market interaction among firms extends over a number of periods, there is the real possibility that cartel members are able to retaliate against defectors. Because potential defectors will rationally anticipate such retaliation, this punishment threat is a deterrent—stopping the noncooperative behavior before it starts.

The formal description of a strategy for a repeated game is quite complicated because current and future actions are now conditional on past actions. That is, a firm's action today depends critically on what has happened in previous plays of the game. To get some idea of how rapidly the complexity grows, consider the simple Cournot game in Table 14.3(a). Suppose that this game, which we will call the stage game, is played three times in succession. At the end of the first round there are four possible outcomes, that is, four possible histories. At the end of the second round, we have sixteen possible game histories—four second-round outcomes for each of the first-round results. By the third round, sixty-four game histories are possible—and this assumes that there are only two players with two possible actions to take in each round. Because, formally speaking, a strategy must define how a player acts at each round of play depending on the precise history of the game to that point, the complexity introduced by considering repeated games is formidable.

There are, fortunately, a few mental shortcuts available to us. The critical concept in this regard is the familiar one of Nash equilibrium. It is possible to identify the Nash equilibrium or equilibria for a repeated game relatively quickly if one keeps a few key principles clearly in mind. We can best illustrate these by working through our Cournot example.

Recall that when this game is played once its only equilibrium is that both firms defect. This is referred to as the "one-shot" equilibrium. Our interest is to see what happens when the firms interact with each other over and over again. We shall show that the key factor is whether the interaction is repeated over a finite (though perhaps large) number of periods or whether it goes on forever indefinitely. In other words, we can separate repeated games into two classes: (1) those in which the number of repetitions is finite *and known to the potentially colluding firms*, and (2) those in which the number of repetitions is infinite.

14.2.1 Finitely Repeated Games

When is it reasonable to assume that the number of times that the firms interact is finite *and known to both firms*? At least three situations come to mind. First, it may be that the firms exploit an exhaustible and nonrenewable resource such as oil or natural gas with a given total supply that will definitely be exhausted beyond a certain date. Secondly, the firms might operate in a market with proprietary knowledge protected by patents. Because all patents are awarded for a finite period, say, twenty years, the date of patent expiration can mark the date at which many new entrants emerge and cooperation ceases. For example, the antipsychotic drugs, *Zyprexa* and *Seroquel*, have recently dominated the market for treatment of schizoprenia, bipolar disorder, and other severe mental illnesses. Protected by their patents from any new rivals, the makers (Eli Lilly and AstraZeneca) of these two drugs could act as duopolists and perhaps work out a tacit collusive agreement. That becomes much less likely once the patents expire and new entrants can compete away the profits of those firms.

Finally, while we conventionally equate the players in the game with firms, the truth is that it is ultimately individuals who make the output or price decisions. The same management teams can be expected to be around for only a finite number of years. When there is a major change in management at one or more of the firms the initial game will likely end and this end can often be foreseen.

It turns out that what happens in a one-shot or stage game gives us a very good clue to what is likely to happen in a repeated game when the number of repetitions is finite. After all, a one-period game is just one that is very finite. Consider a simple extension of our Cournot game from one-period to two and determine what the equilibrium will be in this limited but nonetheless repeated setting.[6] When we do this we find that the two-period repeated game will have the same noncooperative outcome in each round as the one-shot game. To see why, consider the following alternative strategy for firm 1:

First play: Cooperate

Second play: Cooperate if firm 2 cooperated in the first play, otherwise Defect.

The idea behind this strategy is clear enough. Start off on a friendly footing. If this results in cooperation in the first round, then in the second round, firm 1 promises to continue to cooperate. However, should firm 2 fail to reciprocate firm 1's initial cooperation in the first round, that "triggers" firm 1 to then take "take the gloves off" and fight back in the second round. For this reason, this sort of strategy is called a "trigger" strategy.

The problem with this strategy is that it suffers from the same basic credibility problem that afflicted many of the predatory threats that we discussed in the preceding chapters. To see why, suppose firm 2 chooses to cooperate in the first round. Now think of firm 2's position at the start of its second and last interaction with firm 1. The history of play to that point is one in which both firms adopted cooperative behavior in the first round. Further, firm 2 has a promise from firm 1 that, because firm 2 cooperated in the first round, firm 1 will continue to do so in the second. However, this promise is worthless. When firm 2 considers the payoff matrix for the last round, the firm cannot fail to note that—regardless of firm 1's promise—the dominant strategy for firm 1 in the last round is not to cooperate. This breaks firm 1's promise, but there is nothing firm 2 can subsequently do to punish firm 1 for breaking its promise. There is no third round in which to implement such punishment. Firm 2 should rationally anticipate that firm 1 will adopt the noncooperative behavior in the last round.

Firm 2 has just discovered that any strategy for firm 1 that involves playing the cooperative strategy in the final round is not credible, i.e., it is not subgame perfect. The last round of the game is a subgame of the complete game, and a strategy that calls for firm 1 to cooperate in this last period cannot be part of a Nash equilibrium in that period. No matter what has transpired in the first round, firm 1 can be counted upon to adopt noncooperative

---

[6]   Even though the game lasts for two market periods, we will keep things simple and assume that profits in the second period are not discounted. In other words, we will assume that the discount factor $R = 1$ or, equivalently, the interest rate $r = 0\%$. See the discussion of discounting in Chapter 2.

behavior in the final period of play. Of course, the same is true when viewed from firm 1's perspective. Firm 2's best strategy in the last round is likewise not to cooperate. In short, both firms realize that the only rational outcome in the second round is the noncooperative equilibrium in which each earns a profit of $1,600.

The fact that we have identified the equilibrium in the final round may seem like only a small part of the solution that we were originally seeking—especially if the game has 10 or 100 rounds instead of just 2. However, as you may recall from the Chain-Store Paradox in Chapter 11, the outcome for the terminal round can lead directly to a solution of the entire game. Consider again our two-period repeated game. In the first round, firm 1 will now see that firm 2's best first-round strategy is not to cooperate. The only reward that firm 1 can offer to persuade firm 2 from such noncooperative action in the first round is the promise of cooperation in the future in return for firm 2 cooperating today. Yet such a promise is not credible. No matter how passionately firm 1 promises to cooperate tomorrow in return for cooperation today, firm 2 will recognize that when tomorrow actually comes, firm 1 will not cooperate. It follows that the only hope firm 1 had of dissuading firm 2 from noncooperative action in the first round is gone.

Again symmetry implies the same reasoning holds true for any hope firm 2 had of inducing cooperation from firm 1. Hence, we have identified the subgame perfect equilibrium for the entire game. Both firms adopt strategies that call for noncooperative behavior in *both* period one and period two. In other words, running the game for two periods produces outcomes identical to those observed by playing it as a one-period game.

14.2

Consider our first example, but now assume that the interaction between the firms extends to three periods. What will be the outcome in the final period? What does this imply about the incentive to cooperate in period two? If both firms believe that there will be no cooperation in either period two or period three, will either cooperate in period one?

Practice Problem

We have identified the subgame perfect equilibrium for our example when the game is played for two periods. However, as Practice Problem 14.2 illustrates, our reasoning also extends to a solution for the game whether it is played two, three, or any finite number of periods, T. In all such cases, no strategy that calls for cooperation in the final period is subgame perfect. Therefore, no such strategy can be part of the final equilibrium. In the last period, each firm always chooses not to cooperate regardless of the history of the game to that point. But this means that the same noncooperative behavior must also characterize the penultimate, or $T - 1$, period. The only possible gain that might induce either firm 1 or firm 2 to cooperate in period $T - 1$ is the promise of continued cooperation from its rival in the future. Because such a promise is not credible, both firms adopt noncooperative-behavior in both period $T - 1$ and period T. In other words, any strategy that calls for cooperative behavior in either of the last two periods can also be ruled out as part of the final equilibrium. An immediate implication is that a three-period game must be one in which the players simply repeat the one-shot Nash equilibrium three times.

We can reiterate this logic for larger and larger values of T. The outcome will always be the same Nash equilibrium as in our first example no matter how many times it is played, so long as that number is finite and known. The one-shot Nash equilibrium is just repeated T times, with each firm taking noncooperative action in every period.

The foregoing result is by no means a special case. Rather, that analysis is an example of a general theorem first proved by Nobel Prize winner Reinhard Selten (1973):

Selten's Theorem: If a game with a unique equilibrium is played finitely many times, its solution is that equilibrium played each and every time. Finitely repeated play of a unique Nash equilibrium is the Nash equilibrium of the repeated game.[7]

Introducing repetition into a game theoretic framework adds history as an element to the analysis. When players face each other over and over again, they can adopt strategies that base today's action on the behavior of their rivals in previous periods. This is what rewards and punishments are all about. What Selten's Theorem demonstrates is that history, or rewards and punishments, really do not play a role in a finitely repeated game in which the basic one-shot game has a unique Nash equilibrium.

14.2.2   Infinitely or Indefinitely Repeated Games

As noted above, there are situations in which the assumption of finite repetition makes a great deal of sense and therefore to which Selten's Theorem applies. However for many, and perhaps most, situations, firms are better regarded as having an infinite or, more precisely, an indefinite life. Google may not last forever, but nobody inside or outside this giant telecommunications firm knows of a date T periods from now at which point Google will cease to exist. Our assumption that everyone knows the final period with certainty is therefore likely to be too strong. The more likely situation is that after any given period, the players see some positive probability that the game will continue one more round. So, while firms may understand that the game will not last forever, they cannot look ahead to any particular period as the last.

Why is this important? Recall the argument that we used to show that finite repetition will not lead to cooperation in a Cournot or Bertrand game. Cooperation is not an equilibrium in the final period T, and so is not an equilibrium in $T - 1$, and so in $T - 2$, and so on. With infinite or indefinite repetition of the game this argument fails *because there is no known final period*. So long as the probability of continuing into another round of play is positive, there is, probabilistically speaking, reason to hope that the next round will be played cooperatively and so reason to cooperate in the present. Whether that motivation is strong enough to overcome the short-run gains of defection, or can be made so by means of some reward-and-punishment strategy will depend on certain key factors that we discuss below. We will see that once we permit the possibility that strategic interaction will continue indefinitely, the possibility of successful collusion becomes a good bit more real.

In developing the formal analysis of an indefinitely repeated game, we must first consider how a firm values a profit stream of infinite duration. The answer is simply that it will apply the discount factor R to the expected cash flow in any period. Suppose that a firm knows that its profits are going to be π in each play of the game. Suppose also that the firm knows that in each period there is a probability p that the market interaction will continue into the next period. Then starting from an initial period 0, the probability of reaching period 1 is p, the probability of reaching period 2 is p^2, of reaching period 3 is p^3, … of reaching period t is p^t and so on. Accordingly, the profit stream that the firm actually expects to receive in period t is $p^t \pi$.

---

[7]   A formal proof can be found, for example, in Eichberger (1993).

Now apply the firm's discount factor is R. The expected present value of this profit stream is given by:

$$V(\pi) = \pi + pR\pi + (pR)^2\pi + (pR)^3\pi + \dots + (pR)^t\pi + \dots \tag{14.1}$$

To evaluate $V(\pi)$ we use a simple trick. Rewrite equation (14.1) as:

$$V(\pi) = \pi + pR\left(\pi + pR\pi + (pR)^2\pi + (pR)^3\pi \dots + (pR)^t\pi + \dots\right) \tag{14.2}$$

Now note that the term in brackets is just $V(\pi)$ as given by (14.1), so (14.2) can be rewritten:

$$V(\pi) = \pi + pRV(\pi)$$

Solving this for $V(\pi)$ then gives:

$$V(\pi) = \frac{\pi}{1 - pR} = \frac{\pi}{1 - \rho} \tag{14.3}$$

where $\rho = pR$ can be thought of as a "probability-adjusted" discount factor. It is the product of the discount factor reflecting the interest rate and the belief the firm holds regarding the probability that the market will continue to operate from period to period.

As suggested above, repetition allows history to play a role in strategy making. In fact, many variants of the trigger strategy that would not work in the finitely repeated game will work in the infinitely repeated one. We focus on perhaps the simplest of these in which each player promises to play the cooperative action upon which all players have agreed as long as the history of the game to that point does not reveal any defections. However, if any player should deviate from the agreement then our trigger-strategy player promises to revert to the one-shot Nash equilibrium forever.

Consider again our simple duopoly example for both the Bertrand and Cournot case.[8] Suppose that the firms formulate a price-fixing agreement that gives them both profits of π^M (one half each of the combined monopoly profit). Each firm knows that if it deviates optimally from this agreement it will earn in that period of deviation a profit of π^D. Finally, denote the noncooperative Nash equilibrium profit to each firm as π^N. Common sense and our Cournot and Bertrand examples of Table 14.3 tell us that $\pi^D > \pi^M > \pi^N$.

Now consider the following trigger strategy:

Period 0: Cooperate.

Period $t > 1$: Cooperate if both firms have cooperated in every previous period. Switch to the Nash equilibrium forever if either player has defected in any previous period.

A firm whose rival is following this strategy then faces the following choice. Continue to cooperate and earn π^M or defect from cooperative play and earn π^D for one period but only π^N in every subsequent period because that defection will trigger the rival to move to the noncooperative equilibrium permanently in that following period.

---

[8]   Our analysis generalizes to an n-firm oligopoly as we note below.

The only way to compare the gain with the loss is in terms of present values. The present value of profits from sticking to the agreement is, using equation (14.3):

$$V^C = \pi^M + \rho\pi^M + \rho^2\pi^M + \ldots = \frac{\pi^M}{1-\rho} \tag{14.4}$$

In contrast, the present value of firm 2's profits if it deviates is:

$$V^D = \pi^D + \rho\pi^N + \rho^2\pi^N + \rho^3\pi^N + \ldots$$

$$= \pi^D + \rho[\pi^N + \rho\pi^N + \rho^2\pi^N + \ldots] = \pi^D + \frac{\rho\pi^N}{1-\rho} \tag{14.5}$$

Cheating on the cartel is not profitable, and so the cartel is *self-sustaining* provided that $V^C > V^D$, which requires that:

$$\frac{\pi^M}{1-\rho} > \pi^D + \frac{\rho\pi^N}{1-\rho} \tag{14.6}$$

Multiplying both sides by $(1-\rho)$ and simplifying gives:

$$V^C > V^D \Rightarrow \pi^M > (1-\rho)\pi^D + \rho\pi^N \Rightarrow \rho(\pi^D - \pi^N) > \pi^D - \pi^M$$

In other words, the critical value of ρ above which defection on the cartel does not pay leading firms to voluntarily stick by the cartel agreement is:

$$\rho > \rho^* = \frac{\pi^D - \pi^M}{\pi^D - \pi^N} \tag{14.7}$$

Equation (14.7) has a simple underlying intuition. Cheating on the cartel yields an immediate, one period gain of $\pi^D - \pi^M$. However, starting the next period and continuing through every period thereafter, the punishment for cheating is a loss of profit of $\pi^M - \pi^N$. The present value of that loss starting next period is $(\pi^M - \pi^N)/(1-\rho)$. Its present value as of today when the profit from cheating is realized is $\rho(\pi^M - \pi^N)/(1-\rho)$. Cheating will be deterred if the gain is less than the cost when both are measured in present value terms, i.e., if $\pi^D - \pi^M < \rho(\pi^M - \pi^N)/(1-\rho)$. It is easy to show that this condition is identical to that in equation (14.7). Because $\pi^D > \pi^M > \pi^N$ it follows that $\rho^* < 1$. Hence, *there is always a probability-adjusted discount factor above which a cartel is self-sustaining.*

Consider our two examples in Table 14.3. In the Bertrand case $\pi^D = 3,600$, $\pi^M = 1,800$, and $\pi^N = 0$. The critical probability adjusted discount factor above which our Bertrand duopolists can sustain their cartel is $\rho_B^* = 0.5$. In the Cournot case we have $\pi^D = 2,025$, $\pi^M = 1,800$, and $\pi^N = 1,600$. Substituting into (14.7) the critical probability adjusted discount factor above which our Cournot duopolists can sustain their cartel is $\rho_C^* = 0.529$. Practice Problem 14.3 below asks you to prove that these critical discount factors hold for *any* Cournot or Bertrand duopoly with linear demand and constant, equal marginal costs.

Suppose that both firms playing the Cournot game believe that their interaction will always be repeated with certainty, so that $p = 1$. Then the critical probability adjusted discount factor ρ_C^* corresponds to a pure discount factor of $R = 0.529$. That is, if $p = 1$, neither firm will deviate so long as the firm's interest rate r does not exceed 89 percent. Now suppose instead that both firms perceive only a 60 percent probability that their interaction lasts from one period to the next, i.e., $p = 0.6$. Now the cartel agreement is self-sustaining only when the pure discount factor $R > 0.529/0.6 = 0.882$. That is, successful collusion now requires that the interest rate r does not exceed 143.4 percent, which is a less restrictive requirement. This example points to a general result. An indefinitely lived cartel is more sustainable the greater is the probability that the firms will continue to interact and the lower is the interest rate.

14.3

Assume a duopoly and let demand be given by $P = A - bQ$. In addition, let both firms have the same marginal cost c. Show that:

a. If the firms compete in quantities, the probability adjusted discount factor must satisfy $\rho_C^* \geq 0.529$ for collusion to be sustained; and
b. If the firms compete in prices, the probability adjusted discount factor must satisfy $\rho_B^* \geq= 0.5$ for collusion to be sustained.

Practice Problem

14.3 THE FOLK THEOREM AND FACTORS THAT FACILITATE COLLUSION

Our analysis easily extends to cases where the number of firms is more than two. All we need do is to identify the three firm-level profits $\pi^D > \pi^M > \pi^N$ for each firm. Substituting these values into equation (14.7) then yields the critical probability-adjusted discount factor for each firm.

14.3.1 The Folk Theorem

Yet despite its general application, the success of the trigger strategy discussed above is far from guaranteed. To begin with, any trigger strategy is rooted in the assumption that cheating on the cartel agreement is detected quickly and that punishment is swift. If instead, detection and punishment of cheaters takes time then sustaining the cartel becomes more difficult because it allows the defecting firm to enjoy the gains for more periods and this raises the incentive to defect.

A further and related issue is that the trigger strategy employed above is potentially too harsh and unforgiving for a world of uncertainty and miscommunication. For example, suppose that market demand fluctuates within some known bounds, as shown in Figure 14.1, and that the cartel has agreed to set a price P^C or has agreed to production quotas that lead to that market price. In this setting, a cartel firm that observes a decline in its sales cannot tell whether this reduction is due to cheating by one of its partners or to an unanticipated reduction in demand. Yet under the simple trigger strategies we have been discussing, the firm is required quickly and permanently to move to the retaliatory behavior. Clearly, this will lead to some regret if the firm later discovers that its partners were innocent and that it has needlessly unleashed a damaging price war.[9]

In general, these obstacles to the use of a trigger strategy are important but they can in principle be overcome. Even if detection and punishment is not swift, it can still be effective

---

[9] Two different views of oligopolistic behavior with uncertain demand that makes detection difficult may be found in Green and Porter (1984) and Rotemberg and Saloner (1986).

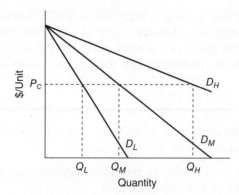

Figure 14.1 Cartel maintenance with uncertain demand
If demand is uncertain and varies between D_L and D_H with a mean of D_M, cartel members will not be able to tell whether a variation in their output is the result of normal variation in the market or cheating by other cartel members.

if the probabilistic discount factor is sufficiently large, i.e., if firms place a sufficiently large weight on the future monopoly profits that cooperation makes possible. Likewise, the issue of uncertainty can be met by adopting a modified trigger strategy. For instance, the firm might only take retaliatory action if sales or price fall outside some agreed range, i.e., the firm refrains from retaliation against minor infractions. A different modification would impose punishment swiftly after any deviation, including a minor one, is observed but limit the period of punishment to a finite period of time. Thus, we can envision a trigger strategy of the form "I will switch to the Nash equilibrium for $\tau \geq 1$ periods if you deviate from our agreement but will then revert to our agreed cooperative strategies." This approach may mistakenly punish innocent cartel members but, by limiting the period of such punishment, it permits reestablishment of the cartel at a later date.

The point is that in an infinitely repeated game there are many trigger strategies that allow a cartel agreement to be sustained. Indeed, in some ways, there are almost too many. This point is made clear by what is known as the *Folk Theorem* for infinitely repeated games (Friedman 1971):[10]

> *Folk Theorem*: Suppose that an infinitely repeated game has a set of payoffs that exceed the one-shot Nash equilibrium payoffs for each and every firm. Then any set of feasible payoffs that are preferred by all firms to the Nash equilibrium payoffs can be supported as subgame perfect equilibria for the repeated game for some discount rate sufficiently close to unity.

We can illustrate the Folk Theorem using our Cournot example. If the two firms collude to maximize their joint profits, they share aggregate profits of $3,600. If they act noncooperatively they each earn $1,600. The Folk Theorem says that any cartel agreement in which each firm earns more than $1,600 and in which total profit does not exceed $3,600 can, at least in principle, be sustained as a subgame perfect equilibrium of the infinitely repeated game. The shaded region of Figure 14.2 shows the range of profits for this example that can be earned by each firm in a sustainable cartel.

---

[10]   The term "Folk Theorem" derives from the fact that this theorem was part of the "folklore" or oral tradition in game theory for years before Friedman wrote down a formal proof.

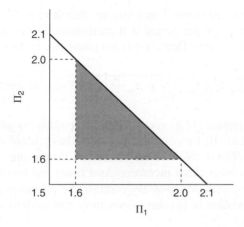

Figure 14.2   The Folk Theorem
Any distribution of profits in the shaded area can be supported by a trigger strategy for some discount factor sufficiently close to unity.

A qualifying note should be added here. The Folk Theorem does not say that firms can always achieve a total industry profit equal to that earned by a monopoly. It simply says that firms can do better than the noncooperative, Cournot–Nash or Bertrand-Nash equilibrium. The reason that exact duplication of monopoly may not be possible is that the monopoly outcome always results in the highest possible price relative to marginal cost. At such a high price, any cartel member can earn substantial short-term profit with even a small deviation from the cartel agreement. Consequently, duplicating the monopoly outcome gives members a tremendous incentive to cheat unless the probability adjusted discount factor is fairly large. Yet the incentive to deviate and break the monopoly agreement does not mean that no cartel can be sustained. Firms can still earn profits higher than the noncooperative equilibrium by means of a sustainable cartel agreement, even if they cannot earn the highest possible profits that the industry could yield. This is what the Folk Theorem says.

14.3.2   Factors Facilitating Collusion

In sum, the Folk Theorem tells us that some collusion is always a possiblility subject to two qualifications. First, the probabilistic discount factor must be sufficiently close to unity. Second, while collusion may be possible, the profit resulting from it may not be very large relative to the noncooperative outcome. It is natural then to ask under what conditions these qualifications will be important. That is, what factors make successful and profitable collusion likely?

While a complete list of all the factors that make successful collusion more likely would be very long, we concentrate here on seven factors that are particularly important. These are 1) high concentration/small number of firms; 2) barriers to entry; 3) frequent and regular orders; 4) rapid market growth; 5) technology and cost similarities; 6) product homgeneity; and 7) multimarket contact. We discuss each of these in turn.

Concentrated Markets/Small Number of Firms

We are more likely to find collusion in more concentrated markets for at least two reasons. First, increased concentration typically reduces the critical probability-adjusted discount factor ρ^*. Take our Bertrand model[11] and assume that there are n identical firms in the market. Each has profit π_m/n per period if it participates in the cartel and one-off total monopoly profit π_m if it deviates. Deviation is not profitable, therefore, if

$$\frac{\pi_m}{n}(1 + \rho + \rho^2 + \ldots) = \frac{\pi_m}{n(1 - \rho)} > \pi_m \Rightarrow \frac{1}{n} > 1 - \rho \Rightarrow \rho(n) > 1 - \frac{1}{n} \qquad (14.8)$$

Note that if $n = 2$, equation (14.8) gives the critical probability adjusted discount factor $\rho^*(2) = 0.5$ found earlier. If, by contrast, $n = 4$ we have $\rho^*(4) = 0.75$ and if $n = 10$ we have $\rho^*(10) = 0.9$. The intuition is easy to see. A firm in the cartel has to share the cooperative profits with other cartel members. As a result, the returns to collusion fall as the number of cartel members increases. By contrast, the returns to deviation typically do not decrease with n. Deviation is, in other words, more profitable as industry concentration falls, i.e., as n increases.

Hay and Kelley (1974) provide compelling support for this proposition that successful cartels are more likely in concentrated industries. Their analysis of the prosecutions of sixty-two cartels by the US Department of Justice from 1963–1972 is summarized in Table 14.4 below. These data show a direct correlation between the four-firm concentration ratio and the likelihood of cartel formation.[12]

Significant Entry Barriers

Easy entry undermines collusion because one of two things must happen when a new firm enters a cartelized market. Either the entrant does not join the cartel and then is free to compete against the cartel members forcing them to act more competitively, or the entrant joins the cartel so that the cooperative profits must now be shared across more members. In either case, the profitability of the cartel and therefore the motivation to maintain cooperative behavior is diminished.

Frequent and Regular Orders

An industry in which firms receive infrequent orders will not be one conducive to price-fixing. When orders are infrequent, it takes longer to punish a firm that cheats on the

Table 14.4 Cartels and industry concentration

Number of Conspirators	2	3	4	5	6	7	8	9	10	11–15	16–20	21–25	> 25	Total
Number of Cases	1	7	8	4	10	4	3	5	7	5	2	–	6	62
Trade Association	–	–	1	–	4	1	–	1	3	1	1	–	6	18

	Four–Firm Concentration Ratios				
Concentration (percentage)	0–25%	25–50%	51–75%	76–100%	Total
Number of Cases	3	9	17	21	50

Source: Hay and Kelley (1974)

---

[11] In the exercises, you are asked to conduct the same analysis for Cournot competitors.
[12] Concentration ratios were available for only fifty of these cartels. We comment on the importance of trade associations below. See also Posner (1970).

Reality Checkpoint

European Cartel Was, Like, Totally Tubular!

As noted in the text, the €1.5 billion fine imposed by the European Commission in December 2012 is the largest single price-fixing fine ever imposed by the Commission and the firms involved include some of world's largest electronics firms, such as LG Electronics, Philips, Samsung, Panasonic, and Toshiba. Contrary to our suggestion that market growth facilitates collusion, the cartels in this case were formed to manage a declining market, namely, the market for old-fashioned cathode ray tubes (CRT) used in TVs and computer monitors before the advent of plasma and liquid crystal display technologies. While the market for CRT tubes was still strong in 1996 when the cartel was first started, it went into decline in 2000–2001 in the wake of a general recession and the growing use of the newer display technologies. Nevertheless, the cartel survived for at least another five years and likely would have lasted longer had the Commission not begun unannounced inspections of the companies' offices and documents in 2007.

The success of the two cartels is likely due to the high degree of organization each exhibited. For the ten years of their operation, officials from each firm met regularly to fix prices, allocate market shares and specific customers, set capacity and output levels at each firm, and exchange other sensitive information. The colluders also carefully monitored each member's compliance with the agreement by reviewing production and sales at each firm and even by visiting each other's plants to insure production capacity was being held in check.

These implementation meetings also reflected the deep involvement of almost all management officials in a carefully orchestrated hierarchy of regular meetings. Top officials would meet regularly to set the main points of the agreements at golf events that to the outside eye might appear to be benign social get-togethers. Conspirators therefore referred to these top-level meetings as "green(s) meetings." This distinguished them from the meetings of lower-level management held to implement the agreements, referred to as "glass meetings," and that were held on a much more frequent monthly and sometimes even weekly basis in both Asia and Europe.

Participants in both "greens" and "glass" meetings clearly knew what they were about and that it was illegal. One uncovered document reviewing the price-setting discussion included the mandate that: *"producers need to avoid price competition through controlling their production capacity."* Another document began with the explicit warning that: *"Everybody is requested to keep this a secret as it would be serious damage if it is open to customers or European Commission,"* and many documents included the instruction: *"Please dispose the following document after reading it."*

As noted, the fines imposed are the largest the European Commission has ever levied as a price-fixing punishment. However, unlike the United States, the European Commission has no ability to level criminal charges against specific individuals and seek personal fines or imprisonment against them. Many lawyers and public policy experts consider this a major weakness in the European system.

Source: J. Kanter, "Europe Fines Electronics Makers $1.92 Billion," *New York Times* 5 December 2012, B3; and European Commission Press Release, Antitrust, "Commission Fines Producers of TV and Computer Monitor Tubes € 1.47 Billion for Two Decade-Long Cartels," http://europa.eu/rapid/press-release_IP-12-1317_en.htm, December 5, 2012.

cartel agreement and this obviously makes cheating more attractive. The math behind this intuition is straightforward. The critical discount factor ρ^* is a per period discount factor (day, week, month …) that can be converted into an annual discount factor if we know the relevant time period. The longer the time between orders, the higher the critical factor will be. Imagine, for example, that orders are monthly and $\rho^* = 0.9$. This is equivalent to an annual discount factor of $0.9^{12} = 0.28$. By contrast, if the period between orders is six months, then the annual discount factor is $0.9^2 = 0.81$. Simply put, less frequent orders implies that it takes longer to detect and punish a firm that cheats on the cartel agreement.

Irregularly sized orders also hamper collusive efforts. Take our Bertrand case, but suppose that in the current period ($t = 0$) a large order is received that has profit $\lambda\pi_m$, with $\lambda > 1$, while all later profits are expected to return to π_m per period. A slightly modified equation (14.8) gives the condition for the cartel to be self-sustaining in the face of this large order:

$$\frac{\pi_m}{n}(\lambda + \rho + \rho^2 + \ldots) = \frac{\pi_m}{n}\left(\lambda + \frac{\rho}{(1-\rho)}\right) > \lambda\pi_m \Rightarrow \lambda + \frac{\rho}{(1-\rho)} > \lambda n \qquad (14.9)$$

Solving this for ρ gives the critical probability-adjusted discount factor

$$\rho^*(\lambda, n) = \frac{\lambda(n-1)}{1 + \lambda(n-1)} \qquad (14.10)$$

Suppose that $n = 2$ and $\lambda = 1$ (no large orders). Then we have the earlier Bertrand condition that the probability-adjusted discount factor necessary for collusion must exceed $\rho(1, 2) = 0.5$. If, by contrast, $n = 2$ and $\lambda = 2$, then the critical discount factor necessary for collusion is $\rho > \rho(2, 2) = 2/3$. From equation (14.10), it is easy to show that the critical discount factor $\rho^*(\lambda, n)$ is increasing in the parameter λ. Again, the intuition is clear. The temptation to "steal" the profits from a one-time extra large order can be sufficiently great to undermine what otherwise would have been a successful cartel.[13]

Rapid Market Growth

Cartels are more likely to be sustainable in growing markets and more likely to be unstable in declining markets. Once again, the intuition is simple to see. Take the case where the market is expected to grow over time. Deviation "early" in the market's growth generates profits as usual but now runs the risk of sacrificing the larger profits that the cartel will generate as the market grows. The opposite argument applies, of course, if the market is expected to decline over time. In this case, there is a stronger temptation to cheat and get out now while the gains from doing so are reasonably good.

Technological or Cost Symmetry

Symmetry among industry firms in terms of technology and costs is another market feature that can support cartel formation. Our earlier analysis suggests one reason why this should be the case. When two firms have different costs it will be more difficult to formulate a collusive agreement that they both find satisfactory. A firm is more able to formulate a collusive agreement with a firm that "looks like" it does rather than one that does not. In

[13]   The same argument applies regarding demand uncertainty. With random demand, there will occassionally be a positive demand shock and this is essentially equivalent to a large unexpected order.

addition, detailed negotiations over prices and market shares are much more straightforward when firms are similar.

To see this point more formally, think of a Bertrand model in which each firm has a marginal cost that rises with its output. At any price set by the cartel, the firms whose marginal cost rises fastest will have the smallest output in the cartelized equilibrium. Let there be n firms in the cartel and denote the profit of firm i as firm i's share s_i times the total industry profit π_m, i.e., as $s_i \pi_m$, we can number the firms in decreasing order of their profit shares, so that $s_1 \geq s_2 \geq s_3 \geq \ldots \geq s_i \geq \ldots \geq s_n$ with, of course $s_1 + s_2 + \ldots + s_n = 1$. For firm i to be willing to remain in the cartel the condition is:

$$s_i \pi_m (1 + \rho + \rho^2 + \ldots) = \frac{s_i \pi_m}{(1 - \rho)} > \pi_m \Rightarrow s_i > 1 - \rho \Rightarrow \rho(s_i) > 1 - s_i \qquad (14.11)$$

If all the firms have equal profit shares $s_i = 1/n$ this simplifies to our "standard" Bertrand case of equation (14.8). By contrast, when profit shares are different, the firm with the lowest profit share determines the binding probability-adjusted discount factor used in equation (14.11). The smaller the share of the smallest firm, the higher that discount factor has to be for collusion to be sustainable.

Multi-Market Contact

The fact that the same firms in an industry meet many times, i.e., the fact that the game is repeated, is perhaps the crucial element facilitating collusion. It is therefore tempting to suspect that a similar force is at work when rival firms compete in several distinct markets. That is, competing against the same set of rivals in many markets at one point in time is similar in some respect to competing against the same set of rivals in one market over several periods. Cheating in one period risks punishment and the loss of cartel profits in many subsequent periods, whereas cheating in one market could risk punishment and the loss of cartel profits in the other markets. This intuition would suggest that multi-market contact should again be a feature that facilitates collusion.

Unfortunately, the foregoing intuition is somewhat misleading because time is in fact different from space. In the multi-market case a firm can cheat on all of its collusive arrangements across different markets at the same point in time whereas it requires the passage of time to cheat across different time periods. Nevertheless our intuition may well be correct when the colluding firms have asymmetric market shares in the different markets in which they compete.[14]

For example, suppose that two firms A and B each operate in two markets, 1 and 2. Let aggregate cartel profits in each market be π_m per period. The profit share for firm A in each of these markets is s_{A1} and s_{A2}, respectively, and we assume that $s_{A1} > 1/2$ while $s_{A2} < 1/2$. Hence, for firm B $s_{B1} = 1 - s_{A1} < 1/2$ and $s_{B2} = 1 - s_{A2} > 1/2$. In other words, firm A is the "large" firm in market 1 and firm B is the "large" firm in market 2. As an example, A might be a US firm and B a European firm with market 1 being the US and market 2 being the EU. To keep matters simple, further assume that the two firms have the same time preferences and the same discount rates. In other words, they have the same probability-adjusted discount factors. Finally, assume that in each market competition, if it occurs, is in prices (Bertrand).

[14] See Bernheim and Whinston (1990) for a more complete analysis of this insight.

If we treat the two markets separately, we know from our discussion in the previous section that collusion is sustainable in market 1 only if the probability-adjusted discount factor for each firm is greater than $1 - s_{B1} > 1/2$ and in market 2 only if the probability-adjusted discount factor for each firm is greater than $1 - s_{A2} > 1/2$. Now consider the two markets together. Take firm A. Firm A knows that if it deviates from the collusive agreement in either market then it will be punished in both. If firm A is contemplating deviation it should deviate in both markets. In these circumstances, for deviation *not* to be profitable it must be that:

$$(s_{A1} + s_{A2})\pi_m(1 + \rho + \rho^2 + \dots) = \frac{(s_{A1} + s_{A2})\pi_m}{(1 - \rho)} \geq 2\pi_m$$

$$\Rightarrow (s_{A1} + s_{A2}) > 2(1 - \rho) \Rightarrow \rho(s_{A1}, s_{A2}) \geq 1 - \frac{(s_{A1} + s_{A2})}{2} \qquad (14.12)$$

The analogous result applies for firm B: $\rho(s_{B1}, s_{B2}) \geq 1 - \frac{(s_{B1} + s_{B2})}{2} \rho(s_{B1}, s_{B2}) \geq 1 - \frac{(s_{B1} + s_{B2})}{2}$.

To see the point about multi-market contact let's make it simple and suppose that firm A has profit share $s_{A1} = s$ in market 1 and $1 - s$ in market 2, with $s > 1/2$ to reflect asymmetric positions. Analogously, firm B has profit share $s_{B1} = 1 - s$ in market 1 and s in market 2. From (14.12) the cartel between firms A and B is sustainable when they operate in both markets for any probability-adjusted discount factor greater than or equal to 1/2 (which is the standard Bertrand result again). However, the probability adjusted discount factor would have to be greater than s, which by assumption is greater than 1/2, if the firms collaborate in only one market. Multi-market contact can then support cooperation. What is necessary is first, that the colluding firms have asymmetric positions in the markets in which they jointly operate and second, that the asymmetry is reduced when all the markets in which they compete our considered. In our example, each firm had a share in excess of 1/2 in any one market. However, aggregated across both markets each firm has a share of 1/2.

Product Homogeneity

The empirical evidence reported in Hay and Kelley (1974) and the conventional wisdom of government authorities and the courts is that collusion is easier to sustain when the cartel members produce homogeneous or nearly homogeneous products. Again, there is an intuitive basis for this finding that stems from the complexity of the cartel agreement. First, homogeneous products implies that a price-fixing cartel has to set and monitor only one price, while by contrast, collusion in pricing differentiated products requires agreeing on and monitoring a different price for each product. This raises a second issue. Setting such a set of distinct prices when the products are differentiated requires that the cartel members agree on just how much differentiation there really is. This is a far from simple matter especially as its resolution will largely determine each firm's share of the cartel profits. Thirdly, punishment of deviation becomes more complex in a differentiated products context. Should all non-deviating firms punish a deviant or should punishment be confined to those whose products are the closest substitutes to the deviant's product? If the latter, can punishment be targeted to affect only the deviant firm or will there be spillover effects to other members of the cartel?

It should be noted, however, that there is a potential advantage to product differentiation for cartel sustainability. When the cartel members sell differentiated brands, each of which has substantial brand loyalty, then the temptation to cheat falls. If consumers exhibit considerable loyalty to their favorite brand then a deviant firm will find it hard to win much business even when it secretly cuts its price. However, the weight of the evidence suggests that cartels will be more successful—and therefore more likely—when they offer fairly homogenous products.

Other Factors

Several other important factors facilitate the formation and continuation of cartel agreements. Monitoring the cartel agreement is easier when prices are *observable*. Factors that facilitate a cartel's task of monitoring its members and responding to transgressions swiftly therefore favor collusion. Regulations that require government agencies to publish the bids they have received assist price monitoring by bid-rigging cartels. On private sector contracts, a *trade association* among the companies can help to facilitate collusive bidding behavior. The Hay and Kelley study noted above (Table 14.4) provides evidence of the importance of such trade associations in sustaining "large number" cartels.

In many consumer product markets *most-favored-customer* and *meet-the-competition clauses* can help to maintain a price-fixing agreement among firms.[15] *Most-favored-customer clauses* guarantee that if the seller offers the same product to another buyer at a lower price, the first buyer will receive a rebate equal to the difference in the two prices, whereas *meet-the-competition clauses* guarantee that a firm will match any lower price offered by another seller. It might seem surprising to think of these clauses as being anti- rather than pro-competitive but a moment's thought should indicate how they each can work to maintain cartel discipline.

The *most-favored-customer clause* severely restricts the temptation of any seller to reduce its price because the price reduction has to be offered to all previous buyers as well. Similarly, *meet-the-competition clauses* make the process of detecting cheating particularly effective, because now the firms offering these guarantees have vast numbers of unpaid market watchers in the person of every consumer who has bought the product. At the same time, such clauses effectively bind the hands of the firms that offer them.

If meet-the-competition clauses have anticompetitive effects why are consumers lured by such guarantees? A price-matching clause is valuable to any one buyer who is assured of getting the very best deal possible. However, because that buyer then becomes implicitly a monitor of prices on behalf of the colluding firms, there is an externality to the buyer's purchase of which the buyer may be unaware. Moreover, such monitoring will lead to prices being set higher (albeit identical) for all consumers. So, in fact, the equilibrium outcome will be one in which all buyers are worse off.

Meet the competition clauses can also strengthen the trigger strategies that support collusive behavior among firms. To get some idea as to just how powerful this effect can be, consider a simple one-period pricing game between two firms. The payoff matrix shown in Table 14.5 describes this prisoners' dilemma game. The one-shot nature of the game leads the firms to the only Nash equilibrium in which both firms price low. Now consider what happens when we permit both firms to publish meet-the-competition guarantees that are

[15]   See Salop (1986) for more details on these competition clauses.

Table 14.5   Pay-off matrix for a 2x2 pricing game

		Strategy for Firm 2	
		Price High	Price Low
Strategy for Firm 1	Price High	(12, 12)	(5, 14)
	Price Low	(14, 5)	(6, 6)

legally and instantaneously binding.[16] These guarantees render the off-diagonal price pairs in Table 14.5 unattainable. There is no opportunity to undercut one's cartel partner when each firm has announced a meet-the-competition policy that goes into effect immediately. Because the combinations of one firm pricing low and the other firm pricing high are unattainable, neither firm has any incentive to deviate from the Price High policy. The cartel works even in this simple one-period setting.

One way for a cartel in an unstable market to reinforce the trigger strategy is to establish a *centralized sales agency*, as in the famous De Beers diamond cartel, or a trade association. Either institutional arrangement can monitor and report upon both market conditions and individual firm performance. Monitoring may be further facilitated by agreements to divide the market explicitly, say by percentage of total sales or by geographic territory.

To summarize, cooperative price-fixing agreements are facilitated when an industry exhibits characteristics that make the detection and the deterrence of cheating easier. Such factors include the presence of only a few firms selling homogeneous products on a reasonably frequent basis and under relatively stable market conditions. All of these factors have been found to be present in the prosecution of numerous recent international cartels.[17] Agreements on market division, whether by geography or sales, also make it easier to monitor the behavior of cartel members. The potential for punishment, in some cases, violence, is greatly enhanced by such features and should never be understated.[18]

The number of price-fixing conspiracies prosecuted each year suggest that the conditions described above are often met. In turn, this is clear support for the Folk Theorem. Cartels happen. Moreover, we only know about the cartels that are detected. There may be many more collusive agreements that we do not (yet) know. The next question then becomes how policy and policy makers should deal with the potential for collusion.[19]

14.4   COLLUSION: THE ROLE OF THE ANTITRUST AUTHORITIES

While cartels may eventually fail as a result of their inherent internal conflicts, the evidence of active cartels makes it clear that the authorities cannot rely on this force alone if they wish to limit collusive agreements. Indeed, Levenstein and Suslow (2006) note in a recent survey of various cartels that "in many case studies . . . cheating was simply not a problem for the cartel" (78). Hence, the authorities will have to take explicit action themselves if they wish to limit cartel formation.[20]

---

[16]   This is perfectly legal because the price-matching guarantees are offered to buyers rather than communicated to other sellers.

[17]   See Connor (2001) for a detailed and very readable analysis of these cartels.

[18]   A number of cartels in New York City have used violence to enforce their market power.

[19]   *The Informant* (2000) by Kurt Eichenwald provides an informative and amusing illustration of the lysine
cartel that operated in the 1990s and the difficulties this case raised for the antitrust authorities.

[20]   Kaplow (2011) provides an excellent discussion of policy with respect to cartels.

14.4.1   Antitrust Enforcement: Detection and Fines

Common to all law enforcement effort, antitrust officials enforcing the prohibition of price-fixing agreements have essentially two distinct but related tools. The first of these is detection (which we will take to include successful prosecution). Stricter enforcement can take the form of closer monitoring thus increasing the probability q that the cartel will be uncovered and successfully prosecuted in any period: but only, of course, at an increased cost associated with stricter enforcement. (Such costs are why the authorities are unlikely to set q $= 1$.) The second tool is the penalty F applied when a cartel is uncovered and brought to justice. Rather than expend resources to increase the probability q that this happens, the authorities can instead raise the penalty F paid by guilty conspirators.

Modeling antitrust enforcement in terms of the detection rate q and the penalty F that is paid upon successful detection may seem quite limiting. The justification for this simplification though is that it permits the role of detection and fines to be illustrated by a reasonably simple modification of our earlier analysis. Assume that the authorities set the probability of detection q. Cartel investigation takes one period. If detected by the end of period t the cartel is disbanded at the end of the period and the firms return to the noncooperative game permanently. Detection in period t also leads to the imposition of a fine F, where F is set by the antitrust authorities. It is convenient to think of F as being backdated to the beginning of period t. We assume that the basic probability that the game will continue is as before as given by p and that this is independent of the detection probability.

Now consider what happens at the beginning of some initial period, $t = 0$. With probability $(1-q)$ the cartel is not detected in which case the cartel operates in that period and continues to period 1 with probability p. Expected profit is:

$$V_1 = (1 - q)(\pi^M + \rho V^C)$$

The first term in the second bracket is profit in the current period (0) given that the cartel is not detected. The second term uses the same reasoning as we used to derive equation (14.3). Given that cartel is not detected in period 0 the "cartel game" begins again in period 1 and so has expected profit V^C, which has to be probability discounted one period.

With probability q the cartel is detected by the end of period 0, in which case each cartel member has to pay the fine F, the cartel stops operating but the firms continue to compete in each subsequent period with probability p. Expected profit in this eventuality is:

$$V_2 = q \left(\pi^M - F + \frac{\rho}{1 - \rho} \pi^N \right)$$

Putting these equations together, the expected present value of profit for a cartel member is $V^C = V_1 + V_2$:

$$V^C = (1 - q)(\pi^M + \rho V^C) + q \left(\pi^M - F + \frac{\rho}{1 - \rho} \pi^N \right) \tag{14.13}$$

Solving for V^C gives:

$$V^C = \frac{\pi^M - qF + \left(\dfrac{\rho q}{1 - \rho} \right) \pi^N}{1 - \rho(1 - q)} \tag{14.14}$$

As before, this must be compared with the gains from defecting from the cartel, namely, $\pi^D + \dfrac{\rho}{(1-\rho)}\pi^N$. A little more algebra then reveals that the condition required for the cartel to succeed now is:

$$\rho \geq \rho^* = \frac{\pi^D - \pi^M}{(1-q)(\pi^D - \pi^N)} + \frac{qF}{(1-q)(\pi^D - \pi^N)} \tag{14.15}$$

It is straightforward to see that equation (14.15) collapses to our earlier condition (14.7), as both the probability q of uncovering the cartel and the fine F paid by price conspirators goes to zero. As both q and F rise, however, equation (14.15) shows that the critical discount factor ρ^* also rises. Yet while both q and F are important, they are not symmetric. It does not matter how large the fine F is if q equals zero because then there is zero chance of having to pay the fine. The implication of F falling to zero, though, is less severe. This would mean that the second term in (14.15) vanishes, but from the first term we can see that increases in q still work to raise ρ^*. This is because while detection does not lead to a fine any longer, it does still impose a cost on the cartel in that once uncovered, we have assumed that the cartel must revert back to the noncooperative equilibrium.

While the foregoing model is relatively simple, it does carry one very important point. This is that the role of antitrust policy is not to remedy collusive activity after it has happened but to prevent it from happening in the first place. By raising the discount factor necessary for successful cartelization, it becomes less likely that the cartel members can refrain from cheating. Take our Bertrand example. We know that $\pi^M = 1,800$, $\pi^D = 3,600$, and $\pi^N = 0$, so that in the absence of any enforcement policy, i.e., if $q = F = 0$, the critical probability factor is $\rho^* = 0.5$. However, if q alone is increased to 0.25, we then have $\rho^* = 0.67$. If, in addition, we add a penalty F equal to the firm's collusive profit of \$1800, ρ^* rises further to 0.8333. Moreover, the reality may be that the probability of detection q itself depends on how aggressively the cartel pursues monopoly profits, as noted early on by Block, Nold, and Sidak (1981). If so, then to avoid detection the cartel may need to collude on a price that, while greater than the noncooperative price, is still well below that of pure monopoly. In this case, the threat of antitrust action has a doubly preventive effect. First, by limiting the profit from collusion, it again makes collusion less likely. Second, by inducing cartel members to collude on a lower price, antitrust policy limits the harm from collusion should it still occur.

Which tool—fines or increased probability of apprehension and conviction—should the authorities use? Uncovering and prosecuting price-fixing conspiracies requires careful surveillance and legal work, which is expensive. In contrast fines may be imposed rather costlessly. This suggests that a heavy reliance on substantial punishment is likely to be the more cost-effective strategy. In turn, this helps to explain why the law imposes treble damages in private antitrust lawsuits. The general rule is that some reliance on both detection and fines is appropriate, though the latter may play the dominant role.

14.4.2   Detecting Collusion

As just noted, uncovering a price-fixing conspiracy is difficult. Knowing the conditions that make collusion more likely can help the authorities focus their scarce resources in the right places but even then detection is not easy. In practice, most detection is the result of complaints by customers and, increasingly, by one member of the cartel "finking" on its partners so as to escape or limit its own prosecution. In addition, the authorities sometimes get lucky and the conspiracy will be revealed by firms in the industry who have been unhappy either with the shares that they have been allocated in the cartel or because they have been excluded altogether.[21] However, such luck cannot be counted on as a practical procedure.

The difficulty is that detection in our sense means more than simply uncovering cartel-like behavior. It means legally proving that a collusive agreement existed. This is harder than it may at first appear because the cartel members have one very powerfull advantage over government prosecutors: they are the ones with the true information about the nature of market demand and production and transportation cost. Indeed, even if one firm admits to colluding the others can still plead not guilty. The best the authorities can do is to review market data and internal firm documents and so present as compelling a case as possible. An obvious obstacle in such effort though is that much of that data will be provided by the very same firms who are being investigated. In this setting, a collusive outcome can be made to appear to be competitive. This problem has been termed the *indistinguishability theorem* by Harstad and Philips (1990).[22]

To show the indistinguishability theorem in action, we consider a case in which the European Commission ultimately rendered a verdict against ICI and Solvay, the two firms that control the European market for soda ash, which is a raw material used in glass manufacture. ICI and Solvay had operated a number of cartel agreements for many years. Solvay supplied continental Europe while ICI supplied the United Kingdom, Ireland, and the British Commonwealth. These explicit agreements terminated in 1972, but there was no subsequent market interpenetration by the two producers. In the 1980s, prices in the United Kingdom rose some 15 to 20 percent above those in continental Europe, which the Commission argued was greater than the transport costs across the English Channel. The Commission judged that the lack of market invasion by either firm into the other's historic regional market—especially in the face of such price differentials—was strong evidence of continued tacit collusion by the two firms.

While the Commission's judgment may appear to be sound, there is a counter argument. If each firm has the same marginal cost schedule and if each sets its price equal to marginal cost plus the cost of transportation across the Channel, no cross-market penetration will ever occur. Such pricing behavior would reflect true rivalry, would lead to prices well below the collusive level, and yet there would be no market invasion of one firm by the other. Unless the regulatory agency has independent data on transportation costs, the nature of demand on each side of the Channel, and also on production costs, it cannot make a definitive case that the continued market segmentation is the result of collusive action. Given the available information, authorities may have great difficulty distinguishing between the collusive and competitive explanations of the observed data.

The situation facing government authorities is not hopeless. Careful analysis of the data can provide evidence sufficiently convincing that either a conviction or a settlement in which the cartel members agree to desist will result. Otherwise, we would see no successful price-fixing prosecutions at all. Studies by Porter and Zona (1993) and (1999) are good illustrations

---

[21] A classic example of this is the garbage-hauling business in New York, which was controlled by a trade association between firms who carved up the city between them. If a firm in the cartel took business away from another member, then the association forced the offending company to pay compensation amounting to "up to forty times the monthly pickup charge." Any firm attempting to enter the industry was met by arson and physical violence. Ex-mobsters who had been the victims of the financial penalties and violence provided some of the evidence necessary to break the cartel. (S. Raab, "To Prosecutors, Breakthrough After 5 Years of Scrutiny," *The New York Times*, June 23, 1995, p. 3)

[22] For a much more detailed exposition of the indistinguishability theorem see Philips (1995a). See also LaCasse (1995).

of the kind of hard and thoughtful work that is necessary. Both of these studies use differences between the bidding behavior of cartel members and non-cartel members to identify the former. The first of these concerned a cartel of construction firms involved in bidding on highway paving projects on Long Island in the early 1980s. Here Porter and Zona (1999) found that the while non-cartel members with losing bids had bids that were closely related to their costs, this was not true of cartel members who submitted losing bids. Similarly, Porter and Zona (1999) looked at school milk procurement auctions in which a cartel was active, but in which there were also non-cartel members bidding in the auctions. Here they found that non-cartel members' bids increased with distance from the firm to the school district, as would be expected, while cartel members' bids often decreased with distance.

Osborne and Pitchik (1987) propose a capacity-based test for detecting collusion. Recall our discussion in Chapter 12 of the Spence (1977) and Dixit (1980) models in which a large firm invests in extra capacity as part of its strategy toward rivals. Osborne and Pitchik argue that extra capacity may play a similar disciplinary role in cartels. In the case of Bertrand price competition, for example, only a firm with a large capacity can threaten retaliation against cartel cheaters. Hence, there is a reason for cartel members to acquire large amounts of capacity even if it will not be used if a collusive agreement is reached and output is held well below capacity. Yet, as Osborne and Pitchik (1987) note, it is likely that the firms choose their capacities before the collusive agreement is implemented and that therefore it is unlikely that each will choose exactly the same amount of capacity. Accordingly, when collusion subsequently begins, the price versus marginal cost distinction may be the same for each firm but the profit per unit of capacity will be greater for the firm with the smaller amount of capacity. Not only will the smaller firm have a higher profit per unit of capacity, but Osborne and Pitchik (1987) also show that this difference will increase as the total amount of excess capacity grows.[23] Philips (1995b) subsequently used this result to confirm the suspicion voiced by a number of British analysts, namely that there was a collusive agreement between the two main British producers of white salt, British Salt (BS) and ICI Weston Point (WP). He found that the BS profit per unit of capacity varied from 30 percent to over 100 percent more than the WP profit per capacity, and that this multiple increased precisely as the ratio of industry sales per unit of capacity rose.

Some recent papers suggest that a little significant price variation both across firms and over time may signal collusive activity.[24] Athey, Bagwell, and Sanchirico (2004) show that while random cost shocks would lead Bertrand competitors to change their prices from one period to the next, colluding firms will hold prices steady if they are sufficiently patient, i.e., if the discount factor is close to one.

Harrington and Chen (2006) offer a different model that has a similar result in which colluders are aware that their customers may recognize that a cartel has formed. In their model, prices rise relative to cost as the cartel forms and then stabilize with very little response to cost shocks. Here again, the collusive price tends to be somewhat rigid.

Abrantes-Metz, Froeb, Geweke, and Taylor (2006) look at a cartel comprised of suppliers of "fin-fish" (cod, haddock, perch, and flounder) to US Army bases from 1984–89. That cartel collapsed at the end of this period at which point, the average price fell by 16 percent.

---

[23]   Davidson and Deneckere (1990) offer a similar analysis.

[24]   The recent papers are similar in spirit to Sweezy's (1939) paper suggesting that each colluding firm faces a "kinked" demand curve at the cartel price. A firm that raises its price even a bit will find itself the high-priced firm and lose much of its market—the firm's demand curve is relatively flat. Yet if the firm reduces it price, it will launch a price war in which all firms cut price with little increase in the amount sold by any one firm—the firm's demand curve is relatively steep. As a result, firms tend to keep prices unchanged even in the face of shocks.

More critically, these authors note that with the cartel over, the variation in prices across firms and types of fish increased by nearly three-fold as measured by the coefficient of variation (the standard deviation divided by the mean). This tends to confirm the theoretical arguments that a lack of price variation can serve as a marker for collusive activity.

In a similar vein, Marshall, Marx, and Raiff (2008) study the famous lysine cartel of the 1990s. They find that the creation of the cartel was accompanied by a change in the nature of price announcements. Prior to the cartel, price announcements were made by different firms at different times and were close to simultaneous with the date of the price change in itself. Once the cartel was established, however, price announcements were made at much more regularly timed intervals and quickly supported by all firms. These announcements were now made with substantial lead time before the price actually changed and they seemed to bear little relation to cost.

These studies are all useful in alerting authorities to possible clues regarding the existence of a collusive agreement. Empirically however, they all have the advantage of reviewing a cartel that has already been discovered. It is the question of how best to do this that lies at the heart of the issue.

14.4.3 Leniency (Amnesty) Programs and Cartel Detection

Interestingly enough, many if not most of the antitrust success against cartels in recent years has come about as the result of a member of the cartel confessing to the authorities. The reason for this is clear. An increasing number of regulatory authorities have enacted leniency or amnesty programs as a way of combating cartels. While the actual programs enacted in different regions differ in their details, they typically have the form: "The first member of a cartel to provide evidence that leads to successful prosecution of the cartel receives lenient treatment. Everybody else is subject to heavy fines." Since 1993, the US authorities have granted complete immunity to the first firm to come forward if the authorities have not yet started to investigate. However, even if an investigation has been started, a lighter sentence or even total amnesty might still be offered. This granting of total amnesty to the first confessing firm in the absence of an active investigation has also recently been introduced in Europe and has proven central to successful prosecution of the cartels.[25] Such new programs have been wildly successful in the eyes of the authorities. As the Antitrust Division of the US Department of Justice has said:

> Today, the Amnesty Program is the Division's most effective generator of large cases, and it is the Department's most successful leniency program. Amnesty applications over the past year have been coming in at the rate of approximately two per month—a more than *twenty-fold increase* as compared to the rate of applications under the old Amnesty Program. Given this remarkable rate of amnesty applications, it certainly appears that the message has been communicated. (http://www.usdoj.gov/atr/public/speeches/2247.htm)

Why has granting amnesty proven so successful in breaking cartels? One reason is that such a program encourages finking by cartel members if they believe that an investigation has been started. Leniency programs effectively put the prisoners' dilemma to work on behalf of the authorities. However, as Motta and Polo (2003) and Spagnolo (2004), among others, have pointed out, that explanation cannot be the whole story. For while leniency

---

[25] For further details of the precise conditions under which amnesty might be granted, see the speech by the Deputy Assistant Attorney General at http://www.usdoj.gov/atr/public/speeches/2247.htm.

encourages confessions once an investigation is under way, it also raises the possibility of getting out of the cartel free of prosecution and thereby increases the expected net gains from starting a cartel in the first place.

The fundamental difficulty is really one that bedevils all attempts to measure the impact of deterrence efforts. One only sees the outcome when deterrence fails, i.e., when a cartel is formed—and caught. One does not know how many cartels are formed but escape detection and, even more important, how many cartels might have been formed but were not because of the threat of being caught and fined.

Miller (2009) addresses precisely these issues in a very original and important paper. He develops a stochastic model of endogenous cartel information and then examines what happens when an amnesty program is introduced. The model makes two very clear predictions. The first is that the introduction of the amnesty program should, if it leads to increased detection, cause an immediately noticeable rise in the number of cartels detected and prosecuted. The second prediction is that if the first prediction is validated—if the number of cartels detected rises significantly with the introduction of the amnesty

---

Reality Checkpoint
Leniency Program Succeeds—Only Too Well

The Competition Directorate of the European Commission introduced its leniency program in 2002 and updated the program in December 2006. The new program guidelines include the following provisions:

- Fines are up to 30 percent of the sales value affected by the cartel, multiplied by the number of years over which the cartel operated;
- Cartel members will also be fined an "entry fee" for joining the cartel, which will be between 15 and 25 percent of annual sales in the sectors affected by the cartel;
- Repeat offenders can have their fines doubled for a second offence, tripled for a third offence, and so on;
- Fines can be further increased for companies that do not cooperate with the Commission's investigation and for the ring-leader in the cartel;
- Fines can be decreased if a company fully cooperates with the cartel investigation.
- Companies that "blow the whistle" on the cartel receive full immunity from punishment.

The problem is that this policy appears to be almost too successful. The lure of immunity has generated more than 200 applications since 2002. While this has led to a series of high-profile successes, it also runs the risk of overwhelming the seventy specialist investigators. Even with evidence provided by immunity applicants, cartel investigations currently take at least three years to complete. The flood of immunity applications threatens to drag this out even more. In response, the competition commissioner Neelie Kroes has floated the idea of offering "direct settlements": reduced fines in return for cooperation with the cartel investigation and the promise not to appeal the Commission's final ruling. However, this proposal faces many practical and legal obstacles. So, for the time being, it looks as if the investigators will have to soldier on with their increased workload unless, of course, some of the rapidly growing revenues from fines are used to hire additional investigators!

Source: "Cartels Feel Pain of Kroes Crusade," *Financial Times*, Companies International, March 29, 2007.

program—and then falls to a rate below that observed before the amnesty program began, then one can infer with certainty that the program is deterring cartel formation. Working with US data, Miller's (2009) simulations suggest that the US amnesty program may have cut the rate of cartel formation by roughly 40 percent. That would certainly justify the claims of success for this program made by antitrust officials.

14.5 EMPIRICAL APPLICATION: ESTIMATING THE EFFECTS OF PRICE-FIXING

As noted earlier in this chapter, detecting and prosecuting price-fixing agreements requires real resources. Indeed, much of the analysis above makes clear just how difficult and therefore expensive it is to achieve a serious rate of detection. Even if cartels would otherwise be relatively common—and we think the evidence is that they would be—it may still not be cost effective to allocate any significant amount of scarce resources to combating them if they only raise prices a small amount. Moreover, the fines to be imposed on successful cartel members should in principle be related to the damage that they cause. For both reasons, we need to have estimates of the price effects of collusive agreements. In turn, this requires that the authorities, or more properly their expert econometric witnesses, estimate three sets of outcomes: the duration of the cartel, the price(s) charged and quantity (or quantities) sold by the cartel during the period the cartel is active, and the price(s) that the cartel would have charged if there had been no cartel—the "but for" price(s).

Of these, undoubtedly the most challenging is determining the "but for" price because this requires estimating something inherently unobservable in any direct manner. Several approaches have been suggested for estimating the "but-for" price. First, we could estimate key demand and cost parameters and use these to simulate a model of noncooperative behavior, thereby obtaining the "but for" price from the simulated market equilibrium. Second, we could use a before-and-after approach. That is, identify a period during which the cartel was not active and generate a measure of the prices charged in that period relative to the price observed during the operation of the cartel. Third, we could specify and estimate a reduced-form, time-series econometric model to estimate demand and supply interactions in the market and include a dummy or other variable to capture the impact of the cartel. Of these, the second and third are the most commonly used.[26]

The econometric method is typically applied[27] by estimating a reduced-form price equation of the form:

$$P_{it} = \alpha + \beta \mathbf{y}_{it} + \gamma \mathbf{w}_{it} + \delta \mathbf{s}_{it} + \lambda \mathbf{D}_{it} + \varepsilon_{it} \tag{14.16}$$

Here, P_{it} is price in region i at time t, $\mathbf{y}_{it}$ is a vector of variables that affect demand (income, prices of other goods), $\mathbf{w}_{it}$ is a vector of variables that affect supply (factor prices), $\mathbf{s}_{it}$ is a vector of market structure variables (concentration, some measure of the strength of economies of scale), $\mathbf{D}_{it}$ is a vector of dummy variables intended to capture the impact of the cartel, and ε_{it} is an error term. This is referred to as a reduced form equation because it is derived from an equilibrium condition equating demand and supply functions, which are functions themselves of underlying structural parameters that are not directly estimated.

---

[26] Connor (2001) provides a detailed discussion of the use of the before-and-after method in estimating impact of the lysine cartel.

[27] Baker and Rubinfeld (1999) discuss the use of this method.

A potential drawback of this approach is, of course, that it is very demanding on data. There needs to be sufficient "before and after" the cartel observations to give reliable estimates of the dummy variable coefficients and some of the variables in $\mathbf{w}_{it}$ such as factor costs can only be obtained with the consent of the firms that are accused of being parties to the cartel. There will often also be problems with endogeneity of the right-hand side variables requiring an instrumental-variables estimation technique, with the "correct" choice of instruments.

There are, however, examples where a variant of the econometric technique has been used with great effect. One such example is Kwoka (1997), who estimated the price impact of a long-running cartel to rig prices in a particular set of real estate auctions held in the District of Columbia.

The auctions related to properties that were either foreclosed as a result of mortgage default or were being sold under court supervision: the latter are referred to as nisi auctions. The cartel members constituted a relatively small and stable set of real estate investors who specialized in the purchase and subsequent resale of this type of property. They operated the cartel by designating a bidder who would submit an agreed winning bid at the auction while the other cartel members either did not bid or deliberately bid low. A non-cartel member who turned up at such an auction was discouraged in various ways. For example, the cartel members might make negative remarks about the property, or the non-member might be paid not to bid or might be allowed to purchase just one property. One measure of the success of this cartel at deterring entry and sustaining the cartel is that the cartel appears to have operated successfully for roughly fourteen years, from January 1976 to August 1990.

At the end of each public auction the cartel members then conducted a second, private, "knockout" auction among themselves to determine the final ownership of the property. Because this auction was conducted as a normal ascending bid auction, the property went to the high bidder: presumably the cartel member who valued the property most highly. The winner of the public auction would then be reimbursed for the price that had been paid, and the remaining difference between the public auction price and the knockout auction price would be distributed as side payments to the members of the bidding ring.

To see how this collusive arrangement works among N members in the bidding ring, we denote the true value of the property by V, the public auction-winning bid by P, and the knockout auction bid by K. Only P and K are observable. There are $N-1$ losing bidders who each receive a pay-off of S where

$$S = \frac{K - P}{N - 1} \tag{14.17}$$

Every member of the ring knows that a member will be paid at least S if the member loses in the knockout auction. The winner of the knock out gets $V-K$ and so in equilibrium $S = V-K$. In other words, the true value of the property is $V = K + S$. Using equation (14.17) this condition implies gives:

$$V = K + \frac{K - P}{N - 1} = \frac{N}{(N - 1)}K - \frac{P}{(N - 1)} = P + \frac{N}{(N - 1)}(K - P) \tag{14.18}$$

Kwoka adds a bit more structure to the model by assuming that the fixed public auction price P on which the bidding ring agreed was a "constant fraction of a property's competitive valuation." If this fraction is m then $m = V/P$. Substituting $V = mP$ in (14.18) and solving for K we have the reduced form equation to be estimated:

$$K = P + (m - 1)P\frac{(N - 1)}{N} \tag{14.19}$$

where the independent variables in the regression are P and $P(N-1)/N$ and m is to be estimated.

Members of the cartel kept detailed records of the identities of all the bidders in each auction and the payoffs made to each losing bidder. These records were central to the eventual prosecution of the cartel. They are also essential to the estimation of the cartel's impact on prices. However, of the twelve individuals that were charged with Sherman Act violations, ten pleaded guilty before trial. Because of this, data are unavailable for these cases. This left Kwoka with data for thirty of the 680 properties affected by the cartel, all of which were auctioned between 1980 and 1988.

Summary statistics for these auctions are reported in Table 14.6. The average number of bidders was 4.6 and ranged from 2 to 9. The average knockout price was 28 percent in excess of the public auction price, or, alternatively, the rigged public auction price was on average 22 percent less than the knockout price.

This is not, however, the full impact of the cartel, because we know that $V = K + S$. Moreover it can be seen from Table 14.6 that there is considerable variance in K/P. Kwoka, therefore, estimated equation (14.19) directly, obtaining the results in column (a) of Table 14.7.

In the first regression in column (a), observe that the coefficients on the two terms P and $P(N-1)/N$ are significant and have the expected signs and the fit is remarkable. In addition, the coefficient on P is (just) insignificantly different from unity, as required by equation (14.19). The coefficient on $P(N-1)/N$ is an estimate of $m-1$, giving $m = 1.86$. Because $P/V = 1/m$, this tells us that $P/V = 0.54$. In other words, the cartel results in public bid prices 46 percent lower than the true valuation of the properties being auctioned.

Kwoka then estimated two refinements on the simple model of equation (14.19). First, of the thirty properties in his sample, nineteen were foreclosure auctions and eleven were nisi auctions. Because the latter are held under court supervision it is possible that the cartel members would be more careful in their public auction bidding. Suppose, therefore, that on nisi actions we have that $V/P = m-d$. Introduce a dummy variable D that takes the value of unity for nisi auctions and zero otherwise. Then the reduced form to be estimated becomes:

$$K = P + (m - 1)P\frac{(N - 1)}{N} - dDP\frac{(N - 1)}{N} \tag{14.20}$$

The results are given in column (b) of Table 14.7. The coefficient on $DP(N-1)/N$ is the estimate of d. It has the correct sign (negative) but is statistically insignificant.

Table 14.6 Summary statistics for the auction cartel

	Mean	Minimum	Maximum
P	$25,800	$8,800	$44,800
K	$30,500	$10,800	$47,300
N	4.63	2	9
K/P	1.28	1.02	2.46

Table 14.7   Regression results

	(a)	(b)	(c)
P	0.519	0.520	0.703
	(2.18)	(2.15)	(4.47)
$P(N-1)/N$	0.860	0.879	0.481
	(2.58)	(2.58)	(2.01)
$DP(N-1)/N$		−0.045	0.014
		(0.51)	(0.23)
UNEQUAL			3501
			(3.08)
R^2	0.979	0.980	0.995
S	667	433	694

The second refinement modifies the mechanism by which losing bidders in the cartel were compensated. In some auctions, losing bidders were compensated equally while in others the compensation was based on each losing bidder's final but losing bid. The impact of unequal compensation is potentially ambiguous. On the one hand, it might make bidders more aggressive to secure themselves a higher share. On the other hand, aggressive bidding might result in a bidder winning an auction the bidder did not want to win. To test for this impact, Kwoka added a dummy variable UNEQUAL to equation (14.20) and ran the regression for the eighteen auctions in which it was possible to distinguish the compensation mechanism.

The results are given in column (c) of Table 14.7. The coefficient on UNEQUAL is positive and significant, implying that unequal compensation increased the subsequent knockout price. Moreover, the coefficient on $P(N-1)/N$ gives a revised estimate for m of 1.48, implying that the cartel rigged the public auction prices to 32.5 percent below the true property values. From this and the rest of Kwoka's (1997) results, this cartel is seen to have had an unambiguous and significant impact on the prices at which these properties were traded in the public auctions.

Kwoka's (1997) findings are broadly consistent with those of many other researchers. For example, Froeb, Koyak, and Werden (1993) found that a price-rigging scheme involved in supplying frozen fish to the US military raised prices by 23 to 30 percent. Connor (2001) found that the lysine cartel raised the market price by 17 percent, while Morse and Hyde (2000) argue the effect was twice as high at 34 percent. In two exhaustive reviews of the evidence, Lande and Connor (2005) and Connor and Bolotova (2006) find that the median cartel price effect over all time periods and across all cartel types is on the order of 22 to 28 percent, with the effect higher for international rather than purely domestic cartels.[28] All of these suggest that the losses associated with price fixing are substantial and well worth trying to combat—especially given the additional finding by Connor and Bolotova (2006) that the typical cartel lasts eight to nine years.

---

[28]   Sproul (1993) is the one contrary study, finding that industry prices rise slightly *after* an indictment, which he interprets as evidence that cartels keep costs low. Apart from notable data problems, Sproul's (1993) analysis suffers from the difficulty that indictments only come after a long investigation. If the investigation itself triggers a breakdown in the cartel, then prices will fall long before the indictment. What happens at the indictment date then gives little guidance as to the actual cartel price effect.

Summary

At least since the time of Adam Smith, there has been the fear that firms in the same industry may collude and raise prices above the level that would otherwise prevail. The good news over the last dozen years or so is that a large number of such collusive cartels have been caught and successfully prosecuted in the courts both in Europe and North America. The bad news is that this same evidence also reveals that collusion remains a real problem. Somehow firms are able to work out and implement cooperative strategies rather than noncooperative ones. So, while the competition authorities can feel good about the cartels that have been broken, they must also worry that there are many other price-fixing agreements that they have not uncovered.

It is the repetition of strategic interaction that makes cartels possible. Firms rarely meet on the corporate battlefield just once. Instead, they can expect to meet many times, and perhaps in many other markets as well. When a game is played only once, each firm has a strong incentive to cheat on the collusive agreement. Because the agreement is not legally enforceable, there is little any firm can do to deter others from cheating. However, when the game is played repeatedly over a number of periods, the scope for cooperation widens considerably. This is because a firm can threaten to "punish" any cheating on the collusive agreement in one period by being more aggressive in the subsequent periods.

While repetition of the game is necessary for firms to collude successfully, it is not by itself sufficient. In addition to the game being repeated, it must have an indefinite end point. That is, in any given period, there is always a positive probability that the game will be played one more time. Absent these conditions, Selten's Theorem makes clear that a finitely repeated game with a unique noncooperative Nash equilibrium will simply result in that Nash equilibrium being the outcome in each period. However, for repeated games that go on indefinitely, the Folk Theorem makes clear that collusion that allows for all firms to gain relative to the one-shot Nash equilibrium is possible.

We have further shown that an active antitrust policy reduces the likelihood of a cartel being self-sustaining. However, this by no means guarantees that cartels will not be formed. Based on the historical evidence, it appears that the conditions for successful collusion are often met and that when they are formed, cartels significantly raise prices—typically on the order of 20 to 30 percent above the price that competitive behavior would yield. Antitrust concern with price fixing agreements thus appears justified. In this connection, the recent tactic of granting amnesty to the first cartel member who discloses the collusive agreement to the authorities appears to have been very helpful in detecting and deterring collusive behavior.

Problems

1. Suppose that two firms compete in quantities (Cournot) in a market in which demand is described by: $P = 260-2Q$. Each firm incurs no fixed cost but has a marginal cost of 20.
   a. What is the one-period Nash equilibrium market price? What is the output and profit of each firm in this equilibrium?
   b. What is the output of each firm if they collude to produce the monopoly output? What profit does each firm earn with such collusion?

2. Return to the cartel in Problem 1. Suppose that after the cartel is established, one firm decides to cheat on the collusion, assuming that the other firm will continue to produce its half of the monopoly output.
   a. Given the deviating firm's assumption, how much will it produce?
   b. If the deviating firm's assumption is correct, what will be the industry price and the deviating firm's profit in this case?

3. Suppose that the market game described in Problems 1 and 2 is now repeated indefinitely. Show that the collusive agreement can be maintained so long as the probability adjusted discount factor, $\rho > 0.53$.

4. Suppose again that market demand is given by $P = 260-2Q$ and that firms again have

a constant marginal cost of 20, while incurring no fixed cost. Now, however, assume that firms compete in prices (Bertrand) and have unlimited capacity.

a. What is the one-period Nash equilibrium price? Assuming that firms share the market evenly any time they charge the same price, what is the output and profit of each firm in this market equilibrium?

b. What will be the equilibrium output and profit of each firm if each agrees to charge the monopoly price?

5. Return to Problem 4. Assume that the cartel is established at the monopoly price. Suppose one firm now deviates from the agreement assuming that its rival continues to charge the monopoly price.

a. Given the deviating firm's assumption, what price will maximize its profit?

b. If its assumption is correct, how much will the profit of the cheating firm be? How much will be the profit of its non-cheating rival?

6. Return again to the cartel in Problems 4 and 5. Now suppose that the market game is repeated indefinitely. What probability adjusted discount factor is necessary now in order to maintain the collusive agreement?

7. Compare your answers in Problems 3 and 6. Based on this comparison, which market setting do you think is more amenable to cartel formation, one of Cournot competition or one of Bertrand competition?

8. Once again, assume Cournot competition in an industry in which market demand is described by $P = 260-2Q$ and in which each firm has a marginal cost of 20. However, instead of two firms, let there now be four.

a. What is the one-period Nash equilibrium market price? What is the output and profit of each firm in this equilibrium?

b. What is the output of each firm if they collude to produce the monopoly output? What profit does each firm earn with such collusion?

9. Return to Problem 8. Suppose that one firm decides to cheat on the collusion, assuming

that each of the three other firms continue to one-fourth of the monopoly output.

a. Given the deviating firm's assumption, how much will it produce?

b. Assuming that its assumption is correct, what will be the industry price and the deviating firm's profit?

10. Consider again your results in Problems 8 and 9. Suppose that the market game is repeated indefinitely. Show that the collusive agreement can be maintained so long as the probability adjusted discount factor, $\rho > 0.610$.

11. Compare your answers in Problems 10 and 3. Based on this comparison, what do you infer about the ability of firms to sustain a collusive agreement as the number of firms in the industry expands?

12. Imagine that in the 1990s, the market demand for the food additive, lysine, had a price elasticity of 1.55. The structure of that market and the (assumed to constant) marginal cost per pound for each firm are shown below:

Firm	Market Share	Marginal Cost
Ajinomoto	32%	$0.70
Archer Daniels Midland	32%	$0.70
Kiyowa Hakko	14%	$0.80
Sewon/Miwon	14%	$0.80
Cheil Sugar	4%	$0.85
Cargill	4%	$0.85

a. Use elasticity, market share, and cost data above to determine the weighted average industry equilibrium price if the firms are competing in quantities.

b. During the 1990s, the lysine producers formed a (now famous) cartel that maintained the shares shown in part a. Under the cartel, the world price of lysine rose to an average of $1.12 per pound. Total world production at this time was about 100 thousand metric tons per year. A metric ton = 2,200 pounds. What was the total additional profit that the industry earned as a result of the cartel?

13. Suppose that a cartel has just been created and it includes both large and small firms,

each having different average and marginal costs curves. The cartel agreement is for each member to reduce its output by 20 percent from the current level. Suppose that the current level of industry output approximates the competitive output level. Will this 20 percent reduction rule maximize the cartel's profit? Explain why or why not.

14. It has often been noted that cartel firms tend to maintain excessive capacity. This is true, for example, in the case of OPEC (especially for Saudi Arabia). It was also true in the electric turbine conspiracy of the 1950s and, more recently, the international lysine conspiracy of the 1990s, among others. One explanation of this is that the success of the cartel inevitably leads the members to reinvest their profits in new capacity. In this view, the cartel sews the seeds of its own destruction. Based on the analysis of this chapter, can you give an alternative explanation? What implications does your explanation have for the long-run viability of the cartel?

References

Abrantes-Metz, Froeb, Geweke, and Taylor. 2006. "A Variance Screen for Collusion," *International Journal of Industrial Organization* 24 (November): 467–86.

Athey, S., K. Bagwell, and C. W. Sanchirico. 2004. "Collusion and Price Rigidity," *Review of Economic Studies* 71 (April): 317–49.

Baker, J. B., and D. L. Rubinfeld. 1999. "Empirical Methods in Antitrust Litigation: Review and Evidence," *American Law and Economics Review* 1 (Fall): 386–435.

Bernheim, B. D., and M. D. Whinston 1985. "Common Marketing Agency as a Device for Facilitating Collusion." *Rand Journal of Economics*, 16 (Summer), 269–81.

Block, M., F. Nold, and J. Sidak. 1981. "The Deterrent Effect of Antitrust Enforcement," *Journal of Political Economy* 89 (June): 429–45.

Davidson, C., and R. Deneckre 1990. "Excess Capacity and Collusion," *International Economic Review* 31 (May): 521–41.

Dixit, A. 1980. "The Role of Investment in Energy Deterrence." *Economic Journal* 90 (January): 95–106.

Connor, J. M. 2001. *Global Price Fixing: Our Customers Are the Enemy*, Boston: Kluwer Academic Publishers.

Connor, J. M., and Y. Bolotova. 2006. "Cartel Overcharges: Survey and Meta-Analysis," *International Journal of Industrial Organization* 24 (November): 1109–37.

Eichberger J. 1993. *Game Theory for Economics*, New York: Academic Press.

Eichenwald, K. 2000. *The Informant*, New York: Random House.

Friedman, J. 1971. "A Non-Cooperative Equilibrium for Supergames," *Review of Economic Studies* 38 (January): 1–12.

Froeb, L., R. Koyak, and G. Werden. 1993. "What Is the Effect of Bid Rigging On Prices?" *Economics Letters*, 42 (April), 419–23.

Green, E. J., and R. Porter. 1984. "Noncooperative Collusion Under Imperfect Price Information," *Econometrica* 52 (January): 87–100.

Harrington, J., and J. Chen. 2006. "Cartel Pricing Dynamics with Cost Variability and Endogenous Buyer Detection," *International Journal of Industrial Organization* 24 (November): 1185–212.

Harsanyi, J. C. 1973. "Games with Randomly Distributed Payoffs: A New Rationale for Mixed Strategy Equilibrium Points," *International Journal of Game Theory* 2 (December): 1–23.

Harstad, R. M., and L. Phlips, 1990. "Perfect Equilibria of Speculative Futures Markets", in R. Selten, eds. *Game Equilibrium Analysis*, *Vol. II*. Berlin: Springer, 289–307.

Hay, G., and D. Kelley, 1974. "An Empirical Survey of Price-Fixing Conspiracies". *Journal of Law and Economics*, 17 (April), 13–38.

Kaplow, L. 2011. "An Economic Approach to Price Fixing," *Antitrust Law Journal* 77: 343–49.

Kwoka, J. 1997. "The Price Effect of Bidding Conspiracies: Evidence from Real Estate 'Knockouts,'" *Antitrust Bulletin* 42 (Summer): 503–16.

Lande, R., and J. Connor. 2005. "How High Do Cartels Raise Prices?" Implications for

Reform of the Antitrust Sentencing Guidelines". *Tulane Law Review*, 80 (November), 513–70.

LaCasse, C. 1995. "Bid Rigging and the Threat of Government Prosecution". *Rand Journal of Economics*, 26 (Autumn), 398–417.

Levenstein, M., and V. Suslow. 2006. "What Determines Cartel Success?" *Journal of Economic Literature*, 44 (March), 43–95.

Marshall, R. C., L. Marx, and M. E. Raiff. 2008. "Cartel Price Announcements—The Vitamins Industry," *International Journal of Industrial Organization* 26 (May 2008): 762–802.

Miller, N. 2009. "Strategic Leniency and Cartel Enforcement," *American Economic Review* 99 (June): 750–68.

Morse, B. A., and J. Hyde. 2000. "Estimation of Cartel Overcharges: The Case of Archer Daniels Midland and the Market for Lysine," Purdue University, Department of Agricultural Economics, Staff Paper 00-8.

Motta, M., and M. Polo, 2003. "Leniency Programs and Cartel Prosecution," *International Journal of Industrial Organization* 21 (March): 347–49.

Osborne, M. J., and C. Pitchik. 1987. "Cartels, Profits, and Excess Capacity." *International Economic Review*, 28 (June), 413–28.

Phlips, L. 1995a. *Competition Policy: A Game-Theoretic Perspective*. Cambridge, England: Cambridge University Press.

Porter, R. H., and J. D. Zona. 1993. "Detection of Bid Rigging in Procurement Auctions." *Journal of Political Economy*, 101 (June), 518–38.

Posner, R. 1970. "A Statistical Study of Cartel Enforcement," *Journal of Law and Economics* 13 (October): 365–419.

Rotemberg, J., and G. Saloner, 1986. "A Supergame Theoretic Model of Price Wars During Booms," *American Economic Review* 76 (June): 390–407.

Salop, S. 1986. "Practices that (Credibly) Facilitate Oligopoly Coordination." *New Developments in the Analysis of Market Structure*, J. Stiglitz and F. G. Mathewson, Cambridge: MIT Press, 265–90.

Schelling, T. 1960. *The Strategy of Conflict*, Cambridge: Harvard University Press.

Selten, R. 1973. "A Simple Model of Imperfect Competition Where 4 Are Few and 6 Are Many," *International Journal of Game Theory* 2 (December): 141–201. Reprinted in R. Selten, 1988. *Models of Strategic Rationality*, Amsterdam: Kluwer Academic Publishers.

Spagnolo, G. 2004. "Divide et Impera: Optimal Deterrence Mechanisms Against Cartels and Organized Crime", CEPR Discussion Paper No. 4840.

Spence, A. M. 1979. "Entry, Investment, and Oligopolistic Pricing". *Bell Journal of Economics*, 8 (Spring, 1979), 1–19.

Sproul, M. 1993. "Antitrust and Prices," *Journal of Political Economy* 101 (August): 741–54.

Sweezy, P. 1939. "Demand Under Conditions of Oligopoly" *The Journal of Political Economy* Vol. 47, (August), 568–73.

Part Five
Contractual Relations Between Firms

In this part, we examine the various ways in which firms may interact that involve formal and legally enforceable contracts. Such formal relationships employ strategic considerations just as much as do the pricing and production decisions considered in the last several chapters. However, the manifestation of these tactical issues is more nuanced because, by its very nature, a formal contract involves some elements of cooperation as well as the usual ingredient of self-interest.

Chapters 15 and 16 explore the implications of the most binding of all contracts, the marriage agreement, which in the corporate world translates into the merger (or acquisition) agreement. Chapter 15 explores the issues surrounding the merger of two firms that formerly competed against each other in the same product market, a horizontal merger. We show that these happen with greater frequency than simple oligopoly models predict, and some time is taken to determine why. Of course, a merger between two former rivals may be motivated by a desire to reduce competition. Therefore, the antitrust authorities and the courts must often evaluate such mergers and try to forecast the post-merger market outcome. The empirical application in this chapter aims at illuminating recent merger simulation techniques used to evaluate the impact of proposed mergers.

Chapter 16 continues with the merger theme, this time in a vertical or conglomerate setting. Mergers between upstream and downstream firms raise interesting questions of organizational strategy and antitrust policy, such as the double-marginalization question, foreclosure of rivals, and strategic commitment. We end with a discussion of the Hortaçsu and Syverson (2007) study of vertical integration in the ready-mixed concrete industry.

In Chapter 17, we consider vertical price restraints wherein one firm, say an upstream manufacture, imposes either an upper or lower limit on the price that the retailer selling its product can charge. We show that such agreements can be potentially welfare-enhancing for both producers and consumers, but that there is also a chance that they can foster collusion and harm welfare. As an empirical analysis we offer the recent study by Smith and MacKay (2007) on the impact of the *Leegin* decision removing the *per se* illegality of vertical price restraints.

Last, in Chapter 18, we consider non-price vertical restrictions such as exclusive territories, exclusive agency contracts, and the after-market issues raised by the 1992 Kodak case. We also discussion divisionalization. We then use the Sass (2005) study of the US beer industry to provide some evidence on common non-price vertical restrictions.

15

Horizontal Mergers

The merger mania that transformed much of corporate America through the 1990s largely disappeared in the wake of the terrorist attack of September 11, 2001, the corporate scandals at Enron, Tyco, HealthSouth, and WorldCom, and the bursting of the dot.com bubble. There was a resurgence in merger activity from 2004—2008 but that also disappeared with the financial crisis that continues to affect economic activity in the United States. Despite the recent downturn in merger activity, however, there were over 9,500 new merger deals with a total value of $840 billion struck in the year ended 05/31/2011 and over 9,000 merger deals with a total value of $759 billion struck in the year ended 05/31/2012. The urge to merge may not be as strong as it was in the 1990s, but it is by no means absent.

The organization and reorganization of firms brought about by mergers and acquisitions raises several issues. Perhaps the most important of these is: why merge? What is the motivation behind the marriage of two (or more) firms? One possible answer is that a merger creates cost savings by eliminating wasteful duplication or by improving information flows within the merged organization. Similarly, a merger may lead to more efficient pricing and/or improved services to customers. This is the case when two firms producing complementary goods such as nuts and bolts merge.[1]

If the primary motivation for mergers is to reduce costs or rationalize complementary production, mergers are likely to be beneficial to society as well as to the merging firms and ought not to be discouraged. However, mergers can also be viewed as an attempt to create legal cartels. The merged firms come under common ownership and control. Hence, the new corporate entity coordinates what were formerly separate actions with a view to achieving the joint profit-maximizing outcome. By placing such coordination within the boundaries of one firm, a merger legitimizes precisely the kind of behavior that would have been illegal had the two firms remained separate. In this light, mergers can be seen as an undesirable attempt to create and exploit monopoly power in a market.

Mergers pose a difficult challenge for antitrust policy because policy makers need to be able to distinguish between anticompetitive mergers, on the one hand, and those that are not injurious to competition, on the other. This tension is openly acknowledged in the Overview to the Merger Guidelines. "While challenging competitively harmful mergers,

---

[1]   See Section 8.3 in Chapter 8.

the Agency seeks to avoid unnecessary interference within the larger universe of mergers that are either competitively beneficial or neutral."[2]

We explore these issues in this chapter and the next. We examine what economic theory can tell us about the profit rationale for mergers and whether the enhanced profit stems from greater efficiency or from enhanced monopoly power. While the relevant theory is mainly an extension of the Cournot and Bertrand models, we warn the reader in advance that it is nevertheless somewhat challenging. The rewards of a deeper understanding of mergers and merger policy justify, we hope, the necessary extra effort you will have to put in.

Before proceeding further, it is useful to classify merger types because not all mergers are alike. An important source of distinction is the nature of the relationship that exists between the merging firms prior to their combination. This gives rise to three different kinds of mergers. First, there are horizontal mergers. These occur when the firms joining together in the merger were formerly competitors in the same product market. A horizontal merger involves two or more firms that, so far as their buyers are concerned, market substitute products. The proposed 2011 merger of the mobile telecommunications carriers AT&T and T-Mobile is one example of a horizontal merger. The 2008 merger of Delta and Northwest Airlines is another.

Vertical mergers are the second type. Such mergers typically join firms at different stages in the vertical production chain. Consider the proposed purchase by Google of Motorola. These two firms are not direct competitors. Google is primarily a software and services producer, whereas Motorola is a hardware company making products designed to run, among others, Google software. The 2006 purchase of Murphy Farms, a major hog farming enterprise by Smithfield Foods, the largest pork company in the world, is a similar vertical combination. Vertical mergers include more than mergers between upstream-downstream firms. They also include any combination of firms that, prior to the merger, produced complementary goods. The merger between Hewlett-Packard, primarily a producer of software, printers, and scanners, and Compaq, a major personal computer firm, would fall in the vertical category. The merger of CSX and Conrail, two large freight rail companies in the eastern United States, provides another example. An important rationale for this merger was that the two firms provide complementary services to customers who wish to transport goods on one continuous system from the southeast of the United States to the northeast.

Finally, conglomerate mergers involve the combination of firms without either a clear substitute or a clear complementary relationship. General Electric, a firm that produces aircraft engines, electric products, financial services, and through its subsidiary NBC television programming, is one of the world's most successful conglomerate firms. Recent examples of conglomerate mergers include, (1) the purchase of Duracell Batteries by Gillette, (2) the purchase of Snapple (iced tea) and Gatorade (a sports drink) by Quaker Oats, and (3) the merger of CUC International, a health and home-shopping company with HFS, a major hotel firm.

In this chapter, we focus on horizontal mergers. Because these reflect combinations of two or more firms in the same industry, they raise the most obvious antitrust concerns. Vertical and conglomerate mergers are discussed in Chapter 16.

---

[2]   The DOJ/FTC Merger Guidelines can be read at http://www.ftc.gov/bc/docs/horizmer.htm. Section 2 on the potential adverse effects of mergers is particularly relevant.

15.1   HORIZONTAL MERGERS AND THE MERGER PARADOX

As we noted above, horizontal mergers replace two or more former competitors with a single firm. The merger of two firms in a three-firm market changes the industry to a duopoly. The merger of duopolists creates a monopoly. The potential for a merger to create monopoly power is clearly an issue in the horizontal case. Our first order of business is therefore rather surprising. It is to discuss a phenomenon known as the *merger paradox*. The paradox is that it is, in fact, quite difficult to construct a simple economic model in which there are sizable gains for firms participating in a horizontal merger *that is not a merger to monopoly*.[3] We illustrate the paradox using the Cournot model of Section 9.4.[4]

Let's start with a simple example. Suppose we have three firms, each with a constant marginal cost of $c = \$30$ and jointly facing an industry demand curve given by: $P = 150 - Q$. The Cournot equilibrium results in each firm producing one-fourth of the competitive output, or 30, so that total output is 90. The price therefore is $P = \$60$ and each firm earns a profit of $30(\$60 - \$30) = \$900$.

What happens if two of these firms merge? In the wake of a two-firm merger, the industry contains two firms, each of which produces one-third of the competitive output, or 40, so that total output now falls to 80. The price rises to $70 and each of the two remaining firms earn a profit of $1,600.

What is the market impact of the merger? First, note that the merger is bad for consumers. Output falls and price rises. Second, the merger is good news for the firm that *did not* merge. The merger allows it to expand its output to 40 units and to sell these at a higher price than previously so that it enjoys a profit increase of $1,600 - \$900 = \$700$. Finally, we come to the central element in the merger paradox. For the two firms that merge, the merger does not pay off. Previously, each firm produced 30 units and earned a profit of $900 for a combined pre-merger output and profit of 60 units and $1,800, respectively. In the post-merger market, however, these two firms have a combined output of only 40 and a total profit of $1,600. The merger has hurt the firms that merged and brought benefits to their rival. If this example is reflective of a more general result, then we ought not to observe many horizontal mergers. Of course, the paradox is that we do observe such mergers all the time.

Even more paradoxically, the foregoing example is far from being a special case. It is in fact easy to show that a merger will almost certainly be unprofitable in the basic Cournot model so long as the merger does not create a monopoly. To see this more general result, start by assuming a market of $N > 2$ firms, each of which produces a homogeneous product and acts as a Cournot competitor. The firms have identical costs given by the total cost function

$$C(q_i) = cq_i \qquad \text{for i} = 1, .., N, \tag{15.1}$$

where q_i is an output of firm i. Market demand is linear and, in inverse form, is given by the equation

$$P = A - BQ = A - B(q_i + Q_{-i}), \tag{15.2}$$

---

[3]   A merger to monopoly is when all the firms in an industry combine into a single monopoly producer.
[4]   The paradox was first formalized in a slightly different form by Salant, Switzer, and Reynolds (1983).

where Q is aggregate output produced by the N firms and Q_{-i} is the aggregate output of all firms except firm i; that is,

$$Q_{-i} = Q - q_i$$

The profit function for firm i can then be written as

$$\pi_i(q_i, Q_{-i}) = q_i[A - B(q_i + Q_{-i}) - c]. \tag{15.3}$$

In a Cournot game, firms choose their output levels simultaneously to maximize profit. The resulting profit to each firm in a Cournot equilibrium is

$$\pi_i^C = \frac{(A-c)^2}{B(N+1)^2} \tag{15.4}$$

Suppose now that $M \geq 2$ of these firms decide to merge. To exclude the case of merger to monopoly, we assume that $M < N$. Such a merger leads to an industry that contains $N - M + 1$ firms. Because all firms are the same, we can think of the merged firm as comprised of firms 1 through M.

The new merged firm picks its output q_m to maximize profit, which is given by

$$\pi_m(q_m, Q_{-m}) = q_m[A - B(q_m + Q_{-m}) - c] \tag{15.5}$$

where $Q_{-m} = q_{m+1} + q_{m+2} + \ldots + q_N$ denotes the aggregate output of the $N - M$ firms that have not merged. Each of the nonmerged firms chooses its output to maximize profit given, as before, by

$$\pi_i(q_i, Q_{-i}) = q_i[A - B(q_i + Q_{-i}) - c]. \tag{15.6}$$

In this case, the term Q_{-i} now denotes the sum of the outputs q_j of each of the $N - M$ nonmerging firms excluding firm i, plus the output of the merged firm q_m.

The only difference between equations (15.5) and (15.6) is that in the former we have a subscript m while in the latter we have a subscript i. In other words, a crucial implication of equations (15.5) and (15.6) is that, after the merger, *the merged firm acts just like any one of the other firms in the industry*. This means that all of these $N - M + 1$ firms, each having identical costs and producing the same product, must in equilibrium produce the same amount of output and therefore earn the same profit. In other words, in the post-merger Cournot equilibrium, it must be the case that the output and profit of the merged firm, q_m^C and π_m^C, are the same as the output and profit of each nonmerged firm. Using the Cournot output and profit equations for a market with $N - M + 1$ firms, these are, respectively:

$$q_m^C = q_{nm}^C = \frac{A-c}{B(N-M+2)} \text{ and } \pi_m^C = \pi_{nm}^C = \frac{(A-c)^2}{B(N-M+2)^2} \tag{15.7}$$

where the subscript m denotes the merged firm and nm a nonmerged firm.

Equations (15.4) and (15.7) allow us to compare the profit of the nonmerging firms before and after the merger. The first point to note is the free-riding opportunity afforded to the nonmerging firms when other firms merge. We know that in the Cournot model as the number of firms decreases industry output falls and price rises. Of course, a merger does just that. It reduces the number of firms. So the price rises for all firms, including those that did not merge. Moreover the merger allows those firms to gain market share while also benefiting from the increase in the market price.

What about the merging firms? There are M of these and, prior to the merger, each one earned the profit shown in equation (15.4). Hence, the aggregate profit of these firms taken together is M times that amount. After the merger, the profit of the merged firm is the profit shown in equation (15.7). Is the profit of the merged firm greater than the aggregate profit earned by the M firms before the merger? For the answer to be yes, it must be the case that

$$\frac{(A-c)^2}{B(N-M+2)^2} \geq M\frac{(A-c)^2}{B(N+1)^2} \tag{15.8}$$

This requires

$$(N+1)^2 \geq M(N-M+2)^2 \tag{15.9}$$

Note that equation (15.9) does not include any of the demand parameters or the firms' marginal costs. In other words, equation (15.9) tells us about the profitability of *any M* firm merger. All that is required is that demand is linear and that the firms each have the same, constant marginal costs.

In our example in which the number of firms is $N = 3$ and the number of firms merging is $M = 2$, it's easy to see then that the inequality in (15.9) is not satisfied. In other words, in a three-firm market satisfying our demand and cost assumptions *no two-firm merger is profitable.*

Condition (15.9) is much more general than this and turns out to be very difficult to satisfy even when more than two firms merge, as long as the merger does not result in a monopoly. To see this, suppose that we substitute $M = aN$ in equation (15.9), with $0 < a < 1$. That is, a is the fraction of firms in the industry that merge. We can then work out how large a has to be for the merger to be profitable. A little manipulation of condition (15.9) shows that for a merger to be profitable, we must have $a > a(N)$ where:[5]

$$a(N) = \frac{3+2N-\sqrt{5+4N}}{2N} \tag{15.10}$$

Table 15.1 gives $a(N)$ and the associated minimum number of firms $\underline{M}$ that have to merge for the merger to be profitable for a range of values of N, the number of firms in the industry.

Equation (15.10) and Table 15.1 illustrate what has come to be termed the 80 percent rule. For a merger to be profitable in our simple Cournot world of linear demand and identical constant costs, it is necessary that at least 80 percent of the firms in the market merge. The problem is that a merger of this magnitude would almost never be allowed by the antitrust authorities.

Table 15.1 Necessary condition for profitable merger

N	5	10	15	20	25
$a(N)$	80%	81.5%	83.1%	84.5%	85.5%
$\underline{M}$	4	9	13	17	22

[5]   You can check this equation by direct substitution of $a(N)$ in equation (15.9).

15.1

Suppose that demand for carpet-cleaning services in Dirtville is described by $P = 130 - Q$. There are currently twenty identical firms that clean carpets in the area. The unit cost of cleaning a carpet is constant and equal to \$30. Firms in this industry compete in quantities.

a.   Show that in a Cournot–Nash equilibrium the profit of each firm is $\pi = 22.67$.
b.   Now suppose that six firms in the industry merge. Show that the profit of each firm in the post-merger Cournot game is $\pi = 39.06$. Show that the profit earned by the merged firm is insufficient to compensate all the shareholders/owners who owned the six original firms and earned profit from them in the pre-merger market game.
c.   Show that if fewer than seventeen firms merge, the profit of the merged firm is not great enough to buy out the shareholders/owners of the firms who merge.

The merger paradox is that many, if not most, horizontal mergers are unprofitable when viewed through the lens of our standard Cournot model. Yet, as the events of the 1990s and even of more recent years tell us, horizontal mergers appear to happen all the time. What aspect of real-world mergers has the simple Cournot model failed to capture? Alternatively, what aspect of the Cournot model is responsible for this prediction that seems at odds with reality?

The critical aspect of the Cournot model that gives rise to the merger paradox is not difficult to find. When firms merge in the Cournot model, the new combined firm behaves after the merger just like any of the remaining firms that did not merge. Thus, if two firms in a three-firm industry merge, the new firm competes as a duopolist. The nonmerging firm in this case has, after the merger, equal status to the merged firm even though it now faces the combined strength of both of its previous rivals.

One cannot help but suspect that, for a merger of any substantial size, either the newly merged firm is different in some material sense from its unmerged rivals, or the overall market has changed in a way that alters rivals' behavior. In the next three sections, we explore such possible modifications while staying within the basic homogeneous good Cournot framework. In the subsequent section, we consider mergers in a market with differentiated products.

15.2   MERGERS AND COST SYNERGIES

In presenting the merger paradox, we assumed that all firms in the market have identical costs and that there are no fixed costs. What happens if we relax these assumptions? It seems reasonable to suppose that if a merger creates sufficiently large cost savings it should be profitable. In this section, we develop an example to show that this can indeed be the case.[6]

---

[6]   This is a special case of a much more sophisticated analysis by Farrell and Shapiro (1990) who show in a general setting that for consumers to benefit from a profitable horizontal merger of Cournot firms the merger has to create substantial cost synergies.

Suppose that the market contains three Cournot firms. Consumer demand is given by

$$P = 150 - Q \qquad (15.11)$$

where Q is aggregate output, which pre-merger is $q_1 + q_2 + q_3$. Two of these firms are low-cost firms with a marginal cost of 30, so that total costs at each are given by

$$C_1(q_1) = f + 30q_1; \, C_2(q_2) = f + 30q_2 \qquad (15.12)$$

The third firm is potentially high-cost with total costs given by

$$C_3(q_3) = f + 30bq_3 \qquad (15.13)$$

where $b \geq 1$ is a measure of the cost disadvantage from which firm 3 suffers. In these cost functions f represents fixed costs associated with overhead expenses such as those for marketing or for maintaining corporate headquarters. We now consider the effect of a merger of firms 2 and 3.

15.2.1   The Merger Reduces Fixed Costs

Consider first the case in which $b = 1$ so that all firms have the same marginal cost of 30. Suppose, however, that after the merger, the merged firm has fixed costs af with $1 \leq a \leq 2$. What this means is that the merger allows the merged firms to economize on overhead costs, for example by combining the headquarters of the two firms, eliminating unnecessary overlap, combining R&D functions, and economizing on duplicated marketing efforts. These are, in fact, typical cost savings that most firms expect, or at least state they expect, to result from a merger.

Because the merger leaves marginal costs unaffected, this is similar to our first example, only now firms also have fixed costs. Accordingly, we know that in the pre-merger market each firm earns a profit of $\$900 - f$. In the post-merger market with just two firms, the nonmerged firm earns a profit of $\$1,600 - f$ while the merged firm earns $\$1,600 - af$. Hence, for this merger to be profitable, it must be the case that $\$1,600 - af > \$1,800 - 2f$ which requires that $a < 2 - 200/f$. What this says is that a merger is more likely to be profitable when fixed costs are relatively high and the merger gives the merged firm the ability to make "substantial" savings in these costs. Note, however, that even if the merger is profitable for the merging firms, consumers are actually worse off as a result of the higher equilibrium price. That same higher price also raises the profit of the nonmerged firm. Moreover, it is still the case that the merged firm loses market share after the merger.

15.2.2   The Merger Reduces Variable Costs

Now consider the case in which the source of the cost savings is not a reduction in fixed costs but instead a reduction in variable costs which we capture by assuming that $b > 1$. In other words, firm 3 is a high variable cost firm. It follows that after a merger of firms 2 and 3, production will be rationalized and the high-cost operations will be shut down (or redesigned to operate the low cost technology). To make matters as simple as possible, we assume that there are no fixed costs ($f = 0$).

Once again, we assume a Cournot framework. The outputs and profits of the three firms prior to the merger are:

$$q_1^C = q_2^C = \frac{90 + 30b}{4}; \quad q_3^C = \frac{210 - 90b}{4} \text{ and}$$

$$\pi_1^C = \pi_2^C = \frac{(90 + 30b)^2}{16}; \quad \pi_3^C = \frac{(210 - 90b)^2}{16} \tag{15.14}$$

The equilibrium pre-merger price is[7] $P^C = \dfrac{210 + 30b}{4}$. Total output is $Q = \dfrac{390 - 30b}{4}$ with each of the low cost firms, 1 and 2, producing a greater amount than their high cost rival, firm 3.

Now, as before, suppose that firms 2 and 3 merge. Because for any $b > 1$, it is always more expensive to produce a unit of output at firm 3 than it is at firm 2, all production will be transferred to firm 2's technology. The result is that the market now contains two identical firms, 1 and 2, each with marginal costs of \$30. Accordingly, in the post-merger industry, each firm produces 40 units, the product price is \$70 and each firm earns \$1,600.

Is this a profitable merger? For the merger to increase aggregate profit of the merged firms it must be the case that

$$1600 - \left(\frac{(90 + 30b)^2}{16} + \frac{(210 - 90b)^2}{16} \right) > 0 \tag{15.15}$$

You can check that this simplifies to

$$\frac{25}{2}(7 - 3b)(15b - 19) > 0 \tag{15.16}$$

The first bracketed term in equation (15.16) has to be positive for firm 3 to have been in the market in the first place. (See footnote 7.) So the merger is profitable provided that the second bracket is also positive, which requires that $b > 19/15$. In other words, *a merger between a high-cost and a low-cost firm is profitable provided that the cost disadvantage of the high-cost firm prior to the merger is "large enough."* In the case at hand, large enough means that firm 3's unit cost is at least 25 percent greater than firm 2's unit cost. However, as we have already demonstrated, whether the merger is profitable or not, price rises and consumers are made worse off.

Together, our analysis of a merger that generates fixed cost savings and one that generates variable cost savings makes clear that mergers can be profitable when the cost savings are great enough. However, there is no guarantee that consumers gain from such a merger. Admittedly, the merger removes a relatively inefficient technology but it also reduces competitive pressures between the remaining firms. Farrell and Shapiro (1990) demonstrate that in the Cournot setting used here, the cost savings necessary to generate a gain for consumers are much larger than those needed simply to make the merger profitable. In turn, this suggests that we should be skeptical of cost savings as a justification of the benefits to consumers of horizontal mergers.

---

[7] Note that this equilibrium exists only if there is a limit on the disadvantage b for firm 3. Specifically, firm 3's pre-merger output in equation (15.14) will be positive only if $b < 210/90 = 7/3$, otherwise it will not operate in this market in the first place.

Research by both Lichtenberg and Siegel (1992) and Maksimovic and Phillips (2001) finds that merger related productivity gains and therefore marginal cost savings, while real, are typically no more than 1 to 2 percent. Salinger (2005) expresses even more doubt that fixed cost savings are substantial. Beyond all this, it is also worth noting that even with cost savings, part of our initial paradox still remains because large profit gains continue to accrue to the firms that do not merge. Why should a firm incur the headaches of merging if it can enjoy many of the same benefits by free-riding on other mergers?[8]

15.2

Practice Problem

Return to the market for carpet-cleaning services in Dirtville, now described by the demand function $P = 180 - Q$. Suppose that there are currently three firms that clean carpets in the area. The unit cost of cleaning a carpet is constant and equal to $30 for two firms and is $30b$ for the third firm, where $b \geq 1$. In addition, all firms have fixed overhead costs of $900. Firms in this industry compete in quantities.

a. What is the Cournot–Nash equilibrium price and what are the outputs and profits of each firm? What is the upper limit on b for the third firm to be able to survive?
b. Now suppose that a low-cost firm merges with the high-cost firm. In doing so, the fixed costs of the merged firm become $900a$ with $1 \leq a \leq 2$. What is the post-merger equilibrium price? What are the outputs of the nonmerged and the merged firms?
c. Derive a relationship between a and b that is necessary to guarantee that the profit earned by the merged firm is sufficient to compensate all the shareholders/owners who owned the two original firms and earned profit from them in the pre-merger market game. Comment on this relationship.

15.3   THE MERGED FIRM AS A STACKELBERG LEADER

If cost efficiencies are not a promising way to resolve the merger paradox, then perhaps a resolution can be found in some other change that gives the merged firm an advantage. One possibility is that merged firms become Stackelberg leaders in the post-merger market.[9] Recall from our discussion in Section 11.1 that the source of a Stackelberg leader firm's advantage is its ability to commit to an output before output decisions are taken by the follower firms. This permits a leader to choose an output that takes into account the reactions of the followers.

Let us assume that a merged firm acquires a leadership role and see whether the commitment power associated with market leadership can resolve the merger paradox. Certainly, such a role seems plausible. After all, the new firm has a combined capacity twice that of any of its nonmerged rivals, and so might well be able to act as a Stackelberg leader. Will this be enough to make a merger profitable? If so, what will be the response of other firms? Will they also have an incentive to merge? If they do, will their merging undo the profitability of the first merger and thereby, if firms are foresighted, discourage them from merging in the first place?

---

[8] Perry and Porter (1985) assume that each firm's cost schedule declines with the total amount of capital it owns. Hence, by merging and gaining more capital, a firm lowers its costs. The scarcity of capital makes it difficult for other firms to do this and, because of rising costs, to free-ride as much on the merger of rivals.

[9] This analysis draws on the model of A.F. Daughety (1990), who suggested this role for the merged firms.

Suppose that demand is of the usual linear form: $P = A - BQ$. There are $N + 1$ firms in the industry and each of the $N + 1$ firms has a constant marginal cost of c. We know from the standard Cournot model that the equilibrium is described by the following equations:

$$q_i = \frac{A - c}{(N + 2)B} \Rightarrow Q = \frac{(N + 1)(A - c)}{(N + 2)B} \text{ and } P = \frac{A + (N + 1)c}{N + 2} \tag{15.17}$$

The profit of each firm, $(P - c)q_i$ is therefore:

$$\pi_i = \frac{(A - c)^2}{B(N + 2)^2} \tag{15.18}$$

Suppose now that two of these firms merge and, as a result, become a Stackelberg leader. The market now contains $F = N - 1$ follower firms and one leader firm so that we now have N firms in total. Of course, the Stackelberg leader is able to choose its output first in a two-stage game. In stage one, the leader chooses its output Q^L. In the second stage, the follower firms independently choose their outputs in response to that chosen by the leader.

To find the equilibrium, we work through the game backwards. Consider the second stage of the game in which the follower nonmerged firms make their output decisions in response to the output choice Q^L of the leader or merged firm. We use the notation Q_{F-f} to denote the aggregate output of the follower firms *other than* f, and denote the output of follower firm f by q_f. Then aggregate output of *all* firms is $Q = Q^L + Q_{F-f} + q_f$. Moreover, the residual demand for firm f, which is the demand left after taking into account the outputs of the leader and the followers other than firm f is:

$$P = [A - B(Q^L + Q_{F-f})] - Bq_f \tag{15.19}$$

Marginal revenue for firm f is, therefore,

$$MR_f = [A - B(Q^L + Q_{F-f})] - 2Bq_f. \tag{15.20}$$

Equating this with marginal cost gives the best response function for firm f:

$$A - 2Bq_f - BQ^L - BQ_{F-f} = c \Rightarrow q_f^* = \frac{A - c}{2B} - \frac{Q^L}{2} - \frac{Q_{F-f}}{2} \tag{15.21}$$

Equation (15.21) is the best response of a follower firm to both the output of the leader and the output of all the other follower firms. Because all follower firms are identical, symmetry demands that in equilibrium the output of each of the follower firms must be identical. The group of followers excluding firm f has $F - 1 = N - 2$ firms. Therefore, $Q_{F-f}^* = (N - 2)q_f^*$. Substituting this into equation (15.21) and simplifying gives the optimal output for each nonmerged follower firm as a function of the aggregate output of the leader pair of merged firms:

$$q_f^* = \frac{A - c}{BN} - \frac{Q_L}{N} \tag{15.22}$$

The aggregate output of all followers as a function of the output of the leader is then

$$Q^F = (N-1)q_f^* = \frac{(N-1)(A-c)}{BN} - \frac{(N-1)Q^L}{N} \tag{15.23}$$

We can use the same basic technique to determine the output for the leader firm in stage one of the game. The residual inverse demand function for the leader firm is dependent upon the output of all the other firms, which is given by equation (15.23). So, the demand function facing leader firm l is:

$$P = A - B(Q^F + Q^L) = A - B\left[\frac{(N-1)(A-c)}{BN} - \frac{(N-1)Q^L}{N}\right] - BQ^L$$

$$P = A - \frac{(N-1)(A-c)}{N} - \frac{B}{N}Q^L \tag{15.24}$$

Its associated marginal revenue function is:

$$MR_l = A - \frac{(N-1)(A-c)}{N} - \frac{2B}{N}Q^L \tag{15.25}$$

Equating this marginal revenue with marginal cost allows us to solve for the leader firm's optimal output:

$$MR_l = c \Rightarrow Q^L = \frac{A-c}{2B} \tag{15.26}$$

You should by now recognize that the output level in equation (15.26) is just the output level chosen by a uniform-pricing monopolist. This is, of course, a standard result for a single leader model with linear demand and constant costs. In turn, this implies the following industry equilibrium values:

$$q_f^* = \frac{A-c}{2BN}; \, Q^F = \frac{(N-1)(A-c)}{2BN}; \, Q = Q^L + Q^F = \frac{(2N-1)(A-c)}{2BN};$$

$$P = \frac{A+(2N-1)c}{2N} \tag{15.27}$$

Profits for the leader and for each follower firm are then:

$$\pi^L = \frac{(A-c)^2}{4BN} \text{ and } \pi^F = \frac{(A-c)^2}{4BN^2} \tag{15.28}$$

Comparison of equation (15.28) with (15.18) reveals that for any industry initially comprising three or more firms and characterized by symmetric Cournot competition, a two-firm merger that creates a Stackelberg leader is profitable for the merged firms. This seems to resolve the merger paradox. However, equations (15.28) and (15.18) also show that the unmerged firms who have become followers are definitely worse off as a result of the merger. We may therefore expect some response from these firms.

Furthermore, if we compare the market price and output in (15.17) with that in (15.27), we find that while the merger has raised the profit of the merging parties, it also has lowered price. Hence, the merger is good for consumers. We seem to have replaced one paradox with another. We now have a model in which a merger is profitable, but that model also removes a principal reason why the antitrust authorities should object to such a merger.

However, we need to consider the response of other firms to the merger. Because leadership confers additional profit, they, too, have an incentive to merge and become leaders. This raises the question as to what happens if there is more than one two-firm merger. Daughety's (1990) model answers this question by assuming that there can be more than one leader firm and merging is the ticket to entry into the club of such leaders. That is, imagine a market that may be divided into two groups of firms: followers and leaders. The first of these groups acts just as the followers did in the preceding analysis. They compete as Cournot rivals over the demand remaining after the leaders make their output decisions. The group of leaders understands this reaction. They compete as Cournot rivals *against each other* in the knowledge that they act first and the followers take their production decisions as given.

To analyze this two-stage competition, we can use the model derived above. In particular, instead of assuming N firms with one leader and $N - 1$ followers, we can assume that there are N firms with L leaders and $N - L = F$ followers. The detailed calculations for this version of the model are presented in the Appendix. Here we concentrate on the resulting price and profit equations. These imply that in an industry comprised of N firms in total, L of which are leaders, the price-cost margin $(P - c)$, the profits for the typical leader firm $(P - c)\, q_l^*$, and typical follower firm $(P - c) q_f^*$ are:

$$P(N, L) - c = \frac{A - c}{(L + 1)(N - L + 1)} \tag{15.29}$$

$$\pi^L(N, L) = \frac{(A - c)^2}{B(L + 1)^2(N - L + 1)} \tag{15.30}$$

$$\pi^F(N, L) = \frac{(A - c)^2}{B(L + 1)^2(N - L + 1)^2} \tag{15.31}$$

You can readily confirm that the profit values shown in equations (15.30) and (15.31) for the general case of N total firms with L leaders yields the same profits as those given in equation (15.28) for the special case of N total firms and $L = 1$ leader.

It is clear from these profit equations that the leader firms are individually more profitable than the nonmerged followers. However, that is not the real issue facing two firms that are contemplating merger. The question is whether *one more merger* is profitable, given that there will then be one more leader, two fewer followers, and one less firm in total. This is why we have written the profit expressions as functions of N and L. The point is that an additional merger creates two countervailing forces. On the one hand, there are fewer firms in total, which ought to increase profits, but there are also more leaders, which ought to decrease the profits of the leaders. Which force is greater?

Suppose there is an additional merger of two followers, so that the newly merged firm and all other leaders earn profit given by equation (15.30) with N replaced by $N - 1$ and L replaced by $L + 1$ to give $\pi^L(N - 1, L + 1)$. For there to be an incentive to merge, this profit must exceed the combined profit earned by the two follower firms prior to the merger. This latter profit is $2\pi_j^F (N, L)\, 2\pi_f^F (N, L)$. So, the merger will be profitable if the following condition is satisfied:

$$\pi^L(N - 1, L + 1) = \frac{(A - c)^2}{B(L + 2)^2(N - L - 1)} > 2\pi^F(N, L) = \frac{2(A - c)^2}{B(L + 1)^2(N - L + 1)^2}$$

(15.32)

This simplifies to the condition

$$(L + 1)^2(N - L + 1)^2 - 2(L + 2)^2(N - L - 1) > 0$$

(15.33)

Note that this condition does not include the demand parameters A and B or the marginal cost c. In other words, the profitability or otherwise of this type of merger depends only on the number of leaders and followers, not on the precise demand and cost conditions.

We show in the Appendix that the condition in (15.33) is always met.[10] In other words, starting from any configuration of leaders and followers, *an additional two follower firms always wish to merge.*

This result is encouraging. It says that the Daughety model offers one way to resolve the merger paradox. A merger raises the profit of the two merging firms by allowing them to take a position as one of, perhaps several, industry leaders. Moreover, the fact that such a merger is always profitable also helps us to understand better the domino effect so often observed within an industry. Once one firm merges and becomes a leader, the remaining firms will wish to do the same rather than watch their output and their profits be squeezed.

15.3

Practice Problem

Return again to the town of Dirtville where the inverse demand for carpet-cleaning services is described by $P = 130 - Q$. Once again assume that there are twenty identical firms that clean carpets in the area, and the unit cost of cleaning a carpet is constant and equal to $30. Firms in this industry compete in quantities.

a. Show that in a Cournot equilibrium the aggregate number of carpets cleaned is $Q = 95.24$. What is the equilibrium price?

b. Suppose that five two-firm mergers occur, that these five merged firms become leader firms, and the remaining ten nonmerged firms are followers. Now there are fifteen firms in the industry. Work through the model just described and show that in the two-stage game a leader firm cleans 16.67 carpets and each follower firm cleans 1.51 carpets. Leadership certainly has its benefits! Show that the total industry output in this case will be $Q = 98.45$. What is the equilibrium price now?

c. If after the five two-firm mergers took place there were no leadership advantages conferred to the merged firms, then we would have fifteen firms competing like Cournot firms in the market. Show that in this case aggregate output is $Q = 93.75$.

---

[10] We are grateful to our colleague Professor Boris Hasselblatt of the Tufts University Mathematics Department for this proof.

While the Daughety model can resolve the merger paradox, it does leave unanswered the question as to whether such mergers are in the public interest. Is there some point at which further mergers are harmful to consumers? The answer to this question can be most easily derived from the price-cost margin $P(N, L) - c$ shown in equation (15.29). Because marginal cost c is constant, any rise or fall in $P(N, L)$ will be reflected in a rise or fall of $P(N, L) - c$.

With L leader merged firms and $N - L$ follower nonmerged firms, the price-cost margin is $\dfrac{A - c}{(L + 1)(N - L + 1)}$. An additional two-firm merger increases L to $L + 1$ and decreases N to $N - 1$, so that the price-cost margin is now $\dfrac{A - c}{(L + 2)(N - L - 1)}$. Thus for this additional merger to benefit consumers it must be the case that:

$$\frac{A - c}{(L + 2)(N - L - 1)} < \frac{A - c}{(L + 1)(N - L + 1)}$$

$$\Rightarrow (L + 1)(N - L + 1) < (L + 2)(N - L - 1) \Rightarrow N - 3(L + 1) > 0 \qquad (15.34)$$

What this tells us is that an additional two-firm merger benefits consumers only if $N > 3(L + 1)$ or, equivalently, $L < N/3 - 1$. In other words, *a two-firm merger that increases the number of leaders benefits consumers only if the current group of leaders contains fewer than a third of the total number of firms in the industry.* We know from equation (15.33) that a two-firm merger that creates a leader will always be profitable. Yet, as we have also just shown, such a merger will be harmful to consumers once the leader group includes one-third or more of the industry's firms. In other words, some mergers are bad—at least for consumers. Accordingly, we now have a model that both resolves the merger paradox and explains why the antitrust authorities are correct to worry about anticompetitive mergers.

For example, return to Practice Problem 15.3 in which we had five leader firms and ten follower firms cleaning carpets in Dirtville. In that scenario, we know that the equilibrium price for cleaning a carpet is \$31.55. Now suppose that two additional firms merge to join the leadership group. We then have a market structure of six leaders and eight followers. In this case, the equilibrium price for cleaning a carpet is \$31.60. This merger harms the consumers in Dirtville.

Daughety's model solves the merger paradox and gives rise to a merger wave by assuming an asymmetry between newly merged firms and their remaining unmerged rivals. The former gain membership in the club of industry leaders. However, this is a rather strong assumption. While some mergers may create corporate giants with an ability to commit to large production levels, it is far from obvious that every two-firm merger should have this leadership role regardless of which two firms are joined and irrespective of the number of leaders already present. In principle, Daughety's model implies that in an industry of ten firms there could be, say, eight leaders. It seems odd to imagine a configuration with so many leaders and so few followers. Moreover, it leaves unanswered the question as to what happens if two leaders merge. Does this merger create a super-leader?

It is also worth noting that while output decisions are sequential in Daughety's model, merging is not. While leader firms choose production first, it is not accurate to describe the decision to merge in a sequential way. The model simply says that for any market configuration, if a two-firm merger creates an industry leader, all follower firm pairs will

Reality Checkpoint

At First Gush: Merger Mania and Spinoffs in the Oil Industry

In August of 1998, British Petroleum or BP announced plans to merge with Amoco, another large oil firm although not quite as large as BP. The price tag was $48.2 billion making it, at the time, the biggest industrial merger ever. The new BP-Amoco would control more oil and gas production within North America than any other firm. It would also be the third-largest publicly traded oil firm in the world. (The largest firm of all, Saudi Aramco, is not publicly traded.)

Reaction from the rest of the oil industry came swiftly. Within a year, Exxon and Mobil merged in a deal worth $73.7 billion to become the largest publicly traded firm on earth. That was quickly followed by the merger of Phillips Petroleum and Conoco. Almost simultaneously, Paris-based Total acquired both PetroFina and Elf to create TotalFinaElf. Soon after, Chevron acquired Texaco for $36 billion. BP then went a step further and acquired Arco for $27 billion. The oil merger wave subsided with the economic decline of 2000–2001 but, even then, did not die altogether. Chevron acquired Unocal in 2005.

This wave of merger activity concentrated oil and gas refining and marketing into the hands of a noticeably smaller number of firms relative to the situation prior to BP's purchase of Amoco. The BP-Amoco merger was then the catalyst for a major wave of mergers and consolidations. In turn, this suggests that a common motive must be behind all these mergers. Yet whether this common factor was the naked pursuit of market power or simply the profit-maximizing response of firms to similar problems is difficult to say. The mergers were taken at a time when energy prices were quite low. Oil, for example, was selling at less than $12 per barrel in 1998. Oil prices and profits have risen dramatically since that time and, correspondingly, energy sector merger activity has stalled and, in come cases, been reversed. Indeed, in 2011, ConocoPhillips de-merged itself by spinning off its oil exploration and production activities from its oil refining and distribution activities—selling off the latter as an independent firm. In so doing, ConocoPhillips was following the decision of Marathon Oil to do the same thing earlier that year. This pattern of oil mergers and de-mergers across the energy sector suggests that the major motivation is a common technical factor—not market power.

Sources: Jim Wells, "Energy Markets: Factors Contributing to Higher Gasoline Prices," Statement of Director of Natural Resources and Environment, General Accounting Office, to US Senate Judiciary Committee, 1 February 2006; and B. Bahree, C. Cooper, and S. Liesman, "BP to Buy Amoco in Biggest Industrial Merger Ever," *Wall Street Journal*, August 12, 1998, p. A1; R. Beales and J. Bush, "The Advantages of Breaking Up," *New York Times*, August 31, 2011, p. B2.

wish to merge as well. One pair does not merge only after it sees another pair merge. Instead, at any single point in time, merging is a dominant strategy and, absent any antitrust intervention, all follower firms will pursue it. Again, this is not because of any new cost savings or product development. It is simply because merging confers leadership status. Daughety's model does not give rise to the sporadic merger waves that we often see as much as it suggests an ever-present tendency for the industry to become more concentrated.

15.4   SEQUENTIAL MERGERS

To capture the idea that merger decisions may be explicitly sequential, i.e., that the decision of one firm pair to merge is a catalyst for another pair to do the same, a number of papers including Nilssen and Sørgaard (1998), Fauli-Oller (2000) and Salvo (2010) have presented models in which a sudden change in cost or product qualities gives rise to merger opportunities that are only profitable if other mergers also occur. It is difficult for this to happen in a simultaneous game because each potential merger pair cannot be sure if others will also merge. However, in a sequential game, some firms get to make their merger decision knowing for certain that others have already merged. This greatly enhances the likelihood of a successful merger.

We illustrate the sequential merger model with a simplification of the Fauli-Oller (2000) model. Consider a four-firm industry characterized by Cournot competition. Initially, all of these firms are high-cost firms with constant unit cost $c^h = c$. Suppose that two firms have had a technical breakthrough that allows them to become low-cost firms with low constant unit cost $c^l = 0$. Industry demand is described by: $P = A - Q$.

Now consider the following sequential scenario. In period 1, low-cost firm 1 decides whether to merge with one of the high-cost firms 3 and 4. Without loss of generality, suppose that firm 1 chooses whether or not to merge with firm 3. In period 2 low-cost firm 2, having observed firm 1's decision, decides whether or not to merge with the remaining high-cost firm 4. The game ends after period 2. To determine the subgame perfect equilibrium we need the pay-offs detailed in Table 15.2. Clearly, for these to make sense we must have $A > 3c$ otherwise a high-cost firm cannot be active in the no-merger case.

Rather than work with this general case, we consider a specific example in which $A = 100$ and $c = 10$. This gives the profits reported in Table 15.3.

First note that a merger in period 1 by firms 1 and 3 *not* followed by a merger of firms 2 and 4 is unprofitable for the merged firms. Merger gives them a combined profit of $756.25 whereas not merging gives aggregate profit to these two firms of $(576 + 196) = $772.

Table 15.2   Pay-offs for the sequential merger game

Number of Mergers	Profit of Low-Cost Firm	Profit of High-Cost Firm
No Mergers	$\dfrac{(A + 2c)^2}{25}$	$\dfrac{(A - 3c)^2}{25}$
One Merger	$\dfrac{(A + c)^2}{16}$	$\dfrac{(A - 3c)^2}{16}$
Two Mergers	$\dfrac{A^2}{9}$	NA

Table 15.3   Pay-offs for the sequential merger game

Number of Mergers	Profit of Low-Cost Firm	Profit of High-Cost Firm
No Mergers	$576	$196
One Merger	$756.25	$306.25
Two Mergers	$1,111.11	NA

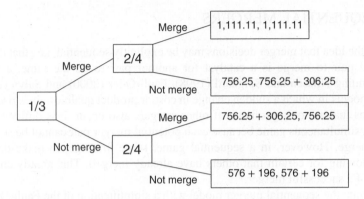

Figure 15.1 Sequential mergers

What we now show is that assuming mergers to be sequential actually leads to merger being profitable in our example.

The extensive form of the game is illustrated in Figure 15.1. In formulating the game, we assume that a merger offer will not be made unless the post-merger profit of the merged entity is greater than the aggregate profit of the two firms pre-merger. If this were not the case, no merger offer could be made that is satisfactory to both firms. Thus the pay-offs in Figure 15.1 for a pair of unmerged firms are aggregate profits As usual we solve this game backwards.

Suppose first that firms 1 and 3 choose to merge. If firms 2 and 4 choose not to merge they earn aggregate profit \$(756.25 + 306.25) = \$1062.50 whereas if they merge they earn profit \$1,111.11. They will choose to merge. Suppose instead that firms 1 and 3 choose not to merge. If firms 2 and 4 also choose not to merge they earn aggregate profit \$(576 + 196) = \$772 whereas if they merge they earn profit \$756.25. They will choose not to merge.

Firms 1 and 3 can now see that if they merge this will be followed by a merger of firms 2 and 4, with the result that firms 1 and 3 as a merged entity earns profit \$1,111.11. By contrast, if firms 1 and 3 do not merge, firms 2 and 4 will also choose not to merge, with the result that firms 1 and 3 earn aggregate profit of \$772. Firms 1 and 3 will therefore choose to merge, in the knowledge that their merger will be followed in the next period by a merger of firms 2 and 4. As a result, we can expect a merger wave in which first one pair merges and then the second pair merges. In other words, conditional on the first merger taking place, the second merger is profitable. In effect, the sequential nature of the game allows the first pair to commit credibly to merging. In turn, this means that the second merger pair does not have to worry that in merging they may be acting alone.

Such a merger wave is, however, not good for consumers. Prior to either merger talking place price is $(A + 2c)/5 = \$24$ whereas after the merger wave it is $A/3 = \$33.33$.

The foregoing story is not limited to just two mergers or to models of Cournot competition. Once cost asymmetries or product quality differences are introduced, we can construct sequential merger models that lead to merger waves for a large number of firms in a variety of settings, e.g., Nilssen and Sørgaard (1998) and Salvo (2006), and these mergers are also anticompetitive. This approach offers another resolution to the merger paradox not simply because it demonstrates why mergers may happen but, in addition, why they often happen in sequential waves. As with Daughety's (1990) model, these models also justify concern over the impact that mergers may have on consumer prices.

15.5   HORIZONTAL MERGERS AND PRODUCT DIFFERENTIATION

Our analysis of mergers has so far been set in the Cournot framework of identical products and quantity competition. However, many firms expend considerable effort differentiating their products and this differentiation gives them some latitude in setting their price. Accordingly, we also need to consider the incentives for and the impact of mergers in industries in which firms produce and market differentiated products.

It is particularly important to explore the merger phenomenon in differentiated product markets for at least two reasons. First, firms are often price setters in such markets and the nature of competition is different with price competition than with quantity competition. In quantity competition, firms' best response functions are downward sloping, i.e., quantities are strategic substitutes. Thus, when merging occurs, the nonmerged firms want to *increase* their outputs in response to the lower output produced by the merger. This response undermines the effectiveness of the merger. By contrast, with price competition, best response functions are upward sloping: prices are strategic complements. A merger leading to an increase in the merged firms' price(s) will encourage the nonmerged firms also to increase their prices, potentially strengthening the effectiveness of the merger.

Second, we saw that one reason for the merger paradox under Cournot competition is that the merged firm looks no different from a nonmerged firm. If m firms merge, effectively $m - 1$ of them disappear. This is not the case with differentiated products. Merger allows coordination of the prices of the products offered by the merged firm *and also* allows the merged firm to keep all m products on the market.

We develop this intuition more explicitly using two different approaches to product differentiation. The first approach is to extend our standard linear demand representation of consumer preferences to incorporate product differentiation. The second is to adopt the spatial model of horizontal differentiation, which we first introduced in Chapter 4 and then revisited in Chapter 10.[11]

15.5.1   Bertrand Competition and Merger with Linear Demand Systems

Suppose that there are three firms in the market, each producing a single differentiated product.[12] Inverse demand for each of the three products is assumed to be given by:

$$p_1 = A - Bq_1 - s(q_2 + q_3)$$
$$p_2 = A - Bq_2 - s(q_1 + q_3) \qquad (0 \leq s < B)$$
$$p_3 = A - Bq_3 - s(q_1 + q_2) \tag{15.35}$$

In these inverse demand functions, the parameter s measures how similar the three products are to each other. If $s = 0$ the products are totally differentiated. In this case, each firm

---

[11]   The spatial model was first formulated in Hotelling (1929), and subsequently extended in Schmalensee (1978) and Salop (1979). We saw in Chapters 4, 7, and 10 that this sort of spatial model has proven insightful in analyzing a variety of topics in industrial organization, including brand proliferation in the ready-to-eat breakfast cereal industry, Schmalensee (1978), and the effects of deregulation of transport services such as airlines or passenger buses, Greenhut, Norman, and Greenhut (1991). It is not surprising that the spatial model is also useful in analyzing mergers of firms selling differentiated products.

[12]   An excellent development of the full analysis can be found in Deneckere and Davidson (1985).

is effectively a monopolist. By contrast, as s approaches B the three products become increasingly identical, moving us closer to the homogeneous product case. We also assume that the three firms have identical marginal costs of c per unit. Finally, assume that the three firms are Bertrand competitors, i.e., they compete in prices and set their prices simultaneously.

We show in the Appendix to this chapter that when these firms compete they each set a price of $p_{nm}^* = \dfrac{A(B - s) + c(B + s)}{2B}$ and each sell quantity $q_{nm}^* = \dfrac{(A - c)(B + s)}{2B(B + 2s)}$. Profit of each firm is

$$\pi_{nm}^* = \frac{(A - c)^2(B - s)(B + s)}{4B^2(B + 2s)} \tag{15.36}$$

Now suppose that firms 1 and 2 merge but that the merged and nonmerged firms continue to set their prices simultaneously. The two previously independent, single-product firms are now product divisions of a two-product merged firm, coordinating their prices to maximize the joint profit of the two divisions. The result is that the merged firm sets its product prices to $p_1^m = p_2^m = \dfrac{A(2B + 3s)(B - s) + c(2B + s)(B + s)}{2(2B^2 + 2Bs - s^2)}$ while the remaining nonmerged firm 3 sets its product price as $p_3^{nm} = \dfrac{A(B + s)(B - s) + cB(B + 2s)}{(2B^2 + 2Bs - s^2)}$.

It is straightforward to confirm that the merger increased the prices of all three products, as we might have expected because the merger reduces competitive pressures in the market. However, there remains the question of the merger's profitability. The profits of each product division (1 and 2) of the merged firm, and the profit of the independent nonmerged firm 3 are, respectively:

$$\pi_1^m = \pi_2^m = \frac{(A - c)^2 B(B - s)(2B + 3s)^2}{4(B + 2s)(2B^2 + 2Bs - s^2)^2}; \pi_3^m = \frac{(A - c)^2(B - s)(B + s)^3}{(B + 2s)(2B^2 + 2Bs - s^2)^2} \tag{15.37}$$

In comparing equations (15.37) and (15.36), we can simplify matters by normalizing $A - c = 1$ and $B = 1$, so that profits are functions solely of the degree of product differentiation s. It is then easy to confirm that this two-firm merger is profitable for the merged firm *and* for the nonmerged firm. More generally, Deneckere and Davidson (1985) show that in a market containing N firms, any merger of $M \geq 2$ firms is profitable for the merged firms and for the nonmerged firms. This simple framework of price setting in a product differentiated market avoids the merger paradox, suggesting that mergers are both profitable and of potential concern to antitrust authorities unless accompanied by cost efficiencies.

15.5.2   Mergers in a Spatial Market

In the spatial model, a merger between two firms may well bring increased profit for reasons similar to those in the previous section. Although merging means that the firms lose their separate identity, they do not lose the ownership or control of the product varieties they offer. For example, the merger of two major banks, Bank of America and Fleet Bank, results in a single new corporate entity. Yet it does not require that the new firm give up any of the locations at which either Bank of America or Fleet currently operate—or that it lose control over the choice of moving some of those locations. Similarly, the acquisition many years ago of American Motors by Chrysler did not mean that the Jeep product line disappeared.

When we consider a firm's product lines, there is a second source of potential profit increase. The merged firms can now coordinate not just the prices but also the design of their product line, or in the context of the spatial model, their location choices. Chrysler can redesign the Jeep line to fit better in its overall range of models. Similarly, Bank of America and Fleet can change the locations of their branches in those areas where each formerly operated an outlet quite close to the other.

To investigate the impact of a merger in the spatial model, we begin by recalling the basic setup of the model.[13] There is a group of consumers who are uniformly distributed over a linear market of length L. Again, we can think of this as Main Street in Littlesville. However, one small problem with the Main Street analogy is that outlets at either end of the market can only reach consumers on one side. This restriction introduces an asymmetry in the model, which we would like to avoid. To make the product differentiated market symmetric, we can bend the ends of the line around until they touch each other, and replace our straight line of length L with a circle of circumference L. For example, if we use the spatial model to represent departure times in the differentiated passenger airline market, the circle represents the twenty-four hours of the day over which consumers differ in terms of their most preferred time of departure. In all other respects, the spatial model remains as before.

Each consumer has an "address" indicating the consumer's location on the circle and, hence, the consumer's most preferred product type. Each consumer is also willing to buy at most one unit of a particular good. The consumer's reservation price for the most preferred good is denoted by V. Different varieties of the good are offered by the firms that are also located on Main Street—or, more appropriately, Main Circle.[14] A consumer buys from the firm that offers the product at the lowest price, taking into account the costs of transporting the good from the firm's address to the consumer's. We assume that these transport costs are linear in distance. If the distance between a firm and a consumer is d, the transport costs from the firm to the consumer are td, i.e., t is the transport cost per unit distance. Recall that in the nongeographic interpretation of the model, transport costs become the consumer's valuation of the loss of utility incurred by consuming a product with characteristics that are not the consumer's most preferred characteristics.

Suppose that there are five firms selling to a group of N consumers who are distributed evenly around the circle of circumference L. A firm is differentiated only by its location on the circle, and we assume that the distance between any two neighboring firms is the same and equal to $L/5$. Each firm has identical costs given by $C(q) = F + cq$, where F is fixed cost and c is (constant) marginal cost. In contrast to our earlier merger analysis, we do not set F, the fixed cost, equal to zero, but instead set unit cost $c = 0$. This simplifies the analysis without losing any generality. What it does do is make it easy to talk about the price-cost margin, which is now just price, denoted by m for mill price.[15]

No Price Discrimination

We start by considering the case in which firms do not engage in price discrimination. This means that each firm sets a single mill price m that consumers pay at the firm's store

---

[13] A more general, but much more complicated version of this analysis can be found in Brito (2003).

[14] It bears repeating that the spatial or geographic interpretation of this model is only the most obvious one.

[15] If the reader is interested in working out the outcome for the case of $c \neq 0$, then we note here that in each case that we examine, the equilibrium price m^* that we derive should be replaced by $c + m^*$.

or mill location. The consumer then pays the fee for transporting the product back to the consumer's location. The full price paid by a consumer who buys from firm i is $m_i + td_i$, where m_i is firm i's mill price and td_i is the consumer's transport cost (or the utility lost by this consumer in buying a product that is not "ideal"). Because marginal cost is zero, the net revenue or profit margin earned by firm i on every such sale is m_i. Consumers buy from the firm offering the product at the lowest full price. As a result, for any set of mill prices across our five hypothetical firms $(m_1, m_2, m_3, m_4, m_5)$ the market is divided between the firms, as illustrated in Figure 15.2. The dotted lines indicate the market division between the firms. Firm 1, for example, supplies all consumers in the region (r_{15}, r_{12}).

When the firms set their prices noncooperatively and the maximum willingness to pay V is relatively large, the market is completely covered. That is, every consumer buys from some firm. Hence, the marginal consumer for any firm is the one who is just indifferent between buying from that firm and buying from one of the firm's neighbors.[16] We show in the Appendix to this chapter that in equilibrium the mill price set by each firm is $m_i^* = tL/5$. At this price, the profit earned by each firm is

$$\pi_i^* = \frac{NtL^2}{25} - F \tag{15.38}$$

The market outcome is illustrated in Figure 15.3, in which we have "flattened out" the circular market to simplify the geometry; that is, firm 1 is to the left of firm 5 and firm 5 is to the right of firm 1. In Figure 15.3, the vertical distance is the effective price—mill price plus transport cost—that each buyer pays. The sloped lines show that this price rises for consumers who live farther from a firm.

Now consider a merger between some subset of these firms. The first point to note is that, taking store locations or product choice as given, *such a merger will have no effect*

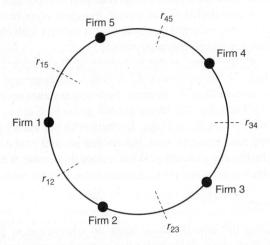

Figure 15.2   Product differentiation—no price discrimination

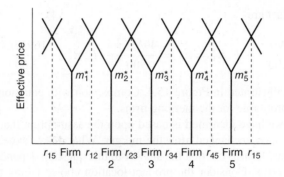

Figure 15.3   Price equilibrium without a merger

unless it is made between neighboring firms. A merger, for example, between firms 2 and 4 leaves prices and market shares unaffected. More generally, this suggests that a merger has no effect on the market outcome unless the market areas of the merging firms have a common boundary. The reason is straightforward. The merging firms hope to gain by softening price competition between them. This will happen only if, prior to the merger, they actually compete directly for some of the same consumers. For example, the merger of the two investment firms Wells Fargo and Morgan Stanley was not for the most part regarded as anticompetitive because the two firms market their services to different, or non-neighboring customers of households and businesses.

Mergers between neighboring firms, however, *do* alter the market outcome. Consider a merger between firms 2 and 3. Suppose that after the merger, the firms do not change either the locations of their existing products or the number of products they offer. Acting now as a single corporate firm with stores in two locations, the merged firm has an incentive to set prices to maximize the joint profits of both products 2 and 3, while the remaining firms continue to price noncooperatively. Of course, firms 1, 4, and 5 also take account of the fact that the merger has taken place. Because firms 2 and 3 are now cooperating divisions of the merged firm they no longer compete for the consumers located between them and so have an incentive to raise the prices of products 2 and 3.[17] This will likely lead to the loss of some consumers, namely, those just on the boundaries identified by the points r_{12} and r_{34}. But provided that the merged firm does not raise prices too much, the loss of market share will be more than offset by the increased profit margins on their "captive" consumers—the consumers between the two merging firms. Moreover, the increased prices set by the merged firm will induce a similar increase in prices set by firms 1, 4, and 5. Such a response reduces the loss of market share that the merged firm actually suffers making the price increase all the more profitable.

Again we show in the Appendix that the merger leads to a new equilibrium with the following prices:

$$m_2^* = m_3^* = \frac{19tL}{60}; m_1^* = m_4^* = \frac{14tL}{60}; m_5^* = \frac{13tL}{60} \tag{15.39}$$

---

[17]   If the merger leaves products 2 and 3 under the control of separate, competing product divisions, prices will not change. The merged firms need to exploit the opportunity they now have to coordinate their prices.

Profits to each product are

$$\pi_2^* = \pi_3^* = \frac{361NtL^2}{7,200} - F; \pi_1^* = \pi_4^* = \frac{49NtL^2}{900} - F; \pi_5^* = \frac{169NtL^2}{3,600} - F \qquad (15.40)$$

This equilibrium is illustrated in Figure 15.4. Comparison with equation (15.38) confirms that this merger is profitable for the merging firms.

The equilibrium we have identified is based upon the assumption that the merged firms leave their product lines unchanged after the merger. What do we expect to happen if we relax this assumption? It turns out that the answer to this question depends upon the precise nature of transport costs. Consider the product location choice facing the newly merged firm 2 and firm 3. The firm faces a trade-off. On the one hand, relocating products 2 and 3 nearer to products 1 and 4, respectively, gives the merged firm two advantages. First, it softens the competition between the merged firm's own two product lines, so that when the firm tries to reach out to customers near the boundary with a lower price, there is less of a fear of simply "robbing Peter to pay Paul." Second, the move also makes it easier for the firm to steal some customers away from its true rivals, firms 1 and 4.[18] On the other hand, relocating products 2 and 3 further from products 1 and 4 offers potential advantages. Admittedly this gives up market share to the rivals but such a move also softens price competition, leading to increased prices by all firms. In our example with linear transport

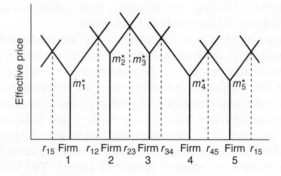

Figure 15.4 Price equilibrium—after merger of firms 2 and 3

---

[18] There is one complication that we have ignored in this discussion. Judd (1985) argues that a merger that creates a multiproduct firm, as for example a merger of firms 2 and 3, may not be sustainable. The intuition is as follows: Assume that an entrant comes in exactly at firm 3's location after the merger of firms 2 and 3. Price competition will drive the price for this product down to marginal cost, in which case the entrant and the incumbent earn zero profits at this location (ignoring fixed costs). But the merged firm also loses money at the neighboring location 2 because the price war with the new entrant forces it to reduce the price there as well. If the merged firm were to close down its location 3 product, the entrant will raise price above marginal cost, and so the merged firm can raise the price at location 2. There is, in other words, a stronger incentive for the merged firm to exit location 3 than for the entrant to do so. Hence, this kind of multiproduct merger may not be sustainable because it is not credible. This argument turns, however, on two important assumptions: that entry costs are not recovered on exit and that the merged firm has no incentive to try to develop a reputation for toughness. Note that in a vertically differentiated context, it may turn out that the merging firms cease producing some versions of the good. See Norman, Pepall, and Richards (2002).

costs, it turns out that the merged firm will wish to relocate its products closer to the rivals 2 and 3. On the other hand, if transport costs were quadratic, of the form td_i^2 the merged firms would actually want to relocate *further* from their rivals.[19]

A merger between two firms in our spatial market is clearly advantageous to the merging firms but is disadvantageous to consumers because a merger tends to raise prices throughout the industry. Both merged and unmerged firms enjoy greater profit and consumers obtain less surplus. There is a possible gain that could benefit consumers: when the merger leads to cost savings that permit lower prices. Remember that the two products that are merged, while not identical, are close substitutes. They could be, for example, low-sugar and high-sugar versions of a soft drink. We might expect there to be some cost complementarities in the production of these products. If so, then production of both goods by one firm will be cheaper than production of both by two separate firms. In short, we should not be surprised if in a product-differentiated market, production of many closely related product lines exhibits economies of scope.[20]

Scope economies provide a strong incentive to merge. The merger allows the new firm to operate as a multiproduct company and thereby exploit the cost-savings opportunities this generates. These savings may be reflected in a reduction in fixed costs. For example, the firms can combine their headquarters, research and development, marketing, accounting, and distribution operations. If, in addition, the merger leads to a reduction in variable costs of production, then this change will be reflected in lower prices. Moreover, even if scope economies are not present, it is still possible that one of the merging firms has a more effective purchasing division or a superior production technology that, following the merger, will be extended to its new partners. The greater such cost synergies are, the more likely it is that consumers will benefit from the merger.

Price Discrimination

Firms that operate in a spatial or product-differentiated setting clearly have some monopoly power. Yet if firms have monopoly power, we might expect them to use discriminatory pricing strategies to exploit this power. In particular, we might expect these firms to adopt some of the price discrimination strategies that we developed in earlier chapters. We now turn to the analysis of how price discrimination affects the incentives for and the impact of mergers in a product differentiated market.

Suppose that firms adopt first-degree or personalized discriminatory pricing policies but maintain at the same time the remaining assumptions of our spatial model in the no–price-discrimination case. The noncooperative price equilibrium is then easy to identify. Remember that firms compete in prices for customers. Accordingly, they set the price as low as need be—at the margin—to attract customers, so long as that price covers their marginal cost. As a result, the equilibrium must be characterized by the following condition. Suppose that firm i is the firm that can supply consumer location s at the lowest unit cost, say $c + ts$ (the marginal production cost plus transport fee), and that firm j is the firm that can supply this location at the next cheapest unit cost, $c + ts + e$, where e is a measure of how much closer the consumer is to firm i than it is to firm j. The Bertrand–Nash equilibrium price to consumer s will be for firm i to charge one cent or epsilon less than the cost of firm j to supply consumer s; that is, to charge just less than $c + ts + e$.

---

[19]   A formal proof for the case of three firms is provided by Posada and Straume (2004).
[20]   Refer to Section 4.3 of Chapter 4 for a definition and explanation of economies of scope.

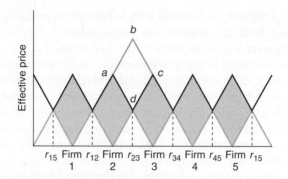

Figure 15.5   Price equilibrium with price discrimination

The heavy shaded line in Figure 15.5 illustrates this price equilibrium. Firm 2 is the lowest-cost supplier (including transport cost) for all consumers in the region (r_{12}, r_{23}). Therefore, firm 2 supplies all consumers in this market region, charging its consumers on the left one cent less than firm 1's costs of supplying them, and its consumers to the right one cent less than firm 3's costs of supplying these consumers. By adopting this pricing strategy, each firm earns a gross profit (profit before deducting fixed cost) given by the shaded areas for their market regions in Figure 15.5.

An interesting feature of this set of discriminatory prices is that the highest price now paid by any consumer is $c + tL/5$. This was the *lowest* price paid by any consumer when firms did not practice price discrimination! Price discrimination in this oligopolistic market unambiguously benefits consumers. Why is this?[21] With nondiscriminatory pricing, when a firm reduces the price to one consumer, it has to reduce the price to every consumer—an expensive prospect. With discriminatory pricing, by contrast, a firm can lower price in one location without having to lower its prices elsewhere. But this means that price discrimination weakens each firm's ability to commit to a set of higher prices, making price competition between the firms much fiercer and so leading to the lower prices that we have just identified.

Now consider the effect on this equilibrium of a merger between two of these firms, say firms 2 and 3, as before. Two points should be clear. First, as in the no–price discrimination case, a merger of non-neighboring firms has no effect. Second, the merged firm's ability to coordinate the formerly separate pricing strategies is particularly valuable in this discriminatory setting. This is because prior to the merger these firms were engaged in what is nearly cutthroat price competition. By merging, the two firms can avoid this expensive conflict, at least with respect to each other.[22] From the perspective of the merged

[21]   This is discussed in Norman and Thisse (1996). They show that with a given number of firms, discriminatory pricing always benefits consumers. They also show, however, that the much more competitive environment of discriminatory pricing may cause enough firms to want to leave the market that prices actually increase for some consumers. See also Reitzes and Levy (1995).

[22]   There is a further important feature of this type of merger. The potential problems that we discussed previously in footnote 18 cannot arise when firms charge discriminatory prices. Consider, for example, an entrant coming in at product 3's location. This would lead to the pre-merger price equilibrium in Figure 15.5 whether or not the merged firm removes its product at this location. There is, in other words, no benefit to the merged firm in exiting from this market. Because a potential entrant can correctly anticipate this, no such entry will take place.

firm, the nearest competitor for consumers in the region between firm 2's location and r_{23} is now firm 1. Similarly, for consumers in the region between firm 3's location and r_{23}, the nearest competitor is now firm 4. As a result, the merged firm can raise prices to all consumers located between firms 2 and 3, as indicated by the line *abc* in Figure 15.5. A merger of firm 2 and firm 3 increases the profits of the merging firms by an amount given by the area *abcd*. One further effect of this type of merger, which is not quite so intuitive, is that when firms practice price discrimination the merger only benefits the merging firms. Prices and profit increase only for those consumers who were served by the merged firm prior to the merger. All other prices are unaffected, and so the profits of the nonmerging firms are unaffected by the merger.

We could also consider issues regarding the merged firm's product location strategies. However, the basic point has been made. Our conclusions for the no–price discrimination case hold all the more strongly when firms engage in discriminatory pricing practices. Prices to consumers rise and the merging firms are more profitable. There is absolutely no paradox about merging in this price discrimination case. From the viewpoint of the merging firms a merger can be a highly profitable venture.

There is one final point to emphasize. Why is it that mergers with price competition in a product-differentiated market do not run into the merger paradox that so bedeviled our earlier analysis with homogenous products and quantity-setting firms? The first part of the answer has already been suggested. Prices are strategic complements whereas quantities are strategic substitutes. With price competition, therefore, the strategic responses of nonmerged firms are potentially beneficial to the merged firms whereas with quantity competition they are potentially harmful.

The second part of the answer is equally important and is related to the notion of credible commitment. The reason why mergers are profitable in the spatial or differentiated products context is that the merged firms can credibly commit to produce some particular *range* of products—that is, the commitment required in the spatial context is a commitment to particular locations or to continue marketing the products of the previously independent firms. By contrast, the commitment necessary with homogenous products and quantity competition must be in terms of production *levels*. The merging firms must be able to commit to a high volume of output following the merger. Generally, this is not credible because such a high volume of production is not the merged firm's best response to a Cournot output decision by the other firms. If, however, the merged firm becomes a Stackelberg leader then the commitment to a high level of post-merger output is credible.

15.6   PUBLIC POLICY TOWARD HORIZONTAL MERGERS

US public policy with respect to horizontal mergers has changed dramatically over the last forty years. To a large extent, this change is reflected in the differences between the first Merger Guidelines issued by the Justice Department in 1968 and the Merger Guidelines currently in force. While it is tempting to summarize these differences as a move from a very strict regime to a more permissive one, it is more accurate to describe the evolution of merger policy as one that has increasingly become more sophisticated and that gives greater recognition to the complexity of corporate organizations in the real world.

The 1968 Merger Guidelines relied heavily on market structure—particularly the four-firm concentration ratio—to determine the legality of a proposed merger. Mergers would be challenged in any industry in which the four-firm concentration ratio exceeded 75 percent and the merging firms each had a market share of as little as 4 percent. In markets with a four-firm concentration ratio below 75 percent, mergers would be challenged if the two firms each had market shares of 5 percent or more. Thus, under the 1968 Guidelines, a combined share of as little as 10 percent would be sufficient in many cases for the government to challenge a merger.

While the approach taken in 1968 reflected many years of empirical work within the Structure-Conduct-Performance framework, its rigidity led to increasingly questionable decisions culminating in perhaps one of the most controversial merger cases ever, *U.S. v. Von's Grocery* (1966) in which the Supreme Court upheld the government's prohibition of a merger between two grocery store chains in Los Angeles that, in combination, had less than 10 percent of the market.

Ironically, courts began to deviate from the rigid, structure-based guidelines of 1968 almost as soon as they were adopted. One early such case was the acquisition by General Dynamics of another coal producer, which was ultimately allowed by the Supreme Court in 1974 despite the fact that the combined market shares of the two firms clearly exceeded the permissible levels set forth by the then 1968 Merger Guidelines. As the courts permitted a number of similar mergers, it soon became clear that the 1968 Guidelines were no longer compelling. This eventually led to the Justice Department issuing of a new set of Merger Guidelines in 1982.

Under the new rules, reliance on the four-firm concentration ratio was abandoned in favor of the Herfindahl-Hirschman Index (HI). The threshold for intervention now became an HI of 1,800 (a little more concentrated than an industry comprised of six, equally large firms). Mergers in less concentrated industries would only be challenged if they raised the HI by more than one hundred points and even then, only if the industry HI already exceeded 1,000. Subsequent amendments to the Guidelines in 1984, 1992, and 1997 relaxed even more the constraints on mergers by specifying and enlarging the ability of merger-generated cost efficiencies as a merger justification.[23]

Underlying these developments was an increasing awareness of modern industrial organization theory as well as a growing body of empirical data that suggested many mergers did not threaten competition as much as the Structure-Conduct-Performance paradigm implied. Moreover the evidence on profitability of mergers was mixed as well. Quite a long list of studies including Mueller (1982); Ravenscraft and Scherer (1989); Lichtenberg and Siegel (1992); Loughran and A. Vijh (1997); Andrade, Mitchell, and Stafford (2001), and Maskimovic and Phillips (2001) have found that mergers are not terribly profitable—especially for the acquiring firm. Indeed, many acquisitions are later reversed by "spin-offs."

The change in attitude reflected by the 1982 guidelines has led to many more mergers being permitted. These have included such major consolidations as Union Pacific and Southern Pacific (railroads), AOL and Time Warner (telecommunications), Chase Manhattan and J.P. Morgan (finance), Exxon and Mobil and also British Petroleum and Amoco (both petroleum mergers), Westinghouse and Infinity Broadcasting (radio), Aetna and US Healthcare (health services), MCI and WorldCom (telecommunications), Maytag and Whirlpool (laundry machines), and XM and Sirius (satellite radio) among others. Many of these mergers were controversial and virtually all raised some competitive concerns, nevertheless these were approved.

---

[23] For work on a theoretical approach to formulating generalized merger policy rules, see Nocke and Whinston (2013) and works cited therein.

Public policy on mergers has increasingly made use of sophisticated empirical techniques to estimate key market parameters and then to use these parameters to model the most likely post-merger scenario. We briefly describe this process of merger simulation in the next section. As developed by Werden and Froeb (1994, 2002) and extended by Epstein and Rubinfeld (2002) merger simulation has become an important, albeit somewhat controversial tool in merger policy. [See Slade (2007).]

In addition to a greater reliance on econometric evidence and economic modeling, policy makers have taken two additional steps that permit horizontal mergers to be approved despite some clear antitrust concerns. First, the antitrust authorities have increasingly used a "fix-it-first" approach regarding proposed mergers. This procedure usually centers on divestiture of some of the assets of the merging parties to another, third firm so as to ensure that competitive pressures are maintained. If, for example, the two firms operate in several towns across the country, but in one town they are the only two such suppliers, then the government may permit the merger so long as one of the firms sells off its operations in the town in question to a new, rival entrant firm. This principle was applied to approve the 2013 beer industry merger of Anheuser Bush Inbev and Grupo Modelo. It is often used in the case of media mergers where newspaper and broadcasting firms have ben required to sell their operations in certain locations before being permitted to conclude a merger.

Divestiture does have some problems. Cabral (2003) notes that divestiture allows the merging firms to dictate the entry position for new rivals. If we think of the circle spatial model described above, if two firms merge but sell the location of some of their stores to a formerly excluded entrant, it means that entrant enters at the same location at which the initial stores existed rather than at other locations on the circle that would be better for consumers. Further, firms can act strategically to reduce the competitive threat presented by divested stores. This occurred in 1995 when Schnucks Markets, a supermarket chain, acquired National Food Markets, which was the major competitor of Schnucks in the St. Louis area. The merger was approved when Schnucks agreed to divest twenty-four supermarkets in the St. Louis area over the next year. However, no immediate buyer was named. Schnucks then took the stores to be divested and proceeded to run them into the ground. It closed departments. It kept the stores understaffed, and referred customers to the other Schnucks stores that were not being divested. Soon, sales at the divesting stores had declined by about one-third and, as a result, they posed less of a competitive threat to the stores that the new Schnucks/National firm continued to operate. It was partly a response to this case that led the FTC to require that the buyer of the divested plants be named in advance and that the firm be one that has the industry knowledge to be an effective competitor. This remedy does not, however, correct for the problems identified by Cabral (2003).

A second, alternative procedure has been to approve mergers subject to behavioral constraints on the merging firms, and then to follow this agreement with active monitoring by government agents. Typically, these consent agreements require the firms to take specific actions and to avoid engaging in certain practices. In monitoring these agreements, the regulatory agencies can always count on a reliable source of outside help, namely, the customers of the merged firms and all parties who opposed the merger. They are always quick to report violations of the consent agreement. Since 1992, the number of consent decrees issued by the FTC and the Justice Department has dramatically increased.

In addition to these procedural changes, the FTC and the Justice Department have also continued to adjust the merger guidelines themselves. In this connection, an important recent modification is the 1997 expansion of Section 4 of the guidelines to permit greater reliance on documented cost savings as a justification of a merger. With this change, the antitrust authorities have indicated an increased willingness to judge a merger to be pro-competitive if it generates cost savings that are likely to translate into lower consumer prices. As we have already noted, however, most analysis finds that the cost savings necessary to generate lower prices are substantial. Hence, the full implication of the 1997 cost efficiencies amendment is yet to be seen.

We should also note that merger-generated cost efficiencies are not necessarily completely beneficial once entry possibilities are considered. If a merger generates lower marginal costs, then any potential entrant will know that *if it enters* price competition will be relatively fierce. If the entrant has fixed costs, this will mean that the market will need to be larger for entry to be profitable. In other words, for a given market size, merger-generated cost efficiencies make post-merger entry less likely. Thus, cost savings can have two price effects. One is the downward pressure on prices exerted by lower costs while the other is the upward pressure exerted by the reduced likelihood of rival entry. Cabral (2003) shows that it is possible that the former outweighs the latter.

15.7   EMPIRICAL APPLICATION: EVALUATING THE IMPACT OF MERGERS WITH COMPUTER SIMULATION

In recent years, the important new tool of merger simulation has emerged to assist with the evaluation of mergers. Merger simulation as pioneered by Werden and Froeb (1994, 2002) and extended recently by Epstein and Rubinfeld (2002) works in two steps. The first is to obtain relevant information on such variables as firms' costs, prices, and demand elasticities, among others. This is usually accomplished with the aid of modern econometric techniques. The second step is to use this evidence to run computer-simulated models of the market in question both before and after a proposed merger. In effect, merger simulation allows economists to conduct laboratory experiments to examine a merger's likely effects. While not necessarily conclusive, such experiments can be very helpful as an evaluative tool.

To understand merger simulation better, consider an industry with four firms, each of which produces a differentiated product and competes in prices against its rivals. For any one firm, the first-order condition for profit maximization is effectively the Lerner condition. That is,

$$\frac{p_i - c}{p_i} + \frac{1}{\eta_{ii}} = 0 \qquad i = 1 \text{ to } 4 \tag{15.41}$$

Here, η_{ii} is the (negative of) the elasticity of the firm i's demand with respect to its own price. If we denote the price-cost margin term as μ_i; firm i's market share as s_i; and then multiply through by the elasticity of demand, equation (15.41) becomes:

$$s_i + s_i \eta_{ii} \mu_i = 0 \tag{15.42}$$

If two firms merge, however, the first-order condition will change as we saw in Section 15.5. Now, the merged firm will coordinate the prices of its two separate products by taking account of the cross demand effects between the two products. Specifically, assume that firms 1 and 2 merge. Then it is straightforward to show that for the merged firm, the first-order condition is:

$$s_1 + s_1 \eta_{11} \mu_1 + s_2 \mu_2 \eta_{21} = 0$$

$$s_2 + s_2 \eta_{22} \mu_2 + s_1 \mu_2 \eta_{12} = 0 \qquad (15.43)$$

where η_{ij} is the cross-elasticity of good i with respect to the price of good j. It is clear from equations (15.42) and (15.43) that measures of the own and cross-price elasticities for each good are critical to estimating the impact of a proposed merger. Indeed, once these elasticities are known, it is relatively straightforward to work out the implied post-merger equilibrium and, therefore, the post-merger prices.

In order to estimate the elasticities, one needs a model of market demand. One commonly used model is derived from what is referred to as the Almost Ideal Demand System (AIDS) as first described by Deaton and Mulbauer (1980). Essentially, such a system describes the demand facing each firm as a function of its own price and the prices charged by other firms, similar to the linear demand that we used to describe our initial model of Bertrand competition with differentiated products. In the case of our four-firm example above, a conventional approach would be to describe market demand with a system of equations something like the following:

$$s_1 = a_1 + b_{11} \ln p_1 + b_{12} \ln p_2 + b_{13} \ln p_3 + b_{14} \ln p_4$$

$$s_2 = a_2 + b_{21} \ln p_1 + b_{22} \ln p_2 + b_{23} \ln p_3 + b_{24} \ln p_4$$

$$s_3 = a_3 + b_{31} \ln p_1 + b_{32} \ln p_2 + b_{33} \ln p_3 + b_{34} \ln p_4$$

$$s_4 = a_4 + b_{41} \ln p_1 + b_{42} \ln p_2 + b_{43} \ln p_3 + b_{44} \ln p_4 \qquad (15.44)$$

The b_{ij} coefficients in the above system are directly linked to the demand elasticities needed to run the merger simulation. Thus, econometric estimation of those coefficients is the first step in obtaining a simulated outcome.

Not counting the a_i coefficients or intercepts, this still leaves 16 b_{ij} coefficients to estimate even in our small four-product example. In general, unless some restrictions are imposed on the nature of the own and cross-price effects, there will be on the order of n^2 coefficients to estimate in a general n-product demand system of the type illustrated above. This is a rather large number of estimates to make with any degree of precision. To simplify matters, it is common to impose restrictions that reduce the number of parameters to be estimated directly.

For example, suppose that our four-firm example is characterized by $q_1 = 250$; $q_2 = 100$; $q_3 = 100$; and $q_4 = 50$, or $s_1 = 50$ percent; $s_2 = s_3 = 20$ percent; and $s_4 = 10$ percent. One way to proceed is to calibrate the model under the assumption of proportionality. As developed by Epstein and Rubinfeld (2002), Proportionally Calibrated AIDS (PCAIDS) assumes that the output loss for good 1 caused by an increase in p_1 will be allocated to the other products in proportion to their market shares. Suppose that the overall elasticity of market demand $\eta = -2$ and the own price elasticity of good 1 is $\eta = -4$. If we think of the overall industry price as the share-weighted average price across the four firms, then a 1 percent increase in firm 1's price p_1 translates into a $1/2$ percent increase in the industry price, all else equal. Firm 1's price increase will then reduce industry output by $1/2$ of 2 percent, or by 1 percent, which in this case is five units. Firm 1's own output will fall by 4 percent, or ten units. Thus, five of these ten units will be picked up in the demand for the other firms if the net industry demand decline is to be just five units. The proportionality assumption is that $[0.2/(0.2 + 0.2 + 0.1)] \times 5$ or 2 units will be diverted to each of firms 2 and 3, while the remaining one unit will be diverted to firm 4. Note that this implies that a 1 percent increase in firm 1's price will raise the demand at each of the other firms by 2 percent, i.e., the cross elasticities η_{21}, η_{31}, and η_{41} are -2 in each case.

What we have just shown is that with the proportionality restriction, the knowledge of just the market demand elasticity and firm 1's own price elasticity has permitted us to deduce three other of the elasticity measures needed for simulation. As it turns out, we can go much farther. In fact, the proportionality assumption permits the complete derivation of all the relevant elasticities once the elasticity is known for the market and for one firm. To put it slightly differently, knowing the market elasticity and own-price elasticity of one firm permits complete calculation of all the b_{ij} coefficients in equation (15.44). The proportionality assumption reduces the number of parameters to be estimated from n^2 to just 2. Once that estimation is complete, we may use the resulting elasticity and market share data to solve the first-order conditions in (15.42) and (15.43) for both the pre-merger and post-merger market. We can then evaluate the price effects of the merger.

Of course, proportionality is a strong assumption. Other techniques for simplifying the estimation procedure also exist. Unfortunately, which technique is chosen can affect the predicted post-merger price change by a factor of ten, as Slade (2007) in particular, has emphasized. Moreover, even if proportionality is assumed there are still two elasticity parameters to be estimated. There is ultimately no way to avoid the use of some econometric analysis in the merger evaluation process.

Efforts to estimate the relevant parameters from a demand system such as the one in (15.44) are tricky at best. Even if only a few parameters are required, there remain difficult measurement questions. And while the specification in (15.44) is common it is not the only way to structure market demand. Alternative specifications will imply different functional forms and cross-product elasticity restrictions that in turn will have different effects on the post-merger equilibrium. For example, the linear demand function that we use in most of the examples in this text implies that demand becomes more elastic as prices rise. This imposes a constraint on post-merger prices even if a merger raises market power because it means that consumers become increasingly sensitive to such price increases. In contrast, a log-linear demand function implies a constant price elasticity of demand that will yield a notably higher price rise for the same market power increase. Yet it is often far from clear what precise specification is most appropriate.

A firm's market share will depend heavily on the definition of the market employed. Yet as we can see from the first-order conditions (15.41–43), these share values are crucial to understanding market dynamics. Indeed, they are crucial to understanding whether or not the merger raises antitrust concerns in the first place.

The difficulties posed by the econometrics in merger analysis were dramatically illustrated by the proposed 1996 merger of two office superstore chains, Staples and Office Depot.[24] Along with Office Max, the merging firms dominated the office superstore retail market. Of course, these three firms are not the only retailers of office supplies. While Staples and Office Depot had between 70 and 75 percent of the market defined by office superstores alone, their combined share of the retail sales of office supplies by all stores, including large

---

[24]   For a more complete discussion of the econometric evidence in this case, see Ashenfelter et al. (2004).

discounters such as Wal-mart, drug store chains, and stationary stores, was probably under 10 percent. Accordingly, the question of whether the merger even crossed the threshold of concern established by the Merger Guidelines had to be addressed.

Moreover, even within the category of office superstores, market definition remains problematic. In the Staples case, it was widely agreed that there was not one national market but many local ones. In principle, this means that estimation of a demand structure like that in equation (15.44) would have to take the specific nature of each localized market into account. That is, account would need to be taken of variation across locations in the extent of competition. How should this variation be modeled?

The government argued that the local market boundaries were those of the Metropolitan Statistical Area (MSA) used by the Census Bureau. For any Staples store, competitors included all other Office Depot and Office Max stores in the same MSA. In contrast, the merging firms argued that there was a difference within an MSA depending on the actual distance between rivals. That is, an Office Depot store exerted greater price pressure on a Staples store if it were only five miles away than if it were ten, or twenty miles away. Again, these seemingly small changes in specifying the competitive interaction can (and did) have a large effect on the results. Just this one alteration led to more than a 3 percentage point difference between the firms' prediction that the merger would raise prices by about 0.8 percent and the government's estimate of a rise of 4.1 percent. Together, these and other modest econometric modifications meant that the range in predicted price increases varied from less than 1 percent to almost 10 percent.

In short, simulating merger effects inevitably requires different estimation techniques and structural demand assumptions that vary according to the conceptualization of the market environment. Assumptions to ease the estimation burden do not alleviate other measurement and econometric issues. We can expect self interest to lead each side in a merger case to choose the framework and associated econometric techniques that yield parameter values and other evidence most favorable to its own objective. Unfortunately, it is typically the case that each approach has some objective justification. It becomes very difficult even for economists to separate the truth from self-interest in interpreting the results. It is even more difficult for the courts to resolve such debates. One of the striking features of the Staples case is that the final court decision never mentions the econometric evidence despite the fact that this case probably involved more econometric presentation than virtually any prior merger litigation.

Summary

Horizontal mergers are combinations of firms that are rivals within the same industry. Because they result in the joining of firms that were previously competitors, horizontal mergers raise obvious antitrust concerns. Such mergers may, in fact, be a means to create a legal cartel. One major puzzle in economic analysis is the merger paradox. This paradox reflects the fact that many commonly used economic models suggest that a merger is not profitable for the merging firms and that the true beneficiaries of a merger are the nonmerging firms.

The clue to resolving the merger paradox is to find some means of credibly committing the newly merged firm to a profit-enhancing strategy. One way to do this in quantity-setting models is to permit the merged firm to take on the role of Stackelberg leader whose increased production is credible. Another way is to consider merger decisions sequentially. Either of these approaches is capable of generating profitable mergers that also have adverse consequences for consumers. The sequential merger approach can also help explain the "domino effect" often observed, by which a merger of two firms in an industry is quickly followed by similar marriages among other firms in the same industry.

The merger paradox does not arise in markets where firms offer differentiated products and compete in price for customers. In these markets, the merging firms can easily make a convincing commitment to specific locations or product designs—namely, those used by the firms before they merged. The ability to make such a commitment is sufficient to make merger profitable.

The ambiguous effects of mergers found in economic theory are also found in empirical analysis. To date, there is little clear evidence that horizontal mergers have resulted in legalized cartels with significant monopoly power. Instead, what is clear is that the combination of theoretical and empirical ambiguity has led the legal authorities to take a much less aggressive and much less rigid stand against proposed mergers, a point to which we return in the policy discussion of the next chapter.

Policy also increasingly includes formal attempts to model the post-merger market and to evaluate mergers on a case-by-case basis. The theory behind this approach builds on the first-order conditions for profit maximization and uses these along with the estimates of the relevant price elasticities to analyze the optimal pricing decisions of the merged firm and its rivals in the post-merger market. In practice, this is hard work and typically requires a number of simplifying assumptions to identify the needed parameters. However, there appears to be little alternative.

In sum, there is no general rule regarding the impact of mergers. The merger paradox suggests that only mergers that are associated with large cost efficiencies will be profitable. Because firms do not pursue unprofitable opportunities, this suggests that any proposed merger must have very large cost efficiencies and, perhaps, should be approved. On the other hand, we know if merged firms can acquire the ability to commit to a production level before others, then the merger can be profitable without cost savings and thus, would be anticompetitive. Antitrust authorities cannot rely solely on economic theory to determine whether or not a specific merger should be challenged. This is an area where empirical work based on advanced econometrics can be predicted to play an important role.

Problems

For problems 1, 2, 3, and 4 consider a market containing four identical firms, each of which makes an identical product. The inverse demand for this product is $P = 100 - Q$, where P is price and Q is aggregate output. The production costs for firms 1, 2, and 3 are identical and given by $C(q_i) = 20q_i$; $(i = 1, 2, 3)$, where q_i is the output of firm i. This means that for each of these firms, variable costs are constant at \$20 per unit. The production costs for firm 4 are $C(q_4) = (20 + \gamma)q_4$, where γ is some constant. Note that if $\gamma > 0$, then firm 4 is a high-cost firm, while if $\gamma < 0$, firm 4 is a low-cost firm ($|\gamma| < 20$). Note also that $Q = \sum_{i=1}^{4} q_i$.

1. Assume that the firms each choose their outputs to maximize profits given that they each act as Cournot competitors.
   a. Identify the Cournot equilibrium output for each firm, the product price, and the profits of the four firms. For this to be a "true" equilibrium, all of the firms must at least be covering their variable costs. Identify the constraint that γ must satisfy for this to be the case.
   b. Assume that firms 1 and 2 merge and that all firms continue to act as Cournot competitors after the merger. Confirm that this merger is unprofitable.
   c. Now assume that firms 1 and 4 merge. Can this merger be profitable if γ is positive so that firm 4 is a high-cost firm? What has happened to the profits of firm 2 as a result of this merger?

2. Now assume that each firm incurs fixed costs of F in addition to the variable costs noted above. When two firms merge the merged firm has fixed costs of bF where $1 \le b \le 2$.
   a. Suppose that firms 1 and 2 merge and that $\gamma > 0$. Derive a condition on b, F, and γ for this merger to be profitable. Give an intuitive interpretation of this condition.

b. Suppose by contrast that firms 1 and 4 merge. Repeat your analysis in (a).

c. Compare the conditions derived in (a) and (b). What does this tell you about mergers that create cost savings?

3. Assume that if two firms merge, the merged firm will be able to act as an industry leader, making its output decision before the non-merged firms make theirs. Further assume that $\gamma = 0$ so that the firms are of equal efficiency.

a. Confirm that a merger between firms 1 and 2 will now be profitable. What has happened to the profits of the non-merged firms and to the product price as a result of this merger?

b. Confirm that the two remaining firms will also want to merge and join the leader group given that the leaders act as Cournot competitors with respect to each other (hint: this merger will create a leader group containing two firms and a follower group containing none). What does this second merger do to the market price?

4. Continue with the conditions of question 3 but now suppose that for a merger to be undertaken, the merging firms each have to incur a fixed cost, f (this might include costs of identifying a merger partner, negotiating the terms of the merger, legal fees, and so on).

a. How high must f be for the merger between firms 1 and 2 to be unprofitable?

b. How high must f be for the subsequent merger between firms 3 and 4 to be unprofitable?

5. In this chapter it was shown that for a two-firm merger to be profitable, the following condition must be satisfied:

$$\pi_l^L(N-1, L+1) = \frac{(A-c)^2}{B(L+2)^2(N-L-1)}$$

$$> 2.\pi_f^F(N, L) = 2\frac{(A-c)^2}{B(L+1)^2(N-L+1)^2}$$

Assume as in questions 1 and 2 that $A = 100, B = 1, c = 20$. Further assume that $\gamma = 0$.

a. Assume that the number of firms in the market is ten, that is, $N = 10$, and that, as in question 4, a two-firm merger requires that each of the merging firms incurs a fixed cost of f prior to the merger. Derive a relationship, $f(L)$, between f and the size of the leader group, L, such that if $f > f(L)$, the two-firm merger will be unprofitable. Calculate $f(L)$ for $L = 1, 2, 3, 4,$ and 5 to confirm that $f(L)$ is decreasing in L. Interpret this result.

b. Now assume that there are eight firms in the market, that is, $N = 8$. Repeat your calculations in part (a) to show that the function $f(L)$ rises as N falls. Interpret this result.

6. Normansville consists of a single High Street that is one mile long and has 100 residents uniformly located along it. There are three independent video rental stores located in the town at distances 1/6, 1/2, and 5/6 of a mile from the left-hand edge of Normansville. Each resident rents one video per day provided that the price charged is no more than \$5. If a consumer is located s miles from a store, the transport costs of getting a video from that store is \$0.50s. Suppose first that the two stores do not price discriminate.

a. What rental charge will the three stores set given that they act as price competitors?

b. What profits do they earn?

7. Suppose that two neighboring stores in Normansville merge.

a. What does this do to prices and profits?

b. Recalculate your answers to and 7(a) assuming that the stores can perfectly price discriminate.

8. Recall that the first-order condition for maximizing profit may be written as: $p = \dfrac{\varepsilon - 1}{\varepsilon} c$; where ε is the absolute value of the firm's elasticity. Show that this result implies that, as an approximation, the proportional change in a firm's price as a result of a merger can be written as: $\dfrac{\Delta p}{p} = \dfrac{\Delta h}{h} + \dfrac{\Delta c}{c}$; where $h = \dfrac{\varepsilon - 1}{\varepsilon}$. Suppose that as a result of a

merger and decline in competitive pressure, a firm's demand elasticity falls by the proportion δ, i.e., $\varepsilon' = (1 - \delta)\varepsilon$. Show that we may write $\dfrac{\Delta h}{h} = \dfrac{\delta}{(1 - \delta)\varepsilon - 1}$.

9. Use your results in question 8 to determine the necessary degree of cost efficiencies

(i.e., the value of $\dfrac{\Delta c}{c}$), for the firm's price not to rise if its initial elasticity is $\varepsilon = 2$, and if as a result of a merger, its demand elasticity falls by 10 percent, i.e., $\delta = 0.1$. That is, by what proportion will costs have to decline in this case to keep p constant?

References

Andrade, G., M. Mitchell, and E. Stafford. 2001. "New Evidence and Perspectives on Mergers," *Journal of Economic Perspectives* 15 (Spring),: 103–20.

Ashenfelter, O., D. Ashmore, J. Baker, S. Gleason, and D. Hosken. 2004. "Econometric Methods in *Staples*," in Princeton Law & Public Affairs Paper No. 04-007.

Baker, J. 2004. "Efficiencies and High Concentration: Heinz Proposes to Acquire Beech-Nut (2001)" in J. Kwoka and L. White, eds. *The Antitrust Revolution*, Oxford: Oxford University Press, 150–69.

Brito, D. 2003. "Preemptive Mergers Under Spatial Competition," Working Paper, FCT, Universidade Nova de Lisboa.

Cabral, L., 2003. "Horizontal Mergers with Free Entry: Why Cost Efficiencies May Be a Weak Defense and Assets Sales a Poor Remedy," *International Journal of Industrial Organization* 21 (May): 607–23.

Daughety, A. F. 1990. "Beneficial Concentration," *American Economic Review* 80:1,231–7.

Deneckere, R. and Davidson, C. 1985. "Incentives to Form Coalitions with Bertrand Competition", *Rand Journal of Economics* 16 (Winter): 473–486.

Deaton, A., and J. Mulbauer, 1980. "An Almost Ideal Demand System," *American Economic Review* 70 (June): 312–26.

Epstein, R., and D. Rubinfeld, 2002. "Merger Simulation: A Simplified Approach with New Applications," *Antitrust Law Journal* 69: 883–920.

Farrell, J., and C. S. Shapiro, 1990. "Horizontal Mergers: An Equilibrium Analysis," *American Economic Review* 80:107–26.

Fauli-Oller, R. 200. "Takeover Waves." *Journal of Economics & Management Strategy* 9 (Summer), 189–210.

Gandhi, A., L. Froeb, S. Tschantz, and G. Werden. 2008. "Post-Merger Product Repositioning." *Journal of Industrial Economics* 41 (March), 49–67.

Greenhut, J., G. Norman, and M. L. Greenhut. 1991. "Aspects of Airline Deregulation," *International Journal of Transport Economics* 18:3–30.

Hotelling, H. 1929. "Stability in Competition," *Economic Journal* 39 (January): 31–47.

Judd, K., 1985. "Credible Spatial Preemption," *Rand Journal of Economics* 16:153–66.

Lichtenberg, F., and D. Siegel. 1992. "Takeovers and Corporate Overhead," in F. Lichtenberg, ed., *Corporate Takeovers and Productivity*, Cambridge: MIT Press.

Loughran, T., and A. Vijh. 1997. "Do Long-Term Shareholders Benefit from Corporate Acquisitions?" *Journal of Finance* 52: 1765–90.

Maskimovic, V., and G. Phillips. 2001. "The Market for Corporate Assets: Who Engages in Mergers and Assets Sales and Are There Efficiency Gains?" *Journal of Finance* 56 (December): 2019–65.

Mueller, D. C., 1982. "A Theory of Conglomerate Mergers," *Quarterly Journal of Economics* 82: 643–59.

Nilssen, T., and L. Sorgard. 1998. "Sequential Horizontal Mergers." *European Economic Review*. 42 (November), 1683–1702.

Nocke, V., and M. Whinston. 2013. "Merger Policy with Merger Choice." *American Economic Review* 103 (April), 1006–1033.

Norman, G., L. Pepall, and D. Richards. 2005. "Product Differentiation, Cost-Reducing Mergers, and Consumer Welfare," *Canadian Journal of Economics* 38 (November)

Norman, G., and J. F. Thisse. 1996. "Product Variety and Welfare under Soft and Tough Pricing Regimes," *Economic Journal* 106:76–91.

Perry, M., and R. Porter. 1985. "Oligopoly and the Incentive for Horizontal Merger," *American Economic Review* 75:219–27.

Posada, P., and O.D. Straume. 2004. "Merger, Partial Collusions and Relocation," *Journal of Economics* 83: 243–265.

Ravenscraft, D. J., and F. M. Scherer. 1989. "The Profitability of Mergers," *International Journal of Industrial Organization* Special Issue (March):101–16.

Reitzes, J. D., and D. T. Levy. 1995. "Price Discrimination and Mergers," *Canadian Journal of Economics* 28:427–36.

Salant, S., S. Switzer, and R. Reynolds. 1983. "Losses from Horizontal Merger: The Effects of an Exogenous Change in Industry Structure on Cournot–Nash Equilibrium," *Quarterly Journal of Economics* 98:185–213.

Salinger, M., 2005. "Four Questions about Horizontal Merger Enforcement," *Remarks to ABA Economic Committee of Antitrust Section, 14* September.

Salop, S. C., 1979. "Monopolistic Competition with Outside Goods," *Bell Journal of Economics* 10 (Spring):141–56.

Salvo, A. 2010. "Sequential Cross-Border Mergers in Models of Oligopoly." *Economica* 77 (April), 352–83.

Schmalensee, R. 1978. "Entry Deterrence in the Ready-to-Eat Breakfast Cereal Industry," *Bell Journal of Economics* 9 (Autumn): 305–27.

Slade, M. 2007. "Merger Simulations of Unilateral Effects: What Can We Learn from the UK Brewing Industry?" forthcoming in B. Lyons, Ed., *Cases in European Competition Policy: The Economic Analysis*, Cambridge: Cambridge University Press.

Werden, G., and L. Froeb. 1994. "The Effects of Mergers in Differentiated Products Industries: Logit Demand and Merger Policy," *Journal of Law, Economics, and Organizations* 10 (October): 407–26.

Werden, G., and L. Froeb. 2002. "The Antitrust Logit Model for Predicting Unilateral Competitive Effects," *Antitrust Law Journal* 70: 257–60.

Appendix

STACKELBERG LEADER-FOLLOWER MODEL WITH SEVERAL LEADERS

Instead of assuming N firms with one leader and $N - 1$ followers, let us assume N firms with L leaders and $N - L = F$ followers. Equation (15.21) still describes the best response of the typical follower firm. Because there are $N - L$ such firms, a little algebra quickly reveals that total follower output Q^F is then:

$$Q^F = (N - L)q_f^* = \frac{(N - L)(A - c)}{B(N - L + 1)} - \frac{(N - L)Q^L}{(N - L + 1)} \tag{15A.1}$$

Denote the output of any one leader firm as q^l and that of all the leaders *other than firm l*, Q_{L-l}. The residual demand function for firm l is then:

$$P = [A - B(Q^F + Q_{L-l})] - Bq_l \tag{15.A2}$$

Substituting for total follower output Q^F from equation (15A.1) and re-arranging yields the typical leader's demand:

$$P = \frac{A + (N - L)c - BQ_{L-l}}{(N - L + 1)} - \frac{B}{(N - L + 1)}q_l \tag{15.A3}$$

Hence, the associated marginal revenue function is

$$MR_l = \frac{A + (N - L)c - BQ_{L-l}}{(N - L + 1)} - \frac{2B}{(N - L + 1)}q_l \qquad (15.A4)$$

Equating this marginal revenue with marginal cost gives the leader firm l's best output response to the output produced by all the other leader firms, Q_{L-l}:

$$MR_l = \frac{A + (N - L)c - BQ_{L-l}}{(N - L + 1)} - \frac{2B}{(N - L + 1)}q_l = c \Rightarrow q_l^* = \frac{A - c}{2B} - \frac{Q_{L-l}}{2} \qquad (15.A5)$$

By symmetry, all leader firms produce the same output in equilibrium. Hence, $Q_{L-l}^* = (L - 1)q_l^*$ substituted into equation (15A.5) then yields the stage-one output chosen by each merged leader firm:

$$q_l^* = \frac{A - c}{2B} - \frac{(L - 1)}{2}q_l^* \Rightarrow q_l^* = \frac{A - c}{B(L + 1)} \text{ and } Q^L = Lq_l^* = \frac{L(A - c)}{B(L + 1)} \qquad (15.A6)$$

Substituting Q^L into equation (15.A.1), total follower output Q^F and individual output for each follower $q_f^* = Q^F/(N - L)$ are:

$$q_f^* = \frac{A - c}{B(L + 1)(N - L + 1)} \text{ and } Q^F = \frac{(N - L)(A - c)}{B(L + 1)(N - L + 1)} \qquad (15A.7)$$

Total market output Q and the equilibrium price P:

$$Q^T = Q^L + Q^F = \frac{(N + NL - L^2)(A - c)}{B(L + 1)(N - L + 1)} \text{ and } P = \frac{A + (N + NL - L^2)c}{(L + 1)(N - L + 1)} \qquad (15A.8)$$

The price-cost margin and profit for the typical leader firm and typical follower firm are:

$$P - c = \frac{A - c}{(L + 1)(N - L + 1)}; \pi^L(N, L) = \frac{(A - c)^2}{B(L + 1)^2(N - L + 1)}; \text{ and}$$

$$\pi^F(N, L) = \frac{(A - c)^2}{B(L + 1)^2(N - L + 1)^2}. \qquad (15A.9)$$

PROOF THAT AN ADDITIONAL MERGER IS PROFITABLE IN THE LEADER-FOLLOWER MODEL

From (15.33), the necessary condition for two firms to merge and join the leader group is

$$(L + 1)^2(N - L + 1)^2 - 2(L + 2)^2(N - L - 1) > 0 \qquad (15A.10)$$

Define $x = L + 1$ and $y = N - L - 1$. Then we need to show that

$$x^2(y + 2)^2 \geq 2(x + 1)^2 y$$

Note that $d(y + 4 + 4/y)/dy = 1 - 4/y^2$ is negative for $0 < y < 2$. For $y > 2$ we have

$$Y + 4 + 4/y \geq 2 + 4 + 4/2 = 8$$

with equality only for $y = 2$. For $x \geq 1$ this inequality can be rewritten

$$(y + 2)^2 \geq 8 \geq 2(1 + 1/x)^2 y = 2((x + 1)/x)^2 y$$

giving $x^2(y + 2)^2 \geq 2(x + 1)^2 y$ as required.

BERTRAND COMPETITION IN A SIMPLE LINEAR DEMAND SYSTEM

Start with the inverse demand system of equations (15.35):

$$p_1 = A - Bq_1 - s(q_2 + q_3)$$
$$p_2 = A - Bq_2 - s(q_1 + q_3) \quad (s \in [0, B))$$
$$p_3 = A - Bq_3 - s(q_1 + q_2) \tag{15A.11}$$

Inverting and manipulating this demand system yields:

$$q_1 = \frac{A(B - s) - (B + s)p_1 + s(p_2 + p_3)}{(B - s)(B + 2s)}$$

$$q_2 = \frac{A(B - s) - (B + s)p_2 + s(p_1 + p_3)}{(B - s)(B + 2s)} \quad (s \in [0, B))$$

$$q_3 = \frac{A(B - s) - (B + s)p_3 + s(p_1 + p_2)}{(B - s)(B + 2s)} \tag{15A.12}$$

The Pre-Merger Case

We begin by identifying the equilibrium when each firm acts independently. Profit to firm 1 is

$$\pi_1 = (p_1 - c)q_1 = (p_1 - c)\left[\frac{A(B - s) - (B + s)p_1 + s(p_2 + p_3)}{(B - s)(B + 2s)}\right] \tag{15A.13}$$

Differentiating with respect to p_1 and simplifying gives the first-order condition for firm 1:

$$\frac{\partial \pi_1}{\partial p_1} = \frac{A(B - s) - 2(B + s)p_1 + s(p_2 + p_3) + c(B + s)}{(B - s)(B + 2s)} = 0 \tag{15A.14}$$

Defines firm 1's best response function. Imposing a symmetric $p^*_1 = p^*_2 = p^*_3 = p^*_{nm}$, substitution into (15A.14) gives: $\dfrac{A(B - s) - 2Bp^*_{nm} + c(B + s)}{(B - s)(B + 2s)} = 0$. Implying equilibrium prices:

$$p^*_{nm} = \frac{A(B - s) + c(B + s)}{2B} \tag{15A.15}$$

Equilibrium output for each firm is therefore $q_{nm}^* = \dfrac{(A - c)(B + s)}{2B(B + 2s))}$ which, in turn, (15A.13) implies that no-merger profit for each firm of:

$$\pi_{nm}^* = \frac{(A - c)^2(B - s)(B + s)}{4B^2(B + 2s)} \tag{15A.16}$$

Merger of Firms 1 and 2

This post-merger profit-maximizing first-order conditions are

$$\frac{\partial(\pi_1 + \pi_2)}{\partial p_1} = \frac{A(B - s) - 2(B + s)p_1 + 2sp_2 + sp_3 + cB}{(B - s)(B + 2s)} = 0$$

$$\frac{\partial(\pi_1 + \pi_2)}{\partial p_2} = \frac{A(B - s) - 2(B + s)p_2 + 2sp_3 + sp_3 + cB}{(B - s)(B + 2s)} = 0 \tag{15A.17}$$

$$\frac{\partial \pi_3}{\partial p_3} = \frac{A(B - s) - 2(B + s)p_3 + s(p_1 + p_2) + c(B + s)}{(B - s)(B + 2s)} = 0$$

Solving these for the equilibrium prices gives $p_1^m = p_2^m = \dfrac{A(2B + 3s)(B - s) + c(2B + s)(B + s)}{2(2B^2 + 2Bs - s^2)}$ for the merged firm and $p_3^{nm} = \dfrac{A(B + s)(B - s) + cB(B + 2s)}{(2B^2 + 2Bs - s^2)}$ for the nonmerged firm. Hence profits are:

$$\pi_1^m = \pi_2^m = \frac{B(A - c)^2(B - s)(2B + 3s)^2}{4(B + 2s)(2B^2 + 2Bs - s^2)^2} ; \pi_3^m = \frac{(A - c)^2(B - s)(B + s)^3}{(B + 2s)(2B^2 + 2Bs - s^2)^2} \tag{15A.18}$$

Comparison of the Pre-Merger and Post-Merger Cases

Define $\sigma = s/B$, where σ lies in the interval $(0, 1)$ since we have that $0 \leq s < B$:

$$\pi_{nm}^* = \frac{(A - c)^2(B - s)(B + s)}{4B^2(B + 2s)} = \frac{(A - c)^2 B^2(1 - \sigma)(1 + \sigma)}{4B^3(1 + 2\sigma)} = \frac{(A - c)^2(1 - \sigma^2)}{4B(1 + 2\sigma)} \tag{15A.19}$$

Profit of each division of the merged firm is:

$$\pi_1^m = \pi_2^m = \frac{B(A - c)^2(B - s)(2B + 3s)^2}{4(B + 2s)(2B^2 + 2Bs - s^2)^2}$$

$$= \frac{B^4(A - c)^2(1 - \sigma)(2 + 3\sigma)^2}{4B^5(1 + 2\sigma)(2 + 2\sigma - \sigma^2)^2} = \frac{(A - c)^2(1 - \sigma)(2 + 3\sigma)^2}{4B(1 + 2\sigma)(2 + 2\sigma - \sigma^2)^2} \tag{15A.20}$$

Without loss of generality, normalize $(A - c)^2/B$ in unity. Profits are then a function solely of σ. A plot of (15A.19) and (15A.20) in the interval $\sigma \in [0,1)$ confirms that the merger raises profits for all firms.

EQUILIBRIUM PRICES IN THE SPATIAL MODEL WITHOUT A MERGER

Consider firm 3 as a representative firm. Demand for this firm from its left is Nr_{23}, where r_{23} is the marginal consumer given by

$$m_3 + tr_{23} = m_2 + t\left(\frac{L}{5} = r_{23}\right) \Rightarrow r_{23} = \frac{m_2 - m_3}{2t} + \frac{L}{10} \tag{15A.21}$$

Similarly, demand from consumers to the right of firm 3 is Nr_{34}, where r_{34} is

$$r_{34} = \frac{m_4 - m_3}{2t} + \frac{L}{10} \tag{15A.22}$$

Firm 3's profit is, therefore,

$$\pi_3 = Nm_3(r_{23} + r_{34}) = Nm_3\left(\frac{m_2 - m_3}{2t} + \frac{m_4 - m_3}{2t} + \frac{L}{5}\right) \tag{15A.23}$$

Differentiating this with respect to m_3 to give the first-order condition for firm 3:

$$\frac{\partial \pi_3}{\partial m_3} = N\left(\frac{m_2 + m_4}{2t} - \frac{2m_3}{t} + \frac{L}{5}\right) = 0 \tag{15A.24}$$

Since firms are identical, equilibrium requires $m_3 = m_2 = m_4$. Hence, the Nash equilibrium prices is

$$m^* = tL/5 \tag{15A.25}$$

EQUILIBRIUM PRICES IN THE SPATIAL MODEL AFTER FIRMS 2 AND 3 MERGE

Conveniently changing the firms' "labels" in equation (15A.23) we have:

$$\pi_1 = Nm_1\left(\frac{m_5 - m_1}{2t} + \frac{m_2 - m_1}{2t} + \frac{L}{5}\right)$$

$$\pi_2 = Nm_2\left(\frac{m_1 - m_2}{2t} + \frac{m_3 - m_2}{2t} + \frac{L}{5}\right)$$

$$\pi_3 = Nm_3\left(\frac{m_2 - m_3}{2t} + \frac{m_4 - m_3}{2t} + \frac{L}{5}\right) \tag{15A.26}$$

$$\pi_4 = Nm_4\left(\frac{m_3 - m_4}{2t} + \frac{m_5 - m_4}{2t} + \frac{L}{5}\right)$$

$$\pi_5 = Nm_5\left(\frac{m_4 - m_5}{2t} + \frac{m_1 - m_5}{2t} + \frac{L}{5}\right)$$

The merged firm chooses m_2 and m_3 to maximize aggregate profit $\pi_2 + \pi_3$. Nonmerged firms choose profit-maximizing prices as before. The first-order conditions are:

$$\frac{\partial \pi_1}{\partial m_1} = N\left(\frac{m_5 + m_2}{2t} - \frac{2m_1}{t} + \frac{L}{5}\right) = 0$$

$$\frac{\partial (\pi_2 + \pi_3)}{\partial m_2} = N\left(\frac{m_1 + m_3}{2t} - \frac{2m_2}{t} + \frac{L}{5}\right) + N\frac{m_3}{2t} = 0$$

$$\frac{\partial (\pi_2 + \pi_3)}{\partial m_3} = N\left(\frac{m_2 + m_4}{2t} - \frac{2m_3}{t} + \frac{L}{5}\right) + N\frac{m_2}{2t} = 0 \qquad (15A.27)$$

$$\frac{\partial \pi_4}{\partial m_4} = N\left(\frac{m_3 + m_5}{2t} - \frac{2m_4}{t} + \frac{L}{5}\right) = 0$$

$$\frac{\partial \pi_5}{\partial m_5} = N\left(\frac{m_4 + m_1}{2t} - \frac{2m_5}{t} + \frac{L}{5}\right) = 0$$

Solving these equations simultaneously gives the prices in the text. As noted, we assume that no firm i ever finds it profitable to price so low that it actually competes with firms beyond $i - 1$ and $i + 1$.

16

Vertical and Conglomerate Mergers

In the fall of 2000, General Electric and Honeywell International announced that the two companies would merge with GE acquiring Honeywell. GE is a very well-known firm with annual revenues well over $100 billion. Its businesses are involved in everything from lighting and appliances to television programming (it owns NBC) and financial services. GE is also a major supplier of jet engines for commercial aircraft for which its chief competitors are Rolls Royce and Pratt-Whitney. Honeywell was originally a leader in temperature and environmental controls but has, over time, developed into a major aerospace firm whose products include electric lighting, ventilation units, and braking systems for aircraft and also starter motors for aircraft engines of the type GE builds. The deal was approved in the United States. However, in July of 2001, the European Commission following the recommendation of Competition Commissioner, Mario Monti, blocked the merger.

The proposed GE-Honeywell merger was a marriage of firms making complementary products. The more aircraft engines GE sells, the more starter motors and other related aircraft items Honeywell could sell. As a result, the proposed merger of GE and Honeywell can be thought of as being equivalent to a vertical merger. Most often vertical mergers combine firms operating at different levels of the production chain, say, a wholesaler and a retailer. However, the connection between an upstream and a downstream firm is qualitatively the same as the relation between Honeywell and GE, or that between computer hardware and software, nuts and bolds, or zinc and copper, which are combined to make brass. In all of these cases, two or more products are combined to yield the final good or service. Because an upstream-downstream relationship is just one of the many types of complementary relationships that may exist between firms, the term vertical merger has come to have the more general interpretation of a merger between any firms that produce complementary products.

We showed in Chapter 8 that the separate production of complementary goods—each one produced by a firm with monopoly power—reduces the joint profit of the two firms and imposes an efficiency loss on both firms and consumers. The intuition behind this result is straightforward. Each firm's pricing decision imposes an externality on the other firm. A high price for computer hardware reduces demand for PCs. It also reduces demand for programs and operating systems. The hardware manufacturer takes the first effect into account, but not the second. The same is true, of course, in reverse. The software manufacturer does not take into account the impact its price choice has on the demand for hardware. In the non-cooperative Nash equilibrium, the prices of both goods are too high. If, say, the hardware firm were to cut its price, this would generate additional demand and additional profit for the software firm. However, because the hardware firm does not receive any of this additional profit, its incentive to reduce price is weakened. This suggests that, with cooperation, both firms will lower their prices and be better off. Consumers, too, will gain as a result of lower prices and expanded output.

One way to achieve the profit and efficiency gains of cooperation is for the two firms to merge. Such a merger creates a single decision-making entity and, therefore, permits the externality to be internalized. The combined hardware and software firm maximizes its total profit by reducing the prices of both complementary goods so as to maximize the joint profit from each. Whenever firms with monopoly power produce complementary products, they have a strong incentive either to merge or to devise some other method to ensure cooperative production and pricing of the complementary products.

Precisely the same issues of cooperation arise when the complementary relationships arise because the firms occupy different levels in the vertical production chain. This is important because it sheds light on how vertical mergers affect competition and so consumer welfare. In the 1980s, the realization that vertical mergers can generate efficiency gains led to something of a revolution in antitrust policy related to vertical mergers. In the decades prior to 1980, vertical mergers were often seen as anticompetitive because of the fear that such mergers would facilitate foreclosure. That is, the upstream merger partner would, after the merger, refuse to supply its product to other downstream firms and thereby either drive them out of the market or create barriers to entry that adversely affect them.

Economists primarily associated with the Chicago School challenged this negative view of vertical mergers. They argued that vertical mergers could also achieve complementary efficiencies and that "vertical integration was most likely pro-competitive or competitively neutral" (Riordan 1998, 1232). By the 1980s, the Chicago School approach began to gain in the courts and vertical mergers were treated increasingly favorably by the antitrust authorities. However, by the mid-1990s the pendulum once more began to swing the other way. A post-Chicago approach has now emerged that employs game theoretic tools to build new and logically consistent models of vertical mergers in which once again the potential for consumer harm is real. This counter-revolution has led to a detailed scrutiny of a number of vertical combinations, most notably, those in the telecommunications sector.

We begin this chapter by developing an analysis of vertical mergers based on the proposition that these are pro-competitive and correct market inefficiencies. In section 2, we consider some of the more recent analysis suggesting that such mergers might adversely affect competition in final product markets. Section 3 presents a simple formal model to illustrate this phenomenon.

Section 4 turns to the third and final type of mergers. These are conglomerate mergers involving the combination of firms without either a clear substitute or a clear complementary relationship. Examples include the purchase of Duracell Batteries by Gillette, the purchase of Columbia Pictures by Sony, and the series of acquisitions in 1986 by Daimler-Benz, a luxury car and truck manufacturer, which turned it into Germany's largest industrial concern, producing everything from aerospace to household goods. Finally, section 5 presents a brief overview of antitrust policy with respect to different types of mergers.

16.1   PRO-COMPETITIVE VERTICAL MERGERS

When firms occupy different stages of the production stream the convention is to label those firms farthest from the final consumer of the product as upstream and those closest to that consumer as downstream. Film production companies and movie theaters are an example.

In this case, the production company is the upstream firm and the theater that shows the film is the downstream firm. Manufacturers and retailers have a similar upstream–downstream relationship. All such relationships can be usefully viewed as being complementary to each other. Each firm in the vertical chain provides an essential service to other firms in the chain. Our first order of business is to show that vertical relationships between two firms, each with monopoly power, lead to a loss of economic efficiency in the absence of some mechanism to coordinate the decisions of the two firms. In the case of vertically related firms, this is referred to as the problem of *double marginalization*.

Suppose that we have a single upstream supplier, the manufacturer, who sells a unique product to a single downstream firm, the retailer. The manufacturer produces the good at constant unit cost, c, and sells it to the retailer at a wholesale price, r. The retailer resells the product to consumers at the market-clearing price, P. For simplicity, we assume that the retailer has no other retailing costs. Consumer demand for the good is described by our familiar linear inverse demand function $P = A - BQ$, and we assume of course that $c < A$.

Given that the retailer purchases Q units from the manufacturer at wholesale price r and resells these Q units to consumers at price $P = A - BQ$ the retailer's profit is

$$\Pi^D(Q, r) = (P - r)Q = (A - BQ)Q - rQ \tag{16.1}$$

The retailer maximizes profit by equating marginal revenue with marginal cost. Marginal revenue is $MR = A - 2BQ$ and marginal cost is r. Equating these two terms yields the optimal downstream output,

$$Q^D = (A - r)/2B \tag{16.2}$$

Substituting this expression into the demand function gives the market-clearing retail price $P^D = (A + r)/2$. From equation (16.1) the retailer's profit is, therefore, $\Pi^D = (A - r)^2/4B$. Figure 16.1 illustrates these results.

What about the manufacturer? What wholesale price should be charged? It is clear from equation (16.2) that the wholesale price determines the number of units the upstream

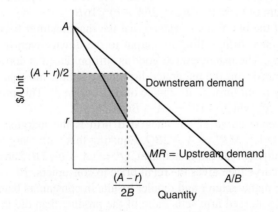

Figure 16.1   Independent retailer's optimal pricing as a function of manufacturer's wholesale price, r

At wholesale price r the retailer will set retail price $P = (A + r)/2$ to maximize profit. Total retail profit is indicated by the shaded region.

supplier is able to sell to the retailer. At the wholesale price r the retailer chooses to sell $Q^D = (A - r)/2B$ units. The retailer must purchase this number of units from the manufacturer. In other words, $Q = (A - r)/2B$ is the demand curve that the upstream manufacturer faces. It describes the relationship between the wholesale price r set by the manufacturer and the quantity of the product demanded by the retailer. But this means that *the inverse demand facing the upstream manufacturer at wholesale price r is $r = A - 2BQ$, which is also the marginal revenue function facing the retailer.*[1]

Practice Problem

16.1

The inverse market demand curve facing a monopoly retailer of gold bracelets is described by $P = 3{,}000 - Q/2$. The retailer buys gold bracelets at a wholesale price, r, set by the manufacturer. Show that the inverse demand curve facing the manufacturer is $r = 3{,}000 - Q$. Suppose instead that the retailer has additional marginal costs (labor etc.) of c^D. Show that the inverse demand curve facing the manufacturer is $r = (3{,}000 - c^D) - Q$.

We can now derive the profit-maximizing price that the manufacturer charges for its product. Very simply, the manufacturer equates marginal cost with marginal revenue. The inverse demand curve for the manufacturer is $r = A - 2BQ$, so the marginal revenue curve for the manufacturer is $MR = A - 4BQ$. Equating this with marginal cost c yields the profit-maximizing output and wholesale price. These are, respectively,

$$Q^U = \frac{A - c}{4B} \text{ and } r^U = \frac{A + c}{2} \tag{16.3}$$

This analysis is illustrated in Figure 16.2. When the upstream manufacturer sets the price $r^U = (A + c)/2$, the downstream retailer charges a price $P^D = (A + r^U)/2 = (3A + c)/4$. The retailer sells $Q^D = (A - c)/4B$ units, which is, of course, precisely the amount the upstream manufacturer anticipated it would sell when it set its upstream price $r^U = (A + c)/2$ in the first place. The profit of the manufacturer, shown in Figure 16.2 as the darkly shaded area $wrgv$, is $\Pi^U = (A - c)^2/8B$. The profit of the retailer, shown as the lightly shaded area $refg$, is $\Pi^D = (A - c)^2/16B$. The combined profit of the two firms is, of course, just the sum of these two areas, $3(A - c)^2/16B$.

Suppose now that the two firms merge so that the manufacturer becomes the upstream division of an integrated firm, selling its output to the downstream retail division of the same parent company. The manufactured good is still produced at constant marginal cost, c. This effectively transforms the integrated firm into a simple monopoly whose goal is to maximize monopoly profit through its choice of retail price P. This profit is total revenue PQ minus total cost cQ, which is $\Pi^I = (A - BQ)Q - cQ$.

The marginal revenue curve of the integrated firm is the marginal revenue curve of the nonintegrated retailer, $MR^I = A - 2BQ$. Equating this with marginal cost c gives the profit-maximizing output of the integrated firm, $Q^I = (A - c)/2B$. Substitution of this into the inverse demand curve then gives the retail price to consumers, $P^I = (A + c)/2$.

The merger of the manufacturer and retailer results in consumers being charged a lower price. As a result, the merged firm sells more of the product than did the two independent

---

[1] If, by contrast, the retailer has additional marginal costs of c^D then the inverse demand facing the manufacturer is $(A - r - c^D) - 2BQ$: see Practice Problem 16.1.

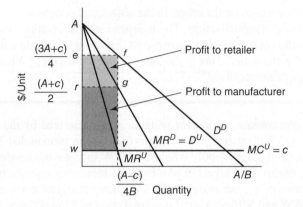

Figure 16.2   Upstream and downstream profit maximization without vertical integration
The retailer's marginal revenue curve MR^B is the manufacturer's demand curve D^U. Double marginalization results when the manufacturer sets its optimal wholesale price $r = (A + c)/2$ above marginal cost c, after which, the retailer adds a further markup by setting retail price $P = (3A + c)/4$. Retail profit is area *refg* The manufacturer's profit is area *wrgv*.

firms. But is this merger profitable? Yes! The profit earned by the integrated firm is $\Pi^I = (A - c)^2/4B$. This is 33.3 percent greater than the aggregate premerger profit of the manufacturer and the retailer, which we saw was $3(A - c)^2/16B$. From a social welfare point of view, *integrating the two monopoly firms has benefited everyone.* Total profit is increased *and* consumer surplus is increased with more of the good being sold at a lower price.

The gains from this vertical merger are illustrated in Figure 16.3. The retailer's premerger profit, area *refg*, is redistributed to consumers as consumer surplus. In addition, consumers gain the area *fgi*. The manufacturer's profit has doubled from area *wrgv* to *wrib* and this more than offsets the loss of the retailer's profit.

Merger of vertically related firms generates an all around efficiency gain because it allows the separate but related activities to be coordinated and, thereby, to internalize the

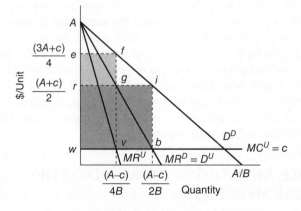

Figure 16.3   Upstream and downstream profit maximization with vertical integration
An integrated manufacturer-retailer sets a retail price to consumers at $P = (A + c)/2$. The area *refg* that would have been profit for a non-integrated retailer now becomes part of consumer surplus. However, the increased sales volume generates a more than offsetting profit gain of area *gjbv*. Total profit for the integrated firm is *rjbw*.

externality that each imposes on the other. In the absence of coordination, the final product price reflects a double marginalization. The independent manufacturer marks up its price to the retailer who then compounds that price-cost distortion by adding a further markup in setting a price to the consumer. This is the basis of the old saying, "What is worse than a monopoly? A chain of monopolies!"

Practice Problem

16.2

Suppose that the downstream market for widgets is characterized by the inverse demand curve $P = 100 - Q$. Widget retailing is controlled by the monopolist WR Inc., which obtains its widgets from the monopoly wholesaler WW Inc. at a wholesale price of w_w per widget. WW Inc. obtains the widgets in turn from the monopoly manufacturer WM Ltd. at a manufacturing price of w_m per widget. WM Inc. incurs marginal costs of $10 per unit in making widgets. WW and WR each incur marginal costs of $5 in addition to the prices that they have to pay for widgets.

a. What is the equilibrium widget price to consumers, P, the equilibrium wholesale price w_w, and the equilibrium manufacturing price w_r? What is the profit earned by each firm at these prices?

b. Show that vertical integration by any two of these firms increases profit and benefits consumers.

c. Show that integration of all three firms is even more beneficial.

There are, of course, several qualifications to this analysis that we should mention. Some are noted in the accompanying Reality Checkpoint regarding the auto industry. In addition, it is important to note that the benefits of the vertical merger just described assume that the downstream firm uses a fixed amount of the upstream firm's product for every unit of output that the downstream firm sells. In our example of a manufacturer and a downstream retailer, this assumption makes sense. The retailer has to have one unit of the manufacturer's product for every unit it sells to its customers. But in other situations this assumption could be too strong. For example, if the upstream firm is a steel producer and the downstream firm is an automobile manufacturer, the steel firm's decision to charge the car manufacturer a price that includes a high markup may induce the automaker to reduce its use of steel in favor of aluminum or perhaps fiberglass. In such a case, the potential gains of the car manufacturer integrating backwards into the steel market are less clear-cut.

In summary, vertical integration of a chain of producers, each of which has monopoly power, is likely to benefit both firms and consumers by correcting the market failure associated with double (and triple and quadruple . . .) marginalization. These benefits are more likely to arise when the technology operated by downstream firms offers limited opportunities for substitution into other inputs.

16.2   POSSIBLE ANTICOMPETITIVE EFFECTS OF VERTICAL MERGERS

The merger analysis of the previous section suggests that the antitrust authorities should be less concerned about the welfare impact of vertical mergers than the impact of horizontal mergers. However, the analysis is based upon some important assumptions that drive the

Reality Checkpoint
Vertical Disintegration in the Automobile Industry

Our analysis of vertical integration has stressed the gains of eliminating "the middle man" and the problem of double-marginalization. If this were all there were to it, we would see much more vertical integration and very little outsourcing. Quite to the contrary, however, the business news over the last decade has been filled with stories of outsourcing and vertical *dis*integration as firms has spun off their former internal divisions. Nowhere has this phenomenon been more dramatic than in the US automobile industry.

Until the 1990s, the organizational design pioneered by the General Motors Corporation founder, W. C. Durant, and his protégé Alfred Sloan, was the dominant model. The logic of avoiding double-marginalization and other organizational advantages led US car companies to vertically integrate from the development and control of electronics and other parts, to the production of engines and car bodies, to the full assembly of ready-to-ship cars and extending down to official dealerships. In fact, the US firms integrated even further in the 1980s by acquiring rental car firms. Chrysler bought both Thrifty and Dollar Rent-A-Car. Ford bought Hertz and GM acquired a half interest in National.

Over the years, however, problems with this organizational strategy emerged. One stemmed from the incentives it created. To the extent the firms bought virtually all their parts internally, the parts divisions had no outside competition to spur efficiency. Closely related to the incentive problem was the fact that once parts-makers and other units were fully part of GM, Ford, and Chrysler, they gained representation by the United Auto Workers. This typically meant higher wages so these supplies became more expensive after incorporation into the parent carmaker. Often, buyers at the automaking divisions did not even know the names of alternative suppliers.

By the mid 1990s, the car companies began to reverse their vertical integration strategy. They all sold off the car rental companies. In addition, GM spun off its parts division as the independent parts firm, Delphi Automotive Systems. In 1999, Ford followed quickly and spun off its parts division as Visteon Corporation.

Further retrenchment followed. In 2006, both firms began withdrawing from the downstream business of financing car purchases by dealers and customers. GM, for example, sold off a majority interest in its banking operation known as the General Motors Acceptance Corporation (GMAC), which then became Ally Financial. Subsequently, in the wake of bankruptcy and reorganization, both firms greatly reduced their downstream dealer operations. GM closed over 1,000 dealerships including all those associated with the discontinued *Hummer*, *Saab*, and *Saturn* lines. Chrysler terminated over 700 dealerships as well. In addition, exclusive dealerships selling just one brand, e.g., Chevrolet, nearly vanished.

Source: J. Schnapp. "Lesser Than the Sum of Its Parts," *Wall Street Journal*, April 4, 2006, p. 18; J. B. White, "How Automakers Keep You Coming Back," *Wall Street Journal*, January 22, 2013, p. B1.

results. In particular, we have assumed that there is a single market in which the final output is sold and that there is monopoly at each stage in the vertical chain. Before coming to the general conclusion that "vertical mergers are good for firms and consumers," we should check on the effects of relaxing these assumptions.

16.2.1   Vertical Merger to Facilitate Price Discrimination

While life is good for a monopolist, it is even better for a monopolist who price discriminates. This is equally true for an upstream monopolist selling to a number of downstream firms. Moreover, there are many cases in which those downstream firms differ in their willingness to pay for the upstream firm's product. Examples include a wholesaler supplying retailers in different cities, a manufacturer of motorcar parts supplying automakers in different countries, a consultant advising different firms in different industries, and so on. In these circumstances, the upstream firm would like to charge a high price for its product or service to those firms whose demand is inelastic and a low price to those whose demand is elastic.

Our earlier discussion of price discrimination showed, however, that successful price discrimination has two requirements. First, the firm must be able to identify which buyers have elastic and which have inelastic demand. Second, the firm must somehow prevent resale of its product among its buyers. Such arbitrage would clearly undo any price discrimination efforts. We will assume that the firm has somehow solved the identification problem. The question then becomes, what strategies can the firm use to surmount the arbitrage problem?

The simplest approach would be for the upstream firm to write a no-resale contract with its buyers. In many circumstances, however, such contracts are unenforceable—for example when the client firms are in different legal jurisdictions—in which case some other approach is necessary. One such approach is for the upstream firm to merge with some or all of its downstream customers.

Suppose that the upstream firm supplies a series of downstream firms and that, because of financial constraints, the upstream firm can integrate forwards with only some of the downstream firms. Then, as Practice Problem 16.3 shows, *it should merge first into markets with the highest elasticities of demand*. Because the merger allows the upstream firm to prevent resale, it also allows the firm to charge high profit-maximizing prices in the other, low-demand-elasticity markets. Is such a merger pro- or anti-competitive? Successful price discrimination can improve economic efficiency. When success is achieved by means of a vertical merger the effect on economic efficiency is, however, ambiguous. The reason is that while the merger increases profits and removes double marginalization in one group of markets, the merger also leads to increased prices in the remaining markets. In other words, some consumers gain and others lose from the vertical merger. The overall effect is uncertain and can be resolved only when we have more information on the precise nature of demand in the various markets.

16.3

Practice Problem

Assume that Widget International supplies widgets to Gizmo Inc. in Boston, where the demand for gizmos is $P_{gb} = 1 - Q_{gb}$, and TruGizmo Inc. of New York, where demand for gizmos is $P_{gn} = 0.5 - 0.2Q_{gn}$. Assume that WI's marginal costs of supplying both markets is \$0.1 per widget and that both Gizmo Inc. and TruGizmo Inc. need exactly one widget for every gizmo they sell. Both gizmo dealers have other costs of production that amount to \$0.1 per gizmo.

a.   What are the profit-maximizing prices for widgets and gizmos in these two markets if Widget International cannot price discriminate? What are the profits of the three firms?

b.   What are the profit-maximizing prices for widgets and gizmos in these two markets if Widget International can price discriminate? What are the profits of the three firms?

c. Show that if WI can merge with either Gizmo Inc. or TruGizmo Inc., it prefers to merge with TruGizmo Inc.
d. What is the effect of the merger on consumer prices and consumer surplus when WI (i) cannot and (ii) can price discriminate pre-merger?

16.2.2   Vertical Merger, Oligopoly, and Market Foreclosure

Now consider the second important assumption underlying the analysis in Section 16.1. The gains from the merger hinge crucially on the fact that prior to the merger there is monopoly at both levels of activity, manufacture and retail. Suppose, instead, that we start with either a competitive manufacturing sector upstream selling to a monopoly downstream, or a monopoly upstream firm selling to a competitive retail sector. In the former case, price competition upstream among manufacturers leads to a wholesale price equal to marginal cost. In the latter, competition among retailers downstream drives the retail price equal to the upstream price P^U plus any downstream cost c_D. In either case, no double marginalization can occur, and there is no efficiency gain to vertical integration.

It could be argued, of course, that assuming perfect competition rather than monopoly in either the upstream or downstream market merely replaces one extreme assumption by another. We now turn, therefore, to the more realistic case in which both upstream and downstream markets are oligopolies. This raises another important issue that needs to be considered explicitly. Beyond the desire to reduce or eliminate double marginalization, there is an additional motive for vertical integration that is more clearly anticompetitive. The motive is the possibility of *market foreclosure*. That is, the merger of vertically related firms might result in an upstream–downstream company that can either deny downstream rivals a source of inputs, or upstream competitors a market for their products.

Consider a hypothetical case in which two suppliers of computer chips compete for sales to two downstream computer manufacturers who in turn sell to the general public. The chips of the two upstream firms are identical so that, if the two suppliers compete in price, they must sell at marginal cost. Hence, only the two downstream firms earn any economic profit. Suppose now that one of the chip manufacturers and one of the computer firms merge. The argument that this merger may be anticompetitive goes roughly as follows. The upstream chip division of the newly merged firm no longer offers to sell any chips to the remaining independent computer firm, that is, it forecloses sales of its product to this downstream rival. Why? The answer is that such foreclosure leaves the independent computer firm with only one supplier, namely, the remaining independent chip firm. That independent chip producer now has monopoly power vis-à-vis the independent computer firm and, accordingly, sets a monopoly wholesale price for its chips. In turn, this raises the costs of the independent computer firm relative to the pre-merger situation and makes it less able to compete with the downstream computer division of the integrated firm. As a result, the merged firm can raise the price of its computers and earn more profit. Because the upstream market was initially competitive there was no double-marginalization and because there are no other cost savings as a result of the merger, this vertical integration is clearly anticompetitive.[2] The merger raises the cost of the nonintegrated rivals on the supply side and thereby leaves them at a disadvantage relative to the integrated firm.

The telecommunications industry is one in which foreclosure concerns have been quite real for regulatory authorities in both the United States and in Europe. In this industry, the local telephone network has generally been monopolized by a firm that also competes in the more competitive long-distance market. Because a long-distance provider, such as Sprint or say 1st Family, has to gain access to its potential customers by connecting to the local network, the local network provider has the potential to price its long-distance competitors out of the market by charging them a very high price for network access or, in an extreme case, denying them access to the network at all. Accordingly, a major concern of the regulatory authorities has been the prices that suppliers of local telephone networks are allowed to charge for access to the local network.

Alcoa has been accused of subjecting its rivals to a similar price squeeze, both by making contractual arrangements with power companies to prevent them from supplying vital electricity to competing aluminum producers and by charging very high prices for aluminum ingots that were used by rivals that competed with Alcoa in downstream markets such as the aluminum sheet market. In short, foreclosure arguments suggest that monopoly power in one, say upstream, market may be leveraged into power in another, downstream market.

16.4

Practice Problem

Suppose that the downstream market for widgets is perfectly competitive and characterized by the inverse demand curve $P = 100 - Q$. Retailers have zero production costs, but do incur a fee, r, for every unit sold. This fee is the payment that retailers must pay to the only manufacturer of widgets, the monopolist Widget International (WI). WI bears no fixed cost. It does, however, have a constant marginal cost of $10.

a.   What is the equilibrium price to consumers, P, and fee to retailers, r? What is the profit earned by retailers and WI at these prices?
b.   Show that vertical integration by which WI becomes the single producer and retailer of widgets does not raise WI's profit and does not lower the price to consumers.
c.   What is the price to consumers if both widget manufacturing and retailing are competitive?

16.3   FORMAL OLIGOPOLY MODELS OF VERTICAL INTEGRATION

The conventional foreclosure argument that we just presented is compelling, particularly when buttressed by the accompanying examples. However, there are also some clear weaknesses in the argument that need to be confronted. The local phone network and Alcoa examples are different from our hypothetical computer chip story in that these real world cases begin with something less than competition in the upstream market. We have not

---

[2]   For a description many ways in which an integrated firm can impose a cost squeeze, see Krattenmaker and Salop (1986).

identified why this may be the case. Apart from this practical consideration, the logic of the argument is still incomplete. We have not explained why the integrated firm will definitely stop selling chips to the independent downstream computer firm. Nor have we considered an obvious response by the remaining independent firms, namely, to merge and similarly enjoy the benefits of vertical integration. In the next section, we describe two models of foreclosure through vertical integration that address these concerns. One is due to Salinger (1988) and is based on Cournot competition. The other is due to Ordover, Saloner, and Salop (1990) and is rooted in price competition.

16.3.1   Vertical Integration and Foreclosure in a Cournot Model

To illustrate Salinger's (1988) basic contribution we return to our basic Cournot model except that we now assume that Cournot competition applies both in an upstream market populated by two firms and in a downstream market, also with two firms. The upstream firms produce a homogeneous intermediate good that is used by the downstream firms to make a homogeneous good for final consumption. One unit of downstream output requires exactly one unit of the intermediate product. Each upstream firm has constant marginal costs of c^U per unit and each downstream firm has constant marginal costs, excluding the cost of the intermediate good, of c^D per unit. Inverse demand for the final consumption good is:

$$P = A - BQ = A - B(q_1 + q_2) \tag{16.4}$$

The market game has two stages. In the first stage, the two upstream firms compete in quantities, generating a price P^U for the intermediate product. In the second stage, the downstream firms compete in quantities taking the upstream price P^U as given. Consider first what happens when there is no vertical merger and then compare this outcome with what happens when there is vertical merger. Such a comparison is easier to make when we have a specific numerical example and so later we will use the values: $A = 100$; $B = 1$; and $c^U = c^D = 23$.

(i) No Vertical Mergers

Cournot competition upstream in the first stage leads to a market-clearing intermediate product price of P^U so that each downstream firm in the second stage faces marginal cost $P^U + c^D$. Cournot competition downstream leads each downstream firm to produce:[3]

$$q_1^D = q_2^D = \frac{A - P^U - c^D}{3B} \tag{16.5}$$

and to earn a downstream profit of

$$\pi_1^D = \pi_2^D = \frac{(A - P^U - c^D)^2}{9B} \tag{16.6}$$

We can use equation (16.5) to identify the *derived demand* that the upstream firms face. Aggregate downstream output is $Q^D = 2(A - P^U - c^D)/3B$. Because each unit of final

---

[3]   See Chapter 9 for the derivation of the Cournot equilibrium.

product output requires one unit of the intermediate product, this is also the aggregate demand, $Q^U = Q^D$ for the intermediate product, which we can write in inverse form as:

$$P^U = (A - c^D) - \frac{3B}{2} Q^U \qquad (16.7)$$

The next step in the analysis is simplified once we recognize that this is in standard linear form $P = a - bQ$, where $a = A - c^D$ and $b = 3B/3$. In the first stage of the game, the Cournot equilibrium output of each upstream firm is, therefore:

$$q_1^U = q_2^U = \frac{a - c^U}{3b} = \frac{(A - c^D) - c^U}{9B/2} = \frac{2(A - c^U - c^D)}{9B} \qquad (16.8)$$

It follows that aggregate output in the upstream market is $Q^U = 4(A - c^U - c^D)/9B$. Substituting this into the upstream demand of equation (16.7) gives the equilibrium upstream price for the intermediate product:

$$P^U = (A - c^D) - \frac{3B}{2} \times \frac{4(A - c^U - c^D)}{9B} = \frac{(A - c^D + 2c^U)}{3} \qquad (16.9)$$

Profit of each upstream supplier is $(P^U - c^U)q_i^U$, which from (16.8) and (16.9) gives

$$\pi_1^U = \pi_2^U = \frac{2(A - c^U - c^D)^2}{27B} \qquad (16.10)$$

Finally, substituting the upstream price into equations (16.5) and (16.6) gives the equilibrium output and profit for each downstream firm:

$$q_1^D = q_2^D = \frac{2(A - c^U - c^D)}{9B} \qquad (16.11)$$

$$\pi_1^D = \pi_2^D = \frac{4(A - c^U - c^D)^2}{81B} \qquad (16.12)$$

It is easy to check that, as we would expect, aggregate downstream demand equals aggregate upstream output. Using the numbers from our specific example, total output is 24 units. The wholesale price is \$41 and the price to consumers is \$76. Each upstream firm earns \$216 in profit and each downstream firm earns \$144.

(ii) Vertical Integration of an Upstream and Downstream Firm

Now consider what happens if one of the downstream firms $D1$ and one of the upstream firms $U1$ merge. Assume for the moment that this newly merged firm refuses to supply the independent downstream firm at all. Hence, the downstream firm $D2$ has to turn to the remaining independent wholesaler $U2$ for its input supply, *and U2 knows this*. It follows that the upstream firm $U2$ has monopoly power over $D2$ and will set a price to $D2$ of $P^U > c^U$. As a result, $D2$ has marginal cost $P^U + c^U$ while $D1$ has marginal cost $c^U + c^D$. In other words, the integrated firm has removed the double-markup in its pricing. As a result, it now competes in the downstream market as a low-cost competitor vis-à-vis $D2$.

Applying the standard Cournot equations, we know that the post merger equilibrium outputs of the two firms downstream are:

$$q_1^D = \frac{A - 2(c^U + c^D) + (P^U + c^D)}{3B} = \frac{A - 2c^U - c^D + P^U}{3B}$$

$$q_2^D = \frac{A - 2(P^U + c^D) + (c^U + c^D)}{3B} = \frac{A - 2P^U - c^D + c^U}{3B} \qquad (16.13)$$

and their equilibrium profits are:

$$\pi_1^D = \frac{(A - 2(c^U + c^D) + (P^U + c^D))^2}{9B} = \frac{(A - 2c^U - c^D + P^U)^2}{9B}$$

$$\pi_2^D = \frac{(A - 2(P^U + c^D) + (c^U + c^D))^2}{9B} = \frac{(A - 2P^U - c^D + c^U)^2}{9B} \qquad (16.14)$$

Equation (16.13) confirms that, under our foreclosure assumption, the downstream division of the integrated firm has a greater output than its non-integrated rival.

How does $U2$ set P^U? We can use (16.13) to identify the derived demand, $q_2^U = q_2^D$ facing the independent upstream firm. Again writing this in inverse form we have

$$P^U = \frac{A - c^D + c^U}{2} - \frac{3B}{2} q_2^U \qquad (16.15)$$

This is in the form $P = a - bq$ and we know that with this demand function the monopoly output is $(a - c^U)/2b$, where $a = (A - c^D + c^U)/2$ and $b = 3B/2$. This gives the equilibrium output for upstream firm 2:

$$q_2^U = \frac{A - c^U - c^D}{6B} \qquad (16.16)$$

The equilibrium price for the intermediate product is, therefore

$$P^U = \frac{A - c^D + c^U}{2} - \frac{3B}{2} \times \frac{(A - c^U - c^D)}{6B} = \frac{(A + 3c^U - c^D)}{4} \qquad (16.17)$$

Profit of the independent upstream firm is $(P^U - c^U)q_2^U$, which from (16.16) and (16.17) is

$$\pi_2^U = \frac{(A - c^U - c^D)^2}{24B} \qquad (16.18)$$

Finally, we can substitute the equilibrium intermediate product price into equations (16.13) and (16.14) to identify the equilibrium outputs, prices, and profits in the downstream market:

$$q_1^D = \frac{5(A - c^U - c^D)}{12B}$$

$$q_2^D = \frac{(A - c^D - c^U)}{6B} \qquad (16.19)$$

$$P^D = \frac{5A + 7c^U + 7c^D}{12}$$

(16.20)

$$\pi_1^D = \frac{25(A - c^U - c^D)^2}{144B}$$

$$\pi_2^D = \frac{(A - c^D - c^U)^2}{36B}$$

(16.21)

The downstream division of the integrated firm is noticeably larger and more profitable than its independent downstream rival. This is the result of the foreclosure of supply to $D2$, which gave $U2$ monopoly power that $U2$ thereafter exploited by setting a high upstream price. Again, using our specific numbers, the upstream price to $D2$ is \$36.5. Because the integrated retailer buys its input at cost, it sells 22.5 units downstream while its independent rival sells just 9 units. The resulting retail price is \$68.5. Prior to the merger, $D2$ earned a profit of \$144. That has now been reduced to \$81. The merging firms, however, have benefited. Their combined profit before the merger was \$360. It has risen through integration to \$506.25.

Two points need to be considered. First, does our assumption of foreclosure make sense? Is it profit-maximizing for the integrated firm not to sell any inputs to its independent downstream rival? This is where Salinger's (1988) argument comes into play. The integrated firm has a total input cost of $c^U + c^D$. It therefore earns $P^D - (c^U + c^D)$ on each unit that it sells downstream. Further, we know that for the rival $D2$ to be in business, it must be the case that $P^D > (P^U + c^D)$. Suppose that the integrated firm did sell one unit of its intermediate good to its independent rival $D2$ at price P^U. What would happen if instead it withdrew this unit and sold it internally to the downstream division so that the total output and therefore the price in the downstream market remain unchanged? In withdrawing the unit originally sold to $D2$, the integrated firm loses profit $P^U - c^U$. However, it then gains a profit $P^D - (c^U + c^D)$ that it makes on every internal sale. It will therefore be profitable to stop selling to the downstream rival or to foreclose if $P^D - (c^U + c^D) > P^U - c^U$. This condition simplifies to $P^D > (P^U + c^D)$, which we know has to hold given that the downstream rival is in business. In other words, if the integrated firm were selling to $D2$ then it could always do better by withdrawing those units and instead sell them internally to increase its own downstream production. In our numerical example, the integrated firm ultimately earns \$68.5 − \$23 − \$23 = \$22.5 for every upstream unit sold internally. By contrast, it would earn only \$36.5 − \$23 = \$13.5 on upstream sales to $D2$. Therefore, foreclosure of sales to downstream rivals does seem to be optimal.

The second feature worth noting is that the vertical merger brings benefits to consumers despite the foreclosure that also accompanies it. In our numerical example, the vertical integration of firms $U1$ and $D1$ causes the price in the downstream market to fall from \$76 to \$68.5. The elimination of double marginalization by the integrating firms benefits consumers. Salinger (1988) shows, however, that this need not be the case. The competitive effect of a vertical merger is determined by the balance between two forces. On the one hand, vertical merger and market foreclosure reduce the number of independent upstream suppliers and so reduce the competitive pressure on upstream—and downstream—prices. On the other hand, a vertical merger eliminates double marginalization for the merged firms and, by reducing their input costs, makes them fiercer competitors in the downstream market, tending to reduce consumer prices. It is difficult to predict how this will play out.

What is likely to be the case is that the anticompetitive effect will be weak if the number of independent upstream competitors remains large.

Moreover, there is an important strategic issue that is not addressed by the Salinger (1988) model. The independent downstream firms that are foreclosed upon may well have an incentive to react to integrated rivals by merging with upstream firms themselves. If vertical integration brings business advantages, then all firms should have an incentive to pursue them. Policy should not penalize any one firm because it happens to be first in line in this process. To address this point, as well as to explore other features of vertical mergers, we now consider the model of Ordover, Saloner, and Salop (1990) (OSS).

16.3.2   Vertical Mergers in a Differentiated Products Setting

The OSS model is in some ways simpler and in others more complex than the Salinger model. It is simpler in that we assume Bertrand competition with homogenous upstream products implying marginal cost pricing. It is more complex in that we treat the relationships between upstream and downstream firms more strategically.

The upstream firms incur constant marginal cost c^U. One unit of the upstream product is needed for every unit of downstream production; the downstream firms have no other production costs. In contrast to the Salinger model, firms sell differentiated products and compete in prices in both markets. The upstream product of the two firms is homogeneous but the downstream products are differentiated. We capture this feature by letting the demand for downstream products 1 and 2 be respectively:

$$
\begin{aligned}
q_1^D &= A - p_1^D + B(p_2^D - p_1^D) \\
q_2^D &= A - p_2^D + B(p_1^D - p_2^D)
\end{aligned}
\quad (0 < B < \infty)
\tag{16.22}
$$

In equation (16.22), B is an inverse measure of the degree of product differentiation in the downstream market. If $B = 0$, the two products are totally differentiated. However, as B approaches infinity the two products become increasingly similar. To keep the analysis as simple as we can, we normalize $A = 100$ and $c^U = 0$ without loss of generality, and we assume that $B = 1$.[4]

In order to consider the explicitly strategic aspects of vertical mergers, OSS develop a four-stage game. In the first stage, one of the downstream firms can choose to acquire one of the upstream suppliers. If such a merger takes place we assume, without loss of generality, that it is between $U1$ and $D1$ and results in the merged firm $F1$.

In the second stage, input prices are set. If no merger occurs then the upstream firms compete in prices. If a merger has occurred then in the second stage two possibilities are considered. First, $F1$ refuses to supply $D2$, i.e., foreclosure. Second, $F1$ sets an upper bound on the input price to be paid by $D2$ by offering to supply it at price c_{12}, with $F1$ setting c_{12} before $U2$ sets its input price. This allows $U2$ to undercut $F1$ in this stage by setting its price "just less" than c_{12}. In the third stage, if there has been a merger in the first stage firms $U2$ and $D2$ decide whether or not to merge. We then proceed to the fourth stage. Here, downstream prices are set given the input prices and organizational structures that have been determined in the previous stages. As usual, we solve this game by working backwards from stage 4.

[4]   The choice of B does affect profits but does not actually affect the equilibrium that emerges from the model.

To specify the extensive form of this four-stage game, we need to identify the pay-offs under the different strategy combinations that can occur.

We begin with the most general case in which firm $D1$ pays c_1 and firm $D2$ pays c_2, respectively, for the upstream product. Our demand equations then imply marginal revenue for each downstream firm given by:

$$MR_1 = 50 + \frac{p_2}{2} - q_1$$

$$MR_2 = 50 + \frac{p_1}{2} - q_2 \tag{16.23}$$

Equating each firm's marginal revenue with its upstream marginal cost yields the best response functions:

$$p_1 = 25 + \frac{p_2}{4} + \frac{c_1}{2}$$

$$p_2 = 25 + \frac{p_1}{4} + \frac{c_2}{2} \tag{16.24}$$

Solving these for p_1^D and p_2^D gives the downstream prices:

$$p_1^D(c_1, c_2) = \frac{2}{15}(250 + 4c_1 + c_2)$$

$$p_1^D(c_1, c_2) = \frac{2}{15}(250 + 4c_1 + c_2) \tag{16.25}$$

As we might expect, both prices are increasing in the costs of the upstream inputs. Substituting these prices into the downstream demand functions of equations (16.22) gives the equilibrium downstream outputs of:

$$q_1^D(c_1, c_2) = \frac{2}{15}(500 - 7c_1 + 2c_2)$$

$$q_2^D(c_1, c_2) = \frac{2}{15}(500 - 7c_2 + 2c_1) \tag{16.26}$$

Each firm's downstream output is decreasing in its own costs but increasing in the rival's costs.

If we now solve for each downstream firm's profits, it is straightforward to show that these are:

$$\pi_1^D(c_1, c_2) = \frac{2}{225}(500 - 7c_1 + 2c_2)^2$$

$$\pi_2^D(c_1, c_2) = \frac{2}{225}(500 - 7c_2 + 2c_1)^2 \tag{16.27}$$

An important point to note for subsequent analysis is that the profit of downstream firm i is decreasing in its own input cost c_i and increasing in its rival's input cost c_j.

Now consider the third stage. If there is no merger in stage 1, there is no merger in stage 3 and the independent upstream firms, acting as Bertrand competitors, supply the upstream product at marginal cost $c^U = 0$. In this case, the upstream firms just break even, while equation (16.27) with $c_1 = c_2 = 0$, implies aprofit for each downstream firm of:

$$\pi_1^D(0,0) = \pi_2^D(0,0) = 2,222.22 \tag{16.28}$$

Suppose by contrast that there has been a merger of $U1$ and $D1$ in stage 1 to form firm $F1$. As we noted above, we then consider two possibilities in stage 2 of the game. The first of these is that $F1$ forecloses on $D2$. The second is that $F1$ sets its input price c_{12} before $U2$ sets its input price.

Suppose that $F1$ forecloses in stage 2. If in stage 3 firms $U2$ and $D2$ do not merge, this effectively makes $U2$ a monopoly supplier to $D2$ (in much the same way as we saw in the Salinger model). Because one unit of the upstream product is required to make one unit of the final product, profit of $U2$ if it sets input price c_m is $\pi_2^U(c^U, c_m) = (c_m - c^U)q_2^D(c^U, c_m)$, where $q_2^D(c^U, c_m)$ is given by (16.26) with $c_2 = c_m$ and $c_1 = c^U = 0$. In other words:

$$q_2^D(0, c_m) = \frac{2}{15}(500 - 7c_m); \quad \pi_2^U(0, c_m) = \frac{2}{15}c_m(500 - 7c_m) \tag{16.29}$$

Inverting U2's demand curve to solve for its marginal revenue and then setting this to its assumed marginal cost of 0 yields the optimal upstream price c_m:

$$c_m = 250/7 = \$35.71 \tag{16.30}$$

Substituting this price into (16.27) and (16.29) gives the profit for $U2$ of $25,000/21$ and for $D2$ of $5000/9$. In other words, aggregate profit of $U2$ and $D2$ if they do not merge in response to merger and foreclosure by $F1$ is

$$\pi_2^A(0, c_m) = 110,000/63 = \$1,746.03 \tag{16.31}$$

Profit to $F1$ from this foreclosure strategy is:

$$\pi_1^D(0, c_m) = 1,280,000/441 = \$2,902.49 \tag{16.32}$$

Now consider what happens if instead $U2$ and $D2$ merge to form firm $F2$. Both $F1$ and $F2$ then obtain the upstream product at marginal cost. As a result, the profits of $F1$ and $F2$ are each given by equation (16.28), that is, $\$2,222.22$. Comparison with (16.31) and (16.32) indicates that if $F1$ forecloses on $D2$ then $U2$ and $D2$ will merge, significantly reducing the profit of $F1$.

As we suggested near the end of our discussion of the Salinger model, those who belong to the club of vertically integrated firms may wish to exclude others from joining. Facing vertically integrated rivals means competing against firms with low input costs and this can lead to intense price competition. So, suppose that $U1$ and $D1$ have merged to form $F1$ but want to prevent $U2$ and $D2$ from doing the same thing. Is there a strategy that might work to achieve this goal? OSS suggest that there is, indeed, such a strategy.

Suppose that in stage 2, $F1$ does not foreclose but instead offers to supply $D2$ at unit input price $c_{12} > c^U$. As we noted above, we assume that $F1$ sets c_{12} before $U2$ sets its input price, so clearly $U2$ can win $D2$'s business by just undercutting c_{12} and has an incentive to do so because $c_{12} > c^U$. However, by committing to price c_{12}, $F1$ puts a ceiling on the price that $U2$ can charge $D2$ and thereby limits the gains from a merger of $U2$ and $D2$. To see this more clearly consider the following analysis.

Profit to $D2$ given that $F1$ supplies its own downstream division at marginal cost $c^U = 0$ and that $U2$ just undercuts c_{12} in supplying $D2$ is given by equation (16.27) with $c_1 = 0$ and $c_2 = c_{12}$:

$$\pi_2^D(0, c_{12}) = \frac{2}{225}(500 - 7c_{12})^2 \tag{16.33}$$

Profit to $U2$ given that it supplies $D2$ at input price c_{12} is $c_{12}q_2^D(c^U, c_{12})$ where $q_2^D(c^U, c_{12})$ is given by equation (16.26) with $c_2 = c_{12}$ and $c_1 = c^U = 0$:

$$\pi_2^U(0, c_{12}) = \frac{2}{15}c_{12}(500 - 7c_{12}) \tag{16.34}$$

Aggregate profit of $U2$ and $D2$ is therefore is $\pi_2^A(0, c_{12}) = \pi_2^U(0, c_{12}) + \pi_2^D(0, c_{12})$ which, from (16.33) and (16.34) is:

$$\pi_2^A(0, c_{12}) = \frac{8}{225}(62{,}500 + 125c_{12} - 14c_{12}^2) \tag{16.35}$$

This aggregate profit is quadratic in c_{12}. It is easy to see that when $c_{12} = c^U = 0$ $\pi_2^A(0,0) = 20{,}000/9 = \$2{,}222.22$. Moreover, it is straightforward to show that $\pi_2^A(0, c_{12})$ is increasing in c_{12} when $c_{12} = 0$. Finally, $\pi_2^A(c^U, c_m) = 110{,}000/63 < \pi_2^D(c^U, c^U)$ from equations (16.30) and (16.35). In other words, $\pi_2^A(c^U, c_{12})$ can be illustrated as in Figure 16.4.

It follows from these results that there is always an input price $c_{12} < c^*$ that $F1$ can set to make $U2$ and $D2$ jointly more profitable as separate firms than they would be if they merged: in our example $c^* = \$8.83$. In preventing their merger, $F1$ not only preserves itself as the lone vertically integrated firm but also ensures that it continues to face a high-cost rival in the downstream market rather than the low cost one it would face if $U2$ and $D2$ merged. In other words, $F1$ has an incentive to set c_{12} as high as possible while preventing

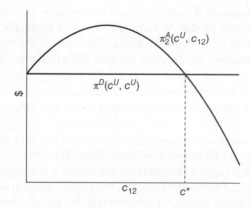

Figure 16.4 Strategic supply price
If $F1$ offers to supply $D2$ at any input price less than c^*, Firms $U2$ and $D2$ will prefer not to merge.

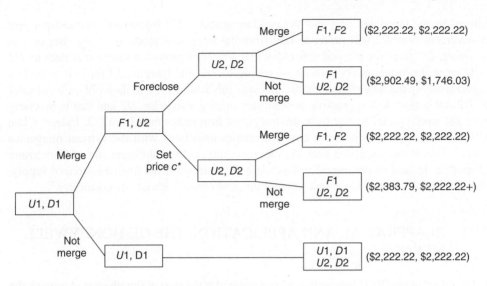

Figure 16.5   The OSS extensive-form game with $c_{12} = c^*$

the merger of $U2$ and $D2$. From equation (16.27) profit of $F1$ when it offers to supply $D2$ at input price c^* (which is just undercut by $U2$) is $\pi_1^D(0, c^*) = \$2,383.79$.

The OSS analysis just outlined is illustrated in Figure 16.5 where we show the extensive form of the four-stage game.

Suppose that $U1$ and $D1$ merge in stage 1 to form $F1$. If $F1$ chooses to Foreclose in stage 2 then $U2$ and $D2$ will choose to merge in stage 3 as a result of which $F1$ has profit $\pi_1^D(c^U, c^U) = \$2,222.22$. Suppose, by contrast, that $F1$ sets c^*, which $U2$ just undercuts. By construction of c^* we know that $\pi_2^A(c^U, c^* - \varepsilon) > \pi_2^D(c^U, c^U)$ so $U2$ and $D2$ choose not to merge. As a result, $F1$ has profit \$2,383.79. It follows that $F1$ prefers to set price $c_{12} = c^*$ than to Foreclose. So if $U1$ and $D1$ Merge in stage 1 the merged firm will offer to supply $D2$ at price c^* in stage 2, as a result of which $U2$ and $D2$ choose not to merge in stage 3 and $F1$ earns $\pi_1^D(c^U, c^*) = \$2,383.79$.

Now suppose that $U1$ and $D1$ choose not to merge in stage 1. Then the upstream firms compete in prices and set input price at marginal cost c^U, as a result of which the downstream firms, in competing in prices, earn $\pi_1^D(c^U, c^U) = \pi_2^D(c^U, c^U) = 2,222.22$. Clearly, $U1$ and $D1$ prefer to merge.

To summarize, the subgame perfect equilibrium to the OSS four-stage game is that firms $U1$ and $D1$ merge in stage 1 to form $F1$. Then $F1$ offers to supply $D2$ in stage 2 at input price c^*, as a result of which $U2$ and $D2$ do not merge in stage 3.

Note among other things that the strategy of offering to supply its rival at price $c_{12} > c^U$ is much closer in spirit to the "squeeze" pricing that phone companies and Alcoa have been accused of than is outright foreclosure. Note too that by preventing the merger of $U2$ and $D2$, and thereby preserving the existence of double marginalization and a high cost rival, $F1$'s strategy of offering to sell to $D2$ at price c_{12} leads to higher prices for consumers. It is an action designed to thwart the outbreak of competition and is therefore truly anti-competitive. In all these ways, the OSS model has an air of realism about it.

Chen (2001) extends the OSS analysis, starting from the empirical regularity that foreclosure seems to be a rarity in practice. He shows that whenever the wholesale price offered by the integrated firm and independent producer $U2$ is the same, the independent downstream firm $D2$ will prefer to buy from the integrated producer. Why? Because in so doing, $D2$ gives the integrated firm another source of profit—a source that rises as $D2$ sells more downstream. As a result of selling to $D2$, the integrated firm will price less aggressively in the downstream market because this would cut into its profit on input sales to $D2$. Of course, less aggressive downstream pricing also helps $D2$ and that is precisely why $D2$ would prefer to buy from the integrated firm rather than from $U2$. Indeed, Chen (2001) suggests that if there are cost efficiencies associated with the vertical merger so that c^U falls at the integrated firm, the merger could lead to a different sort of foreclosure altogether. Instead of cutting off independent downstream firms from a source of supply, the vertical merger may leave independent upstream firms without any customers.[5]

16.4   REAPPRAISAL AND APPLICATION: THE GE-HONEYWELL MERGER

Let us return to the GE-Honeywell merger described at the start of this chapter. As noted, the European Commission eventually ruled against the merger. Their reasoning is summarized in the following extract from the Commission's report (paragraph 355):

> Because of their lack of ability to match the bundle offer . . . [independent] suppliers will lose market shares to the benefit of the merged entity and experience an immediate damaging profit shrinkage. As a result, the merger is likely to lead to market foreclosure on the existing aircraft platforms and subsequently to the elimination of competition in these areas.[6]

There are several points to make in regard to this judgment. First, the "bundling" and unfair competitive advantage that the commission feared would give GE-Honeywell a competitive advantage is nothing more than the elimination of the double marginalization that we have described above. Eliminating double marginalization gave a similar advantage to the integrated firms in the oligopoly models that we have studied in this chapter. Packaging jet engines with engine starter motors is economically equivalent to combining the upstream manufacturing with the retail services of a downstream dealer. Thus, there is some legitimacy in the Commission's fear that GE-Honeywell would gain some advantage over independent rivals.

Whether the merger would lead to foreclosure and whether, if it did, this would raise prices is another matter. In part, that would depend on the nature of initial competition. If the market were very competitive with lots of jet engine firms and avionics companies, then the merger could have very little anticompetitive impact. The nature of competition in both the upstream and the downstream affects the likelihood of foreclosure and its ultimate impact. In short, some understanding of the real world market place is necessary to make an informed judgment regarding this merger.

---

5   Pepall and Norman (2001) offer a similar analysis to Chen (2001) in which vertical foreclosure is never an equilibrium precisely because, again, this leads to competition between multiple vertically integrated firms.

6   The full decision is available at: *http://ec.europa.eu/comm/competition/mergers/cases/decisions/ m2220_en.pdf*.

It is fair to say that neither pre-merger market was competitively structured. Estimates of GE's share of the jet engine market for large commercial aircraft range from 28 to 52 percent, and it had just two major rivals, namely, the Pratt-Whitney division of United Technologies and the Rolls Royce Group. Likewise, Honeywell's share of the avionics market was on the order of 50 percent, and it had just three rivals: Rockwell Collins (25 percent), Thales (15 percent), and Smiths Industries (5 percent). In reaching its decision, the European Commission appears to have been persuaded that the preeminence of GE and Honeywell made subsequent integration by their rivals impossible. As a result, and as the quote above makes clear, the Commission feared foreclosure of GE's competitors and the ultimate loss of competition in the jet engine market.

The Commission is implicitly claiming that rivals could not integrate as well and this would need to be documented. More importantly, we should in this case show that even with foreclosure, the resulting market outcome is worse than the pre-merger case. This was *not* the case in our numerical example of the Salinger (1988) model. In that example, integration by one firm did lead to foreclosure of its rival. Nevertheless, the post-merger downstream price of $68.5 was still well below the pre-merger price of $76. As a review of that example will quickly reveal, even if the foreclosure eventually led the integrated firm to enjoy a complete downstream monopoly, the retail price would still decline to $73. This is, of course, a stylized example. Nevertheless, it reveals just how large the inefficiencies of double-marginalization could be, and perhaps why many economists thought the ruling a mistake.[7]

16.5   CONGLOMERATE MERGERS

The final type of merger to consider is a conglomerate merger. Such mergers bring under common control firms whose products are neither direct substitutes nor complements. The outcome is to join a set of firms producing a diversified range of products with little or nothing in common. While conglomerate companies have been with us for some time, the US merger wave starting in the 1960s and continuing into the early 1980s is, particularly in the earlier years, when many of the conglomerates that we see today were formed. The question is whether we can develop a convincing economic rationale for these mergers. If not, then we should think of conglomerates as an accident of history that are being gradually corrected through corporate downsizing and the focus on "core businesses," strategies that appear to characterize corporate change in the new millennium. A number of reasons have, however, been advanced to support the emergence of conglomerate firms. We examine these in turn.

16.5.1   Possible Economies Associated with Conglomeration

Scope economies and saving on transactions costs are two possible advantages that may accrue to conglomerate firms. By scope economies we mean that a variety of products or services are more cheaply produced by one firm than by two or more firms. By transaction

---

[7]   Nalebuff (2004) offers a similar analysis of the GE-Honeywell case set in a framework of differentiated products. To be fair, the Commission noted other fears besides foreclosure. One was that GE also had an unfair advantage in that its large financial operations allowed it to package financing with jet aircraft in a way that Pratt-Whitney and Rolls Royce could not. There was also a horizontal element to the case as GE and Honeywell were the only two suppliers of regional jet engines.

Reality Checkpoint
Going Whole Hog on Vertical Integration

Nowhere have the strategic advantages of vertical integration been more aggressively pursued in recent times than in meat and poultry markets. Firms in these markets have made a concerted effort to control all aspects of production from the farm to the store counter or, as they say in the pork business, from "birth to bacon and squeal to meal."

The largest pork producer in both the United States and the world is Smithfield Industries with 26 percent of the US market. Smithfield owns or operates thousands of hog farms and has contractual decision-making rights over every single stage of the production chain. It even owns the DNA line for the hogs that it uses and the feed that they eat.

The advantages of such control are clear. Vertical integration allows Smithfield to direct insemination and breeding and thereby maintain a supply of litters without threatening its herd sustainability. Feed and genetic control allow the firm to standardize the leanness and other quality features of its hogs.

Integration also permits Smithfield to design the warehouse barns in which the hogs are raised, ensuring that the hogs will mature and be ready for slaughter on a schedule that permits the most efficient plant utilization rate.

While Smithfield is the world's largest pork producer, annually slaughtering close to 20 million hogs to turn out over 5 billion pounds of pork, it is not alone in its organizational strategy. Tyson, which produces both poultry and beef as well as pork and which is the world's largest meat producer overall, is also highly integrated. So are other pork firms such as ConAgra and Swift. In the pork business, vertical integration is the swine of the times.

Source: S. Kilman, "Smithfield to Buy Hog Farmer Premium Standard," *Wall Street Journal*, September 19, 2006, p. A4; and S. Martinez, 2002. "A Comparison of Vertical Coordination in the US Poultry, Egg, and Pork Industries," *Current Issues in Economics of Food Markets* Agriculture Information Bulletin, AIB-747–05 (May).

costs we mean the costs that are incurred by firms when they use external markets in order to exchange goods and services.[8] These include, for example, the costs of searching for the desired inputs, negotiating supply contracts, monitoring and enforcing these contracts, and the risk associated with unforeseen changes in supply conditions.

Scope economies derive primarily from the ability of the firm to exploit common inputs in the manufacture of a range of products. The same production line can be used for several products, marketing efforts can promote the whole range of goods a firm produces, and the fruits of research and development may extend to a number of diverse products. Advertising and promotional activities also frequently exhibit scope economies across a variety of activities. This line of argument implies that for scope economies to be an important element in conglomerate mergers it is necessary that the firms that merge are related in some respect. Either they sell in similar markets or they have similar production technologies. The data on conglomerates do not appear to be consistent with this hypothesis. A detailed study by Nathanson and Cassano (1982) concludes that there are at least as many conglomerate firms that produce goods with little in common, whether this be technology or the markets at which they are targeted, as there are firms that have relatively low product and market diversity.

[8]   For an excellent discussion of transaction costs, see Besanko, Dranove, and Shanley (2009).

Transactions costs are particularly significant when specialized or knowledge-intensive assets are traded. Consider a specialized asset, such as a sophisticated machine that is specifically designed to produce two goods, A and B. Let us also suppose that the markets for A and B are highly concentrated with a small number of producers, and that the owner of the machine has spare capacity if the machine is used only to produce A. This might arise, for example, if demand for A is limited relative to the productive capacity of the machine. If such spare capacity exists, the owner of the machine may wish to use it to produce B goods as well. A conglomerate merger or the machine owner merging together A and B production is one way that this can happen. However, as Teece (1982) and others have argued, conglomeration is not strictly necessary. The machine owner, a producer of A, can instead simply lease the spare capacity to B producers.

There is a potential problem with the leasing arrangement, however. Because the number of B producers is small, each will have some monopoly power in bargaining over the terms of the lease. As a result, the machine owner may find that the costs and risks associated with the negotiations between the interested parties are large as each side tries to get the best possible deal. Conglomeration may be a means of avoiding such costs. By using the machine to produce both A and B within the same firm, the machine owner avoids all the bargaining hassles. There is no longer any conflict over how to divide the gains from using the machine because those gains all go to the same owner.

Transaction cost problems are particularly important when the asset involved is knowledge or information intensive. The knowledge of such matters as organizational routines or specialized customer needs is generally embodied in specific individuals or teams employed by the company. It is difficult to envision contracts to "lease" such personnel.

In short, the effort to minimize the transactions costs associated with contracting between firms may explain conglomerate mergers to some extent. Nevertheless this motivation seems unlikely to be the major factor behind such mergers. The reason is that here again, we are talking about some asset that is common to all the lines of production operated by the conglomerate, and such commonality in productive assets does not seem to be a feature of conglomerate firms.

16.5.2   Managerial Motives

The skepticism surrounding the explanations based on scope economies, transaction cost savings, and other arguments why conglomerate mergers improve production efficiency has led some to postulate a different, less benign motivation. The alternative motive is that it is in the interest of management even if it is not in the interest of shareholders. Because management calls the shots, it is the managerial interest that prevails.

In any reasonably large public company, ownership, which essentially resides with the shareholders, may be separated from control, which essentially resides with the management team. This separation would not matter too much if management performance could be perfectly observed and monitored by shareholders. Yet perfect monitoring is rare, and absent such monitoring, management can pursue its own agenda at least to some extent. This would not matter so long as the best interests of management are served by maximizing shareholder wealth. It is precisely the attempt to secure this harmony of interest that lies behind the use of performance-related clauses and payment in stock options in many executive compensation schemes. Still, the match between the interests of shareholders and management is rarely perfect, leaving management with at least some ability to pursue goals other than maximization of shareholders' returns.

Suppose that management compensation is based upon company growth.[9] Growth is far from easy to generate internally. It requires that market share be won from competitors who can hardly be expected to sit passively by when they lose customers. Nor is it easy to buy growth through horizontal mergers because this is the kind of acquisition that is watched by the antitrust authorities. In these circumstances, we should not be surprised to find management supporting a conglomerate merger, even if this is not necessarily in the best long-term interests of shareholders. Such a merger offers management the desired growth while avoiding antitrust problems. In this light, it is, perhaps, significant that the greatest wave of conglomerate mergers in the United States coincided with a period in which the antitrust authorities were particularly fierce in their examination of mergers between related companies.

Management may also pursue conglomeration as a means to minimize risk. When a firm is involved in many distinct markets it avoids putting all its eggs in one basket. Such diversification may be important to management.[10] Shareholders often use compensation schemes that closely tie management's pay to the firm's profit performance.[11] Yet while these practices work to align management's interests more closely to those of the stockholders, they also increase the risk that management faces. As profits go up and down, management's compensation rises and falls irrespective of whether the profit results were management's fault or not. To protect against such fluctuations, management may seek to diversify the sources of the firm's income by pursuing conglomeration. This smooths the firm's income stream because with many product lines operating, positive and negative shocks tend to cancel each other out. The derived income stream of the firm's executives is also smoother. Even shareholders might prefer this approach if, in the absence of such diversification, the firm would have to pay its executives higher salaries to compensate them for the greater risk. This may be particularly true for managers who are heavily invested in the firms so that not only their labor income but also their capital income is subject to the same risk.

Some evidence in support of diversification as a means of diversifying managerial risk is found in studies by Ahimud and Lev (1981) and by May (1995). The first of these studies finds that when no shareholder owns 10 percent or more of the stock and management control is high, firms tend to be more diversified. May (1995) finds that a comparison of CEOs in terms of the proportion of their wealth invested in the firm reveals that as this proportion rises, CEOs tend to favor conglomeration.

There are also less attractive or more self-serving managerial goals that may be pursued through conglomeration. These include entrenchment and rent-seeking. It may be more difficult to replace managers who run more complicated firms. Obvious candidates to replace the existing CEO and other executives may be hard to find when the firm is a complex conglomerate. Similarly, the more complex the organization, the more difficult it is for shareholders to monitor management and to guard against managers skimming off profits to their own benefit. These problems are sufficiently real that shares in a conglomerate are often considered low-priced and subject to a conglomerate discount [Aggarwal and Samwick (2003)].

---

[9] This analysis is treated in detail in Mueller (1982).
[10] For a detailed discussion of these ideas, see Ahimud and Lev (1981).
[11] For example, Boeing Corp. linked its annual award of stock options to its 1,500 top executives to the performance of the company's share price over the next five years. See F. M. Biddle, "Boeing Links Managers' Stock Options to Five-Year Performance of Shares," *The Wall Street Journal*, February 26, 1998, p. B12.

16.6   A BRIEF DIGRESSION ON MERGERS AND THE THEORY OF THE FIRM

A merger involves the acquisition of one company by another. As a result of that purchase, the acquiring firm gets the physical capital—buildings, equipment, and land—and perhaps certain intangible assets, such as reputation or brand name, that formerly belonged to the acquired company. The ultimate question raised by any merger is, what does the change in ownership permit the merged firm to do that could not be done before?

In the case of a horizontal merger, the possibility of enhanced market power is clearly part of the motivation. Yet we often see horizontal mergers in which such an increase in market power may not occur. The merger paradox discussed in the last chapter suggests that increases in market power as the result of a merger could be rare. In the case of a vertical merger, the market power motivation is even more suspect. If the upstream and downstream firms each had 5 percent of their respective markets before the merger, little seems changed by moving the ownership of those market shares from two different firms to two different divisions of the same firm.

With upstream-downstream firms, there is the issue of double marginalization. We have suggested a vertical merger as a response to that problem. It is not the only response, however. Various contracts between two vertically related firms could be written to overcome the problem of double marginalization, and these contracts do not require integrating the two firms into one. We will examine such contracts in depth in the next chapter. Here we simply want to raise the question as to why firms merge rather than make use of such contracts. Alternatively, why don't more firms merge? What in fact limits the size of a firm? What stops firms from merging into bigger and bigger firms?

This question is really about what determines the boundaries of a firm. What is the difference between organizing the production of a commodity through many independent companies, on the one hand, and organizing that production through many divisions of the same company, on the other? Viewing the matter in this light makes transparent that what determines the boundaries of the firm is an important question for industrial organization theory.

Many alternative theories of the firm have been developed since the late 1970s. There is sufficient work in this area now for it to make up a course, or a field in itself. Our aim here is not to cover this material in depth. Instead, we wish simply to offer a brief discussion of the limits on firm size. Now seems a particularly appropriate point to raise this topic because a merger, by definition, is a transaction that increases a firm's size.

Neoclassical theory does not tell us much as to what such a transaction gains for the parties. Nor does it tell us why firms operate internal divisions rather than "spinning them off" into individual companies. However, neoclassical theory is not alone in this regard. Other approaches to the theory of the firm also fall short of a complete answer. Take, for instance, the agency view of the firm. Under this view, a firm is an organization designed to generate the proper incentives when the various parties engaged in the production process have different and private information. For example, a supplier of glass may contract with an automobile producer to provide windshields of a particular quantity and quality according to a particular schedule. Obviously, the actual quality of such windshields is beyond the complete control of the glass supplier but the supplier does know whether it exerted its full effort to supplying the specified quality. The automaker, though, is not so well informed. It cannot be sure whether a batch of low-quality glass is due to bad luck or, instead, bad faith on the part of its supplier. Agency theory has generated extremely useful insights into the types of contracts that might be used to surmount such informational problems and provide the proper incentives for both parties to live up to their contractual obligations. Yet it does not tell us whether such contracts must be between two separate firms, as in the automaker and the glass supplier of our story, or whether the contract could simply be the incentive scheme offered to the windshield division of a giant car manufacturer.

Similar problems arise with the transactions cost approach to the firm. Under that approach, the firm is viewed as an organization designed to minimize the costs of negotiating, interpreting, enforcing, and renegotiating contracts. However, the precise mechanism by which this cost reduction is achieved is not typically spelled out. There is no reason, *a priori*, to assume that haggling is less of a problem between two divisions within one firm than between two separate firms.

The issue of corporate mergers reveals a weakness in economic theory regarding the limits or boundaries of a firm's activities. Why is it that we observe General Motors supplying autobodies internally rather than purchasing them from an independent supplier? What advantages are gained and then lost when these divisions are instead independent firms?

One answer is provided in the work of Hart (1995) and centers on the issue of ownership. A merger changes the ownership of assets and ownership gives control. The carmaker that owns its own windshield supply unit is in a position to resolve, by itself, any dispute between its assembly line and the glass unit. This does not necessarily minimize the cost of haggling. However, common ownership may permit investments that increase efficiency that would be less likely to occur otherwise.

Suppose that there is specific machinery that can be used to produce, inexpensively, windshields of a quality and style unique to the automaker in question. An independent glass company might not invest in such equipment because it ties the glassmaker too closely to supplying the particular auto firm. If the glass supplier did make the investment, its bargaining position in disputes with the automaker would be weak because it has no other buyer for the one product that this machinery permits it to make. From the perspective of the glass supplier, it is less risky to use more general equipment that makes it easy to produce glass products for other firms as well. This is true even though the use of such generic processes requires the firm to incur an extra cost to mold the windshield to the specific dimensions specified by the carmaker.

A merger or acquisition of the glass company by the automaker offers a way out. By operating windshield production as a unit within its own firm, the automaker removes the potential conflict. Now, the specialized machinery can be bought and the windshields produced at lower cost because there is no longer any friction over how the gains from this investment will be shared. They all go to the one, common owner of the assets.

In other words, common ownership is desirable whenever there are complementarities—or synergies—between different assets. As a result, we should expect firms to combine whenever such complementarities are present—and to split apart if such complementarities vanish. Because technological changes are ever present, and because such innovations are constantly altering the extent of production complementarities, we should also expect a constant fluctuation in the size and organization of firms. This approach may help explain the recent wave of mergers in the telecommunications industry where rapid innovations have greatly altered the production technology.

16.7   EMPIRICAL APPLICATION: VERTICAL INTEGRATION IN THE READY-MIXED CONCRETE INDUSTRY

Ready-mixed concrete is one of the most widely used construction materials. It consists mainly of cement, water, and aggregates such as sand and gravel. Of these, cement is clearly crucial as the binding agent that hardens the aggregates into a solid mass. Almost invariably, cement makes up 12 percent of the concrete mixture by weight. Hence, cement and ready-mixed concrete match the assumptions of the Salinger (1988) and Ordover, Saloner, and Salop (1990) models in that cement is an upstream product used in fixed proportion per unit of the downstream product, ready-mixed concrete. This makes it an ideal industry in which to study the effects of vertical integration.[12]

Ali Hortaçsu and Chad Syverson (2007) point out that there is a further aspect of the concrete business that makes studying vertical integration in that industry interesting. This is the fact that the different phases of antitrust policy over the late twentieth century were very much evidenced in the ready-mixed concrete market. In the 1960s, cement makers were interested in integrating forward into ready-mixed concrete and the percentage of vertically integrated plants rose steadily throughout the decade. Fearing that these consolidations would lead to foreclosure and anticompetitive price squeezes, the Justice Department filed fifteen antitrust cases in this industry and each one led to divestiture. This vigorous policy also deterred further mergers with the result that during the 1970s, the fraction of cement firms that were vertically integrated fell noticeably. Then came the 1980s and rise of the "Chicago School" approach to antitrust policy, which viewed vertical integration much more favorably. There was a new wave of mergers that again sharply increased the extent of vertical integration in the concrete market. Finally, in the 1990s, the "post-Chicago" school began to make its influence felt and antitrust policy became less lenient. Vertical integration in concrete again declined. This pattern is shown in Table 16.1 below.

Of course, transport costs are far too high for there to be one, national market for ready-mixed concrete. Using Commerce Department data, Hortaçsu and Syverson (2007) identify 348 local markets over the years 1963 to 1997. They then use this data to determine whether the differences in ready-mixed concrete prices across markets are systematically related to the extent of vertical integration in those markets. A simple regression aimed at answering this question might have the form: $P_{it} = A + \beta VI_{it} + e_{it}$, where P_{it} is the average concrete price (measured in logs) in market i in year t; A is an intercept term; VI_{it} is the market share of output accounted for by vertically integrated firms in market i in year t; and e_{it} is a random error term centered on zero. Such a simple model, though, leaves out

Table 16.1   Vertical integration in cement/ready-mixed concrete market

Year	1963	1967	1972	1977	1982	1987	1992	1997
Fraction of Cement Sales Accounted for by Vertically Integrated Firms	25.2	51.2	48.4	41.0	49.5	51.3	75.1	55.4

[12]   See Chipty (2001) for a study of vertical integration in cable television.

many other variables that are likely to be important in determining concrete prices in any given market-year, and therefore would lead to a biased estimate of the coefficient β.

To begin with, the average price over time might be different in each market. There might be something about the Chicago market, for example, that makes its price of cement always relatively high. This effect can be handled by letting the intercept term vary across each market. Then too, industrial organization theory suggests that market structure, as measured by the Herfindahl Index (HI), could also be important for the behavior of prices, as might be the level of demand coming from the local construction industry in that year. In fact, given our discussion of antitrust policy, we might also think that the precise year is important as well because firms might try to keep prices low in years when antitrust pressure is more intense than in years when it is lenient. We need to control for such time-specific factors and the many other forces that could affect concrete prices if we are to isolate the influence of changes in vertical integration alone. The easiest way to do this is to include measures of concentration and local demand and put in a dummy variable for each market and each year.

Hortaçsu and Syverson (2007) make the foregoing adjustments and some others as well to estimate regressions explaining the variation in concrete prices across markets and time. Their central results are shown in Table 16.2 below.

In all the regressions, results for the time and market dummies are suppressed, as are those for the HI and construction demand, which are never significant. The first column shows the results when, apart from the control variables just mentioned, the only explanatory variable is the extent of vertical integration in the local market. This effect is both negative and statistically significant. It is also economically meaningful. For their entire sample, Hortaçsu and Syverson (2007) find that on average, vertically integrated firms account for 31.5 percent of the typical market. The estimated coefficient shown in the first column then implies that ready-mixed concrete prices would be 4 percent lower in such a market than they would be in a market with no vertically integrated firms. Thus, this result suggests that the efficiency results of vertical integration typically outweigh any anticompetitive effects so that consumers benefit.

The next two columns test additional variables that may be important for concrete prices. In column 2, a second independent variable is added for the fraction of firms that operate more than one plant. This includes all the vertically integrated firms plus all those that operate multiple plants horizontally. Including this variable is a means of testing whether

Table 16.2 Results for regressions explaining ready-mixed concrete prices in the US

Independent Variable	Dependent Variable: Weighted Average Market Price (log)	Dependent Variable: Weighted Average Market Price (log)	Dependent Variable: Weighted Average Market Price (log)
Market Share of Vertically Integrated firms	−0.090* (0.041)	−0.086* (0.041)	−0.043 (0.039)
Market Share of Multiple Plant Firms	____	−0.015 (0.022)	0.001 (0.024)
Weighted Average Total Factor Productivity	____	____	−0.293* (0.054)
R^2	0.433	0.434	0.573

*Significant at five percent level.

the vertically integrated variable is really capturing efficiencies that come from coordinating different plants, e.g., better-timed production, lower transport costs, rather than from vertical integration *per se*. However this variable is insignificant and does not materially affect the results in column 1.

The third column is perhaps the most interesting. Here, Hortaçsu and Syverson (2007) include as an additional regressor a measure of average productivity in the local market. This is clearly an important variable. Including it reduces the magnitude of the effects of vertical integration and eliminates their statistical significance. What are the implications of this finding?

First, it makes intuitive sense that concrete prices will be lower in markets where firms are more productive. In this sense, the results in column 3 are not surprising. Second, we should recall that vertical integration has potentially two effects, a price-reducing effect due to greater efficiency and a price-increasing effect due to foreclosure-type forces. Including the productivity variable should control for any efficiency effects so that the vertical integration term now picks up only the price-increasing impact of vertical mergers. The findings in column 3 suggest that once this control for efficiency effects is included, the price-increasing effects appear very weak. Finally, Hortaçsu and Syverson (2007) produce other evidence to show that vertically integrated firms have higher productivity. If vertical integration in this industry has an impact on prices, it does so through the efficiency effect. Overall, these results imply that vertical integration has been welfare-enhancing and good for consumers, at least in the ready-mixed concrete business.

Summary

We have considered two broad types of merger in this chapter: vertical and conglomerate. A vertical merger typically involves the merging of companies operating at different stages of production in the same product line. A conglomerate merger is a merger of two firms that have little or no common markets or products.

Vertical mergers raise complicated issues. On the one hand, such mergers can benefit firms and consumers by eliminating double marginalization. On the other hand, they may be a means to foreclose either upstream or downstream markets to rivals, and to facilitate price discrimination. There is no simple way of determining which of these forces is likely to be the stronger. Some argue that the negative impact of potential vertical foreclosure itself sets up a countervailing force that will induce remaining independent companies to integrate as well. If so, this can reduce inefficiencies still further. However, we have seen that the vertically integrated firm may have both the means and the motive to prevent such subsequent mergers. Resolution of these issues in any particular case must, as always, depend on careful evaluation of the realities of the specific situation.

It is worth noting, however, that even when foreclosure and a price squeeze for independent rivals does happen, it may nonetheless be the case that final consumers are made better off with the vertical merger. Policy makers should therefore not be too hasty in condemning a vertical merger simply because it disadvantages rival firms. The goal of antitrust policy is to preserve the benefits of competition, not the fortunes of competitors.

Conglomerate mergers probably raise the fewest problems from an antitrust perspective. However, for this very reason, the motivation for such mergers can be difficult to identify. They may reflect an attempt to minimize risk either for stockholders or managers. But there would seem to be other means to achieve these same ends.

The ambiguous effects of mergers that characterize our economic models are also found in empirical analysis. To date, there is little clear evidence that vertical mergers have led to significant increases in monopoly power. A recent study of the ready-mixed concrete industry suggests that such vertical integration tends to bring greater productive efficiency and lower consumer prices. The combination of ambiguity in the theory and, if anything, favorable empirical evidence has led the legal authorities to take a much less aggressive and much less rigid stand against proposed vertical mergers. Today these are inevitably handled on a case-by-case approach. In the absence of definitive results—either from economic theory or economic data—this is the best approach to follow.

Problems

1. Norman International has a monopoly in the manufacture of *whatsits*. Each *whatsit* requires exactly one *richet* as an input and incurs other variable costs of $5 per unit. *Richets* are made by PepRich Inc., which is also a monopoly. The variable costs of manufacturing *richets* are $5 per unit. Assume that the inverse demand for *whatsits* is:

   $$p_w = 50 - q_w$$

   where p_w is the price of *whatsits* in dollars per unit and q_w is the quantity of *whatsits* offered for sale by Norman International.

   a. Write down the profit function for Norman International assuming that the two monopolists act as independent profit-maximizing companies, with Norman International setting a price p_w for *whatsits* and PepRich setting a price p_r for *richets*. Hence, derive the profit-maximizing price for *whatsits* as a function of the price of *richets*, and use this function to obtain the derived demand for *richets*.

   b. Use your answer in (a) to write down the profit function for PepRich. Hence, derive the profit-maximizing price of *richets*. Use this to derive the profit-maximizing price of *whatsits*. Calculate the sales of *whatsits* (and so of *richets*) and calculate the profits of the two firms.

2. Now assume that these two firms merge to form NPR International.

   a. Write down the profit function for NPR given that it sets a price p_w for *whatsits*. Calculate the postmerger profit-maximizing price for *whatsits*, sales of *whatsits*, and the profits of NPR.

   b. Confirm that this merger has increased the joint profits of the two firms while reducing the price charged to consumers. By how much has consumer surplus been increased by the merger in the market for *whatsits*?

   c. Assume that the two firms expect to last forever and that the discount factor R is 0.9. What is the largest sum that PepRich would be willing to pay the owners of Norman International to take over Norman International? What is the lowest sum that the owners of Norman International would be willing to accept? (Hint: Calculate the present value of the profit streams of the two firms before and after the merger, and notice that neither firm will want to be worse off with the takeover than without it.)

3. Now assume that PepRich gets the opportunity to sell to an overseas market for *whatsits*, controlled by a monopolist FC Hu Inc., which has the same operating costs in making *whatsits* as Norman International. PepRich knows that it will have to pay transport costs of $2 per *richet* to supply the overseas market. Inverse demand for *whatsits* in this market is

   $$p_w = 40 - q_w/2$$

   a. Repeat your calculations for question 1(a).

   b. The authorities in the overseas market are contemplating taking an antidumping action, accusing PepRich of dumping *richets* into its market. They calculate that by doing so, they will induce PepRich to offer to take over FC Hu. Assume that PepRich has limited access to funds, so that it can take over only one of the two firms Norman International and FC Hu. Are the overseas authorities correct in their calculations? (Hint: Compare the maximum amounts that PepRich would be willing to pay for Norman International and FC Hu.)

4. Go back to the conditions of question 1, so that PepRich is supplying only Norman International. But now assume that the manufacture of each *whatsit* requires exactly one *richet* and one *zabit*. Zabits are made by ZabCor, another monopolist, whose variable costs are $2.50 per *zabit*.
   a. Assume that the three firms act independently to maximize profit. Calculate the resulting prices of *richets*, *zabits*, and *whatsits* and the profits of the three firms.
   b. Assume an infinite life for all three firms and a discount factor $R = 0.9$. PepRich and ZabCor are each contemplating a takeover of Norman International. Which of these two companies would win the bidding for Norman International? What will be the effect of the winning takeover on consumer surplus in the market for *whatsits*?

5. As an alternative to buying Norman International, the owners of PepRich and ZabCor contemplate merging to form PRZ, which will control the manufacture of both *richets* and *zabits*.
   a. Calculate the impact of this merger on (1) the prices of *richets*, *zabits*, and *whatsits*, (2) the profits of these firms, and (3) consumer surplus in the *whatsit* market.
   b. Which merger will be preferred
      i. by consumers of *whatsits*?
      ii. by the owners of PepRich and Zab-Corp.?
      iii. by the owners of Norman International?

6. (More difficult) Ginvir and Sipep are Bertrand competitors selling differentiated products in the carbonated drinks market. The demands for the products of the two firms being given by the inverse demand functions:

   $$p_G = 25 - 2q_G - q_S \text{ for Ginvir and}$$
   $$p_S = 25 - 2q_S - q_G \text{ for Sipep.}$$

Both companies need syrup to make their drinks; the syrup is supplied by two competing companies, NorSyr and BenRup. These companies incur costs of $5 per unit in making the syrup. Both Ginvir and Sipep can use the syrup of either supplier.
   a. Confirm that competition between NorSyr and BenRup leads to the syrup being priced at $5 per unit.
   b. What are the resulting equilibrium prices for Ginrip and Sipep and what are their profits?

7. Now suppose that Ginvir and NorSyr merge and that NorSyr no longer competes for Sipep's business.
   a. What price will Benrup now charge Sipep for the syrup?
   b. What are the resulting profits to the three post-merger companies?
   c. Do Benrup and Sipep have an incentive also to merge?

8. Return to the model of Cournot competition presented in Section 16.3. Show that when both pairs of upstream-downstream firms vertically integrate, total industry profit falls below what it was with no vertical integration.

9. [Hart and Tirole (1990)]. Consider a monopolist upstream supplier $U1$ selling to two downstream producers $D1$ and $D2$ engaged in Cournot competition. Downstream demand is described by: $P = 100 - Q$ and marginal cost is zero at both the upstream and downstream level.
   a. Show that the monopoly level of output is 50 and that monopoly profit is $2500.
   b. Imagine a contract by which $U1$ sells 25 units as a package to each of $D1$ and $D2$ at a price of $1,250. Each firm can either accept the package or reject it. Show that if decisions are made simultaneously, and each firm has full information about the other's actions, the Nash Equilibrium is for each to accept this offer.

10. Imagine now that deals between $U1$ and $U2$ are done in secret. This can be thought

of as raising the possibility that one player goes first. If that player accepts 25 units at a package price of $1,250, $U1$ can then offer a second package to the other retailer.

a. Show that in a sequential setting the first downstream firm will never accept $U1$'s offer.

b. Show that by vertically integrating with one of the downstream firms and foreclosing the other, $U1$ can earn the monopoly profit of $2,500.

References

Aggarwal, R. K., and A. Samwick, 2003. "Why Do Managers Diversify Their Firms? Agency Reconsidered," *Journal of Finance* 58 (February): 71–118.

Ahimud, Y., and Lev, B. 1981. "Risk Reduction as a Managerial Motive for Conglomerate Mergers," *Bell Journal of Economics* 12:605–17.

Besanko, D., D. Dranove, and M. Shanley. 2009. *Economics of Strategy (5th ed.)*, New York: John Wiley and Sons.

Best, M. 1990. *The New Competition: Institutions of Corporate Restructuring*, Cambridge: Harvard University Press.

Chen, Y. 2001. "On Vertical Mergers and Their Competitive Effects." *Rand Journal of Economics*, 32 (Winter), 667–85.

Chipty, T. 2001. "Vertical Integration, Market Foreclosure, and Consumer Welfare in the Cable Television Industry," *The American Economic Review* 91 (June): 428–53.

Hart, O. 1995. *Firms, Contracts, and Financial Structure*, Oxford: Oxford University Press.

Hart, O., and J. Tirole. 1990. "Vertical Integration and Market Foreclosure,". *Brookings Papers on Economic Activity Special Issue* (February): 205–76.

Hortaçsu, A. and C. Syverson. 2007. "Cementing Relationships: Vertical Integration, Foreclosure, Productivity, and Prices," *Journal of Political Economy* 115 (April): 250–301.

Krattenmaker, T., and S. Salop. 1986. "Anticompetitive Exclusion: Raising Rivals' Costs to Achieve Power Over Price," *Yale Law Journal* 96:209–95.

May, D. O. 1995. "Do Managerial Motives Influence Firm Risk-Reduction Strategies?" *Journal of Finance*, 50 (November):1291–1308.

Nalebuff, B. 2004. "Bundling: GE-Honeywell," in J. Kwoka and L. White, eds. *The Antitrust Revolution*, Oxford: Oxford University Press, 4th ed, 388–412.

Nathanson, D. A., and J. Cassano. 1982. "What Happens to Profits When a Company Diversifies?" *Wharton Magazine* 24:19–26.

Ordover, J. A., G. Saloner, and S. Salop. 1990. "Equilibrium Vertical Foreclosure," *American Economic Review* 80:127–42.

Pepall, L., and G. Norman. 2001. "Product Differentiation and Upstream Downstream Relations," *The Journal of Economics and Management Strategy* 10: 201–233.

Salinger, M. A. 1988. "Vertical Mergers and Market Foreclosure," *Quarterly Journal of Economics* 103:345–56.

Teece, D. 1982. "Towards an Economic Theory of the Multiproduct Firm," *Journal of Economic Behavior and Organization* 3:39–63.

17

Vertical Price Restraints

You may never have heard of Seagate or Western Digital. Yet, chances are, you have used their products. Together, these two firms produced roughly 90 percent of the hard drives used in computers, including laptops and the computers that run the "cloud." This means that the customers to whom Seagate and Western Digital sell are firms such as Apple, Dell, and Hewlett-Packard. In turn, these firms assemble their desktop and laptop computers and sell them to retailers including Best Buy and Staples. Apple, of course, maintains its own retail outlets as well.

Vertical chains such as that connecting the hard drive maker to the computer retailer are common. ArcelorMittal and other steel companies sell their product to auto manufacturers (among others) who, in turn, assemble finished auto products and distribute these to dealers for final retail sales. Mattel Toys sells its *Barbie* doll, *Fisher-Price*, and *Hot Wheels* products through retailers such as Toys 'R' Us and Wal-Mart. Kellogg's sells its ready-to-eat cereals through supermarkets such as Kroger and Safeway. Relations at each step require contracts. Seagate and Western Digital sign contracts with Apple, Dell, and Hewlett-Packard and these firms in turn have contracts governing their relations with Best Buy, Staples, and other retailers. The steel firms sign contracts with the auto companies who in turn sign contacts with the car dealers and so on.

The contracts signed by the firms in these production and distribution chains inevitably impose restrictions on the signatory parties. Suppliers may be required to guarantee quality and to help with final sales promotion. Retailers may be required to display the product prominently and to offer various services. Because they take place in the context of the vertical supply chain, these restrictions are typically referred to as vertical restraints. While they may help the firms better coordinate their efforts they can also restrict competition on two levels. First, there is the possibility that vertical restraints may be used to suppress competition between different manufactured goods. That is, the fact that Apple, Dell, and Hewlett-Packard all sell through Best Buy may enable these firms to suppress competition between their different brands, i.e., it may suppress interbrand competition. Alternatively, the fact that different Best Buy establishments are each selling, say, Dell computers may allow for the coordination of Dell pricing thereby suppressing intrabrand competition.

Traditionally, concerns with the competitive effects of vertical restraints have distinguished between those constraints that focus on price and those that focus on non-price decisions. We follow this dichotomy here. In this chapter, we examine vertical price restraints. We investigate the effects of vertical non-price restraints in the following chapter.

17.1   ANTITRUST POLICY TOWARD VERTICAL PRICE CONSTRAINTS: HISTORY AND THEORY

The principle type of retail price restriction is Resale Price Maintenance (RPM). Under such an agreement, the upstream firm such as the manufacturer imposes either an upper level that the retail price cannot exceed, or a floor price that the retail price cannot fall below. Because they are explicitly an agreement on price, all such contractual provisions were for many years considered to be a *per se* violation of the US antitrust laws beginning with the *Dr. Miles* case decided by the US Supreme Court in 1911.[1] This was true regardless of whether the contract specified a minimum or a maximum downstream price.

However, exceptions to this blanket approach crept in rather quickly. In the *Colgate* case of 1919, the Supreme Court ruled that if a producer unilaterally announced that it would terminate any firm that sold below a specified retail price, it could then proceed to do just that and to cut off downstream firms that violated that pricing policy because the unilateral quality of the decision meant that there really was no price agreement.[2] Then in the wake of the Great Depression, the US Congress passed the Miller-Tydings Act of 1937, which explicitly exempted RPM agreements from antitrust prosecution. This was later followed by the 1952 McGuire Act, which permitted the enforcement of an RPM agreement even on firms who had not signed on to the arrangement, provided at least one retailer and manufacturer had agreed to it.

The one loophole in the Miller-Tydings and McGuire legislation was that it required participation by state legislatures to make it effective. Some states, however, continued to prohibit RPM agreements so that in th se states, RPM agreements did not become legal. Over time, this led to a discrepancy between prices in those states in which RPM was legal and those in which it was not. In 1975, in the wake of the substantial inflation induced by OPEC's four-fold increase in the price of crude oil, both the Miller-Tydings and the McGuire Acts were repealed. This reestablished the strong presumption of illegality applying to all RPM agreements. It did not remove the ability of manufacturers to cut off discount dealers established by the *Colgate* decision.

Three subsequent legal cases have greatly expanded the ability of manufacturers to impose retail price restrictions. In the *Sharp Electronics* case,[3] the Court broadened its *Colgate* exception by permitting the manufacturer to terminate a discount dealer even if this termination was the result of other dealers' complaints. Then, in the 1997 *State Oil vs. Khan* case, the Court moved to renounce explicitly any *per se* illegality for RPM agreements establishing a *maximum* price or a price ceiling. Most recently, in the *Leegin* case of 2007, the Court reversed the *Dr. Miles per se* ruling and held that all resale price agreements, maximum or minimum, should be subject to a rule of reason test. In short, despite the initial *Dr. Miles* 1911 ruling, exceptions and exemptions to that *per se* approach have always been part of the legal framework governing RPM agreements. With the *Khan* and *Leegin* cases,

---

[1]   *Dr. Miles Co. v. John D. Park and Sons, Co.*, 220 U.S. 373 (1911).

[2]   *United States v. Colgate & Co.*, 250 U.S. 300 (1919). This exception is often referred to as the *Colgate Doctrine*.

[3]   *Business Electronics Corp. v. Sharp Electronics Corp.* 488 U.S. 717 (1988).

Reality Checkpoint
Yesterday's News

Resale price maintenance contracts have both a variety of motivations and a variable legal history. The 1968 case *Albrecht v. The Herald Co.* makes clear, however, that preventing the extra high retail price that results from double marginalization is a central motivation. In that case, the Herald Co., the publisher of the St. Louis *Globe Democrat*, was taken to court by Albrecht, one of the many independent carriers it hired to deliver the morning paper, each exclusively to a specific territory.

Herald printed its suggested retail price for the *Globe Democrat* on each paper. In 1961, Albrecht began charging his customers a price above that recommended by Herald. The company quickly objected, but Albrecht would not relent. Finally, Herald took decisive action. It offered to deliver the paper to Albrecht's customers at the lower recommended price by using another carrier to "invade" Albrecht's exclusive territory. Albrecht sued citing Herald's efforts as attempted price-fixing. When the case finally made it to the US Supreme Court in 1968, the court found in Albrecht's favor. It agreed that that the Herald's efforts to force a specific price on Albrecht amounted to price-fixing and was therefore *per se* illegal. There was no defense.

The *Albrecht* case did not sit well with many economists. Others also recognized

the double-marginalization problem and the possibility that some vertical price arrangements might benefit consumers. Gradually, this learning spread to the courts but the major break came with the ruling in *State Oil v. Khan*.

Barkat Khan was a Midwestern gasoline dealer supplied by State Oil. The oil firm required that all dealers who set a markup of more than 3.25 cents per gallon would have to rebate the excess markup to the company, itself. Khan began to exceed this maximum and when State Oil complained, Khan filed suit, again, claiming price-fixing much like Albrecht. In its dramatic 1997 ruling, the court not only found in favor of State Oil but also made an explicit statement that vertical price agreements stipulating *maximum* prices would no longer be *per se* illegal. Instead, they would be permitted if it could be shown that there was a legitimate justification for their use and if they did not substantially lessen competition. The Albrecht case was yesterday's news.

Sources: *Albrecht v. The Herald Co.*, 390 U.S. 150 (1968), and *State Oil v. Khan*, 522 U.S. 3 (1997). See also, L. Greenhouse, "High Court, in Antitrust Ruling, Says Price Ceilings Are Allowed," *The New York Times*, November 5, 1997, p. A1.

those exceptions have become the rule, so that RPM agreements are now evaluated using a rule of reason approach.

17.2   VERTICAL PRICE RESTRAINTS AS A RESPONSE TO DOUBLE-MARGINALIZATION

As noted, vertical price restraints can enable the vertically linked firms to better coordinate their decisions. This can benefit consumers as well as the firms. The most prevalent example of such a positive effect of an RPM is the double-marginalization problem discussed in the last chapter. Recall the basic argument. A monopoly manufacturer with constant marginal cost sells to a monopoly retailer whose only marginal cost is assumed, for simplicity, to be the upstream or wholesale price P^U. Given retail demand of $P^D = A - BQ$, the retailer maximizes profit by setting a retail price of $P^D = (A + P^U)/2$. In order for the upstream manufacturer to earn a profit, however, the wholesale price must include a markup m above cost, i.e., $P^U = c + m$. Accordingly, the retail price will be: $P^D = (A + c + m)/2$. Yet the retail price that maximizes upstream and downstream profit combined is: $P^{D*} = (A + c)/2$. Thus, unless the manufacturer foregoes all profit and sets m equal to zero—unless it resolves the double markup problem by removing one of the markups—the downstream price will be higher than the price that maximizes the total profit of the two firms.

In Chapter 16, we demonstrated that this double-marginalization issue could be addressed by a vertical merger. However, an RPM agreement offers an alternative resolution. Under an RPM agreement, the manufacturer can stipulate a maximum retail price equal to the joint-profit-maximizing price of $P^{D*} = (A + c)/2$. If the manufacturer also sets the wholesale price at this level—if it sets $m = (A - c)/2$ —then the manufacturer can in principle appropriate the entire maximum profit. In reality, this may be difficult and the manufacturer may have to settle for a smaller markup while still keeping the price at $P^{D*} = (A + c)/2$. The crucial point to make is that P^{D*} is not only the retail price that maximizes the total profit pie going to the manufacturer and retailer, and therefore one that any RPM should specify; it is also a lower retail price than would occur in the absence of an RPM. Hence, the RPM agreement benefits producers, dealers, *and* consumers.

Note though that there is an alternative solution to the manufacturer's problem. This is to use a two-part pricing contract similar to those discussed in Chapter 6. Specifically, the manufacturer could sell to the retailer at a wholesale price r equal to marginal cost c. This would induce the retailer to set the monopoly profit-maximizing price of $P^D = (A + c)/2$ and earn the maximum profit $(A - c)^2/4B$, which the manufacturer can then capture with an up-front fee. We return to this point later in the chapter.

17.1

Practice Problem

Tiger-el is an upstream manufacturer of electric trains that sells wholesale to The Great Toy Store, the only such store in the area. Demand for the trains at the retail store level in inverse form is $P = 1000 - 2Q$, where Q is the total number of trains sold. The Great Toy Store incurs no service cost in selling the trains. Its only cost is the wholesale price it pays for each train. Tiger-el incurs a production cost of $40 per train.

a. What wholesale price should Tiger-el charge for its trains? What price will these trains sell for at retail? How many trains will be sold?
b. What profit will the toy store and the retailer earn under the pricing choices found in part (a)?
c. What would be the retail price and the quantity sold if Tiger-el sold the trains to the toy store at cost but received a 66.67 percent sales royalty on every train sold? What would each firm's profit now be?

17.3   RPM AGREEMENTS AND RETAIL PRICE DISCRIMINATION

As we saw early in this book a retailer that is able to determine "who is who" on its demand curve and separate consumers into different groups will find it profitable to charge the different groups different prices, with the highest prices charged to those customers with least elastic demand. Coupons, quantity discounts, variations in quality in which the price difference does not match the cost difference, and market segmentation are all mechanisms by which a retailer may price discriminate. However, while such price discrimination can enhance retail profits, it can make life difficult for the upstream manufacturer.

To see how retail price discrimination can raise problems for the manufacturer, consider the following simple example. A retailer serves two separate markets. In each market, retail demand is characterized by $P = 100 - Q$ and, again, the only retail cost is the wholesale price per unit r set by the manufacturer. In one market, the retailer is a monopolist. In the other, the retailer faces Bertrand competition from a rival who also buys at r per unit from the manufacturer. The retailer can add a markup to the wholesale price r in the first market, but in the second, Bertrand competition forces the retail price to be equal to r. We assume that the manufacturer's unit cost is $c = \$20$.

Although one retailer sells in two markets, we assume that the manufacturer cannot sign a separate contract with that retailer for the goods sold in each market. We also assume that where there is more than one retailer, the manufacturer must offer each the same terms. In other words, while a retailer may be able to discriminate, the manufacturer cannot. To avoid the double-marginalization problem, we will allow this one contract to specify both a wholesale price r and an up-front franchise fee T. The manufacturer's problem is to choose T and r to maximize its total profit. A little algebra quickly reveals that the profit-maximizing monopoly price in each market is $60. If this price can be made to stick, each market will generate $1,600 in profit.

Without an RPM agreement, the manufacturer's choice of r and T imposes a clear tradeoff. The conventional strategy of setting r equal to marginal cost $c = \$20$ and using the fixed fee T to claim the profits this strategy generates works well in the monopolized market. There, the retailer facing $r = c = \$20$, will set price $P^D = \$60$ and the maximum monopoly profit of $1,600 will be achieved. However, competition in the remaining market will mean that the wholesale price will also be the retail price in that market, $P^D = r$, because both retailers buy upstream at price r. As a result, there will be no profit to be claimed in this market by any fixed payment T. The only two-part tariff that can work for both markets is one with $T = 0$, which is really just a single-part tariff. Recognizing this, the manufacturer will find it profitable simply to set $r = \$60$ (and $T = 0$). In this case, the competitive market price is also $60 and the manufacturer earns $1,600 in that market. Unfortunately, with $r = \$60$, the retailer will set a price of $P^{D-} = \$80$ in its monopolized market so that only 20 units are sold. The manufacturer will then earn only $(\$60 - \$20) \times 20 = \$800$ in profit from this market—half of the expected $1,600.

In the Appendix to this chapter, we show that, without an RPM agreement, the best that the manufacturer can do in this case is to set a wholesale price of $52, which results in a combined profit from both markets of $2,304. The retail prices in the monopolized and competitive market are then, respectively, $76 and $52. Relative to the profit maximizing retail price of $60 in each market, the price is too high in the monopolized market and too low in the competitive market.

The appeal of an RPM agreement in this setting should be clear. The manufacturer can continue to forego the fixed fee (set $T = 0$) but now set a wholesale price of $r = \$60$ while imposing an RPM agreement that the retail price can never exceed this amount. This will lead to the desired retail price of $60 in each market and of course, the maximum manufacturer total profit of $3,200.

While the two-market story told above is somewhat contrived, it nonetheless serves as a useful illustration of a general principle. Whatever the source of a retailer's ability to discriminate in prices, such discrimination makes it difficult for the upstream manufacturer to establish a wholesale contract that maximizes the total, manufacturing, and retail profit unless that agreement includes an RPM provision. Without an RPM agreement, there will be a tendency for the retail price to be too low to consumers with more elastic demand and too high to those whose demand is less elastic.[4]

As noted in the Reality Checkpoint above, the Supreme Court's ruling in the *State Oil vs. Khan* case removed the *per se* presumption against RPM agreements specifying a maximum price. In this case, State Oil Co. had imposed a maximum retail price on its distributors and one of these, Barkat Khan, tried to exceed that price *to premium buyers*. At the same time, he wanted to keep a low price to consumers of regular grade fuel. That is, Khan wanted to price discriminate. The RPM agreement subsequently legitimized by the Supreme Court appears to have been motivated in part by State Oil's need to prevent such price discrimination. In turn, this suggests that this motivation may well be important in promoting RPM contracts more generally.

17.4   RPM AGREEMENTS TO INSURE THE PROVISION OF RETAIL SERVICES

In the preceding two sections, we have investigated the use of an RPM agreement to set a ceiling on the price consumers pay. Note that even in the price discrimination case, double-marginalization plays a critical role. The difficulty is that the retailer will always want to add a higher, second markup to the price charged to the less elastic market segment. As the *Albrecht* and *Khan* cases (see above Reality Checkpoint) illustrate, this need to set an upper limit on retail prices is clearly one of the forces behind such vertical restraints. However, there are a number of reasons to doubt that double-marginalization and the need to limit downstream markups can be the sole or perhaps even the major explanation for observed RPM agreements.

First, note that the double-marginalization problem only arises when both the upstream and the downstream market are characterized by imperfect competition. If the downstream market is competitive, the manufacturer can set an upstream price of $PU = P^{D*}$ without fear of a second markup further distorting this price. Likewise, if the upstream market were competitive, the wholesale price would be equal to marginal cost c, and any downstream markup would never result in a price greater than P^{D*}.

Moreover, even when market power exists in both the upstream and downstream markets, there will often remain other, non-RPM solutions to the double-marginalization problem. As we noted in our single-market case of section 17.2, a two-part tariff can often resolve the problem. Even in the price discrimination case, an alternative contract based on a *minimum* retail price can do the trick. Specifically, the manufacturer could set a wholesale price of $20 and impose an RPM requirement that the retail price never fall *below* $60. This will lead to a competitive market price of $60 by virtue of the RPM price floor. It will also lead to a retail price of $60 in the monopolized market by virtue of retail profit monopolization. The manufacturer can then claim the $1,600 via an upfront fee of $T = \$1600$.[5]

Finally, the historical evidence is that it has primarily been the retail lobby that has consistently led the fight to legalize and enforce RPM agreements at both the federal and state levels. In addition, as documented by both Overstreet (1983) and Steiner (1985), the vast majority of RPM court cases have been ones in which the issue was the setting of a

---

[4]   See Chen (1999).

[5]   See O'Brien and Schaffer (1994) for further theoretical analysis. See Lafontaine (1992, 1993, and 1995) for evidence on non-price vertical restraints. See also Mathewson and Winter (1998) for a useful review.

minimum retail price, not a maximum price. Similar evidence for the United Kingdom has been presented by Pickering (1966).

A clue to why our analysis so far has not emphasized RPM minimum price restraints is that we have only viewed retailing as an extra stage that occurs between production and final consumption. While insightful, this approach fails to incorporate any actual positive role for retailers. Yet retailers such as supermarkets, discount chains, and department stores provide many services that are valuable to manufacturers. Not only do they gather information about customer satisfaction and desired changes in the manufacturer's product, but they also provide such valuable services as the provision of desirable shelf space, large displays, advertising, and product demonstration. These services can be crucial to the marketing and sales of the manufacturer's product.

Consider the magazine industry. Supermarkets and discount chains presently account for over 60 percent of single-copy sales of US magazines. Because such sales are made at the full, nonsubscription price, they are profitable and quite important to publishing firms. Yet the publishers must rely heavily on the efforts of the retailers to sell their magazines. A prominent display near the checkout register, for example, can greatly increase sales. So can advertising or a promotional visit to the store by a celebrity. Publishers have a deep interest in making sure that the retailers undertake such efforts. Historically, publishers of *People* and other magazines, such as *Cosmopolitan* and *Harper's Bazaar*, have had tense negotiations with retailers such as Wal-Mart and Winn Dixie supermarkets over the display and promotion of various issues of these publications.[6]

A complete model of the relationship between a manufacturer and its retailers should therefore address the upstream manufacturer's interest in the provision of retail services, and the motivation for the retailer to incur the expense of such services. Promotion, product demonstration, and simply providing a pleasant place to shop are costly. Moreover, it is extremely difficult for the manufacturer to monitor the provision of such services. Taken together, these two facts mean that a manufacturer cannot simply specify the level of retail services that it wants for its product and assume that it will be provided. What is required is an enforceable contract that specifies the obligations of both the manufacturer and the retailer. It is this aspect of the vertical contract—that pertaining to the provision of retail services—that we now wish to examine.

Let us begin by describing how demand is affected by retail services. Denote by $D(p, s)$ the amount of the good demanded at price p with retail service level s. Increases in the level of services s raise the quantity demanded at any price or, alternatively, raise the willingness to pay of each consumer. We assume that this effect takes the form shown in Figure 17.1. In this case an increase in the service level from, say, s_1 to s_2 raises the willingness to pay of the marginal consumer. An example of a demand curve that captures this effect is $Q(p, s) = s(A - p)N$, where N is the number of consumers in the market. In inverse form, this is: $p = A - Q/sN$. The top price anyone is willing to pay for the product is $\$A$, no matter the service level, s, but more is bought as s rises.

Providing retail services is costly. Let the cost of supplying s retail services per unit of the good sold be described by a function $\varphi(s)$. We will assume that the provision of retail services is subject to diminishing returns so that raising the service level s raises the cost of providing such services and does so at an ever-increasing rate. (In calculus terms, this means that both $\varphi'(s)$ and $\varphi''(s)$ exceed zero.) For a given level of services, s, the retailer's

---

[6]   G. Knecht, "Big Chains Get Advance Looks at Magazine Contents," *Wall Street Journal* 22 Oct. 1997, p. A1; C. Johnson-Greene "Walmart Cuts Magazine Shelf Space." www.foliomag.com, Sept. 9, 2009.

marginal cost of selling the manufacturer's product is $r + \varphi(s)$. This is the sum of the wholesale price paid to the manufacturer r plus the cost of providing s retail services per unit sold, $\varphi(s)$.

We now consider the provision of retail services under a variety of circumstances. We point out in advance that this presentation is a little advanced. For those who wish to skip this section, our main result is that, in the absence of vertical price restraints, it is unlikely that a retailer will provide the manufacturer's preferred level of service. The intuition behind this argument is straightforward. The manufacturer wants a high level of service because this will raise the price consumers are willing to pay and, hence, the manufacturer's profit. Yet while the profit gain of better service flows at least in part to the manufacturer, the cost of providing such service falls entirely on the retailer. Accordingly, the retailer's incentive to offer such service is reduced. Vertical restrictions such as a resale price maintenance agreement may be a way to overcome this difficulty, at least in part.

17.4.1   Optimal Provision of Retail Services versus Vertically Integrated Monopoly

Let's start by figuring out what is the efficient level of services from the viewpoint of society overall, i.e., the level that would maximize the combined consumer and producer surplus. Recall that efficiency in a market requires that price equal marginal cost. Because marginal cost for a given level of services is constant, we have that $p = c + \varphi(s)$, which means that there is no producer surplus. As shown in Figure 17.1, the social surplus at any price equal to $c + \varphi(s)$ is just the triangular area above the cost line but below the demand curve. Accordingly, the optimal choice of service level s is the level of s that maximizes the area of this triangle. By definition, this area is given by $\{A - [c + \varphi(s)]\}^2(Ns)/2$. We show in the Appendix that the service level s^* that maximizes this area must satisfy:

$$(A - c)/2 = \varphi(s^*)/2 + \varphi\prime(s^*)s^* \tag{17.1}$$

where $\varphi\prime(s^*)$ is the marginal impact of services on cost.

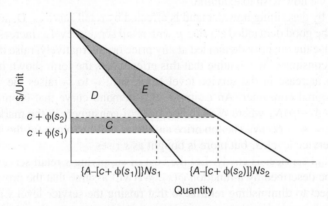

Figure 17.1   The effect of services on demand, costs, and the social surplus

Demand is given by $P = A - Q/sN$. This means that as the level of services rises from s_1 to s_2 the demand curve rotates up and to the right. At service level s_1, marginal cost $= c + \varphi(s_1)$. If price equals marginal cost, total demand is $\{A - [c + \varphi(s_1)]\}Ns_1$, and social surplus is the sum of areas C and D. At service level s_2, marginal cost $= c + \varphi(s_2)$. In this case, equality of price and marginal cost implies that total output $= \{A - [c + \varphi(s_2)]\}Ns_2$, and the social surplus is $D + E$.

Given a service level that satisfies (17.1), the socially optimal price is just the marginal cost of providing the output *plus* that service. Suppose for instance that $N = 100$, $c = 5$, $A = 10$, and that $\varphi(s) = s^2$ so that $\varphi\prime(s^*) = 2s^*$. A small bit of algebra then reveals that the social optimum calls for a service level of $s^* = 1$. (Remember, s is an index and so it is measured in arbitrary units.) At this level of service, optimality would require that the price be equal to $c + \varphi(s^*) = \$6$.

Now consider what the outcome will be if the product is provided by a vertically integrated monopolist producer and retailer. The profit of this integrated firm depends upon the price it sets and the service level it provides, and is:

$$\pi(p^I, s) = p^I(A - p^I)Ns - [c + \varphi(s)](A - p^I)Ns \tag{17.2}$$

Again, the derivation is provided in the Appendix but it is straightforward to show that the integrated monopolist's optimal service level must satisfy:

$$(A - c)/2 = \varphi(s^I)/2 + \varphi\prime(s^I)s^I \tag{17.3}$$

At this service level, the integrated monopolist will set a retail price of:

$$p^I = [A + c + \varphi(s^I)]/2 \tag{17.4}$$

We of course assume that $c + \varphi(s^I) < A$, so that the optimal price insures positive demand. A little reflection on equation (17.4) will reveal that it embodies our usual monopoly relation of price to marginal cost except that now marginal cost includes the service cost $\varphi(s^I)$ as well as the production cost c. As usual, the integrated monopolist will set a price of obtaining a unit of the good along with a given service level that exceeds the marginal cost of providing the good and the associated service cost $c + \varphi(s)$. This is shown in Figure 17.2.

Comparing equations (17.4) and (17.1), it is clear that they are the same. Although the integrated monopoly firm sets too high a price, the service level s^I that it chooses is the same as the socially optimal service level s^*. Returning to our numerical example, with $N = 100$, $c = 5$, $A = 10$, and $\varphi(s) = s^2$, we find that the integrated monopolist will set $s^I = 1$, but set a retail price of $p^I = \$8$. This price combined with a service level of $s = 1$, will yield a total market demand of 200 units, each of which incurs a \$5 production cost and a \$1 service cost. So, the integrated monopolist will earn a profit of $(\$8 - \$6) \times 200 = \$400$.

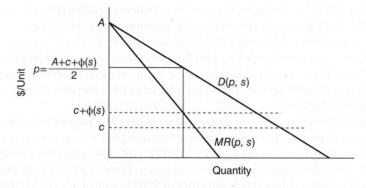

Figure 17.2   The integrated firm's optimal price as a function of the service level, s

As it turns out, the specific result that the integrated monopolist chooses the socially optimum service level reflects the particular demand and cost relationships that we assumed, and is not fully general. Nevertheless, the result is useful because it does show a rather general interest that the manufacturer has in providing retail services. As we shall shortly see, this is why vertical price restrictions establishing a minimum price can play a potentially welfare enhancing role.

17.4.2   The Case of a Monopoly Retailer and a Monopoly Manufacturer

Let's next examine the case where the retailing of the good is done by an independent monopoly downstream retailer. The manufacturer sells the product to the monopoly retailer at price r, after which the retailer sells the good to final consumers at retail price p^D and provides s^D retail services. In accordance with the notation used above, the retailer's profit downstream is

$$\Pi^D(p^D, s^D, r) = [p^D - r - \varphi(s^D)]D(p^D, s^D) = [p^D - r - \varphi(s^D)] s^D N(A - p^D).$$

(17.5)

As in the case of the integrated firm, the retailer must choose the two strategic variables, retail price p^D and the level of retail services s^D. Note though that the retailer in this case has exactly the same profit-maximizing problem as did the integrated firm of the previous discussion, except that the retailer faces a marginal cost r that may differ from the true production cost c, depending on the upstream firm's wholesale price choice. So, we can work out the monopoly retailer's choices just by replacing c with r in equations (17.3) and (17.4). This yields the choices s^D and p^D satisfying

$$(A - r)/2 = \varphi(s^D)/2 + \varphi\prime(s^D)s^D$$

(17.6)

and

$$p^D = \frac{A + r + \varphi(s^D)}{2}$$

(17.7)

Because $r > c$ if the manufacturer is to earn any profit, the price implied by equation (17.7) exceeds that implied by equation (17.5). This is simply the double-marginalization problem again. At any given service level, the monopoly retailer adds the monopolist's markup to the markup already reflected in the manufacturer's wholesale price. Yet as a comparison of equations (17.6) and (17.4) also makes clear, having $r > c$ means that this double-markup is now compounded by a further problem, namely, a suboptimally low level of retail services. For any wholesale price $r > c$ the level of retail services chosen by the retailer s^D is less than the level s^* that is optimal from the viewpoint of both society and the upstream manufacturer.

Again, using the values from our numerical example, it is tedious but straightforward to show that if the manufacturer chooses the wholesale price r to maximize its profit, the outcome will be: $r = \$7$; $p^D = \$8.8$; and $s = 0.775$. Not only is the price too high, but the service level is too low relative to the social optimum. Profit is \$186 for the manufacturer and \$112 for the retailer, so the combined profit of \$298 is well below the \$400 profit of the integrated firm. The intuition behind this outcome is also straightforward. Providing retail services is costly and this, along with the fact that the manufacturer charges a wholesale price r above marginal production cost, puts the squeeze on the retailer's profit. In response, the retailer tries to recapture some of the surplus by cutting back on services.

A two-part pricing agreement can resolve this issue. As usual, the manufacturer should sell to the retailer at marginal cost c, at which point the retailer's profit maximization problem becomes identical with that of the fully integrated firm. This will induce the retailer to provide the optimal service level s^* and price p^I that generate the maximum profit. The manufacturer can then claim all or part of that profit by its choice of the fixed fee T. Returning to our numerical example, $s^* = 1$, $r = c = \$5$, and $p^D = p^I = \$8$ and $\$298 < T < \$400$.

17.2

Assume as in the example in the text that $c = 5$ while $\varphi(s) = s^2$, so that $\varphi\prime(s) = 2s$. Assume that the manufacturer sells through a monopoly retailer and initially sets a wholesale price, r equal to \$6. Assume that retail demand is $Q(p, s) = s(10 - p)100$.

a. What will be the retail service level and the retail price? How much output will be sold at this price and service level combination? What will be the manufacturer's profit?
b. Compare the manufacturer's profit at $r = \$6$ rise with its value at $r = \$7$. What does this increase in r do to the level of retail services?

Practice Problem

17.4.3   The Case of Competitive Retailing

Let's now consider the case of a competitive retailing sector. This is often the more realistic case. It is also a market structure that should work to the manufacturer's benefit. When there is only one retailer, the manufacturer's reach into the retail market is limited, as is its bargaining power with respect to claiming any of the additional profit that coordination yields. When there are many retailers, both the manufacturer's reach and bargaining power are enhanced. Competition among the retailers downstream will bring the retail price-cost margin to zero, and therefore, minimize the problem of double marginalization. The issue of the provision of promotional or retail services, though, still remains. We want to determine the level of services s^c provided by a competitive retail sector and compare that level with the manufacturer's preferred amount, s^*.

We assume that all the downstream retailers are identical. Each buys the manufacturer's product at a wholesale price r and incurs the cost $\varphi(s)$ per unit of output for retail service s. A little thinking leads us to two quick results. First, we know that retail competition will drive the retail price down to marginal cost. In other words, the price to final consumers will have to be $p = r + \varphi(s)$. Second, that same competitive pressure will also force every retailer to offer at that price, the level of services most preferred by consumers. Any retailer who offered a lower service level would quickly lose all its customers. Accordingly, competitive pressure will lead each and every retailer to offer the same retail price and the same service package. The competitive retail price will be $p^C = r + \varphi(s^C)$, and the competitive service level s^C will be the level that maximizes consumer surplus given the price p^C. In Section 17.4.1 we showed that when the price of the good is equal to its true marginal cost, i.e., when $p = c + \varphi(s)$, consumer surplus is $\{A - [c + \varphi(s)]\}^2 Ns/2$.

Reality Checkpoint
Leather Cuts All Too Deep

When the US Supreme Court agreed on December 7, 2006, to hear the case, *Leegin Creative Leather Products, Inc. v. PSKS, Inc.*, No. 06A179, it meant that the court was ready to consider a further major revision of its policy toward vertical price restraints.

In 1997, the women's leather accessories firm, Leegin, had initiated a new marketing policy designed to encourage retailers to promote its brand in a separate section of their stores. In order to participate in this program, retailers had to pledge to adhere to Leegin's suggested prices at all times. PSKS was one of the retailers who agreed to participate in Leegin's program. In 2002, however, faced with disappointing sales, PSKS sharply discounted the Leegin price. Leegin then suspended its shipments to PSKS and the parties went to court.

Similar to Albrecht and Khan, PSKS argued that the Leegin agreement was *per se* illegal and therefore an invalid price-fixing agreement. In the initial trial, PSKS won an award that totaled $1.2 million in damages, which was then trebled. Leegin appealed and directly challenged the *per se* rule to vertical minimum resale price maintenance. When the appellate court affirmed the district court's decision, Leegin appealed to the Supreme Court.

While the *State Oil v. Khan* decision had removed the *per se* prohibition against maximum resale price agreements, it left intact the *per se* unlawful status of *minimum* price restraints. On June 28, the Supreme Court issued its decision. In *Leegin Creative Leather Products, Inc. v. PSKS, Inc.*, 551 U.S. (2007) the court overturned the nearly century-old *Miles* case precedent. Henceforth, in the United States (but not generally in Europe), both minimum and maximum RPM agreements would be subject to a rule of reason test.

Source: S. LaBaton, "Century-Old Ban Lifted on Minimum Retail Pricing," *New York Times*, June 29, 2007, p. A1.

It follows that when price $p = r + \varphi(s)$ consumer surplus is just $\{A - [r + \varphi(s)]\}^2 Ns/2$. Maximizing this with respect to s (see Appendix) yields the service level under competitive retailing, s^C

$$(A - r)/2 = \varphi(s^C)/2 + \varphi\prime(s^C)s^C \tag{17.8}$$

where as before $\varphi\prime(s^C)$ is the marginal effect of service on cost(measured at the value s^C).

Comparison of the value s^c that satisfies equation (17.8) with the manufacturer's preferred efficient level of services (s^* in equation (17.1) or s^I in (17.3)) reveals that the competitive outcome will again provide too low a level of services so long as the wholesale price r exceeds the production cost c. This time though, the reduction in services is not really the result of retailers trying to cut services so as to increase their margin over cost. To the contrary, retailers compete vigorously in providing services. Instead, the problem is that there is in fact no "margin." Competition drives the retail price to be precisely enough to cover the wholesale price plus service cost and no more. While consumers like retail services, they also like low prices and the competitive retail sector tries to give them a bit of both. Thus, for example, if the manufacturer sets $r = \$7$, retailers will now provide services of $s^C = 0.775$ at a cost of \$0.60. This is less than the service the manufacturer would prefer but it allows the retailers to keep the price to consumers down to \$7.60.

The manufacturer earns a profit of \$371.81, which turns out to be the best that can be done in this case if we limit the manufacturer's choice simply to choosing its own markup and the implied wholesale price r.

A solution to the problem must recognize two facts. First, a two-part tariff strategy is no longer workable because there is no retail profit to extract via a lump sum fee T. Second, this is a case in which the retail price is too *low*— \$7.60 in our example relative to the \$8 price set by the integrated monopolist. Together, these two facts suggest that an RPM agreement is needed and that in this case, the agreement should specify a *minimum* price. In particular, the manufacturer can employ an RPM setting a price floor equal to that chosen by the integrated monopolist p^I and then set the wholesale price r just high enough to cover the cost of the optimal service level s^I, that is, $r = p^I - \varphi(s^I)$. Unable to compete by further price reductions, the competitive retailers will focus totally on service and compete away all retail profit by providing exactly s^I just as the manufacturer wishes. Returning to our example, the manufacturer should impose an RPM agreement setting a price floor of \$8 but continue to set a wholesale price of \$7. Retail competition in services will then proceed until $s^C = 1$ and $\varphi(s^C) = 1$ as well so that the downstream price $p^D = r + \varphi(s^C)$. It is easy to verify that doing this will restore the manufacturer's profit to \$400—the same profit as the fully integrated firm.

17.4.4 RPM Agreements, Service, and Free-Riding

One moral of the two cases just considered is that once the costly provision of customer services is included in the analysis, an RPM agreement with a *minimum* price becomes more necessary to insure proper service provision as the downstream market becomes more competitive. There is in fact another reason why this is likely to be the case. This is because many customer services—particularly informational services such as advice on different price and quality combinations, best use practices, and so forth—have the quality of a public good. They are difficult to charge for and easily shared. As with all public goods, provision of these services is likely to be too low.

Think about it for a moment. A consumer electronics shop may keep experts on hand to assist a customer in choosing the digital camera that best meets the customer's needs in terms of portability and convenience, works most effectively with the customer's computer and other peripherals, and fits best within her budget. Similarly, wine shops may employ personnel to advise customers regarding the quality of a particular vintage or the food that best accompanies a given wine.

Providing such presale or point of sale services is costly. Unfortunately, there is no obligation for the consumer, once educated by the store's expert staff, to buy from that specific establishment. Quite to the contrary, once fully informed, the consumer has a strong incentive to go to the "no frills" electronics shop down the street or to the discount wine shop around the corner and purchase what the consumer now knows to be the proper digital camera and the appropriate wine at a lower price. Even worse, the consumer is free to share this information with friends who can then use this knowledge to bypass the specialty shops altogether and go directly to the low-price, low-service outlets.

Because information is a public good, it is hard to deny it even to those who do not pay for it. The low-price discount dealers in our two simple examples are "free riding" on the specialty shops. We call this behavior free riding because the discounter benefits from the activities of the specialty shop but does not pay for them. The scenarios above indicate the likely outcome of this problem. Specialty shops that incur the cost of providing in-store demonstrations and consultations will lose market share to the "no frills" discount stores. As such discount stores come to dominate the retail market, few retail services will be provided overall.

At this point, the advantage of an RPM agreement should be clear. It prevents one retailer from undercutting another and, hence, stifles the emergence of discount stores. In turn, this implies that consumers will visit the retailer who provides the best services because they will not find a lower price elsewhere. By putting a freeze on price discounting, the effect of an RPM agreement is to foreclose discount outlets, resulting in a possibly higher average retail price. Yet this price effect and the loss it imposes on consumers may be offset by the gains that the provision of retail services generate, not only for consumers but for the manufacturer as well.[7]

Moreover, the free-riding justification for RPM applies to more than just purely informational services. For example, higher-end stores such as Bloomingdales, Neiman-Marcus, and Bergdorf Goodman play an important role in identifying and then selling "what's hot" or in fashion. Here again though, providing this service is not cheap. These stores must spend considerable resources to build up their reputation for being on the "cutting edge" of fashion trends. Just by carrying the line of a specific manufacturer, such stores identify the top brands and fashions. Manufacturers need retailers to play this role. Yet if a consumer can go window shopping at a prestigious store to find out "what's in" this season and then buy the apparel at a discount store, we again have the problem of free riding and, along with that, a potential justification for the use of an RPM agreement specifying a floor price.[8]

17.5   RETAIL PRICE MAINTENANCE AND UNCERTAIN DEMAND

We have been discussing in the preceding two sections the way in which competitive pressures in the retail market can reduce the profit of the manufacturer and the welfare of consumers by creating disincentives to provide customer services. However, retail competition can be destructive in other ways as well. Deneckere et al. (1997) demonstrate how uncertain retail demand can produce such an outcome. [9]

Goods are not sold continuously. Instead, retailers place orders with manufacturers and then hold an inventory stock to buffer against movements in demand. As a result, each retailer faces a dilemma in determining how much output to stock for sale to final consumers. On the one hand, the retailer will wish to have the amount on hand necessary for profit maximization during periods when demand is strong. On the other hand, if demand is weak, retailers with a lot of stock will have to do one of two things. Either they try to sell the output or they can absorb the extra output (or simply throw it away) and thereby keep the price high.[10]

It is in this situation that the behavior of the monopolist and the competitive firm will differ. Faced with weak demand, the monopolist will tend just to dispose of (or just hold indefinitely) a good bit of its excess inventory because the monopolist recognizes that every

---

[7]   Tesler (1960) first articulated this view. See also Bork (1966). For an opposing view see Steiner (1985).

[8]   Mathewson and Winter (1983) make a similar argument that resale price maintenance can benefit consumers by economizing on consumer search costs because consumers will no longer spend time trying to find out which retailer sells at the lowest price.

[9]   See also Marvel and McCafferty (1984).

[10]   We assume that inventories cannot be stored. Either they physically perish or become worthless due to the introduction of new goods.

extra unit sold lowers the price on all units. A firm in a competitive retail sector, however, will do the opposite. Under competition, each retailer perceives that its own sales have no or little effect on the market price. Accordingly, each such competitive retailer will try to sell all of its stock. After all, it has already paid for it and it may as well try to get something for it rather than throw any of it away. The problem is that if all retailers act this way the market the price will fall, possibly quite far.

The fact that competition induces sharp price-cutting during periods of weak demand has two implications. First, a manufacturer selling through a competitive retail sector will not earn the profit of an integrated firm. Second, the manufacturer will also find it difficult to induce retailers to hold any sizable inventory because retailers will recognize that they might end up getting rid of that inventory at a very low price. An RPM agreement that establishes a minimum retail price can solve the manufacturer's problem. The reason is straightforward. Setting a minimum price at which the good can be sold ensures that in periods of low demand, retailers will deal with excess inventory exactly the way that an integrated manufacturer would choose. They will throw away the amount that cannot be sold at the specified retail price.

We illustrate the essential insight of the Deneckere et al. argument in Figure 17.3. The figure shows the price and profit outcome for an integrated monopolist manufacturer facing variable demand. As usual, we assume a constant unit cost, c. With probability one-half, demand is strong and the demand curve is D_H. Similarly, with probability one-half, demand is weak and the demand curve is D_L. The integrated monopolist then faces a two-stage problem. In stage one, the firm must choose how much to produce, Q. Once the firm has produced this amount, it will have incurred a cost, which is now sunk, equal to cQ. Afterwards, demand will be either strong or weak, D_H or D_L. At that point, the firm will have no additional cost and will simply have to choose how much of the output in its inventory that it actually wants to sell. Of course, the integrated firm can sell no more than it originally produced, Q. Subject to this constraint, however, it will simply sell the amount that maximizes its revenue conditional upon demand. Because all its costs are sunk, revenue maximization and profit maximization amount to the same thing in the second stage.

The integrated firm will never initially produce more than the amount that would maximize profit if it knew for sure that demand would be high. This is an amount at which the marginal revenue when demand is D_H equals marginal production cost, c. It is shown as Q^{UPPER} in Figure 17.3. To produce more than this level would guarantee that the firm

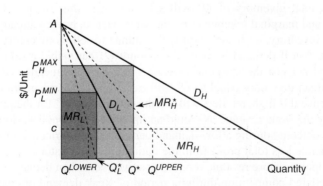

Figure 17.3   Resale price maintenance and variable demand

earns a marginal revenue below its production cost even in the best of demand conditions. Similarly, the firm will never produce for inventory an amount less than Q^{LOWER}, the amount it would produce if it were certain demand would be low. To do so would guarantee too little inventory even in the weakest of markets. The firm must produce somewhere between Q^{LOWER} and Q^{UPPER}. Within this interval, optimization requires that it choose an amount whereby its marginal cost c equals its expected marginal revenue, or one-half times the marginal revenue in a high-demand state plus one-half times the marginal revenue in a low-demand state (which is bounded by zero).

As we have drawn Figure 17.3, the optimal amount of initial production is Q^*. Note that in this figure, demand is quite variable. As a result, in order to come even close to the true profit-maximizing level in a high-demand state, the amount produced for inventory Q^* would be enough to drive the price to zero if it is all sold in a weak-demand state.

If demand is strong, the firm will sell the entire amount Q^* at the price P_H^{MAX}. If demand is weak, an inventory of Q^* is excessive. Because the integrated firm has already incurred its production cost, all it can do then is maximize its revenue. It will do this by selling the amount Q_L^* at the price, P_L^{MIN}. This is an output at which marginal revenue is zero. Weak demand does not lead the firm to try to liquidate its entire inventory, as such an action would drive the price to zero. Instead, the firm throws away the amount $Q^* - Q_L^*$. When demand is weak, the firm drives its marginal revenue to zero. However, because this occurs where the price is still positive, the firm's total revenue remains greater than zero even in the face of weak demand. Its marginal revenue when demand is strong is the marginal revenue at Q^*, shown here as MR_H^*. Its expected marginal revenue is therefore $MR_H^*/2$ which is an amount just equal to c.

The integrated monopolist firm will expect to earn a positive profit in this story. Its total cost is cQ. Its revenue in a low demand period is $P_L^{MIN} Q_L^*$. This is the lightly shaded rectangle in Figure 17.3. Its revenue in a high-demand period is $P_H^{MAX} Q^*$. This is the sum of the darkly shaded rectangle and the lightly shaded region in the figure. The expected profit for the integrated firm, Π_I^e is therefore

$$\Pi_I^e = \frac{1}{2}P_H^{MAX}Q^* + \frac{1}{2}P_L^{MIN}Q_L^* - cQ^*. \tag{17.9}$$

Now consider what happens under competitive retailing. If competitive retailers stocked the optimal amount Q^*, they would earn less total profit than that shown in equation (17.9). The reason is the nature of competition. In a low-demand period, the integrated firm sells only up to the point at which its marginal revenue is zero. However, competitive firms holding a total inventory of Q^* will sell more than this amount. Each such firm perceives price and marginal revenue to be the same. Hence, having already sunk the cost of acquiring its inventory, each such firm will continue to sell its inventory so long as the price is positive. Yet if demand is weak, the amount Q^* can only be sold by driving the retail price—and not just the marginal revenue—to zero. This means that a competitive retail sector with an inventory equal to Q^* will earn no revenue when demand is low. Of course, when demand is high, retailers will sell the entire stock Q^* for the price P_H^{MAX} and generate exactly the same revenue as would an integrated monopolist. However, because the competitive outcome during a low-demand period is a zero price, competitive retailers will always generate less total profit from the optimal inventory stock, Q^*, than would an integrated monopolist whose revenue remains positive even when demand is weak.

In short, unfettered competition during a period of weak demand dramatically reduces the revenue retailers can expect to earn. Accordingly, a manufacturer can only persuade retailers to stock the optimal amount Q^* by selling to them at a sufficiently low wholesale price P_W, so that retailers can still expect to break even. Because retailers only earn positive revenue when demand is high, $P_W Q^*$ must equal the revenue earned by retailers in a high-demand period, times the probability that such a period occurs. Therefore, $P_W Q^*$ must equal $P_H^{MAX} Q^*/2$, implying that $P_W = P_H^{MAX}/2$. In turn, this implies an expected profit, Π^e, for the manufacturer without an RPM agreement of

$$\Pi^e = \left(\frac{1}{2} P_H^{MAX} - c \right) Q^*. \tag{17.10}$$

A comparison of equations (17.9) and (17.10) shows that the profit of the manufacturer in this case will be less than that earned by its integrated counterpart by an amount equal to $P_L^{MIN} Q_L^*/2$. However, an RPM agreement can save the day. The necessary features of such an agreement are suggested by Figure 17.3. That figure shows that the integrated firm never sells at a price below P_L^{MIN}. So, the nonintegrated manufacturer should negotiate an RPM agreement that likewise prohibits anyone from selling below this price. In addition, it should charge a wholesale price P_W^*, satisfying

$$P_W^* Q^* = \frac{1}{2} P_H^{MAX} Q^* + \frac{1}{2} P_L^{MIN} Q_L^*. \tag{17.11}$$

In turn, this implies that

$$P_W^* = \frac{1}{2} P_H^{MAX} + \frac{1}{2} P_L^{MIN} \frac{Q_L^*}{Q^*}. \tag{17.12}$$

At this wholesale price, the competitive retail sector will in fact buy and inventory the optimal amount, $Q*$. Why? When they buy this amount, retailers know that their expected revenue, $P_H^{MAX} Q^*/2 + P_L^{MIN} Q_L^*/2$, just equals their expected cost, $P_W^* Q^*$. Hence, the inventory of Q^* is exactly the amount that leads to an expected profit of zero for retailers. This of course is the equilibrium requirement for a competitive retail sector. Moreover, because retailers buy the amount Q^* at this wholesale price, the manufacturer's expected profit, Π_{RPM}^e, with an RPM is

$$\Pi_{RPM}^e = P_W Q^* - cQ = \frac{1}{2} P_H^{MAX} Q^* + \frac{1}{2} P_L^{MIN} Q_L^* - cQ^* \tag{17.13}$$

A comparison of equations (17.9) and (17.13) quickly reveals that this RPM agreement permits the manufacturer in this case to earn the same profit as that earned by an integrated firm.

It is important to note that it is not just the manufacturer who may benefit from the RPM agreement just described. Such an agreement can potentially also enlarge the expected consumer surplus. This is easiest to see by recognizing that absent an RPM agreement, retailers may not be willing to offer the product to consumers at all. More generally, competitive retailers will buy less inventory in equilibrium without an RPM agreement than they will buy with one. As a result, the price during a period of strong demand will be higher without an RPM contract. This price increase hurts consumers and may more than offset the gains consumers enjoy from permitting prices to fall quite far when demand is weak. Hence, under uncertain demand in a competitive retail sector, both the manufacturer and consumers can benefit from an RPM agreement.[11]

17.3

Suppose that demand is either strong (with probability one-half) and described by $Q = (10 - p)100$, or weak (with probability one-half) and described by $Q = (10 - p)30$. To simplify further, assume that the manufacturer's unit cost is constant at $c = 0$.

a. Show that the revenue-maximizing price is $5 regardless of whether demand is weak or strong.

b. Assume that the firm produces 500 units prior to learning the strength of demand. How much of this will it sell when demand is strong? How much will it sell when demand is weak? What is the firm's expected profit?

c. Suppose now that the firm sells the 500 units through a competitive retail sector. If retailers buy and stock the entire 500 units, what will be the retail price when demand is strong? What will be the retail price when demand is weak?

d. In light of your answer to (c), what wholesale price will induce the retailers to purchase initially an inventory of 500? What will be the manufacturer's profit at this price?

Practice Problem

17.6 RPM AGREEMENTS AND COLLUSION

We noted at the beginning of this chapter that while academics and the courts have varied in their views of non-price vertical restraints (next chapter), there is a long tradition that views vertical restrictions on prices—particularly RPM agreements—much more negatively. Indeed, until quite recently, all such agreements were held to be *per se* illegal. Given that the examples thus far considered in this chapter point to a positive role for RPM agreements, one might wonder why the suspicion of RPM agreements has been so persistent and so long-lasting.

The critical element contributing to the negative view of vertical price restraints is the suspicion that these agreements substantially raise the possibility that firms can collude, i.e., that they facilitate the suppression of interbrand competition. The US Supreme Court was explicit on this point. In the *Business Electronics v. Sharp Electronics* case (1988), the Court wrote that "there is a significant distinction between vertical price and vertical non-price restraints." The Court continued by noting that there has long been a presumption that "vertical price restraints reduce interbrand competition because they 'facilitate cartelizing.'"[12] Yet while the fear that RPM might facilitate collusion may be legitimate, formal analysis of this hypothesis has been limited. However, two recent papers illustrate why this concern may be legitimate.

The first of these is Jullien and Rey (2007). The intuition in this paper is quite straightforward. Consider two manufacturers, each of whom sells a differentiated product

---

[11] The manufacturer always gains from the specified RPM agreement. The outcome for consumers depends on just how variable is demand. If demand is highly variable, consumers are probably hurt by the agreement. However, if demand is only moderately variable, consumers may well benefit from the agreement.

[12] *Business Electronics Corp. v. Sharp Electronics*, 485 U.S. 717 (1988). The Court's statement refers to its earlier analysis in *Continental T.V. Inc. v. GTE Sylvania Inc.* 433 U.S. 36 (1977).

and who compete in prices as described in Chapter 10. Each manufacturer sells to final consumers through its own exclusive retailer at a wholesale price w_i who, in turn, sets the final retail price p_i. It is, of course, that pair of final prices that determines the sales of the upstream producers. Marginal cost is assumed to be zero. The retail demand facing each is:

$$p_i = A - q_i + \beta p_j + \varepsilon_i \quad i, j = 1,2 \; i \neq j \quad 0 < \beta < 1 \tag{17.14}$$

Here, ε_i is a random shock term reflecting the variation in retail demand q_i. Such shocks occur after the wholesale price has been set but before the retail price is determined. Critically, firm j and its retailer can observe only the price p_i that retailer i sets in response to manufacturer i's wholesale price w_i, and the demand shock ε_1. From Chapter 10 we know that i's best response, given its observed ε_1 shock and its expectation for firm j's price p_j^e, is to set $p_i = \left(\dfrac{A + w_i + \varepsilon_i}{2}\right) + \left(\dfrac{\beta}{2}\right) p_j^e$. Since this implies that the expected value of $p_i = p_i^e = \left(\dfrac{A + w_i}{2}\right) + \left(\dfrac{\beta}{2}\right) p_j^e$, equation (17.14) can be rewritten as:

$$p_i = p_i^e + \frac{\varepsilon_i}{2} \quad i, j = 1,2; \; i \neq j \tag{17.15}$$

In other words, firm i's retailer would adjust its retail price in response to demand shocks to be different from what was initially expected. This flexibility however makes collusion more difficult. It means that if firm i observes a low retail price p_j being charged by its rival, it cannot tell whether that is due to a negative demand shock, a move on i's part to price more aggressively or, in the context of collusion, to cheat on the cartel. Consequently, cheating detection is difficult, and, as we know, this makes it more difficult to sustain a cartel.

Matters change with an RPM agreement. Now, any change in the retail price can only occur if the upstream manufacturer changes the RPM price bound. Accordingly, the RPM agreement facilitates collusion. It is not a perfect outcome. The fact that retail prices are pre-set now means that they cannot react to demand shocks and this is a true cost. In addition, because collusion with an RPM agreement permits pushing the price closer to the joint monopoly price than collusion without an RPM agreement does, the one-period gain from cheating is larger when RPM agreements are employed. This of course makes the cartel less sustainable. Still, Jullien and Rey (2007) show that the detection effect will often win out. When it does, firms will find it profitable to adopt RPM agreements that lead to retail prices close to the joint-profit-maximizing level, and that leave consumers worse off.

More recently, Rey and Vergé (2010) offer an alternative model of RPM-facilitated collusion in which, contrary to the case above, manufacturers sell through the same distributors. To take the simplest case, imagine two upstream manufacturers, A and B, and initially, just one downstream retailer that we will call retailer 1. This retailer then sells two differentiated goods that we will call A1 and B1. If retailer 1 could buy at cost from each producer it would then set prices p_{A1}^* and p_{B1}^* that would maximize its joint profit from the two products. That is, retailer 1 would internalize the competition between the two products and so coordinate their prices to earn the maximum profit possible in this market. The prices p_{A1}^* and p_{B1}^* are, in fact, precisely the prices that would be set by the manufacturers themselves if they were fully integrated firms and were cooperating with each other.

The outcome just described is in fact achievable by each manufacturer using a two-part contract in which each sells to the retailer at cost and then claims its share of the resultant profit for itself via the fixed fee. To see this, suppose that firm A adapts such a two-part pricing scheme in which it sells to retailer 1 at a price per unit equal to marginal cost and then takes a chunk of profit by way of a fixed fee F_A. Given that, the best that firm B can do is to work out a contract that will maximize the retailer's profit net of its payment to firm A, and then claim that profit with a fixed fee F_B. The way to do this is again to price at marginal cost. No RPM agreement is necessary to achieve the joint (three-way) maximum profit when both producers sell through a single retailer.

Matters change though if the two producers also sell through a second downstream firm, retailer 2. The reason is that there is now retail competition as well as upstream competition. Analogous to p_{A1}^* and p_{B1}^*, denote now the prices p_{A2}^* and p_{B2}^* as the monopoly profit-maximizing prices that would be set if both producers sold only through retailer 2. Suppose for example that both manufacturers adopt the foregoing two-part pricing at both downstream retailers in the hope that this will yield the four final market prices, p_{A1}^*, p_{B1}^*, p_{A2}^*, and p_{B2}^*. Because the retailers are buying at cost, however, setting these prices implies that each retail price reflects the highest possible markup. As a result, each retailer will find that it can increase its profit significantly by cutting either of its retail prices and stealing business from its rival. Indeed, each producer will be tempted in this way as well.

To put it another way, the pair of prices p_{A1}^* and p_{B1}^* are not retailer 1's best response to a choice by retailer 2 to charge the prices p_{A2}^* and p_{B2}^*. Because each manufacturer is selling at cost, the margin on additional retail sales is very large—creating an equally large incentive to cut retail prices. Manufacturers can dull this incentive by instead selling at a wholesale price r that exceeds marginal cost. Yet this runs into two problems. The first is the familiar one of double-marginalization. The second is the related one that if producer A sets a wholesale price above marginal cost, producer B has an incentive to undercut this so that its products will sell at lower retail prices. In other words, for feasible contract types the retail competition is likely to extend upward to wholesale price competition between the manufacturers. Rey and Vergé (2010) show that in the absence of any RPM agreements, the market outcome is likely to be fairly competitive.

The appeal of RPM agreements now is clear. They suppress retail competition. If for example retailers are perfect Bertrand competitors, wholesale prices map one for one into retail prices and manufacturers compete directly with each other via wholesale prices. RPM agreements weaken this link by allowing a positive retail margin (and can never do worse than a no RPM strategy).[13]

17.7   EMPIRICAL APPLICATION: RPM AND PRICES—EVIDENCE AFTER LEEGIN

Vertical price restraints have been the subject of both considerable academic debate and spirited as well as evolving legal controversies. The recent court decisions in *State Oil v. Khan* and, even more particularly, *Leegin* however mark a clear shift in antitrust doctrine towards more acceptance of vertical price restraints, including RPM agreements, in the recognition that the coordination such restraints make possible may well work to the benefit of consumers. Yet it seems clear that there are potential pitfalls in this approach and that tolerance of RPM agreements can yield results inimical to consumers and economic efficiency.

[13]   Rey and Vergé (2010) make clear that the joint monopoly outcome is just one of a continuum of possible equilbria, with each equilibrium corresponding to a different wholesale price. In many ways, the Rey and Vergé (2010) analysis is a generalization of the earlier analysis in Bernheim and Winston (1985).

An interesting paper by Smith and MacKay (2013) explores the effect of RPM on prices by considering the effect of the *Leegin* decision across different states. While the *Leegin* decision made clear that the federal courts would now treat RPM agreements more leniently, the impact on state laws and legal practices was less clear. Many states, such as Texas, do include formal statements in their business and commercial codes that they will be guided by and follow closely federal precedent where applicable. In these states, the change in the federal approach to a rule-of-reason treatment of RPM agreements that *Leegin* introduced would likely liberalize their legal treatment of such agreements as well. On the other hand, there are a number of states, such as California, in which the state antitrust laws and court precedents indicate a very strong presumption that RPM contracts are a *per se* violation of the antitrust laws. To the extent that antitrust litigation is rooted in local courts, the *Leegin* ruling might not have very much impact on these states.

Smith and MacKay (2013) use the foregoing logic to frame a natural experiment designed to reveal the impact of RPM agreements. Based on their legal and legislative history they identify a group of twenty-four states in which the *Leegin* decision would likely lead to a more legally tolerant view of RPM contracts, and a group of eleven states in which the *Leegin* decision is unlikely to change the (much harsher) legal treatment of these agreements. They then use data from a relatively new data set collected by Nielsen on actual weekly purchases by consumers of literally thousands of items over the years 2004–09. While this includes 1.4 million separate products, Nielsen groups these products in 1,025 modules such as "brandy" or "sleeping aids." Smith and MacKay (2013) were able to examine 1,025 of these.

Smith and MacKay (2013) then construct a weighted price (in logs) for each product sold by each retailer in each state in each week t. For each of the 1,025 product modules, they then estimate the following regression:

$$\ln P_{jrst} = \alpha + \beta_1 RoR + \beta_2 L_t + \beta_3 (L \times RoR_S)$$
$$+ \text{Other characteristics and Fixed Effects} + \varepsilon_{jrst}$$

Here, $\ln P_{jsrt}$ is the log price of product j sold by retailer r in state s and week t; RoR_S is an indicator variable that takes the value of 1 if that state s is in the Rule of Reason group, and 0 for the control group comprised of those states with strong *per se* presumptions of illegality in which *Leegin* is expected to have little effect. L is an indicator variable that takes the value 1 if the observation is in a week t that is after the *Leegin* decision on 28 June 2007 but 0 before that date. Finally, $L*RoR_t$ is an interactive term that is 1 in all weeks after the *Leegin* decision but only for the Rule of Reason groups of states. In all other cases it is 0.

It is the coefficient β_3 on the third term that is most critical. The coefficient β_1 indicates the general difference in prices between the *RoR* group and the control group of *per se* states. The coefficient β_2 reflects the general effect that the *Leegin* decision had on both groups of states. It is the coefficient β_3 though that captures the difference in the effect that the *Leegin* decision had on the RoR group *relative* to the control group. Thus, the coefficient β_3 is really the "difference-in-difference" estimator discussed earlier in Chapter 10. That is, it will capture how much more (if any) prices have risen in the Rule of Reason states after *Leegin* than in the control group of *per se* states.

Nielsen categorizes each of the 1,025 product modules as being in one of ten product departments. It is useful to summarize the results for each of the 1,025 regression by this department type. This is shown for the most basic Smith and MacKay model in Table 17.1.

The results shown in Table 17.1 are somewhat striking. In 61 percent of the products studied, the estimate of β_3 was positive. It was significantly so in over 15 percent and significantly negative in less than 6 percent. The median price effect in the states historically leaning toward a Rule of Reason approach ranges from a low of 1.3 percent to a high of 8.6 percent. Moreover, these increases are typically associated with declines in the quantity sold. This strongly suggests that the greater national legal tolerance of minimum RPM agreements following *Leegin* has led to tighter supplies and higher retail prices in the Rule of Reason states.

Smith and MacKay (2013) recognize that higher prices by themselves do not necessarily mean that consumers are worse off. In the absence of RPM agreements, retailers might not hold sufficient inventory of high-cost branded goods as suggested above in Section 17.5 but, instead, hold more low-cost private label (unbranded) products. If this is so, then the market share of branded products in the Rule of Reason states should have increased after *Leegin* relative to that in the *per se* states. Yet Smith and MacKay (2013) estimate a second difference-in-difference effect to show that this has *not* been the case. In short, the Smith and MacKay (2013) study offers fairly strong evidence that the relaxation of the *per se* illegality rule for RPM agreements has led as many feared to less competitive pricing. Their evidence from market simulations suggests that this has reduced consumer surplus by about 4 percent on average.[14]

Table 17.1   Regression results for estimates of difference-in-difference parameter, β_3 (fixed effects)[15]

Product Department	Number of Regressions	Number of Regressions with $\beta_3 > 0$ (Significant)			Number of Regressions with $\beta_3 < 0$ (Significant)			Percent Positive in Total
		Count	Percent	Median	Count	Percent	Median	
Health & Beauty Aids	165	24	14.5%	3.9%	13	7.9%	−4.7%	59.6%
Dry Grocery	406	67	16.5%	4.2%	23	5.7%	−4.5%	63.5%
Frozen Food	81	23	28.4%	3.4%	1	1.2%	−6.7%	70.7%
Dairy	43	5	11.6%	3.1%	3	7.0%	−2.8%	59.1%
Deli	16	2	12.5%	2.6%	0	0.0%	—	75.0%
Packaged Meat	12	3	25.0%	1.3%	2	16.7%	−12.6%	66.7%
Fresh Produce	21	2	9.5%	8.6%	0	0.0%	—	61.9%
Non-Food Grocery	122	16	13.1%	1.8%	7	5.7%	−4.5%	53.6%
Alcohol Beverages	30	3	10.0%	4.0%	2	6.7%	−3.8%	43.3%
General Merchandise	129	12	9.3%	4.1%	7	5.4%	−4.1%	58.3%
Total	**1025**	**157**	**15.3%**		**58**	**5.7%**		**61.0%**

[14]   Smith and MacKay (2012) run similar regressions using quantity as the dependent variable. Here, the difference-in-difference estimator is expected to be negative as actions that raise price lower the quantity demanded. This too is exactly what they find to roughly the same extent that they find the positive price effects.

[15]   The significance level is 5% for the above regressions. Standard errors are clustered at the state level interacted with a dummy for post-Leegin to allow for arbitrary serial correlation. The authors have a more recent version of the paper in which they calculates significance via bootstrapping. Source: Calculated based on data from The Nielsen Company (US), LLC.

Summary

Because a manufacturer relies on retailers to get its goods to the market, the manufacturer must hope that the retailers will share its views about the appropriate price to consumers and the proper amount of promotional and other services to provide. Unfortunately, this is rarely the case. Double-marginalization and other problems lead to a divergence of interests between the manufacturer and the retailer. However, contractual agreements governing this vertical relationship can resolve some of these differences. Yet such agreements can also facilitate price collusion either among manufacturers or retailers. As a result, public policy regarding vertical restraints is complicated.

In this chapter, we have focused on one particular type of vertical restraint—a resale price maintenance or RPM agreement. Such agreements may specify a maximum price above which a retailer may not charge, or a minimum price that the retailer cannot discount. For many years, RPM agreements were considered anticompetitive and treated as *per se* illegal. However, starting as early as 1919, the courts have chipped away at this strict view so that now RPM agreements and behavior that closely duplicates such a contract even when the contract itself does not formally specify a retail price, are subject to a more flexible rule of reason. With *State Oil v. Khan* and with *Leegin*, the status of RPM agreements has changed from *per se* illegal to legal if reasonably justified. This is true whether the agreement imposes either a maximum or minimum resale price.

The reason that the courts have moved to a more lenient attitude toward RPM agreements is straightforward. Increasingly, economists and policy makers have understood that without such agreements, problems such as double-marginalization, insuring the provision of services to consumers, and dealing with demand uncertainty, work against consumer as well as producer interests. This is not to say that the concern that vertical price restraints may be anticompetitive is unwarranted. It does suggest, though, that a proper adjudication of the issues cannot be made until all the facts are known. In some ways, this is exactly what the courts recognized in moving from a *per se* illegal judgment to one based on a "rule of reason."

At the same time, the potential anticompetitive effects of RPM contracts are clear. Indeed, the supposition that such effects are dominant is heightened by the fact that historically, it has been retailers and not manufacturers who have lobbied most consistently against the *per se* treatment that dominated the first century of antitrust cases. It has also been these same retailers who have supported legislation such as the Miller-Tydings and McGuire Acts permitting such vertical price restraints. Recent empirical work by Smith and MacKay (2012) finds that the *Leegin* case has led to higher product prices precisely in those states that were predisposed to adopt the more tolerant federal court guidelines suggests that these anticompetitive concerns may be justified.

Problems

1. Suppose that a car dealer has a local monopoly in selling *Volvos*. It pays w to *Volvo* for each car that it sells, and charges each customer p. The demand curve that the dealer faces is best described by the linear function $Q = 30 - p$, where the price is in units of thousands of dollars.
   a. What is the profit-maximizing price for the dealer to set? At this price, how many *Volvos* will the dealer sell and what will the dealer's profit from selling the cars be?
   b. Now let us think about how the situation looks from the car manufacturer's point of view. If *Volvo* charges w per car to its dealer, calculate how many cars the dealer will buy from *Volvo*. In other words, what is the demand curve facing *Volvo*? Suppose that it costs *Volvo* \$5,000 to produce each car. What is the profit-maximizing choice of w? What will *Volvo*'s profits be? What price p will the dealer set and what profit will the dealer earn at *Volvo*'s

profit-maximizing choice of wholesale price w?

2. Suppose in problem 1 that *Volvo* operates the dealership itself and sells directly to its customers.

    a. What will be *Volvo's* profit-maximizing price *p*? What will *Volvo's* profit be? Compare your answer to the answer you worked out in 1(b). Give an intuitive explanation for why the answers differ.

    b. Suppose instead that *Volvo* can impose an RPM agreement on its independent retailers. Will *Volvo* set a maximum or minimum retail price? What price will *Volvo* actually set?

3. ABC, Inc. is a monopolist selling to competitive retailers. It faces a constant marginal cost of 10. Demand at the retail level is described by $P = 50 - Q$.

    a. What wholesale price will maximize ABC's profit? What retail price will this imply?

    b. What will be the value of consumer surplus if ABC sets a profit-maximizing wholesale price?

    c. What will be the value of ABC's maximum profit?

4. ABC is still a monopolist selling to competitive retailers but it now discovers that if retailers supply customer services, demand shifts to: $P = 90 - Q$. Each retailer can provide the required services at a total cost of $400.

    a. ABC decides now to implement an RPM agreement with retailers. Under this agreement, what retail price should ABC specify? How many units will retailers sell at this price?

    b. What is consumer surplus under the RPM agreement?

5. Under the RPM agreement and the price specified in 4(a), what is the maximum wholesale price that ABC can set? What will its profit at this wholesale price be? Did adoption of the RPM agreement improve social welfare?

6. A significant number of the resale price maintenance cases that have been the subject of antitrust policy involve the pricing of such simple consumer products as Russell Stover candy, Levi's jeans, Arrow shirts, and Colgate toiletries. Who has the incentive for resale price maintenance for these products? Explain why.

7. In the antitrust case *Albrecht v. Herald Co.*, the successive monopoly problem was created by the publisher granting an exclusive territory to the distributor. Could the problem have been solved by opening up home delivery to competition among several distributors?

References

Bernheim, D., and M. Whinston. 1985. "Common Marketing Agency as a Device for Facilitating Collusion," *Rand Journal of Economics* 16 (Summer): 269–81.

Bork, R. 1966. "The Rule of Reason and the Per Se Concept: Price Fixing and Market Division," *Yale Law Journal* 75 (January): 399–441.

Chen, Y. 1999. "Olgiopoly Price Discrimination and Resale Price Maintenance," *Rand Journal of Economics* 30 (Autumn): 441–55.

Deneckere, R., H. P. Marvel, and J. Peck, 1997. "Demand Uncertainty and Price Maintenance: Markdowns as Destructive Competi-tion," *American Economic Review* 87 (September): 619–41.

Jullien, B., and P. Rey, 2007. "Resale Price Maintenance and Collusion," *Rand Journal of Economics* 38 (Winter): 983–1001.

Lafontaine, F. 1992. "Agency Theory and Franchising: Some Empirical Results," *Rand Journal of Economics* 23 (Summer): 263–83.

Lafontaine, F. 1993. "Contractual Arrangements as Signaling Devices: Evidence from Franchising," *Journal of Law, Economics, and Organization* 9 (October): 256–89.

Lafontaine, F. 1995. "Pricing Decisions in Franchised Chains: A Look at the Restaurant and Fast-Food Industry," Mimeo, University of Michigan, (April).

Marvel, H., and S. McCafferty, 1984. "Resale Price Maintenance and Quality Certification," *Rand Journal of Economics* 15 (Autumn): 346–59.

Mathewson, G. F., and R. A. Winter, 1983. "The Incentives for Resale Price Maintenance under Imperfect Information," *Economic Inquiry* 62 (June): 337–48.

O'Brien, D. P., and G. Schaffer. 1994. "The Welfare Effects of Forbidding Discriminatory Discounts: A Secondary Line Analysis of Robinson-Patman," *Journal of Law, Economics, and Organization* 10 (October): 296–318.

Overstreet, T., 1983. *Resale Price Maintenance: Economic Theories and Empirical Evidence*, Washington, DC: Federal Trade Commission Bureau of Economics Staff Report (November).

Pickering, J. F. 1966. *Resale Price Maintenance in Practice*, New York: August M. Kelley Publishers.

Rey, P., and T. Vergé. 2010. "Resale Price Maintenance and Interlocking Relationships," *Journal of Industrial Economics* 58 (December): 928–61.

Smith, D., and A. MacKay, 2013. "The Empirical Effects of Minimum Resale Price Maintenance on Prices, Output, and Consumer Welfare," Working Paper, Department of Economics, University of Chicago, (May).

Steiner, R. L. 1985. "The Nature of Vertical Restraints," *Antitrust Bulletin* (Spring): 143–97.

Tesler, L., 1960. "Why Should Manufacturers Want Free Trade?" *Journal of Law and Economics* 3 (October): 86–105.

Appendix

MANUFACTURER'S OPTIMAL CONTRACT WHEN SELLING TO A PRICE-DISCRIMINATING RETAILER

We consider the optimal wholesale price r and fixed fee T that a manufacturer should select to maximize total profit when the retailer sells in two identical markets, one of which is a monopoly but the other of which is constrained by potential entry to sell at a price equal to the wholesale price. Given that there is competition in one market, $T = 0$, as any value of $T > 0$ would drive competitive retailers from the market. The problem is then the profit-maximizing choice for the wholesale price r. Recall that demand in each market is given by: $P = A - BQ$. Manufacturing cost is c. The retail cost is just r. Retailer profit maximization in the monopoly case implies:

$$Q_M = \frac{A - r}{2B} \tag{17.A1}$$

and a retail price P^D of

$$P^D = \frac{A + r}{2} \tag{17.A2}$$

The retailer's profit Π^R in this market will therefore be:

$$\Pi_M^R = \frac{(A - r)^2}{4B} \tag{17.A3}$$

Absent any franchise fee T, the manufacturer's profit Π_M^M derived from sales in the retailer's monopoly market will be:

$$\Pi_M^M = \frac{(r-c)(A-r)}{2B} \tag{17.A4}$$

In the competitive market, the price to consumers will be r and retail profit is zero. Output will be given by:

$$Q_C = \frac{A-r}{B} \tag{17.A5}$$

The manufacturer's profit Π_C^M from the retailer's sales in this competitive market is:

$$\Pi_C^M = \frac{(r-c)(A-r)}{B} \tag{17.A6}$$

For a given r at which retailers buy goods in both markets, the total manufacturer combined profits are:

$$\Pi = \Pi_C^M + \Pi_M^M + \frac{(A-r)^2}{4B} = \frac{(r-c)(A-r)}{B} + \frac{(r-c)(A-r)}{2B} + \frac{(A-r)^2}{4B} \tag{17.A7}$$

Maximizing this with respect to r yields the following necessary condition:

$$r = \frac{4A+6c}{10} \tag{17.A8}$$

with $A = 100$ and $c = \$20$, this yields the value of $r = \$52.0$ reported in the text.

EFFICIENT SERVICE PROVISION AND PROFIT MAXIMIZATION AT THE INTEGRATED FIRM

Total surplus from services is $\{A-[c+\varphi(s)]\}^2(Ns)/2$. The surplus-maximizing or efficient value of services s^* must therefore satisfy:

$$(A-c)/2 = \varphi(s^*)/2 + \varphi\prime(s^*)s^*. \tag{17.A9}$$

The integrated firm's profit is:

$$\pi(p,s) = p(A-p)Ns - [c+\varphi(s)](A-p)Ns \tag{17.A10}$$

Necessary conditions for maximizing the integrated firm's profit are then the joint first-order conditions:

$$\frac{\partial \pi(p,s)}{\partial p} = (A-2p)Ns + [c+\varphi(s)]Ns = 0 \tag{17.A11}$$

and

$$\frac{\partial \pi(p,s)}{\partial s} = p(A-p)N - [c+\varphi(s)](A-p)N - Ns\varphi\prime(s)(A-p) = 0 \qquad (17.A12)$$

Equation (17.A11) implies $p^I = [A+c+\varphi(s)]/2$. Substituting this price into (17.A12) yields:

$$(A-c)/2 = \varphi(s^I)/2 + \phi\prime(s^I)s^I \qquad (17.A13)$$

The service level satisfying (17.A13) is the same as that satisfying (17.A9), that is, $s^I = s^*$.

SERVICE PROVISION AND PROFIT MAXIMIZATION BY COMPETITIVE RETAILERS

At any retail price $p = r + \varphi(s)$ consumer surplus is $\{A-[r+\varphi(s)]\}^2 Ns/2$. Maximizing this with respect to s then yields the service level under competitive retailing, s^C

$$(A-r)/2 = \varphi(s^C)/2 + \varphi\prime(s^C)s^C \qquad (17.A14)$$

Because $r > c$ and $\varphi\prime > 0$, $s^C < s^I = s^*$. Competitive retailers provide less service than either the integrated firm or the socially optimal level.

18

Non-Price Vertical Restraints

In May 2012, Penn State University completed an agreement that assigned Pepsi the exclusive "pouring rights" at every fountain and vending machine at each of the university's nineteen campuses across the state of Pennsylvania. For the next ten years, the only soft drinks served at every athletic event, theatrical performance, university ceremony, and in every university-authorized dining service, snack bar, and vending machine at every Penn State school will be *Pepsi Cola* and other Pepsi products such as *Mountain Dew*, *Lipton* iced teas, *SoBe*, *Aquafina*, *Propel Zero*, and *Gatorade*. The agreement followed a similar agreement between Pepsi and the University of Delaware, and is one of a number university "pouring rights" contracts that Pepsi has collected. Coca-Cola plays this game, too. It has recently concluded similar exclusive beverage contracts with the University of Minnesota and Ohio State University. These cola wars do not stop at the college level. By some estimates, 80 percent of public schools have exclusive "pouring contracts" with either Coke or Pepsi, and these extend not just to vending machines, cafeterias, and sports events but even to the drinks offered at fundraisers such as bake sales and book fairs.[1]

The "pouring rights" contracts between schools and beverage companies are examples of non-price vertical restraints. In this case, the upstream manufacturer imposes a restriction on the downstream distributor. As noted in the previous chapter, non-price vertical constraints are traditionally analyzed separately from vertical price restrictions (and historically treated differently in the courts). Whether or not this distinction is legitimate, there is little doubt that non-price restraints are the more common. Lafontaine and Slade (2007) estimate that some sort of exclusive dealing covers one-third of sales by independent retailers in the US. Other non-price vertical restraints such as exclusive territories are also frequently observed. Yet while they have typically been analyzed separately, it is readily apparent that non-price restrictions raise basically the same issues as the vertical price restrictions present. On the one hand, these restrictions can serve as useful arrangements that enhance product quality (including services) and efficiency. On the other hand, they have an obvious potential for weakening competition. In this chapter we focus on the main vertical restrictions: exclusive dealing, exclusive selling and territories, and aftermarket restrictions.

---

[1] T. Philpott, "80 Percent of Public Schools Have Contracts with Coke or Pepsi," *Mother Jones.com* 15 August 2012; http://www.motherjones.com/tom-philpott/2012/08/schools

18.1   UPSTREAM COMPETITION AND EXCLUSIVE DEALING

As the soft drink and school examples above illustrate, exclusive dealing is a contractual agreement that restricts the behavior of the retailer. Essentially, the retailer is not allowed to buy (and then resell) brands that may compete with those of the manufacturer. Justifications for exclusive dealing agreements are typically based on the presence of conflicting interests between the manufacturer and the retailer. Unless some vertical restrictions can be imposed, such conflicts may lead to outcomes that hurt consumers as well as firms.

To understand this concern, we should first recognize that manufacturers often expend considerable resources promoting their products. Household products companies such as Procter and Gamble, cosmetic manufacturers such as Revlon, and appliance firms such as Whirlpool/Maytag, are just some of the many manufacturers that extensively advertise their products. Such advertisements may well increase demand for the manufacturer's brand. They may also increase demand for the product category in general.

Consider, for example, advertisements for *Tylenol*, the well-known non-aspirin pain reliever. Undoubtedly, such advertising helps raise the consuming public's awareness of both *Tylenol*, in particular, and of the benefits of non-aspirin pain relievers in general. Such advertising is expensive. To recover the cost of the advertising, Johnson & Johnson, *Tylenol's* manufacturer will have to raise *Tylenol's* price. We can easily imagine the following transaction between a pharmacy owner and a customer searching for *Tylenol*. When asked why she wants *Tylenol* the consumer will say because she needs non-aspirin medication for pain and fever. The pharmacist may say that *Tylenol* will work fine but that the pharmacy also can offer a lower-cost, unadvertised brand that is the chemical equivalent of *Tylenol*. The price of this alternative may not be a lot below the *Tylenol* price—just enough to persuade the customer to switch to this brand.

It is precisely because the pharmacist can sell the alternative non-aspirin pain reliever at a price relatively close to the price of *Tylenol* that the pharmacist has an incentive to inform the consumer of the alternative. From the perspective of *Tylenol*, however, the pharmacist is free riding on *Tylenol's* advertising. *Tylenol* now makes no sale even though it was the *Tylenol* advertising that may have induced the customer to ask for a non-aspirin pain reliever in the first place. There is then a vertical externality in which actions by the retailer have consequences that can adversely affect the manufacturer and vise-versa.

An exclusive dealing agreement offers a solution to this problem because it permits the manufacturer to prevent the retailers of its product from making such substitutions.[2] This is particularly important in the case of goods in which the retailer plays a role something similar to that of a doctor whose recommendation acts like an informal guarantee of the product's quality. Many intermediate goods sold between firms, e.g., chemical products, may have this feature. At the retail consumer level, automobile dealers are among retailers who may serve this function.

From an antitrust perspective, however, exclusive dealing can also be a means of suppressing competition. We showed in Chapter 13 one way that this could happen. There we discussed the Rasmussen, Ramseyer, and Wiley (1991) model illustrating how exclusive dealing requirements can prevent entry when there are important scale economies in upstream production. However, entry prevention is not the only way that exclusive dealing can limit competition. Such contracts can also be used to limit competition between

---

[2]   Marvel (1982) is among those who have stressed this argument.

existing manufacturers. Foreclosure of a rival's product can give a manufacturer increased market power.[3]

The manufacturer will have to share the profit from that power with the retailer. In order to get the exclusive contract in the first place, a manufacturer will have to offer the retailer as much profit as its rival can offer. As Mathewson and Winter (1987) show, this consideration can greatly complicate the analysis of exclusive dealing. In particular, the manufacturer that gets the exclusive contract may only do so by offering to sell to the retailer at a very low wholesale price. In turn, this low wholesale price will translate into a low retail price. One issue is whether the fall in the retail price is sufficient to compensate consumers for the loss of the alternative products. In principle, welfare could improve despite the fact that the exclusive deal eliminates a rival product line from the market.[4]

Exclusive dealing can also serve to limit competition among retailers and manufactures, simultaneously. For example, suppose that there are two manufacturers selling to two retailers who are spatially separated but still operate within a given territory. Without any exclusive dealing, each retailer may offer both products. As a result, price competition between the two products or interbrand competition, will be quite fierce at each retail location. However, if each manufacturer signs one of the retailers to sell its product by means of an exclusive contract, then interbrand competition can be softened. Effectively, the exclusive dealing does not foreclose either good but it does inject an element of spatial differentiation between the two goods that did not previously exist.[5]

18.2   EXCLUSIVE SELLING AND TERRITORIAL ARRANGEMENTS

We now turn to a different aspect of exclusive selling that relates to territorial restrictions. These cases differ from our soft drink and school example in two important respects. Whereas the restrictions in that example were aimed at limiting *interbrand* competition between rival soft drink companies, exclusive selling and territorial arrangements are aimed at limiting *intrabrand* competition between downstream dealers. In this case, the manufacturer agrees not to sell the product through other retailers. For example, under an exclusive selling agreement, Wal-Mart might obtain the rights to be the only retailer permitted to sell Nuance speech recognition software *Dragon*. Similarly, in an exclusive territorial arrangement, Toyota may sign agreements with a number of Lexus dealers that it will not open a new outlet in within a given distance of these dealers. Note that in both cases, the restriction now falls on the upstream firm.

We know that retail competition can help manufacturers in so far as it reduces or even eliminates the double-marginalization problem. We may well wonder then why a manufacturer would ever sign a contract that limits such retail competition. However, the rationale behind such restrictions is relatively intuitive.

---

[3]   The foreclosure analysis here and in Section 18.3 overlaps with models from Chapter 16. Similarly, the weakened price competition achieved by RPM agreements overlaps with our Chapter 14 analysis.

[4]   The foreclosure argument has been a recurrent topic in industrial organization. Bernheim and Whinston (1990) show that when there are two brands produced by two upstream firms and a single retailer, there are no incentives to adopt exclusive dealing. The retailer will always be a common dealer of both products. In the case of several retailers, O'Brien and Schaffer (1994) and Besanko and Perry (1994) find that exclusive dealing is always adopted. However, in the last two models, foreclosure is explicitly ruled out.

[5]   See Besanko and Perry (1994) for a model along these lines.

Consider a simple case of a single manufacturer that sells to two downstream retailers. In addition, we assume, not unreasonably, that while the manufactured product is the same, the retailers are differentiated at least by location if by no other attribute. In other words, consumers do not view the purchase of the good at each retailer as perfect substitutes so that retail competition is not perfect.

In this context, a horizontal externality emerges in promotion and other services. If one retailer incurs the expense of advertising or providing informational services, it benefits the other retailer as well. For example, if one Lexus dealer runs Lexus commercials on local TV, it potentially raises the demand for all Lexus dealers in the area. Similarly, if one camera store provides information to customers on how to get the best pictures with a Canon digital camera, those customers may then make their final camera purchase from a discount Canon retailer who does not offer such services. In short, there is a temptation for each retailer of a specific brand to free ride on the services provided by other sellers of that brand. As a result, the level of such services will very likely be too low. Moreover, because consumers value such services, this externality not only reduces the profit available to the manufacturer and the retailer, but reduces consumer surplus, as well.[6]

It should be clear how exclusive selling and territorial agreements may remedy the foregoing externality problems. Effectively such contracts limit the number of sellers of the manufacturer's good to just one within any given region or product line. As a result, each retailer reaps a far greater portion of any benefits its services generate. Further, by giving the dealer some monopoly power and therefore some monopoly profit, these restrictions serve to create a real loss if the dealer is found by the manufacturer to be providing too little service and the contract is terminated. [Klein and Murphy (1988).] Hence, exclusive selling and territorial restrictions can serve to raise the service level associated with the manufacturer's good, thereby raising their joint profit and, depending on price effects, possibly consumer surplus as well.

Exclusive selling and territorial arrangements have two other potentially important effects in addition to those just described. Because these contracts result in a single dealer being the only seller of a specific product in its area, the dealer's willingness to dump its merchandise on the market when demand is weak is reduced. This effect can be important in getting dealers to stock an appropriate amount of the manufacturer's good in the first place.[7] The other effect is that an exclusive selling or territorial agreement creates in each region a monopoly upstream supplier selling to a monopoly downstream retailer. This makes the use of a two-part tariff or franchise fee attractive as a tool to prevent the double marginalization and low service problems. Viewed in this light, it should not be surprising that we usually observe selling and franchise fees in the same contract.[8]

So far we have only considered exclusive selling and territorial arrangements in the context of a single manufacturer. When there is more than one upstream manufacturer, these contracts can be used to reduce interbrand competition—to the detriment of consumers. Suppose that there are two upstream manufacturers producing products that are imperfect substitutes. Imagine as well that the two manufacturers sell to a competitive retail sector. If the two manufacturers have identical costs and symmetric demand, then they will set the same wholesale price w^C, which will also be the retail price because competition eliminates

---

[6]   This case differs from those considered in Chapter 17 in which downstream competition helped solve the double marginalization problem because here, the retailers sell differentiated products.

[7]   See Chapter 17 for an analysis of uncertain demand and its potentially negative impack on retailer behavior.

[8]   See Chapter 17 and Lafontaine (1993).

any retail markup. Hence, all downstream retailers will earn zero profit. More importantly, this means that every increase in the wholesale price will be one-for-one translated into an equivalent increase in the retail price.

Now, following Rey and Stiglitz (1995) let us imagine that the market for these products can be divided into regions or territories. Suppose further that each manufacturer grants an exclusive territory to a retailer in each territory, giving that retailer the exclusive right to sell its product in that region. As a result, within any given territory each manufacturer's product will be sold by a retail monopoly. We know that selling to a monopoly retailer will give rise to the double-marginalization problem. Why then should the two manufacturers decide to do this? The answer, in part, is that it softens the intensity of the competition between the two brands. It does so because it weakens the link between the wholesale price and the retail price. From the perspective of each retailer, the wholesale price is a cost. Suppose then that one of the manufacturers raises its wholesale price. For the dealer selling this product, costs have risen. The dealer will want to pass on this increase by means of a higher retail price. Competition with the other retailer will limit how much the dealer can do this. However, now under exclusive territories prices are strategic complements. As the rival retailer sees the first dealer's price rising, the rival retailer will see an opportunity to raise its price without losing customers even though its wholesale cost has not risen. Thus, when a manufacturer raises its wholesale price it will no longer lose as many customers as it did when there was competition without exclusive territories. Even though the rival manufacturer does not raise its wholesale price, the rival retailer does raise the retail price.

Of course, both manufacturers realize the foregoing logic. By each granting an exclusive territory, they weaken retail interbrand competition, which feeds back to weaker wholesale competition. As a result, the granting of exclusive territories will lead to higher prices at both the retail and the wholesale level. Whether the agreement will increase manufacturer profit is another question. It might not because even though wholesale prices are higher, the double-marginalization problem means that the quantity sold is lower than it would be if retailing remained competitive. However, if the double-marginalization problem is not too large (as would be the case if the two goods are fairly close substitutes), the exclusive territorial arrangement will also lead to higher upstream profits. If the manufacturing firms can also adopt a two-part tariff arrangement, the double-marginalization problem can be overcome altogether.[9]

It may even be possible to use exclusive selling arrangements to achieve monopoly profit in what would otherwise be a competitive industry. To see this, suppose that the products of the two manufacturers are perfect substitutes. With a competitive retail sector, neither manufacturers nor retailers will make any profit. However, suppose that the two manufacturers coordinate so that within any territory they give the exclusive rights to their products to the same retailer, each agreeing not to sell to other dealers in that region. The lucky retailer in any region is thereby transformed into a monopolist who can set the monopoly retail price. Because monopolies make extra profit, the lucky downstream retailer in any region will be happy with this scheme.

What about the manufacturers? To some extent, their situation is unchanged. Each still produces a good for which there is a very close substitute. Hence, competition between the two should still be fierce. Of course, if this happens, all the monopoly profit will accrue to the retailer. If competition is less than fierce then the manufacturers can extract some of

---

[9]   The mechanism by which exclusive territories soften interbrand price competition described in Rey and Stiglitz (1995) is conceptually quite similar to the argument in Bonanno and Vickers (1988).

that profit by means of a two-part tariff. In fact, manufacturers may be able to extract profit even without using two-part tariffs. For instance, manufacturers can offer an exclusive sales contract only if the retailer also agrees to a purchase a minimum amount from the manufacturer even if that manufacturer charges a wholesale price higher than the rival's price. This technique—known as a quantity-forcing requirement—again has the effect of softening wholesale price competition. When each manufacturer does this, each can raise wholesale price above cost without fear of losing sales to the rival. As a result manufacturers now earn some profit.[10] Of course, the higher wholesale prices will translate into higher retail prices. That is, this arrangement does not enhance efficiency. The profit gain of the manufacturers is more than offset by a reduction in retailer profit and a fall in consumer surplus. Yet at the same time, it must be recognized that quantity-forcing can also be used to impose a maximum resale price and, thus limit double-marginalization problems. Thus, such vertical contracts can be socially beneficial but there clearly is a downside risk in that they can often be used to soften competition.

18.3   VERTICAL RESTRAINTS AND MARKET FORECLOSURE

Most of the foregoing analysis has considered the potential anticompetitive effects of vertical restraints in terms of their ability to reduce either interbrand or intrabrand competition. However, the primary concern in antitrust policy has been the potential for one firm to use such restraints to foreclose markets entirely to its rivals. In this view, exclusivity restraints have the potential to be used as a predatory instrument that eliminates either upstream or downstream rivals similar to the Rasmussen, Ramseyer, and Wiley (1991) model already noted. Here we focus on two models explicitly set in a vertical context.

18.3.1   Private Contracts

Imagine a monopoly manufacturer selling to n downstream retailers who compete as Cournot competitors. We will initially assume that $n = 2$ and, for convenience, also assume that the only retail cost is the wholesale price W. Ideally, the manufacturer would like to achieve the monopoly outcome, which we will designate as an output of Q^M selling at retail price P^M. Hence, it would like each retailer to sell $q_1 = q_2 = Q^M/2$. It could do this by a quantity-forcing agreement that sells to each the amount $Q^M/2$ at a wholesale price W^M equal to marginal cost and using a fixed fee F to collect the resultant monopoly profit for each firm. For example, if the inverse demand is: $P = 140 - Q$ and marginal cost is $c = \$20$, then the manufacturer could enter a fixed-quantity contract of $q_1 = q_2 = 30$. Selling at marginal cost c will then result in a price of $P = \$80$ and operating profit at each retailer of \$1,800, which the manufacturer can capture by setting $F = \$1,800$.

However, if the contracts between the manufacturer and each retailer are not public, there is a difficulty in achieving the above outcome. Suppose that the monopolist signs a contract with retailer 1 as specified above, i.e., a quantity-forcing agreement in which retailer 1 takes possession of (and sells) 30 units at wholesale price $W = c = \$20$, and agrees to pay a fixed fee of $F1 = \$1800$, with a view to doing the same with retailer 2. The problem is that having signed this contract with retailer 1, the manufacturer will now no longer wish

---

[10]   Note that in the final equilibrium the quantity constraint does not need to be binding.

to do the same with retailer 2. Why? Because we know from studying the Cournot model in Chapter 9 that retailer 2's best response function with $W = c = \$20$ is:

$$q_2^* = \frac{140 - W}{2} - \frac{q_1}{2} = \frac{140 - c}{2} - \frac{q_1}{2} = 60 - \frac{q_1}{2} \tag{18.1}$$

Hence, given an output of 30 units by retailer 1, retailer 2's best response is *not* 30 units but 45 units when $W = c = \$20$. Thus, in its secret dealing with retailer 2, the manufacturer would now wish to sell a quantity-forcing contract for 45 units. Combined with the 30 units sold by retailer 1, this will drive the retail price to \$65 at which price, retailer 2 will earn \$2,025 in operating profit (given that it too buys at cost c) that again will be collected by a fixed fee $F_2 = \$2,025$. By exploiting retailer 1 who now suffers a \$450 loss, the manufacturer has raised its profit to $\$2025 + \$1800 = \$3825$; \$225 more than the \$3,600 pure monopoly profit. The result would obviously be the same if the manufacturer had first signed an agreement with retailer 2.

Of course, each retailer can foresee the possibility of the manufacturer's exploitation. As a result, each will be reluctant to sign any contract calling for half of the monopoly output and a fixed fee of \$1800 knowing that the manufacturer may secretly try to undermine this deal in its negotiations with the rival retailer. In fact, a little intuition suggests that the only credible outcome is for the manufacturer to offer contracts that essentially duplicate the Cournot outcome with each retailer selling 40 units. By extension, the equilibrium outcome with $n = 3$ retailers would be that each sells 30 units. More generally, our result from Chapter 9 that with linear inverse demand of $P = A - Q$, and marginal cost c the symmetric Cournot outcome with n firms is that each produces $\dfrac{A - c}{n + 1}$ units, implies that in this example, each retailer sells $120/(n + 1)$ so that total output increases as equilibrium, n, gets larger and larger and with it, so does the profit loss the manufacturer suffers due to its lack of credibility. The Reality Checkbox concerning the contract between Macy's and Martha Stewart illustrates that fears of producer secret deals are quite legitimate.

In this setting, the attraction of an exclusive retail contract that designates just one retailer as the manufacturer's selling agent is clear. Committing to selling through just one retailer prevents the manufacturer from exploiting its downstream partner. As a result, it can obtain a contract to sell the monopoly output of 60 units exclusively to one retailer leading to the monopoly price of \$80 and monopoly profit of \$3,600, again collected through a fixed fee F.[11]

18.3.2   Slotting Allowances and Exclusion

As noted above, vertical restraints can be imposed on either the upstream or downstream firm and while early attention focused on the restrictions imposed on dealers, increasing attention has been paid to the restraints on the upstream firm's behavior. Such restraints have become somewhat more common in recent years with the rise of very large retail chains such as Wal-Mart, whose size gives them significant if not dominant bargaining power with their suppliers. One manifestation of such retailer power is the increasing use of slotting allowances or fees by which retailers claim an up front payment from the producer in return for shelf space.

---

[11]   This basic argument was first presented by Hart and Tirole (1990) and refined and extended by O'Brien and Shaffer (1992). See also Comanor and Rey (2000).

Reality Checkpoint

Macy's Wants to Take Penney's from Martha Stewart

In January 2012, Ron Johnson, the newly hired chief executive for the department chain J. C. Penney, announced a bold new makeover for the struggling retailer. Johnson had formerly been a chief executive for Apple and his plan was to transform the Penney's experience by making it much more like a visit to an Apple retail store. Frequent sales promotions would be eliminated in favor of three standard prices—everyday, monthly sales, and clearance prices. More importantly, the plan called for each of the vast majority of Penney's stores to be remodeled and divided into 100 small boutiques with a service center. The hope was to get shoppers into the store by giving them a hands-on experience with products and having specialized experts available to talk with about the pros and cons of each item. This also meant lining up specialized, attractive brand name products, including many offered by Martha Stewart Omnimedia Living. That's where the trouble started.

It turned out that Macy's already had signed a 12-year exclusive agreement with Martha Stewart Living that gave it the sole rights to manufacture and sell the Martha Stewart-branded goods until 2018. The announcement by Penney's of its plans came on the heels of the company's purchase of 16.6 percent of Martha Stewart stock for 38.5 million. Macy's claimed that this was part of a secret deal by which Penny's would invest in Martha Stewart in return for that company's agreeing to breach its contract with Macy's and selling its products in J. C. Penney stores.

Martha Stewart of course denied these charges. It said that the goods it would sell at Penney's were not the ones it agreed to sell exclusively at Macy's. It also claimed that Macy's had mainly used the Martha Stewart agreement to get customers in its store and then promoted other goods instead. The case, in which courts have so far tended to support Macy's, involves many of the issues common to vertical restraint contracts, including adequate retail service concerns and fears of secret deals that possibly renege on previous agreements. Whatever the final outcome, however, the fact that the new business plan called for remodeling the 700 largest of Penney's 1,100 stores means that more than a few Penney's are at stake.

Sources: S. Clifford, "J. C. Penney to Revise Pricing Methods and Limit Promotions," *New York Times*, January 25, 2012, p. B1; and "J. C. Penney is Sued over Martha Stewart Deal," *New York Times*, August 16, 2012, p. B3.

In the context of large, imperfectly competitive retailers, Shaffer (1991) has argued that such slotting fees may be a means by which these firms soften both downstream and upstream price competition. Roughly, the argument is that the fees enable the retailers to pay high wholesale prices that, in turn, limit the incentive to cut retail prices at the margin. Essentially, having collected their profit up front via the slotting fees means that the retailers compete less aggressively at the margin on price.

In addtion, there is again a major concern that slotting allowances will lead to market exclusion. Recall our observation in Chapter 12 that firms with market power will typically be willing to spend more to protect it than an entrant will be willing to spend to break into the market. Slotting fees may be an explicit illustration of this point in which upstream producers with market power outbid smaller entrants for the scarce shelf space.[12] In this case, smaller producers are foreclosed access to the retail market.

[12]   For evidence on this point, see the Federal Trade Commission report, *Slotting Allowances in the Retail Grocery Industry: Selected Case Studies in Five Product Categories*, 2003.

Alternatively, slotting fees can be part of an exclusive relation that forecloses access to manufactured goods to some retailers, as shown by Marx and Shaffer (2007). Their model is one of three stages. In the first stage, retailers offer contracts to producers with three critical parameters. The first is the slotting fee S that must be paid to the retailer immediately upon the contract's signing. The second and third parameters are the familiar fixed fee F and wholesale price W paid to the manufacturer but *only* if the retailer actually sells any positive amount so that it actually buys goods from the producer.

To get a rough sense of the Marx and Shaffer (2007) model, return to our Cournot example above. Because demand is given by $P = 140 - Q$, and the producer's marginal cost is $c = \$20$, we know that the monopoly outcome for an integrated firm and hence the overall profit maximum is $Q^M = 60$ and $P^M = \$80$, so that the maximum industry profit is $\Pi^M = \$3,600$. To achieve this symmetrically, contracts in which each firm faces a wholesale price $W = \$50$ is required. At this wholesale price, substitution into the best response function (18.1) along with the symmetry requirement that $q_1 = q_2$ results in both firms producing 30 units so that total output is 60 and the retail price is $80 as in the integrated monopoly case. Note that if this equilibrium were to occur, each retailer would earn an operating profit of $(\$80 - \$50) \times 30 = \$900$. Likewise, the upstream manufacturer would earn an operating profit of $(\$50 - \$20) \times 60 = \$1800$. How this total of $\$3,600$ in operating profit is ultimately shared will then depend on the slotting allowances S and lump sum procurement fee F in each contract.

In considering the determination of S and F, we need to recognize two features of the bargaining environment. First, the retailers have the initiative. Each makes a "take it or leave it" contract offer to the manufacturer. Hence, the manufacturer will always say yes to a contract that raises its profit above what would be earned if it says no. Second, the manufacturer does not have to say yes to both retail contracts. It can choose one and not the other in which case we have one retailer foreclosed.

For example, suppose that as suggested above each retailer offers a contract to the manufacturer with a wholesale price $W = \$50$, a slotting fee $S = \$500$, and a lump sum fee paid to the manufacturer $F = \$100$. Acceptance of both of these contracts by the manufacturer will result in each retailer ordering and selling 30 units, earning $\$900$ in operating profit plus $\$500$ in slotting allowances less $\$100$ in fixed production fees for a total profit at each retailer of $\$1,300$. The manufacturer would then earn an operating profit of $\$1,800$ plus $\$200$ in production fees less $\$1,000$ in slotting payments for a net profit of $\$1,000$.

So, if the manufacturer accepts both contracts, the outcome mimics the integrated monopoly maximum. Yet this *cannot be* an equilibrium because each retailer would have an incentive to raise its slotting fee. Suppose for example that retailer 1 raises S_1 to $\$540$. If the manufacturer accepts this and continues to supply retailer 2 as well, the only change is a transfer of $\$40$ in net profit to retailer 1 at the expense of the manufacturer who now earns just $\$960$. Of course, the manufacturer could reject retailer 1 and work only with retailer 2 with $W_2 = \$50$, $S_2 = \$500$ and $F_2 = \$100$ as before. In that case though, retailer 2 becomes a retail monopoly who, with $W_2 = \$50$, will sell 45 units at a price of $\$95$ each, implying a total operating profit of $\$1,350$ for the manufacturer. In addition, the manufacturer earns a $\$100$ lump sum fee from retailer 2 but pays a $\$500$ slotting fee as before. Hence, rejecting retailer 1 and working only with retailer 2 will cause the manufacturer's net profit to fall to $\$950 - \$10$ less than if it accepts retailer 1's offer and works with both. Knowing the manufacturer will accept, retailer 1 will raise its slotting fee to $\$540$ or even higher.

Of course, retailer 2 also understands the situation. It too has an incentive to request higher slotting fees perhaps even higher than $540. In this regard, it is instructive to consider the case in which both retailers set $S_1 = S_2 = \$550$. With all other contract features the same, the manufacturer continues to sell 30 units to each retailer and earn total operating profit of $1,800. It also collects a combined $200 in lump sum payments but now pays $1,100 in slotting fees so that its total net profit is $900. Yet again the manufacturer cannot do better by accepting only one of the contracts. That one lucky retailer would have a monopoly and sell 45 units. The manufacturer then earns $1,350 in operating profit plus

Reality Checkpoint

Mylan's Antianxiety Drug Pricing Caused a Lot of Anxiety

In July 2000, the Federal Trade Commission reached a record $147 million settlement with Mylan Pharmaceuticals and three other firms: Cambrex, a New Jersey chemical supplier; Profarmaco, an Italian drug supplier owned by Cambrex; and Gyma Laboratories of America, Profarmaco's American distributor. The case centered on the FTC's allegation of an explicit attempt by Mylan to foreclose competitors to the key ingredients in two major antianxiety drugs, lorazepam and clorazepate.

Lorazepam is the generic form of *Ativan* and clorazepate is the generic form of *Tranxene*. Through the early to mid 1990s, increasing competition among generic manufacturers forced the prices of these drugs down. By 1997, both lorazepam and clorazepate prices were at essentially competitive levels. Towards the end of that year, the generic manufacturer, Mylan, entered into exclusive licenses with Profarmco, Cambrex, and Gyma, under which Mylan agreed to share the profits from its lorazepam and clorazepate sales with these three firms in return for their agreeing to supply Mylan exclusively with the key active ingredient in each drug. As these firms controlled virtually all of the available North American supply of these ingredients, Mylan's competitors soon found they could not compete in either product market. Mylan then acted. In January 1998, Mylan raised the wholesale price of clorazepate from $11.36 to $377.00 for a 500 dose bottle. A few

months later, it raised the wholesale price of lorazepam from $7.30 to $190 for a 500-dose bottle. Because doctors at that time were writing over 20 million prescriptions per year for these drugs, these price increases had a major shock effect. Consumer and doctor outrage were particularly strong because these drugs are often used to calm patients suffering from protracted illnesses, including those with Alzheimer's and related dementia, and the terminally ill.

Mylan executives never admitted any wrongdoing. They said that they were settling because otherwise the case would drag on and create lots of uncertainty and more costs for them. Under the proposed settlement, $100 million will be paid in a fund shared by all fifty states. An additional $35 million will be used to settle private lawsuits brought by some large health care institutions, and $12 million will be paid to the government and private lawyers to cover legal costs. The vast bulk of these payments is meant to "disgorge" Mylan of the illegal profits it earned as a result of its foreclosing the market for these antianxiety drugs to other competitors.

Source: S. Labaton, "Generic Drug-Maker Agrees to Settlement in Price-Fixing Case," *New York Times* 13 July 2000, front page; and Federal Trade Commission, "FTC Reaches Record Financial Settlement to Settle Charges of Price-fixing in Generic Drug Market," 29 November 2000, http://www.ftc.gov/opa/2000/11/mylanfin.shtm

$100 as a lump sum less $550 in slotting fees for a net profit of $900—exactly the same as if it accepts both contracts.

The foregoing example is no coincidence. In any conceivable equilibrium in which the manufacturer accepts the contract offer of both firms, it must be the case that it would earn exactly the same profit by accepting only one of those contracts and letting the winner act as a retail monopolist. Otherwise, at least one retailer will want to demand more in slotting fees.

The insight of the Marx and Shaffer (2007) analysis readily follows because it is clear that an equilibrium in which the manufacturer supplies both retailers is not really possible. While the manufacturer may be indifferent between supplying one or both retailers, the retailers themselves are not. Suppose, for instance, that we reach the point just described with each retailer setting $S_i = \$550$, $W_i = \$50$, and $F_i = \$100$. While the manufacturer neither gains nor loses if it supplies only one retailer under these terms, the retailer who gets the monopoly clearly gains. While a downstream duopolist earns net profit of $1350, a retail monopoly earns $2475. The downstream firms will therefore compete for the manufacturer's exclusive supply by offering more generous contracts.

In our symmetric example, equilibrium is reached when each retailer charges a slotting fee of $S_i = 0$; a wholesale price of $W_i = \$20$; and a lump sum payment of $F_i = \$3600$. More generally, one retailer is likely to have some cost or other advantage over its rival. Suppose then that retailer 1 can generate $3700 in operating profit when it buys at $W_1 = \$20$ as opposed to the $3600 assumed for retailer 2. In that case, competition between the two retailers to be the exclusive dealer will end with retailer 2 offering a slotting fee of $S_2 = 0$; $W_2 = \$20$; and $F_2 = \$3600$, while retailer 1 wins the contract with $S_1 = \$99.99$; $W_1 = \$20$ and $F_1 = \$3700$. Retailer 1's advantage allows it to win the bidding by just slightly beating retailer 2's offer but it must do this in a precise way. Specifically, retailer 1 cannot win with the contract $S_1 = \$0$; $W_1 = \$20$ and $F_1 = \$3600.01$ even though that results in the same manufacturer net profit because that contract—once it is signed—permits retailer 1 to operate profitably even if firm 2 enters and produces some small amount. That is, retailer 2 will find it profitable to offer a contract other than $S_2 = 0$; $W_2 = \$20$; and $F_2 = \$3600$, that the manufacturer will accept with the result that retailer 1's operating profit falls below $3700. In contrast, the contract $S_1 = \$99.99$, $W_1 = \$20$, and $F_1 = \$3700$ is only profitable if the manufacturer does not sell to retailer 2. The up-front slotting fee S_i thus dictates that the winning contract must be one that impels an exclusive manufacturer-dealer relation. In general, this exclusivity will imply a welfare loss, e.g., if the two retailers sell differentiated products so that variety falls when one retailer is excluded. In sum, while exclusive contracts can promote services and efficiency, they can also be used to soften price competition and foreclose markets.

18.4   VERTICAL RESTRICTIONS IN AFTERMARKETS

The vertical restrictions that we have examined so far primarily reflect constraints on the sale of the same product as it moves through the chain from the upstream producer to the downstream dealer. In recent years, a different kind of vertical restriction has caught the interest of economists and policy makers alike—one that is closely related to the tying arrangements that we considered in Chapter 13. This restriction effectively involves an excusive selling arrangement in what are known as aftermarkets.

The key legal case in the aftermarkets debate is the *Kodak* case. The specifics of that case are as follows. Kodak was one of a number of manufacturers of micrographic equipment—used for creating, viewing, and printing microfilm and microfiche—and office copiers. This was the primary, or foremarket. However, Kodak also provided repair parts and services to these machines through a nationwide network of technicians. Kodak advertised the quality of this network as a means of persuading consumers to buy its machines in the first place. Because no one needs micrographic or copier parts and services if they have not already purchased a micrographic machine or copier, the parts and services market is referred to as the aftermarket.

Just as in the foremarket, Kodak had competition in the aftermarket. There were many independent firms providing parts and services to firms using Kodak's office machines. However, to the extent that these independent firms needed replacement parts, they relied on Kodak to provide them. Kodak was happy enough to do so until it lost a service contract with Computer Service Corporation (CSC) to an independent firm, Image Technical Services (ITS). After that, Kodak announced a new policy of not providing replacement parts to any independent service provider. Effectively, Kodak imposed a monopoly in the servicing of its machines by exclusively selling the necessary parts to only Kodak technicians. Without those parts, independent repair services would find it impossible to make such repairs. As Kodak enforced the new policy more and more strictly, ITS and other independents filed a lawsuit contesting Kodak's action.

In court Kodak asked for a summary dismissal of the plaintiffs' case. Kodak's basic argument ran along the following lines. There were many other producers of photographic office equipment implying that Kodak faced competition in the foremarket. As a result, Kodak argued it could not possibly exert monopoly power in the aftermarket. Before making a purchase in the foremarket, consumers consider the full cost of, say, a copier—both the price at the initial time of purchase and the price of services later. If Kodak were to try to charge a high price in the aftermarket for services, it would only attract foremarket customers if it reduced its machine prices by a corresponding amount. Hence, Kodak argued that it could not impose monopoly pricing in the aftermarket. The Supreme Court rejected Kodak's contention. Later, a jury turned in a verdict against Kodak.

The Kodak case was followed by a number of similar cases. Again, the central issue is whether and how a firm can exercise monopoly power in the aftermarket if it does not have such power in the foremarket. To illustrate the issues, consider the following simple example in which we assume the interest rate r is zero so that discounting can be ignored. Two firms, Kodak and Lexsung, each sell a machine that lasts potentially for two periods, which is the same time frame as the typical consumer's horizon. While the machines may look physically different they are identical in the eyes of consumers, each of whom values the services of the machine at \$50 per period. We designate the prices of a new Kodak and Lexsung machine as P_M^K and P_M^L, respectively. Competition is in prices (Bertrand), so the assumption that consumers view the machines as perfect substitutes implies that the price will fall to marginal cost, which we here assume to be $P_M^K = P_M^L = \$50$.

While each machine runs perfectly well during the first period, there is a 50 percent chance that each will break down and need repairs in the second period. In principle, consumers whose machine breaks down can do one of two things. They can either return to the foremarket and buy a new machine for \$50 (with a view to selling it as a used machine after one period) or, they can buy repair services from a competitive repair market. In this case, repair prices could never exceed \$25—the net cost of buying either a new or used machine. However, we will rule out the first alternative by assuming that once a particular machine has been bought, consumers are "locked in" to that brand, perhaps because they have made investments in training to use that brand or because they have bought peripheral equipment that only works with that brand. This "lock-in" means that for the 50 percent of consumers whose machine breaks down, the only option is to have it repaired. Moreover, as in the original Kodak case, repair requires Kodak parts. That is, the "lock in" effect applies to both the original machine and repair services and it is the latter that enable Kodak to monopolize the repair of its own machines. Initially, however, we assume a competitive repair market for both types of machines and, for convenience, a marginal cost of 0 for repairs. Hence, competition implies that the initial repair price is also zero.

Kodak's basic defense is easy to see. Suppose that at the start of the first period Kodak had imposed an aftermarkets restriction that only Kodak technicians can repair Kodak machines. Given that they would be locked in after purchasing a machine, and given that in the face of such a breakdown, a Kodak consumer would be willing to pay as much as $50 for a one-period repair, Kodak could in principle charge very close to that amount for its monopoly repair service. However, any first-period buyer of a Kodak machine would then recognize that if he or she buys a machine from Kodak at price P_M^K the buyer will later face with probability 0.5 a second-period repair cost of $50. Thus, the anticipated price of a Kodak machine over for two periods would be $P_M^K + 0.5 * \$50 = P_M^K + \$25$. In contrast, the price of a Lexsung machine over two periods would be P_M^L because it costs zero to repair. Because the two machines are perfect substitutes, Bertrand competition will force P_M^L to $50 as before. Yet given its monopoly repair price of $50, this means that Kodak will lose all its customers unless P_M^K falls to $25, so that $P_M^K + \$25 - \$50$, matching its rival whose machines are viewed as functionally identical to Kodak's. At this price, Kodak will lose $25 on every new machine it will sell. To be sure, it will later earn $50 in repair profit on half of these but this does no more than just offset the loss incurred on every new machine. More generally, the simple analysis suggests that any increase in Kodak's repair price translates one-for-one into an offsetting reduction in its machine price with the result that monopolizing the repair market does not increase its profit.

There are, however, counter arguments to Kodak's argument. The simplest is that there are likely some consumers who do not fully incorporate subsequent repair costs into their equipment purchasing calculations. This assumption might not seem terribly realistic in the context of our simple two-period example. Yet the reality of durable machines is that they often last for far more than two periods and there are multiple repair issues that can arise. As a result, it may be difficult for some consumers to form rigorous expectations of later repair costs and they may therefore just ignore these. Moreover, even if consumers can look far ahead over the lifetime of a machine they would still need a fair bit of information to make a sensible forecast of later repair costs. If that information can only be acquired at great cost, then it may not be worth getting so that again, consumers ignore later repair expenses.

Take our example above. Initially, both Kodak and Lexsung are selling their machines at a price of $50 each and consumers face a later repair price of 0. Let us assume that in this market outcome each firm serves 100 new customers each period. Suppose that if Kodak now monopolizes the market for repairing its machines and sets a price of $50 for repairs it will lose 98 but not all 100 of its new machine customers unless it also lowers its price by an amount equal to the expected repair cost of $25. Losing those 98 customers does not really hurt Kodak, however, because in the initial equilibrium it was not earning any profit from them in any case. In contrast, Kodak will earn an average of $50 of extra profit from the two consumers who do remain. It will earn five times that amount if in contrast to retaining only 2 percent of its customers it retains 10 percent. Thus, if information is incomplete for at least some consumers then monopolization of the aftermarket can be profitable. Moreover, Gabaix and Laibson (2006) suggest that the presence of some unsophisticated consumers can interact with the lock-in effects just described to make firms unwilling to announce low aftermarket prices even when they can and even when competition is strong.[13]

A second motivation to pursue the aftermarket monopoly is sometimes referred to as installed base opportunism. Even if we assume that the information issue is not important so that consumers who have not yet purchased a machine can incorporate aftermarket prices into their purchase decisions, Kodak can still take advantage of those who have already bought its machine. That is, we may envision the market as one with waves of overlapping cohorts of consumers so that at any time there are new consumers about to buy a machine for a two-year horizon and old consumers who bought a new machine one year earlier and are now only seeking a final year's worth of service from the machine. Imagine now that these old consumers bought the Kodak machine for the initial equilibrium price of $50 and that it was only at the end of the first period that Kodak instituted its monopoly repair strategy. While new machine sales of Kodak machines will have to be at a price of $25 per unit, these older consumers have already paid $50 and cannot undo that purchase. They will be taken by surprise by the Kodak move and, as they are locked into the Kodak brand, they will be forced to pay the higher Kodak repair prices.

However, the gain from exploiting its previously installed base is essentially a one-time gain. It only extracts profit from those consumers who paid an initial high machine price *before* Kodak monopolized the repair service (or before it exercised its monopoly power) and therefore expected to pay only the marginal cost. Once Kodak makes its monopolizing move, all future consumers will purchase machines elsewhere unless Kodak reduces the price or unless it restores competitive pricing for its services. Moreover, such opportunism is likely to have a negative impact on Kodak's reputation in the foremarket. Unless the opportunity for future profits is small—perhaps because the market is in decline—the short-run gain may not be worth this cost.

At the same time, it is important to recognize that to the extent Kodak keeps prices close to marginal cost, that temptation to exploit those second-stage consumers who are locked in will always be present. That is, it will be difficult if not impossible for Kodak to commit credibly to a policy of always setting its repair price at marginal cost. There is no profit foregone if one loses customers who are only paying a marginal cost price while there is a bound to be some profit available from charging those locked in customers a price above cost, but this can only be accomplished if Kodak has monopoly power in the repairs market. If it does, Borenstein, MacKie-Mason, and Netz (2000) demonstrate that the only aftermarket prices to which Kodak can commit to keep constant through time are prices that exceed marginal cost—and that therefore eliminate this temptation. The equilibrium can then be one of inefficiently high aftermarket prices and somewhat inefficiently low foremarket prices, with the result that consumers replace their machines too frequently.

In short, whenever there are lock-in effects, the potential for aftermarket profits via exclusionary restraints cannot be ruled out by economic theory as Kodak originally asked.[14]

---

[13] In the Gabaix and Laibson (2006), the interaction between the lock-in and the presence of some unsophisticated consumers induces firms to charge super-competitive prices to aftermarket products, e.g., hotel phone use and rental car insurance, and low prices for the foremarket goods, rooms, and rented cars.

[14] Chen and Ross (1993) explore the case in which the foremarket is imperfectly competitve so that firms can use the aftermarket products as part of a tying price discrimination strategy of the type discussed in Chapter 5. Note too that Miao (2010) shows that if consumers are myopic and firms are simultaneously active in both the foremarket and the aftermarket, Kodak's argument is invalid because it implies a pricing inconsistency.

At the same time, it is prudent to recognize that there are practical limits on firms pursuing such profits. Companies may be reluctant to exploit any aftermarket power for fear of the damage this brings to their reputation—a damage that may extend to all their products and not just those for which there are important aftermarkets. Consumers may be able to avoid being locked in by renting instead of buying. Firms may compete by offering more complete information or long-term service contracts. Further, contrary to our simplifying assumptions, access to a used equipment market may place a further constraint on any aftermarket monopoly profits.

Because the aftermarket scenario applies to a wide variety of products—automobiles, consumer appliances, office and medical equipment, to name just a few—the *Kodak* case

---

Reality Checkpoint
Aftermarkets After Kodak

The controversy over the aftermarkets issue raised in the Kodak case has continued to this day. However, while early cases such as *Allen-Myland v. IBM* 33 F.3d 194 (3rd Cir. 1994) were very much in keeping with the initial Kodak finding the courts have increasingly restricted the applicability of the "Kodak doctrine".

The Allen-Myland case involved the market for maintaining and upgrading IBM mainframe computers—at the time a market almost as valuable as the mainframe market itself. Allen-Myland had a large share of this business until IBM began to offer lower installation prices for firms promising to use only IBM's upgrade services. IBM then also required customers to return used parts so as to dry up a potential alternative part sources. Allen-Myland sued and won.

In *PSI v. Honeywell*, 104 F.3d 811 (6th Cir. 1997), the Court considered the case of another computer systems repair firm PSI. When Honeywell began prohibiting computer chip makers from selling Honeywell parts to independent repair services such as PSI, PSI sued contending that this practice was precisely that found to be illegal in the *Kodak* case. However, PSI lost largely because the Court rejected the repair lock-in argument.

Most recently, the district court in Maryland held in favor of Océ North America

against an allegation of illegal aftermarket monopolization made by MCS Services (*Océ North America, Inc. v. MCS Services, Inc.*, D.Md., No. 1:10-CV-984-WMN, 6/14/11). Océ manufactures high-speed continuous form printers. Using very large spools of perforated paper, these printers can run off over a thousand pages per minute and typically cost several hundred thousand dollars. Along with MCS, Océ and other firms offered both maintenance services as well as replacement of the toner the printers used. Servicing the printers though required access to Océ software and Océ stopped providing that to rivals. In addition, Océ began to require that its customers use only Océ-approved toner. The court rejected MCS's allegation of monopoly on two grounds. First, it said that Kodak did not apply to intellectual property such as the Océ software. Second, the court argued that the technical sophistication required to use the printers meant that the customers were sophisticated buyers who would demand a discount in the printer price if the service and toner prices ever rose.

Sources: G. Graham, "IBM Sent Back by Appeals Court to Face Retrial in Anti-Trust Suit," *Financial Times*, August 18, 1994, p. 6; D. Goldfine and K. Vorrasi, 2004. "The Fall of the *Kodak* Aftermarket Doctrine: Dying a Slow Death in the Lower Courts" *Antitrust Law Journal* 72 (January): 209–31.

has deservedly received much attention from academics, lawyers, and policy-makers. The consensus that seems to have emerged over time is that while it was right to deny Kodak's initial request for dismissal, i.e., economic theory does not rule out gains from aftermarket monopolization even when the foremarket is highly competitive, it is difficult in practice for the courts to determine clearly the extent of consumer harm in such cases. As a result, application of the *Kodak* doctrine has waned over time. (See Reality Checkpoint.)

18.5   PUBLIC POLICY TOWARD VERTICAL RESTRAINTS

Non-price vertical agreements can have both positive and negative effects. Accordingly, a "rule of reason" approach has dominated the legal cases in this area. The outcome in the courts typically reflects the court's balancing of the conflicting pro- and anti-competitive forces. Not all analysts agree on the wisdom of this approach. For some, such as Posner (1981), the potential efficiency gains of exclusive selling and territorial agreements are likely to be sufficiently large that all such vertical restrictions ought to be considered *per se* legal under the antitrust laws. The argument is essentially that vertical restrictions must at least benefit the upstream and downstream firms that have agreed to such restraints. They may, as we have seen, benefit consumers as well. Attempting to use a rule of reason and judge each situation on a case-by-case method will, in this view, be very difficult and produce a large number of inconsistent and quite possibly wrong decisions. Accordingly, the wisest course for antitrust policy is simply to let all vertical restrictions alone. The US Justice Department came close to adopting such a view in its Vertical Restraints Guidelines of 1985, and there was little prosecution of vertical arrangements for the next several years. However, those guidelines were rejected in 1993 and the antitrust authorities have since taken a still tolerant but somewhat less generous attitude towards vertical restraints.

A similar fluctuation in policy has been observed in Europe. Up until the late 1990s, the approach taken by the European Union was largely one of condemnation for any type of non-price vertical restraint in general, coupled with broad exemptions for specific arrangements, especially franchise contracts. However, in 1999 as economic integration became more complete, the European Union adopted its own Vertical Restraint Guidelines that applied a much more lenient treatment of vertical restraints again based on a rule-of-reason approach.

A good bit of tolerance toward non-price restrictions is probably warranted. While there are many well justified concerns about the potential for these restraints to exert anticompetitive effects, the great bulk of the empirical evidence is that such restraints are usually good for producers and have either positive or at least no negative consequences for consumers.[15] Moreover, when studies do find negative consequences for consumers, it is usually because they find a rise in retail prices. Yet this may occur for benign reasons. Recall the free-riding problem in our earlier *Tylenol* example. Because the cost of *Tylenol's* advertising is reflected in its price, the more free-riding is a serious problem, the more we would expect Johnson & Johnson to seek an exclusive dealing contract or other vertical restraint. In other words, it is likely that we will observe vertical restrictions most in precisely those markets where manufacturers have to make serious investments in advertising or quality improvement that need to be protected. Because the expense of those investments will be reflected in the product price, this also means that the use of those restrictions will be associated with higher prices. Yet the restriction is not the cause of the

---

[15]   See Lafontaine and Slade (2007).

higher price and its use does not necessarily hurt consumers. When the possible endogeneity of vertical restraints is recognized, the accumulated empirical evidence implies even more strongly that the use of such restraints has generally been beneficial.

Sometimes non-price vertical restraints are imposed by the government and sometimes these restraints have a negative effect. For example, in many states, independent opticians have been prohibited from fitting contact lenses. Instead, lens wearers have been required to see an ophthalmologist or optometrist, thereby effectively tying the purchase of lenses to the services of these professionals. Hass-Wilson (1987) found that such policies raised consumer prices without any improvement in quality. They also diminished the variety of consumer choices. Such findings are not unusual in the case of state-imposed vertical restrictions.[16]

The efforts of policy makers to balance anticompetitive effects such as entry deterrence against the efficiency gains that exclusive dealing can generate are illustrated by a US case involving the two principal manufacturers of the water pumps used by fire engines. Hale Products, Inc., and Waterous Company, Inc. were the pump-makers in question. Each manufactured the water pump that is installed on fire trucks in the United States. Each sold its pumps directly to the makers of such fire trucks through exclusive dealing contracts. Those fire truck manufacturers who bought from Hale agreed not to buy from any other pump-maker, and likewise for those who agreed to purchase their pumps from Waterous. In determining the effect of these agreements, the FTC noted that together the two firms accounted for 90 percent of the US market for water pumps and had done so for nearly fifty years, with the remainder accounted for by a small third firm, W. S. Darley & Company. During that time, no new entrant had come into the market. This was taken as evidence by the FTC that the exclusive dealing agreements had effectively blocked such entry. In addition, the FTC alleged that the agreements also worked to reduce competition between Hale and Waterous. Documents were presented indicating that each firm realized that so long as it dealt only with its half of the engine manufacturers, it did not need to fear competition from the other. Further, the FTC noted that neither pump-maker would wish to cheat on this tacit agreement because such cheating would be quickly detected. Waterous would know immediately that if it lost a pump customer it was likely won by Hale. The same would be true for Hale. Ultimately, the FTC prevailed and the two firms agreed to cease the exclusive dealing arrangements.[17]

The above procedure illustrates how a rule of reason operates in practice. The threshold issue is the fraction of the market such agreements cover. Unless that fraction is large, the agreements are presumed not to weaken competition in any meaningful way and are therefore deemed legal. Even if the threshold is reached however, that merely sets the stage for subsequent investigation. The question then becomes whether the restrictions are substantially harmful to competition. Here, factors such as the history of entry, the behavior of prices, and the potential for free-riding problems need to be examined. This is a complicated process and the *per se* presumption of legality suggested by Posner (1981) is understandably tempting. Our view is that there are sufficient grounds for concern that the continued use of a rule of reason approach is warranted despite the difficulties that entails.

---

[16] States occasionally issue blanket prohibitions on vertical restraints, e.g., bans on direct ownership of service stations by oil refineries. Such restraints on organizational choices can create difficulties. See, e.g., Blass and Carlton (2001). See Steiner (1985) for a general discussion of vertical restraint policy.

[17] See Federal Trade Commission, Decision and Order, In the Matter of Hale Products Inc., Docket No. C-3694, November 22, 1996; and Decision and Order, In the Matter of Waterous Company, Inc., Docket No. C-3694, November 22, 1996.

18.6   A BRIEF DISCUSSION OF FRANCHISING AND DIVISIONALIZATION

Our discussion of vertical relations has often included references to franchising. In fact, probably the bulk of vertical restrictions arise in the context of franchising agreements because these cover a large fraction of retail sales, roughly over a third. As a result, franchising merits some individual attention of its own.

There are two basic types of franchising agreements. Under the traditional type observed with soft drinks, gasoline, and car dealerships, the upstream franchisor sells its branded product to the downstream franchisee, which then resells this good either to other firms or consumers. More recently, a second type of franchising known as business format franchising has emerged. Here, the franchisee buys the right to a brand name and a complete business plan. Food establishments such as McDonald's and hotel chains such as Marriott are examples of this latter type. Business format franchising has grown rapidly and now accounts for over a quarter of all franchising.[18]

The proliferation of franchised outlets reflects a number of forces. To a large extent, it reflects an effort to internalize the externalities noted above. An advertisement by the McDonald's parent corporation will benefit all McDonald's restaurants. This effect may be particularly important in the modern era of brand proliferation and the resulting consumer need for recognizable brand names that reduce uncertainty about quality and save on shopping time. For the same reasons, franchising also permits the exploitation of scale economies in advertising and the purchase of supplies. However, even after the decision to establish new outlets has been made, a franchisor still has an organizational choice to make. In particular, it has to determine whether it wishes to operate the outlet as a company-owned operation managed by a salaried employee or as an independent franchise run by a profit-maximizing owner.

There are two countervailing forces that affect this choice. On the one hand, a salaried employee running a company-owned outlet may not have strong incentives to put forth effort and maximize profit whereas the franchisee as residual claimant does have incentives much more closely aligned with those of the franchisor. On the other hand, the company-owned outlet can perhaps be more easily monitored and controlled to make sure that it works cooperatively with others in pursuit of the franchisor's goals. In contrast, while an independent franchise owner may have a strong incentive to innovate and earn the maximum profit yielding more for its owner, we need to recognize that maximizing the outlet's profit and maximizing the franchisor's profit can be two different matters. For example, an independent franchisee may not support the promotional and service efforts that maximize the joint profit of all the company's outlets but, instead, free-ride on the efforts of others. Of course, if all outlets do this, promotional and service levels may fall far below the level that maximizes joint profit.

We have seen that vertical restrictions such as exclusive territorial rights may help resolve the incentive conflicts between franchisors and franchisees. Further, by granting a local territorial monopoly, the franchisor may induce franchisee owners to pay a higher initial franchise fee. However, once that fee has been collected, a further potential conflict arises between franchisor and franchisee. The franchising firm may have an incentive to open additional outlets that crowd in on the territory of the initial franchisee.

---

[18]   See Lafontaine (1993), Lafontaine and Shaw (1999) and Blair and Lafontaine (2005).

There are at least three reasons for a franchisor to wish to have a large number of franchisees. From a spatial perspective, operating many outlets means that the franchisor is better able to meet the specific preferences of each individual customer. This enables the franchise operation to extract more surplus by charging each customer an amount much closer to a customer's maximum willingness to pay for the most preferred variety. In short, operating many outlets may enhance the franchisor's ability to price discriminate.

In addition, the operation of a large number of outlets may be a means for firm to overcome asymmetric information and attendant moral hazard problems. With just one outlet, the franchisor cannot tell whether a low-profit outcome is due to bad luck—which could happen to anyone—or to the outlet's poor management. With many outlets, it is less likely that they all will have bad luck at the same time. Hence, the average performance of a large number of outlets may serve as a benchmark against which to measure the performance of each franchise individually.

Both of these are perfectly plausible explanations for why franchising is a popular business model and also for why companies might wish to establish various operating divisions as independent profit centers. A third motivation is also possible, however. It is that, operating a large number of independent franchises (or divisions) may be a way for a firm to commit to a large total output. This is the approach taken by Baye, Crocker, and Ju (1996) who analyze the implications of this motive for franchising, or divisionalization, using a two-stage model. In the first stage, there are two independent franchisors, each of which chooses the number of independent franchises that it wishes to establish. In the second stage, the franchises from both franchisors compete in a Cournot quantity-setting game.[19]

Suppose that the franchises of both firms produce a homogeneous product at a constant marginal cost of c. The inverse demand for the product in the downstream market is described by our usual linear function, $P = A - BQ$, where Q is total market output.

In stage one of the game, let n_1 and n_2 denote the number of franchisees established by franchisors 1 and 2, respectively. A franchisor incurs a sunk cost K in the first stage when it sets up a franchise. In stage two, all of the franchisees act as independent players in a simultaneous-move Cournot game. By that we mean that each franchise acts like an independent profit-maximizer.

To solve this game we begin with the stage-two competition. Let q_{ij} denote the output chosen by the ith franchise of firm j, where i runs from 1 to n_j and j is equal to 1 or 2. Let Q_{-ij} describe the total output of all franchises except the ith franchise of firm j. The profit of this franchise π_{ij} can then be written as

$$\pi_{ij}(q_{ij}, Q_{-ij}) = [A - B(Q_{-ij} + q_{ij})]q_{ij} - cq_{ij} \tag{18.2}$$

where total market output Q is equal to $\sum_{j=1}^{2} \sum_{i=1}^{n_j} q_{ij}$.

The ith franchise of firm j chooses output q_{ij} to maximize its profit. This, of course, requires setting its marginal revenue to its marginal cost. This implies in turn that the optimal output of any franchise q_{ij}^* satisfies

$$A - BQ_{-ij} - 2Bq_{ij}^* = c \tag{18.3}$$

---

[19]   Rather than franchises, these could be divisions of the company provided that the divisions are established as independent profit centers.

Because all franchises are identical, they must all choose the same optimal output in equilibrium—that is, $q_{ij}^* = q^*$ for all i, j. This greatly simplifies matters. Because there are $n_1 + n_2$ franchises in total, Q_{-ij} must equal $(n_1 + n_2 - 1)q^*$. Substitution into equation (18.3) then yields

$$q^* = \frac{A - c}{(n_1 + n_2 + 1)B} \qquad (18.4)$$

from which it follows that the total industry output Q and associated market price P in stage two are

$$Q = \left(\frac{n_1 + n_2}{n_1 + n_2 + 1}\right)\left(\frac{A - c}{B}\right) \text{ and } P = \frac{A + (n_1 + n_2)c}{n_1 + n_2 + 1} \qquad (18.5)$$

At this price, each franchise will earn a stage-two profit π_{ij} given by

$$\pi_{ij} = \frac{(A - c)^2}{B(n_1 + n_2 + 1)^2} \qquad (18.6)$$

The two franchisors who anticipate competition among franchises in stage two along the lines just described must decide in stage one how many franchises to set up. Firm 1's profit can be written as $\pi_1 = \sum_{i=1}^{n_1} \pi_{i1} - Kn_1$ where K is the cost of establishing a franchise at either firm. Because equation (18.6) shows the profit earned by each of firm 1's n_1 franchises in stage two, we can rewrite firm 1's overall profit as

$$\Pi_1(n_1, n_2) = n_1 \frac{(A - c)^2}{B(n_1 + n_2 + 1)^2} - Kn_1 \qquad (18.7)$$

Firm 1 chooses its total number of franchises n_1^* so as to maximize its profit $\Pi_1(n_1, n_2)$ when firm 2 has n_2 franchises of its own. In other words, firm 1 wants to choose a best response n_1^* to the number of franchises, n_2, that firm 2 has. It is straightforward to show that this best response function satisfies[20]

$$\frac{(A - c)^2}{B(1 + n_1^* + n_2)^2}\left(1 - \frac{2n_1^*}{(1 + n_1^* + n_2)}\right) - K = 0 \qquad (18.8)$$

Because firm 2 is identical to firm 1, we have a symmetric condition for n_2^*. Therefore, using the notation that $n_1^* = n_2^* = n^*$ and recognizing that this symmetry implies that $n_1^* + n_2^* = 2n^*$, we can solve for n^*. This solution is

$$n^* = \frac{1}{2}\left[\left(\frac{(A - c)^2}{BK}\right)^{1/3} - 1\right] \qquad (18.9)$$

---

[20]   The response function in equation (18.8) is derived by taking the derivative of the profit function (18.7) with respect to n_1 and setting it to zero. This technique assumes that we can ignore the constraint that n_1 be an integer.

Equation (18.9) shows that the greater is $(A - c)$ and/or the smaller is K, the greater is the number of franchises chosen by firm 1 and firm 2 in stage one of the game. Recall that the difference between price and cost is $(A - c)/2$ if the market is monopolized. One implication of this model is that firms will create more franchises the greater the price-cost differential would be under a monopoly. However, having more franchises is tantamount to having more Cournot-type units, and this brings us closer to the competitive equilibrium. Hence, the greater the possible markup under a monopoly, the greater the number of franchises the two firms operate, and the more closely they end up approximating the competitive equilibrium. The firms are locked in a "prisoners' dilemma" in which the best response of each firm acting separately is not optimal from the standpoint of the two firms collectively. The firms independently open up more franchises than they would if they cooperated or colluded.

In short, an additional reason for franchise growth may be that it permits aggressive efforts to claim market share. This encourages firms both to adopt the franchise format and, having chosen that format, to expand the number of franchisees. This results in many more franchises than the number that would maximize industry profits. Moreover, while expanding the number of franchises may be hard on firm profits, it can be especially hard on the profits earned by each individual franchisee. This reflects another case of incentive conflicts that beset vertical relations.[21]

18.1

Practice Problem

Assume two firms confront each other in an industry in which the inverse demand is $P = 100 - Q$. Let marginal cost be constant at $c = 25$, and let the sunk cost of setting up a franchise be $K = 45$.

a. According to equation (18.9), how many franchises will each firm operate?
b. According to equation (18.7), what profit will each firm make if each operates the number of franchises derived in part (a)?
c. According to equation (18.5), what will be the industry price, P, and output, Q?
d. Calculate the industry output, price, and profit earned by a pure monopolist. Compare this with your answers in part (b).

18.7   EMPIRICAL APPLICATION: EXCLUSIVE DEALING IN THE US BEER INDUSTRY

The impact of exclusive dealing and exclusive territorial contracts has been the subject of many studies. The emerging consensus from these studies is that such contracts are beneficial, both for firms and for consumers, when they are not mandated by the

---

[21]   While we have cast our example in terms of the operation of independent franchisees, it could equally well be cast in terms of operating independent divisions such as the different divisions run by major auto makers such as GM and Ford. Here again, the outcome may be too many divisions from the viewpoint of maximizing industry profits, but with no real way for any one car firm to reduce the number of divisions unilaterally. This may ultimately be why in the wake of the Great Recession and industry reorganization of 2007–09, GM eliminated its *Saturn* and *Pontiac* divisions and Ford eliminated its *Mercury* division.

government but instead, the result of private negotiations. A recent study by Tim Sass (2005) on exclusive dealing in the US domestic beer market is an example of the kind of study that finds support for private vertical contracts.

The US has a three-tiered beer market. At one end of the stream are the beer producers or breweries, such as Anheuser-Busch (AB—now Anheuser-Busch InBev), Miller, and Coors. In the case of a foreign beer, the domestic firm importing that beer plays the role of a producer. Besides producing the beer, brewers also engage in a good bit of advertising and product promotion.

The brewers sell to the next tier, which comprises distributors. These sales are usually made at a constant price per unit, i.e., they typically do not set franchise fees or use two-part tariffs. The distributors warehouse the product, do local advertising and promotion, and also monitor local beer quality. They sell to the third tier, the retailers from whom consumers make their purchases of beer. Again, sales to retailers usually employ linear pricing.

All of the major breweries have exclusive dealing contracts with at least some of their distributors. They also typically assign exclusive territories. The latter means that there is little *intra*brand competition among distributors. However, there is a fair bit of *inter*brand competition. It is very rare that a single distributor possesses a monopoly in a regional market.

Sass (2005) first tries to determine what factors lead to the use of exclusive contracts in the beer market. Data from a *1996/1997 Distributor Brand-Equity Survey* provides evidence on 381 distributor contracts, 69 of which include an exclusive dealing clause (most of these are AB distributors). If foreclosure is a motivation for such contracts, then they should become less likely as market size grows. This is because foreclosure works by denying the rival a sufficiently large sales base to permit exploiting scale economies, and this is harder to do when the market is large. Sass (2005) uses two variables to capture potential market size. One is the population (*POP*) of the distribution region. The other is the state-level market share (*MSD*) of the brewery that is the primary supplier of the distributor.

Another factor has to do with the local market information that the distributor has acquired. A distributor who has a lot of information about local consumer tastes and price responsiveness will likely be less willing to sign an exclusive dealing contract because this limits that distributor's ability to profit from its information. Sass (2005) proxies this information by the number of years (*YRS*) that the distributor has been owned by the same family.

Finally, brewers may want to have exclusive dealing when they have large promotional expenses themselves that raise retail demand for beer in general but which, in the absence of an exclusive arrangement, the distributor might meet by selling an alternative brand. To capture the importance of such non-brand specific advertising, Sass (2005) uses the national advertising of the brewer's primary supplier (*ADS*) and a 1,0 variable indicating whether or not there is a state ban on billboard or sign advertising (*BAN*). If protecting its advertising against free riding is a motivation for the brewer, the first should have a positive effect and the second should have a negative effect.

Because a contract is either classified as an exclusive deal or not, the independent variable in the econometric specification is a 1,0 variable and Sass (2005) estimates this regression using the Probit procedure that we described in the Empirical Application in Chapter 13 regarding the Ellison and Ellison (2006) study of entry into generic drug markets. This means that the estimated coefficients indicate how much a change in the explanatory variable would raise or lower the *probability* of using an exclusive contract. The results are shown in Table 18.1 below.

Overall, the evidence on the determinants of where exclusive dealing contracts are used in the US beer market implies that these contracts are not used to harm competition. Instead, they appear to be used for the beneficial reason of protecting brewers' investments in their own product promotion. For example, increases in market size as measured by both *POP* and *MSD* raise the likelihood of an excusive dealing clause and the t-statistics indicate that both of these effects are statistically significant. This suggests that these contracts are not being used to foreclose markets to rivals. There is some evidence that the real motive is to protect the brewer's generalized advertising efforts against free riding. While *ADS* is not statistically significant, the presence of a ban against beer advertising on billboards and signs does have a negative effect on exclusive dealing. When there is less promotion, there is less need to protect it with an exclusive dealing contract. Finally, there is also evidence that as distributors gain experience and knowledge of the local market, they are less willing to sign an exclusive dealing contract that might restrict their ability to profit from that information. The coefficient on *YRS* is negative and significant.

Having examined the factors that lead to exclusive dealing, Sass (2005) then turns to examining the market effects that such contracts have. He considers four possible variables that might be affected. These are: 1) the average price paid by the distributor to brewers, *PB*; 2) the price the distributor charges retailers for its primary brand, *PD*; 3) the quantity of the primary brand sold, *QPRIMARY*; and 4) the quantity of all brands sold, *QTOTAL*, each measured in logarithms.

Prices of course, should reflect both supply (i.e. cost) and demand pressures. Assuming that production costs are roughly the same for the brewers, the cost differences in supplying a distributor will reflect shipping costs or the distance from the nearest plant *DIST*; the level of excise taxes *TAX*; and possibly, the presence of a ban on outside advertising *BAN*, which could raise promotional costs. If these variables affect the price paid by the distributor then they should also affect the price paid by the retailer. That price in turn should affect both sales of the primary brand and of all brands. Thus, these three variables belong in all four equations.

To capture demand effects, Sass (2005) uses three variables. These are: 1) per capita income in the distribution territory, *INC*; 2) population in the distribution territory, *POP;* and the percent of the population that is of prime drinking age, *AGESHARE*. Of course, the primary variable of interest is whether or not the distributor in question operated under an exclusive dealing contract, *EXDEAL*. This is a binary variable equal to 1 if there was an exclusive dealing contract and 0 if there was not.

Table 18.1   What explains the use of exclusive dealing in US beer distributor contracts?

Explanatory Variable	Estimated Coefficient	t-Statistic
POP	0.0001	(1.87)
MSD	0.0079	(2.79)
YRS	−0.0017	(−2.10)
ADS	−0.0002	(−0.38)
BAN	−0.0955	(−2.12)

The four regressions suggested by the variables just described are:

$$PB = CONSTANT + a_1EXDEAL + a_2DIST + a_3TAX + a_4BAN + a_5INC$$

$$+a_6POP + a_7AGESHARE + \varepsilon_{PB}$$

$$PD = CONSTANT + b_1EXDEAL + b_2DIST + b_3TAX + b_4BAN + b_5INC$$

$$+b_6POP + b_7AGESHARE + \varepsilon_{PD}$$

$$QPRIMARY = CONSTANT + c_1EXDEAL + c_2DIST + c_3TAX + c_4BAN + c_5INC$$

$$+c_6POP + c_7AGESHARE + \varepsilon_{QPRIMARY}$$

$$QTOTAL = CONSTANT + d_1EXDEAL + d_2DIST + d_3TAX + d_4BAN + d_5INC$$

$$+d_6POP + d_7AGESHARE + \varepsilon_{TOTAL}$$

Basically, these are the regressions that Sass (2005) estimates. However, in both the first and the fourth equations, he also includes market share data for three of the major brands to see how the extent of their presence affects the brewer's price to the dealer and final total sales. Sass (2005) also recognizes that the distributor's costs, and therefore price to retailers, may reflect both the distributor's business savvy as captured by the number of years the same family has owned the distributorship, and an additional cost factor based on the average number of retailing stops the distributor must stop at per week. Hence, Sass's final set of regressions are as follows:

$$PB = CONSTANT + a_1EXDEAL + a_2DIST + a_3TAX + a_4BAN + a_5INC$$

$$+a_6POP + a_7AGESHARE + MARKET\ SHARE\ EFFECTS + \varepsilon_{PB}$$

$$PD = CONSTANT + b_1EXDEAL + b_2DIST + b_3TAX + b_4BAN + b_5INC$$

$$+b_6POP + b_7AGESHARE + OTHER\ COST\ FACTORS + \varepsilon_{PD}$$

$$QPRIMARY = CONSTANT + c_1EXDEAL + c_2DIST + c_3TAX + c_4BAN + c_5INC$$

$$+c_6POP + c_7AGESHARE + \varepsilon_{QPRIMARY}$$

$$QTOTAL = CONSTANT + d_1EXDEAL + d_2DIST + d_3TAX + d_4BAN + d_5INC$$

$$+d_6POP + d_7AGESHARE + MARKET\ SHARE\ EFFECTS + \varepsilon_{TOTAL}$$

We are mainly interested in the impact of exclusive dealing. Before discussing that effect, however, it is worth noting two features of this system. These are reduced form equations. That is, they are not equations that describe the full supply and demand structure. Instead, they describe the outcome for the dependent variable in terms of the basic factors that underlie supply and demand. In each case, the final term represents the influence of random factors that may affect the brewer's price, the distributor's price, primary brand sales, or total brand sales.

In principle, each of these regressions could be run alone using ordinary least squares (OLS). However, it seems likely that the random factors that, say, raise total demand may also affect primary brand demand and, in turn, feed into prices. In other words, while the regressions may seem independent of each other, there is a correlation between the random forces affecting each one, i.e., ε_{PB}, ε_{PD}, $\varepsilon_{QPRIMARY}$, and ε_{TOTAL} may all be correlated. If they are, then information about the nature of this correlation can be used to estimate the regression coefficients more precisely. To do this, Sass (2005) employs a regression technique known as Seemingly Unrelated Regression. This approach estimates the four regressions simultaneously by applying an estimate of the correlation across the error terms to construct generalized least squares (GLS) coefficient estimates. The implied effect of exclusive dealing in each of the four regressions is shown Table 18.2 below:

In every case, the effect of an exclusive dealing clause is positive and highly significant. It raises the unit price set by brewers by about 6 percent and the price set by distributors by about 5 percent. Despite these increases, final sales of both the primary producer's brand and of all brands also rise under exclusive dealing. These effects are particularly large. Demand for the brewer's product rises by 32 percent as the result of exclusive dealing. Yet this does not come at the expense of other brands. Instead, their sales rise as well by over 28 percent. In further regressions, Sass (2005) finds that exclusive dealing by one brewer (AB, in particular) does not significantly decrease rival brewers' prices.

The implications of these findings are relatively straightforward. The fact that exclusive dealing rises with the size of the market seems inconsistent with the idea that it is used as an anticompetitive foreclosure device. This inference is strengthened by the finding that such restrictions also do not tend to force rivals to lower their prices. Instead, the fact that exclusive dealing restraints rise with both market size and the presence of restrictions on outdoor advertising is more consistent with the notion that such contracts are used to mitigate conflicts between the brewery and its distributors.

Because the price to the distributor and the distributor's price to the retailer rise while sales volume also rises, there is no doubt that the surplus of brewers and distributors is enhanced by exclusive dealing. What happens to retailers and consumers is less clear. However, the rise in sales volume is sufficiently large that there is a strong supposition that their surplus also goes up. In short, the results of Sass (2005) strongly indicate that exclusive dealing in the US beer industry is welfare enhancing.

Sass's (2005) results are not unusual. For example, Zanarone (2009) examines the impact of 2002 European regulations that made exclusive territories and minimum quantity purchases unlawful. Analysis of thirty-eight contracts—half written before 2002 and half after—shows a systematic shift in decision rights. After the regulations are imposed, auto manufacturers are much more likely to write contracts that allow the manufacturer to: 1) impose a maximum resale price; 2) require minimum contributions to the manufacturer's national advertising budget; and 3) require that dealers implement a customer satisfaction survey and achieve minimum standards in those surveys. Thus, like Sass (2005), the evidence in Zanarone (2009) is again consistent with the idea that the exclusive territories and minimum quantities of the earlier contracts were meant to prevent too high a retail markup and too low a provision of retail services.

Table 18.2 Effect of exclusive dealing on market outcomes

PB Equation		PD Equation		QPRIMARY Equation		QTOTAL Equation	
EXDEAL		EXDEAL		EXDEAL		EXDEAL	
Coefficient	t-statistic	Coefficient	t-statistic	Coefficient	t-statistic	Coefficient	t-statistic
0.0630	(2.73)	0.0368	(2.13)	0.3241	(3.09)	0.2816	(2.74)

Summary

Contracts between manufacturers and the various retailers that sell the manufactured products directly to consumers include a variety of non-price restrictions. These may include an exclusive dealing restriction that prevents the retailer from selling the products of any other manufacturer, or exclusive selling and territorial arrangements that restrain the manufacturer from allowing any other retailer to sell its product. They can also include slotting fees that producers must pay for access to retail distribution. Because these restrictions so clearly have the appearance of a restraint on trade, they fall under suspicion as anticompetitive.

In reality, however, there may be many efficiency gains that lie behind such restrictions. Often they may serve to ensure adequate promotional activities and other consumer services. They may also be useful in creating an environment in which retailers can better handle demand shocks. Yet the fear that these restrictions can be used either to soften competition or to eliminate competitors altogether via restrictions that lead to foreclosure are also justified. In this respect, there seems little alternative to evaluating each case on its own merits.

For the most part, public policy towards vertical restraints has increasingly recognized their potential benefits. This largely reflects the accumulating empirical evidence that these restrictions generally help producers and may help, or at least not hurt consumers. However, the potential for the abuse of market power seems clear, especially when the restrictions apply to a large fraction of the existing market. For this reason, authorities have continued to take a rule-of-reason approach to non-price vertical restraints rather than a *per se* legal one.

Before concluding we note that, in many respects, the retailer acts as an agent on behalf of the manufacturer. It learns about consumer tastes, makes promotional and other service decisions, and, of course, sets the final consumer price. Consequently, the vertical relationship between the producer and the retailer is a principal-agent relationship akin to the relationship between a client and lawyer, or between shareholders and management. The contractual issues that arise between manufacturer and retailer are therefore part of a broader set of questions that arise in connection with contracts that govern all principal-agent relationships. These are important issues in the theory of the firm. For example, what is the difference between a producer connected to its retailer by means of a formal contract and a producer that simply is fully integrated into the retail market; or, for that matter, a producer that operates a retail division? Why do firms choose one form of organization over another? We do not answer these questions here. However, we do want to acknowledge that the issue of vertical relationships is really part of a larger question regarding the boundaries of the firm.

Problems

1. Most beer companies impose an exclusive dealing clause on the supermarkets that sell their products. Discuss whether you think this practice will yield efficient market outcomes.

2. General Motors, Ford, and Daimler-Chrysler all operate many divisions of automobile lines, e.g., *Chevrolet*, *Cadillac*, and *Buick*. Discuss the motivation for this practice. Who do you think this practice benefits the most, automakers or consumers?

3. In Europe, automobile dealers have traditionally been granted exclusive territories. Do you think that this practice should be legal?

4. Review the model of Rasmussen, Ramseyer, and Wiley (1991) from Chapter 13. Why are scale economies important for this argument that exclusive dealing can deter entry?

5. Who would be willing to pay more for the right to use the McDonald's name—an outlet located in the center of Centerville, or one that would do the same amount of business at the interstate turnpike?

6. What are the incentives for McDonald's to require franchisees to buy hamburger buns, meat, napkins, and other supplies from it rather than from other, possibly lower-cost local suppliers, other than the incentive of removing double-marginalization?

References

Aghion, P., and P. Bolton. 1987. "Contracts as a Barrier to Entry", *American Economic Review* 77, (June): 388–401.

Bonanno, G., and J. Vickers, 1988. "Vertical Separation," *Journal of Industrial Economics* 36 (March): 257–65.

Borenstein, S., J. Mackie-Mason, and J. Netz, 2000. "Exercising Market Power in Proprietary Aftermarkets," *Journal of Economics and Management Strategy* 9 (Summer): 157–88.

Baye, M., K. Crocker, and J. Ju. 1996. "Divisionalization, Franchising, and Divestiture Incentives in Oligopoly," *American Economic Review* 86 (March): 223–36.

Bernheim, B. D., and M. Whinston, 1990. "Multimarket Contact and Collusive Behavior," *Rand Journal of Economics* 21 (Spring): 1–26.

Besanko, D., and M. K. Perry, 1994. "Exclusive Dealing in a Spatial Model of Retail Competition," *International Journal of Industrial Organization* 12 (Fall): 297–329.

Blair, R.D., and F. Lafontaine, 2005. *The Economics of Franchising*, Cambridge University Press: New York, NY.

Blass, A. A., and D. W. Carlton, 2001. "The Choice of Organizational Form in Gasoline Retailing and the Cost of Laws that Limit that Choice," *Journal of Law and Economics* 44 (October): 511–24.

Chen, Z., and T. Ross, 1993. "Refusals to Deal, Price Discrimination, and Independent Service Organizations," *Journal of Economics and Management Science* 2 (Summer): 593–614.

Comanor, W., and P. Rey, 2000. "Vertical Restraints and the Market Power of Large Distributors," *Review of Industrial Organization* 17 (Spring): 135–53.

Ellison, G., and S. Ellison. 2011. "Strategic Entry Deterrence and the Behavior of Pharmaceutical Incumbents Prior to Patent Expiration." *American Economic Journal* 3 (January), 1–36.

Federal Trade Commission Staff Report, 2003. *Slotting Allowances in the Retail Grocery Industry: Selected Case Studies in Five Product Categories.* http://www.ftc.gov/os/2003/11/slottingallowancerpt031114.pdf.

Gabaix, X., and D. Laibson 2006. "Shrouded Attributes, Consumer Myopia, and Information Suppression in Competitive Markets."

Quarterly Journal of Economics, (May): 505–40.

Goldfine, D., and K. Vorrasi, 2004. "The Fall of the *Kodak* Aftermarket Doctrine: Dying a Slow Death in the Lower Courts" *Antitrust Law Journal* 72 (January): 209–31.

Hart, O., and J. Tirole, 1990. "Vertical Integration and Market Foreclosure," *Brookings Papers on Economic Activity (Microeconomics)*: 205–85.

Hass-Wilson, D. 1987. "Tying Requirements in Markets with Many Sellers: The Contact Lens Industry," *Review of Economics and Statistics* 69 (February): 170–75.

Klein, B., and K. Murphy. 1988. "Vertical Restraints as Contract Enforcement Mechanisms." *Journal of Law & Economics* 31 (October): 265–97.

Lafontaine, F., 1992. "Agency Theory and Franchising: Some Empirical Results," *Rand Journal of Economics* 23 (Summer): 263–83.

Lafontaine, F., and M. Slade, 2007. "Exclusive Contracts and Vertical Restraints: Empirical Evidence and Public Policy," Forthcoming in P. Buccirossi, ed., *Handbook of Antitrust Economics*, Cambridge: MIT Press.

Lafontaine, F., and K. Shaw, 1999. "The Dynamics of Franchise Contracting: Evidence From Panel Data," *Journal of Political Economy* 107 (October): 1041–80.

Lafontaine, F., and K. Shaw. 1993. "Contractual Arrangements as Signaling Devices: Evidence from Franchising," *Journal of Law, Economics, and Organization* 9 (October): 256–89.

Marvel, H. 1982. "Exclusive Dealing," *Journal of Law and Economics* 25 (April): 1–25.

Mathewson, G. F., and R. A.Winter, 1987. "The Competitive Effects of Vertical Agreements: Comment," *American Economic Review*, 77: 1057–62.

Miao, C. 2010. "Consumer Myopia, Standardization, and Aftermarket Monopolization." *European Economic Review* 54 (October): 931–46.

Marx, L., and G. Shaffer, 2007. "Upfront Payments and Exclusion in Downstream Markets," *Rand Journal of Economics* 38 (Autumn): 823–43.

O'Brien, D. P., and G. Shaffer. 1992. "Vertical Control with Bilateral Contracts," *Rand Journal of Economics* 23 (Autumn): 299–308.

O'Brien, D. P., and G. Shaffer. 1994. "The Welfare Effects of Forbidding Discriminatory Discounts: A Secondary Line Analysis of Robinson-Patman," *Journal of Law, Economics, and Organization* 10 (October): 296–318.

Posner, R. 1981. "The Next Step in the Antitrust Treatment of Restricted Distribution: Per se Legality," *University of Chicago Law Review* 48: 6–26.

Rasmussen, E., J. Ramseyer, and J. Wiley. 1991. "Naked Exclusion," *American Economic Review* 81 (December): 1137–45.

Rey, P., and J. Stiglitz. 1995. "The Role of Exclusive Territories in Producer Competition," *Rand Journal of Economics* 26 (Fall): 431–51.

Sass, T., 2005. "The Competitive Effects of Exclusive Dealing: Evidence from the US Beer Industry," *International Journal of Industrial Organization* 23 (April): 203–25.

Shaffer, G. 1991. "Slotting Allowances and Resale Price Maintenance: A Comparison of Facilitating Practices," *Rand Journal of Economics* 22 (Spring): 120–35.

Steiner, R. L. 1985. "The Nature of Vertical Restraints," *Antitrust Bulletin* (Spring): 143–97.

Whinston, M. 1990. "Tying, Foreclosure, and Exclusion," *American Economic Review* 80 (September): 837–59.

Zanarone, G. 2009. "Vertical Restraints and the Law: Evidence from Automobile Franchising," *Journal of Law & Economics* 52 (November): 691–700.

Part Six
Non-Price Competition

So far, most of our analysis has focused on interfirm competition centered on quantity or price. However, firms compete in many other dimensions, as well. Two such competitive mechanisms are advertising and innovative effort. These are the topics addressed in Part Six.

Advertising has long been an issue of both academic and popular concern. Initially, economists focused on the use of advertising to build brand loyalty and thereby to soften price competition between different brands. However, subsequent analysis has focused on the informational role of advertising. By helping consumers learn what alternatives are available and at which prices, by informing consumers about the appropriate uses of a new product and its overall quality, and in numerous other ways, advertising can play a useful role in improving the welfare of both producers and consumers. In Chapter 19 we examine many economic models of advertising. We also present Ackerberg's (2001) empirical paper offering evidence on the critical role that advertising plays as information regarding what products are being sold and what their critical features are.

In Chapter 20, we consider the general issues of innovation and Schumpeterian competition. Chapter 20 begins with a presentation of a well-known set of propositions typically referred to jointly as the Schumpeterian hypotheses. This is that large firms and concentrated industries are necessary for technological innovation. This chapter explicitly addresses the nature of R&D competition and precisely the sort of market structure that most encourages technical progress. We also explore the potential gains and losses when firms cooperate on R&D activity, and review empirical evidence on the Schumpeterian hypotheses. We conclude with a consideration of the evidence on the spillovers from one firm's R&D to another's as found in the empirical work of Keller (2002).

In Chapter 21, we consider public policy designed to encourage R&D, especially patent policy. Such policy must walk a thin line between granting wide access to available technologies and yet also giving innovators the rights to restrict such access so as to earn a return on their inventions. We discuss recent patent policy developments and, in particular, the rise of the so-called "patent thicket." We also note the issues that arise in a patent system when patents are issued sequentially, and all patents are needed to pursue further innovation. The empirical study for this chapter is the Hall and Zedonis (2001) paper on innovation in the semiconductor industry.

19

Advertising, Market Power, and Information

Large retail stores that sell many different kinds of goods and many different brands of each good are a relatively recent phenomenon in the history of commerce. A customer buying, say, a pair of shoes in the early twentieth century would have faced a different shopping experience from the one faced today. The consumer would have been restricted to making a purchase in a specialized shoe store carrying only one or at most two brands, or possibly a cobbler's shop that made its own shoes. In addition, the consumer of a hundred years ago would have had to consult with the store proprietor, and would not have been able to examine and compare the merchandise directly.

How different the modern shopping experience is from the practices of the not-so-distant past. Today's consumer can go to a shoe or department store and see a whole range of different brands. Once there, the consumer can personally handle and inspect each different style without any need to deal with a store employee. Only when the consumer decides actually to try a specific pair of shoes on will the assistance from a store employee be required—and even that is not always necessary. Consumers now may choose directly from an even wider range of different brands and never deal with a sales representative when they purchase shoes over the web.

What has made this dramatic change in the nature of retailing possible? Our reference to the web provides a clue. The retailing revolution of the twentieth century that has continued to the digital commerce of the twenty-first owes much to the advent of mass media. Beginning with radio, then television, and now the Internet, technological change in telecommunications has made it possible for manufacturers to reach their consumers en masse and promote their products directly to the public. With wide scale advertising, manufacturers themselves can promote their products directly to a wide target audience. In turn, this has facilitated the formation of large-scale retail establishments such as department stores, discount stores, and web-based retailers like Amazon, each selling several varieties of hundreds of different kinds of goods. Mass communication and large-scale advertising have developed hand-in-hand, leading to a sustained dramatic change in the way consumers learn about the products that are out there waiting for them to buy.[1]

---

[1] For a good discussion of this revolutionizing effect of modern advertising and other aspects of advertising and promotional activities, see D. Pope, *The Making of Modern Advertising*, (1983).

Yet while it is clear that the emergence of large-scale advertising has played a crucial role in the development of retailing, the full nature of advertising's impact remains a puzzle. We do not know exactly how advertising affects the consumer's decision of whether to buy and if so, what brand to buy. Consider, for example, television ads for Nike shoes. These ads often say little about the nature of the shoes and instead just feature a collage of images accompanied by the Nike Company's famous "swoosh" logo. How does this affect a consumer's decision to buy? In some Nike ads the company expressly points out that it is a corporate sponsor and apparel provider for the US Olympic team. How does this affect the consumer's decision of whether to purchase Nike shoes?

The question as to how ads like those run by Nike actually work is important for many reasons. To begin with, Nike is not alone. Its promotional efforts are typical of many firms marketing consumer products and these efforts are very costly. Advertising on network television, for example, can cost millions of dollars for a single minute of airtime. For the 2013 Super Bowl the average price of a 30-second spot was a record-breaking $3.75 million, with some spots going for over $4 million and all spots sold more than a month before the Super Bowl itself.[2] Still, Anheuser-Busch InBev, Frito-Lay, Pepsi-Cola, Proctor & Gamble, and others all bought spots for that game. We would like to understand first how advertising works in order to understand the incentives for these firms to incur such costs. At that point we can examine the decisions of firms to promote their products and why firms in some industries do much more advertising than those in others. Understanding how advertising works allows us to move on to investigate how advertising affects the strategic interaction between firms, and what this means for the consumer.

Our goal in this chapter is to understand the role of advertising and the implications that this carries for strategic interaction in the market place and consumer welfare. Advertising is provided by both manufacturers, e.g., Nike, and by retailers, e.g., Target. As a result, the provision of promotional services involves many of the vertical incentive conflicts that we have discussed in the previous two chapters. For the most part, we will suppress the distinction between manufacturer and retailer and focus on how advertising affects consumer buying decisions and the strategic interaction among firms competing for the consumer's patronage. We are interested in how advertising works, what information or other features advertising provides that induces consumers to buy the advertised brand, and what impact advertising has on the market.

Advertising could be viewed as an integral element of competition among firms that sell different brands of the same good. In this case, high advertising could be considered a sign of good health—a way to increase consumer awareness of different brands and therefore a vital component of healthy competition. In contrast, advertising could be seen as a way to differentiate one manufacturer's brand from another and thereby weaken competition by making it less likely that a consumer will switch brands. High advertising in this case would be a sign of market power. There is a long-standing policy concern that advertising expenditures overall could be socially wasteful (see Reality Checkpoint and Appendix)—in that each firm's effort to switch consumers to its brand just offsets its rivals' so that these expenditures yield no net gain to any firm. Our analysis should provide a better understanding of this issue as well. However, gaining insight into whether there is too much or too little advertising requires that we learn the underlying economic logic behind advertising. Why do firms do it and how does it work?

---

[2]   S. Elliott, "Super Bowl Commercial Time is a Sellout," *New York Times*, January 8, 2013, p. B3.

Reality Checkpoint
The Brush War in Hog Heaven

Perhaps one of the clearest examples of a "prisoners' dilemma" advertising war comes from the 1990's rivalry between Braun and Optiva, the two biggest makers of electric toothbrushes. While the rivalry between these two firms has witnessed many intense episodes over the years, perhaps none was so extraordinary than that in late 1999. In an effort to win market share for its *Sonicare* brand, Optiva hired a crack dental research team to conduct tests showing that *Sonicare* toothbrushes were both less abrasive and better at attacking bacteria below the gum line than Braun's *Oral B Plaque Remover* model. This was quite expensive because the tests were conduced by repeatedly brushing the teeth of 3,000 dead pigs, which required the purchase of the pig heads from slaughterhouses and then arranging for the transportation and refrigeration of those heads in storage.

Braun responded quickly. It sent a team of scientists to Kansas to brush the teeth of a large number of *living* pigs. To do this, it not only had to pay the farmers but also arrange for the sedation of the swine because hogs are not eager to have their teeth cleaned electronically.

The whole affair was very expensive. Indeed, the resultant claims and counter claims ultimately led to a court battle and more costs. In truth, it is hard to know how relevant the brushing of pigs' teeth is to human oral hygiene. It was easy to see though that this war was bad for the health of both firms' profits.

Source: M. Maremount, "Braun, Sonicare Brush Up on their Legendary Feud," *The Wall Street Journal*, April 30, 1999, p. A1.

19.1   ADVERTISING: PRACTICE AND THEORY

The phenomenon of advertising is something of a paradox. Promotional efforts such as TV commercials are often barely tolerated by social critics. Advertising is frequently disparaged as something that is wrong with contemporary society—something that tricks us into wanting and even buying things we don't need. At the same time, advertising is ubiquitous. It airs on our television sets and radios, accounts for many of the pages in magazines and daily newspapers, dots the landscape and cityscape with billboards, and even shows up on our T-shirts and other apparel. However, much one might be critical of advertising, it seems that we can hardly live without it.

The magnitude of the advertising phenomenon as reflected in total dollars of expenditure is substantial. From the 1950s to 2008, total expenditure on advertising in the United States has consistently amounted to roughly 2 percent of the gross domestic product.[3] This has fallen somewhat in the wake of the Great Recession that began in late 2007. Thus, in 2011, while total US advertising expenditures were a quite substantial $250 billion, that amounted to only 1.65 percent of that year's GDP. Of this amount, nearly two-thirds was for measured media advertising. This includes spending on nationwide broadcast and cable television networks, radio networks, national magazines, newspapers, yellow pages, and the Internet. The other one-third is non-measured, or only indirectly measured media spending. This category includes expenditures on direct mailings, promotions, coupons, catalogs, business

---

[3]   Data on advertising expenditures are from Advertising Age Data Center, adage.com.

publications, and the sponsorship of special events. Retail advertising is often more heavily concentrated in non-measured media spending.[4]

Firms differ substantially in their advertising behavior. Based on measured media advertising in the United States, Procter & Gamble was the largest 2011 advertiser, spending $2.9 billion. However, telecommunications firms such as AT&T, Verizon, and Comcast all spent well over $1 billion, as did the reborn car makers General Motors and Chrysler, and each of these firms was among the top ten advertisers of 2011. In contrast, Apple computers was some way down the list with total expenditures of $62 million.[5]

In order to compare advertising efforts across firms of different sizes we typically compute advertising expenditure as a percentage of sales revenue. Even looking at this fraction—the advertising-to-sales ratio—still leaves considerable variation among firms, however. In 2011, the ratio for Procter & Gamble was about 11 percent, whereas for Apple computer it was closer to 1 percent. For most automakers, the advertising-to-sales ratio is on the order of 2 to 3 percent. Within the pharmaceutical industry, Pfizer's measured advertising spending came close to 9 percent of its sales revenue. Yet its rival Merck was closer to 3 percent. Johnson & Johnson, which is both a pharmaceutical maker and medical equipment manufacturer, had a 2011 advertising-to-sales ratio of about 5.2 percent.[6]

In sum, we see significant differences in advertising intensity between industries and even between firms in the same industry. The clear implication is that advertising is a strategic variable chosen by individual firms in response to their perceived strategic environment. To understand that choice—and its implications—we need to consider that environment and precisely how advertising works in that setting.

19.2   ADVERTISING AND MARKET POWER

As we noted earlier, economic research on advertising has been a long-running enterprise. Indeed, even Alfred Marshall (1890) devoted some consideration to advertising and its ability to facilitate the exploitation of scale economies.[7] Much of the earliest work, however, came in the early post World War II period and this drew a fairly negative assessment that advertising is a socially wasteful way for firms to compete that tends to foster market power [Kaldor (1950), Galbraith (1958), Solow (1967)].[8] One notable study in this last regard is that by Nichols (1951) of the American cigarette market. Nichols provides statistical evidence that the major brands relied heavily on advertising to differentiate their products and thereby soften price competition, especially that of "penny cigarettes."

Two further studies that were particularly influential—both with deep roots in the Structure-Conduct-Performance framework—were those of Bain (1956) and Comanor and Wilson (1967). Bain (1956), found that both concentration and profitability were positively linked and that, in turn, the central factor preserving concentration was the barrier to entry provided by intense advertising that differentiated incumbent products from those of potential new entrants. Similarly, using a somewhat more sophisticated regression analysis, Comanor and Wilson (1967) found that industries with high profitability are

---

[4]   Expenditures on measured media is tracked by TNS Media Intelligence.

[5]   Advertising Age, 2013 Annual.

[6]   Ibid.

[7]   A modern exposition of this view is found in Bagwell and Ramey (1994).

[8]   Viewed in this light, advertising is much like rent-seeking behavior. See, for example, Posner (1975).

closely associated with those that have a high advertising to sales ratio. This result was soon replicated in several similar studies for different time periods and different countries.[9]

However, in examining any link between advertising and market structure, we again need to remember that both are potentially endogenous variables. Advertising may foster concentration and market power but market power may equally be at least as an important determinant of advertising. We therefore need to separate out the causality in understanding any connection between the two. Moreover, if advertising does work by changing consumer tastes then calculating its effects requires that we think carefully about how it does this and what this implies for the benefits that consumers derive from the product.

19.3   THE MONOPOLY FIRM'S PROFIT-MAXIMIZING LEVEL OF ADVERTISING

Rational firms will only expend considerable resources on advertising if it is profitable to do so. Because advertising is costly, this means that it must generate revenue to cover those costs. In other words, advertising must affect demand. It is useful in this respect to recall that any firm with market power faces a downward sloping demand curve. The firm is interested in pushing its demand curve out and selling more at the same price rather than selling more by lowering its price and moving down along the existing demand curve. So, one way of thinking of how advertising works is that advertising shifts the firm's demand curve. In other words, demand depends not only upon the price the firm sets but also upon the amount of advertising that the firm chooses. This can be described by the general inverse demand function: $P = P(Q, \alpha)$ where P is the product price and α is the amount of advertising, measured for example as seconds of television or radio time, or perhaps as page space in newspapers or magazines per period. As usual, we assume that for a given level of advertising, the firm's demand falls as the price P rises, i.e., to sell more output Q requires that the price P fall. Consistent with our assumption that advertising shifts the demand curve outward, this means that we may assume that for a given output Q, the price consumers are willing to pay rises as the amount of advertising increases. The inverse demand function $P = \alpha(A - BQ)$ is an example of a demand relation that would satisfy these requirements.

Whatever the specific demand function, the ability of advertising to increase demand is the "good news" of advertising. The "bad news" is that advertising is costly. We will assume that every unit of advertising or advertising message costs the firm c_α[10] and that every unit of production costs the firm c_G. It then follows that the firm will earn a total profit $\pi(Q, \alpha)$ given by:

$$\pi(Q, \alpha) = [P(Q, \alpha) - c_G]Q - c_\alpha \alpha \tag{19.1}$$

The firm's profit maximization strategy now involves two choices. It must pick a both a level of output Q and a level of advertising α that together maximize profit. Yet while the profit-maximization decision now has two dimensions, we can still use some of our basic insights from our earlier work to determine the implications of such profit-maximizing

---

[9]   See, for example, Lambin (1976), Geroski (1982), and Round (1983).

[10]   This assumption may not always hold. Often there is considerable quantity discounting when air time, network time, or magazine space is purchased by a firm for advertising.

behavior. To begin with, we know that given an optimal amount of advertising α^*, the firm's optimal output Q^* will need to satisfy the requirement that given that advertising level, marginal revenue equals marginal production cost c_G at Q^*. In turn, we know from our work in Chapter 4 that this implies that the firm's price-cost margin as measured by the Lerner Index be equal to the inverse of the price elasticity of demand. That is, a necessary condition for the firm to be setting the optimal price P^* (producing the optimal output Q^*) is:

$$\frac{P^* - c_G}{P^*} = \frac{1}{\varepsilon_P} \tag{19.2}$$

where $\varepsilon_p = \frac{\Delta Q/Q}{\Delta P/P} = \frac{P}{Q}\left(\frac{\Delta Q}{\Delta P}\right)$ is the price elasticity of demand evaluated at the firm's optimal price choice P^* and conditional, as noted, on the given level of advertising α.

Now consider the monopoly firm's optimal amount of advertising, or α^*. At any given price P the firm's corresponding output Q will rise if advertising α also increases, i.e., $\frac{\Delta Q}{\Delta \alpha} > 0$. This extra output will generate additional profit of $(P-c)$ per unit. So, the total net revenue from an increase in advertising α is just: $(P - c_G)\frac{\Delta Q}{\Delta \alpha}$. The firm will therefore wish to keep raising its advertising, keep raising α, up to the point where this net revenue increase just covers the marginal cost. Therefore, an additional condition that the firm must meet is that it choose an optimal amount of advertising such that:

$$(P - c)\frac{\Delta Q}{\Delta \alpha} = c_\alpha \tag{19.3}$$

If we now divide both sides of equation (19.3) by total sales PQ and multiply both sides by total advertising α, we then obtain:

$$\frac{(P - c_G)}{PQ}\frac{\Delta Q}{\Delta \alpha}\alpha = \frac{c_\alpha \alpha}{PQ} \tag{19.4}$$

Note that the right-hand side of equation (19.4) is the ratio of total advertising expense $c_\alpha \alpha$ to total sales PQ, i.e., the standard advertising-to-sales measure of the firm's advertising intensity. We may get some insight into the left-hand-side by rewriting equation (19.4) as follows:

$$\left(\frac{P^* - c_G}{P^*}\right)\frac{(\Delta Q/Q)}{(\Delta \alpha/\alpha^*)} = \frac{c_\alpha \alpha}{PQ} = \frac{advertising\ expense}{total\ sales} \tag{19.5}$$

where we have now indicated that this condition must also hold when the firm chooses both the optimal price P^* and the optimal advertising effort α^*. From equation (19.2) we know that at this optimum the first term on the left-hand side of (19.4) is the inverse of the price elasticity of demand ε_p.

Now consider the second left-hand-side term $\frac{(\Delta Q/Q)}{(\Delta \alpha/\alpha^*)}$. As a little thought quickly reveals, this term captures the proportional change in the quantity demanded $(\Delta Q/Q)$ in response to a proportional change in advertising effort $(\Delta \alpha/\alpha^*)$ measured at the optimal level of α. Hence, it is naturally interpreted as the elasticity of demand with respect to advertising ε_α. Thus, we may now write equation (19.5) quite simply as:

$$\frac{\varepsilon_\alpha}{\varepsilon_P} = \frac{advertising\ expense}{total\ sales} \tag{19.6}$$

We now have a key result. The firm with market power maximizes profit by choosing a price (or output level) and a level of advertising such that the ratio of advertising expenditure to sales is just equal to the ratio of the advertising elasticity of demand to the price elasticity of demand. This result is usually referred to as the Dorfman-Steiner condition after the pioneering paper on advertising written by Dorfman and Steiner in (1954).[11] It makes clear that whatever effect advertising efforts may have in creating and preserving market power, basic theory implies that there is a direct causal link between a firm's market power as measured by its Lerner Index and the amount of advertising the firm does. Specifically, firms with greater market power facing less elastic demand and therefore able to set a higher markup of price over cost will be firms that do more advertising. In turn, this means that any positive correlation we see in the data between a measure of market power and a measure of advertising intensity does not by itself mean that the higher advertising is causing the greater market power. Instead, it may well be the case that it is the greater market power leading to the greater advertising. Think of it this way. A perfectly competitive firm is a price-taker that faces an infinitely elastic demand. Equation (19.6) therefore implies that such a firm should have an advertising-to-sales ratio of zero, i.e., it should do no advertising. The underlying intuition is that the perfectly competitive firm can sell all that it wants to at the current price. It does not need to advertise and "push out" its demand curve to sell more. It is only those firms with less elastic demand that, in the absence of increased advertising, can only sell additional units by lowering the price that have the real incentive to advertise.

19.1

Practice Problem

Suppose that a monopoly firm faces an inverse demand curve described by $P(Q, \alpha) = 100 - \frac{1}{\sqrt{\alpha}} Q$. The firm has a constant marginal production cost equal to 60. Each advertising message costs the firm $1.

a. What is the slope of the demand curve when $\alpha = 100$? When $\alpha = 1000$? Illustrate your answers.

b. Suppose that firm decides to send $\alpha = 2500$ advertising messages.

   i.   What is the monopolist's marginal revenue curve?
   ii. What will be the monopolist's profit-maximizing price and output values?
   iii. What is the price elasticity of demand at this price and output combination?

c. The demand function is such that the advertising elasticity of demand is constant at $1/2$. Do the price and output combination derived in part (b), satisfy the Dorfman-Steiner condition?

---

[11]   Dorfman, R. and P. Steiner, 1954. "Optimal Advertising and Optimal Quality," *American Economic Review* 44: 826–36.

19.4   THE ECONOMIC ROLE OF ADVERTISING

It is clear from the foregoing that the market environment is a key determinant of firms' advertising choices. Yet as noted, there is a long intellectual tradition arguing the reverse—that advertising itself has an important impact on the competitive setting, especially as it affects barriers to entry. Whether and if this is the case, depends in important ways on just precisely how advertising works to increase consumer demand. Does it truly alter consumer preferences? Or does it merely provide information about the availability and price of goods?

19.4.1   Advertising as Consumer Persuasion

As noted, a very common view of advertising is that it actually changes consumer preferences in favor of the advertised good. Consumers are thereby induced to purchase more of a particular brand than they would have in the absence of advertising. This is reflected in an outward shift in the demand curve for the advertised good.

Evaluating the impact of persuasive advertising is tricky on several counts. To begin with, some of the persuasion may be based on fraudulent claims. Indeed, an important reason for the creation of the Federal Trade Commission (FTC) was to protect consumers against false or deceptive advertising characteristic of "snake oil" sales pitches of the late nineteenth and early twentieth century. Even today, the FTC's Consumer Protection Division is one of its busiest. In 2012, the division forced Oreck to cease advertising its claim that its vacuum cleaners and air purifiers could prevent the flu, and required Nivea to halt advertising that its *My Silhouette!* skin cream could help users lose weight. Both Oreck and Nivea paid fines as well. In the case of the shoe company, Reebock, the FTC not only forced the firm to stop advertisements that claimed its "toning shoes" provided extra tone and strength to leg and buttock muscles, but also required the firm to issue $25 million in customer refunds. As these were just some of the hundreds of deceptive advertising complaints that the FTC handled, it seems clear that fraudulent persuasive advertising is a real phenomenon. In these cases, any outward shift in the demand curve is likely to prove temporary as consumers learn of the product's true qualities.[12] We return to this issue below in our discussion of advertising as information (or misinformation).

More importantly, the view that advertising changes consumer preferences raises difficult issues in economic analysis as the usual assumption is that preferences are given. That is, we usually assume that the consumer has a given utility function that reflects tastes and that determines the consumer's willingness to pay for different goods and services. If we are to assert that advertising can change these tastes, then the calculation of consumer surplus and welfare measures becomes complicated.

Two approaches are described in Dixit and Norman (1978). Both may be illustrated by Figure 19.1. Here D_0 is the demand curve that reflects consumers' innate tastes before any advertising, while D_1 is the demand curve that reflects those tastes as altered by

---

[12]   The demand shift may last longer in some cases. For example, in the case of negative options such as used by book clubs and credit card protection services, among others. In these cases, the advertiser persuades the consumer to make an initial purchase, e.g., to try 30 days of credit card protection. The catch is that after 30 days, the customer continues to receive and to pay for the service unless the customer explicitly indicates that it is no longer wanted.

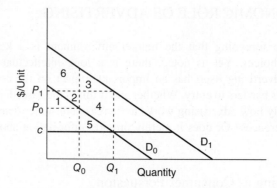

Figure 19.1   Welfare analysis of persuasive advertising

persuasive advertising. As shown, the advertising has shifted out the demand curve and led to both an increase in price (from P_0 to P_1) and an increase in the quantity purchased (from Q_0 to Q_1).

Suppose we take the view that it is the original demand curve D_0 that is the relevant one for analyzing welfare. In this view, the advertising clearly makes consumers worse off. They now paymore for the initial amount that they were buying—a loss captured by the sum of areas 1 and 2 in the figure. In addition, they now buy an additional Q_1-Q_0 goods at price P_1 that they do not truly value at that price. This loss is reflected in area 4. Thus, in total, consumers lose areas $1 + 2 + 4$. Note though that this sum also reflects an equal gain in producer surplus. That is, areas $1 + 2 + 4$ reflect not a deadweight loss but, instead, a transfer from consumers to producers. In addition, producers now also earn the further amount captured by area 5. This additional profit does not come free, however. The cost of obtaining it is the cost of the advertising itself. Let us assume that the advertising cost is A dollars. The net welfare gain or loss for society will then be area $5-A$.

One can immediately see that the above case suggests that firms with market power will advertise excessively. For the firm, the net profit gain from spending A on advertising is $1 + 2 + 4 + 5-A$. For society though, the net gain is simply area $5-A$. The former will often be positive even when the latter is negative and firms will advertise too much.

Do matters change if we instead base our surplus calculations on the demand curve D_1, which reflects consumers' preferences after being exposed to advertising? The answer is, a little but not much. If we use the demand curve D_1 consumers still lose areas $1 + 2$ from their initial surplus. However, area 4 is no longer a loss as consumers now value these additional units at least as much as the price P_1 that they are paying for them. From consuming $Q1$ units of the goods, consumers now gain additional surplus represented by areas $6 + 3$. The net change in consumer surplus is then area $3 + 6$ less area $1 + 2$. For the firm though the profit gain is the same, namely the sum of areas $1 + 2 + 4 + 5$.

Thus, using the post-advertising demand curve suggests that advertising may be less hurtful to consumers and more beneficial overall. Ultimately, however, it will still tend to be excessive. To see why, it is easiest if we assume advertising is subject to diminishing returns so that the same expenditure A pushes the demand curve out by smaller and smaller amounts. In the limit, few additional units are sold and areas 3, 4, and 5 become increasingly small. The price effects, though, that permit a rise in the price consumer pays for the initial Q_0 units are first order effects. Even as consumers begin to cut back on their purchases, the firm can still gain area 1 in profit. Yet because this comes at consumers' expense, it does not represent a net social gain that would justify the additional advertising expense.[13]

Our analysis so far has not addressed the competitive impact of persuasive advertising. This is in fact not easy. Clearly, if one firm can use advertising to increase the demand for its product at the expense of a rival, the rival ought to be able to counteract that with advertising of its own. If advertising is truly uninformative and merely an effort in persuasion, this will yield excessive advertising at the industry if not the firm level as a "war of wasteful advertising" breaks out. The view of Bain (1956) and others, though, is that advertising competition is not typically this symmetric. In particular, incumbent firms may have the advantage of spreading the cost of advertising over an existing large volume of output relative to smaller new entrants. This will be especially true if advertising is not continuous but must be purchased in indivisible chunks. However, the competitive impact of advertising may be greatly altered if advertising conveys useful information.

19.4.2   Informative Advertising

There are many ways that advertising can provide useful information. It may for instance inform potential customers what the product does, as in medical products advertising or, relatedly, useful characteristics of the product, as in a digital camera's ability to interact with the Internet or an automobile's safety features. To the extent that such information enhances the demand for the product it works to shift in much the same way as the persuasive advertising illustrated in Figure 19.1.

Informative Advertising and Signaling

One difficulty with understanding advertising as an effort to provide consumers with information is that, as noted earlier, much advertising includes little or no information about the product. Yet even here it is possible that advertising nevertheless conveys useful information as two very influential articles by Nelson (1970, 1974) argue cogently.

Nelson (1970, 1974) began by raising the following question. "What do consumers *know* about a product *before* they purchase it?" More specifically, Nelson (1970, 1974) asked, "Can consumers identify the quality or other characteristics of the product before they try it?" For certain goods, specifically goods such as basic table salt or perhaps sunglasses, the answer is largely, "yes." There is very little variation in table salt and eyeglasses can be tried on and sampled before any purchase is made. These goods are examples of what are often called *search goods* in that the primary objective in shopping for them is to seek out where they are offered at the lowest price. However, Nelson argued that many for other goods,

---

[13]   Fisher and McGowan (1979) criticize the Dixit and Norman (1978) approach by arguing that the truly relevant comparison is one between the pre-advertising equilibrium using pre-advertising tastes and the post-advertising equilibrium using post-advertising tastes. This would mean that area 6 in Figure 19.1 would have to be included in the latter. Because this is not appropriated by the firm, its inclusion could easily yield the contrary result that the firm's advertising is below the socially optimal level. To some extent, however, this introduces the familiar problem of interpersonal comparison of utility levels. Note too that if there are strong scale economies, the increased output that advertising induces may lead to declining cost and price. This would complicate the welfare analysis further.

such as medications and personal computers, the answer was largely, "no." These goods fall into a category that might be called *experience goods*, for which consumers cannot know the quality of the product—especially its quality in terms of the specific setting of a particular consumer—until after they have bought and used the product. However, the manufacturer of the product knows from the start whether it is a high-quality or low-quality product.

Nelson's argument regarding the role of advertising in the case of experience goods is then quite straightforward. Once a consumer buys an experience good, the consumer will learn through use what sort of quality it is. To make matters a little more concrete, we will suppose that if it is a low-quality product, its value to the consumer is zero whereas if it is high-quality, its value is $40. This quality is a random event based on the success of the product's design with the probability being 80 percent that the design will work well. The actual production cost per unit is $16 regardless of the kind of good being produced and the elasticity of demand is constant at $\varepsilon_D = 3$, regardless of the size of the market. As a result, we know from Chapter 4 that the firm's optimal price is (from the Lerner Condition) $P^* = \$24$. Both the firm and consumers have a two-period horizon.

We will assume that the total demand for the product at the profit-maximizing price $P^* = \$24$ depends on the perceived quality of the good. If consumers know nothing more than the fact that there is a 20 percent chance of the product being low-quality, enough are sufficiently risk averse that only X consumers will purchase the product. However, if a product is known to be a high-quality good, demand rises by the proportionate amount α to $(1 + \alpha)X$. Finally, first-time sales only occur in the first period. The only buyers in the second period are those consumers who bought in the first period and, because of their experience, buy again in period 2 if the product is high-quality.

Note that regardless of whether the firm has a high-quality or low-quality product to offer, it will want to sell to as many first-period consumers as possible because it earns a profit of $24–$16 = $8 on every unit. Thus, regardless of its type, the firm would definitely like to claim that it is offering a high-quality product and expand first-period demand from X to $(1 + \alpha)X$. For this reason, just announcing that it is selling a high-quality good will not be enough to distinguish a high-quality firm from a low-quality one in the eyes of consumers.

However, there is one key difference between the two types of firms that may be exploitable. This is the fact that whatever customers it captures in period 1, a firm selling a high-quality good will gain all consumers back in the second period as repeat customers whereas one selling a low-quality product will not. For the moment, let us assume that if a firm adapts a first-period advertising program that costs $A, consumers will regard it as selling a high-quality product. In that case, the firm making a high-quality product has the following choice. If it does not advertise, it will earn profits over the two periods with a present value V^H of:

$$V^H = \$8X + R\$8X = \$8(1 + R)X; \ 0 < R < 1 \tag{19.7}$$

where R is the discount factor discussed in Chapter 2. Alternatively, the firm selling a high-quality good can spend $A on an advertising campaign and earn two-period profit with present value V_A^H:

$$V_A^H = \$8(1 + \alpha)X + \$8R((1 + \alpha)X - A = \$8(1 + R)(1 + \alpha)X - \$A \tag{19.8}$$

Thus, if consumers view advertising as a signal of high quality, a high-quality firm will find it profitable to advertise if $V_A^H > V^H$, i.e., if $\$8(1 + R)\alpha X > \$A$ or:

$$\frac{A}{8\alpha X} < 1 + R \qquad (19.9)$$

Of course, if spending $\$A$ on an advertising campaign induces more first-period consumers to buy then a low-quality firm has some incentive to do this, too. If this turns out to be profitable, if both a low-quality and a high-quality firm gain from first-period advertising, then consumers cannot use the fact of advertising to indicate quality. Thus, we must make sure that this is not the case if advertising is to play a quality-signaling role in equilibrium.

Recall though that a low-quality firm will never make any second-period sales. Hence, it earns a profit of $\$8X$ if it does not advertise and a profit of $\$8(1 + \alpha)X - \$A$ if it does. Therefore, a low-quality firm will not advertise if:

$$\frac{A}{8\alpha X} > 1 \qquad (19.10)$$

Putting conditions (19.9) and (19.10), we have the following result. Consumers will be right to assume that a firm is selling a high-quality product if it is spending an amount $\$A$ on advertising that satisfies:

$$1 + R > \frac{A}{8\alpha X} > 1 \qquad (19.11)$$

Because the discount factor R always exceeds 0, there will always be some value of A—some level of advertising spending—that a high-quality firm can profitably do that would not be profitable for a low-quality firm to imitate. That is, there will always be some value of A that separates a high-quality firm from a low-quality one and that, therefore, consumers can use the level of advertising as an accurate signal indicating they are buying a high-quality product. For instance, suppose that $X =$ one million, $\alpha = 0.25$, and the discount factor is $R = 0.9$ (corresponding to an interest rate of about 11 percent). Then an advertising budget of a little over $10 million (but less than $19 million) will do the trick.

The important point to note about Nelson's (1970, 1974) insight is that the advertising itself does not have to contain much information. It is simply the fact that the firm is spending $\$A$ on advertising that provides the signal. The underlying intuition behind this result should be clear. Advertising is an investment and the payoff to that investment depends critically on the number of repeat customers a firm obtains. It is precisely because high-quality firms win more repeat business that they can afford to make a more sizable advertising investment. In turn, it is precisely the fact that only high-quality firms can afford heavy advertising expenses that consumers can use that expense itself (and not the actual information content) as a signal of high quality.

Nelson's (1970, 1974) insight is important. Yet it is worth noting that Nelson's original work makes some important but not always explicit assumptions and its conclusion does not always survive changes in those assumptions. For example, the illustrative model above assumed that the price-cost margin was the same regardless of product quality, but this might not be the case as Schmalensee (1978) early demonstrated. For example, it may that a high-quality pain reliever can be produced at a cost of twenty cents per dosage while a worthless pain reliever costs only a penny per dose to make. Then a firm offering the worthless painkiller may find that it can earn a very high markup on a very large volume even if no repeat purchases occur—enough to justify a heavy advertising campaign if that is what it takes to persuade first-time consumers that the product is high-quality. Again though, if low-quality firms find it worthwhile to advertise as much as high-quality ones do, then the signaling ability of advertising is lost.

Some further difficulties are also worth noting. Perhaps the most obvious of these is that if advertising expense really is an indicator of product quality, then we should observe firms simply announcing their advertising expenditures. That they do not suggests that the model has some important limitations. In addition, there is the fact that Nelson's (1970, 1974) model really applies best to so-called experience goods. Many well-known goods though such as a Ralph Lauren *Polo* shirt or a pair of Calvin Klein jeans can be tried on and inspected for fit, comfort, and appearance before purchase. Thus, they qualify more as search goods. Nevertheless, both firms advertise these products heavily contrary to what Nelson's (1970, 1974) analysis suggests.

Further, to the extent that Nelson's model applies to experience goods as a general category, it should apply to such goods regardless of the type of buyer. Yet in practice, advertising expenditure-to-sales ratios are markedly higher for experience goods that are marketed to consumers than for those that are marketed instead to other firms, i.e., intermediate or producer goods. Even within the consumer goods category advertising expenditures are also relatively high for search goods as well as experience goods.

Despite its limitations, the possible role for advertising as a quality signal is nevertheless a very important insight. Nelson's (1970, 1974) papers were among the first to raise this issue and, more generally, the problem firms face in trying to communicate credibly with consumers. As a result, this issue has generated much investigative research.[14]

Among the more important papers in this literature are those by Kihlstrom and Riordan (1984) and Milgrom and Roberts (1986). Kihlstrom and Riordan (1984) develop a two-period model in which a firm's advertising alone in the first period determines whether consumers believe the good to be a high- or low-quality product. Given consumer beliefs about quality, prices are then determined in a traditional demand and supply manner. The important result of the Kihlstrom and Riordan (1984) study is that they too find a strong incentive for high-quality producers to lure "repeat buyers" by advertising heavily in the first period, just as Nelson (1970 and 1974) found in his earlier analysis. The contribution of Milgrom and Roberts (1986) is to show that pricing can serve as a quality signal as well as advertising can. If both advertising and pricing can indicate quality though, the extent to which either is used is complicated. Using a high price to signal quality is a cheaper alternative for the firm than advertising, with the result that the Milgrom and Roberts (1986) paper weakens the theoretical link between advertising and product quality. The Milgrom and Roberts signaling model is, however, a monopoly or single firm model. Fluet and Garella (2001) show instead that when the firm competes in price with other firms it may be necessary to use advertising, and not price, to signal quality.

The large volume of papers on the signaling theory of advertising and prices has generated empirical research as well. In general, this research has tried to provide evidence on the extent to which the quality of a good is linked with the manufacturer's advertising-to-sales ratio, or price. Of course, one obvious issue is that the task of empirically measuring quality is far from easy. The truth is that quality has many dimensions and it is not clear how to combine the many dimensions into a single index. Nevertheless, broad rankings of product

---

[14] See also Bagwell and Riordan (1991) and Schwartz and Wilde (1985).

quality are regularly published by Consumers Union. An important early study using this data was done by Reisz (1978) on over 10,000 brands of 685 products. He found, however, only a weak correlation between price and product quality.

If high prices do not necessarily signal high quality, what about advertising? Kotowitz and Mathewson (1986) examined this relationship for both automobiles and whole-life insurance. They did not, however, find evidence that the higher the advertising the better the deal. Similarly, Archibald, Haulman, and Moody (1983) examined running shoes and again found that neither price nor advertising levels for 187 brands were strongly correlated with the quality rankings, which were published in the magazine *Runner's World*. However, these authors did find that the magazine's quality ratings, once publicized and circulated, were very positively correlated with the extent of advertising done *after* those rankings were published. Firms with a high ranking were anxious to let consumers know this fact, while those with a low ranking were less interested in displaying their product's deficiencies.[15]

A study of 196 different industries by Caves and Green (1996) finds few discernible tendencies in the relationship between advertising and brand quality. For many industries, these authors find that the quality-advertising expenditure correlation approaches a negative one—the exact opposite of Nelson's prediction. They do, however, find a positive relationship between advertising and quality in the case of new or innovative goods. They also find a weaker but still positive correlation between advertising and the quality of those goods in their sample that might be called "experience goods." The Caves and Green evidence on Nelson's hypothesis may then be best described as mixed.

Non-Informative Informative Advertising

As noted above, an attractive feature of the signaling view of advertising is that the advertising itself does not need to include any obvious or specific information. It is the fact of advertising itself that communicates product quality. This part of the theory definitely does find confirmation in the data. Much advertising seems to leave out important information such as price, quality of materials used, and so on. An alternative approach to the information content of advertising that offers a different explanation for this lack of advertising content has been offered by Anderson and Renault (2006). We explore their argument briefly, here.

The Anderson and Renault (2006) model starts by recognizing that once the consumer has traveled to a particular store, that travel cost is sunk. This can lead to a so-called "hold-up" problem for consumers. Recall the 1990s fad of Beanie Babies. Suppose that different consumers value the Beanie Babies differently. Some are willing to pay $25 for *Crunch the Shark* whereas others do not value *Crunch* at all. Instead, they prefer *Chilly the Polar Bear*. If there are any transport costs, a retailer that advertises that it is selling *Crunch the Shark* will only attract the first group. Hence, the dealer may prefer to advertise that it has Beanie Babies in general and suppress the information that its inventory is *Crunch* in particular. The retailer knows—and consumers know that it knows—that anyone coming to the store and asking for *Crunch the Shark* values *Crunch* at $25. Because the transport cost is sunk at that point, the retailer will have a strong incentive to "hold up" consumers and charge them the full $25—ultimately deterring such buyers from responding to an ad.

Somewhat more formally, let there be three consumer types, 1, 2, and 3, and let us now just consider a relatively generic good called widgets that comes in three colors, red, blue,

---

[15]   Note that *Runner's World* allows manufacturers to quote their rankings in advertisements.

and yellow. Consumer type 1 values red widgets at $40, yellow widgets at $20, and blue widgets at $15. Type 2 values red widgets at $15, yellow widgets at $40, and blue widgets at $20. For type 3, the respective valuations are $20, $15, and $40. The willingness to pay values for each consumer (which all consumers know) are shown in the Table 19.1 below.

We assume that each consumer also incurs a transport cost of $5.01 to visit the store. Once a consumer actually visits a store, that transport cost is sunk. In the absence of knowledge of a store's actual stock, consumers rightfully believe that a store is equally likely to have either red, yellow, or blue widgets. Hence, if consumers know only that a store has widgets, they infer a probability of one-third that the store has widgets of any specific color. To keep things really simple, we also assume that the store incurs zero cost per widget.

Consider two advertising strategies for a store that has only red widgets. The store can advertise that it has red widgets or the store can advertise simply that it has widgets. Which strategy will the store prefer? First observe that the store will never set a widget price below $15, the minimum valuation of any consumer. Now consider the first strategy of advertising that the store has only red widgets. If the retailer does this, consumer types 2 and 3 will not come to the store. The $5.01 in transport cost will mean that the effective price for them will never be less than $20.01. So, it is not worthwhile for either of these two types to come. Of course, the store knows this, too. So, if it advertises its "Red Widgets" alone, it knows that the only buyers who show up are type 1 consumers. Because, for these consumers, the $5.01 in transport cost is a sunk cost once they are at the store, the owner can then charge them their full willingness-to-pay of $40 for the widgets. Foreseeing this outcome, type 1 consumers will not respond to a red widget advertisement either. Advertising that the store only has red widgets will therefore not attract customers at all.

However, if the shop announces that it simply has widgets in general, consumers can reason as follows. Faced with a crowd of all consumer types but not knowing who is who, the shopkeeper will set a price of $15 per widget. This will permit the store to sell one (red) widget to each type and earn a profit of $45 from each threesome rather than set a price of $40 and sell only to one type or a price of $20 and sell to types 1 and 3 (each of which yields profit of $40 per threesome). Moreover, because consumers infer that the probability associated with each color is one-third, all three types will in fact respond to the ad by showing up at the store knowing that when this happens, the store owner will keep the price at $15. Consumer i will work out that for a price of $15 and a transport cost of $5.01, consumer i will receive either a red, yellow, or blue widget (each with probability 0.3333) whose value therefore is: $0.3333(\$40 + \$20 + 15) = \$25$, implying a net value of $5 regardless of what consumer i's most preferred type is.

There are a number of features of the foregoing outcome worth noting. First, the store suppresses some information in its advertising. Specifically, it does not reveal that its inventory is just red widgets. The store also does not need to mention the price in its ads. Consumers can work out that the profit-maximizing price to set is $15. It is the presence

Table 19.1   Consumer type

		Consumer 1	Consumer 2	Consumer 3
Widget Type	Red	$40	$15	$20
	Yellow	$20	$40	$15
	Blue	$15	$20	$40

of a variety of consumer types—due to precisely the vagueness of the advertisement—that supports this outcome. Because some of the consumers attracted to the store do not value red widgets very highly, the storeowner is motivated to keep the price low. We have a market outcome in which advertising deliberately does not mention either the specific attributes of the product for sale or its price.

Perhaps most surprising of all, the suppression of this informational content can raise welfare. To see this, observe that advertising red widgets led to a complete breakdown of the market whereas advertising widgets in general leads to trades from which everyone potentially can gain.[16] In other words, a law requiring full disclosure by the retailer would make things worse.

Ellison and Ellison (2005) present a somewhat related argument regarding search engines on the web. In principle, search engines increase the competitive pressure on Internet firms. Moreover, the search engine can claim for itself some of the profit that would have gone to the firm in return for providing consumers with the relevant price information. Thus, an e-commerce company has some reason to thwart the search engine even though it may like the fact that the search engine or shopbot brings customers to its site. It can do this in a variety of ways. For example, it can list a low product price that the search engine sees but charge a very high transport price that the search engine does not see, or similarly offer only very slow delivery. Again, once the consumer has invested in the search cost and arrived at the firm's website, the firm may find that it can charge the consumer a very high price for the product that the consumer really wants, e.g., one with quick delivery. Here again, e-tailers are happy to list some information to entice the search engine but simultaneously to keep too much information from being revealed.

The point is then that advertising can play a useful role even when its information content is limited. In fact, it can do so even when firms deliberately suppress or obscure some of the information content. Such strategic choices enable firms to attract—and to serve—a wider range of customers than they would get if they offered complete information, and this may be necessary for the market to function at all.

Advertising, Information, and Price Competition

While much advertising may contain little concrete information, there is also no denying that a good bit of advertising *is* informative. Newspapers and magazines are filled with ads announcing sales, television commercials for cars typically mention explicit financing/lease terms and fuel mileage, airlines' and hotels' Internet spots mention availability and price, and this list does not even include the many informative advertisements in trade magazines. Moreover, even advertisements that do not include such explicit information serve the purpose of making the consumer aware of the product. As a result, advertising can be directly informative to consumers about the existence and features of alternative goods. Because it is difficult for a seller to sell a product at a high price when consumers are aware that a perfect or at least a good substitute may be available, truly informative advertising can be a highly useful and pro-consumer force that works to intensify market competition.

To see formally how advertising can intensify price compeition we consider the Grossmand and Shapiro (1984) reworking of the spatial Bertrand model of Chapter 10. Let there

---

[16] Not counting (sunk) transport costs, all consumers and the seller are better off in the limited information equilibrium. Including sunk costs, type 2 consumers are (trivially) worse off but the gains for all other participants are enough that these consumers could be compensated while others would still be better off.

be two rival firms each located at either end of a unit long segment with a uniformly distributed population of N potential consumers. Each consumer will buy at most one unit of the good if their willingness to pay V exceeds the lowest price p_i plus transport cost t (per unit of distance) that they must pay to obtain it and if they know of that purchasing opportunity. Unlike that earlier model, however, we will assume that such knowledge is not complete. In particular, for each firm there is a fraction of the N consumers s_i who are only partially informed in that they know only of firm i's product. There is also a fraction S_{ij} of fully informed consumers that knows of both products. Clearly, this latter fraction is the same for both firms, i.e., $S_{12} = S_{21}$. For simplicity, we will extend this symmetry to the fraction that knows only of one firm's product so that we also have: $s_1 = s_2$. In addition, we note the condition that $0 < s_i + S_{ij} \leq 1$, which implies also that $0 < s_j \leq 1$ and $0 < S_{ij} \leq 1$, as well as the fact that if $s_i(S_{ij}) = 1$, then $S_{ij}(s_i) = 0$. In other words, because the shares of either partially or fully informed consumers can never be negative, if one is unity the other must be zero. The $s_i N$ partially informed consumers and the $S_{ij} N$ fully informed consumers are also assumed to be uniformly distributed over the interval separating the two firms. Finally, each firm has a constant marginal cost c per unit.

We will assume that each consumer's willingness to pay V for the most preferred version of the good is reasonably high such that each firm has a captive demand of $s_i N$ from its partially informed consumer base. These consumers will buy from their preferred retailer even if it does not have the lowest (net-of-travel-cost) price. However, the firm also confronts a group of $S_{ij} N$ fully informed consumers who will only buy from the firm with the lowest price plus transport cost. We know from our work in Chapter 10 that for this group, the marginal consumer who is just indifferent between buying from either firm 1 or firm 2, has location (measuring from left (west) to right (east)) of $x^M = \dfrac{p_2 - p_1 + t}{2t}$. Hence, for firm 1 located at the left or western end of the segment, total demand is given by:

$$q_1 = s_1 N + S_{12} N \left(\frac{p_2 - p_1 + t}{2t} \right) \tag{19.12}$$

Hence, firm 1's inverse demand curve is given by:

$$p_1 = \left(\frac{s_1}{S_{12}} \right) 2t + p_2 + t - \left(\frac{2t}{S_{12} N} \right) q_1 \tag{19.13}$$

It follows that firm 1's marginal revenue curve is:

$$MR_1 = \left(\frac{s_1}{S_{12}} \right) 2t + p_2 + t - \left(\frac{4t}{S_{12} N} \right) q_1 \tag{19.14}$$

Equating MR_1 with the firm 1's marginal cost c and solving for firm 1's optimal output conditional on p_2 yields:

$$q_1^* = \left(\frac{s_1}{2} \right) N + \left(\frac{S_{12}}{4t} \right) N(p_2 + t - c) \tag{19.15}$$

Substituting the above result into equation (19.13) then yields firm 1's best response function to any price p_2 set by its rival:

$$p_1^* = \frac{c}{2} + \left[\left(\frac{s_1}{S_{12}} \right) + \left(\frac{1}{2} \right) \right] t + \frac{p_2}{2} \tag{19.16}$$

Hence, our symmetry assumption that $p_1^* = p_2^*$ implies that the equilibrium price p for both goods will be:

$$p = c + \left(\frac{2s_1 + S_{12}}{S_{12}} \right) t \tag{19.17}$$

It is easy to verify that when the entire market is fully informed so that $S_{12} = 1$ and $s_1 = s_2 = 0$, equation (19.17) implies an equilibrium price of $p = c + t$, exactly as found in Chapter 10. It is equally easy to see that as S_{12} falls below this value, the equilibrium price rises.[17] The underlying intuition is also straightforward. Firms compete for the fully informed consumers but charge the same mill price to all. As more consumers become fully informed, each firm has a greater incentive to lower its price a bit and win more of this larger market share. Hence, the greater the proportion of potential consumers who know of both products and can therefore do comparison shopping, the more intense the price competition grows.

Advertising is of course a way for firms to inform consumers of their products. Indeed, each firm must advertise if it is to reach any consumers at all. Therein lies the rub. Each firm needs to advertise if any consumers are to be informed either partially or fully. Yet neither firm can be sure that its advertisements will simply reach those consumers who are unaware of the rival's products. To the contrary, the greater the effort each makes to reach some consumers, the more likely it becomes that an important segment of the market is aware of both goods and it is competition over that segment that drives the equilibrium price progressively lower.

In the Appendix, we present a simple version of the foregoing model in which firms choose their advertising effort as reflected in the fraction of consumers they try to reach as well as select their profit-maximizing price. The general point should be clear, though. To the extent that advertising does provide consumers with information about alternative products, it tends to intensify price competition to the benefit of the consumer. Note, however, that this does not mean that the market becomes more competitively structured or that more firms enter the market. Quite to the contrary, the intensified price competition that advertising induces can easily serve to limit entry and to foster a more concentrated industry.

While we noted the potentially negative anti-competitive effects that early researchers such as Bain (1956) found, the fact is that there is much empirical evidence to support the view that advertising prices and retail locations intensifies price competition. Early on, Telser (1964) showed that greater advertising intensity was associated with more volatility in market shares, leading him to conclude that advertising promoted competition. More explicitly, Benham (1972) showed that the average price of eyeglasses was significantly

---

[17]   If S_{12} gets very small, the price is limited by consumers' maximum willingness to pay V. The Grossman-Shapiro (1984) is just one model of advertising and consumer search. Others include: Stigler (1968), Butters (1977), and Clark and Horstmann (2005).

higher in states where advertising the prices and retail locations of opticians' services was prohibited. Similar price effects when advertising is restricted were found by Cady (1976) in the market for prescription drugs. [See Milyo and Waldfoget (1995) for related evidence from the retail liquor industry.]

Glazer's (1981) study of the New York City newspaper strike provides three connected but chronologically distinct bits of the pro-competitive role of advertising. That strike, which ran for nearly three months starting in August, 1978 shut down each of the three major New York City newspapers, *The New York Times*, *The New York Post*, and *The Daily News*, and thereby greatly reduced the access that city residents had to any advertising of supermarket food prices. However, within a few weeks of the strike's beginning, a number of interim papers emerged that potentially filled this informative role, although

Reality Checkpoint
Everyday Lowe's Prices

Lowe's is the second biggest home improvement retailer in North America and one of the country's fifty largest firms with annual revenues of nearly $50 billion. Even so, it lags well beyond its main rival, Home Depot, whose revenues are roughly twice as large. Home Depot has traditionally been seen as having consistently lower prices and better services.

These competitive pressures have prompted Lowe's to move away from a strategy of typically setting high prices but periodically holding sales with steep discounts to an Everyday Low Pricing (EDLP) strategy that sets a low price continuously. The EDLP approach was pioneered by Wal-Mart and offers a number of advantages in that it enables retailers to reduce inventory costs, better coordinate supply chains, and reduce the risk of stock shortages by smoothing the demand variability induced by frequent sales. On the other hand, the former high-low pricing strategy permits the revenue gains of price discrimination. In addition, holding sales on specific items from time to time attracts consumers to a store where they may see—and purchase—items that are not on sale.

To improve service, Lowe's introduced a web-based tool called My Lowe's. This permits individuals to set up individualized histories of what they have previously bought at Lowe's. In turn, this makes it easier for replacements and repairs to match original models, and permits customers to upload photographs and then use computer visualization techniques to see the effects of different colors, materials, and designs on the final outcome of a home improvement project. Ultimately, the My Lowe's site became accessible via a mobile app, as well.

To get the word out about its pricing and new service, Lowe's launched an expensive new advertising campaign, "Never Stop Improving," stressing the need for continued home modifications over a typical family's lifespan and encouraging consumers to establish the My Lowe's profiles. This suggests that aggressive advertising is complementary to low prices, and that both reflect a move towards more intense competition. Such increased competitive intensity may have been the result of the steep drop in construction activity and therefore the drop in demand for home improvement projects in the wake of the deep recession that began in late 2007.

Source: Associated Press, "Lowe's Says Price Cuts Helped Lift Its Profit," *New York Times*, February 26, 2013 p. C4.

their circulation was much smaller. These events make for a natural comparison with nearby Nassau County on Long Island, which suffered no real break in the publication of its local newspapers. Glazer (1981) therefore compares the food prices in Queens (one of the New York's five boroughs) with those in neighboring Nassau county over each of three periods: 1) the early part of the strike when Queens residents had little food price information; 2) the latter part of the strike when Queens residents had some information from interim papers; and 3) the post-strike period when Queens residents were once again presumably as well informed about local food prices as were residents in neighboring Nassau. The basic results were that food prices rose about 3.4 percent *more* in Queens during the first period; rose no further during the second period; and then rose 8 percent *less* than Nassau prices in the last period. In other words, the basic pattern was that Queens' food prices became more competitively priced relative to Nassau prices the more advertising information Queens residents had.

More recently, two closely related papers by Slade (1995) and Pinkse and Slade (2007) analyze the joint advertising and pricing decisions of rival supermarket firms. Focusing on saltine crackers, Slade (1995) finds that each supermarket tends to advertise more when its rivals raise their price and, conversely, that each tends to cut its price in response to a rise in rivals' advertising. Both effects suggest that advertising fosters price competition. Working with the same data, Pinkse and Slade (2007) find that the advertising effort is complementary to price reductions, i.e., firms advertise more heavily to spread the word about a recent reduction in price. This too suggests a pro-competitive effect for advertising although the longer-run dynamics are more complicated as rivals respond to these strategic choices. Relatedly, Nevo (2001) shows that advertising plays a key competitive role in the ready-to-eat breakfast cereal market.

19.5   ADVERTISING: COMPLEMENTS, COORDINATION, AND INDUSTRY DYNAMICS

In this section we offer some further considerations regarding how advertising works and its impact on industry outcomes. One possibility—raised early by Stigler and Becker (1977) but presented more formally by Becker and Murphy (1993)—is that advertising works because consumers value it as a complement to the advertised good. An analogy that Becker and Murphy (1993) use is that advertising is much like the television or newspaper coverage of a local sports team. The report of a game's outcome and recap of the key events may neither change consumers' tastes, as in the persuasive view, nor add useful information (especially to those who were at the game), as in the informative view. Nevertheless, such coverage raises consumer interest in and demand for attending team games.

In the Becker and Murphy (1993) view, advertising can work in this same complementary way to raise the demand for the advertised good. Of course, informative advertising can act as a complement as well. The value of the Becker and Murphy (1993) approach is that this conceptualization makes it easy—at least in theory—to work out whether or not advertising is excessive without any need to worry about whether to use pre- or post-advertising demand curves. The question boils down to whether the extra value that advertising brings to consumers plus the extra profit it brings to producers (all at the margin) covers the advertising marginal cost. In this respect, it is entirely possible that advertising may work to raise the elasticity of the firm's demand. If so, then as the total amount of the advertised good that is sold rises, the price must fall because $(p-c)/p = 1/\varepsilon_P$ is a necessary condition for profit maximization. In turn, Becker and Murphy show that this implies there will be *too little* advertising as it means that the advertiser will not take the greater product value that consumers get from the product into account in deciding how much advertising to do.

Pastine and Pastine (2002) offer a different role for advertising in markets where each consumer wants to purchase the same brand as most other consumers. In such markets, there are network effects (see Chapter 22) that reflect an externality on the demand side—the more people that buy a specific brand, the more valuable that brand is to each consumer. Network markets are typically characterized by multiple equilibria and some equilibria—often those in which all or virtually all consumers purchase the same brand—raise welfare higher than other equilibria. In their model then advertising plays a useful, welfare-enhancing role even though it does not change consumer tastes, provide information, or serve as a complement to the good itself. Instead, advertising is helpful because it can serve as a device for coordinating consumer purchasing decisions. With each consumer forming the expectation that the brand other consumers will buy will be the one that is most heavily advertised, that expectation can become self-fulfilling and therefore rational. On the supplier side, Pastine and Pastine (2002) assume a duopoly model in which each firm chooses its advertising level for two periods with one firm choosing in period t and the rival choosing in period $t + 1$. This means that in any specific period, one firm's advertising is pre-set while the rival gets to re-set its choice from two periods earlier. The firm that is free to choose its advertising in any period then has an incentive to out-advertise its rival precisely because consumers are using that advertising to coordinate their decisions—thereby reinforcing the self-fulfilling expectational equilibrium. This leads to interesting dynamics over time as an advertising war breaks out in which each firm increases its advertising every two periods until a maximum is reached. At that point it becomes worthwhile to reduce the advertising effort back to a low level from which the process can start all over again. The model also helps to explain why much advertising is directed at young people for whom peer pressure and "being in" may be most important.

Finally, a recent article by Dinlersoz and Yorukoglu (2012) builds on the point made at the beginning of this chapter that breakthroughs in information technology and the ability to reach consumers with advertising can have a dramatic effect on the evolution of an industry. In their model, firms advertise prices and more efficient firms can advertise lower prices. As a result, more efficient firms grow in size and less efficient firms shrink and exit. (Firm growth is therefore *not* independent of firm size in contrast to the assumption of the Gibrat process discussed in Chapter 12.) Because consumers tend to repurchase from firms from which they recently bought, relatively more efficient firms will also tend to win more repeat sales and therefore become relatively larger firms over time. Hence, their model predicts a positive relation between a firm's advertising effort and its size as noted earlier in this chapter. More importantly, when there is a decline in the cost of advertising, e.g., the information revolution reflected in the rapid extension of the Internet, information dissemination will accelerate to the benefit of the most efficient firms with the result that concentration will increase even as price competition intensifies. Dinlersoz and Yorukoglu (2012) present evidence that this is exactly what has happened in industries with significant web-based sales, such as bookstores, camera and photo stores, and travel agents. Apart from providing a rich description of market evolution, the Dinlersoz and Yorukoglu (2012) study serves again to remind us that market structure is endogenous and not necessarily a good proxy for the intensity of price competition.[18]

19.6   EMPIRICAL APPLICATION: ADVERTISING, INFORMATION, AND PRESTIGE

There has been considerable debate over the role that advertising plays in influencing consumer demand. Advertising could offer basic information, signal quality, or provide a complementary aspect of social status or prestige to the advertised product. While important insights come from exploring each of these approaches, the question of advertising's actual role may be ultimately an empirical one. It is difficult, however, to come up with good clean empirical evidence that identifies the nature of advertising's role. A paper by Daniel Ackerberg (2001), though, does offer some interesting and promising results.

Ackerberg's (2001) paper studies the introduction of a new yogurt product by Yoplait, the second largest yogurt firm in the United States. In April of 1987, the company introduced *Yoplait 150* as its first entry into the low-calorie and low-fat yogurt product line. This period falls within the time frame of data collected by the A. C. Nielsen Co. for just under 2,000 households split roughly evenly between Sioux Falls, South Dakota and Springfield, Missouri. That data included scanner readings used to monitor the shopping trips and purchases of these households. It also included recordings from TV meters installed in the consumers' homes that allowed Nielsen to monitor their television viewing and, hence, their exposure to *Yoplait 150* advertising over the twelve months starting three months after the *Yoplait 150* introduction, i.e., from July of 1987 to July of 1988. Thus, the data are a panel of observations covering consumers in two cities at weekly intervals over a one-year period.

Ackerberg (2001) considers two broad effects that advertising could have. The first of these is an information effect. Advertising may either inform consumers of the good's existence, as in Grossman and Shapiro (1984), or signal quality or other information about the product's attributes, as in Nelson (1970) and Kihlstrom and Riordan (1984). In contrast, the Becker and Murphy (1993) model of complementary advertising and the advertising as persuasion models suggest that the role of advertising is not informative but instead one that confers a separate recognition or prestige effect of its own. Ackerberg (2001) argues that if advertising plays an informational role then it should have little effect on experienced consumers. This is particularly the case if the relevant information is simply about the existence and availability of the good. Once a consumer has bought it, they presumably know these facts so further advertising exposure will have no impact on them if, of course, this is the way advertising works.

This is also true but to a lesser extent if the information is about the quality of the product. *Yoplait 150*, for example, came out in many different flavors. It may take consumers a few tries to determine whether there is a flavor that they really like or not. In this case, advertising about alternative flavors will still have some effect on consumers over time,

---

[18]   Bagwell and Ramey (1994) derive a similar outcome when the demand-raising effects of advertising permit scale economies and so lower prices even as concentration rises. All these studies on advertising and industry dynamics recall the critical work of Sutton (1991).

but one that should definitely diminish as they become more experienced with the product. However, if advertising confers a recognition effect then there should be little distinction between its impact on experienced and inexperienced consumers. The complementary gains in consuming a well-recognized product should, on average, be the same whether a consumer is enjoying it for the first time or the tenth.

Ackerberg (2001) hopes to identify the role of advertising by distinguishing between its effects on experienced and inexperienced buyers. Two preliminary ordinary least squares (OLS) regressions suggest that this strategy may work. In these regressions, he looks at the total *Yoplait 150* purchases over specific days in his sample and then divides these into two types. In one group are the sales that reflect first-time purchases. In the other group, are the sales that reflect repeat purchases, each measured as a fraction of the number of shopping trips that day. Ackerberg (2001) then creates separate time series of first-time sales and repeat sales on specific market days over the twelve-month period. For each of those making either a first or a repeat purchase, Ackerberg (2001) also has data on the average *Yoplait 150* price for each market day (PRICE), and, for each purchase, the number of *Yoplait 150* TV ads the buyer was exposed to in the last four days (ADS). Because *Yoplait 150* generally sold much better in Springfield, he also includes a dummy variable (MARKET) equal to 1 if the data are from Springfield but 0 if they are from Sioux Falls. These preliminary results are shown in Table 19.2 below:

Observe first that the price effects are negative and statistically significant. Likewise, there is clearly a stronger preference for *Yoplait 150* in Springfield than there is in Sioux Falls. Of most importance, however, is the differential effect of advertising on the two types of expenditures. Recent advertising exposure has a far greater positive effect on first-time buyers of *Yoplait 150*. In fact, the effect on repeat purchases is not statistically significant from zero. Thus, this evidence gives rough support to the idea that advertising provides information in that it has little effect on experienced consumers who, presumably already know of the existence and quality (taste) of *Yoplait 150*.

To get a deeper understanding of the role that advertising plays, Ackerberg (2001) exploits more fully the panel nature of his data and the variation among consumers that this implies. His approach, with some simplification, is to hypothesize that the propensity of consumer i in period t to purchase *Yoplait 150* (y_{it}^*) is a linear function of k different exogenous variables X_{it} and a random factor ε_{it}. That is

$$y_{it}^* = \sum_{j=1}^{k} \beta_j X_{jit} + \varepsilon_{it} \tag{19.18}$$

Table 19.2   Preliminary results

| Independent Variables | Dependent Variable | | | |
| | Initial Purchases | | Repeat Purchases | |
	Coefficient	Std. Error	Coefficient	Std. Error
PRICE	−0.038	(0.013)*	−0.029	(0.014)*
ADS	0.030	(0.015)*	0.014	(0.017)
MARKET	0.002	(0.001)*	0.006	(0.001)*

*Indicates significant at the 5 percent level.

However, one does not observe y_{it}^* directly. All one actually observes is whether consumer i at time t buys *Yoplait 150* ($Y_{it} = 1$) or does not ($Y_{it} = 0$). The standard assumption in this case then is that we observe $Y_{it} = 1$, when $y_{it}^* \geq 0$, and $Y_{it} = 0$ when $y_{it}^* < 0$. This implies that the probability of observing a purchase $Y_{it} = 1$ is given by

$$\text{Prob}(Y_{it} = 1) = \text{Prob}\left[\sum_{j=1}^{k} \beta_j x_{jit} + \varepsilon_{it} \geq 0 \right]$$

$$= \text{Prob}\left[\varepsilon_{it} > -\left(\sum_{j=1}^{k} \beta_j x_{jit} \right) \right] = 1 - F\left[-\left(\sum_{j=1}^{k} \beta_j x_{jit} \right) \right] \qquad (19.19)$$

where $F()$ is the cumulative distribution of ε_{it}. It is convenient to assume that $F()$ has a symmetric distribution so that $1 - F(-Z_{it}) = F(Z_{it})$. Then we have

$$\text{Prob}(Y_{it} = 1) = F\left(\sum_{j=1}^{k} \beta_j x_{jit} \right) \qquad (19.20)$$

Clearly, much depends on the choice of the distribution of the random term ε_{it}. If ε_{it} is assumed to be distributed normally[19] one gets the Probit estimation procedure. A popular alternative is to assume instead that ε_{it} has a logistic cumulative distribution in which case:

$$F(Z_{it}) = \frac{e^{Z_{it}}}{1 + e^{Z_{it}}} \qquad (19.21)$$

The reason for the popularity of this distribution is that this transformation implies that:

$$\ln\left[\frac{F(Z_{it})}{1 - F(Z_{it})} \right] = Z_{it}$$

In other words,

$$\ln\left[\frac{F\left(\sum_{j=1}^{k} \beta_j x_{jit} \right)}{1 - F\left(\sum_{j=1}^{k} \beta_j x_{jit} \right)} \right] = \ln \frac{\text{Prob}(Y_{it} = 1)}{\text{Prob}(Y_{it} = 0)} = \sum_{j=1}^{k} \beta_j x_{jit} \qquad (19.22)$$

The ratio of the probability $Y_{it} = 1$ to the probability that $Y_{it} = 0$ is known as the odds ratio. By assuming a logistic distribution for ε_{it}, the logit estimation procedure assumes that the log of the odds ratio is a linear function of the key exogenous variables. This is a very convenient feature for estimation purposes.

Ackerberg (2001) presents a number of regressions based on the above logit procedure. The independent variables X_{it} include: 1) the amount (in time) of *Yoplait 150* advertising the household has seen up to that time divided by the total time spent watching television,

---

[19]   This assumption was made in the empirical applications in Chapters 13 and 19.

ADS; 2) the price of *Yoplait 150* in the relevant market at that time, OWN PRICE; 3) a comparable measure of the average competitor's price, RIVAL PRICE; 4) the number of times (possibly zero) the household had purchased *Yoplait 150* previous to that time, NUMBER PREV; and 5) the key 1,0 variable indicating whether the household had any previous purchases of *Yoplait 150*, EXPERIENCED or INEXPERIENCED.[20] Some of his main results are summarized in Table 19.3 below.

Consider the first regression results. Advertising has an important impact, but only for those who have not yet tried the new product. Again, this implies that advertising mostly plays an informative role. Specifically, the coefficient on the interactive term, ADS*EXPERIENCED captures the impact of advertising on consumers who know the quality of *Yoplait 150* and therefore should reflect only complementary prestige or recognition effects. This coefficient is not statistically different from zero. In contrast, the coefficient on ADS*INEXPERIENCED reflects both prestige and information effects. It *is* statistically different from zero and this suggests that the information effect is behind this because our estimate of prestige effects is not distinct from zero.[21]

The second regression tries to discriminate more between the two types of information that advertising provides. In the first regression, the assumption is that a household becomes fully informed after just one purchase of *Yoplait 150*. This would likely be the case if the important information provided by advertising were simply knowledge of the good's existence and availability. Once a household has bought the product, it presumably knows these features of the product. Learning brand characteristics such as taste, calories, and so on may take a little longer and may be facilitated by continuing advertisements. For this reason, the regression includes ADS alone as an independent regressor, but then also includes this variable in an interaction term with NUMBER PREV, the number of prior purchase of the *Yoplait 150*. The idea is that the pure effect of advertising measured by ADS will decline as the consumer's experience grows. The more rapidly this decline occurs, the more likely it

Table 19.3   Effect of advertising in the low-fat yogurt market dependent variable: purchase (or not) of *yoplait 150* by household *i* at time *t*

Independent Variable	Coefficient	Std. Error	Coefficient	Std. Error
ADS*INEXPERIENCED	2.306	(0.776)*	—	—
ADS*EXPERIENCED	0.433	(1.212)	—	—
ADS	—	—	2.014	(0.790)*
ADS*(NUMBER PREV)	—	—	−0.356	(0.108)*
NUMBER PREV	−0.267	(0.093)*	−0.270	(0.092)*
(NUMBER PREV)^2	0.009	(0.001)*	−0.001	(0.001)
OWN PRICE	−5.584	(0.350)*	−5.616	(0.356)*
RIVAL PRICE	0.761	(0.217)*	0.768	(0.219)*

*Indicates significant at the five percent level.

[20]   Household size and income and, as before, a market dummy for Springfield households were also included. Ackerberg (2001) also includes a random, household-specific intercept to control for household heterogeneity in time-persistent preferences for the product.

[21]   To be precise, the difference between the two coefficients, ADS*INEXPERIENCED and ADS*EXPERIENCED is a direct estimate of the pure information effects. Standard techniques yield a t-statistic for this difference of about 1.5.

is that the primary information obtained from advertising is existence and availability. The more slowly it declines, the more likely that the information provided concerns product attributes that take time to learn. Sure enough, the coefficient on ADS*(NUMBER PREV) is negative but a relatively small −0.36. This implies that it takes six or seven purchases of *Yoplait 150* before the advertising information is no longer useful. As noted, this implies that part of the information advertising provides concerns product attributes.

Are these coefficient estimates sensible? It is difficult to say immediately because the coefficients in the logit model relate to the effect of advertising on the *probability* of purchase and not directly to demand. However, there are some aspects of the results that give us confidence in the findings. First, in each case, the price of *Yoplait 150* had a strong negative impact and the rival's price a strong positive effect on a household's purchase decision. Second, one can simulate the model to see what overall demand features the price and advertising coefficients imply. When Ackerberg (2001) conducts such simulations with the full model he finds that, taken at the mean, the own-price elasticity of demand is 2.8—a fairly elastic response. He also finds that the elasticity of demand with respect to advertising is 0.15. Taken together, the advertising and price elasticities would imply, by virtue of the Dorfman-Steiner condition, an advertising-to-sales ratio of $0.15/2.8 = 0.054$ or 5.4 percent. This is a quite reasonable result given that Yoplait's overall advertising-to-sales ratio was reported at the time to be about 7 percent. Overall, then, Ackerberg's (2001) findings seem to be quite plausible.

In short, the evidence from Ackerberg (2001) is that the primary role of advertising is to provide consumers with information. Some of this information is simply making consumers aware of the product's availability, but some of it concerns educating consumers about the product's key features. There is little evidence that in this particular market advertising provides prestige or complementary effects. The data are based, however, on a perishable consumer food product purchased with some frequency. Whether it applies to other more durable consumer goods, or to goods such as medications that consumers buy less frequently, merits further investigation.

Summary

Advertising plays a role in informing consumers of the availability of a product, its brand image, and sometimes product attributes. This role can be played even when the actual information content of the advertising message is low. When consumers are uncertain about product quality, the very fact that a product is advertised heavily may convey information. When advertising informs consumers of the availability of substitute products, it also tends to increase price competition. In competing for customers, advertising in equilibrium may be socially wasteful or excessive if each firm spends substantial but mutually offsetting amounts that, on net, leaves customer patronage unchanged.

However, we should not infer that advertising is socially excessive from the fact that consumers often receive advertising at zero cost. Advertising may be viewed as a complement to the product advertised. As with any complement, an increase in the supply of advertising raises the demand for the promoted product. In this view, what really matters is the total price that consumers pay for the product and the advertising together. It is important, however, to recognize as well the competition-enhancing effects of advertising in assessing its welfare effects.

There is considerable empirical evidence that advertising does in fact provide information to consumers—especially for search goods. Nevertheless, we should not necessarily take this to imply that advertising will foster less concentrated industries. We should in fact expect more advertising by firms with market power and also by firms with low costs. In fact, the more intense competition that advertising may induce can serve to deter entry and to enable more efficient firms to grow large so that industrial concentration rises.

Problems

1. Suppose that the demand for a new wrinkle cream is described by a nonlinear demand function $Q(P, A) = P^{-1/2}A^{1/4}$. Show that the price elasticity of demand is $\eta P = 1/2$ and that the advertising elasticity of demand is $\eta A = 1/4$. What do you predict the advertising-to-sales ratio would be in this industry? Does it depend on how costly it is to advertise for this product?

2. A firm has developed a new product for which it has a registered trademark. The firm's market research department has estimated that the demand for this product is $Q(P, A) = 11,600 - 1,000P + 20A^{1/2}$ where Q is annual output, P is the price, and A the annual expenditure for advertising. The total cost of producing the new good is $C(Q) = .001Q^2 + 4Q$. The unit cost of advertising is constant at $m = 1$.

   a. Calculate the optimal output level Q^*, price P^*, and advertising level A^* for the firm.

   b. What is firm profit if it follows this optimal strategy?

   c. What is consumer surplus if the firm adopts this strategy?

3. Imagine that there are 1,000 consumers. For each consumer, the willingness to pay for a widget is distributed uniformly over the interval [0,1] depending on the style of the widget. A retailer with a particular style of the good knows this distribution. Its costs are zero. Consumers do not know the style that the retailer has stocked and each incur a transport or search cost of $T = 0.125$. Once this cost is incurred it is sunk. At that point, a consumer in the retailer's store will purchase the product so long as the consumer's valuation is greater than or equal to the price charged by the retailer.

   a. Show that facing a random selection of customers, the retailer's profit maximizing price is $p = 0.5$.

   b. Show that with $T = 0.125$, all consumers will come to shop expecting a price of 0.5. What would happen if $T = 0.15$?

4. Suppose that the retailer in question 3 could communicate in some way to those customers with valuations less than 0.5 of the style that it has in stock and tell them that it is not worth coming. If the retailer keeps the price at 0.5, how large can the transport cost T now be before the market collapses? Will the retailer keep the price at $p = 0.5$?

5. Let there be two firms, 1 and 2. Each firm sells a product of with material quality $Z = 1$ and each chooses its price, p_1 and p_2, respectively. However, firm 1 also gets to choose an advertising level a_1. Consumers perceive the overall product quality to be the product's advertising level times its material quality. In other words, consumers perceive product 1 to be of quality a_1 and product 2 to be of quality 1. Consumers are indexed by v distributed continuously from zero to 1, where v_i is consumer i's willingness to pay for quality. Consumer i's net gain from consuming product 1 is $v_i a_1 - p_1$, while consuming product 2 generates a net gain of $v_i - p_2$. There is no production cost; however, firm 1 incurs advertising cost of $(a_1/2)^2$.

   a. Assume all N consumers always buy the product of either firm 1 or firm 2, i.e., the market is always covered. Derive the condition for the marginal consumer v^m satisfies and the demand facing each firm.

   b. Derive the equilibrium values of p_1, p_2, and a_1.

   c. Suppose firm 2 is permitted now to advertise at any positive level a_2 between 0 and 0.5. What level of advertising will it choose if it takes firm 1's choice a_1 as given?

6. You have been hired to market a new music recording that is expected to have target sales of $20 million for the coming year. The marketing department has estimated that a 1 percent increase in advertising the recording would increase the recordings sold by about 0.5 percent, and that a 1 percent increase in the price of the recording would reduce the number sold by about 2 percent. How much money should you commit to advertising the recording in the coming year?

7. How could you explain the different advertising-to-sales ratios of the following firms:

Firm	Main Products	Advertising/Sales
Philip Morris	Tobacco, food, beer	7
Procter & Gamble	Soaps, paper, food	5.3
General Motors	Autos	3.5
Kodak	Photo supplies	9
Johnson & Johnson	Pharmaceuticals	11
Pepsico	Soft drinks, snacks	5.2
Sears, Roebuck	Retailing	3.4
American Home Products	Pharmaceuticals	17.3

References

Anderson, S., and R. Renault. 2006. "Advertising Content," *American Economic Review* 96 (March): 93–113.

Ackerberg, D. 2001. "Empirically Distinguishing Informative and Prestige Effects of Advertising," *Rand Journal of Economics* 32 (Summer): 316–33.

Archibald, R., C. A. Haulman, and C. E. Moody. 1983. "Quality, Price, Advertising, Published Quality Ratings," *Journal of Consumer Research* 9 (March): 347–53.

Bagwell, K., and M. Riordan. 1991. "High and Declining Prices Signal Product Quality," *American Economic Review* 81 (March): 224–39.

Bagwell, K., and G. Ramey, 1994. "Coordination Economies, Advertising, and Search Behavior in Retail Markets," *American Economic Review* 84 (June): 498–517.

Bain, J. S. 1956. *Barriers to New Competition: Their Character and Consequences in Manufacturing Industries*, Cambridge, MA: Harvard University Press.

Becker, G., and K. Murphy. 1993. "A Simple Theory of Advertising as a Good or Bad," *Quarterly Journal of Economics* 108 (August): 941–64.

Benham, L. 1972. "The Effect of Advertising on the Price of Eyeglasses." *Journal of Political Economy*, 15 (October), 337–52.

Butters, G. 1977. "Equilibrium Distribution of Sales and Advertising Prices," *Review of Economic Studies*, 44 (June): 465–91.

Cady, J. F. 1976. "An Estimate of the Price Effects of Restrictions on Drug Price Advertising," *Economic Inquiry* 14 (July): 493–510.

Caves, R. E., and D. P. Green. 1996. "Brands' Quality Levels, Prices, and Advertising Outlays: Empirical Evidence on Signals and Information Costs," *International Journal of Industrial Organization* 14 (1996): 29–52.

Clark, C., and I. Horstmann, 2005. "Advertising and Coordination in Markets with Consumption Scale Effects," *Journal of Economics and Management Strategy* 14 (June): 377–401.

Comanor, W. S., and T. A. Wilson. 1967. "Advertising Market Structure and Performance," *Review of Economics and Statistics* 49 (November): 423–40.

Dinlersoz, E., and M. Yorukoglu. 2012. "Information and Industry Dynamics." *American Economic Review*, 102 (April), 884–913.

Dixit, A., and V. Norman, 1978. "Advertising and Welfare," *Bell Journal of Economics* 9 (Spring): 1–17.

Dorfman, R., and P. O. Steiner, 1954. "Optimal Advertising and Optimal Quality," *American Economic Review* 44 (December): 826–36.

Ellison, G., and S. Fisher Ellison. 2005. "Search, Obfuscation, and Price Elasticities on the Internet," Working Paper, MIT Department of Economics.

Fisher, F., and J. J. McGowan. 1979. "Advertising and Welfare: Comment," *Bell Journal of Economics* 10:726–7

Fluet, C., and P. Garella. 2001. "Advertising and Prices as Signals of Quality in a Regime of Price Rivalry." *International Journal of Industrial Organization* 20 (September): 907–30.

Galbraith, J. K. 1958. *The Affluent Society*, Boston: Houghton-Mifflin.

Geroski, P. 1982. "Simultaneous Equations Models of the Structure-Performance Paradigm," *European Economic Review* 19 (September): 145–58.

Glazer, A. 1981. "Advertising, Information, and Prices: A Case Study," *Economic Inquiry* 19 (October): 661–71.

Grossman, G. M., and C. Shapiro. 1984. "Informative Advertising with Differentiated Products," *Review of Economic Studies* 51 (February): 63–81.

Kaldor, N. V. 1950. "The Economic Aspects of Advertising," *Review of Economic Studies* 18 (February): 1–27.

Kihlstrom, R., and M. Riordan. 1984. "Advertising as a Signal," *Journal of Political Economy* 92 (June): 427–50.

Kotowitz, Y., and G. F. Mathewson. 1986. "Advertising and Consumer Learning," in P. M. Ippolito and D. T. Schefman, eds., *Empirical Approaches to Consumer Protection Economics,* Federal Trade Commission. Washington, D.C.: U.S. Government Printing Office.

Lambin, J. J. 1976. *Advertising, Competition, and Market Conduct in Oligopoly over Time.* Amsterdam: North-Holland.

Marshall, A. 1890. *Principles of Economics*, London: MacMillan and Co.

Milgrom, P., and J. Roberts, 1986. "Price and Advertising Signals of Product Quality," *Journal of Political Economy* 94 (August): 796–821.

Milyo, J., and J. Waldfogel. 1995. "The Effect of Price Advertising on Prices: Evidence in the Wake of 44 Liquormart," *American Economic Review* 89 (December): 1081–96.

Nelson, P. 1970. "Information and Consumer Behavior," *Journal of Political Economy* 78 (May): 311–29.

Nevo, A. 2001. Measuring Market Power in the Ready-to-Eat Cereal Industry. *Econometrica*, 69 (March), 307–42.

Nichols, W. H. 1951. *Price Policy in the Cigarette Industry*, Nashville: Vanderbilt University Press.

Pastine, I., and T. Pastine. 2002. "Consumption Externalities, Coordination, and Advertising," *International Economic Review* 43 (August): 919–43.

Pinkse, J., and M. Slade. 2007. "Semi-Structural Models of Advertising Competition," *Journal of Applied Econometrics* 22 (December): 1227–46.

Pope, D. 1983. *The Making of Modern Advertising*, New York: Basic Books.

Reisz, P. 1978. "Price versus Quality in the Marketplace," *Journal of Retailing* 54 (Winter): 15–28.

Round, D. K. 1983. "Intertemporal Profit Margin Variability and Market Structure in Australian Manufacturing," *International Journal of Industrial Organization* 1 (June): 189–209.

Schmalensee, R. 1978. "A Model of Advertising and Product Quality," *Journal of Political Economy* 86 (June): 485–503.

Schwartz, A., and L.L Wilde. 1985. "Product Quality and Imperfect Information," *Review of Economics Studies* 52: 251–262.

Slade, M. 1995. "Product Rivalry with Multiple Strategic Weapons: An Analysis of Price an Advertising Competition," *Journal of Economics and Management Strategy* 4 (September): 445–76.

Solow, R. M. 1967. "The New Industrial State or Son of Affluence," *Public Interest* 9 (Fall): 100–108.

Stigler, G. 1968. "Price and Non-Price Competition," *Journal of Political Economy* 76 (February): 149–54.

Stigler, G., and G. Becker. 1977. "De Gustibus Non Est Disputandum," *American Economic Review* 67 (March): 76–90.

Sutton, J. 1991. *Sunk Costs and Market Structure.* Cambridge, MA: The MIT Press

Telser, L. 1964. "Advertising and Competition," *Journal of Political Economy* 72 (December): 537–62.

Appendix

We present here first a model of excessive advertising competition and, second, a simplified version of the advertising information and differentiated product competition model developed by Grossman and Shapiro (1984).

WASTEFUL COMPETITION

Assume a duopoly with each firm's profit given by:

$$\pi_1 = Z(1 + A_1 - bA_1A_2 - 0.5A_1^2)$$
$$\pi_2 = Z(1 + A_2 - bA_1A_2 - 0.5A_2^2) \tag{19.A1}$$

where A_i is the level of advertising effort of firm i measured as the advertising-to-sales ratio, and Z and b are positive parameter a with $0 < b < 1$.

The first-order conditions then yield the following best response functions:

$$A_i = 1 - bA_j \quad i, j = 1, 2 \text{ and } i \neq j \tag{19.A2}$$

Hence in equilibrium:

$$A_1 = A_2 = \frac{1}{1 + b} \tag{19.A3}$$

and

$$\pi_1 = \pi_2 = Z\left[1 + \frac{0.5}{(1 + b)^2}\right] \tag{19.A4}$$

The cooperative advertising choices that maximize the sum, $\pi_1 + \pi_2$, are:

$$A_1^C = A_2^C = \frac{1}{1 + 2b} \tag{19.A5}$$

This yields a cooperative π_i^C profit to each firm of

$$\pi_1^C = \pi_2^C = Z\left[1 + \frac{0.5 + b}{(1 + 2b)^2}\right] > \pi_1 = \pi_2 = Z\left[1 + \frac{0.5}{(1 + b)^2}\right] \text{ for } 0 < b < 1 \tag{19.A6}$$

INFORMATIVE ADVERTISING AND PRICE COMPETITION

We assume a set of N consumers continuously distributed along a line segment of unit length. Firm 1 is at the left end of the segment and firm 2 is at the right end. Each consumer buys at most one unit of the good and receives surplus net of travel cost x_i equal to

$$U_i = V - p_1 - tx_i \text{ if the consumer buys from firm 1; and}$$
$$U_i = V - p_2 - t(1 - x_i) \text{ if the consumer buys from firm 2} \qquad (19.\text{A7})$$

Each firm i chooses a level of advertising aimed at informing a fraction θ_i of the N consumers. Hence, $\theta_1(1-\theta_2)N$ know only of brand 1; $\theta_2(1-\theta_1)$ know only of brand 2; $\theta_1\theta_2 N$ know of both goods; and $(1-\theta_1)(1-\theta_2)$, know of either good. We assume that both θ_1 and $\theta_2 < 1$.

Among the $\theta_1\theta_2 N$ consumers informed about both products the marginal consumer indifferent to either good has address $x^m(p_1, p_2) = \dfrac{(p_2 - p_1 + t)}{2t}$. Demand for firm 1 is made up of two parts. The first part is the $\theta_1(1-\theta_2)N$ consumers who know only of firm 1's brand. The second part comes from the $\theta_1\theta_2 N$ consumers who know of both brands. Hence, the total demand for firm 1 is:

$$q_1(\theta_1, \theta_2 p_1, p_2) = \theta_1(1 - \theta_2)N + \theta_1\theta_2 x^m N = \left[\theta_1\left(1 - \theta_2\right) + \theta_1\theta_2\frac{(p_2 + t - p_1)}{2t}\right]N$$

$$(19.\text{A8})$$

We assume a quadratic advertising cost function:

$$A(\theta_1)N = \frac{1}{2}\alpha\theta^2 N \qquad (19.\text{A9})$$

Firm 1's profit function is therefore:

$$\pi(\theta_1, \theta_2, p, p_2) = (p_1 - c)\left[\theta_1\left(1 - \theta_2\right) + \theta_1\theta_2\frac{(p_2 + t - p_1)}{2t}\right]N - \frac{1}{2}\alpha\theta_1^2 N \quad (19.\text{A10})$$

The two first-order conditions necessary for profit maximizaiton are:

$$\frac{\theta_1\theta_2(p_2 + -p_1)N}{2t} + \theta_1(1 - \theta_2)N - \frac{\theta_1\theta_2(p_1 - c)N}{2t} = 0$$

$$(p_1 - c)\left[\left(1 - \theta_2\right) + \theta_2\left(\frac{p_2 + t - p_1}{2t}\right)\right]N - \alpha\theta_1 N = 0 \qquad (19.\text{A11})$$

By symmetry, $p_1 = p_2 = p^*$ and $\theta_1 = \theta_2 = \theta^*$. Hence, the first of the two-first order conditions is:

$$p^* - c = -t + \frac{2t}{\theta^*} \qquad (19.\text{A12})$$

Similarly, the second first-order condition now is:

$$(p^* = c)\left(1 - \frac{\theta^*}{2}\right) = \alpha\theta* \qquad (19.A13)$$

These two conditions may then be jointly solved to yield:

$$p^* = c + \sqrt{2\alpha t} \qquad (19.A14)$$

and

$$\theta^* = \frac{2}{1 + \sqrt{\dfrac{2\alpha}{t}}} \qquad (19.A15)$$

Because we assumed that some consumers remain uninformed, $\theta^* < 1$, we assume that that $\alpha > t/2$. Equation (19.A14) then implies an equilibrium price $p^* > c + t$. Each firm's equilibrium profit π^* is:

$$\pi^* = \frac{2\alpha}{\left(1 + \sqrt{2\alpha/t}\right)^2} \qquad (19.A15)$$

20

Research and Development

The final results of the human genome project indicate that we humans are not as complicated as we thought we were. Rather than consisting of the approximately 100,000 genes that were initially predicted, it appears that we have only 30,000 genes, more but less than twice as many as the humble roundworm with its 19,098 genes.[1] This finding is important for many reasons. From our perspective, there is an important economic aspect to this result. It is well understood that genes are a crucial factor in predicting and curing many diseases. Therefore, identifying and understanding the workings of each gene could lead to the creation of a new family of custom-made drugs. The rough equation quoted by the pharmaceutical companies was "one gene, one patent, one drug."[2] If, as initially expected, there were 100,000 genes then there was potentially a vast number of revenue-generating patents. The finding that the actual number of genes is far less than 100,000 has suggested to many that genes hold many fewer of the keys to the treatment of disease. As a result, understanding genes and their functions may offer a much less lucrative source of new patentable treatments.

However, all is not lost. It is being suggested that much of human biology is determined at the protein level rather than at the DNA level, and we have well over 1,000,000 different proteins in our bodies. So now we have a whole new science, proteomics—studying how genes control proteins—as a method for creating tailored drugs. Proteomics is being pursued by an increasingly wide number of companies and institutions: Harvard University, for example, has created a new Institute of Proteomics.

The race to understand the proteomic causes of diseases and to develop new drugs targeted at those diseases will not come as a surprise to anyone familiar with the popular business literature of the past twenty years. That literature is characterized by the dominant theme that the most successful firms find new ways of doing things, or develop new products and new markets.[3] The now prevalent view is that firms become industry leaders

---

[1] If you are interested, the complete human genome is available as a free download from http://gdbwww.gdb.org/.

[2] "Scientists, Companies Look to the Next Step After Genes," *The New York Times* 13 February 2001.

[3] This is virtually the mantra in the best-selling book by Peters and Waterman, 1982. *In Search of Excellence: Lessons from America's Best Run Companies*. However, the argument is repeated frequently in other business books, including, as noted herein, Porter's (1990) encyclopedic volume.

by conducting research and development (R&D), leading to innovations in their production technologies or the products they provide. Michael Porter's *The Competitive Advantage of Nations* (1990) serves to make the point. Porter writes that any theory of competitive success

> must start from the premise that competition is dynamic and evolving.... Competition is a constantly changing landscape in which new products, new ways of marketing, new production processes, and whole new market segments emerge.... [Economic] theory must make improvement and innovation in methods and technology a central element. (Porter 1990, 20).

Porter's quote could almost have been taken verbatim from Joseph Schumpeter's classic work written almost fifty years earlier. Schumpeter was both an economist and a historian. He brought a historical perspective to his study of competition and the rise and fall of corporate empires. The following dramatic passage appears in his book *Capitalism, Socialism, and Democracy* first published in 1942.

> [I]t is not ... [price] competition which counts but competition from the new commodity, the new technology, the new source of supply, the new type of organization ... competition which commands a decisive cost or quality advantage and which strikes not at the margins of the profits and outputs of existing firms but at their foundations and very lives. (Schumpeter 1942, 84).

Interest in the forces behind innovative activity is perhaps stronger today than it was when Schumpeter wrote.[4] An important issue, raised by Schumpeter, concerns the market environment most conducive to R&D activity. Schumpeter conjectured that R&D efforts are more likely to be undertaken by large firms than by small ones. He speculated secondly that monopolistic or oligopolistic firms would more aggressively pursue innovative activity than would firms with little or no market power. Accordingly, Schumpeter argued that the benefits of an economy made up largely of competitive markets populated by small firms reflected the rather modest gains of allocating resources efficiently among a *given set of goods and services produced with given technologies*. In contrast, the benefits of markets dominated by large firms, each with sizable market power, stems from the much larger dynamic efficiency gains of developing new products and new technologies. As Schumpeter wrote, "a shocking suspicion dawns upon us that big business may have had more to do with creating (our) standard of life than with keeping it down" (p. 88).

The validity of Schumpeter's ideas—which have come to be jointly referred to as the Schumpeterian hypothesis—is the key issue addressed in this chapter. Do larger firms do more R&D? Does a concentrated market structure provide a better environment for the development of new innovations than a competitive structure?

Table 20.1 lists the ten companies awarded the most patents by the US Patents and Trademark Office (USPTO) in 2011 as well as their ranks in 2010 and 2009. Each of these is a large company. Most operate in oligopolistic markets with only a few large competitors. Moreover, there is considerable stability in the rank ordering, at least over these three years. It is tempting to conclude on the basis of such data that Schumpeter was right and that large firms in concentrated markets are more innovative. However, great care is needed before

---

[4] For example, see the story by C. J. Whalen, "Today's Hottest Economist Died 50 Years Ago," *Business Week* 11 December 2000. Ever since Solow's (1956) classic work, macroeconomists studying growth have also focused intensively on technological progress and innovation as the primary source of improved living standards over time. See, e.g., the books by Barro and Sala-I-Martin (1995) and Romer (2006).

Table 20.1   Top ten patent-receiving firms in 2011 and rank in 2010 and 2009

Company	# of patents 2011	Rank in 2010	Rank in 2009
International Business Machines	6,148	1	1
Samsung Electronics	4,868	2	2
Canon Kabushiki Kaisha	2,818	4	4
Panasonic Corporation	2,533	5	5
Toshiba Corporation	2,451	6	6
Microsoft Corporation	2,309	3	3
Sony Corporation	2,265	7	7
Seiko Epson Corporation	1,525	12	9
Hitachi	1,455	11	13
General Electric	1,444	14	15

Source: USPTO

reaching that conclusion. Rather than implying that large firms do more R&D, these results could imply that firms that do more R&D become large.

The most active areas for research activity are likely to vary over time. Table 20.2 lists the top patent-receiving industries or research areas in 2010 and 2011. It also shows the cumulative patents in that area up to that year. While there is some consistency across the three columns there is also considerable variation. Thus, while multiplex communications have led the patent parade in recent years, bio-science drugs, semiconductor devices, solid state devices, and molecular chemistry have accounted for many more patents in total over time.

Introducing a new product can often undermine the marketability of the firm's existing products. Similarly, the development of a new production process requiring new equipment reduces the value of existing productive capacity. Because introducing new products

Table 20.2   Top patent receiving sectors in 2011 and cumulative patents to that year

Industry Class	2010	2011	Total
Multiplex Communications	7415	7720	57275
Active Solid-State Devices (e.g., Transistors, Solid-State Diodes)	6901	7028	74029
Semiconductor Device Manufacturing: Process	6143	5909	81088
Telecommunications	4311	5578	44707
Electrical Computers and Digital Processing Systems: Multicomputer Data Transferring	4647	4877	31663
Drug, Bio-Affecting, and Body Treating Compositions	4712	4597	94335
Data Processing: Database and File Management or Data Structures	4452	4245	27382
Data Processing: Financial, Business Practice, Management, or Cost/Price Determination	4056	4062	20460
Image Analysis	3370	3744	33340
Chemistry: Molecular Biology and Microbiology	3711	3733	64819
Computer Graphics Processing and Selective Visual Display Systems	3321	3525	39756
Pulse or Digital Communications	3024	3073	34123

Source: USPTO

Reality Checkpoint

Creative Destruction in the Pharmaceutical Industry: Will the Prozac Work if the Viagra Fails?

The pharmaceutical industry offers perhaps the best examples of Schumpeter's "creative destruction." Consider the market for antidepressants. For several years after its introduction in 1987 by Eli Lilly & Co., *Prozac* dominated this market. Originally envisioned as a treatment for high blood pressure and, when that failed, an anti-obesity drug, Lilly was pleasantly surprised when hospital tests on mildly depressed patients showed a marked and widespread positive effect. Lilly took its fluoxetine drug as it was then called, and asked Interbrand, one of the major branding companies in the world, to develop a new name and sales campaign. *Prozac* was born and soon it dominated the antidepressant market. By the early 1990s, *Prozac* accounted for nearly a quarter of Lilly's $10 billion revenue.

Competition came quickly. In 1992 Pfizer, Inc., introduced *Zoloft*, which quickly jumped to a third of the market. SmithKline Beecham's *Paxil* followed shortly and soon had 20 percent. All three drugs increased levels of the neurotransmitter, serotonin, but all three had slightly different chemical bases and different side effects. When the *Prozac* patent expired in 2001, prescriptions for generic fluoxetine grew rapidly. Within a year, Lilly had lost 90 percent of its *Prozac* prescriptions. Lilly countered with a new drug, *Cymbalta* that works on two neurotransmitters, serotonin and norepinephrine.

Originally known as sildenafil citrate, *Viagra*, was first envisioned as a treatment for high blood pressure and angina. Even though it failed in that regard, its many male users reported a dramatic increase in sexual function. Pfizer received approval from the Food and Drug Administration (FDA) to market the drug as a treatment for erectile dysfunction (ED) and re-launched the drug under the name, *Viagra*, in 1998. Sales topped $1 billion within a year.

Once again, success brought competition. By 2003, two new ED drugs appeared. *Levitra* (made by Bayer and GlaxoSmithKline) worked twice as fast as *Viagra*, while *Cialis* (developed by ICOS but marketed by Lilly) lasted far longer. Within the United States, the two new drugs combined quickly for as much as 40 percent of the market. In countries such as Australia and France, *Cialis* alone claimed 40 percent of the market within its first year. Once again, generic competition threatens these market positions. Pfizer's UK patent expired in June, 2013. Its US patent survived one court challenge from Teva that barred doctors from prescribing generic substitutes as an ED treatment until 2019 but not as a treatment for hypertension. Some medical analysts are forecasting a significant increase in the number of men reported to be suffering from high blood pressure over the next few years.

Sources: R. Langreth, "High Anxiety: Rivals Threaten Prozac's Reign," *Wall Street Journal*, May 9, 1996, p. A4; A. Pollack, "Lilly Pays Bid Fee Up Front to Share in Rival of Viagra," *New York Times*, October 2, 1998, p. C1; S. Carey, "Lilly Reports 22% Decline in Net Income as Generics Hurt Sales of Prozac," *Wall Street Journal*, April 16, 2002, p. C2; and "Viagra Rival Cialis Wins up to 40 Percent Market Share," *Reuters News Wire*, March 23, 2004; P. Loftus, "Pfizer Viagra Patent Upheld," *Wall Street Journal*, August 15, 2011, p. C1.

or processes inevitably means the destruction of old ones, Schumpeter dubbed such competition by innovation "creative destruction." In addition, because some of the products and processes that are made obsolete may well be those of the innovating firm itself, we can ask our central question in a somewhat different way. Why do firms undermine existing activities (including their own ones) in this way? More generally, what are the incentives to engage in innovative activity and how do these vary with firm size and market structure?

Both the professional and the popular business literature have had much to say on the Schumpeterian hypothesis in recent years. In this chapter, we approach this topic using the tools of economic analysis and strategic interaction that we have built throughout the book. However, before we begin a more formal analysis, we need to establish some definitions or classifications to which we can easily refer.

20.1   A TAXONOMY OF INNOVATIONS

Research and development consists of three related activities. The first is *basic research*. This includes studies that will not necessarily lead to specific applications but, instead, aim to improve our fundamental knowledge in a manner that may subsequently be helpful in a range of activities. The derivation and validation of the theory of laser technology is a good example. A second category is *applied research*. Such research generally involves substantial engineering input and is aimed at a more practical and specific usage than basic research. The creation of the first laser drill for dentistry would be an example of applied research. Finally, there is the *development* component of R&D. Here, the goal is to move from the creation of a prototype to a product that can be used by consumers and that is capable (to some extent at least) of mass production. To continue our analogy, the transformation of the first laser drill into a small, handheld product that is affordable and usable by a large number of dentists would be an example of the development stage. For the most part we shall be concerned with applied research rather than development, but we shall touch upon some of the important issues that characterize the decision to move from research to development.

In considering the output of R&D, it is common to distinguish between two kinds. *Process innovations* are discoveries of new, typically cheaper methods for producing existing goods. *Product innovations* are the creation of new goods. For the most part, we shall concentrate on process innovations, but we shall also present examples showing how the analysis can be extended to product innovations.

Finally, with respect to process innovations, there is a further distinction that can be made. This is the division of innovations into *drastic* or major innovations, and *nondrastic* or minor innovations. Roughly speaking, drastic innovations are ones that reduce a firm's unit cost to such an extent that even if it charges the profit-maximizing monopoly price associated with that low cost, it will still undercut all competitors. Hence, a drastic innovation creates a monopolist unconstrained by any fear of entry or price competition—at least for some time. By contrast, a firm making a nondrastic innovation may gain some cost advantage over its rivals but not one so large that the firm can price like a monopolist without fear of competition.

The formal distinction between drastic and nondrastic innovations is illustrated in Figure 20.1. Assume that demand for a particular product is given by $P = 120 - Q$ and that before the innovation all firms can produce the product at a constant marginal cost of \$80. Assume also that the existing firms are Bertrand competitors so that the price is \$80 and total output is 40 units.

Now suppose that one firm gains access to a process innovation that reduces its marginal costs to \$20 as in Figure 20.1(a) and that, perhaps because of a patent, this firm is the only

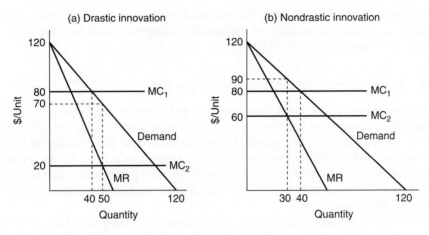

Figure 20.1   Drastic and nondrastic process innovations

one able to use the new low-cost technology. If this innovator were alone in the market, it would set the monopoly price corresponding to its new, lower marginal costs of $20. Given our demand function we know that marginal revenue is $MR = 120 - 2Q$. Equating this with marginal cost of $20 gives an output of 50 units and a monopoly price of $70. Setting this monopoly price forces all the other firms out of the market. The innovation is a drastic one because the reduction in cost is so great that the innovating firm can charge the full monopoly price associated with the new low cost and still be able to undercut the marginal costs of all other firms.

Suppose by contrast that the innovation reduces marginal costs to $60 as in Figure 20.1(b). By exactly the same argument as above, the innovating firm acting as a monopolist wants to produce an output of 30 units and set a price of $90. The problem is that this will not work. The remaining firms can profitably undercut this price. So the best that the innovating firm can do now is to set a price of $80 (more accurately, $79.99) and an output of 40 units. This still eliminates the other firms but only by the innovator lowering the price that it charges. Hence, this is a nondrastic innovation.

Assume that demand in a competitive market is given by the linear function: $P = 100 - 2Q$ and that current marginal cost of production is constant at $60. Now assume that there is a process innovation that reduces marginal cost to $28. Show that this is a nondrastic innovation. How much would the innovation have to lower marginal costs for it to be drastic?

20.2   MARKET STRUCTURE AND THE INCENTIVE TO INNOVATE

We now turn to some of the basic questions economists have asked regarding how the incentives to spend on R&D are affected by market structure.[5] We assume the demand for a particular good is linear. Specifically, the inverse demand curve is again assumed to be

---

[5]   This analysis owes much to Nobel Prize winner Kenneth Arrow's path-breaking work (1962).

given by the equation $P = 120 - Q$. We also assume that each producer of the good has a marginal cost of \$80. Accordingly, if the market is competitive and there are many such producers, the current price is also \$80.

20.2.1   Competition and the Value of Innovation

Suppose that a research firm, not involved in the actual manufacture of this good, discovers a new production process by undertaking research at some cost K. Using the notation from above, we consider the case of a nondrastic process innovation that reduces the marginal production cost to \$60. We further assume that the innovation is protected by a patent of unlimited duration that cannot be "invented around" by other potential or actual firms. What benefits does the innovation bring, and does the market mechanism work to convey such incentives to the research firm?

Let us first consider how society as a whole values the innovation. Imagine a social planner whose goal is to maximize total social surplus (producer surplus plus consumer surplus) and, moreover, who has the power to command that prices be set at whatever level the planner requests. Such a benevolent dictator would reason as follows: With or without the innovation, optimality requires that price be set to marginal cost. The per-period value that the social planner places upon the innovation is the increase in consumer surplus when price equals (constant) marginal cost as then there is no producer surplus. Prior to the innovation, consumer surplus at a price of \$80 is \$800. After the innovation, when firms set the price equal to the new lower marginal cost of \$60, consumer surplus increases to \$1,800.[6] The increase in consumer surplus is \$1,000, the shaded area in Figure 20.2(a). This additional surplus will be realized not just in one period but also in all subsequent periods following the innovation. Hence, using the discounting techniques discussed in Chapter 2, the total present value of the additional surplus created by the innovation is $V^p = 1000/(1 - R)$ where $R = (1 + r)^{-1}$ is the discount factor and r is the interest rate. The more this value exceeds the cost K, that is, the more it exceeds the present value of the expenses associated with discovering the process, the more desirable is the innovation.

Of course, we don't have a social planner, and if we did it is doubtful that the planner would succeed in maximizing social welfare. What we have are markets. The issue is how the structure of the market affects the realization of the value of this innovation. What is the incentive of a research firm to pursue the innovation if when it is successful it can auction the rights to the innovation to a competitive industry comprised of many firms? Prior to the innovation all firms sell at a price equal to the marginal cost of \$80 and earn zero profit. Total output each period prior to the innovation is just 40 units.

Now consider the behavior of a firm that has the rights to the innovation. Quite evidently, its best strategy is to undercut its erstwhile competitors just slightly, driving them out of the market and giving it an effective monopoly. The firm that wins the rights will set a price that is one cent less than the old competitive price, \$80. At this price, the industry's total output remains identical to what it was prior to the adoption of the innovation. Consequently, the firm will earn per-period profit of $\$(80 - 60) \times 40 = \$800$. This is illustrated by the shaded rectangle in Figure 20.2(b). The present value that a competitive firm places on the innovation is the maximum amount it willingly bids for the rights to it and this is $V^c = 800/(1 - R)$. This is less than the social value of the innovation. The reason is simple: the competitive firm only considers the profit it can earn as a result of

---

[6]   Given our demand function $P = 120 - Q$ and assuming that $P = MC$, consumer surplus is the area of a triangle with height $120 - MC$ and base $120 - MC$. That is, $CS = (120 - MC)^2/2$.

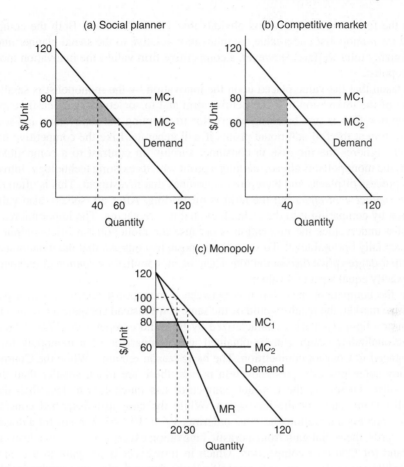

Figure 20.2   Market structure and the incentive to innovate

the innovation. It ignores the additional benefit from increased consumer surplus that the innovation brings.

Now consider the potential value when it is a monopolist who has the rights to the innovation and who faces no threat of entry. For such a firm, the gain from introducing the innovation is the additional profit it makes as a result of being able to produce at a lower marginal cost. Because the monopolist maximizes profit by setting marginal revenue equal to marginal cost, we can measure this gain by comparing the monopolist's per-period profit at its current marginal cost with its per-period profit at the lower marginal cost that the innovation permits. This is illustrated in Figure 20.2(c).

Given our demand function we know that marginal revenue is $MR = 120 - 2Q$. So, prior to the innovation, the monopolist produces an output of 20 units, sets a price of $100 and earns profit per period of $400. After the innovation output is increased to 30 units, price is reduced to $90 and per-period profits are $900. As a result, the per-period value placed by the monopolist on the innovation is $500—the difference between profits with and without the innovation. This is illustrated by the shaded area in Figure 20.2(c).[7] In turn, the total present value the monopolist places on the innovation is $V^m = 500/(1 - R)$.

---

[7]   This is derived from the property that one way to represent the monopolist's profit is the area between the monopolist's MR and MC curves.

From the foregoing analysis, it is obvious that $V^p > V^c > V^m$. Both the competitive firm and the monopolist undervalue the innovation relative to the social planner interested in maximizing total welfare. However, a competitive firm values the innovation more than the monopolist.

The reason that the value placed upon the innovation by the monopolist is smaller than the value of the innovation to a competitive firm and to society is again easily explained. A competitive firm is just breaking even prior to adopting the innovation and so values the innovation at the full additional profits it will generate. Like the competitive firm, the monopolist ignores the increase in consumer surplus. In contrast to a competitive firm, however, the monopolist is already earning a profit with its existing technology. Introducing the new process displaces and therefore undermines that investment. This is often referred to as the *replacement effect* but the term is misleading. After all, society also values the innovation by comparing it to the technology that it is replacing. The important reason the monopolist undervalues the innovation is because the monopolist restricts output to less than the socially optimal level. To see why suppose, by contrast, that the monopolist could employ first-degree price discrimination. Then the monopolist's valuation of the innovation would exactly equal society's valuation.

While the comparison just drawn is between a monopolist and a firm in a perfectly competitive market, the results would be the same if we instead compare a monopolist with a firm in an oligopoly market characterized by Bertrand competition. (Why?) Moreover, the same qualitative result will be obtained in a comparison of a monopoly firm with firms engaged in Cournot competition. The basic reason remains. While the Cournot firm does enjoy some positive, pre-innovation profits, these are much smaller than those of a monopolist. Therefore, the Cournot competitor has much less to lose than does the monopolist from pursuing the innovation. While the case just described considered a nondrastic process innovation, the same ordering, $V^p > V^c > V^m$, holds for a drastic one. In other words, the social gain from a drastic innovation exceeds the gain to a firm engaged in Bertrand (or Cournot) competition, which in turn exceeds the gain to a monopolist. Finally, while our analysis assumes a specific linear demand, the same results are obtained for any demand function even if it is nonlinear.[8]

20.2

Practice Problem

Assume that demand for a homogeneous good is $P = 100 - Q$, where P is measured in dollars, and that a process innovation reduces marginal costs of production from $75 to $60 per unit. Assume that the discount factor is $R = 0.9$.

a.   Confirm that this is a nondrastic innovation and that marginal costs would have to be reduced to less than $50 per unit for the innovation to be drastic.

b.   Calculate the maximum amount that a monopolist is willing to pay for the innovation. Now assume that the market is served by Cournot duopolists who have identical marginal costs of $75 prior to the innovation.

c.   Confirm that the pre-innovation price is $83.33 and that at this price each firm has profits per period of $69.44.

d.   Confirm that if one of these firms is granted use of the innovation, the price will fall to $78.33.

e.   Show that this firm is willing to pay more for the innovation than the monopolist.

---

[8]   Gilbert (2006) shows that our results generalize to any demand function.

20.2.2 Preserving Monopoly Profit and the Efficiency Effect

The analysis in the previous section assumed that the only innovator is a lab outside the industry. If that laboratory company does not innovate, no one does. This does not truly capture the spirit of Schumpeter's contention. Instead, Schumpeter's point is precisely that firms *compete* by means of innovation. This means that firms have their own labs and that each firm is a potential innovator. As a result, even if one firm does not innovate, another might. This can reverse the previous results.[9]

Suppose that demand is given by $P = 120 - Q$ and that the current technology allows production at a marginal cost of $60. An incumbent monopolist and a potential entrant play the following three-stage game. In stage 1 the incumbent decides whether or not to undertake R&D, which we assume reduces marginal cost to $30. In stage 2 a potential entrant decides whether or not to enter. If the incumbent has not undertaken R&D, the entrant then chooses whether or not to undertake R&D. Without R&D, either firm's marginal cost is $60 and with it marginal cost is $30. No matter who innovates, the innovation is protected by a patent of unlimited duration that cannot be "invented around" by other potential or actual firms. If entry occurs then in stage 3 the entrant and the incumbent act as Cournot competitors. Using the standard Cournot equations gives the extensive form of this game illustrated in Figure 20.3.

As usual we solve this game "backwards." Suppose that the incumbent has undertaken R&D. Then the entrant will enter with a cost of $60. The incumbent earns per period profit of $1,600 and the entrant earns per-period profit of $100. (This assumes, of course, that there are no sunk costs of entry. We return to this point below.) Now suppose that the incumbent does not innovate. The entrant will certainly enter. Innovation by the entrant gives the entrant per-period profit of $1,600 while no innovation leads to per-period profit of $400.

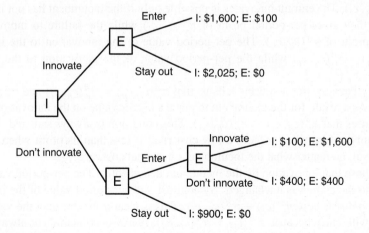

Figure 20.3 Extensive form for the innovation and entry game

---

[9] The underlying analysis can be found in Gilbert and Newbery (1982). Reinganum (1983) shows, however, that this conclusion might not hold when the timing of the successful breakthrough is uncertain. The incumbent monopolist might delay innovation in order to enjoy its current profits. A potential entrant has no such incentive to delay its innovative activity.

We can now calculate how much the innovation is worth to the incumbent and to the entrant. For the entrant, innovation increases per-period profit from \$400 *to* \$1,600. Accordingly the present value of the innovation to the entrant is $V^e = \$1,200/(1 - R)$. What about the incumbent? No innovation by the incumbent will lead to innovative entry provided only that the cost of the innovation is less than \$1,200/$(1 - R)$. In that case, the incumbent then earns per-period profit of \$100. By contrast, if the incumbent innovates and pre-empts innovation by the entrant the incumbent earns per-period profit of \$1,600. As a result, the value of the innovation to the incumbent is $V^i = \$1,500/(1 - R)$. Clearly this exceeds the value placed on the innovation by the entrant. Hence, the monopolist has the stronger incentive to innovate.

Our analysis illustrates the potential for innovation to deter entry, protecting the incumbent's monopoly position and profit. Suppose that sunk entry costs S are such that $\$100/(1 - R) < S < \$400/(1 - R)$. That is, imagine that sunk costs are greater than the profit that the entrant expects to make if the incumbent innovates but less than the profit that the entrant expects to make if neither entrant nor incumbent innovates. The value of the innovation to the entrant is unchanged at \$1,200/$(1 - R)$. This is not the case for the incumbent. Now innovation deters entry, allowing the incumbent to maintain its monopoly position with per-period profit of \$2,025. Failure to innovate, by contrast, leads to innovative entry and per-period profit to the incumbent of \$100. The value of the innovation to the incumbent is now even greater at $V^m = \$1,925/(1 - R)$.

The foregoing result is not peculiar to the numbers we have assumed. It is in fact quite general. Suppose first that innovation by the incumbent does not deter entry. Denote the per-period duopoly profit of the incumbent as $\pi_i^d(c_i, c_e)$ and of the entrant as $\pi_e^d(c_i, c_e)$, where c_i is marginal cost of the incumbent and c_e is marginal cost of the entrant. Innovation reduces marginal cost from c_h (high) to c_l (low). The incumbent knows that innovation gives per-period profit $\pi_i^d(c_l, c_h)$ while failure to innovate leads to innovative entry and profit $\pi_i^d(c_h, c_l)$. The entrant innovates is possible only if the incumbent has not innovated. Innovation then gives per-period profit of $\pi_e^d(c_h, c_l)$ while the failure to innovate gives per-period profit of $\pi_e^d(c_h, c_h)$. The per-period value of the innovation to the incumbent is $\pi_i^d(c_l, c_h) - \pi_i^d(c_h, c_l)$ while the per-period value of the innovation to the entrant is $\pi_e^d(c_h, c_l) - \pi_e^d(c_h, c_h)$.

Symmetry between the two firms tells us that $\pi_i^d(c_l, c_h) = \pi_e^d(c_h, c_l)$ and $\pi_e^d(c_h, c_h) = \pi_i^d(c_h, c_h)$. As a result, for the incumbent to place a higher value on the innovation than the entrant requires that $\pi_i^d(c_h, c_l) < \pi_i^d(c_h, c_h)$. This condition is always satisfied. The profit of the incumbent firm when it faces a low-cost rival is less than its profit when it faces a high-cost rival, no matter what the incumbent's marginal costs are.

Now suppose that innovation by the incumbent deters entry. The per-period value of the innovation to the entrant is unchanged. By contrast, the per-period value of the innovation to the monopolist is now $\pi^m(c_l) - \pi_i^d(c_h, c_l)$. This is clearly greater than the value of the innovation with entry because $\pi^m(c_l) > \pi_i^d(c_l, c_h)$. A low-cost incumbent always prefers monopoly to sharing the market, even when the sharing is with a high-cost rival.

To summarize, no matter whether innovation by an incumbent monopolist maintains that monopoly or not, the incumbent firm values the innovation more highly than a potential entrant. Replacing oneself is better than being replaced by a newcomer. This effect is called the *efficiency effect*.

20.3   A MORE COMPLETE MODEL OF COMPETITION VIA INNOVATION

What drives the efficiency effect is the fact that the cost of not innovating becomes higher once we recognize that it is precisely in this case that a rival may innovate. Such an increase in the opportunity cost of non-innovation makes the incumbent monopolist much more willing to pay for the innovation. Clearly, the strategic interaction from potential entry through innovation seems closer to the view Schumpeter (1942) presents.

We can get even closer to the Schumpeterian spirit by making the decision to spend on R&D an explicit part of a firm's strategy. The simplest model in this spirit is one due to Dasgupta and Stiglitz (1980). Their model is attractive both for its key insights and because it builds on the Cournot model developed in Chapter 9. We present the essentials of their analysis here.

Dasgupta and Stiglitz assume an industry comprised of n identical Cournot firms, each of which has to determine the level of output, q_i it will produce and the amount, x_i, that it will spend on R&D. While R&D is costly, the benefit of R&D spending is that it lowers the firm's unit cost of production, c. Specifically, each firm's unit cost is a decreasing function of the amount it spends on R&D, $c_i = c(x_i)$ and $dc(x_i)/dx_i < 0$. Total net profit for any firm, π_i, is:

$$\pi_i = P(Q)q_i - c(x_i)q_i - x_i \tag{20.1}$$

Suppose that each firm spends a specific amount, x^*, on research. Each firm then has a unit cost of $c(x^*)$. Accordingly, if we know the value of x^*, we know each firm's unit cost, and we can work out the equilibrium output for the individual firm and the industry in total using the analysis from Chapter 9.[10] In particular, we know that the outcome in this symmetric, n-firm Cournot model is an equilibrium price-cost margin, or Lerner Index, given by

$$\frac{(P - c(x^*))}{P} = \frac{s_i}{\eta} \tag{20.2}$$

Here, P is the industry price, s_i is the ith firm's share of industry output, η is the elasticity of market demand, and x^* is the amount that each firm spends on R&D in equilibrium. We have dispensed with the subscript on the term x^* because for identical firms the amount chosen is the same in equilibrium for each firm. We can simplify further by recognizing that because all firms are identical, s_i is just $1/n$. So, equation (20.2) can be written as

$$P\left(1 - \frac{1}{n\eta}\right) = c(x^*) \tag{20.3}$$

Equation (20.3) does not by itself tell us the amount of R&D expenditure, x^* that each firm will find optimal. To determine that value we must add a second equilibrium condition. That condition must reflect a choice x^* consistent with profit maximization. Let $-\Delta c$ be the

---

[10]   If we set the derivative of equation (20.1) with respect to q_i to zero, taking the production of all firms other than the ith, Q_{-i} as given, and then solve for q_i we obtain each firm's best response function.

reduction in unit cost that results from a small increase Δx in R&D spending. Since that unit cost reduction applies to all q_i units, the marginal benefit of R&D spending is:

$$\text{Marginal Benefit of R\&D Spending} = -\frac{\Delta c}{\Delta x_i} q_i \qquad (20.4)$$

Of course, the marginal cost of an extra dollar of R&D spending is just 1. Profit maximization then requires:

$$\text{Marginal Benefit} = \text{Marginal Cost OR} \ -\frac{\Delta c}{\Delta x_i} q_i = 1 \qquad (20.5)$$

No equilibrium can exist that has obvious ways in which firms—or even just one firm—can raise profit. So, the profit-maximizing condition expressed in equation (20.5) must hold for each firm i, in any equilibrium. Symmetry then implies that we can drop the i subscripts and simply write $-\Delta c/\Delta x = 1$ as the generic representation at each firm.

What are the implications of the equilibrium conditions of equations (20.3) and (20.5)? The most obvious conclusion is that an increase in the number of firms in the industry will decrease the amount that each firm is willing to spend on R&D. An increase in the number of firms in the industry decreases the amount that each firm will choose to produce. This is, actually, a direct implication of equation (20.3). But equation (20.5) makes clear that the marginal benefit of extra R&D spending is directly proportional to a firm's output. Hence, the reduction in a firm's output that results from increasing the number of firms also reduces the marginal benefit that R&D spending yields to an individual firm. It follows that the equilibrium level of such spending per firm, x^*, will fall as the number of firms rises.

This does not necessarily imply, however, that the total industry spending on R&D, which is nx^*, will also fall. It is perfectly possible that each firm spends less on R&D but total R&D spending increases. Dasgupta and Stiglitz show that aggregate spending on R&D may actually either increase or decrease as the number of firms in the industry increases. The key point is that for aggregate R&D spending to increase, the elasticity of market demand must be fairly large. When demand is relatively elastic, the expansion of industry output resulting from a greater number of firms will not decrease the price too much and, as a result, will not decrease the marginal revenue of equation (20.3) very much either. Because this difference between price and cost is what finances a firm's R&D expenditure, such expenditure can be expected to rise in total with the number of industry firms so long as η is relatively large. If, however, the elasticity of market demand declines as output expands (as is the case with linear demand curves), then increasing the number of firms will, beyond some point, lead to a reduction in total R&D efforts. Even for a relatively small number of firms in the market adding one more firm induces a decline in total R&D spending. Therefore, the Dasgupta and Stiglitz model may be taken as partial support for the Schumpeterian hypothesis that concentration fosters innovation.

The foregoing does not explain what determines the number of firms in an industry. Dasgupta and Stiglitz invoke a third equilibrium condition that, in the long run, free entry will lead to an increase in the number of firms until each firm makes zero profit. In other words, industry structure is determined endogenously by the firms' output and R&D expenditure decisions. The zero profit condition, when applied to equation (20.1), tells us that

$$P(Q^*)q^* - c(x^*)q^* - x^* = 0 \qquad (20.6)$$

Aggregating this over the equilibrium number of firms in the industry, n^*, gives

$$P(Q^*)Q^* - c(x^*)Q^* - n^*x^* = 0 \tag{20.7}$$

which implies that $(P(Q^*) - c(x^*))Q^* = n^*x^*$. Now because each of the n firms is of the same size, each has a market share equal to $1/n$. By equation (20.2) we know that $P - c(x^*) = P/n^*\eta$. Using this substitution, the equilibrium R&D outcome derived by Dasgupta and Stiglitz is

$$\frac{n^*x^*}{P(Q^*)Q^*} = industry\ R\&D\ spending\ as\ a\ share\ of\ industry\ sales = \frac{1}{n^*\eta} \tag{20.8}$$

Comparing across industries, equation (20.8) suggests that the share of an industry's total sales revenue that will be devoted to R&D is likely to be smaller in less concentrated industries. In other words, those industries with a naturally more competitive structure will undertake less R&D effort, all else equal. This may then be seen as offering fairly strong theoretical support for Schumpeter's basic claim that imperfect competition is good for technical progress and more imperfect competition is even better.

20.4   EVIDENCE ON THE SCHUMPETERIAN HYPOTHESIS

The debate over the Schumpeterian hypothesis cannot be resolved by an appeal to economic theory alone. We must also consider empirical evidence. To date, a number of statistical studies relating R&D effort to firm size and industry structure have been conducted. While these studies are far from uniform in their results, one general finding does emerge. R&D intensity does appear to increase with increases in industrial concentration but only up to a rather modest value after which R&D efforts appear to level off or even decline as a fraction of firm revenue.

Some of the earliest studies exploring the link between industry structure and R&D were those of Scherer (1965, 1967). His basic finding was that while firm size and concentration are each positively associated with the intensity of R&D spending, these correlations diminish beyond a relatively low threshold. That is, once firms reach a relatively small size and/or markets reach a relatively low level of concentration, any positive effects of firm size or market concentration on innovative activity tend to vanish. Subsequent studies, including those of Levin and Reiss (1984); Levin, Cohen and Mowery (1985 and 1987); Levin, Klevorick, Nelson, and Winter (1987); Lunn (1986); Scott (1990); Geroski (1990); and Blundell, Griffith and Van Reem (1995) have tended to confirm Scherer's (1965) basic finding.[11]

In examining the influence of firm size and market structure on innovative activity, a number of important issues must be addressed. The first of these is that in comparing R&D efforts across markets, we should control for the "science-based" character of each industry: recall the very different patent activity by industry category noted in Table 20.2. Markets in which the member firms produce goods such as chemical products or computer hardware have such a strong technical base that general advances in scientific understanding can rapidly translate into either product or process innovations. Other markets, however, such as

[11]   See Cohen and Levin (1989) for an early summary.

those for haircuts or hairstyling, have limited ability to make use of scientific breakthroughs and have less direct contact with universities and research laboratories. It turns out that measures of such technological opportunities tend to be highly correlated with the degree of industry concentration. In other words, while the simple correlation between concentration and innovation may be positive, this correlation reflects the positive effects on innovation that come with increases in an industry's opportunity for technical advances. The more recent studies cited above demonstrate that controlling for this factor is very important.

A second factor is the distinction between R&D expenditures and true innovations as perhaps measured by patents. While innovative effort can be measured by the ratio of R&D spending to sales, this approach really measures the inputs to the innovative process. Presumably though, what we are really interested in are the outputs of that process—the true number of innovations as perhaps measured by the number of patents a firm acquires. Even though different firms do the same amount of R&D spending, the Schumpeterian hypothesis might be validated if size or concentration leads that spending to be more productive. The studies cited above do in fact look at the patent output of firms. Here again, however, little evidence is found in support of the Schumpeterian claims. Cohen and Klepper (1996) conclude that the general finding is that large firms do proportionately more R&D than smaller firms but get fewer innovations from these efforts. A notable exception in this regard, however, is Gayle (2002) who finds that firms in concentrated industries do generate many more patents when patents are not simply counted but, instead, are measured on a citation-weighted basis.[12]

Finally, a third issue is the endogeneity of market structure. Some firms, for example Alcoa or Microsoft, came to dominate their industry on the basis of a dramatic innovation. In the case of Alcoa, it was its unique process for refining aluminum. In the case of Microsoft, it was its unique *Windows* operating systems for personal computers. In these and other cases, the key technology that led to the firm's dominant position was associated with a number of patents. If this experience is pervasive, a naïve researcher may find that large, dominant firms are also firms with many patents and wrongly conclude that the Schumpeterian hypothesis is validated. In these cases, it is the innovative activity that leads to market power and not the other way around. If the firms that come to dominate their markets start out as small operations and then grow on the basis of entrepreneurial skill and technical breakthroughs, the implication would be quite to the contrary of Schumpeter's model.[13]

20.5   R&D COOPERATION BETWEEN FIRMS

Our final topic in this chapter is the issue of cooperation on R&D efforts among firms. Two features of the innovative process make such efforts attractive from the viewpoint of economic efficiency. First, modern technology is very complicated and often draws on different areas of expertise and experience. Because it is doubtful that the scientists

---

[12]   When a patent application is filed, the applicant must cite all the prior patents related to the new process or product. It is plausible that the most important patents are those that are cited most frequently. Hence, in evaluating a firm's true innovative output, one may want to control for how often the firm's patents are cited.

[13]   Generally, market structure and innovative activity evolve together. For example, if experience raises R&D productivity then older firms will tend to do more innovation because it has a higher return for them, so that early entrants will tend to dominate an industry over time. See Klepper (2002) for an analysis along these lines.

and engineers in one firm possess all this know-how, it is desirable that firms share their experiences, experimental results, and design solutions with each other so as to realize fully the benefits from scientific study. Second, there is a potential for wasteful R&D spending as firms duplicate each other's efforts in a noncooperative R&D race.

We do have explicit evidence on this score. In the 1980's, steel minimills emerged as one of the most dynamic sectors in the US economy. These firms rely on small-scale plants using electric arc furnaces to recycle scrap steel. They became widely regarded as world leaders and have outperformed even the Japanese steel firms once thought to be invincible. Through a series of interviews, von Hippel (1988) found that these firms regularly and routinely exchanged technical information with each other. In fact, sometimes workers of competing firms were trained (at no charge) by a rival company in the use of specific equipment. Such exchanges of information and expertise were made with the knowledge and approval of management even though they had the effect of strengthening a competitor.

To analyze the implications of research spillovers, we again make use of the Cournot duopoly model, similar to the Dasgupta and Stiglitz (1980) model except that we now explicitly permit one firm's research to benefit others.[14] We address three issues. First, how do technical spillovers affect the incentives firms have to undertake R&D? Second, what is the impact of such spillovers on the effects of R&D? Finally, what are the benefits to be gained from allowing firms to cooperate in their research, for example, by forming research joint ventures (RJVs)? Are these benefits worth the risk that cooperation in R&D might facilitate collusion between the same firms in the final product markets?

To begin, suppose that the demand for a homogeneous good is linear and given by $P = A - BQ$. Two firms, each of which has constant marginal costs of c per unit, manufacture the good. These costs can be reduced by research and development activity, but it is possible that the knowledge developed by one firm can spill over to its rival. This can happen, for example, because the firms fund common sources of basic research such as universities or research laboratories; or because the research direction that one firm is taking becomes known to its rival; or because some of the preliminary results of research effort leak out; or, of course, because of industrial espionage.

Specifically, if firm 1 undertakes R&D at intensity x_1 and firm 2 undertakes R&D at intensity x_2, the marginal production costs of the two firms become

$$c_1 = c - x_1 - \beta x_2$$
$$c_2 = c - x_2 - \beta x_1 \qquad\qquad (20.9)$$

Here $0 \leq \beta \leq 1$ measures the degree to which the R&D activities of one firm spill over to the other firm.[15] If $\beta = 0$, there are no spillovers—firm 1's research effort x_1 yields benefits only to firm 1 itself. If $\beta = 1$, spillovers are perfect—every penny of cost reduction that x_1 brings to firm 1, it also brings to firm 2. For the intermediate case of $0 < \beta < 1$, spillovers are only partial—if firm 1's research lowers its own cost by one dollar per unit, it will lower firm 2's cost by some fraction of a dollar per unit.

---

[14]   The model is developed in d'Aspremont and Jacquemin (1988). A more general version of this type of investigation can be found in Kamien et al. (1992).

[15]   We confine our attention to the case in which the spillovers are positive. It is, however, possible that there might be negative spillovers. For example, firms might spread misinformation about their research or claim that they have made a breakthrough in order to discourage rivals from continuing with a particular line of research.

Research is, of course, costly. Indeed, not only is it costly, but we assume that R&D activity exhibits *diseconomies* of scale, i.e., it becomes more costly the more research the firm does. Specifically, we assume that research costs are the same for both firms and given by the research cost function

$$r(x_i) = \frac{x_i^2}{2}, \quad i = 1,2. \tag{20.10}$$

Thus, if the R&D intensity is $x_i = 10$, then the research budget $r(x_i) = 10^2/2 = \$50$. If the R&D intensity doubles to $x_i = 20$, the budgetary expense climbs to $20^2/2 = \$400$. A doubling of R&D effort therefore leads to a quadrupling of the R&D cost. This is an example of what we mean by a scale diseconomy.

20.5.1 Noncooperative R&D: Profit, Prices, and Social Welfare

Consider first what happens when firms do not cooperate on research. Suppose that we have a two-stage game and in the first stage, each firm chooses its research intensity x_i. In the second stage, each firm acts as a Cournot competitor in choosing its output. As usual, this game is solved backwards. Again, from Chapter 9 we know the Cournot equilibrium outputs for given values of c_1 and c_2 are

$$q_1^C = \frac{(A - 2c_1 + c_2)}{3B}$$

$$q_2^C = \frac{(A - 2c_2 + c_1)}{3B} \tag{20.11}$$

and the firm profits after paying the research costs are

$$\pi_1^C = \frac{(A - 2c_1 + c_2)^2}{9B} - \frac{x_1^2}{2}$$

$$\pi_2^C = \frac{(A - 2c_2 + c_1)^2}{9B} - \frac{x_2^2}{2} \tag{20.12}$$

We also know from equation (20.9) that $c_1 = c - x_1 - \beta x_2$ and $c_2 = c - x_2 - \beta x_1$. This allows us to express the final equilibrium outputs directly as a function of each firm's choice of R&D effort and the degree of spillover from one firm's findings to the other firm's costs. The resultant Cournot–Nash equilibrium outputs for each firm are

$$q_1^C = \frac{(A - c + x_1(2 - \beta) + x_2(2\beta - 1))}{3B}$$

$$q_2^C = \frac{(A - c + x_2(2 - \beta) + x_1(2\beta - 1))}{3B} \tag{20.13}$$

and their profits are

$$\pi_1^C = \frac{(A - c + x_1(2 - \beta) + x_2(2\beta - 1))^2}{9B} - \frac{x_1^2}{2}$$

$$\pi_2^C = \frac{(A - c + x_2(2 - \beta) + x_1(2\beta - 1))^2}{9B} - \frac{x_2^2}{2} \tag{20.14}$$

Equation (20.13) indicates that the output of each firm is an increasing function of its own R&D expenditures x_i. Such expenditures reduce a firm's costs and thereby make higher output more profitable. By contrast, the effect of the *rival's* R&D effort on a firm's production can go either way. Consider firm 1. On the one hand, the R&D activity of firm 2 spills over and lowers firm 1's costs, which has an expansionary effect on firm 1's own output. On the other hand, firm 2's R&D reduces firm 2's cost. This makes firm 2 more competitive and permits it to expand its output leaving less market available to firm 1. The net result of these two countervailing forces is ambiguous. This ambiguity is reflected in the coefficient on x_2 in the q_1 equation and the coefficient of x_1 in the q_2 equation. In both cases, this coefficient, $2\beta - 1$, is positive only when the degree of spillover is large, that is, when $\beta > 0.5$. When spillovers are small, that is, when $\beta < 0.5$, a firm's output and profit are decreasing functions of the R&D expenditures of its rival. The same ambiguity appears in the profit equations (20.14).

We know that each firm will choose the level of research activity that maximizes its profit given the research effort of its rival. For every choice of effort that firm 2 makes, firm 1 will choose its own profit-maximizing response. The same is true for firm 2 in reverse. So we can in principle identify the best response or *research intensity reaction function* for each firm.

This is done in the Appendix to this chapter, allowing us to specify the research intensity reaction functions as follows:

$$R_1 : x_1 = \frac{2(2 - \beta)[A - c + x_2(2\beta - 1)]}{[9B - 2(2 - \beta)^2]} \text{ and } R_2 : x_2 = \frac{2(2 - \beta)[A - c + x_1(2\beta - 1)]}{[9B - 2(2 - \beta)^2]}$$

$$(20.15)$$

Inspection of these functions confirms an intuitive result that follows from our previous discussion. When research spillovers are low, the research intensity reaction functions for the two firms are downward sloping, indicating that the research expenditures of the two firms are *strategic substitutes*—more research by one firm reduces the amount done by the other. That is, research activity by one firm substitutes for research activity by the other. The intuition is that in this case the increased research effort by one firm primarily reduces its costs and so gives it a competitive advantage with respect to the other rival firm. In turn, this results in a reduction in the profitability of the rival firm, which can be offset only by the rival reducing its expenditure on research.

By contrast, when spillovers are high, the research intensity reaction functions are upward sloping, meaning that the research expenditures of the two firms are *strategic complements*. When spillovers are this high, an increase in research intensity by one of the firms induces an increase in research intensity by the other. In this case the intuition is that if one firm opts for a high level of R&D effort, the benefits of that activity spill over to the other firm to such an extent that the other firm's profit increases, providing that firm with the funds and the incentive to increase its own R&D spending. Figure 20.4 illustrates typical research intensity reaction functions.

However, determining whether the reaction functions slope downward or upward—whether the two firms' R&D efforts are strategic substitutes or complements—does not tell us what the equilibrium level of R&D spending is. In particular, there can be no presumption that the presence of large R&D spillovers and hence the case of strategic complements will

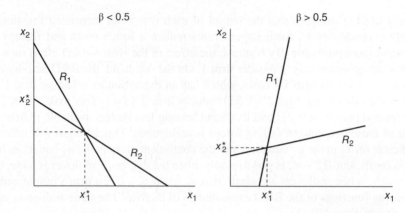

Figure 20.4   Best response functions for research intensity in the noncooperative R&D game

result in a higher equilibrium level of R&D spending than the case in which such spillovers are low. The Nash equilibrium occurs at the intersection of the two response functions, and the case in which this point is farthest from the origin is far from obvious.

In order to illustrate this last point, we focus for the remainder of our discussion on a numeric example. The Appendix gives a more general mathematical analysis. Let demand for the good be $P = 100 - 2Q$, and each firm's marginal production cost currently be \$60. The firms can choose two levels of research intensity: $x_i = 10$ or $x_i = 7.5$. Further, we assume that the degree of research spillover (which is outside the control of the two firms) takes one of two values: a low value of $\beta = 1/4$ or a high value of $\beta = 3/4$.

Consider first the low-spillover case and assume that firm 2 chooses the high research intensity of $x_2 = 10$. If firm 1 also chooses high research intensity, its output and profits will be, from equations (20.13) and (20.14)

$$q_1^C = \frac{(40 + 17.5 - 5)}{6} = 8.75; \pi_1^C = \frac{(40 + 17.5 - 5)^2}{18} - \frac{100}{2} = \$103.13$$

By contrast, if firm 1 chooses the low research intensity, its output and profits will be

$$q_1^C = \frac{(40 + 13.125 - 5)}{6} = 8.02; \pi_1^C = \frac{(40 + 13.125 - 5)^2}{18} - \frac{56.25}{2} = \$100.54$$

Now assume that firm 2 chooses the low research intensity of $x_2 = 7.5$. If firm 1 chooses the high research intensity, its output and profits will be

$$q_1^C = \frac{(40 + 17.5 - 3.75)}{6} = 8.96; \pi_1^C = \frac{(40 + 17.5 - 3.75)^2}{18} - \frac{100}{2} = \$110.50$$

By contrast, if firm 1 chooses the low research intensity, its output and profit will be

$$q_1^C = \frac{(40 + 13.125 - 3.75)}{6} = 8.23; \pi_1^C = \frac{(40 + 13.125 - 3.75)^2}{18} - \frac{56.25}{2} = \$107.31$$

Table 20.3(a)   Payoff matrix with low R&D spillovers, $\beta = 0.25$

		Firm 2	
		Low Research Intensity	High Research Intensity
Firm 1	Low Research Intensity	$107.31; $107.31	$100.54; $110.50
	High Research Intensity	$110.50; $100.54	$103.13; $103.13

Table 20.3(b)   Payoff matrix with low R&D spillovers, $\beta = 0.75$

		Firm 2	
		Low Research Intensity	High Research Intensity
Firm 1	Low Research Intensity	$128.67; $128.67	$136.13; $125.78
	High Research Intensity	$125.78; $136.13	$133.68; $133.68

The same calculations apply to firm 2. We then have the payoff matrix of Table 20.3(a). *The Nash equilibrium in this case of low spillovers is for both firms to adopt high research intensities.*

When the degree of R&D spillover is high, with $\beta = 0.75$, the same calculations lead to the payoff matrix of Table 20.3(b). *The Nash equilibrium in this case is for both firms to adopt low research intensities.*

An increase in the degree of R&D spillover causes the two firms to reduce their research intensities. Why? Consider first the case in which R&D spillovers are weak. In this case the more firm 1 spends on R&D, the less firm 2 will spend because the primary effect of such spending is to strengthen the competitive position of firm 1. Yet somewhat paradoxically, this gives each firm an incentive to spend aggressively on R&D so as to avoid being the loser in this competition. If firm 1 spends a lot on R&D and firm 2 spends nothing, virtually all the benefits of firm 1's spending stay with firm 1. Firm 2 would find itself losing significant market share and profit to a much lower-cost competitor. When each firm tries to avoid falling behind in this manner, the net result can be a substantial amount of R&D effort, both at each firm and in total.

Just the opposite holds in the case of large spillovers. Yes, the more firm 1 spends on R&D, the more firm 2 is induced to spend by virtue of the strategic-complements setting, but this relation is a two-edged sword. Even if firm 1 spends only a little on R&D it knows that this will still induce firm 2 to do a fair bit of research activity. Moreover, the research activity at firm 2 will bring substantial benefits to firm 1 by virtue of the large spillovers. In this setting, the incentive for either firm to spend much on R&D can be quite small as each firm seeks to free ride on the other's efforts.

Where graphs fail to give clear results, algebra can often save the day. That this is true here is shown in the Appendix. The Nash equilibrium level of research intensity is:

$$x_1^C = x_2^C = \frac{2(A - c)(2 - \beta)}{9B - 2(2 - \beta)(1 + \beta)} \tag{20.16}$$

The amount of research done by each firm *decreases* as β, the degree of R&D spillover, increases—the free-riding effect to which we have just referred.

20.5.2   Technology Cooperation

We now consider two other possible arrangements between the duopoly firms that can alter the outcome from that described above. The first possibility is that the two firms agree that while each will continue to do its own R&D, they will coordinate the extent of such research effort. Thus, the two firms now choose x_1 and x_2 to maximize their joint profit. They continue to recognize that they will compete as Cournot firms in the product market. The other possibility we consider is that the firms explicitly share their R&D activities by setting up a Research Joint Venture (RJV). One way this scenario might work in practice would be for the two firms to jointly set up a laboratory for experimentation and analysis with all the discoveries made at that laboratory to be made fully available to both firms.

We introduce this RJV arrangement into the model by letting the two firms pick x_1 and x_2 cooperatively but by adding the further assumption that the degree of spillover is complete, that is, $\beta = 1$. Whatever is learned in the research lab—whether discovered by a firm 1 scientist or a firm 2 scientist—reduces the cost of both firms by the same amount.

We start with the simple coordination case. What we want to do is to pick the values of x_1 and x_2 that maximize the sum of the individual profit expressions shown in equation (20.14). The mathematical solution, as in the previous section, is developed in the Appendix to this chapter. The equilibrium research intensity is:

$$x_1^{RC} = x_2^{RC} = \frac{2(A - c)(1 + \beta)}{9B - 2(1 + \beta)^2} \tag{20.17}$$

We shall concentrate once again on our simplified example as given by the payoff matrices of Tables 20.3(a) and 20.3(b). When the firms coordinate their research efforts they choose the combination of R&D intensities that maximizes the sum of the profits in the cells of the relevant payoff matrix. *When R&D spillovers are low, coordination leads each of the firms to choose the low R&D intensity.* Cooperation then increases each firm's profits from \$103.13 to \$107.31. By contrast, *when the R&D spillover is high, coordination leads each firm to choose the high R&D intensity,* increasing their profits from \$128.67 to \$133.68.

What our example and the more detailed analysis in the Appendix show is the following. First, it is now the case that the higher is the level of R&D spillover—the larger is β—the more each firm spends on research: this follows directly from equation (20.17). This is because the agreement between the two firms to set their R&D efforts jointly explicitly forces each firm to internalize the external benefits that such spending has upon its rival. In turn, this eliminates the free-riding problem that characterizes R&D competition when there are high spillovers. The ability to avoid this problem also means that the two firms will each enjoy a profit at least as great as that which they would have earned in the absence of such cooperation.[16]

The second point to note is that the outcome under the simple coordination plan may not necessarily be good for the consumer. In particular, consumers are hurt by the technology cooperation when $\beta < 0.5$ and the extent of spillover is small. The reason is straightforward. When β is small, then without cooperation each firm tends to do a fair bit of research. It does so because a low value of β means that most of the benefit from its innovative efforts will accrue to it alone and because it knows that its rival is proceeding along the same line of

---

[16]   For $\beta = 0.5$ each firm earns exactly the same profit under uncoordinated R&D spending as each does with an R&D cartel. For all other values of β each firm's profit is higher with the R&D cartel.

attack. From the viewpoint of consumers, this is great because there has been considerable cost reduction and therefore a sharp decline in the price they pay. If, in this setting, we now introduce a cooperative R&D agreement, the two firms realize that their best bet is to reduce R&D intensity, which otherwise simply makes competition tougher in the product market. By decreasing R&D intensity, the firms increase their profits. Unfortunately, the lower rate of innovation also implies a higher price to consumers.

By contrast, when the degree of R&D spillover is high ($\beta > 0.5$), both firms and consumers benefit from a cooperative R&D agreement. This happens because now the primary effect of the R&D cooperation is to correct a market failure. In the absence of cooperation, a large degree of spillover leads each firm to free ride on the R&D efforts of its rivals and to take no account of the beneficial effects its own R&D expenditures have on the costs and profits of other firms. R&D cooperation internalizes these effects because it forces the cooperating firms to look at the impact their R&D expenditures have on aggregate profit rather than merely on their individual profit.

What about a research joint venture? As noted, an RJV can be best thought of as a case in which the firms take actions not only to coordinate their research expenditures but also to ensure that the spillover from one firm's research to the other's is complete, that is, so that $\beta = 1$. A little thought should convince you that an RJV will likely yield the maximum benefits to both firms and consumers. As we just saw, coordination of R&D levels benefits both producers and consumers whenever $\beta > 0.5$. Moreover, the profit outcomes in Tables 20.3 indicate that if the firms could find some way of increasing the technology spillover from $\beta = 0.25$ to $\beta = 0.75$, they would both benefit at *any* research intensity. We can make this discussion even more general. In the Appendix we show that an increase in the spillover parameter β increases the research intensity and the profits of each firm *and* increases the output that each firm brings to the market. In other words, *both firms and consumers benefit from an increase in β*. The RJV takes this to its logical conclusion by ensuring that $\beta = 1$, its highest possible value. The equilibrium research intensity with $\beta = 1$ is:

$$x_1^{RJV} = x_2^{RJV} = \frac{4(A - c)}{9B - 8} \tag{20.18}$$

The RJV gives higher profits *and* lower prices than any other arrangement.

In our example, the benefits of an RJV are easily confirmed. Consider the case in which both firms choose the high degree of research intensity. Thus, with perfect R&D spillover, the profits to each firm are $(40 + 10 + 10)^2/18 - 50 = \$150$, while if each chooses the low research intensity, the profits to each firm will be $(40 + 7.5 + 7.5)^2/18 - 56.25/2 = \$139.93$. Clearly, the RJV will go for the high research intensity leading to the lowest costs. In turn, this will translate into the lowest consumer prices that these Cournot firms will offer.

The intuition behind the foregoing analysis is as follows. First, by maximizing the extent of spillovers, the RJV also maximizes the benefits of R&D. Every discovery is spread instantly to all firms in the industry. Second, despite this perfect spillover, the free-riding problem is now avoided. Because the two firms have agreed to coordinate their research efforts they fully internalize the otherwise external effects of research. Thus, firms will pursue extensive research, which, partly because of the perfect spillover effect of sharing, will lead to a sizable reduction in costs for every firm. This substantial cost reduction translates into an equally impressive reduction in the price to consumers.[17] The policy

---

[17]   While we have derived this result for a duopoly, Kamien et al. (1992) show that it extends to an *n*-firm oligopoly.

implication of this is obvious and important. Research joint ventures should be encouraged because they benefit both consumers and producers so long as the antitrust authorities can ensure that such cooperation on research effort does not also extend to cooperation in production and prices, that is, to a price-fixing cartel.

The potentially large benefit from technology cooperation is undoubtedly the reason that research joint ventures—unlike price-fixing agreements—are not treated as *per se* violations by the antitrust authorities. Instead, they are evaluated on a rule of reason basis. Indeed, the US Congress passed legislation in 1984 to require explicitly the application of a reasonability standard in the specific case of RJVs.

20.6   EMPIRICAL APPLICATION: R&D SPILLOVERS IN PRACTICE

R&D spillovers suggest a diffusion-like process. The greater the spillover, the more rapid or the more complete is the diffusion of technological advances in one firm to the productivity of other firms. We might also suspect that a similar process is at work at a national and even international level. In particular, it seems likely that the R&D efforts of one country could spill over to enhance the productivity of its neighbors. Here again, the extent of such spillover is of interest. If technical advances in one country spread quickly to others, β will be high. In a world in which the international transfer of technical knowledge is weak, β will be low.

Wolfgang Keller (2002) explores the extent of international technical spillover by looking at data covering twelve broadly defined manufacturing industries from fourteen countries over the years, 1970–95. To understand his basic approach, consider a simple Cobb-Douglas production function (see Section 4.5) for industry i in country c.

$$Q_{ci} = K_{ci}^{1-\sigma} L_{ci}^{\sigma} \tag{20.19}$$

Here Q_{ci} is output (value added) and K_{ci} and L_{ci} are capital and labor inputs, respectively, in industry i in country c and σ is the share of costs accounted for by labor. Taking logarithms then yields:

$$\ln Q_{ci} = (1 - \sigma) \ln K_{ci} + \sigma \ln L_{ci} \tag{20.20}$$

For industry i, we define $\ln \overline{Q}_{ci}$ to be the average log of output across all countries. Similarly, for industry i, let $\ln \overline{K}_{ci}$, and $\ln \overline{L}_{ci}$ be the average amount of capital and labor inputs (again in logs), respectively, across all countries. If we define total factor productivity, TFP_{ci}, in industry i and country c as the difference between the log of output and the weighted average level of inputs, i.e., $TFP_{ci} = \ln Q_{ci} - (1 - \sigma)n K_{ci} + \sigma \ln L_{ci}$, then the *relative* (to the mean) factor productivity F_{ci} of industry i in country c at a point in time is:

$$F_{ci} = (\ln Q_{ci} - \ln \overline{Q}_{ci}) - (1 - \sigma_{ci})(\ln K_{ci} - \ln \overline{K}_{ci}) - \sigma_{ci}(\ln L_{ci} - \ln \overline{L}_{ci}) \tag{20.21}$$

where we now let the cost share of labor σ_{ci} vary across countries and industries. Equation (20.21) is a measure of the extent to which output in industry i in country c remains above average even after correcting for any above average use of inputs. It is thus a measure of the productivity advantage (or disadvantage) in industry i in country c at any point in time. This is why it is called *relative* productivity. Of course, this will probably change over time due to R&D and other factors. For this reason, Keller (2002) measures relative productivity for each year from 1970 to 1995. This means that for each of the twelve industries in each of the fourteen countries, Keller (2002) has a measure of relative productivity in each year, 1970 to 1995. Because we are now measuring this term over time as well as over industries and across countries, relative factor productivity now has an additional time subscript, i.e., F_{cit}. It is this series of relative productivity measures that Keller seeks to explain.

Because, by construction, variations in the relative productivity measure F_{cit} reflect variations in factors other than capital and labor inputs, it is natural to identify these remaining differences as those due to differences in technology. In turn, these technical differences ought to reflect differences in R&D. Keller's (2002) approach in this respect is to distinguish between R&D done domestically in industry i and that done abroad. The first research question is whether foreign R&D spills over to domestic productivity. The second is whether these spillovers are greater for countries that are closer to each other.

The fourteen countries in Keller's (2002) sample are: Australia, Canada, Denmark, Finland, France, Germany, Italy, Japan, the Netherlands, Norway, Spain, Sweden, the United Kingdom, and the United States. Five of these countries—France, Germany, Japan, the United Kingdom, and the United States—account for over 92 percent of all the R&D in the sample. Hence, Keller (2002) treats these G5 countries as the potential engines of technical change and examines how their R&D affects productivity in the remaining nine. Specifically, he estimates the parameters of the following equation:

$$ F_{cit} = \alpha_{ci} + \alpha_t + \lambda \ln \left[S_{cit} + \gamma \left(\sum_{g \in G5} S_{git} e^{-\delta D_{cg}} \right) \right] + \varepsilon_{cit} \tag{20.22} $$

Here, F_{cit} is the relative productivity measure derived above for industry i in country c in year t, measured for each of the nine countries examined. The first term is a country and industry specific constant that permits for a time-independent productivity advantage or disadvantage for that sector in that country. The second is meant to pick up productivity increases over time that affect all firms in all countries in common. The key parameters are embedded in the next term. S_{cit} is a measure of the R&D done in industry i in country c up to time t. In contrast, S_{git} is a measure of R&D in that same industry but in one of the G5 countries and D_{cg} is the distance of that country from the domestic country in question. ($D = 1$ implies a distance of 235 kilometers.) Together, S_{cit} and the summation term for the G5 countries are meant to capture the R&D relevant to productivity in the domestic industry i at time t.

The effect of that combined industry-based R&D on productivity in that same industry in the domestic country is captured by the parameter λ. However, two adjustments are included to distinguish the impact of foreign R&D from that of domestic R&D. To understand the first of these adjustments suppose that all G5 countries were right next to the domestic country in question ($D_{cg} = 0$). Then the contribution of their R&D on domestic productivity in industry i to total industry-relevant R&D is adjusted by the parameter γ (taken to be same for all G5 countries). That is, if $\gamma < 1$, foreign R&D contributes less than the full effect of domestic R&D in adding to the knowledge relevant to a particular domestic industry's productivity. In many ways then, γ is comparable to the β of our industry analysis above. However, Keller (2002) also introduces a second source of distinction between domestic and foreign research lies in the distance term, D_{cg}. As this distance grows, the contribution of that G5 country's R&D to domestic productivity diminishes further if the parameter δ is positive. In short, the specification permits both for the possibility that simply by being foreign R&D may contribute less to domestic technology than home-grown research, and also for the more complicated fact that spillovers from foreign R&D grow smaller as the source of that R&D is farther away. Of course, the error term ε_{cit} picks up any remaining random factors that affect productivity.

The specification in equation (20.22) assumes that the decay parameter δ is the same throughout the time period. Keller (2002) recognizes, however, that increased globalization over the twenty-five years of his sample suggests that δ will decline over this period. He therefore estimates an alternative specification given by:

$$F_{cit} = \alpha_{ci} + \alpha_t + \lambda \ln \left[S_{cit} + \sum_{g \in G5} \gamma_G \left(1 + \psi_F I_t \right) S_{git} e^{-\delta(1+\psi_D I_t)D_{cg}} \right] + \varepsilon_{cit} \qquad (20.23)$$

In this equation, I_t is a 1,0 dummy variable equal to zero over the first half of the sample to 1982 and then 1 in the thirteen years thereafter. The coefficient ψ_F permits the effect of G5 R&D to have a different effect on domestic productivity in the second half of the sample than it does in the first, holding the distance between the domestic and G5 countries constant. Similarly, the coefficient ψ_D permits the extent to which spillovers decline with distance to change from the first half of the sample to the second half. Note too that this specification allows the effect of G5 R&D to differ across each G5 country by permitting a different coefficient γ_G for each one. This is reasonable as the different languages in these countries may affect the ease with which a technology can be transferred.

Because the contribution of foreign R&D to the total relevant measure of R&D depends on the parameters γ (or γ_G) and δ that are also to be estimated, equations (20.22) and (20.23) cannot be estimated by ordinary least squares. Instead, a nonlinear least squares estimation is required. In this procedure, we begin with a starting value for the nonlinear parameters and then estimate the regression with OLS. We may then use these estimates to reiterate the process until the coefficient estimates stop changing and converge to stable values. Table 20.4 shows the key parameter estimates and their standard errors that Keller (2002) obtains from this maximum likelihood process for both specifications.

Table 20.4   Regression estimates of international R&D spillovers

Parameter	Specification 1		Specification 2	
	Parameter Estimate	Standard Error	Parameter Estimate	Standard Error
λ	0.078	(0.013)	0.096	(0.008)
δ	1.005	(0.239)	0.384	(0.047)
γ	0.843	(0.059)	—	—
γ_J	—	—	1.000 (set)	set
γ_{US}	—	—	1.031	(0.059)
γ_{UK}	—	—	0.863	(0.060)
γ_{GER}	—	—	1.157	(0.060)
γ_F	—	—	1.011	(0.060)
ψ_D	—	—	−0.784	(0.068)
ψ_F	—	—	−0.061	(0.108)

The estimates in Specification 1 suggest that technical spillovers are strongly localized. The cumulative productivity effect of overall R&D is to raise productivity by 7.8 percent. However, foreign (G5) R&D contributes only 84 percent to the technical base that domestic research does and that is only if the domestic country is right next to the G5 source nation so that $D = 0$. The estimate of $\delta = 1.05$ though, indicates that that contribution dies out rapidly. Half of it is gone when $D = 0.69$ or at a distance of 162 kilometers (100 miles), and the rest is virtually eliminated once the source country of the foreign R&D is more than 400 miles away.

However, the results from Specification 2 qualify the foregoing findings. It is useful to first note that the estimate of ψ_F is insignificantly different from zero. Hence, correcting for distance and country of origin, the contribution of a G5 country's R&D on domestic technical know-how is pretty much the same throughout the sample years and, on average, not too different from the 84 percent found in Specification 1 when the distance to the G5 country is $D = 0$. The real change comes in the extent to which the impact of G5 R&D declines with distance. Now the estimate of δ is a much smaller 0.384, indicating that the effect declines much more slowly with distance, even in the first half of the sample when $I_t = 0$. Over the latter half, though, when I_t is 1, the estimate of $\psi_D = -0.784$ indicates that this small rate of decline is even smaller from 1983 to 1995 than it was previously. Together, these estimates indicate that at least half of the effect that a G5 nation's R&D would have had if the domestic country had been right next to it ($D = 0$) is still there as far out as 424 kilometers (263 miles) from 1970 to 1982, and is felt as far out as 1,963 kilometers (1,217 miles) after 1983. This implies a larger and growing degree of technical spillovers between industries in different nations.

Because Keller's spillover estimates apply to whole sectors separated by national boundaries there may well be a lower bound for the extent of such spillovers between firms within the same domestic industry. If this is so, then these empirical estimates when taken together with our analysis of the noncooperative outcome with high spillovers suggest that the market will likely be characterized by inefficiently low R&D. If that is the case, then the argument for permitting R&D cooperation and/or joint ventures becomes noticeably more compelling.

Summary

Research and development is the wellspring of technical advancement. Such advancement is the key source of the gain in per capita income and living standards that has characterized the developed economies for almost all of the past 200 years. Firms often compete by investing in R&D projects in the hope of uncovering cost-saving innovations and new consumer products. Such competition in R&D raises the question as to whether the market will yield efficient R&D outcomes. It also raises a potential tension between allocative efficiency at a point in time and dynamic efficiency over time.

The tension between the gains from competition and the gains from innovation, i.e., the tension between the replacement effect and the efficiency effect is unavoidable. It has led economists to consider which market environment—competitive or monopolistic—will foster greater research and development. The Schumpeterian hypothesis is, broadly speaking, that oligopolistic market structures are best in this regard.

Both theory and empirical data give ambiguous evidence as to the market structure most conducive to R&D effort. Competitive markets can sometimes fail to be as innovative as their less-competitive counterparts but a surprising number of key inventions have come from small firms. Policy has a role to play here, too. One role for policy is to encourage cooperation in research efforts. Empirical evidence suggests that we live in an increasingly interconnected world in which the benefits from one firm's R&D spill over to other firms including, in particular, its rivals. In such a world, the noncooperative outcome is likely to be one with too little R&D effort. Policy that fosters research cooperation among firms can be helpful in this setting. Yet caution is also necessary. The trick is somehow to foster cooperation on R&D without simultaneously inducing collaboration on prices and product design.

A similar tension arises in the role of patent policy. Patents can enhance the incentives for firms to pursue technological innovations. Yet, by temporarily granting monopoly power, patents can also weaken competitive forces and reduce consumers' access to those breakthroughs. We consider patents and related policy issues in the next chapter.

Problems

1. Assume that inverse demand is given by the linear function $P = A - BQ$ and that current marginal costs of production are c.

   a. By how much would an innovation have to reduce marginal cost for it to be a drastic innovation?

   b. Use your answer to derive a condition on the parameters A, B, and C that determines whether a drastic innovation is feasible. (Hint: costs cannot be negative.)

For Problems 2 through 5 assume the following: Inverse demand is given by $P = 240 - Q$. The discount factor is 0.9. Marginal production costs are initially $120:

2. Calculate the market equilibrium price, output, and profits (if any) on the assumption that the market is currently

   a. monopolized;
   b. a Bertrand duopoly;
   c. a Cournot duopoly.

3. Suppose that a research institute develops a new technology that reduces marginal costs to $60.

   a. Confirm that this is not a drastic innovation in either the Bertrand or Cournot cases.

   b. Calculate the new market equilibrium price, output, and profits for the monopolist and each duopolist, given that in the duopoly case the innovation is made available to only one firm.

   c. How much will the monopolist and duopolist each be willing to pay for the innovation?

4. Now assume that there is a potential entrant in the monopolized case and that the research institute is considering offering the innovation to this firm as well as to the monopolist. How does this affect the amount that the incumbent monopolist will be willing to pay for the innovation?

5. Now return to the duopoly case but assume that the research institute is considering whether it should actually sell the innovation to both firms. Will it wish to do so

   a. in the Bertrand duopoly?
   b. in the Cournot duopoly?

6. Assume that annual inverse demand for a particular product is $P = 150 - Q$. The product is offered by a pair of Bertrand competitors, each with marginal costs of $75. The discount factor is 0.9. What is the current equilibrium price and total surplus?

7. Return to Problem 6. Assume now though that if R&D is conducted at rate x, it incurs one-off costs of $r(x) = 10x^2$ and reduces marginal costs to $(75 - x)$. Suppose that one firm decides to conduct R&D at rate $x = 10$. This research will be protected by a patent of T years.

   a. What profit (ignoring the one-off costs of R&D) does the innovating firm make each year during the period of patent protection?

   b. What is the new equilibrium price and total surplus once patent protection expires?

8. Use your answers to 7(a) and 7(b) to write the total net surplus from the innovation as

a function of the period of patent protection. Use a spreadsheet program to derive an approximation to the socially optimal period of patent protection.

9. How are your answers to 7(a) and (b) affected if the innovating firm conducts research at rate $x = 15$?

10. Why might industries facing less elastic demand do proportionately more R&D [Dasgupta and Stiglitz (1980)]?

References

Arrow, K., 1962. "Economic Welfare and the Allocation of Resources for Inventions," in R. Nelson, ed., *The Rate and Direction of Inventive Activity: Economic and Social Factors*. National Bureau of Economic Research. Princeton: Princeton University Press.

Barro, R., and X. Sala-i-Martin. 1995. *Economic Growth*, New York: McGraw-Hill.

Blundell, R., Griffith, R., and Van Reenen J., 1995. "Dynamic Count Data Models of Technological Innovation," *Economic Journal* 105 (March): 333–344.

Cohen, W., and Levin, R. 1989. "Empirical Studies of Innovation and Market Structure," in R. Schmalensee and R. Willig, eds., *Handbook of Industrial Organization, Vol.* 2. Amsterdam: North-Holland, 1059–98.

Cohen, W., and S. Klepper. 1996. "A Reprise of Size and R and D," *Economic Journal* 106 (July): 925–951.

Dasgupta, P., and J. Stiglitz. 1980. "Industrial Structure and the Nature of Innovative Activity," *Economic Journal* 90 (January): 266–93.

d'Aspremont, C., and A. Jacquemin. 1988. "Cooperative and Noncooperative R&D in Duopoly with Spillovers," *American Economic Review* 78 (September): 1133–7.

Gayle, P., 2002. "Market Structure and Product Innovation," Working Paper, Department of Economics, Kansas State University.

Geroski P., 1990. "Innovation, Technology Opportunity and Market Structure," *Oxford Economic Papers* 42 (July): 586–602.

Gilbert, R. J. 2006. "Competition and Innovation," *Journal of Industrial Organization Education*: Vol. 1: Issue 1, Article 8. Available at: http://www.bepress.com/jioe/vol1/iss1/8.

Gilbert, R. J., and D. M. G. Newbery. 1982. "Preemptive Patenting and the Persistence of Monopoly," *American Economic Review* 72 (June): 514–27.

Kamien, M. I., E. Muller, and I. Zang. 1992. "Research Joint Ventures and R&D Cartels," *American Economic Review* 82 (December): 1293–306.

Keller, W. 2002. "Geographic Localization of International Technology Transfer," *American Economic Review*, 92 (March): 120–42.

Klepper, S. 2002. "Firm Survival and the Evolution of Oligopoly," *Rand Journal of Economics* 33 (Spring): 37–61.

Levin, R., and P. Reiss. 1984. "Tests of a Schumpeterian Model of R and D and Market Structure," in Z. Griliches, ed., *R and D, Patents and Productivity*, Chicago: NBER University of Chicago Press.

Levin, R., W. Cohen, and D. C. Mowery. 1985. "R and D Appropriability, Opportunity, and Market Structure: New Evidence on Some Schumpeterian Hypotheses," *American Economic Review, Papers and Proceedings* 75 (May): 20–4.

———. 1987. "Firm Size and R&D Intensity: A Reexamination," *Journal of Industrial Economics* 35 (June): 543–65.

Levin, R., A. Klevorick, R. Nelson, and S. Winter. 1987. "Appropriating the Returns from Industrial Research and Development," *Brookings Papers on Economic Activity: Microeconomics* 2: 783–822.

Lunn, J. 1986. "An Empirical Analysis of Process and Product Patenting: A Simultaneous Equation Framework," *Journal of Industrial Economics* 34 (February): 319–30.

Markides, C., and P. Geroski. 2005. *Fast Second: How Smart Companies Bypass Radical Innovations to Dominate New Markets*, San Francisco: Jossey-Bass.

Peters, T., and R. Waterman. 1982. *In Search of Excellence*. New York: Harper & Row.

Porter, M. 1990. *The Competitive Advantage of Nations*, New York: The Free Press.

Reinganum, J. 1983. "Uncertain Innovation and the Persistence of Monopoly." *American Economic Review*, 73 (September): 741–48.

Romer, D. 2006. *Advanced Macroeconomics*, New York: McGraw-Hill/Irwin, 3rd ed.

Scherer, F. M. 1965. "Firm Size, Market Structure, Opportunity and the Output of Patented Innovations," *American Economic Review* 55 (September): 1097–125.

Scherer, F. M. 1967. "Market Structure and the Employment of Scientists and Engineers," *American Economic Review* 57 (June): 524–31.

Schumpeter, J. A. 1942. *Capitalism, Socialism, and Democracy*, New York: Harper.

Scott, J. T. 1990. "Purposeful Diversification of R&D and Technological Advancement," in A. Link, ed., *Advances in Applied Microeconomics*, Vol. 5. Greenwich, Conn., and London: JAI Press.

Solow, R., 1956. "A Contribution to the Theory of Economic Growth," *Quarterly Journal of Economics* 70 (February): 65–94.

von Hippel, E., 1988. *The Sources of Innovation*, New York: Oxford University Press.

Appendix

EQUILIBRIUM NONCOOPERATIVE R&D EFFORT IN THE PRESENCE OF SPILLOVERS

Differentiation of the profit equation (20.14) with respect to research effort of firm i and Solving for x_i implies best response curves R_1 and R_2 for firm 1 and firm 2 of:

$$R_1 : x_1 = \frac{2(2 - \beta)[A - c + x_2(2\beta - 1)]}{[9B - 2(2 - \beta)^2]}. \tag{20.A1}$$

and

$$R_2 : x_2 = \frac{2(2 - \beta)[A - c + x_1(2\beta - 1)]}{[9B - 2(2 - \beta)^2]}. \tag{20.A2}$$

These slope upward if $\beta > 0.5$ and downward if $\beta < 0.5$. In any equilibrium $x_1 = x_2$ by symmetry. Substitution then yields the Nash equilibrium research intensity, output, and profit levels:

$$x_1^C = x_2^C = \frac{2(A - c)(2 - \beta)}{9B - 2(2 - \beta)(1 + \beta)} \tag{20.A3}$$

$$q_1^C = q_2^C = \frac{3(A - c)}{9B - 2(2 - \beta)(1 + \beta)} \tag{20.A4}$$

$$\pi_1^C = \pi_2^C = \frac{(A - c)^2[9B - 2(2 - \beta)^2]}{[9B - 2(2 - \beta)(1 + \beta)]^2} \tag{20.A5}$$

Equation (20.A3) is decreasing in β. Higher research spillovers decrease research intensity.

EQUILIBRIUM R&D EFFORT WITH R&D COOPERATION

With cooperation, each firm's optimal research intensity maximizes the sum of the two firms' profits, given noncooperative output determination in stage two. From equation (20.14) aggregate profit is:

$$
\pi_1^C + \pi_2^C = \frac{[A - c + x_1(2 - \beta) + x_2(2\beta - 1)]^2}{9B} - \frac{x_1^2}{2}
$$
$$
+ \frac{[A - c + x_2(2 - \beta) + x_1(2\beta - 1)]^2}{9B} - \frac{x_2^2}{2} \tag{20.A6}
$$

Differentiating and imposing symmetry, yields the first order condition:

$$
\frac{2(1 + \beta)[A - c + x^{RC}(1 + \beta)] - 9Bx^{RC}}{9B} = 0 \tag{20.A7}
$$

(where the superscript RC denotes "R&D cooperation"). The equilibrium R&D intensity then is:

$$
x_1^{RC} = x_2^{RC} = \frac{2(A - c)(1 + \beta)}{9B - 2(1 + \beta)^2} \tag{20.A8}
$$

This is increasing in β. Output and profit levels may be obtained by substitution into equations (22.13) and (22.14) and simplifying to yield:

$$
q_1^{RC} = q_2^{RC} = \frac{3(A - c)}{9B - 2(1 + \beta)^2} \tag{20.A9}
$$

$$
\pi_1^{RC} = \pi_2^{RC} = \frac{9B(A - c)^2}{[9B - 2(1 + \beta)^2]^2} \tag{20.A10}
$$

EQUILIBRIUM R&D EFFORT WITH A RESEARCH JOINT VENTURE (RJV)

An RJV agreement amounts to cooperation with 100 percent R&D spillovers, i.e., $\beta = 1$ in equations (20.A8)–(20.A10) above. Thus:

$$
x_1^{RJV} = x_2^{RJV} = \frac{4(A - c)}{9B - 8} \tag{20.A11}
$$

$$
q_1^{RJV} = q_2^{RJV} = \frac{3(A - c)}{9B - 8} \tag{20.A12}
$$

$$
\pi_1^{RJV} = \pi_2^{RJV} = \frac{9(A - c)^2}{(9B - 8)^2} \tag{20.A13}
$$

An RJV gives the highest per-firm profits and the lowest consumer prices of any arrangement.

21

Patents and Patent Policy

In 1769, an English inventor, Richard Arkwright, patented a spinning frame that would revolutionize the production of cotton cloth. Two years later, in 1771, Englishman James Hargreaves introduced another invention, the spinning jenny. With these inventions, Britain entered the Industrial Revolution. Equally important, the inventions allowed Arkwright and Hargreaves to establish a commanding position in the production of cloths and, more generally, textile products. This allowed the inventors to reap large profits and to sell at a high price in the American colonies even after these became independent states.

The British energetically protected their monopoly position. Westbound ships out of London were searched thoroughly to make sure that no passenger was a former Arkwright or Hargeaves employee or had a copy of the design plans for the Arkwright–Hargreaves machines that firms outside of Britain might copy. Such restrictions along with the high textile price for British textiles vexed many Americans. Consumers did not like paying the monopoly prices and firms were eager to get some version of the machines that would permit them to compete with the British producers. Some firms offered ":bounties" for English apprentices who would be able to obtain the necessary information. Finally, in 1789, an enterprising young Englishman and former Arkwright partner, Samuel Slater, responded to just such a bounty offer. After completely memorizing the engineering details of the Arkwright-Hargreaves machines, he disguised himself as a common laborer and set sail for America. Shortly thereafter, Slater arrived in Pawtucket, Massachusetts and established the first of many New England textile mills consolidating the region's manufacturing base and finally breaking the British monopoly.

The issues raised by Slater's entrepreneurship (what some might call theft) lie at the heart of this chapter. The central question is how strongly a firm's innovation should be protected from imitative competition. On the one hand, information about an innovation is a public good so that once the information is produced, efficiency requires that access to this information, i.e., new production techniques and new products, should be unrestricted to prevent the rise of monopoly. On the other hand, if the government does not protect innovators against imitation, there may be little incentive to do the hard work that led to the invention in the first place.

The patent system was designed to create incentives for innovative activity. Patents and copyrights confer ownership to new inventions, new designs, and new creative works. In turn, those property rights permit innovators to restrict the use of their ideas just as the British restricted the flow of information on their textile technology. The patent holder can act as a monopolist regarding its discovery and earn a monopoly profit as a result. Yet while that profit may create an incentive to undertake R&D efforts, the monopoly that generates the profit reduces the total surplus below what it could be given that the invention has occurred.

Getting this balance right is not easy. We can imagine just how much less productive the economy would be if the science behind electric lighting, the aerodynamics of airplanes, and semiconductors had never been developed. Or how much less healthy we would be without drugs to lower cholesterol and combat polio and malaria. However, society would also be less productive and less healthy were those same technologies not now widely available to all firms and consumers. At some point, policy must shift from a stance of protecting innovators from imitation to one of permitting the use of the innovation on as wide a basis as possible. The sixty-four-million-dollar question is, exactly where does that point arise? When has protection of the innovator extended sufficiently far that we ought to start thinking about protection of consumers?

The issue as to how far patent rights should extend has two dimensions. First, what is the length of time for which any patent rights ought to last? Second, to what range of products should the patent apply? Should the developer of a new AIDS treatment based on a special combination of protease inhibitors be protected against a rival's later development of an alternative AIDS treatment based on a different combination of protease inhibitors? What about a new AIDS treatment that is not based on protease inhibitors? Or what if a protease inhibitor treatment originally created as a treatment for AIDS is now applied as a treatment for multiple sclerosis? These issues—typically referred to as patent length and patent breadth—are the central questions in patent policy.

21.1   OPTIMAL PATENT LENGTH

Current patent law establishes a patent duration that varies from country to country. In the United Kingdom and the United States, patent law grants protection for twenty years from the date of filing the application. In both countries it is up to the patent holder to ensure that the patent is renewed during its life and to ensure that the patent is not infringed.

Economic theory can provide some insights as to whether that duration makes sense. The key is to find a balance between the innovator's ability to earn a return on its R&D investment and the benefits that accrue to consumers once the patent expires and competition emerges. The basic model, which is due to Nordhaus (1969), is presented below.

Imagine a competitive industry in which each firm is pursuing a nondrastic innovation. Innovative efforts incur costs. Each firm's unit operating cost is currently c. If a firm invests in R&D at some intensity x, it expects to reduce its unit operating costs from c to $c - x$. The cost of undertaking R&D at intensity x is $r(x)$. We assume that such costs rise as the level of research intensity increases and that they do so at an increasing rate. Formally, this means that $dr(x)/dx > 0$ and $d^2r(x)/dx^2 > 0$. Thus, R&D is expensive to do and exhibits decreasing returns in that a doubling of research intensity will give less than double the reduction in operating costs.

Our assumption of a competitive market implies that price equals marginal cost, which means that the initial market price is c and that the output level is Q_0^C. This is shown in Figure 21.1. A successful innovator will be able either to produce at the lower unit cost of $c - x$ and drive out all its rivals by setting a price just one penny less than the current price, or to license its discovery to its competitors for a fee of $c - x$ per unit produced. Either way, the current market price and volume of output remain unchanged. The innovator,

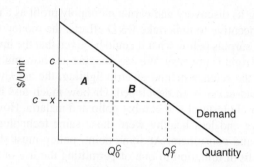

Figure 21.1   Innovation gains during period of patent protection (T years) and after patent protection

The innovator receives profit of area A for the T years that the patent is in effect. When the patent expires, competition lowers the price to $c - x$. Consumers gain the former profits A and also area B as consumer surplus. However, only the area B is a net increase in welfare.

however, earns a profit equal to area A in Figure 21.1. Assuming that the life of the innovator's patent is T years, this profit will last for T years as well.

When the patent expires, all firms will have access to the technology for free. Competition will reduce the price to $c - x$, and output will expand to Q_T^C. The profit that the innovator used to earn becomes consumer surplus. This is simply a transfer from a producer to consumers and so does not reflect a net gain. However, the expansion of industry output to the higher level Q_T^C does bring such a net benefit by virtue of the additional consumer surplus this generates. This additional surplus is shown in Figure 21.1 as area B.

The longer the duration of the patent (the higher is T), the longer is the time over which the innovator earns the profit A and the greater is the innovator's incentive to do costly R&D. Denote the per period profit flow to the innovator (area A in Figure 21.1) as $\pi^m(x; T)$ and the discount factor as R. The present value of the innovator's profit from R&D is[1]

$$V_i(x; T) = \sum_{t=0}^{T-1} R^t \pi^m(x; T) = \frac{1 - R^T}{1 - R} \pi^m(x; T) \qquad (21.1)$$

Therefore, the R&D has a net value to the innovator of

$$V_i(x; T) - r(x) \qquad (21.2)$$

For a given value of T chosen by the patent office, the innovator selects a level of R&D activity, $x^*(T)$, that maximizes this expression. This choice just balances the marginal gain of additional discounted profit against the marginal cost of doing more R&D work.

Of course, a rational patent office recognizes that its choice of patent life T affects the firm's choice of R&D effort. We suppose that the patent office can work out this relationship precisely. In other words, the patent office can determine the innovator's profit-maximizing research intensity, $x^*(T)$, as a function of T. To choose T optimally, the patent office

---

[1]   This result uses the following equation in calculating discounted value. Assume that a sum A is to be received each period for T periods, and recall from Chapter 2 that $R = (1 + r)^{-1}$ where r is the interest rate. Then the discounted value of these cash flows is $S = A + RA + R^2A + R^3A + \ldots + R^{T-1}A = A(1 + R + R^2 + \ldots + R^{T-1}) = A(1 - R^T)/(1 - R)$.

wishes to pick the patent duration that maximizes the net social gain to both consumers and producers given how firms choose their research intensities. Let us denote by $cs(x; T)$, the per-period increase in social surplus that the innovation generates once it becomes freely available, which as we have seen is the area $A + B$ in Figure 21.1. The present value of this increase in surplus is then

$$CS(x; T) = \sum_{t=T}^{\infty} R^t cs(x; T) = \frac{R^T}{1 - R} cs(x; T) \qquad (21.3)$$

The total net social surplus from the innovation is

$$NS(x^*(T); T) = V_i(x^*(T); T) + CS(x^*(T); T) - r(x^*(T)) \qquad (21.4)$$

and the objective of the patent office is to choose the patent duration T^* that maximizes this net surplus. This is a complicated expression but we can develop an intuitive argument to support a very important proposition, namely, that *the optimal patent duration is finite*.

To see why, note that as the patent office initially increases patent duration it induces greater R&D effort and, at first, a greater discounted net surplus to producers and consumers. If patent duration is zero, the returns to an innovator are also zero because the results of the innovation will be imitated immediately. Accordingly, there is no R&D and no change in the social surplus. If we now increase the patent length to a value $T > 0$, we induce some innovation and, thereby, some increase in the total surplus. Beyond some point, however, continued increases in T reduce net social surplus even though they lead to more R&D and therefore greater reductions in production cost. Two forces work to limit the optimal value of T. The first is our assumption of diminishing returns to R&D activity. Because it becomes progressively more expensive to lower production costs, it takes progressively greater increases in T to achieve a given additional cost saving. The second force limiting optimal patent duration is the fact of discounting. The consumer benefits shown as area B in Figure 21.1 are not realized until after the patent expires. If the patent office chooses a very long duration time T the present value of those benefits is very small indeed.

This is particularly important because it has sometimes been argued that innovation should be granted patent protection forever. Such a long patent duration puts far too heavy a value on the monopoly profits that patent protection generates and gives too little consideration to the additional consumer surplus that emerges only after the patent protection has expired.[2]

21.1

Let the inverse demand function for a particular product be $P = 100 - Q$, and let it be provided by a group of competitive firms, each with an identical marginal (and average) cost of $70 per unit.

a. Show that the current market output and price are, respectively, $Q = 30$ and $P = \$70$.
b. Imagine that one firm can conduct R&D at a pace x, at a cost of $r(x) = 15x^2$. Let the interest rate, r, be 10 percent so that the discount factor, R, is 0.9091. Show that a patent length of 25 years will induce the firm to pursue R&D at a level of approximately

Practice Problem

---

[2] Author Mark Helprin has similarly argued for an infinite copyright for creative works: "A Great Idea Lives Forever, Shouldn't Its Copyright?" *New York Times* 20 May 2007. Note, the argument for an infinite patent life is moot if there is continual innovation that effectively limits the economic life of any one patent.

$x = 10$. Note that if $x = 10$, the firm's research activity will reduce the unit cost from $70 to $60.

c. Would the firm's R&D effort increase or decrease if patent duration was reduced to 20 years?

d. Would total social welfare increase or decrease if patent duration was reduced to 20 years?

21.2   OPTIMAL PATENT BREADTH

The question of the optimal patent breadth is trickier than that of patent length, mainly because there is no universally accepted measure of breadth comparable to time as a measure of duration. Conceptually, the idea is to set a minimum amount by which a new innovation must differ from an existing process (or good) in order for the new one either to avoid infringement on an existing patent or to be itself patentable. The larger this required minimal degree of difference, the more difficult it is for other firms to "invent around" the patent and to cut into the inventor's profit. We could in principle work out the optimal patent breadth just as we worked out the optimal patent length. But the lack of a clear method for measuring breadth makes implementing this plan very difficult.

This lack of precision is reflected in the language of the patent office. Each application for a patent is required to specify all the "related" existing patents and to indicate not only how the patent being applied for is a discovery distinct from those already patented, but also to show that the discovery is "novel, nonobvious, useful." Such language leaves the patent office a lot of discretion regarding how it rules in any particular case.

What makes the question of the optimal patent breadth even more difficult is that it cannot be divorced from the question of optimal duration. Patent policy must set both dimensions of patent protection. Typically, this amounts to choosing between a system in which patents should have a short duration but a broad coverage, the "short and fat" approach, or a long duration combined with a very narrow coverage, the "long and thin" solution. As always, these choices involve balancing the need to maintain the incentive to innovate against the need to distribute the benefits of innovation as widely as possible.

The complications that arise when a second dimension of breadth is introduced into patent policy can be seen in a number of formal models. Consider for instance the analysis of Gilbert and Shapiro (1990). They define patent breadth in terms of the extent to which the patent-holder can charge a price above marginal cost. Broader patents decrease consumer substitute options and permit a higher price-cost margin. This margin of course is the source of the patent-holder's profit. Suppose that we know the desired innovative effort level x, and hence the cost $r(x)$ necessary to achieve that effort. The trick then is to do this with a patent design that produces the necessary (discounted) profit at the lowest possible social cost. That is, we may frame the objective as choosing patent breadth and length so as to minimize the deadweight loss per unit of innovator profit subject to that profit level being sufficient to undertake the desired inventive activity.

Given the social objective and their definition of patent breadth, Gilbert and Shapiro (1990) then demonstrate that the optimal patent is to have very narrow but infinitely long patents. Why? The underlying intuition is as follows. If we think of time as a sequence of equally long intervals, then each interval may be thought of as a separate market. A standard condition for welfare maximization is that it should not be possible to raise welfare by shifting production from one market to another, i.e., the net marginal value of an extra unit should be the same in each market or, in our case, in each period. A finite patent does not typically satisfy this condition. During the patent life, the price is high due to the patent-holder's monopoly power. Once the patent has expired, however, the price falls to marginal cost. The only way to avoid this discontinuity is to keep the price above marginal cost in all markets, i.e., for all time periods into the infinite future, while limiting the accompanying distortion that this brings by restricting the patent's breadth so that price is just enough above cost permanently that the necessary profit level is achieved. In other words, optimal patent policy induces small but equal price distortion for many periods rather that a few large distortions in some periods and none in others.

However, the Gilbert and Shapiro (1990) approach is not the only way to model patent breadth. Klemperer (1990) for example offers an alternative approach that relates patent breadth more directly to product differentiation. If we think of a Hotelling line segment of finite length, Klemperer's view is that a useful definition of patent breadth is the fraction of the line segment that is covered by the patent. Again assuming that the goal is to minimize the ratio of social cost to innovator profit subject to covering desired innovation costs, Klemperer (1990) then shows that there are cases in which optimal patent design is just the opposite of that implied by the Gilbert and Shapiro analysis. That is, it is often the case that the best patent design is one of broad patents that are short-lived.

To understand Klemperer's (1990) argument, consider a simple example. Suppose that the new good costs nothing to produce (all the costs are sunk design costs) and that there are ten potential customers for the product. Assume further that each customer values the good at $10. If there were no other substitutes available, the monopolist firm would then simply set a price of $10, sell one unit to each of the ten consumers, and claim all of the $100 surplus from the market. There would be no consumer surplus but also no welfare loss. Total output would also have been ten had the monopolist priced at marginal cost ($= 0$).

Now suppose that the transport cost of buying an alternative legal substitute is different for each of the ten consumers. Specifically, let one consumer incur a transport cost of $1 per unit of distance the substitute is from the product; a second incur a transport cost of $2 per unit; and so on. In this setting, patent breadth w is interpreted as how far consumers have to travel to obtain a legal alternative brand. A very wide breadth or high value for w effectively puts one back in the setting of no alternatives. Hence, if w is very broad, the market outcome will again be a price of $10, and there will be no deadweight loss. Now, however, consider what happens if we limit the patent width to $w = 1$ (or just a bit less). In this case, at any price $p \geq \$1$, the patent holder loses some customers. At a price of $1, the patent holder loses one client. At a price of $2, a second is lost, so on. The best option (assuming whole-dollar prices) is then to set a price of $5, in which case the patent holder sells five units and earns profit of $25. Now there is a deadweight loss. Real resources are being used to produce the less desired substitutes into which consumers are shifting. Consumers are incurring transport costs, as well. In other words, the narrower is the patent the greater is the deadweight loss, implying the need for broad patents. Patent length should then be set at the minimum necessary to achieve the desired innovative expenditure.

As noted, Klemperer's (1990) analysis also yields conditions under which a narrower but longer-lived patent is preferred. This occurs for example when, unlike the case above, it is the transport cost that is the same for all and the valuation that varies across consumers. However, the crucial result is that when consumer variation primarily reflects differences in transport cost or strength of preference for the brand of the new good and not in the basic valuation of that good, broad patents of relatively short derivation are preferred.

Gallini (1992) provides a further reason why short-lived broad patents may be best. She makes the point that imitators can often get around patent protection if they spend enough money to imitate the product without infringement. They will be particularly encouraged to do so when patents are long because otherwise, entry into the market will be greatly delayed. When patents are short, imitation is less attractive because firms now find it cheaper simply to wait for the patent to expire than to engage in costly efforts to imitate legally now. In other words, Gallini (1992, 2002) makes the important point that costly imitation efforts also need to be accounted for in considering any welfare effects. If these imitation costs are sizeable, then broad but short-lived patents are preferable.

Denicolò (1996) synthesizes many of these features in a framework that also incorporates the extent of market competition. He finds that "Loosely speaking, the less efficient is the type of competition prevailing in the product market, the more likely it is that broad and short patents are socially optimal" (264). By "efficient," Denicolò means roughly the extent to which competition drives firms close to the competitive ideal. Denicolò's statement implies that markets in which firms have a greater degree of monopoly power will do best with the "short and fat" approach, while markets characterized by a good bit of competition will do best with patents that are "long and thin."

As a policy recommendation, a major drawback of Denicolò's proposal is that it seems to suggest applying different standards to different innovators depending on the structure of the innovator's basic industry. In reality, the rule of law cannot be applied so selectively without risking serious inconsistency. Even apart from that consideration, there is a further difficulty in implementing any of the proposed standards. The problem again is that it is not always easy to make the concept of patent breadth operational. We do not have an easy way to translate real markets into a spatial representation and no obvious measure of distance. Indeed, as Scotchmer (2004) has noted, Klemperer's (1990) horizontal concept of breadth is itself too limiting. There is also a vertical component reflecting how much better (or how much worse) a rival's product has to be before it does not infringe on the patented good. Recognizing this second dimension of patent breadth makes its measurement all the more difficult from a practical perspective. While it is probably fair to say that we will not go too far wrong if we adopt a one-size-fits-all policy of granting patents with "reasonable" breadth but constrained length, precisely what this means in practice is a lot less clear.

21.3   PATENT RACES

Our discussion of market structure and innovative activity was largely motivated by Schumpeter's observation that innovation is a crucial and different kind of competition. The Schumpeter vision is one in which firms vie with each other by racing to develop new technologies or new goods and in which this sort of rivalry is potentially deadly for those who come up short. This is particularly true when innovations are eligible for patent protection. With patents, coming in first is all that matters whether one wins by several lengths or by just a nose. The first firm to discover a cure for male baldness or to engineer a successful system for producing "talking" pictures leaps far ahead of its rivals and stays there for some time by virtue of patent or copyright protection. Patent awards have a "winner-take-all" feature so that finishing second is no better than finishing third or fourth or, for that matter, tenth.

Innovative competition can be regarded as a race in which one player's success is the other player's serious defeat. The loser of a patent race may see years of investment and hard work wiped out overnight when the rival announces its breakthrough. We now turn to some of the issues that arise when we consider the implications of a patent system that generates races in which finishing first is all that matters. What are the consequences of such races? Do they lead to inefficient investment in R&D? Does the innovative activity generated by the race influence market structure?

Consider a patent race between two firms that can choose to invest in research with a view to developing a new product. The first to make the breakthrough wins the race and files a patent giving that firm exclusive rights to its invention. This is what gives the race its winner-take-all aspect. The loser walks away less than empty-handed, having expended resources on R&D with no return.

Let there be two firms, BMI and ECN, who both are considering doing the R&D necessary to create a new product. They each estimate that if the innovation is successful they can produce this new product at a marginal cost of c and that demand for the new good is $P = A - BQ$. They are also confident that the new product is a sufficiently radical departure that it will have a negligible impact on their existing businesses and so will not affect their existing profits—that is, there is no replacement effect.

The R&D effort by each firm requires establishment of a research division that costs a fixed sum, K. This sum covers both the costs of research and of development if the research is successful and, once sunk, can never be recaptured. Given that such a division is established, the probability of a successful innovation is ρ. If only one firm is successful in its R&D efforts, we assume that the innovation is protected from imitation, perhaps by a patent or by some other means so that the successful innovator earns the monopoly profit. If both are successful simultaneously, both firms file a patent application and we assume that each firm has a 50 percent probability of its patent application being successful, in which case this firm earns the monopoly profit. To keep matters reasonably simple, we assume that both firms discount the future heavily—that is, the interest rate r is so large that the discount factor $R \approx 0$.

In order to identify the incentives each firm has to establish the research division, we need to identify their profits with and without a successful innovation. If neither firm attempts to develop the new product, neither firm enters this new market. As a result, each earns zero profit in this new market.

If both firms undertake R&D but only one firm, say BMI, is successful in its R&D efforts while ECN is not, then BMI will be a monopolist in the new product market earning the monopoly profits. ECN will earn nothing from the new market. The profits of the two firms in this case, again ignoring the costs of establishing the R&D division, become

$$\pi_b = \frac{(A - \underline{c})^2}{4B} \; ; \; \pi_e = 0 \tag{21.5}$$

Of course, if ECN is successful but BMI is not, these profits are reversed.

Conversely, if both firms undertake R&D and both are successful in making the innovation, each has a 50 percent probability of being awarded a patent, so that expected profit, ignoring the costs of establishing the R&D division, is

$$\pi_b = \pi_e = \frac{(A - \underline{c})^2}{8B} \tag{21.6}$$

We can now calculate the expected profit for each firm depending on whether or not it establishes a research division. If neither firm sets up such a division, neither innovates and each earns zero profit in this new market. Now consider the expected profit if only one firm, say BMI, establishes an R&D division. For BMI expected profit is made up of two components:

1. profit if the R&D division is unsuccessful, which is zero and occurs with probability $(1 - \rho)$;
2. profit if the R&D division is successful, which is the monopoly profit $(A - c)^2/4B$ and occurs with probability ρ.

As a result, the expected *net* profit of BMI if it is the only firm to establish an R&D division is

$$\pi_b = \rho \frac{(A - c)^2}{4B} - K \tag{21.7}$$

Of course, the expected profit of ECN, given that only BMI has established an R&D division, is zero. By symmetry, we reverse these payoffs to get expected profits if ECN is the only firm to establish a research division.

If both firms establish R&D divisions, the expected profit to either firm is given by

1. profit if the firm's R&D division is successful and the rival's is not, which is $(A - c)^2/4B$, and occurs with probability $\rho(1 - \rho)$;
2. profit if both R&D divisions are successful and the firm wins the patent application, which is $(A - c)^2/8B$, and occurs with probability ρ^2.

Of course if neither firm is successful in R&D they earn nothing from the new market. This means that the expected *net* profit of each firm, given that they both operate R&D divisions, is

$$\pi_b = \pi_e = \rho(1 - \rho)\frac{(A - c)^2}{4B} + \rho^2 \frac{(A - c)^2}{8B} - K = \frac{(A - c)^2}{8B}\rho(2 - \rho) - K \tag{21.8}$$

Before we put these payoffs into a payoff matrix, we can do a bit of simplifying. The profit equations share a common expression, the monopoly profit, which we denote as $M = (A - c)^2/4B$. We can use this to define a parameter $S = K/M$, which is the share of the monopoly profits that are needed to establish the R&D division. With the substitution of S and M, the expected profits are summarized in the payoff matrix of Table 21.1 (below). This matrix allows us to identify the possible Nash equilibria for this R&D game. As we shall see, these are dependent upon the relative magnitudes of the two parameters, S and ρ.

There are three possibilities that have to be considered:

1. *Neither Firm Wishes to Establish an R&D Division.* For this to be a Nash equilibrium, the payoff to BMI, for example, from not having an R&D division, given that ECN also has no R&D division, must be greater than the expected profit from investing in R&D,

Table 21.1   Payoff matrix for the duopoly patent race

		BMI	
		No R&D Division	R&D Division
ECN	No R&D Division	$0, 0$	$0, M(\rho - S)$
	R&D Division	$M(\rho - S), 0$	$M\left(\dfrac{\rho(2 - \rho)}{2} - S\right), M\left(\dfrac{\rho(2 - \rho)}{2} - S\right)$

again given that ECN does not. In other words, BMI expects to make more profit from the strategy combination (No R&D, No R&D) than from the combination (No R&D, R&D). This requires that $M(\rho - S) < 0$, which implies that $S > \rho$, the probability of success is less than the fraction of monopoly profit required to fund the R&D. This expression is illustrated by the line 0A in Figure 21.2. All parameter combinations above 0A give the Nash equilibrium (No R&D, No R&D).

2. *Only One Firm Wishes to Establish an R&D Division.* Assume that the firm that establishes the R&D division is BMI. Then for the strategy (No R&D, R&D) to be a Nash equilibrium, two conditions must be satisfied:

    a. BMI expects its expenditure on R&D to be profitable, given that ECN is not investing in R&D—that is, BMI expects to make more profit from the strategy combination (No R&D, R&D) than from the strategy combination (No R&D, No R&D). This is just the opposite of the expression derived in part 1. It requires that $S < \rho$.

    b. ECN does not expect its expenditure on R&D to be profitable, given that BMI is investing in R&D—that is, ECN prefers the strategy combination (No R&D, R&D) to (R&D, R&D). For this to be the case, the following must be true: $M\left(\dfrac{\rho(2-\rho)}{2} - S\right) < 0$ which requires that $S > \dfrac{\rho(2-\rho)}{2}$ This relationship is illustrated by the curve 0B in Figure 21.2. All parameter combinations that lie between 0A and 0B are such that only one of the firms will establish an R&D division.

3. *Both Firms Wish to Establish an R&D Division.* For this to be a Nash equilibrium, the payoff to, for example, BMI from having an R&D division, given that ECN also has an R&D division, must be greater than the expected profit from not investing in R&D, again given that ECN does. In other words, BMI expects to make more profit from the strategy combination (R&D, R&D) than from the strategy combination (R&D, No R&D). For this to be the case we must have that

$$M\left(\frac{\rho(2-\rho)}{2} - S\right) > 0 \text{ which requires that } S < \frac{\rho(2-\rho)}{2}$$

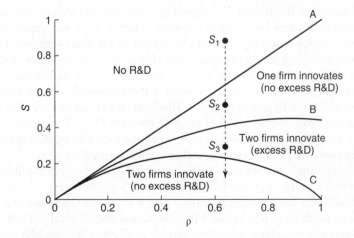

Figure 21.2   A patent race with a duopoly

Of course, exactly the same condition guarantees that ECN prefers the strategy combination (R&D, R&D) to the strategy combination (No R&D, R&D). Thus, all parameter combinations below 0B are such that both firms will establish an R&D division.

One question about patent races is whether the potential profit from successful innovation can lead the two firms to overinvest in R&D. Neither of the firms establishes an R&D division unless this division is expected to be profitable. For the strategies (R&D, No R&D), (No R&D, R&D), and (R&D, R&D) to be equilibria, they must each give positive expected profits to the two firms. This tells us that no equilibrium in which only one firm invests in R&D is characterized by "excessive" R&D in the sense that the firms would be better off without the R&D. The question that is left is whether there is "too much" R&D when both firms establish R&D divisions. Are there situations in which the strategy combination (R&D, R&D) is a Nash equilibrium but generates less aggregate profit than the strategy combinations (R&D, No R&D) or (No R&D, R&D)? For this to be the case, it must be that

$$2M \left(\frac{\rho (2 - \rho)}{2} - S \right) < M(\rho - S) \text{ which requires that } S > \rho(1 - \rho)$$

This is illustrated by the curve 0C in Figure 21.2. All parameter combinations between 0C and 0B lead to excessive R&D as the two firms race to be first to discover and introduce the new product.

Our simple model delineates three distinct possibilities. First, neither firm will invest in R&D unless it is expected to be profitable. Hence R&D must have a reasonably low cost relative to the monopoly profits that it might generate (low S), or a reasonably high probability of success. Second, for any given probability of success, a larger number of firms will establish R&D facilities when there is a lower cost of R&D relative to the profit the innovation is expected to generate. Thus, for any given probability of success ρ, the equilibrium number of firms with R&D divisions increases from zero to one and finally to two as S is reduced. Third, there is an intermediate range of values for the cost of R&D in which there is excessive R&D in that both firms establish R&D divisions although this reduces their aggregate profits. In this range, the lure of profit from innovation involves the firms in a competitive R&D race that they would be better to avoid.

So far, we have only considered the gain that research brings in terms of the expected profit of the two firms. From a public policy perspective, however, increased profit is not the only potential benefit of innovation. We should also consider the gain in consumer surplus that development of this new product will generate. While we have just shown that the level of R&D activity can be excessive from the viewpoint of the firms' combined profits, we have not demonstrated that this is the case when viewed with the objective of maximizing the total gain of profit plus consumer surplus. The R&D which seems excessive to the firms may still be worthwhile to society overall if the additional consumer surplus more than offsets the reduction in aggregate profit. However, R&D can be excessive even when evaluated with this broader criterion, (see Practice Problem 21.2). The patent race can lead both firms to establish research divisions even when the total cost of such divisions is not justified by the sum of expected producer and consumer surplus.

Even more interesting is that we can easily show that the possibility of too little R&D—as judged from a social welfare perspective—is quite real. Suppose that $S > \rho$, in which case neither firm undertakes R&D. Suppose further that S is so close to ρ that one firm could almost expect to break even if it pursued the innovation and its rival did not. If the new product generates any significant consumer surplus at all, then it is socially desirable that the research takes place. The value of the expected consumer surplus more than provides the extra funds needed to ensure that the innovator breaks even. However, in the absence of government intervention, the fact that $S > \rho$ means that no such R&D efforts will occur.[3]

This brings us back to the role of patent length in influencing innovative activity. Recall that $S = K/M$ and relax our assumption that the discount factor is zero. Then we can rewrite S as $S(T) = K/M(T)$, where $M(T)$ is the discounted value of monopoly profits with a patent of length T. Clearly, S gets smaller as T increases. (Formally, $dS(T)/dT < 0$.) This brings attention to the obvious parameter that the Patent Office can influence in $S(T)$ is patent length as measured by T. Suppose first that T is "short," giving $S(T) = S_1$ in Figure 21.2. Then there is no innovation to develop the new product. If, however, patent length is increased, giving $S(T) = S_2$ in Figure 21.2, one firm will be induced to undertake the innovation. Because this is profitable for the firm *and* is likely to generate consumer surplus even during the period of patent protection, this can be expected to be socially desirable.

So far so good. Note, however, that if patent length is increased still further, giving $S(T) = S_3$ in Figure 21.2, both firms will be induced to undertake the innovation and we have socially wasteful innovation. In other words, we have yet another reason for being cautious in the design of patent policy. Very lengthy patents are attractive to firms and so may induce socially wasteful patent races.

21.2

Practice Problem

Consider the BMI–ECN example of a patent race. Assume that demand for the new good is $P = 100 - 2Q$, and that each firm believes that it will be able to produce this good at a unit cost of $c = \$50$. Assume further that the discount factor R is so small that each firm cares only about the one-period profit it will make. (Alternatively, assume that one period is of a very long duration, say, thirty years or more.) The probability that such a lab will be successful and actually produce a discovery is $\rho = 0.8$.

a. Show that if one firm is successful in introducing the product, it will have a monopoly price of $75, sell 12.5 units, and earn monopoly profits (before paying for the research) of $M = \$312.50$. Show also that consumer surplus is $156.25.

b. Show that if each firm sets up a lab and if both labs are successful, then each firm will earn a profit (before paying for the research) of $138.89. Consumer surplus in this case will be $277.78

c. Now show that the expected profit to BMI (or ECN) if it is the only firm to establish an R&D division is $250 - K$ while the expected profit to each firm if they both establish R&D divisions is $138.89 - K$. Use these results to construct the payoff matrix for this case, now including the cost, K, of establishing an R&D division.

d. Show that if K, the cost of setting up the research lab, is such that $K > \$250$, neither firm will set up a lab, while if $K < \$138.89$, both firms will set up a lab.

e. Show that expected social surplus ignoring research costs if one firm establishes a research lab is $375, and if two research labs are established, is $416.67. Hence, show that the second lab is socially desirable only if $K < \$141.67$.

We have focused on the risk that patent races may yield either too much or too little R&D investment. Another issue to consider is the possibility that patent races lead firms to pursue more risky innovations. The intuition behind this argument can be illustrated fairly simply.

[3] See Reinganum (1989) for a masterful survey of patent races and the timing of innovation, including the consequences for social welfare.

Suppose that firms can choose to invest either in a relatively safe R&D route that has an expected discovery time uniformly distributed between one and three years or a more risky route that has an expected time of discovery uniformly distributed between zero and four years. Both discoveries are equally costly, and both are expected to become redundant or worthless in five years' time. We also assume that each discovery generates the same profit of $1 million per period during the time that it is utilized and is protected from imitation by a patent.

Because the expected date of discovery is the same, namely two years for both routes, then assuming neither firm had any competition, a risk-neutral firm considering them would be indifferent between the two options, and a risk-averse firm would go for the less risky route. However, when firms are involved in a patent race, competition between the firms may lead them to choose the more variable or risky route in which success can come anytime between zero and four years.[4] The reason is once again that when innovation is protected from imitation, all that matters is winning the race. The second-place firm loses the same amount no matter how close it is behind the winner. In our example, if my rival chooses the less risky R&D route, I have an incentive to choose the more risky route, because this offers the possibility of success and a quick victory right away. Similarly, if my rival adopts the risky strategy, I can see that unless I do the same there is a real possibility that I will be left behind in the race. Of course, my rival can work out all this too. The result is that both of us choose the more risky route.

21.4   MONOPOLY POWER AND "SLEEPING PATENTS"

Another way in which the patent system and innovative competition can interact to affect market structure is through "sleeping patents." Many students at first find it puzzling that firms may hold a large number of patents all related to the same process or product, many of which are never acted upon. (Return to Table 21.1 for some evidence on this point.) What possible reason can a firm have to earn patent rights to products and processes that it never uses, that is, what could be the rationale for a firm to create and hold what is called a "sleeping patent"?

One important motivation for holding a sleeping patent is to create a buffer of protection for the monopoly profits generated by the truly valuable patent. Legal history and economic analysis have both documented that the protection granted by a single patent is often very limited. Edwin Mansfield and his associates (1981) found in a study of forty-eight patented new products, that 60 percent were imitated within four years of their introduction. Firms often can and do "invent around" patent protection, as we discussed earlier in the case of pharmaceuticals. Frequently, there are several technical solutions to a particular problem such as is the case for the production of the whitening agent, titanium oxide. Each such alternative production technique is a threat to the firm holding a patent on a particular process or product. Hence, by patenting as many of these alternatives as it can, a firm increases the protection it has in using whatever process it actually decides upon.

Suppose, for example, that market demand is given by $P = 100 - Q$ and that the incumbent firm has a proprietary technology with a constant marginal cost of $c_I = \$20$. The firm has a patent that protects its technology. Let us also suppose that this technology is so efficient that entry is not possible, and thus the incumbent is free to set the monopoly price

---

[4]   This type of case is discussed in Klette and de Meza (1986).

and earn a monopoly profit each period of $\pi^m(c_I = 20)$. To be precise, the monopolist will sell 40 units at a price of $60 and earn a profit of $1,600.

Assume now that there is also an alternative technology that the monopolist has discovered, which permits production at the higher constant marginal cost of $c_E = \$30$. Clearly, the monopolist has no incentive to switch to this technology. However, if $30 is a low enough unit cost so that another firm could acquire this technology and enter the industry, then the incumbent's current monopoly would be eroded. The entrant would either be the high-cost member of a Cournot duopoly or, if Bertrand competition prevailed, the entrant's cost based on using this alternative technology would at least establish a clear upper bound of $30 on the incumbent's price—one that we know (by construction of the example) is below the incumbent's current monopoly price.

It is easy to see that the incumbent has an incentive to patent the higher-cost technology as well as the lower-cost one, even though it will never use this alternative, higher-cost technology. By acquiring this patent and letting it lie dormant or sleep, the incumbent strengthens its hold on its monopoly position. The question is whether the incumbent's incentive to acquire the higher-cost technology is so strong that it actually exceeds the incentive of the entrant to acquire the technology and enter.

The surprising answer is yes. Acquiring a patent to the high-cost technology is worth more to the incumbent monopolist than to its potential rival. This is obvious in the case of Bertrand competition. In that case, the rival's entry with a high unit cost of $30 would provoke a price war in which the incumbent would have to lower its price from its current monopoly level to the marginal cost of the entrant, namely, $30. Of course, when this happens, the entrant earns nothing. The incumbent, however, because of its lower cost, will still earn $30 − $20 = $10 per unit. At this price, the incumbent will now sell $70 units and earn a profit of $700. This is less than what it earned previously but still better than nothing. From this it should be clear why the monopolist places a greater value on discovering the alternative process than does the entrant. Under Bertrand competition, the entrant never earns any money with this innovation. Hence, for the entrant, discovering the process is worthless. Yet, even though the entrant cannot make money with this higher-cost process, it can put pressure on the incumbent. Specifically, discovery of the process by the entrant imposes a limit of $700 on the incumbent's profit. So, it is worth $900(= $1600 − $700) to the incumbent to acquire the process first and thereby prevent the imposition of this profit ceiling.

The same basic result holds in a Cournot model. The gain to the monopolist from acquiring the second, sleeping patent on the high-cost process is the profit earned as a monopoly firm using the low-cost technology, $\pi^m(c_I = 20) = \$1600$, less the profit earned as a duopoly firm with the low-cost technology facing a rival with the high-cost technology, or $\pi_I^d(c_I, c_E) = \pi_I^d(20,30) = \$900$. So, the total net gain to the monopolist is $\pi^m(c_I = 20) - \pi_I^d(20,30) = \$700$. In contrast, the gain to the potential entrant is the profit earned as the high-cost firm in a duopoly, $\pi_E^d(c_I, c_E) = \pi_E^d(20,30) = \$400$ less its current profit, taken to be zero.[5] Therefore, the entrant's net gain from developing the technology is $400. Hence, in the Cournot case also, the gain to the monopolist incumbent exceeds that of the potential entrant.

The reason that the incumbent monopolist is more willing than a potential rival to develop the high-cost process and patent it is now familiar. It is because the monopolist has a lot more at stake. If it wins the race, it gets to keep its current monopoly position. If the entrant

---

[5]   We leave it to the reader to show that the Cournot equilibrium has the incumbent producing 30 units and the entrant producing 20 units implying the profit amounts we have used here.

Table 21.2   Patent use by inventor's employer

	Internal Use	Licensing	Cross-Licensing	Licensing & Use	Blocking Competitors	Sleeping Patents
Large companies	50.0%	3.0%	3.0%	3.2%	21.7%	19.1%
Medium sized companies	65.6%	5.4%	1.2%	3.6%	13.9%	10.3%
Small Companies	55.8%	15.0%	3.9%	6.9%	9.6%	8.8%

Source: Giuri, P., Mariani, M., et al (2005) p. 20.

wins the race, the best the entrant can hope for is to be the high-cost member of a duopoly. The incumbent acquires the patent on the high-cost process to make sure that nobody else will use it. Viewed in this light, acquiring "sleeping patents" amounts to broadening the patent's width.

The data in Table 21.2 provide some empirical support for this proposition. These data are drawn from a PatVal-EU survey of 9,017 patents issued by the European Patent Office between 1993 and 1997 to individuals located in France, Germany, Italy, the Netherlands, Spain, and the United Kingdom.[6] The survey asked the inventors to rate the importance that they put on different motives for patenting.

In this table, "blocking competitors" refers to sleeping patents that are used specifically for the strategic reasons we have been discussing in this section (what the researchers term sleeping patents are patents that, according to the respondents, were not used for any of the other six purposes identified in the table). As can be seen, large companies used fewer of their patents and used a higher proportion of patents for blocking purposes than did medium sized or small companies, consistent with our "protecting monopoly power" analysis.

Historic examples of an incumbent using a "sleeping patent" strategy to inhibit rival expansion are common. Alcoa achieved its dominant market position largely on the strength of Charles Martin Hall's electrolytic process for the reduction of aluminum bauxite ore. Fifteen years after it was formed, the company bought up the competing Bradley patents on an alternative reduction process—one that Alcoa never used. Similarly, Du Pont's patent of the synthetic fiber nylon was accompanied by the company's filing of literally hundreds of other patents all based on variants of the same molecule. Perhaps the best example of the use of sleeping patents comes from Hollywood. Film companies regularly buy the film rights to books, stage plays, and submitted screenplays knowing that many of these script ideas will never be turned into a final product. In part, each film company simply wants to make sure that a rival producer does not get the chance to make a film based on this material.

21.5   PATENT LICENSING

Efficiency requires that the existing stock of information should be available to all buyers at the marginal cost involved in sharing such knowledge. However, because this implies a "price for information" of near zero, it leaves little incentive for anyone to produce new

---

[6]   For a detailed description and analysis of these data see Giuri and Mariani, 2005. "Everything you always wanted to know about inventors (but never asked): evidence from the PatVal-EU survey," available at http://www.lem.sssup.it/WPLem/files/2005-20.pdf.

information as embodied in new goods or new technologies. Patent protection is an effort to cut a middle path between these two pressures. The firm receiving the patent is protected (to some extent) from sharing its discovery with others for free. In fact, it does not have to share it at all.

One interesting possibility is that an innovating firm might be willing to share its technical advance with other firms for a price. When this happens, it results in a licensing agreement between the patent owner and the patent user. Not sharing the patent at all can be interpreted as charging a very high (perhaps infinite) licensing fee. Actual licensing reflects a movement away from such a high fee and toward a price for information that is closer to—if still some way off—the efficient charge of near zero. In this sense, the licensing of a patent is unambiguously a good thing. The question is, does an innovating firm have a profit incentive to license its discovery?

The most obvious case in which a firm would prefer to license an innovation is if the licensee operates in a totally different market from the licensor. For example, a US firm that has a patent on a particular product or process innovation may prefer to license a foreign firm to use this patent (for a fee, of course) rather than setting up a foreign subsidiary or exporting. About the only reasons for not licensing are, first, that the licensor may not be able to secure a satisfactory payment for the license except after extensive bargaining. If such negotiations will be prolonged, either or both parties may decide that it is simply not worthwhile. Second, the licensor may fear that, ultimately, the foreign licensee will produce in some market where it competes directly with the licensor. Finally, there is the fear that the licensee may—by acquiring rights to use the new process or product—improve its ability to develop the next generation of this technology by itself and thereby enhance its future ability to compete.

While these fears are undoubtedly real, there are considerable offsetting benefits to licensing agreements. Licensing gains revenue for the innovator today. Because the cost of sharing the information is low, any such revenue translates into profit.

What about cases, though, where the licensor and licensee are not separated by large geographic distance but instead are competitors in the same market? Will an innovating firm license its patented discovery for use by some or all of its rivals? The answer depends on market structure and the strength of competition in the market.

21.5.1 The Incentive for an Oligopolist to License a Nondrastic Innovation

Consider the toughest type of competition—price competition between firms making identical products. A firm that obtains a patent on a new technology that permits it to sell at a lower cost has little incentive to license the process to a competitor. Suppose, for example, that both firms are currently selling at a price equal to their (constant) marginal cost of $15 and that one firm has discovered a way to reduce this cost to $12. Without licensing its rival, the innovating firm can supply the entire market at $14.99 and drive its competitor from the market while earning a $2.99 profit on every unit sold. If it tries to sell a license to its rival, the only sensible royalty rate is $2.99 per unit. The rival firm will pay no higher royalty because then it will be unable to compete as its cost will be $12 plus the royalty, which is no better than its current cost of $15. At any lower royalty, the rival will force the innovating firm to lower its price below the current $14.99. But at a royalty of exactly $2.99, both firms will sell at $14.99 and split the market. The licensing firm loses $2.99 on those units it would have sold if it had not licensed but stayed a monopolist. It then gains the $2.99 back as a royalty payment on each of those same units now sold by its rival. In short, licensing gains the innovator nothing. Hence, the incentive to license is very small when the competition is Bertrand.[7]

By contrast, consider a market in which firms are Cournot competitors. In this case, a patent holder has a strong incentive to license, as a simple example shows. Assume that demand for the product in question is $P = 120 - Q$ and that there are three firms in the market, each with constant marginal costs of $60. Then we know from our earlier analysis that the Cournot equilibrium output of each firm is 15 units, total output is 45, the equilibrium price is $75, and each firm earns a profit of $225.

Suppose now that one firm makes a nondrastic process innovation lowering its cost to $40 per unit, while the other two firms continue to produce at the higher value of $60 per unit. If the innovating firm does not license the innovation, then the Cournot–Nash equilibrium price falls to $70. The innovating firm increases its output to 30 units, while the other, high-cost firms reduce their outputs to 10 units each. Profit to the innovating firm increases to $900 while profit to each of the other firms falls to $100.[8]

Now assume that the innovating firm agrees to license the innovation to its rivals at a fee of $10 per unit that each rival produces. This means that the innovator's costs are $40 per unit and the other firms' costs are $50 per unit. At the post-licensing equilibrium the innovating firm's output is 25 units while the other firms produce 15 units each so that price is $65. The profit of the innovating firm is now $25 per unit on its own sales plus $10 per unit on the sales of its two rivals, giving a total profit of $925. For each non-innovating firm, profit is $15 per unit, giving each firm profit of $225. The rivals' profits are just as high and the innovator's profit is higher with licensing rather than without it.

Licensing is, indeed, potentially quite profitable. Moreover, the licensing fee of $10 that we have chosen is not the best that the innovating firm can do.[9] We show in the Appendix that the innovator should actually push the license price as close as possible to the difference in costs that the innovation generates—in our example, as close as possible to $20. Suppose for example that the innovator charges a royalty rate of $20 per unit (more accurately, $19.99). This restores the equilibrium with the innovation but without licensing. The innovator produces 30 units and each non-innovating firm 10 units, giving a product price of $70. Profit of each non-innovating firm is, once again, $100 because their costs are $60 per unit. By contrast, profit of the licensing firm is $30 per unit on its own output and $20 per unit on the output of its rivals, giving the licensor a total profit of $1,300. The message then is clear. For a Cournot firm with a nondrastic innovation, licensing its discovery is very attractive.

---

[7]   For the patent holder that is selling in a *differentiated products market*, the analysis is a bit more complicated. Here, each additional license has three effects. First, it adds licensing revenue. Second, however, it makes the market more competitive and hurts the patent holder in its product market. Third, and as a result of the second effect, each additional license sold drives down the market value of licenses in general. In other words, the demand curve for licenses will be downward sloping because the more that are sold, the more competitive is the market and therefore the less any licensee can afford to pay for a license. Because the patent holder is the monopoly supplier of such licenses, its marginal revenue curve for selling will lie below the demand curve for licenses.

[8]   These numbers come from simple application of the equations for the Cournot-Nash equilibrium that we have developed in previous chapters.

[9]   For details see Katz and Shapiro (1985).

21.5.2   Licensing, Drastic Innovations, and Monopoly Power

What if the innovation had been drastic? Or what if the industry had been a monopoly instead of an oligopoly? Consider each question in turn. If one firm in a Cournot oligopoly patents a drastic innovation, it will not want to license its discovery. Take the simple case of a duopoly. Without licensing, the innovating firm becomes a monopoly. The innovation offers such a dramatic reduction in cost that even when it sets the monopoly price associated with that cost, it still underprices its old duopolist rival, while earning considerable monopoly profit. Here, nothing can be gained by licensing. If the rival is permitted to compete, the market returns to being a duopoly except at lower cost. The most the rival would ever pay for the license is therefore its share of the duopoly profit. Combining this with the innovator's share would yield the innovator a total profit with licensing equal to the profit earned by two duopoly firms. Yet we know that—because the firms cannot collude—this is generally a smaller amount than the innovating firm could earn as a pure monopolist without licensing. Accordingly, a Cournot firm that makes a drastic innovation will not share its discovery with rivals even for a fee. Of course, this is also true for firms engaged in Bertrand competition. In all such cases, the oligopolist that makes a truly dramatic breakthrough may be expected to emerge as a monopolist driving its former competitors from the field.

Turning next to the case of monopoly in the first place, we now have to permit the innovation to take place at an outside firm or laboratory if we are to consider any licensing. (If the monopolist makes the innovation itself, there is no other firm to which it can license!) It should be clear that in such cases the innovating firm will license the monopolist. Because the patent holder is not active in the market, the only way it can obtain any revenue from its discovery is to sell or license it to the monopolist.

The interesting point in this case is the precise form that such a licensing contract should take. Should the licensor charge a royalty of X per unit? Or should it charge a fixed fee independent of output? Or should it use some combination of both? You should recognize that charging a per unit royalty—while it has the advantage that it relates revenue directly to usage—runs into the familiar problem of double-marginalization (see Chapters 16, 17, and 18). It raises the licensed firm's marginal cost so that—after that firm adds its markup—the price to the final consumer is doubly distorted and sales volume is restricted. In this light, it should not be surprising that the innovating lab will do best by using a two-part tariff. The principal part of this scheme will be a fixed fee (per month or per year). The second part will be a small royalty per unit reflecting any per unit cost the patent holder incurs in licensing its technology. For a transfer of pure information, this per unit charge will be zero. But if the patent holder needs to offer services or technical advice that increases with the frequency with which the technology is used, this fee will be positive. The licensing contract is much like a franchising contract. In principle, the inventor can appropriate all the increased profit that the invention brings if the contract is written correctly, that is, with a fixed fee exactly equal to that additional profit. In practice, however, the patent holder's bargaining position will usually not be strong enough to achieve this outcome. When the manufacturer has a monopoly in the product market, the inventor needs the manufacturer just as much as the manufacturer needs the inventor.

Patent Licensing, Social Welfare, and Public Policy

The foregoing cases indicate that most of the time an innovator has an interest in licensing its discovery. This is a reassuring result because our intuition is that licensing is typically a desirable outcome. Katz and Shapiro (1985) have provided a formal argument that licensing nearly always increases social welfare. Specifically, they show that licensing is socially desirable if total output increases as a result of the licensing activity. To see why, note that licensing will not occur unless it raises profit for both the innovating firm and in total. The license agreement will not be signed unless the licensees see some benefit from it and will not be offered unless the licensor also sees some benefit from it. If, in addition to this mutual gain in profit, the license agreement increases total output, then the price will be lower and consumer surplus will be increased too. In other words, if the license agreement increases total output, both consumers and producers gain from the agreement, and so the agreement is socially desirable. Yet even if this fails to happen—even if the industry output is unchanged—licensing is still likely to be socially beneficial because the licensing revenue at least increases producer surplus. Somebody then, either a producer or a consumer or both, is made better off by licensing.

Moreover, licensing may have other beneficial effects. First, if a firm knows that it is going to gain profits from licensing its research findings as well as (or instead of) exploiting the research itself, this should increase the incentive to undertake research. Further, the possibility that a firm can obtain a license to use a particular innovation reduces wasteful R&D that either duplicates existing research efforts or is intended merely to invent around an existing patent.

Consider an entrant whose profit (in present value terms) under duopoly is $5 million but in order to enter has to incur an R&D expenditure of $3 million to develop its own product alternative. In the absence of any licensing, the entrant will pursue this investment because it yields a net gain of $2 million. Yet if this is the case, then the monopolist firm knows that whether it licenses or not, it will soon be a duopolist. If the monopolist firm licenses its technology to the entrant for $3 million, the entrant is just as well off and the monopolist now gets the licensing revenue. In addition, society avoids the unnecessary expenditure of $3 million that the entrant would otherwise have made. The moral of this section therefore seems quite clear. Public policy should actively encourage the licensing of innovations as much as possible.

There is, however, need for a cautionary note. Licensing might involve some risks. First, consider the risks associated with licensing based upon an output-related royalty. Imagine as well that the licensing agreement holds for the outstanding duration of the patent that is being licensed because, after that, the information becomes publicly available. If the royalty rate extracts almost all of the additional profits that the licensee might expect to make, there is the risk that the licensee will take the license in order to gain experience with the technology but then actually produce very little during the period of the license agreement, which means, of course, that very little is actually paid for the license. Alternatively, if output is difficult to monitor, the licensee has the incentive to lie about how much is actually being produced. What may be necessary is that the licensor tie the license agreement to some agreed minimum level of output on the part of the licensee, but even this is not always easy to negotiate or enforce.

A further risk in licensing is that it can be difficult to write enforceable contracts that limit the ways in which licensees can use the license. Typically, the licensor wants to limit the markets into which the licensee can sell, for example, to avoid direct competition with the licensor or with other licensees. This may be possible within a particular jurisdiction such as the United States, although even here antitrust laws may prevent such market-limiting agreements. But it is almost impossible to write binding contracts that limit the international markets in which licensees can operate. In addition, access to a particular process or product technology may enhance the ability of a licensee to develop related technologies that are not covered by the patent being licensed. Once again, it is almost impossible to write enforceable contracts that protect the licensor from such imitation or at least give the licensor some return from the new technologies that licensees develop.

Licensing raises public policy issues that suggest caution in favoring and promoting every licensing agreement. One danger is that licensing contracts include restrictions on price or geographic territory that create monopolies with exclusive territories—monopolies that would otherwise be illegal under the antitrust laws. Matters become particularly complicated when, as often happens, one patent leads to another, complementary development. One firm creates, say, a new antibiotic that has some occasional and serious side effects. Then another firm develops a means to undo the side effects of the first firm's drug. The two firms may strike a deal that licenses each to produce the other's product. Yet it is easy to see that this agreement may often include terms that exclude other firms. Such dangers are recognized by US policy, which tends to limit severely the ability of reciprocal licensing agreements to include exclusive provisions. Still, the example serves to make clear that the tension between promoting licensing and realizing its associated benefits, on the one hand, and the potential risk of collusion that licensing may foster, on the other, is real.

21.5.3   Patent Thickets and Sequential Innovation

Indeed, the increasing complexity of technical advances has resulted in what some call a "patent thicket." [See Shapiro (2000).] As advance builds on advance, and technical progress increasingly draws from learning in different fields, the technology involved in bringing a new product to market may be built upon a host of patented techniques, each of which is owned by a different entity. The innovator may then need to get the approval of each of the individual patent holders before proceeding. In turn, this can involve the coordination difficulties of complements that we described in Chapters 8 and 16, among others.

To understand the patent thicket issue better consider a product that is produced competitively but requires the input of three different patented inputs. That is, one unit of each input is required to make the final product. While each input is freely available on the market at cost c, the patent owner establishes a patent fee per f_i unit of the associated input, so that the final price for each input to the producers: $p_1 = f_1 + c$; $p_2 = f_2 + c$; and $p_3 = f_3 + c$. Demand for the final product is linear and given by $P = A - BQ$. Because the product is produced competitively, the final product price $P = p_1 + p_2 + p_3$. We may thus write the demand equation as: $p_1 + p_2 + p_3 = A - BQ$

We imagine that each patent holder takes the price of its rivals as given. Because every unit of final product demand translates into exactly one unit of patented input demand for each input we may write the inverse demand facing each patent holder as:

Patent Holder 1 : $p_1 = A - p_2 - p_3 - BQ$

Patent Holder 2 : $p_2 = A - p_1 - p_3 - BQ$

Patent Holder 3 : $p_3 = A - p_1 - p_2 - BQ$ (21.9)

It follows that the profit from patent license fees for each patent holder is:

$$\pi_1 = f_1 q_1 = f_1 Q = (p_1 - c)Q$$
$$\pi_2 = f_2 q_2 = f_2 Q = (p_2 - c)Q$$
$$\pi_3 = f_3 q_3 = f_3 Q = (p_3 - c)Q \qquad (21.10)$$

The usual profit-maximizing condition that marginal revenue equal marginal cost must apply. So, we can write

$$MR_1 = A - p_2 - p_3 - 2BQ = c$$
$$MR_2 = A - p_1 - p_3 - 2BQ = c$$
$$MR_3 = A - p_1 - p_3 - 2BQ = c \qquad (21.11)$$

If we sum up the three equations in (21.11), we then have:

$$3A - 2p_1 - 2p_2 - 2p_3 - 6BQ = 3c = \overline{c} \qquad (21.12)$$

where $\overline{c}$ is the actual unit cost of producing the product in the absence of any patent fees. Given the inverse demand and the fact that competition implies $2(p_1 + p_2 + p_3) = 2P$, we may rewrite equation (21.12) as

$$3P - 2P - 3BQ = P - 3BQ = \overline{c} \qquad (21.13)$$

Hence, we have:

$$\frac{P - \overline{c}}{P} = 3B \left(\frac{Q}{P} \right) = 3 \frac{\Delta P}{\Delta Q} \left(\frac{Q}{P} \right) = \frac{3}{\varepsilon} \qquad (21.14)$$

Equation (21.14) says that the industry price-cost margin as measured by the Lerner Index introduced in Chapter 4 will be three times the inverse of the market elasticity of demand ε. Yet we know from that chapter as well as from our work in Chapter 16 that an integrated firm that owned all three patents would set a price such that the Lerner Index would be:

$$\frac{P - \overline{c}}{P} = \frac{1}{\varepsilon} \qquad (21.15)$$

In other words, with three independent patent owners each holding a critical patent, the final markup is three times that which would maximize the industry's joint profit. Of course, this much higher price hurts consumers as well. Moreover, the result in equation (21.14) readily generalizes. If n firms each hold an essential patent, then the final price-cost margin rises to n/ε or n times the optimal amount. Clearly, this patent thicket creates a major obstacle to production.

There are a number of responses to the patent thicket. One is to permit the patent holders to form a patent pool that permits others to acquire the use of all the patents for one overall fee—in effect, producing the integrated solution. Another is to permit cross-licensing agreements by which firms agree to license their patents to each other. However, these all run the risk of permitting cooperation beyond the technological sphere and giving the parties a chance to wield their technological power collectively against potential entrants. Beyond these cooperative arrangements, though, another alternative is simply to recognize that the intricate web of interconnected patents may be the result of policy that grants patents too liberally. Hence, it may be that a weak patent policy in which patents are only granted for the clearest and most dramatic of innovations is best. Such a weak patent policy becomes even more attractive when patents are sequential so that each patent builds on an earlier one as argued by Bessen and Maskin (2009).[10]

---

[10]   See Lerner and Tirole (2004).

To get a sense of the Bessen and Maskin (2009) model, we consider the case of a three-period duopoly under two regimes—one with clear and strongly enforced patents and one with no patents in which case competitive imitation is quick to emerge. We will imagine that a firm that does R&D in any period incurs a cost of c and, with probability p, creates an innovation that raises the market value of a product by V. This is true in each period. Thus, if R&D is successful in period 1, it creates a total additional value of V. A second innovation in period 2 would then add a further V in value *if combined with the product now enhanced by the first innovation*. Thus, the sequential nature of the innovative process is embodied in the fact that no innovation can take place in period $t + 1$ (or later period) *unless* there is an innovation in period t, e.g., digital music players and "Bluetooth" digital music speakers cannot be created unless someone first creates a process for digitalizing music.

To keep matters concrete, we will work with a numerical example in which V is \$200; the probability of successful R&D by any one firm is $p = 0.5$; and that the cost of R&D is $c = \$25$. Thus, the net expected social value of one firm doing R&D is $pV - c = \$75$.

To drive the point home as clearly as possible, we assume that under a patent regime the first patent winner has to be paid for rights to use the enhanced product and all bargaining power resides with this original innovator so that it can claim as payment the value of any subsequent improvement. For example, suppose that firm 1 (alone) successfully innovates in period 1. If firm 2 then makes a breakthrough in period 2 worth V dollars, it would only be able to apply this innovation to the product by also employing firm 1's patent for which it would have to pay a fee. Because firm 2 has already sunk the R&D cost of c, there is nothing to prevent firm 1 from setting a fee equal to the full value V of the new innovation. Yet that would mean that firm 2 would foresee that its risky research effort would ultimately not be profitable and therefore not engage in research. The implication is that in our model, a patent regime results in just one firm doing R&D once a breakthrough has been made.[11]

Now consider the first of our three periods and assume there is a breakthrough. If there is a patent regime, then as just noted, the innovating firm will be the only firm that then does R&D in either period 2 or period 3. What if there are no patents?

In the case of no patents, we assume that any innovation by one firm is followed immediately by imitation by its rival leading to competition and that each firm receives the payoff SV, where $S < 0.5$ to reflect the fact that competition results in some of the surplus going not to the firms but to consumers. For our purposes, we will assume that $S = 0.4$.

We start with the third and final period. At that time, each firm will have to decide whether to incur a cost $c = \$25$ to engage in research with a potential social payoff of $V = \$200$ and for which no prior inventor can claim any fee. However, if a breakthrough is made by say firm 1, then the rival firm 2 imitates and competes with the result that the revenue flow to both firms is $SV = \$80$. Because $pSV - c = \$15$, we know that at least one firm will find it profitable to pursue the innovation. Is there a possibility that both firms will do so?

Recalling that if it fails, a second innovator can still copy rival success and letting either firm's R&D success be independent and equal to 0.5, the answer is no. If a second firm spends \$25 on R&D, it will be successful half the time and earn \$80. It will fail the other half but in half of these cases it can copy its successful rival. So the expected net gain of a second firm's R&D expense is:

$$[p + p^2]SV - c = 0.75 \times 0.4 \times \$200 - \$25 = \$35 \tag{21.16}$$

---

[11] More generally, firm 1 will only permit firm 2 to use its patent if the joint profit of both firms with both patents in use exceeds firm 1's monopoly profit and there is no reason to assume that this is the case.

However, with no patents, instead of spending on R&D like its rival, a firm can choose not to do so and simply imitate any successful innovation that the rival develops. In this case, the imitating firm has expected profit

$$pSV = 0.5 \times 0.4 \times \$200 = \$40 \tag{21.17}$$

As the payoff is greater to imitating rather than being a second innovator, the period 3 outcome in the no-patent regime must be one in which one firm does R&D and the other does not. There are of course two such equilibria—one in which firm 1 does the R&D and one in which firm 2 does the R&D. We will imagine that this choice is made by random assignment, i.e., a coin toss.

Now consider period 2. In that period, we know that at least one firm will innovate because again, $pSV - c = \$15$. In considering whether a second firm will innovate or simply imitate though, the calculation now is a little changed. This is because a breakthrough in the second period helps *both* firms in the third period because that is what makes possible an innovation at that later time. Suppose for example that firm 1 pursues R&D in period 2, but firm 2 does not. Then firm 2's expected profit over both periods 2 and 3 is:

$$E(\pi_2) = 0.5 \times 0.4 \times \$200 + 0.5 \times 0.5[(0.5 \times 0.4 \times \$200 - \$25) + (0.5 \times \$0.4 \times \$200)]$$

$$= \$53.75 \tag{21.18}$$

Firm 2's expected profit if it imitates in period 2 has two parts. The first is the probability that firm 1 makes a breakthrough in period 2, which happens with probability 0.5 and in which case firm 2 imitates and earns $80. The second term is firm 2's expected third-period gain. Getting to that period with any opportunity for further innovation is simply the probability $p = 0.5$ that firm 1 is successful in period 2. In that third period however, we know that only one firm pursues R&D. Given that the chances of success are $p = 0.5$, that firm has expected profit of $0.5 \times 0.4 \times \$200 - \$25$, and its rival has expected profit $0.5 \times 0.4 \times \$200$. Of course, firm 2 has a fifty percent chance of being either one of these firms in period 3.

If on the other hand, firm 2 decides to follow firm 1 and pursue R&D in period 2, its expected profit over the remaining two periods is:

$$E(\pi_2) = 0.75 \times 0.4 \times \$200 - \$25 + 0.75 \times 0.5[(0.5 \times 0.4 \times \$200 - \$25) + (0.5 \times \$0.4 \times \$200)]$$

$$= \$55.625 \tag{21.19}$$

Here again, firm 2's expected profit has two components. The first is the now higher probability that there is a breakthrough in period 2 times the revenue that brings and less the cost of doing research *plus* the also higher probability that there is opportunity for a further breakthrough in period 3 times the expected net gain for firm 2 in that period which depends on whether it is the one firm then doing any R&D.

As can be seen, firm 2 does better by investing in research in period 2 and thereby adding its innovative efforts to those of firm 1 rather than simply imitating its rival. Thus, conditional on a breakthrough in period 1, the no-patent regime leads to both firms doing research in period 2 and only one doing it in period 3 while the patent regime leads to only one firm doing research in both periods 2 and 3, i.e., the no-patent regime yields more R&D following the initial period than the patent regime does. Moreover, this result easily generalizes to periods 2 and 3 in a four-period model; periods 2, 3, and 4 in a five-period model; and so on. The intuition is straightforward. By adding to the innovation effort of its rival, firm 2 not only increases the chance of an innovation in that period but also to the chance of an innovation later which helps firm 2 even if it plans only to imitate at those later times. This makes doing R&D more profitable.

We have not addressed the first period. It is easy to guess though that a strong patent system will generate as much if not more R&D effort as a weak one in that first interval. However, the sequential nature of innovation suggests that once an innovation occurs, the obstacles that a strong patent system and associated patent thicket creates may well lead to *less* innovative activity in every subsequent period. This conclusion follows directly from the sequential nature of innovation. Hence, to the extent that innovation has that sequential feature, there is again concern that recent patent policy has erred too strongly in the protection of intellectual property.

21.3

Practice Problem

Two firms compete in a Cournot-type duopoly. The industry demand is given by $P = 100 - 2Q$. Each firm has a constant average and marginal cost of $60.

a. What is the current equilibrium price and quantity in the industry?
b. Suppose that one firm discovers a procedure that lowers its average and marginal cost to $50.

    i.   If the innovator does not license its product but simply competes as the low-cost firm in a Cournot duopoly, what will be the innovator's profit?

    ii. What will be the innovator's profit if it licenses the technology to its competitor at a royalty rate of $10?

    iii. Suppose instead that the innovator licenses the technology for a fixed fee. What is the highest fee that the non-innovator will be willing to pay? What will the innovator's profits be if it can charge the highest possible such fee?

21.6   RECENT PATENT POLICY DEVELOPMENTS

In the first half of the 1980s, a number of events occurred that, together, greatly increased the legal protection of patent rights in the United States. The first and perhaps most crucial step was a legal reorganization that gave the Court of Appeals for the Federal Circuit (CAFC), in Washington, D.C., exclusive jurisdiction over patent appeals in an effort to unify the legal treatment of patent rights. This court is widely considered to have a very "pro-patent" view and, until recently, its decisions were left unquestioned by the US Supreme Court. The CAFC emerged as the final and sole arbiter of patent disputes and its pro-patent views became widely reflected in lower court cases. Just how much stronger patent protection was to become became apparent in the 1986 patent infringement suit filed by Polaroid against Kodak regarding Kodak's production and sale of an instant-film and instant-picture camera.

Prior to that decision, losers in a patent infringement case had typically paid small penalties and been permitted to continue to produce so long as they paid appropriate royalties to the winner. However, when Polaroid won the suit Kodak was required to pay very large penalties and, most importantly, forced to stop producing its instant camera. Because shutting down a high volume production line is very expensive—even if only

---

Reality Checkpoint

Patent Policy in the Information Age: Getting One (click) Up On the Competition

The most valuable real estate lots bordering the information superhighway may be ideas for using the Internet profitably. These business method innovations differ from manufacturing technological advances but may be even more valuable ever since the granting of patent protection to business methods with the 1998 U.S. Court of Appeals ruling that legitimized Signature Financial Group's patent for an algorithm to manage mutual fund investments [*State Street Bank and Trust Co., Inc. v. Signature Financial Group*, 149 F.3d 1368, Fed. Cir (1998)].

Consider the on-line giant Amazon, for example. Its customers shop the site and list the items that they wish to purchase. At the end of their visit, customers simply make one click of their mouse and their order is processed. Amazon actually received a patent for this 1-Click feature and touts it to all potential customers. How effective that patent is was revealed in 1999 when traditional "brick and mortar" bookseller, Barnes & Noble, added internet selling and included a one-click feature in its web Express Lane checkout. Amazon successfully sued for patent infringement and Barnes & Noble had to move to finalizing an order in two clicks.

The 1-Click case is not unique. A customer at Burger King, for instance, might order a Whopper, an order of french fries, and a small salad for a total of $7.14. When checking out, the cashier might say, "for just 86 cents more, you can also have a soft drink that regularly sells for $1.29." If the customer agrees to this so-called upsale, Burger King receives more revenue. Yet, a good chunk of the extra funds will go to Walker Digital as a licensing fee because Walker owns a patent on this process.

In the wake of the *State Street* decision, filings for business method patents nearly tripled. Many economists, including Gallini (2002) and Hall (2003), suspect business method patents may slow down technical progress. It would be ironic if at the same time that technical breakthroughs made information cheap, expanded business method patents made information more expensive to exploit.

Sources: S. Hansell "Barnes And Noble Injunction Lifted," *The New York Times*, February 15, 1991, C1; and J. Angwin "Business Method Patents, Key to Priceline, Draw Growing Protest," *The Wall Street Journal*, October 3, 2002, p. B1.

---

for a few weeks—the fact that the courts were now willing to impose such an outcome put all firms on notice that patent infringement cases were serious business. Moreover, the Kodak/Polaroid case was quickly followed by very aggressive behavior on the part of one firm, Texas Instruments (TI), in filing infringement suits (mostly against foreign firms) and raising royalty fees that also served to put high technology firms on notice. In the technology sector, where reverse engineering has always been important, TI was so aggressive that its royalty fees and court awards began to outstrip its production activities as a source of revenue.

In short, a new legal environment of much stronger protection for patent-holder rights emerged in the United States in the 1980s. It may not be surprising then to discover that there was an explosion of patent activity over the next several years. Between 1983 and 2000, the annual number of patent applications doubled while the annual number of patents actually granted rose by an even greater 170 percent.

There has been increasing concern that the strengthened protection of patent rights has become too aggressive. To begin with, recent empirical evidence casts considerable doubt that stronger patent enforcement yields better innovation results. Drawing on a range of sources, Lerner (2000) identified 177 distinct patent policy changes in 60 countries over 150 years such as those that lengthened or broadened patents, those that reduced the patent filing fee, those that required compulsory licensing, and so forth. He then examined the effect of these changes on the rate of patenting. He found that increased patent protection sharply increased patenting by foreign firms but decreased patenting by domestic innovators. The overall effect was positive. However, the inference is that foreign companies used patents to protect themselves against domestic competitors. Hence, while patents may have enhanced international trade, their effect on innovation was negligible.

Moser (2005) constructed internationally comparable data using the catalogues of two 19th century world fairs: the Crystal Palace Exhibition in London, 1851, and the Centennial Exhibition in Philadelphia, 1876. These included innovations that were not patented, as well as those that were, and innovations from countries both with and without patent laws. He found no evidence that patent laws increased levels of innovative activity. Instead, they simply affected the direction of innovation. Relative to countries with strong patent protection, inventors in countries without such protection simply concentrated their efforts in industries where secrecy was easily maintained, leaving the overall rate of innovative efforts unchanged. Similarly, Sakakibara and Branstetter (2001) found no evidence that a strengthening of Japanese patent laws in 1988 led to any increased R&D spending or innovative output.

Fears that patent protection had gone too far reached a dramatic high point in February 2007 when the three million customers of the BlackBerry wireless e-mail service were threatened with a shutdown due to a patent dispute. A small Virginia firm, NTP, had developed and patented the technology for a wireless e-mail device in 1990. However, NTP never produced a product nor did it make any effort to license the technology to others. In 1998, the Canadian firm, Research In Motion (RIM), unveiled its first wireless e-mail device. Sales took off sharply. Although RIM claimed that it had developed the technology on its own, NTP filed suit against BlackBerry in 2001. In 2002, a US jury found the Canadian firm guilty of sixteen counts of patent infringement. On appeal, seven of these were dismissed in 2004 but that still left nine outstanding. In 2005, RIM offered a $450 million to NTP to settle the case, but that settlement was rejected by the trial judge. In January 2006, the Supreme Court refused to hear any further appeal and a hearing to order a shutdown of the BlackBerry service was scheduled for Friday, February 24, 2006. The hearing did not reach a final decision. However, after further negotiations, RIM and NTP reached a settlement in which RIM made a one-time payment of $615 million to the Virginian firm for unfettered use of the technology. The agreement came even as the US Patent and Trademark Office (USPTO) was conducting a review of the legitimacy of NTP's patents. Many felt that the strong pro-patent laws had effectively allowed NTP to extort the payment from RIM and forced it to rush to a settlement before the USPTO completed its review.

In April of 2007, the Supreme Court served notice that it too was concerned about excessive patent protection. (See Reality Checkpoint.) In *KSR International vs.Teleflex, Inc* the court ruled that new products that combine elements of pre-existing inventions and that result from nothing more than "ordinary innovation" with no more than predictable results were not entitled to patent protection. The decision was notable both for its unanimity and for its clear concern that patent system abuse could undermine innovation. As a result, most experts believe that the decision raised the bar substantially for future patent applications. It also opened the door to a re-examination of existing patents and gave judges much more

Reality Checkpoint

It Was Patently Obvious and Therefore, Not Patent Worthy

In April, 2007, the US Supreme Court issued an important ruling that substantially raised the bar for patents on new products that combine elements of pre-existing inventions. The case involved a patent infringement lawsuit filed by Teleflex, Inc. against KSR International over the development of an adjustable gas pedal for use on cars and trucks equipped with electronic engine controls. The position of the accelerator pedal in many cars is not adjustable. Instead, the driver adjusts the position of the seat until the pedal is a comfortable distance away. However, in the 1970s, a number of inventors began to develop adjustable pedals that could slide forward or backward without changing the effect of depressing the pedal a specific amount. KSR won a 1999 contract with General Motors to provide such an adjustable pedal with an electronic sensor on GM vehciles. Teleflex, which had a patent for a specific type of electronic pedal sensor claimed infringement and demanded royalties. KSR refused to pay arguing that the Teleflex patent was invalid because it combined elements of exisiting sensors in an obvious manner. KSR won in District Court but lost on Tlelefex's appeal to the CAFC, the main patent appellate court.

Although the Supreme Court had a history of letting CAFC judgments stand unreviewed, in this case the Court took issue with the CAFC and especially, its use of the so-called "teaching, suggestion, or motivation" test (TSM test). This test only finds an invention obvious if "some motivation or suggestion to combine the prior art teachings" can be found in the previous work. Thus, the TSM test would imply that even when a new device yields very predictable results that any professional could logically foresee, the device would nonetheless be patentable unless that expecation had actually been tested in practice. The Supreme Court found that this test awarded protection too easily. It reversed the CAFC judgment and found in favor of KSR.

Because most inventions combine previously known elements, the decision in the *KSR v. Teleflex* case was widely recognized as a signal that two decades of aggressive patent enforcement were coming to an end. Indeed, it was accompanied by a second very similar decision in which the court found for Microsoft against a charge of patent infringement by AT&T.

Sources: *KSR International Co. vs. Teleflex Inc.*, 550 U.S. 398 (2007); *Microsoft Corporation v. AT&T Corp.* 550 U.S. 437 (2007); and L. Greenhouse, "High Court Puts Limits on Patents," *New York Times* 1 May 2007.

leeway to dismiss patent infringement suits. Further evidence that the Court had moved to a less protective patent policy came in June, 2013 when it rules that firms could not legally patent human genes.

21.7   EMPIRICAL APPLICATION: PATENT LAW AND PATENT PRACTICE IN THE SEMICONDUCTOR INDUSTRY

The semiconductor industry was not immune to the patent fever that spread through America in the last part of the 20th century. As Hall and Ziedonis (2001) document, patent awards per million dollars of R&D spending in this industry doubled in the ten years following 1982.

What makes this increase particularly striking is that semiconductor industry representatives have been surveyed repeatedly and consistently reported that patents are not a very effective way to appropriate the returns on R&D investments. Because the semiconductor industry is one of rapid technological change where product life cycles are short, semiconductor firms have instead relied on lead time, secrecy, and product design tactics to reap the profits from their innovations. What then is the reason for the increased patent activity by semiconductor firms? How is it related to the changed legal environment?

Hall and Ziedonis (2001) examine the patent explosion in the semiconductor industry using data from 95 industry firms covering the years 1979 to 1995. These firms were awarded over 17,000 patents in this period. Hall and Ziedonis (2001) model these successful patents as the outcome of a patent production process that relates the ith firm's production of patents in year t or p_{it} to a set of variables X_{it} including the firm's R&D spending and its overall size. However, they recognize that p_{it} is what is called a count variable. That is, it counts the number of successes that take place during a time interval of given length. Thus, p_{it} can only take discrete integer values and often will be zero. If we consider p_{it} to have a random component, then we need to assume a probability distribution that recognizes these features. The natural choice for this purpose is the Poisson distribution, which gives the probability $f(\lambda, p)$ that there are p occurrences of a random variable in a fixed time interval as:

$$f(\lambda, p) = \frac{e^{-\lambda} \lambda^{p}}{p!} \tag{21.20}$$

The Poisson distribution has a very nice feature in that it is fully characterized by the parameter λ, which is both its mean and its variance. Thus, Hall and Ziedonis (2001) model patent production as a Poisson process that has a conditional mean λ_{it} that is an exponential function of X_{it} as follows:

$$E(p_{it}|X_{it}) = \lambda_{it} = \exp(X_{it}\beta + \gamma_t) \tag{21.21}$$

where γ_t is a 1,0 dummy variable for each year reflecting factors in that year that are common to the patenting activity of all semiconductor firms. Of course, we can linearize this relationship by taking logs to yield:

$$\ln \lambda_{it} = X_{it}\beta + \gamma_t \tag{21.22}$$

Hall and Ziedonis (2001) measure p_{it} as the number of patents per employee. The variables in X_{it} include: 1) the log of firm R&D spending per employee; 2) a 1,0 dummy variable equal to one if the firm reported no R&D spending that year and zero otherwise; 3) the log of firm size measured as the number of employees in thousands; 4) the log of the plant and equipment value per employee as a measure of the capital intensity of the firm's production; 5) a 1,0 dummy variable equal to 1 if the firm entered the market after 1982 and zero otherwise; 6) a 1,0 dummy variable equal to 1 if the firm is a design firm that does no fabrication and zero if it is a manufacturing firm; 7) a 1,0 dummy variable equal to 1 if the firm is Texas Instruments and zero otherwise; and 8) the log of the firm's age.

The first three variables reflect the standard view of patents as the output of a process in which R&D is the input and in which there may be scale economies. The fourth variable allows Hall and Ziedonis (2001) to test the hypothesis that part of the increased patenting following the change in the patent enforcement environment reflects the decision by firms with large sunk costs who cannot afford to get "held up" in a patent dispute, to expand their patent portfolio rapidly to guard against such "hold ups." The fifth and sixth variables allow them to test a second hypothesis, namely, that another reason for the rise in patent activity was that the new legal environment made it attractive for design firms who, unlike semiconductor manufacturers, rely heavily on patents to enter the market, and thereby they change the mix of firms in the semiconductor industry to one more likely to patent. The seventh variable captures the well-known super-aggressive patenting strategy adopted by TI, while the age variable allows for firm-specific learning.

Hall and Ziedonis (2001) observe the annual number of patents p_{it} by firm i in year t for 95 semiconductor firms from 1979 to 1995, and use these to estimate a Poisson process in which the mean λ is taken to be conditional on a set of firm characteristics X_{it} and time dummies γ_{it}. Because they are estimating a Poisson distribution, the assumptions of Ordinary Least Squares (OLS) do not hold. Instead, Hall and Ziedonis use Maximum Likelihood Estimation (MLE). Because λ is both the mean and the variance of the Poisson distribution, comparing the variance of the data with the mean is a natural test for the appropriateness of the underlying Poisson specification. The results of their two regressions that do best on this test are shown in Table 21.3, below.

The estimates in both regressions for the first four variables imply roughly constant returns to scale in patent production. As firm size (measured by the number of employees) grows, semiconductor firms tend to increase their patent output proportionately. This is similar to the finding of other researchers, e.g., Hall, Griliches, and Hausmann (1986). It is also clear that TI has a markedly higher propensity to patent than do other semiconductor firms consistent with TI's well-known aggressive patenting policy during these years.

Most importantly, both of the key hypotheses are supported by these data. Firms with capital-intensive production as measured by the amount of plant and equipment per employee do significantly more patenting than others do. In addition, it appears that the firms that entered the industry following the 1982 centralization of patent law cases at the CAFC were much more likely to patent than the firms that were already in the industry. The coefficient on the post-1982 entry variable is highly significant in both regressions. While the coefficient on the design firm variable is not significant in the second regression, it is if the post-1982 entry variable is omitted indicating that the entry variable reflects mostly entry by design firms.

Table 21.3   Parameter estimates for expected patent output by semiconductor firms

Variable	Estimated Coefficient	Standard Error	Estimated Coefficient	Standard Error
Log R&D per Employee	0.190	(0.084)	0.196	(0.117)
Dummy for No Reported R&D	−1.690	(0.830)	−1.690	(0.840)
Log Firm Size	0.854	(0.032)	0.850	(0.034)
Log Firm P&E per Employee	0.601	(0.113)	0.603	(0.114)
Dummy for Post-1982 Entry	0.491	(0.169)	0.491	(0.199)
Dummy for Design Firm			−0.130	(0.185)
Dummy for Texas Instruments	0.799	(0.111)	0.798	(0.115)
Log of Firm Age			0.220	(0.146)

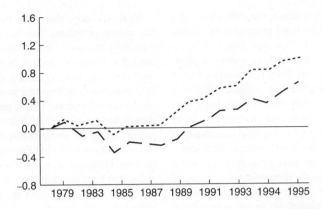

Figure 21.3   Pattern of regression time coefficients in semiconductor patent behavior

In sum, Hall and Ziedonis (2001) interpret their results as indicating two major reasons for the jump in patenting efforts in the semiconductor industry after 1983. One is that the new pro-patent environment and the prospect of having production actually stopped by legal injunction was particularly threatening to capital-intensive firms with heavy sunk costs. The result was that they responded strategically by rapidly accumulating a portfolio of patents to protect their products and processes. The second was that the changed legal environment also induced entry of purely design firms that have an inherently greater propensity to patent their findings in any case.

There is also a third effect revealed by the Hall and Ziedonis (2001) findings. This is that the changed legal framework led all semiconductor firms to patent more. The evidence for this is in the time dummies (not shown). Normalizing so that the effect is zero in 1979, the pattern of these coefficients is shown in Figure 21.3. Here, the dotted line reflects the time dummy coefficients from the first of the two regressions above, while the dashed line reflect the same coefficients in the second regression estimates.

What both sets of estimates clearly show is that after 1986, even after controlling for the mix of semiconductor firm characteristics, there was a steady increase in the proclivity to patent with each successive year. The new pro-patent environment is the most obvious explanation for this rise that is common to all semiconductor firms.

Summary

By giving innovators a legally enforceable means of earning a return on their discoveries, patents and copyrights do provide incentives for innovative activity that might otherwise not be undertaken. Yet patents also confer monopoly power on the patent holder, with all the price distortions that such power entails. In addition, patent rules may enhance the ability of existing monopolies to maintain their current dominant position against would-be entrants. One mechanism by which this may occur is through the use of "sleeping patents" designed to buffer the invention against any and all attacks from rival innovations that might permit an entrant to "invent around" the original patent.

Licensing agreements by which firms permit the use of their patented knowledge for a fee can help ameliorate the patent tension. This is because such agreements both permit wider use of the innovation and also allow an innovator to earn a greater return on its R&D investments than it otherwise would receive. However, licensing contracts can be difficult to enforce except by imposing restrictions that can be harmful to competition.

Within the United States, the 1980s marked a sharp increase in the legal protection of patents against infringement. This was followed by an equally sharp increase in both patent applications and patent grants. Empirical evidence from the semiconductor industry suggests that this reflects in part the desire of firms with large sunk investments in products and processes to avoid disruption of their production by accumulating a large patent portfolio. It also reflects the encouragement of entry by new firms that rely more heavily on patents to appropriate the gains of their innovations. That evidence also confirms that there was a general rise in patent proclivity across all semiconductor firms at that time.

More recently, there has been concern that US patent protection has been overly strong, especially because there is little evidence that it has led to faster innovation. In particular, patent decisions may have created a thicket of necessary approvals and fees that strongly deters new product development. This is particularly true if patents have a sequential feature such that one patent builds on those before it. Accordingly, recent court decisions have pared back these protections. However, as our discussion of licensing and recent legal developments makes clear, there is no easy way to eliminate the tension between allocative and innovative activity that a patent system is meant to balance.

Problems

1. Let the inverse demand for a particular product be given by $P = 250 - Q$. The product is offered by two Cournot firms, each of which has a current marginal cost of $100. Both firms can invest a sum K to establish a research facility to develop a new process with lower marginal costs. The probability of success is ρ.

   a. Assume that the new process is expected to have marginal costs of $70. Derive a relationship between K and ρ under which

      i. neither firm establishes the research facility;

      ii. only one firm establishes a research facility;

      iii. both firms establish a research facility.

   b. Can there be "too much" R&D? Illustrate your answers in a diagram with ρ on one axis and K on the other.

   c. Now assume that the marginal costs of the new process are expected to be $40. How does this affect your answers to 1(a)?

2. In the text of this chapter we considered sleeping patents in the context of a process innovation. The same principles apply in the case of a product innovation. To see why, consider the following example: Assume that there are 100 aspiring Olympic swimmers whose tastes for low-water-resistance

colored swimming suits are evenly distributed over the color spectrum from black to yellow. The "length" of this spectrum is normalized to be one unit. Each of these swimmers values the loss of utility from being offered swimming suits in other than their favorite color at $10 per unit of "distance." Each swimmer will buy exactly one swimming suit per period provided that the full price for the suit—the price charged by the firm plus the value of utility loss if there is a color difference between the suits on offer and the swimmer's favorite color—is less than $100 (these are very keen swimmers!). Production of low-water-resistance swimming suits is currently feasible only in black and is controlled by a monopolist who has a patent on the production of the black material. The marginal cost of making a swimming suit is $25.

   a. What is the current profit-maximizing price per suit and what are the monopolist's per-period profits?

      Now assume that research can be conducted that will allow the swimming suits also to be manufactured in yellow at the same marginal cost of $25.

   b. If the monopolist undertakes the research and introduces the new color what will be the resulting equilibrium prices of black and yellow swimming suits? What is the impact on the monopolist's per-period profit, ignoring research costs?

c. If a new entrant undertakes the research and introduces the new color, what will be the resulting equilibrium prices of black and yellow swimming suits? What will the entrant's per-period profit be, again ignoring research costs?

3. Return to Problem 2, above.

a. Confirm that the incumbent monopolist will be willing to spend more on researching the new color than the potential entrant.

b. Assume that the research costs can be split into some amount R, which is pure research cost, and another amount D, which is development cost—the cost of transforming a successful innovation into a viable product. Calculate limits on R and D such that the monopolist will be willing to undertake the research into manufacture of yellow swimming suits and patent it but then leave the patent sleeping.

4. Consider a Cournot duopoly in which inverse demand is given by $P = 120 - Q$. Marginal cost of each firm is currently $60.

a. What is the Cournot equilibrium quantity for each firm, product price, and profit of each firm?

   Now assume that one of the firms develops a new technology that reduces marginal cost to $30.

b. If it keeps control of this innovation itself, what will be the new Cournot equilibrium outputs, product price, and profits of the two firms?

c. If it licenses the innovation to its rival at some per unit fee r, calculate the innovator's profit as a function of r. What is the profit-maximizing value of r for the licensor?

5. Return to problem 4, above. Assume now that the innovator licenses the innovation to its rival for a fixed fee of L. What is the maximum fee that it can charge? Will the innovator prefer to set a per-unit license fee or a fixed license fee? What kind of licensing arrangement would consumers prefer?

6. Consider the same Cournot duopoly as in question 4, but now assume that the research has been conducted by an outside research firm. Suppose that this firm agrees to license the technology at a per unit fee of r. What license fee will the research firm charge

a. if it licenses to only one of the duopolists?

b. if it licenses to both?

c. How are your answers to (a) and (b) affected if the research firm chooses instead to charge a fixed fee of L for the license?

References

Bessen, J., and E. Maskin, 2009.

Denicolò, V. 1996. "Patent Races and Optimal Patent Breadth and Length," *Journal of Industrial Economics* 44 (March): 249–65.

Gallini, N. 1992. "Patent Policy and Costly Imitation," *Rand Journal of Economics* 23 (Spring): 52–63.

Gallini, N. 2002. "The Economics of Patents: Lessons from Recent U.S. Patent Reform," *Journal of Economic Perspectives* 16 (Spring): 131–154.

Gilbert, R., and C. Shapiro, 1990. "Optimal Patent Length and Breadth," *Rand Journal of Economics* 21 (Spring): 106–12.

Giuri, P., et al., 2005. "Everything You Always Wanted to Know about Inventors (But Never Asked): Evidence from the PatVal-EU Survey," Working Paper 2005/20, Laboratory of Economics and Management, Sant'Anna School of Advanced Studies, Pisa, Italy.

Hall, B. H., Z. Griliches, and J. Hausmann. 1986. "Patents and R and D: Is There a Lag?" *International Economic Review* 27 (June): 265–83.

Hall, B., and R. H. Ziedonis. 2001. "The Patent Paradox Revisited: An Empirical Study of Patenting in the U.S. Semiconductor

Industry, 1979–1995," *Rand Journal of Economics* 32 (Spring): 101–28.

Katz, M., and C. Shapiro. 1985. "On the Licensing of Innovation," *Rand Journal of Economics* 16 (Winter): 504–20.

Klemperer, P. 1990. "How Broad Should the Scope of Patent Protection Be?" *Rand Journal of Economics* 21 (Spring): 113–30.

Klette, T., and D. de Meza. 1986. "Is the Market Biased against R&D?" *Rand Journal of Economics* 17 (Spring): 133–9.

Lerner, J. 2000. "150 Years of Patent Protection," Harvard Business School Working Paper No. 00–039.

Lerner, J. and J. Tirole. 2004. "Efficient Patent Pools," *American Economic Review* 94 (June): 691–711.

Moser, P. 2005. "How Do Patent Laws Influence Innovation? Evidence From Nineteenth-Century World Fairs," *American Economic Review* 95 (September): 1214–36.

Nordhaus, W. 1969. *Invention, Growth and Welfare*, Cambridge: MIT Press.

Reinganum, J. 1989. "The Timing of Innovation: Research, Development, and Diffusion," in R. Schmalensee and R. Willig, eds., *The Handbook of Industrial Organization*. Amsterdam: North-Holland, 849–908.

Sakakibara, M., and L Branstetter, 2001. "Do Stronger Patents Induce More Innovation? Evidence From the 1998 Japanese Patent Law Reforms," *Rand Journal of Economics* 32 (Spring): 77–100.

Scotchmer, S. 2004. *Innovation and Incentives*. Cambridge: MIT Press.

Shapiro, C. 2000. "Navigating the Patent Thicket: Cross Licenses, Patent Pools, and Standard Setting," in *Innovation Policy and the Economy*, A. Jaffe, J. Lerner, and S. Stern, eds. National Bureau of Economic Research, 1190–1250.

Appendix

Here, we derive the optimal license fee for the simple case in the text. Demand is $P = A - BQ$, the initial marginal cost is c' and the innovation lowers marginal costs to c. For any royalty per unit $r \leq c' - c$. the innovator's profit is:

$$\pi = \frac{(A - Nc + (N - 1)(c + r))^2}{B(N + 1)^2} + r(N + 1)\frac{(A - Nc + (N - 1)(c + r))}{B(N + 1)} \qquad (21.A1)$$

Since $(A - Nc + (N-1)(c + r)) = A - c + (N-1)r$, it is evident that the expression in (21.A1) is increasing in r. Hence, profit maximization implies raising r as high as possible until the maximum $c' - c$ is reached.

Part Seven
Networks, Auctions, and Strategic Policy Commitment

In this final part of the text, we explore topics that do not fit easily within our earlier classifications. The first of these is network externalities, which are the topic of Chapter 22. For many goods, such as telephones, the value of the product to any one consumer rises as additional consumers buy it. Such network effects greatly alter both the nature of industry competition and the characteristics of the market outcome. Often, network externalities and the complementarities that underlie them give rise to multiple equilibria with no guarantee that the actual equilibrium chosen will be the best of these. Further, because network externalities act much like scale economies except that they work on the demand side, they create strong incentives for firms to operate on a large scale with the result that the market will inevitably be dominated by those few firms that survive. In turn, because not just some profit but a firm's very survival may be at stake, competition in industries with important network effects can be incredibly fierce. We explore these issues in some detail. We also include a discussion of Gandal's (1994) empirical study that tries to identify network characteristics in the market for computer spreadsheets.

In Chapter 23, we switch gears somewhat and turn to the topic of auctions. It has only been in recent years that auctions have re-emerged as a common market arrangement, especially for government privatization efforts and private exchanges on the Internet. Our analysis begins with a review of Vickery's (1961) classic piece leading to the Revenue Equivalence Theorem, which says that, under certain rather broad conditions, the final auction price is independent of the auction design. We then examine various ways in which this outcome might break down when bidders have affiliated values or signals. Perhaps most importantly, we show that the insights of auction theory may be usefully applied to industrial organization topics such as Bertrand pricing. We subsequently offer the Porter and Zona (1999) study of Ohio school milk auctions as an example of careful application of auction models to uncovering collusive behavior.

Finally, Chapter 24 applies the insights of industrial organization to international trade. We explore how knowledge of the Cournot and Bertrand models can help to develop strategic trade policies that depart from the economist's traditional free trade recommendations. This analysis allows us to make clear the critical role of commitment in any strategic setting. We conclude with an investigation of the use of strategic trade policy by the Canadian Wheat Board along the lines of a Cournot model as suggested by Hamilton and Stiegert (2002).

22

Network Issues

On Thursday, November 15, 2001, Microsoft CEO Bill Gates introduced the video game console, *Xbox*. Many questioned the decision to launch this new entry in a market that was then dominated by Sony and Nintendo, and that also included Sega, another firm with a sizable installed base. Today, however, the *Xbox* brand is still very much alive. The *Xbox 360* (introduced in 2005) is the best-selling video game console in the world and claims a 47 percent share of the North American market—well above rivals Sony (*PS3*) and Nintendo (*Wii*). Sega has exited the market altogether. All of the current ten best-selling games from *Mass Effect* to *Kingdoms of Amalur* to *Just Dance* are available in *Xbox* format. In 2011, *Xbox* consoles sales totaled $2.1 billion alone, and Microsoft earned an additional $4.6 billion from sales of games and accessories. Current estimates imply that 67 million *Xboxes* have been sold since that November 2001 launch.

The *Xbox*, of course, is just one of many computer-based success stories associated with Microsoft. Unlike most of these, however, the *Xbox* is a hardware product. Rather than Microsoft, the major providers of the software that runs on the *Xbox* platform are game development firms such as Electronic Arts and Activision Blizzard. Indeed, both the game developers and Microsoft are tied in a sort of "chicken-and-egg" relationship. There is no way to market *Xboxes* successfully unless developers produce games for that console. Yet there is no reason for developers to produce games for the *Xbox* unless a lot of *Xboxes* are sold. Put differently, the more *Xboxes* are sold, the more game-makers want to develop *Xbox* compatible games, and the more *Xbox* compatible games there are the more consumers want to buy the *Xbox*. There is then an external effect to the consumers' decision. As more consumers buy the *Xbox*, more games are developed for that platform, raising the value of the *Xbox* for everyone.

When the value of a product to any one consumer increases as the number of other consumers using the product increases, we say that the market for that product exhibits network externalities or demand-side scale economies. Video game consoles exhibit such network effects but they are far from the only such goods and services. Telephone systems are perhaps the most obvious of the other examples. By itself, one person's ownership of a telephone is not very valuable. Yet as more and more phone users hook into the system, the value of a connected phone rises for all. The online auction firm eBay offers yet another illustration of network effects. Prior to the 1990s, direct trade in many items, especially collectibles, had been limited because of the extreme cost of matching a potential buyer with a potential seller. eBay founder, Pierre Omidyar, was among the first to recognize the enormous potential of the Internet—which makes it easy to disseminate a vast amount of information to a large number of buyers and sellers in a very short time—to solve this problem. As more buyers came to look for goods on eBay, more sellers found it worthwhile to sell there which, in turn, attracted more buyers and so on.

The telephone and eBay cases are examples of what are typically called *direct* network effects. In contrast, the video game console market illustrates an *indirect* network effect. Operating systems such as *Windows* and *Mac* also benefit from indirect network externalities. Analogous to the console, these systems become more popular as more software is developed to run on them while, in turn, more compatible software is developed as the systems become more popular. The difference between direct and indirect network effects should thus be clear. In the direct case, the effects pertain directly to the good or service, e.g., the telephone, itself. In indirect case, the network effect is mediated by a complementary good. In this chapter, we investigate these issues and the equilbria that are likely when important network effects are present.[1]

22.1   MONOPOLY PROVISION OF A NETWORK SERVICE

An early but insightful analysis of network issues is that provided by Rohlfs (1974). Rohlfs' approach is quite straightforward and draws attention to the main issues that arise in network settings. It simplifies the supply side by assuming a monopoly so that the analysis can focus on the central demand-side aspects that give rise to network effects. We present a modified version of Rohlfs model here.

Assume that the monopolist, say a telecommunications firm, charges an access fee but does not impose a per usage charge. That is, the consumer is charged a single price p for "hooking up" to the network but each individual call is free, perhaps because the marginal cost of a call is zero.[2] We will also assume that there is a maximum size of the market, say one million, reflecting the maximum number N of consumers who would ever willingly buy the product even if the access fee were zero. By fixing the total amount of potential customers at N, we can talk interchangeably about the fraction f of the market and the actual number of customers fN served. That is, if the maximum size of the market is one million, we can characterize a market outcome in which 100,000 purchase the service either in terms of the fraction $f = 0.10$ or the number of customers $fN = 100,000$ served.

Consumers all agree that the service is more valuable the greater the fraction f of the market that signs up for it. However, even if everyone acquires the service ($f = 1$), consumers would still vary in their valuation or willingness to pay for the service. Specifically, we denote the valuation of the ith consumer when $f = 1$, as v_i. These valuations or v_is are assumed to be uniformly distributed between 0 and $100. For example, the 1 percent of consumers who most value the service (roughly about 10,000 individuals in our case) would willingly pay close to $100 for it if they knew that all other consumers would also acquire it. Unfortunately, when the consumer signs on, the consumer does not know the actual fraction f of potential users that will sign on to the network. Instead, the consumer's willingness to pay depends on the fraction f^e of users the consumer *expects* to sign on in that the *i*th consumer's willingness to pay for network membership is assumed

---

[1]   For a formal but very readable introduction to network externalities, see Economides (1996).
[2]   Note that this pricing policy is essentially that of a two-part tariff as described in Chapter 6.

to be given by $f^e v_i$. Each consumer will buy either one or no units of the good depending on how the price p compares with the consumer's willingness to pay $f^e v_i$. Specifically, the demand by consumer i for a hook up to the communications service is assumed given by

$$q_i^D = \begin{cases} 0 \ \text{if} \ f^e v_i < p \\ 1 \ \text{if} \ f^e v_i \geq p \end{cases} \tag{22.1}$$

Equation (22.1) makes clear that consumer i's willingness to pay for the service $f^e v_i$ increases with the fraction of potential buyers f^e that are expected to buy it. It is this interdependence between the willingness to pay and the fraction of the market that one expects to be served that leads to network externalities. Note that all potential users of the network consider only the value to themselves of joining the network. In particular, they do not take into account the fact that by joining they will improve the usefulness of the network to all of the other users because now the network is bigger.

We can use equation (22.1) to calculate the actual fraction f of consumers who buy into the service at any given price p. As usual, we start by focusing on the marginal consumer denoted by the reservation valuation $\tilde{v}_i$. This is the consumer who is just indifferent between buying into the service network and not buying into it, so that $\tilde{v}_i = p/f^e$. All consumers with a valuation less than $\tilde{v}_i$ will not subscribe to the service. The remainder will subscribe. Because v_i is distributed uniformly between 0 and 100, the fraction of consumers with a valuation below $\tilde{v}_i$ is simply $\tilde{v}_i/100$. Hence, the fraction of consumers f with valuations greater than $\tilde{v}_i$ and who therefore acquire the service is

$$f = 1 - \frac{\tilde{v}_i}{100} = 1 - \frac{p}{100 f^e} \tag{22.2}$$

If we now solve for p we obtain the inverse demand function confronting the monopolist expressed in terms of the fraction f of the maximum potential number of customers who actually buy the service as

$$p = 100 f^e - 100 f^e f = 100 f^e (1 - f) \tag{22.3}$$

It may help to express equation (22.3) in terms of actual demand Q. Recall that the total number of potential customers is N. Hence, $Q = fN$ implying that $f = Q/N$. We may therefore rewrite equation (22.3) as:

$$p = 100 f^e - 100 f^e Q/N \tag{22.4}$$

For a given expected fraction f^e (assumed common to all consumers), a given maximum valuation of \$100, and a given potential market size N, the demand equation (22.4), which is mathematically equivalent to (22.3), describes a conventional downward-sloping inverse demand curve with price intercept of $100 f^e$ and slope of $-100 f^e/N$. Note though that the position of the curve depends critically on the fraction expected f^e to buy into the service. That is, for any price p the actual fraction of the N consumers that buy into the service will change as the faction f^e expected to buy into it changes.

Because the demand curve depends critically on the expected fraction f^e of service users, we need to have some way of resolving the value of this parameter if we are to determine the equilibrium outcome. For this purpose, we will assume that a full equilibrium requires that the expected and actual fraction of users be equal $f = f^e$, otherwise rational individuals would be changing their expectations to eliminate their forecast error. This requirement implies that in a full, rational expectations equilibrium, equation (22.3) may be rewritten as:

$$p = 100f - 100f^2 = 100f(1 - f) \tag{22.4}$$

This expectations equilibrium demand curve is illustrated in Figure 22.1. This diagram also includes a horizontal line through the value $p = \$22.22$, which we shall explain later.

The curve shown in Figure 22.1 is interesting in a number of respects. Note first that for all prices greater than \$25, no equilibrium with a positive value of f exists. If for some reason, the monopolist must charge a price greater than \$25, perhaps to cover fixed costs, then the network will simply fail. This is true even though the network might be socially efficient.

To illustrate, suppose that the monopolist incurs a fixed cost of \$15 million to set up the system but that the marginal cost of one more customer signing in is zero. This means that when half the market ($f = 0.5$) or 500,000 consumers are served, the firm has an average cost of $\$15/0.5 = \$30$ per customer. We also know, however, that if half the population were to buy the product, it would be those consumers with v_i values in the range of \$50 to \$100. The average $v_i = \left(\dfrac{1}{50}\right) \displaystyle\sum_{I=51}^{100} v_i$ value for this group is therefore \$75. Hence, with $f = 0.5$, the average actual willingness to pay across these consumers would be $\$75/2 = \$37.50$—enough it would seem to cover the \$30 cost per consumer.

Yet as we have stated and as Figure 22.1 illustrates, the network will not be viable at a price of \$30. Why? Because while the average consumer valuation at $f = 0.5$ is \$37.50, there are some current consumers (those for whom $\$50 \le v_i < \$60$) whose willingness to pay is less than \$30. As the price rises toward \$30, these consumers drop the service. Some (those for whom $\$50 \le v_i < \$52$) drop as soon as the price rises to \$26, more drop as it hits \$27, and so on. The loss of these consumers, however, reduces the value of the network to

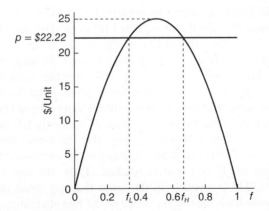

Figure 22.1   Demand to a monopoly provider of a network service
At price p if fewer than f_L consumers subscribe to the network, the equilibrium will fall to $f = 0$. If more than f_L consumers subscribe to the network, the equilibrium will rise to f_H.

those remaining. Those who were previously just willing to pay $30 when the service had 500,000 subscribers, no longer will be willing to do so now that fewer people are signed on. These consumers will also cease to purchase the product, reducing still further the network's value to the now even fewer customers left behind. This process will continue until the entire market unravels and the network fails. Here, one can see the externality quite explicitly. A consumer does not consider the impact of her choice to join or to leave the network has on the value of the network to others.

We have not of course shown that $25 is the firm's profit-maximizing price. All we have shown is that no rational expectations equilibrium exists with $p > \$25$ and that the market can suboptimally fail. Determining the monopolist's profit-maximizing price (or output) is tricky in this case because the quadratic quality of the demand curve means that we cannot simply apply our standard twice-as-steep rule to determine marginal revenue. However, as we show in the Appendix to this chapter, simple calculus quickly reveals that the optimal price is $22.22. This points to a second common feature of network markets, namely, the existence of multiple equilibria, with the result that one cannot be sure which outcome will obtain.

As noted earlier, the horizontal line in Figure 22.1 is drawn through the value $p = \$22.22$, i.e., through the monopolist's profit-maximizing price. This line indicates the three rational expectations equilibria associated with this price. The first is where the line intersects the vertical axis at $f^e = f = 0$. If no one expects anyone else to subscribe to the service, no one does. The second is where the line intersects the demand curve at $f^e = f = 0.333$, an outcome we will refer to as the low-fraction equilibrium $f_L(p)$. The final possible equilibrium occurs where price is again $p = \$22.22$ and $f^e = f = 0.667$, an outcome we will refer to as the high-fraction equilibrium $f_H(p)$. Which of these three might we expect to occur?

Rohlfs points out that the low-fraction equilibrium is actually unstable. To see what this means, consider, for example, a case in which the market is at this equilibrium with $p = \$22.22$ and $f = f^e = f_L(p) = 1/3$. Suppose that starting from this point, there is a small increase in the expected fraction f^e to 0.40. At this value of f^e, the marginal consumer is now given by: $\widehat{v_i} = p/100 f^e = 22.11/0.40 = 55.5$. Because all consumers with v_i values greater than this buy into the service, this implies that the actual fraction f of subscribers would rise to $f = (100 - 55.5)/100 = 0.445$. In other words, the expectation that $f^e = 0.40$ would lead to an actual proportion $f = 0.445$ even higher than expected. This difference between the actual and expected network size cannot persist as it is not an equilibrium. Sooner or later the reality of the higher actual fraction f would lead consumers to raise their expectations f^e further as well. In turn, this would raise the actual proportion f higher still. This process will continue until the high proportion equilibrium $f^e = f = f_H(p) = 0.667$ is reached at which point the expectation that 2/3 of the population will subscribe induces precisely the same actual fraction of consumers to subscribe. Analogously, if the expected fraction f^e suddenly fell to 0.25, $\widehat{v_i}$ would fall to $\widehat{v_i} = p/100 f^e = 22.22/0.40 = 0.888$, implying that the actual fraction of subscribers would fall below f^e to $f = 0.112$. Once again, this process would continue until the alternative equilibrium of $f^e = f = 0$ is reached. Thus, the low fraction equilibrium $f^e = f = f_L(p) = 0.3333$ is unstable in the sense that any small deviation away from $f^e = 0.333$ immediately leads the market to one of the two alternative equilibria.

It is straightforward to show that in contrast to the low-fraction equilibrium, both the zero fraction and high fraction equilibria are stable. That is, deviations away from these equilibria set in motion forces that tend to restore them. Therefore, it seems likely that one of these two must ultimately prevail. Because there is no consumer or producer surplus when $f^e = f = 0$, the high-fraction surplus of $f^e = f = f_H(p) = 0.667$ is obviously preferable. There is however no guarantee that it will be reached. Yet if the market can somehow reach the low-fraction equilibrium $f^e = f = f_L(p)$, then it seems virtually certain that the high-fraction equilibrium will be attained because only a trivial increase in f^e (or a trivial decrease in p) is necessary to do so. For this reason, Rohlfs refers to the fraction $f_L(p)$ as a "critical mass" for the network. If $f_L(p)$, can be established, the network will grow to contain the high fraction, $f_H(p)$, of the population.

The critical mass $f_L(p)$ is a key feature confronting firms in network markets. When network firms compete, those that do not reach the critical mass are not just smaller. They fail to survive at all. An important question therefore is whether and how the monopolist can reach the critical mass. One possibility is to provide the service free for a limited period of time, perhaps by bundling the service with some other product. Another option is to lease the equipment to potential users with a promise to cancel the service with no penalty if it does not achieve critical mass. A further possibility, one used when fax machines were first marketed, would be to target groups of large users first. In this regard, national and multinational companies or government agencies are the obvious examples of institutions that might want to operate their own internal networks. Once the network comes into common use for internal company communications, there may well be a demand for it to be extended to those with whom the company does business. Before long, this may grow into a demand by company users of the service for it to be available in their homes.

How do the monopolist's choices of $p = \$22.22$ and $f = 2/3$ compare with the social optimum? Because that optimum requires that the market be as large as possible at a price equal to marginal cost, it requires in this case that all N consumers should be served, i.e., $f = 1$. Clearly then the monopolist sets too high a price and serves too small a market. Because we know that monopolies typically restrict output, this result should come as no surprise. In this case though, there is a second reason for the market to be suboptimally small, namely, the presence of the network externality. The fact that each consumer ignores the impact of the decision to subscribe on the service valuation of other consumers, market demand tends to be too low at any price. Even a competitive market will tend to under produce a network good. Indeed, competitive firms may have difficulty coordinating on the collective actions necessary to push demand beyond the critical mass.

22.1

Imagine that consumer valuations v_i are distributed uniformly between 0 and 100. Each consumer will buy at most one unit of the good depending on his or her willingness to pay. However, that willingness to pay depends on the fraction f of population that buys the good. In particular, consumer i will buy one unit of the good only if $(0.4 + 6f^2)v_i \geq p$. Otherwise, consumer i buys zero.

a. Assume that the price is $p = \$50$. Show that the marginal consumer has basic valuation $v^M = 50/(0.4 + 6f^2)$.

b. Show that at this price, two non-zero market equilibria are possible: one with $f = 0.1905$ and one with $f = 0.906$. Which, if either of these, is stable?

Practice Problem

22.2   NETWORKS, COMPETITION, AND COMPLEMENTARY SERVICES

While the Rohlfs (1974) model focuses on the provision of network services by a monopolist, it makes clear many of the major difficulties that network externalities raise when competition is considered. The market will generally be too small and could fail altogether. Alternatively, there could be more than one equilibrium outcome and there is no guarantee that the market will choose the best one. Indeed, the multiplicity of equilibria may rise once competition is permitted. Further, and perhaps more importantly, competition in network markets tends to be particularly fierce owing to the fact that gaining just a few more customers raises the value of a firm's network to all potential subscribers. We illustrate these points below.

For example, suppose that there are two firms, firm A and firm B, competing for the 1,000,000-customer market above. Suppose further that while fixed costs are zero, each firm now has a positive marginal cost of $11.11. Consumers buy the service of the network that gives them the biggest net surplus, $f_A v_i - p_A$, and $f_B v_i - p_B$, respectively. In the case of a tie, consumers are split randomly between the two services. One possible equilibrium occurs with each firm setting a price $p_A = p_B = $ marginal cost $= \$11.11$ and two-thirds of the market being served. The firms offer identical products and, given the tie-breaking assumption, each serves half of the consumers ranging from valuations $33.33 and up. However, because each firm individually serves only one-third of the market, the valuation of the least valuable consumer in each case is $f v_i = 0.333 \times \$33.33 = \$11.11$. Neither firm has an incentive to raise its price unilaterally. This would only lose customers and make its network even less valuable to consumers. Nor does either firm have an incentive to lower its price. While this may give it an edge in attracting customers, each one served now involves a loss as the firm would be selling below cost. Hence, $p_A = p_B = \$11.11$ and two-thirds of market being served is one possible equilibrium.

However, there are a number of other possible outcomes. Clearly, one possibility is that neither firm's network attracts any customers at prices $p_A = p_B = \$11.11$. Again, no one will subscribe to a network to which no one else is expected to belong, and neither firm has an incentive to sell below marginal cost. Yet two alternative equilibria also occur. They arise when either firm A or firm B has a monopoly with respect to all consumers actually subscribing to a network at the monopoly price while its rival has zero customers at a price equal to or greater than marginal cost. We show in the appendix, for example, that with a marginal cost of $11.11, the monopoly price would be $23.89 and that at this price, the monopolist would serve about 60.5 percent of the market and earn a profit of $12.78 on each customer. Suppose that firm A is doing precisely this while firm B is charging a lower price but has zero consumers. Clearly, firm A has no incentive to raise or lower its price because it already has set a price that maximizes its profit. Firm B has no incentive to change its price either. Raising it surely will not help it attract any customers. Yet lowering it won't either because no one will choose a network that has no other customers regardless of the price.

Price competition is also more intense in network markets. To see this, consider our linear Main Street market with two firms located at either end of the one mile long street and N consumers distributed uniformly between them. Firm A is located at the west end of town ($x = 0$) and firm B is located at the east end of town ($x = 1$). Each firm has a constant marginal cost of c. Each consumer buys at most one unit of the good either from firm A or firm B and incurs a cost of t per unit of distance travelled. Absent network effects, the net surplus earned by a consumer at location x is: $V - tx - p_A$ if the consumer buys from firm A, and $V - t(1 - x) - p_B$ if the consumer buys from firm B. V is large enough that consumers always buy from one of the two firms, i.e., the market is covered. Firms compete in prices, p_A and p_B, respectively. The location of the marginal consumer who is just indifferent between the two products is identified by x^m. Because this consumer gets the same surplus whether goods are bought from firm A to the west or firm B to the east, we must have: $V - tx^m - p_A = V - t(1 - x^m) - p_B$. In turn, this implies that $x^m = \dfrac{1}{2} + \dfrac{p_B - p_A}{2t}$. Because firm A's demand $q_A = x^m N$ and firm B's demand is $(1 - x^m)N$, the inverse demand curve facing each firm is:

Inverse Demand for firm A: $p_A = t + p_B - \dfrac{2t}{N}q_A$

Inverse Demand for firm B: $p_B = t + p_A - \dfrac{2t}{N}q_B$ $\hspace{2cm}$ (22.5)

By the twice-as-steep rule, the marginal revenue curve for each firm is therefore:

marginal Revenue for firm A: $MR_A = t + p_B - \dfrac{4t}{N}q_A$

marginal Revenue for firm B: $MR_B = t + p_A - \dfrac{4t}{N}q_B$ $\hspace{2cm}$ (22.6)

Equating marginal revenue with marginal cost, firm A's optimal output is: $q_A = \dfrac{N(t + p_B - c)}{4t}$. Likewise, firm B's optimal output is: $q_B = \dfrac{N(t + p_A - c)}{4t}$. Substituting these values back into the inverse demand functions then yields the best price response curve for each firm:

Best Response for Firm A: $p_A = \dfrac{c + t + p_B}{2}$

Best Response for Firm B: $p_A = \dfrac{c + t + p_B}{2}$ $\hspace{2cm}$ (22.7)

From equations (22.7), it is easy to determine that without the further pressure of any network effects, the equilibrium prices in this market are:

$p_A = p_B = c + t$ $\hspace{2cm}$ (22.8)

Now consider the same market when network effects are present. To capture these, we assume that a consumer's surplus depending on the consumer's location x is $V + ks_A^e - tx - p_A$ if the consumer buys from firm A, and $V + ks_B^e - t(1 - x) - p_B$ if the consumer buys from firm B. Here s_A^e and s_B^e are, respectively, the market shares of consumers that the typical consumer *expects* to purchase good A and good B. To operationalize this expectation, we impose the same rational constraint that we did earlier, namely, $s_A^e = x^m$ and $s_B^e = 1 - x^m$. In other words, we impose the constraint that the expected market share equal the actual market share for each firm. Substitution of these values into the consumer surplus measures then quickly reveals that the location of the marginal consumer x^m is now given by: $x^m = \dfrac{1}{2} + \dfrac{p_B - p_A}{2(t - k)}$.

It is easy now to repeat the logic of the no-network case. The inverse demand functions are:

Inverse Demand for firm A: $p_A = t - k + p_B - \dfrac{2(t - k)}{N} q_A$

Inverse Demand for firm B: $p_B = t - k + p_A - \dfrac{2(t - k)}{N} q_B$ \hfill (22.9)

Using the twice-as-steep rule to derive the marginal revenue functions, solving for the optimal output of each firm, and substituting this result back into the demand curves then yields the following best response functions when network effects are present:

Best Response for Firm A: $p_A = \dfrac{c + t - k + p_B}{2}$

Best Response for Firm B: $p_A = \dfrac{c + t - k + p_B}{2}$ \hfill (22.10)

In turn, this implies that the price equilibrium when there are network effects is:

$$p_A = p_B = c + t - k \quad [0 < k < t] \hspace{2cm} (22.11)$$

Comparison of equation (22.8) with (22.11) shows that equilibrium prices are definitely lower when network effects are present. The reason is clear. The value to a firm of gaining additional customers from one's rival now is enhanced as that makes consumers more willing to pay for the firm's service. Competition between two or more firms to establish the network can be particularly fierce if it is possible that only one firm or network survives, that is, when the market has a "winner-take-all" feature. The winning network claims the entire (served) population and the loser gets nothing. The market is "tippy" in that once a firm starts to lose customers, the value of its product to the remaining customers falls, causing it to lose more customers, its value to fall further, and so on. In such a setting, more than market share is at stake. Survival itself is on the line. Moreover, while this "winner-take-all" feature would greatly intensify the competition by itself, coupling it with an environment in which pricing below cost may be necessary just to get any network started, makes the competition truly nasty. Some economists have argued that it was precisely this dynamic that was at work in the Microsoft versus Netscape case and that what may look like predatory behavior when applied in other markets is really just normal competition when applied in a setting of network goods.[3]

Market problems become particularly difficult when the network is a system comprised of complementary components and when we consider what happens over time. Suppose for instance that the network in question involves the market for Digital Versatile Disc (DVD) movies. The two components to this network are the DVD player and the movie discs themselves. This complementary relationship complicates the network effect. The desired

---

[3]   See Schmalensee (2000) for a clear statement of the view that competition in network or, (what he calls) "winner take most" markets is likely to be extremely fierce and easily mistaken for predatory conduct when practiced by a dominant incumbent.

outcome is for sufficiently wide use of DVD players and discs to achieve what appear to be rather sizable scale economies that characterize production, especially disc-making. However, no firm or group of firms will sink the large up-front costs necessary to produce a lot of DVDs unless they are sure that there will be a substantial number of DVD players. Yet consumers may be reluctant to purchase a DVD player until they are sure that there will be a large number of films translated to DVDs for playing. In such a setting, one possibility is that the market fails completely because of self-fulfilling expectations. If no consumer expects DVD films to be widely available (or available at a low price), no one will invest in buying a DVD player and, as a result, no firm will produce many DVD films. In turn, this outcome will confirm the initial expectations, justifying the decision not to purchase a DVD player. On the other hand, an alternative outcome is that each consumer expects others to purchase DVD players and therefore anticipates that firms will find it worthwhile to put films on DVDs. In this case, each consumer will purchase a player, inducing firms to produce movie discs, which now confirms this more optimistic expectation. The network externality in this case is reflected in the fact that as I buy a DVD player, I enhance the value of your DVD machine because I increase the likelihood that there will be firms that find it worthwhile to produce DVD films.

The DVD example also highlights another aspect of the multiple equilibria problem, namely, the possibility that the particular equilibrium realized may be one in which the market is "locked" into the wrong or an inferior technology. From a durability and volume of information viewpoint, the DVD technology is an undoubtedly superior and less costly way to provide movie rentals than is the VHS technology based on videocassettes and VCRs. However, because the two systems are substitutes and because VHS was the first system to get established, the DVD system needed to attract customers away from VHS in order to gain a footing. It might have been the case that the number of customers so attracted was not sufficiently large for the DVD manufacturers to exploit the available scale economies and avoid losses. To reach that volume, each potential DVD consumer needed not only to be convinced of the superiority of the DVD system but also to be sure that others shared that conviction and were willing to act on it. In this case, purely by the historical accident that the videocassette system was developed first, consumers could have been locked into the inferior system.[4]

To put it somewhat differently, there is "path dependence" so that whichever system eventually claims the market is the result of an arbitrary process, but one that "locks in" that outcome for a considerable period of time. Instead of the VHS versus DVD example just given, consider a closely related one from the earlier days of home video, namely, the VHS versus Betamax versions of Video Cassette Recorders (VCRs). Imagine that 40 percent of the population has a slight preference for VHS machines *if* the price and market share of these machines are identical to the price and market share of Betamax based products. Similarly, the remaining 60 percent have a slight preference for Betamax. However, these slight preferences can be overcome if one firm has a much larger market share because, again, no one really wants to buy a network product if it does not have a very large network of users. Finally, we assume that all consumers are not initially aware of the general home

---

[4]   David (1985) has argued that the standardized QWERTY keyboard used initially by typewriters and now by all PC keyboards is an example of path dependent lock-in to an inferior technology, with the superior one being the Dvorak keyboard. While Liebowitz and Margolis (1990) cast considerable doubt on this argument, the case nevertheless makes clear that such market failure is a real possibility. See also, Arthur (1989).

video market. Instead, they learn of it over time. Each week a few more consumers randomly find out about home videos and decide to buy a VCR of either a VHS or Betamax type.

On average, we would expect each new wave of new consumers to be made up of 60 percent Betamax preferring consumers and 40 percent VHS preferring consumers. However, it is quite possible that, picking randomly, one could get a batch of new consumers who were comprising, say, 90 or even 100 percent of those who prefer VHS. Starting from a point in which each system has equal market penetration, such a random draw could easily tip the market heavily in favor of VHS. Once that happens, then even those with a slight preference for Betamax will, in subsequent rounds, choose to buy a VHS machine because that network is so much larger that many more films are going to be printed for it. Hence, the small random draw favoring VHS may tip the entire market in favor of this technology forever even though, at base, Betamax is the superior technology in that most consumers favor it over VHS when all else is equal.

Similarly, Microsoft's dominance may reflect just plain good luck as much as it does superior technology. A key development in this regard came in 1980 when IBM decided to enter the personal computer market in a major way. IBM awarded the contract for its disc operating system to Microsoft and *MS-DOS* was born. Some analysts think that Microsoft did not have the best product at that time. Yet having the support of IBM was clearly a major advantage in establishing a network of *MS-DOS* users. Note that the network effect gives Microsoft a strong defense against *Linux* or *Apple* or some other product even if it is a better operating system than *Windows*. Again, the lock in effect raises the possibility that the market may adopt the inferior technology.

22.3   SYSTEMS COMPETITION AND THE BATTLE OVER INDUSTRY STANDARDS

Competition between networks does not always leave just one survivor. The US has four major credit card firms (Visa, Amercian Express, MasterCard and Discover). There is about the same number of major wireless phone service provides (Verizon, AT&T, Sprint, and T-Mobile). When we allow for the coexistence of two or more firms, each operating its own network, a number of additional features enter into the analysis. In such cases, there is the important issue of compatibility. To what extent will the industry adopt a standard product design that enables consumers to "plug in" to any network? If a standard is adopted, what standard will it be? In this section, we address these and related questions using a simple illustrative model described below.

Consider, for example, the question of technology adoption. Assume that two firms have to decide on whether to stick with their individual, existing technology or switch to a new one. To be specific, suppose that the firms estimate the payoffs to their choices to be those shown in Tables 22.1(a) and 22.1(b). The distinction between these two matrices is that in (a) sticking with the old technology is less profitable jointly than incurring the installation costs of switching to the new technology, while in case (b) both firms switching reduces their joint profits.

The payoff received for either firm depends critically on what choice its rival makes. However, there is also a further complication, namely, the issue of compatibility. Suppose that the old technology and the new technology are incompatible in the sense that they cannot be used together. This means that if each firm makes a different choice, they do not derive any network benefits from being interchangeable with each other. By contrast,

Table 22.1 Excess inertia and excess momentum with network externalities (in US dollars, millions)

		Firm 2	
		Old technology	New technology
Firm 1	Old technology	5, 4	3, 2
	New technology	3, 3	6, 7

(a) The new technology is Pareto superior to the old. A Nash equilibrium with both firms staying with the old technology exhibits excess inertia.

		Firm 2	
		Old technology	New technology
Firm 1	Old technology	6, 7	3, 2
	New technology	3, 3	5, 4

(b) The old technology is Pareto superior to the new. A Nash equilibrium with both firms adopting the new technology exhibits excess momentum.

if they choose the same technologies—whether old or new—then they do enjoy network externalities. Such positive network externalities mean that the payoff to each firm if they choose the same technology is greater than if they choose different technologies. This is illustrated in the payoff matrices by the fact that the payoff to either firm when both firms choose the same technology, no matter which, is greater than the payoff to either firm when they choose different (incompatible) technologies.

Regardless of whether both would do best by switching to the new technology [Table 22.1(a)], or both would do best by avoiding the cost of installing the new equipment and sticking with the existing technology [Table 22.1(b)], it can be seen that there are two Nash equilibria: one in which the two firms stay with the old technology, and the other in which they both switch to the new technology. There is no simple way to pick between these two equilibrium outcomes. If the payoffs are as in Table 22.1 (a) and so both switching is efficient, each firm may nevertheless choose not to switch from fear of moving alone into an incompatible technology. Farrell and Saloner (1985) refer to this as a case of excess inertia. Alternatively, with the payoffs of Table 22.1(b), we might find excess momentum with both firms making a costly switch to the new technology out of fear of being stranded alone with the old technology.

There are, of course, ways by which the firms can attempt to avoid either of these unsatisfactory outcomes. For example, the firms might be able to communicate their proposed technology choices—and they have the incentive to do so honestly because lying actually hurts both firms. Coordination may also be more likely if we extend this game over many periods, because then a firm has the potential to correct a "wrong" choice, i.e., one different from that of its rival. Nevertheless, even in these more general settings, Farrell and Saloner show that firms may in particular delay switching technology longer than they should. That is, rather than move promptly to introduce new technology soon, they may wait unduly long until a sufficiently large "bandwagon" has built-up. Thus, some theater owners and film producers in the 1920s did not invest in the equipment to show or to make "talking pictures" until they were certain that the new phenomenon would catch on. As a result, the advent of "talkies" may have been suboptimally delayed.

Compatibility is clearly an important factor in technological choice. However, there is a drawback to compatibility. When each firm adopts the same technical standard, their products become very close substitutes, and so price competition is likely to be intense. Hence, while product differentiation by means of different technologies incurs the cost of foregoing possible network effects it has the benefit of softening price competition. Firms therefore have to make a judgment in this regard. Choosing the same technology will lead the firms into direct, intratechnology competition of the type discussed throughout the earlier chapters of this book—that is, competition on price, quality, and service. By contrast, the choice of different technologies will lead the firms into intertechnology competition.

Of course, if a firm can establish its technology as the industry standard, the rewards from this kind of competition are likely to be very large indeed. When firms choose to compete in different technologies, each is hoping that its technology will someday win the market and become the industry standard. Think of Sony's *PlayStation*, Nintendo's *Wii*, and Microsoft's *Xbox*. These three firms apparently regard the advantages of compatibility to be more than offset by the disadvantages that it would bring in terms of intensified price competition. As a result, the three systems are totally incompatible. Yet each hopes to win the market and to establish its technology as the standard for which all applications, i.e., games are written.

There is no *a priori* means of determining whether rewards will be greater under intratechnology competition "within the market" or intertechnology competition "for the market." There are, however, three main possibilities that we should consider. We illustrate these with three simple games: (1) Tweedledum and Tweedledee, (2) The Battle of the Sexes, and (3) Pesky Little Brother.[5]

22.3.1   Tweedledum and Tweedledee

Assume that the payoffs for this game of technology choice are given in Table 22.2. There are two Nash equilibria, in each of which the firms prefer to adopt incompatible technologies. This implies that the firms believe that network externalities are not particularly strong and that any gains from adopting a common technology will be more than offset by the fact that this will lead to particularly fierce intratechnology price competition. They also believe that a battle to establish the industry standard will not significantly delay its adoption by potential consumers and so offers large rewards.

With these payoffs, each firm willingly enters into a battle to have its technology established as the dominant one, i.e., each will push for the Nash Equilibrium that favors its own product. In terms of the game matrix, firm 1 will fight to establish its technology as

Table 22.2   Tweedledum and tweedledee (in US dollars, millions)

		Firm 2	
		Technology A	Technology B
Firm 1	Technology A	3, 2	8, 4
	Technology B	4, 8	2, 3

---

[5]   This analysis is developed in depth in Besen and Farrell (1994). The language that follows is also borrowed from their discussion.

the "A" technology, thereby defining firm 2's as the lesser "B" technology, and firm 2 will do exactly the same. Besen and Farrell (1994) suggest four forms that this battle can take:

1. *Build on an Early Lead.* If there are any network externalities at all associated with a particular technology of the type we have discussed, there is considerable benefit to a firm that succeeds in establishing a large installed base of current users. These users will be reluctant to switch to a different technology. At the same time, the existence of such a large installed base makes the technology attractive to new users. (Just think of the choice that a new computer user has to make between buying an IBM compatible running the *Windows* operating system against a similar machine running *Linux* or an Apple computer with the *Apple* operating system.) Under this scenario, there will be intense price competition in the early stages of new technologies as each firm attempts to capture as many customers as possible. Firms will also reveal and perhaps exaggerate their sales figures in order to persuade potential buyers that a large installed base already exists.

2. *Attract Suppliers of Complements.* As we have pointed out many times, the attractiveness of a product is affected by the number of complementary products that are also available. A computer is of little use except to the most advanced users unless there is a wide range of computer software that will run on it. A Nintendo game machine becomes more attractive as Nintendo or other firms expand the number of games it can play. There is little point in owning a CD player unless recording companies offer a wide range of recordings in CD format.

   Owners of a primary technology such as Dell or Microsoft will likely encourage software developers to produce a wide range of programs that will run on their platform. Indeed, one reason that Apple lost its early lead in personal computers may well have been its reluctance to have its operating system installed in clones. This restriction limited the market penetration of Apple's system and consequently reduced the incentives of software developers to produce Apple-compatible software.

3. *Product Preannouncement.* The owner of a particular technology can try to slow the growth of a rival network by regularly "preannouncing" new products in advance of their actual introduction. The idea is to discourage new buyers from choosing the rival's product with the promise of new "goodies" to come. The long-advertised arrival of Microsoft's *Vista* program from 2004 to 2007 may have been in part an effort to attract new buyers who might otherwise have started out buying an alternative operating system. Such a strategy is not without risk, however. Announcing that a new version of a dominant product that is just round the corner may not just cause some new customers to delay their purchase of a rival's product. It may also cause customers already favorable to one's existing product to delay their purchases as well.

4. *Price Commitments.* A contractual commitment to achieve and maintain low prices over the long term is a fourth method by which new consumers can be persuaded to adopt a particular technology. This will be especially beneficial if the firm offering the commitment knows that there are significant economies of scale or learning economies in the manufacture of the primary product. In such circumstances, building a large installed base early generates cost reductions that allow the firm to deliver on its low price while maintaining its profitability.

In short, when rival firms compete to establish an industry standard, a variety of strategies and outcomes emerge. Here again we find that such markets are 'tippy,' with multiple equilibria in which the coexistence of incompatible products may be unstable. The tide of battle can turn rapidly and quite suddenly a dynamic can develop that leads to a single winning standard dominating the market. Moreover, there is no guarantee that the winner will offer the best technology.

22.3.2   The Battle of the Sexes[6]

Rather than fight to have their own technology adopted as the industry standard, firms may agree on the adoption of a common technology. The payoff matrix in this case is as in Tables 22.3(a) and (b). The simplest case is that illustrated in Table 22.3(a). Here, both firms are agreed that they should adopt technology 1. Accordingly, they should be able to establish this technology as a common standard by simple communication between them.

In the case of Table 22.3(b), however, there is no such agreement. The firms would prefer a common standard but they are not agreed on which of the two technologies the standard should be. Firm 1 will fight to establish technology 1 as the standard, and firm 2 will fight to establish technology 2. This is another instance in which commitment plays a crucial role. Firm 1, for example, may be able to persuade firm 2 to accept technology 1 as the standard by irrevocably committing itself to this technology. It could, for example, build an installed base rooted in technology 1. Alternatively, it could invest in production capacity to build more units embodying this technology, or establish a large R&D program devoted to improving this technology. The common intent here is to broadcast the clear message that firm 1 will never give in on its demand that technology 1 be the standard because to do so would cost firm 1 too much.

Other possible commitments take the form of concessions rather than threats. Thus, firm 1 could offer to license technology 1 to firm 2 for a low fee in return for firm 2 agreeing that technology 1 will be the standard. Alternatively, firm 1 can promise to develop the

Table 22.3   The battle of the sexes (in US dollars, millions)

		Firm 2	
		Technology 1	Technology 2
Firm 1	Technology 1	10, 10	5, 4
	Technology 2	6, 5	8, 8

(a) Agreement on compatible standard and choice of standard.

		Firm 2	
		Technology 1	Technology 2
Firm 1	Technology 1	10, 7	5, 4
	Technology 2	6, 5	8, 12

(b) Agreement to be compatible but disagreement on standard.

---

[6]   This title comes from a well-known game in which two individuals, perhaps husband and wife, in choosing their entertainment for the night, agree that they would rather be together than apart, but put very different valuations on the entertainment they might share. These could be, for example, going to a ball game or to an opera.

technology jointly, or it can suggest that the two firms develop a hybrid technology that combines the best features of each.

22.3.3 Pesky Little Brother

In the "Tweedledum and Tweedledee" case, the two firms pursue inter-technology competition rather than adopt a common technology and confront each other in the market with technologically undifferentiated products. In the "Battle of the Sexes," each firm prefers competition between technically compatible products, but the question of which technology is the appropriate standard remains an issue. What these two cases have in common is that there is some degree of consensus, if only on the terms on which competition between the firms will occur. If, however, there are asymmetries between the firms, it may be impossible for them to reach even this limited kind of consensus.

Assume, for example, that firm 1 has established a dominant position with a large installed base and a powerful reputation. It will prefer incompatibility with a small rival in order to hold its customers. The smaller rival, firm 2, will prefer compatibility in order to derive benefits from the network that the larger firm has established. As Besen and Farrell indicate, "The firms' problem is like the game between a big brother who wants to be left alone and a pesky little brother who wants to be with his big brother."

The payoff matrix now looks something like Table 22.4. There is no Nash equilibrium (in pure strategies) to this game if the firms make simultaneous choices—the two firms' strategic choices are inconsistent.[7] Resolution of the game then comes down again to a question of timing and commitment.

Suppose that the dominant firm must commit to its technology choice first. This is perhaps the most plausible assumption, given that we have motivated the game by describing firm 1 as a preexisting firm with a large installed base. In this case, the smaller firm 2 may actually enjoy a second-mover advantage. If firm 1 is committed to its existing technology either because it is costly to change or because such change would lose firm 1 the guaranteed patronage it now enjoys from its customers, it may be unable to prevent firm 2 from following. In this case, firm 2's clear choice will be to follow with a compatible system, precisely the outcome firm 1 had hoped to avoid.

Two tactics might be available to firm 1 that would prevent firm 2 from imitating its lead and offer firm 1 relief from its "pesky little brother." These are: (a) aggressive protection of its property rights and (b) changing its technology frequently. The first tactic relates to

Table 22.4 The pesky little brother (in US dollars, millions)

		Firm 1	
		Technology 1	*Technology 2*
Firm 1	*Technology 1*	12, 4	16, 2
	Technology 2	15, 2	10, 5

There is no (pure strategy) Nash equilibrium in simultaneous play. Firm 1, the dominant firm (or big brother) prefers that the technologies be incompatible. Firm 2 (the little brother) prefers that they be compatible.

[7] With a game of this type with a finite number of strategies, there is always a Nash equilibrium in mixed strategies in which the firms randomize their choice of technologies, but we shall not consider this equilibrium.

the use of patents. If the technology the dominant firm has built up is protected by patents, then imitation may be preventable through strict enforcement of the protection such patents give and by building up a stock of sleeping patents that make it difficult for a smaller firm to invent around the current technology.

Alternatively, firm 1 can try to hamper firm 2's imitation efforts by changing its technology frequently. This, of course, can be expensive and runs the risk of alienating users of the existing installed base unless they can be protected by, for example, being given favorable access to the new generation of products. The advantage to this approach is that the target at which the smaller rival is aiming is constantly shifting in ways that are difficult for the small firm to predict. If you really want to avoid your pesky little brother, don't tell him where you are going!

In short, competition over technology has a variety of implications. Often, there may be large social gains from all firms adopting a common technical approach. But the incentive for firms to differentiate their products, as well as the rivalry over which technology should become the industry standard, can frequently thwart the realization of such gains. While the gains from price competition are generally clear, the network externality effects make the gains from technology competition more ambiguous.

22.4   NETWORK GOODS AND PUBLIC POLICY

Our analysis of network services suggests many ways in which the market mechanism may fail to produce an efficient outcome. In some cases, a socially desirable service may fail to be provided. In other cases, multiple possible outcomes raise the possibility that the market may choose the wrong equilibrium and lock into an inferior technology. Competition may not be a feasible market structure. Moreover, even where feasible, competition may not be a remedy for these failures. To the contrary, competition may intensify the rush to a particular standard or technology, which later is realized to be inferior. Competition may also lead firms to reject compatibility even when it might actually be desirable. When the market will only support one system or network, competition is likely to be very intense and border on predatory conduct. How should public policy deal with these issues?

It is important to understand that in many respects, the problems raised by network effects are not new. The presence of dramatic scale economies and externalities have long been recognized as potential sources of market failure. Large scale economies make marginal cost pricing unlikely because such large scale economies means that marginal cost is below average cost over a wide range of production. Further, even when it is possible to operate at a sufficiently large size that all the scale economies are exploited, doing so will likely imply that there is room for only a few firms. Similarly, externalities always imply a divergence between private and social benefit (or cost) with the result that market outcomes based on the maximizing choices of individuals and firms are not likely to be optimal.

Saying that the problems raised by network effects are not new, however, is not the same thing as saying that they are easy. Three problems are particularly difficult in the case of network goods. The first of these is the problem of detecting or proving anticompetitive behavior. The second is the difficulty of devising an appropriate remedy once anticompetitive actions have been identified. The third is determining the proper role that the government should play in coordinating the technology choices of different firms with a view towards achieving standardization.

Reality Checkpoint
The Battle over High Standards

In the late 1970s, Sony introduced the Beta-Max technology for videocassette recorders (VCRs) and thereby initiated the war with the Video Home System (VHS), initially engineered by JVC Corporation, over the format standard for VCRs. VHS eventually won this war leaving Sony and many consumers with worthless BetaMax machines.

Thirty years later, Sony had to fight this war all over again, as the rise of affordable high definition TVs and disc players in the early 2000s, raised the issue of the industry standard disc format. Sony was the developer and primary proponent of the Blu-Ray technology. Its chief rival was Toshiba, the developer and main advocate for an alternative format known technically as the Advanced Optical Disc (AOD) format, but commonly referred to as HD DVD. Both technologies used a short wavelength blue-violet laser technology employing a very fine laser beam that permitted storing a great amount of information on a single disc.

Because each side had a considerable investment at stake, each fought hard to win. Among film companies, Sony persuaded Columbia, Disney, and Fox to use Blu-Ray. Toshiba won the support of Paramount, Universal, and Warner Brothers. Each also lined up support from other electronics firms such as Hitachi, Samsung, Dell, and Hewlett Packard (Sony), and NEC, RCA, Microsoft, and Intel (Toshiba). This of course created difficulties for retailers and consumers uncertain about which machines and DVD's to buy or stock.

As the battle raged on it became increasingly bloody. Sony took the very costly but important strategic step of building the Blu-Ray technology into its *Play Station 3* game consoles. Toshiba brokered a deal to sell its machines through Wal-Mart, the largest DVD retailer, for under $200. The decisive moment came in January 2008, when Warner Brothers announced that it would switch to Blu-Ray. Although Toshiba cut prices another 40 percent, Wal-Mart announced in February that it would phase out HD DVD within six months. The battle was over. Toshiba suspended HD DVD in March. Sony's Blu-Ray won albeit at a cost of much red ink.

Source: N. Wingfield, "Format Face-Off: Bringing the DVD War Home," *The Wall Street Journal*, June 20, 2006, p. D1; W. Mossberg, "Don't Get Caught in a Losing Battle over DVD Technology," *The Wall Street Journal*, March 8, 2007, p. B1.; and M. Fackler, "Toshiba Concedes Defeat in the DVD Battle," *New York Times*, February 20, 2008, p. C1.

Consider the problem of determining anticompetitive tactics. The presence of network externalities requires that the developer of a new product such as a facsimile machine sell to a large number of consumers in order to establish any market at all. In turn, this may well mean pricing below cost, at least initially. This may result in a competitor being driven out of the business. When later, the winning firm raises its price so as to earn a return on its investment, the historical record of selling below cost, eliminating a rival, and then raising price looks a lot like a case of predatory pricing. Indeed, such a record is essentially the evidence called for by Baumol (1979) to determine predation. (See Chapter 12.) Yet such a finding may simply reflect the need to price low so as to penetrate the market and the fact that the market can only support one supplier.

Similarly, the developer of a platform such as *Windows* or *Wii* or a DVD player requires that there be a large number of applications (programs, games, or films) available at a low cost in order to gain wide acceptance of the overall system. One way to achieve this aim is to produce and market such complementary goods itself. Yet to the extent that one can only play Nintendo *Wii* cartridges on a Nintendo *Wii* machine the market outcome begins to look like illegal tying or possibly an attempt at foreclosure. To borrow from an example earlier in the text, Microsoft's *Windows* almost certainly gained from the availability of a compatible, low-cost web browser. Yet Microsoft's decision to bundle its *Explorer* browser with *Windows* raised substantial concerns of tying with a view to driving Netscape out of the browser business.[8]

With regard to technology adoption and product improvement, the case of Microsoft is again relevant. Sun Microsystems' *Java* programming language offered the possibility of greatly enhancing the functionality of *Windows*. However, this required that *Windows* be made compatible with *Java*. Microsoft was generally reluctant to do this at least in part because there was a widespread view that *Java* could provide the basis for an alternative applications platform if it ever became widely accepted. Making it compatible with *Windows* would have this effect. So, while providing that compatibility might greatly improve the technology available for PC users, it might also provide an opportunity for entry to a new rival. Does Microsoft's reluctance in this case reflect an illegal effort to deter entry?[9]

As difficult as it is to identify anticompetitive behavior in network or systems markets, devising an appropriate remedy when such actions are discovered is perhaps even more problematic. The just mentioned case of Microsoft and Sun Microsystems is instructive in this connection. Is the appropriate policy to force Microsoft to make *Windows* compatible with *Java*? Adoption of such a policy would place the government in the awkward position of pushing a particular technology, and it is far from clear that the government has the skill to do this well. What if *Java* really does not offer any real improvement on the *Windows* product? Indeed, what if there is an alternative programming language that would offer much greater enhancement? That alternative may never break through if antitrust officials require that *Windows* work with *Java*. In other words, antitrust policy may also result in an inferior technology lock-in.

This raises the general question as to the proper role for the government in coordinating the technology choices of different firms with a view toward achieving widespread standardization. Consider the market for mobile telephone service. Relatively early on, the European Telecommunications Standards Institute (ETSI) imposed a requirement that cell phone service providers adopt GSM as the 2G standard to be used throughout Europe. Consequently, a British resident traveling on the continent was able to use a mobile phone to make calls in Italy just as easily as at home in the United Kingdom. This was much less feasible for US residents at that time, in part, because no centralized authority had acted to coordinate the digital standards of American mobile phone companies. Instead, US mobile service providers initially adopted four different standards that left interservice communication quite difficult, if not impossible. However, competition between these different standards spurred further technical development. Indeed, this advantage was implicitly recognized by ETSI when it later chose to adopt the American-based CDMA standard for 3G systems. [See Cabral and Kretschmer (2007).]

---

[8]　This point was made forcibly by Schmalensee (2000). See Fisher (2000) for an opposing point of view. Note that if Schmalensee's argument is that in some industries, e.g., web browsers, only one firm can survive, this is really a statement that such a market is a natural monopoly. The only difference is that here the scale economy lies on the demand side via the network externality. See also Eisenach and Lenard (1999).

[9]　Microsoft and Sun eventually did reach an agreement of sorts, but Sun was never happy with it and the agreement was later abandoned.

22.5 EMPIRICAL APPLICATION: NETWORK EXTERNALITIES IN COMPUTER SOFTWARE—SPREADSHEETS

As noted earlier, computer software such as operating systems and web browsers are likely to exhibit important network effects. Users care about being able to run their programs on the computers of their friends or business associates. The more people using a specific software package or the more compatible a software package is with add-on programs, the more valuable it should be. Gandal (1994) offers empirical evidence of this phenomenon from the early days of desktop computing.

A spreadsheet was initially a pencil-and-paper operation. Essentially, it was a large sheet of paper with columns and rows organizing all the relevant data about a firm's transactions. Its name comes from the fact that costs or revenues connected to a specific operation were spread or displayed over the sheet in a manner allowing sums over a given row or column. In that way, management is able to focus on a specific factor, say energy costs, in making an informed decision about company operations. The advantage of a spreadsheet format is that if a given cost factor or revenue assumption is changed, decision makers can trace through the implications of this change rather quickly. However, there is a natural limit to the speed of such adjustments when spreadsheets are "hard copy" and changes must be made by hand.

Beginning about 1980, electronic spreadsheets suitable for use on desktop computers began to make their commercial appearance. The first of these was *VisiCalc (Visible Calculator)*. Computerization greatly enhanced the speed with which managers could assess the impact of cost or revenue changes. It thereby greatly increased the usefulness of spreadsheets in daily operations. Demand for such products grew and so did the supply. Soon, there were a number of spreadsheet programs including *SuperCalc, VP Planner, PlanPerfec, Quatro Pro, Multiplan, Excel*, and *Lotus 1-2-3*.

These early products differed both from each other and over time. The earliest versions had very limited, if any, graphing abilities. Some could link entries in one spreadsheet to others in another spreadsheet. Some could not. Only a few were able to link with external data and incorporate that data into the spreadsheet cells directly. The most flexible of all was the *Lotus 1-2-3* program. Throughout the late 1980s and into the 1990s, this was the dominant product. Indeed, an important attribute of other spreadsheet programs was whether or not they were *Lotus* compatible.

Gandal (1994) notes that spreadsheet demand will likely exhibit network effects for a number of reasons because users like to be able to share their information and the results of their spreadsheet analyses with each other. Gandal then identifies three features of a spreadsheet program that should promote such networking. The first is whether or not the program was compatible with *Lotus 1-2-3*, the dominant product. This is measured by a variable *LOCOMP* equal to 1 if the program is *Lotus* compatible and 0 if it is not. The second network attribute is *EXTDAT*. This is a variable that takes on the value 1 if the program can import files from external data sources and 0 if it cannot. The final network feature is another 1, 0 variable *LANCOM* that indicates whether or not the program can link independent users through a local area network.

Gandal (1994) hypothesizes that if network externalities were present in the early spreadsheet market, then a program's market price will be higher if it has any of the three features just described, i.e., when for that product, any of the variables *LOCOMP, EXTDAT*, or *LANCOM* is positive. A function that specifies how product price changes as the product's attributes change is known as an hedonic function. Estimating such functions is usually done by ordinary least squares (OLS) in an hedonic price regression. Gandal (1994) gathered data for ninety-one computerized spreadsheet products over six years: 1986 through 1991. His basic regression equation is:

$$\ln p_{it} = \alpha_0 + \alpha_1 TIME87_t + \alpha_2 TIME88_t + \alpha_3 TIME89_t + \alpha_4 TIME90_t + \alpha_5 TIME91_t$$
$$+ \beta_1 LMINRC_{it} + \beta_2 LOTUS_{it} + \beta_3 GRAPHS_{it} + \beta_4 WINDOW_{it}$$
$$+ \gamma_1 LOCOMP_{it} + \gamma_2 EXTDAT_{it} + \gamma_3 LANCOM_{it} + \varepsilon_{it}$$

The dependent variable is the natural log of the price of spreadsheet model i in year t. Not including the constant, the first five variables are time dummy variables equal to 1 in the year that is indicated by the dummy and zero otherwise. These variables pick up the pure effects of time on spreadsheet program prices while holding the quality attributes fixed. The next four variables are variables that pick up specific features that should add to the value of a spreadsheet program. *LMINRC* is the natural log of the minimum number of rows or columns that the spreadsheet can handle. This is meant to capture the sheer computing power of the program. *LOTUS* is a 1, 0 dummy variable indicating whether the product is a *Lotus* spreadsheet. This term captures any brand premium that *Lotus* enjoyed during these years. GRAPHS is a 1, 0 dummy variable indicating whether or not the program can construct pie, bar, and line graphs. *WINDOW* indicates the number of windows a program can handle on a screen simultaneously. Of course, the final three variables are the networking effects described earlier. If there are network externalities, the coefficients on these variables should be significantly positive.

Gandal's (1994) results are presented in Table 22.5, shown below. The first regression shown is the estimated hedonic equation described above. Note that all the attributes hypothesized to raise the value of a spreadsheet program do in fact exert a significantly positive effect on its price. There is a strong brand premium for *Lotus*. There is an almost as strong premium for programs that have graphing abilities. Most important of all, however, the three networking variables are very strongly positive. *LOCOMP*, *EXTDAT*, and *LANCOM* all have a substantial positive effect on a program's price.

Regression 2 shows the effects of allowing the coefficients to change over time. Gandal (1994) splits the sample in half and adds as regressors, values of the independent variables multiplied by 1 if the observation comes in the second half of the sample. Most of these interacted variables are not significant. However, the coefficients on both *MINRC and LINKING* do change over time as indicated by the coefficients on *TMINRC and TLINKING*. These coefficients are interpreted as the difference between the marginal value of these features in the first half of the sample and that value in the second half of the sample. Note that this regression includes *TLANCOM* but not *LANCOM*. This is because connecting to local area networks was generally not possible for any program prior to the second half of the sample.

Gandal (1994) prefers Regression 2 as the better specification of the hedonic price equation. Note again that it implies strong network externalities. The coefficients on *LOCOMP*, *EXTDAT*, and *TLANCOM* are all very significantly positive. Consumers are willing to pay a lot extra for spreadsheets that others can use either because they are *Lotus*-compatible, can easily import data from external programs, or can exchange information over a local area network. These effects are powerful. Because the dependent variable is the log of the price, the coefficient is easily interpreted as the percentage increase in price

Table 22.5 Hedonic regression results for spreadsheet programs, 1986–91

Variable	Regression 1		Regression 2	
	Coefficient	t-statistic	Coefficient	t-statistic
CONSTANT	3.76	(12.31)	3.12	(9.50)
TIME87	−0.06	(−0.38)	−0.07	(−0.43)
TIME88	−0.44	(−2.67)	−0.45	(−3.03)
TIME89	−0.70	(−4.20)	0.92	(1.71)
TIME90	−0.79	(−4.90)	0.90	(1.67)
TIME91	−0.85	(−5.30)	0.85	(1.59)
LMINRC	0.11	(1.59)	0.26	(3.24)
LOTUS	0.56	(4.36)	0.46	(3.62)
GRAPHS	0.46	(3.51)	0.52	(4.18)
WINDOW	0.17	(2.14)	0.14	(1.92)
LINKING	0.21	(1.91)	0.26	(2.00)
LOCOMP	0.72	(5.28)	0.66	(5.17)
EXTDAT	0.55	(4.05)	0.57	(3.93)
LANCOM	0.21	(1.65)		
TLANCOM			0.61	(3.28)
TLMINRC			−0.34	(−3.07)
TLINKING			−0.31	(−1.49)

a consumer would pay for that feature. Thus, being *Lotus*-compatible raised the price of a spreadsheet program by 66 percent according to Gandal's (1994) estimates. A program's ability to import data from an external source raised the price by 57 percent.

A frequent use of hedonic price regressions is to construct price indices that trace the movement of a commodity's price over time. This is often difficult to do because we do not have an easy way to adjust for quality. A television set today may cost much more that a television set from ten years ago. However, it would be wrong to interpret all of that price increase as inflation because today's television set has many more features than that of an earlier set such as high definition, DVD compatibility, and a flat screen, to name just a few. Because the hedonic regression controls explicitly the value of quality features, it permits the easy construction of a quality-corrected price index by focusing on the changes that are due simply to the passage of time, i.e., holding quality constant. In Regression 1, these changes are fully captured by the year specific dummies. Because the dependent variable is $\ln p_{it}$, the predicted price for a spreadsheet of constant quality in any year: $p_{it} = e^{\alpha_t YEAR_t}$ so the $YEAR_t$ variable is the dummy for that observation and α_t is the coefficient estimated for that dummy. If we normalize so that the price index P_t is 1 in the first year of 1986, then equation 1 says that the price index will be $e^{-0.06}$ in 1987; $e^{-0.44}$ in 1988; and so on. For Regression 2, constructing the quality-adjusted price index is slightly more complicated because the value of the some of the attributes also changes over time, but the basic idea is the same. We present Gandal's (1994) estimated spreadsheet price indices for both regressions in Table 22.6, below. It indicates that over the six-year period for which Gandal (1994) collected data, the quality-adjusted price of spreadsheet programs—like the price of much software and hardware in this time period—declined substantially. Here, the decline exceeded 50 percent.

Table 22.6   Quality adjusted price indices for spreadsheet programs, 1986–91

	1986	1987	1988	1989	1990	1991
Price Index from Regression 1	1.00	0.94	0.64	0.49	0.45	0.42
Price Index from Regression 2	1.00	0.93	0.64	0.50	0.48	0.46

Summary

In this chapter, we have focused on the product markets exhibiting important "network externalities." In such markets, the value of the good or service to any one consumer increases as the total number of consumers using the product increases. Services with important network effects, such as telecommunications and home electronics, play an increasingly large role in modern economies.

Markets with strong network effects present special problems. Competition to establish a network service can be unusually fierce, leading to low prices that can be difficult to distinguish from predation. Often, such competition will result in only one firm surviving so that the market's ultimate structure is one of monopoly. There is also a nontrivial risk that the service will be underdeveloped or not developed at all. Similarly, the course of technical development exhibits a path dependency in which the market may eventually lock into an inferior technology.

There are no easy solutions to the problems raised by network goods. On the one hand, the possibilities for anticompetitive outcomes seem sufficiently clear that such markets necessarily invite examination by the antitrust authorities. Yet it must also be acknowledged that it is not easy either to identify anticompetitive actions clearly or to devise workable remedies to the market failures to which network services are prone. Such tensions have dominated the debate over policies regarding the telecommunications industry and other "new economy" markets in the past. They will no doubt continue to be important in the future.

Problems

1. Two banks compete for the checking and savings deposit business of a small town. Each bank has its own ATM network that works only on its own bankcards, but bank 1 has three times as many ATM machines as bank 2. Depositors value a bank's services as an increasing function of the number of machines on the network. Bank 2 approaches bank 1 and suggests that they merge their ATM networks so that depositors of either bank can use either bank's machines.

    a. Is this merger in the interest of deposit consumers in general?
    b. Do you think that bank 1 will agree with bank 2's proposal?

2. Assume that consumers contemplating buying a network service have reservation prices uniformly distributed on the interval $[0, 50]$ (measured in dollars). Demand by a consumer with reservation price w_i for this service is

    $$q_i^D = \begin{cases} 0 \text{ if } fw_i < p \\ 1 \text{ if } fw_i \geq p \end{cases}$$

    a. Calculate the demand function for this service.
    b. What is the critical mass if price is set at $5?
    c. What is the profit-maximizing price for the service?

3. Many social customs exhibit network effects. To this end, consider a party given by a group of individuals at a small university. The group is called the Outcasts and has twenty members. It holds a big party on campus each year. These parties are good, but are

especially good the more people are in attendance. As a result, the number of people who
actually come to the Outcasts party depends
on how many people are expected to attend.
The more people that are expected to attend,
the more fun it will be for each attendee
and, hence, the more people who actually
will come. These effects are captured by
the following equation: $A = 20 + 0.95A^e$.
Here, A is the number of people actually
attending the party. This is equal to the 20
Outcast members plus 0.95 times the number
of partygoers A^e that are expected to go.

a.   If potential party attendees are sophisticated and understand the equation
describing actual party attendance, how
many people are likely to attend the
Outcasts party?

b.   Suppose that each party attendee costs
the Outcasts \$2 in refreshments so that
the Outcasts need to charge a fee p for

attending the party. Suppose as well that when
going to the party requires paying a fee, the
equation for attendance is: $A = 20 + 0.95A^e - p$. What value of p should the Outcasts set
if they want to maximize their profit from the
party? How many people will come to the party
at that price?

4.   Two firms are competing in their choice of
technologies. The payoff matrix for the game
between them is given below:

a.   Identify constraints on the payoffs a–h
that are such that the firms' choices
reflect network externalities.

b.   Assume that the constraints in (a) are
satisfied. Identify further constraints that
must be satisfied for the game between
the two firms to be of the form

  i.   Tweedledum and Tweedledee;
  ii.   The Battle of the Sexes;
  iii.   The Pesky Little Brother.

		Firm 2	
		Technology 1	Technology 2
Firm 1	Technology 1	a, b	c, d
	Technology 2	e, f	g, h

References

Arthur, W. Brian, 1989. "Competing Tech-
nologies, Increasing Returns, and Lock-in by
Historical Events," *The Economic Journal* 99
(March): 116–31.

Besen, S. M., and J. Farrell, 1994. "Choosing
How to Compete: Strategies and Tactics in
Standardization," *Journal of Economic Per-
spectives* 8 (Spring): 117–31.

Cabral, L., and T. Kretschmer. 2007. "Standards
Battles and Public Policy." In S. Greenstein
and V. Stango, eds. *Standards and Public Policy*. Cambridge: Cambridge University Press,
329–44.

David, P. A., 1985. "Clio and the Economics
of QWERTY," *American Economic Review,
Papers and Proceedings* (May): 332–37.

Economides, N. 1996. "The Economics of Networks," *International Journal of Industrial
Organization* 14 (October): 673–99.

Eisenach, J. A., and T. M. Lenard. 1999. *Competi-
tion, Innovation and the Microsoft Monopoly:
Antitrust in the Digital Marketplace*, Kluwer
Academic Publishers.

Farrell, J., and G. Saloner, 1985. "Standardization, Compatibility and Innovation," *Rand
Journal of Economics* 16 (Spring): 70–83.

Fisher, F., 2000. "The *IBM* and *Microsoft* Cases:
What's the Difference?" *American Economic
Review* 90 (May): 180–83.

Gandal, N., 1994. "Hedonic Price Indexes for
Spreadsheets and a Test for Network Externalities," *Rand Journal of Economics* 25 (Spring):
160–70.

Liebowitz, S. and S. Margolis, 1990. "The Fable
of the Keys," *Journal of Law and Economics*
33 (April): 1–26.

Rohlfs, J., 1974. "A Theory of Interdepen-
dent Demand for a Communications Service,." *Bell Journal of Economics* 5 (Spring):
16–37.

Schmalensee, R., 2000. "Antitrust Issues in
Schumpeterian Industries," *American Economic Review, Papers and Proceedings*
90 (May): 192–96.

Appendix

The Profit-Maximizing Network Access Price for a Monopolist

PRICE FOR A MONOPOLIST

Let N potential consumers be ranked in terms of their valuation v_i for a good when all consumers are expected to buy, with v_i distributed in the interval [0,100]. The anticipated surplus any buyer receives given the expected fraction f^e of subscribers is: $S_i^e = f^e v_i - p$. Equation (22.3), then implies:

$$p = 100 f^e - 100 f^e f \qquad (22.A1)$$

The monopolist's revenues $pQ = R(Q)$, and costs $C(Q)$ are given respectively by:

$$R(Q) = 100 f^e fN - 100 f^e f^2 N \text{ and } C(Q) = F + cQ = F + cfN; F, c \geq 0 \quad (22.A2)$$

In any full expectations equilibrium we have $f^e = f$, so that $R(Q) = 100 f^2 N - 100 f^3 N$. Combining equations (22.A1) and (22.A2) with $f = f^e$, implies profit of:

$$\pi(f) = 100 f^2 N - 100 f^3 N - F - cfN$$

The necessary first-order condition for profit maximization is:

$$\frac{d\pi(f)}{df} = 0 \Rightarrow 200 f - 300 f^2 - c = 0$$

When $c = 0$, the solutions are: $f = 0$; and $f = 2/3$. When $c = \$11.11$, they are: $f = 0.0612$ and $f = 0.6055$.

23

Auctions: Basic Theory and Applications

Historians of the Roman Empire often refer to the year 193 AD as the year of the five emperors.[1] Following the death (by assassination) of Emperor Commodus in 192, the famed Praetorian Guard had arranged for the appointment of Pertinax as the new Roman emperor. However, Pertinax proved to be more honest and more devoted to the ascetic ways of former emperor, Marcus Aurelius, than the Guard had expected. In particular, Pertinax did not give the Guard the generous financial reward they deemed appropriate in return for proclaiming him emperor. Dissatisfaction grew quickly. Although he escaped an initial coup, his inability to placate the Guard led to a final confrontation on March 28, 193, in which Pertinax was killed. Then followed what Roman consul and historian, Dio Cassius, called "a most disgraceful business" in which "both the City and its entire empire were auctioned off."[2] The winner of this auction was Didius Julianus who ruled as emperor for an equally short time until his own assassination and decapitation prior to the ascension of Emperor Septimus Severus.

Of course, auctioning off cities and empires is a rare event. These days, however, the use of auctions is widespread. From the sale of master art works to the market for government bonds to the millions of transactions at on-line sites such as e-Bay, the auction process has become an increasingly common mechanism for awarding ownership and contracts. Indeed, it is probably the leading example of the market mechanism and economics articles and textbooks frequently refer to the "Walrasian auctioneer."[3]

It is somewhat surprising then that development of the formal theory of auctions and auction behavior is comparatively recent. However, the last two decades have made up for this with an explosion of auction research. In this chapter, we review some of the basic results of auction theory. We then show that analysis of auctions offers more than just formal theoretical insights into auction design and bidding strategies. It also offers some deep insights into imperfect competition.[4]

---

[1] See Scarre (1995), 150–223.
[2] See *Dio's Roman History, Book LXXIV*, translated by Earnest Cary (1960).
[3] See, for example, Loertscher (2008).
[4] Krishna (2010) provides an excellent and rigorous survey of modern auction theory. Klemperer (2003) surveys key results and their critical implications for industrial economics.

23.1   AUCTIONS: A TAXONOMY

Auctions may be categorized along two dimensions. One dimension concerns the auction design—the rules regarding bidding and what the winning bidder pays. The second dimension concerns the nature of the bidder valuations of the item(s) being auctioned. One possibility is that these valuations are totally private. Each individual bidder has his or her own willingness-to-pay for the item, totally unrelated to what others are willing to pay for it. The alternative is a common value auction. In this case, each individual may have an independent idea regarding an item's true worth, but ultimately that item has a market value that is common to all buyers.

Regarding auction design, there are four basic types: the English or ascending auction, the Dutch or descending auction, the first-price sealed bid auction, and the second-price sealed bid auction. This last case is sometimes referred to as a Vickrey auction in honor of the pioneer of auction theory, Nobelist William Vickrey. The rules for each of these auction designs are described below.

The English, or ascending, auction is essentially the type used by the Praetorian Guard. Bidders call out ever increasing bids until just one bidder remains. The last bidder then wins the auctioned good. The Dutch, or descending, auction is similar except that it works in reverse. In this case, the auctioneer starts with a high price and continues to lower it until a buyer is found. Both the English and Dutch auctions are open in the sense that bidders can observe each other' actions.

In contrast, the first-price and second-price sealed bid auctions are closed auctions. In each of these cases, bidders submit sealed or private bids for the item and the highest bid wins. In neither case do bidders observe the bids of others. The difference between the two is that in the first-price sealed bid auction, the winner pays precisely what was bid, while in the second-price case, the winning bid pays an amount only so high as the second-highest bid.

23.2   PRIVATE VALUES AUCTIONS AND THE REVENUE
EQUIVALENCE THEOREM

All auctions, but perhaps most especially English ascending auctions are characterized by strategic interaction. Every bidder knows that the chances of winning the auction and the price that will be paid if the bidder does win is profoundly affected by the bids made by others. Precisely for this reason, it is natural to view auctions through the prism of game theory and to determine the auction's outcome by determining the Nash equilibrium strategy combination for this game. This is the approach adopted here.

We begin with the study of auctions in which bidders have independent private values. This analysis is relatively straightforward but it does require some work. That effort is worthwhile because the insights from private value auctions are substantial. Further, it is much easier to understand the key features of common value auctions once one has a foundation in auctions with private values.

23.2.1   Equilibrium Bidding Strategies in English and Second-Price
Private Value Auctions

It is readily apparent that if bidders bid their true valuations, the English ascending auction and the second-price or Vickrey auction are formally identical. Suppose for example that there are five people bidding for a vintage baseball card and that the value v_i that each places on the card is, in increasing order: $100, $200, $300, $400, and $500. Let's denote the bid of each player as b_i. If each player adopts the rule $b_i = b(v_i) = v_i$, then in a second price auction the winning bid will be $b_i = $500, and the winner will pay the second-highest bid value of $b_i = $400. Likewise, in an English auction once the bid rises to an arbitrarily small amount above $400, all bidders except the one with the highest valuation will have exited. Once again, if all bidders follow the rule $b_i = b(v_i) = v_i$, that is, if all bidders bid their true value, the card will go to the bidder with the highest valuation at a price equal to second-highest willingness to pay, namely, $400 in this case.

A question that immediately arises then is whether it makes sense for each bidder to bid a true valuation in both an English or second-price auction. Another way to put this is to ask whether the strategy $b_i = v_i$ for each player simultaneously constitutes a Nash equilibrium in these settings. To see that it does, it is helpful to recognize that in both the English and second-price sealed bid auctions, what one bids determines only whether or not one wins—not what one pays.

Returning to our example, suppose realistically that bidders know their own valuation of the baseball card but not the valuations of others. All a bidder knows in this latter regard is that the other bids are drawn randomly from a very large pool of potential bidders, each drawn from a uniform distribution with a range of $0 to $600. Now suppose again that all bidders are following the strategy of bidding their true valuation so that $b_j = v_j$ for each. Can any one bidder alter her behavior in a way that improves her expected outcome?

To see that the answer is no, think about a specific bidder, such as bidder 4. Suppose that she lowers her bid to $390—$10 below her valuation. Even without knowing the other valuations, she can foresee that this will lead to one of two outcomes. One of these is that all the other bidders had lower valuations and that the next highest bid was less than $390. In this case, the change has no effect on her chances of winning or what she pays. The other possibility is that she had the highest valuation but that the next highest exceeded $390, e.g., $395. In that case, the fact that other bidders are bidding their true valuations will mean that bidding $390 will result in bidder 4 losing the chance to buy a baseball card she values at $400 for less than that amount. In short, bidder 4's decision to reduce her bid below $400 will definitely not lead to any gain and may result in a possible loss.

The foregoing reasoning also applies to a decision by bidder 4 to raise her bid above $400—say to $410. If the winning bid was greater than this amount, e.g., $500, then again bidder 4's increase to $410 has no effect. However, if the winning bid was between $400 and $410, e.g., $405, then bidder 4's decision to bid $410 will mean she buys the baseball card at a price that exceeds her personal valuation. Once again, the choice to alter her bid—this time to raise it slightly—cannot improve her outcome but may lead to a loss.

We can repeat the foregoing analysis for each bidder. It then becomes clear that with all other bidders following the strategy $b_i(v_i) = v_i; i \neq j$, the best response for bidder j is to bid her valuation and set $b_j(v_j) = v_j$, as well. Thus, the symmetric Nash equilibrium in a second-price sealed bid auction is for each player to submit a bid equal to her true valuation. The winning bid will then pay an amount equal to the second-highest valuation. As noted, this is also exactly what would happen in an oral English auction. These two auctions are functionally equivalent.

Because the actual amount paid in English and second-price auctions is equal to the second-highest valuation, it is interesting to determine what the expected winning price will be. For this purpose, we need the concept of an order statistic. For a random sample of n from a given population, the kth order statistic is the value of the kth smallest value. For example, in our sample of $n = 5$ bidders with valuations $100, $200, $300, $400, and $500, respectively, the first order statistic $v(1)$ is the smallest value, or $100. The second order statistic is $v(2) = 200. Because we know that both a second-price sealed bid auction and an English auction both result in a winning payment equal to the second-highest valuation among the sample of bidders, we can work out the expected winning bid for any sample of size n by working out the n-1th order statistic, e.g., for a random sample of five bidders, the expected actual payment is the expected fourth-smallest valuation or the fourth order statistic $v(4)$. For the uniform distribution between 0 and V^{Max}, this is given by:

$$\text{Expected Value of } k\text{th Order Statistic with Sample Size } n = \text{E}[v(k)] = \frac{k}{n+1} V^{Max}$$

(23.1)

Thus, for our five bidder case with bids drawn randomly from a uniform distribution with a maximum valuation of $V^{Max} = 600, we would expect that in a sample of five, the second-highest (fourth-smallest) value and therefore the price paid by the winning bidder would be $\text{E}[v(4)] = \left(\frac{4}{6}\right) $600 = 400. This is also the revenue that the seller of the baseball card should expect.

Note that as the number of bidders rises, the relevant order statistic also increases. If instead we had a sample of ten bidders drawn from this same uniform distribution, we would be interested in the ninth order statistic or the expected value of $v(9)$. This would be given by: $\text{E}[v(9)] = \left(\frac{9}{11}\right) $600 = 490.91. For the general case of n bidders drawn from a uniform distribution ranging from $0 to V^{Max}, we have the expected winning price p as the n-1th order statistic or:

$$\text{E}[v(n-1)] = \text{E}(p) = \left(\frac{n-1}{n+1}\right) V^{Max}.$$

(23.2)

More bidders means that it is more likely that the pool will include buyers with very high valuations. As a result, the expected price or revenue to the seller rises closer and closer to the maximum valuation among all potential bidders.

Show that a dominant bidding strategy in an English auction is to continue bidding as long as the price in the auction is less than your true value of the good.

23.2.2   Equilibrium Bidding Strategies in Dutch and First-Price Private Value Auctions

We now turn to the Dutch descending auction and the first-price sealed bid auction. A little thought quickly reveals that these two auction types are also equivalent because the essential strategic choice is the same in each. In each case, bidder i must decide on a strike price at which he or she will claim the item. The remaining question is what that strike price or bid should be. The answer is suggested by the central difference between our two broad auction types—the Dutch and first-price auctions on the one hand, and the English and second-price auctions discussed above, on the other. This difference is that unlike our earlier cases, the price the bidder pays in either a Dutch or first-price auction *is* determined by the bid he makes rather than the next highest bid. This immediately rules out ever bidding more than one's valuation. Instead, the fact that bidders in a Dutch or first-price auction pay precisely what they bid instead of the next-highest bid, suggests that they may want to shade their bids a bit relative to bidders in an English or second-price auction. The issue then becomes the extent of such shading. How far below their private valuation should bidders in a Dutch or first-price sealed bid auction bid?

Let's start by focusing on a sealed bid auction for the rare baseball card imagined above but also by simplifying that example by assuming just two random bidders. Bidder 1 personally values the card at \$200 while bidder 2 values it at \$400. However, the bidders only know their own valuation. As before, all bidder i knows about bidder j's valuation is that it is drawn randomly from a uniform distribution ranging from 0 to \$600. Because we are explicitly interested in bidding rules that may yield a bid lower than the bidder's true valuation, we will consider proportional rules of the form $b_i(v_i) = \lambda v_i$, where $0 \le \lambda \le 1$. When $\lambda = 1$, bidders bid their full valuation $b_i = v_i$. For smaller values of λ bids are only a fraction of that valuation.

Suppose that both bidders choose $\lambda = 0.9$, that is, each bids 90 percent of their true valuation. Because these bids are strictly proportional to the underlying valuations, the probability of having the highest bid is exactly the same as the probability of having the highest valuation. For bidder 1, given her value of \$200 and what she knows about the distribution of her rival's valuation, she can work out that she has a one-third chance of being the highest bidder. Similarly, bidder 2 can determine that he has a two-thirds chance of being the highest bidder. Is this a Nash equilibrium?

Consider bidder 1 first. Right now, she is bidding $0.9v_1 = 0.9 \times \$200 = \$180$. While she does not know her rival's valuation, she knows that her rival is also submitting a bid of $0.9v_2$. So, as noted, bidder 1's chance of submitting the winning bid is one-third. Because she only gains if she is the winner, bidder 1's expected outcome $E[Y_1]$ in the current setting is:

$$E[Y_1] = 0.3333 \times [\$200 - \$180] = \$6.67 \tag{23.3}$$

Suppose now that instead of continuing to bid 90 percent of her valuation, bidder 1 reduces her bid still further, say to 80 percent. This has the advantage of greatly increasing the gain if she is in fact the high bidder. However, she is now bidding sufficiently low that her chance of being the high bidder has also fallen. With a little effort, we can in fact determine how this tension works out.

By bidding only 80 percent of her valuation, bidder 1 reducers her bid to \$160. Hence, if she wins the auction, she now gains \$40 instead of only \$20. What is the probability with which this happens?

To answer this question first note that if bidder 1 were to subit a bid of \$160 when *all* bidders including bidder 1 bid 90 percent of their valuation, it would imply that bidder 1 had a true valuation of $v_1 = \$160/0.9 = \$177.78$. In reality, this is not her true value. But this thought experiment is nevertheless instructive. In a world in which all other bidders are bidding 90 percent of their true value, bidder 1's decision to submit a bid equal to 80 percent of her true $200 value gives her the same chance of winning as if she had continued to bid 90 percent of her value but had a value of only $177.78. Specifically, her chance of winning now given her rival's strategy is $177.78/$600 = 0.296. As expected, this is a lower chance than before, but this fall in the likelihood of winning is more than offset by the increased gain of winning. Bidder 1's expected outcome now is:

$$E[Y_1] = 0.296 \times [\$200 - \$160] = \$11.84 \tag{23.4}$$

From this it is clear that the strategy combination of each bidder shading his or her bid to 90 percent of its true value is *not* a Nash equilibrium. If bidder 2 were to do this, bidder 1 would do better by unilaterally reducing her bid to 80 percent of its true value. Moreover, this result is symmetric. If bidder 1 were submitting a bid equal to 90 percent of her true value, bidder 2 could likewise do better by shading his bid more deeply as well.

We have just seen that $\lambda = 0.9$ is too high a proportional bid to be consistent with a Nash equilibrium. It is pretty clear however that some choices of λ would be too small. For example if both bidders set λ arbitrarily close to zero, either one could virtually assure herself of winning the auction by increasing its bid a little while still enjoying a very sizable gain after the auction is won. The issue is then whether we can find a λ value that is neither too small nor too large—one that if used by both bidders implies that neither can gain by raising or lowering his or her bid a small amount. As it turns out, we can and for this simple two-bidder case, the Nash equilibrium is for each bidder to submit a bid that is one half of the true value, i.e., $b(v_i) = 0.5v_i$. In this case, the expected gain for each bidder is

$$E[Y_1] = 0.3333 \times [\$200 - \$100] = \$33.33$$

$$E[Y_2] = 0.6667 \times [\$400 - \$200] = \$133.33 \tag{23.5}$$

To illustrate that $b(v_i) = 0.5v_i$ constitutes a Nash equilibrium for both bidders, we work through the logic of our earlier example and ask whether a small rise in the bid of either bidder would yield a gain given that the rival bidder continues to set $b(v_i) = 0.5v_i$.

Consider bidder 1. With $b(v_i) = 0.5v_i$, she bids $100 so that $33.33 is her expected win. If she raises her bid to $110, her chances of winning rise to $\left(\dfrac{110/0.5}{600}\right) = 0.367$. Her gain if she wins is then ($200-$110) = $90. So, her expected win if she increases her bid to $110 while bidder 2 still plays $b(v_i) = 0.5v_i$ is

$$E[Y_1] = 0.367 \times [\$200-\$110) = \$33 \tag{23.6}$$

This is less than the expected win if she continues with the strategy $b(v_i) = 0.5v_i$. Accordingly, it does not pay to raise her bid.

Now consider what happens if bidder 1 lowers her bid, say to $90. In this case, her chances of winning the auction fall to $\left(\dfrac{90/0.5}{600}\right) = 0.30$. Her expected win as a result becomes:

$$E[Y_1] = 0.3 \times [\$200-\$90) = \$33 \tag{23.7}$$

Just as she has no reason to raise her bid, bidder 1 has no reason to lower it either.

What about bidder 2? The same calculations show that he too has no reason to deviate from the strategy $b(v_i) = 0.5v_i$, given that bidder 1 has not done so. With both bidders setting $b(v_i) = 0.5v_i$, he has a 0.67 chance of winning \$200 for an expected payoff of \$134. If he raises his bid to \$220, he will increase his chance of winning to $\left(\dfrac{220/0.5}{600}\right) = 0.733$, but lower the gain from winning to \$400–\$220 = \$180. His expected payoff now given that bidder 1 still plays $b_i(v_i) = 0.5v_i$ declines to

$$E[Y_2] = 0.733 \times [\$400{-}\$220) = \$132 \tag{23.8}$$

Similarly, if bidder 2 lowers his bid to \$180, his gain if he wins rises to \$220 but his chances of winning fall to $\left(\dfrac{180/0.5}{600}\right) = 0.60$. Hence, his expected payoff in this case is again:

$$E[Y_2] = 0.60 \times [\$400{-}\$180) = \$132 \tag{23.9}$$

As \$132 again implies a fall in bidder 2's expected gain, it appears that with two bidders submitting sealed bids in a first-price auction, there is a symmetric Nash equilibrium in which each bidder submits a bid equal to one-half of his or her private evaluation given that the valuation of the rival bidder is drawn from a uniform distribution. We have not proven this formally here (the proof is in the appendix), yet the heuristic analysis is compelling. We therefore assert the result here. In particular, we assert that:

> If two bidders, each with a private valuation drawn randomly from an identical uniform distribution, compete in a first-price, sealed-bid auction the symmetric Nash equilibrium bidding strategy is for each bidder to bid exactly one half of his or her true value, v_i, i.e., $b(v_i) = 0.5v_i$.

What happens if there are more than two bidders? We already have some intuition regarding the answer. In our discussion of English and second-price auctions we learned that as the number of bidders increased, the bidding became more competitive and the winning bid rose higher toward its maximum possible value. It is reasonable to assume that that same competitive pressure also holds in Dutch and first-price auctions. It follows that as the number n of bidders rises above two, that we should expect to see bidders offering to pay a higher fraction—choose a higher λ value—as part of their bidding strategies.

As it turns out, the foregoing intuition is exactly right. As we show in the Appendix to this chapter, for bidders in a first-price or Dutch auction, the optimal value of λ for the general case of n bidders with independent private value drawn from a common uniform distribution is $\lambda = \dfrac{n-1}{n}$. Again, the proof is given in the appendix but the insight is reflected in the following result:

> In a Dutch or first-price auction with n bidders with independent private values v_i drawn from a common uniform distribution, the symmetric equilibrium bidding is for each bidder to submit a bid given by: $b(v_i) = \dfrac{(n-1)}{n}v_i$.

Once again, it is useful to determine the expected winning bid or equilibrium price that will be paid for the auctioned item. For this purpose, we recall the order statistics for the uniform distribution. Because both the winning bid and the actual payment are equal to the highest bid submitted, the expected price is just equal to the bid generated by the above equilibrium bidding strategy when applied to the nth highest expected value v_i from a random sample of n bidders whose values are drawn independently from a uniform distribution ranging from 0 to V^{Max}. That nth smallest value is given by $\left(\dfrac{n}{n+1}\right) V^{Max}$ so that the expected winning bid or price is:

$$E(p) = \left(\frac{n-1}{n}\right)\left(\frac{n}{n+1}\right) V^{Max} = \left(\frac{n-1}{n+1}\right) V^{Max} \tag{23.10}$$

23.2

You are bidding for an original John Lennon hat in a sealed bid first-price auction. You are one of eight bidders in this auction and the most you would be willing to pay for this hat is $200. Show that your optimal strategy is to submit a bid of $175.

23.2.3   The Revenue Equivalence Theorem

We are now in a position to state what may be the most famous result in all of auction theory. A comparison of equations (23.2) and (23.10) reveals that they are identical. That is, the expected price ultimately paid by the winning bid in an English or second-price auction is exactly the same as the expected price paid in either a Dutch or first-price auction. That is, from the standpoint of the seller, all auction designs yield the same expected revenue. This result, originally due to Vickrey (1961), is known as the Revenue Equivalence Theorem. We have shown it here for the specific case of the uniform distribution. However, it is a quite general result that holds across different distributions of individual private values. We state this theorem below:

Revenue Equivalence Theorem: *Any auction in which the item goes to the highest bidder and in which risk neutral bidders have private values drawn independently from an identical and continuous distribution and in which the expected payment from a bidder with value 0 is 0, will yield the same expected revenue to the seller.*

The Revenue Equivalence Theorem is a remarkable result.[5] It also applies when more than one unit is being auctioned so long as each bidder wants only one unit and the auction gives the m units being sold to the m highest bidders. There are, of course, important situations in which Revenue Equivalence will not hold. In particular, it will not hold when any of the assumptions on which it relies such as risk-neutrality are not satisfied.[6] Yet in such cases it is precisely the ability of the theorem to identify the reason that revenue equivalence fails that makes the theorem so useful.

---

[5]   The initial observations behind the theorem are due to Vickrey (1961). The formalization of the theorem itself is typically credited to both Riley and Samuelson (1981) and Myerson (1981).

[6]   Recall that bidders in the first-price auction take some risk of being outbid by a lower-valuation bidder in that each bidder shades his bid below his personal valuation. If bidders are risk averse, they will shade their bids less (buy insurance with a higher bid), in such cases leading to a higher overall revenue in first-price auctions.

23.3   COMMON VALUE AUCTIONS AND THE WINNER'S CURSE

In the baseball card example above, we assumed that each bidder had his or her own private value of the card, independent of what other bidder's valued it. This may well be the case for certain heirloom items, memorabilia, or art objects and similar items. Yet for many items, the ultimate worth to the buyer depends on how much the item can be sold for later, i.e., on its worth to others. Thus, when two companies bid for drilling rights on a particular tract of land, or the legal rights to a specific patent, and when two bidders bid for a jar with an undisclosed amount of quarters in it or perhaps even for a vintage baseball card, what they truly care about is the item's true market value or the price at which it can be sold—a common value for which each bidder may only have a private estimate.

For example, suppose that we again have n bidders interested in buying a vintage baseball card, not as a personal prize but as an investment. As a result, each is interested in the card's true market value V^*, which is a random variable. After doing some research, the bidders obtain an estimate v_i of V^* that is related to their estimate by an error ε_I as follows:

$$v_i = V^* + \varepsilon_i \tag{23.11}$$

where the ε_i term is distributed uniformly from $-\$100$ to $+\$100$. This means that for any bidder, v_i is an unbiased estimate of the true value $V^* : E(v_i) = V^* + E(\varepsilon_i) = V^*$. Each bidder of course only sees v_i—not its decomposition into V^* and ε_i. Yet given that the expected value of ε_i is 0, a bidder who receives information that the baseball card is worth $\$400$, i.e., one for whom $v_i = \$400$, can reasonably take this value as an unbiased estimate of the true value V^*. As a result, each bidder may well be tempted to bid up to the bidder's observed v_i value in order to procure the card.

Unfortunately, bidding v_i is likely to lead to overpaying in these situations. This is because the winner will be the bidder for whom ε_i was greatest. In other words, the auction winner will likely be one whose value estimate v_i included a large positive value of ε_i. When the true market value V^* is revealed, this winner will discover that she has overpaid. This phenomenon is known as "the winner's curse." The problem is that the bidder is interested in more than just an unbiased expectation of V^*, which in fact is provided by her observed v_i. What the bidder is really interested in is the expected value of V^* *conditional on her having the winning bid*. It is clear in this regard that the winning bidder will be the one whose individual estimate v_i included the highest value of the error term ε_i. That is, each bidder can foresee that if she wins, it will be because her v_i estimate was the most optimistic and likely overstates the true market value V^*. Rational bidders need to take this into account and again shade their bids to minimize the winner's curse.

Once again we can work out the optimal amount of shading using the order statistics. Effectively, the v_i are random observations drawn from a uniform distribution ranging from $V^*-\$100$ to $V^* + \$100$. We know that if there are n bidders, the expected value of the highest bidder's observed v_i lies a fraction $n/(n + 1)$ of this distance from the lower bound. That is:

$$E[n\text{th order statistic}] = V^* - \$100 + \left(\frac{n}{n + 1}\right)\$200$$

$$= V^* - \left(\frac{n + 1}{n + 1}\right)\$100 + \left(\frac{n}{n + 1}\right)\$200 = V^* + \left(\frac{n - 1}{n + 1}\right)\$100. \tag{23.12}$$

Equation (23.12) says that, conditional on winning, each bidder can infer that he was the highest of the n bidders in which case his observed value v_i is $\left(\dfrac{n-1}{n+1}\right)$ $100 above the true value V^*. Thus each bidder should shade his bid below v_i by this amount. If there are just two bidders, this shading amounts to bidding $33.33. If there are three bidders, the optimal shading rises to $50. It continues to rise with the number of bidders and asymptotically reaches $100.

The reason that the optimal shading increases with the number of bidders is that the winner's curse does as well. When there are many bidders, the bidder who finds himself with the top estimate v_i has a very good reason to believe his estimate is an outlier. By analogy, consider a student in a classroom who wants to ask a question. If there are just a few other students, the student might not be too worried about raising his hand. However, if there are many students, the student might rationally infer that if it were a good question, someone else would have asked it. By the same logic, it is natural for any bidder to take a very high estimate of the baseball card's true value with several grains of salt if there are a lot of other bidders interested in it as well.[7]

Note that in terms of the impact of the number of bidders n, the winner's curse phenomenon in common value auctions cuts against the insight of equation (23.10) that large numbers lead to higher bids. Economists are naturally drawn to the idea that more bidders means more competition and that this will bid prices up. When there is a "winner's curse" possibility, though, as there is in common value auctions, having many bidders can work in the opposite direction to lower the equilibrium price.[8]

23.3

Practice Problem

Suppose your local town is auctioning off a franchise to sell hot dogs at the July 4th celebration. You and your partner decide to bid for the franchise. Including your partnership there are eight groups bidding in the auction. Your market research on expected attendance, hot dog consumption, and costs suggests that the franchise is worth $20,000. You know that this value is an unbiased estimate of the true value but that it includes an error distributed uniformly between −$3000 and +$3000. What is your expected monetary "curse" if you bid $20,000 for the concession?

23.4   AFFILIATED VALUES

The private value and common value cases represent the two polar auction cases. The intermediate case involves elements of both. Thus, to return to our baseball card analogy, it is possible that each bidder has his or her own private value for the card but that this private value is nevertheless influenced by the values assigned to the card by other bidders. This seems the most realistic assumption for many cases. Even devoted art collectors who know and love specific artists or styles will likely care about the resale value of their acquisitions notwithstanding their passionate views on an item's worth. Conversely, while homebuyers

---

[7] Revenue Equivalence can still hold in a common value auction if buyers' signals are completely independent.

[8] For examples in which the winner's curse hedging is the dominant force, see Bulow and Klemperer (2002).

clearly care about the market value of their property, each may differ on the utility or psychic income that a specific parcel yields depending on how much it "speaks" to them.

When the values of each bidder are affiliated, it means that it is a little unclear what we mean by the bidder's privately observed value because for any given signal, the true value is known to be affiliated with others' observed signals. As a result, there is some ambiguity regarding what is meant by a bidding rule that says the bidder should bid her own valuation, i.e., $b_i = v_i$. A good rule of thumb however is that bidders should bid their valuation as if the next highest bidder had observed the same signal. This will still lead to differential bids because each bidder observes her own individual signal or value v_i. Moreover, the fact that the v_i are affiliated means that if one bidder observes a fairly high value or v_i, others are more likely to observe high values as well. The winner's curse effect may thus be mitigated in affiliated auctions but it is not in general eliminated.

The selection bias that leads to the winner's curse phenomenon means that whenever players' signals are not independent, revenue equivalence will not hold. It follows that if some auction designs are better than others in reducing the winner's curse, such auctions will also lead to less shading and higher equilibrium prices. In this respect, both an open English auction and a second-price auction are likely to lead to higher equilibrium prices than either a Dutch of first-price auction. Further, an English auction is likely to yield a higher price than a second-price auction. The intuition behind these results is straightforward. The open English auction limits the winner's curse because bidders can see the bids and therefore infer the signals received by other bidders. This gives more probabilistic support to their own estimated value and reduces the possibility that they will greatly overbid. Likewise, the second-price or Vickrey auction helps to reduce the winner's curse because as noted earlier, the bid determines only whether one wins. What one pays is decided by the next highest bid. So, some protection against the winner's curse is already built into the auction process. The reason that an English auction dominates or, at least, can never yield a lower price than the second price auction is that it naturally includes the second-price mechanism in its final stage. That is, after $n - 2$ bidders have dropped and there are just two bidders remaining, the open English auction is equivalent to the second-price auction with the winner paying a price equal to the value at which the next-to-last bidder quits.

Incidentally, this seems like a good moment to make clear a vital point. The winner's curse is an outcome that *can* happen—the winner will regret how much she paid—if bidders are irrational and do not shade their bids properly. If bidders are rational however, they will make the appropriate adjustments such that the winning bid will not be too high, on average. The winner's curse should not be a commonly observed event in real auctions. To the extent that it is observed (recall that Didius Julianus totally lost his head in winning the Roman Empire), it calls into question bidder rationality—not the rationality of the bidding strategies analyzed here.[9]

23.5   AUCTIONS AND INDUSTRIAL ORGANIZATION

What are the implications of auction theory for industrial organization? The study of auctions is a relatively new field. Despite Vickrey's (1961) path-breaking early work, it is only in the last twenty years that the applications of auction theory have begun to be widely

---

[9]   Thaler's (1992) well-known piece renewed interest in the winner's curse by providing evidence that it was frequently real.

Reality Checkpoint
You're Watched and Wanted

Log on to a web page. Chances are you will see in the margin or elsewhere on the site one or more product advertisements. What may be more surprising is that if you then go to a different website, you may seem many of the same ads. This is no accident. Your time and attention and, ultimately, your money, are wanted.

Digital advertising space—what the industry calls an impression—is valuable. For any would-be advertiser, however, just how valuable an impression is depends critically on the type of consumer seeing it—their age, their gender, their income, their location, what other sites they visit, and so forth. Cookies and other tracking mechanisms allow this information to travel with you each time you visit a site. In a manner of milliseconds, this information can be recorded and decoded so that each potential advertiser can very quickly know who is visiting a particular site.

This is where modern advertising exchanges such as Yahoo's *Right Media*, Google's *AdEx*, and the *Rubicon Project* come into the picture. These firms act as auctioneers gathering all the information on each particular impression visitor and then auctioning off that particular digital spot to the highest bidder. The bidders themselves are either firms trying to sell a product or their marketing agents. These firms in turn rely on complicated algorithms to respond with a bid to the various attributes the exchange reports. Again, all this happens at a speed so fast that you, the Internet user, will never know it is happening.

The real time technology allows advertisers to reach highly targeted audiences rather than simply buy a space on a website based on the general characteristics of its visitors. The auction process for allocating these impression rights should further serve to insure that those firms that place the highest value on getting access to your digital persona will be the ones whose ads you see. Your cyber self is being sold almost every second you are on the web.

Source: N. Singer, "Your Online Attention, Bought in an Instant," *New York Times*, November 18, 2012, p. B1.

understood. While the insights from auction theory for economic analysis are numerous and growing, we focus here on two that are particularly relevant to industrial organization. The first of these has to do with oligopoly pricing. The second has to do with market asymmetries, perhaps most notably, those between an entrant and an incumbent.

23.5.1   Auctions and Oligopoly Pricing

Consider the simple Bertrand model, in which two firms sell an identical product. Let us start with a simple case. There is a buyer willing to pay at most V for exactly one unit of the good and each firm has a constant and identical marginal cost c_i with $0 \leq c_i < V$. To make matters specific, let us assume that $V = \$110$, $c_1 = \$10$, and $c_2 = \$15$. In this initial case, we will assume that all of the foregoing is common information known to all participants. The market interaction then proceeds as follows. Each firm is asked to post a price at which it will sell and the buyer chooses the firm that offers the lowest price. In this case, it is easy to see that the Nash equilibrium requires that each firm will quote a price equal to $c_2 = \$15$. If either firm ever expected the other to quote a price above $15, say $16, the other would win the competition by offering a price of \$15.99. Yet this would mean that the high-price firm would want to change its price quote, i.e., it would not meet the Nash equilibrium criterion. Yet firm 2 will also never set a price below \$15. If it does, it may win the competition but it will lose money on the sale. The only possible Nash equilibrium for this game is $p = c_2 = \$15$, with firm 1 winning the bid. As is usual with Bertrand pricing, we get price equal to the second-lowest marginal cost even though there are only two firms. Indeed, adding a third or fourth with costs $c_3 = \$20$ and $c_4 = \$25$ would not change the outcome.

Let us now, however, change the model slightly by altering the information structure. In particular, let us assume that there are just the original two firms and that each firm knows its own marginal cost c_i, but does not know the rival's marginal cost. Instead, it knows only that its rival's marginal cost is distributed uniformly between 0 and \$100. What price should a firm post in this market setting?

The answer to this question comes from auction theory. The difference is that unlike the analysis in Section 23.2, we are now considering a selling auction rather than a buying auction. Nevertheless, the underlying principles are the same. Each firm will adopt a pricing rule $p_i = p(c_i)$ that determines the price that will maximize its expected profit from the sale of the one unit to be bought given the firm's observed cost c_i. We show below that the pricing rule that achieves this outcome is:

$$p(c_i) = c_i + \frac{100 - c_i}{2} = \frac{100 + c_i}{2} \qquad (23.13)$$

Equation (23.13) says that in this duopoly case, each firm sets its price equal to its own cost c_i plus an amount equal to half the difference between this cost and the maximum cost (\$100) possible. This result is just the mirror image of our earlier work on bidding in a second-price auction. The underlying logic is that this rule still implies that the firm with the lowest cost will post the lowest price. It follows that the probability that firm i wins the sale is exactly the same as the probability that it has the lowest cost c_i.

In other words, if both firms follow the pricing rule, then

$$prob(b_i < b_j) = prob(c_i < c_j); \ i = 1, 2; \ i \neq j.$$

Given the uniform distribution of c_i between 0 and \$100, this probability is equal to:

$$prob(c_i < c_j) = \frac{100 - c_i}{100} = 1 - \frac{c_i}{100}; \ i = 1, 2; \ i \neq j.$$

The cumulative distribution of c_i at some value c_1 is just the probability of the random variable c_i being less than or equal to c_1, and for the case at hand, this is given by $c_1/100$. Therefore the probability of some randomly chosen c_i variable being greater than c_1 is just 1 minus the cumulative distribution at c_1 or $1-c_1/100$.

For example, if firm 1 has a marginal cost of $c_1 = \$10$, it would know that 90 percent of the time its rival will be a firm with a higher marginal cost given that the marginal cost is distributed between 0 and \$100. If both firms follow the pricing rule of equation (23.13), this will also then be the probability with which firm 1 wins the sale. Recall that pricing rule calls for firm 1 to set a price $p_1 = \$55$, that is (\$100–\$10)/2 = \$45 above cost. Firm 1 will then have an expected profit $E(\pi)$ of

$$E(\pi) = prob(p_1 < p_2)(p_1 - c_1) = 0.9(\$45) = \$40.50 \qquad (23.14)$$

Suppose instead that firm 1 set a price of $65. This will obviously increase its profit margin but also decrease its chance of winning if firm 2 continues to follow the pricing rule specified by equation (23.13). Specifically, by working that equation backward, we can determine that if firm 1 sets a price of $65, it is acting as if its cost is $30. Firm 1's chance of winning the sale therefore becomes equivalent to the probability that its rival has a cost greater than $30, namely, 70 percent. Hence, firm 1's expected profit under this alternative strategy becomes:

$$E(\pi) = prob(\$30 < c_2)(p_1 - c_1) = 0.7(\$65 - \$10) = \$38.50 \tag{23.15}$$

Similarly, if firm 1 decreased its bid to $50, it would be pricing as if it had a marginal cost of $c_1 = \$0$. It would raise its chance of winning the sale to 100 percent. Yet while it would win with certainty, it would only earn $50–$10 = $40, which is still less than the $40.50 earned using the optimal bidding strategy. In short, given that firm 2 is pricing according to the rule specified in equation (23.13), the profit-maximizing choice for firm 1 is to follow this rule as well. Obviously, the same is true in terms of firm 2's best response if firm 1 follows that pricing rule. Thus, with each firm pricing as indicated by equation (23.13), each will be making its best response to the other, i.e., the market will be in a Nash equilibrium. While we have demonstrated this result here only by example, a general proof is provided in the appendix.

There are a number of points worth noting about the Bertrand pricing equilibrium just described. First, it generalizes to the case of $n = 3, 4$, or more competitors. That is, for the general case of n firms the Nash equilibrium pricing rule is:

$$p_i(c_i, n) = c_i + \frac{100 - c_i}{n} = \frac{100}{n} + \frac{(n-1)}{n}c_i \tag{23.16}$$

Thus, as the number of firms n rises, the Bertrand pricing outcome now gets closer and closer to the competitive outcome of $p = c = $ marginal cost. Firms optimally reduce the margin of their posted price over cost as they face more competitors.

Second, it is worthwhile to determine the expected price that will be paid in this Bertrand market. For this purpose, it is helpful to recall the first two order statistics for the uniform distribution between 0 and 100—the expected value of the lowest and second-lowest of n random draws. These are:

$$C^1 = \frac{100}{n+1} \quad \text{and} \quad C^2 = \frac{200}{n+1} \tag{23.17}$$

Thus, with $n = 2$ firms the lowest expected cost in our example is $C^1 = \$100/3 = \$33.33$ while the second-lowest expected cost is $C^2 = \$200/3 = \$66.67$. It follows that when $n = 2$, as in our example, we would expect *ex ante* that the lowest cost firm would have $c_i = \$33.33$. The pricing rule in (23.16) then implies that such firm would set a price equal to $(\$100 + \$33.33)/2 = \$66.67$. Note that this expected price in the duopoly case is exactly equal to C^2 or the expected value of the second-lowest cost. This is no accident. It follows directly from the Revenue Equivalence Theorem. If we were to hold a Dutch auction and keep lowering the price until just one firm remained, we would expect that on average the price at which one firm dropped out would be $C^2 = \$66.67$.

Moreover, this result generalizes to all values of n. For example, when n rises to 3, the first order statistic falls to $C^1 = \$25$. In this case, the pricing formula of equation (23.16) says that the expected market price is then:

$$E(p,n) = \frac{\$100}{n} + \frac{(n-1)}{n}C^1 = \frac{\$100}{3} + \frac{2}{3}\$25 = \$50 \text{ when } n = 3 \qquad (23.18)$$

From equation (23.17) we know that when $n = 3$, the second order statistic C^2 and the expected winning bid = $\$200/4 = \$50$, as well. We can repeat this for all values of n. However, simple algebra makes clear that with $C^1 = \$100/(n+1)$, the pricing formula of equation (23.16) will always yield an expected winning price of C^2. Again, this is really just an example of the Revenue Equivalence Theorem. The more important point here is that even though we have Bertrand competition and identical products, we nevertheless get a result in which the expected price generally exceeds the lowest marginal cost but moves asymptotically closer to it as the number of firms n rises. Market structure matters.

23.5.2 Auctions, Asymmetries, and Firm Rivalry

Thus far we have assumed that the bidders in auctions are symmetric. They may each realize a different draw from a random distribution but each draws from the same distribution with the same probabilistic parameters, and the price or payoff, conditional on that expectation, is the same. Yet we know that in many real strategic settings, the players may not be equal. For example, the gain to an incumbent firm from a new patent that partially replaces the profit from its existing intellectual property may be less than the gain that the new patent would yield to a new firm. Auction theory offers a powerful insight into the analysis of these econometric cases as well.[10]

To understand the role of asymmetry, consider the following somewhat contrived but revealing example. An incumbent, firm 1, dominates a local market but does face some competition from a small, high-cost rival R with a loyal following. More threatening to firm 1 is the potential entry of a highly efficient rival, firm 2. However, given the setup costs of entering and establishing its own brand, firm 2 can only enter by buying the existing rival R and transforming R's operations with firm 2's significantly more cost-effective technology and management. The dominant incumbent can stop this, however, if it beats firm 2 to the punch and acquires R for itself. Hence, firm 1 and firm 2 will each be interested in buying R—the latter with a view to entering the market and the former with a view to blocking such entry.

In bidding for R each firm makes use of the information that it has on the benefits and costs of successful entry. This information is structured as follows. Based on its years of experience of actual market operations, firm 1 knows that it will lose at least G_1 in profit if firm 2 enters. However, it may lose an additional but uncertain amount G_2 depending on

---

[10]   See Klemperer (1998) and Maskin and Riley (2000) for formal analysis of the role of asymmetry in auctions.

firm 2's cost-effectiveness and marketing skills. From firm 1's perspective, G_2 is distributed continuously between 0 and a large number. Conversely, firm 2 knows its cost-efficiency and marketing skills and therefore knows that it will gain at least G_2 if it enters. It may also gain the (to firm 2) unknown amount G_1 depending on key features of the market known to firm 1. Here again, firm 2 knows only that G_1 is distributed continuously between 0 and a much larger value.

In short, both firms face an expected gain of $G_1 + G_2$ from buying R. For firm 1, this total includes a known part G_1 and an unknown component G_2, and reflects the profit gain from keeping firm 2 out of the market. For firm 2 the total is comprised of an uncertain amount G_1 and a certain component G_2. This total reflects the entrant's potential profit gains from successful entry. The firms bid for R in an English auction and the bidding stops when one firm drops out.

How much should each firm bid? It is straightforward to show that firm 1 should bid up to $2G_1$ while firm 2 should spend up to $2G_2$. That this is a Nash equilibrium can be seen as follows. Given that both firms are following this strategy, firm 2 will drop out (forego entry) as soon as the required expenditure reaches $2G_2$. If this happens, firm 1 will claim R and the total gain $G_1 + G_2$ for an expense of $2G_2$. Given the hypothesized bidding rule however, this only happens when $G_1 > G_2$. As a result, firm 1 will know that with this strategy combination, any time that it wins the auction, it gains $G_1 + G_2 - 2G_2 = G_1 - G_2 > 0$ precisely because $G_1 > G_2$ whenever firm 1 wins. Analogously, firm 2 will know that if it wins it does so at a commitment of $2G_1$. Yet for this to be a winning bid means that $G_2 > G_1$ which, in turn, means that when firm 2 wins, it gains $G_1 + G_2 - 2G_1 = G_2 - G_1 > 0$. Clearly, there is no sense in either firm i committing to a higher expenditure strategy as this will not increase its chances of winning when $G_i > G_j$ but will result in firm i enjoying a smaller gain when it does win. Likewise, there is no sense in either firm adopting a lower expense strategy. This will only result in a lost opportunity for a net gain, on average. In this setting, we should therefore envision an equilibrium in which each firm i will bid up to $2G_i$ to buy the target firm R as a means of either invading or defending the market. The winning bid will therefore be equal to $2 \times \text{Minimum}[G_1, G_2]$.

As structured, the entry game just described is a common value auction in which each player has specialized information about a common value $G_1 + G_2$ but in which the bidders are symmetric in that there is no reason to believe that either one will consistently face an essentially different payoff. Because it is a common value auction, we know that any bidding strategy combination that is sensible must somehow involve a degree of optimal shading to avoid the winner's curse. The shading here is reflected in the fact that once the bid reaches say $2G_1$ firm 1 will accede to firm 2's entry even though firm 1 then knows, by virtue of the very fact that firm 2 has pushed the bidding up to $2G_1$, that G_2 must be at least as large as G_1 and may well be larger. Nevertheless, firm 1 does not increase its bid any higher than $2G_1$ because, again, again, firm 1 (and firm 2 as well) is not interested in the expected value of the total gain but that expected value conditional on its winning the bid.

Now consider one small change to the above scenario. Specifically, let us make use of what we know to be generally true in entry games, namely that the gain to the incumbent of keeping the entrant out exceeds the gain to the entrant of successfully coming into the market. This extra gain does not need to be large. Indeed, the main point of the exercise is to show that even a small asymmetry can have very large consequences.

A numerical example may help. Let us imagine that G_1 and G_2 both vary between 0 and $25 (million), and that when firm 2 wins the bidding for R it gains as before the sum, $G_1 + G_2$. However, due to the asymmetry, if firm 1 outspends firm 2, it gains $G_1 + G_2 + \$1$ (million). How does this change the outcome?

Suppose that firm 2 continues to bid up to the value $2G_2$. In that case, the incumbent firm 1 will find it advantageous to bid up to the value $2(G_1 + 1)$ (in millions). If firm 1 wins, it must be because $G_1 + 1 > G_2$. In this case, firm 1 buys R at a price of $2G_2$ and gains $G_1 + 1 + G_2$ for a net gain of $G_1 + 1 - G_2 > 0$. For example, if $G_2 = \$20$ million and $G_1 = \$19.05$ million, firm 1 will bid up to $2 \times (\$19.05 + 1) = \$40.1$ million. Because $G_2 = \$20$ million, firm 1 will win the bidding at a price of $40 million and gain $0.1 million.

If, however, firm 1 adopts the bidding rule of bidding up to $2(G1 + 1)$ for R, firm 2 will quickly find that bidding $2G_2$ is no longer optimal. The more aggressive bidding by firm 1 now increases the winner's curse facing firm 2. Suppose again that firm 1 knows that $G_1 = \$19.05$ million and therefore bids up to $40.1 million for R. This time though, let firm 2 know that $G_2 = \$20.051$ million and therefore bid up to $40.102 million. It will find it gains only $\$19.05 + \$20.051 = \$40.101$ million, implying a loss of $0.001 million or $1,000$. Firm 2 can avoid this loss and the enlarged winner's curse by shading its bid further. In particular, firm 2 should set its top bid equal to $2(G_2 - 1)$. In that case, it will only win if $G_2 - 1 > G_1 + 1$ or $G_2 > G_1 + 2$, given that firm 1's top bid is $2(G_1 + 1)$. Hence, this means that firm 2 will now pay $2(G_1 + 1)$ for a gain of $G_1 + G_2$ or a net gain of $G_2 - G_1 - 2 > 0$ if $G_2 > G_1 + 2$.

Unfortunately, the revised bidding strategy on firm 2's part is not the end of the story. This is because firm 2's decision to bid less aggressively lowers the potential winner's curse for firm 1 and therefore encourages firm 1 to bid even higher. Specifically, if firm 2's top bid is $2(G_2 - 1)$, then firm 1 will now find it optimal to set a top bid of $2(G_1 + 2)$. Firm 1 will then find that it wins the bid whenever $G_1 + 2 > G_2 - 1$, i.e., whenever $G_1 > G_2 - 3$. When it wins, firm 1 will gain $G_1 + G_2 + 1$ for a payment of $2(G_2 - 1)$, and therefore a net gain of $G_1 - G_2 + 2 + 1$, which of course is positive whenever the condition $G_1 > G_2 - 3$ is satisfied. In turn though, this more aggressive bidding by firm 1 will induce firm 2 to reduce its bid for R still further. Where will the process end?

It should be clear that firm 2 will never bid less than G_2 to acquire R. No matter what firm 1's bidding strategy is, firm 2 cannot lose with a winning bid of G_2 because it knows that the entry access that ownership of R confers is always worth at least this much. Yet the surprising logic of our analysis above is that in equilibrium, the small asymmetry that we have assumed also means that firm 2 will never bid *more* than G_2. Any higher bid will put it at risk. Thus, in the usual case in which the incumbent's gain G_1 asymmetrically exceeds the entrant's gain G_2, the incumbent will have a strong advantage in bidding for R.

There are two lessons from the foregoing example. First, the fact that asymmetries transform common value auctions into almost-common value auctions, means that auction design again becomes important in such settings. In particular, the Revenue Equivalence Theorem will no longer hold necessarily.

The second insight, though, is the one more important one from an industrial organization perspective. This is the fact that even small advantages can have major implications for the outcomes in imperfectly competitive markets. Thus, the advantages of say incumbency—even if they are small—may have a major effect not just for entry battles but also for patent races, advertising rights, and a host of other non-cooperative games.

23.6   EMPIRICAL APPLICATION: SCHOOL MILK AUCTIONS, COMPETITION, AND COLLUSION

Each summer, public school districts around the country run an auction to solicit bids for providing school lunch milk. Ohio is no exception to this rule. Unfortunately, Ohio is also not an exception to the rule that school lunch auction bids often reflect collusion instead of competition. The predictability and relatively inelastic demand for school milk coupled with the homogeneity of the product, and therefore, the similarity of cost structures across producers, facilitates collusive bidding. In addition, the fact that the districts announce the identity of the winning bidder and the amount of the wining bid along with that fact that the game is repeated each year so that any firm that does not cooperate can be punished soon also make it easier to monitor and enforce collusive agreements. Consequently, it is not surprising that collusion in school milk markets is relatively common, especially because milk transport costs mean that the number of firms that could potentially serve a given school district is typically small. Over the past twenty-five years, more than two dozen states have launched investigations of price fixing in school milk auctions and guilty pleas have been entered in over half of these cases.

Definitive legal proof of price-fixing is, however, difficult. Somehow, overt collusion must be distinguished from the normal rivalry, which includes imperfect competition. This is particularly true when conspirators engage in what is commonly referred to as complementary or courtesy bidding. In such cases, the colluding firms submit bids to a wide variety of buyer auctions in an effort to give the appearance of competition. In reality though, the bids are deliberately set too high to provide any real competitive pressure and thus allow the designated conspirator to win a particular auction at a high price. Nevertheless, a sensible use of auction theory may help provide such compelling evidence. Economists Robert Porter and J. Douglas Zona (1999) attempted to do just that and later reviewed their findings in the paper "Ohio School Milk Markets: An Analysis of Bidding."

The case investigated by Porter and Zona (1999) stemmed from state investigations that led in 1993 to confessions by two Cincinnati dairies, Meyer and Coors Brothers, to participation in bid-rigging schemes. Executives from both companies described a collusive bidding ring that included a third Cincinnati dairy, Louis Trauth, in which different school districts were allocated to each specific dairy with the other two dairies agreeing to submit bids so as to give the appearance of competition but bids that, in actuality, were excessively high bids so that the chosen dairy would still win the bidding with a profitable price. In other words, the Myers and Coors executives described a standard case of complementary bidding. Despite the confessions of Myers and Coors, Trauth maintained its innocence. The case then proceeded as the state of Ohio pursued collusion charges against a number of dairies.

Porter and Zona (1999) review bids from the roughly sixty different firms in 509 Ohio school districts over the eleven years, 1980–90. With these data, they construct a control group of the vast majority of dairy distributors and processors presumed innocent of any bid rigging. They then attempt to identify collusive bidding by testing for any differences between the actual bidding practices of Meyer, Coors, and Trauth and the bidding practices that these firms would have exhibited if they behaved like the competitive control group firms.

Porter and Zona (1999) break the bidding process into two steps. First, there is the decision simply to submit a bid. That is, each supplier has to determine whether or not to submit a bid to any particular district. Second, conditional on submitting a bid to a particular district, the firm has to determine how much to bid, i.e., what price it should ask for should it indeed be the winning bidder.

The authors therefore start by using data from the control group to estimate a model of the probability that a specific district receives a bid from a specific firm in a particular year. Their findings may be briefly summarized as follows. First, processing firms that actually transform raw milk into a finished product are more likely to submit bids to any given district than are distributor firms that simply distribute processed milk. Second, all milk sellers are more likely to submit bids in one direction from their base rather than in multiple directions. Third, all sellers are more likely to submit bids in a nearby districts rather than ones far away. Finally, fewer bids are submitted to those districts requiring that complementary goods such as straws be provided along with the milk.

Turning to the price quoted in the bid given that a bid is submitted, the most important finding is that the level of the bid rises as the distance between the bidder and the district increases. However, Porter and Zona (1999) also find that distributors tend to submit higher bids than do processing firms and that bids that have an escalator clause allowing for the price to increase over the life of the contract, are also lower.

All of the foregoing results are quite plausible. Because processors often serve many milk demands, they have more routes and therefore a greater likelihood of serving a route that includes a school. Similarly, it is easier to serve schools that lie along an existing route structure that runs, say, from east to west, rather than to serve a school along a new route running from, say, south to north. Because transport costs are very significant, it makes sense that firms will tend to submit bids in closer districts. Likewise, because providing straws and other services (e.g., coolers) is expensive, districts that require these items should also expect to get fewer bids.

The bid level results are also consistent with expectations. Again, the presence of significant transport costs implies that a dairy firm's bid should rise the further the dairy has to transport the milk to delivery. Because distributors buy their milk from processors, one would again expect that distributors would ask for a higher price, all else equal. Finally, if a firm is protected against cost increases over time by means of an escalator clause, we would expect that the firm can submit a lower bid free from any need for a premium to protect against such risk.

In sum, there is ample reason to suspect that the behavior of the control group captures the normal workings of Ohio's imperfectly competitive school milk markets. In light of these results, Porter and Zona (1999) then seek to determine whether and in what ways the behavior of the three main alleged conspirators—Meyer, Coors, and Trauth—is different from that of the control group.

Table 23.1 demonstrates one clear difference. Relative to the typical dairies in the control group, the three accused firms submit bids much more frequently in nearby markets—markets not far from any of the firms. Thus, the third row of the table indicates that considering districts twenty to thirty miles from the dairy's office, Coors submits 22.9 percent more bids, Meyer submits 18.5 percent more bids, and Louis Trauth submits 20.6 percent more bids than would the typical competitive firm draws from the control group analysis. Moreover, many of these differences are statistically significant.

The true importance of the foregoing finding though only emerges when Porter and Zona (1999) investigate the actual prices that the accused firms submit when they do bid. In contrast to the behavior of the control group firms, the delivered milk prices offered by the three Cincinnati firms *fall* with distance. That is, these firms tend to offer a lower milk price to school districts farther away even though shipping milk this distance incurs much

Table 23.1   Accused conspirators' difference in bidding propensity from control group by distance

Distance in Miles	Coors Brothers	Meyer	Louis Trauth
0–10	24.1% >	5.6% >	7.0% >
10–20	42.9% >	8.2%	15.2% >
20–30	22.9% >	18.5% >	20.6% >
30–40	−17.1% <	18.6% >	0.1%
40–50	−9.5% <	−2.2%	−4.3%
50–60	−6.0%	−5.5%	6.9%
60–70	−6.0%	−18.6% <	47.1% >
70–80	−4.9% <	−25.0% <	10.0% >
80–90	−2.4% <	−17.5% <	−2.5% <
90–100	−1.7% ·	−7.7% <	11.8% <
100–110	−1.3%	30.7% >	8.7% >
110–120	−0.6%	0.5%	−4.2% <
120–130	−0.5%	−0.9%	−3.6% <
130–140	−0.2%	−0.3%	−2.0%
140–150	−0.2%	−0.1%	−1.2%

> Indicates statistical significance

higher transportation costs. This pattern is especially evident for Meyer and Trauth who, as Table 23.1 shows, were the two of the three firms who submitted a lot of bids far away. Taken together then, these findings reveal a pattern in which the Coors, Myer, and Trauth submitted lots of bids in school districts close to their home town of Cincinnati where they were in most direct competition. These bids were relatively high while the prices offered to more distant school districts were noticeably lower. This of course is very consistent with the practice of complementary bidding to which the Meyer and Coors executives had confessed.

In addition to the above finding, Porter and Zona (1999) also offered further evidence of bid rigging. First, the bids of the indicted conspirators were significantly lower in 1983 and 1989, the two years in which the Meyer and Coors executives testified that there was a breakdown in the cartel. More formally, Porter and Zona (1999) examine two correlation measures among the accused firms. Briefly put, if the three firms are truly submitting bids in an independent fashion, then the fact that, say, Meyer bid unexpectedly in a particular district should be totally uncorrelated with whether either Coors or Trauth also bid unexpectedly in that district. However, complementary bidding would imply that these unexpected bids would be positively correlated. In agreement with Meyer and Trauth, Coors would submit bids in the same districts these firms did more often than not. Similarly, independence would imply that in a district in which say, Coors submitted an unexpectedly high price, we would not expect the bids of either Meyer or Trauth to show any pattern. In contrast, a complementary bidding scheme would suggest that in such districts, Meyer and Trauth would, if they bid at all, also submit bids that are unexpectedly high.

Porter and Zona (1999) therefore also consider the correlation between: 1) the unexpected bid propensity measured as the unexplained residuals for the three firms from the regression predicting their bidding submission; and 2) the unexpected level of the bid again measured

Table 23.2   Pair-wise correlation coefficients on unexplained propensity to bid and unexplained bid price

	Coors & Myer	Meyer & Trauth	Trauth & Coors
Propensity to Bid	0.58	0.54	0.43
Bid Price	0.66	0.67	0.54

as the unexplained residuals now taken from the pricing equation estimated for the three firms. Table 23.2 displays the pairwise correlations for each case.

As Table 23.2 indicates, the correlations are all positive and in each case, the estimated correlation is significantly different from zero. In districts where one of the three firms unexpectedly submitted a bid, the other two were statistically very likely to do the same. Further, when bidding, if one of the three firms submitted an unexpectedly high bid, the others were very likely to do so as well. Coupled with the earlier evidence, these findings strongly reject the hypothesis of independent bidding. They are instead very consistent with the complementary bidding scheme that was alleged.

Overall, Porter and Zona (1999) estimate that on average, the collusion raised prices by 6.5 percent over what they otherwise would have been. For some school districts—particularly those in which one of the three alleged conspirators already had a contract and in which therefore the other two were strongly encouraged not to undercut that incumbent's prices—the bid-rigging is estimated to have raised school milk prices by as much as 49 percent.

Summary

The common use of auctions for all sorts of market transactions raises many important questions. One of the most important is the impact of auction design. That is, are the market outcomes different for English or Dutch or first-price or second-price sealed-bid auctions? Vickrey's (1961) path-breaking work provides a key answer. His main result, typically referred to as the Revenue Equivalence Theorem, is that the expected price or revenue is the same under each auction design *provided* that the bidders' values are independent.

Apart from auction design, auctions also differ depending on whether the item(s) being sold has only a purely private value or, instead, a common value that will be revealed after the auction is completed. A common value auction—in which the item(s) being sold ultimately have a true market value common to all bidders but unknown to any bidder prior to the bidding—has the potential for a "winner's curse." Bidders in auctions for real estate, oil tract rights, radio spectra, and so on know that their signal or guess as to what the item is truly worth is based on the information that they happened to observe. Therefore, any bidder who wins a common value auction can infer that he or she must have had the most optimistic signal or estimate of the item's true market value. Unless bidders shade their bids below the value implied by the information they have they will find that they have paid more than the item's true value. If bidders shade their bids optimally, they will avoid the "winner's curse" of paying too much in a common value auction.

When the signals of bidders are affiliated, the potential for a "winner's curse" and other features imply that auction design does matter. In general, the ranking is that an open English or ascending auction leads to a higher price than does a second-price auction. In turn, a second-price auction yields a higher selling price than does a first-price, sealed bid auction.

Auction theory offers many insights for industrial organization analysis. It provides an alternative interpretation of the Bertrand price competition model in which the number of competitors does matter. It also makes clear how market asymmetries can have a lasting impact on market outcomes.

Equally important, auctions markets are subject to the same industrial organization influences as are other markets. In such markets, there still remains the temptation for firm imperfect competitors to collude. Examination of the auction markets for school milk in Ohio using standard microeconomic concepts to determine non-collusive bidding strongly implies that some firms in Ohio did collude. They bid too much, too high, and offered bids that declined with distance despite the fact of very high transport costs for processed milk. In short, auction theory has become an important part of both the theory and practice of industrial organization.

Problems

1. Suppose that there are six bidders in an English auction for an antique 1950s Vaporizer. Each has his or her own private value for the vintage machine. In ascending order, these values are $50, $60, $70, $80, $90, and $100. What will be the winning bid?
   a. What will be the winning bid if the highest three bidders collude?
   b. What will be the winning bid if the middle three bidders collude?

2. Imagine that you are an educational consultant and that you have been asked to submit a bid for a month-long project by a small liberal arts college. You know that the college's willingness to pay for your service is uniformly distributed between $5,000 and $15,000. Assuming that you have other earning opportunities for that month for which you would be paid $5,000, what should you bid?

3. In a "war of attrition" two bidders with valuations drawn independently from the same uniform distribution ranging from 0 to $10, bid for an object but in this case, *both* pay the losing bid. Derive the equilibrium for this game. [Hint: Use the Revenue Equivalence Theorem.]

4. The wallet game is a well-known common value auction. In this game, two players are each given a chance to bid for a total amount equal to the sum of the money they are carrying in their wallets. For example, if the amount in player 1's wallet w_1 is $20 and the amount in player 2's wallet w_2 is $45, the total prize is $65. Of course, each bidder only knows the amount in his or her own wallet. Player 1 knows w_1 and player 2 knows w_2. Show that each player following the bidding rule $b(w_i) = 2w_i$ is a (Nash) equilibrium.

5. Up until the 1990s, the US Treasury has auctioned off its debt instruments of Treasury bills and notes using a discriminatory format. Under this procedure, the supply of securities would be auctioned off in lots at different prices until the available supply was purchased. That is, bidders submit bids indicating both the price they will pay and how many securities they wish to buy at that price. In response, the Treasury fills the demand of the highest priced bidder first. It then moves on to the demand of the second-highest bidder, and so on until all the supply of Treasury securities is sold. However, in the 1990s the Treasury moved to a uniform price auction in which roughly the above procedure was followed except that now, all bidders paid the same price—namely the lowest price at which the supply cleared. Why might the uniform price auction have encouraged more bidders to participate in Treasury auctions?

References

Cary, E. 1960. *Dio's Roman History: Translation by Earnest Cary*, London: J. Heineman.

Bulow, J., and P. Klemperer. 2002. "Prices and the Winner's Curse," *Rand Journal of Economics* 33 (Spring): 1–21.

Klemperer, P. 1998. "Auctions with Almost Common Values: The Wallet Game and Its Applications," *European Economic Review* 42: 757–69.

Klemperer, P. 2003. "Why Every Economist Should Learn Some Auction Theory," in *Advances in Economics and Econometrics* (Volume 1 of Eighth World Congress—Econometric Society Monograph), M. Dewatripont, L. Hansen, and S. Turnovsky, eds., 25–35. Cambridge: Cambridge University Press.

Krishna, V. 2010. *Auction Theory*, 2nd edition. Amsterdam: Elsevier.

Loertscher, S. 2008. "Market Making Oligopoly," *Journal of Industrial Economics* 56 (June): 263–89.

Maskin, E., and J. Riley. 2000. "Asymmetric Auctions," *Review of Economic Studies* 67 (July): 439–54.

Myerson, R., 1981. "Optimal Auction Design," *Mathematics of Operations Research* 6 (February): 580–73.

Porter, R., and J. D. Zona. 1999. "Ohio School Milk Markets: An Analysis of Bidding," *Rand Journal of Economics* 30 (Summer): 263–88.

Riley, J., and W. Samuelson. 1981. "Optimal Auctions," *American Economic Review* 71 (June): 381–92.

Scarre, C., 1995. *Chronicle of the Roman Emperors: The Reign-by-Reign Record of the Rulers of Imperial Rome*, London: Thames & Hudson.

Thaler, R. 1992. *The Winner's Curse: Paradoxes and Anomalies of Economic Life*, New York: Simon & Schuster.

Vickrey, W. 1961. "Counterspeculation, Auctions, and Competitive Sealed Tenders," *Journal of Finance* 16 (March): 8–37.

Appendix

OPTIMAL BIDDING IN FIRST-PRICE AUCTIONS

We show that optimal bidding in a sealed-bid first price auction with n bidders with valuations v_i drawn from a uniform distribution ranging from 0 to V^{Max} is for each bidder i to bid $b_i = \dfrac{(n-1)}{n} v_i$. We assume that any equilibrium bidding rule $b(v_i)$ adopted by all bidders must imply $b(v_i) > b(v_j)$ if $v_i > v_j$, i.e., the bidder with the highest value v_i will have the highest bid. Bidder i's expected gain is then:

$$\text{Prob } (v_i > v_j \text{ for } j = 1, \ n \text{ and } j \neq i) \times [v_i - b(v_i)] \tag{23.A1}$$

Uniformity implies that the probability that any randomly drawn valuation will have a value less than v_i is v_i / V^{Max}. In a sample of n bidders with independent valuations the probability that all of the $n-1$ valuations are below v_i is $\left(\dfrac{v_i}{V^{Max}}\right)^{n-1}$. Hence, any admissible bidding rule $b(v)$ in (23.A1) implies:

$$\text{Expected Gain for Bidder } i = \left(\frac{v}{V^{Max}}\right)^{n-1} [v_i - b(v)] \tag{23.A2}$$

Taking the derivative with respect to v and setting it to zero at $v = v_i$ we have:

$$[v_i - b(v_i)](n - 1)\frac{(v_i^{n-2})}{(V^{Max})^{n-1}} - \left(\frac{v_i}{V^{Max}}\right)^{n-1} b'(v_i) = 0 \tag{23.A3}$$

Simplifying, we than obtain the differential equation:

$$b'(v_i) = (n - 1)\left[1 - \frac{b(v_i)}{v_i}\right] \tag{23.A4}$$

For which the solution is readily confirmed to be:

$$b(v_i) = \left(\frac{n-1}{n}\right) v_i \tag{23.A5}$$

When $n = 2$, each bidder bids an amount equal to $0.5v_i$. As n grows ever larger, bidding becomes more competitive. In the limit, $b_i \Rightarrow v_i$ as $n \Rightarrow \infty$.

OPTIMAL BIDDING IN OLIGOPOLISTIC BERTRAND COMPETITION WITH INCOMPLETE INFORMATION

We assume n firms competing in price to sell a good for whom the consumer has valuation V and each firm has cost c_i drawn from a uniform distribution ranging from 0 to C^{Max}. The probability that c_i is the lowest cost is $\left(1 - \dfrac{c_i}{C^{Max}}\right)^{n-1}$. Given a pricing function $p(c_i)$ that preserves this ranking, firm i's expected net gain is:

$$\mathrm{E(Gain}_i) = \left(1 - \frac{c}{C^{Max}}\right)^{n-1} [p(c) - c_i] \tag{23.A6}$$

Therefore, the optimal pricing function must satisfy:

$$\left(1 - \frac{c}{C^{Max}}\right)^{n-1} p'(c_i) = \frac{(n-1)}{C^{Max}} \left(1 - \frac{c_i}{C^{Max}}\right)^{n-2} [p(c_i) - c_i] \tag{23.A7}$$

Simplifying equation (23.A7) then yields:

$$(n-1)[p(c_i) - c_i] = p'(c_i)[C^{Max} - c_i] \tag{23.A8}$$

The pricing function that satisfies this differential equation for all permissible values of c_i is:

$$p(c_i) = \frac{C^{Max}}{n} + \left(\frac{n-1}{n}\right) c_i \tag{23.A9}$$

24

Strategic Commitments and International Trade

The first US Secretary of the Treasury was the brilliant but prideful Alexander Hamilton whose picture still adorns the US ten-dollar bill. Hamilton came to his position just as the new country was struggling with a host of financial issues accumulated from its long war for independence and the somewhat chaotic financing that had thereafter characterized the eight years under the Articles of Confederation. Of crucial importance to Hamilton was the young country's international profile. He was convinced that America had to establish its identity in international markets. In particular, Hamilton argued forcefully that America had to raise sufficient taxes to pay off its accumulated foreign debt and eliminate any fear of default. Yet Hamilton's vision did not stop there. He also had a very clear idea about the sort of taxes that would best serve the United States in its quest for a respected place in the international community. In Hamilton's view, the United States had to have an internationally competitive manufacturing sector. Therefore, in his *Report on Manufactures* (1791), Hamilton argued strongly for tariffs on manufacturing imports. This would help raise the revenue necessary for debt service and, by discouraging imports, encourage the development of US manufacturing that Hamilton viewed so central to the country's future economic success. In fact, he also recommended the establishment of a Society for Useful Manufactures to subsidize certain key industries that he saw as critical to a vibrant manufacturing sector.

The issues raised by Hamilton's analysis have carried forward to this day. As this text is going to press, the countries of the Euro zone are struggling with the issue of credible debt reduction. Simultaneously, countries around the globe are concerned about the trade policies that will best insure the health of their manufacturing sector, especially in light of the rapid emergence of manufacturing bases in China and other newly industrialized nations.

As it turns out, these issues have a significant industrial organization component. The gains from strategic trade policy depend critically on both the element of commitment that they introduce into trade models and also on the nature of competition in those trade sectors. In this chapter, we use the tools developed earlier to explore industrial competition in an international context.[1]

---

[1] Many authors have contributed to the strategic trade literature. Central contributions include Spencer and Brander (1983), Brander and Spencer (1985), Eaton and Grossman (1986), and Krugman (1986). Fudenberg and Tirole (1984) offer a classic analysis of strategic commitment.

24.1   STRATEGIC COMMITMENTS IN INTERNATIONAL MARKETS

We begin with a simple numerical illustration. Assume that Boeing and Airbus are the only two international producers of large passenger aircraft. Assume that each is considering a major investment in the development of a new super jumbo jet capable of carrying over 500 passengers. Both recognize that the size of the jet may make it economical but also limit its market to routes connecting airports that have both the demand for and the facilities needed to handle such a large passenger load. As a result, there is really only room for one firm to develop the aircraft successfully. If a firm sinks the development costs and is not the firm to survive it will suffer a major loss. This is illustrated in Table 24.1 below in which all payoffs are in millions of Euros.

As can be seen, this simple game has two Nash equilibria. In one of these, Airbus develops the new superjumbo jet. In the other, Boeing does. Absent some explicit coordination or other device, there is no way to determine which of these two equilibria will prevail. We could imagine a probabilistic equilibrium where each firm develops the new plane with a probability of, say, one-third, but does not with a probability of two-thirds. Instead, however, let's assume that the European Union commits to financing Airbus's R&D in the amount of €3.5 billion. With this change, the payoff matrix is now that of Table 24.2.

Now Airbus has a dominant strategy, namely, to develop the new aircraft. The Nash equilibrium therefore becomes one in which Airbus develops the plane and Boeing stays out of the race. As a result, Airbus earns a surplus of €9500 *million*. Assuming these funds accrue to Europeans, the Union as a whole has gained from its commitment to Airbus. The subsidy of €3500 million has been worthwhile.

24.1.1   Strategic Subsidies in an International Cournot Model

To investigate the role of R&D subsidies more formally, suppose that there are two countries, A and B, in each of which there is a domestic monopoly firm, a and b, respectively. However, while firms a and b do not compete with each other in their home markets, they do compete in other markets which we shall simply designate as the

Table 24.1   The strategic R&D game without subsidies

		Boeing	
		Don't Develop	Develop
Airbus	Don't Develop	0,0	0,€6000
	Develop	€6000, 0	−€3000, −€3000

Table 24.2   The strategic R&D game with a subsidy for airbus

		Boeing	
		Don't Develop	Develop
Airbus	Don't Develop	0,0	0, €6000
	Develop	€9500, 0	€500, −€3000

international market. Demand in this market is given by $P = A - Q$, and each firm has a constant marginal cost $c > 0$. Hence, from Chapter 9 we know that the equilibrium quantity and profit of each firm are: $q_1 = q_2 = (A - c)/3$; and $\pi_a = \pi_b = (A - c)^2/9$.

Now imagine that firm a persuades its government to subsidize its costs to the extent of s per unit. As a result, firm a now faces a reduced constant marginal cost of $c - s$. Its profit function will therefore be:

$$\pi_a = (A - q_a - q_b - c + s)q_a \tag{24.1}$$

As we saw in Chapter 9, firm a's best response function is now:

$$q_a = \frac{(A - c + s)}{2} - \frac{q_b}{2} \tag{24.2}$$

Of course, because it receives no subsidy, firm b's best response function is given by equation (24.2) with $s = 0$. Combining these two equations, we then have the new equilibrium outputs in the international market:

$$q_a = \frac{(A - c + 2s)}{3}; q_b = \frac{(A - c - s)}{3}; Q = \frac{2(A - c) + s}{3}; P = \frac{A + 2c - s}{3} \tag{24.3}$$

In turn, this implies that firm a earns profit:

$$\pi_a = \frac{(A - c + 2s)^2}{9} \tag{24.4}$$

In the absence of any subsidy, $s = 0$ and firm a earns the standard Cournot duopoly profit $\pi_a = \frac{(A - c)^2}{9}$. Therefore, the profit increase $\Delta\pi$ for firm a that the subsidy generates is:

$$\Delta\pi = \frac{(A - c + 2s)^2}{9} - \frac{(A - c)^2}{9} = \frac{4(A - c)s + 4s^2}{9} \tag{24.5}$$

The total cost $TC(s)$ of the subsidy is s times the number of units firm a produces. Hence:

$$TC(s) = s\frac{(A - c + 2s)}{3} = \frac{3(A - c)s + 6s^2}{9} \tag{24.6}$$

Hence, the net benefit of the subsidy $NB(s)$ is:

$$NB(s) = \Delta\pi - TC(s) = \frac{(A - c)s - 2s^2}{9} \tag{24.7}$$

The subsidy should of course be chosen so as to maximize the net benefit shown in equation (24.7). A straightforward application of calculus then yields the optimum per unit subsidy s^*:

$$s^* = \frac{A - c}{4} \tag{24.8}$$

However, an alternative derivation of (24.8) is perhaps more insightful if more involved. As we know from Chapter 9, any increase in s will shift firm a's best response curve out and slide it along the best response curve of firm b. Symmetry and equation (24.2) tell us that response curve has slope -0.5, i.e., a small increase in q_a will lead to a reduction of 0.5 units in q_b. Since the demand curve has slope -1, this implies a consequent price increase of 0.5. Thus, as a first approximation, a small unit increase in q_a will raise the price at which all existing q_a units sell by 0.5, so that the marginal revenue from that small increase is approximately $0.5q_a$. The marginal cost of subsidizing one more unit is of course just s. The optimal subsidy s^* balances the marginal revenue against the marginal cost. With $q_a = (A - c + 2s)/3$, the optimal subsidy must therefore satisfy:

$$s^* = 0.5q_a = \frac{(A - c + 2s)}{6} \tag{24.9}$$

From which it follows that $s^* = \dfrac{A - c}{4}$ just as in equation (24.8).

Two key results may now be derived. First, substitution of the optimal subsidy value s^* from equation (24.8) into the net benefit $NB(s)$ function of equation (24.7) quickly reveals that when done optimally, the net benefit is positive and equal to

$$NB(s^*) = \frac{(A - c)^2}{72} \tag{24.10}$$

Second, substitution of the optimal subsidy s^* into equation (24.3) shows that firm a's output $q_a(s^*)$ is:

$$q_a(s^*) = \frac{A - c}{2} \tag{24.11}$$

This last expression should look familiar to you. It is the output that would be chosen by a Stackelberg leader when both firms have identical unit costs. As we emphasized in Chapter 12 (recall Dixit's (1980) model of entry deterrence), however, achieving the Stackelberg leader first-mover advantage requires the ability to credibly commit to that higher output level. This is the insight of the strategic trade literature. Government intervention—here in the form of a subsidy—acts as such a commitment in a manner that Alexander Hamilton would have readily understood. As a result of that subsidy and the production commitment it enables firm a to make, the additional profit more than covers the subsidy cost and overall benefits are positive for Country A.

24.1

Practice Problem

Imagine an international market shared by two firms, each from a different country, A and B. Demand in the market is described by the equation $P = 1000 - Q$. Each firm has a constant marginal cost of $c = 400$.

a.   What is the Nash equilibrium output and profit of each firm in the absence of any subsidy?

b.   If Country A subsidizes its "national champion" optimally, what is i) firm A's profit? ii) the cost of the subsidy? and iii) the net gain from the subsidy?

24.1.2 Strategic Tariffs and Scale/Scope Economies

The foregoing analysis of a strategic subsidy captures much in the spirit of Alexander Hamilton's goal of assisting the domestic industry. However, because he was interested in raising tax revenue and paying off the debt, Hamilton focused more on protective tariffs to encourage the expansion of domestic manufacturing. As it turns out, the use of tariffs as the strategic weapon actually adds a further dimension to the analysis that is worth exploring.

We again assume a Cournot model with two firms, firm a and firm b, from Country A and Country B, respectively, and assume that each country functions as a separate market, perhaps because the goods produced for A and B are not identical. That is, the firms are competing for the Country A widget market in which demand is described by $Q = A - P$, and the Country B gadget market, in which demand is again described by $Q = A - P$. To simplify the impact of a tariff, we also assume that each firm has a unit cost of not c but $c - s$.

From our earlier work, it is straightforward to work out the equilibrium in each case. Within each country the firms a and b produce and earn profit as shown in Table 24.3 below.

Firm a sells $(A - c + s)/3$ in Country A and also sells $(A - c + s)/3$ in Country B. The same is true for firm b. Now suppose that Country A puts a tariff of s per unit on imports. Effectively, this translates into a cost increase of s for firm b on all units sold in Country A. In other words, firm b now has a cost of c per unit within Country A. From the previous section, we know that this results in a reduction in firm b's output and profit in Country A and a corresponding rise in these values for firm a. If this were the end of the story, the new output and profit configuration would be as described in Table 24.4 below.

Table 24.3 Production and profit in the two-country Cournot game

	Country A		Country B	
	Production	Profit	Production	Profit
firm a	$\dfrac{(A - c + s)}{3}$	$\dfrac{(A - c + s)^2}{9}$	$\dfrac{(A - c + s)}{3}$	$\dfrac{(A - c + s)^2}{9}$
firm b	$\dfrac{(A - c + s)}{3}$	$\dfrac{(A - c + s)^2}{9}$	$\dfrac{(A - c + s)}{3}$	$\dfrac{(A - c + s)^2}{9}$

Table 24.4 Production and profit in the two-country Cournot game with a tariff on firm b in country A

	Country A		Country B	
	Production	Profit	Production	Profit
firm a	$\dfrac{(A - c + 2s)}{3}$	$\dfrac{(A - c + 2s)^2}{9}$	$\dfrac{(A - c + s)}{3}$	$\dfrac{(A - c + s)^2}{9}$
firm b	$\dfrac{(A - c - s)}{3}$	$\dfrac{(A - c - s)^2}{9}$	$\dfrac{(A - c + s)}{3}$	$\dfrac{(A - c + s)^2}{9}$

The outcome described in the table above implies that the tariff does not have any impact on the rivalry between the two firms in Country B. In that country, the two firms produce and earn profit just as before. The tariff so far affects only the market outcomes in Country A.

As Krugman (1986) shows, however, the foregoing results change if there are scale or scope economies. The reduction in firm b's output in Country A is also a reduction in its total output globally. If there are scale or scope effects such that a firm's unit cost rises as its output across the two markets declines, the production decline for firm b will mean that its unit cost is no longer $c - s$ but something higher. Likewise, the expansion in firm a's output may allow it to achieve even lower costs.

To work out the complete equilibrium would require that we fully specify the nature of the scale or scope effects and determine the Cournot equilibrium as those effects grow or diminish. Instead we adopt a convenient short cut here and simply assume that scale effects are exhausted for firm a so that its unit cost remains $c - s$, but that as the result of its output reduction firm b does experience a cost rise to c per unit in both countries. The consequent output and profit levels are shown in Table 24.5 below.

A comparison of Tables 24.5 and 24.3 shows that firm a's total profit has increased by $6s(A - c) + 11s^2$, while total output in Country A has fallen by $2s/3$. Given that aggregate demand in Country A is $Q = A - P$, this means that $2s/3$ measures the rise in price in Country A. Hence, Country A suffers a consumer surplus loss of $2s^2/9$. However, firm a now earns $[2s(A - c) + 3s^2]/9$ more in profit in Country B than it did previously. This is more than enough to compensate for the domestic welfare loss. Moreover, there is the additional profit firm a now earns in its home country that previously went to firm b. The tariff does more than protect domestic production. It acts as a commitment that firm a will be advantaged in Country A and therefore larger globally than its rival firm b. It is therefore a commitment to insure that firm a will have a lower unit cost than firm b. This leads firm b to lose additional market share and profit to firm a in *both* countries A and B."

The commitment role of the tariff merits emphasis. As Hamilton implicitly understood, the tariff allows Country A to insure that firm a will operate on a relatively large scale in its home market. Because that market is an oligopoly, that commitment acts as a non-negotiable claim for a larger share of the domestic oligopoly profit. Credibility of the commitment is cemented by the fact that it also prevents firm b from enjoying scale economies. Hence firm a is also advantaged in Country B further offsetting the tariff cost.

Table 24.5   Production and profit in the two-country Cournot game with a tariff on firm b in country A and scale economies

| | Country A | | Country B | |
	Production	Profit	Production	Profit
firm a	$\dfrac{(A - c + 3s)}{3}$	$\dfrac{(A - c + 3s)^2}{9}$	$\dfrac{(A - c + 2s)}{3}$	$\dfrac{(A - c + 2s)^2}{9}$
firm b	$\dfrac{(A - c - 3s)}{3}$	$\dfrac{(A - c - 3s)^2}{9}$	$\dfrac{(A - c - s)}{3}$	$\dfrac{(A - c - s)^2}{9}$

24.2

Solve the foregoing tariff model with demand in each country given by: $Q = 100 - P$, and the constant marginal cost given by $c - s = \$12$. Assume that if country A imposes a tariff of \$2 per unit, the loss in production raises firm b's unit cost to \$14 everywhere. Determine the net change in consumer and producer surplus in Country A as a result of the tarrif.

24.1.3 Strategic R&D Subsidies

One problem with either the direct subsidy or the tariff policy just described is that each violates the international trade laws negotiated by the World Trade Organization (WTO) to promote free, unfettered trading arrangements. As a result, they are likely to lead to punishments and trade sanctions that will undermine their net benefits. We return to consider the WTO and trading policies later. At this point, we wish to explore an alternative and slightly less direct route to assist the domestic firm, namely, to subsidize its R&D.

There are many ways to subsidize R&D. Large grants to universities and hospitals, the provision of information to farmers about crop rotation and other techniques, and the award of production grants that permit firms to work their way down the learning curve may all be viewed as government support for the creation and dissemination of technical information. While each of these may be justified for other reasons, there can be little doubt that each may also provide advantages to domestic firms. American pharmaceutical and bioengineering firms likely benefitted from the research support provided to university medical schools and faculty. American farmers clearly benefitted from the Agriculture Department's Extension Service, and Boeing's strong position in the aircraft market may well reflect the head start it received from developing aircraft for the US military. The same assertions could be made regarding firms in most other countries as well. In general, R&D subsidization of some sort is common. Indeed, this is what makes R&D subsidization so difficult to monitor as an unfair method of trade competition. It is difficult to distinguish policies meant purely to give a domestic firm an advantage over foreign rivals from policies to promote economic growth.

Modeling the impact of a strategic R&D subsidy requires modeling the impact of R&D on the firm's production technology as well as the cost of doing that R&D. This is complicated and we save the details for the Appendix. However, the intuition can be readily understood.

We will continue to assume a Cournot duopoly with quantity competition. When it comes to R&D, we will now make the further assumption that while R&D spending works to lower a firm's unit production cost c, this effect is subject to diminishing returns. As a result, the R&D cost of reducing c grows quickly as one tries to push it lower and lower with more and more R&D. In this plausible scenario, the R&D spending choices for the two firms are, like their output choices, strategic substitutes. As *firm a* increases its R&D spending x_a, firm b's best response is to curtail its own x_b.

The market outcome is now described by Figures 24.1 and 24.2. In the first of these, the best response function for each firm in terms of its R&D is shown by the heavy black curves. In the absence of any subsidies, the Nash equilibrium would be where these curves intersect at A. However, if Country A subsidizes firm a's R&D, its best response curve shifts out as shown by the dashed curve, and the new equilibrium now moves to B. Notice that in this equilibrium, firm b now does less R&D.

Because the subsidy changes the R&D level at both firm a and firm b, it also alters their unit costs and, hence, their equilibrium outputs. Figure 24.2 illustrates these effects.

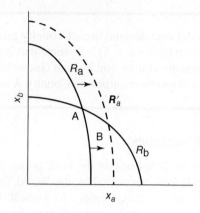

Figure 24.1

Competition in R&D spending levels

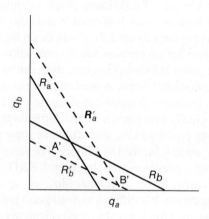

Figure 24.2

Competition in output levels

In the absence of any subsidy, the R&D equilibrium at A in Figure 24.1 would yield symmetric research efforts and therefore identical unit costs at the two firms. In Figure 24.2, the resultant Cournot equilibrium is where the two heavy black best response functions intersect at A'. The subsidy though has a double barrel effect of both lowering firm a's cost and, by way of less R&D, raising firm b's cost. This is shown in Figure 24.2 by the outward shift of firm a's best response function and the inward shift of firm b's best response function. The result is a two-fold assault on firm b's output, which now shrinks dramatically as the equilibrium in Figure 24.2 moves from A' to B'.

24.2   TRADE AGREEMENTS AS COMMITMENT DEVICES

We have now worked through three separate cases in which a country may enjoy net gains by intervening in international markets so as to advantage the domestic firm vis-à-vis foreign rivals. A natural question that arises in this context is why Country B should not react to Country A's intervention by doing the same thing. What happens if both impose tariffs or subsidize domestic firms?

Essentially, these questions point to a deeper level game than the ones we have so far considered. This is the game between the governments of each country in which the variable of strategic choice is either a tariff, or production cost subsidy, or R&D subsidy. In general, the Nash equilibrium of this game has a prisoners' dilemma in which both countries subsidize or impose tariffs to a greater extent than they would if they played cooperatively. Absent any formal agreement mechanism, however, cooperative play is not feasible.

This is where international trade agreements and organizations such as the WTO have become important. By joining such institutions, the member countries pledge themselves not to give in to the short-run temptation of intervening on behalf of domestic firms. Two features make this commitment more credible. First, such organizations act to police and to punish members who violate their free trade promises. In this view, organizations such as the WTO may be analyzed using the same logic that we used to discuss the ability of firms to cooperate in Chapter 14. The necessary elements are an ability to detect violations and then to punish them. In this respect, one feature that is helpful in the case of the WTO is that while violations are typically directed by one country at another, punishment is meted out by all members. Thus, if the United States imposes tariffs or intervenes to aid domestic producers of LCD screens against the Korean giant, Samsung, and if this action is deemed a violation of the WTO agreement, the penalty may include restrictions on US exports to all member nations and not just South Korea.

A second source of credibility is that to some extent, joining the international agreement insulates domestic politicians from political pressure. When pressured by domestic industry representatives for unfair assistance, the domestic authorities can respond by saying that while they would like to help, the rules of membership are clear and "their hands are tied." The strengths of such commitment devices should not be minimized. A central feature of the US Constitution was that it reserved jurisdiction over interstate commerce to the federal government. Prior to the Constitution's adoption, when the US government was organized under the Articles of Confederation, the states had considerable power to levy taxes and otherwise hinder the products of other states in an effort to protect their own. The result was a nightmare web of barriers to trade and inefficiencies as each state tried to protect its industry and raise revenue to pay its debts by taxing the products of out-of-state producers. In this light, the interstate commerce clause may be seen as a conscious effort to bind the states more fully to their commitment to trade freely with each other. Perhaps it is no wonder then that it was that student of commitment, Alexander Hamilton, who was one of the leading advocates for the Constitution's adoption.

24.3   EMPIRICAL APPLICATION: STRATEGIC SUBSIDIES AT THE CANADIAN WHEAT BOARD

We have seen that strategic intervention by a government can, in the case of imperfectly competitive international markets, serve as a commitment that enhances the competitive position of domestic firms. In turn, the additional profit that this allows the domestic firm(s) to earn can more than offset the cost of the intervention, e.g., more than offset the cost of a subsidy to production or research. A compelling example of such intervention may be the case of the Canadian Wheat Board (CWB), as work by Hamilton and Stiegert (2002) reveals.

Reality Checkpoint
Subsidizing the Dream

The international market for commercial jet aircraft is dominated by two firms, Boeing and Airbus (part of the European Aeronautic Defense and Space Company (EADS) N.V group). In addition to producing for the commercial aircraft market, however, both firms have extensive operations supplying equipment for military use, space exploration, and other government-funded activities. Indeed, EADS is partly owned by a consortium of European governments. Hence, it is not surprising that both firms have close governmental relations.

The perception of those ties has historically led each firm to claim that its rival has benefitted from unfair subsidies for research and development. These claims and counterclaims have been litigated at the World Trade Organization (WTO). In the most recent case, Airbus complained that Boeing received explicit subsidies from both the US Defense Department and the National Aeronautics and Space Administration to develop lightweight carbon composite materials that the manufacturer subsequently used in 50 percent of the main structure of its newest, most-fuel efficient jet, the Boeing 787, nicknamed the *Dreamliner*. Ultimately, the WTO agreed finding that the implicit subsidies Boeing received in government contracts since the late 1970s amounted to about $5 billion. This prompted one European official to refer to the 787 as "the Subsidy Liner."

Yet while the finding was a blow to Boeing, its advocates still claimed victory in that the amount of subsidy found by the WTO was much less than that originally alleged by Airbus. Perhaps more importantly, the $5 billion in subsidies the WTO found went to Boeing was much less than the $15 billion that the WTO had earlier found that Airbus had received in grants and below-market interest rate loans in its development of the A380 superjumbo jet. Therefore, both sides have claimed victory.

In both cases, WTO rules require that the firms document new procedures to end the subsidies. Otherwise, the rival's home country can impose tariffs and other trade measures as a punishment. Boeing claims to have done this. Airbus has yet to make a full response. Airbus may have less to worry about though than it seems. Since its commercial introduction, the Boeing 787 has been plagued with technical failures and the airline has currently grounded these aircrafts. Boeing's subsidies may have been funding a pretty scary dream.

Source: C. Drew and N. Clark, "In Appeal, W.T.O. Upholds a Decision against Boeing," *New York Times*, March 12, 2012, p.B7.

The CWB is an example of State Trading Enterprise (STE). STE's are either explicitly government agencies or quasi-public agencies closely associated with government policy designed to control either exports or imports or both of a particular set of commodities. In the case of the CWB, the central commodity is durum wheat for which the CWB has total monopoly power. In brief, the CWB buys wheat from Canadian producers at a specified price w and then acts as the sole exporter of wheat from Canada to the rest of the world. Canadian producers are expected to meet the production demands of the CWB at price w, knowing that the CWB will subsequently distribute the profits from its sales back to the producers based primarily on each producer's share of the production.

A moment's thought will reveal how the CWB payment system may be structured to achieve precisely the subsidy effect discussed earlier in this chapter. By setting w below marginal cost, the input price to the CWB is lowered. The agency's best response function shifts out accordingly with the result that Canadian wheat exports expand while those of other producers shrink. If the market behaves as in our earlier analysis and if w is chosen correctly, then the resultant increase in total profit is more than enough to compensate wheat producers for their initial selling at a price below marginal cost.

Hamilton and Stiegert (2002) collect data on wheat prices (\$/ton) and quantities for the period 1972 through 1995, which they use to estimate a model of the world wheat market with more general demand and supply behavior and more than two firms. The underlying intuition of the model, though, is the same as outlined above. These data allow the authors to calculate estimates of both the actual implicit subsidy and the theoretically optimal subsidy in each of the twenty-four years. How well these two values match then provides a test of the extent to which the CWB structured its payments to Canadian wheat producers so as to maximize their net surplus.

We need to note first, however, that our derivation of the optimal implicit subsidy s was based on a standard assumption reflected in all Cournot best response functions of which equation (24.2) is a good example. The standard Cournot best response function for any firm is derived under the assumption that the output of the rivals is given, i.e., that the firm's action will not induce further responses. Another way to say this is that in the standard Cournot game, each firm believes that a change in its own output will map one-for-one into a change in total market output as no other firms will react. In turn, this means that the optimal subsidy we derived is predicated on the assumption that for any one firm $\Delta Q = \Delta q_i$. Of course, this may not be the case. In the wheat market, for example, the CWB may anticipate that its best response will induce further output changes from rivals. This means that any test of the CWB price-setting is really a test that of the assumption that $\Delta Q = \Delta q_C$ as well as a test of strategic subsidization given that assumption. For this reason, Hamilton and Stiegert (2002) structure their analysis so that it also yields an estimate of the parameter λ in the equation:

$$\Delta Q = \lambda \Delta q_c \tag{24.12}$$

Here, λ is the conjectural variations parameter described in Chapter 9. It measures how much the CWB conjectures the production of other exporters will respond to the CWB's choices.

The key results of the Hamilton and Stiegert (2002) analysis are shown in Table 24.6, below. We first show the estimated value of the conjectural variations parameter λ, along with its standard error. We then display the observed and estimated optimal value of the subsidy for each year in the data.

The first thing to notice is that Hamilton and Stiegert (2002) estimate of the conjectural variations parameter λ is very close to 1. In fact, the hypothesis that it is equal to 1 cannot be rejected by the data implying less than fully independent production choices. Thus, we can now turn to comparing the observed subsidy against the hypothetically optimal subsidy assuming that λ is in fact 1 just as the Cournot model predicts.

In this respect, note that while the observed unit subsidy s and the optimal unit subsidy s^* are notably different in a few specific years, they are generally close in most years and also close—judging by the mean and the median—over the entire twenty-four year sample period. Hamilton and Stiegert (2002) test this similarity further using nonparametric tests such as the Wilcoxen signed rank and Spearman coefficient of rank tests that do not assume

Table 24.6   Estimated conjectural variations parameter λ and actual and optimal implicit CWB price subsidies by year

λ (*Complete Sample*) = 1.058 (*Standard Error* < 0.52)

Year	Observed Subsidy s	Optimal Subsidy s*
1972	42.08	14.18
1973	88.22	76.58
1974	74.55	63.82
1975	18.00	32.29
1976	30.22	19.02
1977	16.54	24.60
1978	17.07	12.19
1979	33.82	21.47
1980	0.49	32.43
1981	21.79	18.11
1982	8.74	22.74
1983	17.54	22.46
1984	17.13	15.54
1985	13.66	8.97
1986	13.18	8.36
1987	44.02	13.65
1988	10.11	10.99
1989	9.91	15.94
1990	0.00	13.48
1991	30.61	13.51
1992	28.80	8.88
1993	34.27	32.44
1994	36.04	38.74
1995	17.98	82.29
Mean	**26.03**	**25.95**
Median	**17.99**	**18.56**

the underlying distributions to be normal. Here, again, they cannot reject the null hypothesis that s and s^* are the same over the sample period.

In short, the evidence in Hamilton and Stiegert (2002) is broadly consistent with the view that during the years 1972 through 1995, the CWB structured its payments to Canadian wheat producers so as to subsidize exports implicitly and thereby to appropriate additional rent or surplus from the world wheat market. The observed annual subsidy implicit in the initial below-market price to wheat producers is close to the estimated optimal value each year. It therefore appears that the behavior of the CWB in these years is exactly what strategic trade theory predicts.[2] The implication, then, is that while Canadian consumers may have been hurt by higher prices, the gains to Canadian wheat farmers and to the CWB may have been enough to more than offset consumers' loss.

[2]   It is important that the analysis ends in 1995 as that is about the time that the World Trade Organization emerged along with stricter rules on the behavior of State Trading Enterprises.

Summary

Threats or promises can only be effective if the threats are credible, i.e., part of a subgame perfect strategy. In many cases, this credibility can only be obtained by making some commitment that binds the player to carrying out that threat or promise in the event that a rival takes the action that the threat or promise was designed to prevent. Commitment is the key to credibility.

International trade is an area in which understanding the role of commitment can have dramatic implications for public policy. In particular, the economist's traditional admonition that tariffs and other trade interventions will be detrimental to domestic welfare may be overturned when one allows for imperfect competition and therefore a role for strategic commitment. Imperfect completion and economies of scale and scope offer a role for the strategic use of trade barriers and subsidies to domestic firms that enable them to claim more of the surplus from international commerce. Such tactics effectively commit the domestic firm to an aggressive strategy that often results in a gain similar to a first-mover advantage.

Unfortunately, other countries will likely pursue the same policies and the non-cooperative outcome of this game between nations will typically exhibit a prisoners' dilemma feature in which both countries are worse off than if neither had intervened. In this light, trade institutions like the WTO can be seen as a mechanism by which countries truly commit to their free trade promises. Yet this effort may ultimately trigger retaliation. The success achieved by the US adoption of the interstate commerce clause and by institutions such as the WTO suggests that a commitment to permit free competition may be the best policy both in theory and in practice.

Problems

1. Assume a two-country duopoly market where each country, A and B, is represented by a national champion—firm a for Country A and firm b for Country B. Inverse demand is given by: $P = 100 - Q$ and the marginal cost of each firm is $c_a = c_b = 400$.

   a. Determine the equilibrium profit for each firm if there is no subsidy.
   b. Determine the profit to each firm if Country A optimally subsidizes firm a.
   c. Determine the profit to each firm if both Country A and Country B offer their champion firms the optimal subsidy derived in 1c.
   d. In 1c above is the cost of the subsidy covered by the change in profit that results from the no-subsidy setting?

2. California Instruments manufactures musical equipment for the North American market. Its major rival is H. Hill Products located in Iowa. Demand facing the two firm is described by: $P = 100 - Q$, and each has a marginal cost of 20.

3. Consider the "Battle of the Sexes" technology game in which each of the two firms agree that compatibility is best but differ over which technology should be the standard as shown below. Firm 1 is from Country 1 and firm 2 is from Country 2. What sort of strategies might Country 1 choose in order to commit to its particular technology?

		Firm 2	
		Technology 1	Technology 2
Firm 1	Technology 1	8, 5	3, 3
	Technology 2	3, 3	4, 10

References

Brander, J., and B. Spencer. 1985. "Export Subsidies and International Market Share Rivalry," *Journal of International Economics* 18 (February): 83–100.

Dasgupta, P., and J. Stiglitz. 1980. "Industrial Structure and the Nature of Innovative Activity," *Economic Journal* 90 (January): 266–93.

Dixit, A. 1980. "The Role of Investment in Entry Deterrence," *Economic Journal* 90 (January): 95–106.

Eaton, J., and G. M. Grossman. 1986. "Optimal Trade and Industrial Policy under Oligopoly," *Quarterly Journal of Economics* 100 (May): 383–406.

Fudenberg, D., and J. Tirole. 1984. "The Fat Cat Effect, the Puppy Dog Ploy, and the Lean and Hungry Look," *American Economic Review (Papers and Proceedings)* 74 (May): 361–66.

Hamilton, A., 1791. "Report on Manufactures," in *American State Papers*, volume 9, W. Lowrie and M. St. Clair Clarke, eds. Washington, D.C.: T. B. Wait & Sons.

Hamilton, S.F., and K. Stiegert. 2002. "An Empirical Test of the Rent-Shifting Hypothesis: The Case of State Trading Enterprises," *Journal of International Economics* 58 (October): 135–57.

Krugman, P. 1986. *Strategic Trade Policy and the New International Economics*, Cambridge: MIT Press.

Spencer, B., and J. Brander. 1983. "International R&D Rivalry and Industrial Strategy," *Review of Economic Studies* 50 (October): 707–22.

Appendix

Formal Analysis of Research Subsidies & International Trade

Here, we present formally the strategic subsidy model originally due to Spencer and Brander (1983). We again assume a Cournot duopoly in which there is now just one international market with inverse demand $P = A - Q$. The output and profit of firm a and firm b initially are:

$$q_a = \frac{(A - 2c_a + c_b)}{3}; q_b = \frac{(A + c_a - 2c_b)}{3} \tag{24.A1}$$

$$\pi_a = \frac{(A - 2c_a + c_b)^2}{9}; \pi_b = \frac{(A + c_a - 2c_b)^2}{9} \tag{24.A2}$$

As in the Dasgupta and Stiglitz (1980) model (Chapter 20), each firm's unit cost c is a function of its R&D spending x, i.e., $c = c(x)$, with $c'(x_a) < 0$ and $c''(x_a) < 0$. We therefore rewrite equations (24.A1) and (24.A2) as follows:

$$q_a = \frac{[A - 2c(x_a) + c(x_b)]}{3}; q_b = \frac{[A + c(x_a) - 2c(x_b)]}{3} \tag{24.A3}$$

$$\pi_a = \frac{[A - 2c(x_a) + c(x_b)]^2}{9} - x_a; \pi_b = \frac{[A + c(x_a) - 2c(x_b)]^2}{9} - x_b \tag{24.A4}$$

Because each firm's unit cost, output, and profit depends on its R&D spending, that spending is the ultimate strategic variable. Differentiating equation (24.A4) with respect to x_a yields the following first-order condition, which implicitly defines a's best R&D response function:

$$[A - 2c(x_a) + c(x_b)]c'(x_a) = -\frac{9}{4} \qquad (24.A5)$$

The slope of the implicit best response function dx_a/dx_b is:

$$\frac{dx_a}{dx_b} = \frac{-c'(x_a)c'(x_b)}{[A - 2c(x_a) + c(x_b)]c''(x_a) - 2[c'(x_a)]^2} \qquad (24.A6)$$

The numerator of equation (24.A6) is definitely negative. The denominator will be positive so long as $c''(x_a)$ is relatively large, which we assume here. Hence, the best response function for firm a (and by symmetry firm b) slopes downward in a curve as shown in Figure 24.1. The positions of the output best response functions, shown in Figure 24.2 depend on the unit cost of each firm and therefore the R&D equilibrium. An R&D subsidy in Country A, shifts out firm a's best R&D response and commits the firm to a level of R&D that it could not credibly threaten on its own. Because R&D levels are strategic substitutes, firm b now does less R&D. The resultant increase in the equilibrium value of x_a lowers c_a. The decrease in x_b has the opposite effect for firm b. Output market equilibrium moves from A' to B'. Spencer and Brander (1983) show that the optimal R&D subsidy is always positive.

Answers to Practice Problems

Chapter 1

No Practice Problems in this chapter.

Chapter 2

2.1 a. Profit Maximization implies $MC = 2q + 10 = P$. Hence, $q = (P - 10)/2$.
  b. With 50 firms, horizontal summation of the individual marginal cost curves yields: $Q^S = 50(P - 10)/2 = 25P - 250$.
  c. Equilibrium: $P = \$30$ and $Q = 500$.
  d. $q = (P - 10)/2 = 10$. Revenue $= Pq = \$300$. Total cost $= 100 + q^2 + 10q = \$300$. Profit $= 0$.

2.2 a. Inverse demand curve is: $P = (6{,}000 - 9Q)/50$. Hence, $MR = 120 - (18Q/50) = 120 - (9Q/25)$.
  b. $MC = 10 + Q/25$. Equate with MR to obtain: $Q = 275$. At this output, $P = \$70.50$.
  c. Total revenue $= \$19{,}387.50$. Each plant produces 5.5 units and incurs a total cost of $\$185.25$. Each plant earns a revenue of $\$387.75$. Profit at each plant is $\$202.50$.

2.3 a. Consumer surplus is the area of the triangle above the equilibrium price but below the demand curve $= (1/2)(\$120 - \$30)500 = \$22{,}500$. Producer surplus is the area of the triangle below the equilibrium price but above the supply curve $= (1/2)(\$30 - \$10)500 = \$5{,}000$. Total Surplus $= \$22{,}500 + \$5{,}000 = \$27{,}500$. Note: Surplus is a marginal concept. Producer fixed cost is not considered.
  b. Total surplus falls by area of deadweight triangle. Height of triangle is given by reduction in output which is $500 - 275 = 225$. Marginal cost at $Q = 275$ is $\$21$. Base of triangle is given by price less marginal $= \$70.50 - \$21 = \$59.50$. So deadweight triangle has area equal to: $= (1/2)(\$49.50)225$ or $\$5{,}568.75$. The new total surplus is the competitive surplus less the deadweight loss $= \$27{,}500 - \$5568.75 = \$21{,}931.25$.

2.4 a. Efficiency requires $P = MC$. Marginal cost is $\$10$. So, $P = \$10$ $(Q = 30)$ is efficient outcome.
  b. Profit maximization requires setting the monopoly price. Because inverse demand is $P = 25 - Q/2$, $MR = 25 - Q$. Equating MC and MR then yields $10 = 25 - Q$ or $Q = 15$ and $P = \$17.5$ is profit maximizing output and price.
  c. Welfare loss is $WL = 0.5(\$17.5 - \$10)(30 - 15) = \$56.25$.

2.5 a. Present value of incremental cash flows from driving out Loew $= -\$100,000 + \dfrac{R}{1-R}$
$\$10,000 = -\$16,629$. Driving out Loew is not a good investment.

b. Present value of incremental cash flows from buying Loew $= -\$80,000 + \dfrac{R}{1-R}$
$\$10,000 = \$3,330$. This is a good investment.

Chapter 3

3.1 a. $CR4^A = 70\%$; $CR4^B = 76\%$. $HI^A = 2698$; $HI^B = 1660$. Industry A has one firm that dominates the industry. Industry B has five firms that control 90 percent of the production. But these five firms may compete fiercely. The Herfindahl-Hirschman index seems to better capture the greater potential for monopoly power in Industry A.

b. With the merger of the three, second largest firms in Industry A, the new values are: $CR4^A = 80\%$; $HI = 2992$. Both measures rise.

Chapter 4

4.1 In this case, we have discrete and not continuous changes in output. Hence we have to use the average value of marginal cost at output 11. This is calculated as the average of the marginal cost of increasing output from 10 to 11 units ($137) and the marginal cost of increasing output from 11 to 12 units ($165), which is just $151. Average or unit cost at 11 units is equal to $1407/11 = \$127.91$. Hence, $S = AC/MC = \$127.91/151 = 0.847 \approx 0.85$.

4.2 a. $AC = TC/q = 50/q + 2 + 0.5q$. $AC(q = 4) = 16.5$; $AC(q = 8) = 12.25$; $AC(q = 10) = 12$; $AC(q = 12) = 12.167$; $AC(q = 15) = 12.833$.

b. $MC = \Delta TC$ per unit change. For decreases: $\Delta TC = 50 + 2q + 0.5q^2 - [50 + 2(q - 1) + 0.5(q - 1)^2] = 2 + q - 0.5$. For increases: $\Delta TC = 50 + 2(q + 1) + 0.5(q + 1)^2 - [50 + 2q + 0.5q^2] = 2 + q + 0.5$. The average of these two value is $2 + q$.

c. $S > 1$ for $q < 10$; $S = 1$ for $q = 10$; $S < 1$ for $q > 10$.

Chapter 5

5.1 a. Total moviegoers is the sum of daytime and evening moviegoers. Note that we assume the price is the same in the daytime and in the evening. This allows us to derive an overall demand function for daytime and evening, which is $Q_{Total} = 100 - 10P_D + 140 - 10P_E = 240 - 20P$. The monopolist maximizes the profit function $\Pi = Q(P - c) = (240 - 20P)(P - 3)$, where $d\Pi/dP = 300 - 40P = 0$. Solving leads to $P = 7.5$, $Q_D = 25$, $Q_E = 65$, and $\Pi = 405$.

b. With third-degree price discrimination the monopolist treats daytime and evening as two separate markets, so P_D and P_E can vary. Profit for the daytime is $\Pi_D = Q_D(P_D - c)$ and profit for the evening is $\Pi_E = Q_E(P_E - c)$. Plugging in the demand equations, we get $\Pi_D = (100 - 10P_D)(P_D - 3)$ and $\Pi_E = (140 - 10P_E)(P_E - 3)$. Setting $d\Pi_D/dP_D = 0$ and $d\Pi_E/dP_E = 0$, we find $P_D = 6.5$, $P_E = 8.5$, $Q_D = 35$, $Q_E = 55$, $\Pi_D = 122.5$, $\Pi_E = 302.5$. Total attendance is 90 as in part (a), but aggregate profit is now 425.

5.2 a. The chowder is being sold in three distinct markets. To solve, we can find separate equilibria for each market. First define the profit function for each market, which is just $\Pi_i = Q_i(P_i - c_i)$. Substitute in the demand equation and the marginal cost for each market. For Boston this is $\Pi_B = (10,000 - 1,000P_B)(P_B - 1)$, for New York it is $\Pi_{NY} = (20,000 - 2,000P_{NY})(P_{NY} - 2)$, and for Washington it is $\Pi_W = (15,000 - 1,500P_W)(P_W - 3)$. Take the first derivative $d\Pi_i/dP_i$ and set it equal to 0 to find the profit maximizing prices. For Boston this is $5.50, for New York it is $6, and for Washington it is $6.50. Plugging price back into the demand equation gives the equilibrium daily quantity. These are $Q_B = 4500$, $Q_{NY} = 8000$, $Q_W = 5250$. Quantities are given in units per day.

b. Plug price and quantity back into the profit equations to find the daily profit in each market. $\Pi_B = \$20{,}250$, $\Pi_{NY} = \$32{,}000$, $\Pi_W = \$18{,}375$.

5.3 Total welfare is the sum of consumer surplus and producer surplus (profit). Consumer surplus is the total amount "saved" by all consumers who paid less than they were willing to pay for the movie. Geometrically, on a graph of price and quantity in the movie market, consumer surplus is the triangle bounded on the left by the y-axis (the line $Q = 0$), on top by the demand curve, and on the bottom by the price curve ($P = P$).

In the non-discriminatory market, the theater's profit $\Pi = 405$. Inverse demand curves are $P_D = 10 - Q_D/10$ and $P_E = 14 - Q_E/10$. From these curves it is clear that the reservation price of the consumers with greatest willingness to pay in the daytime and evening markets are 10 and 14, respectively. The consumer surplus is sum of the areas of the triangles with heights $(10 - 7.5)$ and $(14 - 7.5)$ and bases 25 and 65. Total consumer surplus is $1/2(10 - 7.5)(25) + 1/2(14 - 7.5)(65) = 242.5$. Total surplus is $405 + 242.5 = \$647.5$.

In the discriminatory market, consumer surplus is once again the sum of the consumer surpluses in the daytime and evening markets. Total consumer surplus is $1/2(10 - 6.5)(35) + 1/2(14 - 8.5)(55) = 212.5$. Total surplus is $425 + 212.5 = 637.5$, which is $10 less than the non-discriminatory total surplus.

Chapter 6

6.1 a. Because the demand curve is linear, it must be the line that passes through the two points, (5, $40) and (10, $25). The slope of this line is $(\$40 - \$25)/(5 - 10) = -3$, so $P = -3Q + b$. Plug in a point and solve for b to find the inverse demand equation, $P = 55 - 3Q$. The reservation price of the consumer with the greatest willingness to pay is $55, the price when quantity is 0. At this point, the good is at its scarcest, so only the consumer with greatest willingness to pay will buy the good.

b. We can think of total demand as being the sum of demand for a first unit and demand for a second unit. Because every consumer is willing to pay $8 less for the second unit, the demand curve for a second unit is just the demand for the first unit shifted down by $8, or $P = 47 - 3Q_2$. Plugging in $P = 34$, we find 7 first units will be sold and 4.333 second units will be sold, for a total of 11.333 units sold.

6.2 a. The price per ride should be set at marginal costs, which is $k + c$ so $p = k + c$. The number of rides bought at this price is q_1. The admission fee T should be set to consumer surplus at this price p, which is the area under the demand curve and above $k + c$.

b. The price per ride $p = 0$ at which price the number of rides bought is q_2. The admission fee should be set to consumer surplus at this price, which is the total area under the demand curve.

c. In Policy A, the park's profit per customer is T. The price per ride just covers costs. In Policy B, the park's profit per customer is T' minus the cost of q_2 rides. However, the cost of each ride is only c, because there is no need to issue tickets. Total profit will be the area under the demand curve minus a box of dimensions c by q_2. Which policy is better is uncertain without further information. Policy B gains profit whose area is the trapezoid bounded by c, $k + c$, and the demand function, but loses profit given by the triangle above the demand curve and below c.

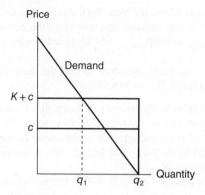

6.3   a.

	Low Demand Customers			High Demand Customers		
Number of Units in the Package	Charge for the Package*	Profit per Package	Consumer Surplus from Low-Demand Package	Maximum Willingness to Pay for 12 units	Charge for Package of 12 Units	Profit from Each Package of 12 Units
0	0	0	0	$120.00	$120.00	$72.00
1	$11.50	$7.50	$4.00	$120.00	$116.00	$68.00
2	$22.00	$14.00	$8.00	$120.00	$112.00	$64.00
3	$31.50	$19.50	$12.00	$120.00	$108.00	$60.00
4	$40.00	$24.00	$16.00	$120.00	$104.00	$56.00
5	$47.50	$27.50	$20.00	$120.00	$100.00	$52.00
6	$54.00	$30.00	$24.00	$120.00	$96.00	$48.00
7	$59.50	$31.50	$28.00	$120.00	$92.00	$44.00
8	$64.00	$32.00	$32.00	$120.00	$88.00	$40.00
9	$67.50	$31.50	$36.00	$120.00	$84.00	$36.00
10	$70.00	$30.00	$40.00	$120.00	$80.00	$32.00
11	$71.50	$27.50	$44.00	$120.00	$76.00	$28.00
12	$72.00	$24.00	$48.00	$120.00	$72.00	$24.00

b.   If the number of high- and low-demand customers is the same, then for each high-demand customer there is one low-demand customer. Thus, for each pair, the profit is profit from a low-demand package plus profit from a high-demand package. This sum is greatest when the low-demand package has 4 units and the high-demand package has 12 units, so that combined profit is $24 + $56 = $80.

c.   For each high-demand customer, there are now two low-demand customers. We want to pick the low-demand package to maximize 2*profit low + profit high. This is maximized when the low-demand package has 6 units, so the profit from 2 low-demand customers and 1 high-demand customer is $108.

d.   From the table, the profit maximizing prices would be $54 for the low-demand package, and $120 for the high-demand package. We want to know at what ratio the profit from only selling the high-demand package exceeds that of selling the high- and low-demand packages. This is equivalent to asking when $72*$N_{High}$ > $44*$N_{High}$ + $31.50 \times N_{Low}$. This equality reduces to $N_{High}/N_{Low} > 1.125$. Therefore, the monopolist should only offer the high-demand package when the ratio of high-demand to low-demand customers is greater than 1.125.

Chapter 7

7.1   He should locate in the middle, where he will have the greatest access to consumers. Consumers will buy from Henry as long as the price plus the travel cost is less than the reservation price, or $P + .5d < 10$, where d is the distance from Henry's in tenths of a mile. The marginal consumer will be located where $P + .5\underline{d} = 10$, or $\underline{d} = 20 - 2P$. The number of customers is just $2\underline{d}$, because people come to Henry's from both directions. However, $2\underline{d}$ cannot exceed 21, because that is the maximum number of people in the town. Henry's profit is $\Pi = 2\underline{d} (P - c) = 2(20 - 2P)(P - 2)$. To maximize profit, we set $d\Pi/dP = 0$ and solve for P, which in this case is $P = \$6$. At this price, $\underline{d}$ is 8 so the total number of customers supplied is 16, and $\Pi = \$64$.

   With the mobile smithy, Henry can charge every customer their \$10 reservation price, but the travel cost of \$0.75 per tenth of a mile cuts into his profits. Henry will visit consumers as long as $.75^*d + 2 < 10$, so $\underline{d} = 10.67$. This would imply Henry would service 21.33 customers, but because there are only 21 customers, Henry just serves everyone in the town. He earns \$10 in revenue from the person at his position, \$9.25 from the two next nearest consumers, \$8.50 from the two second-nearest consumers ... giving him revenue minus transport costs of $\$10.00 + 2(9.25 + 8.50 + 7.75 + \ldots + 2.50) = \$127.50$ and profit of $\$125.50 - \$42 = \$85.50$. The profit from traveling is clearly greater than the profit from staying in the same place, so Henry should travel.

7.2   a.   The demand curve for a given quality is a line with slope $-1/z$, crossing the y-axis at $P = 4$. As z increases, the lines become shallower as the slope gets closer to 0, but always cross the y-axis at the same point.

   b.   For $z = 1$, $P = 4 - Q$ and $C = 1$. Profit $\Pi = Q(4 - Q) - 1$. The profit maximizing output is $Q = 2$. For $z = 2$, $P = 4 - Q/2$ and $C = 4$. Profit $\Pi = Q(4 - Q/2) - 4$. The profit maximizing output is $Q = 4$. For $z = 3$, $P = 4 - Q/3$ and $C = 9$. Profit $\Pi = Q(4 - Q/3) - 9$. The profit maximizing output is $Q = 6$.

   c.   For $z = 1$, $P = 2$ and $\Pi = 3$. For $z = 2$, $P = 2$ and $\Pi = 4$. For $z = 3$, $P = 2$ and $\Pi = 3$. The quality choice of $z = 2$ leads to the highest profits.

7.3   a.   Both type A and type B customers are willing to pay more as quality z increases. The firm should set z as high as possible, so $z = 2$. The firm should then set price to extract all the indirect utility, so $P_A = 20(2 - \underline{z}_1)$ and $P_B = 20$.

   b.   The firm should offer two products only if $20N_a > 10(N_a + N_b)$, or $N_a > N_b$. We know $N_a = \eta N$ and $N_b = (1 - \eta)N$. Substituting in, we see that the firm should offer two products only if $\eta > 1/2$. If this is the case, the firm should offer a high-quality and a low-quality product. Quality for type A $z_a = 2$, and quality for type B $z_b = 20 z_1/(20 - 10) = 2z_1$. $P_a = 20(2 - \underline{z}_1)$ and $P_b = 20^*10\underline{z}_1/(20 - 10) = 20\underline{z}_1$. For the $\eta < 1/2$ case, the firm produces only one good and $z_a = z_b = 2$. The firm will price to sell to both types of consumers.

   c.   If $\underline{z}_1 = 0$, then the only restriction on type A customers is that they will only buy a product whose quality is greater than 0. This restriction is implicit for type B customers as well. Profits are still increasing in z, though, so the firm should sell only one product at quality $z = 2$. At this quality, type A customers are willing to pay \$40 and type B customers are willing to pay \$20. The price should be $P = \$40$ if $40\eta N > 20(1 - \eta)N + 20N$, or $\eta > 2/3$. If $\eta < 2/3$, the price should be $P = \$20$.

Chapter 8

8.1   a.   The cable operator should set the price to maximize profits from each service. The profit maximizing prices are \$11 for the Basic Service and \$15 for the Disney Channel. If the price for the Basic Service is \$11, then families, hotels, and pensioners subscribe, and the cable operator makes profit $\Pi = 11*3 - 3*3 = 24$. If the price for the Disney Channel is \$15, then students, schools, and young adults subscribe, and profit is $\Pi = 15*3 - 3*3 = 36$.

b. The bundled service is the Basic Service and the Disney Channel together. Notice that the reservation prices for the bundled service for students, families, hotels, schools, young adults, and pensioners, are respectively \$20, \$20, \$20, \$20, \$17, and \$17. Thus, the price of the bundle should be \$20. The prices of individual items must be \$17, so that young adults and pensioners will still buy the individual services. The profit from mixed bundling is $\Pi = 20*4 + 17*2 - 8*3 - 2*3 = \$84$. Students, families, hotels, and schools buy the bundled service. Young adults only buy Disney, and pensioners only buy Basic. The cable company is clearly better off with the mixed bundling strategy.

c. The best that the cable operator can do with mixed bundling is price the bundle at \$20 and the individual services at \$17, as in part (b). This generates zero profit from sales of the bundle, because the marginal cost of the bundle is \$20 and \$7 each from sales of Disney to young adults and Basic Service to pensioners, giving a total profit from mixed bundling of \$14. The best that the cable operator can do is price the Basic Service at \$14, selling this to hotels and pensioners, and the Disney Channel at \$15, selling this to students, schools and young adults. Profit from this strategy is $\Pi = 14*2 - 2*10 + 15*3 - 3*10 = \$23$.

8.2 If film is sold separately from the camera, then the price charged to low- and high-demand customers must be the same. We can find the overall demand $Q_{Total} = Q_{High} + Q_{Low} = 28 - 2P$. Notice the profit is composed of two parts: Profit from the film and profit from leasing the camera. The profit from film is $\Pi_{film} = 1000*(16 - P)(P - 2) + 1000*(12 - P)(P - 2)$. The fee for leasing the camera is what would have been consumer surplus for the low-demand customers, but all 2,000 customers now have to pay it, so $\Pi_{camera} = 2000* \frac{1}{2}(12 - P)^2$. Total profit is $\Pi = 1000(-P^2 + 8P + 88)$, so $d\Pi/dP = 1000(-2P + 8) = 0$, and $P = 4$.

With the 8- and 14-shot varieties, there is no charge for film and all profit comes from the lease. The 8-shot camera lease must be priced so as to leave no surplus for the low-demand customers but be less attractive to high-demand customers than the 14-shot variety. Likewise, the 14-shot variety must not generate surplus for the low-demand customers, and must be attractive to high-demand customers. When the low-demand customers take 8 shots, they are effectively paying a price of \$4 per shot, and are receiving \$32 in surplus. Thus the price of the 8 shot camera should be $\$32 + \$4*8 = \$64$. At this price, all of the consumer surplus is extracted from the low-demand customers and turned into profit. However, high-demand customers can buy this package and get $\$8*8 + \$32 - \$64 = \$32$ of surplus, because 8 shots are worth \$8 apiece to a high-demand customer. That means that the 14-shot camera must be priced to leave high-demand customers with at least \$32 of surplus if they are to choose it over the 8-shot. 14 shots are worth \$2 apiece to the high-demand customer, and after paying $\$2*14$ they also get \$98 of consumer surplus. Therefore, the price for the 14-shot should be just less than $\$98 + \$2*14 - \$32 = \$94$, so the 14-shot should be priced at \$93.99 to ensure the high-demand customers will buy. Notice that the high-demand customer still makes \$32.01 of consumer surplus from buying the 14-shot camera. Profit is $\Pi = 1000*(\$64 - 8*\$2) + 1000*(\$93.99 - 14*\$2) = \$113,990$.

a. If there are 1,000 low-demand customers and N_h high-demand customers, then from the text we know the profit from selling the 14-shot and 10-shot varieties is $\Pi = 1000*(\$70 - 10*\$2) + N_h*(\$88 - 14*\$2) = \$50,000 + N_h*\$60$. If only the 14-shot is offered, then cameras are only sold to the high-demand customers, but the price does not have to be discounted to make sure there is at least \$32 of surplus, so profit is $\Pi = N_h*(\$126 - 14*\$2)$. Rowling will only sell the 14-shot variety if $98N_h > 50000 + 60N_h$, which is true when $N_h >\approx 1316$.

b. For the 14-shot and 8-shot varieties, profit from selling the 14-shot and 8-shot is $\Pi = 1000*(\$64 - 8*\$2) + N_h*(\$93.99 - 14*\$2) = \$48,000 + N_h*\$65.99$. If only the 14-shot is offered, then once again the price does not have to be discounted to make sure there is at least \$32 of surplus, so profit is $\Pi = N_h{}^*(\$126 - 14{}^*\$2)$. Rowling will only sell the 14-shot variety of $98N_h > 48000 + 65.99N_h$, which is true when $N_h >\approx 1500$.

Chapter 9

9.1   The unique Nash equilibrium is: (Suspense, Suspense). In each of the other three possible outcomes (Romance, Romance), (Romance, Suspense), and (Suspense, Romance), at least one firm has an incentive to switch its strategy.

9.2   Best Response: $q_1 = 22.5 - q_2/2$, and vise-versa for q_2. Hence, $q_1 = q_2 = 15$. $Q = 30$; $P = \$40$; and $\pi_1 = \pi_2 = \$450$.

9.3   Best response function for Untel: $q_U = 2.5 - q_C/2$; best response for Cyrox: $q_C = 2 - q_U/2$. $q_C = 1$; $q_U = 2$; $Q = 3$; $P = \$60$; $\pi_C = \$20$ million; $\pi_U = \$80$ million. If $c_C = \$20$, then $q_1 = q_2 = 1.67$; $P = \$53.33$. Hence, $\Pi_U = \Pi_C = \$55.55$ million.

Chapter 10

10.1   a.   Best response function for q_1 is: $q_1 = 45 - q_2/2$. By symmetry: $q_2 = 45 - q_1/2$. Hence, in equilibrium: $q_1 = q_2 = 30$. Therefore, market price is: $P = \$20 - \$Q/5 = \$8$. $\pi_1 = \pi_2 = \$180$.
   b. $P_1 = P_2 = P = \$2$; and $\pi_1 = \pi_2 = 0$.

10.2   Market output $Q = q_S + q_R$. At price $P = \$110$, $Q = 2400$, which is the combined capacity of the two resorts. If Pepall Ridge sets a price $p_{SR} = \$110$, the residual demand curve for Snow Richards is $Q = 8000 - 60p_{SR}$, or $p_{SR} = 133.33 - Q/60$. The marginal revenue curve is MR $= 133.33 - Q/30$. On the interval $0 \le Q \le 1400$, marginal revenue is greater than marginal cost, so Snow Richards would increase production to its capacity of 1400. Conversely, if Snow Richards sets its price $p_{SR} = \$110$, the residual demand curve facing Pepall Ridge is $Q = 7600 - 60P$, or $P = 126.67 - Q/60$. The marginal revenue curve is MR $= 126.67 - Q/30$. Marginal revenue is greater than marginal cost on the interval $0 \le Q \le 1000$, so Pepall Ridge will increase production to its capacity of 1,000. Therefore, in the capacity constrained Nash equilibrium: $p_S = p_R = \$110$; $q_{PR} = 1000$; $q_{SR} = 1400$; and $\pi_{PR} = (\$110 - \$10) \times 1000 = \$100,000$; $\pi_{SR} = (\$110 - \$10) \times 1400 = \$140,000$.

10.3   a.   Assume the entire market is served. Best response function for Cheap Cuts: $p_{CC} = \dfrac{p_R + c_{CC} + t}{2}$. Likewise, best response function for the Ritz is: $p_R = \dfrac{p_{CC} + c_R + t}{2}$. With $t = \$5$ and $c_{CC} = \$10$, Cheap-Cuts has a best-response function of $p_{cc} = 0.5p_R + \$7.50$. In contrast, The Ritz has a best-response function given by: $p_R = 0.5p_{CC} + \$12.50$. For every \$1 in one firm's unit cost the rival's optimal price rises by 50 cents.
   b.   Equilibrium prices: $p_{CC} = t + \dfrac{2}{3}c_{CC} + \dfrac{1}{3}c_R = \$18.33$; $p_r = t + \dfrac{1}{3}c_{CC} + \dfrac{2}{3}c_R = \$21.67$. When the two firms had the same unit cost $c = 10$, then $p_{CC} = p_R = \$15$. Prices rise now because c_R has risen and this induces a rise in p_R. In turn, because prices are strategic complements, the rise in p_R permits a similar rise in p_{CC}.

Chapter 11

11.1   a. $q_2 = 70 - q_1/2$.
   b. $q_1 = 70$; $q_2 = 35$; $P = \$95$; profit to firm 1 (leader) $= \$2,450$; profit to firm 2 (follower) $= \$1,225$.
   c. $q_1 = q_2 = 46.67$; $Q = 93.33$; $P = \$106.67$. Profit to firm 1 $=$ profit to firm 2 $= \$2,177.77$. Firm 1 loses and firm 2 gains as game becomes Cournot rather than Stackelberg. Consumers enjoy more output and lower prices under Stackelberg.

11.2 a.   West End will be on its best response function: $p_{WE} = (p_{EE} + c + t)/2$. Demand for East End is: $p_{EE} = (p_{WE} - p_{EE} + t)N/2t$. Substitution and profit maximization then yields: $p_{EE} = c + 3t/2$ while $p_{WE} = c + 5t/4$, or: $p_{EE} = \$17.50$ and $p_{WE} = \$16.25$. Because of its higher price, East End will serve only 3/8 of the 100 potential customers or 37.5. It earns a profit of $\$7.5 \times 37.5 = \$281.25$. West End serves 62.5 customers and earns a profit of $\$6.25 \times 62.5 = \$390.63$.

  b.   Prices in this sequential price game are higher than they are in the simultaneous game. Prices are strategic complements. With sequential price setting, the firms can exploit this complementarity and coordinate prices to some extent. Note, however, that going first is a disadvantage in this game. While both firms earn more profit than when play is simultaneous, the firm setting its price second earns the most.

11.3 a.

		Player 2	
		Take All	Share
Player 1	Wait	(0, 3)	(1.5, 1.5)
	Grab	(1, 0)	

  b.

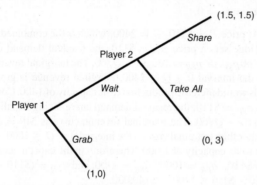

  c.   Take All is a dominant strategy for Player 2. The promise to play Share is not credible. Anticipating this, Player 1 will Grab the dollar.

Chapter 12

12.1 a.   Entrant's residual demand described by: $q = (100 - Q_0) - P$ or, in inverse form: $P = (100 - Q_0) - q$.

  b. $q = 30 - Q_0/2$.

  c.   Entrant profit $= (P - c)q - 100 = [100 - Q_0 - q - 40]q - 100$ Substituting in for q, entrant profit $= (30 - Q_0/2)^2 - 100 = 0$ if entry is to be deterred. $Q_0 = 40$, which implies that the price with optimal production by the entrant $[q = 30 - Q_0/2] = 10$, is $P = \$50$. The entrant will then earn only $\$10$ on each of its 10 units, leaving no profit after the $\$100$ sunk cost. So, the limit output is $Q = \overline{Q} = 40$ as this output removes any incentive to enter.

12.2 a.   Because inverse demand is $P = 120 - (q_1 + q_2)$, the incumbent's marginal revenue is $MR_1 = 120 - q_2 - 2q_1$. the incumbent's marginal cost for output less than $\overline{k}_1$ is 30, hence, equating marginal revenue and marginal cost yields its best response function for this range of output of: $q_1 = 90/2 - q_2/2 = 45 - q_2/2$. For output greater than or equal to

$\overline{K}_1$, the incumbent's marginal cost is 60. Hence, equating marginal revenue and marginal cost for this range of output, yields a best response of: $q_1 = 30 - q_2/2$.

b. The entrant's marginal revenue is likewise: $MR_2 = 120 - q_1 - 2q_2$. However, the entrant's marginal cost is always 60. So, its best response function is always $q_2 = 30 - q_1/2$.

c. For monopoly, profit $= (P - c)q_1 - 30K_1 - \$200 = (120 - q_1 - 30)q_1 - 30K_1 - \$200 = (90 - q_1)q_1 - 30K_1 - \$200$. However, a monopoly firm will not keep capacity unused so long as MR > MC, so it will choose K such that $K_1 = q_1$. Hence, profit $= (90 - q_1)q_1 - 30q_1 - 200 = (60 - q_1)q_1 - \$200$. Maximization then yields, $60 = 2q_1$ or $q_1 = 30$. Entrant's best response implies that if $q_1 = 30, q_2 = 15$. Total output $= 45$.   Price $= \$75$.   Incumbent profit $= \$(75 - 30)30 - \$30 \times 30 - \$200 = \$250$. Entrant's profit $= \$(75 - 60)15 - \$200 = \$25$.

d. With $K_1 = 32 =$ committed value of q_1, then entrant's best response is $q_2 = 16$. Total output $= 48$ and price is $\$72$. Entrant's profit after entry cost is: $(\$72 - \$60) \times 16 = \$192$. Fixed cost is $\$200$, so net profit is $\$192 - \$200 < 0$. Because the entrant cannot earn a positive profit, there will be no entry. The incumbent will produce at capacity because at q_1 and no rival, marginal revenue at $K_1 = 32 = q_1$, is $\$56 >$ marginal cost $= \$30$. However, beyond that output of $q_1 = 32$, marginal cost rises to $\$60$, so the incumbent will produce no more than $q_1 = 32$. At this output level, P $= \$88$. Profit $= (\$88 - \$60)32 - \$200 = \$696$. Because this exceeds the Stackelberg profit, entry deterrence is worthwhile.

12.3 a. The incumbent will fight if $3 > 4 - C$ or if C > 1.

b. For C > 1, the initial expenditure of C implies the incumbent will always fight any entry, so entry does not occur. The incumbent therefore earns $\$(8 - C)$ by expending C. If C is not spent, entry will occur and the incumbent earns $\$4.50$. Expenditure C is only worthwhile if $\$(8 - C) > \$4.50$. If C > 3.50, this condition is not satisfied.

Chapter 13

13.1 The bank would have to ask for at least $\$137.5$ million in a good year, and $\$100$ million in a bad year. It will then earn $\$137.5$ with probability 0.4 and $\$100$ million with probability 0.6 for an average of $\$115$ million. If it needs to earn an additional $\$1.25$ million to cover costs, then the bank can ask for $\$140.625$ in a good year so that its expected gross payment is: $\$116.25$ million. No, there is no change in the incentive for predation. The bank and Newvel can still expect to make a profit by entering in the second period.

13.2 a. $q_L = 45, q_f = 22.5, Q = 67.5, P = \$32.5; \pi_L = \$1,012.5; \pi_f = \$506.25$.

b. If the firms play the standard Stackelberg game in each period, then the leader earns $\$1,012.5$ each period or $\$2,025$ in total (we assume the discount factor is 1). If instead the leader predates, then in first period, $q_L = 90$ and $\pi_L = 0$. In second period, $q_L = 45$ and $\pi_L = \$2,025$. The leader does not gain from this strategy (and will actually lose if the discount factor $R > 1$ as all of the gains from this strategy come in the second period).

c. Offer entrant $\$506.25$ to stay out in 1st period. Earn $\$2,025 - \$506.25 = \$1,518.75$ in 1st period; $\$2,025$ in 2nd period.

13.3 The expected predation gain $=$ the increased probability of Newvel failure times the value of Microhard's gain when this happens. Hence, the gain from predation is: $(\Delta\text{prob}) \times (\$325 - \$150)$ million. This must cover the cost of predation $= \$30$ million. Solving for Δprob yields the lowest increase Newvel's failure probability consistent with Microhard pursuing predatory practices is $\Delta\text{prob} = 17.14$ percent.

Chapter 14

14.1   (Confess, Confess) is the unique Nash Equilibrium.

14.2   The third period outcome must be the one-period Nash equilibrium with both producing 40 (thousand) and earning $1.6 million each. Foreseeing the inevitability of this outcome will thwart any cooperation in period and 2. Hence, both will produce 40 (thousand) units in that period as well. In turn, foreseeing no cooperation in either period 2 or period 3, each firm will also produce 40 (thousand) units in period 1. The three-period game will simply be played as three one-period games.

14.3   a.   If the firms collude they share the monopoly profit, so if the cartel is sustained we have $\pi^M = \dfrac{(A - c)^2}{8b}$. If the cartel fails, per-period profit is the Cournot-Nash profit $\pi^N = \dfrac{(A - c)^2}{9b}$. Now suppose that one firm sticks by the cartel agreement to produce $(A - c)/4b$ while the other cheats on the agreement. The cheating firm's best response is to produce $3(A - c)/8b$, with profit $\pi^D = \dfrac{9(A - c)^2}{64b}$. Substituting into equation (14.7) and simplifying gives the critical probability-adjusted discount factor $\rho_C^* = \dfrac{9/64 - 1/8}{9/64 - 1/9} = \dfrac{9}{17} = 0.529$.

    b.   If the firms collude they each earn π^M per-period as in part a. If the cartel fails we have $\pi^N = 0$. A firm that cheats on the cartel earns $\pi^D = \dfrac{(A - c)^2}{4b}$. Substituting into equation (14.7) and simplifying gives the critical probability-adjusted discount factor $\rho_B^* = \dfrac{1/4 - 1/8}{1/4 - 0} = \dfrac{1}{2} = 0.5$

Chapter 15

15.1   a.   If demand is $P = A - BQ$ and there are N identical firms each with constant marginal cost of c, we know that the Cournot-Nash equilibrium profit is $\pi^C = \dfrac{(A - c)^2}{B(N + 1)^2}$. Substituting $N = 20$, $A = 130$, $B = 1$ and $c = 30$ gives profit to each firm of $22.67.

    b.   If six firms merge this reduces the number of firms in the industry to fifteen. Substituting $N = 15$ gives profit to each firm of $39.06. So the merged firm earns profit post-merger of $39.06 whereas as six independent firms they earn 6*$22.67. This merger is not profitable.

    c.   From the text we know that the fraction of firms that have to merge for the merger to be profitable for the merged firms when there are N firms in the industry pre-merger is $a(N) = \dfrac{3 + 2N - \sqrt{5 + 4N}}{2N}$. Substituting $N = 20$ gives $a(20) = 0.8445$, so that at least 16.89 firms have to merge. That is, at least seventeen firms must merge. This can be double checked. If sixteen firms merge this leaves five firms in the industry, each with profit of $277.78, whereas aggregate profit of these firms pre-merger is 16*22.67 = $362.81. By contrast if seventeen firms merge this leaves four firms in the industry, each with profit of $400 whereas aggregate profit of these firms pre-merger is 17*22.67 = $385.49.

15.2   a.   The general equation for output of a Cournot firm when there are N firms in the industry, when the marginal cost of firm i is c_i ($i = 1, .., 20$) and when market demand is $P = A - B.Q$ is $q_i^C = \dfrac{A - (N+1) \times c_i + \sum\limits_{j=1}^{N} c_j}{B(N+1)}$, the equilibrium price

is $P = \dfrac{A + \sum\limits_{i=1}^{N} c_i}{N+1}$, and profit to firm i is $\pi_i^C = \dfrac{\left(A - (N+1) \times c_i + \sum\limits_{j=1}^{N} c_j\right)^2}{B(N+1)^2}$.

In our example $A = 180$, $B = 1$, $N = 3$, $c_1 = c_2 = 30$, $c_3 = 30b$. This gives

$q_1^C = \dfrac{180 - 4.30 + (30 + 30 + 30b)}{4} = \dfrac{120 + 30b}{4}$; $\quad q_2^C = \dfrac{120 + 30b}{4}$; $\quad q_3^C =$

$\dfrac{180 - 120b + (30 + 30 + 30b)}{4} = \dfrac{240 - 90b}{16}$. Profit of the three firms, ignoring

overhead costs, is $\pi_1^C = \dfrac{(120 + 30b)^2}{16}$; $\pi_2^C = \dfrac{(120 + 30b)^2}{16}$; $\pi_3^C = \dfrac{(240 + 90b)^2}{16}$. The

equilibrium price is $P = \dfrac{180 + 30 + 30 + 30b}{4} = \dfrac{240 + 30b}{4}$. For firm 3 to be able to

survive it is necessary that $240 - 90b > 0$ or $b < 2.67$.

b. The merger leads to the closure of firm 3, resulting in a duopoly with each duopolist

having constant marginal cost of \$30. Output of each firm is $q_1^C = q_2^C = \dfrac{180 - 30}{3} =$

50. The equilibrium price is $P = \dfrac{180 + 30 + 30}{3} = \$80$. Profit of the merged firm is

\$2500 $- 900a$ and of the nonmerged firm is \$2500 $- 900 = \$1400$.

c. The merger is profitable if $2500 - 900a > \dfrac{(120 + 30b)^2}{16} + \dfrac{(240 - 90b)^2}{16} - 1800$. This

requires that $a < \dfrac{1}{72}(-16 + 180b - 45b^2)$.

15.3 a. This is just an application of the standard Cournot equation $q_i^C = \dfrac{A - c}{B(N+1)} =$

$\dfrac{130 - 30}{21} = \dfrac{100}{21}$. So, total output $Q = 20 \times (100/21) = 95.24$. The equilibrium price

is \$34.76.

b. Apply the equations from the text. Output of a leader firm is $q_l^* = \dfrac{A - c}{B(L+1)} =$

$\dfrac{130 - 30}{6} = 16.67$. Output of a follower firm is $q_f^* = \dfrac{A - c}{B(L+1)(N-L+1)} =$

$\dfrac{100}{6 \times 11} = 1.51$. Total output is $5 \times 16.67 + 10 \times 1.51 = 98.45$. The equilibrium price is

\$31.55, lower than the price pre-merger.

c. This is just an application of the standard Cournot equation. With fifteen firms, total

output is $(15/16)$ of the competitive output, or $(15/16) \times 100 = 93.75$.

Chapter 16

16.1 The retailer's marginal revenue curve is $MR = 3{,}000 - Q$ and the retailer maximizes profit
by equating MR and MC, giving $r = 3{,}000 - Q$, which is also the manufacturer's demand
curve. If the retailer has additional marginal costs of c^D then profit maximization gives
$3{,}000 - Q = r + c^D$, which gives $r = (3{,}000 - c^D) - Q$ as the manufacturer's demand
curve.

16.2 a. Profit maximization by WR implies $100 - 2Q = 5 + W_W \Rightarrow W_W = 95 - 2Q = $ WW's demand curve. Profit maximization by WW implies: $95 - 4Q = 5 + W_M \Rightarrow W_M = 90 - 4Q = $ WM's demand curve. Profit maximization by WM implies: $90 - 8Q = 10 \Rightarrow Q = 10$; $W_M = \$50$; $W_W = \$75$; $P = \$90$. $\pi_{WM} = \$400$; $\pi_{WW} = \$200$; $\pi_{WR} = \$100$; total profit $= \$700$.

   b. If WM and WW merge, then their cost of combined operation is \$15. Demand curve facing merged firm is $W_W = 95 - 2Q$. Profit maximization implies: $95 - 4Q = 15 \Rightarrow Q = 20$. Wholesale price to retailer falls to \$55. Price charged to consumers falls to \$80. Profit of the merged firm is $(55 - 15) \times 20 = \$800$. Profit of the retailer is $(80 - 60) \times 20 = \$400$. Total profit has increased, the merged firm has greater profits and the retailer has greater profits. Consumers are offered lower prices.

   If WW and WR merge, WW will supply WR at marginal cost, which is $5 + w_m$. WR then equates MR with MC giving $100 - 2Q = 10 + w_m$ giving the demand function for WM of $w_m = 90 - 2Q$. Equating MR with MC gives $90 - 4Q = 10$ or $Q = 20$. This gives $w_m = \$50$. Profit to WM is \$800. The final product (retail) price is \$80. Profit to the merged firm is $\$(80 - 10 - 50) \times 20 = \$400$.

   c. If all three firms merge, total cost of bringing good to market is \$20. Merged firm faces retail demand of $P = 100 - Q$, hence, $MR = 100 - 2Q = 20$ implies $Q = 40$ and $P = 60$. Merged firm profit is: $\$1600 > \$1200$ above.

16.3 a. Suppose that WI sets a wholesale price of w. GI maximizes profit by setting $MC = 0.1 + w = MR = 1 - 2Q_{gb}$ so $Q_{gb} = 0.45 - w/2$. TI maximizes profit by setting $0.1 + w = 0.75 - 0.4Q_{gn}$, so that $Q_{gn} = 1.625 - 2.5w$. This gives aggregate demand for WI of $Q = 2.075 - 3w$ or $w = 2.075/3 - Q/3$. Marginal revenue for WI is then $MR = 2.075/3 - 2Q/3$ and $MC = 0.1$. This gives profit maximizing total output $Q = 0.8875$. The wholesale price is $w = \$0.396$. Sales in Boston are 0.252 and in New York are 0.635. The price of gizmos in Boston is \$0.748 and in New York is \$0.623. Profits are: WI $= \$0.263$; GI $= \$0.063$; TI $= \$0.081$.

   b. Suppose that WI sets a price w_b for widgets in Boston and w_n for widgets in New York. GI sets $MR = 1 - 2Q_{gb} = MC = 0.1 + w_b$, giving derived demand to WI of $w_b = 0.9 - 2Q_{gb}$. Marginal revenue is $MR = 0.9 - 4Q_{gb}$. Equating with MC of 0.1 gives $Q_{gb} = 0.2$. The wholesale price is $w_b = \$0.5$. The Boston gizmo price is \$0.8. Profit of GI is \$0.04. Profit of WI in Boston is \$0.08. Similarly, derived demand for WI in New York is $w_n = 0.75 - 0.4Q_{gn}$. Equating $MR = 0.75 - 0.8Q_n$ with $MC = 0.1$ gives $Q_n = 0.8125$. Wholesale price is \$0.425. The New York gizmo price is \$0.5875. Profit of TI is \$0.051 and of WI from sales in New York is \$0.264. Profit for WI increased and for TI and GI decreased.

   c. Suppose that WI merges with GI in Boston. Widgets are supplied to GI at marginal cost. GI equates $MR = 1 - 2Q_{gb} = MC = 0.2$, giving $Q_{gb} = 0.4$. Price of gizmos in Boston $= \$0.6$, profit of the merged firm from Boston is \$0.16, aggregate profit is \$0.349. Now suppose that WI merges with TI in New York. Widgets supplied to New York at marginal cost. GI sets $MR = 0.75 - 0.4Q_{gn} = MC = 0.2$, giving $Q_{gn} = 1.375$. Price of Gizmos in New York \$0.475. Profit of the merged firm is \$0.458. So merger with TI is preferred.

   d. i.   Price in Boston rises and in New York falls. There is the opposite effect on consumer surplus.

      ii. Price and consumer surplus in Boston are unaffected. Price in New York falls and consumer surplus increases.

16.4 a. Competitive price is equal to marginal cost equals r. Demand facing WI is $r = 100 - Q$, so $MR = 100 - 2Q = 10$ for profit maximization, or: $Q = 45$ and $r = P = \$55$. WI profit is \$2,025. Competitive retailers earn zero profit.

b.   WI is already earning the maximum profit possible in this industry (absent price discrimination). Therefore, integration with one or even many downstream retailers cannot raise WI's profits or price P to consumers. Even if WI bought all downstream retailers, it would still maximize profits by setting P = $55, selling 45 units, and earning $2,025 in profit.

c.   Competitive manufacturing price = marginal cost = $10. Competitive retail price = manufacturing price = $10.

Chapter 17

17.1   a.   The Great Toy Store's marginal revenue curve is $MR^R = 1,000 - 4Q$ and the Toy Store maximizes profit by equating MR and MC, giving $r = 1,000 - 4Q$, which is also Tiger-el's demand curve. Tiger-el therefore has a marginal revenue curve of $MR^M = 1,000 - 8Q$. Equating this with the Tiger-el's marginal cost $c = \$40$ yields $Q = 120$. From the Tiger-el demand curve, $r = 1000 - 4Q$, this implies a wholesale price of $r = \$520$. From the retail demand curve facing the Great Toy Store, $P = 1,000 - 2Q$, the retail price will be $760.

b.   The Great Toy Store will earn profit of ($760 − $520) × 120 = $28,800. Tiger-el will earn profit of ($520 − $40) × 120 = $57,600.

c.   Tiger-el receives $c = \$40$ for each unit plus a sales royalty of 2/3 of all sales. Hence, Tiger-el's total revenue is $(c + 0.667P)Q = \$40Q + 0.6667 \times PQ = (\$40 + 666.67 - 1.333Q)Q$. Its marginal revenue is therefore $706.67 - 2.667Q$. Equating this with its marginal cost $c = \$40$ yields an optimal output of: $Q = 250$. The retail price will therefore be $P = 1,000 - 500 = \$500$. Total Toy Store revenue will be $125,000. The Toy Store keeps one-third of this less wholesale costs = 0.3333 × $125,000 − $40 × 250 = $41,666.67 − $10,000 = $31,666.67 as retail profit. Tiger-el keeps the remainder = $93,333.33 as its revenue leaving it $83,333.333 as profit after production costs.

17.2   a.   From equation (17.6) we have $(10 - 6)/2 = s^2/2 + 2s^2 + (17.7)$. Hence, $s = \sqrt{(2/2.5)} = 0.894$. From equation (17.7), $P = (10 + 6 + s^2)/2 = \$8.4$. From the demand curve, $Q = 0.894(10 - 8.4)100 = 143.4$. Hence, the manufacturer's profit is: ($6 − $5) × 143.4 = $143.4.

b.   If the wholesale price $r = \$7$, then the service level s falls to $s = \sqrt{(1.5/2.5)} = 0.775$. In turn, this implies a retail price of $P = (10 + 7 + 0.775^2)/2 = \$8.80$. The total amount sold falls to $0.775(\$10 - \$8.80)100 = 93$.

17.3   a.   Because marginal cost $c = 0$, profit maximization is the same as revenue maximization, i.e., the firm will wish to produce where marginal revenue $MR = 0$. When demand is strong, the inverse demand is: $p = 10 - Q/100$. Hence $MR^S = 10 - Q/50$. The revenue-maximizing choice of Q is therefore $Q = \$500$ implying a retail price of $5. When demand is weak, the inversed demand is: $p = 10 - Q/30$, so that marginal revenue in this case of $M^W = 10 - Q/15$ which, in turn, implies an optimal output of $Q = 150$. Substitution of this into the weak case inverse demand curve then implies a price of $5 again.

b.   If the 500 units have already been produced then their production cost is sunk. As a result, the firm's marginal cost is zero and it will wish to sell either the full capacity of 500 units or to the point where $MR = 0$, depending on which constraint binds first. When demand is strong and $MR^S = 10 - Q/50$, the firm will wish to sell all 500 units. When demand is weak and $MR^W = 10 - Q/15$, the firm will wish to sell only 150 units. In the first case, the retail price is $5 and the firm earns a profit of $2,500. In the second case, the retail price is again $5, but the firm earns a profit of only $750. Because these cases occur with equal probability, the expected profit conditional on having produced 500 units is ($2500 + $750)/2 = $1,625.

c. Once bought as a block of 500 units, competitive retailers treat the wholesale cost as sunk. Therefore, their marginal cost is 0. Because they will sell so long as price exceeds marginal cost, competitive retailers will sell all 500 units at the market-clearing price of $5 if demand is strong. When demand is weak, they will continue selling until the number of units sold is 300 and the retail price as fallen to 0.

d. Let w be the implicit wholesale price per unit when a block of 500 units is initially sold. In the competitive retail sector case, retail profits net of initial wholesale costs are $2,500 less w500 when demand is strong and 0 less w500 when demand is weak. Hence, expected retail profits are $0.5 \times \$2500 + 0.5 \times 0 - w500$. Because competitive retailers need to expect to break even, the wholesale price necessary to induce competitive retailers to stock 500 units is $w = \$2.50$. If the manufacturer sets this price, competitive retailers as a group can be persuaded to stock 500 units. Accordingly, the manufacturer will earn a profit of $2.50 \times 500 = \$1,250$.

Chapter 18

18.1 a. $n^* = 2$.

b. q per division = 15. Profit per division = $225. Profit per firm = $450 less ($90 in sunk division costs) $360.

c. $Q = 60$; $P = \$40$.

d. Pure monopoly: $P^M = \$62.50$; $Q^M = \$37.50$; $\Pi^M = \$1406.25$ less $45 (sunk cost for $n = 1$ division) = $1361.25

Chapter 19

19.1 a. $a = 100$ implies $dP/dQ = -0.1$; $a = 1,000$ implies $dP/dQ = -0.0316$.

b. i. $MR = 100 - 0.04Q$.

ii. $P = \$80$; $Q = 1,000$.

iii. Price elasticity (absolute value) = 4. Elasticity of sales with respect to advertising = 1/2.

c. At $a = 2,500$, $P = \$80$; $Q = 1,000 \Rightarrow$ Advertising/Sales Ratio $= a/PQ = 0.03125$. Dorfman-Steiner condition requires Advertising/SalesRatio $= (1/2)/4 = 1/8$, is not satisfied here. Optimal advertising rate that does satisfy Dorfman-Steiner condition yields: $a = 40,000$; $P = \$80$; $Q = 4,000$.

Chapter 20

20.1 With a marginal cost of $28, the monopolist would like to price such that MR = MC. This implies $100 - 4Q = 28$, or $Q = 18$. At this quantity, price would be $P = 100 - 2(18) = \$64$. However, the current market price with Bertrand competition is $60. Because the innovator's ideal monopoly price is greater than the current market price, this is a non-drastic innovation. The innovator has to reduce the price to $59.99 in order to capture the market.

Say the innovator's new marginal cost of production is c_M. Then we want to choose a c_M such that $P_M < 60$. We know MR = MC and $100 - 4Q_M = c_M$, so $Q_M = 25 - c_M/4$, and $P_M = 100 - 2(25 - c_M/4) = 50 + c_M/2..$ Monopoly price $P_M < 60$ implies $50 + c_M/2 < 60$, which in turn implies $c_M < 20$. In order for the innovation to be drastic, c_M must be less than $20.

20.2   a.   The innovation is non-drastic if the monopolist's ideal price is greater than the competitive price, $P_M > P_C$. Because the firms compete in price, $P_C = c_C = 75$. The monopolist would profit-maximize by setting $MR = MC$, or $100 - 2Q_M = 60$, so $Q_M = 20$ and $P_M = 80$. Because $80 > 75$, this is a non-drastic innovation. If the innovation reduces cost to c_M, equating MR with MC gives $100 - 2Q = c_M$ which gives $Q = 50 - c_M/2$ and $P = 50 + c_M/2$. For this to be a drastic innovation requires that $50 + c_M/2 \leq 75$ or $c_M \leq \$50$.

       b.   If the market is a monopoly the monopolist sets $MR = MC$, or $100 - 2Q = 75$, or $Q = 12.5$ and $P = \$87.5$ prior to the innovation, earning profit of \$156.25 per period prior to the innovation. With the innovation $MC = 60$ and so the monopolist sets $100 - 2Q = 60$ or $Q = 20$ and price $P = 80$. Profit after the innovation is therefore $\$(80 - 60) \times 20 = \$400$ per period. The monopolist values the innovation at $V_M = \$(400 - 156.25)/0.1 = \$2,437.50$.

       c.   Cournot duopolists facing the same marginal cost each produce output $Q_D = (A - c)/3B = 25/3 = 8.33$. Aggregate output is 16.67 and so price is \$83.33. Profit to each duopolist is $\$(83.33 - 75) \times 8.33 = \$69.44$.

       d.   Now we suppose firm 1 has innovated, so its marginal cost is $c_1 = 60$, but firm 2 has not innovated and still has marginal cost $c_2 = 75$. Output of firm 1 is the duopoly output $Q_1 = (A - 2c_1 + c_2)/3B = 18.33$ and of firm 2 is $Q_2 = (A - 2c_2 + c_1)/3 = 3.33$. Aggregate output is 21.67 so price is \$78.33.

       e.   Profit to innovation, the innovating firm is $\$(78.33 - 60) \times 18.33 = \$336.11$. The innovating Cournot duopolist values the innovation at $V_D = \$(336.11 - 69.44)/0.1 = \$2,666.67$. Because $V_D > V_M$ this confirms that the duopolist values the innovation more than the monopolist.

Chapter 21

21.1   a.   If the firms compete in price, then price is driven to marginal cost, so $P = \$70$ and $Q = 30$.

       b.   If the firm chooses research activity x its marginal cost becomes $70 - x$. Assuming that the innovation is non-drastic, the innovating firm will set price \$70 and sell 30 units. The resulting profit per period while the patent is in force is then $\$(70 - 70 + x)30 = 30x$. Aggregate profit over the life of the patent is then $V(x; 25) = \dfrac{1 - 0.9091^{25}}{1 - 0.9091} 30x - 15x^2 = 299.57x - 15x^2$. This equation is maximized when $dV/dx = 299.57 - 30x = 0$, or when $x \approx 10$.

       c.   If the patent duration is reduced to twenty years, then $V(x; 20) = \dfrac{1 - 0.9091^{20}}{1 - 0.9091} 30x - 15x^2 = 280.97x - 30x_2$ so $dV/dx = 280.97 - 30x = 0$, and. $x \approx 9.4$ Because of the decrease in the patent duration, the firm's R&D effort is decreased.

       d.   The total net surplus $TS(x; T) = V(x, T) + CS(x; T) - r(x)$. Consumer surplus is $CS(x; T) = \dfrac{1 - R^T}{1 - R} CS_P + \dfrac{R^T}{1 - R} CS_{NP}$ where $CS_P = (100 - 70)^2/2 = \$450$ is the consumer surplus per period while the innovation is on patent and $CS_{NP} = (100 - (70 - x))^2/2 = (30 + x)^2/2$ is the consumer surplus when the innovation goes off patent. Note: Consumer surplus is the triangle with height $100 - P$ and base $Q = 100 - P$. When the innovation comes off patent $P = c - x$. While on patent, $P = 70$. For $T = 25$, we know from part (c) that $x \approx 10$ and $TS(10; 25) = 2995.7 + (1 - 0.9091^{25})/(1 - 0.9091)*30^2/2 + 0.9091^{25}/(1 - 0.9091)*40^2/2 - 15*10^2 = \$6,801.61$. If we have $T = 20$, then $x \approx 9.4$, so $TS(9.4; 20) = 2809.7 + (1 - 0.9091^{20})/(1 - 0.9091)\frac{1}{2}*30^2 + 0.9091^{20}/(1 - 0.9091)*\frac{1}{2}*(30 + 9.4)^2 - 15*9.4^2 = \$6799.66$. Thus, total welfare decreases approximately $2 if the patent life is decreases from 25 to 20 years.

21.2 a. If only BMI innovates, then ECN is shut out of the market and BMI monopolizes. Facing a demand curve of $P = 100 - 2Q$, a marginal cost of $c = 50$, and a fixed cost for setting up a lab of K, BMI maximizes the profit function $\Pi = Q(P - c) - K = Q(100 - 50 - 2Q) - K$. This function is maximized when $\partial\Pi/\partial Q = 50 - 4Q = 0$, which is when $Q = 12.5$ and $P = 100 - 2*12.5 = 75$. Monopoly profits are $\Pi = 12.5(75 - 50) - K = \$312.5 - K$. Consumer surplus is the area of the triangle with height $100 - P$ and base Q, so $CS = \frac{1}{2}*25*12.5 = \$156.25$.

b. If both BMI and ECN successfully innovate, then the two firms will compete, Cournot-style. Output of each firm is $Q_i = (A - c)/3B = 8.33$. Price is $\$66.67$ and profit of each firm including the cost of setting up a lab, $\Pi_1 = \Pi_2 = 8.33(66.67 - 50) - K = \$138.89 - K$. Consumer surplus is once again the area of the triangle with height $100 - P$ and base Q, so $CS = \frac{1}{2}*(100 - 66.67)*16.67 = \$277.78$.

c. If only one firm sets up a lab, then likelihood that the lab is successful and the firm innovates is $\rho = 0.8$, and the likelihood that the lab is unsuccessful is $(1 - \rho) = 0.2$. Expected profit is $0.8(\$312.50) - K = \$250 - K$. If both firms set up a lab, then there are four possible outcomes for each firm. These are

i.   BMI successfully innovates and ECN does not, with probability 0.8×0.2;

ii.   both successfully innovate with probability 0.8×0.8;

iii. ECN successfully innovates while BMI does not, with probability 0.2×0.8;

iv.   neither successfully innovate with probability 0.2×0.2.

In each of the last two cases, BMI makes no profit. So, its expected profit is: $0.8 \times 0.2 \times \$312.50 + 0.8^2 \times \$138.89 - K = \$138.89 - K$. The payoff matrix is:

		BMI	
		No R&D Division	R&D Division
ECN	No R&D Division	0, 0	0, $250 – K
	R&D Division	$250 – K, 0	$138.89 – K, $138.89 – K

d. For (No R&D, No R$D) to be a Nash equilibrium $\$250 - K < 0$ or $K > \$250$. For (R&D, R&D) to be a Nash equilibrium $\$138.89 - K > 0$ or $K < \$138.89$. For $\$138.89 < K < \$250$ only one firm will do R&D.

e. The expected social surplus with only one lab is $0.8(\$312.50 + \$156.25) - K = \$375 - K$. With two labs it is $2 \times 0.8 \times 0.2 \times (\$312.50 + 156.25) + 0.8 \times 0.8 \times (138.89 + 277.78) - 2K = \$416.67 - 2K$. Two labs are optimal if $\$416.67 - 2K > \$375 - K$ or $K < \$41.67$.

21.3 a. With Cournot competition, firms choose quantity as the strategic variable. Each firm wants to maximize the profit function $\Pi_i = q_i(100 - 2(q_i + q_{-i}) - c) = q_i(40 - 2q_i - 2q_{-i})$. This function is maximized when $\partial\Pi_i/\partial q_i = 40 - 4q_i - 2q_{-i} = 0$, which is when $q_i = 10 - q_{-i}/2$. Because costs are symmetrical, $q_i = q_{-i}$, so both firms are on their best response functions when $q_i = q_{-i} = 6.67$ and $Q = 13.33$, so price is $P = 73.33$.

b. i. The two firms will still engage in Cournot competition, except that now the innovator's marginal cost is 50 and the non-innovator's is still 60. Say firm 1 is the innovator and firm 2 is the non-innovator, then $\Pi_1 = q_1(100 - 2q_1 - 2q_2 - 50)$ and $\Pi_2 = q_2(100 - 2q_2 - 2q_1 - 60)$. This leads to best response functions Firm 1: $q_1 = 12.5 - q_2/2$ and Firm 2: $q_2 = 10 - q_1/2$. Both firms are on their best response functions when $q_1 = 10$ and $q_2 = 5$, so $Q = 15$ and $P = 70$. Firm 1's profit is $\Pi_1 = 10(70 - 50) = \$200$ and firm 2's profit is $\Pi_2 = 5(70 - 60) = \$50$.

ii.   If firm 1 licenses the invention to firm 2 at $10 per unit, then firm 2's marginal produc-
tion cost will be $50 because of the innovation, but there is a $10 royalty fee on each
unit, so the overall marginal cost is still $c_2 = 50 + 10 = 60$. However, firm 1 also
makes a profit of $10 on every unit firm 2 sells, so the new profit functions
are $\Pi_1 = q_1(50 - 2q_1 - 2q_2) + 10q_2$ and $\Pi_2 = q_2(40 - 2q_1 - 2q_2)$. This, however, leads to the same best response functions, because firm 1 does not have control
over q_2, so the equilibrium quantities are still $q_1 = 10$, $q_2 = 5$, and $Q = 15$, and the
equilibrium price is still $P = 70$. Firm 1's profit is $\Pi_1 = 10(70 - 50) + 5{*}10 = 250$
and firm 2's profit is $\Pi_2 = 5(70 - 50) - 5{*}10 = 50$.

iii. Say that firm 1 licenses the product to firm 2 for a fee K. Then both firms will
take advantage of the innovation and have a marginal cost $c = 50$. Profits are
$\Pi_1 = q_1(P - 50) + K$ and $\Pi_2 = q_2(P - 50) - K$. Best response functions are
now Firm 1: $q_1 = 12.5 - q_2/2$ and Firm 2: $q_2 = 12.5 - q_1/2$. Both firms are
on their best response functions when $q_1 = q_2 = 8.33$, $Q = 16.67$, and price
is $P = 66.67$. Profits are $\Pi_1 = 8.33(66.67 - 50) + K = 138.89 + K$ and $\Pi_2 =$
$8.33(66.67 - 50) - K = 138.89 - K$.

Firm 2 will be willing to pay the licensing fee as long as the profit from buying
the license and using the innovation is greater than the profit from part (i), where
it didn't have the license. Thus, as long as $138.89 - K > 50$, firm 2 will buy the
license. This requires $K < 88.89$.

Firm 1 should price the license so that it is just marginally better for firm 2
to buy the license, so the price should be $K = 88.88$. Firm 1's profits will be
$\Pi_1 = 138.89 + 88.88 = \$227.77$. Firm 2's profits will be $\Pi_2 = 138.89 - 88.88 =$
$\$50.01$. Note that in this example the innovator would prefer the royalty to the fixed
fee.

Chapter 22

22.1 a.   The consumer who is indifferent between buying the good and not buying is has basic
valuation v_i satisfying the condition $(0.4 + 6f^2)v^M = p$. Hence, with $p = 50$, we have:
$v^M = p/(0.4 + 6f^2) = 50/(0.4 + 6f^2)$.

b.   The market fraction f that is served is given by $f = 1 - v^M/100$. Hence we have
$f = 1 - 0.5/(0.4 + 6f^2)$. This equality holds when either $f = 0.1905$ or $f = 0.906$.
The second solution is stable.

Chapter 23

23.1 A dominant strategy is one that gives you a payoff greater than any other strategy regardless
of what is chosen by other players. Clearly it does not pay to bid more than your willingness
to pay. You will lose anytime that you win. The other strategy you could choose is to stop
bidding when the price is less than your true valuation. Suppose that the auction price is p and
your true valuation is V. If $p < V$ and you stop bidding your payoff is 0, whereas if you bid
$p + \varepsilon < V$ then your payoff is $V - (p + \varepsilon) > 0$. So, for any $p < V$, continuing to bid is a
dominant strategy. Because you also cannot gain but may lose if you bid $V + \varepsilon$, bidding V is
a dominant strategy.

23.2 Your best strategy here is to assume that you are the one with the highest valuation. In
other words you assume that the other seven bidders have valuations drawn from a uniform
distribution over the interval [0, 200]. If we assume that these bids are evenly spaced out over
the interval then the lowest would be 25($=1/8{*}200$), the next 50($=2/8{*}200$), the next 75,
the next 100, the next 125, the next 150, and finally the highest bid from the other bidders will
be 175($=7/8{*}200$). You should submit a bid of $175 to win the auction.

23.3   Your $20,000 estimate is likely too high by the amount $\left(\dfrac{n-1}{n+1}\right)\$3000 = \left(\dfrac{8-1}{8+1}\right)\$3000 =$ $2,333.33 If you bid $20,000 that is the amount you are likely overbidding.

Chapter 24

24.1   a.   The marginal revenue for firm A is: $MR_A = 1000 - q_B - 2q_A$. Setting this equal to marginal cost $MC_A = 400$ yields firm A's best response function: $q_A = 300 - q_B/2$. By symmetry, firm B's best response is: $q_B = 300 - q_A/2$. Hence, the Nash equilibrium is: $q_A = q_B = 200$, implying $Q = 400$; $P = \$600$; and profit to each firm $\pi_A = \pi_B = \$40,000$.

   b.   From equation (24.8) or (24.9), the optimal subsidy $s^* = (A - c)/4$. Here we have $A = \$1000$ and $c =$ marginal cost $= \$400$. Hence the optimal subsidy is $s^* = \$150$. It follows from equation (24.3) that $q_A = (1000 - 400 + 2s^*)/3 = 300$. Firm B's best response function in turn implies that: $q_B = 300 - q_A/2 = 150$. Because total output is $Q = 450$, the market price is $550.

      i.   Firm A's profit is: $(\$550 - c + s^*)q_A = \$300 \times 300 = \$90,000$.
      ii.   The cost of the subsidy is $s^*q_A = \$150 \times 300 = \$45,000$.
      iii.   The net gain from the subsidy is $90,000 - \$45,000 = \$45,000$

24.2   In general, we know from Chapter 9 that the Cournot model with cost differences implies the following output levels: $q_A = (A - 2c_A + c_B)/3$; and $q_B = (A + c_A - 2c_B)/3$. Before the tariff, the marginal cost for each firm is $c_A = c_B = 12$. Hence, prior to the tariff, each firm had output: $q_A = q_B = 88/3$. So, total output was $Q = 58.67$ implying a price $P = \$41.33$. Pre-tariff profit to firm A is: $29.33^2 = \$860.44$. Consumer surplus in Country A in the no-tariff case is: $0.5 \times (100 - 41.33) \times 58.67 = \$1720.89$. After the tariff, firm A still has a marginal cost of $c_A = 12$. However, firm B loses scale economies and so has an increase in the marginal cost of production to $s_B = 14$. To this higher marginal cost, we must add the additional 2-dollar tariff. Hence, within country A, firm faces an implicit marginal cost—production plus tariff—of $14 + 2 = 16$ for units sold in country A. It follows that after the tariff, each firm's output will be: $q_A = (100 - 24 + 16)/3 = 92/3$; and $q_B = (100 + 12 - 32)/3 = 80/3$. Hence, total output is $Q = 57.333$, implying a price of $P = \$42.67$. Firm A's profit is now: $(\$42.67 - \$12) \times 92/3 = \$940.455$. Consumer surplus in Country A is now: $0.5 \times (100 - 42.67) \times 57.33 = \$1643.46$. Producer surplus has increased by $940.44 - \$860.44 = \$80$. Consumer surplus has decreased by $1720.89 - \$1643.46 = \$77.33$.

Index